Lecture Notes in Computer Science 2888

Edited by G. Goos, J. Hartmanis, and J. van Leeuwen

W0235181

Springer-Verlag Berlin Heidelberg GmbH

Robert Meersman   Zahir Tari
Douglas C. Schmidt et al. (Eds.)

On The Move to Meaningful Internet Systems 2003: CoopIS, DOA, and ODBASE

OTM Confederated International Conferences
CoopIS, DOA, and ODBASE 2003
Catania, Sicily, Italy, November 3-7, 2003
Proceedings

 Springer

Series Editors

Gerhard Goos, Karlsruhe University, Germany
Juris Hartmanis, Cornell University, NY, USA
Jan van Leeuwen, Utrecht University, The Netherlands

Volume Editors

Robert Meersman
STAR Lab, Vrije Universiteit Brussel
Pleinlaan 2, Gebouw G-10, 1050 Brussels, Belgium
E-mail: Robert.Meersman@vub.ac.be

Zahir Tari
RMIT University
School of Computer Scienc and Information Technology
GPO Box 2476V, Melbourne, Victoria 3001, Australia
E-mail: zahirt@cs.rmit.edu.au

Douglas C. Schmidt
University of California at Irvine
Electrical and Computer Engineering Department
Irvine, CA 92697-2625, USA
E-mail: schmidt@uci.edu

Cataloging-in-Publication Data applied for

A catalog record for this book is available from the Library of Congress.

Bibliographic information published by Die Deutsche Bibliothek
Die Deutsche Bibliothek lists this publication in the Deutsche Nationalbibliografie;
detailed bibliographic data is available in the Internet at <http://dnb.ddb.de>.

CR Subject Classification (1998): H.2, H.3, H.4, C.2, H.5, I.2, D.2.12, K.4

ISBN 978-3-540-20498-5   ISBN 978-3-540-39964-3 (eBook)
DOI 10.1007/978-3-540-39964-3

This work is subject to copyright. All rights are reserved, whether the whole or part of the material is
concerned, specifically the rights of translation, reprinting, re-use of illustrations, recitation, broadcasting,
reproduction on microfilms or in any other way, and storage in data banks. Duplication of this publication
or parts thereof is permitted only under the provisions of the German Copyright Law of September 9, 1965,
in its current version, and permission for use must always be obtained from Springer-Verlag. Violations are
liable for prosecution under the German Copyright Law.

Springer-Verlag is a part of Springer Science+Business Media

springeronline.com

© Springer-Verlag Berlin Heidelberg 2003
Originally published by Springer-Verlag Berlin Heidelberg in 2003

Typesetting: Camera-ready by author, data conversion by PTP-Berlin, Protago-TeX-Production GmbH
Printed on acid-free paper   SPIN: 10970614   06/3142   5 4 3 2 1 0

DOA 2003

Bernd Krämer
Maarten van Steen
Steve Vinoski

ODBASE 2003

Roger (Buzz) King
Maria Orlowska
Rudi Studer

CoopIS 2003

Elisa Bertino
Dennis McLeod

OTM 2003 General Co-chair's Message

We as General Chairs are rather proud to announce that the conference series we started in Irvine last year proved to be a concept that continues to attract a representative selection of today's research in distributed, heterogeneous yet collaborative systems, of which the Internet and the WWW are its prime examples.

Indeed, as large, complex and networked intelligent information systems become the focus and norm for computing, software issues as well as methodological and theoretical issues covering a wide range of topics, such as data and Web semantics, distributed objects, Web services, databases, workflow, cooperation, ubiquity, interoperability, and mobility for the development of Internet- and Intranet-based systems in organizations and for e-business, need to be addressed in a fundamental way. The second, 2003 edition of the "On The Move" (OTM) federated conference event provided an opportunity for researchers and practitioners to understand and publish these developments within their respective as well as within their broader contexts. It co-located the three related, complementary and successful conference series: DOA (Distributed Objects and Applications), covering the relevant infrastructure-enabling technologies, OD-BASE (Ontologies, DataBases and Applications of SEmantics) covering Web semantics, XML databases and ontologies, and CoopIS (Cooperative Information Systems) covering the application of these technologies in an enterprise context through, for example, workflow systems and knowledge management. Each of these three conferences treated its topics within a framework of theory, conceptual design and development, and applications, in particular case studies and industrial solutions.

In 2003 we also invited a number of workshop proposals to complement the more archival nature of the main conferences with research results in a number of selected and more avant garde areas related to the general topic of distributed computing. For instance, the so-called Semantic Web has given rise to several novel research areas combining linguistics, information systems technology, and artificial intelligence, such as the modeling of (legal) regulatory systems and the ubiquitous nature of their usage. One such event was continued from last year, a so-called "Industry Program" workshop soliciting relevant case studies and best practice results from industry in the areas covered by On The Move 2003.

All three conferences and the associated workshops therefore shared the distributed aspects of modern computing systems, and the resulting application pull created by the Internet and the so-called Semantic Web. For DOA 2003, the primary emphasis stayed on the distributed object infrastructure; for OD-BASE 2003, it became the knowledge bases and methods required for enabling the use of formal semantics; and for CoopIS 2003, the main topic was the interaction of such technologies and methods with management issues, such as occur in networked organizations. These subject areas naturally overlap and many submissions in fact also treat an envisaged mutual impact among them. As for the 2002 edition in Irvine, the organizers wanted to stimulate this cross-pollination with a program of shared famous keynote speakers (this year we got Sycara, Goble, Soley and Mylopoulos!), and encouraged multiple attendance by providing authors with free access to another conference or workshop of their choice.

We received an even larger number of submissions than last year for the three conferences (360 in total) and the workshops (170 in total). Not only can we therefore again claim a measurable success in attracting a representative volume of scientific papers, but such a harvest allowed the program committees of course to compose a high-quality cross-section of worldwide research in the areas covered. In spite of the increased number of submissions, the Program Chairs of the three main conferences decided to accept only approximately the same number of papers for presentation and publication as in 2002 (i.e., around 1 paper out of every 4–5 submitted). For the workshops, the acceptance rate was about 1 in 2. Also for this reason, we decided to separate the proceedings into two volumes with their own titles, and we are grateful to Springer-Verlag for their collaboration in producing these two books. The reviewing process by the respective program committees was very professional and each paper in the main conferences was reviewed by at least three referees. The On The Move federated event organizers therefore also decided to make both (sizeable) books of proceedings available to all participants of the conferences and workshops. Even though this meant that participants had extra weight to carry home.

The General Chairs are especially grateful to all the many people directly or indirectly involved in the setup of these federated conferences, and who in so doing made then a success. In particular we thank our eight conference PC co-chairs (DOA 2003, Bernd Krämer, Maarten van Steen, and Steve Vinoski; ODBASE 2003, Roger (Buzz) King, Maria Orlowska, and Rudi Studer; CoopIS 2003, Elisa Bertino and Dennis McLeod) and our 13 workshop PC co-chairs (Angelo Corsaro, Corrado Santoro, Priya Narasimhan, Ron Cytron, Ernesto Damiani, Brian Blake, Giacomo Cabri, Mustafa Jarrar, Anne Salaun, Elizabeth Chang, William Gardner, Tharam Dillon, and Michael Brodie), our publicity chair (Guillaume Pierre) and our publication chair (Kwong Lai), who together with their many PC members did a superb and professional job in selecting the best papers from the large harvest of submissions.

We do hope that again the results of this federated scientific event may contribute to your work and that we may see you all again, as well as many others, for next year's edition!

August 2003   Robert Meersman, Vrije Universiteit Brussel, Belgium
                              Zahir Tari, RMIT University, Australia
                  Douglas Schmidt, University of California at Irvine, USA

Organizing Committee

The OTM (On The Move) 2003 Federated Conferences, which involve CoopIS (Cooperative Information Systems), DOA (Distributed Objects and Applications) and ODBASE (Ontologies, Databases and Applications of Semantics) 2003, are proudly supported by RMIT University (School of Computer Science and Information Technology) and Vrije Universiteit Brussel (Department of Computer Science).

Executive Committee

OTM 2003 General Co-chairs	Robert Meersman (Vrije Universiteit Brussel, Belgium), Douglas Schmidt (UCI, USA) and Zahir Tari (RMIT University, Australia)
CoopIS 2003 PC Co-chairs	Elisa Bertino (University of Milan, Italy) and Dennis McLeod (University of Southern California, USA)
DOA 2003 PC Co-chairs	Bernd Krämer (FernUniversität in Hagen, Germany), Maarten van Steen (Vrije Universiteit of Amsterdam, The Netherlands) and Steve Vinoksi (Iona, USA)
ODBASE 2003 PC Co-chairs	Roger (Buzz) King (University of California, USA), Maria Orlowska (University of Queensland, Australia) and Rudi Studer (University of Karlsruhe, Germany)
Publication Chair	Kwong Yuen Lai (RMIT University, Australia)
Local Organizing Chair	Corrado Santoro (University of Catania, Italy)
Publicity Chair	Guillaume Pierre (Vrije Universiteit of Amsterdam, The Netherlands)

CoopIS 2003 Program Committe

Dave Abel	Anne Doucet	Yahiko Kambayashi
Naveen Ashish	Marie-Christine Fauvet	Latifur Khan
Karin Becker	Klaus Dittrich	Roger (Buzz) King
Klemens Boehm	Elena Ferrari	Steven Laufmann
Mic Bowman	Timothy Finin	Qing Li
Omran Bukhres	Avigdor Gal	Cha-Hwa Lin
Tiziana Catarci	Mohand-Said Hacid	Toshiyuki Masui
Ming-Syan Chen	Joachim Hammer	Claudia Medeiros
Umesh Dayal	Arthur ter Hofstede	Ben Chin Ooi
Alex Delis	Michael Huhns	Christine Parent

Evaggelia Pitoura
Allessandro Provetti
Tore Risch
Marek Rusinkiewicz
Felix Saltor
Cyrus Shahabi

Antonio Si
Susan Urban
Athena Vakali
W.M.P. van der Aalst
Kyu-Young Whang
Mike Wooldridge

Jian Yang
Kokou Yetongnon
Arkady Zaslavsky
Roger Zimmermann

DOA 2003 Program Committee

Gul Agha
Matthias Anlauff
Egidio Astesiano
Ozalp Babaoglu
Jean Bacon
Mark Baker
Sean Baker
Roberto Baldoni
Guruduth Banavar
Judith Bishop
Gordon Blair
Michel Chaudron
Shing-Chi Cheung
Francisco (Paco) Curbera
Wolfgang Emmerich
Pascal Felber
Mohand-Said Hacid
Daniel Hagimont
Franz Hauck
Arno Jacobsen
Mehdi Jazayeri

Fabio Kon
Doug Lea
Hong Va Leong
Peter Loehr
Joe Loyall
Frank Manola
Keith Moore
Priya Narasimhan
Andry Rakotonirainy
Heinz-Walter Schmidt
Richard Soley
Jean-Bernard Stefani
Joe Sventek
Stefan Tai
Guatam Thaker
Nalini Venkatasubramanian
Norbert Voelker
Andrew Watson
Doug Wells
Shalini Yajnik

ODBASE 2003 Program Committee

Aberer, Karl
Bussler, Christoph
Carlis, John
Catarci, Tiziana
Chen, Arbee
Colomb, Bob
Dayal, Umeshwar
Decker, Stefan
Delis, Alex
Drew, Pamela

Euzenat, Jérôme
Fensel, Dieter
Gal, Avigdor
Gil, Yolanda
Goble, Carole
Green, Peter
Guarino, Nicola
Kashyap, Vipul
Klas, Wolfgang
Lenzerini, Maurizio

Lee, Dik
Li, Qing
Liu, Chengfei
Liu, Ling
Ling, Tok Wang
Maedche, Alexander
Mark, Leo
Marjanovic, Oliviera
McLeod, Dennis
Mendelzon, Alberto
Missikoff, Michele
Mylopoulos, John

Navathe, Sham
Neuhold, Erich
Papazoglou, Mike
Rosemann, Michael
Sadiq, Shazia
Sadiq, Wasim
Schulz, Karsten
Sheth, Amit
Sycara, Katia
Sure, York
Zeleznikow, John

Table of Contents

Agent Systems and Applications

Cooperation and Evolution in Innovative Applications

Peer-to-Peer Systems

Processing, Availability, and Archival for Cooperative Systems

Trust Management

Advances in Workflow Systems

Information Dissemination Systems

Data Management on the Web

Ontologies, Databases, and Applications of Semantics (ODBASE) 2003 International Conference

Keynotes

Web Services

The Semantic Web

Data Mining and Classification

Ontology Management and Applications

Temporal and Spatial Data

Data Semantics and Metadata

Distributed Objects and Applications (DOA) 2003 International Conference

Keynote

Real-Time

Ubiquitous Systems

Adaptibility and Mobility

Systems Engineering

Software Engineering

Transactions

Author Index

Tenth Anniversasy of CoopIS: Cooperative Information Systems Then and Now

John Mylopoulos

University of Toronto
jm@cs.toronto.edu

Abstract. The idea of focusing research on a new type of information system was launched with a series of workshops, held at IJCAI'91 in Sydney (Australia), Niagara-on-the-Lake (Canada), Como (Italy) and Dagstuhl (Germany). This idea gained a foothold in the research establishment with the First International Conference on (Intelligent and) Cooperative Information Systems (CoopIS for short) held in Rotterdam in 1993, and never looked back since then.
We review some of the early proposals put forward in those early days, and how these have evolved over the years. We also outline our current work, which assumes that cooperative information systems of the future will be agent-oriented software systems combining some of the features of multi-agent systems in AI with methodological principles and down-to-earth constructs from Software Engineering.

Biography

John Mylopoulos received his PhD degree from Princeton University in 1970, and is now Professor of Computer Science at the University of Toronto. John's research interests include Requirements Engineering, Databases, and Knowledge-Based Systems. John was a co-recipient of the most influential paper award at the International Conference on Software Engineering (1994), is serving as president of the Very Large Databases Endowment (1998–2002, 2002–2006), and is a fellow of the American Association for Artificial Intelligence.

R. Meersman et al. (Eds.): CoopIS/DOA/ODBASE 2003, LNCS 2888, p. 1, 2003.
© Springer-Verlag Berlin Heidelberg 2003

PC Co-chairs' Message

Elisa Bertino and Dennis McLeod

The Cooperative Information System (CIS) paradigm has been growing and gaining substantial importance the support of information and service interoperation and integration. CoopIS is the leading conference for researchers and practitioners in CIS. CoopIS brings together researchers from a variety of disciplines such as database modeling and integration, collaborative work, Internet data management, electronic commerce, human-computer interaction, agent technologies, and software architectures (particularly middleware). CoopIS has always had an interdiscipliary focus, and papers that explore applications in these areas are also included.

CoopIS 2003 is a joint event with two other conferences organized within the global theme "On the Move to Meaningful Internet Systems 2003"; these two other associated conferences are "Ontologies, Databases and Applications of Semantics (ODBASE)" and "Distributed Objects and Applications (DOA)". All three events will be hosted in Sicily November 3-7, 2003.

CoopIS 2003 has the theme "Cooperation in Ubiquitous Computing". We see an increasing number of computing systems and devices connected everywhere. The central issue in this vision is the need for these computing systems and devices to cooperate. The key areas covered include:

- **Software and information services for CIS**
  Web information systems and services
  Middleware technologies, mediators, and wrappers
  Interoperability, XML, semantic interoperability
  Multi-databases and workflow
  Mobile and wireless systems and protocols
  Ubiquitous computing environments and tools
  Human-Computer Interactions

- **Agent technologies, systems and architectures for CIS**
  Markets, auctions, exchanges, and coalitions
  Negotiation protocols, matchmaking, and brokering
  Multi-agents and agent societies
  Self-organizing systems, service description
  Learning, perception, and actions in agents
  Distributed problem solving, peer-to-peer cooperation

- **CIS applications and modeling**
  E-commerce, e-government, supply chain
  Use of information in organizations
  Computer-supported cooperative work
  Enterprise knowledge management

R. Meersman et al. (Eds.): CoopIS/DOA/ODBASE 2003, LNCS 2888, pp. 2–3, 2003.
© Springer-Verlag Berlin Heidelberg 2003

Data and knowledge modeling

- **Trustworthy CIS**
  Security, privacy, and quality of information
  Trust models and trust management
  Cooperative access control policies, models, and mechanisms
  Security in dynamic coalitions

This year, CoopIS received approximately 140 original submissions. We were able to accept 32 full papers, and 12 poster papers. Each submitted paper was assigned for review by three program committee members. The accceptance rate for full papers is therefore approximately 23%. We hope that you will find this program rich in research results, ideas and directions and that CoopIS will provide you opportunities to meet researchers from both academia and industry with whom to share your research perspectives.

Many people contributed to CoopIS. Clearly, first thanks go to the authors of all submitted papers. It is, after all, their work that becomes the conference program. The increased number of submissions, compared to the previous years, has shown that CoopIS is increasingly attracting interest from many researchers involved in both basic and applied research. We are grateful for the dedication and hard work of all program committee members in making the review process both thorough and effective. We also thank external referees for their important contribution to the review process.

In addition to those who contributed to the review process, there are others that helped to make the conference a success. Special thanks go to Kwong Yuen Lai for his invaluable help in the review process and program preparation. We would like also to thank Robert Meersman, Douglas Schmidt, Zahir Tari - General co-chairs of CoopIS - for their constant advice and support.

Elisa Bertino, University of Milan, Italy Dennis McLeod, University of Southern California, USA (CoopIS 2003 Program Committee Co-Chairs)

August 2003   Elisa Bertino, University of Milan, Italy
Dennis McLeod, University of Southern California, USA
(CoopIS 2003 Program Committee Co-Chairs)

"Almost Automatic" and Semantic Integration of XML Schemas at Various "Severity" Levels

Pasquale De Meo[1], Giovanni Quattrone[1], Giorgio Terracina[2], and
Domenico Ursino[1]

[1] DIMET, Università Mediterranea di Reggio Calabria, Via Graziella, Località Feo di
Vito, 89060 Reggio Calabria, Italy,
{demeo,quattrone}@ing.unirc.it, ursino@unirc.it
[2] Dipartimento di Matematica, Università della Calabria, Via Pietro Bucci, 87036
Rende (CS), Italy
terracina@mat.unical.it

Abstract. This paper presents a novel approach for the integration of a
set of XML Schemas. The proposed approach is specialized for XML, is
almost automatic, semantic and "light". As a further, original, peculiar-
ity, it is parametric w.r.t. a "severity" level against which the integration task is performed. The paper describes the approach in all details,
illustrates various theoretical results, presents the experiments we have
performed for testing it and, finally, compares it with various related
approaches already proposed in the literature.

1 Introduction

The Web is presently playing a key role for both the publication and the exchange of information among organizations. As a matter of fact, it is becoming
the reference infrastructure for most of the applications conceived to handle
interoperability among partners.

In order to make Web activities easier, W3C (World Wide Web Consortium)
proposed XML (eXtensible Markup Language) as a new standard information
exchange language that unifies representation capabilities, typical of HTML, and
data management features, typical of classical DBMS.

The twofold nature of XML allowed it to gain a great success and, presently,
most of the new documents published on the Web are written in XML. However,
from the data management point of view, XML documents alone have limited
and primitive capabilities. In order to improve these capabilities, in such a way
to make them similar to those typical of classical DBMS, W3C proposed to associate XML Schemas with XML documents. An XML Schema can be considered
as a sort of catalogue of the information typologies that can be found in the
corresponding XML documents; from another point of view, an XML Schema
defines a reference context for the corresponding XML documents.

Certainly, XML exploitation is a key step for improving the interoperability of
Web information sources; however, that alone is not enough to completely fulfill
such a task. Indeed, the heterogeneity of data exchanged over the Web regards

R. Meersman et al. (Eds.): CoopIS/DOA/ODBASE 2003, LNCS 2888, pp. 4–21, 2003.
© Springer-Verlag Berlin Heidelberg 2003

not only their formats but also their semantics. The use of XML allows format heterogeneity to be faced; the exploitation of XML Schemas allows the definition of a reference context for exchanged data and is a first step for handling semantic diversities; however, for a complete and satisfactory management of these last, an integration activity is necessary.

This paper provides a contribution in this setting and proposes an approach for the integration of a set of XML Schemas. Our approach behaves as follows: first it determines interscheme properties [2,7,11,17,15], i.e., terminological and structural relationships holding among attributes and elements belonging to involved XML Schemas. After this, some of the derived properties are exploited for modifying involved Schemas in order to make them structurally and semantically uniform. The modified Schemas are, finally, integrated for obtaining the global Schema.

Let us now examine the peculiarities of our approach in more detail. First, it has been specifically conceived for operating on XML sources. In this sense it differs from many other approaches already presented in the literature which integrate information sources having different formats and structure degrees (e.g., relational databases, XML documents, object-oriented sources and so on). Generally, such approaches translate all involved information sources into a common representation and, then, carry out the integration activity. On the contrary, our approach is specialized for integrating XML Schemas. With regard to this, it is worth pointing out that: *(i)* the integration of XML Schemas will play a more and more relevant role in the future; *(ii)* the exploitation of generic approaches designed to operate on information sources with different formats, for performing the integration of a set of XML Schemas (i.e., a set of sources having the same format), is unnecessarily expensive and inefficient. Indeed, it would require the translation of involved XML Schemas in another format and the translation of the integrated source from such a format back to XML.

Our approach is almost automatic; in this sense it follows the present trend relative to integration techniques. Indeed, owing to the enormous increase of the number of available information sources, all integration approaches proposed in the last years are semi-automatic; generally, they require the human intervention for both a pre-processing phase and the validation of obtained results. The overwhelming amount of sources available on the Web leads each integration task to operate on a great number of sources; this requires a further effort for conceiving more automatic approaches. The approach we are proposing here provides a contribution in this setting since it is almost automatic and requires the user intervention only for validating obtained results.

Our approach is "light"; with regard to this we observe that most of the existing approaches are quite complex, based on a variety of thresholds, weights, parameters and so on; they are very precise but difficult to be applied and fine tuned when involved sources are numerous, complex and belonging to heterogeneous contexts. Our approach does not exploit any threshold or weight; as a consequence, it is simple and light, since it does not need a tuning activity.

Our approach is semantic in that it follows the general trend to take into account the semantics of concepts belonging to involved information sources during the integration task [2,4,7,11]. Given two concepts belonging to different information sources, one of the most common way for determining their semantics consists of examining their neighborhoods since the concepts and the relationships which they are involved in contribute to define their meaning. As a consequence, two concepts, belonging to different information sources, are considered semantically similar and are merged in the integrated source if their neighborhoods are similar.

We argue that all the peculiarities we have examined above are extremely important for a novel approach devoted to integrate XML Schemas. However, the approach we are proposing here is characterized by a further feature that, in our opinion, is extremely innovative and promising; more specifically, it allows the choice of the "severity level" against which the integration task is performed. Such a feature derives from the consideration that applications and scenarios possibly benefiting of an integration task on the Web are numerous and extremely various. In some situations (e.g., in Public Administrations, Finance and so on) the integration process must be very severe in that two concepts must be merged only if they are strongly similar; in such a case a high severity degree is required. In other situations (e.g., tourist Web pages) the integration task can be looser and can decide to merge two concepts having some similarities but presenting also some differences. At the beginning of the integration activity our approach asks the user to specify the desired "severity" degree; this is the only information required to her/him until the end of the integration task, when she/he has to validate obtained results. It is worth pointing out that, to the best of our knowledge, no approaches handling the information source integration at various "severity" levels have been previously presented in the literature. Interestingly enough, a classical approach can be seen as a particular case of that presented in this paper in which a severity level is fixed and all concept merges are performed w.r.t. this level.

2   Neighborhood Construction

In this section we formally introduce the concept of neighborhood of an element or an attribute of an XML Schema. As pointed out in the Introduction, this concept plays a key role in the various algorithms which our approach consists of. Preliminarily we introduce the concept of x-component which allows both elements and attributes of an XML document to be uniformly handled.

Definition 1. Let S be an XML Schema; an *x-component* of S is either an element or an attribute of S. □

An x-component is characterized by its name, its typology (indicating if it is either a complex element or a simple element or an attribute) and its data type.

Definition 2. Let S be an XML Schema; the set of its x-components is denoted as $XCompSet(S)$. □

We introduce now some boolean functions that allow to determine the strength of the relationship existing between two x-components x_S and x_T of an XML Schema S. They will be exploited for deriving interscheme properties and, ultimately, for integrating XML Schemas. The functions are:

- $veryclose(x_S, x_T)$, that returns *true* if and only if: *(i)* $x_T = x_S$, or *(ii)* x_T is an attribute of x_S, or *(iii)* x_T is a simple sub-element of x_S;
- $close(x_S, x_T)$, that returns *true* if and only if *(i)* x_T is a complex sub-element of x_S, or *(ii)* x_T is an element of S and x_S has an $IDREF$ or an $IDREFS$ attribute referring x_T;
- $near(x_S, x_T)$, that returns *true* if and only if either $veryclose(x_S, x_T) = true$ or $close(x_S, x_T) = true$; in all the other cases it returns *false*;
- $reachable(x_S, x_T)$, that returns *true* if and only if there exists a sequence of *distinct* x-components $x_1, x_2, \ldots, x_n$ such that $x_S = x_1, near(x_1, x_2) = near(x_2, x_3) = \ldots = near(x_{n-1}, x_n) = true, x_n = x_T$. $\square$

We are now able to compute the connection cost from x_S to x_T.

Definition 3. Let S be an XML Schema and let x_S and x_T be two x-components of S. The Connection Cost from x_S to x_T, denoted by $CC(x_S, x_T)$, is defined as:

$$CC(x_S, x_T) = \begin{cases} 0 & \text{if } veryclose(x_S, x_T) = true \\ 1 & \text{if } close(x_S, x_T) = true \\ \mathcal{C}_{ST} & \text{if } reachable(x_S, x_T) = true \text{ and } near(x_S, x_T) = false \\ \infty & \text{if } reachable(x_S, x_T) = false \end{cases}$$

where $\mathcal{C}_{ST} = min_{x_A} (CC(x_S, x_A) + CC(x_A, x_T))$ for each x_A such that $reachable(x_S, x_A) = reachable(x_A, x_T) = true$.

We are now provided with all tools necessary to define the concept of neighborhood of an x-component.

Definition 4. Let S be an XML Schema and let x_S be an x-component of S. The jth neighborhood of x_S is defined as:

$$neighborhood(x_S, j) = \{x_T | \ x_T \in XCompSet(S), CC(x_S, x_T) \le j\}$$

$\square$

The construction of all neighborhoods can be easily carried out with the support of the data structure introduced in the next definition.

Definition 5. Let D be an XML document and let S be the corresponding XML Schema. The *XS-Graph* relative to S and D is an oriented labeled graph defined as $XG(S, D) = \langle N(S), A(S, D) \rangle$. Here, $N(S)$ is the set of nodes of $XG(S, D)$; there is a node in $XG(S, D)$ for each x-component of S. $A(S, D)$ is the set of arcs of $XG(S, D)$; there is an arc $\langle N_S, N_T, f_{ST} \rangle$ in $XG(S, D)$ for each pair (x_S, x_T) such that $near(x_S, x_T) = true$; in particular, N_S (resp., N_T) is the node of $XG(S, D)$ corresponding to x_S (resp., x_T) and $f_{ST} = CC(x_S, x_T)$. $\square$

The following proposition measures the computational complexity of the construction of $XG(S, D)$.

Proposition 1. Let D be an XML document and let S be the corresponding XML Schema. Let n be the number of x-components of S and let N_{inst} be the number of instances of D. The worst case time complexity for constructing $XG(S, D)$ from S and D is $O(max\{n, N_{inst}^2\})$.   □

With regard to this result we observe that, in an XML document, in order to determine the element which an IDREFS attribute refers to, it is necessary to examine the document, since neither the DTD nor the XML Schema provide such an information. As a consequence, the dependency of the computational complexity from N_{inst} cannot be avoided. However, we point out that the quadratic dependency from N_{inst} is mainly a theoretical result; indeed, it derives from the consideration that each IDREFS attribute could refer to N_{inst} components. Actually, in real situations, each IDREFS attribute refers to a very limited number of instances; as a consequence, the dependency of the computational complexity from N_{inst} is generally linear.

The next theorem determines the worst case time complexity for computing all neighborhoods of all x-components of an XML Schema S.

Theorem 1. Let $XG(S, D)$ be the XS-Graph associated with an XML document D and an XML Schema S and let n be the number of x-components of S. The worst case time complexity for computing all neighborhoods of all x-components of S is $O(n^3)$.   □

Example 1. Consider the XML Schema S_1, shown in Figure 1, representing a shop. Here *customer* is an x-component and its typology is "complex element" since it is an element declared with a "complex type". Analogously *SSN* is an x-component, its typology is "attribute" and its data type is "string". All the other x-components of S_1, the corresponding typologies and data types can be determined similarly.

In S_1, *veryclose(customer, firstName)* = *true* because *firstName* is a simple sub-element of *customer*; analogously *veryclose(customer, SSN)* = *true* and *close(customer, musicAcquirement)* = *true*. As for neighborhoods, we have that:

$$neighborhood(customer, 0) = \{customer,\ SSN,\ firstName,\ lastName,\ address,$$
$$gender,\ birthDate,\ profession\}$$

All the other neighborhoods can be determined similarly.   □

3   Extraction of Interscheme Properties

In this section we illustrate an approach for computing interscheme properties among x-components belonging to different XML Schemas. As pointed out in the Introduction, their knowledge is crucial for the integration task. The interscheme properties considered in this paper are *synonymies* and *homonymies*. Given two

```
<?xml version="1.0" encoding="UTF-8"?> <xs:schema
xmlns:xs="http://www.w3.org/2001/XMLSchema">
    <!-- Definition of attributes -->
    <xs:attribute name="SSN" type="xs:string"/>
    <xs:attribute name="code" type="xs:ID"/>
    <xs:attribute name="acquiredBooks" type="xs:IDREFS"/>
    <xs:attribute name="acquiredMusics" type="xs:IDREFS"/>
    <xs:attribute name="acquirementDate" type="xs:date"/>
    <!-- Definition of simple elements -->
    <xs:element name="firstName" type="xs:string"/>
    <xs:element name="lastName" type="xs:string"/>
    <xs:element name="address" type="xs:string"/>
    <xs:element name="gender" type="xs:string"/>
    <xs:element name="birthDate" type="xs:date"/>
    <xs:element name="profession" type="xs:string"/>
    <xs:element name="artist" type="xs:string"/>
    <xs:element name="author" type="xs:string"/>
    <xs:element name="title" type="xs:string"/>
    <xs:element name="pubYear" type="xs:integer"/>
    <xs:element name="publisher" type="xs:string"/>
    <xs:element name="genre" type="xs:string"/>
    <xs:element name="support" type="xs:string"/>
    <!-- Definition of complex elements -->
    <xs:element name="bookAcquirement">
        <xs:complexType>
            <xs:attribute ref="acquirementDate"/>
            <xs:attribute ref="acquiredBooks"/>
        </xs:complexType>
    </xs:element>
    <xs:element name="musicAcquirement">
        <xs:complexType>
            <xs:attribute ref="acquirementDate"/>
            <xs:attribute ref="acquiredMusics"/>
        </xs:complexType>
    </xs:element>
    <xs:element name="customer">
        <xs:complexType>
            <xs:sequence>
                <xs:element ref="firstName"/>
                <xs:element ref="lastName"/>
                <xs:element ref="address"/>
                <xs:element ref="gender"/>
                <xs:element ref="birthDate"/>
                <xs:element ref="profession"/>
                <xs:element ref="bookAcquirement"
                    minOccurs="0" maxOccurs="unbounded"/>
                <xs:element ref="musicAcquirement"
                    minOccurs="0" maxOccurs="unbounded"/>
            </xs:sequence>
            <xs:attribute ref="SSN" use="required"/>
        </xs:complexType>
    </xs:element>
    <xs:element name="music">
        <xs:complexType>
            <xs:sequence>
                <xs:element ref="artist" maxOccurs="unbounded"/>
                <xs:element ref="title"/>
                <xs:element ref="pubYear"/>
                <xs:element ref="genre"/>
                <xs:element ref="support"/>
            </xs:sequence>
            <xs:attribute ref="code" use="required"/>
        </xs:complexType>
    </xs:element>
    <xs:element name="book">
        <xs:complexType>
            <xs:sequence>
                <xs:element ref="author" maxOccurs="unbounded"/>
                <xs:element ref="title"/>
                <xs:element ref="publisher"/>
                <xs:element ref="pubYear"/>
                <xs:element ref="genre"/>
            </xs:sequence>
            <xs:attribute ref="code" use="required"/>
        </xs:complexType>
    </xs:element>
    <!-- Definition of root element -->
    <xs:element name="shop">
        <xs:complexType>
            <xs:sequence>
                <xs:element ref="customer" maxOccurs="unbounded"/>
                <xs:element ref="music" maxOccurs="unbounded"/>
                <xs:element ref="book" maxOccurs="unbounded"/>
            </xs:sequence>
        </xs:complexType>
    </xs:element>
</xs:schema>
```

Fig. 1. The XML Schema S_1

x-components x_A and x_B belonging to different XML Schemas, a *synonymy* between x_A and x_B indicates that they represent the same concept; an *homonymy* between x_A and x_B denotes that they indicate different concepts yet having the same name.

Our technique for computing interscheme properties is semantic [2,7,15] in that, in order to determine the meaning of an x-component, it examines the "context" which it has been defined in. It requires the presence of a thesaurus storing lexical synonymies existing among the terms of a language. In particular, it exploits the English language and WordNet[1] [14]. The technique first extracts all synonymies and, then, exploits them for deriving homonymies.

3.1 Derivation of Synonymies

As previously pointed out, in order to verify if two x-components x_{1_j}, belonging to an XML Schema S_1, and x_{2_k}, belonging to an XML Schema S_2, are synonymous, it is necessary to examine their neighborhoods. In particular, our approach operates as follows.

---

[1] Actually, in the prototype implementing our technique, WordNet is accessed by a suitable API.

First it considers $neighborhood(x_{1_j}, 0)$ and $neighborhood(x_{2_k}, 0)$ and determines if they are similar. This decision is made by computing the objective function associated with the maximum weight matching of a suitable bipartite graph constructed from the x-components of $neighborhood(x_{1_j}, 0)$ and $neighborhood(x_{2_k}, 0)$ and their lexical synonymies as stored in the thesaurus (see below for all details). If $neighborhood(x_{1_j}, 0)$ and $neighborhood(x_{2_k}, 0)$ are similar it is possible to conclude that x_{1_j} and x_{2_k} are *synonymous* [2,15]. However, observe that $neighborhood(x_{1_j}, 0)$ (resp., $neighborhood(x_{2_k}, 0)$) takes into account only attributes and simple elements of x_{1_j} (resp., x_{2_k}); therefore, it considers quite a limited context. As a consequence, the synonymy between x_{1_j} and x_{2_k} derived in this case is more "syntactic" than "semantic" [7,2,15].

If we need a more "severe" level of synonymy detection it is necessary to require not only the similarity of $neighborhood(x_{1_j}, 0)$ and $neighborhood(x_{2_k}, 0)$ but also that of the other neighborhoods of x_{1_j} and x_{2_k}. More specifically, it is possible to introduce a "severity" level u at which synonymies are derived and to say that x_{1_j} and x_{2_k} are synonymous with severity level equal to u if $neighborhood(x_{1_j}, v)$ is similar to $neighborhood(x_{2_k}, v)$ for each v less than or equal to u. The following proposition states an upper bound to the severity level that can be specified for x-component synonymy derivation.

Proposition 2. Let S_1 and S_2 be two XML documents; let x_{1_j} (resp., x_{2_k}) be an x-component of S_1 (resp., S_2); finally, let m be the maximum between the number of complex elements of S_1 and S_2. The maximum severity level possibly existing for the synonymy between x_{1_j} and x_{2_k} is $m - 1$.   □

A function *synonymous* can be defined which receives two x-components x_{1_j} and x_{2_k} and an integer u and returns *true* if x_{1_j} and x_{2_k} are synonymous with a severity level equal to u, *false* otherwise.

As previously pointed out, computing the synonymy between two x-components x_{1_j} and x_{2_k} implies determining when two neighborhoods are similar. In order to carry out such a task, it is necessary to compute the objective function associated with the maximum weight matching relative to a specific bipartite graph obtained from the x-components of the neighborhoods into consideration.

More specifically, let $BG(x_{1_j}, x_{2_k}, u) = \langle N(x_{1_j}, x_{2_k}, u), A(x_{1_j}, x_{2_k}, u) \rangle$ be the bipartite graph associated with $neighborhood(x_{1_j}, u)$ and $neighborhood(x_{2_k}, u)$ (in the following we shall use the notation $BG(u)$ instead of $BG(x_{1_j}, x_{2_k}, u)$ when this is not confusing). In $BG(u)$, $N(u) = P(u) \cup Q(u)$ represents the set of nodes; there is a node in $P(u)$ (resp., $Q(u)$) for each x-component of $neighborhood(x_{1_j}, u)$ (resp., $neighborhood(x_{2_k}, u)$). $A(u)$ is the set of arcs; there is an arc between $p_e \in P(u)$ and $q_f \in Q(u)$ if a synonymy between the names of the x-components associated with p_e and q_f holds in the reference thesaurus. The maximum weight matching for $BG(u)$ is a set $A'(u) \subseteq A(u)$ of edges such that, for each node $x \in P(u) \cup Q(u)$, there is at most one edge of $A'(u)$ incident onto x and $|A'(u)|$ is maximum (for algorithms solving the maximum weight matching problem, see [8]). The objective function we associate with the maximum weight matching is $\phi_{BG}(u) = \frac{2|A'(u)|}{|P(u)| + |Q(u)|}$.

We assume that if $\phi_{BG}(u) > \frac{1}{2}$ then $neighborhood(x_{1_j}, u)$ and $neighborhood(x_{2_k}, u)$ are similar; otherwise they are dissimilar. Such an assumption derives from the consideration that two sets of objects can be considered similar if the number of similar components is greater than the number of the dissimilar ones or, in other words, if the number of similar components is greater than half of the total number of components.

We present now the following theorem stating the computational complexity of the x-components' similarity extraction.

Theorem 2. Let S_1 and S_2 be two XML documents. Let x_{1_j} (resp., x_{2_k}) be an x-component of S_1 (resp., S_2). Let u be the selected severity level. Finally, let p be the maximum between the cardinality of $neighborhood(x_{1_j}, u)$ and $neighborhood(x_{2_k}, u)$. The worst case time complexity for computing $synonymous(x_{1_j}, x_{2_k}, u)$ is $O((u+1) \times p^3)$. □

Corollary 1. Let S_1 and S_2 be two XML documents. Let u be the severity level. Let m be the maximum between the number of complex elements of S_1 and S_2. Finally, let q be the maximum cardinality relative to a neighborhood of S_1 or S_2. The worst case time complexity for deriving all synonymies existing, at the severity level u, between S_1 and S_2 is $O((u+1) \times q^3 \times m^2)$. □

3.2   Derivation of Homonymies

After synonymies among x-components of S_1 and S_2 have been extracted, homonymies can be directly derived from them. More specifically, we say that an homonymy holds between x_{1_j} and x_{2_k} with a severity level equal to u if $synonymous(x_{1_j}, x_{2_k}, u) = false$ and both x_{1_j} and x_{2_k} have the same name.

It is possible to define a boolean function $homonymous$, which receives two x-components x_{1_j} and x_{2_k} and an integer u and returns $true$ if there exists an homonymy between x_{1_j} and x_{2_k} with a severity level equal to u; $homonymous$ returns $false$ otherwise.

Example 2. Consider the XML Schemas S_1 and S_2, shown in Figures 1 and 2. Consider also the x-components $customer_{[S_1]}$[2] and $client_{[S_2]}$. In order to check if they are synonymous with a severity level 0, it is necessary to compute the function $synonymous(customer_{[S_1]}, client_{[S_2]}, 0)$. Now, $neighborhood(customer_{[S_1]}, 0)$ has been shown in Example 1; as for $neighborhood(client_{[S_2]}, 0)$, we have:

$$neighborhood(client_{[S_2]}, 0) = \{client_{[S_2]}, SSN_{[S_2]}, firstName_{[S_2]},$$
$$lastName_{[S_2]}, address_{[S_2]}, phone_{[S_2]}, email_{[S_2]}\}$$

The function $\phi_{BG}(0)$ computed by $synonymous$ in this case is $\frac{2|A'(0)|}{|P(0)|+|Q(0)|} = \frac{2 \times 5}{8+7} = 0.67 > \frac{1}{2}$; therefore $synonymous(customer_{[S_1]}, client_{[S_2]}, 0) = true$.

In an analogous way, $synonymous(customer_{[S_1]}, client_{[S_2]}, 1)$ can be computed. In particular, in this case, $\phi_{BG}(1) = 0.43 < \frac{1}{2}$; as a consequence,

---

[2] Here and in the following, we use the notation $x_{[S]}$ to indicate the x-component x of the XML Schema S.

```
<?xml version="1.0" encoding="UTF-8"?>
<xs:schema xmlns:xs="http://www.w3.org/2001/XMLSchema">
  <!-- Definition of attributes -->
  <xs:attribute name="SSN" type="xs:string"/>
  <xs:attribute name="code" type="xs:ID"/>
  <xs:attribute name="purchasedCDDAs" type="xs:IDREFS"/>
  <xs:attribute name="purchasedMiniDisks" type="xs:IDREFS"/>
  <xs:attribute name="purchaseDate" type="xs:date"/>
  <xs:attribute name="quantity" type="xs:integer"/>
  <xs:attribute name="bitRate" type="xs:integer"/>
  <!-- Definition of simple elements -->
  <xs:element name="firstName" type="xs:string"/>
  <xs:element name="lastName" type="xs:string"/>
  <xs:element name="address" type="xs:string"/>
  <xs:element name="phone" type="xs:string"/>
  <xs:element name="email" type="xs:string"/>
  <xs:element name="artist" type="xs:string"/>
  <xs:element name="title" type="xs:string"/>
  <xs:element name="song" type="xs:string"/>
  <xs:element name="year" type="xs:integer"/>
  <xs:element name="genre" type="xs:string"/>
  <!-- Definition of complex elements -->
  <xs:element name="CDDAPurchase">
    <xs:complexType>
      <xs:attribute ref="purchaseDate"/>
      <xs:attribute ref="purchasedCDDAs"/>
    </xs:complexType>
  </xs:element>
  <xs:element name="miniDiskPurchase">
    <xs:complexType>
      <xs:attribute ref="purchaseDate"/>
      <xs:attribute ref="purchasedMiniDisks"/>
    </xs:complexType>
  </xs:element>
  <xs:element name="client">
    <xs:complexType>
      <xs:sequence>
        <xs:element ref="firstName"/>
        <xs:element ref="lastName"/>
        <xs:element ref="address"/>
        <xs:element ref="phone" minOccurs="0"
          maxOccurs="unbounded"/>
        <xs:element ref="email" minOccurs="0"
          maxOccurs="unbounded"/>
        <xs:element ref="CDDAPurchase" minOccurs="0"
          maxOccurs="unbounded"/>
        <xs:element ref="miniDiskPurchase" minOccurs="0"
          maxOccurs="unbounded"/>
      </xs:sequence>
      <xs:attribute ref="SSN" use="required"/>
    </xs:complexType>
  </xs:element>
  <xs:element name="CDDA">
    <xs:complexType>
      <xs:attribute ref="code" use="required"/>
      <xs:attribute ref="quantity"/>
    </xs:complexType>
  </xs:element>
  <xs:element name="miniDisk">
    <xs:complexType>
      <xs:attribute ref="code" use="required"/>
      <xs:attribute ref="quantity"/>
      <xs:attribute ref="bitRate"/>
    </xs:complexType>
  </xs:element>
  <xs:element name="composition">
    <xs:complexType>
      <xs:sequence>
        <xs:element ref="artist" maxOccurs="unbounded"/>
        <xs:element ref="title"/>
        <xs:element ref="song" maxOccurs="unbounded"/>
        <xs:element ref="year"/>
        <xs:element ref="genre"/>
        <xs:element ref="CDDA" minOccurs="0"/>
        <xs:element ref="miniDisk" minOccurs="0"/>
      </xs:sequence>
    </xs:complexType>
  </xs:element>
  <!-- Definition of root element -->
  <xs:element name="store">
    <xs:complexType>
      <xs:sequence>
        <xs:element ref="client" maxOccurs="unbounded"/>
        <xs:element ref="composition" maxOccurs="unbounded"/>
      </xs:sequence>
    </xs:complexType>
  </xs:element>
</xs:schema>
```

Fig. 2. The XML Schema S_2

$synonymous(customer_{[S_1]}, client_{[S_2]}, 1) = false$, i.e. $customer_{[S_1]}$ and $client_{[S_2]}$ cannot be considered synonymous with a severity level 1.

All the other synonymies can be derived analogously. As for these Schemas, no homonymy has been found.   □

4   The Integration Task

In this section we propose an integration algorithm which receives two XML Schemas S_1 and S_2 and a severity level u and returns the integrated XML Schema S_G. The algorithm consists of two steps, namely: (i) construction of a *Merge Dictionary* $MD(u)$ and a *Rename Dictionary* $RD(u)$; (ii) exploitation of $MD(u)$ and $RD(u)$ for obtaining the global Schema.

Preliminarily it is necessary to observe that in XML Schemas there exists a large variety of data types. Some of them, e.g. *Byte* and *Int*, are compatible in the sense that each attribute or simple element whose type is *Byte* can be treated as an attribute or a simple element whose type is *Int*; in this case *Int* is said *more general* than *Byte*. Other types, e.g. *Int* and *Date*, are not compatible. Compatibility rules are analogous to the corresponding ones valid for high level programming languages.

4.1 Construction of MD(u) and RD(u)

At the end of interscheme property derivation, it could happen that an x-component of a Schema is synonymous (resp., homonymous) with more than one x-components of the other Schema. The integration algorithm we are proposing here needs each x-component of a Schema to be synonymous (resp., homonymous) with at most one x-component of the other Schema. In order to satisfy this requirement, it is necessary to construct a *Merge Dictionary* $MD(u)$ and an *Rename Dictionary* $RD(u)$ by suitably filtering previously derived synonymies and homonymies.

The construction of $MD(u)$ begins with the definition of a support bipartite graph $SimG(u) = \langle SimNSet_1(u) \cup SimNSet_2(u), SimASet(u) \rangle$.

There is a node n_{1_j} (resp., n_{2_k}) in $SimNSet_1(u)$ (resp., $SimNSet_2(u)$) for each complex element E_{1_j} (resp., E_{2_k}) belonging to S_1 (resp., S_2). There is an arc $A_{jk} = \langle n_{1_j}, n_{2_k} \rangle \in SimASet(u)$ if $synonymous(E_{1_j}, E_{2_k}, u) = true$; the label of each arc A_{jk} is $f(n_{1_j}, n_{2_k})$ where:

$$f(n_{1_j}, n_{2_k}) = \begin{cases} \phi_{BG}(E_{1_j}, E_{2_k}, u) & \text{if } A_{jk} \in SimASet(u) \\ 0 & otherwise \end{cases}$$

Function f has been defined in such a way to maximize the sum of the similarity degrees involving complex elements of S_1 and S_2.

After this, a maximum weight matching is computed on $SimG(u)$; this selects a subset $SimASubSet(u) \subseteq SimASet(u)$ which maximizes the objective function $\phi_{Sim}(u) = \sum_{\langle n_{1_j}, n_{2_k} \rangle \in SimASubSet(u)} f(n_{1_j}, n_{2_k})$.

For each arc $A'_{jk} = \langle n'_{1_j}, n'_{2_k} \rangle \in SimASubSet(u)$ a pair $\langle E'_{1_j}, E'_{2_k} \rangle$ is added to $MD(u)$.

In addition, let E'_{1_j} (resp., E'_{2_k}) be a complex element of S_1 (resp., S_2) such that $\langle E'_{1_j}, E'_{2_k} \rangle \in MD(u)$ and let x'_{1_j} (resp., x'_{2_k}) be an attribute or a simple element of E'_{1_j} (resp., E'_{2_k}); then $\langle x'_{1_j}, x'_{2_k} \rangle$ is added to $MD(u)$ if *(i)* a synonymy between the name of x'_{1_j} and that of x'_{2_k} holds in the reference thesaurus and the data types of x'_{1_j} and x'_{2_k} are compatible, or *(ii)* x'_{1_j} and x'_{2_k} have the same name, the same typology and compatible data types.

After $MD(u)$ has been constructed, it is possible to derive $RD(u)$. More specifically, a pair of x-components $\langle x''_{1_j}, x''_{2_k} \rangle$ is added to $RD(u)$ if x''_{1_j} and x''_{2_k} are two elements or two attributes having the same name and $\langle x''_{1_j}, x''_{2_k} \rangle \notin MD(u)$.

4.2 Construction of the Global XML Schema

After $MD(u)$ and $RD(u)$ have been derived, it is possible to exploit them for constructing a global Schema S_G. Our integration algorithm assumes that S_1 and S_2 are represented in the *referenced style*, i.e., that they consist of sequences of elements and that each element may refer to other elements by means of the *ref* attribute. Actually, an XML Schema could be defined in various other ways (e.g., with the *inline style*); however, simple rules can be easily defined for translating it in the *referenced style* (see [1] for more details on the various definition styles).

More formally, S_1 and S_2 can be represented as:

$$S_1 = \langle x_{1_1}, x_{1_2}, \ldots, x_{1_i}, \ldots, x_{1_n} \rangle; \; S_2 = \langle x_{2_1}, x_{2_2}, \ldots, x_{2_j}, \ldots, x_{2_m} \rangle$$

where $x_{1_1}, \ldots, x_{1_n}, x_{2_1}, \ldots, x_{2_m}$ are x-components. A first, rough, version of S_G can be obtained by constructing a list containing all the x-components of S_1 and S_2:

$$S_G = \langle x_{1_1}, \ldots, x_{1_n}, x_{2_1}, \ldots, x_{2_m} \rangle$$

This version of S_G could present some redundancies and/or ambiguities. In order to remove them and, consequently, to refine S_G, $MD(u)$ and $RD(u)$ must be examined and some tasks must be performed for each of the properties they store. More specifically, consider $MD(u)$ and let $\langle E_{1_j}, E_{2_k} \rangle \in MD(u)$ be a synonymy between two complex elements. E_{1_j} and E_{2_k} are merged into a complex element E_{jk}. The name of E_{jk} is one between the names of E_{1_j} and E_{2_k}. The set of sub-elements of E_{jk} is obtained by applying the xs:sequence indicator to the sets of sub-elements of E_{1_j} and E_{2_k}; the list of attributes of E_{jk} is formed by the attributes of E_{1_j} and E_{2_k}. Note that, after these tasks have been carried out, it could happen that:

- A tuple $\langle A'_{jk}, A''_{jk} \rangle$, such that A'_{jk} and A''_{jk} are attributes of E_{jk}, belongs to $MD(u)$. In this case A'_{jk} and A''_{jk} are merged into an attribute A^*_{jk}; the name of A^*_{jk} is one between the names of A'_{jk} and A''_{jk}; the type of A^*_{jk} is the most general one between those of A'_{jk} and A''_{jk}.
- A tuple $\langle E'_{jk}, E''_{jk} \rangle$, such that E'_{jk} and E''_{jk} are simple elements of E_{jk}, belongs to $MD(u)$. In this case E'_{jk} and E''_{jk} are merged into an element E^*_{jk}; the name of E^*_{jk} is one between the names of E'_{jk} and E''_{jk}; the type of E^*_{jk} is the most general one between those of E'_{jk} and E''_{jk}; the $minOccurs$ (resp., the $maxOccurs$) indicator of E^*_{jk} is the minimum (resp., the maximum) between the corresponding ones relative to E'_{jk} and E''_{jk}.
- A tuple $\langle E''_{jk}, A''_{jk} \rangle$, such that E''_{jk} is a simple sub-element of E_{jk} and A''_{jk} is an attribute of E_{jk}, belongs to $MD(u)$. In this case, A''_{jk} is removed since its information content is equivalent to that of E''_{jk} and the representation of an information content by means of an element is more general than that obtained by exploiting an attribute.

After this, all references to E_{1_j} and E_{2_k} in S_G are transformed into references to E_{jk}; the $maxOccurs$ and the $minOccurs$ indicators associated with E_{jk} are derived from the corresponding ones relative to E_{1_j} and E_{2_k} and, finally, E_{1_j} is replaced by E_{jk} whereas E_{2_k} is removed from S_G.

After $MD(u)$ has been examined, it is necessary to consider $RD(u)$; in particular, let $\langle x_{1_j}, x_{2_k} \rangle$ be a tuple of $RD(u)$ such that x_{1_j} and x_{2_k} are both elements or both attributes of the same element. In this case it is necessary to modify the name of either x_{1_j} or x_{2_k} and all the corresponding references.

Observe that, after all these activities have been performed, S_G could contain two root elements. Such a situation occurs when the root elements E_{1_r} of S_1 and E_{2_r} of S_2 are not synonymous. In this case it is necessary to create a new root element E_{G_r} in S_G whose set of sub-elements is obtained by applying the xs:all

Table 1. The Merge Dictionary $MD(0)$

x-component of S_1	x-component of S_2	x-component of S_1	x-component of S_2
shop	store	customer	client
music	composition	SSN	SSN
firstName	firstName	lastName	lastName
address	address	code	code
artist	artist	title	title
pubYear	year	genre	genre

indicator to E_{1_r} and E_{2_r}. The occurrence indicators associated with E_{1_r} and E_{2_r} are $minOccurs = 0$ and $maxOccurs = 1$.

As for the computational complexity of the integration task, it is possible to state the following theorem.

Theorem 3. Let S_1 and S_2 be two XML Schemas, let n be the maximum between $|XCompSet(S_1)|$ and $|XCompSet(S_2)|$ and let m be the maximum between the number of complex elements of S_1 and the number of complex elements of S_2. The worst case time complexity for integrating S_1 and S_2 into a global Schema S_G is $O(m \times n^2)$. $\square$

Example 3. Assume a user wants to integrate the XML Schemas S_1 and S_2, shown in Figures 1 and 2, and the severity level she/he specifies is 0. $MD(0)$ is illustrated in Table 1; $RD(0)$ is empty because no homonymy has been found among x-components of S_1 and S_2 (see Example 2). Initially a rough version of S_G is constructed that contains all the x-components of S_1 and S_2; the refined version of S_G is obtained by removing (possible) redundancies and/or ambiguities present therein.

The first step of the refinement phase examines all synonymies among complex elements stored in $MD(0)$. As an example, consider the synonymous elements $customer_{[S_1]}$ and $client_{[S_2]}$; they must be merged in one single element. This task is carried out as follows. First a new element $customer_{[S_G]}$ is created in S_G. The set of sub-elements of $customer_{[S_G]}$ is obtained by applying the xs:sequence indicator to the sets of sub-elements of $customer_{[S_1]}$ and $client_{[S_2]}$; the list of attributes of $customer_{[S_G]}$ is formed by the attributes of $customer_{[S_1]}$ and $client_{[S_2]}$. At the end of this task, $customer_{[S_G]}$ contains two attributes named SSN. Since the tuple $\langle SSN, SSN \rangle$ belongs to $MD(0)$, the two attributes are merged into a single attribute SSN having type "string". An analogous procedure is applied to sub-element pairs $\langle firstName_{[S_1]}, firstName_{[S_2]} \rangle$, $\langle lastName_{[S_1]}, lastName_{[S_2]} \rangle$ and $\langle address_{[S_1]}, address_{[S_2]} \rangle$.

After this, all references to $customer_{[S_1]}$ and $client_{[S_2]}$ are transformed into references to $customer_{[S_G]}$; finally, $customer_{[S_1]}$ is replaced by $customer_{[S_G]}$ where-as $client_{[S_2]}$ is removed from S_G. All the other synonymies stored in $MD(0)$ are handled similarly. Since no homonymy has been found, no further action is necessary. The global XML Schema S_G, obtained at the end of the integration activity, is shown in Figure 3. $\square$

```xml
<?xml version="1.0" encoding="UTF-8"?>
<xs:schema xmlns:xs="http://www.w3.org/2001/XMLSchema">
    <!-- Definition of attributes -->
    <xs:attribute name="SSN" type="xs:string"/>
    <xs:attribute name="code" type="xs:ID"/>
    <xs:attribute name="acquiredBooks" type="xs:IDREFS"/>
    <xs:attribute name="acquiredMusics" type="xs:IDREFS"/>
    <xs:attribute name="acquirementDate" type="xs:date"/>
    <xs:attribute name="purchasedCDDAs" type="xs:IDREFS"/>
    <xs:attribute name="purchasedMiniDisks" type="xs:IDREFS"/>
    <xs:attribute name="purchaseDate" type="xs:date"/>
    <xs:attribute name="quantity" type="xs:integer"/>
    <xs:attribute name="bitRate" type="xs:integer"/>
    <!-- Definition of simple elements -->
    <xs:element name="firstName" type="xs:string"/>
    <xs:element name="lastName" type="xs:string"/>
    <xs:element name="address" type="xs:string"/>
    <xs:element name="gender" type="xs:string"/>
    <xs:element name="birthDate" type="xs:date"/>
    <xs:element name="profession" type="xs:string"/>
    <xs:element name="phone" type="xs:string"/>
    <xs:element name="email" type="xs:string"/>
    <xs:element name="artist" type="xs:string"/>
    <xs:element name="author" type="xs:string"/>
    <xs:element name="title" type="xs:string"/>
    <xs:element name="song" type="xs:string"/>
    <xs:element name="pubYear" type="xs:integer"/>
    <xs:element name="publisher" type="xs:string"/>
    <xs:element name="genre" type="xs:string"/>
    <xs:element name="support" type="xs:string"/>
    <!-- Definition of complex elements -->
    <xs:element name="bookAcquirement">
        <xs:complexType>
            <xs:attribute ref="acquirementDate"/>
            <xs:attribute ref="acquiredBooks"/>
        </xs:complexType>
    </xs:element>
    <xs:element name="musicAcquirement">
        <xs:complexType>
            <xs:attribute ref="acquirementDate"/>
            <xs:attribute ref="acquiredMusics"/>
        </xs:complexType>
    </xs:element>
    <xs:element name="book">
        <xs:complexType>
            <xs:sequence>
                <xs:element ref="author" maxOccurs="unbounded"/>
                <xs:element ref="title"/>
                <xs:element ref="publisher"/>
                <xs:element ref="pubYear"/>
                <xs:element ref="genre"/>
            </xs:sequence>
            <xs:attribute ref="code" use="required"/>
        </xs:complexType>
    </xs:element>
    <xs:element name="CDDAPurchase">
        <xs:complexType>
            <xs:attribute ref="purchaseDate"/>
            <xs:attribute ref="purchasedCDDAs"/>
        </xs:complexType>
    </xs:element>
    <xs:element name="miniDiskPurchase">
        <xs:complexType>
            <xs:attribute ref="purchaseDate"/>
            <xs:attribute ref="purchasedMiniDisks"/>
        </xs:complexType>
    </xs:element>

    <xs:element name="customer">
        <xs:complexType>
            <xs:sequence>
                <xs:element ref="firstName"/>
                <xs:element ref="lastName"/>
                <xs:element ref="address"/>
                <xs:element ref="gender"/>
                <xs:element ref="birthDate"/>
                <xs:element ref="profession"/>
                <xs:element ref="bookAcquirement"
                    minOccurs="0" maxOccurs="unbounded"/>
                <xs:element ref="musicAcquirement"
                    minOccurs="0" maxOccurs="unbounded"/>
                <xs:element ref="phone"
                    minOccurs="0" maxOccurs="unbounded"/>
                <xs:element ref="email"
                    minOccurs="0" maxOccurs="unbounded"/>
                <xs:element ref="CDDAPurchase"
                    minOccurs="0" maxOccurs="unbounded"/>
                <xs:element ref="miniDiskPurchase"
                    minOccurs="0" maxOccurs="unbounded"/>
            </xs:sequence>
            <xs:attribute ref="SSN" use="required"/>
        </xs:complexType>
    </xs:element>
    <xs:element name="CDDA">
        <xs:complexType>
            <xs:attribute ref="code"/>
            <xs:attribute ref="quantity"/>
        </xs:complexType>
    </xs:element>
    <xs:element name="miniDisk">
        <xs:complexType>
            <xs:attribute ref="code"/>
            <xs:attribute ref="quantity"/>
            <xs:attribute ref="bitRate"/>
        </xs:complexType>
    </xs:element>
    <xs:element name="music">
        <xs:complexType>
            <xs:sequence>
                <xs:element ref="artist" maxOccurs="unbounded"/>
                <xs:element ref="title"/>
                <xs:element ref="pubYear"/>
                <xs:element ref="genre"/>
                <xs:element ref="support" minOccurs="0"/>
                <xs:element ref="song"
                    minOccurs="0" maxOccurs="unbounded"/>
                <xs:element ref="CDDA" minOccurs="0"/>
                <xs:element ref="miniDisk" minOccurs="0"/>
            </xs:sequence>
            <xs:attribute ref="code"/>
        </xs:complexType>
    </xs:element>
    <!-- Definition of root element -->
    <xs:element name="shop">
        <xs:complexType>
            <xs:sequence>
                <xs:element ref="customer"
                    maxOccurs="unbounded"/>
                <xs:element ref="music"
                    maxOccurs="unbounded"/>
                <xs:element ref="book"
                    minOccurs="0" maxOccurs="unbounded"/>
            </xs:sequence>
        </xs:complexType>
    </xs:element>
</xs:schema>
```

Fig. 3. The integrated XML Schema S_G

5   Experiments

To test the performances of our approach we have carried out various experiments; these have been performed on several XML Schemas taken from different application contexts. Involved XML Schemas were very heterogeneous in their dimensions; indeed, the number of x-components associated with them ranged from tens to hundreds.

The first series of experiments has been conceived for measuring correctness and completeness of our interscheme property derivation algorithm. In particular, *correctness* lists the percentage of properties returned by our techniques agreeing with those provided by humans; *completeness* lists the percentage of properties returned by our approach with regard to the set of properties provided by humans.

In more detail, we proceeded as follows: *(i)* we ran our algorithms on several pairs of XML Schemas and collected the returned results; *(ii)* for each pair of Schemas we asked humans to specify a set of significant interscheme properties; *(iii)* we computed the overall quality figures by comparing the set of properties obtained as described at points 1 and 2 above.

As for severity level 0, we have obtained a correctness equal to 0.88 and a completeness equal to 1,00.

Actually, the intrinsic characteristics of our algorithm led us to think that, if the severity level increases, the correctness increases as well, whereas the completeness decreases. In order to verify this idea, we have performed a second series of experiments devoted to measure correctness and completeness in presence of variations of the severity level. Table 2 shows obtained results up to a severity level equal to 3; for higher severity levels, variations of correctness and completeness are not significant.

Table 2. Correctness and Completeness of our approach at various severity levels

Severity Level	Correctness	Completeness
Level 0	0.88	1.00
Level 1	0.97	0.81
Level 2	0.97	0.78
Level 3	0.97	0.73

Results presented in Table 2 confirmed our intuitions. Indeed, at severity level 1, correctness increases of a factor of 9% whereas completeness decreases of a factor of 19% w.r.t. correctness and completeness relative to severity level 0. As for severity levels greater than 1, we have verified that correctness does not increase whereas completeness slightly decreases w.r.t. level 1.

In our opinion such a result is extremely relevant; indeed, it allows us to conclude that, in informal situations, the right severity level is 0 whereas, in more formal contexts, the severity level must be at least 1.

After this, we have computed variations of the time required for deriving interscheme properties caused by an increase of the severity level. Obtained results are shown in Table 3. In the table the value associated with severity level i ($1 \leq i \leq 3$) is to be intended as the percentage of time additionally required w.r.t. severity level $i - 1$.

Table 3 shows that the increase of time required for computing interscheme properties when the algorithm passes from the severity level 0 to the severity level 1 is significant. Vice versa, further severity level increases do not lead to

Table 3. Increase of the time required by our approach at various severity levels

Severity Level	Time Increase
Level 1	56%
Level 2	14%
Level 3	20%

significant increases of the time necessary for computing interscheme properties. This observation further confirms results obtained by the previous experiments, i.e., that the most relevant differences in the results obtained by applying our approach can be found between the severity levels 0 and 1.

6   Related Work

In the literature many approaches for performing interscheme property extraction and data source integration have been proposed. Even if they are quite numerous and various, to the best of our knowledge, none of them guarantees the possibility to choose a "severity" level against which the various activities are carried out. In this section we examine some of these approaches and highlight their similarities and differences w.r.t. our own.

In [16] an XML Schema integration framework is proposed. It consists of three phases, namely pre-integration, comparison and integration. After this, *conflict resolution* and *restructuring* are performed for obtaining the global refined Schema. To the best of our knowledge the approach of [16] is the closest to our own. In particular, *(i)* both of them are *rule-based* [17]; *(ii)* both of them assume that the global Schema is formulated in a *referenced style* rather than in an *inline style* (see [1] for more details); *(iii)* integration rules proposed in [16] are quite similar to those characterizing our approach. The main differences existing between them are the following: *(i)* the approach of [16] requires a preliminary translation of an XML Schema into an *XSDM* Schema; such a translation is not required by our approach; *(ii)* the integration task in [16] is graph-based and object-oriented whereas, in our approach, it is directly based on *x-components*;.

In [10] the system *XClust* is presented whose purpose is XML data source integration. More specifically, *XClust* determines the similarity degrees of a group of DTD's by considering not only the corresponding linguistic and structural information but also their semantics. It is possible to recognize some similarities between our approach and *XClust*; in particular, *(i)* both of them have been specifically conceived for operating on XML data sources (even if our approach manages XML Schemas whereas *XClust* operates on DTD's); *(ii)* both of them consider not only linguistic similarities but also semantic ones. There are also several differences between the two approaches; more specifically, *(i)* to perform the integration activity, *XClust* requires the support of a hierarchical clustering whereas our approach adopts schema matching techniques; *(ii)* *XClust* represents DTD's as trees; as a consequence, element neighborhoods are quite different from those constructed by our approach; *(iii)* *XClust* exploits some weights and thresholds whereas our approach does not use them; as a consequence, *XClust* provides more refined results but these last are strongly dependent on the correctness of a tuning phase devoted to set weights and thresholds.

In [13] the system *Rondo* is presented. It has been conceived for integrating and manipulating relational schemas, XML Schemas and SQL views. *Rondo* exploits a graph-based approach for modeling information sources and a set of high-level operators for matching obtained graphs. Rondo uses the *Similarity Flooding Algorithm*, a graph-matching algorithm proposed in [12], to perform schema matching activity. Finally, it merges involved information sources according to three steps: Node Renaming, Graph Union and Conflict Resolution. There are important similarities between *Rondo* and our approach; indeed both of them are semi-automatic and exploit schema matching techniques. The main differences existing between them are the following: *(i) Rondo* is generic, i.e., it can handle various kinds of information sources; vice versa our approach is specialized for XML Schemas; *(ii) Rondo* models involved information sources as graphs whereas our approach directly operates on XML Schemas; *(iii) Rondo* exploits a sophisticated technique (i.e., the Similarity Flooding Algorithm) for carrying out schema matching activities [12]; as a consequence, it obtains very precise results but is time-expensive and requires a heavy human feedback; on the contrary, our approach is less sophisticated but is well suited when involved information sources are numerous and large.

In [6] an XML-based integration approach, capable of handling various source formats, is presented. Both this approach and our own operate on XML documents and carry out a semantic integration. However, *(i)* the approach of [6] operates on DTD's and requires to translate them in an appropriate formalism called ORM/NIAM [9]; vice versa, our approach directly operates on XML Schemas; *(ii)* the global Schema constructed by the approach of [6] is represented in the ORM/NIAM formalism whereas our approach direcly returns a global XML Schema; *(iii)* the approach of [6] is quite complex to be applied when involved sources are numerous.

In [18] the DIXSE (Data Integration for XML based on Schematic Knowledge) tool is presented, aiming at supporting the integration of a set of XML documents. Both DIXSE and our approach are semantic and operate on XML documents; both of them exploit structural and terminological relationships for carrying out the integration activity. The main differences between them reside in the interscheme property extraction technique; indeed, DIXSE requires the support of the user whereas our approach derives them almost automatically. As a consequence, results returned by DIXSE could be more precise than those provided by our approach but, when the number of sources to integrate is high, the effort DIXSE requires to the user might be particularly heavy.

In [4] a *machine learning* approach, named LSD (Learning Source Description), for carrying out schema matching activities, is proposed. It has been extended also to ontologies in GLUE [5]. LSD requires quite a heavy support of the user during the initial phase, for carrying out training tasks; however, after this phase, no human intervention is required. Both LSD and our approach operate mainly on XML sources. They differ especially in their purposes; indeed, LSD aims at deriving interscheme properties whereas our approach has been conceived mainly for handling integration activities. In addition, as far as interscheme property derivation is concerned, it is worth observing that LSD is *"learner-based"* whereas our approach is *"rule-based"* [17]. Finally, LSD requires a heavy human intervention at the beginning and, then, is automatic; vice versa, our approach does not need a pre-processing phase but requires the human intervention at the end for validating obtained results.

In [3] the authors propose COMA (COmbining MAtch), an interactive and iterative system for combining various schema matching approaches. The approach of COMA appears orthogonal to our own; in particular, our approach could inherit some features from COMA (as an example, the idea of operating iteratively) for improving the accuracy of its results. As for an important difference between the two approaches, we observe that COMA is generic, since it handles a large variety of information source formats; vice versa, our approach has been specifically conceived to handle XML documents. In addition, our approach requires the user to specify only the *severity level*; vice versa, in COMA, the user must specify the *matching strategy* (i.e., the desired matchers to exploit and the modalities for combining their results).

7   Conclusions

In this paper we have proposed an approach for the integration of a set of XML Schemas. We have shown that our approach is specialized for XML documents, is almost automatic, semantic and "light" and allows the choice of the "severity" level against which the integration activity must be performed. We have also illustrated some experiments we have carried out to test its computational performances and the quality of results it obtains. Finally, we have examined various other related approaches previously proposed in the literature and we have compared them with ours by pointing out similarities and differences.

In the future we plan to exploit our approach in various other contexts typically benefiting of information source integration, such as Cooperative Information Systems, Data Warehousing, Semantic Query Processing and so on.

References

1. XML Schema Part 1: Structures. W3C Recommendation, http://www.w3.org/TR/xmlschema-1, 2001.
2. S. Castano, V. De Antonellis, and S. De Capitani di Vimercati. Global viewing of heterogeneous data sources. *Transactions on Data and Knowledge Engineering*, 13(2):277–297, 2001.
3. H. Do and E. Rahm. COMA- a system for flexible combination of schema matching approaches. In *Proc. of the International Conference on Very Large Databases (VLDB 2002)*, pages 610–621, Hong Kong, China, 2002. VLDB Endowment.
4. A. Doan, P. Domingos, and A. Halevy. Reconciling schemas of disparate data sources: a machine-learning approach. In *Proc. of the International Conference on Management of Data (SIGMOD 2001)*, pages 509–520, Santa Barbara, California, USA, 2001. ACM Press.

5. A. Doan, J. Madhavan, P. Domingos, and A. Halevy. Learning to map between ontologies on the Semantic Web. In *Proc. of the International Conference on World Wide Web (WWW 2002)*, pages 662–673, Honolulu, Hawaii, USA, 2002. ACM Press.

6. R. dos Santos Mello, S. Castano, and C.A. Heuser. A method for the unification of XML schemata. *Information & Software Technology*, 44(4):241–249, 2002.

7. P. Fankhauser, M. Kracker, and E.J. Neuhold. Semantic vs. structural resemblance of classes. *ACM SIGMOD RECORD*, 20(4):59–63, 1991.

8. Z. Galil. Efficient algorithms for finding maximum matching in graphs. *ACM Computing Surveys*, 18:23–38, 1986.

9. T. Halpin. Object-Role Modeling (ORM-NIAM). In P. Bernus, K. Mertins, and G. Schmidt, editors, *Handbook on Architectures of Information Systems*, chapter 4, pages 81–102. Springer-Verlag, 1998.

10. M.L. Lee, L.H. Yang, W. Hsu, and X. Yang. XClust: clustering XML schemas for effective integration. In *Proc. of the International Conference on Information and Knowledge Management (CIKM 2002)*, pages 292–299, McLean, Virginia, USA, 2002. ACM Press.

11. J. Madhavan, P.A. Bernstein, and E. Rahm. Generic schema matching with Cupid. In *Proc. of the International Conference on Very Large Data Bases (VLDB 2001)*, pages 49–58, Roma, Italy, 2001. Morgan Kaufmann.

12. S. Melnik, H. Garcia-Molina, and E. Rahm. Similarity Flooding: A versatile graph matching algorithm and its application to schema matching. In *Proc. of the International Conference on Data Engineering (ICDE 2002)*, pages 117–128, San Jose, California, USA, 2002. IEEE Computer Society Press.

13. S. Melnik, E. Rahm, and P.A. Bernstein. Rondo: A programming platform for generic model management. In *Proc. of the International Conference on Management of Data (SIGMOD 2003)*, pages 193–204, San Diego, California, USA, 2003. ACM Press.

14. A.G. Miller. WordNet: A lexical database for English. *Communications of the ACM*, 38(11):39–41, 1995.

15. L. Palopoli, D. Saccà, G. Terracina, and D. Ursino. Uniform techniques for deriving similarities of objects and subschemes in heterogeneous databases. *IEEE Transactions on Knowledge and Data Engineering*, 15(2):271–294, 2003.

16. K. Passi, L. Lane, S.K. Madria, B.C. Sakamuri, M.K. Mohania, and S.S. Bhowmick. A model for XML Schema integration. In *Proc. of the International Conference on E-Commerce and Web Technologies (EC-Web 2002)*, pages 193–202, Aix-en-Provence, France, 2002. Lecture Notes in Computer Science, Springer-Verlag.

17. E. Rahm and P.A. Bernstein. A survey of approaches to automatic schema matching. *VLDB Journal*, 10(4):334–350, 2001.

18. P. Rodriguez-Gianolli and J. Mylopoulos. A semantic approach to XML-based data integration. In *Proc. of the International Conference on Conceptual Modelling (ER'01)*, pages 117–132, Yokohama, Japan, 2001. Lecture Notes in Computer Science, Springer-Verlag.

Managing the Evolution of Mediation Queries

Mokrane Bouzeghoub[1], Bernadette Farias Lóscio[2], Zoubida Kedad[1],
and Ana Carolina Salgado[2]

[1] Laboratoire PRiSM, Université de Versailles
45, avenue des Etats-Unis 78035 Versailles, France
{Zoubida.Kedad, Mokrane.Bouzeghoub}@prism.uvsq.fr
[2] Centro de Informática - Universidade Federal de Pernambuco
Av. Professor Luis Freire s/n, Cidade Universitária
50740-540 Recife – PE, Brasil
{bfl, acs}@cin.ufpe.br

Abstract. Previous works in data integration can be classified according to the approach used to define objects at the mediation level. One of these approaches is called global-as-view (GAV) and requires that each object is expressed as a view (a mediation query) on the data sources. One important limit of this approach is the management of the evolutions in the system. Indeed, each time a change occurs at the source schema level, all the queries defining the mediation objects have to be reconsidered and possibly redefined. In this paper, we propose an approach to cope with the evolution of mediation queries. Our claim is that if the definition of mediation queries in a GAV context follows a well-defined methodology, handling the evolution of the system becomes easier. These evolution problems are considered in the context of a methodology we have previously defined for generating mediation queries. Our solution is based on the concept of relevant relations on which propagation rules have been defined.

1 Introduction

The goal of data integration consists in providing a uniform view of data sources (called mediation schema or global schema) and defining a set of queries (called mediation queries or mediation mappings) which define objects of the mediation schema. These queries will later serve to rewrite users' queries prior to their execution. A mediator is a software device that supports a mediation schema [15], i.e., a collection of views over the data sources reflecting users' requirements. Beside the set of mediation queries which define the mediation schema, a set of linguistic mappings specifies correspondences between the mediation schema elements and the local schemas ones.

Previous work in data integration can be classified according to the approach used to define the mediation queries [4, 7, 14]. The first approach, called global-as-view (GAV), requires that each relation (or class) of the global schema be expressed as a view (i.e. a query) on the data sources. In the second approach, called local-as-view (LAV), mediation queries are defined in an opposite way; each relation (or class) in a given source is defined as a view on the global schema. The GAV approach is known

R. Meersman et al. (Eds.): CoopIS/DOA/ODBASE 2003, LNCS 2888, pp. 22–37, 2003.
© Springer-Verlag Berlin Heidelberg 2003

as easy to implement but difficult to evolve; each change raised at a source schema may lead to the redefinition of possibly all the mediation queries. The LAV approach has the opposite feature; each source evolution results into the redefinition of the only mediation queries corresponding to this source, but the implementation of this approach is harder as the rewriting process of user queries is more complex.

This paper addresses the problem of evolution in the context of the GAV approach. As we know, local data sources are often autonomous and may change both in their structures and their concepts. New sources may be added to the system and other sources may be removed from the system either because of their irrelevance or because of their unavailability. We are interested in providing mechanisms to correctly update the mappings between the mediation schema and the distributed sources after source schema changes. Few research have discussed some aspects related to this problem [1, 8, 9]. We will compare our approach to these related works in section 5.

The challenge is to maintain the mediation queries consistent with source evolution. We claim that if the mediation queries are derived following a certain design methodology, the problem of their evolution will be easier to solve. Indeed, prior to the evolution problem, the definition of mediation queries is also a hard problem in the GAV approach, especially in the context of large scale systems. Defining a mediation relation over hundreds or thousands of source schemas is a very hard task, regarding the amount of metadata necessary to determine the queries. In fact, the evolution problem of the GAV approach is also related to the scalability of mediation systems. Evolution of a small-size mediation system is not as crucial as that of a large-size mediation system.

In a previous work, we have proposed a design methodology which generates mediation queries in the context of very large mediation systems based on the relational model [5]. Given a mediation relation, a set of source schemas and a set of linguistic assertions between the mediation schema and the sources schemas, we have defined an algorithm which discovers the mediation queries defining this relation. The evolution process is seen as an incremental execution of this algorithm.

This paper is organized as follows. Section 2 defines the evolution problem and the main notations. Section 3 recalls the principles of our design methodology for determining the mediation queries. Section 4 is devoted to the propagation of source changes to the mediation level using this methodology. Section 5 presents the related works and finally, section 6 concludes with some open problems.

2 Problem Statement

In mediation systems, the evolution problem is mainly related to changes raised at the data source level: adding or removing a relation schema, an attribute or a constraint. The mediation schema itself is supposed to be relatively stable, that is, not subject to intensive changes. Moreover, advantages and drawbacks of GAV and LAV approaches are given with respect to this assumption. Handling source evolution is an essential feature as it implies modularity and scalability of the mediation system. As mentioned before, the GAV approach suffers from the lack of evolution because each change at the source schema level may lead to the reconsideration and possibly the change of all mediation queries. One way to cope with this problem is to isolate only those mediation queries which are impacted by the source change and to automatically redefine these queries by applying only the necessary changes.

In a mediation architecture (as shown in figure 1), a mediation schema represents the reconciliation between users' requirements and the sources capabilities. In other words, if we assume that the mediation schema is expressed using the relational model, it contains all the relations needed in a specific business domain to answer users' queries which can be computed from the data sources. In the GAV approach, each relation R_i in the mediation schema is defined by a mediation query Q_i which computes the relation R_i over a subset of data sources.

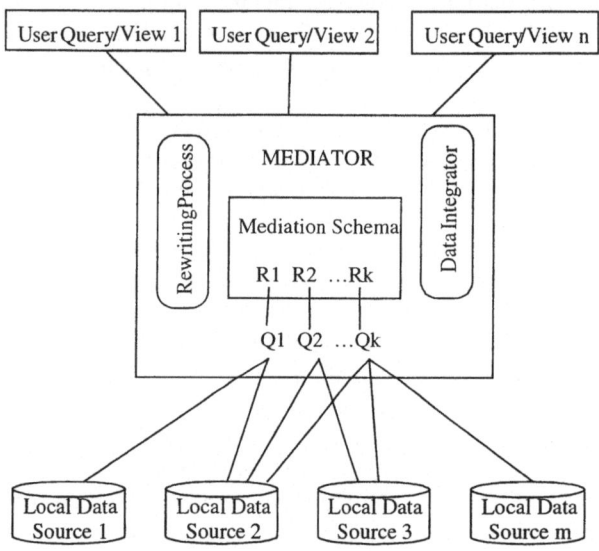

Fig. 1. A mediation architecture

To illustrate the problem we aim to solve, consider the example of two mediation relations R_1 and R_2 having the following schemas: R_1(#K, A, B) and R_2(#K', C, D). These relations are defined over the following source relations: S_1(#K, A, @X), S_2(#X, B), S_3(#K', C, D), S_4(#K', C, D). Primary key attributes are prefixed by # and foreign key attributes are prefixed by @. S_1 and S_2 belong to the same data source 1. S_3 and S_4 belong respectively to data sources 2 and 3. The mediation queries associated with the mediation relations R_1 and R_2 are the following:

$R_1 = \Pi_{K, A, B}(S_1 \bowtie_{S1.X=S2.X} S_2)$ and $R_2 = S_3 \cup S_4$.

Suppose some changes occur at the source level, consisting in removing the source relations S_1 and S_4. Our goal is to propose a methodology allowing to propagate the changes occurring at the source level to the mediation queries. As a consequence of these changes, mediation queries have to be checked, and if possible, to be rewritten. In our example, after the source changes, there is no way to compute the relation R_1 and the associated mediation query becomes invalid. The relation R_2 is still computable, and the new mediation query is $R_2 = S_3$.

The key issues of this process are first, how to propagate a given source change into a single mediation query, which is done through a set of evolution rules; second, how to define the global evolution process, which will consists in propagating a set of changes issued by several data sources to the set of mediation queries defining relations of the mediation schema.

In the following sections, we assume the relational model being the common model for both the local schemas and the mediation schema. We use the following notations to represent relations and attributes.

- S_{ij} denotes a relation i in the data source j.
- R_m denotes a relation of the mediation schema.
- $S_{ij}.A_k$ denotes the attribute A_k of the source relation S_{ij}; similarly, $R_m.A_k$ denotes the attribute A_k of the relation R_m in the mediation schema.

We also assume that some meta data describing the sources and the mediation schema is available. We will use the following definitions:

- Referential constraints: they are defined within a single schema, either the mediation schema or a local source schema; they are denoted $Ri.A \rightarrow Rj.K$.
- Semantic equivalence between attributes: when two attributes A_1 and A_2 represent two equivalent concepts, they are said to be semantically equivalent; this link is denoted $A_1 \cong A_2$ (or $R_i.A_1 \cong R_j.A_1$ to avoid confusions).
- Schema assertions, which are one of the following:

  $\underline{R_1} = \underline{R_2}$ if the schema of the relation R_1 corresponds to the schema of the relation R_2 through a 1:1 mapping such that each attribute of R_1 has a semantically equivalent attribute in R_2 and each attribute of R_2 has a semantically equivalent attribute in R_1.

  $\underline{R_1} \subset \underline{R_2}$ if each attribute of the relation R_1 has a semantically equivalent attribute in the relation R_2.

  $\underline{R_1} \cap \underline{R_2} \neq \emptyset$ if some attributes of R_1 have semantically equivalent attributes in R_2.

  $\underline{R_1} \cap \underline{R_2} = \emptyset$ if there is no attribute in R_1 having a semantically equivalent attribute in R_2.

In the remaining of this paper, equality, union and intersection operations stand for schema assertions when relation symbols are underlined; they stand for regular relational algebra when the relation symbols are not.

3 Generation of Mediation Queries

One of the difficult problems met when designing mediation-based systems is the definition of mediation queries. Indeed, defining queries over tens or hundreds of heterogeneous data sources requires a complete and perfect understanding of the semantics of these sources. In [5], we have proposed an approach which discovers mediation queries over a set of heterogeneous sources in a GAV context. This section recalls, through a simple example, the general principle of the Mediation Query Generation approach (MQG), which will serve as a support to propagate changes from the source level to the mediation level.

3.1 Intuitive Approach

The MQG algorithm can be roughly summarized by three steps: (i) search of contributive sources, (ii) determination of candidate operations, (iii) definition of queries. These steps are illustrated through the following example. Let R_m(#K,A,B,C) be a mediation relation and {S_1,S_2,S_3,S_4} be a set of source relations over which R_m will be defined. S_1(#K,A,@X,Y) and S_2(#X,B,Z) are in source 1, S_3(#B,C,W) is in source 2 and S_4(#B,C,U) is in source 3. Primary key attributes are prefixed by # and foreign key attributes are prefixed by @.

- *Step 1. Search for contributive sources:* The first step consists in finding all possible sources which may contribute to the computation of R_m. Intuitively, a source relation S_{ij} contributes to the computation of a mediation relation R_m if S_{ij} includes some of the attributes of R_m. The notion of *mapping relation* T_{mij} is introduced to group all common attributes between R_m and S_{ij}. To later facilitate the discovery of operations, the definition of a mapping relation is extended with primary keys and foreign keys of its source relation S_{ij}. Figure 2 shows the mapping relations T_1, T_2, T_3, and T_4 derived from source relations S_1, S_2, S_3 and S_4 to compute the mediation relation R_m.

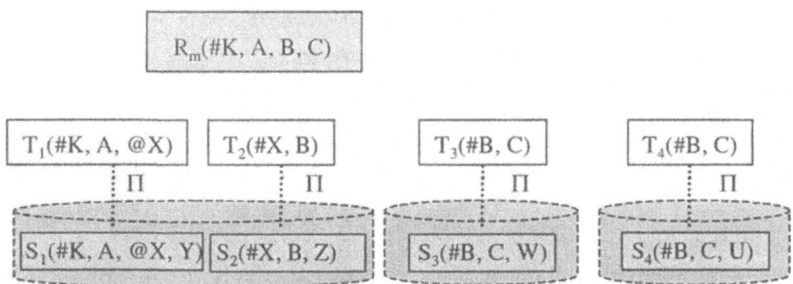

Fig. 2. Example of mapping relations

- *Step 2. Determination of candidate operations:* Given the set of mapping relations {T_1,T_2,T_3,T_4} associated with the mediation relation R_m, the determination of candidate operations depends on operation type (join, union, intersection, difference), relation schemas and links between relations. To illustrate this, we will consider the join and union operations.

  o *The join operation is candidate in two cases:* (i) the two mapping relations are originated from the same source; in this case we consider that a join is possible only if there is an explicit referential constraint between the two source relations; (ii) the two mapping relations are originated from different sources; in this case, we consider that a join is possible if the primary key of one relation has an equivalent attribute in the other relation, either a non-key attribute or a key attribute. We consider the case of a non-key attribute as a kind of implicit referential constraint between the two source relations.

  o *The union operation is candidate if the two mapping relations have the same schema.* We can extend this rule to any intermediate relation obtained by combination of mapping relations.

Figure 3 shows some possible operations between mapping relations of figure 2. The graph of all possible operations is called the operations graph.

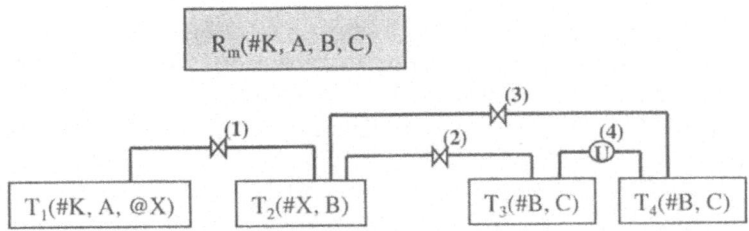

Fig. 3. Example of operations graph

One should remark that, in the case of a join operation, there is not always necessarily an explicit or implicit referential constraint between two source relations. It might be possible to join two source relations S_i and S_j through a third relation S_k which is not directly contributive to the computation of R_m. Our algorithm includes these relations as *transition relations* which contain only necessary primary keys and foreign keys which make possible a join between mapping relations. Obviously, there may exist more than one transition relation between two mapping relations.

- *Step 3. Definition of mediation queries:* Having the operations graph defined between relevant relations (mapping relations and transition relations), it becomes easier to generate mediation queries. For that purpose, we introduce the concept of *computation path*, which is a mapping relation involving all the attributes of R_m, or any connected and acyclic sub-graph of the operations graph which involves all the attributes of R_m. It may occur that no computation path exists in a given operations graph; in such case, no mediation query can be defined. Examples of computation paths in the operations graph given in figure 3 are $C_1 = (4, 2, 1)$ and $C_2 = (1, 2)$. The generation of a relational expression consists in identifying the set of all possible orderings of the operations contained in a computation path. C_1 and C_2 lead respectively to the following expressions:

$E_1 = (T_4 \cup T_3) \bowtie T_2 \bowtie T_1$ and $E_2 = T_1 \bowtie T_2 \bowtie T_3$.

To complete the process, expressions E_1 and E_2 should be rewritten using the definitions of mapping relations and transition relations. E_1 and E_2 become:

$E_1 = \Pi_{K, A, B, C} [((\Pi_{B, C} S_4) \cup (\Pi_{B, C} S_3)) \bowtie (\Pi_{X, B} S_2) \bowtie (\Pi_{K, A, X} S_1)]$ and

$E_2 = \Pi_{K, A, B, C} [(\Pi_{K, A, X} S_1) \bowtie (\Pi_{X, B} S_2) \bowtie (\Pi_{B, C} S_3)]$.

The result of the approach is a set of mediation queries having different semantics. Given this set, one mediation query is selected either by the designer or using some heuristics.

3.2 Definitions

This subsection groups the essential definitions of the MQG algorithm which will serve for evolution purposes. Indeed, propagating changes raised at the source level will mainly consist in redefining relevant relations, operations graphs and computation paths.

Definition 3.1. Mapping relation (m-relation): An m-relation $T_{mij}(K,X,X')$ between a mediation relation R_m and a source relation S_{ij} is defined as a relation having a schema composed of the following attributes: (X,X',K) such that: (i) $X \subseteq R_m$, $X \subseteq S_{ij}$ and $R_m.X \cong S_{ij}.X$, (ii) X' is the foreign key attributes of S_{ij}, and (iii) K is the primary key attributes of S_{ij}.

Definition 3.2. Transition relation (t-relation): A t-relation $T_{mij}(XY)$ is a projection of a non contributive source relation S_{ij} on its primary keys X and foreign keys Y such that: X is a foreign key of a mapping relation or another transition relation of R_m and Y is a primary key of a mapping relation or another transition relation of R_m.

Definition 3.3. Relevant relation (r-relation): A r-relation is either an m-relation or a t-relation.

Definition 3.4. Operations graph: An operations graph is the representation of both the relevant relations and the set of candidate operations. Each relevant relation, either m-relation or t-relation, is represented by a node in the operations graph. An edge between two nodes corresponding to relevant relations represents a candidate relational operation between these relations.

Definition 3.5. Computation path: This concept is used to generate mediation queries. A computation path in the operations graph G_{Rm} associated with the mediation relation R_m is either a relevant relation which involves all the attributes of R_m, or any connected and acyclic sub-graph of G_{Rm} which involves all the attributes of R_m.

4 Propagation of Source Changes to the Mediation Queries

As stated before, the evolution process of a GAV mediation system may take advantage of a rigorous design methodology like the one supported by the MQG algorithm. Propagating changes from the source level to the mediation level consists in detecting new contributive data sources or relations, redefining some mapping relations and/or transition relations, adding or removing operations from operations graphs, detecting new computation paths and selecting appropriate mediation queries. The evolution process consists mainly in adapting the MQG algorithm to make it more modular and more incremental. Hence, the new algorithm, called IMQG (incremental mediation query generation) makes no difference between an initial design based on a modular methodology and an evolution process.

To achieve the goal of a modular and incremental design, we assume that the mediation schema maintains a history of all design choices that have been made in a previous iteration. The operations graph plays a major role as it contains relevant relations, candidate operations, computation paths which have been selected and those which were not. Consequently, further incremental iterations of the algorithm will consist in updating only parts of this operations graph (history) which are precisely dependent of the change events raised at the sources, instead of redefining the whole mediation schema.

In the remaining of this section, we will first present the local schema change operations and the propagation primitives used to update the mediation level, then we will present the set of rules allowing to propagate the source changes into the operations graph, either on the relevant relations or on the associated operations. Finally, we will briefly discuss the global evolution process.

4.1 Local Schema Change Operations

Local schema change operations specify modifications that are performed in the local source schemas and that must be propagated to the mediation level. The possible change operations at the data source level are listed in Table 1.

Table 1. Local Schema Change Operations

Change Operation	Definition
add_relation($\underline{S}_{ij}$)	Adds a new relation schema into the source j
remove_relation($\underline{S}_{ij}$)	Removes an existing relation schema from the source j
add_attribute($\underline{S}_{ij}$, A)	Adds the attribute A into S_{ij}
remove_attribute($\underline{S}_{ij}$, A)	Removes the attribute A from S_{ij}
add_ref_constraint ($S_{ij}.A$, $S_{lj}.K$)	Adds the referential constraint $S_{ij}.A \rightarrow S_{lj}.K$ into S_j
remove_ref_constraint ($S_{ij}.A$, $S_{lj}.K$)	Removes the referential constraint $S_{ij}.A \rightarrow S_{lj}.K$ from S_j

Note that the removal or the addition of a data source can be represented in terms of a set of change operations, for example, the addition of a source can be considered as a set of *add_relation* operations and the removal of a data source can be considered as a set of *remove_relation* operations. In this paper, we will restrict ourselves to handle only some of the changes described in table 1.

4.2 Propagation Primitives

We consider that each mediation relation R_m is associated with an operations graph G_{R_m} corresponding to the mediation query defining R_m. If a change occurs in the data sources, some checking operations have to be performed on this graph to test if the computation path and therefore the mediation query associated with R_m are still valid. If not, new computation paths have to be searched and a new query has to be defined. A given computation path is invalid if one or more operations in this path is no longer valid. For example, if this path contains a join operation and if an attribute involved in the join predicate is removed from the data source, the join and consequently the computation path become invalid.

The propagation primitives presented in Table 2 specify modifications and verifications which must be performed in the operations graphs and the corresponding mediation queries to reflect local schema change operations.

Table 2. Mediation queries propagation primitives

Propagation Primitive	Definition
valid_operation_graph(G_{Rm})	Checks the validity of the operations graph G_{Rm} associated with the relation R_m and removes the invalid operations.
search_operation(G_{Rm})	Searches new operations for combining pairs of relevant relations in the operations graph G_{Rm}.
remove_operation(G_{Rm}, T_{ij}, A)	Removes all edges in the operations graph G_{Rm} that become invalid because of the removal of the attribute A from the relevant relation T_{ij}.
add_relevant_relation(T_{ij}, G_{Rm})	Adds relevant relation T_{ij} into the operations graph G_{Rm}.
remove_relevant_relation(T_{ij}, G_{Rm})	Removes relevant relation T_{ij} from the operations graph G_{Rm}.
search_relevant_relation(G_{Rm}, S)	Searches new relevant relations associated with relation R_m from the set of data sources S.
search_computation_path(G_{Rm})	Determines the computation paths associated with the operations graph G_{Rm}.
generate_query(G_{Rm}, Q)	Generates the set Q of relational expressions to compute relation R_m using the operations graph G_{Rm}.
select_query(Q, q)	Takes as input a set of possible queries Q and produces as output a single query q (the choice is made either by the designer or using some heuristics)

4.3 Evolution Rules for Relevant Relations

Given a source change represented by one of the local schema change operations described in section 4.1, we will first propagate these changes into the set of relevant relations associated with each mediation relation. To specify this propagation, we use event-condition-action (ECA) rules. The rules are classified according to the type of local schema change operations. Each rule has a name and a parameter denoted R_m which represents a mediation relation. G_{Rm} represents the operations graph associated with R_m. Table 3 gives a sample of such rules that we will discuss hereafter. Due to space limitations, only some of the evolution rules are presented in this table. A complete description is given in [3].

Table 3. Evolution rules

Rule 1 (R_m) **Event**: add_attribute($\underline{S}_{ij}$, A) **Condition**: $A \in \underline{R}_m$ $\exists T_{ij} \in M_{Rm} \mid \underline{T}_{ij} \subseteq \underline{S}_{ij}$ /*M_{Rm} is the set of relevant relations corresponding to the relation R_m */ **Action**: $\underline{T}_{ij} := \underline{T}_{ij} \cup \{A\}$, valid_operation_graph($G_{Rm}$), search_operation($G_{Rm}$).	**Rule 2 (R_m)** **Event**: add_attribute($\underline{S}_{ij}$, A) **Condition**: $A \in \underline{R}_m$ $\nexists T_{ij} \in M_{Rm} \mid \underline{T}_{ij} \subseteq \underline{S}_{ij}$ **Action**: /* X is the set of key attributes and foreign keys of S_{ij} */ $T_{ij} = \Pi_{X \cup A} S_{ij}$, add_relevant_relation($T_{ij}$, G_{Rm}), search_operation(G_{Rm}).
Rule 3 (R_m) **Event**: remove_attribute($\underline{S}_{ij}$.A) **Condition**: $\exists T_{ij} \in M_{Rm} \mid \underline{T}_{ij} \subseteq \underline{S}_{ij}$ $A \in \underline{T}_{ij}$ **Action**: $\underline{T}_{ij} := \underline{T}_{ij} - \{A\}$, remove_operation($G_{Rm}$, T_{ij}, A).	**Rule 4 (R_m)** **Event**: add_relation($\underline{S}_{ij}$) **Condition**: $\exists A \in \underline{S}_{ij} \mid A \in \underline{R}_m$ **Action**: /* X is the set of key attributes and foreign keys of S_{ij} */ $T_{ij} = \Pi_{X \cup A} S_{ij}$, add_relevant_relation($T_{ij}$, G_{Rm}), search_operation(G_{Rm}).
Rule 5 (R_m) **Event**: remove_relation($\underline{S}_{ij}$) **Condition**: $\exists T_{ij} \in M_{Rm} \mid \underline{T}_{ij} \subseteq \underline{S}_{ij}$, **Action**: remove_relevant_relation(T_{ij},G_{Rm}).	**Rule 6 (R_m)** **Event**: add_ref_constraint(S_{ij}.A, S_{kj}.K) **Condition**: $\exists T_{ij} \in M_{Rm} \mid \underline{T}_{ij} \subseteq \underline{S}_{ij}$ $\exists T_{kj} \in M_{Rm} \mid \underline{T}_{kj} \subseteq \underline{S}_{kj}$ $A \in \underline{T}_{ij}$ **Action**: search_operation(G_{Rm}).

- *Adding an attribute into a relation of a local schema:* Rules 1 and 2 update the relevant relations corresponding to the mediation relation R_m after the insertion of a new attribute A into a local source relation S_{ij}. The Rule 1 checks if the new attribute A belongs to the set of attributes of R_m and if there is a relevant relation T_{ij} associated with R_m over S_{ij}. If the attribute A belongs to the relation R_m, this means that there is at least one relevant relation T_{xy} containing the attribute A and derived from a source relation S_{xy} which is distinct from S_{ij}. If the conditions are true, the attribute A must be inserted into the relevant relation T_{ij}. As a consequence of this, the operations graph G_{Rm} must be validated and new operations must be searched.

The validation of the operations graph consists in verifying the validity of the existing operations after the insertion of the attribute A into the relevant relation T_{ij}, and removing the invalid operations. The Rule 2 checks if the new attribute A belongs to the set of attributes of R_m and if there is no relevant relation T_{ij} derived from the source relation S_{ij}. In this case, a new relevant relation should be added to the operations graph G_{Rm}. As a consequence of this, new operations must be searched in G_{Rm}.

- *Removing an attribute from a relation of a local schema:* Rule 3 updates the set of relevant relations and the set of candidate operations that define the mediation relation R_m after the deletion of the attribute A from the local relation S_{ij}. The condition part checks if there is a relevant relation T_{ij} associated with R_m over S_{ij} and if the removed attribute A belongs to the relevant relation T_{ij}. The attribute A must be removed from the relevant relation T_{ij} and all edges in G_{Rm} representing operations which are no longer valid must be removed. It may occur that no computation path can be found after the propagation; in such case, the mediation relation R_m becomes no longer computable.

- *Adding a relation into a local schema:* Rule 4 updates the set of relevant relations defining the mediation relation R_m after the addition of a local relation S_{ij}. The condition part checks if there is a set of attributes A in the source relation S_{ij} that belongs to the schema of R_m. If such set exists, then a relevant relation T_{ij} must be added into the operations graph G_{Rm}. As a consequence of this, new operations must be searched in G_{Rm}.

- *Removing a relation from a local schema:* Rule 5 updates the set of relevant relations associated with the relation R_m in the mediation schema after the deletion of a local relation S_{ij}. The condition part checks if there is a relevant relation T_{ij} associated with R_m over S_{ij}. To reflect the deletion of the local relation S_{ij}, the corresponding relevant relation T_{ij} must be removed from the operations graph G_{Rm}, along with all the operations involving T_{ij}. It may occur that no computation path can be found after the propagation; in such case, the mediation relation R_m becomes no longer computable.

- *Adding a referential constraint involving two relations in the same data source:* Considering that the constraint involves the source relations S_{ij} and S_{kj}, rule 6 checks if there are two mapping relations T_{ij} and T_{kj} derived from S_{ij} and S_{kj} respectively and if the attribute A belongs to T_{ij}. In such case, new operations are searched between the two mapping relations.

The propagation of source changes in the relevant relations and the query generation are the two main steps of the global evolution process which is described in the next section.

4.4 The Global Evolution Process

This section describes the global evolution process used in our approach to propagate source schema changes to the mediation level. A general overview of this process is presented in figure 4.

The global evolution process receives events (*e*) representing source schema changes and propagates them to the mediation level. An event is a source change represented by one of the local schema operations described in section 4.1. We consider that the events are produced by the data sources participating in the data integration system (or by a specific process called *Lookup* which detects these changes automatically).

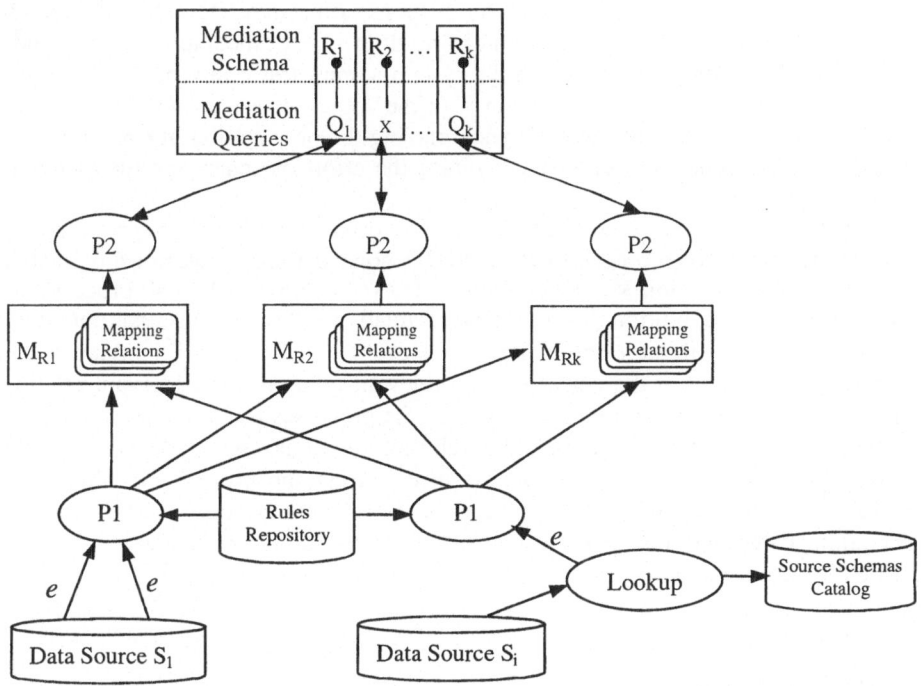

Fig. 4. Global Evolution Process

The evolution process can be divided into two main steps: a relevant relation evolution step and a mediation queries generation step. The relevant relations evolution consists in propagating source schema changes to the relevant relations associated with each mediation relation using the set of ECA rules described in section 4.3. This step is executed by a set of processes, where each process, called relevant relations evolution process and denoted *P1* is associated with a distinct data source S_i and is responsible for updating the relevant relations derived from S_i. In this way, different processes can be executed concurrently updating distinct sets of relevant relations.

The mediation queries generation step consists in generating a mediation query for each mediation relation when the corresponding set of relevant relations is modified. Each mediation relation R_m is associated with a process, called mediation queries generation and denoted $P2$, which is responsible for generating the mediation query used to compute R_m. Note that a mediation relation may become invalid after a source change; in figure 4, the symbol X linked to a mediation relation represents the fact that no mediation query has been found for this relation. There are two possible strategies for the global evolution process: (i) *Query driven evolution*, in which new mediation queries are generated when user queries are posed to the system and (ii) *Source driven evolution*, in which new mediation queries are generated when a set of changes is notified by a data source.

One of the problems in the query driven strategy is that, since the new mediation query is generated at evaluation time, the response time may increase. Besides, the process of mediation queries generation can result in a set of mediation queries, and it is therefore necessary to interact with the system administrator in order to ask him to choose one of them. The main problem with the source driven evolution strategy is that we have to find the best way of synchronizing the propagation of events notified by different data sources in order to minimize the effort of generating the mediation queries.

In our work, we have adopted the source driven evolution strategy and the synchronization between processes $P1$ and $P2$ is done as follows: we consider that for a given mediation relation R_m, the process $P2$ is executed only when all processes $P1$ have finished the evolution of the relevant relations. This means that the query generation process will start only when all the events notified by all the data sources have been propagated in the corresponding relevant relations. The relevant relations corresponding to the relation R_m are locked by the processes $P1$; when these locks are released, the process $P2$ can lock the relevant relations and start its execution. Another possible strategy would consists in executing the process $P2$ whenever a process $P1$ signals the end of the evolution of the relevant relations. In this case, the generation process will take place as many often as the number of sequences of events notified by the data sources.

5   Related Works

In [1] an approach is presented which minimizes the cost of query processing for a mediator by pre-compiling the source descriptions into a minimal set of integration axioms. An integration axiom specifies a particular way in which available sources can be combined to provide the data for a class belonging to the global model. The current version of the proposed algorithm to discover integration axioms is incremental, which means that when new sources are added, the system can efficiently update the axioms, but no details on how this could be achieved nor examples are given. In the current version of the algorithm, in case of deleting a source the algorithm must start from scratch. A LAV approach is used to define the mappings between the global model an the local sources, while we have adopted a GAV approach in this paper.

The problem of evolution is also discussed in [8], which provides an approach to handle both schema integration and schema evolution in heterogeneous database architectures. The proposed approach is based on a framework for schema transformation, which consists of a hypergraph-based common data model and a set of primitive schema transformations defined for this model. Source schemas are integrated into a global schema by applying a sequence of primitive transformations to them. This set of transformations can also be used to systematically adapt the global schema and the global query translation pathways after changes to the source schemas. Instead of defining mediation queries as in many mediation systems, they use some transformations to automatically translate queries posed to the global schema to queries over the local schemas. In the proposed framework the schemas are defined in a hypergraph-based data model (HDM) and queries are expressed using Datalog.

The work presented in [9] is one of the few which studies the view evolution problem in information integration systems. The authors propose the Evolvable View Environment framework (EVE) as a generic approach to solve issues related to view evolution under schema changes for both view definition adaptation and view extent maintenance after synchronization. EVE uses materialized views for data integration. They propose some view synchronization algorithms to evolve a view definition by finding appropriate replacements for affected view components based on available meta-knowledge, and by dropping non-essential view components. Unlike the strategies proposed for query rewriting using views [6, 13], the proposed algorithms find view rewritings that are not necessarily equivalent to the original definition. Similarly to our approach they use the relational data model as the common data model and they also propose an extended view definition language (derived from SQL), which allows users to explicitly define evolution preferences for changing the semantics of the view. In this way, it is possible to accept view rewritings that preserve only the required attributes if preserving all is not possible.

Our approach differs from the approach proposed in [9], because the modifications are not directly executed in the mediation query definition but in the metadata that describes the mediation query. We consider that a mediation query must be modified as a consequence of every kind of source schema change. In [9], a view must evolve only when a source schema change occurs that can make the view definition obsolete; i.e., only the cases of removal of relations or attributes are dealt with. In the current version of our algorithm, we consider that all attributes of a mediation query are required, i.e., when an attribute cannot be found then the mediation query is invalid.

6   Conclusion

In this paper, we have presented a solution to the problem of evolution of mediation queries in a GAV approach. This solution is an improvement of the MQG algorithm which has been defined to generate mediation queries. The improvement consists in adapting the MQG algorithm to make it more incremental by introducing a set of propagation rules that operate on operations graphs and reflect the changes made at the source schema level. Propagation rules are formalized as event-condition-action (ECA) rules whose events correspond to the change operations and the actions to a set of propagation primitives. Conditions specify the semantic context in which the transformations are valid.

One interesting aspect to investigate in future works is the impact on the mediation level (schema and queries) of user requirements changes. In the same way as changes in the source schemas are, changes in the users' requirements must be reflected in the mediation level. In that case, the assumption on the invariance of the mediation schema is relaxed and the advantage of the LAV approach compared to the GAV approach is lost, because a change in the mediation schema will result in reconsidering and possibly rewriting all the mediation queries. Consequently, the evolution process in this case will mainly concern the LAV approach, because in the GAV approach, a change at the mediation schema results in the redefinition of one mediation query. One perspective of this work in the near-future is to propose an adaptation of our approach to handle user requirements changes in a LAV context.

References

1. J. Ambite, C. Knoblock, I. Muslea and A. Philpot, Compiling Source Description for Efficient and Flexible Information Integration, Journal of Intelligent Information Systems (JIIS), vol. 16, no.2, Mar. 2001.
2. J. Banerjee, W. Kim, H. J. Kim, and H. F. Korth, Semantics and Implementation of Schema Evolution in ObjectOriented Databases, in Proc. of SIGMOD, pp. 311–322, 1987.
3. M. Bouzeghoub, B. Farias-Loscio, Z. Kedad, A.C. Salgado, Design and Evolution of Large Scale Mediation Systems, Technical report, september 2003.
4. Y. Halevy, Theory of answering queries using views, SIGMOD Record, vol. 29, no.4, pp.40–47, 2000.
5. Z. Kedad and M. Bouzeghoub, Discovering View Expressions from a Multi-Source Information System, in Proc. of the Fourth IFCIS International Conference on Cooperative Information Systems (CoopIS), Edinburgh, Scotland, pp. 57–68, Sep. 1999.
6. A. Y. Levy, A. Rajaraman, J. D. Ullman, Answering Queries Using Limited External Processors, in Proc. of Symposium on Principles of Database Systems – PODS, pp. 227–237, 1996.
7. A. Y. Levy, Logic-based techniques in data integration, in J. Minker, editor Logic Based Artificial Intelligence. Kluwer Publishers, 2000.
8. P. McBrien and A. Poulovassilis, Schema Evolution in Heterogeneous Database Architectures, A Schema Transformation Approach, in Proc. of CAiSE'02, pp. 484–499, Toronto, May 2002.
9. A. Nica and E. A. Rundensteiner, View maintenance after view synchronization, in Proc. of International Database Engineering and Application Symposium (IDEAS'99), Apr. 1999.
10. Y. G. Ra and E. A. Rundensteiner, A Transparent Schema Evolution System Based on ObjectOriented View Technology, IEEE Transactions on Knowledge and Data Engineering, pp. 600–624, September 1997.
11. E.A. Rundensteiner, A. Lee, and Y.G. Ra, Capacityaugmenting schema changes on object-oriented databases: Towards increased interoperability, in ObjectOriented Information Systems, 1998.
12. D. Sjoberg, Quantifying Schema Evolution. Information and Software Technology, vol. 35, no.1, pp. 35–54, Jan. 1993.

13. D. Srivastava, S. Dar, H. V. Jagadish, A. Y. Levy, Answering Queries with Aggregation Using Views, in Proc. of 22th International Conference on Very Large Data Bases, pp. 318–329, 1996.
14. J. D. Ullman, Information integration using logical views, in Proc. of ICDT'97, vol.1186 of LNCS, pp.19–40, Springer-Verlag, 1997.
15. G. Wiederhold, Mediators in the architecture of future information systems, IEEE Computer, pp.38–49, Mar. 1992.

Semantics-Based Reconciliation for Collaborative and Mobile Environments

Nuno Preguiça[1], Marc Shapiro[2], and Caroline Matheson[2]

[1] Dep. Informática, FCT, Universidade Nova de Lisboa,Portugal
[2] Microsoft Research Ltd., Cambridge, UK

Abstract. IceCube is a system for optimistic replication, supporting collaborative work and mobile computing. It lets users write to shared data with no mutual synchronisation; however replicas diverge and must be reconciled. IceCube is a general-purpose reconciliation engine, parameterised by "constraints" capturing data semantics and user intents. IceCube combines logs of disconnected actions into near-optimal reconciliation schedules that honour the constraints. IceCube features a simple, high-level, systematic API. It seamlessly integrates diverse applications, sharing various data, and run by concurrent users. This paper focus on the IceCube API and algorithms. Application experience indicates that IceCube simplifies application design, supports a wide variety of application semantics, and seamlessly integrates diverse applications. On a realistic benchmark, IceCube runs at reasonable speeds and scales to large input sets.

1 Introduction

In order for collaborative users to contribute to the common task or coordinate, they must be able to update their replicas of the shared information. Furthermore, in mobile environments, mobile users need to access shared data during disconnection periods or to face slow or expensive networks. Thus local replicas may diverge and need to be *reconciled*. This is not trivial however because of conflicts.

Most existing reconcilers use syntactic mechanisms such as timestamps and drop actions to avoid conflicts. For instance in Figure 1, User 1 is requesting a reservation for room A and also for either B or C. A bit later User 2 requests either A or B. Reconciling in timestamp order reserves A and B for User 1, and User 2 cannot be satisfied. If instead the reconciler ignores timestamps but understands the meaning of "or" it can accomodate both users.

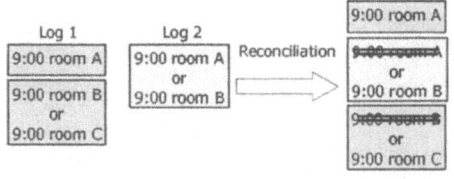

Fig. 1. Syntactic scheduling spuriously fails on this example

The IceCube reconciler constitutes a general-purpose middleware that is flexibly parameterised by application semantics. It works seamlessly across users, applications and objects that need not be aware of each other's existence.

R. Meersman et al. (Eds.): CoopIS/DOA/ODBASE 2003, LNCS 2888, pp. 38–55, 2003.
© Springer-Verlag Berlin Heidelberg 2003

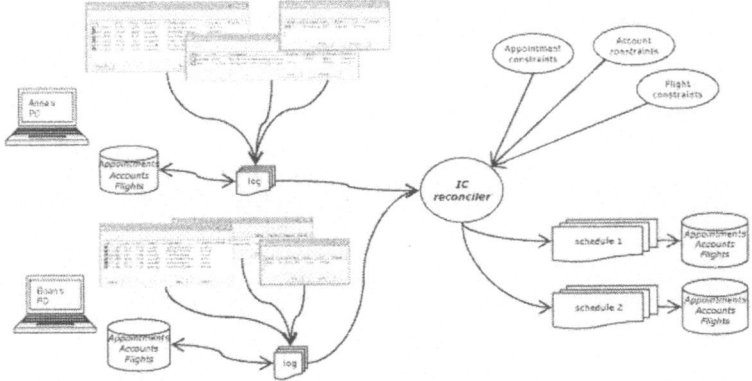

Fig. 2. IceCube system structure

Table 1. Summary of interface between applications and IceCube

Tentative operation App → IceCube	Initialise reconciliation IceCube → App	Compute schedule IceCube → App	Commit IceCube → App
Tentative execution	Collect object constraints	Take checkpoint	Commit actions
Record action in log		Execute action	
Set log constraint		Compensate action	
		Return to checkpoint	

A model IceCube environment is sketched in Figure 2. It shows two computers (Anne's and Brian's PCs), each with its own replicas of shared data (Appointments, Accounts, and Flights). An application can *tentatively* update a local replica [13]. Tentative updates are logged.

IceCube will combine the concurrent logs into sequential executions called *schedules*. In contrast to the inflexible schedulers of previous systems, IceCube obeys the application semantics, expressed by way of so-called *constraints*. Constraints constitute a general and powerful API for applications to express precisely their dependencies and invariants. By viewing scheduling as an optimisation problem, IceCube also avoids dropping actions unnecessarily.

Benchmarks show that IceCube reconciles in reasonable time and scales nicely to large logs, thanks to the following contributions. (i) Our *static* constraints, which incur no runtime cost, are sufficiently expressive for a wide spectrum of applications. (ii) The engine decomposes large inputs into independent subproblems.

The IceCube approach may appear hard to use, but in our experience it is practical. We report on a number of useful applications that we have coded. IceCube simplifies application development. Furthermore, multiple applications and object types will reconcile consistently and seamlessly.

Table 1 summarises the different phases and the interactions between applications and IceCube, to which we will refer in the rest of this paper.

This paper is organised as follows. We present a usage scenario in Section 2. Section 3 discusses the basic data and action abstractions. Section 4 presents our

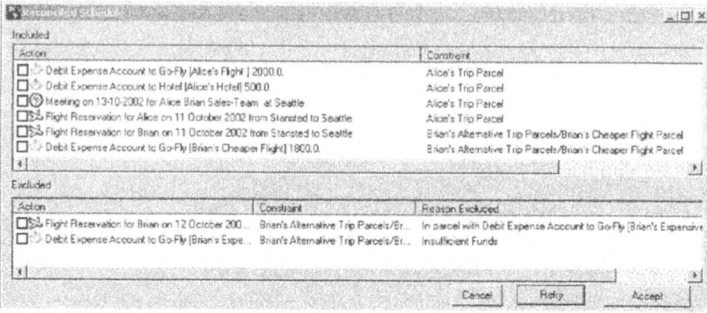

Fig. 3. Possible reconciliation for travel scenario

central abstraction of constraints. The scheduler's algorithms are explained in detail in Section 5. We evaluate performance and quality of IceCube in Section 7. Section 8 discusses related work, and Section 9 summarises conclusions and lessons learned.

2   A Multi-application, Multi-data Scenario

A simple scenario will give a feel of how IceCube operates. Anne and Brian are planning a business trip to meet some colleagues. While away from the network, Anne uses a calendar application to schedule a meeting, a travel application to reserve a flight to get there, and an account manager to pay for the flight. Anne groups her three actions into an atomic "parcel" (to be described shortly), even though they span separate applications.

Anne's machine being disconnected, the local database replicas are necessarily partial and possibly stale. Disconnected updates are only tentative, against the local replicas. However, they will become effective after connecting and reconciling; for instance, her payments will be executed, when, and if, the flights are committed.

In the meantime, Brian wants the system to help him choose between two different possibilities, a convenient but expensive flight on 12 October, and a cheaper but less convenient one on 11 October. He gives a higher value to the former to indicate his preference. The two choices constitute an "alternatives" construct, each of which contains a "parcel" combining reservation and payment.

Other users are similarly updating the databases concurrently. When Anne and Brian reconcile, they may experience conflicts such as double bookings, insufficient funds, or a full flight. Figure 3 presents an output from the reconciler: on top, a suggested non-conflicting schedule; the bottom lists the actions dropped from the schedule with explanations why dropped. In this case, Brian could not pay for the expensive flight, presumably because in the meantime a colleague has spent some of the travel account. The booking action in the same parcel is therefore dropped too. Instead, the cheaper flight alternative is scheduled. If Anne presses "Accept" at this point, the updates are committed to the underlying databases, i.e., the meeting added to the shared calendar, the flights are reserved, and costs are debited. Alternatively she may press "Retry" to ask IceCube to propose a new schedule based on the same inputs, or "Cancel" to exit and reconcile later.

3   Shared Data and Actions

Here we describe the replicated data and action classes; this information will be useful when we come to understanding constraints.

Replicated data is of class ReplicatedState, where applications provede implementations for the abstract checkpoint and returnToCheckpoint methods. This is so that the IceCube engine can undo tentative actions.

An action is an operation that is provided by some application; in effect, a method pointer or a closure. Some important interfaces of actions are in Figures 4, 5 and 6. The application programmer provides implementations for these interfaces, which are invoked by IceCube during reconciliation.

```
interface ActionExecution {
    // test precondition; no side effects
    boolean preCondition (ReplicatedState);
    // update state; return postcondition + undo info
    boolean execute (ReplicatedState, UndoData);
    // undo; return false if can not undo
    boolean compensate (ReplicatedState, UndoData);
}
```

Fig. 4. Action execution interface

The ActionExecution interface of Figure 4 is used to perform an action. IceCube first executes its preCondition method, then execute. The former (which may have no side effects) tests whether the action is valid in the current state. The latter updates the state. If either returns false, this indicates a dynamic constraint (defined shortly) has been violated.

The compensate method rolls back an update, provided undo information that was returned by the corresponding execute.

Not illustrated in the figure, an action has an integer *value*, 1 by default; this conveys user preferences between actions. The remaing interfaces will be detailed in later sections.

4   Constraints

A *constraint* is a correctness condition on schedules. Constraints are our central abstraction for conflict detection and scheduling. A *static* constraint relates two actions unconditionally. An example is the conflict between two appointment requests for Anne at 10:00 in different places. A *dynamic* constraint consists of the success or failure of a single action, depending on the current state. For instance, overdraft of the expense account constitutes a dynamic constraint.

No schedule generated by the engine ever violates a static constraint, therefore static constraints incur no run-time cost. In contrast, dynamic constraints are expensive, as a violation may cause unlimited roll-back. Fortunately, our technique of dividing the work into sub-problems (to be explained later) usually limits roll-backs to a small number of actions.

4.1 Primitive Static Constraints

The static constraints are built upon two primitives, Before, noted $\rightarrow$, and MustHave, noted $\triangleright$. Any schedule s must satisfy the following correctness conditions:

1. For all actions $\alpha, \beta \in s$, if $\alpha \rightarrow \beta$ then α comes before β in the schedule (although not necessarily immediately before),
2. For any $\alpha \in s$, every action β such that $\alpha \triangleright \beta$ is also in s (but not necessarily in that order nor contiguously).

Although the Before relation might be cyclic, a correct schedule may not contain a cycle of Before. The scheduler breaks any existing cycles by dropping actions appropriately. This search for an optimal acyclic sub-graph in a non-binary cyclic graph makes reconciliation an NP-hard problem [4].

4.2 Log Constraints

A *log constraint* is a static constraint between actions of the same log. User and application use log constraints to make their intents explicit. The addLogConstraint API assigns log constraints to an action.

In the current prototype, we have found the following three log-constraint types useful, which are built by composing the primitives. Constraint predSucc(α, β) establishes that action β executes only after α has succeeded (causal ordering). For instance, say a user tentatively updates a file, then copies the new version. To maintain correct behaviour in the reconciliation schedule, the application records a predSucc constraint between the write and the copy. predSucc(α, β) is equivalent to $\alpha \rightarrow \beta \land \beta \triangleright \alpha$.

The parcel log-constraint is an atomic (all-or-nothing) grouping. Either all of its actions execute successfully, or none. parcel(α, β) is equivalent to $\alpha \triangleright \beta \land \beta \triangleright \alpha$.[1] For instance a user might copy two whole directory trees inside a third directory as a parcel. If any of the individual copies would fail (e.g., for lack of space, or because the user doesn't have the necessary access rights) then none of the copies is included in the reconciled schedule.

The alternative log constraint provides choice of at most one action in a set. alternative(α, β) translates to $\alpha \rightarrow \beta \land \beta \rightarrow \alpha$, i.e., a cycle that the scheduler breaks by excluding either α or β (or both) from the schedule. An example is submitting an appointment request to a calendar application, when the meeting can take place at (say) either 10:00 or 11:00. Users use alternative constraints to provide the scheduler with a fallback in case of a conflict.

4.3 Object Constraints

An *object constraint* is a semantic relation between concurrent actions.

In preparation for reconciliation, and for every pair of concurrent actions, IceCube calls the methods in the ActionObjectConstraint interface of Figure 5

---

[1] Unlike a traditional transaction, a parcel does not ensure isolation. Its actions may run in any order, possibly interleaved with other actions (unless otherwise constrained).

to collect its object constraints. The application developper provides implementations for these methods: mutuallyExclusive should return true if both actions cannot be in the same schedule; and bestOrder should return true to indicate a preference for scheduling this action before the other.

```
interface ActionObjectConstraint {
    // test whether this and other action conflict
    boolean mutuallyExclusive (Action other);
    // Favorable ordering of actions
    int bestOrder (Action other);
}
```

Fig. 5. Object constraint interface

Object constraints express static concurrency semantics, similarly to Schwartz [14] or Weihl [18]. For instance, creating a file and creating a directory with the same name is mutuallyExclusive. Another example: an account manager indicates a bestOrder preference to schedule credits before debits. Like alternative, the constraint mutuallyExclusive(α, β) translates to $\alpha \rightarrow \beta \wedge \beta \rightarrow \alpha$. bestOrder$(\alpha, \beta)$ is equivalent to $\alpha \rightarrow \beta$.

Table 2. Account and Calendar constraints

Account	credit/credit	debit/debit	debit/credit
Different accounts	¬overlap	¬overlap	¬overlap
Same account	commute	commute	bestOrder
Dynamic constraint: no overdraft			
Calendar	/add/add	remove/remove	remove/add
Other user, time	¬overlap	¬overlap	¬overlap
Same user & time	Mut.Excl.	commute	bestOrder
Dynamic constraint: no double-booking			

As an example, Table 2 summarises the object and dynamic constraints of the account manager, and a calendar application with actions to add or remove an appointment.

4.4 Explicit Commutativity

Two actions that are not explicitly related by $\rightarrow$ can run in any order. However it is useful to further differentiate pairs of commuting actions that have no mutual side effects. This is important in several places; for instance when rolling back an action, later actions that commute with it do not need to be rolled back.

The ActionEnhancement methods of Figure 6 provide explicit commutativity information; they have priority over mutuallyExclusive and bestOrder.

A *domain* is an opaque hash characterising a set of objects read or written by an action. Get-

```
interface ActionEnhancements {
    // domain identifiers
    long[] getDomain ();
    // do this and other action (same domain) overlap
    boolean overlap (Action other);
    // do this and other (overlapping) action commute
    boolean commute (Action other);
}
```

Fig. 6. Action commutativity interface

Domain returns any number of domains. Actions with no common domain are commutative. For instance the domain of an account manager might be a hash of the account number.

If two actions have a common domain, IceCube calls their overlap method to test whether they overlap; if not, they are commutative. In our accounting example, overlap tests, first if the other action is also a accounting action (because domains are not guaranteed unique), then whether it operates on the same branch and account number.

When two actions overlap, method commute tests whether they commute semantically; if yes they are commutative. For instance, two credits to the same account overlap but commute.

4.5   Dynamic Constraints

To check a dynamic constraint the system must execute the action against the current state. Both preCondition and execute return a boolean value; if either returns false a dynamic constraint has been violated. A preCondition is not allowed to have side effects in order to avoid the cost of rolling back.

These methods can test arbitrary predicates that cannot easily be expressed with static constraints. The typical example is to check that the balance of an account is sufficient before executing a debit action.

It could be argued that dynamic constraints subsume static ones. While it is true that $\rightarrow$ could be checked dynamically, this would be orders of magnitude more expensive than our static scheduling algorithm. Furthermore $\triangleright$ cannot be captured with a dynamic check, which can only look at already-executed actions, not future ones.

5   Reconciliation Scheduler

As the scheduling problem is NP-hard, IceCube explores the space of possible schedules heuristically.

We now present more detail of the heuristics and optimisations. Benchmarks presented in Section 7 show that the algorithm is efficient, scales well and closely approximates the true optimum.

5.1   Partitioning into Sub-problems

For efficiency, we first the search space such that the combined complexity is much smaller than the original problem. IceCube partitions the actions into disjoint *sub-problems*, such that: actions in any sub-problem commute with actions in all other sub-problems, and there are no static constraints connecting actions from different sub-problems. Actions from different sub-problems may be scheduled in arbitrary order, and executing or rolling back an action belonging to some sub-problem does not affect actions of another sub-problem.

Partitioning occurs in three stages. First, actions are partitioned according by domain identifier (see Section 4.4), with a complexity linear in the number of actions. Then, each such domain again subdivided into sets of commuting actions (thanks to the interface of Figure 6), for a complexity quadratic in domain size.

Finally, any of the resulting sets that are connected by a static constraint or have an action in common are joined together, for a complexity proportional to the number of actions. For space reasons, we omit further detail; interested readers are referred to our technical report [11].

5.2   Heuristic Search

The scheduler performs efficient heuristic sampling of small portions of the search space for each sub-problem. If the user requests a new schedule, or the computation hits a dynamic constraint violation, the search restarts over an unrelated portion of the search space.

An exhaustive search has exponential complexity. In contrast, our heuristics have only quadratic cost (in sub-problem size), and have results virtually indistinguishable from exhaustive search. This is confirmed by our benchmarks in Section 7.

Iteratively, the scheduler heuristically selects the best (as defined in the next paragraph) action α from a set of candidates. If executing α violates a dynamic constraint, the scheduler undoes its execution and removes it from the candidate list. Otherwise it adds α to the current schedule, and removes from the candidates any action that conflicts statically with α. This algorithm guarantees that schedules are heuristically optimal and satisfy the constraints.

Given some partial schedule s, each candidate action α is assigned a merit that estimates the benefit of adding α to s, measured by the number of other actions can be scheduled after α. After experimenting, we have found that the following heuristic to be the most effective. The merit of α is:

1. Inversely proportional to the total value of actions β that could have been scheduled only before α, i.e., such that $\beta \notin s \wedge \beta \to \alpha$.

2. Inversely proportional to the total value of alternatives to α.

3. Inversely proportional to the total value of actions mutually exclusive with α.

4. Proportional to the total value of actions β that can only come after α, i.e., such that $\beta \notin s \wedge \alpha \to \beta$.

The above factors are listed in decreasing order of importance.

The merit also takes dynamic constraints into account. When a dynamic constraint is violated, we want to avoid violating it again. It is not known precisely which action(s) caused the constraint to to fail, but it can only be an action of the same sub-problem. Therefore we decrease the merit of the current action and of all actions that precede it in the same sub-problem.

The merit estimator executes in constant time.

Our scheduling algorithm, displayed in pseudo-code in Figure 7, selects, with randomisation, some action among those with highest merit, executes it, and adds it to the schedule if execution succeeds.

```
scheduleOne (state, summary, goodActions) =
  schedule := []
  value := 0
  actions := goodActions
  WHILE actions <> {} DO
    nextAction := selectActionByMerit (actions, schedule, summary)
    precondition := nextAction.preCondition (state)
    IF precondition = FALSE
    THEN // pre-condition false
      // abort partially-executed parcels
      cantHappenNow := OnlyBefore (nextAction, schedule)
      toExclude := MustHaveMe (nextAction)
      toAbort := INTERSECTION (schedule, toExclude)
      IF NOT EMPTY (toAbort)
      THEN // roll back
          SIGNAL dynamicFailure (goodActions \ toExclude)
      ELSE
          summary.updateInfoFailure (actions, toExclude)
          actions := actions \ toExclude \ cantHappenNow
          LOOP
    // pre-condition succeeded; now execute
    postcondition := nextAction.execute (state)
    IF postcondition = TRUE
    THEN // action succeeded
      toExclude := OnlyBefore (nextAction, schedule)
      toExclude := MustHaveMe (toExclude)
      actions := actions \ toExclude
      summary.updateInfo (actions, nextAction)
      schedule := [schedule | nextAction]
      value := value + nextAction.value
    ELSE // post-condition false: roll back
      toExclude := MustHaveMe (nextAction)
      SIGNAL dynamicFailure (goodActions \ toExclude)
  RETURN { state, schedule, value }
```

Fig. 7. Selecting and executing a single schedule

If executing candidate action α violated a dynamic constraint, it will not be scheduled, but the scheduler must roll back any side effects α may have had.[2] Furthermore, if the scheduler previously executed actions β such that $\beta \rhd \alpha$ (for instance, α and β are part of a parcel), then β is removed from the schedule and its side effects rolled back as well.

When adding some action α to the schedule, the engine drops from future consideration any action β that (if scheduled) would violate a static constraint against α. This consists of the sets MustHaveMe(α) = $\{\beta | \beta \rhd \alpha\}$ and OnlyBefore(α, s) = $\{\beta | \beta \to \alpha \wedge \beta \notin s\}$.

The scheduler calls scheduleOne repeatedly and remembers the highest-value schedule. It terminates when some application-specific selection criterion is satisfied — often a value threshold, a maximum number of iterations, or a maximum execution time.

The overall complexity of scheduleOne is $O(n^2)$, where n is the size of its input (a sub-problem). Readers interested in the full algorithm and justification of the complexity estimate are referred to our technical report [11].

---

[2] Selected actions are executed immediately, in order to reduce the amount of roll-back in case of dynamic constraint violation.

6   Calendar Application

To give a flavour of practical usage, we describe the calendar application in some detail (other applications are presented in more detail elsewhere [11]). It an appointment database shared by multiple users. User commands may request a meeting, possibly proposing several possible times, and cancel a previous request. A user command tentatively updates the database and logs the corresponding actions.

Database-level actions add or remove a single appointment. The user-level request command is mapped onto an alternative containing a set of add actions; similarly for cancel. Each such action contains the time, duration, participants and location of the proposed appointment.

Figure 8 contains some relevant code for add andremove. Object constraint and commutativity methods do the following:

1. getDomain: A shared calendar constitutes a domain.
2. overlap: Two actions (of the same calendar) overlap when either time and location or time and participants intersect.
3. commute: Overlapping remove actions commute with one another, since removing a meeting twice has the same effect as once.
4. mutuallyExclusive: if two add actions overlap, they also are mutually exclusive.
5. removes should preferably execute before adds to increase the probability that adds can be accommodated.

The code for add and remove actions implement the action execution methods from Figure 4:

1. preCondition: add.preCondition checks that the appointment doesn't double-book anything currently in the database.[3] remove.preCondition returns true.
2. The execute method updates the database and saves undo information.
3. The compensate method rolls back a previous executeusing the undo information.

Besides the add and remove, it was necessary to create a calendar ReplicatedState (CalendarState) to keep the calendar information (i.e., the scheduled appointments). Finally, a GUI interface allows users to access and modify the shared calendar.

The whole calendar application is very simple, totaling approximately 880 lines of code. This application was used as one of our performance and quality benchmarks, as we report in Section 7.

7   Measurements and Evaluation

This section reports on experiments that evaluate the quality, efficiency and scalability of IceCube reconciliation. Our two benchmarks are the calendar application, described previously, and an application described by Fages [3].

---

[3] The static constraints appear to make this check unnecessary, but it remains necessary in some corner cases.

```
class AddAction extends AbstractAction {
  long []domainId;
  MeetingInfo meeting;

  public boolean preCondition( ReplicatedState s0) {
    CalendaState s = (CalendarState)s0;
    return s.roomFree( meeting.location, meeting.time) &&
           s.peopleFree( meeting.participants, meeting.time);
  }
  public boolean execute( ReplicatedState s, UndoData info) {
    boolean result = ((CalendarState)s).insert( meeting);
    info.set( new Boolean( result));
    return result;
  }
  public boolean compensate( ReplicatedState s, UndoData info) {
    if( ! ((Boolean)info.get()).booleanValue())    // nothing to undo
      return true;
    return ((CalendarState)s).remove( meeting) != null;
  }
  public long []getDomain() {
    return domainId;
  }
  public boolean overlap( Action otherAction) {
    if( otherAction insetanceof AddAction)
      return meeting.overlaps( ((AddAction)otherAction).meeting);
    else
      return meeting.overlaps( ((RemoveAction)otherAction).meeting);
  }
  public boolean commute( Action otherAction) {
    return false;
  }
  public boolean mutuallyExclusive( Action otherAction) {
    return otherAction insetanceof AddAction &&
      return meeting.overlaps( ((AddAction)otherAction).meeting);
  }
  public int bestOrder( Action otherAction) {
    if( otherAction insetanceof RemoveAction &&
      meeting.overlaps( ((RemoveAction)otherAction).meeting))
      return ActionConstants.OTHER_FIRST;
    else
      return ActionConstants.ANY_ORDER;
  }
}

class RemoveAction extends AbstractAction {
  long []domainId;
  MeetingInfo meeting;

  public boolean preCondition( ReplicatedState s0) {
    return true;    //removing a non-existent meeting is not as error
  }
  public boolean execute( ReplicatedState s, UndoData info) {
    MeetingInfo oldMeeting = s.remove( meeting);
    info.set( oldMeeting);
    return true;
  }
  public boolean compensate( ReplicatedState s0, UndoData info) {
    MeetingInfo oldMeeting = (Meeting)info.get();
    if( meeting != null)
      return ((CalendarState)s0).insert( oldMeeting);
    return true;
  }
  public boolean commute( Action otherAction) {
    return otherAction insetanceof RemoveAction;
  }
  public boolean mutuallyExclusive( Action otherAction) {
    return false;
  }
}
```

Fig. 8. Calendar actions (simplified).

The calendar inputs are based on traces from actual Outlook calendars. These were artificially scaled up in size, and were modified to contain conflicts and alternatives and to control the difficulty of reconciliation. The logs contain only Requests, each of which contains one or more add alternatives. We varied the number of Requests and the number and size of possible sub-problems. The average number of add alternatives per request is two.

In each sub-problem, the number of different adds across all actions is no larger than the number of Requests. For instance, in the example of Figure 1, in the three Requests, there are only three different adds ('9am room A', '9am room B' and '9am room C'). This situation represents a hard problem for reconciliation because the suitable add alternative needs to be selected in every request (selecting other alternative in any request may lead to dropped actions).

In these experiments, all actions have equal value, and longer schedules are better. A schedule is called a *max-solution* when no request is dropped. A schedule is optimal when the highest possible number of Requests has been executed successfully. A max-solution is obviously optimal; however not all optimal solutions are max-solutions because of unresolvable conflicts. Since IceCube uses heuristics, it might propose non-optimal schedules; we measure the quality of solutions compared to the optimum. (Analysing a non-max-schedule to determine if it is optimal is done offline.)

The experiments were run on a generic PC running Windows XP with 256 Mb of main memory and a 1.1 GHz Pentium III processor. IceCube and applications are implemented in Java 1.1 and execute in the Microsoft Visual J++ environment. Everything is in virtual memory.

Each result is an average over 100 different executions, combining 20 different sets of requests divided between 5 different pairs of logs in different ways. Any comparisons present results obtained using exactly the same inputs. Execution times include both system time (scheduling and checkpointing), and application time (executing and undoing actions). The latter is negligeable because the add code is extremely simple.

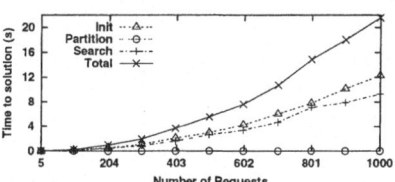

Fig. 9. Decomposition of reconciliation time (single sub-problem).

7.1 Single Sub-problem

To evaluate the core heuristics of Figure 7, we isolate the effects of partionining into sub-problems with a first set of inputs that gives birth to a single sub-problem.

Figure 9 measures the major components of IceCube execution time as log size increases. The "Init" line plots the time to collect object constraints and compute the initial summary of static constraints. "Partition" is the time to run the partitioning algorithm (although the experiment is rigged to generate a

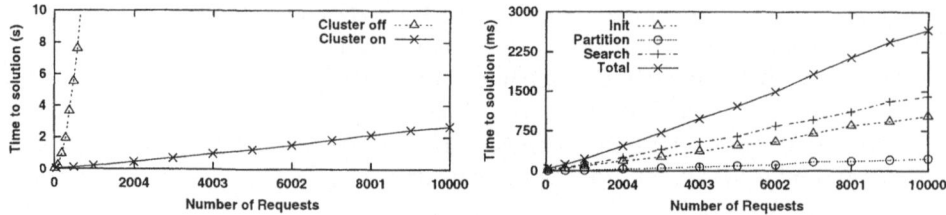

Fig. 10. Performance improvement with partitioning

Fig. 11. Decomposition of reconciliation time with partitioning.

single sub-problem, the partitioning algorithm still runs). "Search" is the time to create and execute schedules. "Total" is the total execution time. As expected, partitioning takes only a small fraction of the overall execution time. Init and Search are of comparable magnitude. The curves are consistent with our earlier $O(n^2)$ complexity estimate.

These experiments are designed to stop either when a max-solution is found, or after a given amount of time. Analysis shows that the max-solution is reached very quickly. The first schedule is a max-solution in over 90% of the cases. In 99% of the cases, a max-solution was found in the first five iterations. This shows that our search heuristics work very well, at least for this series of benchmarks. A related result is that in this experiment, even non-max-solutions were all within 1% of the max size.

Here is how the inputs are constructed. On average, each request is an alternate of h adds; each add in one request conflicts with a single add of another request. A log of x requests contains hx actions. To put the performance figures in perspective, consider that a blind search that ignores static constraints would have to explore a search space of size $(hx)!$ which, for $h = 2$ and $x = 1000$, is of the order of 10^{2061}. A more informed search that takes advantage of commutativity of actions would still have to explore a space of size $2^{hx} \approx 10^{600}$ for $h = 2$ and $x = 1000$. In fact there are only x distinct max-solutions.

7.2   Multiple Sub-problems

We now show the results when it is possible to partition the actions into sub-problems. This is the expected real-life situation.

The logs used in these experiments contain a variable number of Requests, and are constructed to that 25% of the adds can be partitioned alone; 25% of the remaining adds are in sub-problems with two actions; and so on. Thus, as problem size increases, the size of the largest sub-problem increases slightly, as one would expect in real life. For instance, when the logs contain 1,000 actions, the largest sub-problem contains the adds from 12 Requests, and 18 when the logs total 10,000. The number of sub-problems is approximately half of the number of actions; this ratio decreases slightly with log size. The average number of alternatives per request is two.

IceCube always finds a max-solution, whether partitioning is in use or not.

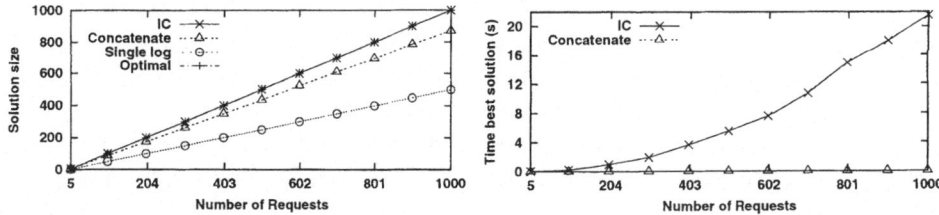

Fig. 12. Syntactic vs. semantic schedule quality.

Fig. 13. Syntactic vs. semantic performance.

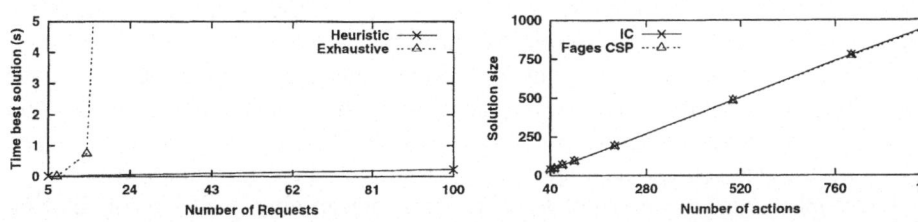

Fig. 14. Exhaustive vs. heuristic search performance.

Fig. 15. IceCube vs. Fages schedule quality (Fages' benchmarks).

Figure 10 shows the time to find a max-solution, with partitioning turned on or off; note the increased scale of the x axis. As expected a solution is obtained much more quickly in the former case than the latter. A running time under 3 s for a log size of 10,000, much larger than expected in practice, is quite reasonable even for interactive use. As the number of sub-problems grows almost linearly with the number of actions and the size of the largest sub-problem grows very slowly, reconciliation time is expected to grow almost linearly. The results confirm this conjecture. Moreover, the decomposition of the reconciliation time of Figure 11, shows that all components of the reconciliation time grow approximately linearly, as expected.

7.3   Comparisons

Here we compare the quality and performance of IceCube to competing approaches. Results in this section pertain to the non-partitioned problems of Section 7.1.

Most previous systems use a syntactic scheduling algorithm such as timestamp order or log concatenation. As these all suffer equally from false conflicts, Figure 12 compares IceCube against the simplest one, log concatenation.

As expected, the results of semantic search are better than syntactic ordering. Whereas log concatenation drops approximately 12% of Requests, semantic-directed search drops close to none (although IceCube's drop rate grows very slightly with size). Remember that dropping a single action may have a high cost.

The baseline for comparison is the line marked "Single log." This scheduler selects all actions from a single log and drops all actions from the other; it is the simplest non-trivial syntactic scheduler that guarantees absence of conflicts.

Figure 13 shows the execution time of our engine versus a log-concatenation (hence suboptimal) scheduler. As expected, IceCube is much slower. This is in line with the expected complexities, $O(n^2)$ in IceCube without partitioning, and $O(n)$ for the syntactic approach.

Figure 14 compares execution time of our heuristic with an exhaustive search algorithm [7]. Given unlimited time, exhaustive search is guaranteed to find the optimal schedule, but the figure shows this is not feasible except for very small log sizes (up to 20 actions or so). When execution time is limited, exhaustive search yields increasingly worse quality solutions as size increases. For instance, exhaustive searches of five different logs, each containing 30 requests, and each admitting a max-solution (size 30), returned schedules of size 28, 17, 6, 30, and 4 (average = 17) when limited to a very generous 120 s. With size 40 the average is 18, and for size 100 the average is only 28, under the same time limit. ·

Fages [3] studies a constraint satisfaction programming (CSP) reconciliation algorithm, with synthetic benchmarks. We now compare the quality of the two approaches by submitting one of Fages' benchmarks to IceCube, and our calendar benchmarks to Fages' system.

Fages' benchmark randomly generates (on average) 1.5 × size Before constraints per node. Figure 15 compares the quality of Fages' CSP solutions with IceCube's. The results are similar, but notice that IceCube appears to perform slightly better on large problems. This shows that the IceCube heuristics perform well on a different kind of input. As Fages' execution environment is very different, it would make no sense to compare absolute execution times; however we note that IceCube's execution time grows more slowly with size than Fages' constraint solver.

When we submit our calendar problems to Fages' system, execution time grows very quickly with problem size. For instance, for only 15 of our requests, Fages cannot find a solution within a timeout of 120 s. The explanation, we suspect, is that Fages' system does not deal well with alternatives.

8   Related Work

Several systems use optimistic replication and implement some form of reconciliation for divergent replicas. Many older systems (e.g., Lotus Notes [5] and Coda [8]) reconcile by comparing final tentative states. Other systems, like Ice-Cube, use history-based reconciliation, such as CVS [2] or Bayou [17]. Recent optimistically-replicated systems include TACT [19] and Deno [6]. Balasubramaniam and Pierce [1] and Ramsey and Csirmaz [12] study file reconciliation from a semantics perspective. Operational Transformation techniques [15] re-write action parameters to enable order-independent execution of non-conflicting actions, even when they do not commute. For lack of space we focus hereafter on systems most closely related to IceCube. For a more comprehensive survey, we refer the reader to Saito and Shapiro [13].

Bayou [17] is a replicated database system. Bayou schedules syntactically, in timestamp order. A tentative timestamp is assigned to an action as it arrives. The final timestamp is the time the action is accepted by a designated primary replica. Bayou first executes actions in their tentative order, then rolls back and replays them in final order. A Bayou action includes a "dependency check" (dynamic constraint) to verify whether the update is valid. If it is, the update is executed; otherwise, there is a conflict, and an application-provided merge procedure is called to solve it. Merge procedures are very hard to program [16]. IceCube extends these ideas by pulling static constraints out of the dependency check and the merge procedure, in order to search for an optimal schedule, reconciling in cases where Bayou would find a conflict. IceCube's alternatives are less powerful than merge procedures, but provide more information to the scheduler and are easier to use.

Lippe et al. [9] search for conflicts exhaustively comparing all possible schedules. Their system examines all schedules that are consistent with the original order of operations. A conflict is declared when two schedules lead to different states. Conflict resolution is manual. Examining all schedules is untractable for all but the smallest problems.

Phatak and Badrinath [10] propose a transaction management system for mobile databases. A disconnected client stores the read and write sets (and the values read and written) for each transaction. The application specifies a conflict resolution function and a cost function. The server serialises each transaction in the database history based on the cost and conflict resolution functions. As this system uses a brute-force algorithm to create the best ordering, it does not scale to a large number of transactions.

IceCube follows on from the work of Kermarrec et al. [7]. They were the first to distinguish static from dynamic constraints. However their engine only supports Before (not MustHave), does not distinguish between log and object constraints, and does not have clean logs. Most importantly, an exhaustive search algorithm like theirs cannot not scale beyond very small log sizes.

9   Final Remarks

Supporting collaboration in mobile computing environments requires that applications and data management system rely on optimistic replication. As uncoordinated contributions (updates) from several users may conflict, the reconciliation mechanism is an important piece in system that support collaborative activities in mobile computing environments.

In this paper, we have presented a general-purpose, semantics-aware reconciliation scheduler that differs from previous work in several key aspects. Our system is the first to approach reconciliation as an optimisation problem and to be based on the true constraints between actions. We present novel abstractions that enable the concise expression of semantics of these constraints. This simplifies the development of applications using reconciliation, as demonstrated by several prototype applications, and enables the reconciler to deliver high-quality solutions efficiently. Although reconciliation is NP-hard, our heuristics find near-optimal solutions in reasonable time, and scale to large logs. Finally, IceCube is application-independent, and bridges application boundaries by allowing actions from separate applications to be related by log constraints and reconciled together.

Our system has made it easier for developers to make their applications tolerant of tentative operation and to reconcile replicated data. Application developers need not develop their own reconciliation logic. The framework design keeps application logic largely independent from the distribution, replication, and reconciliation. For the latter, IceCube provides a general-purpose middleware that applies to a large spectrum of applications. On the other hand, application design for this environment remains a demanding intellectual task.

The source code for IceCube is available from
http://research.microsoft.com/camdis/icecube.htm.

Acknowledgements. We thank François Fages for studying the complexity of reconciliation and proposing alternative solutions. Peter Druschel, Anne-Marie Kermarrec and Antony Rowstron provided much of the initial design and implementation.

References

1. S. Balasubramaniam and Benjamin C. Pierce. What is a file synchronizer? In *Int. Conf. on Mobile Comp. and Netw. (MobiCom '98)*. ACM/IEEE, October 1998. http://www.cis.upenn.edu/~bcpierce/papers/snc-mobicom.ps.
2. Per Cederqvist, Roland Pesch, et al. Version management with CVS, date unknown. http://www.cvshome.org/docs/manual.
3. François Fages. A constraint programming approach to log-based reconciliation problems for nomadic applications. In *Proc. 6th Annual W. of the ERCIM Working Group on Constraints*, June 2001.
4. R.M. Karp. Reducibility among combinatorial problems. In R.E. Miller and J.W. Tatcher, editors, *Complexity of Computer Computations*, pages 85–103. Plenum, New York, 1972.
5. Leonard Kawell Jr., Steven Beckhart, Timoty Halvorsen, Raymond Ozzie, and Irene Greif. Replicated document management in a group communication system. In *2nd. Conf. on Comp.-Supported Coop. Work*, Portland OR (USA), September 1988.
6. Peter J. Keleher. Decentralized replicated-object protocols. In *18th Symp. on Princ. of Distr. Comp. (PODC)*, Atlanta, GA, USA, May 1999. http://mojo.cs.umd.edu/papers/podc99.pdf.
7. Anne-Marie Kermarrec, Antony Rowstron, Marc Shapiro, and Peter Druschel. The IceCube approach to the reconciliation of divergent replicas. In *20th Symp. on Principles of Dist. Comp. (PODC)*, Newport RI (USA), August 2001. ACM SIGACT-SIGOPS. http://research.microsoft.com/research/camdis/Publis/podc2001.pdf.
8. Puneet Kumar and M. Satyanarayanan. Flexible and safe resolution of file conflicts. In *Usenix Tech. Conf.*, New Orleans, LA, USA, January 1995. http://www.cs.cmu.edu/afs/cs/project/coda/Web/docdir/usenix95.pdf.

9. E. Lippe and N. van Oosterom. Operation-based merging. *ACM SIGSOFT Software Engineering Notes*, 17(5):78–87, 1992.
10. Sirish Phatak and B. R. Badrinath. Transaction-centric reconciliation in disconnected databases. In *ACM MONET*, July 2000.
11. Nuno Preguiça, Marc Shapiro, and Caroline Matheson. Efficient semantics-aware reconciliation for optimistic write sharing. Technical Report MSR-TR-2002-52, Microsoft Research, Cambridge (UK), May 2002.
    http://research.microsoft.com/scripts/pubs/view.asp?TR_ID=MSR-TR-2002-52.
12. Norman Ramsey and Előd Csirmaz. An algebraic approach to file synchronization. In *9th Foundations of Softw. Eng.*, pages 175–185, Austria, September 2001.
13. Yasushi Saito and Marc Shapiro. Replication: Optimistic approaches. Technical Report HPL-2002-33, Hewlett-Packard Laboratories, March 2002.
    http://www.hpl.hp.com/techreports/2002/HPL-2002-33.html.
14. Peter M. Schwartz and Alfred Z. Spector. Synchronizing shared abstract types. *ACM Transactions on Computer Systems*, 2(3):223–250, August 1984.
15. Chengzheng Sun and Clarence Ellis. Operational transformation in real-time group editors: issues, algorithms, and achievements. In *Conf. on Comp.-Supported Cooperative Work (CSCW)*, page 59, Seattle WA (USA), November 1998.
    http://www.acm.org/pubs/articles/proceedings/cscw/289444/p59-sun/p59-sun.pdf.
16. Douglas B. Terry, Marvin Theimer, Karin Petersen, and Mike Spreitzer. An examination of conflicts in a weakly-consistent, replicated application. Personal Communication, 2000.
17. Douglas B. Terry, Marvin M. Theimer, Karin Petersen, Alan J. Demers, Mike J. Spreitzer, and Carl H. Hauser. Managing update conflicts in Bayou, a weakly connected replicated storage system. In *Proc. 15th ACM Symposium on Operating Systems Principles*, Copper Mountain CO (USA), December 1995. ACM SIGOPS.
    http://www.acm.org/pubs/articles/proceedings/ops/224056/p172-terry/p172-terry.pdf.
18. W. E. Weihl. Commutativity-based concurrency control for abstract data types. *IEEE Transactions on Computers*, 37(12):1488–1505, December 1988.
    http://www.computer.org/tc/tc1988/t1488abs.htm.
19. Haifeng Yu and Amin Vahdat. Combining generality and practicality in a Conit-based continuous consistency model for wide-area replication. In *21st Int. Conf. on Dist. Comp. Sys. (ICDCS)*, April 2001.
    http://www.cs.duke.edu/~yhf/icdcsfinal.ps.

A Distributed Rule Mechanism for Multidatabase Systems

Vasiliki Kantere[1], John Mylopoulos[1], and Iluju Kiringa[2]

[1] University of Toronto, 40 St George St., Toronto, Canada
{verena,jm}@cs.toronto.edu
[2] University of Ottawa, 800 King Edward, Ottawa, Canada
kiringa@site.uottawa.ca

Abstract. We describe a mechanism based on distributed Event-Condition-Action (ECA) rules that supports data coordination in a multidatabase setting. The proposed mechanism includes an ECA rule language and a rule execution engine that transforms and partitions rules when they are first posted, and then coordinates their execution. The paper also presents a prototype implementation in a simulated environment as well as preliminary experimental results on its performance. This work is part of an on-going project intended to develop data coordination techniques for peer-to-peer databases.

1 Introduction

In the last fifteen years, relational and object-oriented database management systems have been augmented with a mechanism for expressing active behavior to yield active database management systems (ADBMSs). Usually, ADBMSs use Event-Condition-Action (ECA) rules as the standard mechanism for capturing active behavior. Using a set of ECA rules, an ADBMS performs database definition and manipulation operations automatically, without any user intervention. However, ECA functionality has been considered mostly in centralized environments [4]. Some attempts were made to integrate ECA rules in distributed database systems in [18], [6], [7], [1], and [14]. These approaches usually elaborate on some of the aspects of the problem, but do not present a complete solution. A notable exception is the vision for ECA functionality in a distributed setting discussed in [4].

The recent surge of interest in the peer-to-peer (hereafter P2P) architectures of networking should motivate a change in our attitude towards distributed ECA rule mechanisms. Briefly, a P2P architecture is a dynamic node-to-node mode of communication over the Internet. Existing P2P applications support mostly file exchange, and there is no obvious way of performing advanced querying or enforcing consistency on data across peers. Overall, the existing P2P applications do not deal with data management issues. However, many application domains need the kind of advanced data management that would be offered by a P2P system to be able to manage efficiently data residing in peer databases [17], [2], [13]. One such domain is health care, where

R. Meersman et al. (Eds.): CoopIS/DOA/ODBASE 2003, LNCS 2888, pp. 56–73, 2003.
© Springer-Verlag Berlin Heidelberg 2003

hospitals, family doctors, pharmacists, and pharmaceutical companies maintain data-bases about patients and would like to participate in a P2P system in order to exchange information about medical histories, medication, symptoms, treatments and the like for patients. Another example is genomic databases. There are many genomic data sources all over the world, from widely known ones, like GenBank and GDB, to indi-vidual and independent lab repositories [13]. It would be useful for scientists to be able to share such data and exploit information from different databases that is rele-vant to their research. Further domains that would benefit from P2P database technol-ogy are: e-commerce in general (e.g. buyers and sellers with the same business inter-ests would like to share information and build *ad hoc* communities), and news industry (e.g. TV channels, radio stations, and press could set up partnership communities for sharing information).

In this paper we present a prototype distributed rule mechanism for a multidatabase system that we intend to use in a P2P setting. We consider multidatabase systems consisting of autonomous databases that reside on different nodes of a network and intend to exchange information without complying with any central administration. However, for simplicity we assume that the heterogeneity issue is solved through a mapping mechanism (e.g. mapping tables [13]). In particular, we propose an ECA rule language that includes a rich event language for the expression of composite events. We have also designed an execution model that minimizes the number of communica-tion messages among the multidatabases involved in the execution of a rule. The pro-posed evaluation procedure is fully distributed, and involves partial evaluations of rule components in different databases, together with the composition of partial results into a global evaluation. We have also developed a prototype implementation of the pro-posed mechanism and have performed preliminary experiments in a simulated envi-ronment comparing it with a centralized rule execution model.

The next section gives specific scenarios that illustrate the usefulness of the active functionality in a multidatabase environment. Section 3 presents the main features of our ECA rule language. An execution model for the rule language of Section 3 is given in Section 4. Section 5 describes our prototype implementation, and reports on some experimental results. Section 6 discusses related work. Finally, Section 7 con-cludes the paper, and raises issues that need further work, particularly the intended application of our framework in the P2P setting.

2   A Motivating Example

Assume that there is a multidatabase system where the involved multidatabases can be databases of family doctors, hospitals and pharmacists. This example is adapted from [3]. Fig. 1 depicts a subnet of such a system with three multidatabases, on top of which resides a rule management system.

Assume that Dr. Davis is a family doctor and his database, DavisDB, is member of the multidatabase system. DavisDB is acquainted with the database of a pharmacist,

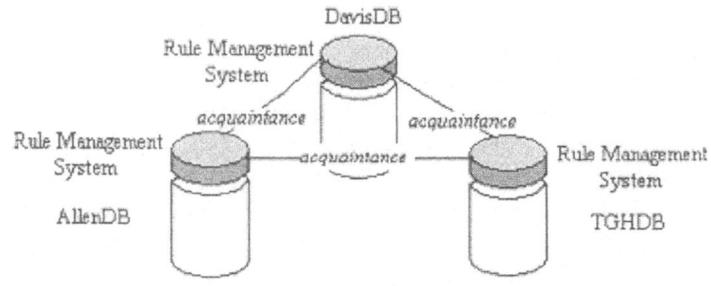

Fig. 1. Acquainted Multidatabases

AllenDB and with the database of the Toronto General Hospital, TGHDB. Also, AllenDB is acquainted with TGHDB. The three databases contain the following tables:
DavisDB:
Visit (OHIP#, Date, Time, Symptom, Diagnosis)
Prescription (OHIP#, DrugID, Date, Dose, Quantity)
DiseaseOccur (OHIP#, Date, DiseaseDescr)
Treatments(DiseaseDescr, TreatmRecord, DrugsRecord)
Allergies (OHIP#, Allergy)
AllenDB:
Presciption (Prescr#, CustName, CustPhone#, DrugID, Dose, Repeats, DiseaseDescr)
Allergies (DrugID, Allergy)
TGHDB:
DiseaseOccur (Date, OHIP#, DiseaseDescr)
Treatment(TreatID, TGH#, Date, DiseaseDescr, TreatDescr, PhysID)
Admission (AdmID, OHIP#, AdmDate, ProblemDesc, PhysID, DisDate)
MedRec (OHIP#, Date, Time, Record)
Medication (OHIP#, Date, Time, DrugID, Dose)

Suppose that Dr. Davis wants to keep track of treatment methods and medications for a number of specific diseases. Thus, he wants to get information about treatments in the hospital and the medication that Mr. Allen is selling after prescription for this disease. The appropriate rule for this is:

Rule 3:
when TGHDB.('insert',
        (Treatment,(_, _, _, <DiseaseDescr_value>, <TreatDescr_value>, _)))
        OR AllenDB.('insert',
        (Prescription,(_,_,_, <DrugID_value>, _, _, <DiseaseDescr_value>))))
if   <DiseaseDescr_value> in DiseaseDescrSet
        (*where* DavisDB.('retrieve',15, {DiseaseDescrSet})
then DavisDB.('update',(Treatments, (<DiseaseDescr_value>, _, _)))

The underscores denote values of the corresponding attributes that are of no interest or computable at runtime. The *where* clause denotes that we get the set of values of the *DiseaseDescr* attribute of the *Treatments* relation by performing the query 15 below on DavisDB:

Query 15:   *Select*   DiseaseDescr
              From   Treatments

Suppose that a patient visits Dr. Davis and the latter suggests that she should be admitted to the hospital for examination. When she is admitted to the hospital, information on the diagnosis of Dr. Davis should be transferred to the TGHDB. To do this, the following rule may be appropriate:

Rule 4:

when   DavisDB.('insert', (Visit, (<OHIP#_value1>,
         <Date_value>,<Time_value>, _,<Diagnosis_value>))) «
         TGHDB.('insert', (Admission, (_, <OHIP#_value2 >, _, _, _, _)))
if   <OHIP#_value1> = <OHIP#_value2>
then   TGHDB.('insert', (MedRec, (<OHIP#_value2>,
                 <Date_value>, <Time_value>, <Diagnosis_value>)))

The symbol '«' means sequence and is introduced explicitly in the next section. This rule denotes that when there is an insertion in the *Visit* relation of DavisDB for a patient, and afterwards there is an insertion in the *Admission* relation of TGHDB for another (possibly different) patient, if the two patients are the same person according to their OHIP#, then insert to the *MedRec* relation of TGHDB a tuple with information about the diagnosis of Dr. Davis for that patient.

3 Distributed ECA Rule Language

The ECA rules have the following general form:
              R: *when <event>,*
                         [if <condition >,]
                         then <action>
where the brackets denote an optional part. Many ECA rule languages have been proposed in the previous decade for centralized environments. Most of them involved event, condition and action languages that provided only basic operators. However, there are some rich event languages in the literature [10]. The main goal in proposing a rule language for a multidatabase environment is to provide clear semantics specifically adapted to the distributed nature of such a system, so that they are able to express events, conditions and actions on more than one databases and that will allow distributed evaluation of rules. Also, such a rule language should be rich enough in order to be suitable for a variety of multidatabase systems, and furthermore, for P2P database systems. As far as we know there are no rule languages for distributed database systems suitable for distributed evaluation. Moreover, the existing ones for centralized environments offer event languages with semantics that cannot be used for partial and asynchronous evaluations of composite events.

In the rest of this section we define the languages that we use in order to declare each one of the three ECA parts, namely event, condition, and action.

Operator	Type	Function	Syntax
∧	Binary	Logical AND	\<event1>∧\<event2>
∨	Binary	Logical OR	\<event1>∨\<event2>
!	Unary	Logical NOT	!\<event>
«	Binary	Loose Sequence	\<event1> « \<event2>
*	Unary	Zero or more occurrences	*\<event>
+	Unary	One or more occurrences	+\<event>
#	Binary	Exact number of occurrences	\<number of occurrences>#\<event>
&	Binary	Maximum number of occurrences	\<number of occurrences>&\<event>
$	Binary	Minimum number of occurrences	\<number of occurrences>$\<event>
>	Binary	Strict sequence	\<loose sequence expression> > \<not expression>

Fig. 2. Event Operators

3.1 Event Language

The event language that we propose provides a set of operators with clear semantics for a multidatabase environment. These semantics allow the construction of a wide variety of composite events. We believe that the high level of expressiveness of the event language makes it suitable for many types of multidatabase systems. A simple or primitive event SE in a database DB, which we denote as DB.SE, can be either a database or a time event. A time event can be an absolute, a relative or a periodic time event. A database event is one of the following four types of primitive database operations: *retrieve, update, insert,* and *delete*. A composite event is an expression that is formed by applying the operators of an event algebra on simple or composite events. An event instance is an occurrence in time of the respective event. Generally, an event instance starts at a time point t_s and ends at a time point t_e. Our convention is that an event instance is instant and occurs at the time point t_e.

The event algebra that we propose for a multidatabase system is shown in the table of Fig. 2. The general form of an operator is $OpType_{ti}$, where $OpType$ is the type of operator and ti is the time interval within which an instance of the composite event specified by the operator should be completed. More specifically, for every instance of a composite event, the earliest simple event instance and the latest one should have a time distance equal or shorter than the time interval denoted by the value of ti. The ti parameter of the operators is the main difference between our event algebra and the ones used for the declaration of composite events in centralized database environments. The time interval of an operator provides reference time points (either relative or absolute) that allow the performance of partial asynchronous distributed evaluations in several sites, which produce partial results (i.e. event instances) that could be used for the detection of an event instance of a global rule.

Let CE(t) denote a composite event instance occurring at the time point t. Also, let E denote an event expression (either simple or composite). Then the following defines the event operators of our language (See Fig. 2)[1].

1. <u>Conjunction</u>: ∧

$CE(t) = (E1 \wedge_{ti} E2)(t) := E1(t_1) \ AND \ E2(t_2)$, where $t_2 = t$ if $t_1 \leq t_2$, or $t_1 = t$ if $t_2 < t_1$. and $t_1, t_2 \in ti$. Thus, the conjunction of E1 and E2 given ti means that both E1 and E2 occur during ti.

2. <u>Disjunction</u>: ∨

$CE(t) = (E1 \vee_{ti} E2)(t) := E1(t_1) \ OR \ E2(t_2)$, where $t_2 = t$

if $t_1 \leq t_2$ or there is no t_1, or $t_1 = t$ if $t_2 < t_1$ or there is no t_2, and $t_1, t_2 \in ti$. Thus, the disjunction of E1 and E2 given ti means that either E1 or E2, or both E1 and E2 occur during ti.

3. <u>Negation</u>: !

$CE(t) = (!_{ti} E)(t) := NOT \ (\exists t' \in ti : E(t'))$. Thus, the negation of E given ti means that E does not occur during ti. Also, t is the end point of ti.

4. <u>Loose sequence</u>: «

$CE(t) = (E1 \ll_{ti} E2)(t) := E1(t_1) \ AND \ E2(t)$, where $t_1 \leq t$ and $t_1, t \in ti$. Thus, loose sequence of E1 and E2 given ti means that E1 occurs before E2 during ti.

5. <u>Strict sequence</u>: >

$CE(t) = ((E1 \ll_{ti} E2) >_{ti} (!_{ti} E3))(t) := E1(t_1) \ AND \ E2(t) \ AND \ (NOT \ E3(t_3))$, where $t_1 \leq t_3 \leq t$ and $t_1, t_3, t \in ti$. Thus, the strict sequence of E1 and E2 given ti and E3 means that E1 occurs before E2 without E3 occurring between them during ti.

6. <u>Zero or more occurrences</u>: *

$CE(t) = (*_{ti} E)(t) := (E(t_1) \ AND \ E(t_2) \ AND \ ... \ AND \ E(t_{m-1}) \ AND \ E(t_m)) \ OR \ true$, where $t_1 \leq t_2 \leq ... \leq t_{m-1} \leq t_m$ and $t_m = t$ and t1, t ∈ ti and $1 \leq m$ and $m \in N$. Thus, 'star' of E given ti means that E either does not occur or occurs one or more times during ti. Note that the goal of the * operator, according to the definition above, is not to search for the validity of the expression $*_{ti}E$, but to keep track of the instances of the event expression E, if there are any. The role of the 'star' operator is associative. It is not used in the declaration of original event expressions, but in the construction of subevents (see Section 4).

7. <u>One or more occurrences</u>: +

$CE(t) = (+_{ti} E)(t) := E(t_1) \ AND \ E(t_2) \ AND \ ... \ AND \ E(t_{m-1}) \ AND \ E(t_m)$, where $t_1 \leq t_2 \leq ... \leq t_{m-1} \leq t_m$ and $t_m = t$ and $t_1, t \in ti$ and $1 \leq m$ and $m \in N$. Thus, 'plus' of E given ti means that E occurs one or more times during ti.

8. <u>Exact number of occurrences</u>: #

$CE(t) = (_m\#_{ti} E)(t) := E(t_1) \ AND \ E(t_2) \ AND \ ... AND \ E(t_{m-1}) \ AND \ E(t_m)$, where $t_1 \leq t_2 \leq ... \leq t_{m-1} \leq t_m$ and $t_m = t$ and $t_1, t \in ti$ and $m \in N$. Thus, given m and ti E occurs exactly m times during ti.

9. <u>Maximum number of occurrences</u>: &

$CE(t) = (_m\&_{ti} E)(t) := E(t_1) \ AND \ E(t_2) \ AND ... AND \ E(t_{m-1}) \ AND \ E(t_m)$, where

---

[1] In all the definitions throughout the paper the symbol N represents the set of natural numbers

$t_1 \le t_2 \le ... \le t_{m-1} \le t_m$ and $t_m = t$ and t_1, $t \in$ ti and $m' \ge m$ and $m', m \in$ N. Thus, given m' and ti E occurs at most m' times during ti.

10.<u>Minimum number of occurrences</u>: $

$CE(t) = (_m\$_{st} E)(t) := E(t_1)$ AND $E(t_2)$ AND ... AND $E(t_{m-1})$ AND $E(t_m)$, where $t_1 \le t_2 \le ... \le t_{m-1} \le t_m$ and $t_m = t$ and t_1, $t \in$ ti and $m' \le m$ and $m', m \in$ N. Thus, given m' and ti E occurs at least m' times during ti.

3.2 Condition Language

The composite condition of the ECA rule is a Boolean expression using the operators of the Boolean algebra, i.e., AND, OR, and NOT. These operators take as operands either composite or simple conditions that can involve more than one database. A simple condition is one of the following:

1. a mathematical expression of the form: $f(X_1, X_2,..., X_n)$ *mop* Y, where *mop* (which stands for mathematical operator) is either $=$, $\ne$, $>$ or $<$; X_1, X_2, ..., X_n, $Y \in \Re$; $n \in$ N; and f is any kind of mathematical function.
2. a logical expression of the form $X == Y$ or $X \ne Y$, where X, Y are strings.
3. an expression of the form $X \in \{X_1, X_2,..., X_n\}$, where X, X_1, X_2,..., X_n are strings, or X, X_1, X_2,..., $X_n \in \Re$.

The symbol $\Re$ in the definitions above represents the set of real numbers. For all three cases: X_i, for i = 1,..,n, X or Y are either variables or constants. If they are variables, they take values either directly from parameters of the simple event instances of the event part of the rule or indirectly from results of queries that are performed in order to evaluate the condition. The definition of such queries is parametrical and can use parameters from the event part of the rule.

3.3. Action Language

The composite action of the ECA rule is a conjunction of simple or composite actions. A simple action is of the form: $DB_i.(Tr)$. Here, the expression DB_i, for $\forall i \in$ N and $1 \le i \le n$, is one of the n-1 acquainted databases to the one on which the rule that contains this specific action is to be installed. The variable Tr comprises the necessary information in order to perform the predefined transaction that is actually the simple database operation (insert, update, delete, retrieve) that we want to perform on DB_i.

3.4 A Further Rule Example

We present a sample rule (from the health care domain of Section 1) emphasizing on the condition part. Suppose that we want to monitor a specific patient in the hospital that has 2 or more epileptic crises in a day. If she is taking a specific drug, <DrugID_value1>, and the dose is more than <constant>, if she is not allergic to drug

<DrugID_value2>, then change the medication to the latter. We assume that the family doctor of the patient is Dr. Davis. The corresponding rule is:

Rule 5:
when $_2\$_{(0, 0, 0, 1-, 0, 0)}$ TGHDB.('insert',('MedRec',
      (<OHIP#_value>, _, _, 'epileptic crisis')))
if (<DrugID_value> == <DrugID_value1>) AND (<Dose_value> > <constant>)
  AND ({<Allergy_value1> ∈ AllergySet1} ≠
          {<Allergy_value2> ∈ AllergySet2})
    (*where* TGHDB.('retrieve', 15, {<OHIP#_value>,
          <DrugID_value>, <Dose_value>})
    and DavisDB.('retrieve',45,{<OHIP#_value>, AllergySet1})
    and AllenDB.('retrieve',17,{<DrugID_value2>, AllergySet2}))
then TGHDB.('insert', ('Medication', (<OHIP#_value>,
    <currentDate>, <currentTime>, <DrugID_value2>, _)))

Query 15:	*Select*	DrugID, Dose
	From	Medication
	Where	OHIP# = <OHIP#_value>, Date = <current date>,
		Time = <most recent time>
Query 45:	*Select*	Allergy
	From	Allergies
	Where	OHIP# = <OHIP#_value>
Query 17:	*Select*	Allergy
	From	Allergies
	Where	DrugID = <DrugID_value2>

In this example, the value (0,0,0,1,_,0,0) denotes the period of one day (the actual set of parameters is (second, minute, hour, day, weekday, month, year). For details on the definition and use of the time interval of an operator see [11]). The 'where' clause in the condition means that we have to perform some queries in order to get the values of the attributes that we want to compare. Thus, we perform query 15 in TGHDB in order to retrieve the drug name and the dose that the patient is receiving currently; we perform the query 45 in DavisDB and the query 17 in AllenDB to retrieve the allergies of the patient and the allergies that the drug <DrugID_value2> can provoke, respectively. The results of queries 45 and 17 are stored in the variables AllergySet1 and AllergySet2 respectively.

4 Processing ECA Rules

When a new rule is created in a database, the latter is responsible for the coordination of the global evaluation of the rule. However, the evaluation of the rule involves other databases with respect to the event, condition and action. This section describes the general evaluation procedure as well as the two basic algorithms that construct the input of the partial evaluations that take place in databases involved in the rule.

NewRule ()

  {   *while* (creation of a new rule)

    { -- decompose the rule into subrules and send

          them to the respective databases

    -- run the evaluation procedure for this rule

    -- run the garbage collection for this rule } }

EvaluationProcedure (Rule newRule)

{   *while* (*true*)

    { -- wait until a subrule instance of this rule is received

      -- *boolean* valid = evaluate the original rule with all the accumulated subrule

        instances

      if (valid)

      {*if* (additional info for the condition is

             needed)

      { -- request additional info for the

        evaluation of the condition

      -- *boolean* newruleinstance = evaluate   the condition with all the

        accumulated info

      if (newruleinstance)

      { -- execute the action part of the global rule

        -- throw away the subrule instances and the additional condition informa-

          tion used to form this rule instance } }

    else

    { -- execute the action part

    -- throw away the subrule instances

      used to form this rule instance } } } }

GarbageCollection (Rule newRule)

{ periodically remove the obsolete subrule instances}

Fig. 3. Evaluation Procedure

4.1 Algorithm for the Global Evaluation

Fig. 3 presents a pseudo code of the general algorithm for the global distributed evaluation procedure. The evaluation procedure is as follows: The new rule, to which we refer as global/original rule, is decomposed into subrules that can be evaluated separately in each one of the databases that are involved in the original rule. We produce one such 'subrule' for each database involved in the event part. For those databases that appear both in the event and the condition parts, we add the appropriate condition expression to their corresponding subrule. This condition expression is a sub-expression of the condition part of the global rule. Each subrule is sent to the database it was made for and is evaluated there. The action part of these subrules is to send the subrule instance to the database responsible for the global evaluation of the rule. The global evaluation of the original event and the original condition expression starts when the local evaluation of one of the created subrules produces an instance that could contribute to the production of an instance of the original-global rule. When such a subrule instance is received in the database where the global rule was created, the procedure tries to find a valid match using the subrule instances that are stored and not used by other rule instances. If a valid match is found, possible additional condition information is requested and gathered. Finally, if the condition instance is true, the action part is executed. The global evaluation procedure aims to minimize the number of messages exchanged among the multidatabases.

The algorithm in Fig. 3 guarantees that the maximum number of messages (that are exchanged among the databases involved in the processing of a rule until the event and the condition expressions are valid and the action part is executed) is the lowest. This number is Max # messages = n+2k+r, where n, k and r is the number of databases involved in the event, condition and action part, respectively (for details see [11]).

4.2 Transformation Algorithm

Before the event expression is decomposed into parts, it is transformed in order to have a form more convenient for decomposition. The goal of the following algorithm is to push the 'not' operators down to the leaves of the tree of the event expression. The evaluation of the 'not' operators is hard and by pushing them down in the event tree, we may be able to eliminate some of them. Moreover, it is possible to give to the rule a form that is more convenient for the evaluation procedure. However, the decomposition of an event expression is possible even without running the transformation algorithm first. The steps of the algorithm are executed multiple times until there are no transformations left to be done. Note that, in case that the operand of the 'not' operator is a composite event, the time interval of the 'not' operator has to be the same as the time interval of the operator of its operand.

transformed = true;
while (transformed)
{   transformed = false;
1. check if there are pairs of consecutive 'not' operators. If there are, eliminate them and set transformed = true.
2. check for the pattern: $!_{ti1}$ (E1 $\wedge_{ti1}$ E2). If found, replace it with the pattern: ($!_{ti1}$ E1) $\vee_{ti2}$ ($!_{ti1}$ E2) and set transformed = true.
3. check for the pattern: $!_{ti1}$ (E1 $\vee_{ti1}$ E2). If found, replace it with the pattern: ($!_{ti1}$ E1) $\wedge_{ti2}$ ($!_{ti1}$ E2) and set transformed = true.
4. check for the pattern: $!_{ti1}$ (E1 $\ll_{ti1}$ E2). If found, replace it with the pattern: ($!_{ti1}$ E1) $\vee_{ti2}$ ($!_{ti1}$ E2) $\vee_{ti2}$ (E2 $\ll_{ti1}$ E1) and set transformed = true.
5. check for the pattern: $!_{ti1}$ ((E1 $\ll_{ti1}$ E2) $>_{ti1}$ ($!_{ti1}$ E3)). If found, replace it with the pattern: ($!_{ti1}$ E1) $\vee_{ti2}$ ($!_{ti1}$ E2) $\vee_{ti2}$ (E2 $\ll_{ti1}$ E1) $\vee_{ti2}$ (E1 $\ll_{ti1'}$ E3 $\ll_{ti1''}$ E2), where ti1' + ti1'' = ti1 and set transformed = true.
6. check for the pattern: $!_{ti1}$ ($+_{ti1}$ E). If found, replace it with: $!_{ti1}$ E and set transformed = true.

7. check for the pattern ! $_{ti1}$ ($_m$ $ $_{ti1}$ E). If found, replace it with: $_{m-1}$ & $_{ti1}$ E, and set transformed = true.

8. check for the pattern ! $_{ti1}$ ($_m$ & $_{ti1}$ E). If found, replace it with: $_{m+1}$ $ $_{ti1}$ E, and set transformed = true.

9. check for the pattern ! $_{ti1}$ ($_m$ # $_{ti1}$ E). If found, replace it with: ($_{m-1}$ & $_{ti1}$ E) ∨ $_{ti2}$ ($_{m+1}$ $ $_{ti1}$ E), and set transformed = true.

10. Change the time interval of 'not' operators that have as operand a composite event to be equal to the time interval of the operator of their operand.

}

In steps 1, 2, 3, 4, 5, 9 of the algorithm above the time interval ti2 of the transformed expressions is of zero length: |ti2| = 0. Also, note that the disjunction operator in step 9 serves as an exclusive OR. Step 10 is associative and adapts the time interval of the 'not' operators to the interval in which the non-occurrence of their operand should be evaluated. After the transformation the 'not' operators have as operands only simple events. The initial event expression is semantically equivalent to the transformed expression. For details about the semantic equivalence of the expressions before and after the transformations see [11].

4.3 Decomposition Algorithm

The transformed event expression is broken into subrules, one for each database involved in the event. Each one is sent and installed in the appropriate database. The following algorithm describes the generation of event expressions of these subrules:
For (each database involved in the event expression)
{   -- In the event expression replace the simple events that do not belong to this database with time variables that represent their time of occurrence.
    -- Simplify the event expression according to the following rules:

1. Eliminate the nodes of all the unary operators that are left with no operand (i.e. their operand is a time variable).

2. Eliminate the nodes of all the binary operators except 'disjunction' that are left with one operand, that is not a composite event of the 'not' operator, and all the binary operators that are left with no operands. For the disjunction cases, substitute the time variable with 'null'.

3. For all operators except 'disjunction' that have operands changed because of elimination, change their time interval, ti, to the sum of their initial ti and the ti intervals of the 'underlying' eliminated operators, (for exceptions see [11]).

4. If there is a 'strict sequence' operator eliminate the part that has no information relevant to this database. Eliminations are performed according to steps 4a, 4b, 4c, (for details see [11]).

5. Change the 'loose sequence' operators that have a binary operator eliminated in their right operand to a 'conjunction' operator.

6. Merge two successive 'plus' operators to one with time interval equal to the sum of their time intervals.

7. Change the 'not' operators to 'star' ones with the same time interval.

}

In the last step of the algorithm above we substitute the 'not' operators with 'star' in order to just gather the necessary information which will be used to evaluate the 'not' operator in the original event expression during the global evaluation. If we try to evaluate the 'not' operators in the partial evaluations of the local subevents, we may loose instances that could form an instance of the event of the global rule. (For details on the semantic equivalence of the expressions before and after the decomposition and on the change of 'not' operators to 'star' see [11]).

A subevent concerning one database matches at least the same combinations of event instances as those matched by the original event expression. Transforming and decomposing the condition of the rule is done in the obvious way of first order logic.

We consider a sample rule from the health care domain of Section 2. Suppose that until the end of the second day of a patient's admission to the hospital we want a trigger when she has not had either a prescription for a specific drug by Dr. Davis in the past 12 days or less than 2 epileptic crises. Then, if the patient has not been under some other medication in the past 12 days, we would like to give this specific drug to the patient. The ECA rule is:

Rule 6:

when TGHDB.('insert', (Admission, (_,<OHIP#_value >, _, _, _, _))) $\ll_{(0, 0, 0, 2,-, 0, 0)}$
     $(!_{(0, 0, 0, 12,-, 0, 0)}((_2 \&_{(0, 0, 0, 2,-, 0, 0)}$ TGHDB.('insert',
     ('MedRec', (OHIP#_value, _, _, 'epileptic crisis')))) $\vee_{(0, 0, 0, 12,-, 0, 0)}$
     DavisDB.('insert', (Prescription, (<OHIP#_value>, <DrugID_value>,_,_,_)))

if   (DrugSet1 = $\varnothing$) AND (DrugSet2 = $\varnothing$)
     (*where* TGHDB.('retrieve', 31, {OHIP#_value, DrugSet1}) *and* DavisDB.
     ('retrieve', 25,{OHIP#_value, DrugSet2})

then   TGHDB.('insert', ('Medication', (OHIP#_value,
          <currentDate>, <currentTime>, <DrugID_value>, _)))

Query 31:   *Select* DrugID,
          From   Medication
          Where   OHIP#=OHIP#_value

Query 25:   *Select* DrugID,
          From   Prescription
          Where   OHIP# = OHIP#_value, Date > <12 days ago>

Here, the information retrieved by query 31 and query 25 is stored in DrugSet1 and DrugSet2, respectively. The generated subrules for TGHDB and DavisDB are:

TGHDB Subrule:

when TGHDB.('insert', (Admission, (<OHIP#_value >, _, _, _, _))) $\wedge_{(0, 0, 0, 2,-, 0, 0)}$
     $(_2 \$_{(0, 0, 0, 2,-, 0, 0)}$
          TGHDB.('insert',('MedRec', (OHIP#_value, _, _, 'epileptic crisis'))))

if   (DrugSet1 = $\varnothing$) where TGHDB.('retrieve', 31, {OHIP#_value, DrugSet1})
then   propagate the subrule instance

DavisDB Subrule:

when $*_{(0, 0, 0, 12,-, 0, 0)}$ DavisDB.('insert', (Prescription, (<OHIP#_value>, <DrugID_value>, _,_,_)))

if   (DrugSet2 = $\varnothing$) where DavisDB.('retrieve', 25, {OHIP#_value, DrugSet2})
then   *propagate the subrule instance*

5 Implementation

The presented algorithms have been implemented to compare our distributed rule mechanism with a naïve implementation in terms of communication messages among the databases. In the naïve case the rule evaluation is centralized: all the simple event instances needed for the evaluation of a specific rule are sent individually, as soon as they occur, to the database that is responsible for the global evaluation of that rule. Also, when an event is instantiated, condition information is requested by the responsible database from the appropriate ones, and the condition instances are sent from the latter to the former. Hence, the naïve case has no partial evaluations of subrules: the database where the global rule resides collects all the necessary information.

5.1 Experimental Setup

We experiment on 4 rules that involve databases DB1 and DB2. The rules are declared in DB1:

Rule r1:
when	DB1.E1 $\wedge_{ti}$ DB2.E2
if	*null*
then	DB1.A1 AND DB2.A2

Rule r2:
when	DB1.E1 $\wedge_{ti}$ DB2.E2
if	DB2.C1
then	DB1.A1 AND DB2.A2

Rule r3:
when	DB1.E1 $\wedge_{ti1}$ (DB2.E2 $\wedge_{ti2}$ DB2.E3)
if	*null*
then	DB1.A1 AND DB2.A2

Rule r4:
when	DB1.E1 $\wedge_{ti1}$ (DB2.E2 $\wedge_{ti2}$ DB2.E3)
if	DB2.C1
then	DB1.A1 AND DB2.A2

In the rules above, DB1.E1 is a simple event in DB1 and DB2.E2, DB2.E3 are simple events in DB2. Also, DB2.C1 is a simple condition evaluated in DB2, Finally, DB1.A1 and DB2.A2 are actions to be executed in DB1 and DB2, respectively.

As we can observe, r1 and r3 have an empty condition part. With them we aim to test how the number of event instances influences the number of communication messages between DB1 and DB2. In rule 1 the event is composed by a simple event from DB1 and a simple event from DB2. Thus, for every event instance of DB2.E2 a new message with this information is sent by DB2 to DB1. In rule 3 there is a simple event from DB1 and a composite (composed of two simple events) event of DB2. Thus, in the case of our rule mechanism, again one message is sent by DB2 to DB1 for every instance of the composite event of DB2. However, in the naïve case one message is sent for every event instance of DB2.E2 or DB2.E3 and the composite event instances of DB2 are formed and validated in DB1. The rules r2 and r4 are similar to r1 and r3, respectively, with a condition part referring to DB2. For these rules, the naïve case has additional messages for the request and the accumulation of condition information.

In the experiments we test the two mechanisms for a total of 10, 100, 200, 300 and 400 maximum *possible* subrule instances. For example, in the first test, for rules r1 and r2 we have 10 event instances 5 instances of DB1.E1 and 5 of DB2.E2. Thus we have exactly 10 subrule instances in total for rule r1 and r2. In fact, the actual number of subrule instances for r1 and r2 is the maximum one. (However, r2 would have a

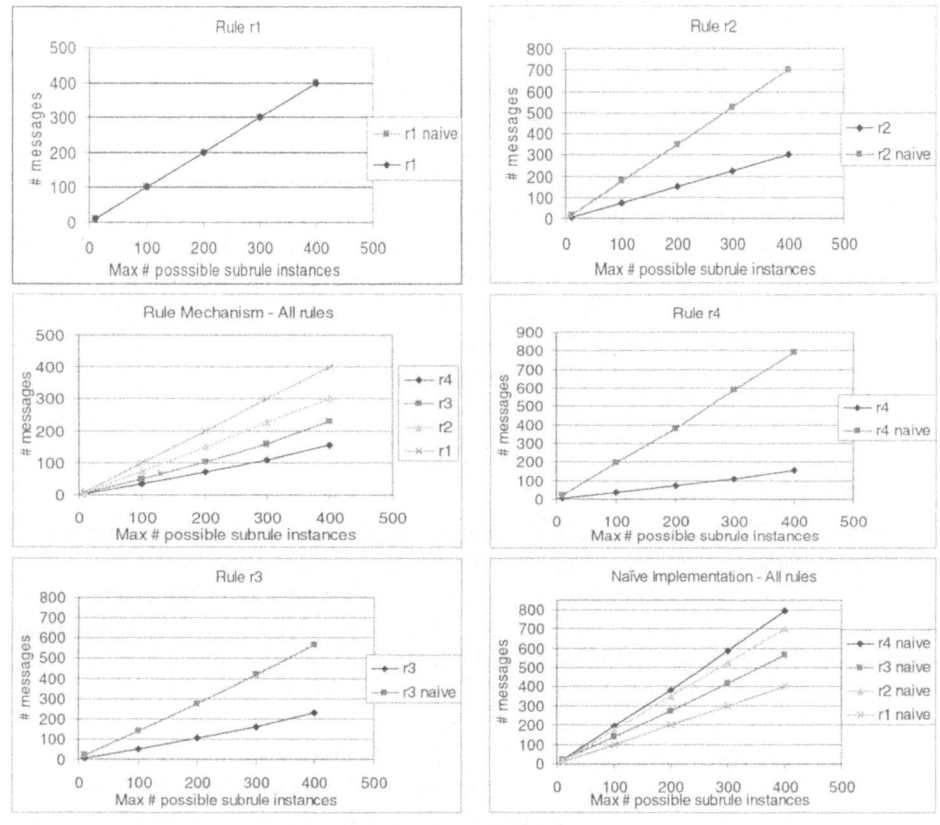

Fig. 4. Experimental results

smaller number if we took into account the form of the condition in order not to communicate subrule instances with an invalid condition). As for rules r3 and r4, the test comprises 15 event instances: 5 of each one of DB1.E1, DB2.E2 and DB2.E3. Nevertheless, the maximum number of possible subrule instances is 10 and depends on the time interval ti2. Consequently, for rules r1 and r2 the maximum number of possible subrule instances coincides with the total number of primitive event instances of DB1 and DB2, whereas, for r3 and r4, given a maximum number of subrule instances d, the total number of event instances involved is 3/2d (d/2 DB1 and d DB2 primitive event instances). The reason why we count the exchanged messages versus the maximum number of *possible* subrule instances and not versus the number of primitive event instances, is because the number of rule instances depends totally on the first, but only partially on the latter. For example, for a total of 100 primitive event instances we could have at most 50 rule instances of rule r1 but only 33 of rule r3, (note that we assume that there are 100/2 instances of events DB1.E1 and DB2.E2 in the first case and 100/3 instances of events DB1.E1, DB2.E2 and DB2.E3, in the second).

For r1 and r2 the time parameter ti is set to a value big enough so that none of the possible composite event instances is rejected by the evaluation procedure because of a difference in the occurrence time of the component simple event instances bigger than ti. The same holds for the parameter ti1 r3 and r4. Yet, in these rules we play with the parameter ti2 of the composite subevent of DB2 in order to observe how the partial evaluations benefit our rule mechanism (in terms of number of messages) versus the naïve implementation. Therefore, we perform the experiments for 3 values of ti2: 0, 5, 15 seconds. When ti2 equals 0, only simultaneous instances of DB2.E2 and DB2.E3 form subevents of DB2 used by the evaluation procedure for r3 and r4. Also, when ti2 equals 15 almost all the instances of DB2.E2 and DB2.E3 participate in subevents of DB2 that are used to form instances of r3 and r4. Additionally, for r2 and r4 we play with the percentage of valid condition instances of DB2.C1 and perform tests for 100%, 60%, 40%, and 0% of valid condition instances. The number of the latter influences the number of global rule instances.

5.2 Experimental Results

The graphs in Fig. 4 show the average number of messages exchanged between DB1 and DB2 versus the number of maximum possible subrule instances for the experiments on rules r1, r2, r3, r4 performed using the implementation of the proposed rule mechanism and the naïve one. For each one of the four rules, for a specific maximum number of subrule instances, we average the number of messages we get from testing all the possible combinations of the values of the parameters ti2 and the percentage of valid condition instances.

The first four graphs of Fig. 4 compare for each one of the rules the results of the proposed mechanism and the naïve implementation. As we can observe, the two rule mechanisms have exactly the same number of exchanged messages for r1, but have great differences for the rest of the rules. Moreover the difference in the number of exchanged messages is big for r3, bigger for r2 and even bigger for r4. A closer observation shows that this occurs because from experiment r1 to r2 or r3 the number of exchanged messages increases for the naïve case whereas it decreases for the proposed mechanism! The reason is that the proposed rule mechanism takes advantage of the limitations imposed by the form of the rule in order to diminish the number of messages during the evaluation. Moreover, in many cases, the rule mechanism communicates groups of DB2 subrule instances instead of sending them one by one. In case of r4, where there are restrictions both in the event and the condition part, the difference in the number of exchanged messages becomes even bigger.

The last two graphs compare the results of all the experiments for the proposed rule mechanism and the naïve implementation. We can certify by them the previous conclusion: for the naïve case the number of exchanged messages augments as the number of primitive event instances increases and when there is a condition part in the rule (r2 and r4), whereas for the proposed mechanism it decreases when there is a condition part or/ and there is a composite event of DB2.

As we can observe, the experimental results on all four rules are linear, which means that the number of messages is proportional to the maximum number of subrule instances. The linearity is due to the fixed percentages of valid condition instances and the fixed values of ti2 (while the frequency of occurrence of the event instances was kept reasonable). The linearity of the results would disappear in case of a real work-load where the number of valid condition instances and the number of composite subevent instances would not depend on the number of primitive event instances.

6 Related Work

Generally, as stated in the introduction, the ECA functionality has been considered mostly in centralized environments as far as databases are concerned. However, there are attempts to integrate ECA rules in distributed environments such as [18], [6], [7], [1], [4],[14], [5], [9], [15] and [8].

In [4], a framework for characterizing active functionality in terms of dimensions of a distributed ECA rule language and its execution model is introduced. The problem of incorporating ECA rules in a distributed environment is properly defined and broken into parts in order to discover how distribution affects the ECA rules and their execution model. The authors try to reconsider the techniques used in centralized databases and decide if and how they can be adapted in order to fit the distributed dimension of the problem.

In [14] an approach for managing consistency of interdependent data in a multidatabase environment is presented. They introduce the 'data dependency descriptors' (D^3s), objects distributed among the databases that describe the consistency constraints among data and the restoration transactions. Contrary to the D^3s mechanism, our approach is more general by providing d-ECA rules as a global means of expressing data coordination, including various degrees of consistency enforcement. In the near future, we plan to complete the implementation of an application showing how to enforce consistency constraints similar to those enforced by the D^3s mechanism.

An interesting work is presented in [6], where local and global events are detected asynchronously in a distributed environment and are spread together with their parameters to sites interested in them. This work is based on the ADBMS Sentinel and its event specification language Snoop. Both are extended to accommodate composite events from various sources and an appropriate execution model. This work is similar to ours in its mechanism for distributed event detection. However, it differs from our work in two ways. First, recall that the database on which a newly created ECA rule resides coordinates the global evaluation process of the new rule. The event and rule managers on this database act as global event and rule managers. Therefore we do not need a dedicated Global Event Manager in the sense of [6] which could cause a bottle-neck in the network. Second, our execution model distributes entire rules to acquainted databases, not only subevents. In fact, the evaluation of the condition together with the respective event is meaningful in order to decide if the event instance is worth of propagation.

A framework with a motivation similar to ours is reported in [5]. Here, however, a distributed service-based mechanism is used to provide an ECA functionality that relies on ontologies known to all participant peers. Instead, our mechanism – as shown in [12] – also uses ingredients known only to acquainted peers such as tables mapping heterogeneous data originating in the acquainted peers [13]. In [9], the idea of adapting ECA functionality to an application profile is similar to our idea of on-the-fly instantiation of ECA rules. However, we show in [12] that such an instantiation is not sufficient, and needs to be complemented by the automatic generation of rules.

The authors in [18] present a method that uses ECA rules in order to maintain global integrity in a federated database system. Unlike our approach, [18] uses a global database of meta information. Our approach deals with such meta information in a distributed fashion. Moreover, in [18] only primitive event instances without any processing are propagated. The system in [18] is similar to the naïve implementation we used for comparison in the experiments of Section 5.

Generally speaking, most of the projects that try to incorporate ECA functionality in distributed environments in order to manage data [5], [15], [8] have not dealt with optimized distributed evaluation of coordination ECA rules. Also, even though people have talked about distributed conditions tied to specific databases, [16] asynchronous evaluation of condition parts is not considered.

7 Conclusions

We have presented a novel distributed ECA rule mechanism for coordinating data in a multidatabase environment. The mechanism consists of a rule language and an execution model that transforms rules to more easily manageable forms, distributes them to relevant databases, monitors their execution and composes their evaluations. The mechanism is designed in a manner that minimizes the number of messages that need to be exchanged over the network. We have also conducted a preliminary experimental evaluation to compare the implementation with a naïve centralized execution model. Our objective is to use this mechanism to support coordination among databases in a P2P network [2], [3]. Unlike conventional multidatabase systems, the set of participating databases in such a setting is open and keeps changing. So are the rules that define the degree of coordination among the databases. Moreover, we assume that there is no global schema, control, coordination or optimization among peer databases. Also, access to peer databases is strictly local. These assumptions violate many of the premises of traditional (multi)database systems, where a global schema is taken for granted, optimization techniques are founded on global control, and database solutions are arrived at design time and remain static during run time.

In the near future we will present a complete SQL extension based on the rule language we propose. Moreover, we will explore the optimization of the number of communication messages based on which database performs the global evaluation of a rule. The presented execution model used the decoupled coupling mode for both pairs of event-condition and condition-action in order to achieve asynchronous event and condition evaluation, and action execution. However, we intend to follow the idea in [18] that tackles the issue of distributed ECA functionality in the context of advanced transactions by systematically studying coupling modes in a distributed context.

References

1. Arizio, B. Bomitali, M.L. Demarie, A. Limongiello, P.L. Mussa. Managing inter-database dependencies with rules + quasi-transactions. In *3rd Intern. Workshop on Research Issues in Data Engineering: Interoperability in Multidatabase Systems*, pages 34–41, Vienna, 1993.
2. M. Arenas, V. Kantere, A. Kementsietsidis, I. Kiringa, R. J. Miller, J. Mylopoulos. The Hyperion Project: From Data Integration to Data Coordination. In *SIGMOD Rec.*, Sep. 2003.
3. P. Bernstein, F. Giunchiglia, A. Kementsietsidis, J. Mylopoulos, L. Serafini. Data Management for Peer-to-Peer Computing: A Vision", in proceedings of the *Second Workshop on Databases and the Web*, 2002.
4. G. von Bültzingslöwen et al. ECA Functionality in a Distributed Environment, in *Active Rules in Database Systems.*Springer Verlag, New York, pages 147–175, 1999.
5. M. Cilia, C. Bornhövd, A. P. Buchmann. Moving Active Functionality from Centralized to Open Distributed Heterogeneous Environments, in proceedings of *Cooperative Information Systems, 9th Conference*, pages 195–210, Trento, Italy, September 5–7 2001.
6. S. Chakravarthy, H. Liao. Asynchronous monitoring of events for distributed cooperative environments. In *Intern. Symp. on Coop. Database Sys. for Advanced Applications,* 2001.
7. S. Chawathe, H. Garcia-Molina, and J. Widom. Flexible constraint management for autonomous distributed databases. In *Bulletin of the IEEE Technical Committee on Data Engineering,* 17(2):23–27, 1994.
8. Collet. The NODS Project: Networked Open Database Services, in proceedings of the *Intern. Symposium on Objects and Databases*, pages 153-169, Sophia Antipolis, 2000.
9. Gatziu S., A. Koschel, G. von Bültzingsloewen, H. Fritschi. Unbundling Active Functionality, *SIGMOD Record 27(1): 35–40*, 1998.
10. Zimmer D., Unland R., On the semantics of complex events in active database management systems. In *Proceedings of the 15th International Conference on Data Engineering,* 1999.
11. V. Kantere, *A Rule Mechanism for P2P Data Management,* Tech. Rep. CSRG-469, University of Toronto, 2003.
12. V.Kantere, I.Kiringa, J. Mylopoulos, A. Kementsietsidis, M. Arenas. Coordinating Peer Databases Using ECA Rules, *in proceedings of the International Workshop on Databases, Information Systems and P2P Computing, Berlin*, September 2003.
13. A. Kementsietsidis, M. Arenas, R. J. Miller. Mapping Data in Peer-to-Peer Systems: Semantics and Algorithmic Issues, in *Proceedings of the ACM SIGMOD Intern.Conference on Management of Data, San Diego, June 2003.*
14. G. Karabatis, M. Rusinkiewicz, A.Sheth. Aeolos: A System for the Management of Interdependent Data. In A. Elmagarmid, M. Rusinkiewicz, A.Sheth (Eds.), *Management of Heterogeneous and Autonomous Database Systems*, Chapter 8, Morgan Kaufmann 1999.
15. A. Koschel, P.C. Lockermann. Distributed events in active database systems: Letting the genie out of the bottle, in *Data & Knowledge Engineering V. 25*, pages 11–28, 1998.
16. L. Lakshmanan, F. Sadri, and S. Subramanian. SchemaSQL: an Extension to SQL for Multidatabase Interoperability. *ACM Transactions on Database Systems*, 26(4), 2001.
17. W.S. Ng , B.C. Ooi, K.L. Tan, and A.Y. Zhou. PeerDB: a P2P-based System for Distributed Data Sharing. Tech. Report, University of Singapore, 2002.
18. C. Turker and S. Conrad. Towards maintaining integrity in federated databases. In *3rd Basque Intern. Workshop on Information Technology* Biarritz, 1997.

Identification and Modelling of Web Services for Inter-enterprise Collaboration Exemplified for the Domain of Strategic Supply Chain Development

Antonia Albani, Alexander Keiblinger, Klaus Turowski, and Christian Winnewisser

Chair of Business Information Systems (WI II), University of Augsburg,
{antonia.albani, alexander.keiblinger, klaus.turowski,
christian.winnewisser}
@wiwi.uni-augsburg.de

Abstract. Web applications are often developed ad hoc with limited systematic approach, inhering the potential risk of applications of poor quality and causing considerable costs for maintenance and evolution. This applies also for Web services, since a lack of common integrative specification standards and methodologies for the design of domain specific Web services diminishes reusability and marketability.

In this paper, we propose a methodology for the identification of Web services suitable for business applications. The methodology is based on a process for the design of domain specific business component applications and has been extended to be applicable to the identification and modelling of Web services. The usability of the proposed methodology is exemplified within the business domain of strategic supply chain development. This domain constitutes an inter-enterprise collaboration problem, which is generally suited for Web services. Core of the concept is the extension of the traditional frame of reference in strategic sourcing from a supplier-centric to a supply-chain-scope including the dynamic modelling of supply-chains. Based on a comprehensive functional decomposition of strategic supply chain development, the proposed methodology is used to identify reusable and marketable Web services.

1 Introduction

With a continuous development of information and communication technologies for the Web, the possibility of developing Web-based business applications supporting inter-enterprise integration, communication and collaboration has been improved. Nevertheless there are still several problems to address in order to satisfy flexibility and security requirements of business partners, before engaging in more dynamic and new forms of cooperation using the Web as collaboration platform.

Web applications are often developed ad hoc with limited systematic approach [11], inhering the potential risk of applications of poor quality and causing considerable costs for maintenance and evolution. There is no stringent systematic approach and the resulting Web applications are dependent on the knowledge and experience of individual developers.

R. Meersman et al. (Eds.): CoopIS/DOA/ODBASE 2003, LNCS 2888, pp. 74–92, 2003.
© Springer-Verlag Berlin Heidelberg 2003

Web services are a new promising paradigm for the development of modular applications accessible over the Web and running on a variety of platforms. The Web service standards are SOAP [30] – supporting platform independency – WSDL [31] – specifying the interfaces and services offered – and UDDI [20] – used for the publication of the Web services offered by a specific company. All standards are based on the eXtensible Markup Language (XML) [6]. An overview of standards and related technologies for Web services is given in [27].

With the use of those standards, business services can be published on the Web enabling universal access for all, end-users, business partners or developers. But why is there still a lack of mature Web services on the market? Wrapping SOAP, WSDL or UDDI layers around existing applications does not guarantee that a reusable, manageable and reliable Web service has been developed. There are two main problems arising with the development of Web services: *the specification of Web services in an unequivocal way* and *the identification of suitable Web services being reusable and marketable*. Not only service providers, but also service requestors need to *specify* the services, respectively the requests, in such a way, that suitable services can be found and used in order to solve specific business problems. Additionally adequate Web services need to be *identified* to ensure that reliable and reusable business services addressing not only to the need of single but of multiple service requestors can be built. The problems of specification and identification need to be addressed in order to build dedicated Web services. In the field of Web services specification important work is ongoing, as for example [15, 3, 9] whereas in the field of identifying reusable and marketable Web services, there is little research initiative to date [33, 21]. The necessity of addressing the problem of Web services identification leads to the contribution of this paper. Based on a proposal [15] of specifying Web services for a specific business domain according to the memorandum for "Standardized Specification of Business Components" and on a derivation process for modelling domain specific business component applications, a modelling and identification process for building reusable and marketable Web services is proposed.

After a short discussion of Web services and business components in section 2 the Web Services Model (WSM) is introduced in section 3. The WSM process is then evaluated in section 4 and 5 for the business domain of strategic supply chain development, explaining the WSM analysis phase in section 4 and the WSM design phase in section 5.

2   Web Services versus Business Components

The problems of specification and identification of suitable services are not new and have already been addressed in the field of component based software development. The experiences made in that field can be useful to Web services design as seen in [11, 10]. But frequently the interfaces that software components realise are too low level and not representative to the actual business service provided. Since Web services perform activities for a specific domain in distributed business applications, there is a need to look at the experiences made in the field of business components which can be useful for the development of reusable, marketable, flexible and extensible Web services.

In [15] Web services and business components are compared on the basis of their definitions, resulting in the notion that a Web service can be regarded as a special kind of a business component. Therefore a comparison of the specification and identification processes of Web services and business components can be applied to gain understanding for the adaptation of those processes to Web services.

The specification of a business component is defined as a complete, unequivocal and precise description of its external view. It describes which services a business component provides under which conditions. Based on the ideas of [4, 29, 28] the memorandum for "Standardized Specification of Business Components" states that the specification of business components is to be carried out on different contract levels – marketing, task, terminology, quality, coordination, behavioural and interface level as shown in Fig. 1. Besides arranging the specifications' contents according to contract levels a specific notation language is proposed for each level of abstraction. Web services as well need to be specified in an unequivocal way, in order to enable customers to decide whether a given service meets the required specification or not.

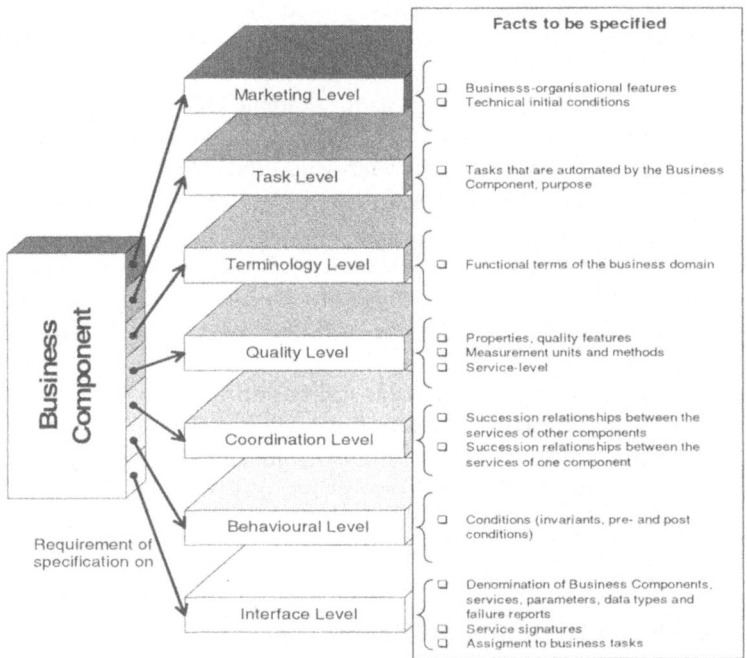

Fig. 1. Software contract levels and facts to be specified

A detailed discussion of the resulting specification comparison for Web services and business component is given in [15]. According to the authors, the necessity for specifying Web services as done for business components has been analysed first. Their result was the notion that a specification for different types of Web services as detailed as for business components is required. The comparison also states that the

Web services specification standards, UDDI and WSDL, do not satisfy a specification on all levels of abstraction as known from the specification of business components. For the interface level WSDL as specification standard is fully satisfactory, whereas UDDI is only satisfactory on the marketing level for simple Web services. For more complex services UDDI needs to be extended in order to satisfy the specification needs. For the other levels – having been identified as prerequisite for obtaining marketable and reusable business components – neither WSDL nor UDDI satisfy the specification standards. The advantages of using a complete, unequivocal and precise formal description for business components have proven beneficial in different applications. Therefore, Web Services being used in lieu of component technology could also benefit from the specification standard used for business components.

Having discussed the specification standards for Web services and business components, the modelling approach for identifying marketable, reusable, flexible and extensible Web components needs to be analysed. Since no standard design methodology and engineering principles exist for the development of applications based on Web services, we propose an adaptation of the Business Component Model (BCM) [1] process, used for identifying business components, for the identification of Web services.

First it needs to be analysed to what extent the BCM methodology is adequate to Web services. Therefore the BCM process is shortly described. In Fig. 2 an overview of the BCM process is given, illustrating the two phases, the component based domain analysis and design phase. A detailed description of the BCM process can be found in [1].

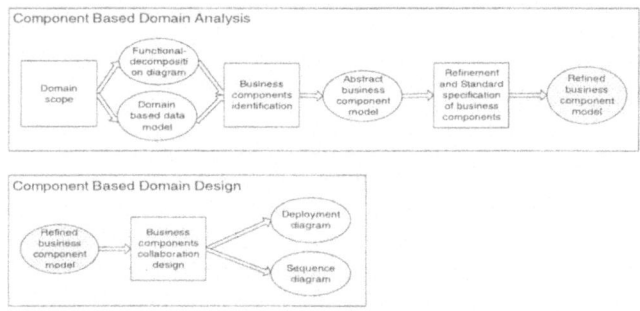

Fig. 2. Business Components Modelling process

To build an application for a given business domain, a functional-decomposition diagram and a data model need to be defined. Based on the defined business tasks and on the identified information objects the Business Component Identification (BCI) process is applied to that data in order to gain a first abstract business component model. This model needs then to be refined and all components which have been identified need to be specified for each contract level, as defined in the memorandum. A refined business component model results, being the output of the component based domain analysis phase. The refined business component model is then used in the design phase to define the collaboration between business components. Two main diagrams need therefore to be designed, the deployment diagram for the deployment of component instances on different systems and the sequence diagrams to visualise communication dependencies between business components.

In general, all BCM sub phases described for the identification and modelling of business components are also applicable to Web services. However one important issue related to Web-based application development is not addressed in the BCM process, namely: what business tasks and what information objects, gained from the functional-decomposition and data model diagrams, are adequate to be provided and accessed through Web services? Despite the fact that more and more business applications are provided over the Web, there are still essential problems which are not adequately solved with existing Web information and communication technologies. The most important ones related to the development of Web services being performance, security, trustability of service providers or trustability of 3rd party service providers. To date, security and privacy in Web services based applications are considered unsatisfactory and research work is ongoing [34, 5]. Even though there are not always good reasons to trust the service providers, to date most services run on the basis of trust. Sabotage, insider break-ins, technical incompetence or changes of the ownership can occur even with service providers with good reputation. Depending on the sensitivity of the data it may not always be worthwhile to make the data available to a service provider.

Considering these problems the BCM process needs to be adapted in such a way, that sensitive data or sensitive tasks, which should not be provided through Web services, can be identified upfront and can be excluded from the Web services identification process. The BCM process adapted for the identification and modelling of Web services is explained in the next section.

3   Web Services Modelling

A precondition to Web-based development of application systems by using Web services is a stable Web services model. In order to obtain stable models, a well defined derivation process is necessary. Since Web services should not only satisfy the requirements for a single application system but rather for a family of systems – and therefore for a certain domain – the derivation process requires throughout all development phases the consideration of the specific business domain.

Domain Engineering [8 , p. 19–59, 23 , p. 159–169] aims at the development of reusable software and a large number of Domain Analysis and Domain Engineering processes exist, among the most important ones being [13, 25]. The methods mentioned contribute to different aspects of the Domain Engineering area as for example in identifying prominent or distinctive features of a class of systems or in defining maintainability and understandability characteristics of family of systems.

Building on the perception of domain engineering, the most important prerequisites for Web services are reusability, maintainability and marketability. Therefore the Web Services Modelling process is introduced as an extension of the Business Component Modelling process, with business components having similar prerequisites as Web services.

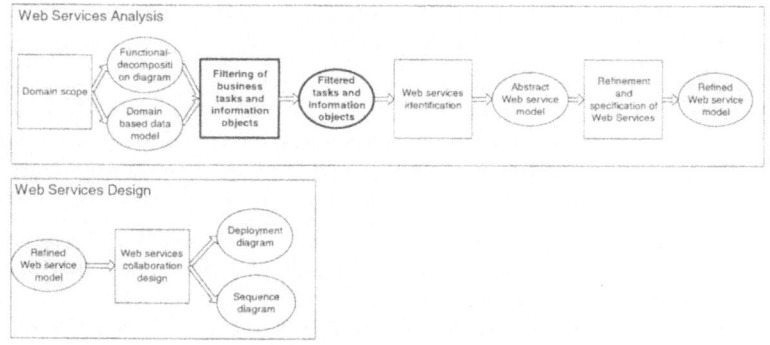

Fig. 3. Web Services Modelling process

An overview of the WSM process focusing on the *Web Services Analysis* and *Web Services Design* phases is given in Fig. 3. Rectangles denote sub phases of the process and ellipses contain the resulting diagrams and models of each sub phase.

In the following the single phases and their performed tasks are explained. During *domain scope* the domain of interest is identified, characterised and business processes with their functional tasks are defined. In addition data is collected to analyse the information objects and their relationships. Possible sources of domain information include existing systems in the domain, domain experts, handbooks, requirements on future systems, market studies, and so on. As a result of the first sub phase a *functional-decomposition diagram* and a *domain based data model* are generated.

Out of these models the information objects and the business tasks to be provided in the Web application are extracted. Since not all business tasks and data are designated to be accessible through Web services – because of security, performance or trust reasons as explained in section 2 – a sub phase for *filtering* this information is necessary. The resulting information is then used for the next sub phase in the WSM process, namely the *Web services identification*.

In order to optimise the process of identifying high quality, reusable and marketable Web services the Business Components Identification (BCI) method is adapted for the context of Web services and is called Web Services Identification (WSI) process in that context.

WSI is based upon the Business System Planning (BSP) [12] method and has been modified for the field of Web services identification. WSI takes as input the filtered business tasks of a specific domain and the domain based filtered data, both obtained from the filtering of business tasks and information objects phase. In a first step a matrix is built defining the relationships between the single business tasks and the information objects. The relationships are visualised inserting "C" and "U" in the matrix. "C" denotes that the data is created by the specific business task, and "U" denotes the usage of informational data by a given task. In changing the order of data and business tasks and placing the "C" as far left and as up as possible in the matrix, groups of relationships can be recognised, see Table 4 and Table 5. These groups identify potential Web services. If some "U"'s are outside of the groups, arrows are used to identify the data flow from one group to the other. The result of the WSI is an abstract Web services model with some already defined dependencies between the single services. In section 4 the WSI method is explained by means of the domain of strategic supply chain development.

In the next sub phase each Web service of the abstract model needs to be *refined* and *specified*. Since no standard specification for Web services exists for the task-, terminology-, quality-, coordination- and behavioural-level, it is suggested that the same specification as stated in the standardised specification of business components document is used. For the marketing and interface levels UDDI and WSDL can be used. The resulting Web service model has all seven contract levels – marketing, task, terminology, quality, coordination, behavioural and interface – specified.

The refined model is the main input for the *Web Services Design* and *Web Services Implementation* phases. The Web services design phase is explained next, whereas the implementation phase is not within the scope of this paper to be defined.

The sub phase *Web services collaboration design* of the design phase is used to define the location of the Web services and the dependencies between single Web services. Web services can be instantiated by a single service provider or e.g. by a 3rd party service provider. Dependencies are defined by single service calls. As a result different kinds of diagrams are produced, e.g. *deployment* and *sequence diagrams*. These diagrams together with the refined Web services model are the outcome of the WSM process and are the main input for developing Web based information systems with high maintainable, reusable and marketable Web services. The complete WSM process is summarised in Table 1.

Table 1. Summary of the WSM Process

WSM Phase	WSM sub phases	Performed Tasks	Results
Web Services Analysis	Domain scope	Identification and characterisation of the domain	Functional-decomposition diagram
		Definition of the business processes and functional tasks of the domain	
		Data collection and definition of information objects	Domain based data model
		Identification of relationships between information objects	
	Filtering of business tasks and information objects	Filtering of business tasks and information objects gained from the functional-decomposition diagram and domain based data model	Filtered tasks and information objects
	Web services identification	Grouping of functional business tasks and informational object for the identification of Web services	Abstract Web services model
	Refinement and specification of Web services	Specification of Web services for all contract levels (marketing, task, terminology, quality, coordination, behaviour, interface)	Refined Web services model
Web Services Design	Web services collaboration design	Definition of the location of Web services (service provider, 3rd party service provider)	Deployment diagram
		Process of service calls	Sequence diagram

To illustrate the process of WSM it is applied in the following sections to the domain of strategic supply chain development detailing both phases, sub phases, tasks and the resulting diagrams and models.

4 Web Service Analysis

The goal of the Web services analysis phase is to generate a refined Web services model with all services being specified.

4.1 Domain Scope – From Strategic Sourcing to Strategic Supply Chain Development

The relevance of the purchasing function in the enterprise has increased steadily over the past two decades. Till the 70ies, purchasing was widely considered an operative task with no apparent influence on long term planning and strategy development [18]. This narrow view was broadened by research that documented the positive influence that a targeted supplier collaboration and qualification could bring to a company's strategic options [2]. In the 80ies, trends such as the growing globalisation, the focus on core competencies in the value chain with connected in-sourcing and out-sourcing decisions, as well as new concepts in manufacturing spurred the recognition of the eminent importance of the development and management of supplier relationships for gaining competitive advantages. As a result, purchasing gradually gained a strategic relevance on top of its operative tasks [14].

Based on these developments, purchasing has become a core function in the 90ies. Current empiric research shows a significant correlation between the establishment of a strategic purchasing function and the financial success of an enterprise, independent from the industry surveyed [7, p. 513]. One of the most important factors in this connection is the buyer-supplier-relationship. At many of the surveyed companies, a close cooperation between buyer and supplier in areas such as long-term planning, product development and coordination of production processes led to process improvements and resulting cost reductions that were shared between buyer and suppliers [7, p. 516].

In practice, supplier development is widely limited to suppliers in tier-1. With respect to the above demonstrated, superior importance of supplier development we postulate the extension of the traditional frame of reference in strategic sourcing from a supplier-centric to a supply-chain-scope, i.e., the further development of the strategic supplier development to a strategic supply chain development. This re-focuses the object of reference in the field of strategic sourcing by analysing supplier networks instead of single suppliers. Embedded in this paradigm shift is the concept of the value network that has been comprehensively described, e.g., [17], [32], [22].

The main reason for the lack of practical implementation of strategic supply chain development can be found in the high degree of complexity that is connected with the identification of supply chain entities and the modelling of the supply chain structure, as well as the high coordination effort, as described by [16].

In a next step the functional tasks of strategic supply chain development have to be defined. Those tasks will be derived from the main tasks of strategic sourcing. The most evident changes are expected for functions with cross-company focus. The functional tasks of strategic supply chain development have been illustrated in a function decomposition diagram (Fig. 4).

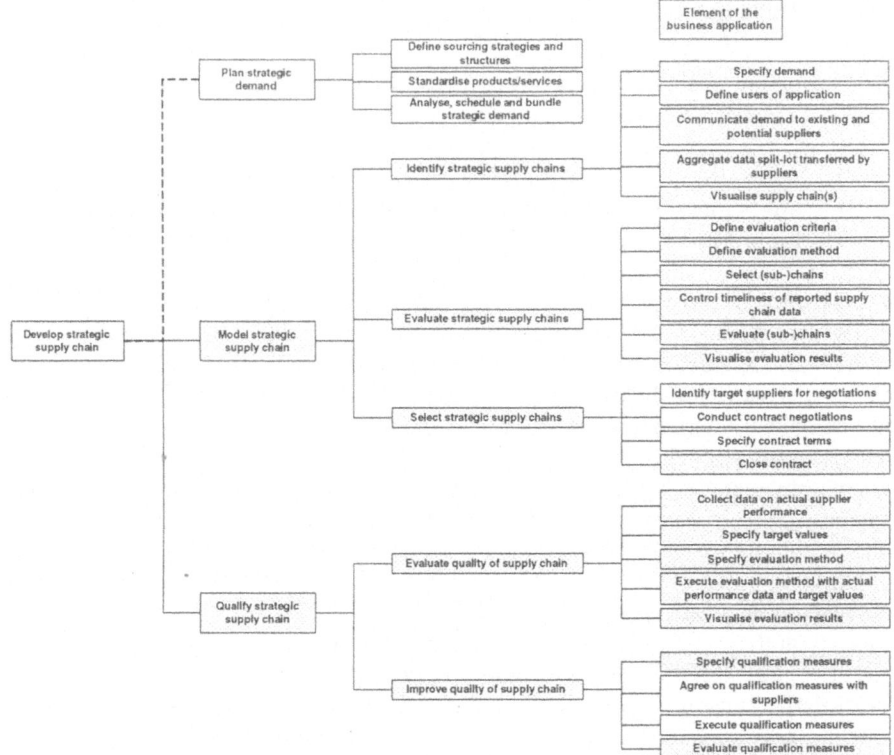

Fig. 4. Functional decomposition diagram for the supply chain development

Processes and tasks that should be automated have been shaded. In the following only selected tasks will be described. The focus will be on changes to current tasks of strategic purchasing.

Task "Model strategic supply chain": The process supplier selection from strategic purchasing undergoes the most evident changes in the shift to a supply chain centric perspective. The expansion of the traditional frame of reference in strategic sourcing requires more information than merely data on existing and potential suppliers in tier-1. Instead, the supply chains connected with those suppliers have to be identified and evaluated, e.g., by comparing alternative supply chains in the production network. As a consequence, the task supplier selection is part of the process that leads to the modelling of strategic supply chains.

The perception of the supply chain as dynamic network constitutes the basis for the identification of strategic supply chains. To visualise the network in a structured way, a specific strategic demand is communicated to existing and/or potential suppliers in tier-1. Subsequently, those tier-1 suppliers report their own demand to their respective suppliers. The requested information are split-lot transferred the other way round, aggregated and finally visualised as supply network, in which each participant of the supply chain constitutes a network hub. Without information technology, such an approach could not be realised.

According to the assumptions described above, the rating of supply chains requires the evaluation of networks instead of single suppliers. There has been preparatory work on evaluation methods for business networks (e.g., [26, 24]) on which we have based initial methods for the described application. However, there is need for further research, especially in the area of aggregation of incomplete information.

Task "Qualify strategic supply chain": In addition to the selection of suitable supply chains and composition of alternative supply chains, the performance improvement of strategically important supply chains is one of the major goals of strategic supply chain development. Main prerequisite is the constant evaluation of the actual performance of selected supply chains by defined benchmarks. The application should support respective evaluation methods and enables the user to identify imminent problems in the supply chain and to initiate appropriate measures for qualification of supply chain partners.

This is important because of the long-term character of strategic supply chain relationships. As a result of the long-term perspective, qualification measures – e.g., along the dimensions product, processes and management abilities – require deployment of resources on the buyer side as well. Because of this effort, problems in the supply chain should be identified proactively and qualification measures should be tracked.

Task "Plan strategic demand": Strategic planning, i.e., analysing, scheduling and grouping of long-term demand, primarily affects intra-company processes that will not change significantly by switching to a supply chain perspective in strategic purchasing and therefore will not be automated in a first step.

Having identified and characterised the domain of strategic supply chain development and defined the business processes and tasks of that domain, it is necessary to determine the relevant information objects involved in the modelling of the strategic supply chain development. The resulting data model is listed as UML class diagram [19 p. 294] in Fig. 5.

Starting from the demand of a *buyer* it is relevant to collect data not only from the suppliers in tier-1, but from all suppliers in tier-n. A *demand* consists of *services, material groups* and more which can be generalised to a *demand category*. To each demand category different *characteristics* can be added, as for example *method of production, service level, time, volume* etc. A whole supply chain specified by a demand is a network of suppliers providing information to the buyer which is used for the development of the supply chain. This network of suppliers is represented in the data model as a *complex monitoring object* whereas a single supplier is represented as an *elementary monitoring object*. With the affiliation of elementary monitoring objects to a complex monitoring object and with the identification of predecessors and successors of such elementary monitoring objects the whole supply chain is defined. At a particular time each elementary object provides information about the *product range, bill of material, financial data* or more. This information is known as *supplier generated data*. In addition the buyer generates own data, called *buyer generated data*, specifying the performance of the supplier, respectively of the elementary monitoring object, as termed in the data model.

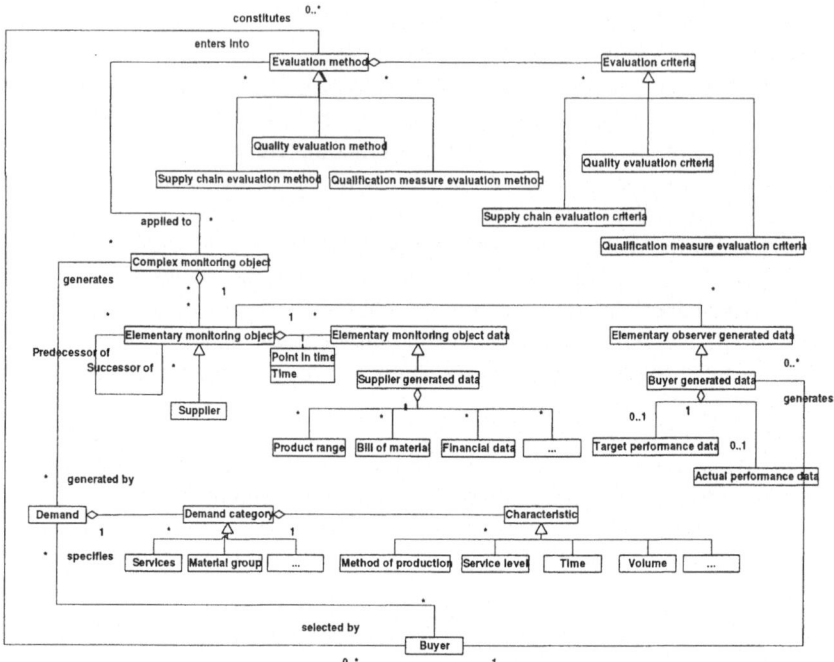

Fig. 5. Data model for the domain of strategic supply chain development

Examples for data generated by the buyer are *target performance* data and *actual performance data*. Target performance data are guidelines for the supplier, and the actual performed data are the work performed measured by the buyer. The buyer holds with the acquisition of supplier generated data and with the definition and the measurements of performance data for all different complex monitoring objects the information needed to evaluate the supply chain. Different *evaluation methods* are defined by different *evaluation criteria*.

The data model and the functional-decomposition diagram derived from the domain scope is the main information needed for the identification of high quality Web services explained in the next subsections.

4.2   Filtering of Business Tasks and Information Objects

The business tasks and the informational data which are gained from the functional-decomposition diagram and from the data model need to be filtered in order to extract the sensitive data before identifying Web services. In Table 2 the business tasks are listed on the left and the application type on top. Two different types of applications are listed: Web services based applications and business components based applications. Web services based applications provide functionality and information which are not sensitive and which can be given to a service provider or to a 3rd party service provider. Whereas the sensitive information and functionality are available through business components which are integrated into the customers own application without having to deal with security and trust problems as is the case by Web services based applications.

Table 2. Filtering of business tasks

Tasks \ Application type	Web service based	Business components based
Define users of application	X	
Specify deman	X	
Communicate demand to existing and potential suppliers	X	
Aggregate data split-lot transferred by suppliers	X	
Visualise supply chain(s)	X	
Define evaluation criteria	X	
Define evaluation method	X	
Select (sub-)chains	X	
Control timeliness of reported supply chain data	X	
Evaluate (sub-) chains		X
Visualise evaluation results		X
Close contract		X
Collect data on actual supplier performance		X
Specify target values	X	
Specify evaluation method	X	
Execute evaluation method with actual performance data and target values		X
Visualise evaluation results		X
Specify qualification measures		X
Evaluate qualification measures		X

The critical business tasks – defined for the domain of strategic supply chain development – listed in Table 2 are the ones which affect the evaluation of supplier's data. That concerns the collection of the supplier's performance data, the execution of the different evaluations and the visualisation of the resulting information. The business tasks mentioned will therefore not enter into the identification process of Web services. The same applies to the information objects, which are related to those sensitive business tasks. The highly sensitive data are actual performance data and target performance data as listed in Table 3.

Table 3. Filtering of information objects

Information objects \ Application type	Web services based	Business components based
Demand	X	
Supplier	X	
Supplier generated data	X	
Evaluation criteria	X	
Evaluation method	X	
Target performance data		X
Actual performance data		X

For the following sub phases we focus on the business tasks and on the information objects which can be accessed through Web applications based on Web services. For the modelling of the sensitive business tasks using business components, we refer to [1]. In the next section the identification methodology for Web services is explained.

4.3 Web Services Identification (WSI)

With the WSI method relationships between the filtered business tasks and the filtered information objects are defined and grouped. In Table 4 the relationships for the domain of strategic supply chain development are shown.

Table 4. Grouping of filtered tasks and information objects

The business tasks are listed left on the table and the information objects on top. Such information objects are demand, supplier, supplier generated data, evaluation criteria and evaluation method. An example relationship would be the usage "U" of supplier generated data for the visualisation of the supply chain. Three areas result for the domain of strategic supply chain development in changing the order of tasks and information objects in the matrix as defined in chapter 3. The three areas represent potential Web services. The first one offers services for the specification of the demand and for the definition of application users. It therefore provides services for the *supply chain development*. The second Web service is responsible for the *supply chain administration and visualisation* in aggregating and managing the data received from the suppliers. The *evaluation administration* Web service provides interfaces to define evaluation methods and criteria. The resulting Web services are shown in Table 5.

Table 5. Web services identified using the WSI method

4.4   Refinement and Standard Specification of Web Services

The Web service *supply chain administration and visualisation* gained from the WSI method needs to be further partitioned in two Web services, the *supply chain administration* and *the visualisation and selection* service in order to separate the administration of data from the visualisation of data. The separation of data and presentation is a common pattern within software development. Two additional Web services are added to the model, namely the *communication manager* and the *communication* services. These ones are attained from inter-enterprise communication requirements and not from business requirements and therefore are not resulting from the WSI method.

The Web services model gained from the WSI method and refined as just mentioned is shown in Fig. 6.

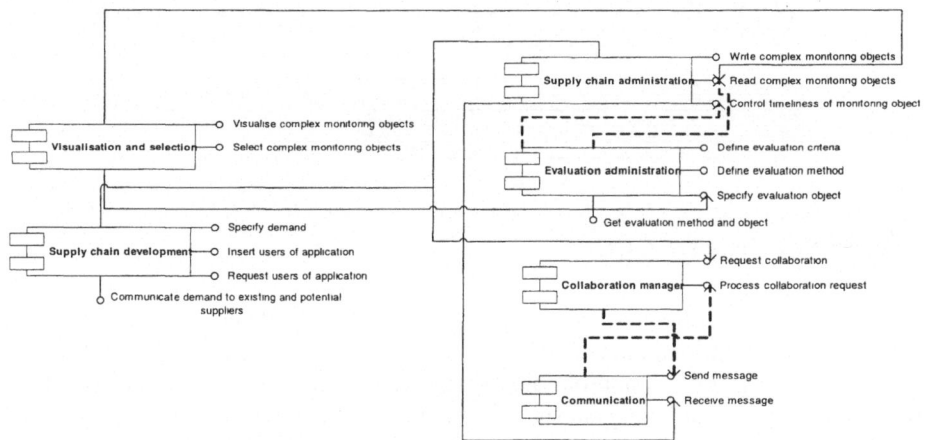

Fig. 6. Refined Web services model

For each Web service listed, a specification for all levels of abstraction – marketing, task, terminology, quality, coordination, behavioural and interface – as defined in section 3 needs to be given. The description of the detailed specification of all levels for each single Web service is not within the scope of this paper.

Interesting for this paper instead is the specification on task level. Single business tasks need to be assigned to Web services interfaces. The mapping for the strategic supply chain development domain is shown in Table 6.

Some business tasks are mapped one to one to Web service interfaces, e.g. specify demand or communicate demand to existing and potential suppliers. However most of the business tasks are mapped to a superordinate more abstract defined interface, e.g. the business task visualise supply chain is mapped to the interface visualise complex monitoring objects.

Fig. 6 shows the refined Web services model with all interfaces defined for each Web service and with the dependencies between the individual Web services represented by arrows. With the definition of a very abstract data model for the strategic supply chain development domain, as given in Fig. 5, powerful and reusable Web services can be identified being used with for different Web application systems.

Table 6. Mapping of business tasks to interfaces of Web services

Task	Service
Define users of application	Insert users of application
Specify demand	Specify demand
Communicate demand to existing and potential suppliers	Communicate demand to existing and potential suppliers
Aggregate data split-lot transferred by suppliers	Process collaboration request
Visualise supply chain(s)	Visualise complex monitoring objects
Define evaluation criteria	Define evaluation criteria
Define evaluation method	Define evaluation method
Select (sub-)chains	Select complex monitoring objects
Control timeliness of reported supply chain data	Control timeliness of monitoring objects
Evaluate (sub-)chains	(executed by business components)
Visualise evaluation results	(executed by business components)
Identify target suppliers for negotiations	(execute manually)
Conduct contract negotiations	(execute manually)
Specify contract termn	(execute manually)
Close contract	(executed by business components)
Collect data on actual supplier performance	(executed by business components)
Specify target values	Define evaluation criteria
Specify evaluation method	Define evaluation method
Execute evaluation mehtod with actual performance data and target values	(executed by business components)
Visualise evaluation results	(executed by business components)
Specify qualification measures	(executed by business components)
Agree on qualification measures with suppliers	(execute manually)
Execute qualification measures	(execute manually)
Evaluate qualification measures	(executed by business components)

5   Web Services Design

The goal of the Web services design is to elaborate different diagrams providing more information about instantiations and collaboration of the different services. Therefore two types of diagrams are appropriate, a deployment and a sequence diagram. Both are presented in the following subsection using the Unified Modelling Language [19, p. 362 and 432] notation.

5.1   Web Services Collaboration Design

A Web based application is in general accessible using a Web browser while having the Web services provided by a service provider, with either services running on the service provider's own system or in composing the application from additional Web service available from 3rd party service providers. Both solutions are possible for the domain of strategic supply chain management.

In Fig. 7 the services are distributed among two service providers. The one provides all Web services related to the development, administration and visualisation of the supply chain. The 3rd party service provider administrates the evaluation methodologies used in order to evaluate the supply chain.

The suppliers access the system e.g., over a Web browser, whereas the producer accesses the Web service interfaces from its own application. The application of the producer includes also the business components which have been derived from the sensitive business tasks and information objects, and which should not be provided as Web services. Since the focus of this paper is on Web services, the detailed composition of the producer's application is not explained in this context.

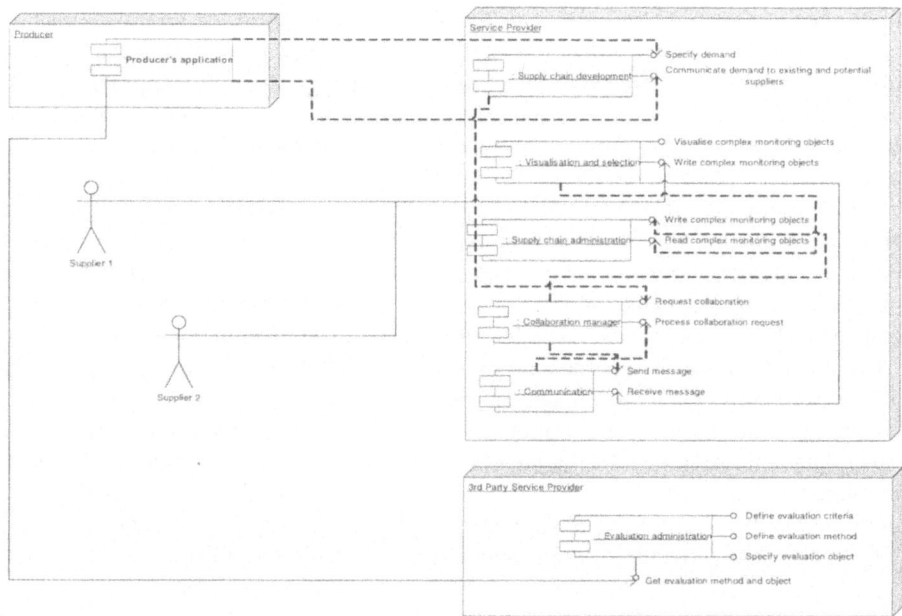

Fig. 7. Instantiation and deployment diagram

For a more coherent display not all Web service interfaces and dependencies are shown. The dependencies and the service calls are presented by arrows. A detailed description of the dataflow is given by means of an example and is illustrated in Fig. 8.

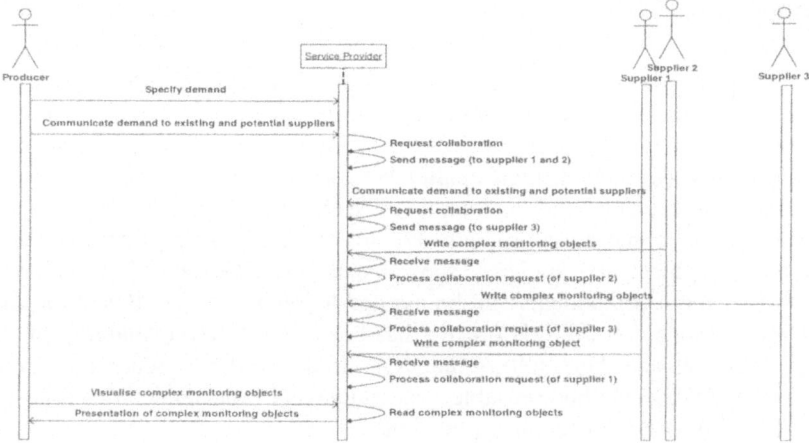

Fig. 8. Sequence diagram

Example: For the strategic development of a supply chain, defined by a demand, it is essential to collect complete data not only from the supplier in tier-1 but also from all suppliers in tier-n in order to be able to model and evaluate existing and alternative supply chains. Using the interfaces of the Web service *supply chain development* a producer is able to specify the demand and to communicate the demand to all suppliers in tier-n. Triggered by that request, the supply chain development service accesses the interface *request collaboration* of the collaboration manager which uses the *send message* interface of the communication component in order to notify the demand to all suppliers in tier-1.

The service calls are visualised in Fig. 8 by arrows. When a supplier has been notified about the need of delivering supplier information, it notifies its own suppliers using the interface *communicate demand to existing and potential suppliers* of the supply chain development Web service. All inter-enterprise communication is established by the Web services collaboration manager and communication.

All suppliers in tier-n use the interface *write complex monitoring objects* of the Web service supply chain administration to provide their own or aggregated data to the supplier in tier-(n-1). The supplier in tier-(n-1) aggregates the data received with its own data and provides it to the supplier in tier-(n-2). In the example the producer communicates the demand to the supplier 1 and 2 in tier-1. The supplier 1 communicates the demand to the supplier 3 in tier-2. The aggregated data of supplier 3 and supplier 1 is provided to the producer together with the information of supplier 2.

The producer, having received all aggregated data of the suppliers in all tiers, can request to visualise the complex monitoring object. The complete supply chain is presented containing all information about the single supplier nodes. The producer is therefore able to evaluate and to develop the complete supply chain according to its requirements.

6   Conclusion

Having illustrated the need of building advanced inter-enterprise information systems using Web services, two main problems have been recognised while developing such Web applications based on Web services. First, Web services need to be *specified* in an unequivocal way. Second, high quality Web services need to be *identified*, such that reusable, marketable and maintainable Web services can be offered on the market. Having seen that those problems are not new to the field of component based software development it has been shown that the concepts of specifying and identifying business components can be applied to Web services. Based on this, the Web Services Modelling (WSM) process has been introduced, explaining the single phases, sub phases and the resulting diagrams used in order to achieve a maximum result. With the WSM method reusable, marketable and expandable Web services can be identified and used in different applications.

The WSM method has been verified for the domain of strategic supply chain development, which extends the traditional frame of reference in strategic sourcing from a supplier-centric to a supply-chain-scope including the dynamic modelling of strategic supply chain. The phases Web services analysis and design with the corresponding sub phases have been detailed for that domain and the resulting diagrams are explained.

Further work for the validation and refinement of the proposed WSM methodology is required. In particular supplementary business domains need to be examined to obtain a broader assessment base. Additionally the criteria for filtering business tasks and information objects that are not suitable for Web services have to be further explored.

References

[1] A. Albani, A. Keiblinger, K. Turowski and C. Winnewisser, *Domain based identification and modelling of business component applications, to appear in Proceedings of the 7th East-European Conference on Advances in Databases and Information Systems (ADBIS'03)*, Dresden, Germany, 2003.

[2] D. Ammer, *Materials Management*, Homewood, 1968

[3] A. Arkin and S. Assaf, *Web Service Choreography Interface 1.0*, 2002, www.sun.com/software/xml/developers/wsci/wsci-spec-10.pdf.

[4] A. Beugnard, J.-M. Jézéquel, N. Plouzeau and D. Watkins, *Making Components Contract Aware*, IEEE Computer, 32 (1999), pp. 38–44.

[5] C. Boyens and O. Günther, *Trust Is not Enough: Privacy and Security in ASP and Web Service Environments, Conference on Advances in Databases and Information Systems (ADBIS 2002)*, Slovakia, 2002.

[6] T. Bray, J. Paoli and C. M. Sperberg-McQueen, *Extensible Markup Language (XML) 1.0*, World Wide Web Consortium (W3C), http://www.w3.org/TR/1999/REC-xml-1998021, 1998.

[7] A. S. Carr and J. N. Pearson, *Strategically managed buyer - supplier relationships and performance outcomes*, Journal of Operations Management, 17 (1999), pp. 497–519.

[8] K. Czarnecki and U. Eisenecker, *Generative programming: methods, tools, and applications*, Addison Wesley, Boston, 2000

[9] M. Duftler and R. Khalaf, *Business Process with BPEL4WS: Learning BPEL4WS, Part 3*, IBM developerWorks, 2002,

[10] M. Gaedke and G. Graef, *Development and Evolution of Web-Applications using the WebComposition Process Model, 2nd Web Engineering Workshop at the 9th International World Wide Web Conference (WWW9-WebE)*, Amsterdam, The Netherlands, 2000.

[11] H.-W. Gellersen and M. Gaedke, *Object-Oriented Web Application Development*, IEEE Internet Computing, 3 (1999), pp. 60–68.

[12] IBM, *Business Systems Planning-Information Systems Planning Guide*, International Business Machines, Atlanta, 1984

[13] K. C. Kang, *Feature-Oriented Domain Analysis (FODA) feasibility study*, Carnegie Mellon University Software Engineering Institute, Pittsburgh, Pa., 1990

[14] L. Kaufmann, *Purchasing and Supply Management – A Conceptual Framework, Handbuch Industrielles Beschaffungsmanagement*, Hahn, D, Kaufmann, L. (Hrsg.), Wiesbaden, 2002, pp. 3–33.

[15] A. Krammer and K. Turowski, *Spezifikationsbedarf von Web-Services*, in E. Ortner and S. Overhage, eds., *1. Workshop Entwicklung von Anwendungen auf der Basis der XML Web-Service Technologie*, TU-Darmstadt, Darmstadt, 2002, pp. 1–14.

[16] D. M. Lambert and M. C. Cooper, *Issues in Supply Chain Management*, Industrial Marketing Management, 29 (2000), pp. 65–83.

[17] T. W. Malone and R. J. Lautbacher, *The Dawn of the E-Lance Economy*, Harvard Business Review (1998), pp. 145–152.

[18] R. McIvor, P. Humphreys and E. McAleer, *The Evolution of the Purchasing Function*, Journal of Strategic Change, Vol. 6 (1997), pp. 165–179.

[19] OMG, *OMG Unified Modelling Language Spezification Version 1.4*, 2001

[20] U. Organisation, *UDDI Version 3.0*, 2002, http://uddi.org/pubs/uddi-v3.00-published-20020719.htm.

[21] M. P. Papazoglou and J. Yang, *Design Methodology for Web Services and Business Processes, Lecture Notes in Computer Science*, Springer-Verlag, 2002, pp. 54 ff.

[22] C. Rautenstrauch, H. Tangermann and K. Turowski, *Manufacturing Planning and Control Content Management in Virtual Enterprises Pursuing Mass Customization*, in C. Rautenstrauch, K. Turowski and R. Seelmann-Eggebert, eds., *Moving into Mass Customization – Information Systems and Management Principles*, Springer-Verlag, Dubai, 2001, pp. 103–118.

[23] J. Sametinger, *Software engineering with reusable components*, Springer, Berlin; New York, 1997

[24] M. Sawhney and J. Zabin, *The Seven Steps to Nirvana: Strategic Insights into eBusiness Transformation*, New York, 2001

[25] M. Simos, D. Creps, C. Klinger, L. Levine and D. Allemang, *Organization Domain Modeling (ODM) Guidebook*, 1996

[26] D. Tapscott, D. Ticoll and A. Lowy, *Digital Capital: Harnessing the Power of Business Webs*, Boston, 2000

[27] A. Tsalgatidou and T. Pilioura, *An Overview of Standards and Related Technology in Web Services - Special Issue on E-Services*, International Journal of Distributed and Parallel Databases (2002), pp. 135–162.

[28] K. Turowski, *Spezifikation und Standardisierung von Fachkomponenten*, Wirtschaftsinformatik, 43 (2001), pp. 269–281.

[29] K. Turowski, *Standardisierung von Fachkomponenten: Spezifikation und Objekte der Standardisierung*, in A. Heinzl, ed., *3. Meistersingertreffen*, Schloss Thurnau, 1999.

[30] W. W. W. C. (W3C), *SOAP Version 1.2 Part 0: Primer*, 2002, http://www.w3.org/TR/2002/CR-soap12-part0-20021219/.

[31] W. W. W. C. (W3C), *Web Services Description Language (WSDL) Version 1.2*, 2003, http://www.w3.org/TR/wsdl12/.

[32] H.-J. Warnecke, *Vom Fraktal zum Produktionsnetzwerk. Unternehmenskooperationen erfolgreich gestalten*, Berlin, 1999

[33] J. Yang and M. P. Papazoglou, *Web Component: A Substrate for Web Serivce Reuse and Composition, Lecture Notes in Computer Science*, Springer-Verlag, 2002, pp. 21 ff.

[34] S. Yang, H. Lam and S. Y. W. Su, *Trust-Based Security Model and Enforcement Mechanism for Web Service Technology, In Proceedings of the 3rd VLDB Workshop on Technologies for E-Services (TES'02)*, China, 2002.

Advertising Games for Web Services[*]

Alessandro Agostini and Paolo Avesani

ITC-IRST Trento
Via Sommarive 18, 38050 Povo, Trento, I
{agostini,avesani}@irst.itc.it

Abstract. We advance and discuss a framework suitable to study theoretical implications and practical impact of language evolution and lexicon sharing in an open distributed multi-agent system. In our approach, the assumption of autonomy plays a key role to preserve the opportunity for the agents of local encoding of meanings. We consider the application scenario of Web services, where we conceive the *problem of advertisement* as a matter of sharing a denotational language. We provide a precise formulation of the agents' behavior within a game-theoretical setting. As an important consequence of our "advertising games," we interpret the problem of knowledge interoperability and management in the light of evolutionary dynamics and learning in games. Our methodology is inspired by work in natural language semantics and "language games."

Keywords: Web information systems and services; semantic interoperability; negotiation protocols; peer-to-peer cooperation.

1   Introduction

The recent trend in the information technology is the promotion of distributed solutions. Web services and peer-to-peer architectures are two of the most representative examples (see for instance [6,8,4,7,12] and the references cited therein). The common objective of these fast-growing research and technological areas is the design and the development of autonomous and distributed systems that overcome the restrictions of client-server architectures. As far as we know, a main challenge of the web services is how to achieve a full interoperability among distributed processes. In particular, the efficient advertisement of a service content is really a crucial task to reach full interoperability, because it addresses the actors concerned to an effective communication based on a shared knowledge representation. Advertisement is in fact the first step in the deployment of a web service. A main purpose of a service provider on the Web is the publishing of the interaction protocol by which information seekers may connect reliably with the provider. Together with the interaction protocol, the service provider

---

[*] This work was partially supported by the *Provincia Autonoma di Trento* Project EDAMOK ("Enabling Distributed and Autonomous Management of Knowledge") under deliberation number 1060-4/5/2001.

R. Meersman et al. (Eds.): CoopIS/DOA/ODBASE 2003, LNCS 2888, pp. 93–109, 2003.
© Springer-Verlag Berlin Heidelberg 2003

communicates the specification of the service content. Usually, understanding of such specification is made easier by assuming that the agents agree on a common ontology, which also fixes the semantic relations involved in the service. This centralized approach, however, is not always sustainable on the large scale (see for instance [3,5] and the references cited there).

From the standpoint of language disambiguation, categorial indeterminacy of service advertisements is an important problem in Web services. Categorial indeterminacy is the name—historically emerged from the community of natural language semantics and situated grounded word semantics (see for instance [21,22]), of a kind of partial incoherence of a set of languages and relations distributed over a possibly huge set of agents. In these distributed environments, most interesting situations apply to agents concerned with the management of rich categorial databases. For example, think of an information agent in the role of a provider as the holder of the directories of *Google*, and of an information agent in the role of a seeker as the holder of the directories of *Yahoo!*. In such situation, it is indeed possible and very common that a particular topic, chosen by the seeker, is conceptualised in very different ways by the provider. A possible consequence is the emergence of polysemy—that is, the same word may be used by the agents to denote different categories or topics. Successful advertisements for a web service often depend on the ability of choosing the "right" denotation among those that would be used by the agents for the same service. A similar ability is related to the problem of guessing the content of an user searching the web, where a common technique is *context guessing* (see for instance [10]; see also [13]). Unfortunately, today web service techniques "by guessing" are limited to cases where potential semantic contents of the required services can be identified on the basis of the keyword query. This is often not the case in the Web search.

The attempts to design solutions to categorial indeterminacy have produced the development of mapping algorithms (see for instance [11,15,16]). A (schema, model, ontology, context) mapping can be effective to support the semantic interoperability between the web services, and it may be possibly used to reduce categorial indeterminacy. However, mappings may be not suitable to face with the assumption of the open World (Wide Web), where new actors join and leave the scenario continuously. A reason is that the strategy to solve the problem of interoperability based on mapping requires to find the relative mapping for each pair of actors. An undesirable consequence is that the deployment of a new actor can be very demanding, especially whenever the actor community is very large.

In this paper, we propose a general approach that exploits the meaning-to-meaning relationships found in many domains of interest, one of them being the Web services. In particular, we define a game suitable to model any domain with meaning-to-meaning relationships. Our solution concept for the problem of semantic interoperability is based on the emergence of a shared language for the advertisement in a system of agents. In other words, our idea is to conceive the problem of knowledge interoperability as a matter of sharing a denotational language. A question we investigate in this paper is whether and how language and expecially language evolution are functional to get an efficient advertising service and, as a consequence, a successful matching between an information seeker and the relevant service provider. Our methodology is inspired by work in natural language semantics and "language games" [17,21]. A similar approach with different assumptions has been adopted in the domain of robotics [18,19], where the notions like "naming game" and "guessing games" have been proposed.

This paper is organized as follows. In Section 2 we advance and discuss some related work, expecially language games. In particular, we compare to our approach "naming games" and their major variant of "guessing games." In Section 3 we illustrate an application scenario in the Web services, which is formalized in Section 4 and further discussed through a detailed analysis of the players' behavior in Section 5. We add some final remarks to discussion in Section 6. We conclude in Section 7 with a summary of the results of this paper.

2   Related Work

Language games have been introduced to study natural language semantics by experimental use of visually grounded robots in a distributed group [18,19]. The problem was to determine the systematic relations between language forms ("words"), their meanings ("concepts")—expecially local meaning assigned to words by a single agent, and their referents ("instances," "objects"). A corollary of the problem solution is the evolution of the agents' language and of their lexicon. This problem is referred to as "the grounding problem" in [20].

A major sub-problem is "naming," that is, how vocabulary and meanings are learned individually and a shared lexicon eventually emerges in a group of agents. The problem of naming may be expressed in game-theoretical terms, and was extensively studied since the *naming games* [18]. In short, each player from a uniform set of agents has a set of words and a set of objects, and randomly associates a word to an object, called "the topic," to form a local lexicon. In a naming game, it is assumed that all the agents gain a positive payoff in cooperating, "but only if they use the same language" [18]; thus, a naming game is a coordination game in the sense of game theory (see for instance [14]). It is repeatedly played among randomly chosen pairs of players and involves a different couple of agents at each repetition of playing. A naming game is adaptive, in the sense that the players in the game can change their internal state. A reason for changing is to be more successful in playing future games.

There are several variations and extensions of a naming game. In relation to the problem of finding successful advertising strategies for the web services, the most interesting to us are all those which consider a player's "guessing" of the semantic content of a publicly played linguistic expression ("query"). This is the case, for example, of the query-answering systems in the Web search [10].

Following [19], a *guessing game* is played between two agents, called "the speaker" and "the hearer." By convention, the speaker always moves first. In its simplest form the game is played in two steps. First, the speaker chooses an object (called "the topic") from other objects in a given context, the hearer attempts to guess it. The context is a fixed set of objects taken from the reality at the very beginning of the game. A context characterizes the domain of a guessing game.

In contrast with the naming games, instead of playing directly the topic, in a guessing game the speaker explicitly plays to the hearer a linguistic hint. Then, the hearer guesses the topic through the verbal description ("verbalisation") provided by the speaker. The game ends in success just in case the hearer's guess is equal to the topic. The game ends in failure otherwise.

Three important points of a guessing game are that (a) topics are hidden, that is, they must be expressed through linguistic acts rather than exchanges of objects; (b) topics are the means not the end to the game playing, since the solution concept aims at discovering *sets* of topics—which are called "concepts" rather than single objects; (c) topics are always played by the speaker as a direct feedback of the hidden concept to guess. As we will see, the framework we are going to present is based on assumptions similar to (a) and (b). In contrast, a main change is about (c). In our "advertising games," in fact, the players' feedback on the meaning to guess is almost always indirect. One essential aspect of the guessing games we modify is that agents become capable of understanding each other by the fact that they are situated in a common environment and each one can detect the actions of the others in this environment. In our model the agents still communicate in a common environment, to be defined as the set of all objects the agents perceive. However, we rely on indirect communication, and the actions that the agents can mutually detect are primarily linguistic.

A remark concerns statistical learning; see for instance [23]. Although our general approach is clearly comparable to statistical learning, in particular to statistical learning under unlimited amount of sample data, we do not know about any work in statistical learning literature which relates to the problem of lexicon evolution and language sharing in the context of the web services.

3   The Application Scenario

Before introducing the formal definition of an "advertising game," we sketch an example of an application scenario in the domain of web services.

Let us imagine a distributed community of actors with the common goal of sharing their effort in building web directories. We image the directories are of the same kind of *Google, Yahoo!* and *Looksmart*'s. The objective of the application is to define an anytime alerting service that informs an actor, who classified a topic according to some category in a given directory, of a new reviewed web page, classified under the same category but in a different directory. We depict a scenario of pairwise interactions between actors, or *peers*, who can play two roles: *the seeker* and *the provider*. The seeker looks for latest news on a given topic, the provider advertises latest news on a given topic. In this scenario, the problem is twofold. On the one hand, the seeker has to find the "right" denotation to formulate the query about a topic of interest that has to be propagated over the network of peers. On the other hand, the provider has to detect whether the broadcasted query is relevant to the local denotation of the news topic. In both cases, an actor faces with the needs of a shared language denotation for the different but similar topics.

```
<TopicAdvertisement>              <TopicQuery>
    <Name>...</Name>                 <Name>...</Name>
    <Topic>...</Topic>               <Topic>...</Topic>
</TopicAdvertisement>             </TopicQuery>
```

Fig. 1. XML Communication Protocol. On the left hand side, a sketch of the protocol to support the advertising of a new topic of interest, i.e. a directory to collect and to share bookmarks according to a predefined category. On the right hand side, a sketch of the protocol to support an inquiry over the network to receive recommendations on related category.

The basic operations, or actions, available to an actor are two: (a) advertising for a new service on a given topic—called the "target topic," and (b) searching for news on a given topic—called the "source topic." The figure illustrates these basic operations as XML schemata (Fig. 1). In terms of role assignments, notice that advertising is primarily an action taken by a provider, while searching is primarily an action taken by a seeker. However, each actor may take both actions, since we have stated that actors are peers by definition. In case (a), the specific issue is to formulate an (extra-linguistic) advertisement by using the linguistic expression choosen by the seeker to communicate the source topic. To be effective, we require the advertisement to be relevant ("similar") to the source topic. In case (b), the issue is finding a language expression ("label," "query") to denote the source topic. This expression must be equivalent to the way the provider advertises the target topic, in a sense we will make precise below. Otherwise, a mismatch between the source and the target topics may occur. The way the provider advertises a service and the seeker formulates a search query are crucial for helping the actors to match.

We imagine that the administrator of *Google*, playing the role of the seeker, has defined a topic in a web directory (Fig. 2). The topic is a category encoded by a node identifier (the pathname /top/home/cooking/soups_and_stews), a mnemonic label to refer to (the syntagm "fish and soup"), and a collection of web locations representative of the topic (bookmarks). Similarly, the *Yahoo!* administrator, playing the role of the provider, defines a topic as a category in the *Yahoo!*'s directories. Now suppose that the administrator of *Google* is interested in finding whether there are other web directory administrators that have collected unknown web references for the topic "fish and soup." Unfortunately, the topic identifier is not suitable for this purpose, because the encoding (i.e., the pathname) depends on the particular web directory. However, the mnemonic label can indeed be effectively used by the administrator, because it can be revised thanks to meaning negotiation. The challenge of a successful application is to bring the administrators of the web directories to converge, by meaning negotiation, towards a common denotation without forcing the alignment of the directories' structure.

```
<topic>

<directory>
   Google:/top/home/cooking/soups_and_stews/fish_and_seafood
<\directory>
      <name>fish and seafood</name>
      <bookmark>
        <uri>
          http://www.fish2go.com/rec_0120.htm
        </uri>
        <excerpt>
          Finnan Haddie and Watercress Soup: made with smoked
          haddock, potatoes, watercress, and milk.
        </excerpt>
      </bookmark>
      <bookmark>...</bookmark>
      ...
      <bookmark>...</bookmark>
</topic>

<topic>

<directory>
   Yahoo:/top/society_and_culture/food_and_drink/cooking/recipes/
         by_ingredient/fish_and_seafood
<\directory>
      <name>beef</name>
      <bookmark>
        <uri>
          http://www.freshfish4u.com/fishnet/recipes
        </uri>
        <excerpt>
          For a range of fish and shellfish species. Alphabetically
          organized.
        </excerpt>
      </bookmark>
      <bookmark>...</bookmark>
      ...
      <bookmark>...</bookmark>
</topic>
```

Fig. 2. Topic XML Schema. A couple of examples of directories extracted from *Google*'s web directories. Each directory is defined by an identifier (in this case the full path), a name that provides a mnemonic support to detect the related category associated to the directory (the local denotation), and a collection of bookmarks.

4   The Framework

We model the foregoing application scenario together with the pairwise interactions of the actors by a kind of language game. More specifically, we introduce the notion of an "advertisement game," where the local representation of a topic is hidden, that is, it is not shared among the actors. In an *advertising game*, the only way to assess whether a seeker's query about some topic matches a provider's advertisement on the same or on a similar topic is to go through an inductive trial and error process. From the standpoint of the game design, our ultimate goal is to reduce the search failures which are the result of a provider's misunderstanding of a seeker's queries. In short, we aim to minimize categorial indeterminacy of service advertising and search.

4.1   Basic Components

In this subsection, we present and discuss the basic elements and properties of an "advertising game." An *advertising game* is defined over a countable (nonempty) collection $\mathcal{D}$ of *objects* shared among a (recursive) set Λ of agents—we call the set $\mathcal{D}$ *game domain*. Intuitively, $\mathcal{D}$ denotes the class of objects in the reality ("universal set") that all players perceive in the same way according to the nature of the game. For example, if the game is used to model information extraction or retrieval, $\mathcal{D}$ is a set of achievable documents.[1] For another example related to the application scenario of Web services (Section 3), $\mathcal{D}$ is the set of documents contained in the nodes of a web directory.

Each agent has a set of words and a set of meanings. In this paper we assume that a word (also "label") is any finite string of symbols from an alphabet of symbols *Sym* without further specification. Intuitively, a meaning is a proper subset of the game domain. For example, if the game domain is information retrieval then a set of documents is a meaning. (We do not discuss here how these are related to each other, since we assume meanings to be primitive elements of our model.) Each agent has a "lexicon." Informally, a lexicon is a set of pairs of the form $\langle word, meaning \rangle$. An agent's lexicon may be either empty (no associations) or incomplete, that is, there may be some word with no meaning or some meaning with no word associated. Polysemy and synonymy, that is, the same meaning may be expressed by the agents through different words, may occur. Notice that there is not one lexicon for all agents, but each agent has his own local lexicon. A general lexicon as a system's component (that is, a global element of the game) can indeed be defined by the union of the agents' lexicon, and we do it below. However, this general component is not necessary in our game construction. A motivation is that we want to deal with locally computable elements, and a global lexicon cannot be computed by any agent, because the set-theoretical operation of union runs over all the agents.

Given a player i, let Lx_i denote the player's *lexicon*. Let $pow(\mathcal{D})$ denote the power set of $\mathcal{D}$. We define Lx_i to be any subset of $\mathcal{L}_i \times \mathcal{C}_i$, where $\mathcal{L}_i$ denotes the language (i.e., a set of "words") of player i, and $\mathcal{C}_i \subseteq pow(\mathcal{D})$ denotes the set of meanings of i (given $\mathcal{D}$). We define the *game lexicon* (written: Lx) by the

---

[1] The *content* of the documents, however, may be perceived in different ways by the players, and in fact this is the main point of this paper: how the agent can compare documents whose content is locally assigned by each player independently?

union of Lx_i over all $i \in \Lambda$. To provide easy starting of the game, for simplicity we assume that

(1) *there is at least a player $i \in \Lambda$ such that $Lx_i \neq \emptyset$.*

In particular, $\mathcal{L}_i \neq \emptyset$ and $\mathcal{C}_i \neq \emptyset$. Only a player i satisfying (1) is allowed to play the role of the seeker at the beginning of the (repeated version of) the advertising game. In other words, (1) is the condition we require to a player to be able to start the game.

Each agent has a *sampling function* that transforms every meaning in the agent's set of meanings into an infinite sequence ("ω-sequence") of nonempty subsets of objects in the game domain $\mathcal{D}$. To define an agent' sampling function we introduce some notation. We write $length(\sigma)$ for the length of a finite sequence. Let N denote the set $\{0, 1, 2, ...\}$ of natural numbers. We write σ_n for the nth element of σ, $0 \leq n < length(\sigma)$.

Definition 1. Let game domain $\mathcal{D}$, player i and meaning $m \in \mathcal{C}_i$ be given. A *sample of m in $\mathcal{D}$ by player i* is an infinite sequence over $pow(\mathcal{D})$ (written: $\mathsf{Sample}^i(m \mid \mathcal{D})$) such that:

(2) $\bigcup_{n \in N} \mathsf{Sample}^i(m \mid \mathcal{D})_n = m$.

We say that the nth element $\mathsf{Sample}^i(m \mid \mathcal{D})_n$ of $\mathsf{Sample}^i(m \mid \mathcal{D})$ is the *sample* ("instance," "example,"...) by player i of m in $\mathcal{D}$ at n.

There are "good" and "bad" samples. For goodness, a necessary (but not sufficient) condition to efficiency is that for every $n \in N$, $\mathsf{Sample}^i(m \mid \mathcal{D})_n$ is finite. For badness, an example is the sample $\langle \emptyset\ m\ \emptyset\ \emptyset\ \emptyset \ldots \rangle$ for m being a meaning with an infinite extension.

Remark 1. A question is why we resort to infinite sequences to define a meaning's sample. The answer is in fact fundamental to understand our approach. We define sampling "in the limit," in the sense that we assume that no finite sampling can capture completely any (sufficiently interesting) meaning. Of course, a sample may be an infinite sequence of a *finite* number of sets (subsets of $\mathcal{D}$) even for meanings with denumerable extension.

We note that the infinite sequence $\mathsf{Sample}^i(m \mid \mathcal{D})$ defines a preference order over samples for m in $\mathcal{D}$. Also observe:

Lemma 1. For all players i and all game domains $\mathcal{D}$, and for every meaning $m \subseteq \mathcal{D}$, $\mathsf{Sample}^i(m \mid \mathcal{D})$ exists if and only if $m \in \mathcal{C}_i$.

Proof: The "only if" direction follows immediately from Definition 1. To prove the "if," suppose that $m \in \mathcal{C}_i$. Observe that the cardinality of m is countable. Then m is a r.e. set and we can list all the members of m according to a recursive procedure. For example, we can produce the first element of the list, say o_1, randomly from m, the second element of the list, say o_2, randomly from $m - \{o_1\}$, the third element of the list, say o_3, randomly from $m - \{o_1, o_2\}$, and so on. For all $n \in N$, define $\mathsf{Sample}^i(m \mid \mathcal{D})_n = o_n$. It is immediate to verify that (2) holds. ∎

Each agent has a *preference relation* ("utility function") over the lexicon. Let Z denote the set of integers (positive, negative, and zero).

Definition 2. Let player i be given. A *utility function* of i is a total computable function from Lx_i to Z.

In other words, a utility function decides what utility a player gets for his choice. Intuitively, negative numbers are bad outcomes, positive numbers are good outcomes, and 0 is the neutral outcome. Big positive outcomes are nicer than small positive outcomes, and similarly for negative numbers. Observe that a utility function is locally computable, that is, each agent computes the utiliy of assigning a meaning to a word over its own lexicon.

We refer to values of a utility function as *payoffs* (or "utilities"). For all pairs $\langle w, m \rangle \in Lx_i$, let $\mathsf{Pref}^i(w, m)$ denote the preference, or utility, of player i to use a word w to communicate a meaning m. If $\mathsf{Pref}^i(w, m) = n$, we say that w is the n-preferred word by player i for m or, equivalently, that m is the n-preferred meaning by player i for w. Since we are interested in the repeated playing of a game, the updating of the players' preferences over time is important. In order to deal with time, we extend Definition 2 over N as follows. Given $t \in N$, let $\mathsf{Pref}^i(w, m, t)$ denote the payoff $\mathsf{Pref}^i(w, m)$ *at time* ("move") t of the game history. To shorten notation, we write $\mathsf{Pref}^i(w, m)$ for $\mathsf{Pref}^i(w, m, 0)$.

Remark 2. An infinite sequence $\mathsf{Sample}^i(m \mid \mathcal{D})$ defines a preference ordering over the samples of m. As a consequence, we have two related kinds of preferences, respectively over meanings with respect to a given word, and over the samples of a given meaning. In an advertising game, the former preferences are properly used by the seeker, who decides what meanings to play; while the latter preferences are properly used by the provider, who uses sampling as a way to communicate the seeker's requests; see the protocols in Section 5 for details.

We are now ready to define a "local similarity relation."

Definition 3. Let player i and game domain $\mathcal{D}$ be given. A *local similarity relation* of i on $\mathcal{D}$ is a recursive relation on $\{i\} \times pow(\mathcal{D})^2$ such that the restricted relation on $pow(\mathcal{D}) \times pow(\mathcal{D})$—called *similarity relation*, is a reflexive, symmetric and transitive binary relation.

Intuitively, given $m, m' \subseteq \mathcal{D}$, $\mathsf{Sim}(i, m, m')$ is true if m and m' are "similar" from the i's viewpoint. Otherwise, $\mathsf{Sim}^i(m, m')$ is false. The simplest example of similarity is equality. Other examples are Notice that this definition of similarity emphasizes the local perspective of individual agents. For notational convenience, from now to the end of this paper we write $\mathsf{Sim}^i(m, m')$ in place of $\mathsf{Sim}(i, m, m')$.

Remark 3. Various aspects of meaning can be used to determine the exact content of similarity, usually depending on the application domain and the appropriate definition of similarity for that domain. When meanings are sets, and this is the case in an advertising game, a similarity relation is identical to an equivalence relation in discrete mathematics. However, we prefer to use a similarity relation rather than an equivalence relation, because one main goal of our research agenda is to lead off to experimental work on the impact of language evolution and lexicon sharing in the Web services. Similarity relations play an important role in our foreseeable experimental work [2]. For a similar reason, notice that often similarity is a continuous measure, rather than a binary relation, so a question arises on motivations. On the one hand, we may extend our definition, for example to integers, denoted by Z, and define the local similarity measure of a player i on game domain $\mathcal{D}$ to be a recursive *function* from $\{i\} \times pow(\mathcal{D})^2$ to Z. (Recall that the relation $\mathsf{Sim}^i(\cdot, \cdot)$ is equivalent to a function with codomain $\{0, 1\}$.) On the other hand, at the present stage of our work we do not need to deal with the additional power but the additional complexity of continuous similarity metrics.

Whatever $\mathsf{Sim}^i(\cdot, \cdot)$ is defined, we require it satisfies the following property. We rely on some notation. Given any (finite, infinite) sequence σ over $pow(\mathcal{D})$, let $content(\sigma)$ denote the union set of elements in σ. For example, take $\mathcal{D}$ be the set of natural numbers and $\sigma = \langle \{0\} \, \{0, 2, 6\} \, \{2, 74, 8, 1\} \, \{1\} \rangle$. Then $content(\sigma) = \{0, 1, 2, 6, 8, 74\}$. Observe that $content(\sigma) \subseteq \mathcal{D}$, so $content(\sigma)$ is a meaning. The announced property follows:

(3) *For all players i, j and for all $m \in \mathcal{C}_i$, $\tilde{m}' \in \mathcal{C}_j$ such that $\mathsf{Sim}^i(m, \tilde{m}')$ is true, there are meaning $m' \subseteq \mathcal{D}$ and $k \in N$ such that:*
  (a) $\tilde{m}' = \mathsf{Sample}^j(m' \mid \mathcal{D})_k$,
  (b) $m \cap content(\mathsf{Sample}^j(m' \mid \mathcal{D})) \neq \emptyset$, and
  (c) $\mathsf{Sim}^i(m, \mathsf{Sample}^i(m \mid \mathcal{D})_n)$ is true for all $n \in N$.

Observe that (3) implies that a strategy to succeed in the game playing is genuinely an inductive process. For example, it may happen that $\mathsf{Sim}^i(m, \tilde{m}')$ is true but $m \cap \tilde{m}' = \emptyset$.

5   Game Protocols – A Result

We now analyze in more detail the behavior of the players in an advertising game. This is controlled by two related kind of rules. We call *game protocol* the computable "rules of the game." In an advertising game there are two kind of rules. First, the rules to govern the mutual inter-actions of the players. Second, the rules to update the players' preferences. We present each set of rules in turn. Notice that a game protocol is shared by all the players, but individual strategic components are present. An individual strategy is basically a set of rules which tells the player who uses it how to move. A strategy may depend on earlier decisions and the opponent's moves taken in the game. A strategy is said to be winning if a player wins every game in which he or she uses it. We will see that the strategies in the protocols below are winning to supply the agents in the repeated playing of the game with a shared lexicon.

5.1   Communication Protocol

We assume that the seeker is chosen from a subset of players whose lexicon is nonempty at time $t \in N$. This guarantees the easy starting of the game, as we

Algorithm 1 "One-shot" playing of an advertising game.

proc $OneShotGame(\mathcal{G}(Sym, \{i, j\}, \mathcal{D}, \rho), t) \equiv$
    i "thinks" to $m \in \mathcal{C}_i^t$ at time t;
    i "plays" $w \in \mathcal{L}_i^t$ to j at time t s.t. $\mathsf{Pref}^i(w, m, t)$ is the maximum over Lx_i^t;
    if $\exists m' \in \mathcal{C}_j^t \langle w, m' \rangle \in Lx_j^t$
        then $M_w^t := \{m \in \mathcal{C}_j^t \mid \langle w, m \rangle \in Lx_j^t\}$;
                j "thinks" to $m' \in M_w^t$ s.t. $\mathsf{Pref}^j(w, m', t)$ is the maximum over Lx_j^t;
                $\tilde{m}' := \mathsf{Sample}^j(m' \mid \mathcal{D})_t$;
                j "outputs" $\tilde{m}'$ to i at t;
                if $\mathsf{Sim}^i(m, \tilde{m}')$ **then**   (* reinforcement *)
                            i "outputs" True to j at t;
                            $PrefUpdating+(\mathcal{G}(Sym, \{i\}, \mathcal{D}, \rho), t, w, m)$;
                            $PrefUpdating+(\mathcal{G}(Sym, \{j\}, \mathcal{D}, \rho), t, w, m')$
                        else i "outputs" False to j at t;
                            $PrefUpdating-(\mathcal{G}(Sym, \{i\}, \mathcal{D}, \rho), t, w, m)$;
                            $PrefUpdating-(\mathcal{G}(Sym, \{j\}, \mathcal{D}, \rho), t, w, m')$
                fi
    else
            j "outputs" ? to i;   (* "call for help" - "?": special symbol *)
            $\tilde{m} := \mathsf{Sample}^i(m \mid \mathcal{D})_t$;
            i "plays" $\tilde{m}$ to j at t;   (* direct feedback *)
            $PrefUpdating-(\mathcal{G}(Sym, \{i\}, \mathcal{D}, \rho), t, w, m)$;   (* adaptation i *)
            $\mathcal{L}_j^{t+1} := \mathcal{L}_j^t \cup \{w\}$;   (* adaptation j *)
            $\mathcal{C}_j^{t+1} := \mathcal{C}_j^t \cup \{\tilde{m}\}$;
            $Lx_j^{t+1} := Lx_j^t \cup \{\langle w, \tilde{m} \rangle\}$;
            $\mathsf{Pref}^j(w, \tilde{m}, t) := 0$;
            $\mathsf{Sample}^j(\tilde{m} \mid \mathcal{D})_t = \tilde{m}$ **fi**.

have said in (1). In the following, we identify the seeker with player $i = 1$ and the provider with player $j = 2$. We illustrate Algorithm 1 by dividing it into four main steps. We call the actions taken by the agents in these steps a *round* (or "play") of the advertising game. Without loss of generality, we describe the algorithm for $t = 0$.

Step 0. The players agree *by convention* to play on a common set of objects $\mathcal{D}$. Moreover, the players agree on the reinforcement parameter $\rho > 0$ to use to update their own preferences.[2]

Step 1. The seeker outputs a word $w \in \mathcal{L}_1$ while internally he plays (interpretes, "conceptualizes" it by) a meaning $m \in \mathcal{C}_1$ with positive preference $\mathsf{Pref}^1(w, m)$. We assume that $\mathsf{Pref}^1(w, m)$ is the maximum over the seeker's lexicon. In this case, we say that m is the most preferred meaning for w or that w is the most preferred word for m.

Comment: If the maximum of $\mathsf{Pref}^1(w, m)$ is not unique, then a user-internal procedure runs to pick out the final best choice. For simplicity, we assume that the

---

[2] Variants of the game are obtained by requiring the players to exchange objects and to communicate explicitly the reinforcement parameter (Step 0).

seeker internal-procedure to rule out optimal preferences among equally desiderable alternatives is the simplest "take it randomly."

Step 2. The provider inputs w. Suppose that w is an entry in the provider's lexicon Lx_2. In other words, suppose that there is $\langle w', m' \rangle \in Lx_2$ such that $w' = w$.[3] Hence, the set $M_w = \{m \in C_2 \mid \langle w, m \rangle \in Lx_2\}$ is nonempty. The provider picks a meaning $m' \in M_w$ with positive preference $\mathsf{Pref}^1(w, m')$. Again, we assume that m' is the most preferred meaning in M_w by the provider. So we assume that $\mathsf{Pref}^2(w, m') > \mathsf{Pref}^2(w, m)$ for all $m \in M_w$. We call m' the provider's *guess* of m (at some time t—we assumed $t = 0$ here). The provider applies his sampling function $\mathsf{Sample}^2(\cdot \mid \mathcal{D})$ to compute $\mathsf{Sample}^2(m' \mid \mathcal{D})$. Observe that $\mathsf{Sample}^2(m' \mid \mathcal{D})$ exists by Lemma 1 and the definition of Lx_2. The provider outputs $\tilde{m}' = \mathsf{Sample}^2(m' \mid \mathcal{D})_0$.[4] If either the provider's lexicon is empty or w is not an entry in the provider's lexicon, then the provider outputs the special word "?". Intuitively, this means that the provider publicly signals misunderstanding, as a "call for help" to the seeker. The game ends in failure. Then the seeker plays $\tilde{m} = \mathsf{Sample}^1(m \mid \mathcal{D})_0$ directly to the provider—"direct feedback" intervenes—and updates her preferences in order to reduce the probability that she uses word w to denote m in playing future "rounds" of the game. The provider updates his language: $\mathcal{L}_2 = \mathcal{L}_2 \cup \{w\}$,[5] adds $\tilde{m}$ to C_2—we refer to $\tilde{m}$ as to the provider's ("special") *guess* of m, and $\langle w, \tilde{m} \rangle$ to his lexicon and sets $\mathsf{Pref}^2(w, \tilde{m}) = 0$ and $\mathsf{Sample}^2(\tilde{m} \mid \mathcal{D})_n = \tilde{m}$ for all $n \in N$.

Comment 1: If m' is not unique, then a provider-internal procedure runs to pick out the final best choice. For simplicity, in this paper we assume that the provider internal-procedure to rule out optimal preferences among equally desiderable alternatives is the simplest "take it randomly."

Comment 2: If the game ends in failure, then there is a different behavior by the seeker as if the game would succeed. Someone could then wonder whether this asymmetry is truly motivated, expecially in the scenario of the web services. According to the protocol, in fact, communication between the agents is pairwise, linguistic and extra-linguistic. In particular, both linguistic queries and objects samples are eventually played by the seeker to the provider. For example, the seeker gives the provider some documents or URL links related to the meaning he is referring to when doing a linguistic query. This would happen in case of game failure, for instance because of the misunderstanding of the query by the provider. Two special words "True" and "False" are allowed. These special words are assumed to be universally understood by the players in the game and provide

---

[3] The model here presents a way of generalization to linguistic analysis, for example by parsing. In other words, the identity between words required at this step of playing may be replaced by an appropriate linguistic equivalence, whose definition, however, is out of the scope of this paper.

[4] In the terminology of infinitely repeated games, we consider one-shot playing of a game to be equivalent to playing the first repetition of the infinitely repeated version of the game. Here, we denoted such first repetition with "0."

[5] For the sake of simplicity, we omitted time-dependent decorations like superscripts on $\mathcal{L}_2$. However, it is important to emphasize that language evolves along time.

Algorithm 2 Preferences updating.

---

proc *PrefUpdating+*$(\mathcal{G}(\,Sym,\{a\},\mathcal{D},\rho\,),t,w,m)$ $\equiv$
  $\mathsf{Pref}^a(w,m,t+1) := \mathsf{Pref}^a(w,m,t) + \rho;$ (* winning association *)
  if $a =$ "**the seeker**"
    then foreach $\langle\,\tilde{w}\,,m\,\rangle \in Lx_a^t$ with $\tilde{w} \neq w$ **do**   (* competing associations *)
        $\mathsf{Pref}^a(\tilde{w},m,t+1) := \mathsf{Pref}^a(\tilde{w},m,t) - \rho$ **od**
  elsif $a =$ "**the provider**"
    then foreach $\langle\,w\,,\tilde{m}\,\rangle \in Lx_a^t$ with $\tilde{m} \neq m$ **do**
        $\mathsf{Pref}^a(w,\tilde{m},t+1) := \mathsf{Pref}^a(w,\tilde{m},t) - \rho$ **od**
  fi.
proc *PrefUpdating-*$(\mathcal{G}(\,Sym,\{a\},\mathcal{D},\rho\,),t,w,m)$ $\equiv$
  $\mathsf{Pref}^a(w,m,t+1) := \mathsf{Pref}^a(w,m,t) - \rho.$ (* wrong association *)

---

the seeker with the way to communicate to the provider the feedback about the meaning he used to interpret the query.

Step 3. The seeker inputs $\tilde{m}' \subseteq \mathcal{D}$. (If the seeker inputs "?" see the adaption mechanism in Step 2.) Two cases arise.

Case 1. Suppose that $\mathsf{Sim}^1(m,\tilde{m}')$ is true.[6] Then the seeker outputs True— the seeker publicly signals agreement. The game ends in success. Observe that it is not necessary for the seeker to compute $\mathsf{Sim}^1(\mathsf{Sample}^1(m \mid \mathcal{D})_0, \tilde{m}')$ rather than $\mathsf{Sim}^1(m,\tilde{m}')$, since we assumed that the seeker "knows" m in full. So, using a sample of m (at step 0) is not easier from the standpoint of the seeker than using the whole meaning m.

Case 2. Suppose that $\mathsf{Sim}^1(m,\tilde{m}')$ is false. Then the seeker outputs False—the seeker publicly signals disagreement. The game ends in failure.

5.2   Preferences Updating Protocol

Both game success and game failure imply learning by updating. The procedures we present are based on simple positive reinforcement of successful moves and on negative reinforcement of competing associations $\langle\,word\,,meaning\,\rangle$. The players' preferences are updated according to the following cases (see Algorithm 2 below). Recall that $\mathsf{Pref}^a(,,t)$ refers to the player a utility function at time $t \in N$, w is a word, and m is a meaning.)

Suppose that the *nth* round of the repeated game has been played.

Case 1. $\mathsf{Sim}^1(m,\tilde{m}')$ is true. Then the seeker increases the value of her preferences over the winning association $\langle\,w\,,m\,\rangle$ she played by a fixed amount $\rho \in N$ (the "reinforcement parameter" of the game), namely, $\mathsf{Pref}^1(w,m,n) = \mathsf{Pref}^1(w,m,n-1) + \rho$. At the same time n, the seeker decreases by the same amount ρ her payoff over competing associations, namely, $\mathsf{Pref}^1(\hat{w},m,n) = \mathsf{Pref}^1(\hat{w},m,n-1) - \rho$ for every pair of the form $\langle\,\hat{w}\,,m\,\rangle$, $\hat{w} \neq w$, in the seeker's lexicon Lx_1. The seeker's motivation to adapt preferences is to play a different word for the same meaning in future playing against the same provider.

---

[6] Recall that m is the meaning for the word played by the seeker at Step 1.

Similarly, the provider increases the value of his preferences over the winning association $\langle w, m' \rangle$ he played by the same amount ρ, namely, $\mathsf{Pref}^2(w, m', n) = \mathsf{Pref}^2(w, m', n-1) + \rho$, and decreases by the same amount ρ the value of his preferences over competing associations: $\mathsf{Pref}^2(w, \hat{m}, n) = \mathsf{Pref}^2(w, \hat{m}, n-1) - \rho$ for every pair of the form $\langle w, \hat{m} \rangle$, $\hat{m} \neq m'$, in the provider's lexicon Lx_2. The provider's motivation to adapt preferences is to play a different meaning for the input word in future playing of the game againts the same seeker.

Case 2. $\mathsf{Sim}^1(\tilde{m}, \tilde{m}')$ is false. Then the players decrease the value of the preferences over their selected associations. In particular, the following updating are computed. For the seeker, $\mathsf{Pref}^1(w, m, n) = \mathsf{Pref}^1(w, m, n-1) - \rho$. For the provider, $\mathsf{Pref}^2(w, m', n) = \mathsf{Pref}^2(w, m', n-1) - \rho$.

6 Discussion

By the foregoing protocols of communication and preferences updating, a shared, preferred lexicon eventually emerges from a system of agents as the result of an "infinite horizon" repeated game. The idea of infinitely repeated advertising game is that players will play the same basic game $\mathcal{G} = \mathcal{G}(Sym, \Lambda, \mathcal{D}, \rho)$ over and over again (see Algorithm 3 below). Each player bases his next move on the prior history of the game to that point. The history in a repeated advertising game is recorded as lexicon evolution and preference updating.

Algorithm 3 An "infinite horizon" repeated advertising game.

---

foreach $a \in \Lambda$ **do**   (* initialization *)
    $\mathcal{L}_a^t := \mathcal{L}_a$;
    $\mathcal{C}_a^t := \mathcal{C}_a$;
    $Lx_a^t := Lx_a$ **od**;
$t := 0$;
Take $i \in \Lambda$ s.t. $Lx_i^t \neq \emptyset$;
$i :=$ "the seeker";
for $t = 0$ **to** $t = l$ **do**   (* repeated playing starts *)
      foreach $j \in \Lambda \setminus \{i\}$ **do**
      $j :=$ "the provider";
      $OneShotGame(\mathcal{G}(Sym, \{i, j\}, \mathcal{D}, \rho), t)$ **od od**.

For a repeated advertising game whose players behave according to the communication and preferences updating protocols we have presented so far, categorial indeterminacy of advertising and search is minimized. Although we have omitted a full theoretical development to support our claim in this paper, we have shown in some detail how we conceive the real setting of an experimental scenario. Experimental work along the direction presented in this paper is available in preliminary form [2], where we have continued the study of the application scenario presented in Section 3.

If an advertising game $\mathcal{G}$ is repeatedly played the resulting infinitely repeated game models a genuine limiting process, say in the spirit of inductive inference [9]. The seeker's feedback might never imply the correct matching of the samples played by the two players at each step of the game history, and the use of game history becomes fundamental. But success in our infinitely repeated advertising games may nevertheless be possible.

In Steels' guessing games, words are associated with *single objects*. In contrast, we associate words with *sets of objects*, namely, meanings. As an important consequence, an advertising game captures a guessing game under the constraint of "complete sampling" of the target meaning at each step of the game. More precisely, this means that if $\tilde{m} = \mathsf{Sample}^i(m \mid \mathcal{D})_t$ is equal to m for each $t \in N$, then for every guessing game there is an equivalent advertising game with the same effects on language and lexicon of the game players. The converse is false.[7]

Related to the previous remark is the cardinality of a single-step sampling $\tilde{m}$, that is, the number of objects in the game domain eventually played at some time by the provider in response to the seeker's query. In Steels' work on guessing games, the learning feedback at some time t in the game history about the hearer's (hidden!) choice of meaning m in a context $\mathcal{D}$ is, when traslated into our framework, $\tilde{m} = \mathsf{Sample}^2(m \mid \mathcal{D})_t$. The strong hypothesis by Steels is that $\tilde{m} = m$. Of course, in the case of a meaning m with very high cardinality, such hypothesis is at least uncomfortable (ineffective). So, our approach differs from Steels' with respect to the ability we allow the players to sample a meaning, in order to obtain a *strictly proper* subset of the target meaning at ever step in the game history (i.e., $\tilde{m} \subset m$) and, possibly, a set of minimal cardinality.

As we have seen, in Steels' guessing games, the feedback allows the hearer to learn, and it implies lexicon evolution (in short, the game evolution). The feedback is played by the speaker through a single object o for which a conceptualization (i.e., a distinctive feature set) has been created (by the speaker). Such feedback is *direct*, in the sense that o is assumed to completely explain the hidden conceptualization (i.e., a distinctive feature set) taken by the speaker in order to play an associated, most preferred word in the lexicon. In contrast, we perceive the seeker's feedback to be *indirect*. This means that the "True/False" response by the seeker on the sample $\tilde{m}' = \mathsf{Sample}(m' \mid \mathcal{D})_t$ refers to elements which do not characterize uniquely the target meaning.

7 Conclusion

We have argued for the evidence that the proposed model is suitable to capture the dynamics of new services advertising in a community of agents. We have viewed communication as a general way of managing a seeker/provider relationships, and we have applied the resulting model to an information retrieval scenario of the Web services. We have been concerned about how to make the meaning relevant to a seeker's needs usable by a potential provider in order to fulfill the seeker's requests. More precisely, we have studied the problem of

---

[7] A formal treatment of this topic is out of the scope of this paper. See [1,2].

how to successfully coordinate a seeker's needs and a provider's ability to fulfill
these needs by means of lexicon sharing. How can the agents establish a common
language semantics over a shared domain that allows them to communicate reliably? How do a common language eventually emerge by meaning negotiation?
Hereby, we have proposed to these related questions an answer important *per
se* that might also be useful to address the more general problem of knowledge
management. In fact, we strongly believe that knowledge management is, essentially, a process whereby knowledge seekers are linked with knowledge sources,
and knowledge is transferred.

To summarise, in this paper we have advanced and discussed a framework
suitable to study both theoretical implications and experimentally grounded
impact of language evolution and lexicon sharing within an open distributed
multi-agent system. In our approach, local meanings of eventually shared linguistic expressions and the positive benefits of the agent cooperation played an
important role. We have considered the application scenario of Web services,
where we defined two main operations on services that each agent may perform:
advertising and search. For these basic actions, we have provided a precise formulation within a game-theoretical setting. We have conceived the problem of
advertisement as a matter of sharing a denotational language. As an important
consequence of our "advertising games", we have interpreted the problem of
knowledge interoperability and management in the light of evolutionary dynamics and learning in games.

In the context of future work, we plan to work the scenario of Web services
up into new experiments and theoretical work. The advertising games we have
defined and discussed in this paper provide, we believe, a fruitful starting point.

Acknowledgments. We thank Alessandra Zecca for proofreading.

References

1. A. Agostini and P. Avesani. Advertising games for the web services. Technical
   report, ITC-irst, Trento, Italy, April 2003.
2. A. Agostini and P. Avesani. A peer-to-peer advertising game. Technical report,
   ITC-irst, Trento, Italy, June 2003.
3. M. Bonifacio and P. Bouquet. Una visione distribuita del sapere organizzativo: il
   ruolo dell' Intelligenza Artificiale. *Sistemi e Impresa*, 653(6), 2002.
4. M. Bonifacio, P. Bouquet, G. Mameli, and M. Nori. KEx: A Peer-to-Peer solution
   for distributed knowledge management. In *Proceedings of the Fourth International
   Conference on Practical Aspects of Knowledge Management (PAKM-02)*, pages
   490–500, Heidelberg, 2002. Springer-Verlag LNAI 2569.
5. M. Bonifacio, P. Bouquet, and P. Traverso. Enabling distributed knowledge
   management. managerial and technological implications. *Novatica and Infor-
   matik/Informatique*, III(1), 2002.
6. E. Christensen, F. Curbera, G. Meredith, and S. Weerawarana. Web services description language. Electronically available at http://www.w3.org/TR/wsdl, 2001.

7. F. Giunchiglia and I. Zaihrayeu. Making peer databases interact: A vision for an architecture supporting data coordination. In *Proceedings of the Sixth International Workshop on Cooperative Information Agents (CIA-02)*, Heidelberg, 2002. Springer-Verlag LNAI 2446.

8. M. Gudgin, M. Hadley, J.-J. Moreau, and H. Frystyk. SOAP messaging framework. Electronically available at http://www.w3.org/TR/, October 2001.

9. S. Jain, D. Osherson, J. Royer, and A. Sharma. *Systems That Learn - An Introduction to Learning Theory, 2nd edition*. The MIT Series in Learning, Development, and Conceptual Change, v. 22. The MIT Press, Cambridge, MA, 1999.

10. S. Lawrence. Context in Web Search. *IEEE Data Engineering Bulletin*, 23(3):25–32, 2000.

11. J. Madhavan, P. A. Bernstein, P. Domingos, and A. Y. Halevy. Representing and reasoning about mappings between domain models. In R. Dechter, M. Kearns, and R. Sutton, editors, *Proceedings of the 18th National Conference on Artificial Intelligence (AAAI-02) and of the 14th Innovative Applications of Artificial Intelligence Conference (IAAI-02)*, pages 80–86, Menlo Park, CA, 2002. AAAI Press/The MIT Press.

12. S. A. McIlraith, T. C. Son, and H. Zeng. Semantic Web Services. *IEEE Intelligent Systems*, 16(2):46–53, 2001.

13. R. Navarro-Prieto, M. Scaife, and Y. Rogers. Cognitive strategies in web searching. In *Proceedings of the Fifth Conference on Human Factors & the Web (HFWEB-99)*. NIST, 1999.

14. M. J. Osborne and A. Rubinstein. *A Course in Game Theory*. The MIT Press, Cambridge, MA, 1994.

15. E. Rahm and P. A. Bernstein. A survey of approaches to automatic schema matching. *VLDB Journal*, 10(4):334–350, 2001.

16. L. Serafini, P. Bouquet, B. Magnini, and S. Zanobini. An algorithm for matching contextualized schemas via SAT. Technical Report 0301-06, ITC-irst, Trento, Italy, January 2003.

17. L. Steels. Perceptually grounded meaning creation. In Y. Demazeau, editor, *Proceedings of the Second International Conference on Multi-agent Systems (ICMAS-96)*, pages 338–344, Los Alamitos, CA, 1996. IEEE Computer Society.

18. L. Steels. Self-organizing vocabularies. In C. Langton and T. Shimohara, editors, *Proceedings of the V Alife Conference*, Cambridge, MA, 1996. The MIT Press.

19. L. Steels. The origins of syntax in visually grounded robotic agents. *Artificial Intelligence*, 103:133–156, 1998.

20. L. Steels. Language games for autonomous robots. *IEEE Intelligent Systems*, 16(5):16–22, 2001.

21. L. Steels and F. Kaplan. Situated grounded word semantics. In T. Dean, editor, *Proceedings of the Sixteenth International Joint Conference on Artificial Intelligence (IJCAI-99)*, pages 862–867, San Francisco, CA, 1999. Morgan Kaufmann.

22. L. Steels, F. Kaplan, A. McIntyre, and J. Van Looveren. Crucial factors in the origins of word-meanings. In A. Wray, editor, *The Transition to Language*, pages 214–217. Oxford University Press, Oxford, UK, 2002.

23. V. Vapnik. *Statistical Learning Theory*. John Wiley & Sons, New York, 1998.

Defining and Coordinating Open-Services Using Workflows

Khalid Belhajjame, Genoveva Vargas-Solar, and Christine Collet

LSR-IMAG, Université de Grenoble
BP 72 38402 Saint-Martin d'Hères, France
{Khalid.Belhajjame, Genoveva.Vargas, Christine.Collet}@imag.fr

Abstract. Recently, workflow technology has been widely accepted as a mean for integrating services to build applications (services). Provided a set of services a workflow is used to coordinate and to synchronize their executions. This paper proposes an approach based on workflow technology and an associated mechanism for defining and coordinating services. Given a *service provider* that exports a set of methods a workflow can be defined for coordinating calls to such methods, in order to program a service. A service definition is decoupled from the capabilities of the *service provider*, thus a service may be adapted according to different application requirements. Services coordination is carried out by an orchestrator workflow that provides a fine control on their executions. Definition and coordination are characterized by a set of properties that ensure the correct behaviour of the resulting application (service).

Keywords: Services integration, workflow management, service definition, services coordination.

1   Introduction

The idea of using workflow technology to build applications out of existing services is not new. Provided a set of services a workflow can be used to coordinate and to synchronize their execution. Activities of such a process are used to control services execution, the controlflow describes dependencies among them, and the dataflow specifies how data are exchanged among them.

The diversity of systems [5,4,12,16] and languages [13,9] that have been recently proposed shows the potential and the relevance of such an approach. Generally speaking, two complementary techniques are used for integrating services: wrapping [5] and coordination [4]. Using the wrapping technique, pre-existing services are wrapped to provide an entry point for activating the service. Wrapped services are then orchestrated by a workflow which is executed by an engine.

Existing technology suffers from some drawbacks. In general, a service is a black box accessible through a method call. There is no mean to suspend, resume, or exchange data with a service during its execution. A service cannot be reconfigured or modified to meet new application requirements. Yet, modifying services can be useful when new requirements have to be considered.

Our research contributes to the construction of open services that can be synchronized for building out new applications or services. This paper proposes an approach based

R. Meersman et al. (Eds.): CoopIS/DOA/ODBASE 2003, LNCS 2888, pp. 110–128, 2003.
© Springer-Verlag Berlin Heidelberg 2003

on workflow technology and an associated mechanism called AEROS, for defining and orchestrating services. It describes how it provides openness to services and fine control on their executions. Furthermore, it discusses properties that have to be verified such that resulting applications can be executed correctly.

Accordingly, the paper is organized as follows. Section 2 gives an overview of our approach. Section 3 presents a service manager, describes the model it supports and characterizes a service through a set of properties. Section 4 presents the orchestrator manager and it shows how it synchronizes services. Section 5 describes AEROS an infrastructure for instantiating Service managers and Orchestrator managers. Section 6 compares our approach with existing works. Finally, Section 7 concludes the paper and gives some research perspectives.

2   Overview of the Approach

The following introduces the notion of open service and shows how autonomous *service providers* (software components) can provide customized services according to different application requirements. It also shows how open services can be finely orchestrated for building applications (services).

2.1   Motivations

Consider a flight booking application built out of the following services. Adventurer manages clients needing to book flights. Payment contacts bank servers for executing billing transactions on given customers accounts. Reservation searches flight offers and manages a flight data base.

Current approaches [4,5,12] assume that services provide an interface of independent methods. Using a service implies executing a method call (service call). Integrating services means ordering method calls in order to build an application. Assuming that getInfo(), reserveFlight() and withdraw() are methods provided respectively by the above services. The resulting application illustrated in Figure 1, consists in calling getInfo() for letting the client express his/her requests about a flight (e.g., *Mexico - Paris, 19 may 2003, Air Mexique*). In response, a list of possibilities is proposed by the service. The client can then choose and reserve a flight calling reserveFlight() offered by the reservation service. Finally, the Payment service is contacted to withdraw() the corresponding amount of money for paying the flight and validating the reservation. Under this strategy, services integration is hard coded at the application level.

Furthermore, the approach used for conceiving services is limited when they need to be configured for fulfilling specific application requirements. For example, assume that the Reservation service returns only flights having available places, and that a client wants to have information even about those flights with no places. In such a case, the service has to be modified but this is often impossible since services are "black boxes"! Suppose now that a client wants to guide the reservation process, for example, to avoid searching flights of a specific airline that he/she does not want to use. In order to enable client interaction, the Reservation service must provide means to control its execution. Again, this implies the re-implementation of the service.

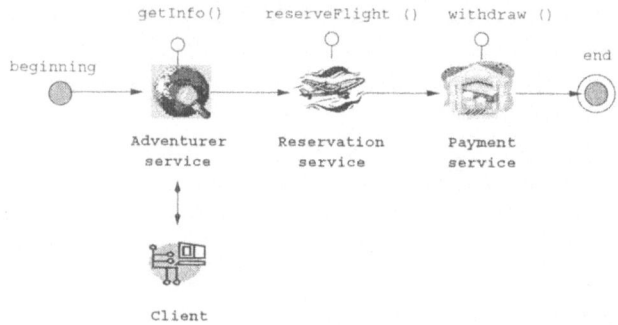

Fig. 1. Booking application

These examples highlight the need of an approach that enables an open definition of a service in order to support (i) customization, (ii) a fine control of its execution and of the way it can be integrated with other services for building applications. In the following we describe an approach that attempts to fulfil these needs.

2.2   Open Service

According to our approach a service is programmed on top of an autonomous *service provider* that provides a set of methods specified in an API. Methods are not independent among each other and their dependencies are defined within the API. Figure 2 illustrates the API of the Payment *service provider*. It is composed of a set of methods. The API also specifies the following relationships among methods. precedence (checkCredit,withdraw) means that withdraw can be called only after checkCredit has been executed. exclusion (withdraw,cancel) means that withdraw and cancel cannot both be executed within the same payment session.

A service is a workflow that specifies the coordination of method calls respecting dependencies specified in the API. Activities in the workflow correspond to method calls on the *service provider* and the control flow defines the execution "semantic" of the service. According to our example, an open Payment service can be specified using such API. In Figure 2 Service 1 is a workflow representing a Payment service. First, payment is initialized (IntializePayment), then, simultaneously (AND-JOIN), the client information (ProcessRequest) and the product purchase amount (GetPurchaseAmount) are requested. If the client has enough money to pay the product then the operation is authorized (GetAuthorization) and the amount is withdrawn from his/her account (Withdraw), otherwise the payment operation is cancelled (Cancel). Finally, the operation is terminated (TerminatePayment).

Furthermore, several services can be programmed on top of the same *service provider*. As shown in Figure 2, a new Payment service (Service 2) can be defined for performing the billing of several purchases instead of one. The amount of each purchase is requested before asking for the billing authorization. This configuration is described by an iterative loop (see Figure 2, Service 2).

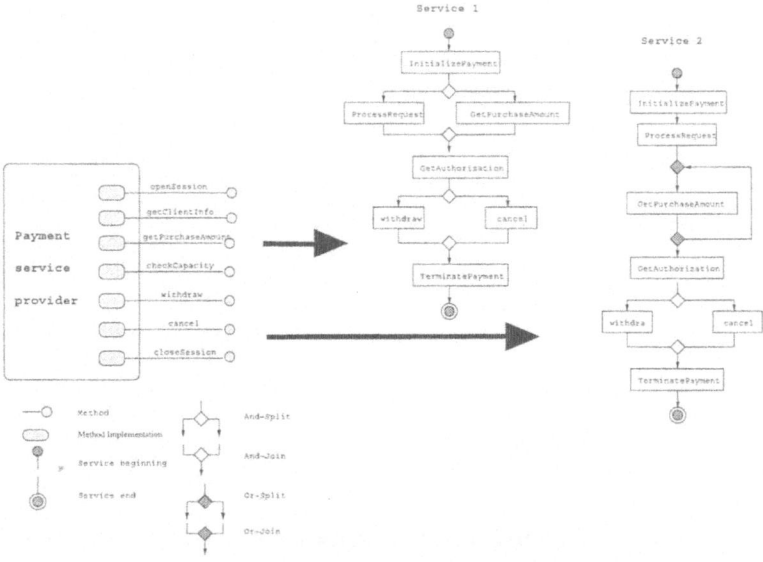

Fig. 2. Customized services

2.3   Services Orchestration

Let us consider a new version of the flight booking application, assuming that services Adventurer, Reservation and Payment have been defined according to our approach (see Figure 3). First the Adventurer service sends information about the customer and his/her destination. Then, the Reservation service replies with a list of available flights. Once the customer has chosen a flight, a request is sent to the Reservation service. The Reservation service contacts the Payment service for executing the payment and waits for an acknowledgment. If the payment operation is accepted then the Reservation service sends reservation details to the Adventurer service, otherwise it sends an acknowledgment notifying the failure of the operation.

Note that services executions cannot be independent and that they have to be synchronized in order to build the application. For example, the execution of the Payment service must be interrupted after its initialization until the orchestrator workflow provides it with information concerning the client and the purchase amount. Therefore, it is necessary to have means to interrupt a service execution so that it can be synchronized to send/receive information to/from another service necessary for continuing the execution of each service and of the application as a whole.

As shown in Figure 4, in our approach, each service provides a set of entry points that act as gateways for controlling its execution and exchanging data with other services (i.e., *interrupt the execution until input data have arrived, continue the execution once input data are delivered*). Such entry points are not hardcoded, they are associated to a service according to the global application characteristics.

Applications (services) is performed according to control flow and data flow implemented by an *orchestrator workflow* (see Figure 4). Activities of the *orchestrator*

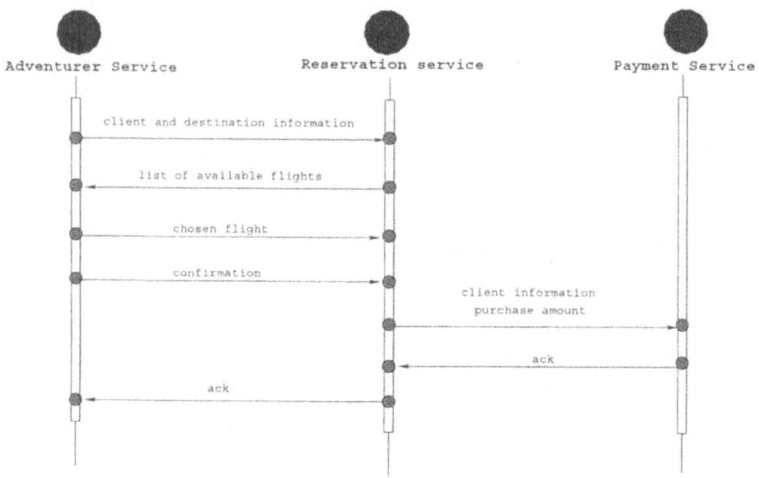

Fig. 3. Flight booking application

workflow are used to control the progress of services execution and they correspond to service calls on entry points. The control flow (activities order) specifies services dependencies, and the data flow specifies input and output data exchanged among them.

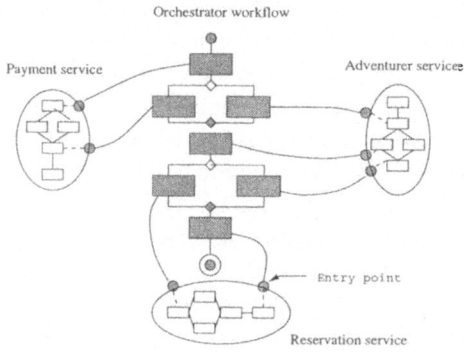

Fig. 4. Services orchestration

2.4 Definition and Orchestration Mechanisms

Services specified under our approach are managed by a service manager. A service manager is a mechanism that orchestrates the execution of a service by interacting with a *service provider*. It also provides interfaces for accessing services definitions and for adapting services: activities can be added or deleted from the service and their dependencies can be modified. Thereby, services definition is open and it can be customized.

An orchestrator manager is specialized for managing an *orchestrator workflow* that synchronizes services executions. Therefore it interacts with existing service managers for exchanging input and output data produced/consumed by services. Given a services orchestration specification, the orchestrator manager contacts the corresponding service managers and specifies entry points that must be associated to a service. At execution time, the orchestrator manager interacts with services managers for instantiating, interrupting and resuming services execution through entry points, thereby acting as an information and control broker among services.

3   Service Manager

A service manager is supported by a service model that characterizes service providers, service activities, and the way they have to be synchronized for defining a service. The following details the service model, it then discusses its properties and describes the architecture of a service manager.

3.1   Service Model

Figure 5 illustrates the UML diagram representing the service model. It is composed of four main classes: Service provider, Method, Dependency and Service.

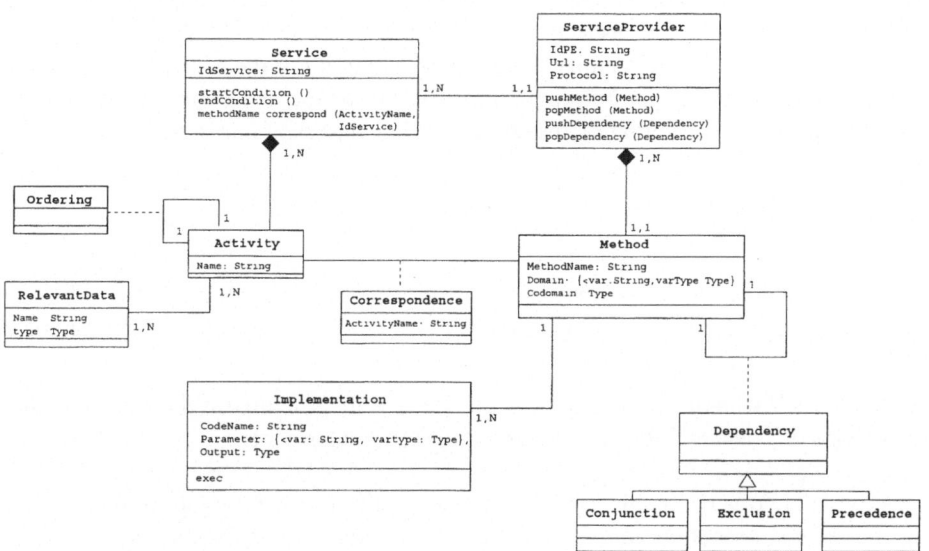

Fig. 5. Service model

Service provider represents a software component characterized by the methods it provides and dependencies among them.

Method characterizes a method by a MethodName, a Domain and a Codomain. The Domain is a Cartesian product of input types (e.g., boolean, integer and string) and a

Codomain corresponding to its output type. A method is associated to an Implementation that represents the physical code that implements it. Several implementations can be associated to the same method. An implementation is characterized by a CodeName representing the name of the file that implements the code [1], input Parameters and an Output type. The method exec is called for executing an Implementation.

Dependency specifies a binary relationship between two methods provided by a Service provider. The service model characterizes three types of dependencies dep(m_i,m_j) where m_i and m_j denote methods and dep one of the following dependency types. (i) precedence, m_j can be called only if m_i has been called before. (ii) conjunction, if m_i is called, m_j must be called too, and vice versa. (iii) exclusion, either m_i or m_j can be called, but not both of them.

For example the model of the *service provider* Bank server is defined by instantiating the corresponding classes of our service model. The Bank server provides a set of methods with the following dependencies. precedence (openSession,closeSession): specifies that closeSession can be called only if openSession has been executed. conjunction (openSession,closeSession): if openSession is called then closeSession must be called too, and vice versa. precedence (checkCredit,withdraw): specifies that money cannot be withdrawn from a bank account unless the credit has been checked (check-Credit). exclusion (withdraw,cancel), specifies that if money has been already withdrawn the transaction cannot be cancelled, and vice versa.

Service specifies the execution order of method calls provided by a Service provider. According to the model, a service is a kind of Workflow where activities correspond to method calls, and the order respects Dependencies associated to Methods. Correspondence represents the relationship associating each activity of the Service to a Method. One or several services can be programmed on top of the same *service provider*. A service is defined by instantiating the corresponding classes of our service model.

3.2   Service Properties

Services specified as workflows must be well structured and well defined. In the following we define such properties and we give an overview of the way they can be verified on a given service.

Definition 3.1. Well structured service. A service is well structured if the workflow that implements it is deadlock free and its execution terminates once.

□

Consider the two versions of the Payment service illustrated in Figure 6. In Figure 6 (a), the service execution cannot progress beyond the first AND-JOIN because both ProcessRequest and GetPurchaseAmount must be completed so that GetAuthorization can be executed. However, according to the workflow, only one of these activities can be executed! Consequently, the service execution does not terminate. The service illustrated in Figure 6 (b) can terminate several times. Note that GetAuthorization activates both Withdraw and Cancel and that both lead to the execution of TerminatePayment.

---

[1] Note that the code is a black box for the service manager and it assumes that it is correctly implemented by the service provider.

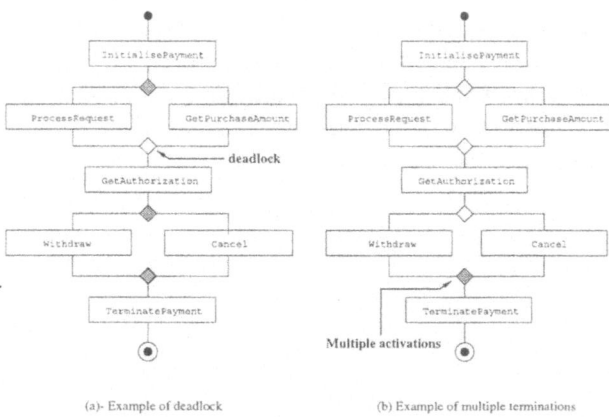

(a)- Example of deadlock   (b) Example of multiple terminations

Fig. 6. Structural Inconsistencies

Service structure verification The verification process adopted is inspired of [21] and it mainly consists in determining whether operators AND-SPLIT (resp. OR-SPLIT) and AND-JOIN (resp. OR-JOIN), are balanced. Intuitively, structural verification of a service is done on the graph representing it. A recursive analysis is applied on such a graph for checking whether every AND-SPLIT (resp. OR-SPLIT) structure is followed by an AND-JOIN (resp. OR-JOIN). If this condition does not hold, an exception is raised.

For example, the Payment service in Figure 6 (a) is not well structured because the first AND-JOIN corresponds to OR-SPLIT while it should correspond to AND-SPLIT. Neither is the Payment service in Figure 6 (b), because the last OR-JOIN corresponds to AND-SPLIT while it should correspond to an OR-SPLIT.

Definition 3.2. Well defined service. Given a *service provider* SP and a service S programmed using the API of SP, S is well defined if:

- S is well structured, and
- every activity of S is associated to a method provided by a SP, and
- the control flow of S respects method dependencies specified by the API of SP.

□

For example, consider again the Payment service illustrated in Figure 6 (b). Note that the service does not respect method dependencies specified by the service provider (i.e., exclusion (withdraw,cancel) is not verified).

Service definition verification Given a reachability graph that represents service state transitions, a static analysis is applied in order to determine whether dependencies among methods hold. Generally speaking, the graph is a direct acyclic graph (DAG) where each node is labelled by a n-tuple $\langle a_1 \ldots a_n \rangle$, where $\forall i \in \{1,\ldots,n\}$ $a_i \in \{0,1\}$ and $a_i = 1$ means that the activity a_i is being executed. An edge of the graph represents a change of a state on some activitie(s) a_i in the tuple. A starting node, called root, and a terminal node are identified within the graph. Figure 7 illustrates the reachability graph of the Payment service where states are labelled with 7-tuple $\langle a_1,a_2,a_3,a_4,a_5,a_6,a_7 \rangle$ [2]. For instance, the tuple $\langle 0,1,1,0,0,0,0 \rangle$ corresponds to the state where the activities ProcessRequest and GetPurchaseAmount are running. A path leading from the root to the terminal node represents a possible execution of a service. For example, Figure 7 shows that there are two possible executions of the payment service.

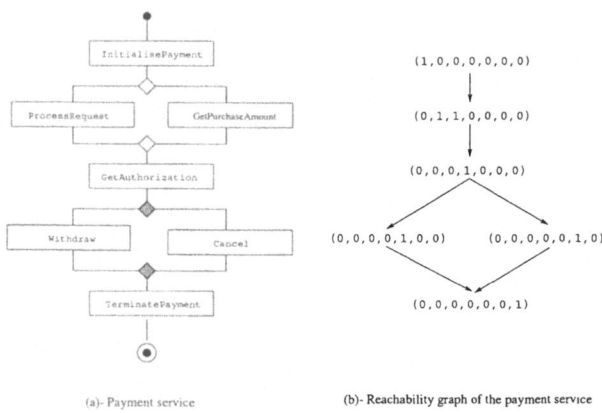

(a)- Payment service   (b)- Reachability graph of the payment service

Fig. 7. Example of a reachability graph

A service is verified as follows. Given two activities a_i and a_j that call the methods m_i and m_j, respectively, the following predicates must be verified. Precedence (m_i,m_j) holds if every path starting at the root and leading to a state where a_j is executed, goes through a state where a_i is executed. In the previous example, precedence (GetAuthorization,Withdraw) holds, since there is only one path leading from the root to a state where Withdraw is executed and it goes through by a state where GetAuthorization is executed (see Figure 8 (a)). Exclusion (m_i,m_j) holds if every path that leads from the root to the end of the reachability graph, and that goes through a state where a_i is executed does not go through a state where a_j is executed and vice versa. For example, exclusion (Withdraw,Cancel) is verified according to only two possible paths, the first going through a state where Withdraw is executed and through no state where Cancel is executed. The second, going through a state where Cancel is executed and through no state where Withdraw is executed (see Figure 8 (b)). Conjunction (m_i,m_j) holds if every path that goes from the beginning to the end and that goes through a state where a_i is executed, goes also through by a state where a_j is executed, and vice versa. Dependency conjunction (InitiatePayment,TerminatePayment) holds. There are two possible paths that link the root of the workflow to the end. Both of them go through a state where InitiatePayment and TerminatePayment are executed (see Figure 8 (c)).

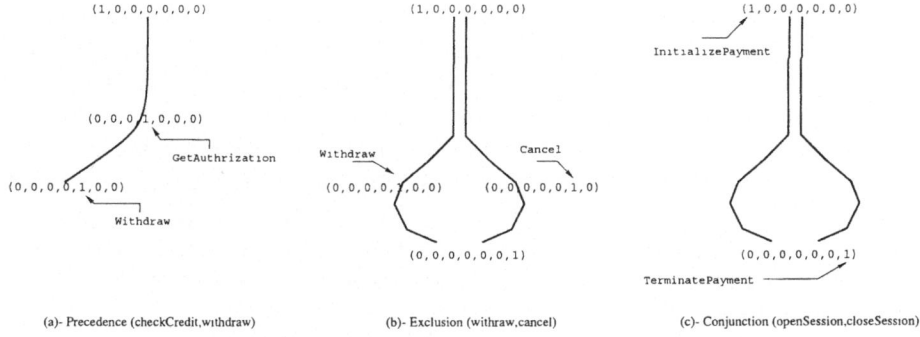

(a)- Precedence (checkCredit,withdraw)   (b)- Exclusion (withraw,cancel)   (c)- Conjunction (openSession,closeSession)

Fig. 8. Examples of dependencies verification

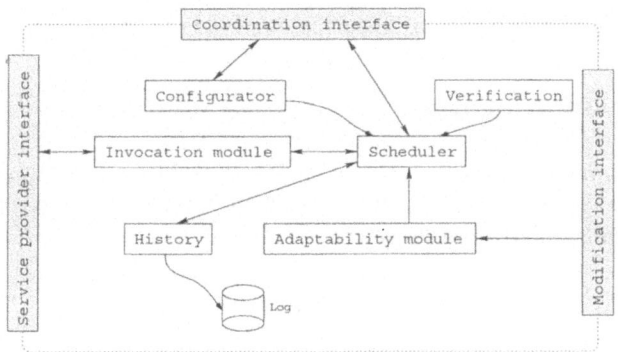

Fig. 9. Service manager architecture

3.3   Service Manager Architecture

Figure 9 depicts the architecture of a service manager. It is composed of set of components and three interfaces. Coordination interface used to interact with the orchestrator manager. Modification interface used by the Instantiation component to notify service provider evolutions. *Service provider* interface used for calling service provider methods and getting results. Components implement manager functionalities: service configuration, scheduling, methods call, service adaptation. Scheduler, coordinates service execution. The service execution is initialized by a Orchestrator manager. The service is then executed according to the service controlflow. Whenever a send entry point is reached, the Scheduler sends the associated context to the orchestrator manager through the Coordination interface. When it reaches a receive entry point, it waits for the authorization of the orchestrator manager to continue the execution. The data produced by activities are stored in a database and maintained using a History module. Invocation module, when the Scheduler triggers an activity, this module calls the corresponding method. Once it receives the execution results it notifies them to the Scheduler that

---

[2] Each attribute a_i in the tuple is associated respectively to activities `IntializePayment`, `ProcessRequest`, `GetPurchaseAmount`, `GetAuthorization`, `Withdraw`, `Cancel` and `TerminatePayment`.

chooses the next activitie(s) to be triggered. Adaptability module is used to adapt the service in response to the evolution of the *service provider* API. Adaptability may imply the modification of the service controlflow. Modifications may occur while a service is being executed. In such a case, this module checks whether current service execution can be modified and the set of changes to be applied (e.g., delete activity, add data). The Verification component is also used to check that the new service is well defined. Configurator is used by the Orchestrator manager for specifying service entry points. It provides methods to add and delete an entry point and to associate it to a context. Once entry points have been specified, the Verification component checks that they are well located within the service.

Different services can be performed using the same Service manager. When a programmer specifies a service, either a new Service manager is instantiated or it is assigned to an existing Service manager. In general, a Service manager is instantiated and associated to every *service provider* for managing its services.

4 Orchestrator Manager

An orchestrator manager is a mechanism in charge of the synchronization of services executions. The following presents the coordination model, its associated properties, and the orchestrator manager architecture.

4.1 Coordination Model

Figure 10 illustrates the UML diagram representing the coordination model composed of two main classes: EntryPoint and Orchestrator workflow.

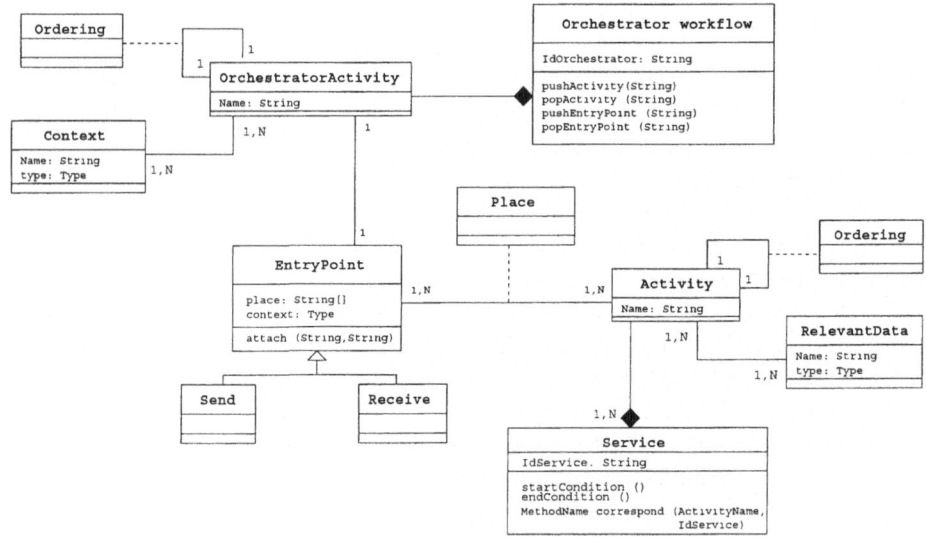

Fig. 10. Coordination model

EntryPoint represents a gateway through which a service execution can be controlled. An EntryPoint can be of type, Send EP or Receive EP. It has an associated *context* that characterizes data to be exchanged through it. Every Entry point is associated to a service. Such an association is described by the relationship Place that represents the location of an EntryPoint within the structure of the workflow that implements its service. The set of entry points placed in a service define the service interface adapted for a given Orchestrator workflow. Let us consider the Payment service and the flight booking application specified in Figure 11. According to the sequence diagram, two entry points are required, one to get the client references and the product price (i.e., *receive entry point*), and the second for notifying payment acknowledgment (i.e., *send entry point*). Entry points are defined as instances of the corresponding class of the services coordination model. Figure 11, shows the entry points associated to the Payment service for building the flight booking application. Note that the first entry point, ReceiveInfo is located after the activity openSession so that input data for activities getClientInfo and getProductPrice can be delivered. The second entry point, SendPaymentStatus is located after activities Withdraw and Cancel. It is used for notifying the status of the payment (i.e., accepted or cancelled). In addition to these entry points, two entry points ReceiveInstantiation and SendTermination are placed at the beginning and at the end of the service. They are used respectively to let the orchestrator workflow initialize the service and to notify it about the termination of the service.

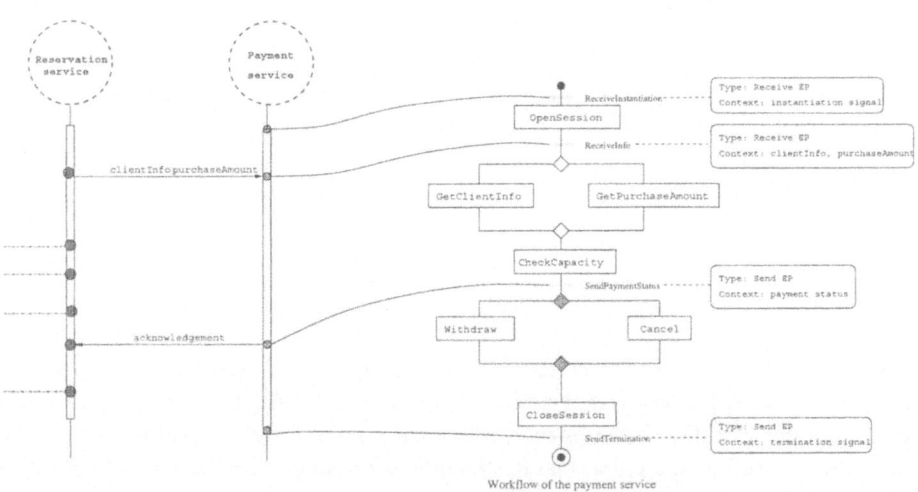

Fig. 11. Entry points in the Payment service

Every Orchestrator activity is associated to a specific Entry point belonging to a service. An orchestrator activity is used to control the progress of a service execution. The model characterizes three types of orchestrator activities. Instantiate: represents an activity that initializes a service execution. Wait: represents an activity that notifies the execution point of a service. Continue: represents an activity that enables continuing the execution of a suspended service.

Figure 12 depicts the Orchestrator workflow of the flight booking application defined as an instance of the model. The orchestrator activities are typed. Each orchestrator activity is associated to an entry point of type *send* or *receive* and that has an associated context (i.e., data to be sent to/from entry points).

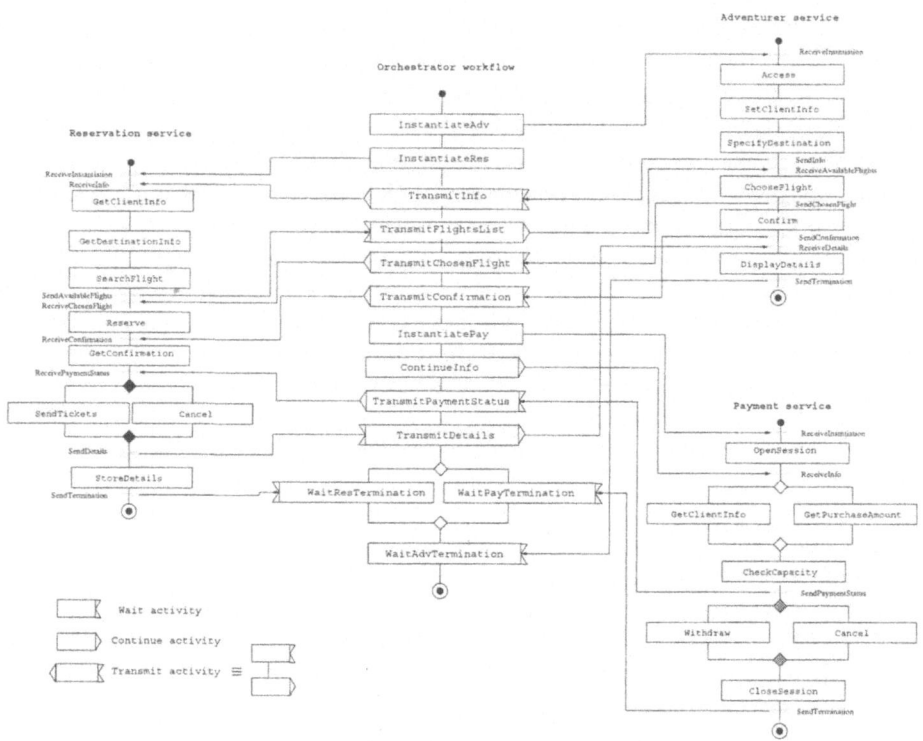

Fig. 12. Flight booking application

Whenever a service execution reaches a *send entry point*, it notifies the orchestrator workflow and sends the associated context. For example, the Adventurer service notifies the orchestrator workflow when it reaches the entry point SendInfo and it sends to the orchestrator workflow the client and destination information. The service execution is suspended when it encounters a *receive* entry point. For example, Adventurer service execution is suspended when it reaches the entry point ReceiveAvailableFlights. Finally, the execution continues until the *continue* entry point is called and input information has been delivered. In the example, Adventurer service execution continues on the reception of the list of available flights.

4.2   Coordination Properties

As explained in the previous sections, every service is associated to a set of entry points enabling its interaction with the orchestrator workflow. Such points are located within a service according to a context they send or receive. A send entry point must be located after the activities that produce information composing its context. Conversely, activities that use the context of a receive entry point must be located after it. These aspects are expressed by the following property.

Definition 4.1. Well located entry point. Given a service S, a send entry point SEP and a receive entry point REP.

- SEP is well located within S, if SEP is reachable from the activities that produce its context.
- REP is well located within S, if the activities that use the context of REP are reachable from REP.

□

Consider the electronic purchase application illustrated in Figure 13 composed of Payment and Purchase services. A client first accesses the catalogue, that advertises a collection of products, and chooses a product (e.g., a lap top) ChooseProduct. She/he specifies his/her references, and the chosen product is packed. Two alternatives are possible, either the stock is updated and the product is delivered or the purchase is cancelled. Whether the purchase is cancelled or should be delivered depends on the status of the payment operation. Finally, an acknowledgment is sent to the client.

The orchestrator workflow that implements the above application consists of 7 activities. Each one corresponds to an entry point of one of the services. Note that the entry point SendPurchaseAmount in Purchase service is not well located because it is located before the activity ChooseProduct which produces its associated context, i.e., purchaseAmount!

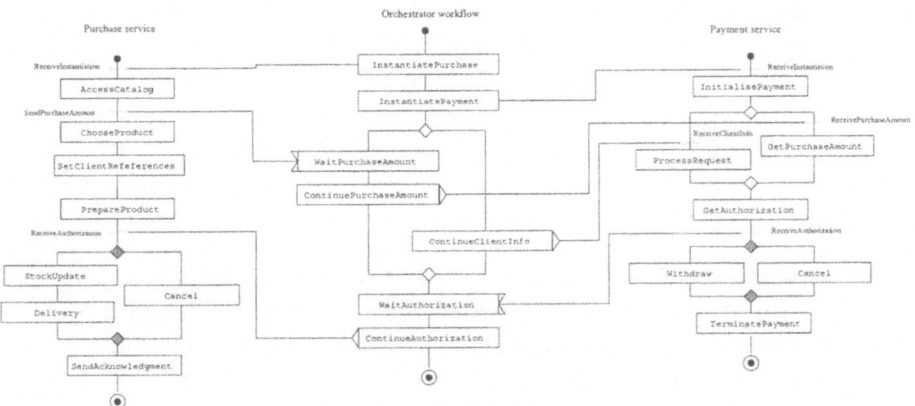

Fig. 13. Purchase application

Definition 4.2. Valid connections. We say that connections between the activities of an orchestrator workflow and their associated entry points are valid, if there is conformance between their types.

□

Figure 14 shows entry point and activity types correspondences. Activities of type Instantiate and Continue are associated to Receive entry points, and activities of type Wait are associated to Send entry points. In our example, the connection that links activity WaitAuthorization to the entry point ReceiveAuthorization is not valid due to type conflicts (i.e., both of them expect a context that they will not receive).

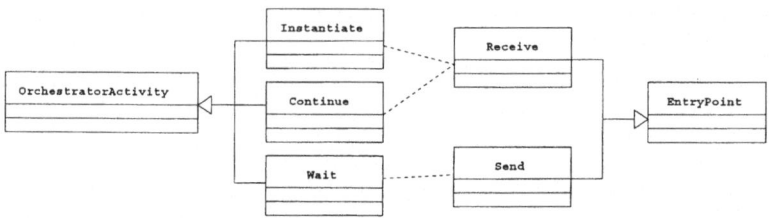

Fig. 14. Correspondences between orchestrator activities and entry point types

Definition 4.3. Well structured orchestrator workflow. We say that and orchestrator workflow is well structured if:

- every service it instantiates terminates before its completion, and
- if every instantiate or continue activity A_i is reachable from wait activities A_1, ..., A_k, $k \geq 1$ such that: $A_i.\text{dataInput} \subseteq \cup_{j \in \{1,...,k\}}(A_j.\text{dataOutput})$

□

According to the definition 4.3, services integrated by an orchestrator workflow must be completed before the last activity of the *orchestrator workflow* has been completed. Furthermore, given an activity A_i that consumes input data coming from other activities A_1, ..., A_k there exists a path within the orchestrator controlflow connecting every activity A_1, ..., A_k to A_i.

Definition 4.4. Well defined application. Consider a set of services $\{s_1, \ldots, s_n\}$ provided respectively by the service providers $\{\rho_1, \ldots, \rho_n\}$. Consider the application Λ built by integrating $s_1, \ldots, s_n$, using the orchestrator workflow θ. Λ is well defined if:

- $s_1, \ldots, s_n$ are well defined, and
- entry points of $s_1, \ldots, s_n$ are well located, and
- connections between θ activities and services entry points are valid, and
- θ is well structured.

□

4.3   Architecture of an Orchestrator Manager

Figure 15 shows that an orchestrator manager is composed of a set of components and two interfaces. Administration interface enables users to monitor and control the progress of the application. Service manager interface used to interact with services managers. The orchestrator manager functionalities are implemented by the following components.

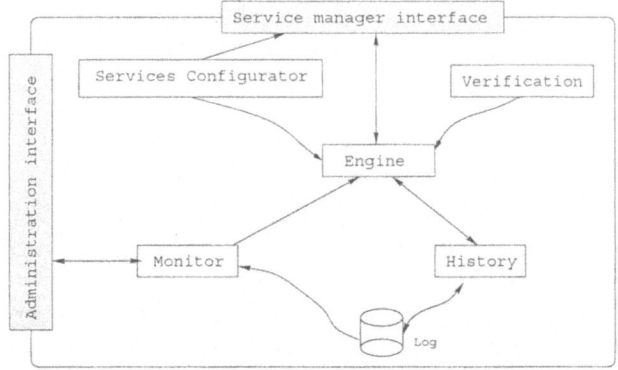

Fig. 15. Orchestrator manager architecture

Services Configurator, interacts with service managers to specify the entry points that are required for synchronizing their executions. The validity of generated connections is verified by the Verification component. Engine, synchronizes services execution by triggering Instantiate, Wait and Continue activities according to the orchestrator workflow definition. Monitor initializes the execution of the application, and observes its progress. Execution data, stored and managed by the History component, are used for such a purpose.

5   Implementation Issues

Service managers and orchestrator managers are instantiated using the framework AEROS. Such a framework is composed of two main components, Subscription and Instantiation. Subscription component receives requests from a *service provider* for defining its API. Such a definition is then stored within the *Service providers* database. Instantiation component is used to instantiate Service managers and orchestrator managers.

The first version of the framework AEROS has been implemented using JAVA as a programming language, RMI and JMS as a communication infrastructure, and FastObjects for data storage.

Service manager provides an interface for specifying service providers capabilities and programming services [23]. An executable workflow is then generated. Activities are JAVA objects that implement method calls, and control flow is implemented by ECA rules [1,2].

Orchestrator manager provides an interface for specifying the sequence diagram representing data exchanged among services. Based on such a diagram, the set of entry points to be located within the service and the orchestrator workflow are instantiated. The application designers should then locate entry points within services. We are currently using the framework AEROS for developing an application for supporting administrative services in a private college [3]. Several services such as registration, admission, resi-

---

[3] Instituto Mexico in Puebla, Mexico, http://www.giga.com/~imex/

dence and payment services, are defined on top of existing database applications and information systems. Such service are made available through WEB interfaces.

6   Related Work

Services integration has been intensively studied in the last few years. In this Section, we analyze proposals that are close to our work, i.e., those using workflow technology to address services integration.

[6,5] proposes eflow, a platform for developing and managing services. It aims at dynamically defining composite services to deal with the emergence of new services and the availability of their providers. Using a service implies calling a service provider through a proxy. Service coordination is defined by a graph specifying the order of service execution. SelfServ [4,3] supports a peer-to-peer coordination of services. Each service is associated with a coordinator that acts as a router and each coordinator calls the corresponding service using a service wrapper. Once a service execution terminates, the control is passed to the next coordinator identified using a routing table. In both eflow and SelfServ, a service provider hides details about services which are considered as atomic activities.

Several languages have been proposed for defining and orchestrating Web services. For example, WSDL [18,10] (Web Service Description Language) defines a service as a collection of ports. Each port provides a set of operations. The coordination of services defined using WSDL can be then specified using languages such as BPEL4WS, or WSFL [19,22]. Similar to eflow and SelfServ, services are not workflows, rather they are stateless and defined as a set of method calls. Besides, as far as we know, there is no mechanisms for verifying the correctness of resulting applications.

Discussion Similar to our approach in CrossFlow [8], PARIDE [14], Mentor [15,17], [20] and Interworkflow [11] a service is a workflow, enabling a fine control of its execution. The problem addressed within Crossflow is that of out-sourcing a service. Given a service, a service provider is chosen for its execution. The service provider communicates the state of the service execution for monitoring purposes. In Mentor, a workflow representing the target application is first specified. It is then split into a set of subworkflows (services). Services interact by exchanging their intermediate results. PARIDE and [15] adopt a similar approach.

Although these systems express a service as a workflow, they do not decouple its definition from the description of provider capabilities. Decoupling is useful because it enables the definition and modification of a service according to the application needs (i.e., service openness).

From the coordination perspective, in the majority of these works services orchestration is not separated from services definition. Consequently, the modification of the services orchestration in not obvious. In fact, it implies revisiting all involved services definitions. In contrast, in our approach we clearly separate orchestration from services definitions thereby enabling to handle more efficiently processing of orchestration changes independently of services.

7   Conclusion and Future Work

This paper introduced our approach for constructing adaptable services that can be finely orchestrated for building applications (services). A service, programmed on top of a service provider (SP), is a workflow that synchronizes method calls executed by the SP. Services with different execution semantics can be defined on top of the same SP. Applications can be built by synchronizing services executions (services coordination). Services coordination is expressed as a workflow that synchronizes data exchange among services (Orchestrator workflow).

The main contribution of the approach is that it decouples service definition from the service provider. Hence, a service can be customized to meet application requirements. A service is defined as a workflow process. Entry points are associated to such a process to enable a fine control of their execution when they are integrated with other services. Finally, services definition and orchestration have been characterized by a set of properties that ensure the correct execution of resulting services and applications. We are currently using AEROS to integrate services defined under NODS project [7]. We are also investigating the evolution of applications built using the proposed approach from different perspectives: service providers capabilities, services definitions and coordination.

References

1. K. Belhajjame, G. Vargas-Solar, and Ch. Collet. A flexible workflow model for process-oriented applications. In *The 2nd International conference on Web Information Systems Engineering, WISE'2001*, Kyoto-Japan, December 2001. IEEE Computer Society.
2. K. Belhajjame, G. Vargas-Solar, and Ch. Collet. Towards an adaptable workflow management system. In *Proceedings of the 17èmes Journées Bases de Données Avancées, BDA'2001*, Agadir-Morocco, October 2001.
3. B. Benatallah, M. Dumas, and Z. Maamar. Definition and execution of composite web services: the self-serv project. *IEEE Data Engineering Bulletin 25*, 2002.
4. B. Benatallah, M. Dumas, M. Shen, and A. H. H. Ngu. Declarative Composition and Peer-to-Peer Provisioning of Dynamic Web Services. In *Proceedings of the 18th International Conference on Data Engineering, San Jose, California, USA*. IEEE Computer Society, 2002.
5. Fabio Casati, Ski Ilnicki, Li jie Jin, Vasudev Krishnamoorthy, and Ming-Chien Shan. Adaptive and dynamic service composition in eflow. In *Advanced Information Systems Engineering, 12th International Conference CAiSE 2000, Stockholm, Sweden, June 5–9, 2000, Proceedings*, 2000.
6. Fabio Casati and Ming-Chien Shan. Dynamic and adaptive composition of e-services. *Information Systems*, 6(3), 2001.
7. C. Collet. The NODS Project: Networked Open Database Services. In *Proc. of the 14th European Conference on Object-Oriented Programming (ECOOP 2000) – Symposium on Objects and Databases*, Cannes, France, June 2000.
8. CrossFlow. Crossflow project web page. http://www.CrossFlow.org.
9. F. Curbera, Y. Goland, J. Klein, F. Leymann, D. Roller, S. Thatte, and S. Weerawarana. Business Process Execution Language for Web Services, 2002.
10. Francisco Curbera, Matthew Duftler, Rania Khalaf, William Nagy, Nirmal Mukhi, and Sanjiva Weerawarana. Unraveling the web services web: An introduction to soap, wsdl, and uddi. *IEEE Internet Computing*, 6(2), 2002.

11. K. Hiramatsu, K. Okada, and H. Hayami. Interworkflow system: coordination of each work-flow system among multiple organizations. IEEE Computer Society, 1998.
12. A. Lazcano, G. Alonso, H. Schuldt, and C. Schuler. The wise approach to electronic commerce, 2000.
13. F. Leymann. Web Services Flow Language (WSFL 1.0), 2001. http://www-3.ibm.com/solutions/webservices/pdf/WSFL.pdf.
14. M. Mecella, B. Pernici, M. Rossi, and A. Testi. A Repository of Workflow Components for Cooperative eApplications. In *Proceedings of the IFIP TC8 Working Conference on ECommerce/EBusiness, Salzburg, Austria*, 2001.
15. P. Muth, D. Wodtke, J. Weissenfels, and A. Dittrich. Weikum: From centralized workflow specification to distributed workflow execution, 1998.
16. O. Mylopoulos, A. Gal, K. Kontogiannis, and M. Stanley. A Generic Integration Architecture for Cooperative Information Systems. In *Proceedings of the First IFCIS International Conference on Cooperative Information Systems (CoopIS'96)*, 1996.
17. G. Shegalov, M. Gillmann, and G. Weikum. XML-enabled workflow management for e-services across heterogeneous platforms. *VLDB Journal*, 10(1):91–103, 2001.
18. A. Tsalgatidou and T.Pilioura. An overview of standards and related technology in web services. *Distributed and Parallel Databases*, 12(3):135–162, 2002.
19. W. van der Aalst. Don't go with the flow: Web services composition standards exposed. *IEEE Intelligent Systems*, 2003.
20. W. van der Aalst and M. Weske. The P2P approach to interorganizational workflows. *Lecture Notes in Computer Science*, 2068, 2001.
21. Wil M. P. van der Aalst. Workflow verification: Finding control-flow errors using petri-net-based techniques. *Lecture Notes in Computer Science*, 1806, 2000.
22. W.M.P. van der Aalst, M. Dumas, A.H.M. ter Hofstede, and P. Wohed. Pattern-based analysis of bpml (and wsci). QUT Technical report FIT-TR-2002-05, Queensland University of Technology, Brisbane, 2002.
23. G. Vargas-Solar, K. Belhajjame, E. E. Castillo-Contreras, and K. J. Peredo-Marquez. Terra-acqua, adaptable and distributed definition and execution of workflows. In *Proceedings of the workshop on Advances in databases and information retrieval, ENC'03*, 2003. To appear.

Keeping Watch: Intelligent Virtual Agents Reflecting Human-Like Perception in Cooperative Information Systems

Pilar Herrero and Angélica de Antonio

Facultad de Informática. Universidad Politécnica de Madrid.
Campus de Montegancedo S/N.
28.660 Boadilla del Monte. Madrid. Spain
{pherrero,angelica}@fi.upm.es

Abstract. A matter pending in Intelligent Virtual Agents Systems (IVAS) and multi-Intelligent Virtual Agents Systems (mIVAS) is to introduce human-like sensitive perception. Within the cognitive research area there are many studies underwritting that human perception can be understood as a first level of an "awareness model" [6,7].Following these researches, we have developed a human-like perceptual model based on one of the most successful awareness models in Computer Supported Cooperative Work (CSCW), called the Spatial Model of Interaction (SMI) [1], which manage awareness in Collaborative Virtual Environments (CVEs) through a set of key concepts. This perceptual model extends the key concepts of the SMI introducing some human-like factors typical from human being perception as well as it makes a reinterpretation with the aim of introducing them as the key concepts of a IVA's human-like perceptual model.

1 Introduction

Over the past years, there has been a growing interest in using human-like embodied virtual agents with varying degrees of intelligence, getting what we call Intelligent Virtual Agents (IVAs). IVAs can inhabit a variety of virtual environments, depending on the application purpose, such as education, entertainment, computer games or communication. Current trends try to introduce on IVAs the appearance and the functions of life, simulating humans beings, making use of positional information, visual information and information about user's awareness and focus of attention to reason about encounters with users (and other agents) in the world and to adapt their information gathering behaviour to the current environment. However, when agents are unable to perceive the environment like human beings, it can be difficult for them to keep in touch with events like a human being inside the environment [20].

The scope of our research is what we call mIVA-VE systems (VEs populated by multiple IVAs). A Virtual Environment (VE) can be defined as *"a computer-synthesized, three-dimensional environment in which a plurality of human partici*

R. Meersman et al. (Eds.): CoopIS/DOA/ODBASE 2003, LNCS 2888, pp. 129–144, 2003.
© Springer-Verlag Berlin Heidelberg 2003

pants, appropriately interfaced, may engage and manipulate simulated physical elements in the environment and in some forms, may engage and interact with representations of other humans, past, present, or fictional, or with invented creatures" [23]. An mIVA-VE is particular type of MAS (Multi-Agent Systems) in which both users and agents are embodied and may interact with each other.

Interactive virtual worlds combined with agents or mIVA-VEs offer an exciting new tool for entertainment, education and training. In the last few years, this new technology has experimented an exciting progress but virtual agents still have a limited range of capabilities. These kinds of systems have an important "physical" component where agents carry on their tasks. In fact, many works in mIVA-VEs have the goal to provide agents with a higher degree of realism, and realism has often been sought providing human-like appearance or behaviour. However, the realism of perception has been ignored for a long time.

One of the most important characteristics of IVAs is the ability to be aware of current situations in the environment where they reside and operate. Situation awareness plays a central role in cognition, which comprises the entire spectrum of cognitive activities from perception, such as lower-level vision activities, to high-level cognition, such as understanding, reasoning, and decision making. We propose a perceptual model, which seeks to introduce more coherence between IVA's perception and human being perception. In this way, the psychological *"coherence"* between the real life and the virtual environment experience will be incremented. Having in mind that the physical perception can be understood as the first level of an "awareness model" [6,7,24] the first goal for our research was to select a model of awareness which could be valid for our purposes.

As the "Spatial Model of Interaction" (SMI) [1] used the properties of the space to get knowledge of the environment, it was based on a set of key awareness concepts – which could be extended to introduce some human-like factors - and it had been tested with successful results in CSCW multi-user environments, this model had the essential qualifications for our purposes and we selected it. The aim of our research is not just to extend the Spatial Model of Interaction to mIVA-VEs, but also to make it more realistic introducing some concepts typical in human-like perception.

In order to get that, we had to make a reinterpretation of the meaning of "awareness" - quite different to the definition used in CSCW literature [5] – as well as a reinterpretation of the key concepts of the SMI to introduce them as key concepts of a perceptual model, applying this model to IVAs.

In this paper we will concentrate on visual perception but we have also designed, developed and implemented a similar model for simulating human-like auditory perception in IVAs[14].

2   Visual Perception in IVAS

Agent perception in this kind of systems has to be mainly *sensorial*, providing the agent with knowledge about its "physical" surroundings. According to the agent's sensory requirements we can classify agent systems and MAS as *sensory systems* and *not sensory systems*.

A general definition of agent's perception, applicable whether the system has sensory information or not, is given by Chenney [3]. He defines the perception of autonomous agents as a process of interaction with the environment to collect and exchange information about the environment and the agent itself, and classifies the perception as: *Active Sensing*: Information is continuously being provided, regardless of the agent being explicitly looking for it or not; *Passive Sensing*: "*Passive sense data is only generated when required*" Passive sensing is generally implemented as a query procedure. Almost all the implemented agent architectures support passive sensing. For example, SodaJack [8] queries a sensing system to determine if goals have been achieved or are achievable. Terzopoulos and Tu [25] use a *focusser*, which is essentially a selective filter, to perform passive sensing; and *Feedback Sensing*: "*Feedback sensing may be considered a special case of passive sensing; however it differs in that it is generally not integrated with the general sensing system. Rather, it is coupled to the motor controllers that require the feedback*".

While some years ago the aim of agent's perception was just seeking information from the environment, requirements have changed and, currently, a wide range of simulation realistic applications has been developed, mainly for training purposes, requiring a relatively high fidelity model of perception.

Many approaches have been employed to implement the visual process of perception in IVAs, oriented to different kind of applications, such as artificial creatures [2,25] or virtual humans [4 ,15,16, 22,26]. Perception in those agents has been modelled in diverse ways, depending on what they were designed for. Basically, the implementation of perception can be focussed on the processing of sensory inputs [26] or on the cognitive process of perception [15]. In this paper we have focused on the sensory inputs of the perceptual model. A classification of current approaches can be found in [12].

3   An Architecture for the Agent's Perception

We have selected a *vertical layering* agent architecture, like the Triple Tower Model of Nilsson [21], as the starting point for our architecture because of its simplicity and flexibility.

Our architecture has three main blocks (figure 1), representing the agent's perception, the agent's central processing and the agent's actions, but we concentrate our attention just on the agent's perception block. This component is concerned with modelling the agent's unique perception of their environment.

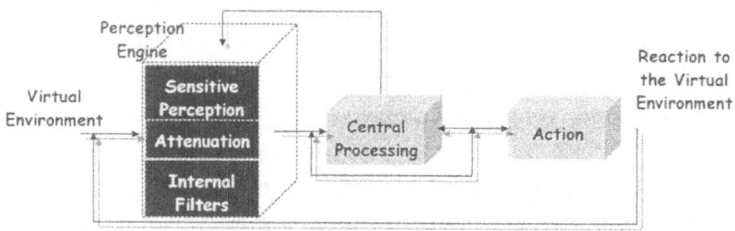

Fig. 1. Agent's Architecture

The perception block, or perception engine, operates concurrently with the central processing block, and some of the interpretations of the perceived data or some of the parameters of the agent's internal model can in turn modify the perceptual process.

The perception engine will deal with the interaction with the environment and it will be composed by the following three modules: *Sensitive Perception, Attenuation and Internal Filtering* [13].

Although in this paper we concentrate on describing the sensitive perception module of this perceptual engine, we also have to bear in mind that perceptual sensations are subjectively attenuated with time. The attenuation module will introduce a reduction experienced by the signal coming from the sensitive perception. On the other hand, the internal filtering module will do the selection of the most relevant objects within the focus of perception.

4   Key Concepts in the Visual Perceptual Model

As we mentioned in previous sections, these key concepts are based on the main concepts of a CSCW awareness model known as *The Spatial Model of Interaction (SMI)* [1].

4.1   Key Concepts in the SMI

The spatial model, as its name suggests, uses the properties of space as the basis for mediating interaction. It was proposed as a way to control the flow of information of the environment in CVEs (Collaborative Virtual Environments). It allows objects in a virtual world to govern their interaction through some key concepts: medium, aura, awareness, focus, nimbus, adapters and boundaries.

Aura is the sub-space which effectively bounds the presence of an object within a given medium and which acts as an enabler of potential *interaction*. In each particular medium, it is possible to delimit the observing object's interest. This area is called *focus* "The more an object is within your focus the more aware you are of it". The focus concept has been implemented in the SMI as an "ideal" cone limited by the object's aura.

In the same way, it is possible to represent the observed object's projection in a particular medium. This area is called *nimbus*: "The more an object is within your nimbus the more aware it is of you". The nimbus concept, as it was defined in the Spatial Model of Interaction, has always been implemented as an sphere in a visual medium. The radio of this sphere has an "ideal" infinite value, although in practice, it is limited by the object's aura.

The implementations of these concepts –focus and nimbus- in the SMI didn't have in mind human aspects, thus reducing the level of coherence between the real and the virtual agent behaviour.

The main concept involved in controlling interaction between objects is *"aware-ness"*. One object's awareness of another object quantifies the subjective importance or relevance of that object. The awareness relationship between every pair of objects is achieved on the basis of quantifiable *levels* of awareness between them and it is unidirectional and specific to each medium. Awareness between objects in a given medium is manipulated via *focus* and *nimbus*. Moreover, an object's aura, focus, nimbus, and hence awareness, can be modified through *boundaries* and some artefacts called *adapters*.

4.2 Making the Visual Perceptual Model More Human-Like

There are many factors that contribute to our ability as humans to perceive an object, some of which are directly working on the mental processes, being not easily modelled or reproduced in a virtual world. We have analysed some human visual perception key concepts to determine which of them could be introduced in our visual agent's perceptual model. These concepts, selected for being the more representative of human visual perception, are [11,12,13,14]:

- **Visual Acuity**: Representing the general "Sense Acuity" in a visual medium, the Visual Acuity is a measure of the eye's ability to resolve fine detail and is dependent upon the person itself, the accommodative state of the eye, the illumination level and the contrast between target and background [17]. Virtual agents that exhibit this property would be able, for instance, to perceive a message, wrote on a notice board, only if the distance from the agent to that notice board is within the visual range of perception.

- **Lateral Vision**: Representing the general "Sense Transition Region" (STR), the Lateral Vision corresponds to the visual perception towards the extremes of the visual focus. Virtual agents should exhibit this characteristic to avoid anomalous behaviours as, for example, those that will happen if an agent is not aware of and can not interact with another agent which is inside the Lateral Vision area but out of the visual focus.

- **Visual Filters**: Allowing the selection, from all the objects in an extensive focus of only those that the agent is especially interested in.

In this paper we concentrate on the two first concepts (visual acuity and lateral vision) but we also had in mind the third one (visual filters) when we developed and implemented our model of human-like visual perception in IVAs.

4.3 Reinterpreting the SMI's Key Concepts

Neither the SMI nor its implementations considered aspects of human perception. Thus, if the SMI were applied just as it was defined by Benford, the level of coherence between real and virtual agent behaviour would be minimum. We have decided to identify the factors concerning human-like perception, which provide more realistic perception and introduce them into the SMI. In this section, we are going to describe the human factors considered and how the key concepts defining the SMI have been modified to introduce these factors.

4.3.1 Visual Focus

Benford introduced the focus concept in 1993 as "*The more an object is within your focus the more aware you are of it*" [1]. This concept meant that the observing object's interest for each particular medium could be delimited. According to this definition, the focus notion is the area within which the agent is perceiving the environment. In previous sections, we have analysed how sensitive perception works in humans beings, and, from this analysis, we have decided to select the physical factors that should have an effect on the physical area delimiting the observing object's interest. These factors are *Sense Acuity* and the *Sense Transition Region*.

Starting from the focus concept in the spatial model, and bearing in mind previous implementations, for example, by Greenhalgh [9], where focus was implemented as a cone, we will introduce sense acuity and sense transition regions. We will define a new mathematical function to represent the human-like focus concept. This mathematical function (Eq. 1) will be described by the following set of variables and parameters and is represented in Figure 2:

- $(\mu_x, \mu_y, \mu_z) \rightarrow$ Represents the agent's eye position in a 3D system of reference.
- $D_m \rightarrow$ Represents the agent's visual resolution acuity distance.
- $(x, y, z) \rightarrow$ Represents any point inside the focus.
- $\theta' \rightarrow$ Represents the angle delimiting human foveal vision.
- $\theta \rightarrow$ Represents the angle delimiting human vision: foveal and peripheral vision.
- $s \rightarrow$ Represents the object's size.

$$\mu_y \leq y \leq \mu_y + D_m$$

$$\left(x - \mu_x\right)^2 + \left(z - \mu_z\right)^2 \leq (tang\ (\theta))^2 * (y - \mu_y)^2$$

$$\left(x - \mu_x\right)^2 + \left(z - \mu_z\right)^2 \leq (tang\ (\theta'))^2 * (y - \mu_y)^2$$

$$D_m \leq \frac{s}{tang\ (MAR)}$$

(Eq. 1)

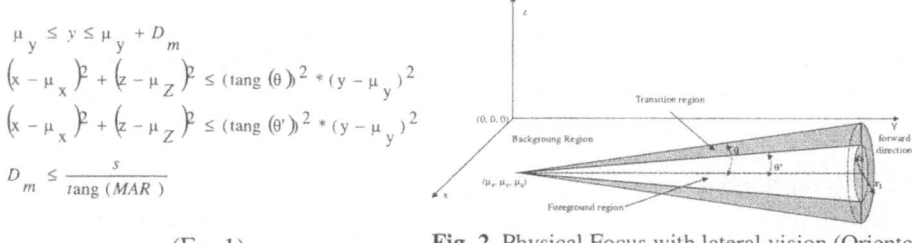

Fig. 2. Physical Focus with lateral vision (Orientation component)

In the implementation of the model, we have separated global focus, which has infinite length, from specific focus, associated with each agent. The length of global focus is limited by the aura, while the length of specific focus is limited by each agent's physical factors.

When the agent perceives an object in the environment, perception will be different depending on the area in which the object is located. Both the object's orientation (Figure 3) and the area in which it is located (Figure 4) play an important role in determining the perception of the object.

As Figure 2 shows, two different cones can be distinguished, the internal cone (with angle θ') represents the agent's field of vision without lateral vision, and the external cone (with angle θ) represents the agent's field of vision with lateral vision (STR). Both cones have been implemented as functions delimiting the agent's visual perception area. Starting from some experiments run for "The Old Man" [10], the origin of the cones will be placed at an eighth part of the object's height (above the nose and in between the agent's two eyes).

In Figure 4, the Area of Perception (AP) indicates whether an object is within the focus, and, in this case, within which area it is located. For our purposes, we have implemented a function that checks whether an object is inside the agent's focus, and if it is, then this function will indicate the area within which the object is located (foreground or transition region). This function will allow us to determine whether the agent can detect an object because it is inside its field of vision. If the agent's objective is not just to detect the object but also to perceive some details of the object, we will be also interested in the clarity of the perception that the agent has of the object.

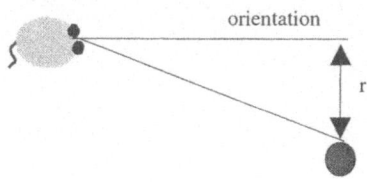

Fig. 3. Agent's eye orientation and object's position

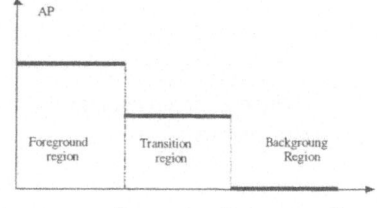

Fig. 4. Physical Focus with lateral vision (Distance component)

Considering medium homogeneity, we find that, while in a homogeneous medium, the focus shape is uniform and corresponds to a cone, whereas, in a heterogeneous medium, it could have discontinuous transitions between regions with different densities. We are not going to deal with heterogeneous media in our model.

Our initial equation considers that the cone orientation is parallel to the y-axis. Otherwise, this approach will be valid subject to the previous rotation of the axes according to Euler's Rotation Theorem.

4.3.2 Visual Nimbus

Benford introduced the nimbus concept in 1993 as *"The more an object is within your nimbus the more aware it is of you"* [1]. This concept meant that the observed object's projection for each particular medium could be delimited.

The nimbus concept, as defined in the Spatial Model of Interaction, has always been implemented as a sphere in both visual and hearing media. The radius of this sphere has an "ideal" infinite value, although, in practice, it is limited by the object's aura. Just as with the above-mentioned focus concept, the nimbus concept in the Spatial Model of Interaction does not consider any human factors, thus hypothetically reducing the level of coherence between real and virtual agent behaviour. We are going to represent the nimbus of an object as an ellipsoid (equation 2)or a sphere (equation 3), depending on the conic by which it is circumscribed (Figure 5), centred on the object's geometrical centre. The way of determining which conic has to be associated with each object in the environment is to look for the bounding box that has been associated to this object in the environment. If the bounding box is a rectangle, we will approximate the nimbus as an ellipsoid; if the bounding box is a circle, then we will approximate the nimbus as a sphere.

The nimbus radius, or its eccentricity if it is an ellipsoid, will depend on two factors: the object's shape and the furthest distance at which a human being would be able to distinguish the object. This distance is determined by visual acuity, which depends on the object's size; thus, indirectly, the nimbus conic will depend on the object's size as well.

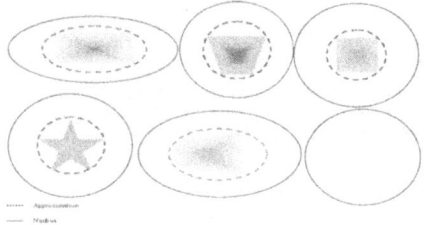

Fig. 5. Nimbus representations for geometric objects

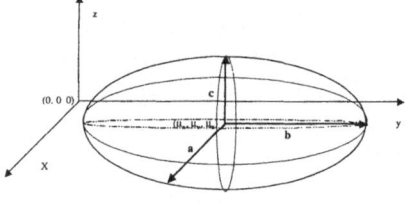

Fig. 6. Physical nimbus representation

$$\left(\left(\frac{x-\mu_x}{a}\right)^2+\left(\frac{y-\mu_y}{b}\right)^2+\left(\frac{z-\mu_z}{c}\right)^2\right)\leq 1 \quad (2) \quad (x-\mu_x)^2+(y-\mu_y)^2+(z-\mu_z)^2\leq R^2 \quad (3)$$

Where (μ_x, μ_y, μ_z) represents the object's geometrical center, (a, b, c) represents the ellipsoid parameters and R represents the radius' sphere (when a = b = c = R).

5   Visual Clarity of Perception

In this section, we concentrate on the sensitive perception block introduced in section 3. The sensitive perception module simulates the typical process by which organisms receive sensations from the environment. Sensation usually refers to the immediate, relatively unprocessed result of stimulation of sensory receptors in the eyes, ears, nose, tongue, or skin. Sensitive perception depends on some relevant sensorial concepts (figure 7): *Human Factors* –such as Visual Acuity, Lateral Vision and Visual Filters-; *Physical Factors* – such as the distance between the object and the position of the agent's eye ($d_{eye-object}$)-; Object's *Factors*; and *Adaptors* [12]. The $d_{eye-object}$ distance, and clarity of perception, in general, should be considered a key concept in agent's perception because it introduces more realism, believability and efficiency. For example, it will be necessary to check its value to know if an agent can read a notice board at a fixed distance. Moreover, making awareness dependent on this factor is totally new, no other model had it in mind before.

Clarity of Perception is a measurement of the ability to perceive an object inside the agent's visual focus, as well as the clearness of this perception. Once an object's nimbus intersects with the agent's focus the sensitive perception module will calculate the *clarity of perception* for this object.

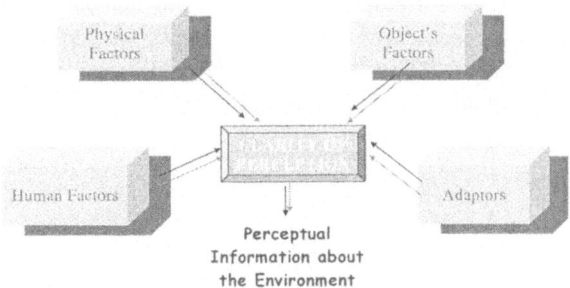

Fig. 7. Sensitive Perception

The process of human visual perception is continuous and the size of the image on the retina will continuously depend on the distance between the eye and the object to be perceived. Therefore, from the sensorial point of view, if clarity of perception is the ability to distinguish what kind of object is being perceived, then it should depend on the object image that we have on the retina. Moreover, as the retinal image decreases continuously with the eye-object distance, then the clarity of perception will decrease continuously with this distance as well. But we are also taking into account the size constancy phenomenon, by means of which the object's size tends to appear constant in spite of it changing with distance. This factor will imply that the clarity of perception will fall still more smoothly. Following the research conducted by Levi et al. [18,19], we propose a Gaussian as the function to describe the variation in the clarity of perception with the eye-object distance (Figue 8, equation 4) for a fixed object's size in the foreground region, where (d_1) represents the minimum distance necessary to have a clear perception of an object and (d_2) represents the maximum distance necessary to have a clear perception of an object. In the figure 7 we can also appreciate that the level of detail starts decreasing (between d_2 and d_3) and starting from (d_4) the eye can not perceive almost any detail from any object. More details are given in [12].

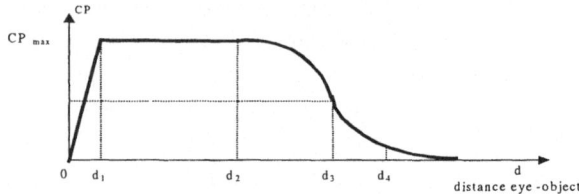

Fig. 8. Clarity of perception relative to distance inside the focus foreground region

$$0.0 \leq d \leq d_1 \quad CP(d) = \lambda d$$
$$d_1 \leq d \leq d_2 \quad CP(d) = CP_{max}$$
$$d \geq d_2 \quad CP(d) = \frac{1}{\sigma * \sqrt{2 * \pi}} * \exp\left\{-\frac{(d-d_2)^2}{2 * \sigma^2}\right\} \tag{4}$$

The clarity of perception function in the transition region has to take into account the presence of peripheral vision. Peripheral vision, as mentioned above, is paying attention to what is happening at the periphery of your field of vision. In this area you may become aware of movement, but you are less aware of colour and contrast distinctions.Following the research by Levi et. al [18,19], we propose another Gaussian function to describe the variation that the clarity of perception has with the distance eye-object (figure 9, equation 5) in the lateral region. More details are given in [12].

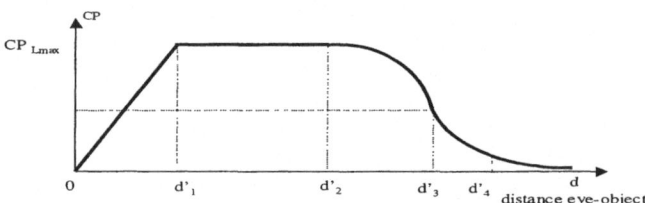

Fig. 9. Clarity of perception relative to distance inside the focus transition region

$$0.0 < CP_{Lmax} < CP_{max}$$
$$d'_1 > d_1 \quad d'_2 < d_2 \quad d'_3 > d_3 \quad d'_4 \approx d_4 \tag{5}$$

6 Perceptual Model Implementation

This model has been implemented in Visual C++, focusing on the construction of a library. This library has been integrated with **MASSIM_AGENT**, a prototype system built using the MASSIVE-3 CVE system and the SIM_AGENT toolkit for developing agents, but the design of this library has been done to be totally independent on any VE system or agent platform. In fact, our next goal is to integrate it with the system being built under a project called MAEVIF (Model for the Application of Intelligent Virtual Environments to Education and Training). This project is part of the R&D Spanish National Plan.

MASSIM_AGENT is the first prototype resulting of the integration of the MASSIVE-3 system and the SIM_AGENT toolkit. MASSIM_AGENT (figure 10) was the result of a collaboration established between the Mixed Reality Laboratory (MRL) at the University of Nottingham and the Universidad Politécnica de Madrid (UPM). SIM_AGENT has its own methods for the agents to get information from the environment. The main problem to integrate it with MASSIVE-3 has been to over-ride these default methods, obtaining the information from the MASSIVE-3 environment. Once SIM_AGENT has enough information from the 3D environment, this informa-tion is used by the SIM_AGENT methods to make their own actions and decisions, updating, subsequently, the MASSIVE-3 environment [20]. Before executing any action, SIM_AGENT has to request permission from MASSIVE-3. If it doesn't raise any objection (for instance, there is not a collision detected) the action can be executed inside the MASSIVE-3 environment, and once it has be done, MASSIVE-3 will send updated information to SIM_AGENT before starting with the next cycle.

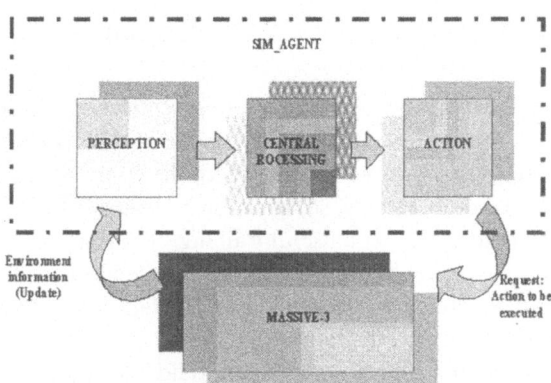

Fig. 10. MASSIM_AGENT communication

In the figure 10, it is possible to appreciate how an agent in MASSIM_AGENT is provided with information about their surroundings by MASSIVE-3. If this happens, an agent in MASSIM_AGENT will be able to experiment, in real-time, any virtual simulated environment. Moreover, the agent will behave and respond to stimuli of their environment, having then the possibility of interacting and communicating rather naturally. This information is related to the objects' physical position in the environ-ment as well as their geometrical data. The research presented in this paper extends the perceptual capabilities of MASSIM_AGENT providing the agent with a more human-like perception of the environment, necessary to behave with more believability, according to some pre-establish rules.

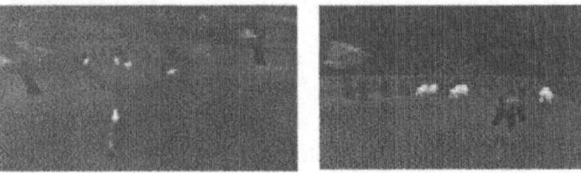

Fig. 11. The sheepdog simulation in MASSIM_AGENT

The first implementation realized in MASSIM_AGENT, called the sheepdog simulation, was developed between the Mixed Reality Laboratory (MRL) at the University of Nottingham and the Universidad Politécnica de Madrid (UPM) [20].The sheepdog simulation (figure 11) consisted of five sheep and a dog, all simulated as distinct agents within a single SIM_AGENT process. Translating the sheepdog simulation into the MASSIVE-3 environment required defining appropriate embodiments for the sheep, the dog and the obstacles and splitting the simulation, so the sheep and the dog were simulated in different SIM_AGENT processes on different machines, communicating via the MASSIVE-3 environment.

7   Some Scenarios for Human-Like Perception

In order to prove the usefulness of the proposed perception model, lets consider that, as it was previously mentioned, mIVA-VE systems can be used to simulate risky situations, as for example, a world-wide war, where the soldiers' training plays a very important role. In this kind of systems, soldiers can be trained for living and surviving the worse real-life situations. To get a useful training, it is important to endow soldier agents with a human-like perception model. Different scenarios and situations can be raised where human-like perception plays a very important role. In this section we are going to describe some of them.

Lets imagine that a soldier agent is at the battlefield. He is placed at a physical position given by the co-ordinates (x,y,z)= (1,0,0) in the space, in meters, with an orientation of 90° related to the x axis of co-ordinates. This soldier is endowed with a visual acuity (in Snellen notation) equivalent to 20/20 and his foreground angle of vision is $\theta=30°$ while his lateral angle of vision is $\theta'=65°$. Lets also imagine that a fighter plane, a Focke-Wulf BMW whose size is (length x wide x height)=(20,15,7), in meters, appears in the air space. Introducing all these values in the implemented visual perceptual model, we get the foreground and lateral soldier's cone of vision following the equation 1 introduced at section 4.3.1 of this paper, providing us with the visual cone of perception. In the same way, we get the nimbus geometry associated to the plane's nimbus, which is this case is an ellipsoid, and he plane's nimbus, following the equation 2 introduced at section 4.3.2 of this paper. In the same way, the perceptual model calculates the maximum distance of resolution, which in this case is 64.20 m. When the plane is placed at co-ordinates (x,y,z)=(1,25,0), in meters, away from the soldier, it is possible to perceive the object in the foreground area of perception. The clarity of perception in this area gets the maximum normalised value 1. The soldier can perceive most of the plain's details. When the plane is placed at co-ordinates (x,y,z)=(-40,25,25), in meters, away from the soldier, it is possible to perceive the object in the lateral area of perception. The clarity of perception in this area is 0.5. The soldier can perceive few details of the plane. The soldier probably will perceive an object but he will not be able to identify its physical details. As the plane is placed in the lateral area of perception, the details that this soldier can get from the plain will be associated to its movement. When the plane is placed at co-ordinates (x,y,z)=(15,70,25), in meters, away from the soldier, it is possible to perceive the object in the foreground area of perception. The clarity of perception in this area is 0.033 (very low). Maybe the soldier can perceive the plain's shape and its movement but this soldier can make a mistake confusing the coming plane with a friendly plane instead of recognising it as the hostile plane that it really is.

Fig. 12. The war scenario in MASSIM_AGENT

Now, lets imagine the following situation, where a soldier agent (A) is placed at a physical position given by the co-ordinates (x,y,z)= (1,0,0), in meters, with an orientation of 90° related to the x axis of co-ordinates. This soldier is endowed with a visual acuity (in Snellen notation) equivalent to 20/25 and, as the previous soldier, his foreground angle of vision is θ=30° and his lateral angle of vision is θ'=65°. The maximum distance of resolution is 3.64 m. Lets also imagine he is walking through a forest looking for the enemy, and while the soldier A is passing close to a tree, an enemy soldier (B), tries to throw towards the soldier A's neck with the aim of killing him. When soldier B is placed at co-ordinates (x,y,z)=(1,-1,0), in meters, away from the soldier A, the soldier B is very close to the soldier A but the soldier A can not be aware of the soldier B's presence because B is not inside neither A's field of foveal vision nor A's field of peripheral vision, and, consequently, the soldier A can not react to the soldier B's attack. The clarity of perception in this situation is null. When the soldier B is placed at co-ordinates (x,y,z)=(1,2,0), in meters, away from the soldier A, the soldier B's is inside the soldier A's foreground area of perception and therefore the soldier A can detect not just the soldier B's movement but also its physical detail. The clarity of perception in this area gets the maximum normalised value 1. When the soldier B is placed at co-ordinates (x,y,z)=(1,4.5,0), in meters, but there is a magnifying window-wall at co-ordinates (1,1,1), which is working as an non obstructive boundary. Without any kind of boundary, the soldier B is placed in the foreground area of perception, the clarity of perception in this area is 0.0.5. The soldier A could perceive the soldier B as an object but he will not be able to identify neither the shape nor the details. But the presence of this magnifying window-wall modifies the process of perception and the clarity associated to this perception will depend on the magnifying power of the materials composing this window. This means that if the magnifying power of the signal processor is high the clarity of perception would get the maximum normalised value 1.This is an example of how boundaries should limit the agent's perception in order to achieve more realism.

8 Conclusions

We have developed a human-like perceptual model based on one of the most successful awareness models in Computer Supported Cooperative Work (CSCW), called the Spatial Model of Interaction (SMI) [1], which manage awareness in Collaborative Virtual Environments (CVEs) through a set of key concepts.

This perceptual model extends the key concepts of the SMI introducing some human-like factors typical from human being perception – such as Visual Acuity, Lateral Vision and Visual Filters - as well as it makes a reinterpretation with the aim of introducing them as the key concepts of a IVA's human-like perceptual model.

We also have introduced a new concept which we have called Clarity of Perception (CP) as a way of having a measurement of the ability to perceive an object inside the agent's visual area of perception, as well as the clearness of this perception.

The final perceptual model allows an IVA to perceive its environment and surrounding objects in real-time with a human-like clarity of perception, giving it the chance to behave and react to stimuli in its environment, as well as to respond to interactions with the real world, making it interactive.

Acknowledgements. The work presented in this paper has been supported by the Communication Research Group (CRG), led by Steve Benford and Chris Greenhalgh at the School of Computer Science and Information Technology in the University of Nottingham. This work has been partially funded by the Spanish Ministry of Science and Technology through project TIC00-1346

References

[1]   Benford, S.D., and Fahlén, L.E. *A spatial Model of Interaction in Large Virtual Environments*. Proc. Third European Conference on Computer Supported Cooperative Work (ECSCW'93), Milano, Italy. Kluwer Academic Publishers, 1993.

[2]   Blumberg, B. *Go with the Flow: Synthetic Vision for Autonomous Animated Creatures*. Proceedings of the First International Conference on Autonomous Agents (Agents'97), Marina del Rey, CA, 1997.

[3]   Chenney Stevephen *Sensing for Autonomous Agents in Virtual Environments*. http://www.cs.berkeley.edu/~schenney/autonomous/sensing.html.1996.

[4]   Chopra-Khullar, S. and Badler, N. *Where to look? Automating attending behaviors of virtual human characters*. Autonomous Agents and Multi-agent Systems 4(1/2), 2001, pp. 9–23.

[5]   Dourish, P., Bellotti, V. *Awareness and Coordination in Shared Workspaces*. Proceedings of the 4th ACM Conference on CSCW. Toronto / Canada, Oktober 1992.

[6]   Endsley. M. *Towards a theory of situation awareness*. Technical report, Texas Technical University, Department of Industrial Engineering, 1993.

[7]   Endsley. M., *Design and evaluation for situation awareness enhancement*. Proceedings of Human Factors Society and Annual Meeting, volume 1, 1988.

[8]   Geib C. W., Levison L., and Moore M. B. *SodaJack: an architecture for agents that search for and manipulate objects*. Tech. Rep. MS-CIS-94-16/LINC LAB 265, Department of Computer and Information Science, University of Pennsylvania, 1994.

[9]   Greenhalgh, C., *Large Scale Collaborative Virtual Environments*. Doctoral Thesis. University of Nottingham. October 1997.

[10] Herrero P. *Awareness of interaction and of other participants*. Technical Report. Amusement Esprit Project 25197. February 1999.

[11] Herrero P., De Antonio A., Segovia J. *Is the Awareness of Avatars in a Virtual World Different from Human Awareness?* Workshop on the Future of Cves: "Voltage in the Milky Night: The Future of CVE's" The Third International Conference on Collaborative Virtual Environments. ACM Collaborative Virtual Environments 2000. San Francisco (California). USA. September 2000.

[12] Herrero P., De Antonio A., *A Human Based Perception Model for Cooperative Intelligent Virtual Agents*. Tenth International Conference on Cooperative Information Systems (CoopIS 2002). University of California, Irvine. October 30–November 1, 2002

[13] Herrero P., De Antonio A., Benford S., Greenhalgh C., *Increasing the Coherence between Human Beings and Virtual Agents*. Proceedings of the First International Joint Conference on Autonomous Agents and Multiagent Systems, Bologna, Italy, July, 2002.

[14] Herrero P., De Antonio A., Benford S., Greenhalgh C., *A Hearing Perceptual Model for Intelligent Virtual Agents*. Proceedings of the Second International Joint Conference on Autonomous Agents and Multiagent Systems, Melbourne, Australia, July, 2003.

[15] Hill, R. Han, C. van Lent, M. *Applying Perceptually Driven Cognitive Mapping To Virtual Urban Environments*. Conference on Innovative Applications of Artificial Intelligence (IAAI-2002) in Edmonton, Canada.2002.

[16] Hill, R. Han, C. van Lent, M. *Perceptually Driven Cognitive Mapping of Urban Environments*. Proceedings of the First International Joint Conference on Autonomous Agents and Multiagent Systems, Bologna, Italy, July, 2002.

[17] Howarth, P. A. and Costello P.J., *Contemporary Ergonomics* 1997, Ed. S.A.Robertson, Taylor and Francis London, 1997, pp 109–116.

[18] Levi, D.M., Hariharan, S. & Klein, S.A. *Suppressive and Facilitatory Spatial Interactions in Peripheral Vision: Peripheral Crowding is neither size invariant nor simple contrast masking.* Journal of Vision, 2, 167–177.2002. http://www.journalofvision.org/2/2/3/

[19] Levi, D.M., Klein, S.A. & Hariharan, S. *Suppressive and Facilitatory Spatial Interactions in Foveal Vision: Foveal Crowding is simple contrast masking.* Journal of Vision, 2, 140–166. 2002. http://journalofvision.org/2/2/2/

[20] Logan, B., Fraser, M., Fielding, D., Benford, S., Greenhalgh, C., Herrero P. *Keeping in Touch: Agents Reporting from Collaborative Virtual Environments.* Artificial Intelligence and Interactive Entertainment: Papers from the 2002 AAAI Spring Symposium, Technical Report SS-02-01, AAAI Press, March 2002.

[21] Nilsson, N. *Teleo-Reactive Programs and the Triple-Tower Architecture.* Electronic Transactions on Artificial Intelligence, Vol. 5, Section B, pp. 99–110. 2001.

[22] Noser, H., A *Behavioral Animation System Based on L-systems and Synthetic Sensors for Actors.* PhD Thesis. École Polytechnique Fédérale De Lausanne. 1997

[23] Nugent, W. R. *Virtual Reality: Advanced Imaging Special Effects Let You Roam in Cyberspace* Journal of the American Society for Information Science, September 1991.

[24] Shively, R. J., Brickner, M., Silbiger J., A *Computational Model of Situational Awareness* Instantiated in MIDAS 1997

[25] Terzopoulos D. and Rabie, T.F. *Animat Vision: Active Vision in Artificial Animals.* Published in Videre: Journal of Computer Vision Research, 1(1):2–19, 1997.

[26] Thalmann, D. *The Foundations to Build a Virtual Human Society.* Proc. Intelligent Virtual Actors (IVA'01), Madrid, Spain. 2001.

BRAIN: A Framework for Flexible Role-Based Interactions in Multiagent Systems

Giacomo Cabri[1], Letizia Leonardi[1], and Franco Zambonelli[2]

[1]Dipartimento di Ingegneria dell'Informazione – Università di Modena e Reggio Emilia
41100 Modena, Italy
{giacomo.cabri, letizia.leonardi}@unimo.it
[2]Dipartimento di Scienze e Metodi dell'Ingegneria – Università di Modena e Reggio Emilia
42100 Reggio Emilia, Italy
franco.zambonelli@unimo.it

Abstract. Agent-based approaches in application development seem to meet the requirements of adaptability, scalability, decentralization, and flexibility imposed by complex software systems. In open applications, interactions among agents are one of the most important issues that must be faced carefully. In this paper we propose the BRAIN framework, which aims at supporting the different phases of the development of interactions in agent-based applications, relying on the concept of role to model agent interactions. Roles carry different advantages in modeling interactions and, consequently, in exploiting derived infrastructures to support multiagent systems. Besides the interaction model, the BRAIN framework includes XRole, an XML-based notation to express roles in an interoperable way, and Rolesystem, an interaction infrastructure that implements the proposed model. An application example shows the advantages of our approach in application engineering.

1 Introduction

Current trends in distributed application development clearly outline the need of new methodologies and tools to face the emerging requirements. Complex software systems call for new approaches that meet such requirements. Current scenarios are *very dynamic, heterogeneous*, and *unpredictable*, and therefore they require *high adaptability, scalability, decentralization*, and *flexible interacting capability*. The agent-oriented approach is emerging as a feasible solution. In fact, agents, thanks to their capability of both executing in a proactive way and reacting to environment changes, can naturally deal with dynamism, heterogeneity and unpredictability [16]. Moreover, the capability of dealing with unexpected situations as part of their intrinsic behavior, rather than in terms of "exceptions", enforces their adaptability to dynamic scenarios. Finally, their sociality leads to autonomy in interactions, allowing scalable decompositions of applications in terms of decentralized multi-agent organizations [10], and enabling interaction among agents not only belonging to the same application, but also to different ones, as happens in the people real world.

In agent-based applications, interactions are an important issue to be faced, both between cooperating agents of the same application and between competitive agents

R. Meersman et al. (Eds.): CoopIS/DOA/ODBASE 2003, LNCS 2888, pp. 145–161, 2003.
© Springer-Verlag Berlin Heidelberg 2003

belonging to different applications. The feature of *mobility*, which allows agents to change their execution environment, adds great flexibility, but also introduces peculiar issues in interactions, such as localization, site and platform dependences [12].

We argue that the following *requirements* must be met in the development of agent interactions:

- *Agent oriented features.* In our opinion, the most important requirement is that interactions have to be modeled following an agent-oriented approach, i.e., all the peculiar features of agents must be considered.
- *Separation of concerns.* We argue that an important aspect in the development of agent applications is the separation of concerns between algorithmic issues and interaction issues. This helps in developing applications because allows facing the two issues separately, leading to a more modular approach.
- *Independence.* It is quite obvious that a model is independent of platforms and applications; moreover, we require using for the interaction development a model that is independent of environments, and that enables a useful notation, which allows interoperability and independence.
- *Concrete usability.* We are not interested in producing a formalism for modeling interactions (such as UML-based approaches for agent oriented software engineering [19]), neither for describing roles (such as the GAIA methodology [21]). Instead, we would like to promote a way to support and simplify the development of interactions in agent-based applications.
- *Promotion of locality.* A trend that has recently appeared and seems to be accepted in the agent area is the adoption of locality in agent interactions, i.e. the environment is modeled as a multiplicity of *local interaction contexts*, representing the logical places where agent interaction activities occur. An agent is situated on a given interaction context (which may change because of mobility) and here is enabled to access local resources and to interact with local executing agents [6].

There have been different proposals in the area of agent interaction and coordination: they have concerned message passing adapted to agents, "meeting point" abstractions, event-channels, and tuple spaces [3]. However, these approaches to agent interactions suffer from being adaptations of older approaches traditionally applied in the distributed system area and do not take into account the new needs. Moreover, traditional approaches often consider agents as bare objects; this implies that the features of agents are managed in a not uniform way, leading to fragmented approaches. Finally, there is no approach that covers all the phases of the software development, leading to fragmentation of the solutions.

In this paper we propose a complete view of the BRAIN (Behavioral Roles for Agent INteractions) framework [2]. BRAIN proposes a new approach where the interactions among agents are based on the concept of *role*. The concept of role is adopted in different areas of the computing systems and we can find role-based approaches also in the area of software development [11, 14, 18]. In BRAIN, a role is defined as a set of capabilities and an expected behavior. The former is a set of actions that an agent playing such role can perform to achieve its task. The latter is a set of events that an agent is expected to manage in order to "behave" as requested by the role it plays. Interactions among agents are then represented by couples *action-event*, which are dealt with by the underlying interaction infrastructure, which can enforce local policies and rules.

The paper is organized as follows. Section 2 introduces the BRAIN framework. Section 3 explains the adopted interaction model based on roles. Section 4 reports XRole, an XML-based notation to express roles. Section 5 details the interaction infrastructure called Rolesystem, that implements the proposed model. Section 6 reports some related work. Finally, Section 7 concludes the paper.

2 The BRAIN Framework

To overcome the limitations of the traditional approaches, the BRAIN framework [2] proposes an approach that relies on a simple yet general role-based interaction model and aims at covering the different phases of the development of interactions in agent-based applications. There are different, well-recognized advantages in modeling interactions by roles and, consequently, in exploiting derived infrastructures. First, it enables a separation of concerns between the algorithmic issues and the interaction issues in developing agent-based applications [5]. Second, it permits the reuse of solutions and experiences; in fact, roles are related to an application scenario, and designers can exploit roles previously defined for similar applications. Finally, roles can also be seen as a sort of design patterns [20]: a set of related roles along with the definition of the way they interact can be considered as a solution to a well-defined problem, and reused in different similar situations.

The BRAIN framework proposes (i) an a simple yet general *interactions model* based on roles, that is exploited at the beginning of the development process to model and design interactions; (ii) an XML-based *notation* to describe the roles, which is flexible enough to allow its exploitation at the different phases of the development; and (iii) implementations of interaction *infrastructures* based on the previous model and notation, which enable agents to assume roles and to control interactions (see Fig. 1). These BRAIN framework components will be detailed in the next sections.

Besides the already mentioned advantages related to roles, BRAIN aims at providing further advantages. In fact, it respects the main features of agents, leading to more agent-oriented solutions. Also, it promotes locality in interactions, by allowing the definition of specific roles and specific behaviors for each logical place where agents interact.

2.1 An Application Example

In the following, we will use an application example to show the concrete exploitation of our approach. This application concerns the management of a conference session by means of agents. We suppose that each attendee has her own agent, which helps its owner in attending the session. As soon as an attendee joins the session (i.e., enters the room where the session occurs) her agent, executing on her laptop or PDA, connects to the local interaction context.

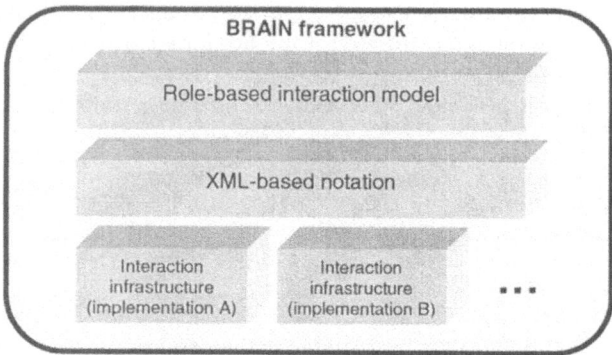

Fig. 1. The BRAIN framework

An attendee can behave differently depending on the (human) role she plays in the session. We can distinguish four main (human) roles:

- *Participant.* A participant is the most common attendee, which (more or less) silently listens to the speakers. Her agent can download the session program and the slides of the current presentation.
- *Speaker.* The speaker is the attendee that currently presents her work. Her agent uploads the presentation slides on the display device, supplies the slides to participants on demand, and manages the incoming questions.
- *Questioner.* A participant can become a questioner when she wants to ask a question to the speaker. Her agent can transmit the question to the chair or directly to the speaker.
- *Chair.* The chair moderates the conference session. Her agent manages the session program; in particular, it keeps the program and schedules the speakers.

In this application, we exploit agent roles that implement participants, speakers, questioners, and chairs. We stress that attendees' agents are not specialized agents (e.g., the agent of a speaker is not a speaker agent), but they are arbitrary agents (for example, personal information manager agents) that assume the appropriate role when required. In this way, the same agent can for instance behave as participant, as speaker and as questioner in different periods of the session. For sake of presentation simplicity, in the following we say "the X agent" (where X can be participant, speaker, questioner, or chair) to mean "the agent playing the X role".

3   Role-Based Interaction Model

In our approach, a role is modeled as a *set of the capabilities* and an *expected behavior* [7] (see Fig. 2). Even if this definition is a little bit different from the classical one based on rights and duties, we think that it better suits the main feature of agents: *proactiveness* and *reactivity*. The former point in our model is that a role is a set of capabilities, i.e., a set of *actions* that agents assuming a role can perform. Since the *proactiveness* feature of agents, they have to perform actions to carry out their tasks, and so, they must be enabled to do it. The latter point in the role definition is that an agent assuming a given role is expected to exhibit a specific behavior. *Since* the agents are *reactive*, they are sensible to what happens in the environment where they live. The "expected behavior" represents the reactions to incoming *events*; it is "expected" because the agent is supposed, at least, to receive events. Therefore, the management of events can well shape the reactivity feature of agents. So, in BRAIN a role is concretely represented by *actions* that agents can perform, and *events* that agents receive and by which perceives the world.

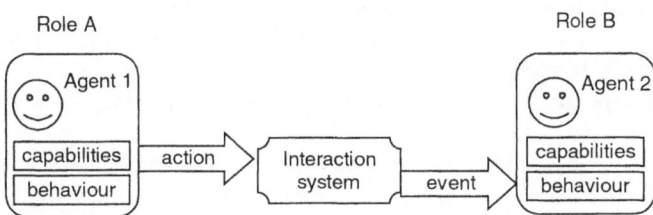

Fig. 2. The models of roles and interactions

There are some characteristics of roles that lead to deal with them separately from the concept of agent. The role is *temporary*, since an agent may play it in a well-defined period of time or in a well-defined context. Roles are *generic*, in the sense that they are not tightly bound to a specific application, but they express general properties that can be used in different applications and then for different agents. Finally, roles are *related to contexts*, which means that each environment can impose its own rules and can grant some local capabilities, forcing agents to assume specific roles.

This model of role leads to a twofold viewpoint of the role: from the application point of view, a role allows a set of capabilities, which can be exploited by agents to carry out their tasks; from the environment point of view, a role imposes a defined behavior to the agents that assume it.

In our framework, an interaction between two agents occurs when one agent performs an action (chosen among the set of capabilities belonging to the role it plays) and such action is translated into an event that is notified to another agent that exhibits the specific behavior. The underlying interaction *infrastructure* provides for the translation from actions to events (see Fig. 2). A possible implementation of the interaction system is presented in Section 5.

In our application example, let us consider the participant role. Possible actions are asking for the program of the session, asking for the slides of the current talk, talking with other participant, and so on. While managed events can be receiving the session program, receiving the current slides, being notified of being the next speaker, listening to another participant that want to talk, etc. Note that some events are the consequence of actions: for instance, the "receiving the program" event is a consequence of an "asking for the program" action. This leads to an interaction between the agents playing the participant and the chair roles.

4   XRole Notation

Starting from the role model of the previous section, the BRAIN framework includes XRole [4], a notation for the definition of roles for agents. The main aim of XRole is to support the different phases of the development of agent interactions.

XRole exploits the XML language to build up definitions of roles. XML, representing information in a tagged form, exhibits the well-appreciated feature of human-readability and platform-independence. This allows a high degree of interoperability and helps in dealing heterogeneous situations.

In XRole, roles are defined by XML documents that respect the XML Schema reported in Fig. 3. It shows that there are three main parts (dashed boxes in Fig. 3) that have to be specified in the definition of a role, following the above-described model:

- *The basic information.* This part includes the pieces of information that are used to identify the role, and to specify an interaction context for such role. A high-level description and some keywords are supplied to let developers understand the role functionalities.
- *The allowed actions.* Each role defines which are the allowed actions. An action is characterized by a name and a high-level description that can be useful for developers. Moreover, the addressee of the action and the content are specified.
- *The recognized events.* These are events that the agent is expected to accept and manage. An event is characterized by a name and a high-level description that is useful to developers. The other two elements specify which role performed the related action – and, consequently, sent the event – and the event content.

The content of an XRole document can be translated into appropriate representations by XSL sheets, for instance into an HTML page or into a piece of code in some programming language. It is worth noting that each different representation derives from the same XRole document, so the different phases of the development of applications relies on the same information, granting continuity during the entire development.

During the analysis phase, the XRole documents can be translated into HTML documents to provide high-level information; in the design phase, the same XRole documents can be translated into more detailed HTML documents to suggest functionalities of the involved entities; finally, at the implementation phase, again the same XRole documents can be exploited to obtain code that implements the role properties.

Fig. 4 reports a fragment of the XRole document that defines the participant role of the conference application example; in particular, the figure reports the role basic information, an example of allowed action, and an example of recognized event.

The advantages of the use of XRole are the following:

- XRole enables a notation for the interaction model introduced in the previous section; thus, it derives all the related advantages.
- XRole supports developers in every phase of the software life cycle. The information can be translated in different ways, depending on the interests of developers. Roles defined by XRole can be read by human people, by automatic tools and by agents themselves. This allows the exploitation of roles even at runtime by agents, which can dynamically search for appropriate roles and assume them.

- XRole grants a high degree of interoperability, since it is based on XML and it is not bound to a given agent system nor to a *given interaction infrastructure*.

```
<?xml version="1.0" encoding="UTF-8"?>
<xsd:schema xmlns:xsd="http://www.w3.org/2000/10/XMLSchema" elementFormDefault="qualified">
  <xsd:element name="role" type="RoleType"/>
  <xsd:complexType name="ContentType">
    <xsd:sequence>
      <xsd:element name="description" type="xsd:string" minOccurs="0"/>
      <xsd:element name="type" type="xsd:string"/>
    </xsd:sequence>
  </xsd:complexType>
  <xsd:complexType name="ActionType">
    <xsd:sequence>
      <xsd:element name="name" type="xsd:string"/>
      <xsd:element name="description" type="xsd:string" minOccurs="0"/>
      <xsd:element name="addressee_role" type="xsd:string"/>
      <xsd:element name="content" type="ContentType" minOccurs="0"/>
    </xsd:sequence>
  </xsd:complexType>
  <xsd:complexType name="EventType">
    <xsd:sequence>
      <xsd:element name="name" type="xsd:string"/>
      <xsd:element name="description" type="xsd:string" minOccurs="0"/>
      <xsd:element name="sender_role" type="xsd:string"/>
      <xsd:element name="content" type="ContentType" minOccurs="0"/>
    </xsd:sequence>
  </xsd:complexType>
  <xsd:complexType name="RoleType">
    <xsd:sequence>
      <xsd:element name="name" type="xsd:string"/>
      <xsd:element name="context" type="xsd:string"/>
      <xsd:element name="description" type="xsd:string" minOccurs="0"/>
      <xsd:element name="keyword" type="xsd:string" minOccurs="0" maxOccurs="unbounded"/>
      <xsd:element name="action" type="ActionType" minOccurs="0" maxOccurs="unbounded"/>
      <xsd:element name="event" type="EventType" minOccurs="0" maxOccurs="unbounded"/>
    </xsd:sequence>
  </xsd:complexType>
</xsd:schema>
```

Fig. 3. The XML Schema followed by roles defined in XRole

5 Rolesystem Implementation

Rolesystem is an interaction infrastructure that implements the interaction model of BRAIN [8]. It is completely written in Java to grant high portability and to be associated with the main agent platforms. The concrete platform we chose to implement Rolesystem is Jade [15], a FIPA compliant agent platform, which allows also mobility of agents.

Fig. 5 reports the architecture of Rolesystem, which is the concrete implementation of the model sketched in Section 3. As shown in the figure, the Rolesystem implementation is divided into two parts: the upper one is independent of the agent platform, while the lower part is bound to the chosen agent platform, in

```
<?xml version="1.0" encoding="UTF-8"?>
<role xmlns:xsi="http://www.w3.org/2000/10/XMLSchema-instance"
xsi:noNamespaceSchemaLocation="roleSchema.xsd">
  <name>participant</name>
  <context>conference</context>
  <description>An agent that attends a conference session</description >
  <keyword>conference</keyword>
  ...
  <action>
    <name>askProgram </name>
    <description>Asks for the program of the current session</description>
    <addressee_role>chair</addressee_role>
  </action>
  ...
  <event>
    <name>receiveProgram</name>
    <description>The participant receives the program of the session</description>
    <sender_role>chair</sender_role>
    <content>
      <type>Program</type>
    </content>
  </event>
  ...
</role>
```

Fig. 4. The XRole document that define the participant role (fragments)

this case Jade. We remark that it is not possible to have a complete independent implementation, but our effort was in the direction of reducing the platform-dependent part.

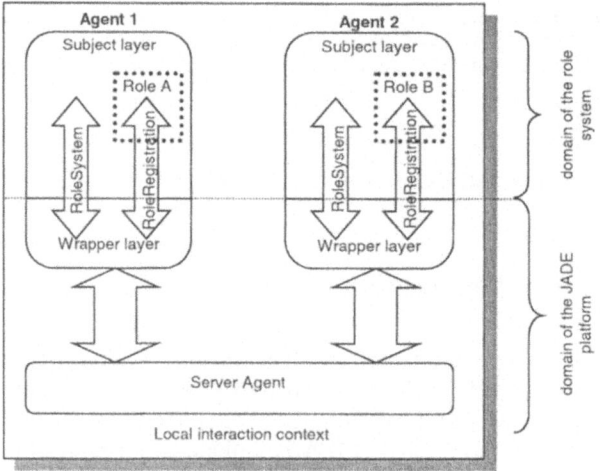

Fig. 5. The Rolesystem architecture

In applications exploiting the Rolesystem infrastructure, agents are composed of two layers: the *subject layer*, representing the subject of the role system independent of the platform, and the *wrapper layer*, which is the implementation entity (e.g., the Jade agent) in charge of supporting the subject layer (see Fig. 5). The implementers, besides the agent classes, must define appropriate classes that implements interfaces to manage roles. A specific agent for each interaction context, called *server agent*, is in charge of managing local roles and their interactions; in this way, it is possible to have different interaction contexts, to enforce locality in interactions.

Therefore, the current implementation consists of several Java classes, both platform-independent and related to Jade. The availability of platform-independent parts and the capability of exploiting local implementations imply that performing an action is a little bit more complex than simply invoking a method, as can be seen in the next subsections.

The connection between the subject layer and the wrapper layer is granted by two Java objects, instances of classes implementing respectively the RoleSystem and RoleRegistration interfaces, which provide methods to register the associations between agents and roles, to search for agents playing a given role, to listen for events and to perform actions. Such interfaces are described in detail in the next subsection.

5.1   RoleSystem and RoleRegistration Interfaces

The RoleSystem interface enables agents to perform preliminary operations needed to assume a role. It provides the following methods: reqRegistration, to register an agent in the system with a specified role; searchForRoleAgent, to search for agents playing a given role.

Note that, when an agent asks for registration, it already knows the class implementing the role; the registration is needed by the role system to know which role such agent plays.

With regard to the presented application example, Fig. 6 shows the code to request for registration of an agent A that wants to assume the *participant* role. The request is made by invoking the reqRegistration method, supplying as parameter the name of the role (the static field ROLE_ID of the Participant class, see Fig. 7). This invocation occurs in the code of the class that implements the subject layer of the agent A.

```
...
RoleRegistration registration;
try {   registration=roleSystem.reqRegistration(Participant.ROLE_ID); }
catch(RoleException re) {   System.err.println(re);   return; }
...
```

Fig. 6. Example of registration request

The RoleRegistration interface enables agents to perform operations on the system after that the agent has assumed a role. The following methods are defined:

- listen, with and without timeout, to listen for occurring events. The operation without timeout is blocking, and returns as soon as an event occurs. The methods return an object of event class, or null.
- doAction, to perform a given action (detailed later).
- whoAmI, to know the associated identifier.
- dismiss, to cancel the registration and leave the corresponding role.

When an agent wants to play a role, the first step its subject layer has to perform is to obtain an object that implements the RoleRegistration interface, invoking the reqRegistration method. The returned object represents the association between the agent and a specific role, i.e., the role assumed. Then, such object can be exploited to perform actions and manage events. As soon as an agent does not need to play the assumed role any more, it releases the role registration via the dismiss method. If the agent wants to assume a role again, it has to require another registration via the reqRegistration method.

5.2 Roles, Actions, and Events

In Rolesystem, a role is implemented by an abstract class, where the features of the role are expressed by static fields and static methods. This class is easily derived from an XRole document, by means of an appropriate XSL document. Note that agent programmers can exploit XRole documents to know about methods and rely on the implementations available on interaction contexts; so they do not need to implement the role classes.

```
package rolesystem.roles.conference;

import rolesystem.core.RoleAction;
import rolesystem.roles.KnownEvent;

/** This role is the participant at a conference session.
 *  Keywords: conference, participant.
 */
public abstract class Participant
{ /** Role identifier.   */
  public static final String ROLE_ID="conference.Participant";
```

Fig. 7. The beginning of the Participant class

The abstract class that implements a role has the same name of the role, and is part of a package that represents the application scenario for such role. A static and final field called ROLE_ID, of type String, is exploited to identify the role; to avoid name conflicts, the value of this field is the concatenation of the name of the package with the name of the role, in the form *package.Role*. In the following, we report some code fragments of the classes belonging to the conference application example. Fig. 7 reports the beginning of the class that represents the participant role.

Each action defined in a role is built by a static method, which is in charge of creating an appropriate instance of the class RoleAction and returning it to the caller. Such a static method has the same name of the corresponding action and one or two parameters: the former one is the agent addressee of the event corresponding to the action; the optional latter parameter is the information content to perform the action. For example, Fig. 8 reports some actions defined in the Participant class of the application example.

To perform an action, an agent playing a given role must obtain the appropriate RoleAction instance, invoking the corresponding static method of the role class. Then, it has to invoke the doAction method of RoleRegistration to actually perform the action, supplying the previously created instance of RoleAction (see Fig. 10 for an example of code). As previously stated, this may seem complex, but is needed to grant uncoupling. Then, when the Server agent of the local interaction context receives the request to perform the action via the wrapper layer, translates it into a known event, and sends it to the addressee agent.

```
...
/** Asks for the program of the current session.
 *  @param addressee Chair
 */
public static RoleAction askProgram (Id addressee)
{    return new RoleAction("askProgram", addressee);   }

/** Talks.
 *  @param addressee Participant
 *  @param content Message.
 */
public static RoleAction talk(Id addressee, String content)
{    return new RoleAction("talk", addressee, content);   }
...
```

Fig. 8. Actions in the Participant class

```
/**  The participant receives the program of the session.
 * Sender role: Chair
 * Content: Program of the session.
 */
public static final KnownEvent KE_receiveProgram=new KnownEvent("receiveProgram",
Chair.ROLE_ID, Program.class);

/** The chair notifies that I am the next speaker.
 *  Sender role: Chair
 */
public static final KnownEvent KE_youNext=new KnownEvent("youNext", Chair.ROLE_ID);

/** Another participant talks.
 * Sender role: Participant
 * Content: Message.
 */
public static final KnownEvent KE_talk=new KnownEvent("talk", Participant.ROLE_ID,
String.class);
}
```

Fig. 9. Events in the Participant class

An (addressee) agent waits for incoming events by invoking the listen method of the RoleRegistration interface. When an event for this agent arrives, the listen method returns an instance of the class RoleEvent, and then the agent can evaluate whether the incoming event is among the recognized ones, which are defined in the role class as instances of the class KnownEvent. This class describes the *name* of the event, the *role* assumed by the sender of the event, and the *class* of the information content of the event. Thanks to the match method of the class KnownEvent, agents can compare the known events (instances of KnownEvent) with the occurred event (instance of RoleEvent); this method returns true if and only if (i) the name of the occurred event is the same of that of the known event, and (ii) the role of the sender agent is the same of that of the known event, and (iii) both the events are without any information content or the information content of the occurred event can be casted to the class of the information content of the known event.

The names of the KnownEvent instances correspond to the names of the events they represent, preceded by the prefix "KE_". Fig. 9 reports some recognized events for the Participant class of the application example. Each event is represented by a static field initialized with the appropriate instance of KnownEvent.

5.3   An Interaction Example

An interaction between two agents occurs when one agent performs an action (chosen among the available to the role it plays) and such action is translated into an event that is notified to another agent that exhibits the specific behavior. The Rolesystem infrastructure provides for the translation from actions into events.

As an example of interaction in the proposed conference application, we show how the chair agent interacts with a participant agent to inform it is the next speaker and must assume the appropriate role. Fig. 10 reports a fragment of the code of the chair agent: it retrieves the identifier of the next speaker from the session program and performs an alertNext action. The Server agent of the Rolesystem infrastructure translates the action performed by the chair agent into an appropriate event. In particular, the alertNext action is translated into a KE_youNext event and sent to the participant agent specified as addressee.

```
// class implementing the agent assuming the chair role
...
// register as chair
registration = roleSystem.reqRegistration(Chair.ROLE_ID);
...
// get the next speaker from the program
Id nextSpeaker = sessionProgram.next();
// if there is a next speaker
if (nextSpeaker != null)
{ // perform an action to alert it
  RoleAction action = Chair.alertNext(nextSpeaker);
  registration.doAction(action);
}
...
```

Fig. 10. Chair-speaker interaction

Fig. 11 shows the behavior of the participant agent. When it receives an event, it evaluates whether one of the known events matches with the incoming event (following the rules reported in the previous subsection). In the depicted case, the received event matches with the KE_youNext event, which means that the chair agent has performed the alertNext action. The participant agent, by managing the incoming event, knows that its user is the next speaker, and then asks for assuming the speaker role (i.e., it requests a Rolesystem registration as a speaker).

The administrator of a site can enforce local interaction laws, by defining which interactions are allowed in the site. In particular, she can set a grid of permissions, which tells who can interact with who, and each interaction permission must specify the sender and the addressee; since the interactions in Rolesystem are asymmetric, it may happen that a role A can interact with role B, but role B cannot interact with role A. An appropriate GUI can be exploited to set permissions. With regard to our application example, we can figure out that there are sessions where participants are not allowed to ask questions directly to the speaker, but they have to involve the chair; in this case, the local administrator have to set permission in the appropriate way, denying interactions where the sender and the addressee are participant and speaker respectively.

```
// class implementing the agent assuming the participant role
...
// register as participant
registration = roleSystem.reqRegistration(Participant.ROLE_ID);
...
// listen for incoming events
event = registration.listen();
// if the occurred event matches an alert action
if(Participant.KE_youNext.match(event))
{ try { // dismiss the participant role
    registration.dismiss();
    // and register as speaker
    registration=roleSystem.reqRegistration(Speaker.ROLE_ID);
  } catch(RoleException re) {    System.err.println(re);    return;    }
  // from now act as a speaker agent
    ...
}
...
```

Fig. 11. A participant manages an event

6   Comparison with Other Approaches

6.1   OO-Based Approach

A traditional OO-based approach implies the definition of methods in the agent code, to interact with other agents (or entities). The mostly adopted model is the message-passing one, usually exploited in a "procedure call" fashion, i.e., the agent invokes a method and expects an answer as return value.

Fig. 12 shows an example of method that manages an interaction between a questioner and a speaker: the method askQuestion of a speaker is invoked by a questioner that wants to ask a question, which is supplied as parameter.

Even if this approach is the simplest one, its main limitation is that the specific features concerning the role played by the agent are not separated from the general features, for instance from the mobility or the planning features. This leads to some important drawbacks. First, interactions are not well integrated with the agent characteristics, since it is difficult to clearly point out how they fulfil the proactiveness and the reactivity. Interactions are more object-oriented than agent-oriented: in particular, interactions and events are dealt with in a different way, leading to a fragmented implementation without a global management of the possible situations. Then, from the Internet site point of view, specific site-dependent code of actions cannot be provided, and agents must embody the code from the beginning.

Moreover, it is not possible to enforce local laws and to control the interactions among them.

```
Presentation myPresentation = ...;
...
public void askQuestion (String question)
{ if (myPresentation.isFinished())
  { // directly report the question to the speaker
    ...
  }
  else
  { // record the question, which will be managed later
    ...
  }
}
...
```

Fig. 12. Traditional OO approach

6.2   Aspect-Oriented Approach

Even if it has not been designed in connection with roles, Aspect Oriented Programming (AOP) seems to provide interesting mechanisms to support the management of roles for agents [9, 17]. AOP starts from the consideration that there are behaviors and functionalities that are orthogonal to the algorithmic parts of the objects. So, it proposes the separate definition of components and *aspects*, to be joined together by an appropriate compiler (the *Aspect Weaver*), which produces the final program. The separation of concerns introduced by AOP permits to distinguish the algorithmic issues from the behavioral issues. Since an aspect is a property that cannot be encapsulated in a stand-alone entity, but rather affects the behavior of components, it is evident the similarity with a role.

Fig. 13 reports an example of use of AOP in our application. The Participant aspect implements the role, and provides the appropriate methods that are embodied in the agent code by the Aspect Weaver; in the Figure they are added to the ag instance of the class MyAgent.

Even if the AOP approach is similar to ours, in our opinion it has some limitations: First, the role/aspect must known the class which is going to modify, for instance, in the Figure the Participant aspect must known the MyAgent class to add the appropriate methods. Then, as a consequence, this approach lacks flexibility in the definition and usage of aspects, and this is due to the fact that AOP focuses on software development rather than addressing the issues of dynamic and wide-open environments, such as the ones considered in this paper. Finally, interoperability among agents of different applications is hard to be achieved, since this approach does not provide an adequate uncoupling of roles from agents.

6.3   Other Role-Based Approaches

In the Object-Oriented area, roles have been proposed to simplify the design phase of complex application. Kristensen and Østerbye propose the *roleification* as an

```
public class MyAgent
{ // intrinsic members of the class
private String question;

...

}

aspect Participant extends Role
{ ...
   // introduce extrinsic member to Agent
   introduce public void MyAgent.askSlides() {}
   // advise weaves impact extrinsic members
   advise public void MyAgent. askSlides()
   {// code of the asking action}
   ...

}

...
// Java code to instantiate MyAgent and Participant
// and to attach ag to the aspect
MyAgent ag = new MyAgent("Bob");
Participant participantAspect = new Participant();
participantAspect.addObject(ag);
// ag asks for slides
ag.askSlides();
...
```

Fig. 13. AOP approach

abstraction process that is similar to specialization and classification, but differs from them because addresses dynamic and temporary properties, which particularly assume importance in the relationships with other objects [18]. Similar to BRAIN, they recognize the advantages of exploiting roles in describing peculiar features that are not intrinsic in objects (agents in BRAIN) and are related to the interactions between them.

The importance of roles is evident starting from the first phases of software development. In describing patterns, Fowler says that roles are "some common behavior" of entities that "do not have the same behavior" [14], and points out that the isolation of such common behavior can simplify the design of applications.

E. Kendall well describes the importance of modeling roles for agent systems [17], and she exploits the AOP to concretely implement the concept of role in agent applications. Another interesting approach is AALAADIN [13], a meta-model to define models of organizations. It is based on three core concepts: *agent, group* and *role*. The ROPE project [1] addressing the collaboration issues and recognizes the importance of defining roles as first-class entities, which can be assumed dynamically by agents. Yu and Schmidt [22] exploit roles assigned to agents to manage workflow processes. They traditionally model a role as a collection of rights (activities an agent is permitted on a set of resources) and duties (activities an agent must perform). An interesting issue of this approach is that it aims to cover different phases of the application development, proposing a *role-based analysis* phase, an *agent-oriented design* phase, and an *agent-oriented implementation* phase.

A comparison between the above approaches and BRAIN shows that none of them exhibits the flexibility of BRAIN, nor provides support for all phases of the software development.

7   Conclusions and Future Work

This paper has presented a new approach to deal with interactions in the development of agent-based applications. Differently from traditional proposals in the area, interactions are modeled and implemented following an agent-oriented approach, i.e., all the peculiar features of agents are taken into account. Our approach enables separation of concerns, independence, and locality.

With regard to future work, we point out some research directions. An interesting issue to be faced is the exploitation of roles at runtime by agents; in particular, we are extending our infrastructure to enable agents to dynamically assume roles. Another interesting issue is security: appropriate mechanisms can be defined to control the requests for registration, to revoke roles by the administrator, and to specify a lease for each registration. Finally, even if the shown application example involves general interaction issues, other application areas must be assumed as test bed to evaluate the usability of our approach, such as agent negotiation and information retrieval.

Acknowledgments. Work supported by the NOKIA Research Center of Boston, by the Italian MIUR and CNR in the "IS-MANET, Infrastructures for Mobile ad-hoc Networks", and by the CNR within the project "Mobile software agents to enable access to multimedia services by mobile users and devices".

References

1. M. Becht, T. Gurzki, J. Klarmann, M. Muscholl, "ROPE: Role Oriented Programming Environment for Multiagent Systems", the Fourth IFCIS Conference on Cooperative Information Systems (CoopIS'99), Edinburgh, Scotland (1999)
2. The BRAIN framework, http://polaris.ing.unimo.it/MOON/BRAIN/index.html
3. G. Cabri, L. Leonardi, F. Zambonelli, "Mobile-Agent Coordination Models for Internet Applications", IEEE Computer, Vol. 33, No. 2, pp. 82–89 (2000)
4. G. Cabri, L. Leonardi, F. Zambonelli, "XRole: XML Roles for Agent Interaction", The 3rd International Symposium "From Agent Theory to Agent Implementation", at the 16th European Meeting on Cybernetics and Systems Research (EMCSR 2002), Wien (2002)
5. G. Cabri, L. Leonardi, F. Zambonelli, "Separation of Concerns in Agent Applications by Roles", the 2nd International Workshop on Aspect Oriented Programming for Distributed Computing Systems (AOPDCS 2002), Wien (2002)
6. G. Cabri, L. Leonardi, F. Zambonelli, "Engineering Mobile Agent Applications via Context-dependent Coordination", IEEE Transactions on Software Engineering, Vol. 28, No. 11, pp. 1040–1056 (2002)
7. G. Cabri, L. Leonardi, F. Zambonelli, "Modeling Role-based Interactions for Agents", The Workshop on Agent-oriented methodologies, at the 17th Annual ACM Conference on Object-Oriented Programming, Systems, Languages, and Applications (OOPSLA 2002), Seattle, Washington, USA (2002)

8. G. Cabri, L. Leonardi, F. Zambonelli, "Implementing Role-based Interactions for Internet Agents", The 2003 International Symposium on Applications and the Internet (SAINT 2003), Orlando, Florida, USA (2003)
9. Communications of the ACM, Special Issue on Aspect Oriented Programming, Vol. 33, No. 10 (2001)
10. Y. Demazeau, A.C. Rocha Costa, "Populations and Organizations in Open Multi-Agent Systems", the 1st National Symposium on Parallel and Distributed Artificial Intelligence (1996)
11. B. Demsky, M. Rinard, "Role-Based Exploration of Object-Oriented Programs", the International Conference on Software Engineering 2002, Orlando, Florida, USA (2002)
12. P. Domel, A. Lingnau, O. Drobnik, "Mobile Agent Interaction in Heterogeneous Environment", the 1st International Workshop on Mobile Agents, Lecture Notes in Computer Science, Springer-Verlag (D), No. 1219, pp. 136–148 (1997)
13. J. Ferber, O. Gutknecht, "A meta-model for the analysis and design of organizations in multi-agent systems", the 3rd International Conference on Multi-Agent Systems (1998)
14. M. Fowler, "Dealing with Roles", http://martinfowler.com/apsupp/roles.pdf (1997)
15. Jade home page, http://jade.cselt.it/
16. N. R. Jennings, "An agent-based approach for building complex software systems", Comm. of the ACM, Vol. 44, No. 4, pp. 35–41 (2001)
17. E. Kendall, "Role Modelling for Agent Systems Analysis, Design and Implementation", IEEE Concurrency, Vol. 8, No. 2, pp. 34–41 (2000)
18. B. B. Kristensen, K, Østerbye, "Roles: Conceptual Abstraction Theory & Practical Language Issues", Special Issue of Theory and Practice of Object Systems on Subjectivity in Object-Oriented Systems, Vol. 2, No. 3, pp. 143–160 (1996)
19. J. Lind, "Specifying Agent Interaction Protocols with Standard UML", the 2nd International Workshop on Agent Oriented Software Engineering (AOSE), Montreal (C) (2001)
20. J. Lind, "Patterns in Agent-Oriented Software Engineering", the 3rd International Workshop on Agent Oriented Software Engineering, Bologna (I) (2002)
21. M. Wooldridge, N. R. Jennings, and D. Kinny, "The Gaia Methodology for Agent-Oriented Analysis and Design", Journal of Autonomous Agents and Multi-Agent Systems, Vol. 3, No. 3, pp. 285–312 (2000)
22. L. Yu, B.F. Schmid, "A conceptual framework for agent-oriented and role-based workflow modelling", the 1st International Workshop on Agent-Oriented Information Systems, Heidelberg (1999)

Profiling and Matchmaking Strategies in Support of Opportunistic Collaboration

Adriana Vivacqua[1], Melfry Moreno[1], and Jano de Souza[1,2]

[1]COPPE/UFRJ – Graduate School of Engineering
[2]Institute of Mathematics
Federal University of Rio de Janeiro
PO Box 68511, Zip Code 21941-972, Rio de Janeiro, RJ, Brazil
{avivacqua, melfry, jano}@cos.ufrj.br

Abstract. With the recent advances in communications technologies and decentralization of work practices, there has been an increase in distributed, remote, computerized work environments. In most systems, individuals work from their personal computer terminals, unaware of their peers. With the change from a physical to a virtual environment, opportunities for collaboration often go unnoticed. In this paper, we focus on how to bring unplanned collaboration about. We present an agent framework to encourage and support unplanned cooperation between people. Agents build user profiles through analysis of their documents and work environment and match them according to their interests, activities and opportunities for collaboration. By matching users' work contexts, needs and resources, we expect to uncover opportunities for collaboration, filter down the information to be provided and determine the moment and recipients of the information. The notification of these opportunities should lead to more frequent collaboration between users. Resource sharing is facilitated in the hopes of stimulating collaboration.

1   Introduction

With recent advances in communications technologies and the widespread adoption of computers by organizations and individuals, new work practices have emerged. It has become more common to encounter individuals working at their computers and remotely collaborating with others. A tendency towards the decentralization of work has also gained strength, as teams come together temporarily to work on projects. As more organizations adopt cooperative work tools, individuals are led to the establishment of remote collaborations and working together in virtual environments.

In these environments, certain opportunities for interaction are lost: informal hallway conversations and impromptu suggestions that may influence one's line of thought or work are no longer present. At the computer, a person's environmental awareness is seriously limited, with the absence of visual, aural and environmental information constituting a major setback. Not only that, but computer-mediated interactions are inevitably poorer that face-to-face interactions. It's not as easy to get

R. Meersman et al. (Eds.): CoopIS/DOA/ODBASE 2003, LNCS 2888, pp. 162–177, 2003.
© Springer-Verlag Berlin Heidelberg 2003

to know and trust someone in the virtual world, or to casually bump into someone you know and might be able to collaborate with.

Instant messaging tools have started changing that somewhat: they provide a means for people to be aware of others they know who are online at the moment and a quick way to contact them if necessary. However, that still requires that users establish the need for communication and actively decide to initiate contact. We believe more can be done to jump start collaboration. Many opportunities for cooperation are lost due to the lack of awareness that they even exist. Individuals don't know of others skills, interests, availability or willingness to participate on a project. User profiling, competence, interest and expertise management and context awareness, are techniques we employ to assist in establishing cooperation opportunities and induce cooperative work. By making users aware of each other, they can better leverage each other's skills, competencies and available time.

Furthermore, individuals very often log on to messaging systems in "invisible mode", so that no one will know they are there or try to contact them. That is an attempt to reduce unwanted conversations, which tend to start when one is caught online (in "available mode"). That points to the fact that messages can be disruptive in a work environment: to a large extent, information about the activities of others is irrelevant in the current working context and only hinders work [33]. This indicates a need for careful control of information flow, to minimize disruption.

Just-in-time information delivery is the study of how to provide information when it is needed, to whoever needs it and in such as way as to not disrupt the individual's work. The "what, when, how and who" questions have grown in importance along with the volume of information available. To address these issues, we employ profiling and matchmaking techniques to filter down the information to be provided and determine the moment and recipients of the information.

In this paper we present Cumbia, an agent-based framework to support awareness and discovery of potential collaboration opportunities. We introduce some background and related work in section 2, move on to describe the CUMBIA framework in section 3, and wrap up in section 4.

2   Background and Related Work

Computer Supported Cooperative Work, or CSCW for short, is a multidisciplinary research area that focuses on effective methods for sharing information and coordinating activities. CSCW systems are often categorized according to the time/location matrix, as found in [16] (synchronous/asynchronous vs. Centralized/distributed). These may be redefined and reorganized to take into account different kinds of cooperative work and the complexity of the processes they involve that need to be supported [6]:

- Ad-hoc cooperative work: brainstorming, cooperative learning, informal meetings, design work, etc. Process modeling support is implemented through awareness triggers.

- Predefined/strict workflow: office automation style systems, represented by simple document/process flow. Examples of such systems are Lotus Notes [28], Active Mail [15] and MAFIA [24].
- Coordinated workflow: as found in traditional centralized software maintenance work consisting of checkout, data processing, check-in, merging, etc. There are several prototypes for systems that support coordinated workflow: EPOS [7], MARVEL [3] and APEL [8].
- Cooperative workflow: decentralized software development and maintenance work conducted in distributed organizations or across organizations. Example of a system supporting distributed organizations and processes is Oz [3].

We are currently looking at supporting ad-hoc cooperative work, such as what happens in unstructured or loosely structured work environments. In these cases, work groups and teams are highly reconfigurable and are not necessarily predefined from the start of the project. The academic environment is one such example: research teams may be engaged in different lines of work and specialists may join the groups and contribute at different points. They may work as a temporary addition to the group (with a the objective of solving a particular problem, for instance) or they may become permanently involved with the project as a whole.

2.1   Awareness Systems

Awareness has received a lot of attention among CSCW researchers in the past few years. Researchers have started to realize the importance of being aware of collaborators in a group work environment. Initially, the focus was on providing video and audio to support cooperation and awareness, but other tools and methods have appeared since.

Several works deal with video interfaces and the use of video to support personal awareness and informal interactions. For instance, CRUISER [30] is a virtual environment that uses audio and video channels to support the dynamic processes of informal social interaction (social browsing). VideoWindow [14] is a teleconferencing system that connects two coffee lounges in different (physically separated) offices. Portholes [9] and Polyscope [5] are media spaces to support shared awareness that can lead to informal interactions.

Some proposals involve motivation, incentives and support for cooperation, such as Pinheiro et al. [29]. They propose a framework to provide past event awareness, where users are informed of past occurrences, results and work history of each other (which includes evolution of shared data, members' actions and decisions, etc.), so as to better collaborate in the present. Prospect awareness systems that allow individuals to envision the potential benefits of collaboration have been proposed, in an attempt to motivate collaboration [17].

Other research focuses on document- or task-based awareness and on providing information to users about who is working on the same document or performing similar tasks at a given moment [18, 25, 26, 27]. Piazza [18], for example, provides awareness information about others who are working on similar tasks when using their computers, exposing an opportunity for interaction or cooperation. It supports intentional contacts and planned meetings as well. The PIÑAS [26, 27] platform provides potential and actual collaboration spaces, as well as services tailored to support collaborative writing on the Web. These are clear attempts at matching individuals at the moment they share a work context. It is important to take the current context into account, as any cooperation will most likely happen within that context. Many recent papers address awareness in mobile computing environments, where location awareness is a central issue for collaboration [2, 13, 22].

The most basic form of awareness, personal awareness, is currently provided by messenger systems (such as Yahoo Messenger, MSN Messenger, AOL Instant Messenger, etc.). A more specialized collaborative tool, GROOVE[1] introduces concept of "shared spaces" to increase the scope of personal awareness. In GROOVE'S shared spaces, users can be aware of what others in that space are doing and on what spaces' objects they are working.

The first step towards successful collaboration is becoming aware of the opportunity to collaborate. We therefore focus on potential collaboration awareness, and provide users' with information on opportunities for collaboration [27] given their current work contexts.

2.2   Unplanned Interactions

A useful classification of the different types of interaction found in work environments is presented by Kraut [23]: Scheduled: conversations previously scheduled or arranged; Intended: the initiator sets out specifically to visit another party; Opportunistic: the initiator had planned to talk to other participants at some point and took advantage of a chance encounter to do so; Spontaneous: a spontaneous interaction in which the initiator had not planned to talk with other participants.

Kraut also points out that the majority of conversations are informal in nature and that these are usually short and build upon previous discussions. Conversations occur because one person happens to be close to another at a time when one wants to ask for or provide information. Studies show that these types of informal interactions play a central role in helping workers learn, understand, adapt and apply formal procedures and processes [19]. Few systems have focused on support for opportunistic and spontaneous interactions.

According to Esborjörnsson and Östergren [13], spontaneous interactions are the actions that take place when human and/or computational participants coincide temporarily at a location and interoperate to satisfy immediate needs. A similar viewpoint is adopted in [2], where co-location is central to spontaneous collaboration. Both works deal with mobile computing environments, but provide useful insight for the implementation of virtual work environments, because they identify important factors for the establishment of interactions. Esborjörnsson and Östergren also point out that users are usually involved in several simultaneous activities, which means that great care must be taken when deciding on the composition of information [13].

Information about knowledge, physical and cognitive skills, distance and psychosocial characteristics like trust and attitudes are important to the establishment of a successful collaboration [2]. According to Aldunate, Nussbaum and González, similarity in activity preferences, basic values, interests, hobbies, culture, common

---

[1] http://www.groove.net

history and trust on the other person are some of the most important predictors of successful contact. Individuals possess mental models of themselves and of others and the closer the models, the more likely they will be to have successful interactions with each other.

Matsuura et al. [25] introduce the concept of virtual proximity, which is defined as situations in which users access the same data or users invoke the same application in the virtual environment. We take a similar approach, using an individual's current work context (what one is currently working on) to inform the search for others with whom it might be interesting to collaborate with.

2.3   Agent-Based Systems

Intelligent agents are entities that perceive its environment through sensors and act upon it [31]. Agent-oriented techniques are being increasingly used in a range of telecommunication, commercial, and industrial applications, as developers and designers realize its potential [20]. Agents are especially suited to the construction of complex, peer-to-peer systems, because they are lightweight and permit parallelization and easy reconfiguration of the system.

It is currently believed that Multi-Agent Systems (MAS) are a better way to model and support distributed, open-ended systems and environments. A MAS is a loosely-coupled network of problem solvers (agents) that work together to solve a given problem [35].

CSCW systems are complex distributed systems and there are many good arguments for the application of an agent-oriented approach for software engineering to deal with this class of systems [20] (for instance, agent-oriented decomposition to handle problem space magnitude and agent-oriented philosophy for modeling and managing organizational relationship). Agents have been used in groupware for a long time due to their social abilities [4]. A recent survey of the application of agents in groupware and CSCW can be found in [10, 34]. NEEM [11], Personal Assistant [12] and COLLABORATOR [4] are some examples of agent approaches used in developing collaborative tools. AwServer, CScheduler and E_Places are good examples of agent-based awareness work [1].

3   The CUMBIA Framework

We have created an agent-supported peer-to-peer architecture where each user has a cluster of agents to assist with knowledge management and collaboration tasks. Agents are in charge of identifying potential cooperation situations and trying to making these come to fruition by providing relevant information in a timely manner. The CUMBIA framework is detailed in the following sections.

3.1   Agent Architecture

Each user has its own "agency" (a group of agent service teams) to assist with knowledge management and cooperation tasks.   There are four agent service teams that interact to perform specific tasks: User Interface Services, Collaboration Services, Awareness & Matchmaking Services and Knowledge Management Services, as shown in Figure 1. Agent service teams and main functionalities are:

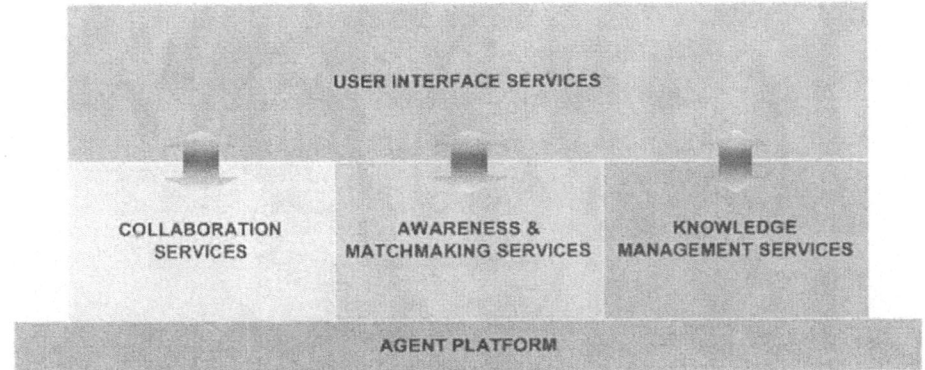

Fig. 1. Agent Architecture

- User Interface Services: information display and allowing the user to specify parameters and information to the other agent teams.
- Collaboration Services: allow for the easy and quick establishment of contact when the possibility for collaboration arises and provide tools for cooperation (forums, messaging, etc.)
- Awareness and Matchmaking Services: search for other users with whom it might be interesting to establish contact, contact other agents for their users' profiles and work contexts, compare user profiles to current context and work environment.
- Knowledge Management Services: manage user's personal data, build initial profiles based upon this data and keep track of document usage, searches, ongoing collaborations and current research.

We created the workspace concept (similar to the multiple desktops found on Linux) to help determine a user's work context. A workspace is a user created work environment: a user can save all the relevant documents, applications, contacts, links, etc. in a workspace when working on a given topic. At any given moment, a user will be working in one of his or her workspaces. A user can easily switch between workspaces, changing work contexts.

In reality, a workspace is only a collection of links, not a representation of physical storage, but a way to determine what resources belong together: documents and links may be saved anywhere on the user's hard disk and be associated with one or more workspaces as shown in Fig. 2. When a user switches to a different context, those documents will be the ones in the most frequent list and the bookmarks saved in that workspace will be the ones first displayed (the user can always have the system "show all" in case he/she wants to retrieve an item from other workspaces).

This effectively creates context-sensitive bookmarks, documents and work environment. Its is important to note that only one workspace can be active at any given time, although users can allocate items to different workspaces by dropping them into the workspace icons.

Fig. 2. Workspace concept

3.2   Knowledge Management Services

The knowledge management agent service team provides profiling functionality to the system. Basic units in the profile are projects and interests, which are interrelated. Part of the profile information has to be explicitly provided (mostly links or interrelations between items), and another part is automatically inferred. Users always have the last say on their profiles, being able to correct the information and determine which information can be made public and which is to remain private. In our environment, we consider that a person is always working within a workspace. Our basic context units are workspace definitions. These contain projects, documents, contacts, etc.

Users' projects are related to documents, people, collaborations and research, but are inherent to each user. So, a cooperative project almost certainly will have two or more different project definitions associated with it, one for each team member. This is in accordance with the fact that individuals have personal views of reality and organize their work accordingly. It is useful, of course, to keep track of the correspondence between individual projects that represent the same group endeavor (this entails keeping track of the different aliases a project might have). Projects are usually related to only one workspace, although it is conceivable that a user may be working on two projects at the same time, in one workspace or may have divided a project into more than one workspace.

Profiling Agents keep track of the following information:

- Contact Information: information necessary for another person, to contact the user: Name, Title, Email, Phone, etc.
- Areas of Interest: general areas in which the user has some interest. These may be automatically or manually setup, and will be ranked by interest and activity level. Areas of interest may be related to projects, people, documents and histories.
- Projects: projects the user is involved with. The user creates these project definitions to help with information organization. Projects are classified according to their activity status: Past (project is finished), Present (project is being worked on at the moment) and Future (these are future projects the user intends to work on at some point). Projects may have deadlines associated with them, which can help prioritize agents' work. All other information may be related or not to projects. Projects may be related to areas of interest, people, documents and histories. Project information is manually provided.
- People: a user's contact list, classified into different categories, such as personal or work contacts, previous, current or potential collaborators, researchers, etc. Some information is inferred from email FROM, TO and CC lists. Contacts are linked to projects in the context of collaborations in progress and are linked to areas of interest when the users have similar interests.
- History: agents track pages the user accesses when navigating the Internet. Histories may also be related to projects and interests. Work activity is also logged to create project and collaboration histories that may inform future interactions.

Rating mechanisms will be put in place so that users can rate other users or resources (sites or documents) according to the relevance to the work or project in progress or to an area of interest, providing more information the system can use.

3.2.1   Batch profiling. When first setting up the environment, agents build initial profiles by scanning all available information as provided by the user. The first step is the processing of textual documents, then web histories and contact networks. The following processes are undertaken:

- Processing textual documents: documents are processed using a text-processing algorithm. Keywords are extracted from each document and relations to the documents are established. Initially, we use TFIDF [32], a well-known keyword extraction algorithm, but we plan on testing other algorithms in the near future.
- Processing bookmarked websites: websites from the user's bookmark lists are visited and processed for keywords as well. Relations are built between the links and the keywords.
- Extraction of web histories: websites visited are extracted from the user's web history and searches are separated from site visits. Multiple sites visits are counted and sites are revisited and processed as above. Keywords are extracted from the searches.

- Extraction of contact networks: email archives are processed, with keywords being extracted from the bodies and contacts from the TO, FROM and CC fields. Contact lists from email and messenger applications are also processed and added to the "master contact list".

Items not classified as belonging to any one workspace are left in a generic workspace, from which they can be retrieved later. This workspace contains documents, links and contacts that haven't yet been assigned their workspaces. Periodically, agents run keyword matches on the generic workspace items and suggest workspace assignments for the unassigned documents. These may or may not be accepted by the user.

3.2.2   Real-time profiling.

When the user is at work, his or her behaviors can be observed to furnish some extra information. As the user works, agents observe his or her behavior and process documents in the same manner as when they are batch processed. The following additional information is extracted from the users' behavior:

- Time spent on documents: total time spent on a document is measured
- Access frequency: the system keeps track of how many times the document has been accessed, and when the last access was.
- Access type: the system logs what type of access was made to each document. Possible access types are read (reading the document), write (writing some text), forward (reading and sending it to others) and publish (writing and sending it out to be read by others).

This information can be used to assign weights to certain documents (to represent relevance or importance in that workspace) that can help improve the matchmaking process. We are currently verifying how these variables factor into the process. The following inferences can be made:

- Needs: information needs are extracted from search keywords and documents or references downloaded, bookmarked or saved. These will then be used to search other users' workspaces for relevant information that can be exchanged.
- Resource use: resources are links and documents a user has at his or her disposal. These can be easily shared with other users. Frequency and length of access (vs. document length) determine how important that document is in that context (is it something that was read over and over or referred to several times? Was it printed?) Distribution also denotes importance or relevance: if a user thought the document was good enough to send it to others, that should also be noted, and the links to the contacts should be established.
- Knowledge: documents written by a user define his or her knowledge and documents read knowledge the user is in the process of acquiring (here the length and frequency of access measurements help determine how well the document was studied).

All profile information is saved in a Knowledge Base. The system logs message exchanges (text, email, discussion) and these are linked to workspaces and active projects, forming a personal work history. This history will inform future discussions, assist users in establishing common understanding, and allow users to "pick up from where they left off" when engaging in new interactions. In addition, it establishes patterns of cooperation, helping with the identification of which users have been cooperative in the past (to possibly favor cooperating with these in the future) and which ones have consistently avoided interaction with the user (to possibly avoid these in the future).

User profiling has been largely explored before, and several sources of information have been identified that can be used to build user profiles. Email, bookmarks, source code and publications read and written are some of them. In many approaches, documents are analyzed for their text content and keywords are extracted. We take an existing approach and build on that for profile construction. We run a keyword extraction algorithm (Term Frequency Inverse Document Frequency - TFIDF) [32] on the user's documents to generate weighted keyword lists. This method has been extensively used with good results, so we expect it will work well in this case as well. We will be testing different algorithms in the near future.

We then rate each document according to its importance to the user. Document rating is based on number of accesses, length of access, type of access (read, write, print), and distribution (whether it was sent to someone else or not), as described above. Thus, documents in users' profiles are ranked by popularity, and keyword importance is calculated accordingly. Links between documents and projects and workspaces are used to determine keyword lists for projects and workspaces. These keyword lists are then used in matchmaking.

3.3 Awareness and Matchmaking Services

Having built user profiles, matches need to be made. Several studies exist in the matchmaking field, especially in relation to recommendation systems. We identify opportunities for collaboration by matching a user's current context (as determined by the workspace) with other users who might have related interests or work.

An opportunity for collaboration is determined by users' contexts: when two users' contexts are similar or related, an opportunity for collaboration might exist. Given the information needs of each user, we look for documents that match those needs in other users' environments. A search, is a clear indicator of a "time of need", therefore the system looks for matches in other users' workspaces whenever a search is performed (the search performed by the user proceeds unencumbered).

The identification of an opportunity for collaboration is a 3-step process:
1. Given the workspace a user is currently working on, look for other users currently in similar workspaces. Look for active workspaces initially. If none are found, look for inactive workspaces as well.
2. Within those found, look for documents in their workspaces that are similar to the document currently being worked on (and that aren't present in the workspace). If searches are being performed, keywords being used for searching can be used to search other users' workspaces. Check to verify if there is a possibility for reciprocity in the exchange.
3. Ask the document owner whether the documents found can be sent and furnish information on the user who will be receiving it. If owner authorizes sending the documents, ask receiver whether he or she wants to

receive them. If no documents are found, inform both users of a potential collaborative opportunity and of similarity in contexts.

This process begins by finding individuals in similar contexts (it is always better not to have the user change contexts) and then finding resources these users should share. Resource exchange is the most direct way of initiating collaboration, since it places few demands on either user. Once the link has been established, users can be directed to collaborate synchronously and exchange thoughts and ideas regarding each other's work.

Matches are made through keyword similarity calculation. Every document has an associated weighted keyword list, as provided by the TFIDF algorithm. These are compared to determine similarity between items and find possible matches.

Matching can be done "online" or "offline": online matching occurs when the user is working, inserted in a context and the system searches for potential collaboration opportunities in real time. Offline matching runs in the background to find users whose workspaces or documents may be related to projects or areas of interest the user is involved in. This is meant to speed up searches: agents independently pre-search the space to build and store simplified models of other users, which are then used to make initial matches and search in more detail for potential collaboration matches.

3.4   Collaboration Services

When an opportunity for collaboration comes up, a user is immediately notified. Opportunities are time sensitive, and the user should be informed of the potential for reciprocity (if any) and should be given information on the other user that includes past partnerships and cooperative behavior. Other useful information, especially for unknown users is to try and find a common link between the two individuals.

After the identification of collaboration opportunity, an individual may become an incidental or an active collaborator in another user's projects. Incidental collaborators provide occasional suggestions and occasionally attend meetings. Active collaborators are inserted in the project and have to deal with schedules and deadlines. It's important to know each participant's status and whether any tasks are dependent on him or her. Project management capabilities are useful in assisting with active collaborations.

The initiation of collaboration should be effortless, so as to create as little overhead to the user as possible. Whenever agents detect some information or document one user has might be useful to another user, they automatically offer to send that user that information, asking only for permission from the owner. In this fashion, a user doesn't have to worry about finding adequate documents, histories or appropriate information to be sent to others. The users may choose to engage in longer interaction, by initiating a chat or message exchange.

All standard collaboration support tools (discussion lists, messaging systems, shared whiteboards, file sharing mechanisms and email) are provided in the system. Most of these exist as modular solutions, which can be plugged in. We concentrate on helping the establishment of first contact and the initiation of collaboration rather than developing new tools. We will progressively add tools and services to the system as they become necessary.

3.5   User Interface Services

User interface agents perform interface related functions, provide information to the users and request information from them. UI agents mediate requests between agents and users. Our basic interface displays little information, so as not to disrupt the user. However, most information is easily accessible with a mouse click or rollover.

Workspaces are accessed and managed through the Cumbia Personal Toolbar. The Cumbia Personal Toolbar is a toolbar that sits on a user's desktop, where users can visualize their available workspaces and switch between them, view their contact list, view associated keywords, links, searches and document lists. Every workspace has a resource briefcase where documents and links are stored, plus an address book with contacts related to the workspace and a document briefcase for documents being edited. There is a message bar for system and other user's messages and two collaboration indicators that flash when an opportunity for collaboration is found: one for incoming collaborations (another user can add to your work) and another for outgoing collaborations (you can contribute to another user's work). There is also a workspace viewer, so that users can easily switch between workspaces. Keyword lists that describe the workspaces can be viewed by rolling the mouse over the icons. Users can add to or modify the workspace definitions at will. Workspaces also have a history log.

Initial definitions and assignments must be made by hand (the user has to drag and drop documents into their workspaces), but afterwards documents are associated with the current workspace as the user works on them. Searches will be logged as part of the current workspace, as will documents being written or downloaded and pages bookmarked. A user can always associate an item with another workspace by dropping it into that workspace. If the item is already saved in the current workspace, the system asks whether it should be moved or copied to the other one. In future versions, agents will be able to decide which are the appropriate ways of displaying information when they receive it and the proper time to display it, thus addressing the problems of what, how and when (given that who is fixed). Relevant work has been done in [1], which we will use and build upon in our system. For the moment, opportunities are displayed as small flashing icons, much in the fashion of current messenger systems. The user has the choice of whether or not to click on the icons, receiving more information on the potential cooperation.

4   Application Scenario

There are three basic types of work environments: structured, loosely structured (or semi-structured) and unstructured. In structured work environments, there is a strict plan that should be followed, a meeting agenda or workflow. In loosely structured ones, there is some structure but it is loose and adaptable, only major outline and breakpoints are in place and it is up to the participants to fill in the blanks, creating their own structure as necessary. In unstructured work environments, there is hardly any structure and what is there is highly changeable: who runs what and how, tasks to be accomplished and steps to that end all depend on the moment and on who's present. Everything is configurable by the participants.

Linux is possibly the most obvious example of unstructured cooperation, as is the whole Open Source initiative. Several studies exist regarding the open source community and how and why it works. We do not presume that this model will work in all environments, but we believe it is important to attempt to identify characteristics that can be replicated in other projects. In the Apache project, for instance, mechanisms were put in place to help with software development, discussion and version control and most issues were resolved through voting.

We are implementing a prototype for an academic knowledge management system. Academic work environments are usually very loosely structured and several opportunities for spontaneous collaboration exist. Groups form as common interests appear and individuals come together to work for a period of time (the duration of a project) and disband later (but ties remain, as does the possibility of further collaboration). Cooperation is often externally triggered as, for instance, with the appearance of a new funding opportunity. External funding agencies provide guidelines for projects (among which there is usually the inclusion of a certain number of qualified specialists): in this case it becomes important to identify and bring together a group of interested, qualified people to form groups and write project proposals to take advantage of the opportunities. This seems like an appropriate application domain, since most of the time, students and academics don't mind sharing resources with each other or entering into collaboration.

We chose JADE (Java Agent Development Framework)[2] to develop our agents. JADE is a software framework fully implemented in Java language. It simplifies the implementation of multi-agent systems through a middle-ware that complies with the FIPA specifications and through a set of tools that supports the debugging and deployment phase. The agent platform can be distributed across machines (which do not need to share the same OS) and the configuration can be controlled via a remote GUI. The configuration can be changed at run-time by moving agents from one machine to another one, as and when required.

JESS[3] is used for inference making, specifically deciding when and how information will be shown to the user. Jess was originally inspired by the CLIPS[4] expert system shell, but has grown into a complete, distinct, dynamic environment of its own. Using Jess, we can build Java software that has the capacity to "reason" using knowledge supplied in the form of declarative rules. Jess is small, light, and one of the fastest rule engines available. The system is currently under implementation, and we expect to initiate testing soon.

5   Conclusion and Further Work

There are six basic functions of informal communication [19]: tracking people, taking or leaving messages, making meeting arrangements, delivering documents, giving or

---

[2] http://sharon.cselt.it/projects/jade/

[3] http://herzberg.ca.sandia.gov/jess/

[4] http://www.ghg.net/clips/CLIPS.html

getting help and reporting progress and news. Most of these can be automated by computers in a cooperative work environment, reducing the need for informal communications. However, informal communication is central to the establishment of a community and strengthening of ties between members. Spontaneous, unplanned interactions are much less frequent in computer based cooperative work environments, where each user works at one station than in offices where users are in physical proximity. We should not be looking to reduce informal communication, we should be trying to increase it.

We have presented an agent-based architecture to support and encourage spontaneous interactions in virtual environments. The first step towards this is identifying potential collaboration situations and making the act of collaboration as effortless as possible. CSCW researchers, recognizing the importance of awareness information, have been striving to provide it in their systems. However, there has been little or no focus as to why it is provided. By focusing on the reasons for providing awareness information, we expect to reduce information flow and create effective mechanisms to encourage collaboration. The workspace metaphor is particularly useful because it helps establish a context for work while assisting the user in the organization of his or her resources.

Two basic problems are always associated with the provision of awareness information: privacy violations and user disruption. Users' privacy may be violated by making details of their activities available that should have been kept private. Every piece of information about a user that is made available to others is a potential privacy violation. Besides, users may be disrupted from their work because unneeded information about others distracts them. For an awareness system to be effectively used, users must trust it. They should be able to understand its limits and capabilities and feel confident that they know what information of their actions can be observed [21]. In our system, the user is allowed to determine what information will be made public, becoming available for awareness purposes. Our system also takes the user's context into account: we provide information that is relevant to the user at the moment, so as to not worsen the problem of information overload or disrupt the user's flow of work or line of thought.

Profiles contain a wealth of information so we can test different matching techniques and variables to determine which work best. There is still much work to be done, namely in the areas of context inference and rule building. We are implementing the first prototype and hope to have some initial results soon. We will be testing and improving on matching and profiling methods as the project evolves.

References

1. Alarcón, R. and Fuller, D. Intelligent Awareness in Support of Collaborative Virtual Work Groups. In: Haake, J. M. and Pino, J. A. (Eds.) CRIWG 2002, LNCS 2440, pp. 147–167, Springer-Verlag, 2002
2. Aldunate, R. Nussbaum, M. and González, R. An Agent Based Middleware for supporting Spontaneous Collaboration among Co-Located, Mobile and not Necessarily Known People. Workshop on Ad hoc Communications and Collaboration in Ubiquitous Computing Environments, CSCW 2002, New Orleans, USA, November 2002.

3. Ben-Shaul, I. and Kaiser, G. A paradigm for decentralized process modeling. Kluwer Academic Publishers, Boston/Dordrecht/London, 1995.
4. Bergenti, F., Garijo, M., Poggi, A., Somacher, M. and Velasco J.R. Enhancing Collaborative Work through Agents. VIII Convegno dell'Associazione Italiana per l'Intelligenza Artificiale, 2002.
5. Bourning, A. and Travers, M. Two approaches to casual Interaction on Computer and Video Networks. Proceedings of International Networking Conference, 1991.
6. C. Liu and R. Conradi. Process View of CSCW. In Proc. of ISFST98, Ocon Technology Application, page 12, Bremen, Germany, 15–17 September 1998. InternationalWorkshop on Intelligent Agents in Information and Process Management.
7. Conradi, R., Jaccheri, M.L, and Mazzi, C. Design, Use and Implementation of SPELL, a language for Software Process Modeling and Evolution. In Proc. Second European Workshop on Software.
8. Dami, S., Estublier,J. and Amiour, M. APEL: A Graphical Yet Executable Formalism for Process Modeling. In Process Technology edited by E. Nitto and Alfonso Fuggetta, pages 61–96, Politecnico di Milano and CEFRIEL, 1998. Kluwer Academic Publishers.
9. Dourish, P. and Bly, S. Portholes: Supporting Awareness in distributed Work Group. Proceedings CHI, 1992.
10. Ellis, C.A. e Wainer, J. Groupware and Computer Supported Cooperative Work. In Weiss, G. (Ed.) Multiagent, Systems, MIT Press, 1999.
11. Ellis, C.A., Barthelmess, P., Quan, B. e Wainer, J. NEEM: An Agent Based Meeting Augmentation System. Technical Report CU-CS-937-02, University of Colorado at Boulder, Computer Science Department, 2002.
12. Enembreck, F. and Barthès, J. P. Personal Assistant to Improve CSCW. Proceedings of the 7th International CSCWD, Rio de Janeiro, 2002, pp 329–335.
13. Esborjörnsson, M. and Östergren, M. Issues of Spontaneous Collaboration and Mobility. Workshop on Supporting Spontaneous Interaction in Ubiquitous Computing Settings, UBICOMP'02, Göteberg, Sweden, 2002
14. Fish, R. S., Kraut R. E. and Chalfonte, B. L. The VideoWindow System in Informal Communications. Proceedings CSCW, 1990.
15. Goldberg, Y., Safran, M., Silverman, W. and Shapiro, E. Active Mail: A Framework for Integrated Groupware Applications. In D. Coleman, editor, Groupware '92, pages 222–224. Morgan Kaufmann Publishers, 1992.
16. Grudin, J. Computer-Supported Cooperative Work: History and Focus. In IEEE Computer, number 5 in 27, pages 19–26, 1994.
17. Hoffman, M and Herrmann, T. Prospect Awareness – Envisioning the Benefits of Collaborative Work. Available online at: http://iundg.informatik.uni-dortmund.de/iug-home/people/MH/ProspectAwareness/PAhome.html
18. Isaacs, E.A., Tang, J.C. and Morris, T. Piazza: A desktop Environment Supporting Impromtu and Planned Interactions. Proceedings of CSCW'96, Cambridge, MA, 1996
19. Isaacs, E.A., Whittaker, S., Frohlich, D. and O'Connail, B. Informal Communication Re-Examined: New Fuctions for Video in Supporting Opportunistic Encounters. In K. Finn, A. Sellen and S. Wilbur (Eds.), Video Mediated Communication, Mahwah, NJ: Lawrence Erlbaum
20. Jennings, N.R. An Agent-Based Approach for Building Complex Software Systems. Communications of the ACM, April 2001/Vol. 44, No. 4
21. Kanerva, A., Koskinen, L. and Pitkäniemi, T. Awareness Support in Virtual Collaborative Systems. University of Helsinki, Department of Psychology and Teamware Group. 2000.
22. Kortuen, G., Gellersen, H.W., Billinghurst, M. Mobile Ad Hoc Collaboration. Proceedings of CHI 2002, April 2002, Minneapolis, USA

23. Kraut, R., Fish, R., Root, B., and Chalfonte, B. Informal communication in organizations: Form, function and technology. In S. Oskamp and S. Spacapan (Eds.), People's reactions to technology in factories, offices and aerospace, The Claremont Symposium on Applied Social Psychology, Sage Publications, 1990. pp. 145–199.
24. Lutz, E., Retzow, H.K. and Hoernig, K. MAFIA – An Active Mail-Filter-Agent for an Intelligent Document Processing Support. In S. Gibbs and A.A. Verrijn-Stuart, editors, IFIP, North-Holland, 1990. Elsevier Science Publishers B.V.
25. Matsuura, N., Fujino, G., Okada, K. and Matsushita, Y. An Approach to Encounters and Interaction in a Virtual Environment. Proceedings of the 1993 ACM Conference on Computer Science, Indianapolis, Indiana, United States, 1993.
26. Morán, A. L., Decouchant, D., Favela, J., Martínez-Enríquez, A. M., González-Beltrán, B. and Mendoza, S. PIÑAS: Supporting a Community of Authors on the Web. Proceedings of Fourth International Conference on Distributed Communities on the Web, Sydney, Australia, April 2002.
27. Morán, A. L., Favela, J., Martínez-Enríquez, A. M. and Decouchant, D. Before Getting There: Potential and Actual Collaboration. In: Haake, J. M. and Pino, J. A. (Eds.) CRIWG 2002, LNCS 2440, pp. 147–167, Spring-Verlag, 2002
28. Orlikowski, W.J. Learning from Notes: Organizational Issues in Groupware Implementation. In Proceedings of the Conference on Computer – Supported Cooperative Work, CSCW'92, pages 362–369, Toronto, Canada, 1992. The Association for Computer Machinery, ACM Press.
29. Pinheiro, M.K., Lima, J.V. and Borges, M.R.S. A Framework for Awareness Support in Groupware Systems. Proceedings of the 7th International Conference on Computer Supported Cooperative Work in Design – CSCWD'2002, Rio de Janeiro, Brazil, September 2002, pp. 13–18
30. Root, R. Design a Multi-Media Vehicle for Social Browsing. Proceedings CSCW, 1988.
31. Russell, S. and Norvig, P. Artificial Intelligence – A Modern Approach. Prentice Hall, Englewood Cliffs, NJ, 1995.
32. Salton, G and McGill, M.J. The SMART and SIRE Experimental Retrieval Systems. In Readings in Information Retrieval. Karen Jones and Peter Willet, eds. Morgan Kaufmann, San Francisco, 1997
33. Sohlenkamp, M. Supporting Group Awareness in Multi-User Environments through Perceptualization. GMD Research Series Report, No 6, 1999. Fachbereich Mathematik-Informatik der Universität – Gesamthochschule, Paderborn, 1998.
34. Wainer, J. and Ellis, C.A. Agents in Groupware Systems. Proceedings CRIWG, Búzios, RJ, Brasil, 1998.
35. Wang, A., Conradi, R., Liu, C. A Multi-Agent Architecture for Cooperative Software Engineering Proceedings of the Third International Conference on Autonomous Agents, 1999

A Strategic Approach for Business-IT Alignment in Health Information Systems

Richard Lenz and Klaus A. Kuhn

Institute of Medical Informatics Philipps-University Marburg
Bunsenstrasse 3   D-35037 Marburg, Germany
{lenzr,kuhn}@mailer.uni-marburg.de

Abstract. Health Information Systems (HIS) are required to flexibly support complex clinical processes involving multiple user groups at different locations throughout a healthcare organization. Healthcare processes, however, are subject to change. A "responsive IT infrastructure" is required as a basis for rapid and effective business-IT alignment. In this article we describe the conditions (available products and standards) under which a strategy for system evolution is to be defined. A strategy based on an application framework and an integrated CASE tool has been elaborated and established at the university hospital in Marburg. Based on XP (extreme programming) and participatory design the software engineering process has been adapted and embedded into a continuous management process in which IT projects are prioritized according to current business needs. The goal is to minimize project risk and to achieve a continuously evolving information system which is driven by the actual needs for process improvement.

1 Introduction

The importance of IT systems in healthcare has been increasingly recognized in recent years, in particular in the context of process support, quality improvement and medical error prevention (e. g. [1,2] etc.). A recent report of the German government stated that insufficient coordination, communication and documentation are among the most important factors contributing to medical errors [3], which is coherent with the results of international studies (e. g. [4,5]). Obviously, integration of healthcare applications both in healthcare facilities and in healthcare networks are core requirements to improve information logistics. Yet, IT projects, and particularly integration projects, continue to fail at a high rate [6,7]. One of the reasons for these failures is, that the healthcare processes are subject to change. Both internal causes (e. g. new diagnostic or therapeutic procedures, change of departmental structure) as well as external causes (e. g. introduction of new policies for hospital reimbursement like Diagnosis Related Groups (DRGs), economic pressure towards hospital mergers and healthcare integrated networks) enforce process changes and create a need to rapidly adapt Health Information Systems (HIS) to the new conditions. Moreover, Berg and Toussaint have pointed out that the organizational processes emerging during

R. Meersman et al. (Eds.): CoopIS/DOA/ODBASE 2003, LNCS 2888, pp. 178–195, 2003.
© Springer-Verlag Berlin Heidelberg 2003

information system deployment are highly unpredictable, and that information system's "requirements" will *necessarily* evolve in this process [8]. Consequently, a responsive IT infrastructure is required in order to be able to rapidly and adequately react to newly arising needs [9,10]. System evolution should thereby be driven by business needs and not by technology capabilities. But how does such a responsive IT architecture look like? How can we establish it with the standards and IT-applications which are available today?

We have developed a system evolution strategy which is based on commercially available products and standards. Continuous improvement is achieved primarily by incrementally adding document based clinical applications to an integrated core system. In addition, as a complementary approach, integration of heterogeneous applications according to established standards is still required, but it is limited to a manageable degree.

2 Background

The IT infrastructure of most healthcare facilities is characterized by a limited number of more or less loosely coupled application systems (3–30). Traditional core systems are Patient Data Management (PDM) providing ADT functionality (Admission, Discharge, and Transfer of patients), and administrative systems for accounting, and controlling. Departmental systems like Laboratory Information Systems (LIS) and Radiology Information Systems (RIS) are also in widespread use, and IT is increasingly being used to support clinical processes. In order to adequately support information flow, in particular order entry and result reporting, systems like LIS and RIS are to be integrated with clinical workstations. Imaging modalities like CT and MRT are also connected to information systems in order to support a seamless information flow. Picture Archiving and Communication Systems (PACS) are commonly used to store large amounts of medical images and the corresponding context information. A typical architecture is shown in Fig. 1.

2.1 Aspects of Integration

The components mentioned in this illustration only represent the most important functional units – many real world systems comprise much more components, e. g. often different systems are used as a clinical workstation in different departments. Integrating these components causes problems on different levels:

Data Integration. The core problem of data integration is semantic heterogeneity, which is a result of the design autonomy of different vendors [11,12, 13]. HL7 ("Health Level 7" according to the application level in the ISO/OSI reference model) is a well established message based standard which contributes to reduce semantic heterogeneity [14]. HL7 is based on a comprehensive catalog of message triggering events and the associated message formats. The standard

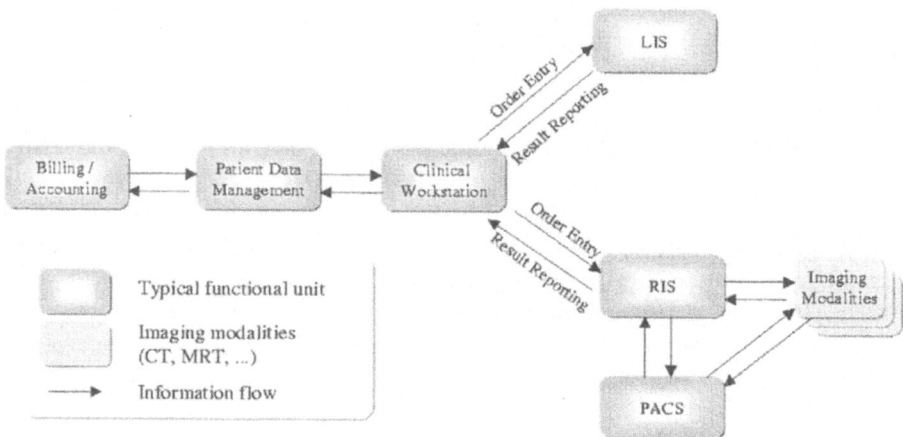

Fig. 1. Typical components of health information systems

particularly specifies the semantics of the data that are to be exchanged. Encoding rules, which are currently being replaced by an appropriate XML format, are of minor importance. Unfortunately HL7 is not a plug-and-play standard: Most vendors only implement a subset of the most frequently required events in their HL7 interface. The standard also allows a variety of integration strategies (e. g. both push strategy and pull strategy can be implemented using HL7 messages) and user specific adaptations of message formats via user defined fields and segments. Synchronization of redundant data stored in autonomous subsystems is another important aspect of data integration. HL7 based integration is typically based on asynchronous messages, which is not suitable to ensure mutual consistency of redundant data. By choosing an appropriate componentization it is possible to reduce the degree of redundancy and the risk of inconsistencies. Thus, data consistency is an important factor for strategic planning of an enterprise architecture (EA).

Functional Integration. Data redundancies are often the result of an insufficient functional integration of different subsystems: Autonomously developed systems usually overlap in their functionality (e. g. basic domain independent functionality like authorization, and also domain specific functionality like patient identification or even procedures like patient admission). A comprehensive system architecture is required which is aimed at an appropriate functional coordination of different system components. This architecture must consider both application requirements (e. g. regular patient admission by administrative personnel, short admission outside usual service hours by department personnel, decentral admission in outpatient departments, and emergency admission with limited possibilities for patient identification and incomplete information) and data consistency requirements (in particular avoiding multiple admission of the same patient under different identifiers and wrong identification). Even in a well organized hospital double Patient-Identifiers will occur – less than 1% might be regarded as a good rate. To minimize this rate and the risk of medical errors that might result it is important to have a "master patient index" as a centralized functionality in order to ensure a unique patient identification.

Presentation Integration. Presentation integration means that the user has the impression to work with a single system (single system image). This includes single sign on and context management, which synchronizes context changes in multiple applications that are active at the same time (e. g. changing the current patient or case). CCOW ("Clinical Context Object Working Group") is an emerging standard for context synchronization including single sign on [15]. Such a standard essentially depends on central components (like a central context manager), and thus necessarily makes assumptions concerning the overall system architecture. CCOW conformant applications must adhere to these assumptions and thus give up their execution autonomy [11] to some degree. Most of today's applications don't have this kind of compatibility yet and are to be modified in order to fit into a predefined architecture.

Process Integration. Process integration is concerned with the coordination of information flow between different application systems according to the requirements that result from the patient treatment process and business processes. A separation of process specification and application is desirable in order to increase adaptability and flexibility. [16] The process of writing a discharge letter, for example, varies in different departments: the physician might directly enter the letter into the system and thereby reuse available reports and laboratory results, or he might prefer to dictate it – on tape or digitally – or use voice recognition to generate it; depending on the strategy different process steps with different responsibilities are to be performed, and a flexible system should be adaptable to this. Today, a process integration that results in flexible process control and adaptation is only rudimentarily possible in distributed environments with autonomous subsystems. The separation of process logic and application logic is difficult to realize, because intra-departmental processes are often coded within the application code, and inter-departmental processes require data integration as a precondition to be solved. Workflow technology is increasingly being used, but in real world hospitals it is mostly limited to homogeneous application suites. [17]

The information flow to and from medical modalities is supported by the DICOM standard (Digital Imaging and Communication in Medicine). [18] The standard comprises an information model for medical image context data as well as a set of communication services (e.g. worklist management) which can be used to prevent redundant data entry at medical modalities. Like HL7, DICOM is not a plug-and-play standard, because it doesn't prevent functional overlapping of different subsystems. The IHE initiative (Integrating the Healthcare Enterprise) is an attempt to improve the compatibility of different healthcare systems by defining integration profiles on the basis of HL7 and DICOM. [19]

2.2   Tools

The typical way to support the integration of heterogeneous components on an HL7 basis is to use an interface engine, a specialized Message oriented Middleware (MoM), which helps to manage interfaced systems. The term "interface" is used here in a very unspecific way: an interface is anything which facilitates the communication between different system components or computer applications. When autonomously developed systems are to be integrated any kind of interface can occur, and an interface engine should offer tools to establish at least "some" communication on the basis of the existing interfaces. This includes a mapping and transformation of different formats and communication protocols, specification of routing information and monitoring. A domain specific MoM usually eases the mapping of interfaces by supporting domain specific standards like HL7, in particular different HL7 versions and appropriate translations between them. At runtime, the interface engine receives messages, stores them in persistent queues, identifies the recipients, translates them and sends them according to the expected format and protocol specified for each recipient.

A PACS-Broker is a more specialized MOM which can be used to coordinate the information flow between HIS, RIS, PACS and medical modalities: The PACS broker receives context data from the HIS and/or the RIS (e. g. patient identification, modality, and procedure identifier), generates a DICOM worklist which is sent to the modality, receives image data from the modality and propagates it together with the context data to a DICOM PACS.

Web servers are frequently utilized for distribution of medical images. Repositories are often used in heterogeneous environments to establish a central reference, e. g. a master patient index, a clinical report reference, or a terminology server.

2.3   Architecture of Health Information Systems

HL7 and DICOM are well established standards which support kind of a bottom up integration strategy. There are also standardization efforts that propagate a top down strategy by specifying an architectural framework in order to avoid functional overlapping and semantic heterogeneity of applications that are conform with this framework. HISA (Healthcare Information Systems Architecture) [20] and its successors are an example, where generic services are built on top of a predefined core database schema. [21,22]

The idea to reduce functional overlapping by domain specific generic services is also a motivation for the CORBAmed initiative of the OMG (e. g. Patient Identification Service, Lexical Query Service, etc.). Unfortunately, these standards have not yet led to a significant increase of product compatibility. However, in some hospitals the developed concepts are already used to direct the specification of a component architecture for a distributed health information system.

2.4   Strategy for System Evolution

A system architecture and a strategy for system evolution are to be defined on the basis of the standards, tools, and products available today. Strategies can be roughly classified in BoB (Best of Breed) and ERP (Enrerprise Resource Planning) approaches. Like in other domains there has been an ongoing debate comparing these strategies for health information systems (e. g. [23,24,25,26]). The ERP approach is motivated by a high degree of integration, in particular a central database which allows consistent sharing of commonly used data from different applications. BoB approaches, in contrast, are primarily motivated by the weaknesses of ERP solutions:

- There is no single ERP suite which offers the best solution for all required application functions.
- Introducing an ERP system is often done in a "big bang" approach with large organizational changes. This implies a high project risk and has often led to project failures in the past. [23]
- The evolution of the system depends on the available components of a single vendor, which limits the possibilities of demand driven system evolution in a specific setting. Software adaptations often lead to long development cycles or high effort custom programming.
- Adaptation to standardized processes coded into an ERP solution bares the risk of losing competitive advantages.
- The commitment to a single vendor also implies an increased risk, because of the dependency of economic development and long term market position of this vendor. [24]

The BoB approach tries to spread the risks over multiple vendors and increase flexibility by purchasing application components from different vendors as required and integrate them into a global system architecture via interfaces. However, some of the disadvantages of ERP approaches also hold for single BoB components, because a departmental BoB application also often has limited capabilities of demand oriented adaptation and evolution. Moreover, the effort for integration should not be underestimated. Improper IS integration and poor compatibility of heterogeneous subsystems are among the most frequently mentioned factors for IS project failures [7,10]. A disadvantage of the BoB approach is its limited capability of supporting inter-departmental processes and the high integration effort needed to consistently interconnect originally unrelated systems. Regardless which integration tool, technique, or infrastructure is used: semantic coordination of heterogeneous applications requires a high manual effort and a deep understanding of the data semantics in all participating system components (in particular: how does the application handle the data, and – even more important – how do the end users interpret the data). As a consequence, implementing and maintaining interfaces (even if HL7 and DICOM are used) requires high personnel costs.[1] An example: The Intermountain Health Care (IHC

---

[1] In this BoB context the term "interface" is commonly used to depict the bilateral communication between two initially unrelated systems; implementing an interface

is a health care delivery system in Salt Lake City Utah, operating 22 hospitals with 2500 beds, 72 clinics, 100,000 in-patients, and more than 3,000,000 ambulatory clinic visits per year) has 19 full time employees who build and maintain interfaces – currently 31 different interface types [24]. The university hospital in Marburg (1200 beds, 45,000 in-patients, 250,000 out patient visits per year) follows a more homogeneous approach: 1 employee is maintaining 2–5 interfaces as one half of his duties. The Marburg approach is aimed at reducing the limitations of traditional ERP solutions by using an integrated generator tool for rapid and demand driven application development.

3   A Responsive System Architecture

The university hospital in Marburg uses an integrated ERP suite as a core system. This system, the Orbis®/OpenMed-system, is in widespread use in Germany, in Austria, and in Switzerland. The installation in Marburg represents one of the most advanced installations of this system, and significant impulses concerning the development, improvement, and use of the integrated RAD tool "OpenMed" (generator tool) have resulted from the Marburg project, which has been described in [27,25]. The core system particularly covers the functionality of a master patient index and an electronic patient record. Autonomous subsystems are still interfaced to this system via standard HL7 interfaces, as usual. The system evolution strategy, however, is to limit the number of interfaced systems as far as possible and incrementally improve the core system by adding integrated generator based applications according to actual process support requirements. Applications built with the generator tool are integrated with the core system from the very beginning, so there is no need for any interface mapping. Figure 2 gives an overview of the software architecture. Within the core system two types of applications interact with a common database. Conventional client-applications covering ADT (admission, discharge, tranfer), billing etc. operate on a database schema which is modeled in a conventional way, i.e. data semantics is reflected by the structure of database tables. Applications built by use of the generator tool are based on a generic Entity-Attribute-Value (EAV) type database schema, i.e. attribute descriptors are entered as data in generic tables [27].

The generator tool supports the construction of paper-like documentation forms, e.g. order entry forms or report forms. Tool generated applications follow a form-oriented user interaction paradigm: users basically fill in instances of paper-like electronic forms. Subsequently we will use the term "electronic document" to depict an instance of an electronic form. Forms are designed by application developers via the generator tool, which offers drag-and-drop design elements for rapid form construction. A field in a form can be connected to the central database, so the application designer can decide to automatically upload

---

then means to establish this communication, which includes the specification of syntactical and semantic mappings but possibly also modifications of the participating systems.

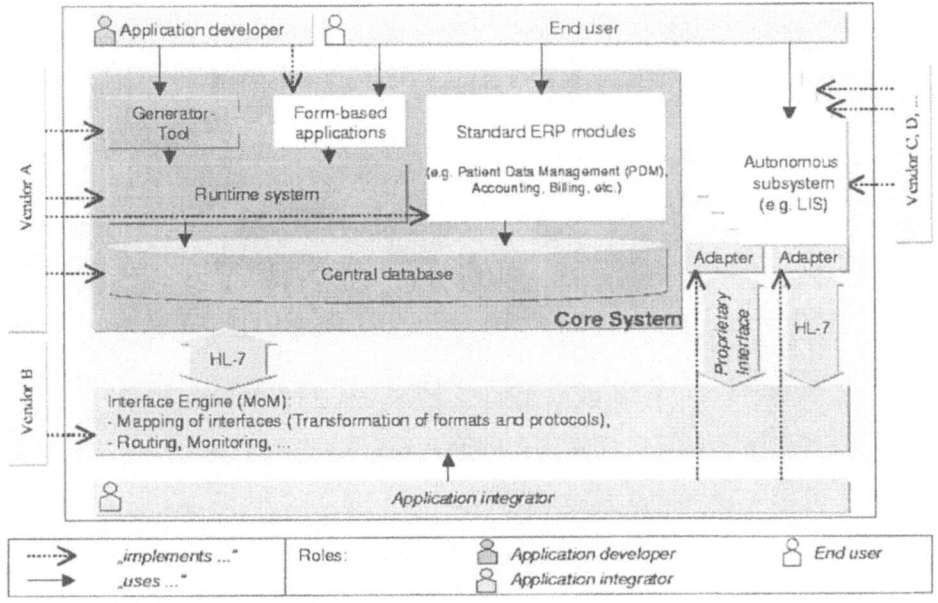

Fig. 2. System architecture of the health information system in Marburg

information from the central database into an electronic form, or to fill some database table via the use of an electronic form.

In addition to electronic forms the generator allows to specify "reference lists". Reference lists are used to provide an overview over available documents. They contain references pointing to documents, where a reference is represented by a short description of the contents of the corresponding document, e. g. "radiology report for patient Jane Doe from Feb 28th, 2002". Patient related reference lists contain references to patient related documents. Examples are the patient history and lists for open requests or new results of a particular patient. Task related reference lists (= work lists) are related to a specific task, e. g. all reports that have to be validated.

Document flow is supported by attributing state variables to forms and by selectively displaying references in different work lists according to the current workflow status of the corresponding documents. As an example, a work list can contain references to all discharge reports of a ward which have been written but not yet validated. After report validation, the state is changed, and the corresponding reference to this report is no longer displayed in this work list.

Technically, forms are event driven programs, interacting with users to display data and to store data input persistently in the underlying common database. However, the specification of these tool generated applications (forms, fields, reference list types) is stored in the common database. An EAV like database schema is used to support system evolution without the need for database schema modification.

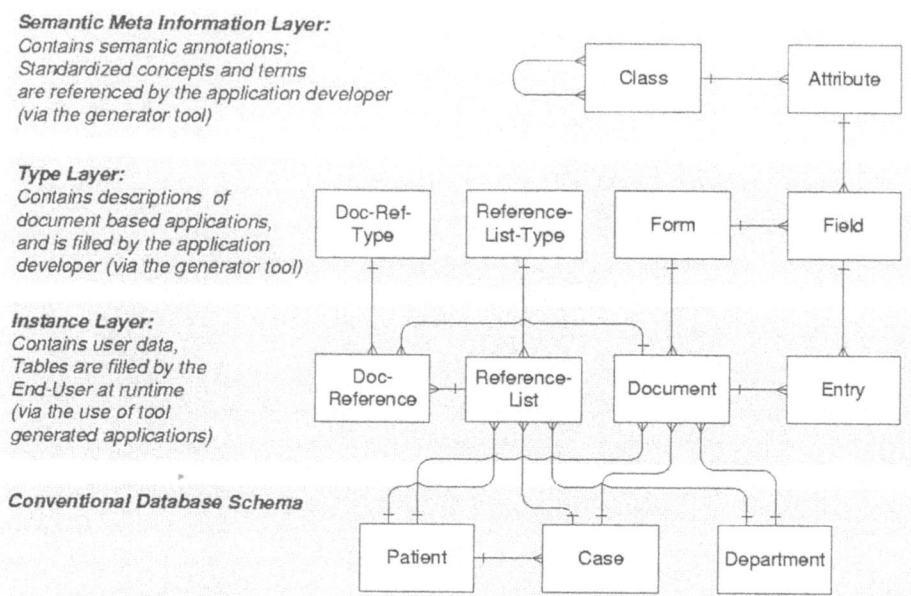

Fig. 3. Entity Relationship diagram of a generic database schema for embedding document based applications. The type layer contains the description of templates for fields, forms, and reference lists. On the corresponding instance or data level, entry is the central (EAV type) database table. Entries are parts of documents, and reference lists are used to reference specific documents (e. g. the patient history referencing reports, letters, diagnoses, appointments etc). [25]

Figure 3 shows a simplified version of the database schema supporting the generator tool approach. The two central layers are the instance layer containing user data, and the type or template layer containing descriptions needed for the applications, e. g. descriptions of forms. This representation follows a material tool metaphor [28] with the instance layer containing material (user data), and the type layer containing tool data (metadata). The basic units of information on the instance level are *entries*, which are part of structured *documents*. On the type level, document templates are called *electronic forms* which contain *fields*. Thus, we refer to an entry as an instance of a field. The *entry* table is an EAV type of database table. A typical EAV table basically contains only three columns – one to specify the entity, one to specify the attribute, and one for the value of the specified attribute [29]. In our case, the columns for entities and attributes are replaced by columns for documents and fields.

In order to link electronic documents to their clinical context it is essential to embed the EAV part of the database schema into the conventional part of the database schema, which contains a central table for patients serving as the master patient index, and tables for cases and for organizational units. We have illustrated this in Fig. 3 by showing typical relationships between documents and their entries to the patients, to cases, and to clinical departments. At runtime linking of electronic documents is done automatically: A user navigates into a specific context by selecting a department, a patient and a case. If he creates an electronic document by instantiating an electronic form, the new document is automatically linked to the context in which it was created.

An EAV type schema results in enhanced flexibility at the cost of lost semantic control. While in a conventional database schema, attribute descriptors are explicitly modeled parts of the data dictionary, they are implicit (and hidden on the data level) in an EAV type approach. To regain semantic control and to control overlaps with the conventional database schema, an additional layer containing annotations (semantic metadata) is needed. This layer does exist, and we have outlined it in Fig. 3; in the current system implementation, its use is still rudimentary. We refer to Nadkarni et al. for a detailed description of relevant aspects concerning EAV type database schemas in general [29]. A more detailed description of the database schema underlying the generator tool is given in [27].

4   Application Design and Software Engineering

In our project, the integrated generator tool for rapidly building workflow-enabled clinical application modules has been one of the central features of the system. A full version of the tool is used by application designers of the vendor company or by hospital IT staff of larger institutions. For both settings, an iterative and participatory software engineering process is an important prerequisite of increasing software quality and adapting application modules to clinical work practice. Customers not using the tool or using a restricted version, depend on the quality of this design process; they may still modify forms or create new forms on the basis of templates according to a predefined workflow. We will describe our perspective of such a software engineering process which has been particularly adapted to the conditions of the generator tool. It has emerged from iterative programming techniques, like the Rational Unified Process [30] and the Extreme Programming approach [31].

4.1   A Participatory and Iterative Software Engineering Process

Programming with the generator tool is different from traditional programming (e. g. object oriented programming), as application developers do not directly edit the JAVA or C++ code of an application. Instead they primarily deal with higher level design primitives like forms, fields, lists of electronic documents ("reference lists"), and so on. The Software Engineering (SE) process, in particular the documentation of tool generated applications, had to be adapted to this kind of programming. UML was only partly suitable, because UML diagrams are not intended to describe the design primitives of this particular high level generator tool. In order to achieve a better business-IT alignment it is also desirable to trigger IT projects on demand out of business process optimization projects; thus, it should be possible to derive the specification of an application directly

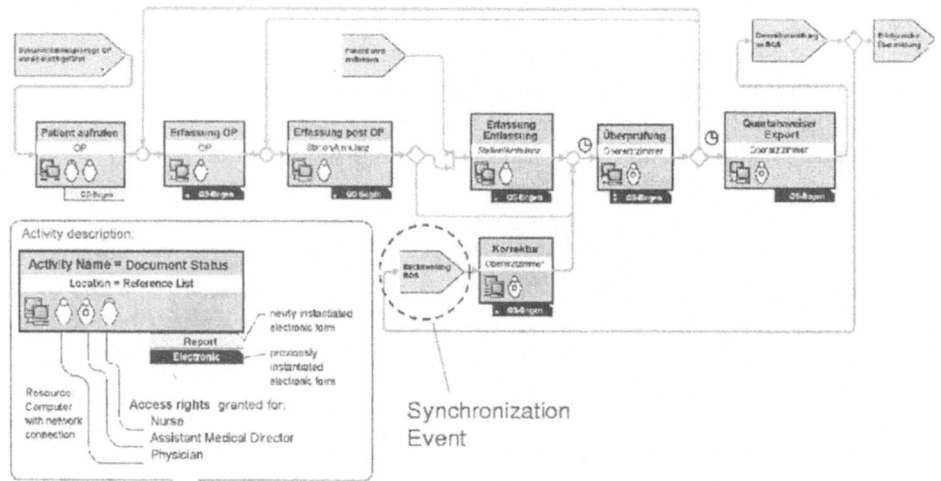

Fig. 4. Mapdoc Target Process Model for an electronic form to support quality assurance in gynecology. Each activity represents a different status in the workflow of the electronic document to be designed.

from an appropriate business process model. We have developed an appropriate healthcare specific business process modeling tool for this purpose. This modeling tool (*"Mapdoc"* – Marburg Process Documentation) [32,33] is based on UML activity diagrams, where each activity is structured according to UML use cases. In addition the model describes which documents are used by which activity, so it also illustrates the flow of electronic documents.

Rapid application development with the generator tool is characterized by iterative development and stepwise improvement of prototypes which are designed, realized, and tested in close cooperation with the end users. The following phases can be distinguished:

Requirements Analysis and Business Process Modeling. By means of interview sessions and observation, the medical domain is analyzed by an application developer in close contact with domain experts. A glossary of relevant terms is built, the needed functionality is specified by means of hierarchically organized use cases. Use cases [30] take a central role, and serve as basic units of the development process. A business process model is constructed which includes an information model. The process model represents the top-level use case incorporating all other use cases, thus helping to verify use case completeness. An example of a model resulting from this step is shown in Fig. 4.

The process model and the set of use cases are important for a common understanding of the application domain: non-technically oriented end users can determine if the domain analyses are complete and correct. In addition, the model helps end users to decide how activities are to be supported by electronic forms and how these forms should look like. Use cases are grouped into work packages according to their scope and their functional relationships; e. g. the use cases "allocation of accession number", "check referrer", and "description of specimen" form the work package "sample acceptance". Implementation priorities are assigned to work packages, to define a top down implementation process proceeding towards iterative refinement. The top level work package containing the process model gets the highest priority.

Application Concept, Including the Design of Work Lists, Forms and States. Different steps of filling electronic forms are described by assigning workflow states to each form. For a pathology documentation form, different documentation steps are "macroscopic description of specimen" and "microscopic description of specimen". Typically, a new state is defined for each activity in which the form is needed. For each state, a work list referencing all documents of this specific state is created, e. g. all documents with macroscopic description already filled in, and microscopic results to be described. If different tasks are performed by the same persons, it may be reasonable to merge the corresponding work lists into one. The application concept is documented in a state diagram, which is derived from the initial process model.

Implementation of a Workflow-Enabled Prototype and End User Verification. On the basis of state diagrams defined in the application concept, a prototype illustrating the flow of documents is implemented. The idea is to give users an impression how forms are filled in incrementally in different states. Provisionary forms without real data are sufficient in this step to help users decide whether the flow model fits their work practice.

Implementation, Tests, and Iterative Refinement. Once the flow model of a form is tested the implementation is completed by adding detailed fields and subforms. According to their priority, further work packages are implemented until the application module reaches a usable state. Each work package is tested by the application designer and by key users. During these tests, use cases may be refined or completely re-written. Functional refinement steps may be altered, so priorities of remaining work packages may need to be changed. If necessary, even new analysis and design phases can be initiated.

End User Test. Before the final training and rollout phase begins, it is important to make sure that a number of users have tested the module and no remaining work flow problems have been found.

End User Training, Rollout, and Iterative Improvement. During routine use, further use cases may be acquired and implemented to refine/modify the functionality and to generate improved versions of the module. This is realized by executing the above steps in an iterative way (which might even include new analysis/design).

4.2   Generator Based Software Development in Practice

The SE process as described above has been elaborated and refined in various software projects. Examples for tool based applications that have been developed from scratch by hospital IT staff are:

- The implementation of a pathology documentation system [25].
- The development of an electronic workflow-enabled quality assessment report for gynecology (process model in Fig. 4).

Today both applications are being used by the vendor company as the basis for generic modules that are parameterized and adapted for use in other hospitals. The gynecology report has been extended to serve as a basis for quality assessment reports in other disciplines.

Examples for IT projects that arose from demand driven incremental improvement of business processes are:

- The optimization of pre-operative autologous blood donation (PABD). PABD is the collection of a patient's own blood prior to elective surgery to be used for his or her own transfusion needs. In the Marburg University Medical Center, PABD is an interdisciplinary process between the clinic for orthopaedic surgery and the institute for transfusion medicine. As the process coordination was found to be inefficient a process analysis was initiated. A process model was developed as the basis for interdisciplinary communication and process optimization [33]. By eliminating redundant activities and reorganizing the workflow the number of activities could be reduced from 15 to 7. After the successful process redesign the optimized workflow could be supported electronically by two simple electronic forms: One for acknowledgement of a performed PABD and one that served as an indication checklist for orthopedists.
- The adaptation of discharge letters is one example out of numerous projects, where an existing application has been substantially improved by adding small but valuable features which helped to improve practitioners work practice. In this case an existing workflow-enabled discharge letter has been improved by providing diagnoses and findings from previous visits for selection and adoption into the new discharge letter.

The vendor company uses the generator tool for developing generic clinical modules for deployment in different health care facilities. These modules are tested and cooperatively improved in our hospital, in order to enhance adaptation to clinical work practice.

5   Summary of Experiences

The generator approach for system evolution has been used in various demand driven projects at the University Medical Center in Marburg. The project scope has ranged from simply parameterizing existing applications to implementing complete departmental systems. The UML modeling techniques were modified in order to achieve a straight forward documentation covering the whole development cycle from the business process model to the system documentation. Use cases, extended activity diagrams (Mapdoc diagrams), class diagrams and state diagrams were useful to some extent. Process modeling was found to be helpful in projects where an organizational redesign was within the project scope. In small projects, where the generator tool was only used for parameterization of existing applications, process modeling was often perceived as a waste of time. However, as a target process model is not only a means to achieve a common understanding but also provides a documentation of the application, it is still desirable to keep the model up to date in order to keep the system maintainable.

The generator approach for system evolution did provide an environment in which a flexible iterative and participatory software development process could be established. To our experiences, the generator and the underlying application framework used in Marburg were still immature in several respects:

- In its current version, the generator tool used in Marburg still has a major drawback that hinders its seamless integration into a semi-formal software-engineering process: It does not support documentation. The Mapdoc tool for documenting business processes has been designed to reflect the artifacts needed for generator based applications, but it is not integrated with the generator tool. In practice this has led to diverging process models and implementation.
- In a layered approach, the lower system levels hide the complexity of generic functionality to the higher levels. Unfortunately, system bugs in the lower system layers often become apparent at the application layer where debugging is difficult, as the application programmer only sees higher level design primitives which hide the underlying code. Such bugs tend to magnify their effect, as generic services are typically reused in multiple tool-generated applications. Thus, there is a high risk if framework stability and robustness is insufficient.
- Another typical effect of using a RAD tool for system development is its reduced expressiveness: Application developers have been limited by the predefined design primitives of the generator tool. If there are requirements that do not fit into this schema, implementation becomes more cumbersome and not as straightforward as described in our SE process.

Despite these deficiencies, the advantages of database integration and the potential to easily support cross departmental workflow did pay off. Information has become easily available within the holistic system: Hospital-wide result reports from ancillary departments, discharge letters written under the generator environment, and ICD codes have become available without the need for any interface mapping [25,34], and order entry has been introduced.

6   Discussion

Loosely coupled component based systems offer an alternative approach for system evolution. Actually, the highly sketchy clinical work practice has often led to heterogeneous systems composed out of multiple small, partial, and ad hoc, but quick solutions. Unfortunately, autonomously developed systems are difficult to integrate. Nevertheless, the idea of combining BoB components still has its attraction and it is even fueled by promising component technologies [35,36] which provide an infrastructure for transparent access to distributed and technically heterogeneous components. Yet, the really hard integration problem is to bridge semantic incompatibilities among independently developed components, which is not solved by any domain independent infrastructure. Healthcare specific standards like HL7 and DICOM did improve the situation, but they are still far from providing commonly accepted ontologies and a common application framework which are needed for open component based systems [37]. Today, integrating heterogeneous and autonomously developed components in healthcare is still a difficult task, and the resulting systems suffer from integrity problems due to semantic mismatches, insufficient synchronization and update procedures, and the like (e.g. [24]). There is still no generally accepted methodology for EAI (Enterprise Application Integration). Available EAI tools (like "integration engines" or "communication servers") typically provide mediator services that ease the management of heterogeneous interfaces, but bridging semantic incompatibilities necessarily has to be done manually which requires a high effort (e.g. [38,39,12]). Packaged ERP systems, on the other hand, still cannot live up with all expectations and are typically interfaced to numerous subsystems [40,24,37]. Moreover, the complexity of these systems makes them inflexible and leads to long development cycles.

The generator approach for continuous system evolution tries to achieve both a high degree of flexibility and of system integrity at the same time. This might contribute to reduce the number of loosely coupled subsystems, as it becomes easier to rapidly implement and adapt integrated components according to end users' needs. The presented approach requires a tight coupling of the generator tool and the underlying application framework, which is only possible with proprietary vendor specific layering, because standard interfaces for layered Health Information Systems like this are not available yet. The high dependency on one vendor is a project risk that should not be underestimated. In particular, there is a high risk if framework stability and robustness is insufficient. Therefore, testing is of paramount importance. Moreover, a close cooperation between application developer and framework vendor is highly recommendable in this kind of projects.

To improve the generator approach it is highly desirable to close the gap between process modeling and application implementation. Smith and Fingar have recognized that "the traditional software development itself creates a discrepancy between business and IT models which are virtually impossible to keep aligned because the relationships between requirements and the associated technical artifacts – components, files, interfaces – are extremely complex and numerous" [9]. Implementing *paper-like* electronic documents is already close to clinical work practice, but process modeling and implementation still tend to diverge as long as they are separated – the goal should be that the process model *is* the implementation. With the emergence of such tools application development and process management are about to grow together. The question arises whether *end users* should use such "process management tools" to design and improve their own processes. We understand process improvement as the task of conjointly restructuring human work tasks, rearranging organizational routines, redesigning paper forms, and – as one facet – introducing new IT functionalities [8]. The development of these IT functionalities should remain in the hands of IT specialists, even when a generator tool or "process management tool" is used. To our experience, physicians want usable systems that seamlessly fit into their work practice, but they do not want to bother configuring and adapting these systems. Application developers, in any case, will still need informatics know how, even if they only deal with process related artifacts. For example, the application programmer must choose the correct data replication and synchronization strategy according to the semantics of the application: in some cases it is necessary to avoid diverging instances of the same data, in other cases it is necessary to avoid undesired updates on validated documents.

Yet, there is a clear shift of skills within the different roles involved in the software engineering approach presented: If the application programmer can more and more rely on a robust domain specific framework, he or she can increasingly concentrate on business process alignment instead of coding and debugging. Thus, the approach presented, fosters the domain specialization of application developers, and it is a step towards a responsive IT infrastructure alleviating a demand driven introduction of IT functionality in the context of cooperative process improvement.

References

1. Bates, D.W., Cohen, M., Leape, L.L., Overhage, J.M., Shabot, M.M., Sheridan, T.: Reducing the frequency of errors in medicine using information technology. J Am Med Inform Assoc **8** (2001) 299–308
2. Kohn, L.T.: To Err Is Human. Building a Safer Health System. National Academy Press, Washington D.C. (2000)
3. Sachverständigenrat für die Konzertierte Aktion im Gesundheitswesen: Finanzierung, Nutzerorientierung und Qualität. Report (2003)
4. Wilson, R.M., Harrison, B.T., Gibberd, R.W., Hamilton, J.D.: An analysis of the causes of adverse events from the quality in australian health care study. Med J Aust **170** (1999) 411–415
5. Wilson, R.M., Runciman, W.B., Gibberd, R.W., Harrison, B.T., Newby, L., Hamilton, J.D.: The quality in australian health care study. Med J Aust **163** (1995) 458–471
6. Dorenfest, S.I.: The decade of the '90s. Healthc Inform **17** (2000)
7. Sauer, C.: Deciding the future for IS failures: Not the choice you might think. In Curie, W., Galliers, R., eds.: Rethinking management information systems. Oxford University Press (1999) 279–309

8. Berg, M., Toussaint, P.: The mantra of modeling and the forgotten powers of paper: A sociotechnical view on the development of process-oriented ICT in health care. Int J Med Inf **69** (2003) 223–234

9. Smith, H., Fingar, P.: Business Process Management: The Third Wave. 1st edn. Meghan-Kiffer Press (2002)

10. Al-Mashari, M., Zairi, M.: BPR implementation process: An analysis of key success and failure factors. Business Process Management Journal **5** (1999) 87–112

11. Sheth, A., Larson, J.: Federated database systems for managing distributed, heterogeneous, and autonomous databases. ACM Computing Surveys **22** (1990) 183–235

12. Colomb, R.M.: Impact of semantic heterogeneity on federating databases. The Computer Journal **40** (1997) 235–244

13. Lenz, R., Kuhn, K.A.: Intranet meets hospital information systems: the solution to the integration problem? Methods Inf Med **40** (2001) 99–105

14. Schadow, G., Fohring, U., Tolxdorff, T.: Implementing HL7: from the standard's specification to production application. Methods Inf Med **37** (1998) 119–123

15. Seliger, R.: Overview of HL7's CCOW standard. Report (2001)

16. Dadam, P., Reichert, M., Kuhn, K.: Clinical workflows – the killer application for process-oriented information systems? Proc. 4th Int. Conf. on Business Information Systems (2000) 36–59

17. Haux, R., Seggewies, C., Baldauf-Sobez, W., Kullmann, P., Reichert, H., Luedecke, L., Seibold, H.: Soarian – workflow management applied for health care. Methods Inf Med **42** (2003) 25–36

18. Bidgood, W.D., Horii, S.C., Prior, F.W., van Syckle, D.E.: Understanding and using DICOM, the data interchange standard for biomedical imaging. J Am Med Inform Assoc **4** (1997) 199–212

19. Wein, B.B.: [IHE (Integrating the Healthcare Enterprise): A new approach for the improvement of digital communication in healthcare]. Rofo Fortschr Geb Rontgenstr. **175** (2003) 183–186

20. Ferrara, F.M.: The CEN healthcare information systems architecture standard and the DHE middleware. A practical support to the integration and evolution of healthcare systems. Int J Med Inf **48** (1998) 173–182

21. Hurlen, P., Skifjeld, K., Andersen, E.P.: The basic principles of the Synapses federated healthcare record server. Int J Med Inf **52** (1998) 123–132

22. Grimson, W., Jung, B., van Mulligen, E.M., van Ginneken, A., Pardon, S., Sottile, P.A.: Extensions to the HISA standard – the SynEx computing environment. Methods Inf Med **41** (2002) 401–410

23. Light, B., C., H., Kelly, S., Wills, K.: Best of breed IT strategy: An alternative to enterprise resource planning systems. Proceedings of the 8th European Conference on Information Systems **1** (2000) 652–659

24. Clayton, P.D., Narus, S.P., Huff, S.M., Pryor, T.A., Haug, P.J., Larkin, T., Matney, S., Evans, R.S., Rocha, B.H., W. A. Bowes, I., Holston, F.T., Gundersen, M.L.: Building a comprehensive clinical information system from components. The approach at Intermountain Health Care. Methods Inf Med **42** (2003) 1–7

25. Kuhn, K.A., Lenz, R., Elstner, T., Siegele, H., Moll, R.: Experiences with a generator tool for building clinical application modules. Methods Inf Med **42** (2003) 37–44

26. Degoulet, P., Marin, L., Lavril, M., Bozec, C.L., Delbecke, E., Meaux, J.J., Rose, L.: The HEGP component-based clinical information system. Int J Med Inf **69** (2003) 115–126

27. Lenz, R., Elstner, T., Siegele, H., Kuhn, K.A.: A practical approach to process support in health information systems. J Am Med Inform Assoc **9** (2002) 571–585

28. Lilienthal, C., Züllighoven, H.: Techniques and tools for continuous user participation. PDC '96 Proc. of the Participatory Design Conference, 1996 (2003) 153–159

29. Nadkarni, P.M., Marenco, L., Chen, R., Skoufos, E., Shepherd, G., Miller, P.: Organization of heterogeneous scientific data using the EAV/CR representation. J Am Med Inform Assoc **6** (1999) 478–493

30. Kruchten, P.: The Rational Unified Process – An Introduction. Object Technology. Addison-Wesley, Canada (2000)

31. Beck, K.: Extreme Programming. Addison-Wesley, München (2000)

32. Hinrichs, F., Lenz, R., Griss, P.: Modellierung und Prozessoptimierung in einer orthopädischen Klinik. Zeitschrift für Orthopädie und ihre Grenzgebiete **139** (2001) 172

33. Lenz, R., Herlofsen, H., Hinrichs, F., Zeiler, T., Kuhn, K.: Abteilungsübergreifende Prozessoptimierung – Ein Anwendungsbeispiel. Informatik Biometrie und Epidemiologie in Medizin und Biologie **33** (2002) 88–90

34. Lenz, R., Elstner, T., Kuhn, K.: Experiences with a holistic information system. J Am Med Inform Assoc (suppl) (2001) 952

35. Gruhn, V., Thiel, A.: Komponentenmodelle – DCOM, JavaBeans, Enterprise Java-Beans, CORBA. 1st edn. Professionelle Softwareentwicklung. Addison-Wesley, München (2000)

36. Szyperski, C.: Component software – beyond object-oriented programming. 1st edn. Addison-Wesley, Harlow, England (1999)

37. Lenz, R., Huff, S., Geissbühler, A.: Report of conference track 2: Pathways to open architectures. Int J Med Inf **69** (2003) 297–299

38. McGoveran, D.: Business semantics. EAI Journal (2000) 10

39. Stonebraker, M.: Integrating islands of information. EAI Journal (1999) 1–5

40. Gell, G., Schmucker, P., Pedevilla, M., Leitner, H., Naumann, J., Fuchs, H., Pitz, H., Kole, W.: SAP and partners: IS-H and IS-H*MED. Methods Inf Med **42** (2003) 16–24

From Where to What: Metadata Sharing for Digital Photographs with Geographic Coordinates

Mor Naaman, Andreas Paepcke, and Hector Garcia-Molina

Stanford University

Abstract. We describe LOCALE, a system that allows cooperating information systems to share labels for photographs. Participating photographs are enhanced with a geographic location stamp – the latitude and longitude where the photograph was taken. For a photograph with no label, LOCALE can use the shared information to assign a label based on other photographs that were taken in the same area. LOCALE thus allows (i) text search over unlabeled sets of photos, and (ii) automated label suggestions for unlabeled photos. We have implemented a LOCALE prototype where users cooperate in submitting labels and locations, enhancing search quality for all users in the system. We ran an experiment to test the system in centralized and distributed settings. The results show that the system performs search tasks with surprising accuracy, even when searching for specific landmarks.

1   Introduction

Organizing digital photographs is a difficult task for many people [1,2]. In many applications, simple text labeling of some photographs will enable much better results when searching or browsing a collection. However, many people do not label more than a few of their photos, or do not invest the effort of labeling their photos at all. Can a cooperative information system enable a solution through sharing of existing labels so that nobody needs to do more work than they do now, yet everyone gains functionality? LOCALE is such a system.

Today's digital cameras add a considerable amount of metadata to an image file, most significantly a timestamp. The timestamp is already being used in photo browser applications. In our previous work [3] we also have shown how timestamps can be used to enhance browsing of a digital photo collection.

We believe that cameras will eventually support a "location stamp", specifying the geographic coordinates where a picture was taken. Two separate hardware advancements support this thesis: the lower cost of GPS chips, and the combination of the inherently location-aware cell phone technology[1] with digital cameras. Even today the standard EXIF header, included in most digital photos, supports location data. High-end cameras such as Nikon D1X have a

---

[1] See http://www.fcc.gov/911/enhanced/ for FCC plan to mandate location capabilities of 50-100mts accuracy for mobile phones by 2005.

R. Meersman et al. (Eds.): CoopIS/DOA/ODBASE 2003, LNCS 2888, pp. 196–217, 2003.
© Springer-Verlag Berlin Heidelberg 2003

direct interface to GPS devices. In addition, off-the-shelf software is available for merging GPS logs and digital photos to create "location-stamped" photos for any camera, without requiring a direct GPS interface.

Using location data as a pivot, we have a good basis for collaborative approaches towards photo management. For example, we can enable the sharing of information about photos: by comparing where photos were taken, we can associate photos from a set of labeled photographs with unlabeled photos from another set. We then associate the corresponding labels with the unlabeled photographs. Physical proximity of photo origin is much easier to evaluate than current image-based proximity measures, like visual similarity, which are still computationally expensive and inaccurate.

We now illustrate the general idea using a simple example. Meet H, an avid photographer. H has taken a photo of Stanford University's Memorial Church. H labeled the photo "Stanford Church" using some desktop software tool such as a photo browser. The label and the coordinates of the photos are submitted to an online repository that H agreed to participate in. Another photographer, M, takes a picture of the church from the same location a day later. Now, M does not have to label the photo: M queries the online repository by the coordinates of M's photo and receives, in reply, the label submitted by H.

Another scenario is for users to perform a *term search* over their own unlabeled collection – without having explicitly associated labels with any of their photos. For example, M submits a "Stanford Church" query to the system. The system finds H's matching label, notes the location where H's church photo was taken, and then searches M's photos for ones taken near the location of H's church photo. The coordinates of M's church photo will be the result of this search.

There are several potential problems to consider. First, H may have given the photo an unhelpful label (e.g., "My Son and I in California"). More confusingly, M may have taken a photo near Stanford's Memorial Church but pointed the camera at an entirely different subject (the Stanford campus offers nice views in many directions). Another potential problem is H using a different, or shortened, name for a photographed object. Of course, H's label can just be plain wrong.

The solution we propose is LOCAtion-to-LabEl (LOCALE), a cooperative information retrieval system. The LOCALE system collects coordinates of photos and their associated labels from participating users, and responds to search queries. LOCALE applies term frequency, weighting and clustering techniques to avoid the problems mentioned above.

There are distributed and centralized modes for search in LOCALE. In centralized mode, the LOCALE server stores the database of photo metadata (photo locations and labels) and handles all the computation, including the process of searching M's photos. Thus, the server has to know the location of all the photos in M's collection for M to be able to perform a search.

In distributed mode, a summarization of LOCALE data is cached on M's machine if M wishes to perform searches. After the information is cached, the term search and ranking of the photos can be performed over the LOCALE cache on M's machine without contacting the server.

Note that in both modes the photos themselves never leave their owner's machine, nor are the identities of the photographers ever needed for operation.

We have implemented LOCALE using three different strategies, in both centralized and distributed modes. The implementation strategies are described in Sect. 2. To test LOCALE, we devised an experiment to acquire geo-referenced, labeled photos from tourists visiting the Stanford campus. In Sect. 3 we present this experiment and the data we collected. The evaluation of search performance is presented in Sect. 4. We also looked at how well LOCALE can automatically assign labels to photos, and discuss some preliminary results in Sect. 5.

Two bodies of related work are image retrieval (overview in [4]) and image labeling ([5] and others) research. We expand on these and future work in Sect. 6.

2   The LOCALE System

The LOCALE (LOCAtion-to-LabEl) system consists of a centralized server with a global photo database DB_s, and users with personal photo databases DB_1, DB_2, etc. The system is illustrated in Fig. 1. The main table in these photo databases is the photos table $P(I, G, L)$ where the columns are image (I), geographic location coordinates (G), and Label (L). In each user u's DB_u, table P_u consists of tuples for u's own photos. The server's table P_s consists of tuples submitted by cooperating users. Null values are permitted: in our implementation, the I values in P_s are always null (the server never requires the submission of *photographs* – users submit $(null, g, \ell)$ tuples). Also, some user databases could lack labels for some, or all, of their photos (L values may be null).

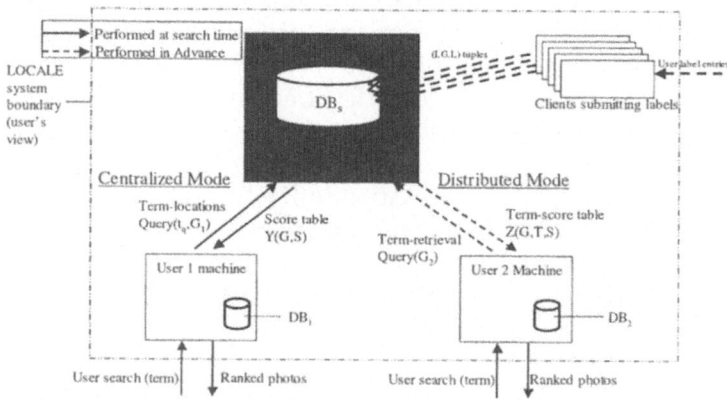

Fig. 1. Architecture of the LOCALE system

Labels can be any type of textual information attached to the photos: keywords, free-form text etc. In our system, labels are broken down into *terms* consisting of a single word or a two-word phrase.

The purpose of LOCALE is to enable a user u to perform term searches over u's collection P_u, even if those photos are not labeled. The user input is a search term t_q and, implicitly, the locations of the user's photos[2] $G_u = \Pi_G(P_u)$. The search output is an ordering of $I_u = \Pi_I(P_u)$ based on relevance to the search term. The search is performed using only the data in P_s. For simplicity, we only consider the case where users performing search, like u, have not labeled any photos (column L in each row of P_u is null). Therefore, we assume a different set of users that contribute labels (see Fig. 1). Optimally, a search will be able to integrate the user's own labels with the LOCALE search based on other users' labels.

User search is handled differently depending on whether LOCALE is in a *distributed* or *centralized* mode. In the following subsection we describe the search process in centralized mode. In the next subsection we describe the distributed mode and note the differences from centralized LOCALE. For each mode, we list three implementation strategies (Weighted Neighbors, Location-Clustered and Term-Clustered). For each mode and strategy we explain the way data is stored and pre-processed and the way queries are handled.

2.1   Centralized Mode

In centralized mode the LOCALE server is contacted at search time and performs most of the search-time computation. User 1 demonstrates the process in Fig. 1. The user search query is translated to a *term-locations* query with parameters $t_q, G_1 = \Pi_G(P_1)$: the search term and the set of coordinates of the user's photos. Recall from the introduction that we postulate digital cameras to provide the coordinates automatically. Searching users are not expected to specify coordinates manually[3]. The LOCALE server ranks G_1 with respect to t_q, using the information in P_s. We implemented this ranking using three different strategies; the details of each are below. At the end of the ranking step, the LOCALE server replies with a table $Y(G, S)$ of geographic locations and the score of their match to term t_q. The user's machine then executes a simple natural join with P_1 to produce a ranking of the user's images $\Pi_I(P_1)$ based on the match to t_q.

We now show how the term-locations queries are handled in each implementation strategy.

Term-Locations Query in Weighted-Neighbors (WN) LOCALE. The process of ranking locations based on their match to the search term is done by finding, for each location, nearby photos in P_s whose labels include the search term. This can be done efficiently if indices for the location and the terms exist

---

[2] We will be using relational algebra operators such as Π, the attribute projection, throughout the paper.

[3] In practice, the coordinates of u's photos may already have been stored in the LO-CALE server's photo table P_s ahead of time. In this case the users will identify themselves to LOCALE at query time using a unique ID.

for P_s. The score for the match between each location and the search term t_q is computed for every $g \in G_1$:

$$Score(g, t_q) = \sum_{(i_s, g_s, \ell_s) \in P_s} IR(t_q, \ell_s) PROX(g, g_s)$$

The function $IR(t, l)$ computes the match between a term and a photo's label, while $PROX(g_1, g_2)$ evaluates the proximity between two photo locations. Our $PROX$ function computes the inverse of the square root of the Euclidean distance between $(g1, g2)$, but we set the value of $PROX$ to 0 if the distance between two locations is greater than a threshold. That is, we are taking into account only photos within a certain radius from g (100mts in our case). We did not use a linear distance measure since that measure assigns too much weight to close-by photos. We also capped the value for $PROX$, assigning equal values to all photos within a minimal distance. This cap avoids disproportionate weight bias induced by very close pictures. For example, a photo taken 20cm away should not be weighted much higher than a photo taken 1m away.

The IR function $IR(term, label)$, for our purposes, is a simple matching function:

$$IR(term, label) = \begin{cases} 1 \text{ if } term, \text{ in singular or plural, in } label \\ 0 \text{ otherwise} \end{cases}$$

For example, when searching for the term "tower" we gave the same score to the labels "Towers" and "The tower - what a tall tower!".

After computing the score for each g value, table Y is constructed: $Y = \left\{ (g, s) | g \in G_1; s = Score(g, t_q) \right\}$. Table Y is the reply of the LOCALE server to the query; as mentioned above, the LOCALE system on the user's machine computes $P_1 \bowtie Y$ to produce a ranking on images instead of locations.

Term-Locations Query in Location-Clustered (LC) LOCALE.
Location-Clustered LOCALE introduces some pre-processing on the location/label data. In this implementation the LOCALE server clusters the P_s table geographically using a hierarchical clustering algorithm. Then, LOCALE uses term-frequency methods to assign probable terms to each cluster in the hierarchy. The output of the pre-processing step is a clusters/terms table $CL(C, E, T, F, P)$ of clusters (C), their geographical extent (E), terms (T), the frequency of the term in pictures of this cluster (F), and the parent cluster (P). For example, many pictures are taken in front of Stanford's Hoover Tower; but at the same location one can turn around and take a photo of Memorial Auditorium. Assuming all these photos are geo-clustered together in cluster c_1, two tuples of the format $(c_1, e_1, \text{"Hoover Tower"}, f_1, p)$ and $(c_1, e_1, \text{"Memorial Auditorium"}, f_2, p)$ will appear in CL. Here, f_1 and f_2 are the frequencies in c_1 of "Hoover Tower" and "Memorial Auditorium", respectively, e_1 is the geographical extent of c_1, and p is the parent cluster of c_1 (for example, p could be a cluster that includes all photos of the campus.)

During search, the ranking of User 1's photos is again computed via a term-locations query with parameters t_q, G_1 to the LOCALE server. For each

$g \in G_1$ the LOCALE server assigns g to the closest leaf cluster c_ℓ. The cluster hierarchy is then ascended. Define c_ℓ's ancestors $ANC(c_\ell)$, and a view $TC_\ell = \sigma_{c \in \{c_\ell\} \cup ANC(c_\ell)}(CL)$. Then

$$Score(g, t_q) = \max_{(c_s, e_s, t_s, f_s, p_s) \in TC_\ell} IR'(t_q, t_s, f_s) PROX'(g, e_s)$$

In other words, the score for the search term and the current geographic location g is taken from the cluster in the hierarchy that maximizes the geographical and text/frequency match to the location g and the search term t_q respectively.

Function $PROX'$ is based on the probability of g belonging to c_s's extent, $Prob(g \in e_s)$, and (inversely) to the area of the cluster (the more broad e_s is, the less we value the match). The extent is represented by a two-dimensional Gaussian distribution. The function IR' is based on the frequency of t_q in tuples of cluster c_s in CL, but takes into account the sum of frequencies over all other terms that appear within c_s: the fewer other terms appear within c_s, the more relevant t_q is. This process is similar to the distributed-mode score computation described below (Section 2.2). The particular hierarchical clustering algorithm we used for LOCALE is agglomerative clustering (see [6]).

As in all other centralized-mode computations, the LOCALE server returns a table $Y = \left\{ (g, s) | g \in G_1; s = Score(g, t_q) \right\}$. This is the reply of the LOCALE server to the query; the LOCALE system on the user's machine computes $P_1 \bowtie Y$ to produce a ranking over images.

Term-Locations Query in Term-Clustered (TC) LOCALE. Under the Term-Clustered LOCALE strategy, the server pre-processes the label/location database to compute the geographical extent, or extents, of every term (one- or two-word phrase) that appears in the labels. For example, the algorithm may determine that the term "Hoover Tower" corresponds to two areas: one adjacent to the tower, and the other at a good viewpoint some 500 meters away from where many photographs of Hoover were taken. We compute the extents using a clustering algorithm. See Fig. 2 for the clusters corresponding to the term "fountain"; for illustration we manually marked the extents of the four main clusters in the figure. At the end of the pre-processing steps, we have a table $TC(T, C, E)$ of terms, their associated clusters, and each cluster's geographical extent described by a two-dimensional Gaussian distribution.

As usual in centralized mode, the user search is translated to a term-locations query with parameters t_q, G_1 and sent to the LOCALE server. For each user photo location $g \in G_1$, the server assigns a score according to the geographical match between g and the clusters of term t_q:

$$Score(g, t_q) = \max_{(t_s, c_s, e_s) \in TC} IR''(t_q, t_s) PROX''(g, e_s)$$

The function $PROX''$ is based on the probability of g belonging to the cluster extent, $Prob(g \in e_s)$. The function IR'' is the equality in singular form ($IR(t_q, t_s) = 1 \Leftrightarrow singular(t_q) = singular(t_s)$). As for the LC strategy, we

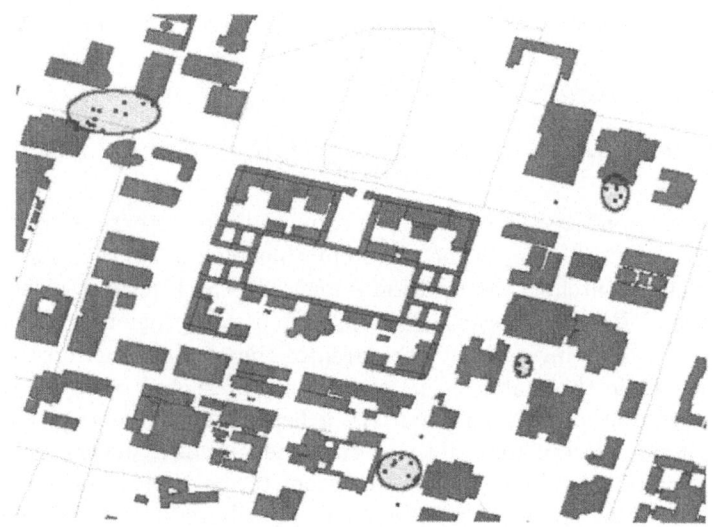

Fig. 2. Map of Stanford campus, with geographical distribution of photographs whose labels contain the term "fountain"

use an agglomerative clustering algorithm. However, since TC required "flat" (one-level) clusters we flattened the cluster tree from the bottom up until we hit sibling clusters that are further than 50 meters away from each other. This provided sufficient results since we found that in the case of terms (like "fountain") that have a number of extents, the extents were distinctly remote from each other.

The LOCALE server then replies with $Y = \left\{ (g, s) | g \in G_1; s = Score(g, t_q) \right\}$. Y is joined with P_1 to produce a ranking of u_1's images.

In the process described above, we generate the clusters and extents for every term, even some terms that are not meaningful geographically. For example, the words "mom", "bicycle", "student" appeared in the labels but are not associated, of course, with a specific location. Indeed, we expected these terms to be randomly distributed around campus. We studied mechanisms to identify such high "entropy" terms, in order to flag those terms as *geographical stop-words* and skip pre-processing for them. We did not find an accurate enough mechanism, mostly, we suspect, because of the limited scope of our experiment. Similarly, we could extend the IR functions to capture the notion of Inverse Document Frequency (IDF), by calculating the number of regions in the map where each term appears. For the scope of our experiment, however, such calculation was not necessary.

2.2   Distributed Mode

In distributed mode (User 2 in Fig. 1), the LOCALE computation is executed in two steps. In the first step, performed in advance, the LOCALE server is used in conjunction with the location data in User 2's collection $G_2 = \Pi_G(P_2)$ to create a new *term-score table* $TS_2(I, T, S)$ of User 2's images (I), possible matching terms (T), and the score (S) of the match between the image and the term. To this end, the user's machine submits a *term-retrieval query* to the LOCALE server with the photo locations G_2. The reply from the LOCALE server consists of a table $Z(G, T, S)$ of locations, terms and scores which is then used to produce TS_2. User 2's machine retains TS_2 (it may also choose periodically to update it).

The details of this location-term score computation are different for each of the three strategies, and are listed below. In all strategies, the terms are picked and their scores are computed based on some notion of geographical closeness. Going back to our early example with users M and H, the reply Z to a query by M's machine, that includes the location of the church photo g_c, may include a tuple $(g_c, \text{"Stanford Church"}, s)$. The reply is based on the label submitted by H earlier, where the score s is based on the distance between H's and M's photos. However, s may also incorporate other photos labeled the same way, and the reply may also include tuples for g_c with other terms.

At the end of this first, advance, step, Z is joined (on attribute G) with User 2's photo table P_2 to generate $TS_2(I, T, S)$. Notice that the geographic information can now be discarded. Also notice that the LOCALE server need not be contacted further after we constructed the TS_2 table.

The second step, the actual search, is the same for all implementation strategies. This step is performed when the user submits a search query for term t_q. The search is done directly on table TS_2 - no other data is required. The system looks for possible matches to the search term t_q in the T column of TS_2. The lookup result, as in the centralize case, is a ranking of the photos $\Pi_I(P_2)$ based on an adjusted score of each image i with respect to the search term t_q. The adjustment is based on the "evidence" in favor of the search term, in contrast to evidence against it for each photo.

Table 1. Sample term-score table TS_M for User M

I	T	S
i_c	Church	30
i_c	Quad	15
i_k	Church	30
i_k	Quad	200

For example, going back to user M – suppose he has taken two images, i_c and i_k. The term-score table for M appears in Table 1. In this example, there are two tuples in TS_M for the "Church" photo i_c. The initial score of 30 for i_c and term "Church" does not tell the entire story. Obviously, it is more likely that i_c is a picture of the church than i_k (which is probably a picture of the Quad). For this reason we use a correction factor, the ratio of the score to the total score of terms suggested for this photo. In this case, the final score for photo i_c and the term "Church" will be $30 \times \frac{30}{30+15}$.

Formally, if a tuple (i_c, t_q, s) appears in TS_2 we adjust s by the total of scores for image i_c. The final score is computed as follows:

$$Score(i_c, t_q) = s \times \frac{s}{s + \sum \Pi_S(\sigma_{i=i_c, t_q \neq t}(TS_2))}$$

The same idea is extended for the case where terms consist of two words, but in this case we exclude terms that match either one of these words from the summation.

Finally, all the images in P_2 are ranked according to their computed match score with t_q, and returned to the user.

As usual in distributed problems, there is a tradeoff between the accuracy of distributed processing and the amount of data stored on users' machines. The good news is that the user's machine does not have to hold all the information available at LOCALE: the information is confined to the areas where the user has taken photos, and summarized as described above. In fact, in our experiments, the term-score table only kept the top 15 terms per photo. We show (Sect. 3) that even with this small amount of data (about 300 bytes per photo) we still achieved search results comparable to the centralized mode.

We now describe how the LOCALE server handles distributed mode term-retrieval queries under the different LOCALE implementation strategies.

Term-Retrieval Query in Distributed Weighted-Neighbors (DWN) LOCALE. Recall that the term-retrieval query parameter includes only the locations of the user's photos $G_2 = \Pi_G(P_2)$. A reply is a table $Z(G, T, S)$ of terms matching each location, and their matching scores. Recall also that the term-retrieval is performed in advance, before the user submits a search.

In Weighted Neighbors LOCALE, we compute Z by selecting possible terms for each location $g \in G_2$ from neighboring photos (photos in P_s taken in proximity to g). More formally, we compute a score for every term t that appears in P_s, with respect to the location g: $Score(g, t) = \sum_{(i_s, g_s, \ell_s) \in P_s} IR(t, \ell_s) PROX(g, g_s)$. The IR and $PROX$ functions are as defined in Sect. 3. The table $Z(G, T, S)$ is then constructed; $Z = \{(g, t, s) | g \in G_2; s = Score(g, t)\}$. As described above, the user's machine joins table Z with P_2 to generate the term-score table TS_2.

For example, say two photos p_j and p_k whose labels include the term "Church" appear in P_s; g_j is 10mts and g_k 15mts away from $g_c \in G_2$. Then $Score(g_c, \text{"Church"}) = IR(\text{"Church"}, \ell_j) PROX(10) + IR(\text{"Church"}, \ell_k) PROX(15)$. The reply table Z will include the tuple $(g_c, \text{"Church"}, Score(g_c, \text{"Church"}))$.

Term-Retrieval Query in Distributed Location-Clustered (DLC) and Distributed Term-Clustered (DTC) LOCALE. In both DLC and DTC strategies, the pre-processing in distributed mode is the same as in the respective centralized mode (Sect. 2.1). For both, the process of generating a term-score table for users in advance is analogous to the process performed by DWN. We therefore skip detailed discussions of these strategies.

3   The Visitor-Center Experiment

We ran an experiment to see if the LOCALE system is effective in terms of executing the following user task: "find among my unlabeled pictures the ones that best match the term t_q". In particular, we sought to determine which implementation strategy offers the best result. We also wished to determine whether the results of the distributed search are comparable to the centralized search. Finally, the experiment would help us tune the system's parameters.

For this experiment we required a data set of labeled, geo-referenced photos. Moreover, we needed a high concentration of such photos in a single geographic area; otherwise it would not be possible to obtain statistically significant results. We therefore limited the data set to a bounded "world" – in our case, the Stanford University campus. Every day, tourists take photos on the campus[4], and we made use of these tourists to collect data for our experiment.

3.1   Experimental Setup

We provided loaner cameras and GPS devices to visitors taking the Stanford Visitor Center's campus tour. Thus, the data set was limited to one part of campus (albeit the most photographed one). We asked for volunteers among the groups that were taking the tour. The volunteers were instructed to take photos at their leisure, as if the loaner were their own camera. The GPS devices continuously tracked and logged their carrier's location. After the tour we collected the cameras and GPS units. Some hours later, the participants were sent an email message that asked them to enter labels underneath their photos on a web page we had prepared for this purpose and that we promised to host for them. Most of the participants completed this task a few hours to one week after the end of the tour, much in the fashion of people labeling their own photos upon return from a trip. The participants were instructed to label their photos for their own use: the labels would be used as captions for their online photos and on a photo CD that we sent them in return for their effort. The hosting of photos and the photo CD served as incentives for people to participate in our experiment and to label their photos. We requested that participants label as many of their photos as they would like, but they were not *required* to label even a single photo.

We used software[5] to "align" the GPS track log and the corresponding tourist's photos via timestamps. We thereby created a geo-referenced collection P_u for each tourist's photos. The procedure produced geo-referenced photos with accuracy of roughly 10mts, limited by the original GPS accuracy and the track logs' time resolution.

---

[4] This fact also demonstrates that many photos are taken by different people in the same place (hence, the ability to share.)

[5] http://www.geospatialexperts.com/

We lent cameras to 52 visitors who took an average of 20 photos each. A total of 37 of the participants visited our web site to submit labels. We collected 761 labeled photos, 460 of them geo-referenced. The primary reasons for unreferenced photos were bad GPS reception (e.g., inside buildings, underpasses) and incorrect handling of the equipment (holding the GPS unit out of clear view of the sky). For those labeled photos that were not referenced due to incorrect handling, we manually added location stamps: our knowledge of campus allowed us to determine where each photo was taken. At the end, we had 672 labeled, geo-referenced photos.

The label/location data was prone to problems, some specific to our experiment and some more general. Specific to our experiment are visitors who clearly labeled the photos for no other reason than pleasing us ("Building 1", "Building 2", "Building 3"). One set of labels was clearly produced this way and was removed from our data. Another problem is introduced by the different use patterns with digital cameras: people take many more photos than a typical film camera owner would take in an hour. In our experiment, this effect sometimes reduces the accuracy of labeling (in real life this may not be the case since people may not label "uninteresting" photos). Other problems may appear under any kind of setting. First, since we did not restrict the labels in any way, some of the labels ("Our tour leader: a fine young woman") do not contribute any geographical information. Second, tourists everywhere tend to be less knowledgeable about landmarks and their names than locals may be. Thus, in many cases the labels were not accurate or just plain wrong. We retained this data since such inaccuracies reflect the realities of collective labeling and were thus pertinent to the experiment.

3.2 Experiment Procedure

We performed keyword searches over various users' collections using our LOCALE database of 672 labeled, geo-referenced photos of Stanford's campus. A human referee decided on the relevance of the retrieved images. Strict relevance measures were applied: a result image was deemed to match a search term if and only if an object described by the search term clearly appears in the image. Fig. 3 shows the three top-ranked results for the query "Hoover Tower" on one of the collections. For the purpose of our experiment, the top two photos were determined relevant to "Hoover Tower"; the third is not relevant even though the tower would be visible from the position where the photo was taken. Incidentally, the third photo's position is right between the locations where the other two photos were taken.

We performed our evaluation for different "scenarios": a *global* and an *individual* scenario, as described below. For each scenario, we require:

- A collection of geo-referenced yet unlabeled photographs on which we can perform search.
- A set of search terms we can test on this collection.

For the global scenario, the collection we used was the set of photographs taken by visitors who never accessed our web site to label their photographs. We

Fig. 3. LOCALE Search results for "Hoover Tower" query

had a total of 253 such photographs. This collection emulates a multi-user pool of photographs such as an image database. The search terms for this collection were chosen from all the *labeled* photographs we collected in the experiment, with two conditions: a) The term appears at least four times in the LOCALE database and b) The term is meaningful in *some* geographical manner. For example, we did not include terms like "car" or "student", but *did* include "fountain" and "mosaic". We also excluded search terms that match all the photos in our collection like "Stanford" or "campus". We retained a total of 27 qualifying terms.

For the individual scenario, we picked user collections that were *labeled*, removed their labels, and used the labels as a source for search terms. Each collection comprised pictures taken by *one* visitor. Search on these user collections better emulates search on a personal collection of photos than the global scenario. The collections we picked for the individual scenario had to have a reasonable number of photos (> 25) and labels that are geographically meaningful. There were 13 such collections in total. For each collection, we removed the collection's photo metadata from the LOCALE database. The search terms for each collection were picked so that they a) appear in the user's own (removed) labels and b) are meaningful geographically as described above. In picking only terms that appear in the user's labels we are able to simulate a "personal search": we search for terms as the user thought about them – for example, someone may want to locate their photo of the "chapel" while most people labeled their photo of the same building "church". An average of 8.7 search terms per collection were picked. A sample of the query terms picked for one collection is: "Hoover, tower, engineering building, fountain, clock fountain, palm, Quad, arches, chapel, mosaic, residence."

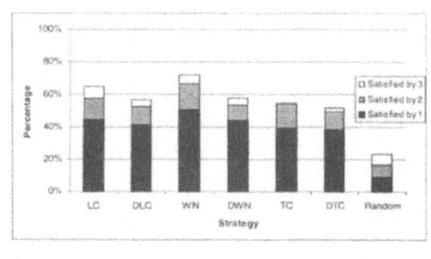 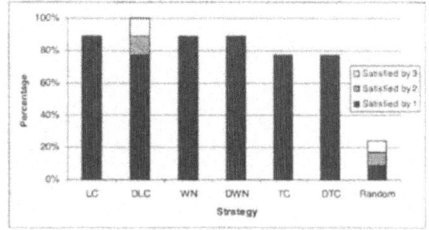

(a) All queries   (b) "Hoover" queries only

Fig. 4. The percentage of queries in every strategy that found a relevant photo within first three results

4   Results

We first discuss the results for the individual scenario. Then we discuss the results for the global scenario.

4.1   Results for the Individual Scenario

As a first step we examine which strategy performs best for the individual scenario, and compare the distributed and centralized implementations. We looked at how many of the queries were *satisfied* – returned at least one relevant photo (a photo matching the search term according to a human referee). We executed the queries as described in Sect. 3.2, while limiting the number of photos retrieved to one, two and three photographs. Often, the actual number of photos with a score greater than 0 was lower than this limit. The results for the different strategies averaged over all collections and queries are shown in Fig. 4(a). On the X-axis we identify the strategy (by acronyms - WN for Weighted Neighbors, DWN for Distributed Weighted Neighbors and so forth). The Y-axis shows the percentage of queries that returned at least one relevant photo within one, two and three retrieved photos. For example, WN produced a relevant photograph within the first three photos retrieved in 72% of the queries. The "random" strategy reflects the expected values when the results are completely random, as is included as a baseline for comparison.

A number of conclusions follow from Fig. 4(a). We can see that all the strategies performed better in centralized mode than they did in the corresponding distributed mode (strategy name starts with 'D'). For example, when the retrieval limit was set to 3, WN satisfied 72% of the queries while DWN satisfied only 58%. Part of this difference can be attributed to the summarization done in the distributed modes, as described in Sect. 2.2. Less popular terms may not score high enough to make it into the summary of a relevant photo, and therefore the photo will not be retrieved. We try to address this issue in more detail with the results of the global scenario.

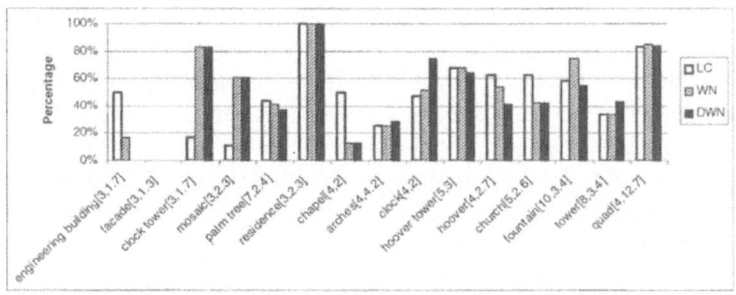

Fig. 5. Average *recall at* $T(t,c)$ for popular query terms

The best performing strategies were WN, LC, and DWN. Incidentally, the percentage of queries satisfied by the first retrieved photo is around 40-50%. This percentage is quite good considering the search terms often included low-frequency terms (e.g., "red fountain"). Compare these numbers to the baseline results of the "random" strategy where the probability that the first retrieved image matches the query is less than 9%. By the third retrieved image, 50-70% of the queries were satisfied (at least one relevant photo was retrieved).

Performance is improved significantly when concentrating on more common terms. To illustrate, Fig. 4(b) shows the same metric limited to queries for the popular terms "Hoover" and "Hoover Tower". Of our 13 collections, our term selection procedure generated "Hoover" or "Hoover Tower" in 9 instances. We used these 9 collections to produce Fig. 4(b). In all the strategies, the first photo retrieved was relevant (a picture of the tower) in 78% of the queries or more. By the third image retrieved, at least one image of Hoover Tower was found in 78-100% of the queries.

Based on the results in Fig. 4 we decided to concentrate on Weighted Neighbors, Distributed Weighted Neighbors, and Location Clustered strategies for the rest of this discussion of the individual scenario.

Instead of the aggregate results presented so far, we now drill down to the level of query terms. We wish to examine the variability between the strategies when handling particular query terms. Figure 5 shows *recall* results for the most popular query terms: the X-axis corresponds to query terms that were used across at least three individual collections. The first number in square brackets next to each term is the number of collections we queried with this term. Remember: for each collection we picked its own query terms from its original labels. For example, the query term "fountain" was picked for search in 10 out of the 13 collections. The second number within the brackets is the average number of relevant photos in these collections. For example, the "fountain collections" have on average 3.4 photos of a fountain. The terms are presented from left to right in order of rising popularity in the label database. "Quad" was the most popular term, appearing 80 times in photo labels.

Recall is usually measured at some pre-defined number of retrieved results: how many of the relevant photos were retrieved when the retrieval is limited to x photos. As mentioned above, the number of relevant photos for each term and collection varied extensively. Thus, we could not use a fixed retrieval limit. We therefore set a different retrieval limit for each term and collection combination – the number of relevant photos. For each collection and term, we manually counted $T(t, c)$ – the total number of photos in collection c which are relevant for term t. Then we submitted the query t over collection c, while limiting the number of retrieved photos to $T(t, c)$. Finally, the recall was computed by dividing the number of relevant photos retrieved by $T(t, c)$[6].

The bars in Fig. 5 group the recall results by term, simply by averaging the computed recall over all collections queried with this term. For example, the average recall at T for the fountain query in LC mode was 60%.

Generally, the performance of all three top strategies based on Fig. 5 is comparable. The average recall at $T(t, c)$ is usually between 25-75%, and on average higher than 45%. The DWN strategy performs almost as well as the centralized WN; in a few cases it even outperforms the centralized implementation. This fact reaffirms our thesis that the unpopular terms are responsible for the lower performance of the distributed strategies in Fig. 4(a). We have no intuition for why WN/DWN perform much better than LC for some terms, and much worse for others.

4.2   Results for the Global Scenario

In the global scenario, we have one collection that is the union of all unlabeled collections. As explained in Sect. 3.2, we had 253 photographs in this collection. We start by comparing the results to the individual scenario. We then compare the different strategies and modes in more depth, and pick three strategy/mode combinations for extended evaluation.

How different is retrieval in the global scenario? Figure 6 compares the number of queries *satisfied*, the same metric used in Fig. 4(a). However, we limited the queries to terms appearing both in the global and in the individual scenario, and we show the stacked results side-by-side for each strategy. The bars corresponding to the global scenario are noted with (G). Again, random retrieval is shown as a baseline.

Interestingly, for most strategies, the first result in the individual scenario was relevant more often than in the global scenario; but by the third result, more queries found a match in the global scenario. The reason for this phenomenon, we believe, is "cluttering" in the global scenario. The individual photos in each collection tend not to be as close to each other as in the global scenario. Take for example the TC strategy described in Sect. 3. Once our system identified geographical extents that correspond to a term, we are likely to find fewer photos in that area in an individual collection than we may find in a global collection. Therefore, the first result is more precise for the individual collection. However, if a match is not found in the first result, there are more match prospects (candidate photos from the same area) in a global collection.

---

[6] Note that when the retrieval is set to $T(t, c)$, the recall is equal to the precision.

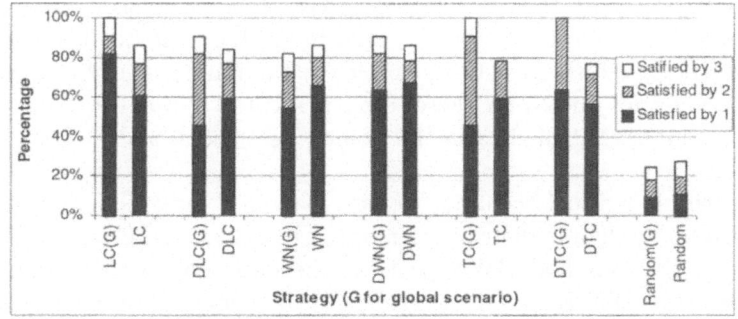

Fig. 6. The percentage of queries in every strategy that found a relevant photo in first three results, for global and individual scenarios

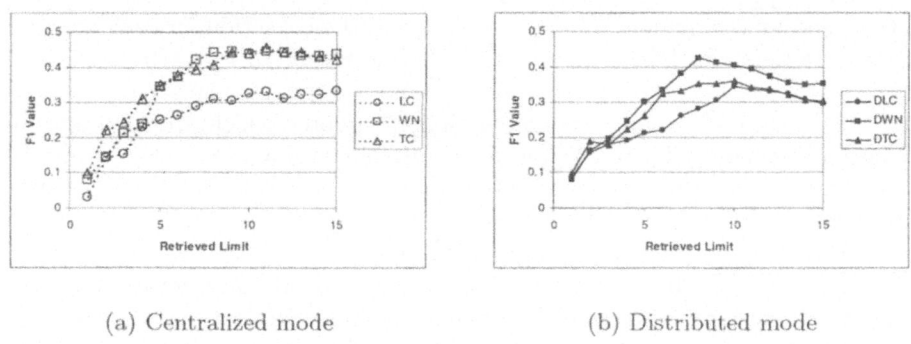

(a) Centralized mode   (b) Distributed mode

Fig. 7. Average F_1 values for least frequent query terms in different strategies, vs. retrieval limit

The previous discussion was limited to a subset of the query terms and a small number of retrieved results, in order to have a base for comparison. To investigate in more depth how the strategies perform in global scenario, we expand on this evaluation. Since our global collection is large, we can now use standard IR measures such as recall, precision, and F_1.

To compare the different mode/strategy combinations, we looked at the F_1 values over varying numbers of retrieved documents (1 to 15), averaged over all queries. The F_1 measure combines precision and recall into a single metric that represents the value of the results to the user. Figs. 7(a) (strategies in centralized mode) and 7(b) (distributed mode) show the F_1 values for the 10 least frequent query terms – the terms used in the global scenario that appear the fewest number of times in the label database. For the 10 *most* frequent terms there were no considerable differences between the strategies, and hence we do not show results for them.

The X-axis in Fig. 7 corresponds to the photo retrieval limit. The Y-axis shows the F_1 value for each strategy. Although values for F_1 range from 0 to 1, the maximum possible F_1 value at each point is not 1, but is dependent on the maximum possible recall/precision at that point. For example, for our data, the best possible F_1 value at 1 is 0.27; at 8 is 0.85 and at 15 is 0.72. As the average number of relevant photos for these terms is 8.1, the optimal F_1 is reached at 8. As seen in the figure, this is also the point where the actual F_1 peaks for most strategies.

As in the individual scenario, we see that all strategies perform better in centralized mode than in distributed mode. The LC and DLC strategies perform the worst while WN and DWN perform the best. For further evaluation, we picked the WN, DWN and TC strategies. As a reminder, WN and DWN were also the choice strategies in the individual scenario (together with LC).

Now that we have limited the discussion to three strategies, we wish to understand the variability between strategies and between queries. We drill down again and list the results by query terms. In Fig. 8 we plot the recall and precision for each search term in WN, DWN and TC LOCALE. The retrieval limit is set to 15 photos. The search terms are displayed in order of popularity, as determined by the number of relevant photos in the collection for each query (in square brackets). In Fig. 8(a) the Y-axis is the recall. In Fig. 8(b), the Y-axis shows the precision. We can see how the more popular term's recall is lower (mainly because there are a lot more than 15 photos which are relevant) and precision is generally higher. While the results for WN and TC are comparable, it seems that recall for the distributed mode (DWN) is higher than the other strategies for the popular terms, yet slightly lower for the unpopular ones. Before we address this, we make a general observation about Fig. 8.

One possible predictor of successful vs. unsuccessful query terms is the concentration of other "interesting" landmarks around the unsuccessful terms. Two interesting outliers in Fig. 8 are "Gates" and "fountain". There are a number of attractions around the Gates building. Thus, in a global collection it may happen that only, suppose, 15% of the photos taken from a Gates viewpoint are indeed pictures of the building; "Gates" retrieval precision is expected to be less than 15%. The term "fountain" offers a contrasting example. People are fascinated with running water, and most of the photos in the areas where fountains are found were, in fact, pictures of the fountains. The precision of fountain is expected to be higher.

As we already hinted above, the problem of "cluttered attractions" was not as acute in the individual collection evaluations. The reason is that in an individual collection there are very few pictures taken at every location. Back to the Gates example, a single person may take one picture of Gates building and one of the other attractions around it; now, when looking for "Gates", the precision should not fall under 50% (compared to the 15% in the global collection).

Going back to the less-popular terms, can we improve on the lower recall of DWN for them? A possible remedy is enlarging the scope of summarization data for each photo. As we explain in Sect. 2.2, in distributed mode we only keep the 15 top matching terms for each photo. We tried the same less-popular term queries when 25 terms are allowed in the term-score table for each photo. Two of the queries, for "clock fountain" and "hall", retrieved three and one (respec-

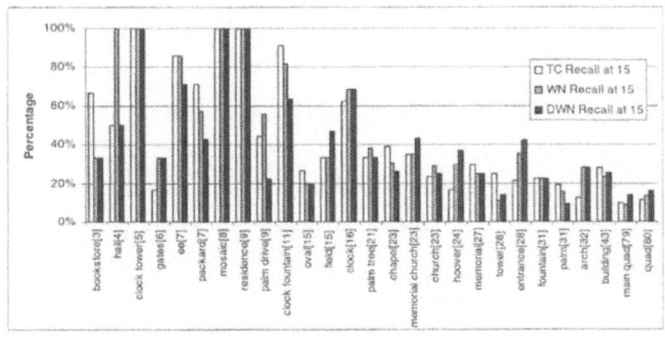

(a) Recall

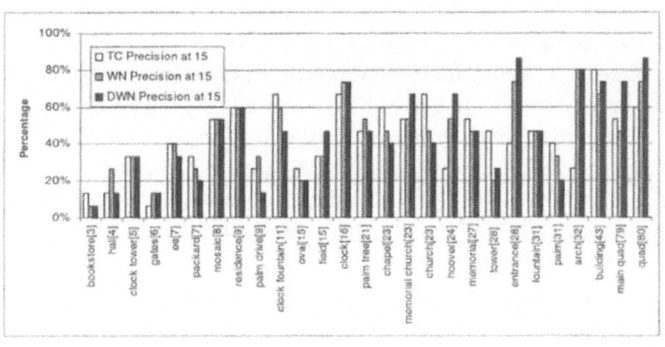

(b) Precision

Fig. 8. Recall and precision at 15 for each query term

tively) more relevant photographs then they did before, while the precision for all the queries did not change (i.e., no negative effect was noted on user query satisfaction). In summary, there seem to be marginal benefits in holding more matching terms for each photo.

5   Automatically Assigning Captions to Photos

For LOCALE's distributed mode, we used term-retrieval queries that collect potentially matching terms for each photo in the user's collection. The system never exposes these suggestions to the users, as these terms are used during search only. But what if it did make these candidate terms available? The system could suggest these terms as a location caption for photos. For example, we could automatically display the top-matching term for every photo as its caption when the user is browsing his collection. Alternatively, our UI design could enable the user to choose the appropriate term from the suggested term list.

Table 2. Photos and suggested terms

Actual Objects in Photo	Suggested Terms
Hoover Tower, Fountain	tower, hoover, hoover tower, tour, fountain.
The Oval	quad, oval, main, main quad, field, the oval.
Clock fountain	building, fountain, clock, Stanford, gates.
Main Quad	church, quad, chapel, Stanford, memorial, memorial church.

Our algorithms were not tuned for this task, but we wanted to examine the prospects of this idea on a sample collection of photos. In Table 2 we show the top 5-6 suggested terms for a few of the photos in one collection. For each photo we list the objects that appear in it on the left, and the suggested terms on the right. The terms were generated by the Distributed Weighted Neighbors implementation.

These sample photos were chosen because the scores for their top suggested terms were especially high. The photos correspond to Stanford's most popular landmarks. The second photo was taken in front of The Oval (an oval-shaped field), but Stanford's Main Quad is right across from it in the other direction. The fourth photo was taken in the Main Quad, in front of the church. Suggested terms for other photos in the collection were not as accurate; but the terms were also scored lower, which demonstrates LOCALE's appropriately low confidence in the match.

Further work is needed to tune the algorithms that suggest terms to users. The thresholds are extremely sensitive, and concerns of exposing private information are greater than in the search scenario. However, we do believe that a reliable system that supports this feature can be implemented.

6   Related and Future Work

Two related fields of research are image retrieval and image labeling. Facilitating efficient labeling of photos has been a focus of research and development in recent years. Ease and automation of the labeling task was the focus of work in [7,5, 8]. For example, [5] proposed a drag-and-drop approach for labeling people in photos. The latest photo browser software packages (Adobe's Photoshop Album, Apple's iPhoto[7] and others) also try to support efficient labeling. In Photoshop Album, labels are divided into categories (e.g., people, places). Such explicit user-entered place labels would simplify the LOCALE analysis. However, we

---

[7] http://www.adobe.com/, http://www.apple.com/

designed the system more generally so that it could utilize any text associated with the photographs.

More relevant to our work is the field of collaborative labeling. In the context of photos, collaboration in labeling has been explicit, and has concentrated on allowing many users to label a shared collection of images. See [9] for details. In contrast, our collaboration is implicit, and users do not need to share images.

In image retrieval, most of the work has been "content based" – using different technologies to extract and query by image features (see [4] for an extensive summary of research in this area). The most interesting future direction for LOCALE may be in augmenting the system with image retrieval and image-analysis tools. Feature extraction will enable better matching of labels and candidate photos. LOCALE can be augmented with systems like Blobworld [10,11] to allow the automatic labeling of objects within images if the image occurs in a certain geographical area.

More internal to the LOCALE implementation, one possible future direction is developing a set of additional techniques to handle larger geographical areas, and higher condensation of data. For example, a LOCALE system covering the entire world should be able to assign not only local labels ("Hoover Tower") but also higher-level labels ("Stanford University"). In addition, we can think about using other data sources such as an "official" gazetteer. However, existing gazetteers (see [12] for example) are usually more reliable in identifying a city/state/country than a landmark related to a single photo. Using additional available metadata is another direction. Examples may be the direction the camera pointed when the picture was taken, or already-captured metadata such as focal point and F-stop. We also consider adding time sensitivity to LOCALE, so it can detect temporal outliers such as "graduation" appearing in an area associated with "Stanford University" during a few days in June. LOCALE should detect such anomalies, remove those labels from the time-neutral dataset, but at the same time suggest these labels for photos taken at the time of the event. Another type of context-sensitivity in LOCALE can be automatic detection of expert users - expert user being one who had contributed many photos of the same geographical area at different times. The expert user's labels may be better trusted based on the assumption that the user knows the mentioned area well. Finally, getting text associated with photos from other sources (web pages, newspaper articles etc.) may be possible as geo-referenced photos become abundant.

7   Conclusions

Our LOCALE cooperative image retrieval system addresses the problems of (a) searching and (b) labeling for global and individual photo collections.

LOCALE shows promising results for keyword search over personal collections of photographs. Even in our limited experiment, the system was able to retrieve and identify landmarks and geographical features with surprising accuracy. On the other hand, the geographic scope of the experiment was small, and the results have to be verified when broader-coverage collections are available.

In addition, our system proved quite useful in a global scenario, providing support for image search on a multi-user database of photos. However, it seems that for such scenarios the system needs to be augmented by other techniques to improve precision. Again, we would like to be able to evaluate the system across broader geographical coverage.

We have also shown satisfying preliminary results for assigning location-related captions to photos, either automatically or semi-automatically with some human assistance (i.e., the user can choose a caption from a few top-scoring candidate terms). Helping users assign labels may assist future search: when users perform searches, their own labels will be more significant matches than labels submitted by others. Ease of labeling will also benefit other cooperating users, as the assigned labels will be submitted and enrich the LOCALE system.

Acknowledgments. This work was made possible by the help of the Stanford Visitor Center. The center's staff was extremely helpful; we would especially like to thank Sean Fenton, Andrea Pazfrost and Lisa Mendelman for their efforts.

References

[1] Kerry Rodden and Kenneth R. Wood. How do people manage their digital photographs? In *Proceedings of the conference on Human factors in computing systems*, pages 409–416. ACM Press, 2003.

[2] David Frohlich, Allan Kuchinsky, Celine Pering, Abbe Don, and Steven Ariss. Requirements for photoware. In *Proceedings of the 2002 ACM conference on Computer supported cooperative work*, 2002.

[3] Adrian Graham, Hector Garcia-Molina, Andreas Paepcke, and Terry Winograd. Time as essence for photo browsing through personal digital libraries. In *Proceedings of the Second ACM/IEEE-CS Joint Conference on Digital Libraries*, 2002. Available at http://dbpubs.stanford.edu/pub/2002-4.

[4] Remco C. Veltkamp and Mirela Tanase. Content-based image retrieval systems: A survey. Technical Report TR UU-CS-2000-34 (revised version), Department of Computing Science, Utrecht University, October 2002.

[5] Ben Shneiderman and Hyunmo Kang. Direct annotation: A drag-and-drop strategy for labeling photos. In *Proceedings of the International Conference on Information Visualization*, May 2000.

[6] A. K. Jain, M. N. Murty, and P. J. Flynn. Data clustering: a review. *ACM Computing Surveys*, 31(3):264–323, 1999.

[7] Allan Kuchinsky, Celine Pering, Michael L. Creech, Dennis Freeze, Bill Serra, and Jacek Gwizdka. Fotofile: a consumer multimedia organization and retrieval system. In *Proceedings of the Conference on Human Factors in Computing Systems CHI'99*, pages 496–503, 1999.

[8] Liu Wenyin, Susan Dumais, Yanfeng Sun, HongJiang Zhang, Mary Czerwinski, and Brent Field. Semi-automatic image annotation. In *8th International Conference on Human-Computer Interactions (INTERACT 2001), 9–13 July 2001, Tokyo, Japan*, 2001.

[9] Bill Kules, Hyunmo Kang, Catherine Plaisant, Anne Rose, and Ben Shneiderman. Immediate usability: Kiosk design principles from the CHI 2001 photo library. Technical Report CS-TR-4293, University of Maryland, 2003.

[10] Chad Carson, Megan Thomas, Serge Belongie, Joseph M. Hellerstein, and Jitendra Malik. Blobworld: A system for region-based image indexing and retrieval. In *Proceedings of the Third International Conference on Visual Information Systems*, June 1999.

[11] Kobus Barnard and David .A. Forsyth. Learning the semantics of words and pictures. In *Proceedings of the IEEE International Conference on Computer Vision*, July 2001.

[12] Linda L. Hill, James Frew, and Qi Zheng. Geographic names – the implementation of a gazetteer in a georeferenced digital library. *CNRI D-Lib Magazine*, January 1999.

Process of Product Fragments Management in Distributed Development

Darijus Strašunskas and Sari Hakkarainen

Dept. of Computer and Information Science, Norwegian Univ. of Science and Technology
Sem Sælands vei 7-9, NO-7491 Trondheim, Norway
{dstrasun; sari}@idi.ntnu.no

Abstract. Management of product constituent fragments is essential for large scale logically or physically distributed projects. Geographically distributed development projects have special settings and needs – special attention has to be given to artifacts management because developers are likely to use different representation formats and a variety of tools for the artifact production. The question is: how can artifacts in different representation formats be related and managed?
Methodological support for artifacts management and traceability is presented in this paper. Product fragments from different development phases (i.e., requirements specification, design, code, test scenarios, and documentation) are interrelated through a conceptual domain model. Domain model is proposed as a means to capture information content despite heterogeneous representation. Given, a domain model with intra-related concepts and artifacts associated to the concepts we are able to interrelate heterogeneous artifacts and to predict and assess how one altered artifact may impact other artifacts. The approach covers the whole lifecycle of a system, enables artifacts' management by associating them according semantics contained inside.

1 Introduction

Information system development is a highly iterative process, in which developers seek to capture the needs and desires of all stakeholders. The goal is to transform the requirements into a complete system, consisting of both manual and computerized parts. The product of a development project undergoes changes because of its iterative nature. Management of the development process imposes requires fine-grained control over all fragments produced throughout whole lifecycle. Traceability facilitates product and process management and control. Traceability is [9] a property of a system description technique that allows changes in one of the system descriptions – requirements specification, design, code, documentation, or test scenarios – to be traced to the corresponding fragments of the other descriptions. Further, such correspondence relationships should be maintained throughout the life time of a system in order to manage the artifact.

Traceability has received attention in the requirements engineering literature [8] [21], where change management requires special efforts because of the highly iterative process and frequent re-conceptualizations. Especially, the pre-requirements traceability has been studied thoroughly [13] [14]. However, there is a lack of traceability tools to support the full life-cycle, starting from artifact inception through for-

R. Meersman et al. (Eds.): CoopIS/DOA/ODBASE 2003, LNCS 2888, pp. 218–234, 2003.
© Springer-Verlag Berlin Heidelberg 2003

malization process to its use. Different representation formats that are used throughout the development process make it complicated to cover the whole life-cycle of an artifact. Given, a single requirement maps to multiple architectural and design concerns which is used to derive, it is difficult to maintain the consistency and traceability. Moreover, an architectural or design component has a number of other relations to various requirements. The task becomes even more difficult in the face of a large system that is build to satisfy thousands of requirements.

System specifications consist of a wide variety of fragments (artifacts), i.e. different kinds of information about system that together comprise a full (or partial) system specification at various levels of abstraction. Some of these artifacts are well structured, textual or graphical documents, while others are more loosely structured. In a geographically distributed project developers may use different tools to create and modify product fragments. The fragments can be refined iteratively and further processed by colleagues. Afterwards produced fragments are interchanged among members of a project, so that is important for colleagues to interpret an artifact correctly. The main challenges are to interrelate and manage all artifacts in different representation formats that are produced in a distributed manner using different tools, and to cover the whole product lifecycle.

The objective of this work is to present an approach to product fragments management during the distributed collaborative development process. The assumptions are that there are intra-related concepts in the problem domain and fragments are mapped to them. Given those conditions, the semantics of an artifact are increased by the artifact mapping to the corresponding concepts, and that enables predicting and assessing fragment change impact on other fragments.

The paper is structured as follows. In section two, related work is analyzed. In section three, the domain model based approach for product fragments management is presented. In section four, a case study is applied and illustrated by using weighted graphs. Finally, in section five, the work is concluded and its possible shortcomings with some insight to how to solve them are discussed.

2 Related Works

Over the recent years, a number of techniques have been proposed to facilitate management of product development through traceability enabling techniques. Some examples are [8] cross referencing schemes, based on some form of tagging, numbering, or indexing; and requirements traceability matrices. Studies in the field of traceability have mainly focused on specific parts of the development process [18] – mostly in the areas of pre-requirements traceability (e.g. [13] [14]) and linking requirements to architectural components (e.g. [10], [15]).

Some of the approaches are based on a specific modeling language and /or a tool. A much cited tool is TOOR (Traceability of Object-Oriented Requirements) [13], which is based on FOOPS, a formal object-oriented language. Integrating textual specifications and UML (Unified Modeling Language) model elements is used by Letelier [11], as a framework for configuring requirements traceability. Both approaches are restricted to FOOPS and UML respectively and can sequentially only be applied to software process based on the same language.

Some approaches establish traceability links after the most of a system is developed (e.g. after producing requirements specification, code, etc.) and, per se, contribute mainly for product maintenance. Frezza et al [7] base their approach on simulation where both the requirements and the implemented system are simulated in order to obtain a set of result data. The data from the requirements and the implementation phase are then compared, which results in a quantitative measure of how accurate the running system implements the requirements. Egyed [5] uses a scenario driven approach to acquire runtime information about a system and relates the information – the footprints - to the requirements and a model of the running system. The footprints are analyzed in a tool, which shows how the components of the system interact when performing specified scenarios. Thus, provides additional trace information on how the running system actually fulfills its requirements and which parts of the design are affected.

Ramesh and Jarke in [16] offer a wide vision about the information that is needed for requirements traceability. Their study is based on an analysis of industrial software development projects. Two segments of traceability users are identified and two corresponding traceability meta-models are suggested. Proposed meta-models are extensive, but nevertheless do not show how different parts of system specification in various representation formats and abstraction levels can be related and traced. For instance, their rationale submodel includes decisions, issues or conflicts, assumptions, alternatives and arguments. This enables very precise description of the change necessity and situation at a particular time. However, recording of rationale has not been widely accepted in the industry due to the disruptive nature of recording the actions as they occur [1].

Hence, in overall, there is a lack of support to the whole product lifecycle. There is also an apparent lack of support for distributed teams that use different tools, representation techniques and notations. There exist development environments (e.g. Rational Suite AnalystStudio [17]), which compound together programs for requirements engineering, design, change management and code repository. Such environments are integrated programs that *a)* do not support collaborative work, *b)* do not support all project phases equally well, *c)* and a customer is bound to one vendor and language (environment) by choosing this kind of tool environment. Below, an attempt to fill in these gaps is presented.

3   Proposed Approach – Mapping to the Domain Concept

In this section we discuss our methodological approach for the artifacts management and traceability. First, the settings of the proposed approach are discussed. Next, functional perspective describes main steps required to enable and apply our approach. Finally, a meta-model describing the scope of the approach is presented and discussed.

3.1   Settings for the Approach

Above, it was argued that it is essential to enable change management and impact prediction through all phases of development in the distributed projects as mentioned above. To cover the whole lifecycle means that different tools and, most likely, different notations are used during the development project. A list of requirements for product development environments in order to enable collaboration in geographically distributed software products development is used in [6]. Here we adopt the requirements as follows.

Requirement 1. Unrestricted product object types – a product development environment should allow the developers to share any type of object that they might find useful for supporting their cooperation.

Requirement 2. Unrestricted relation types – a product development environment should allow the developers to create any type of relation between any two objects of product.

Requirement 3. Incremental product refinement – a product development environment should provide the developers with flexible mechanisms for incrementally refining the product. Hence, the developers should be allowed to start with vague products, and to refine them into more complete and formal ones.

The above three requirements were selected as to cover support for collaboration in distributed projects. Here, the product management and traceability method should meet the requirements 1 – 3 to ensure the applicability of the approach. As this approach is based on the fragments mapping to domain concepts, we say that a `fragment` is a well-defined piece of specification and has semantics, machine readable representation and identity, and supplementary, a `concept` is a well-defined unit of terms found in specific domain description. Further, there are two basic assumptions underlying the approach as follows.

Assumption 1. CASE-tools (Computer Aided Software Engineering) that are used during the product development support XML (eXtensible Markup Language) or XML-dialect format output of developed fragments.

Assumption 2. There is a problem domain and it can be characterized by well-defined, interrelated concepts. Furthermore these concepts are represented as nodes having weighted relationships which show the strength of relationship between the concepts (relatedness of concepts).

The former assumption is reasonable, since most CASE-tools maintain model interchange formats derived from XML and the latter is more restrictive since not all relationships can be easily expressed by weights.

3.2 Functional Perspective of the Approach

Based on above described assumptions, the overall process (see fig.1) consists of four basic steps, where the last three steps are iterative.

Step 1 – Building of conceptual domain specific model. This step consists of two main sub-steps: *(a)* extraction of domain specific concept and *(b)* weighing of relationships between concepts.

Step 1.a – Syntactical analysis of textual documents has been investigated thoroughly in last few decades. Natural language processing is a main technique used to extract more structural information out of documents. Efforts are directed to build models from requirements specification in natural language. The naïve approach is to use nouns as candidates for entities and verbs for relations between entities. However, there is necessity for more sophisticated techniques to handle linguistic variation when proposing model elements when constructing domain models from a large set of documents. [2] proposes approach of natural language analysis for semantic documents modeling, where techniques for domain model construction are discussed. The natural language based approach is adapted for concept extraction.

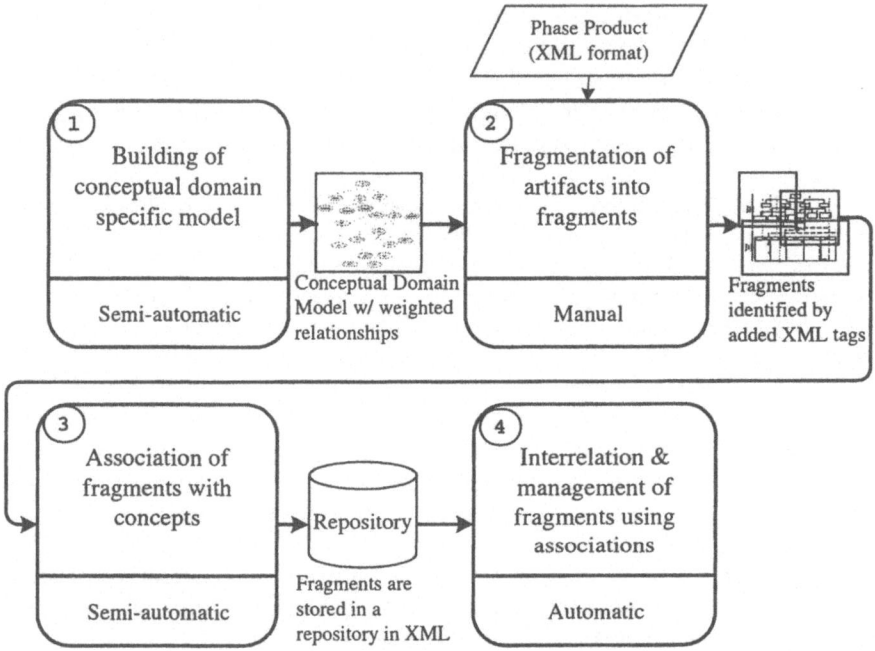

Fig. 1. Main steps to enable fragment management

Step 1.b – Quantification of the relationship between concepts is supported by using linguistics and natural language processing techniques for analyzing the documents from a domain. Collocation technique and text mining are used to evaluate the strength of relationship between concepts. The values should be refined by the domain expert – this reflects domain expert's belief in how much concepts are related in a particular domain. So, these numbers come from either objective data or the experiences of the domain expert accumulated from the development of similar projects. These ranges can be used to represent the high[1] (0.0 to 0.3), medium (0.4 to 0.6) and low (0.7 to 1.0) relatedness degree.

Step 2 – *Fragmentation of artifacts into fragments.* Produced artifact is translated to XML format and logically fragmented according its semantics. Fragmentation is done by a traceability module which gets the XML file as input and provides means for developer to define boundaries of a fragment. An XML file with identifying tags for start and end positions of fragment is produced as output.

Step 3 – *Association of fragments with the concepts.* Candidate concepts form domain model are suggested automatically by processing the fragments. Techniques

---

[1] 'High' means that distance between concept and fragment is short. The values are application sensitive, see a case study in chapter 4.

from *Step 1* are adapted to extract concepts, if possible, from the fragments and propose the closest related concept from domain model to map to it. Fragments can be linked directly to other fragments if developer finds them related or one fragment is part of another (more detailed explanation is provided in the meta-model description below). The weighing scheme is used as described in *Step 1.b*. The mapping rate is revised and confirmed by the developer, who created new or a version of the fragment and checked-in to the repository. The relationship information is encoded using XML tags. Finally, the fragments are stored in a central repository.

Fig. 2 presents a part of RML (Referent Model Language) [20] model in XML format where boundaries of a semantic fragment are identified by the tags `<fragment id="R0012">` and `</fragment>`, and the semantics of the fragments is encoded within the tags `<semantic-association>` and `</semantic-association>` by the associated concepts `<concept id="c17", weight="0.7"/>` and `<concept id="c05", weight="0.9"/>`.

```
<?xml version="1.0" encoding="ISO-8859-1" ?>
<referent-diagram>
  <generator app="refedit" version="Version: 2.3c" ver
    date="Sun 6 Feb 2000">
          <fragment id="R0012">
            <semantic-association>
              <concept id="c017" weight="0.7"/>
              <concept id="c005" weight="0.9"/>
            </semantic-association>
                <content>
                 <referent id="x1">
                    <position x="626" y="83" />
                    <dimension width="109" height="41" />
                  <text>
                    <position x="667" y="98" />
                    <string>Product</string>
                  </text>
                  <aggregation id="x2" idref="x1">
                    <position x="667" y="169" />
                  </aggregation>
                </referent>
              </content>
          </fragment>
    . . .
</referent-diagram>
```

Fig. 2. Cutout of fragmented RML model in XML representation

Step 4 – Usage of the associations for fragments interrelation and management. Domain model is constructed and concepts in the model are intra-related by weighted links according how strongly concepts relate. Those weights are further used to evaluate interrelations between fragments mapped to the domain concepts and to estimate likelihood of impact of one fragment to another.

Thus, association relations are based on the semantics of the artifacts. Fragments are linked to the concepts from the domain model; all selected fragments are mapped and linked through the conceptual domain model as follows.

There exists a set of concepts $\{C_1, C_2, ..., C_n\}$ and a set of fragments $\{F_1, F_2, ..., F_m\}$, then consequently:

- If fragment F_i is mapped to a concept C_i and fragment F_j is mapped to C_i, then transitively F_i also relates to F_j:

$$\left(F_i \to C_i\right) \wedge \left(F_j \to C_i\right) \Rightarrow F_i \to F_j \ . \tag{1}$$

- Given, the related concepts C_i and C_j, and if fragment F_i is linked to a concept C_i and a fragment F_j is linked to C_j, then trace dependency to certain degree exists between F_i and F_j.

$$\left(C_i \to C_j\right) \wedge \left(F_i \to C_i\right) \wedge \left(F_j \to C_j\right) \Rightarrow F_i \to F_j \ . \tag{2}$$

3.3   Meta-model of the Approach

The scope of the approach based on the above settings is specified in a meta-model using RML [19, 20] (see fig. 3). We deal with product development, using system development tools (Syst.Dev.Tool), where a system development tool can also be seen as product, when it is under development. Every product development has a specific lifecycle consisting of different phase type (e.g., business analysis, requirements engineering, design, implementation, testing, etc.). Each phase type has a distinct phase product (e.g. requirements specification, design, code, user manual, and software itself), which is result of particular lifecycle phase. A product is final result of the development project, and it consists of the interrelated phase product.

A fragment is a semantic piece of phase product in a certain level of granularity, e.g., it can be a document, a model, a diagram, a section in a document, a text specifying a non-functional requirement, an use case, a class, an attribute, etc. Fragment can be composed of fragments. Such a fragment is inreflexive, asymmetric, and non-transitive. Fragment can have a direct dependence link to another fragment. Every fragment has semantics, which relate the fragment to one or more concept. A rated mapping relationship is used to distinguish fragment coherency to a particular concept. Semantics of certain fragments can be best described by several concepts or a particular concept cluster, which groups related concepts and composes the domain model. Concepts are connected by an undirected graph with weights (weighted relationship). Weights of those relations are calculated based on the degree of the concept relatedness.

Since recording of rationale is not widely accepted in the industry due to the disruptive nature of recording the actions as they occur [1], the attempt for extensive trace information record can be crucial in huge distributed development projects. Therefore, we expect only vital trace info to be captured. We keep track on the evolution of fragment, the direct relationship between fragments and the relationship between fragment and concept cluster by recording the following information – rationale, change operation (i.e., addition, deletion, altera-

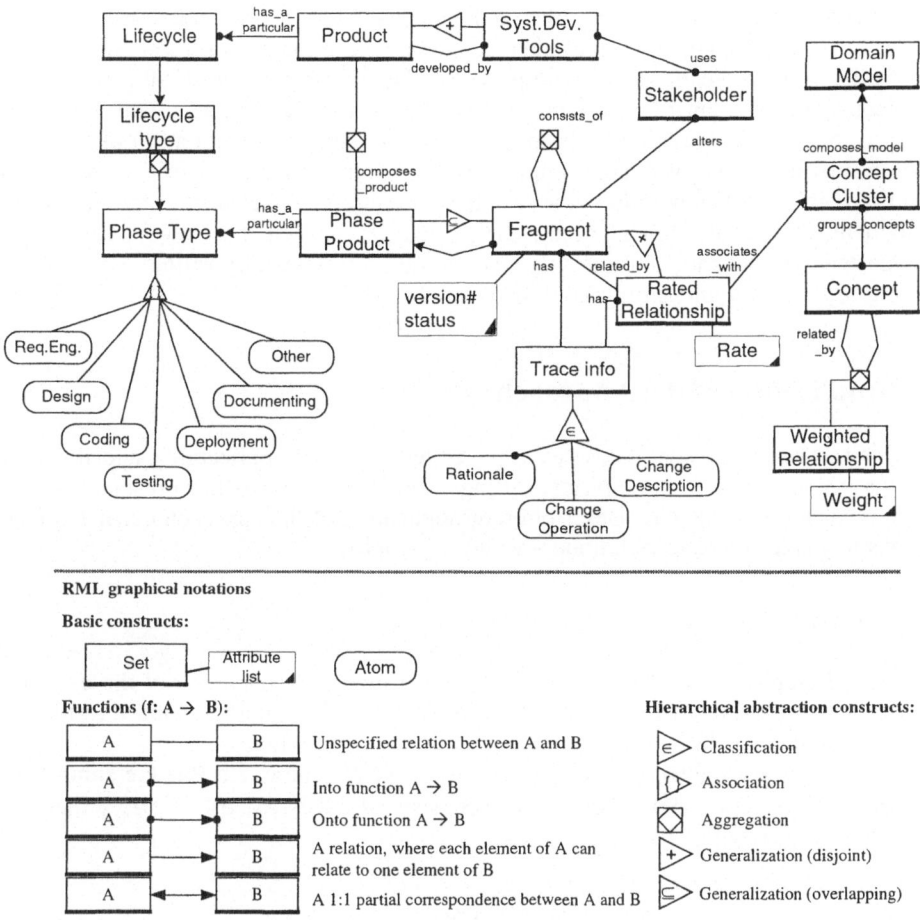

RML graphical notations

Basic constructs:

Set	Attribute list		Atom

Functions (f: A → B):   Hierarchical abstraction constructs:

A — B	Unspecified relation between A and B	∈⊳ Classification
A →• B	Into function A → B	⊏⊳ Association
A •→• B	Onto function A → B	◇ Aggregation
A →• B	A relation, where each element of A can relate to one element of B	+⊳ Generalization (disjoint)
A ←→ B	A 1:1 partial correspondence between A and B	⊆⊳ Generalization (overlapping)

Fig. 3. Meta-model of fragment interrelation and management

tion), and `change description`. Additionally fragment has `version number` and `status`, this information is used for compositional fragment and phase product configuration management. Three configurations are important [18], namely 1) the *latest project-wide*; 2) *latest consistent*; 3) *latest authorized* configuration. The latest project-wide baseline reflects all new developments in the project. Latest baselines are not supposed to be consistent, but all new ideas since the last logon are detected by inspecting this configuration. Latest consistent baselines represent the most recent stable work. These configurations are considered to be candidates for authorization. Latest authorized is the last agreed configuration and it forms the official basis for all subsequent work of the development group.

Fragments interrelationship and trace information are added as metadata (information/data about data) to abstract away from the heterogeneous representation details and capture information content. Association of each product fragment with the corresponding concepts from a domain model enriches its semantic meaning. The intuition is that the more explicit information a fragment conveys, the better the chance that it will be interpreted correctly by other stakeholders. More precise relationship is captured by direct linking between related fragments. Since that is not trivial task even in a smaller scope projects, we see it important to have them at some certain stage of the project. Establishment of direct linking is done in few steps. The initial one is, of course, fragment association with domain concept. Next, by exploitation of those relationships is means for change impact prediction and assessment (see a case study section). When developer alters the fragment because of the change made in another fragment, then establishment of the direct linking between those two fragments is suggested automatically. In this way, we are able incrementally refine and establish fine-grained traceability information between fragments.

4   Application of the Approach

In this section we present a case example to test practical applicability and illustrate the proposed approach in empirical settings. This is done for better presentation and communication of the idea. Description of application of the approach consists of the case study and candidate technique – weighted graphs.

4.1   Weighted Graphs

Weighted graphs are used to represent a concept model. Interrelation of the concepts is depicted as a semantic distance between concepts. The shortest path algorithm is used to predict which fragments are most likely to be impacted.

Given, G is a weighted graph. The length (or weight) of a path P is the sum of the weights of the edges of P. That is, if P consists of edges e_0, e_1, ..., e_{k-1} then the length of P, denoted $w(P)$, is defined as

$$w(P) = \sum_{i=0}^{k-1} w(e_i) \ . \tag{3}$$

The distance from a node v to a node u in G, denoted $d(v, u)$, is the length of a minimum length path from v to u, if such path exists. We calculate a shortest path (i.e., using algorithms for single-source shortest path, for instance, Dijkstra algorithm [4] or Bellman-Ford [3]) from some node v (usually, that is the fragment, which has been altered) to each other node in G, viewing the weights on the edges as distances.

4.2   A Case Study

Domain description. A case study is based on MEIS system, used for the basic course of information systems SIF8035 [12]. MEIS system is used for exercise delivery and evaluation. There exist two groups of users: students (they are also reviewers of others' solutions) and student assistants, who check all deliveries (both solutions to exercise and evaluation of those solutions) and either accept or reject them. Main domain concepts and relationships among them are depicted in the fig.4. Quantification of relationships between concepts (semantic distance) has been performed manually relying on the knowledge of domain. Weights used are from the range $[0.0, 1.0]$, where 0.0 means that concepts have high semantic relatedness in the domain, and the value 1.0 means, that the semantic distance between concepts is very long (concepts are not related at all). For instance, the weight of relationship between 'Student' and 'Reviewer' is equal to 0.0 only in this domain, where students are also reviewers of others' solutions.

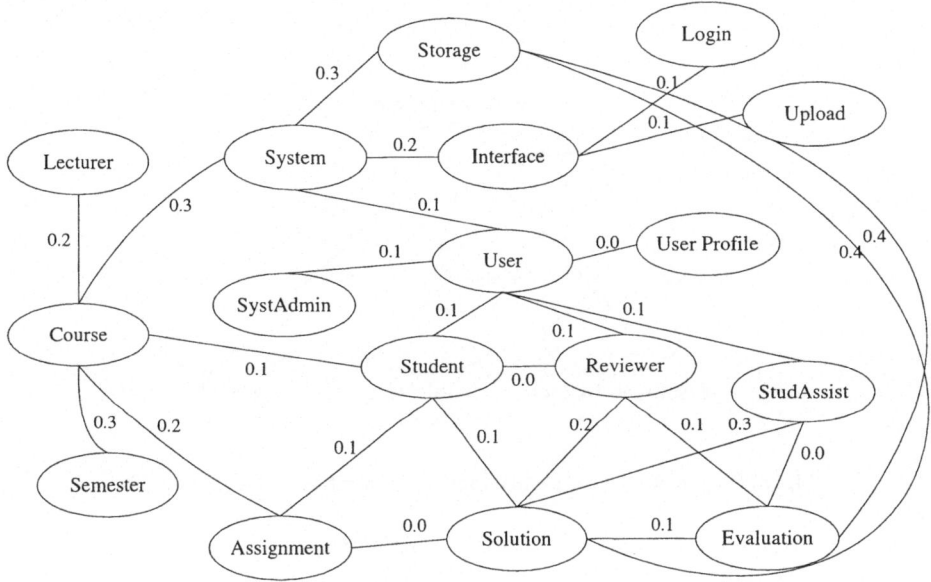

Fig. 4. Domain model for MEIS

Fragmentation. During the development of the MEIS system every requirement was treated as a separate fragment. Some of them are listed below and other kinds of product fragments (use case, code, design, user interface) are presented in figures 5-8. Requirements for MEIS system:

Req.1. It should be possible to create users' profiles from textual file.

Req.2. Student should be able to upload solution:

    Req.2.1. Solution should be stored in the student's folder.

    Req.2.2. Reference (link) to solution1&2 should be kept in the MEIS database.

Req.3. StudAssist should accept/reject a solution1&2.

    Req.3.1. System should provide possibility to reject solution1&2.

Req.4. StudAssist should form a reviewer groups for solution1&2.

    Req.4.1. System should provide to StudAssist a list of students, whose solution was accepted.

    Req.4.2. StudAssist should form a reviewer group.

Req.5. Reviewer should deliver evaluations of solution1 and solution2.

Req.5.1. Reviewer should evaluate DFD/APM model of solution1&2.

Req.5.2. Reviewer should upload Word documents with evaluation for DFD/APM model of solution1&2.

Req.5.3. File with evaluation for DFD/APM model of solution1&2 should be stored in the database.

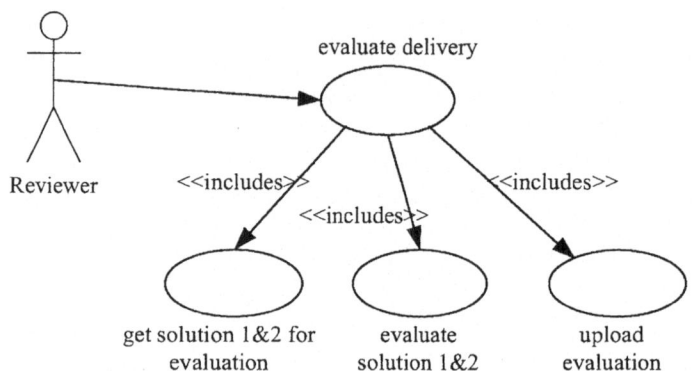

Fig. 5. Fragment – Use Case diagram – reviewer tasks ('UC.1' in fig.9)

```
if ((dbproc = mysql_init(NULL)) == NULL) {
    printf("Unable to init.\n<hr>");
  } else {
    if (mysql_real_connect(dbproc, NULL, "ADMIN_USER",
                    "ADMIN_PASSWORD", "DATABASE_NAME"
                    0, "MYSQL_SOCK", 0) == NULL) {
      printf("Unable to connect.\n<hr>");
    } else {
      if (is_modify) {
        passwd = Find_Value(entries, num_words, "Password1")
        if (passwd == NULL || strlen(passwd) <= 0) {
          sprintf(passwd_buf, "'%s'",
                    Find_Value(entries, num_words, "Password")
        } else {
          sprintf(passwd_buf, "PASSWORD('%s')", passwd);
        }
```

Fig. 6. Fragment – part of code ('Code.1' in fig.9)

Association with a concept. As described in the previous section, developers use the tool for semi-automatic fragments mapping to domain concepts. Additional XML tags are added to keep information about the related concepts and weight of relationship, as a fragment could have one or more related concepts (recall fig. 3). For example, requirement 'Req.5.2: Reviewer should upload Word documents with evaluation for DFD/APM model of solution1/2' provides hints about relation to the concepts 'Reviewer', 'Upload', 'Evaluation' and 'Solution'. Never-

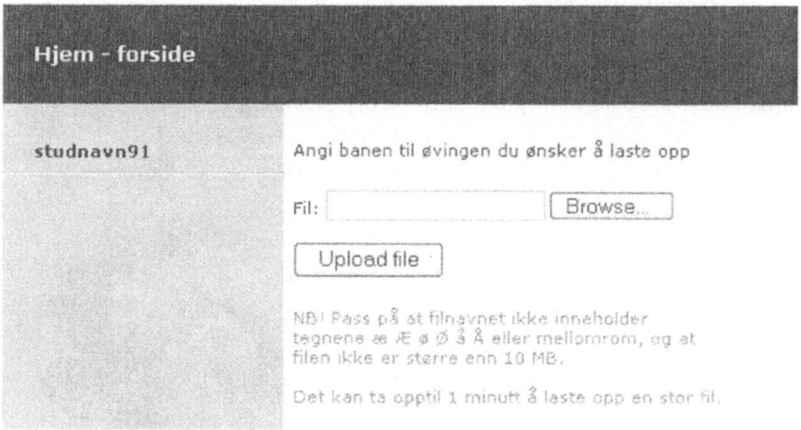

Hjem - forside

studnavn91   Angi banen til øvingen du ønsker å laste opp

Fil: [   ] [Browse...]

[Upload file]

NB! Pass på at filnavnet ikke inneholder
tegnene æ Æ ø Ø å Å eller mellomrom, og at
filen ikke er større enn 10 MB.

Det kan ta opptil 1 minutt å laste opp en stor fil.

Fig. 7. Interface screenshot ('Doc.1' in fig.9)

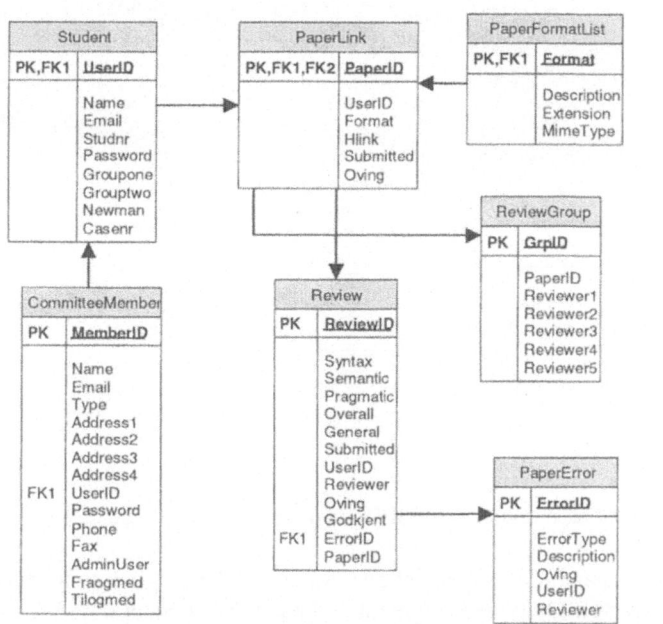

Fig. 8. Fragment – ER diagram of MEIS database ('Dsgn.1' in fig.9)

theless, it is mainly about 'evaluation upload', so this requirement is mapped to the concepts 'Upload' and 'Evaluation' with the assigned weights[2] 0.1 and 0.3 re-

---

[2] Fragment association to concept and weight assignment is more intuition based. Developer knows best the semantics of the fragment. To facilitate the task for developer in assigning the value, only three values are used to identify the relatedness of the concepts – high, medium and low (recall *Step 1.b*)

spectively. Partial[3] graphical representation of the fragments mapped to domain model is depicted in fig.9. The concepts and fragment from above described example are gray shaded. It should be noted that fig. 9 does not imply the way for fragments mapping, but is used here only for explanatory purposes.

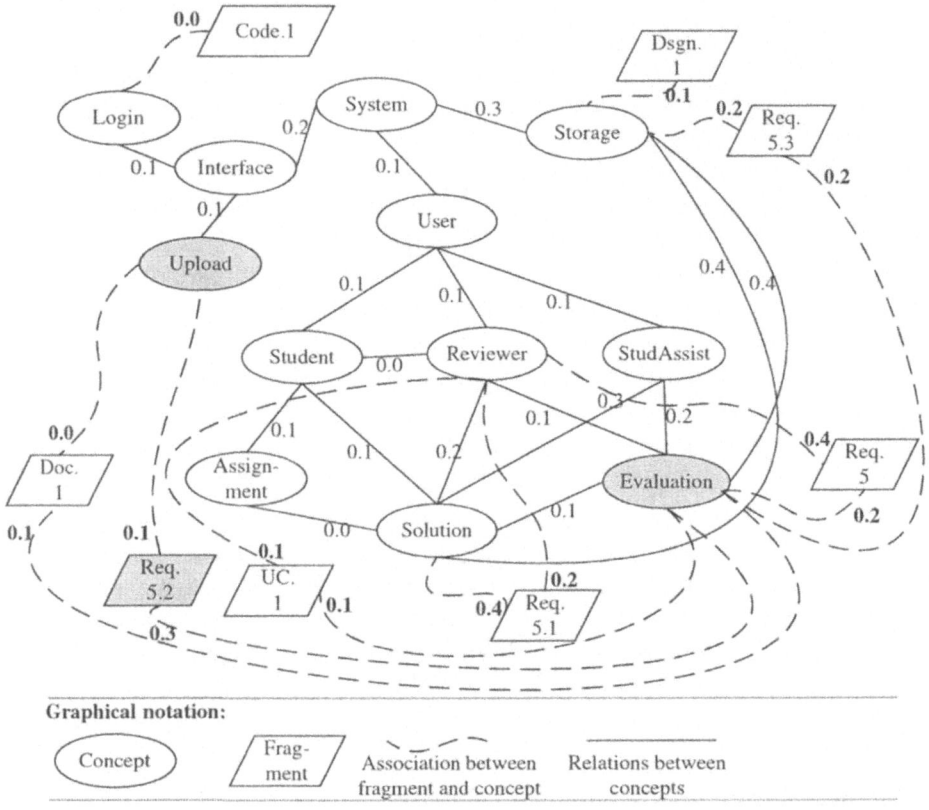

Fig. 9. Graphical representation of MEIS fragments mapping to domain concepts (partial)

For better explanation, table 1 shows mapping the fragments to domain concepts and distance (weight) between fragment and particular concept.

Alteration. During the system development it was decided to make standard web form for evaluation instead of delivering evaluation in Word file. As consequence requirement ('Req.5') has been changed to:

Req.5. Reviewer should be provided 2 (two) web forms for evaluation of each solution1/2.

---

[3] Concepts, which are not associated to any fragment, are removed from fig.9 (in comparison with fig.4) with a reason not to introduce cognitive overload on the reader. As well as partial association of only few fragments is shown.

Table 1. Association and relatedness of the fragments to the concepts

Fragment	Relevant Concepts					
	Storage	Login	Upload	Reviewer	Solution	Evaluation
Req.5				0.4		0.2
Req.5.1				0.2	0.4	
Req.5.2			0.1			0.3
Req.5.3	0.2					0.2
UC.1				0.1		0.1
Dsgn.1	0.1					
Code.1		0.0				
Doc.1			0.0			0.1

This alteration is recorded and saved into the repository. The vital information, which needs to be captured, was discussed in the meta-model description. Fig.10 illustrates this captured trace information, i.e. who altered 'source' fragment, what change operation was performed, what was done and what was rationale behind that change.

```
<fragment id="R005" version="v.1.2" status="authorized">
  <change operation="alteration">
    <user id="dstrasun">
      <rationale> It is necessary to change delivery way in or-
          der to enable automatic comparison of different
          evaluations</rationale>
      <description> Requirement to upload the evaluations in a
          word file was changed to provide web form for
          the evaluation</description>
  </change>
</fragment>
```

Fig. 10. Trace information about the change in XML representation

Assessment of the impact probabilities on other fragments caused by this change is shown in Table 2. Results are calculated applying Eq.3 and using weights between fragments and concepts, and weights between concepts, as a distance between points (nodes). For example, the distance between fragments 'Req.5' and 'UC.1' was calculated in the following way: 'Req.5' is associated with concept 'Evaluation' with a value of 0.2, and 'UC.1' is associated with the same concept with a value of 0.1, so the path (semantic distance) from the altered fragment 'Req.5' to probably impacted fragment 'UC.1' is equal to 0.3.[4]

Since altered fragment is associated with 2 concepts, namely 'Evaluation' and 'Reviewer'. Shortest paths are computed going through both concepts. The purpose for that is to reduce impact probability warnings by allowing developer to specify what part of fragment's semantics was changed. For example, it is obvious that requirement change does not effect reviewer (as he/she still should deliver evaluation),

---

[4] Fragments associated with the same concept, usually will have the shortest path, or semantic distance, as this mapping to the same concept shows that semantics of those fragments are almost the same.

but only the form and way of evaluation. Allowing to developer specify that, we decrease the impact warnings – that means, that only inference through the concept 'Evaluation' should be taken into account and checked (see 2nd column of table 2). It means that developers should go through and check for consistency the top-ranked fragments in 2nd column. If impacted semantics are not specified, then the weighted average can be used.

As all mapped fragments are being assessed, only the ones with the shortest path, i.e. when fragments are very close semantically, should be checked for impact. Of course, there should be defined threshold for notification posting in large development project, threshold value depends on specific project settings and requires attentive empirical study. Defining the threshold to 0.5, these 4 fragments need to be checked for consistency with the change performed: 'UC.1', 'Doc.1', 'Req.5.3', and 'Req.5.2'.

Table 2. Impact assessment based on calculation of shortest path

Fragment	Concepts		
	Evaluation	Reviewer	Average
UC.1	0.3	0.5	0.4
Doc.1	0.3	0.9	0.7
Req.5.3	0.4	1.1	0.9
Req.5.2	0.5	1.0	0.8
Req.5.1	0.7	0.6	0.6
Dsgn.1	0.7	1.0	0.9
Code.1	0.8	0.9	0.9

5   Concluding Remarks and Future Work

In this paper we have described the methodological approach to enable product fragment management in the distributed system development projects. Proposal is based on semantics enrichment of the produced fragments by mapping them to related concepts from specific domain model. These inter-relations are weighted as well as intra-relations among the concepts in a domain model. Weights assigned to relationships suit as basis for impact prediction and assessment.

The approach (a) enables whole lifecycle product management. As nature of collaborative development is usually very iterative, the approach (b) allows relating product fragments at different stages of its incremental refinement (e.g., from abstract sketches to formal representation), (c) does not bind developers to a specific tool and/or modeling language, as far as used tool supports XML output. The use of XML makes it possible to use this approach in settings where the involved artifacts are created and managed by heterogeneous tools, such as text processors and CASE-tools.

Proposal can be beneficial for companies working in the specific domains – a domain model is stable and commonly agreed, expert's knowledge is available. In case of entering new domain the company should work out domain model, which needs to be comprehensible and accepted by all developers. An evolvable domain model is a challenge which should be resolved in future works. Adding or removing some concepts from a conceptual domain model in the middle of project will raise the question what to do with the fragments which are already mapped to that concept. If a new concept is added the relatedness between concept and closest fragments could be automatically calculated and the most related fragments re-mapped. Deletion should not remove the concept from domain model, but lock it not allowing to associate new fragments. This would preserve existing links between the concepts and fragments.

Further, large domain model with thousands of concepts could be real challenge for developers to find relevant concept and to link a fragment in question. This issue can be solved by concepts clustering which could ease the finding the right concept. Development in the area of ontology mapping could also provide useful methods and techniques which could be used both to find the most relevant concept for the fragment and to develop stable and common agreed domain specific model when a domain is new for the developers and several interpretations of domain model exist.

However, the most important contribution of this paper is management of heterogeneous product fragments by interrelating them according their semantics and usage of those interrelations for change impact assessment. Change management and assessment is vital for the large development projects and perhaps the most risky and error-prone task. This approach enables to calculate the probabilities as semantic distance between heterogeneous product fragments – how likely some product fragments will be impacted by the change of 'related' fragment. That value is calculated based on the weighted relations between domain concepts and those weights depends on experts' knowledge of the domain. As the calculation based on those weights is a backbone of this approach, the process of weight assignment should be well reasoned and methodologically described – big challenges for future works lie here.

Direct linking between related fragments would result in more precise relationship and change impact assessment. That is not trivial task even in a smaller scope projects and, certainly, more challenging in distributed development. Thus, we see it being important to refine the mechanism of direct links establishment between related fragments based on change impact history, i.e. when developer alters the fragment because of the change made in another fragment, then establishment of the direct linking between those two fragments should be suggested automatically.

References

1. Arkley, P., Mason, P., Riddle, S.: "Enabling Traceability", in Proceedings of the 1st International Workshop on Traceability, co-located with ASE 2002, Edinburgh, Scotland, UK, September (2002) pp. 61–65
2. Brasethvik, T. and Gulla, J.A.: "Natural Language Analysis for Semantic Document Modeling." In Proceedings of the 5th International Conference on the Application of Natural Language for Information Systems (NLDB'2000) in Versailles, France, June (2000)
3. Cormen, T.H., Leiserson, C.E., Rivest, R.L. and Stein, C.: Introduction to Algorithms, 2nd Edition. The MIT Press and McGraw-Hill, (2001)
4. Dijkstra, E.W.: A note on two problems in connextion with graphs. Numer. Math. 1:269–271, (1959)
5. Egyed, A.: "Reasonings about Trace dependencies in a Multi-Dimensional Space", in Proceedings of the 1st International Workshop on Traceability, co-located with ASE 2002, Edinburgh, Scotland, UK, September (2002) pp. 42–45

6. Farshchian, B.A.: A Framework for Supporting Shared Interaction in Distributed Product Development Projects, PhD thesis, NTNU, Trondheim, Norway, (2001)
7. Frezza, S.T., Levitan, S.P., Chrysanthis, P.K.: "Linking requirements and design data for automated functional evaluation", Computers in Industry, Volume 30, Issue 1, Elsevier Science Publishers B. V., September (1996) pp. 13–25
8. Gotel, O.C.Z., Finkelstein, A.C.W.: "An Analysis of the Requirements Traceability Problem", In Proceeding of the 1st International Conference on Requirements Engineering (ICRE'94), IEEE Computer Society Press, Colorado Springs, Colorado, USA, April (1994) pp. 94–102
9. Greenspan, S., McGowan, C.: Structuring Software Development for Reliability, In Microelectronics and Reliability, 17, (1978) pp. 75–84
10. Grünbacher, P., Egyed, A. and Medvidovic, N.: "Reconciling Software Requirements and Architectures - The CBSP Approach", In Proceedings of the 5th IEEE International Symposium on Requirements Engineering (RE'01), Springer-Verlag, Toronto, Canada, (2001) pp. 202–211
11. Letelier, P.: "A framework for Requirements Traceability in UML based projects", in Proceedings of the 1st International Workshop on Traceability, co-located with ASE 2002, Edinburgh, Scotland, UK, September (2002) pp. 32–41
12. Matulevicius, R.: MEIS requirements specification. Technical report, NTNU, (2003)
13. Pinheiro, F. and Goguen, J.: "An Object-Oriented Tool for Tracing Requirements". *IEEE Software*, 13(2), (1996) pp. 52–64
14. Pohl, K.: "PRO-ART: Enabling Requirements Pre-Traceability", In Proceedings of the Second International Conference on Requirements Engineering (ICSE '96), Colorado, USA, (1996) pp. 76–85
15. Pohl, K., Brandenburg, M., Gülich, A.: "Integrating Requirement and Architecture Information: A Scenario and Meta-Model Based Approach", In Proceedings of the Seventh International Workshop on Requirements Engineering: Foundation for Software Quality (REFSQ'01), Interlaken, Switzerland, (2001)
16. Ramesh, B. and Jarke, M.: "Toward Reference Models for Requirements Traceability". IEEE Transactions on Software Engineering, Vol. 27, No. 1, pp.58–93, January (2001)
17. Rational Suite AnalystStudio. URL: http://www.rational.com/products/astudio/index.jsp
18. Strasunskas, D. "Traceability in a Collaborative Systems Development from Lifecycle Perspective". In Proceedings of the 1st International Workshop on Traceability, co-located with ASE 2002, Edinburgh, Scotland, UK, September (2002) pp. 54–60
19. Solvberg A.: Data and what they refer to. In; Chen, P., Akoka, J., Kangassalo, H., Thalheim, B., (eds.): Conceptual Modeling: Current Issues and Future Trends. LNCS 1565. Springer Verlag (1999)
20. Solvberg, A. and Brasethvik, T.: "The Referent Model Language", Technical Report. NTNU, Trondheim, Norway URL: http://www.idi.ntnu.no/~ppp/referent/
21. Watkins, R., Neal, M.: "Why and How of Requirements Tracing", IEEE Software, 11(4), (1994) pp. 104–106

A Cooperative Approach to the Development of Expert Knowledge Bases Applied to Define Standard of Care in Glaucoma

Mihaela Ulieru and Marcelo Rizzi

Emergent Information Systems Laboratory
Electrical and Computer Engineering Department
The University of Calgary
2500 University Dr. NW
Calgary, Alberta, T2N 1N4 CANADA
Ulieru@ucalgary.ca
http://www.enel.ucalgary.ca/People/Ulieru/Projects/Projects_index.htm

Abstract. In this paper we introduce a methodology for knowledge base creation based on the reconciliation of multiple expert opinions using a fuzzy measure for consensus evaluation determined based on soft competitive learning. Real-life application of our methodology to the establishment of the standard of care in glaucoma monitoring illustrates its practical power. Based on a comparative analysis of expert patterns for glaucoma follow-up and treatment we extract a core rule set on which the experts agree. This exchange of information is supported by an advanced Cyberinfrastructure which enables fast transfer of information (highly accurate image transfer and display from the most complex and sophisticated ophthalmic machines, patient charts, etc.) to enable exchange of expert opinions.

1 Introduction

One of the major problems facing glaucoma specialists in North-America (and not only) is the lack of a standard of care clearly pointing towards follow-up timelines and treatment procedures. Each specialist has its own 'standards' based on their experience and first-hand knowledge acquired from long-term monitoring a particular patient. Extending experience acquired with a patient to another with similar conditions doesn't usually work – as such each case needs as much as possible individual consideration – and this is what makes the task of the specialist so difficult. Even with decades of years of experience glaucoma specialists meet 'new' and 'unknown' cases in which they are confronted with the difficulty (or even impossibility) to make a decision.

In Canada there are absolutely no official standards regarding glaucoma follow [1]. The US *target pressure guidelines* are extremely weak regarding follow-up, as the physician's flexibility ranges from 3 to 24 month, as such not pointing towards any specific responsible decision (given the fact that a patient who needs follow-up in 3 month, would go blind if requested for follow-up in 24 month!) [2].

R. Meersman et al. (Eds.): CoopIS/DOA/ODBASE 2003, LNCS 2888, pp. 235–243, 2003.
© Springer-Verlag Berlin Heidelberg 2003

This strongly points to an immediate need to improve the target pressure guidelines to help glaucoma specialists decide when they should treat and how aggressive they should treat. Besides the main beneficiaries – the glaucoma experts - these improved standards would help all general ophthalmologists (although this is to date an extremely difficult endeavor given the wide range of disagreement in the ophthalmic and glaucoma communities.)

A first step towards defining standards of care in glaucoma follow up is to investigate as much and as widely as possible expert patterns in follow up decisions. For this purpose we have developed an expert system encoding follow up rules acquired with the expertise of Dr. A.C.S. Crichton   [7], [8]. To encode complex linguistic knowledge we have chosen fuzzy technology. To date we have reached a core rule base consisting of about 30 core rules [3]. To expand the current knowledge base encoding Dr. Crichton's patterns of glaucoma follow-up, we have investigated the patterns of other Canadian glaucoma experts (selected from the most reputable internationally recognized ones) joined into what we call the *Canadian Glaucoma Ring*. In the next section we present the methodology by which we have reconciled the other expert opinions into a standard of care for glaucoma follow up.

2   Collaborative Methodology for Embedding Various Expert Patterns into a Knowledge Base

The contribution of several experts to the development of a knowledge base brings enormous value, but at the same time it presents a big challenge to the knowledge engineers. Communication between experts located in different parts of the world has to be supported by an adequate Cyberinfrastructure, various expert opinions have to be reconciled, eliminating contradictions and choosing the most encompassing solution in each case, security issues have to be dealt with adequately, etc. To cope with this we have developed a methodology (Fig. 1) capable to deal with different expert opinions and consolidate the results in a rule set with each rule weighted by the *degree of consensus* reached among the experts. The methodology consists of the following steps:

- *Find the various patterns for each of the experts involved.* Each expert analyzes the existing rules encoding Dr. Crichton's expertise and expresses either agreement or disagreement (arguing wherever possible why they disagree) as well as adding new rules in case the existing ones do not encompass their whole expertise. This will define the respective expert's profile.

- *Investigate the differences and attempt to reconcile them.* Once each expert has defined their profile (that is their own rule base) – we will investigate the differences and attempt to reconcile them as much as possible based on a deeper understanding of each expertise, argumentation, and trying to identify the particularity of each case that led to a different rule/experience/pattern for different experts. To enable this difficult task we have developed a methodology involving a 'consensus analyzer', Fig. 2, to be presented next.

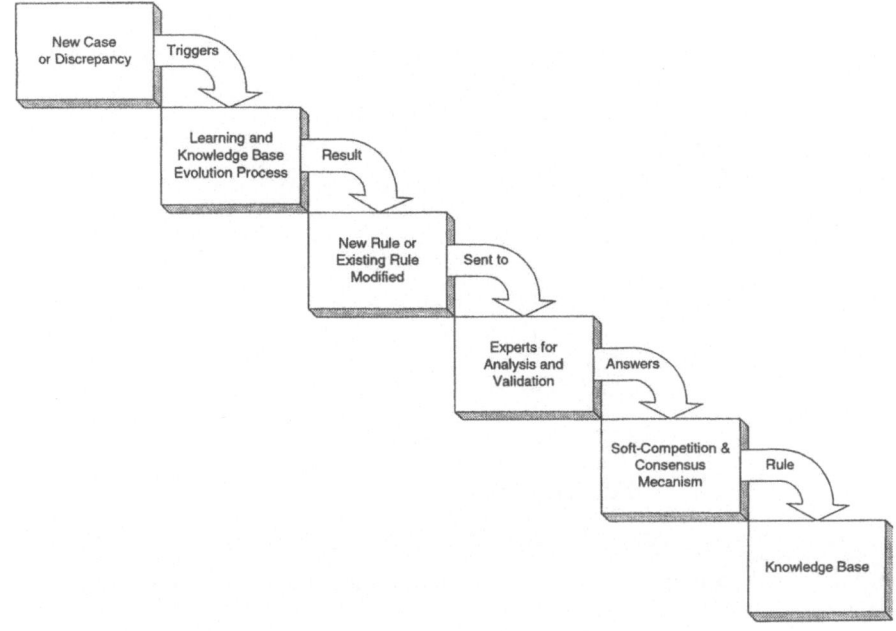

Fig. 1. Embedding various expert views into a knowledge base

- *Determination of the Core Rule Set (Canadian Standard of Care).* The result of this reconciliation process will be a *core rule set* shared by all the experts in the Canadian Glaucoma Ring. However each expert will be able to keep their own variations of the rule set due the particularities of their patients and geographic area. This enables each expert to consult others about how they would treat specific cases and compare the results. This "simulation" characteristic gives to the system a tremendous power when dealing with complex cases.

3   Illustrative Scenario

To illustrate how the consensus mechanism is used to solve the circumstantial expert discrepancies by reaching a consensus between them lets consider the following scenario, Fig 3. When consulting the Glaucoma Expert System to determine the follow-up for the current patient, the expert is faced with a completely new case. Accordingly, the system will inform the user that an accurate follow-up time cannot be determined, so it needs to learn a new rule. To enable this, the expert initiates a set of interaction rounds with other experts connected to the *Canadian Glaucoma Ring*, Fig 3. First the expert facing the case suggests a follow-up based on the current Patient's chart. Then he makes public the to the other experts (via the advanced Cyberinfrastructure [12]) the patient's electronic medical record, the images obtained from the advanced ophthalmic machines and the rule proposed by the expert. After evaluating the data, all the experts are capable to enter their opinions about this new

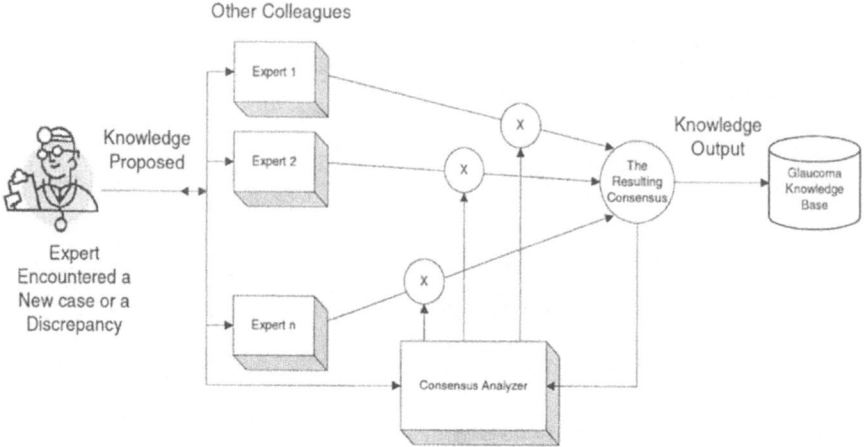

Fig. 2. Expert opinion reconciliation

case, Fig. 3 and participate in discussions until an acceptable degree of consensus is reached.

To avoid deadlocks and long trivial discussions this process is managed and controlled by the consensus mechanism which is detailed in the next Section.

4   The Consensus Analyzer at a Glance

The goal of group decision making typically is to reach a consensus concerning a desired action or alternative from among those considered in the decision process. In this context, consensus is taken to mean *a unanimous agreement by all those in the group concerning their choice*.

Each time a new rule is proposed by an expert or an existing rule needs to be modified as a consequence of an expert's profile discrepancy to reconcile experts disagreement, the rule is presented to all the experts for evaluation. The expert opinions are analyzed by the Consensus Analyzer (Fig. 2) which evaluates the distance between each expert's opinion and the point of minimum consensus [11] (the point of maximum conflict – where the expert opinions are most distant.) To evaluate this distance we use soft competitive learning, a very powerful methodology [9][10] which gives a fuzzy measure of the divergence in the expert opinions.

In contrast to the concept of hard competition that allows only one winner soft competition not only gives a clear winner but more "neighbours" who are winners with a lower degree. The neighbour rules are used as inputs into a consensus procedure (to be presented in the next section) that performs fuzzy measures of the consensus obtained for each rule. Based on this information a decision about the rule

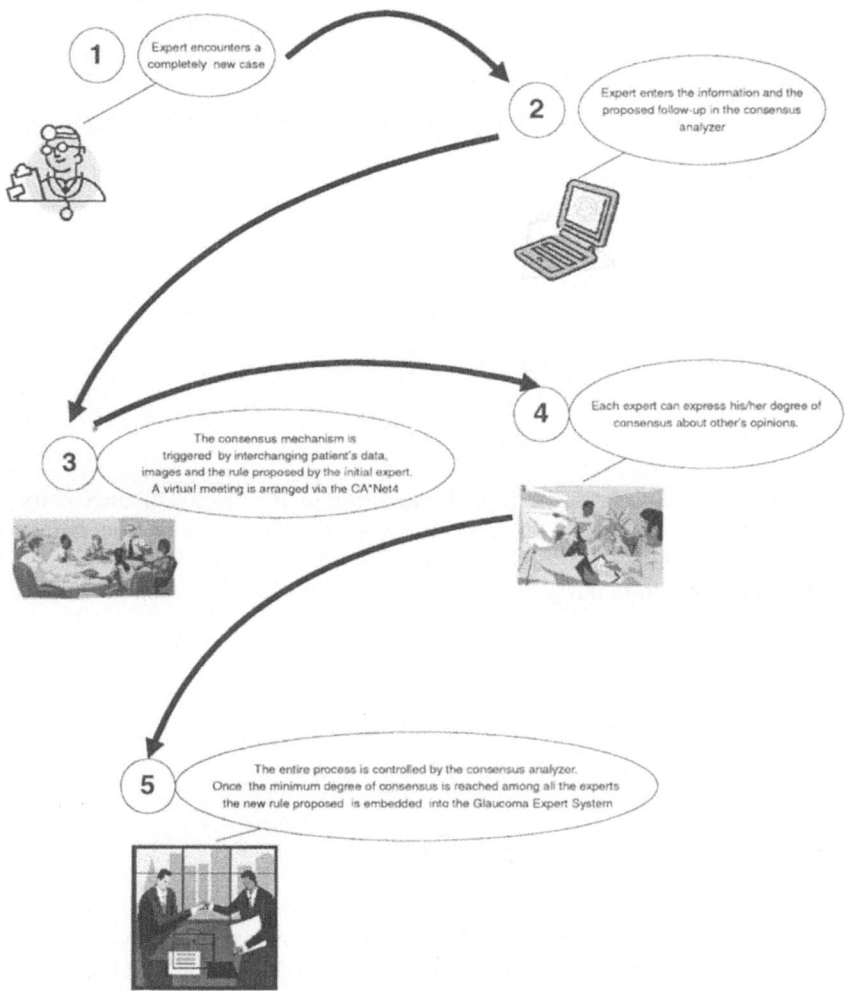

Fig. 3. Consensus Scenario

being considered is made. The rule awarded the highest degree of consensus is selected and then incorporated into the knowledge base. The not neighbours opinions are discarded.

5   Consensus Metrics by Soft Competition

Our goal is to define a typical value of distance to consensus by asking the experts to indicate their preferences for each characteristic of the fuzzy rule, expressing each preference as a fuzzy value.

We will consider the individual preferences as fuzzy relations. Lets suppose we are developing consensus in a universe $X = \{x1, x2, ..., xn\}$; a fuzzy relation **R** of order n will have elements r_{ij} encoding the preferences given to x_i relative to x_j. $r_{ij} = 1$ implies that alternative i is definitely preferred to alternative j. At the other extreme we have maximal fuzziness, where $rij = rji = 0.5$.

Two common measures of preference are defined here as average fuzziness in R and average certainty in R:

$$F(R) = \frac{tr(R^2)}{n(n-1)^{1/2}} \tag{1}$$

$$C(R) = \frac{tr(R \cdot R^T)}{n(n-1)^{1/2}} \tag{2}$$

where tr is the trace and T is the transposed of the matrix.

The measure F(R) averages the joint preferences in **R** over all distinct pairs in the cartesian space X x X. F(R) is proportional to the fuzziness or uncertainty about pairwise rankings. Conversely the measure C(R) averages the individual dominance of each distinct pair of rankings.

The two measures are dependent:

$$F(R) + c(R) = 1 \tag{3}$$

Measures of preference can be useful in determining consensus.

We define three type of consensus as follows:

Type I consensus: There is a clear choice, say alternative i (the ith column is all zeros) and the remaining (n-1) alternatives all have equal secondary preference (i.e 1/2).

Type II consensus: There is one clear choice say alternative i but the remaining (n-1) alternatives all have definite secondary preference (i.e 1).

Type Fuzzy consensus: Occurs when there is a unanimous decision for the most preferred choice, say alternative i but the remaining (n-1) alternatives have infinitely many fuzzy secondary preferences.

From the degree of preferences measures given in previous equations we can construct a distance to consensus metric defined as

$$m(R) = 1 - (2 \cdot C(R) - 1)^{1/2} \tag{4}$$

Where:

$$m(R) = 1 - (2/n)^{1/2} \quad \text{for a Type I consensus relation} \tag{5}$$

$$m(R) = 0 \text{ for a Type II consensus relation} \tag{6}$$

When $n > 2$, the distance between Type I and Type II consensus increases with n as it becomes increasingly difficult to develop a consensus choice and simultaneously rank the remaining pairs of alternatives.

The value of distance to consensus quantifies the dynamic evolution of a group as the group refines its preferences and moves closer to a Type I or Type II or Type Fuzzy consensus. The vast majority of group preference situations eventually develop into Type Fuzzy consensus, Types I and II being typically only useful as boundary conditions.

Based on the consensus metrics the rule base is tuned to embrace all opinions as much as possible (which means that the rules obtained will be positioned in the equidistant point to all expert opinions.) Once the distance to consensus predefined is reached, the rule is integrated in the knowledge base.

6   Enabling Expert Interactions

To enable expert interaction we use a previously developed web-centric extension of the glaucoma expert system [4] [5] [6] (GlaucoMAX[1], Fig. 4) into which we pluged the users interface for the Consensus Analyzer enabling expert opinions reconciliation (Fig. 5).

GlaucoMAX is an interactive portal supporting the web-based accessibility to our Glaucoma Expert System as well as a broader spectrum of services for the glaucoma community such as: discussion groups, forum, document management, community services, E-Pharmacy and lots more.

GlaucoMAX visitors and community members can actively discuss different issues, exchange experiences, meet often and get to know each other better. GlaucoMAX users can collaborate with each other using built-in tools like listings of available communities, threaded discussion groups, live chats, online meetings, event scheduling, online business cards (user profiles), user search, surveys, document folders, special interest groups, and a calendar of all scheduled events.

Exchange of expert information and expertise among the CANARIE Glaucoma Ring for the improvement/validation of the Canadian standard of care (Fig. 5). The initial Core Glaucoma Ring will be subsequently expanded to encompass other Canadian and International glaucoma experts that will join our GlaucoMAX system to benefit from the shared expertise.

---

[1] www.GlaucoMAX.com

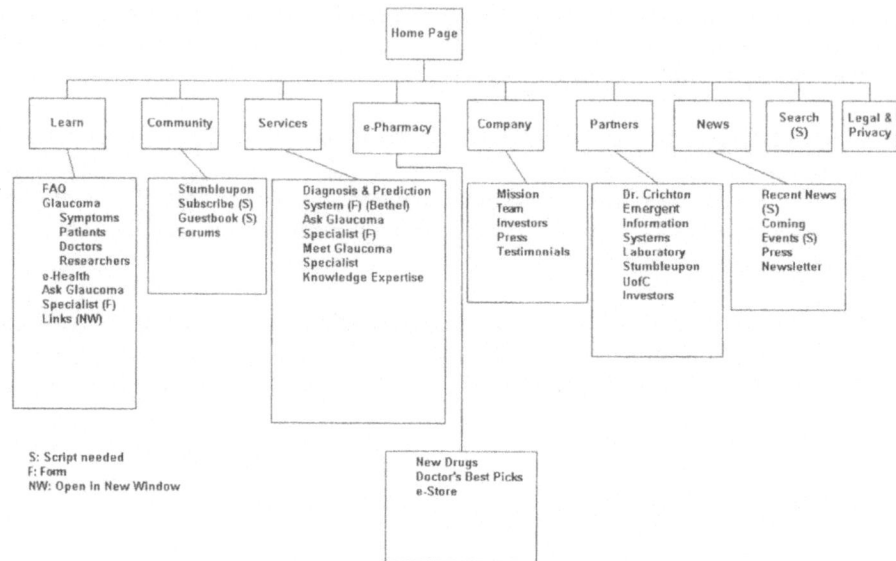

Fig. 4. GlaucoMAX.com: Web-based services for glaucoma communities

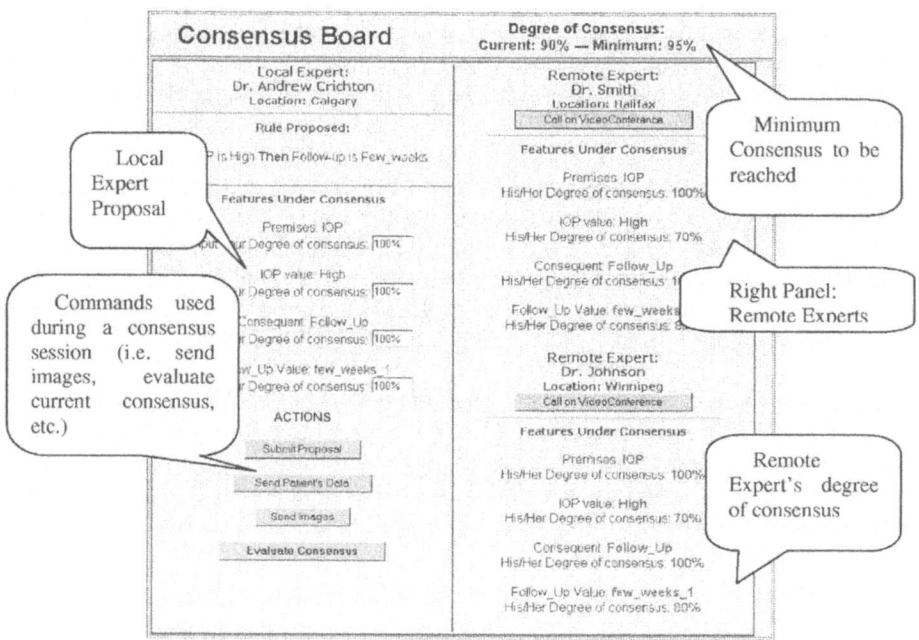

Fig. 5. User Interface Enabling Expert Interaction to Reach Consensus

7 Conclusions

The contribution of several experts to the development of a knowledge base brings enormous value, but at the same time it presents a big challenge to the knowledge engineers. Communication between experts located in different parts of the world has to be supported by an adequate Cyberinfrastructure, various expert opinions have to be reconciled, eliminating contradictions and choosing the most encompassing solution in each case. This paper introduced a methodology capable to deal with different expert opinions and consolidate the results in a rule set with each rule weighted by the *degree of consensus* reached among the experts. Application to the definition of standards of care for glaucoma monitoring and follow-up has proven the success of our methodology.

References

1. Ocular Surgery News. April 1, 2002. 3 Targets, total glaucoma management
2. American Academy of Ophthalmology, the Eye MD Association, Preferred practice pattern. Primary open-angle glaucoma, February 2000
3. Mihaela Ulieru, Andrew C.S. Crichton, Marcelo Rizzi and Cynthia Karanicolas, 'A Fuzzy Model for Glaucoma Follow-Up' International Journal of Soft Computing: A Fusion of Foundations, Methodologies and Applications (Springer) ISSN 1432-7643, 2003 (accepted).
4. Mihaela Ulieru and Alexander Grabelkovsky, "Telehealth Approach to Glaucoma Progression Monitoring", International Journal of Information Theories and Applications 10(3), 2003, ISSN 1310-0513, (in press).
5. Mihaela Ulieru, "Internet-Enabled Soft Computing Holarchies for e-Health Applications", in New Directions in Enhancing the Power of the Internet, (L.A. Zadeh and M. Nikravesh – Editors), Springer Verlag, Berlin, 2003 (in print), 35 pages.
6. Ulieru, M and Geras, A., Emergent Holarchies for e-Health Applications – A Case in Glaucoma Diagnosis, Proceedings of IECON 2002 – 28th Annual Conference of the IEEE Industrial Electronics Society, November 5-8, 2002, Seville, Spain, ISBN 0-7803-7475-4, pp. 2957-2962, (proceedings on CD-Rom, IEEE Catalog Number 02CH37363.)
7. Varachiu, N., Karanicolas, C. and Ulieru, M., Computational Intelligence for Medical Knowledge Acquisition with Application to Glaucoma, Proceedings of the First IEEE Conference on Cognitive Informatics (ICCI'02), Calgary, Canada, August 17-19, 2002, pp. 233-238, IEEE Computer Society Order Number PR01724, ISBN 0-7695-1724-2, Library of Congress # 2002107061.
8. Ulieru M. and Pogrzeba, G. Integrated Soft Computing Methodology for Diagnosis and Prediction with Application to Glaucoma Risk Evaluation, Proceedings of 6th IASTED International Conference on Artificial Intelligence and Soft Computing, July 17–19, 2002, Banff, Canada, pp. 275-280, ISBN: 0-88986-346-6.
9. Jose C Principe, Neil R Euliano, W. Kurt Lefebvre, Neural and adaptive systems. Fundamentals through simulations, John Willey and sons. 2000
10. Ross, T., "Fuzzy Logic with Engineering Applications", McGraw-Hill Inc., 1995
11. Terrence P. Fries, Consensus development in fuzzy intelligent agents for decision making, Proceedings of SSGRR 2001, International Conference on Advances in Infrastructure for Electronic Business, Science, and Education on the Internet, L'Aquila, Italy, Aug 06–Aug 12, 2001, ISBN:88-85280-61-7.
12. http://www.canarie.ca

A Publish/Subscribe Scheme for Peer-to-Peer Database Networks

Jian Yang[1], Mike P. Papazoglou[1], and Bernd J. Krämer[2]

[1] Tilburg University, INFOLAB, P.O. Box 90153, 5000 LE Tilburg, The Netherlands
{jian,mikep}@uvt.nl
[2] FernUniversität Hagen, D-58084 Hagen, Germany
bernd.kraemer@fernuni-hagen.de

Abstract. Peer-oriented computing is a natural way for meeting the data sharing requirements of decentralized, highly dynamic, scalable applications. In this paper we present a framework for data sharing in a peer-to-peer database network. We first introduce a publish/subscribe model where peer groups are formed by matching peer interests (subscriptions) against publications published by relevant peers in the network. We show that queries can be processed on basis of peer collaboration without the need for a global schema.

Keywords: Peer to peer databases, query processing, publish/subscribe models, query transformation.

1 Introduction

Modern data intensive applications, such as web-based information systems, digital libraries, electronic catalogues, and content-based management, require information sharing among different data sources that are heterogeneous by nature and highly dynamic in particular. Heterogeneity implies that the data sources may be based on different data modelling formalisms, they may organize the same kind of data in different formats, and may represent different aspects of the same data elements. In most cases, these data sources either have some data in common or they are complementary to each other, regardless of their heterogeneous nature.

To cope with these challenges, cooperating sites need to share information. The typical solution to this problem is data or schema integration techniques [2, 3]. These techniques distinguish between a mediator schema and a set of local source schemas and specify schema mappings between the local and the mediated schemas. All queries are posed against a mediator schema, which plays the role of a global schema, and are finally processed locally based on schema mappings.

Data integration techniques can be classified according to the way the local data source schemas are related to the global schema. The *global-as-view* (GAV) approach defines a global schema as a view over local schemas. Another approach, known as *local-as-view* (LAV), defines the local sources as views over the global schema [1]. The trade-offs between GAV and LAV are in terms of query

R. Meersman et al. (Eds.): CoopIS/DOA/ODBASE 2003, LNCS 2888, pp. 244–262, 2003.
© Springer-Verlag Berlin Heidelberg 2003

processing and scalability. With the GAV approach, translating global query into sub-queries on the local schemas is straightforward. In the case of LAV, the global query needs to be reformulated in terms of local schema elements. This is known as a hard problem of "rewriting queries using views" [2,4]. Modification of local schemas in the GAV approach involves redesigning the global schema; whereas in the case of the LAV approach, a local change only involves adding, deleting, and updating the local view definitions. As a consequence, the LAV approach scales better.

The ever-increasing need for data sharing between geographically dispersed data sources over the Internet has resulted in loosely coupled, open applications. These require highly dynamic solutions in which the arrangement of data requesters and providers is constantly changing. Schema integration is no solution for such dynamic applications as it does not scale well and requires constant redefinition and updating of the global schema and related schema mappings.

In contrast to LAV or GAV solutions, the dynamic nature of information sharing in an open, distributed environment demands an adaptive, and reconfigurable architectures that are capable of supporting ad hoc collaboration among related data sources and that can also update themselves when data sources join and leave the network. The initial results from peer-to-peer file systems [10,11,12] are very encouraging and inspiring in that regard. These demonstrate that ad hoc sharing of files is achievable in a system with high scalability and resiliency. Peer-to-peer applications rely on equal rights of all network participants to share resources among them. There is no host with special administrative or facilitating roles but all hosts provide the same application logic and perform both client and server roles.

The work presented herein is based on the peer-to-peer communication principle between data sources in a database network. This implies the absence of a global schema or global knowledge. Instead, all peers (data sources) in the network handle queries based on their own schema and may possibly engage acquainted peers (in their group) for processing the query further, if necessary. Peer groups are formed strictly on the basis of publish/subscribe techniques and algorithms are provided for subscribe/publish matching and peer group formation. In particular, we demonstrate how the system scales with respect to peers joining and leaving the network.

The remainder of this paper is organized as follows. Section 2 frames the problem and outlines our proposed solution. In Section 3 we present a publish/subscribe model for P2P database network and define how a peer group is formed. In Section 4 we describe how XML-based queries are distributed among peers and how they are processed. Section 5 discusses related work, while Section 6 presents our summary.

2   Problem Framing and Solution

In this section we introduce an architecture for sharing data among P2P databases. In particular, we explain how peer information is organized and discovered.

2.1   A Motivating Example

This example relates to activities performed in the travel industry. A travel plan could involve air ticket reservation, hotel booking, car rental, and leisure activities. Different peers in a common network compete with each other to provide better quality services to their customers in terms of cheaper prices, better package deals, or comprehensive information. At the same time they also need to share information, collaborate, and form partnerships in order to gain maximum competitive advantages.

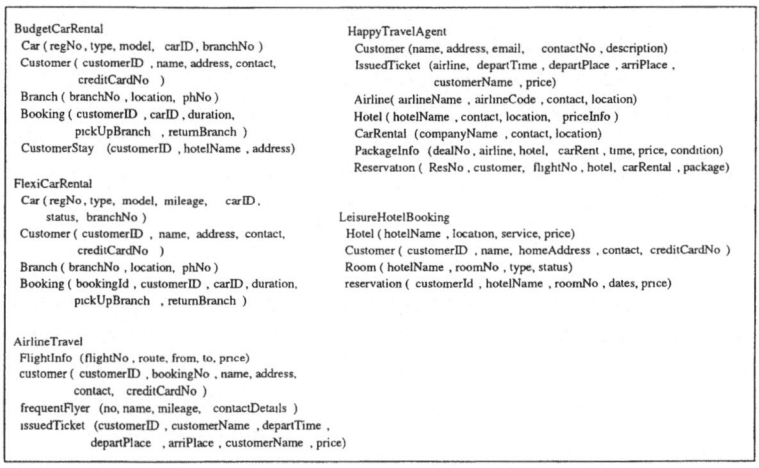

Fig. 1. Example schemas in the travel domain.

We assume that there are five data sources (peers) available in a database network (see Figure 1):

- The `BudgetCarRental` a relational data base that stores information about customers (current and previous), cars for rental purposes, their branches, and booking information.
- The `FlexiCarRental` a relational data base that stores similar information but contains only records of its current customers.
- The `LeisureHotelBooking` a relational data base that stores information about hotels, available rooms, customers and reservations.
- The `AirlineTravel` a relational database that stores information about flights, customers, frequent flyers, and tickets.
- The `HappyTravelAgent` a relational database that stores information about customers, airlines, car rentals, hotels, tickets, reservations, and package deals. The latter may include specific airlines, car rental companies, and hotels under certain conditions.

A travel agency needs to work with airlines, car rentals, hotels, and other travel agents to be able to provide attractive package deals for its customers. On the other hand, a car rental company may wish to work with hotel chains and travel agencies for attracting more customers. Consequently, there is a strong desire for these sources to share and exchange information. In addition, this network is highly dynamic as existing data sources may decide to leave the network or need to get updated, and new data sources may join in, with each peer intent on its own agenda. Bearing all this in mind, we require a system that exhibits the following characteristics:

- all data sources are autonomous, they have total control over their data and decide which of their data other peers in the network can share;
- there is no need for a global schema. When a query is posed against a peer, it will be processed on the basis of the schema of this peer and, at the same time, the query together with relevant schema information will be forwarded to related peers for further processing. This is conducted on the basis of minimal peer information that this specific node has accumulated;
- information about other peers gets updated whenever there are new pertinent peers joining the network, or when existing peers update their shareable data or leave the network.

To support the aforementioned requirements, we employ a publish/subscribe mechanism as the backbone of the peer-to-peer database network. An important requirement of this kind of P2P network is that every time a new peer database joins the network, it has to publish its shareable contents, i.e., its relations and attributes. All peer databases in the network can subscribe to the data contents that are relevant or interesting to them. For example, the FlexiCarRental may choose to subscribe to Car, and Branch data, which is relevant to it, and Hotel data, which although not necessarily relevant, could prove to be interesting for it.

2.2   A P2P Architecture for Data Sharing and Exchange

The P2P database network combines aspects of the directory services P2P model exemplified by Napster [10] and the "pure" P2P architecture exemplified by Gnutella and Freenet [11,12]. It follows a federated approach where a relatively small number of event-servers provide directory services to peer groups. Peers register high-level information about themselves, such as their name, address and names of the data elements they are willing to share with other peers, with an event server. However, they do not use the event-server to locate or communicate with each other. Instead, peers form cohesive groups that provide a common set of information, e.g., hotel accommodation, recreation activities, car rental, etc, depending on their requirements and interests. Each peer builds up a (constantly changing) peer- group of other peers and stores some minimal information about them. Whenever a peer receives a data request it attempts to forward it to appropriate peers within its peer-group for execution. Thus, queries get propagated from peer to peer within a group and responses follow the same path back. The primary advantages of this approach are scalability and lack of logical centralization.

When joining the P2P database network, a peer should first register itself by publishing (public) data items that it is willing to share with other peers. Secondly, it may subscribe to data items that it is interested to know from other peers. All peers can *subscribe* to the data items they are interested in and *publish* those data items they wish to share with other peers. A peer group is formed on the basis of matching a peers' subscription needs against relevant publications that other peers advertise.

Matching between subscription and publication data is the responsibility of a server module, see Figure 2. Whenever a match is detected, the server forwards the publication data and the addresses of relevant peers to all the peers that have subscribed to the published data. As a consequence, each peer contains a set of addresses of the peers that have published information that this peer has subscribed to.

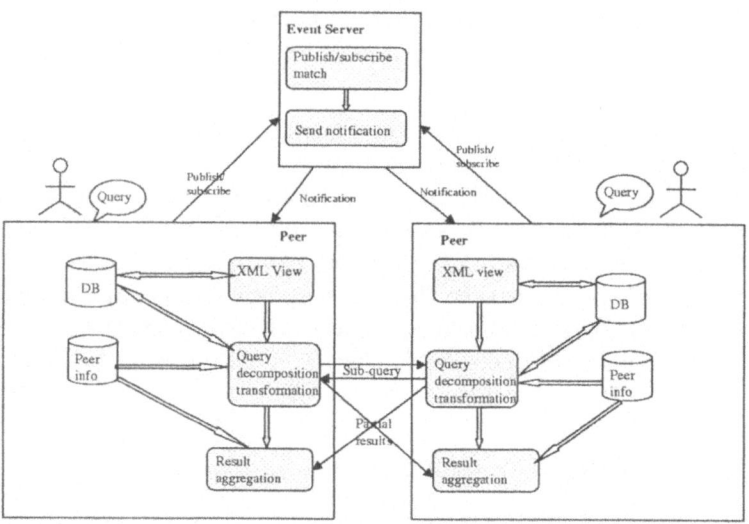

Fig. 2. High-level view of the P2P database network architecture.

The key components of the P2P database network depicted in Figure 2 are as follows:

– **Event Server**: this component is similar to that of a hybrid P2P architecture where indexing is centralized and file exchange is distributed [16]. The event server manages a select set of meta-operations for peers, such as joining/leaving the network, publishing data offerings, and data subscriptions. The event server also performs subscription/publication matching, so that relevant notifications can be sent to interested subscribers (peers).
When the server receives a new publish/subscribe event from a peer that wishes to join the network, it performs two kinds of matching operations.

The first matching operation matches the new peer's publication against all subscriptions that are relevant to it. In this way a notification (regarding the newly published peer) is sent to all peers in the network that have subscribed to data relating to data offered by this new peer. The second matching operation matches all previous publications against the data subscriptions of this new peer. In this way the new peer is informed about existing peers whose publications match its subscription needs and can thus establish its own peer group. Subscribe/publish mechanisms and peer group formation are discussed in section 3.

– **Peer**s: Query processing is performed within peers. For each peer in the network, its peer group is established implicitly by matching its subscription needs against all relevant publications made by other peers in the network. Whenever a match is detected, the event server sends the new peer, say A, a notification containing the address of the matching peers, say peers B and C. Subsequently, peers B and C will be included in the group of peer A, and relevant published data contents of peers B and C will be stored in peer A's *peer information base* (called peer-info in Figure 2). Peers B and C are called *acquaintances* of peer A.

Queries in the P2P database network are handled by the peers where the queries originate. We refer to these peers as *query hosting peers*. If a query-hosting peer detects that a query involves data from other peers in its peer group, the peer first decides which of its acquaintances are the most appropriate for processing segments of the query. This is determined on the basis of peer-acquaintance relevance to the query by analysing this peer's information base. Subsequently, the query-hosting peer will forward the query together with its (partial) schema and a desired result format in XML to relevant peers - acquaintances of a specific peer that may answer parts of the query - in its group. Peer acquaintances reformulate the part of the query they receive according to their own schema and process it. Partial results are then sent back to the query-hosting peer for validation and aggregation.

Query processing in this P2P network is discussed in section 4, where we use the running example of section-2.1 to exemplify how schematic heterogeneity can be resolved and how results from diverse peers are merged.

3   Publish/Subscribe in the P2P Database Network

Publish/subscribe is a communication mechanism that enables the loose coupling of peers in peer-to-peer data exchange networks. The participants of such networks exchange notifications about data publications and subscriptions via asynchronous notifications.

A peer publishes a set of relations[1], each having a set of attributes[2] characterizing the contents published. For a given application domain we assume

---

[1] The term relation is used in a very loose way. It can be relational table in a database or element in XML terms.

[2] The term attribute is also used in a loose way. It can be attribute in a database relation, or a simple element or attribute in XML terms.

that the set of all possible relation and attribute names **R** and **A**, respectively, are well defined. All publications are maintained by an event notification server known to all potential peers **P** (see Figure 2).

In this paper we follow the practices of e-marketplaces, i.e., all the data sources that join an e-marketplace, such as travel industry, chemical, or semi-conductor industry, are forced to use a standard vocabulary and the same naming conventions, when they subscribe and publish information. Accordingly, we are not dealing with terminology fluctuations and semantic mismatches. In addition, we assume that all the peers in the database network employ XML views over the data structures that a peer wishes to make publicly available. For example, the `HappyTravelAgent` may decide to publish only some of its data elements such as `Customer`, `Airline`, `Reservation`, `Hotel` with attributes. In a similar fashion, a subscription can specify a set of contents (e.g., `car`, `branch`) with or without attributes.

3.1   A Model for Publication and Subscription Matching

In this section we introduce a formal model for publication and subscription matching for a given application domain where the sets **R**, **A**, and **P** contain all permissible relation, attribute, and peer names, respectively.

Publication Contexts. A *publication* is a set of pairs (r, A) with $r \in \mathbf{R}$ and $A \subseteq \mathbf{A}$. More concretely, we can express a publication as:

$$\{(r_1, \{a_{r_1,1}, \dots, a_{r_1,k_1}\}), \dots, (r_l, \{a_{r_l,1}, \dots, a_{r_l,k_l}\})\}. \tag{1}$$

The set of all publications known in a specific domain at a particular time is called its *publication context*. Publication contexts and the matching of a subscription against a given publication context can be modelled mathematically in terms of formal concept analysis [18], which relies on the theory of ordered sets and complete lattices.

A publication context can be represented by a matrix that relates a set of peer names with relation names and a set of accompanying attribute names that peers in the P2P network have published. The peer names are represented by rows in the matrix, while the relations and their associated attributes are represented by columns in the matrix. A cross in row p and column r indicates that peer p has published relation r. Table 1 illustrates a publication context for a subset of the relations and attributes used in the example in Figure 1.

Formally a publication context $C := (P, R, I)$ consists of a set $P \subseteq \mathbf{P}$ of peer names, a publication $R \subseteq \{(r, A) \mid r \in \mathbf{R} \wedge A \subseteq \mathbf{A}\}$, and an incidence relation $I \subseteq P \times R$. The fact that a peer p has published a certain relation (r, A) is written as $(p, (r, A)) \in I$. The set of relation names in R is defined by:

$$rel(R) = \{r \mid (r, A) \in R\} \tag{2}$$

and the set of attributes published for some relation name $r \in R$ is defined by:

$$att(r, R) = \{a \mid (r, A) \in R \wedge a \in A\}. \tag{3}$$

Table 1. Example of a publication context for the travel domain depicted in Fig. 1

	Airline()	Booking(pickUpBranch)	Booking(bookingNo,pickUpBranch)	Car(type)	Car(mileage,type)	Customer(address)	Customer(address,description)	Customer(address,creditcardNo)	Hotel(contact,hotelName,location)	Hotel(hotelName,service)	Reservation()	Room()
BudgetCarRental		×		×		×		×				
FlexiCarRental		×	×	×	×	×		×				
HappyTravelAgent	×					×	×		×		×	
LeisureHotelBooking						×		×		×	×	×
Airline						×		×				

The following expression Q' computes the set of *commonly reachable relations* for a set of peers in $Q \subseteq P$:

$$Q' := \{t \in R \mid (p,t) \in I \text{ for all } p \in Q\} \tag{4}$$

Similarly, we define T' as the set of peers that published all relations in a set of relations $T \subseteq R$:

$$T' := \{p \in P \mid (p,t) \in I \text{ for all } t \in T\} \tag{5}$$

When we apply definitions 2, 3, 4 and 5 to the publication context C in Table 1, we obtain:

$$rel(C) = \{\texttt{Airline}, \texttt{Booking}, \texttt{Car}, \texttt{Customer}, \texttt{Hotel}, \texttt{Reservation}, \texttt{Room}\}$$

$$att(\texttt{Customer}, C) = \{\texttt{address}, \texttt{description}, \texttt{creditCardNo}\}$$

$$\{\texttt{Airline}\}' = \{\texttt{Customer(address)}, \texttt{Customer(address, creditCardNo)}\}$$

and

$$\{\texttt{Car(type)}\}' = \{\texttt{BudgetCarRental}, \texttt{FlexiCarRental}\}$$

A simple matrix such as the one illustrated in Table 1 can easily represent the elementary publication context represented by our running example and can be used to compute the results shown in the previous examples. However, for extended publication contexts this procedure is impractical and may lead to errors.

A more elegant way to visualise publication contexts and perform context-based computations, is by means of constructing a *concept lattice* $\mathbf{C}(P, R, I)$ constructed from a given publication context (P, R, I) using an efficient algorithm that relies on the notion of formal concepts and formation of sub-context spaces [19].

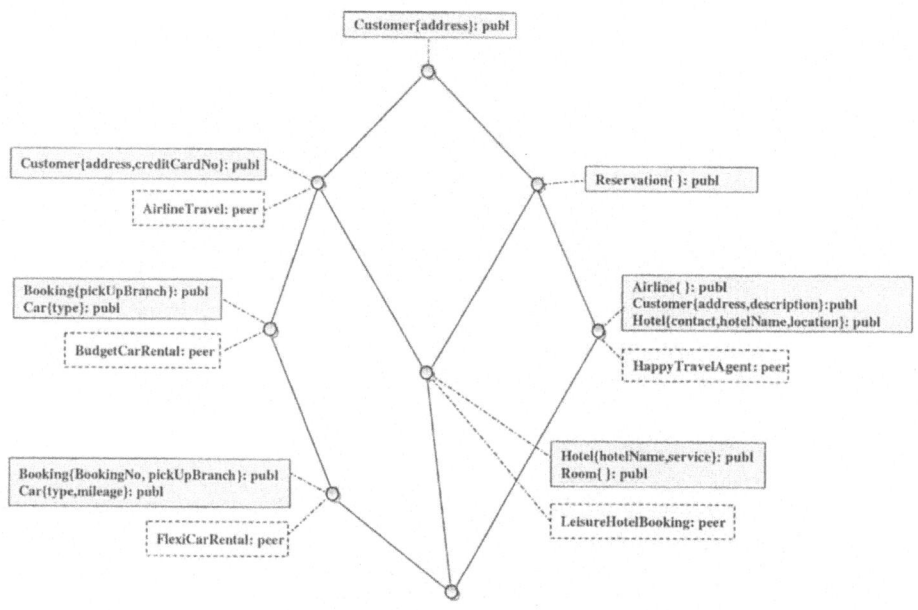

Fig. 3. Concept lattice derived from Table 1

The concept lattice of the sample publication in Table 1 is shown in Figure 3. There are two types of nodes in this lattice: concept (publication) nodes and peer nodes. This concept lattice contains eight concepts (which include the bottom node representing the universal concept) and five peers. All concept nodes reachable upwards from a peer node in the lattice forms the complete concept set that this peer has published. For instance, the node labelled with the peer name `BudgetCarRental` has published:

{ `Booking(pickUpBranch)`, `Car(type)`, `Customer(address,creditcardNo)` ,
                `Customer(address)` }.

Conversely, all the peer nodes reachable downwards from a concept node in the lattice forms the set of peers that have published a common concept. For instance, the concept node `Reservation()` is supported by peer nodes `LeisureHotelBooking, HappyTravelAgent`.

Subscriptions. A subscription S is specified, just like a publication, as a set of pairs (s, A) with $s \in \mathbf{R}$ and $A \subseteq \mathbf{A}$. We say that a peer p *matches* a subscription S if it has published at least the relations listed in the subscription, i.e., $S \subseteq \{p\}'$. All peers of a publication context (P, R, I) that match a subscription form the *acquaintances* of this publication context:

$$[S] := \{p \in P \mid S \subseteq \{p\}'\}. \tag{6}$$

Table 2 shows simple examples of subscriptions and their resulting acquaintances.

Table 2. Examples of subscriptions and their acquaintances

example	subscription	acquaintances
Subscription1	{ Customer(address) }	P
Subscription2	{ Customer(address), Car(type) }	{ BudgetCarRental, FlexiCarRental }
Subscription3	$\emptyset$	P
Subscription4	{ Car() }	$\emptyset$
Subscription5	{ Car(mileage) }	$\emptyset$

These examples show that Subscription 2 extends Subscription 1 by requesting an additional relation to be matched. We observe that Subscription 2 is a superset of Subscription 1, while the acquaintances of Subscription 2 form a subset of the acquaintances of Subscription 1. An empty subscription is matched by all peers, while Subscriptions 4 and 5 yield an empty set of acquaintances because the requested combination of attributes and relation names is not supported.

Intuitively, we want the subscriptions {Car()} and {Car(mileage)} to be inter-related within the publication context in Table 1 since there are two peers, BudgetCarRental and FlexiCarRental, that have published a common part of this relation with some differing attributes. It is thus useful to view the relation Car() as a subtype of the relations Car(type) and Car(mileage,type). In general, we want a subscription element (s, A) to be matched by a peer that has published a relation (r, B) if $s = r$ and $A \subseteq B$.

To achieve this, we extend a given publication context (P, R, I) to the context $(P, \overline{R}, \overline{I})$, where:

$$\overline{R} = \{(r, B) \mid r \in rel(R) \land B \subseteq att(r, R)\} \tag{7}$$

and

$$\overline{I} = I \cup \{(p,(r,B)) \mid \text{ if } (p,(r,A)) \in I \text{ for all } A \subseteq \mathcal{P}(B))\} \tag{8}$$

That is, we supplement the relations $(r, A_1), \ldots, (r, A_n)$ published in R by additional relations (r, B), where B denotes all possible subsets of $A_1 \cup, \cdots \cup A_n$, and we introduce a cross in row p and the new column $(r, A_i \cup \cdots \cup A_k)$ if we find a cross in all columns $(p, (r, A_j))$ in the original publication context (for $j = i, i + 1, \ldots, k)$. Table 3 shows, for illustration purposes, only part of the new matrix resulting from extending Table 1 with definitions 7 and 8. All new columns are marked in a light grey colour. Figure 4 depicts the extended concept lattice corresponding to Table 3. This lattice is stored at the event-server and can be used to assist locating peers related to a query that can not be completely decomposed by its query hosting peer, this is explained in detail in section-4.

Table 3. Example of a publication context for the travel domain depicted in Fig. 1

	Airline()	Booking()	Booking(bookingNo)	Booking(pickUpBranch)	Booking(bookingNo,pickUpBranch)	Car()	Car(mileage)	Car(type)	Car(mileage,type)	Customer()	Customer(address)	Customer(creditCardNo)
BudgetCarRental		×		×		×		×		×	×	×
FlexiCarRental		×	×	×	×	×	×	×	×	×	×	×
HappyTravelAgent	×					×				×	×	
LeisureHotelBooking										×	×	×
Airline										×	×	×

If we now attempt to match Subscriptions 4 and 5 listed in the subscription Table 2 against the extended context $(P, \overline{R}, \overline{I})$, we obtain the acquaintances { BudgetCarRental, FlexiCarRental} and {FlexiCarRental, HappyTravelAgent }, respectively. To exemplify this consider the extended concept lattice shown in Figure 4 and the Subscription Car(). Firstly we need to allocate a concept node that matches this subscription. Then the peer node associated with this concept node (i.e., BudgetCarRental) and all peer nodes associated with the nodes reachable from edges descending from this concept node (i.e., FlexiCarRental) form the acquaintances of this subscription.

We henceforth always refer to the extended publication context and its corresponding concept lattice, when matching subscriptions with publications.

In addition to the above, we also require that a subscription such as $S = \{\texttt{Hotel(), Room(type)}\}$ (partially) matches a certain publication context if at least one of the elements in S is matched against a publication such as $\texttt{Hotel(contact, hotelName)}$. We refer to this type of matching as a *partial match*. A partial match of a subscription S over a publication context $C :=$ (P, R, I), in terms of the function *match*, is defined as follows:

$$match(S, C) = \{p \in P \mid S \cap \{p\}' \neq \emptyset\} \tag{9}$$

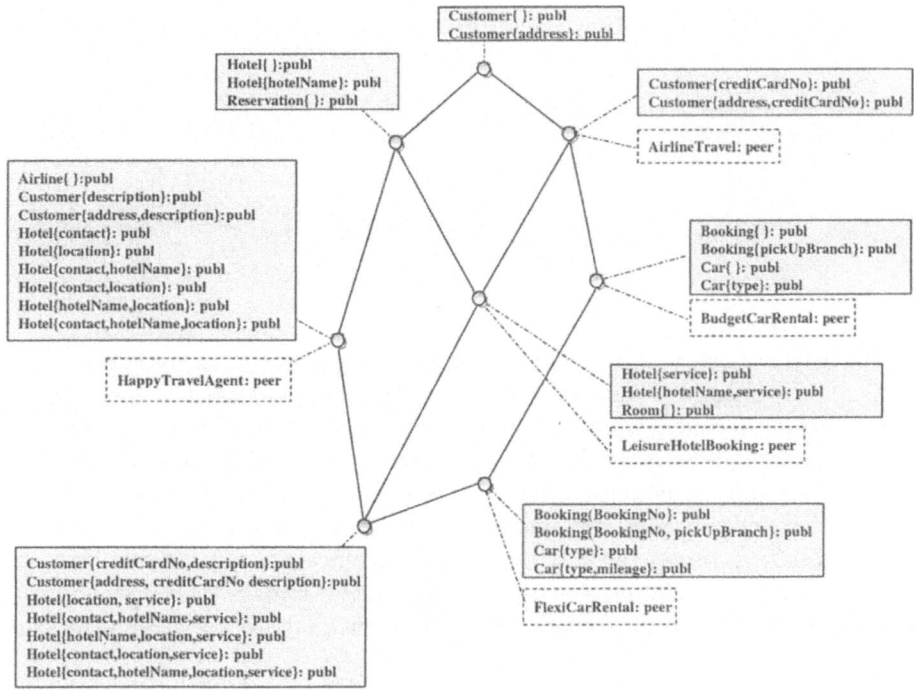

Fig. 4. Concept lattice including subtype relationships among published relations.

3.2   Peer Group Formation and Updating

A peer group is formed by applying the *match* function, defined in section- 3.1, on a peer's subscription against the publication context C. Suppose that the subscription of $\texttt{BudgetCarRental}$ is: $S := \{(\texttt{Car(type), Booking(pickUpBranch)},$ $\texttt{Hotel(hotelName, location, contact)}\}$

A *matched-subscription lattice* for `BudgetCarRental`, shown in Figure 5, is generated by matching its subscription S against the extended publication lattice of the event-server, shown in Figure 4. The matched-subscription lattice is a true subset of the extended publication lattice stored at the event-server and indicates the peers and matching concepts that conform to `BudgetCarRental`'s subscription. This information is stored locally at this peer's site so that it can be used in the future to locate relevant peer acquaintances when attempting to process a query.

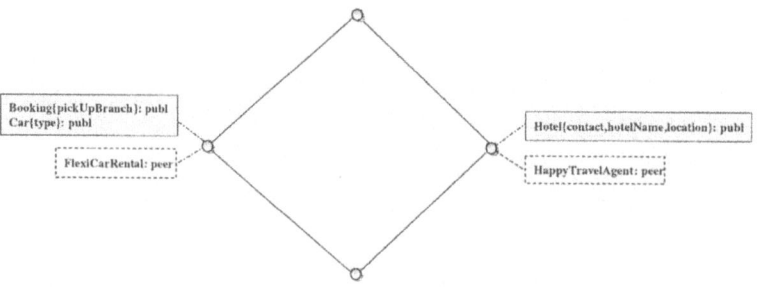

Fig. 5. A matched-subscription lattice for `BudgetCarRental`

Whenever a query is posed at a query-hosting peer, its set of subscriptions needs to be evaluated to determine whether it can support the new query. In case that execution of the new query is not fully supported, then a new subscription (for this peer) will be generated from this query and will be sent to the event-server. Eventually, a new matched-subscription lattice, which satisfies the new subscription, will be generated and sent to the query-hosting peer.

When a peer leaves the P2P network, a notification will be sent from the event- server to all relevant peers, which in turn will update their matched- subscription lattices. This happens in accordance with lattice updating algorithms found in [19].

4   Query Processing

The flexibility and wide-use of XML as a data exchange format makes it a prime candidate for use as a common data model in data integration applications. Using an XML-based schema at the interface level allows to hide the proprietary data elements that the owners of data do not wish to disclose, and allows to adhere to a standard interface without having to migrate existing data.

All peers in the database network expose their own private XML views of their schema and data content. Figure 6 illustrates such an XML view over the `BudgetCarRental` schema and data contents. To query the XML peer views we use XQuery, the standard XML query language proposed by the W3C [20].

```
<BudgetCarRental>
  <Cars>
    <Car>
      <regNo>"BJ100"</regNo><type>"small"</type><model>"MAZDA121"</model>
      <branchNo>"B1"</branchNo><carID>"CA2"</carID>
    </Car>
    <Car>  ..... </Car>
    ...
  <Bookings>
    <Bookong>
      <customerID>"CU1"</customer><carID>"CA2"</carID>
      <pickUpBranch>"Bredasweg 421, Tilburg"</pickUpBranch>
    </Booking>
    <Booking> ... </Booking>
  <Customers> similar to <Cars>    </Customers>
  <Branchs>  similar </Branches>
  <CustomerStays>  similar <CustomerStays>
</BudgetCarRental>
```

Fig. 6. The BudgetCarRental database and its XML view.

Suppose that the following query is issued at the `BudgetCarRental` peer:

"Find the types of all the cars which are picked up at Tilburg and find all the hotels that are close to each car's pick up location."

Figure 7 shows an XQuery corresponding to the previous narrative and formulated on the basis of XML view presented in Figure 6.

```
01 FOR $car in document("BudgetCarRental.xml")//Car {
02  FOR $booking in document("BudgetCarRental.xml")//Booking
03  WHERE $car/carID=$booking/carID
04  AND $booking/pickUpBranch=*Tilburg
05  RETURN
06  <carType type=$car/type/text()}>
07     <hotelNearBy> {
08       FOR $hotel in document ($Hotel)//Hotel
09       WHERE distance ($hotel/location, $booking/pickUpBranch)<=1km
10       RETURN
11       <name>$hotel/name</name>
12       <location>$hotel/location</location> }
13     </hotelNearBy>
14   </carType> }
```

Fig. 7. A query expressed in XQuery

To facilitate query decomposition and subsequent processing of the XQuery and its underlying schema information[3] the XQuery statement is represented by the Document Object Model, or DOM (www.w3.org/DOM). The peer BudgetCarRental generates a tree-like structure against its own XML view of the query in Figure 7 that is illustrated in Figure 8 (a). In addition, all peers in the P2P network represent their XML views also in a DOM tree-like structure. In this way we use the DOM as a common structural substrate for comparison of XQueries and their underlying schema segments against remote peer XML views.

The DOM representation of an XQuery is referred to as the *DOMQuery* for the query-hosting peer. A DOMQuery for the peer BudgetCarRental and XML views on Hotels to which this peer subscribes, is illustrated in Figure 8 (a). Arrows in this figure represent access paths, while dashed thin lines represent predicates or join conditions. A query result DOM structure is also provided, which indicates the tags and values needed to be returned by the query (Figure 8 (b)).

In the following we explain how this DOMQuery can be evaluated against the matched-subscription lattice of a peer (to determine other peers that could potentially contribute towards its processing); how the query is decomposed and transformed according to the DOM structure of the XML view of the remote peers; and how results are aggregated at the query hosting peer BudgetCarRental. The phases of query processing can be describes as follows:

- *Query evaluation:* the query-hosting peer, i.e., BudgetCarRental constructs a DOMQuery (and its resulting DOM structure), for the query it receives and derives its query contents based on its own XML schema (see Figure 8 (a) and (b)). The query content is matched against the matched-subscription lattice of this peer to determine peers that can potentially process the query. In this case, FlexiCarRental and HappyTravelAgent are the two peers that may be able to contribute to the query.
- *Query decomposition:* the query-hosting peer determines which parts of the query these (remote) peers are capable of handling. This is achieved by examining overlaps between their publications (stored in the query-hosting peer's matched-subscription lattice) and the DOMQuery. Subsequently, the DOMQuery is decomposed on the basis of this information into a set of DOM sub- queries that the remote peers are able to process. In this case, the original query-hosting peer DOMQuery and its requested result can be decomposed into two segments highlighted as dashed ellipses in Figure 8 (a) and (b). The query-hosting peer forwards each remote peer the DOM sub-query it has generated for it. See Figure 8 (c-f).
- *Query reformulation:* the DOM sub-query is compared at the remote peer against its own XML view (also expressed in a DOM tree-like structure). The path expressions extracted from these two DOM structures are mapped against each other using transformation rules. Suppose the DOM structure

---

[3] Here we use the term schema loosely to refer to the structure of XML view of the data source.

of the `FlexiCarRental` XML view is as shown in Figure 9 (a), the receiving DOM sub-query (Figure 8 (c)) will be transformed to the one as shown in Figure 9 (b). Some initial results on query reformulation based on XML DTDs can be found in [21].

- *Result aggregation:* finally all results received by the query hosting peer from other peers that have processed segments of the original query are aggregated.

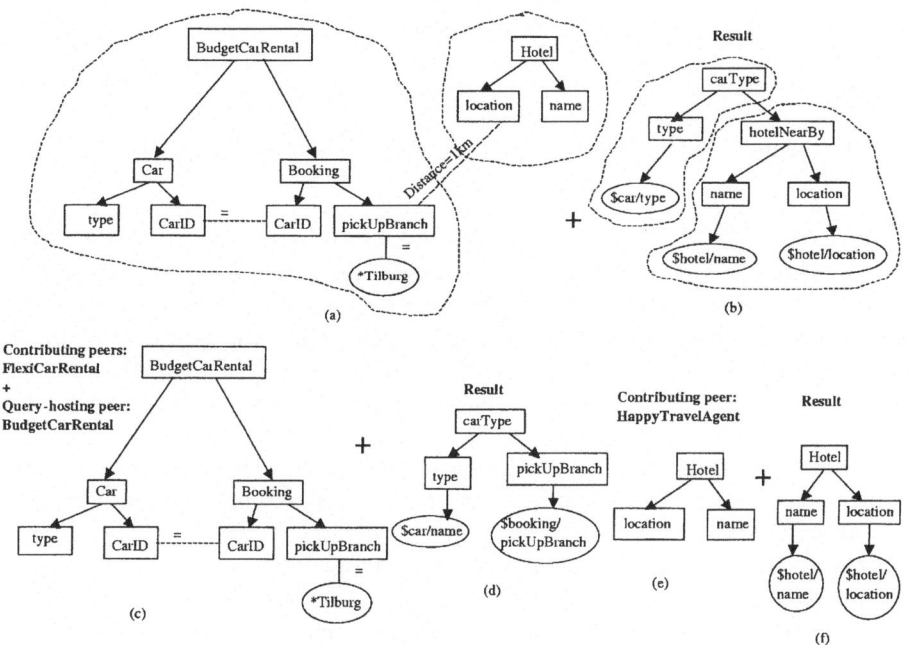

Fig. 8. The DOMQuery corresponding to the XQuery expression in Figure 7.

5   Related Work

Previous work on integration of structured or semi-structured data sources, such as [6,7,8,9], adopts either the GAV or LAV approach. More recently, there were attempts to provide an XML view at the top of databases, and algorithms were presented for query translation and query re- writing for the query on the global schema to that of local schemas [1]. Data integration in the previous work normally involves a global schema (or view) or local views, where constructs in the global schema and local views are tied together using either a GAV or LAV approach. However, these approaches suffer either from scalability problems, or from serious query processing difficulties. In particular, query rewriting could be an NP-hard problem if a LAV approach were used.

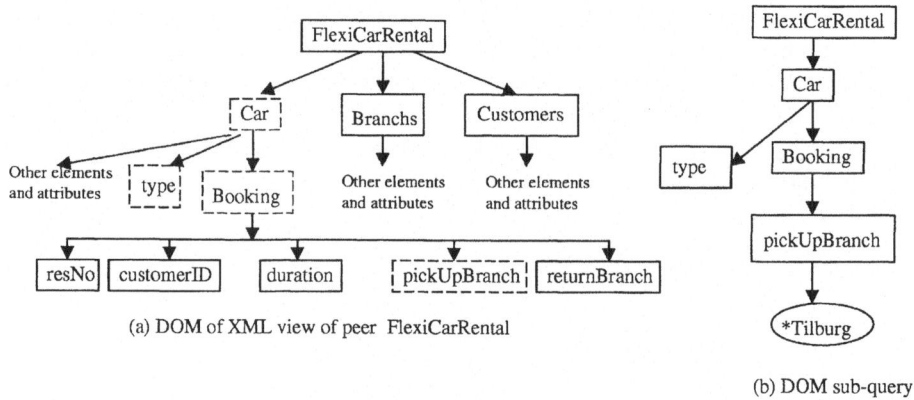

(a) DOM of XML view of peer FlexiCarRental

(b) DOM sub-query

Fig. 9. `FlexiCarRental` DOM-XML View and its DOMQuery

In contrast to the aforementioned research activities, our work is based on peer-to-peer collaboration and exchange of XML-based schema segments rather than the need for a global view, or local view against the global schema. All data sources have their own views and schemas (expressed in XML), and the queries are posed against local schemas and are decomposed and sent to the relevant peers based on knowledge about peers in a peer group. Similar ideas for the query processing part were proposed in [22]. However, this work focused on query translation between different data models based on a semantic translation protocol, while work in this paper deals with query transformation among different XML views with a common data model DOM.

Some interesting ideas in managing p2p database are reported recently. [23, 24] support data sharing without a predetermined schema. They derive keywords from a query and match against the database schemas in order to decide the data sources that can contribute to the query. Work reported in [25] facilitates a super-peer structure that is responsible for indexing and query routing. In [26] a peer index is used to store peer content and select peers when query comes.

On the industrial research side the work that comes closer to the P2P database network reported herein is Sun Microsystem's Project Juxtapose (http://www.jxta.org) – usually referred to as JXTA. JXTA defines a set of XML- based (language and network agnostic) protocols for interoperation and an open network programming platform to enable P2P services and applications. Key entities defined by XML include peers, any entity that can understand protocols required by other peers; messages that are designed as datagrams containing an envelope and a set of protocol headers with associated bodies; identifies to refer top entities such as peers, advertisements and services; and peer groups, which are collections of cooperating peers that provide a common set of circumstances. Currently we are experimenting with the use of JXTA.

6   Summary

In this paper we have presented a framework for data sharing in a peer-to-peer database network based on a publish/subscribe model. In the P2P database network peer groups are formed implicitly by matching peer interests (subscriptions) against publications published by relevant peers in the network. Queries are processed on basis of peer collaboration without the need for a global schema. Each peer builds up a (constantly changing) peer-group of other peers and stores some minimal information about them. Whenever a peer receives a query it attempts to forward it to appropriate peers within its peer-group for execution. A query-hosting peer decomposes a query according to its own perception and sends its segments to peers it "thinks" can contribute towards its processing. Subsequently, the query receiving peers reformulate the segment of the query they receive according to their own schema and process it. Partial results are then sent back to the query-hosting peer for validation and aggregation.

The primary advantages of this approach are scalability and lack of logical centralization.

References

1. I. Manolescu, D. Florescu, D. Kossmann, "Answering XML Queries over Heterogeneous Data Sources", in Proc of VLDB2001, Rome, Septermber, 2001.
2. A. Halevy, "Logic-based Techniques in Data Integration. In Logic Based Artificial Intelegence, 2000.
3. C. Batini, M. Lenzerini, S. B. Navathe. "A Comparative Analysis of Methodologies for Database Schema Integration", ACM Computing Surveys 18(4): 323–364, 1986.
4. A. Levy, A. Mendelzon, Y. Sagiv, and D. Srivastava. "Answering queries using views. In Proc. of PODS, San Jose, 1995.
5. S. Gribble, A. Halevy, Z. Ives, M. Rodrig, D. Suciu, "What Can Peer-to-Peer Do for Databases, and Vice Versa?", In Proc of 4th International Workshop on the Web and Databases (WebDB), 2001.
6. L. Haas, D. Kossmann, E. Wimmers, and J. Yang. "Optimizing Queries across Diverse Data Sources". In Proc. of VLDB Conf., Athens, Greece, 1997.
7. A. Tomasic, L. Raschid, and P. Valduriez. "Scaling Access to Distributed Heterogeneous Data Sources with Disco. IEEE Transaction on Knowledge and Data Engineering, 1998.
8. H. Garcia-Molina, Y. Papakonstantinou, D. Quass, A. Rajaraman, Y. Sagiv, J. Ullman, and J. Widom. "The TSIMMIS project: Integration of heterogeneous information sources". Journal of Intelligent Information Systems, 8(2):117–132, March, 1997.
9. T. Kirk, A. Levy, Y. Sagiv, and D. Srivastava. "The Information Manifold". In AAAI Spring Symposium on Information Gathering, 1995.
10. www.napster.com, 2001.
11. Gnutella Development Home Page. http://gnutella.wego.com
12. Freenet Home Page. http://freenet.sourceforge.com
13. J. Kubiatowicz et al. "Oceanstore: An Architecture for Global-Scale Persistent Storage. In ASPLOS 2000, page 190–201, November 2000.
14. How Entropia Works. www.entropia.com/how.asp, 2000.

15. About LEGION – the Grid OS. www.appliedmeta.com/legion/about.html., 2000
16. Beverly Yang, Hector Garcia-Molina. "Comparing Hybrid Peer-to- Peer Systems". In Procs of VLDB 2001, Roma, September, 2001.
17. A. Carzaniga, D. Rosenblum, and A. Wolf, "Design and Evaluation of a Wide-Area Event Notification Service", in ACM Trans on Computer Systems, Vol. 19, No. 3, Page 332–383, 2001.
18. B. Ganter, R. Wille. *Formal Concept Analysis.* Springer 1999
19. Algorithmen zur formalen Begriffsanalyse. In: B. Ganter, R. Wille, and K.E. Wolff (eds), *Beitrğe zur Begriffsanalyse.* B.I.-Wissenschaftsverlag, Mannheim, 1987, pp. 241–254
20. XQuery 1.0 and XPath 2.0 Data Model, W3C Working Draft 30 April 2002. http://www.w3.org/TR/query-datamodel/.
21. S. Cluet, P. Veltri, and D. Vodislav. "Views in a Large Scale XML Repository", in Procs of 27th VLDB, Italy, Sep 11–14, 2001.
22. M. P. Papazoglou, N. Russell, and D. Edmond. "A Translation Protocol Achieving Consensus of Semantics between Cooperating Heterogeneous Database Systems", in Procs of CoopIS, 1996.
23. W.S. Ng, B.C. Ooi, K-L Tan, and A. Zhou, "PeerDB: A P2P-based System for Distributed Data Sharing", ICDE2003, India, 2003.
24. B.C. Ooi, Y. Shu, and K-L Tan, "Relational Data Sharing in Peer-based Data Management Systems", SIGMOD Record Special issue on p2p, 2003.
25. A. Loser, W. Siberski, M. Wolpers, and W. Nejdi, "Information Integration in Schema-Based Peer-To-Peer Networks", CAiSE03, Velden, June 2003.
26. L. Galanis, Y. Wang, S.R. Jeffery, and D.J. DeWitt, "Processing Queries in a Large Peer-to-Peer System", CAiSE03, Velden, June 2003.

Query Evaluation in Peer-to-Peer Networks of Taxonomy-Based Sources

Yannis Tzitzikas* and Carlo Meghini

Istituto di Scienza e Tecnologie dell' Informazione [ISTI]
Consiglio Nazionale delle Ricerche [CNR], Pisa, Italy
{tzitzik,meghini}@isti.cnr.it

Abstract. We consider the problem of query evaluation in Peer-to-Peer (P2P) systems that support semantic-based retrieval services. We confine ourselves to the case where the peers employ *taxonomies* for describing the contents of the objects, and *articulations*, i.e. inter-taxonomy mappings, for bridging the inevitable naming, granularity and contextual heterogeneities that may exist between the taxonomies of the sources. We identify two basic query evaluation approaches: one based on *query rewriting*, the other based on *direct* query evaluation. For each approach we present a *centralized* and a *decentralized* algorithm for carrying out the query evaluation task. Finally, we present a qualitative comparison of these algorithms and discuss further optimizations. Correctness of the algorithms presented is based on a mathematical analysis of the problem.

1   Introduction

In recent years there has been a growing interest in information integration, whose objective is to access, relate and combine data from multiple sources. This need has stimulated the research on *mediators* (initially proposed in [22]). A model for building mediators over taxonomy-based sources of the kind of Web catalogs has been proposed in [21]. According to this model, each source consists of a taxonomy and an object base, i.e. a database that indexes the objects of the domain under the terms of the taxonomy. A mediator consists of a taxonomy plus a number of *articulations* to the other sources of the network, where an articulation is actually a mapping between the terms of the mediator and the terms of the sources. In this paper we extend this model and study the more general scenario where we have a network of articulated sources. In such a network we can no longer distinguish sources to primary and secondary (i.e. mediators) as we may have mutually articulated sources, thus we actually have a peer-to-peer (P2P) system, i.e. a distributed system in which participants rely on one another for service, rather than solely relying on dedicated and often centralized infrastructure.

Many examples of P2P systems have emerged recently, most of which are wide-area, large-scale systems that provide content sharing [4], storage services

---

* Work done during the postdoctoral studies of the author at CNR-ISTI as an ERCIM fellow.

R. Meersman et al. (Eds.): CoopIS/DOA/ODBASE 2003, LNCS 2888, pp. 263–281, 2003.
© Springer-Verlag Berlin Heidelberg 2003

[13,18], or distributed "grid" computation [2,1]. Smaller-scale P2P systems also exist, such as federated, serverless file systems [7,5] and collaborative workgroup tools [3]. Existing peer-to-peer (P2P) systems have focused on specific application domains (e.g. music files) or on providing file-system-like capabilities. These systems do not yet provide semantic-based retrieval services. In most of the cases, the name of the object (e.g. the title of a music file) is the only means for describing the contents of the object. The advantage of the approach proposed in this paper, is that it also allows describing the contents of the objects with respect to taxonomies. Consequently, we can have enhanced semantic-based retrieval services.

We describe the architecture and the functioning of such a system and we focus on the query evaluation process. We carry out a mathematical analysis of the problem, which leads to the identification of the terms whose interpretation is to be considered in order to evaluate a global query. This result is exploited in the context of two different approaches to query evaluation. In the first approach, which is a kind of query rewriting, a given query is first transformed into a set of local queries, which are then executed in an optimal way to obtain the answer to the original query. In the latter approach, the query is evaluated directly, without any prior consideration of the involved local queries. For each approach, we present a centralized and a decentralized algorithm, capturing the two basic different styles for carrying out a distributed computation. The correctness of the presented algorithms directly stems from the mathematical analysis of the problem.

The remaining of this paper is organized as follows: Section 2 describes the building blocks of a network of articulated sources, i.e. sources, mediators and articulated sources; introduces the notion of network query and answer; and carries out the mathematical analysis of the problem, on which all the algorithms hinge. Section 3 focuses on query evaluation and describes several query evaluation approaches and the corresponding algorithms. It also presents a qualitative comparison of these algorithms and discuses further optimizations. Section 4 describes related work, and finally, Section 5 concludes the paper and identifies issues for further research. For reason of space, proofs are omitted, but the technical ideas behind the most important results (such as Proposition 3) are provided, along with illustrating examples.

2   The Network

Let *Obj* denote the set of all objects of a domain common to several information sources. A typical example of such a domain is the set of all pointers to Web pages. A network of articulated sources over *Obj* is a set of sources $N = \{S_1, ...S_n\}$ where each S_i falls into one of the following categories:

- *Simple sources*: they consist of a taxonomy and an object base, i.e. a database that indexes objects of *Obj* under the terms of the taxonomy. A simple source accepts queries over its taxonomy and returns the objects whose index "matches" the query.

- *Mediators*: they consist of a taxonomy plus a number of articulations to other sources of the network. Again, a mediator accepts queries over its taxonomy but as it does not maintain an object base, query answering requires sending queries to the underlying sources and combining the returned results.
- *Articulated sources*: they are both simple sources and mediators, i.e. they consist of a taxonomy, an object base and a number of articulations to other sources of the network. An articulated source can behave like a simple source, like a mediator, or like a mediator which in addition to the external sources can also use its own simple source during query answering.

Clearly, simple sources and mediators are special cases (or roles) of articulated sources. In order to minimize the number of notions to be introduced, and thus attain clarity, we will first introduce simple sources, and define query-answering on them. Then, articulated sources will be defined, as an intuitive extension, having mediators as special cases.

2.1   Simple Sources

We consider a taxonomy-based conceptual modeling approach. Taxonomies is probably the oldest and most widely used conceptual modeling tool. The advantages of this conceptual modeling approach for the P2P paradigm are discussed in [20].

A simple source consists of two parts: a *taxonomy* and a stored *interpretation*.

Definition 1. A taxonomy is a pair $(T, \preceq)$ where T, the *terminology*, is a finite and non empty set of names, or *terms*, and $\preceq$ is a reflexive and transitive relation over T, modeling *subsumption* between terms.

If a and b are terms of T, we say that a is *subsumed* by b if $a \preceq b$; we also say that b *subsumes* a; for example, Databases $\preceq$ Informatics, Canaries $\preceq$ Birds. We say that two terms a and b are *equivalent*, and write $a \sim b$, if both $a \preceq b$ and $b \preceq a$ hold, e.g., Computer Science $\sim$ Informatics. Note that the subsumption relation is a preorder over T and that $\sim$ is an equivalence relation over the terms T. Moreover $\preceq$ is a partial order over the equivalence classes of terms.

The stored interpretation I of a simple source is a function $I : T \to 2^{Obj}$ that associates each term T of the source terminology with a set of objects (we use the symbol 2^{Obj} to denote the powerset of Obj). Figure 1 shows an example of a source. In this and subsequent figures, objects are represented by natural numbers and their membership to the interpretation of a term is indicated by a dotted arrow from the object to that term; subsumption of terms is indicated by a continuous-line arrow from the subsumed term to the subsuming term, while equivalence is indicated by a continuous non-oriented line segment; finally, for readability, we do not represent the entire subsumption relation but its transitive reduction, in which reflexive and transitive arrows are suppressed. In Figure 1, objects 1 and 3 are members of the interpretation of the term Live. As there are no other objects connected to Live with dotted arrows,

$I(\text{Live}) = \{1, 3\}$. Moreover, the term Metal is subsumed by Rock, while the term Rocky is equivalent to the term Rock. Note that equivalence captures the notion of synonymy, and that each equivalence class simply contains alternative terms for naming a set of objects.

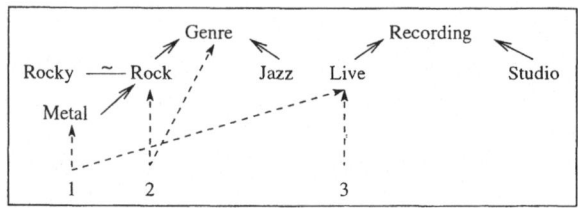

Fig. 1. Graphical representation of a source over a domain of audio files

A simple source responds to queries over its own terminology.

Definition 2. A *query* over a terminology T is any string derived by the following grammar, where t is a term of T: $q ::= t \mid q \wedge q' \mid q \vee q' \mid q \wedge \neg q' \mid (q) \mid \epsilon$. We will denote by Q_T the set of all queries over T.

We now proceed to define the notion of answer to a query. Clearly, a source answers queries based on the stored interpretation of its terminology. However, in order for answers to make sense, the interpretation that a source uses for answering queries must respect the structure of the source's taxonomy in the following intuitive sense: if $t \preceq t'$ then $I(t) \subseteq I(t')$. The notion of model, introduced next, captures well-behaved interpretations.

Definition 3. An interpretation I is a *model* of a taxonomy $(T, \preceq)$ if for all t, t' in T, if $t \preceq t'$ then $I(t) \subseteq I(t')$.

The interpretation of the source illustrated in Figure 1 is not a model of the source taxonomy, as Metal $\preceq$ Genre, and yet $I(\text{Metal}) \not\subseteq I(\text{Genre})$. In order to overcome this problem without altering the contents of interpretations, we need to extend interpretations. However, in so doing, we want to achieve minimality, that is the extension should contain as much data is needed to be a model, and no more. For the term Genre in the source in Figure 1, this amounts to define the extended interpretation I' as $I'(\text{Genre}) = I(\text{Genre}) \cup I(\text{Rock}) \cup I(\text{Rocky}) \cup I(\text{Jazz}) \cup I(\text{Metal})$.

Definition 4. Given an interpretation I of T, the model of $(T, \preceq)$ *generated* by I, denoted $\bar{I}$, is given by: $\bar{I}(t) = \bigcup \{I(s) \mid s \preceq t\}$

In order to show that the generated interpretation satisfies the minimality requirement expressed above, let us order the set of interpretations of a given terminology T by using pointwise set inclusion. Given two interpretations I, I' of T, I is less than or equal to I', in symbols $I \leq I'$, if $I(t) \subseteq I'(t)$ for each term $t \in T$. Note that $\leq$ is a partial order over interpretations. The following Proposition establishes the minimality of generated interpretations.

Proposition 1. If I is an interpretation of T then $\bar{I}$ is the unique minimal model of $(T, \preceq)$ which is greater than or equal to I.

By relying on generated interpretations, we can now define the notion of answer to queries posed against a simple source.

Definition 5. Given a simple source S_i with terminology T and interpretation I, and a query q over T, the *answer to q in S_i*, $ans_i(q)$, is inductively defined as follows: $ans_i(t) = \bar{I}(t)$, $ans_i(q \wedge q') = ans_i(q) \cap ans_i(q')$, $ans_i(q \vee q') = ans_i(q) \cup ans_i(q')$, $ans_i(q \wedge \neg q') = ans_i(q) \setminus ans_i(q')$.

The model defined so far has indeed a logical grounding, which can be disclosed by viewing terms as propositional letters. Then, each subsumption relationship $t \preceq t'$ becomes the conditional $t \rightarrow t'$, the whole subsumption relation $\preceq$ becomes a propositional theory, and the generated interpretation of each object o, $\bar{I}^{-1}(o)$, is the smallest propositional model including $I^{-1}(o)$ and satisfying $\preceq$[1]. A query is a propositional formula q, whose answer is the set of objects o whose propositional model $\bar{I}^{-1}(o)$ satisfies q.

2.2   Articulated Sources

An *articulated source* is a simple source that also maintains a number of *articulations* to other sources. An articulation to a source is a set of relationships between the terms of the articulated source and the terms of that source.

Definition 6. An *articulation* from a taxonomy $(T_i, \preceq_i)$ to a taxonomy $(T_j, \preceq_j)$, denoted by $\preceq_{ij}$, is any nonempty set of relationships $t_j \preceq_{ij} t_i$ where $t_i \in T_i$ and $t_j \in T_j$.

If $t_j \preceq_{ij} t_i$, we say that t_j *articulates* t_i. Articulations bridge the heterogeneities that may exist between two or more sources in order to provide a uniform query interface to these sources. The relationships making up an articulation are defined by the designer and are stored at the articulated source. They can be defined manually, but they can also be constructed automatically or semi-automatically in some specific cases, following a model-driven approach or a data-driven approach In this paper we do not focus on articulation design or construction. We treat this issue in [19].

Definition 7. An *articulated source* M over k sources $S_1, ..., S_k$ consists of: (1) a simple source, comprising a taxonomy $(T_M, \preceq_M)$ and a stored interpretation I_s of T_M, and (2) a set $\{a_{M,1}, ..., a_{M,k}\}$, where each $a_{M,i}$ is an *articulation* from $(T_M, \preceq_M)$ to $(T_i, \preceq_i)$.

An articulated source with an empty stored interpretation, i.e. $I(t) = \emptyset$ for all $t \in T_M$, is called a *mediator*. An articulated source with no articulations and with a nonempty interpretation is a *simple source*.

Figure 2 shows an example of a mediator over two sources that provide access to music files. The articulations $a_{M,1}$ and $a_{M,2}$ shown in this figure are given by:

---

[1]   Note that I^{-1} and $\bar{I}^{-1}$ are functions from Obj to 2^T.

a$_{M,1}$ = {Pop$_1$ $\preceq$ Genre, AlternativeRock$_1$ $\preceq$ Rock, HeavyMetal$_1$ $\preceq$ Metal }
a$_{M,2}$ = {DanceMusic$_2$ $\preceq$ Folk, DanceMusic$_2$ $\preceq$ Greece, Cantriglie$_2$ $\preceq$ Italy }

a$_{M,1}$ demonstrates how articulations can bridge the granularity hetero-geneities that may exist between different terminologies, while a$_{M,2}$ demonstrates how the articulations of the mediator can restore the context of the objects of the sources, here, the fact that the origin of all music files of S_2 is Greece, and that "Cantriglie" also originate from Italy.

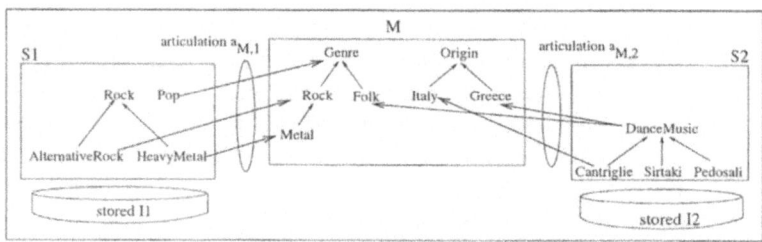

Fig. 2. A mediator over two music sources

Thus a network comprised of simple sources, mediators and articulated sources can be defined in terms of just articulated sources, as follows (two artic-ulated sources are said to be disjoint if their terminologies are disjoint).

Definition 8. A *network of articulated sources,* or simply a *network,* N is a non-empty set of disjoint articulated sources $N = \{S_1, \ldots, S_n\}$, where each source S_i is articulated over some of the sources in $N \setminus \{S_i\}$.

Note that the disjointness of sources can be implemented in practice by, say, prefixing each term by the name of the source in which the term appears. Figure 3 shows an example of a network consisting of four sources $S_1, \ldots, S_4$; two simple sources (S_3 and S_4), one mediator (S_2) and one articulated source (S_1).

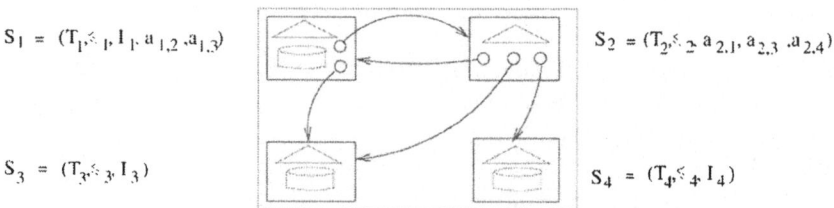

Fig. 3. A network of articulated sources

Networks are set up in order to let users extract information from the member sources. The following questions arise: (a) what queries should users be able to

formulate, and (b) what answer should queries return? Next Section addresses
these questions.

2.3   Network Queries and Answers

From a logical point of view, we can view an entire network $N = \{S_1, \ldots, S_n\}$ as
a single simple source S_N, comprised by a terminology T, a subsumption relation
$\sqsubseteq$ and a stored interpretation I, where:

- $T = \bigcup_{i=1}^n T_i$
- $I = \bigcup_{i=1}^n I_i$
- $\sqsubseteq = (\bigcup_{i=1}^n \sqsubseteq_i)^*$

where $\sqsubseteq_i$ is the *total subsumption* of the source S_i, given by the union of the
subsumption relation $\preceq_i$ with all articulations of the source, that is: $\sqsubseteq_i = \preceq_i$
$\cup\ a_{i,1} \ldots \cup a_{i,n}$ and A^* denotes the transitive closure of the binary relation A.

Accordingly, we can define a *network query* to be a query over T. By so doing,
we have an answer to the first question: users of the network submit network
queries. That is, users can formulate not only queries over the terminology of the
articulated source nearest to them, but also queries over a remote terminology,
or a combination of these two, freely mixing terms from different terminologies
in a single query. In other words, as long as a term is *known* in the network[2], it
can be used to extract information from anywhere in the network.

Following the model developed so far, the answer to a network query q, or
network answer, is given by $ans_N(q)$, which relies, according to Definition 5, on
the model of T generated by I, that is, of each term t in q :

$$\bar{I}(t) = \bigcup\{ I(t') \mid t' \sqsubseteq t\} \tag{1}$$

2.4   Foundations for Answering Network Queries

The formulation of a network answer given in equation 1 does not immediately
lend itself to computation, as it is expressed in terms of the network subsumption
relation, which only exists in fragments. In order to derive a more operational
definition of $\bar{I}(t)$, let us introduce entries.

Definition 9. Given an articulated network $N = \{S_1, \ldots, S_n\}$ and a term $t \in$
T, the *entries of t in N*, $E(t)$, are the terms defined as follows:

$E(t) = \{t\} \cup \{t' \in T \mid \exists t'' \in T : t' \preceq_{ij} t'' \sqsubseteq t \text{ for some } i, j\}.$

The notation $t' \preceq_{ij} t'' \sqsubseteq t$ means that $t' \preceq_{ij} t''$ and $t'' \sqsubseteq t$. For each term t,
the entries of t include t itself and those terms t' which articulate t in the various
sources of the network, either directly or through an intermediate term t'' which
is subsumed by t. For example, in the network shown in Figure 4.(a), the entries
of the term c are given by: $E(c) = \{c, a3, b3, b1\}$ since terms $a3$ and $b3$ articulate
c according to $\preceq_{31}$ and $\preceq_{32}$ respectively, and $b1$ articulates $a3$ (subsumed by c)
according to $\preceq_{12}$.

---

[2] This presupposes that each source knows (or can find) the source that owns every
element of T, or that each term of each submitted query is accompanied by the
identity (address) of its source.

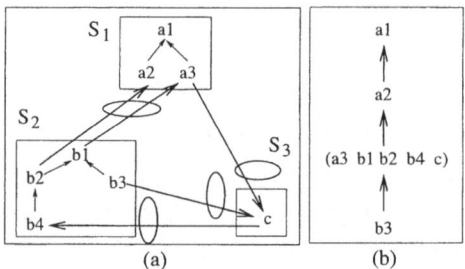

Fig. 4. A network of articulated sources

In the following, if t is a term then we shall use $g(t)$ to denote the subscript of the terminology in which t belongs, e.g. if $t \in T_j$ then $g(t) = j$. As intuition suggests and the following Proposition states, entries are crucial to compute network answers.

Proposition 2. For each term t of a network N, $ans_N(t) = \bigcup\{ ans_{g(t')} \mid t' \in E(t)\}$.

This Proposition represents a first step towards a method for rewriting network queries, in that it maps a network query onto queries to the articulated sources of the network. However, in order to compute entries, knowledge of all articulations and taxonomies is required (*i.e.* $\sqsubseteq$ and $\preceq_{ij}$), and this is feasible only in a client-server architecture, or in a hybrid P2P distributed system (e.g. see [23]), where it is possible to assume that there exists a sort of server node holding this knowledge.

In order to devise a method for a pure P2P architecture, we refine entries to local entries. Our aim is to define equations which can be derived in a single articulated source S_i, by relying on the knowledge of the source subsumption relation $\preceq_i$ and articulations $\preceq_{ij}$.

Definition 10. Given a source S_i in an articulated network N and a term $t \in T_i$, the *local entries of t in N*, $e(t)$, are the terms defined as follows:

$$e(t) = \{t\} \cup \bigcup_{i=1}^{n} \{e(t') \mid t' \sqsubseteq_i t, \ t' \notin T_i\}.$$

By means of recursion, local entries break down the definition of entries into pieces each of which can be computed locally, *i.e.* at a source of the network. We can add subscripts and write $e_i(t) = \{t\} \cup \bigcup_{i=1}^{n}\{e_{g(t')}(t') \mid t' \sqsubseteq_i t, \ t' \notin T_i\}$ in order to indicate the source that performs the computation. To illustrate, let us consider the local entries of term c in the network shown in Figure 4.(a):

$$e(c) = \{c\} \cup e(b3) \cup e(a3) \tag{2}$$
$$e(b3) = \{b3\} \tag{3}$$
$$e(a3) = \{a3\} \cup e(b1) \tag{4}$$
$$e(b1) = \{b1\} \cup e(c)$$

Note that each such equations can be derived in a single articulated source S_i, by relying on the knowledge of the source subsumption relation $\preceq_i$ and articulations $\preceq_{ij}$. Cycles in the network subsumption spanning at least one articulation are reflected into the definition of local entries. As an illustration, a few substitutions in equation 2 yield:

$$e(c) = \{c, b3, a3, b1\} \cup e(c) \tag{5}$$

reflecting the cycle $(a3, c, b4, b2, b1, a3)$ in the subsumption relation graph. This cycle would cause a similar effect on $e(a3)$ and $e(b1)$. Following the classical approach, $e(c)$ in equation 5 can be seen as a function F, mapping sets of terms into sets of terms, defined as: $F(X) \overset{\text{def}}{=} \lambda X.\{c, b3, a3, b1\} \cup X$. The fixpoints of this function are the solutions of the corresponding equation. F is clearly monotonic in the complete partial order $(2^T, \subseteq)$, thus it has unique least fixpoint, i.e. $\{c, b3, a3, b1\}$, and a unique greatest fixpoint, i.e. T. In addition, any set in between these two, according to the $\subseteq$ relation, is also a fixpoint. The selection of a particular fixpoint as the preferred one, is typically based on criteria reflecting the setting in which these equations arise. In our case, we want local entries to be the same as entries, i.e. for all t, $e(t)$ must be the same as $E(t)$. This leads to the selection of the least fixpoint as the preferred solution. In the following, we will generalize these ideas and provide an algorithm for computing local entries.

For convenience, let us define, for a term $t_i \in T_i$, the *index* of t_i as follows:

$$H(t_i) = \{t' \in T \mid t' \sqsubseteq_i t_i,\ t' \notin T_i\}.$$

As a consequence, the definition of the local entries of a term t_i consists, for each term $t_k \in E(t_i)$, of one equation:

$$e(t_k) = \{t_k\} \cup \bigcup \{e(t') \mid t' \in H(t_k)\}, \tag{6}$$

Below we give the index of each term involved in the definition of c in the last Example: $H(c) = \{b3, a3\}$, $H(b3) = \emptyset$, $H(a3) = \{b1\}$, $H(b1) = \{c\}$.

Let us call the *simple unfolding* of one such equations the transformation obtained by adding (in the set-theoretic sense) the definition of each occurring local entry, as given by the appropriate equation, to the right-hand side. For example, the simple unfolding of $e(c) = \{c\} \cup e(b3) \cup e(a3)$, is the addition of the definition of $e(b3)$ and of $e(a3)$ (as given by equations 3 and 4, respectively) to the right-hand side, and yields the equation: $e(c) = \{c, b3, a3\} \cup e(b3) \cup e(a3) \cup e(b1)$. The simple unfolding produces an equation equivalent to the original one, since the union operator is idempotent, that is $A = A \cup A$. In general, an equation of the form (6) can be written as:

$$e(t_k) = A_k \cup \bigcup \{e(t') \mid t' \in B_k\} \tag{7}$$

where A_k and B_k are suitable sets of terms. The simple unfolding of an equation in this form is given by:

$$e(t_k) = (A_k \cup B_k) \cup \bigcup \{e(t') \mid t' \in B_k \cup \bigcup_{t'' \in B_k} H(t'')\}.$$

Now let us call the *unfolding* of an equation, the equation generated by the iterative application of simple unfolding until it produces no change. Formally, the generation of the unfolding can be represented by the evolution of the sets A_k and B_k. Using a superscript to indicate the number of the iteration step in the unfolding, we can derive the initial sets from the equations 6:

$$A_k^0 = \{t_k\}$$
$$B_k^0 = H(t_k)$$

while the (i+1)-th sets, for $i \geq 0$, are obtained by the simple unfolding of the i-th sets, and according to 8 are given by:

$$A_k^{i+1} = A_k^i \cup B_k^i$$
$$B_k^{i+1} = B_k^i \cup \bigcup \{H(t) \mid t \in B_k^i\}. \tag{8}$$

Existence and uniqueness of unfoldings is very simple to prove: at each iteration a few constants and a few recursions are added; since there are only finite terms in $E(t_i)$, the process is bound to converge after at most $|E(t_i)|$ simple unfoldings. Then, let us call $B_k^\star$ the set B_k^m, where m is the smallest number such that: $B_k^m = B_k^{m+1}$. By a simple induction argument, it can be shown that, for all terms t_k and $i \geq 0 : A_k^{i+1} = \{t_k\} \cup B_k^i$. It follows that $A_k^m \neq A_k^{m+1} = A_k^{m+2} = A_k^{m+3} = \dots$, hence analogously to $B_k^\star$, we define $A_k^\star = A_k^{m+1} = \{t_k\} \cup B_k^\star$. It can be shown that:

Proposition 3. For each term t of a network N holds: $E(t) = LFP(e(t)) = A^\star$ where $LFP(F)$ denotes the least fixpoint of F on $(2^T, \subseteq)$.

Table 1 shows the computation of $A_k^\star$ for the term $t_k = c$ in the last Example. It can be verified that $m = 2$, thus $B_k^2 = B_k^\star$ and $A_k^3 = A_k^\star$.

Table 1. Computing $A_k^\star$

i	A_k^i	B_k^i
0	$\{c\}$	$\{b3, a3\}$
1	$\{c, b3, a3\}$	$\{b3, a3, b1\}$
2	$\{c, b3, a3, b1\}$	$\{b3, a3, b1, c\}$
3	$\{c, b3, a3, b1\}$	$\{b3, a3, b1, c\}$

The computation of local entries is an iterative process that mimics the unfolding of the equations 6. At the i-th iteration, the set B^i is computed, until a set B^m is found which is stable and thus is the sought $B^\star$. From $B^\star$, the set $A^\star$, hence $E(t)$, is obtained by just adding the term $\{t\}$. As equation 8 shows, B^i is obtained by adding the index $H(t)$ to B^{i-1}, for each term t in B^{i-1}.

3   Query Evaluation Approaches

We can distinguish query evaluation approaches according to two orthogonal criteria: (a) the number of *stages* of the query evaluation process, and (b) the number of *sources* that control this process.

According to the first criterion we can distinguish the following two approaches:

- The *Rewriting* (or double-stage) approach (denoted by R).

  Here, query evaluation is performed in two stages: in the first, all entries are collected, while in the second the collected entries are sent (probably after a planning stage) to the sources.

- The *Direct* approach (denoted by D).

  Here, both entries and local answers are collected in one stage.

According to the second criterion, assuming that each source can provide the index $H(t)$ for each term t of its taxonomy, we can distinguish two ways of computing B^i : either by sending indexes to a single place where the set B^i is accumulated, or by sending the partial B^i to the sources where indexes are being maintained. Correspondingly, there are two main approaches to the computation of $A^\star$:

- The *single controller* (or centralized) approach (denoted by 1).

  Here, all entries and local answers are accumulated to one source (the original source).

- The *multiple controller* (or decentralized)approach (denoted by m).

  Here, the collection of entries and local answers is done collaboratively by several sources.

Clearly, the above cases can be combined resulting in four different query evaluation approaches, namely $R1$, Rm, $D1$ and Dm. Each approach is discussed in a subsequent section. Of course, all these approaches are subject to several kinds of optimizations which, for reasons of space, are just sketched, in section 3.5.

3.1   The Rewriting – Single Controller ($R1$) Approach

In $R1$ approach, any node of the network receiving a network query q must perform the following steps:

(Stage A)

  1. parsing the query in order to identify the target terms, *i.e.* the terms occurring in q;

  2. executing a single controller algorithm for collecting the entries of each target term;

(Stage B)

  3. sending the entries as queries to be evaluated to the appropriate sources (probably after a planning phase) and derivation of the network interpretation of the target terms by taking the union of the received answers. Then, the network answer is obtained according to Def. 5.

Step 1 is trivial from an algorithmic point of view. Step 3 is also simple although a planning phase can take place for further optimization. Now the algorithm for Step 2, i.e. for collecting the entries of a term t is presented in Figure 5.

Algorithm: *Alg_R1*
Input: a term t
Output: the set $E(t)$
begin
(1) $A := \{t\}$; $C := \{t\}$;
(2)   **repeat**
(3)   change:=FALSE ;
(4) $B := \emptyset$;
(5)   **for each** $t' \in C$ **do** $B := B \cup H_{g(t')}(t')$;
(6)   **If** $B \not\subseteq A$ **then begin**
(7) $C := B \setminus A$;
(8) $A := A \cup B$;
(9)   change := TRUE
(10)   **end**
(11) **until** change = FALSE ;
(12) **return**(A);
end

Fig. 5. Computing local entries in the *R1* approach

It is straightforward to prove that algorithm *Alg_R1* is correct as it implements in a straightforward manner the method described in Section 2.4.

3.2   The Rewriting – Multiple Controller (*Rm*) Approach

Query evaluation in the *Rm* approach can be done as in the *R1* approach with the only difference that here Step 2, i.e. the collection of entries, is done collaboratively by several sources. Specifically, a special data structure D is employed that keeps track of the state of this computation and that is being exchanged by the nodes involved in the process. In particular, the collection of entries is accomplished in the following steps:

1. construction of the data structure D for query evaluation;
2. insertion of D into the P2P network for evaluation;
3. waiting for the result;

For computing the network interpretation of a term t_i the data structure employed by this method is a triple whose first member is the name of the source S_o where the query is posed, followed by two sets of terms C and A explained below. To insert D into the P2P network, means to send this data structure to the source which owns the term t_i. Upon receiving a data structure D, an articulated source S_i executes the Algorithm *Alg_Rm*, illustrated in Figure 6. The set

C is the set of the terms still to be processed, while A accumulates A^*. Initially, the only term to be processed is t_i itself, while A is set to A^0. Upon processing a data structure D, the algorithm focuses on the terms to be processed (*i.e* in C) that are also in the local source terminology T_i. Each such term t is added to A and removed from C. In addition, the algorithm adds to C the terms in $H_i(t)$ *which have not yet been processed*. This last provision prevents redundant computations. Furthermore, it avoids non-termination in presence of cycles in the global subsumption relation. Otherwise, this kind of cycles would cause a phenomenon analogous to that of deadlocks in distributed databases and systems [17,12]. The Algorithm may exit in two different ways: if there are no more terms to be processed (*i.e* C is empty), the data structure D is returned (via *send*) to the originating source S_o, which will find the entries of t_i as the third element of the corresponding triple D. If there are terms still to be processed, the data structure is passed on to a source that owns at least one term in C.

Algorithm: *Alg_Rm*   (for a source S_i)
Input: a data structure $D = (S_o, C, A)$.
Output: an updated data structure sent to another source
begin
(1)   **for each** $t \in C \cap T_i$ **do begin**
(2) $A := A \cup \{t\}$;
(3) $C := (C \setminus \{t\}) \cup (H_i(t) \setminus A)$;
(4)   **end**
(5)   **if** $(C = \emptyset)$ **then** *send(S_o, C, A)*;
(6)   **else begin**
(7)   select a S_j s.t. $\exists\, t' \in C$ where $g(t') = j$;
(8)   *send(S_j, C, A)*;
(9)   **end**
end

Fig. 6. The algorithm for the *Rm* approach

Also in this case, it is not hard to show that: algorithm *Alg_Rm* is correct.

Table 2 shows the application of the *Alg_Rm* algorithm to a query containing just the term c. The first column shows the source at which the algorithm is applied; the second column the resulting triple of the term c. The first line results from the first stage executed at the source S_o where the query is posed.

An important remark that we have to mention here is that the single controller approach is based on the assumption that each source (specifically S_o) knows $g(t)$ for each term $t \in T$. Notice that this is not aligned with the pure P2P paradigm, as this presupposes the existence of a registration server, known to all sources of the network, where all terms are registered to. Notice that the multiple controller approach is not based on this assumption, as each source has to know $g(t)$ only for each term t that appears in its articulation, something quite reasonable even for a pure P2P system.

Table 2. An application of Alg_Rm

Source	(t, C, A)
S_o	$(c, \{c\}, \{\})$
S_3	$(c, \{b3, a3\}, \{c\})$
S_2	$(c, \{a3\}, \{c, b3\})$
S_1	$(c, \{b1\}, \{c, b3, a3\})$
S_2	$(c, \{\}, \{c, b3, a3, b1\})$

From a complexity point of view, note that Alg_R1 operates on a per-term basis, while Alg_Rm operates on a per-source basis. This means that in the worst case, the number of messages that have to be exchanged for computing the entries $E(t)$ of a term $t \in T$ is $2|E(t)| \leq 2|T|$ in $R1$, and k, where k is the number of sources, in Rm.

3.3   The Direct ($D1$ and Dm) Approaches

The algorithms for the direct query evaluation approaches are direct extensions of the techniques presented for query rewriting. The only difference is that now the stored interpretation of each involved term is also collected. Hence, the resulting algorithms return the set $\bar{I}(t)$.

Specifically, an algorithm for the $D1$ approach can be obtained by modifying Alg_R1 as follows:
- add the statement $R := R \cup \bar{I}_{g(t')}(t')$ after the line (8), and
- replace the statement of line (12) with the statement **return**(A).

Analogously, we can obtain an algorithm for the Dm approach by modifying Alg_Rm as follows:
- add the statement $R := R \cup \bar{I}_{g(t')}(t')$ after the line (3), and
- add the statement $Send(So, R)$ after the line 4.

Another algorithm that implements a direct and multiple controller approach is the one presented in [20], which is presented in Figure 7 using the notations employed in the current paper. Notice that cycles in the network subsumption relation may cause endless query loops. According to [20], this phenomenon can be avoided if each source maintains a log file of the received queries . An alternative way, is to add to the parameters of the algorithm a data structure that keeps track of the answered terms (i.e. a data structure like D).

3.4   Comparative Evaluation

The essential difference between the query rewriting and the direct evaluation approach consists in the fact that the former approach is based on the idea of planning the access to local sources, while the latter relies on a simple-minded, straightforward style. None of these two approaches stands out as the best in all cases. Typically, on queries that can be answered with a few accesses to local sources, or producing a small result, planning does not provide any specific benefit, and may indeed result in a slower evaluation procedure. On the

Algorithm: $Alg\_Dm^\beta\_i$ (for a source S_i)
Input: a term t
Output: the set $\bar{I}(t)$
begin
(1) $R_i := \bar{I}_i(t_i)$;
(2)   **for each** $t' \in H_i(t_i)$ **do**
(3) $R_i := R_i \cup Alg\_Dm^\beta_{g(t')}(t')$;
(4)   **return**(R_i);
end

Fig. 7. An alternative algorithm for the Dm approach

other hand, the evaluation of queries requiring a significant number of accesses to local sources, or producing a large result, may indeed greatly benefit from rewriting, for the reason illustrated next. As the application of the Alg_Rm algorithm illustrated in Table 2 shows, it may happen that a source must be accessed more than once during the processing of a query. This is due to the structure of the global subsumption relation, and would occur even if the algorithm Alg_R1 were used. In this case, rewriting can result in a more efficient query evaluation strategy, because sources need to be accessed more than once only in the first stage, when indexes of terms are retrieved. Once the coordinating node knows the local entries of the target terms, it can plan the second stage so that each source is accessed only once for retrieving the data. Instead, in the direct evaluation approach, this optimization is not possible, and the same source may be accessed more than once for retrieving different data. Since indexes are typically much smaller and much faster to obtain than data, multiple accesses to the same source has a less negative impact in the rewriting approach. Another remark is that the multiple controller approach is less robust than the single controller one, because if the node that holds the data structure D disconnects (and note that in P2P systems peers come and go), then the network query will not be answered. Instead, in the single controller approach a query is not answered only if the controller, i.e. the original source, disconnects but in that case there is no need to compute any answer.

Table 3 summarizes the above discussion. In brief, in the rewriting approach more messages have to be exchanged (as there are 2 stages). However, if the size of the local answers is big, i.e. if local answers consist of big number of objects, or if the size of objects is big (e.g. audio/video files), then the rewriting approach is more preferred as planning can be employed in order to reduce the network throughput.

3.5   Optimization Issues

Below we discuss in brief a number of techniques for making the evaluation of queries more efficient.

  – Instead of collecting the entries (and local answers) of one term at a time, we can collect the entries (and local answers) of *all* terms that appear in

Table 3. Comparison of query evaluation approaches

	Query Evaluation Approaches			
	R1	*Rm*	*D1*	*Dm*
number of messages	more more	more	less	less less
size of messages	small	small	big	big
planning	possible	possible	impossible	impossible
robustness	more	less	more	less
applicability	hybrid P2P	pure P2P	hybrid P2P	pure P2P
best if local answers are	big	big	small	small

q. For doing so, we have to modify *Alg_R1* (and *Alg_D1*) so that to take as input a set of terms, and *Alg_Rm* (and *Alg_Dm*) so that the data structure *D* to be a set of triples. In this way we can reduce the number of messages (either local queries or local answers) that have to be exchanged.

– We can exploit parallelism, and thus reduce the latency time of the system, by sending in parallel all *Send* statements (e.g. the calls of line (5) of *Alg_R1*).

– We can increase the robustness of the multiple controller approaches by adopting more than one control structures *D*, or by adopting more sophisticated mechanisms like the those employed by distributed databases.

4   Related Work

Semantic-based retrieval in P2P systems is a great challenge. In general, the language that can be used for indexing the objects of the domain and for formulating semantic-based queries, can be *free* (e.g natural language) or *controlled*, i.e. object descriptions and queries may have to conform to a specific vocabulary and syntax. The first case, resembles distributed Information Retrieval (IR) systems and this approach is applicable in the case where the objects of the domain have a textual content (e.g. [14]). In this paper we have focused on the second case where the objects of a peer are indexed according to a specific conceptual model represented in a data model (e.g. relational, object-oriented, logic-based, etc), and content searches are formulated using a specific query language. This approach, which can be called "database approach", starts to receive noteworthy attention by the researchers, as is believed that the database and knowledge base research has much to contribute to the P2P grand challenge through its wealth of techniques for sophisticated semantics-based data models and query processing techniques (e.g. see [9,6,11]). Of course, a P2P system might impose a single conceptual model on all participants to enforce uniform, global access, but this will be too restrictive. Alternatively, a limited number of conceptual models may be allowed, so that traditional information mediation and integration techniques will likely apply (with the restriction that there is no central authority), e.g. see [16,15]. The case of fully heterogeneous conceptual models makes uniform global access extremely challenging and this is the case that we are interested in.

From a data modeling point of view several approaches for P2P systems have been proposed recently, including relational-based approaches [6], XML-based approaches [10] and RDF-based [15]. In this paper we consider a taxonomy-based conceptual modeling approach. This approach has three main advantages (for more see [20]): (a) it is very easy to create the conceptual model of a source, (b) the integration of information from multiple sources can be done easily, and (c) automatic articulation using data-driven methods (like the one presented in [19]) are possible.

From an architectural point of view, and according to the SIL (Search Index Link) model presented in [8], our networks falls into the case of P2P systems which have only forwarding search links. Specifically, our work specializes content-based queries to taxonomy-based queries. Another distinguishing characteristic, is that in our model a peer does not just forward the received queries to its neighbors, it first translates them. Also note that the relationships stored in the articulations not only determine query translation but also query propagation. Of course, work done on P2P architectures, e.g. [23,8], could be also exploited in our setting in order to enhance the efficiency of a taxonomy-based P2P system. Our approach has some similiraties with Edutella [16,15], an RDF-based metadata infrastructure for P2P systems. However, the mediators of Edutella distribute a query to a peer only if the query can be answered completely by the peer. In contrast, in our model the answers of queries are formed collaboratively. Moreover, in Edutella special servers are devoted for registering the schema that each peer supports. In our model we do not make any such assumption.

An approach for supporting object queries appropriate for domains where no accepted naming standards exist (and thus it generalizes the functionality provided by systems like Napster and Gnutella) is described in [11]. The mapping tables employed there can express only exact mappings, however the open/closed-world semantics that are given are quite interesting and their application to our setting is one topic of our research agenda.

5   Concluding Remarks

In this paper, we focused on query evaluation in P2P systems that support semantic-based retrieval services. We gave four algorithms to carry out this task according to two different approaches (rewriting *vs.* direct evaluation) and computation styles (centralized *vs.* decentralized). Although we adopted a conceptual modeling approach that is based on taxonomies, much of the results presented of this paper (i.e. the query evaluation approaches presented) can be adapted to cases where other conceptual modeling approaches are employed.

For reason of space, we have not considered in depth optimization issues, limiting ourselves to lay down the basics of the four methods. Issues for further research include also query evaluation in cases we have articulations which relate terms with queries.

References

1. "About LEGION - The Grid OS"(www.appliedmeta.com/legion/about.html), 2000.
2. "How Entropia Works"(www.entropia.com/how.asp), 2000.
3. "Groove" (www.groove.net), 2001.
4. "Napster"(www.naptster.com), 2001.
5. T.E. Anderson, M. Dahlin, J. M. Neefe, D. A. Patterson, D. S. Roselli, and R. Wang. "Serveless Network File Systems". *SOSP*, 29(5), 1995.
6. P. A. Bernstein, F. Giunchiglia, A. Kementsietsidis, J. Mylopoulos, L. Serafini, and I. Zaihrayeu. "Data Management for Peer-to-Peer Computing: A Vision". In *Proceedings of WebDB02*, Madison, Wisconsin, June 2002.
7. W. J. Bolosky, J. R. Douceur, D. Ely, and M. Theimer. "Feasibility of a Serveless Distributed File System Deployed on an Existing Set of Desktop PCs". In *Proceedings of Measurement and Modeling of Computer Systems*, June 2000.
8. B. Cooper and H. Garcia-Molina. "Modeling and Measuring Scalable Peer-to-peer Search Networks". Technical report, University of Stanford, September 2002.
9. S. Gribble, A. Halevy, Z. Ives, M. Rodrig, and D. Suiu. "What can Databases do for Peer-to-Peer?". In *Proceedings of WebDB01*, Santa Barbara, CA, 2001.
10. Alon Halevy, Zachary Ives, Peter Mork, and Igor Tatarinov. "Piazza: Data Management Infrastructure for Semantic Web Applications". In *Proceedings of WWW'2003*, May 2003.
11. A. Kementsietsidis, M. Arenas, and R. J. Miller. "Mapping Data in Peer-to-Peer Systems: Semantics and Algorithmic Issues". In *Int. Conf. on Management of Data, SIGMOD'2003*, San Diego, California, June 2003.
12. Edgar Knapp. "Deadlock Detection in Distributed Databases". *ACM Computing Surveys*, 19(4), 1987.
13. J. Kubiatowicz, D. Bindel, Y. Chen, S. Czerwinski, P. Eaton, D. Geels, R. Gummadi, S. Rhea, H. Weatherspoon, W. Weimer, C. Wells, and B. Zhao. "Oceanstore: An Architecture for Global-Scale Persistent Storage". In *ASPLOS*, November 2000.
14. Bo Ling, Zhiguo Lu, Wee Siong Ng, BengChin Ooi, Kian-Lee Tan, and Aoying Zhou. "A Content-Based Resource Location Mechanism in PeerIS". In *Procs of Int. Conf. on Web Information Systems Engineering, WISE 2002*, Singapore, Dec 2002.
15. W. Nejdl, B. Wolf, C. Qu, S. Decker, M. Sintek, A. Naeve, M. Nilsson, M. Palmer, and T. Risch. "EDUTELLA: A P2P networking infrastructure based on RDF". In *WWW'2002*, 2002.
16. W. Nejdl, B. Wolf, S. Staab, and J. Tane. "EDUTELLA: Searching and Annotating Resources within an RDF-based P2P Network". In *Semantic Web Workshop 2002*, Honolulu, Havaii, May 2002.
17. Chia-Shiang Shih and John A. Stankovic. "Survey of Deadlock Detection in Distributed Concurrent Programming Environments and its Application to Real-Time Systems and Ada". Technical Report UM-CS-1991-043, University of Massachusetts, 1991.
18. I. Stoica, R. Morris, D. Karger, M. F. Kaashoek, and H. Balakrishnan. "Chord: A Scalable Peer-to-peer Lookup Service for Internet Applications". In *Procs of the 2001 ACM SIGCOMM Conference*, 2001.
19. Y. Tzitzikas and C. Meghini. "Ostensive Automatic Schema Mapping for Taxonomy-based Peer-to-Peer Systems". In *Int. Workshop on Cooperative Information Agents, CIA-2003*, Helsinki, Finland, August 2003.

20. Y. Tzitzikas, C. Meghini, and N. Spyratos. "Taxonomy-based Conceptual Modeling for Peer-to-Peer Networks". In *Procs of 22th Int. Conf. on Conceptual Modeling, ER'2003*, Chicago, Illinois, October 2003.
21. Y. Tzitzikas, N. Spyratos, and P. Constantopoulos. "Mediators over Ontology-based Information Sources". In *Second International Conference on Web Information Systems Engineering, WISE 2001*, Kyoto, Japan, December 2001.
22. G. Wiederhold. "Mediators in the Architecture of Future Information Systems". *IEEE Computer*, 25:38–49, 1992.
23. Beverly Yang and Hector Garcia-Molina. "Comparing Hybrid Peer-to-Peer Systems". In *The VLDB Journal*, pages 561–570, sep 2001.

An InfoSpace Paradigm for Local and ad hoc Peer-to-Peer Communication

J. Brehm[1], G. Brancovici[1], C. Müller-Schloer[1], T. Smaoui[1], S. Voigt[1], and R. Welge[2]

[1]Institute of Systems Engineering – System- and Computer Architecture, Appelstraße 4, 30167 Hannover, Germany
{brehm, brancovi, cms, smaoui, voigt}@sra.uni-hannover.de
[2]Dpt. of Automation Technology, University of Applied Sciences of NE Lower Saxony Volgershall 1, 21339 Lüneburg, Germany
welge@fhnon.de

Abstract. A key feature of ubiquitous handheld devices will be their simple usability in mobile and highly dynamic ad-hoc peer-to-peer environments. With LINDA, JAVASPACES and TSPACES, shared memory-based communication concepts have been realized on the system level with corresponding APIs. This article proposes to consequently use the same simple communication paradigm also on the user interface level. In this paper we examine existing basic technologies, analyze typical application scenarios and the underlying communication patterns. We discuss in detail, how these patterns can be realized with the InfoSpace mechanism which offers to each user a private local space and a view on a common space shared between all participants. Finally we show an architecture which realizes the InfoSpace infrastructure and report on first experience with a JXTA-based solution.

1 Introduction

The direct interaction between people is helped if not dominated by context information. Clues given by body language like facial expression, gestures, voice melody etc., as well as by the common knowledge of present time and location make otherwise cryptic messages intelligible. Handheld computers so far have very limited sensory equipment. Today, basic context information can be made available with relatively little effort [1]. Examples are location (point in the 3D space), position (vector in the 3D space), time and date, present user, temperature etc. With little effort, also the proximity of one device to another can be detected. Here, the limited range of Bluetooth [2] connections is an advantage.

We make use especially of the latter possibility and will exploit the related context information. Two (or more) devices which find themselves in the same physical space (the extent of which is defined by the radio range) are candidates for local information exchange. They can enter a common information space, an InfoSpace, – provided their respective users choose to do so.

R. Meersman et al. (Eds.): CoopIS/DOA/ODBASE 2003, LNCS 2888, pp. 282–300, 2003.
© Springer-Verlag Berlin Heidelberg 2003

Fig. 1. Human and ubiquitous communication spaces

The mind set of two humans communicating to each other can be described in the same terms: The existence of a physical channel – e.g. audibility plus eye contact – establishes a common information space. Every communication partner is allowed to drop information into this common space, usually guided by synchronization rules (s. fig. 1). Additional partners can be accepted to this space or excluded from it. A user interface which stays as close as possible to these traditional and well accepted patterns has good chances to get adopted.

Projects dealing with information sharing and exchange in the local area have been realized. The 7DS Project [3] of the University of North Carolina is a peer-to-peer system providing distributed information retrieval among (wireless) hosts in the neighborhood. It is based on HTTP request/answer, the GUI for the information retrieval is implemented by a web browser. Each peer stores data in a separate cache. The DataSpace project of Winlab at Rugers is a further example of interesting work concerned with forming information spaces related to physical objects. The spaces (the so-called datacubes) are of different scales. Locality and distance in DataSpace are not defined by the logical structure of the underlying network but rather by geographic space [4]. In this paper we will make clear how our project differs from the above mentioned ones in the underlying architecture as well as in the user interface concept.

This project builds on the JINI, JXTA and tuple space technologies. Tuple spaces are a basic shared memory paradigm proposed by D. Gelernter [5]. JINI and JXTA provide basic functionalities to advertise and discover services. They are alternatives in this project because they provide similar functionality.

JINI [6,8] is a network technology which permits various devices to build an ad hoc network. The devices can offer services over JINI for other devices. JINI has the following characteristics:

- Ad hoc networking: JINI builds connections without any knowledge about the underlying physical network. Hence JINI is prepared for dynamic networks.
- Service Infrastructure: All devices can use and offer services. A typical example is a printer service.
- Connecting heterogeneous systems: JINI is based on JAVA. All devices which support JAVA can participate in a JINI community.
- Leasing: Leasing is an especially important feature in JINI. All Objects in JINI have a validity period. This supports the idea of ad hoc networks and dynamic networking.

JINI was first released in 1999 by Sun. Sun released JXTA two years later. The JXTA project [7,9] started as a research project to address peer-to-peer[1] communication. This project has its roots in programs like Napster and Gnutella which connect particularly in a peer-to-peer mode instead of using connections based on the client-server model. The main target of JXTA is to form a platform which offers all the functionality to work in a peer-to-peer mode. JXTA intends to solve problems like:

- Interoperability: JXTA is designed to enable peers to provide various peer-to-peer services to locate each other and to communicate with each other.
- Platform independence: JXTA does not depend on the programming language, transport protocols and deployment platforms. This is reached with a fortified use of XML.
- Ubiquity: The goal of JXTA is to make any device accessible and allow it to communicate.

The main difference between both architectures is that JXTA only defines a set of protocols, expressed in XML. So it is only defined how to communicate and there is need of equal platforms. JINI uses Java objects to communicate, so the architecture assumes that Java Byte code can be interpreted anywhere. Therefore Jini is protocol independent but is tied to the Java platform.

Further on JINI uses a centralized service location broker. In a JINI community there must be at least one Lookup Service. It is responsible for finding and searching services. In JXTA entities can find other entities without a centralized service.

Each of these architectures works fine as a middleware in an ad hoc community. Due to its basically decentralized architecture and the smaller footprint we have decided in favor of JXTA.

The envisaged InfoSpaces system sketched in fig 1 requires a complex infrastructure which will be described in this article. Chapter 2 will discuss a few application scenarios where InfoSpaces can be used. In chapter 3 we describe the basic interaction patterns necessary for a local peer-to-peer communication between individuals and groups. We will show that a tuple space is well suited for asynchronous communication. The following chapter 4 describes the basic concepts and protocols of our InfoSpace architecture, chapter 5 a mapping between the interaction patterns and some application scenarios and chapter 6 the architecture of the underlying infrastructure. In chapter 7 we report results of a JXTA-based pilot implementation. The final chapter 8 summarizes the article and gives an outlook on future work.

2 Application Scenarios

The following examples serve illustrative purposes. With their help, we will be able to check the suitability of the InfoSpace paradigm for real world applications. Actually, many more application scenarios exist. We will come back to more scenarios in chapter 5 after we will have discussed the mechanism in detail.

---

[1] For clarity we would like to stress that the term „peer-to-peer" in conjunction with InfoSpaces is used to refer to (local) network technologies based on equal peers cooperating with each other for performing a certain task. The term does therefore in our context not mean any of those networks (Gnutella, KaZaa…) which are mostly used for file sharing across the internet.

2.1 Ad hoc Communication

1. A visitor of a computer fair walks from one exhibition area to the next with her handheld device turned on. Thereby she traverses the related potential InfoSpaces offered by the respective exhibitors. If she decides to accept one of the offers she enters the InfoSpace and starts to download information or to upload enquiries.
2. Two visitors meet in a crowd and want to exchange their business cards. Out of the many InfoSpaces offered around them, they choose a private one for themselves and exchange the desired information.

2.2 Interactive Lecture

For an interactive lecture, we assume that all students are physically present in the same room or lecture hall. They are all equipped with notebook computers or tablets, connected to a preferably wireless communication network. Defined by the physical range of wireless communication of their notebook computers, the group members are (physically) eligible for becoming members of the InfoSpace. The teacher might want to restrict access to a smaller (logical) group of members of the InfoSpace. The notebooks provide to each accepted member of the group a common view which can be used for information exchange in a very intuitive manner.

For the presentation, the instructor uses "transparencies" which carry the backbone information of the lecture. There will probably be also some kind of multimedia enhancement like incremental build-up of the transparencies, animations, videos and sounds or illustrative simulations. Two kinds of annotations will be used: The instructor will want to emphasize, add or correct the information on the transparency. The student wants to have copies of these remarks and, in addition, wants to add his own annotations.

A practise phase should interrupt the presentation every 20 – 30 minutes. This can be done by assigning short task assignments to the students. A few multiple choice questions could assist the students in a self test. Also a short simulation carried out by the student is possible. An automatic answering and correction mode keeps this phase from becoming too time consuming.

The students can ask written questions to the instructor anonymously during the presentation or in special Q&A periods. The inhibition of many students to ask possibly silly questions in the public can be overcome this way. On the other hand, there should be a possibility for the instructor to trace questions back to the originator in order to prevent misuse.

The test phase is similar to the practise pattern but requires a collective or individual back channel. An anonymous back channel allows for an aggregate statistical evaluation of the answers which might lead to an adaptation of the presentation speed, stepping back or skipping of parts of the lecture. Individualized task assignments and answers make possible the assignment of micro credit points to the student.

2.3 Project Team

The objective of a project team is learning by doing in a co-operative team environment. An example is the group-oriented development of a computer program. A specific interaction pattern could be the one promoted by "Extreme Programming" [10] proponents.

In a first step, a project team has to be instructed about the task assigned to them. A common workspace is necessary which reflects and co-ordinates changes made by the participants. Notebooks involved will form an ad-hoc community. In addition to the shared development target (the program), a common discussion channel or space has to be provided. In case of a team physically present in one location, the natural voice channel will serve this purpose. Otherwise, a conference-call set-up is necessary which requires means for synchronous communication.

2.4 Infokiosk

An infokiosk is the electronic equivalent of a bulletin board. It is realized through large wall-mounted displays, possibly with touch-sensitive surface. In the simplest case, the user can interact with the information kiosk via fingertip and browser. If the user is equipped with a portable device (PDA, tablet, notebook) she can set up a conversation between her portable device and the infokiosk. This conversation probably will involve some identification of the user. Additional context information 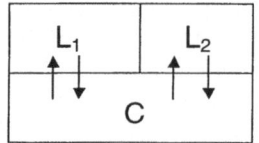 like the location of the infokiosk (in front of the lecture hall or in the student restaurant) can help to pre-select the information offered. This interaction might lead to the download of selected information to the portable device or, vice versa, to the upload (or posting) of information to the bulletin board.

3 Interaction Patterns

We claim that the tuple space paradigm which essentially is a globally shared memory for tuples or – in our case – objects, is sufficient to handle all interaction patterns (I-patterns) typical for peer-to-peer-communication in a local environment. In the following we will analyze such interaction patterns in more detail. The basic operations available to the users are *move* and *copy*. Every user i has a local view L_i holding symbols (i.e. references to objects) stored within his own device, and a common view C shared with all users of the same InfoSpace. The total of the two local spaces L_1 and L_2 and the common space C is one logical Infospace. Each device i sees its device space consisting of the local space L_i and a view of the common space C.

3.1 I-Pattern A

The simplest interaction pattern is a symmetric peer-to-peer-communication between two equal partners. Both partners want to move or copy objects between their respective L-view and C. There is no restriction on the type of objects or the sequence of copies or moves. An example of this type of interaction A(1:1) is the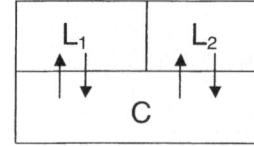

encounter of 2 persons (with their InfoSpace-compatible handheld devices). An InfoSpace is built up with two users, both have write and read access to the common space C. They might use the InfoSpace e.g. to exchange their business cards.

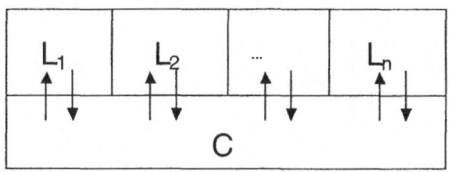

The I-pattern A can be generalized from the 1:1 relationship to an n:n-pattern. n users participate in the same InfoSpace, all of them may write into C or read from it. As in the 1:1 case, there are no restrictions on the type of objects or the sequence of operations.

An example for A(n:n) is a discussion group with free information exchange. Every participant offers and consumes information at the same time. This arrangement requires a certain discipline and trust between the partners in order to avoid overloading of C or e.g. offensive postings. Hence, there has to be an acceptance procedure to become a member of this InfoSpace.

3.2 I-Pattern B (Broadcast)

I-pattern B restricts the access of users to the common space C. It allows one of the users to post information while all the others can only consume it. This I-pattern constitutes a broadcast situation. It generally makes sense only in a 1:n relationship: B(1:n). An example for I-pattern B(1:n) would be the menu in the students' restaurant which is published by the restaurant owner in a dedicated InfoSpace. It is not desirable to let users (students) use this I-Space for their personal postings.

3.3 I-Pattern G (Gathering)

I-pattern G is the inversion of pattern B. Here we have n writers to the common space and (usually) just 1 reader: G(n:1). This type of InfoSpace can be used to collect and later evaluate information from a group of users. An example could be questionnaires filled in by students or answered multiple choice questions. The instructor plays the role of the collector.

3.4 Interaction Matrix

	A	B	G
U_1	RW	W	R
U_2	RW	R	W
U_3	RW	R	W
.			
:			
U_n	RW	R	W

If we denote the right to write into C with W, and the right to read from C with R, the 3 I-patterns can be shown as a table which assigns rights to the users U_1, U_2 ... U_n. Alternatively (and more generally) we can describe the I-patterns in terms of a directed relationship graph or its equivalent interaction matrix M. The users of the InfoSpace are listed as rows and columns of the matrix M. Matrix element $m_{ij} = 1$ if there is a write relationship from user i to user j, otherwise 0.

The matrices for the I-patterns A, B and G take following form:

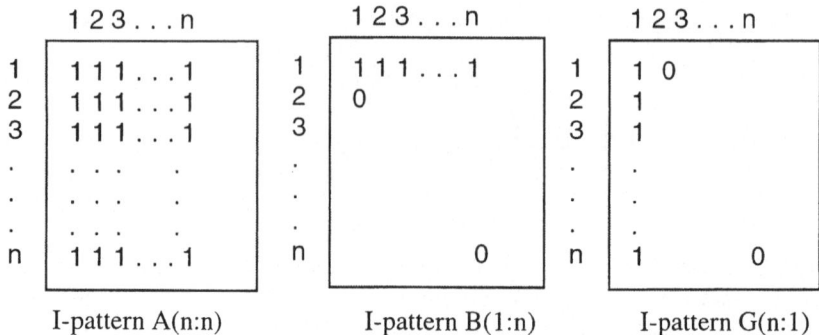

I-pattern A(n:n)   I-pattern B(1:n)   I-pattern G(n:1)

3.5 Complex Interaction Patterns

Obviously the above interaction matrices are just special cases. A general interaction pattern would be represented by an arbitrary distribution of 0's and 1's over the interaction matrix M. Such patterns make sense in special applications and must be supported by the InfoSpace mechanism. We will discuss just one such application as an example taken from the university scenario as sketched in the introduction to this article.

In an interactive lecture, the lecturer will from time to time ask questions to the students in order to get feedback on their progress. The sequence of interactions is the following:

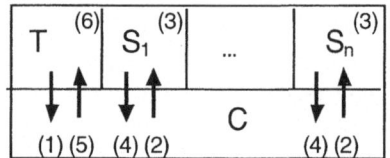

1. Lecturer broadcasts question (same question to all students).
2. Students read the question.
3. Students answer question (local action).
4. Students write answers to C.
5. Lecturer collects answers from C.
6. Lecturer evaluates answers (local action).

Since all participants write and read at some time, we have I-pattern A(n:n). Looking more closely, we have patterns B(1:n) superimposed by pattern C(n:1). This means that, in addition to a general assignment of R and/or W rights to the common space C, we need a more fine grained protection mechanism on the level of the single users vs. the single objects. This solution is based on an access pattern carried by each object, and a capability assigned to each user. This allows us to place objects with different access patterns into the common space C and check capabilities vs. access patterns at access time.

4 InfoSpaces

4.1 Infospace Paradigm

The properties of all tuple space-based approaches (LINDA, JAVASPACES, TSPACES) make them interesting for the realization of InfoSpaces. As the name indicates, an InfoSpace is a common space to share information. In the context of this paper the expression information is used for data and services synonymously. An InfoSpace mimics the communication environment which is set up spontaneously whenever two persons start to interact. It is required to meet the following goals:

1. Simple usability: Only few functions to provide and consume information have to be made available through a graphical user interface.
2. Interoperability: Automatic ad hoc networking between a wide variety of different devices.
3. Service infrastructure: All devices can start and support services. These services can be used by any other device.
4. Data infrastructure: All devices can provide data to and consume data from the InfoSpace.
5. Context sensitivity: The selection process for the shared information should be context driven.

From the user point of view all elements of an InfoSpace are objects ready to be used (in the case of services) or ready to be consumed (in the case of data). The user should not be bothered with configuring network connections, browsing through large file systems, entering network addresses and similarly annoying chores. In contrast, he should be supported by his device to make life easier which is one of the main issues of ubiquitous computing.

The view of user i on an InfoSpace is divided into two parts, a local space L_i and a common space C. The local space contains all data and services provided by the local device (workstation, PC, PDA, mobile phone, etc.). The common space is dynamic in a sense that its data and services are provided in an ad hoc network built from devices with their respective local spaces. We want to emphasize the strict separation between the local space, which is a private area exclusively for the local user's activities without any possibility for other users to access it or change its content, and the common space, which represents a kind of interface between all users that are free to read and write objects into it (copy in/out, move in/out). The result is a peer-to-peer network connection between two devices (fig. 2) creating an InfoSpace consisting of two local spaces (L_1, L_2) and a common space C.

The common space C is symmetric for both devices and users. The information in the common space can be provided and used by both devices. Any information from a local space can be transferred (e.g. by drag and drop) to the common space. It is possible to specify certain attributes (metadata) for the information provided. Examples of metadata are owner, creation date, type, short description, copy counter, leasing time, number of consumers, etc. If nothing else is specified, the information is valid as long as its provider participates in the InfoSpace. If there are more than two devices (fig. 3), an ad hoc network is created with a distributed management of the InfoSpace.

Fig. 2. User views (2 users A and B, 2 devices) on 1 InfoSpace

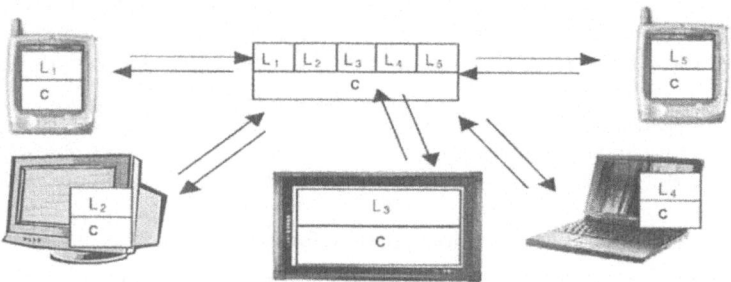

Fig. 3. User views (5 users, 5 devices) on 1 InfoSpace

There are different ways to move information between a local space (L_i) and the common space (C):

1. Manually by the user: Only a few functions to provide and consume information have to be made available through a graphical user interface.
2. Automatically: Each device is aware of the context (e.g. location, time and date, sensor information). Based on these contexts, information can be automatically provided or consumed. Agents are responsible for these tasks on behalf of the user.In any case, information is either copied or moved from L_i to C. The system then updates the common space C to make it consistent between all users. In turn, other users can consume information from C by copy or move operations.

4.2 Information Selection

A user has three possibilities to select the information he wishes to see:

1. By accepting one of several offered InfoSpaces he enters a communication relationship with a certain partner or group. The availability of an InfoSpace is determined by the existence of a physical communication channel between the two devices. E.g. in the wireless case the two or more devices must be in their mutual range of radio signals. After he has selected a specific InfoSpace, he sees all the information that is offered via the common space C corresponding to this InfoSpace.
2. L-space selection: A mapping operation from the local storage area (file system) of user i to the local view L_i selects (e.g. by filtering) objects which are of importance in a certain communication context. An example for such a selection is the set of objects belonging to a specific lecture.

3. C-space filtering: In order to avoid a possibly overloaded C space, additional filtering operations can be applied to the common view. Filters use the metadata information of the objects. It is important to note that filtering is an operation strictly local to the receiving device. This avoids centralized computation on the offering side on behalf of the receivers.

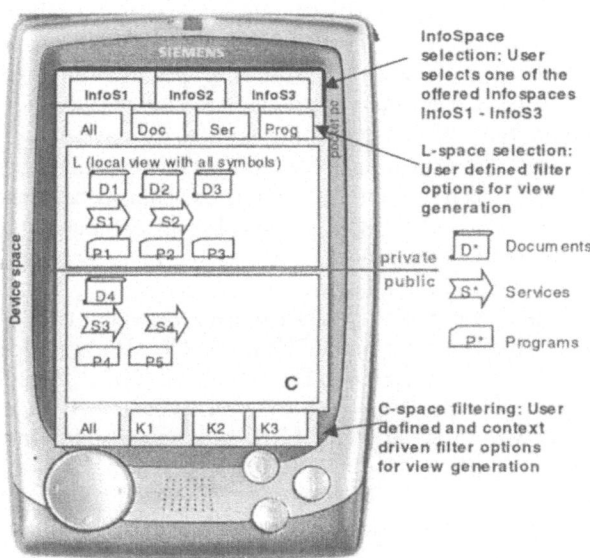

Fig. 4. InfoSpace-capable device with the local view L, the common view C, the InfoSpace selection area (top) and the L-space and C-space filter setting areas

Fig. 4 shows the InfoSpace GUI with the local space L and the common space C. Several symbols representing different objects are shown. A transfer (copy or move, see below) can be carried out by moving the respective symbol. Crossing the L to C borderline constitutes also a transition between the private and the public space. It is guaranteed by the system, that there is no illegal intrusion from a remote device into the private space. All transfers are visible and explicitly initiated by the user. The agents with the task to scan e.g. the common space for certain desired objects constitute the only exception to this rule. The policy in general is: Everything is forbidden unless it is explicitly allowed.

Hence the user has to carry out four types of operations via his GUI:
1. Selection of one of the offered InfoSpaces (top section of the GUI in fig. 4)
2. Selection of information from the local storage to L_i.
3. Information transfer between L_i and C.
4. Setting filter options for C (lower section of the GUI).

We now have to investigate the actions necessary in the InfoSpace infrastructure in order to keep the system consistent. In particular, we have to discuss the movement and visibility of symbols (references) and the corresponding data transfers.

4.3 InfoSpace as an Abstract Communication Mechanism

As already stated, the basic idea of an InfoSpace is to visualize the paradigm of a common globally shared but physically distributed memory on the GUI level and to provide a small number of intuitively simple graphical commands to manipulate information objects in order to make them available to other users or to withdraw them from the common view. In the preceding section we have shown some transfers of objects as seen from the user point of view. At the same time, the InfoSpace can be perceived also as an abstract communication mechanism between applications. The mechanism is then accessed not via (graphical) user commands but through an API. The abstract InfoSpace comes close to the usage other projects like TSPACES and JavaSpaces have made of the tuple space paradigm.

In a strict sense, we have to discriminate between two levels: the abstract InfoSpace and its visualization on the GUI level. The abstract InfoSpace is not visible to the user other than through a GUI. The InfoSpace GUI is a 1:1 visualization of the abstract InfoSpace. Hence, the (human) user is enabled to directly manipulate InfoSpace objects with the help of the GUI. Alternatively, the InfoSpace can also be manipulated (via its API) by application programs. A possible application program can be an agent equipped with a filter or search mask which continually scans the common space C for objects matching its search pattern. In this sense, the InfoSpace GUI resembles the shell of an operating system which allows the human user to access the OS services. The shell also co-exists with other programs which use the operating system via system calls.

4.4 Operations and Protocols on InfoSpaces

When two "InfoSpace-capable" devices meet (i.e. a physical connection is established) they will tell their users that an information partner is present and that an InfoSpace can be used if wanted. When both users agree to participate, the InfoSpace consisting of local spaces (L_1, L_2) and common space C is established (compare fig. 5). Now exactly four basic operations are possible: copy out, move out, copy in, move in. These operations allow the users to share information and services easily by manipulating symbols on the GUI level.

The following copy and move operations are possible if local information from device 1 is to be made accessible for device 2:

– Copy to common (copy out): Symbol A is copied from L1 to C. After the copy out operation, symbol A is visible in the common space on both devices. The reference A points to object A in LS1 (Local Storage 1).

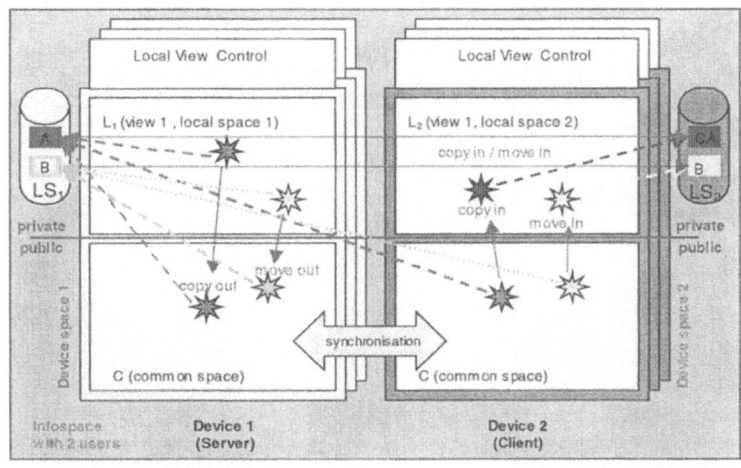

Fig. 5. User views (2 users, 2 devices, 2 device spaces) on 1 InfoSpace, information transfer from LS_1 to LS_2

− Move to common (move out): Symbol A is moved from L1 to C. After the move out operation, symbol A is visible in the common space on both devices. Symbol A is deleted from L1. A symbol A* (grayed out) remains in L1 pointing to a backup copy A* in LS1. The reference A points to object A in LS1.

− Copy from common (copy in): Symbol A is copied from C to L2, a copy of object A in LS1 is transferred to LS2 (Local Storage 2). The reference from the copied symbol A points to object A in LS2.

− Move from common (move in): Symbol A is moved from C to L2, object A is transferred from LS1 to LS2, symbol A is removed from C. After the "move in" operation, symbol A is only visible on device 2, the reference from symbol A in L2 points to object A in LS2. The "move in" operation is potentially dangerous since it results in the deletion of object A in the local storage of device 1. Therefore a user who moves out an object from his local area to C is warned and a backup copy is generated. Despite its dangerous nature we felt that a consequent move operation including the deletion of the source object is necessary to allow for a mutually exclusive update of objects if this is desired by the user.

Since this tuple space based approach is symmetric, local information on device 2 can be made accessible for device 1 in the same way.

The four primitives described above are - as already mentioned - basic (i.e. atomic, not resolvable), so that concurrent access to objects of a common space is impossible. Moreover we do not privilege any device by restricting the execution of a certain primitive to certain devices. I.e. every device in the common space has potentially the right to read or write objects from and into the common space (s. also above: 3.4 Interaction Matrix). Such "device-discrimination" could be very useful for realizing certain application scenarios like the interactive lecture. Such security issues will be subject of future work.

5 Usage Scenarios and Interaction Patterns

After introducing the i-patterns and the InfoSpace paradigm in the last two chapters, we would like to illustrate how these i-patterns could be matched to concrete usage scenarios we are currently working on.

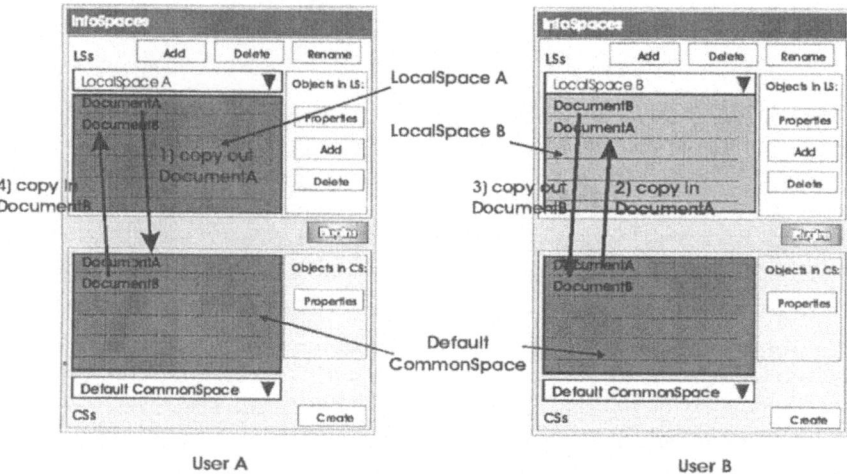

Fig. 6. Object exchange via default common space

5.1 Usage Scenario 1: Data Exchange over the Common Space

This scenario represents the simplest application of the InfoSpaces and in the same time the basis for any other usage. It shows how the InfoSpaces could be used for the spontaneous, intuitive and uncomplicated data (object) exchange between two or more devices in an ad-hoc manner. Suppose two devices running the InfoSpace meet so that the fundamental condition about locality is fulfilled. Without any "extra-effort" (e.g. manual configuration, search...) of the users a (default) common space that comprehends both devices emerges, allowing any user to publish his objects and the others to pick them up. Fig. 6 shows how this could look at the GUI-level.

As – per default – there is no privileged or discriminated entity, we are dealing in this scenario obviously with I-pattern A, where any user can read and write in the common space.

5.2 Usage Scenario 2: The Infokiosk

As introduced above, the infokiosk is a sort of electronic information board. One can make use of infokiosks to realize a dynamic calendar of events of a city or a schedule in a train station or provide students on a campus with information about current lectures and the possibility to access their own examination results. The infokiosk scenario in its simplest form can be realized with the help of an InfoSpace application running permanently. The infokiosk offers a specific common space filled with objects that can be consumed by any user. The user is in this case merely a "silent" participant. He has access to the common space and its objects but cannot change its content (i.e. add or remove objects from it). The infokiosk agent, which is a kind of daemon process, will be the only entity that writes into the common space. This corresponds to I-pattern B.

5.3 Usage Scenario 3: Match-Maker

The idea behind the match-maker scenario is to allow users in a foreign environment to search for adequate fellows or buddies. For that purpose the InfoSpace is supplied with an additional component (agent) which will be responsible for automating certain operations. Users who have joined a dedicated (not the default) common space, let's call it the buddy-search common space, publish (copy out) their profile into the buddy-search common space. An activated agent on a certain user's device will collect all profiles (copy in) and examine according to some (predefined) criteria which one is relevant. If an interesting profile is found, then the match is successful and other actions are triggered. The latter user and the corresponding profile owner can for instance be brought together in a separate common space where they can exchange private data. In this scenario we have obviously the I-pattern G, where many users write their objects (profiles) in the buddy-search common space and one user – with the help of an agent – collects and evaluates them.

6 An InfoSpace Architecture

An architecture to realize InfoSpaces is shown in fig. 7. The InfoSpace Middleware controls the InfoSpaces between the devices. It can be addressed via APIs by applications and through GUIs. To be able to connect a variety of devices it is assumed that communication between devices is possible using the TCP/IP protocol transparently regardless of the physical implementation of the communication channel.

The **InfoSpace Middleware** consists of the following modules (compare fig. 7): View Manager (VM), Connection Scanner (CS), Space Director (SD), Profile manager (PM) and Space Manager (SM). The single modules are briefly characterized in the following.

View Manager VM

The View Manager administrates user defined profiles to set up different views to the local device space (L and C). The default profile shows all symbols available for the basic operations (copy in/out, move in/out). To make it more comfortable the user can define local view profiles to filter symbols. The trigger for the filters can be context driven (location, time, etc.) and/or object driven (to differentiate between documents, programs, services).

Connection Scanner CS

The Connection Scanner is necessary for devices with radio links or optical links such as infrared connections. The CS permanently scans for radio/light signals and checks the signal quality. If the transmission quality is adequate a dialog with the device partner is entered to find out whether the device partner is "InfoSpace compatible". If so, an ID-exchange is carried out automatically and the connection to the InfoSpace is established. The CS is also responsible to disconnect devices from the InfoSpaces if the signal quality is poor or to disconnect devices upon explicit user command.

Space Director SD

The Space Director is informed by the CS about the availability of connections. The SD is responsible for the construction and destruction of common spaces between devices. The SD gets active upon request by the CS. Depending on the context and user demands, the SD initiates the construction of one or more common spaces. If only one communication partner is available, the choice is reduced to one common space. If a group of devices meets it is possible to construct one common space for all devices or to construct bilateral common spaces or to construct groups of common spaces. This decision depends on the needed communication and interaction patterns. To be able to make this decision information has to be exchanged. The SDs of the devices offer their local common spaces to all partners. Depending on profiles from the Profile Manager a decision for the construction of the common spaces can be made. This decision can be automatically (context driven) or user driven. If the user has to decide all offered common spaces are displayed. The SD accepts the user's selection.

The SD also negotiates server/client roles with the partner SD. If new connections are available the SD automatically informs the Space Manager. The SD also deletes users from the common space on explicit demand or upon request from the Connection Scanner.

Profile Manager PM

The Profile Manager administrates local profiles of InfoSpaces. These profiles contain acceptance requirements for establishing InfoSpaces. Thus, the SD is enabled to compare local profiles with offered profiles. Profiles for active partner search or passive acceptance can be set by the user.

Space Manager SM

The Space Manager is responsible for the management of objects in the local device space. It can play a server or client role. There is one SM per device space. The SM can access the local space L and the common space C to copy or delete objects. Thus, the control of the basic operations (copy in/out, move in/out) is carried out by the SM. To correctly perform the basic operations the SM has to communicate with the partner SMs.

The different components described above are realized on the basis of existing class libraries, such as JXTA.

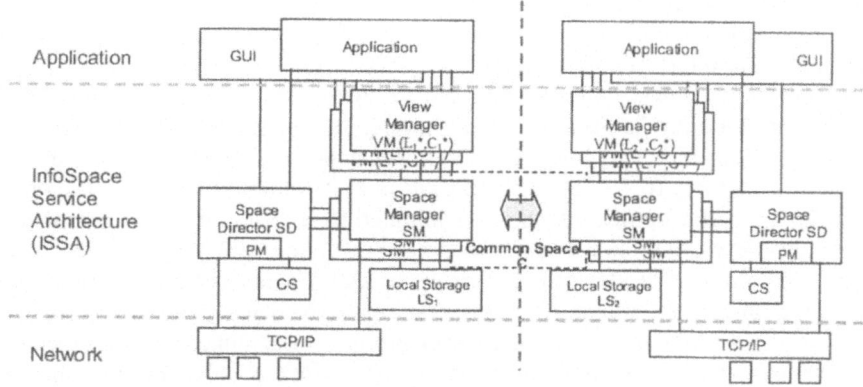

Fig. 7. InfoSpace architecture (CS = Connection Scanner, PM = Profile Manager)

7 Pilot Implementation Using JXTA

Since the release of JXTA, we have been watching the development of the project. Furthermore we have gained some experience by using the platform and its Java reference implementation for developing a demo InfoSpace application. We do not use JXTA as a whole with the complexity of its architecture and its API involved. We rather use specific aspects which serve in particular the ad-hoc and local nature of our InfoSpace Service Architecture (short ISSA). Fig. 8 illustrates the logical architecture of our InfoSpace software. The thickness of every box indicates the importance of the corresponding technology in the model. Notice in particular where JXTA was integrated, namely - apart from the network layer which could be considered as an "external part" of JXTA - at the very bottom level.

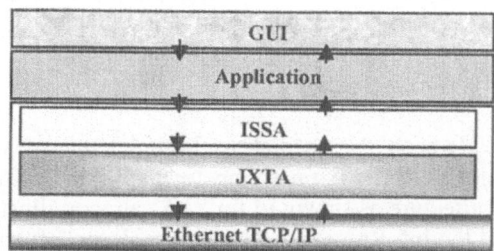

Fig. 8. Architecture of the InfoSpace demo application

Let us describe the architecture bottom-up. The bottom layer depicts the network layer. We have developed the architecture in an Ethernet LAN environment. This is justified by the nature of ISSA, since InfoSpaces will be exclusively deployed between devices that are spatially "close" to each other. This has also a further advantage as far as JXTA is concerned, since JXTA uses different mechanisms for publishing and discovering in LAN and non-LAN (i.e. wide area) environments. Of course those mechanisms designed for LAN are simpler and more reliable. Besides, for this first implementation we have made no assumptions on resources such as computing, storage or network bandwidth in order to concentrate on the JXTA platform and provide a comfortable user interface.

JXTA provides many features which coincide with the ISSA specification. Maybe the most important one is the peer group service. A peer group in JXTA represents a gathering of peers with a common interest. For instance if several peers are interested in a particular service (e.g. content sharing) or in a particular topic (e.g. astronomy) a peer group – given a significant name - is initiated by a peer. Any other peer that can discover this peer group and fulfil its membership policy can apply for membership and enter the group. The idea of membership service represents furthermore an interesting mechanism for building private (password-protected) groups. Due to those properties, it was obvious that the JXTA peer group – in conjunction with other services – could be used to realize the common space. In particular, the fact that peer groups are dynamic and their membership is not stringent is in harmony with our InfoSpace specification. Peer groups can arise ad hoc (default peer group) and vanish autonomously (without a central managing entity) as the last peer leaves the group. Also peers can join and leave a group, without affecting the existence of the group. All these qualities of peer groups are conceived very cleverly by means of advertisements which describe the peer group and which are propagated among peers without the necessity of a coordinating broker service.

Beside the peer group service, we have used extensively the peer discovery service and the corresponding peer discovery protocol (PDP). Both represent the mechanism in JXTA for discovering and publishing resources including peer groups, peers or any other resource "registered" in a JXTA advertisement.

While peer groups merely represent a framework (context) for any kind of activities, other services are responsible for filling the common space with content. Here we have made use of the content management service (CMS). CMS is a JXTA peer group service used for publishing and sharing content on a local peer, demanding a list of shared content from remote peers of the group and retrieving content [7]. Important is that contents are first advertised to the peer group members in form of content advertisements before any actual data transfer takes place. The content advertisement, a kind of identity of the remote peer content, will be collected by every peer in the group (or InfoSpace) and corresponds therefore to the reference to a remote object in our ISSA architecture (compare fig. 5).

Since ISSA has already been described above in this paper, we will confine our description of the third layer in fig. 8 on trying to map JXTA components to certain blocks of our ISSA architecture as shown in fig 7. As already illustrated, the common space which is a part of the InfoSpace is realized through the JXTA peer group service. The functionality of the space manager, particularly with regard to accessing the local storage, managing objects of the local space and publishing them in the common space is covered by the CMS. The role of the space director responsible for the construction of new InfoSpaces is taken by the JXTA platform itself, which constitutes the infrastructure for invoking any other core or middle layer services.

The last two upper layers: Application and GUI realize some other functionalities of the ISSA like the local space and its object references and the defined four primitives copy in/out and move/in out as defined above.

To sum up, JXTA has proved to be appropriate for implementing our demo application, since it specifies useful mechanisms, services and protocols that deal with some of the fundamental aspects that we have standardized. On the other hand, – as result of studying the JXTA standard[2] and its current implementation - we are not planning to deploy JXTA in its "raw" form as delivered from the open source community for the future work. We rather intend to customize certain protocol and service implementations which on the one hand will suit better our ISSA and on the other hand may lead to saving precious resources (bandwidth, compute power, storage) for an optimal and "really" ubiquitous (anywhere, anytime) use of our InfoSpace.

8   Summary and Outlook

We have introduced the concept of InfoSpaces as a new and simple interaction paradigm with ubiquitous devices. InfoSpaces consequently follow the original idea of tuple spaces but raise the scheme to the user level. The very simple interaction via drag-and-drop based on copy and move operations makes InfoSpaces an ideal candidate for small footprint ubiquitous devices.

Analyzing a university application environment as an example we have found a small number of basic interaction patterns between two or more users. Typical applications like an interactive lecture can be mapped to sequences of these basic I-patterns. We have also shown that the InfoSpace paradigm quite naturally lends itself to the implementation of these basic patterns.

The InfoSpace project is building on existing technologies. We have analyzed and compared possible candidates for the implementation of InfoSpaces and decided to use JXTA due to its small footprint and adequate functionality.

The paper has introduced an architecture to realize the InfoSpaces middleware and has shown in some detail the protocols to handle the information transfer.

As a result we think that a JXTA-based realization of InfoSpaces is quite promising. First implementation work resulted in a pilot application.

While the InfoSpace paradigm is already applicable for realizing some scenarios based on locality and context-awareness, there is, however, still space for improvement in terms of security and the use of the common space for collaborative work (e.g. collaborative editing of objects).

We plan to use the InfoSpace technology in the UbiCampus project which aims to provide all our computer science students with notebooks or other mobile devices. We feel that the broad supply of more or less naked notebooks to the students is rather useless unless they are integrated into an easy-to-use infrastructure with a rich set of services. InfoSpaces has been designed to provide exactly this infrastructure which is missing so far.

Finally we want to point out that the envisaged university environment is just one out of many possible application scenarios. Today's more or less complicated and chaotic interactions between wirelessly connected devices during project meetings, conferences or fairs clearly demonstrate the necessity of generally accepted and simple ad hoc peer-to-peer communication mechanisms.

---

[2] JXTA is to be understood as both: a standard and an implementation.

References

1. J. Hightower, G. Borriello: Location Systems for Ubiquitous Computing, IEEE Computer, August 2001, pp. 57–66
2. C. Müller-Schloer, P. Mähönen: The UbiCampus Project: Applying Ubiquitous Computing Technologies in a University Environment, Proc. IDMS 2000, October 2000, University of Twente, Springer, pp. 297–303
3. 7DS: Peer-to-Peer Information Dissemination and Resource Sharing, http://www.cs.unc.edu/~maria/7ds/
4. http://paul.rutgers.edu/~gsamir/dataspace/
5. David Gelernter: Parallel Programming in LINDA, Technical Report 359, Yale University Department of Computer Science, Jan. 1985
6. http://www.jini.org
7. http://www.jxta.org
8. W. Keith Edwards: Core Jini, Prentice Hall, Dezember 2000, 2nd Edition
9. Early Adopter JXTA: Peer-to-peer Computing with Java, Sing Li, Wrox Press Ltd.,Dezember 2001
10. K Beck: „Extreme Programming Explained", Addison-Wesley 2000
11. http://www.almaden.ibm.com/cs/TSpaces/

Digging Database Statistics and Costs Parameters for Distributed Query Processing

Nicolaas Ruberg, Gabriela Ruberg, and Marta Mattoso

Department of Computer Science – COPPE/UFRJ
P.O.Box 68511, Rio de Janeiro, RJ, 21945-970 – Brazil
{nicolaas, gruberg, marta}@cos.ufrj.br

Abstract. Cost parameters and database statistics are the basis of query optimization techniques. However, in distributed and heterogeneous database systems, acquiring and treating information in order to help the optimization process are often tasks of a global query processor, which adapts its functionalities to a specific system architecture. Moreover, this acquisition process involves a large number of parameters and requires customized methods to retrieve data from specific sources. DIG (*Distributed Information Gatherer*) is a provider of data statistics and query costs that, through an independent and flexible service, aims to support global query optimization processing in distributed and heterogeneous database systems over autonomous data sources. We have developed a DIG prototype and experimented it with specific wrappers for a query middleware on both semi-structured data sources and an object DBMS.

1 Introduction

The *Information Age* was marked by the strong dissemination of digital repositories whose databases were spread in computational "islands" interconnected through the World Wide Web. This scenario has evolved, and nowadays we have to face the challenges of the *Knowledge Age*, which emphasis is to integrate and process this huge volume of information in order to reach some useful purpose. In synchronization with such (r)evolution, the techniques for database management have been radically altered since the traditional system architectures are no longer suited for current problems.

Cooperative systems for information integration in the Web have been a hot spot for both database research and industry in the last years. Pushing further the idea of virtual data integration, several Web database projects exploit mediated architectures [28] and, more recently, peer-to-peer (P2P) systems [4] to develop distributed database frameworks [1], [8], [10], [15], [24]. These projects are mostly based on emergent standards for Web services [26], such as XML, SOAP, and WSDL [29].

The performance of query processing in such context is undoubtedly a decisive requirement. Hence, Web query systems have to figure out strategies to efficiently manipulate scattered, miscellaneous databases. However, query optimization

R. Meersman et al. (Eds.): CoopIS/DOA/ODBASE 2003, LNCS 2888, pp. 301–318, 2003.
© Springer-Verlag Berlin Heidelberg 2003

techniques are typically information consumers [20]. Indeed, even heuristic-based approaches for query optimization need basic database information such as the cardinality of data collections. Nevertheless, such supportive information is hidden in diverse Web data sources, and many issues hinder its acquisition. First of all, the distributed, heterogeneous, autonomous and dynamic nature of Web data sources leads to levels of complexity not ever thought of as manageable. Moreover, the service interfaces published in the Web are not enough to capture database statistics and costs parameters. Therefore, Web information systems need mechanisms to help their query processors to identify the data structures and the processing capacity of heterogeneous data sources, and then to define the best alternatives for query execution.

The *Distributed Information Gatherer* (DIG) consists of a service-oriented framework that aims to support the process of query optimization in cooperative information systems by providing database statistics and costs parameters. The DIG architecture defines several software components and connectors, a service catalog, and procedures for the acquisition and publishing of such supportive information. We believe that an independent gathering system, in opposite to the current approaches where the query processor is responsible for the acquisition of query optimization parameters [1], [8], [15], [24], [30], can provide more flexibility to represent the heterogeneity and autonomy of Web data sources, as it allows the information sharing among distinct query systems.

We are concerned in this paper with a twofold problem:

(i) the capture of query-supportive information from diverse autonomous data sources in cooperative information systems over the Web; and

(ii) the publishing of a distributed catalog that represents the collected data in a uniform interface.

Different from traditional database systems, Web data sources are not always associated with a DBMS. Thus, the distributed query processor needs to recognize the real capacity of query processing of each data source. Furthermore, the acquisition of database statistics and costs parameters may be unavailable, and it requires special methods for data inspection and estimates generation [31]. On the other hand, the collected data should not be published at centralized catalogs since they are hard to be maintained up-to-date in distributed settings, and they also restrict the system scalability [6], [16].

The data acquisition and publishing at DIG framework is performed by two basic system components: an information provider, that coordinates the data acquisition, and publishes a catalog of database statistics and costs parameters; and a data collector, that is responsible for the data acquisition on specific data sources. The separation between data acquisition and publishing processes in the DIG architecture contributes to encapsulate the heterogeneity of data sources, and makes it easy to add new participants to the system. Besides that, DIG providers at distinct peers can collaborate to each other by exchanging information about their data sources, thus keeping a dynamic, decentralized information catalog.

The rest of this paper is organized as follows. In Section 2, we address the main issues in the acquisition of database statistics and costs parameters from diverse autonomous data sources to support distributed query processing. Section 3 presents our proposal: the DIG framework, and its components. Section 4 describes an experimental evaluation of the DIG prototype. We discuss the related work in Section 5. Finally, the conclusion of this paper and perspectives for future work are presented in Section 6.

2   Information Gathering to Support Query Processing

A research topic of great concern is the optimization of query processing in cooperative information systems [6], [16]. Whether heuristic or cost based, the current techniques for query optimization are very dependent of information about the databases and the computational resources [20]. However, providing Web query systems with such information is a hard task due to the complexity of data distribution, heterogeneity and autonomy, since [24]:

⇒   The data sources present distinct capacities of query processing;

⇒   The cost of query processing is specific in each data source, therefore it increases the complexity of the cost functions to be evaluated; and

⇒   The local optimization capacity varies in each data source, and is usually limited or non existent.

It is important to point out that in such context the query optimizers are not capable of estimating costs for query execution plans without the cooperation of the data sources. The data autonomy is related to the independence of the data sources to determine which information is published to the distributed system. As a consequence of this characteristic, a data source can restrict the availability of its database statistics and costs parameters, which are needed to the query optimization process.

In a distributed environment, the query execution plans are often represented by trees where the leaf nodes correspond to operators that are executed by specific data sources. In other words, the local processing is pushed to those leaf nodes. Hence, the cost of the inner levels of the query tree can be estimated recursively by the cost of the respective descendent nodes. In order to calculate the sum of the costs and the cardinalities of a distributed query plan, three basic estimates should be obtained for each operator in the execution plan: the total cost, which is the time measured of its first execution; the cost to re-execute, that is the cost of its successive execution; and the resultant cardinality. Nevertheless, the acquisition of costs and statistics is not restricted to these three parameters.

The basic approaches to determine costs parameters of distributed query processing in heterogeneous, autonomous data sources are [31]:

1.   The use of previously informed knowledge about the data sources as well as their external characteristics in order to determine subjectively their costs;

2.   The approach where the data sources are considered as "black-boxes", and some probing queries are executed to measure their performance;

3.   The supervision of the query execution behavior in the data sources, and the dynamic gathering of their cost information.

These approaches can be combined to better represent the diverse data sources.

A traditional catalog of database statistics and costs parameters includes information such as the cardinality of the collections, the number of pages occupied on disk, and the physical characteristics of the database (database page size, data storage policies, etc.). In a distributed and heterogeneous environment, much of this information is hidden in the data sources, and it may be unavailable to the query optimizer. Moreover, the optimization of distributed query processing requires information about the computational resources, such as network latency (e.g., the time to transmit a data packet through the network). Finally, the quality and precision of database statistics and costs parameters are determined by the efforts in their acquisition process [18]. For that reason, and considering that the time spent in the optimization process should not disturb the query execution costs, most of the acquisition of such information should be done previously.

3 DIG Framework

The proposal of this paper consists of a framework to provide descriptive information, database statistics, and costs parameters from autonomous data sources in a distributed and heterogeneous environment. This framework is represented by a distributed system called DIG (Distributed Information Gatherer) whose architecture may be seen as a foundation layer that helps query optimizers to choose the best alternatives to execute distributed queries.

The DIG framework can be visualized according to two dimensions. In a vertical dimension, the DIG architecture is defined by a set of components and connectors that allow the acquisition of information from the data sources that are managed by a single peer. This DIG intra-peer architecture describes a system that harnesses diverse data sources in order to extract information to support query processing optimization in Web query systems. On the other hand, in a horizontal dimension, the DIG framework concerns the exchange of information among several DIG peers, since one peer should not archive much information about data sources located at other peers.

The DIG intra-peer architecture is composed of two basic types of system components: a service named **DIG Provider**, which provides the query optimizers with information about database statistics and costs parameters; and a **DIG Collector**, which interacts with the specific data sources to acquire such costs and statistics. The information captured by the DIG Provider are published at the **DIG Catalog** to the query optimizers. Fig. 1 depicts the DIG intra-peer architecture, with emphasis on the internal and external interfaces of each DIG component.

Some important aspects have guided the outline of the DIG intra-peer architecture. First, we have considered the heterogeneity of the cooperative information systems; a collector mechanism was provided to deal with specific data sources. We have also assumed that there could be data sources without a DBMS. Another important aspect of the DIG architecture project is the design of a flexible information catalog. In order to offer an extensible and uniform interface, the data model of the DIG Catalog

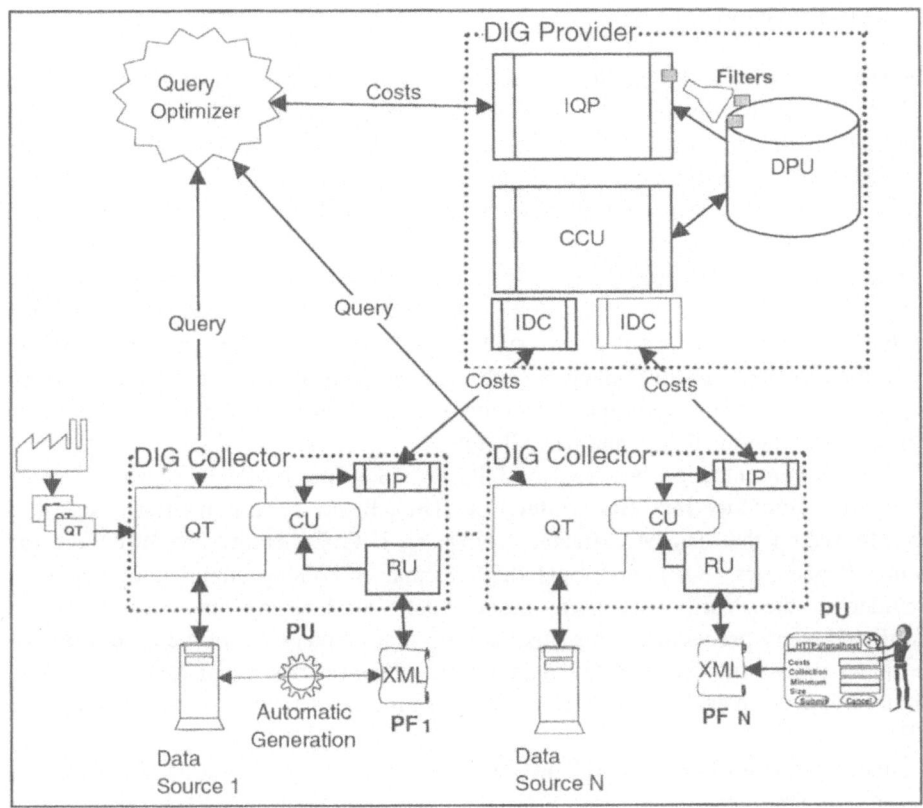

Fig. 1. DIG Intra-peer Architecture

is provided independently from the data sources. Thus, the DIG Catalog can represent information on semi-structured, relational, and/or object-based sources. The model of the DIG Catalog aims to offer a broad service to the distributed query processor, thus a large number of cost information is provided. Furthermore, the DIG intra-peer architecture provides tools to acquire and store information about the execution of methods and programs. Such aspect is very important in Web query systems, since many Web services may be represented as black-box programs, as well as in Grid platforms.

Given that the DIG system is not responsible for the query processing, it is not up to the DIG Provider to deal with issues such as the information redundancy among data sources, and schema extraction (although these issues could be addressed in complementary works). Finally, we assume that the cost of a query operator applied over two or more data sources could be estimated by the costs of its execution in each data source. We have considered that this cost estimation is accomplished by the distributed query processor according to its strategy to traverse the space of possible execution plans.

3.1 DIG Provider

The **DIG Provider** is the module responsible for the management of the information collected from the diverse data sources, and for publishing this information at a standard interface, called DIG Catalog. The DIG Provider has the following components and connectors: a control unit to manage the DIG Collectors; an interface with the DIG Collectors; an interface with the distributed query processors; and a unit to persist the collected data.

The **Collectors Control Unit** (CCU) registers which DIG Collectors can be activated by the DIG Provider. This unit starts the process of information acquisition on the DIG Collectors, and it allows such acquisition to be either specific to a DIG Collector or general to all collectors. The process of information acquisition can be triggered by a command (a request from the distributed query processor) or scheduled to be executed automatically and periodically.

All the communication between the DIG Provider and the DIG Collectors occurs through the **Interface for DIG Collectors** (IDC). Basically, this interface describes the information that can be extracted from each DIG Collector. The **Interface for Query Processors** (IQP) represents the information catalog supplied by the DIG Provider to the distributed environment. Such interface can be accessed by a distributed query processor or any other system that is interested in the description of the query processing on available data sources. **Filters** for special treatment of the acquired data (such as distortion reduction, data mining, etc.) may be associated to the IQP.

Finally, the **Data Persistence Unit** (DPU) stores all the information obtained by a certain DIG Provider. It is the materialized view of the DIG Catalog. This database of statistics and costs can be refined by further processing. For example, more precise database statistics can be supplied based on an historical analysis.

3.2 DIG Collector

One DIG Collector accomplishes the acquisition of database statistics and costs parameters of a specific data source (DBMS, text file, program, etc.), and informs the DIG Provider of what has been collected. The description of the acquisition method in the data sources must be given. The DIG Collector is attached to the Query Translator (QT), and it has the following functional units: a registry unit; a collector unit for the data sources; and an interface for the DIG Provider.

The **Registry Unit** (RU) is responsible for registering all data sources in the DIG Collector, and for the processing of the file containing the description of each data source. This unit contains an XML parser, and functions to extract the description of the acquisition methods.

The **Collector Unit** (CU) can be seen as a "cartridge" of functionalities to be added to the query wrapper. This means that the DIG Collector uses the infrastructure provided by the wrapper to access its respective data sources. Nevertheless, there is no restriction for the DIG Collector to use a wrapper of its own. This unit applies all the methods informed by the Registry Unit to acquire the costs and statistics of a data source. If the Collector Unit is unable to execute the informed acquisition method, or the method result is not valid, then the DIG Collector can associate default values to the respective cost and statistics.

The **Interface for the Provider** (IP) corresponds to counterpart of the IDC module in the DIG Provider. It represents a set of services to trigger the information acquisition in the data sources. Each category of the collected information is represented by a specific service.

It is worth to mention that adding a new data source in the system does not represent a complex task since the set of information to be acquired in a data source can be defined according to the needs/capacity of each DIG Collector. This task is particularly easy if the new data source has the same query language and/or the same data model of the distributed integration system. Moreover, automatic generators may be used to assemble specific wrappers with a minimum set of functions, as proposed in [22].

3.3 The Publishing File

Each DIG Collector reads a plain-text file called **Publishing File** (PF) that registers which data source or data sources should be accessed. The goal of Publishing File is to allow the DIG Collector to identify the particularities of each data source. For example, in this file it could be described how a data object is retrieved, or how a method could be executed, among other operations. The local administrators of each data source must provide the DIG system with a PF describing the information to be gathered.

All the information that can be captured by a DIG Collector from a given data source is described in the Publishing File using the XML format. The several information items (about collections, data types, access methods, etc.) to be monitored in the data sources are represented by XML elements. Each information item must have either: the description of a proper acquisition method that will be used by the DIG Collector; or the declaration of a default value. The first case (using an acquisition method) allows the DIG Collectors to perform a dynamic information gathering.

The acquisition methods can be described, for example, in the query language of the data sources, or even in the language of the query translators, since the definition of a PF does not impose either a canonical data model or a specific query language. When the acquisition methods are used by the DIG Collectors for information gathering, it is up to the query translators to convert (if necessary) from the query language describing them to the specific query language of their data sources, and vice-versa. For example, as shown in the Fig. 2, the query language used to describe the acquisition methods is the SQL3. Note that default values were used in order to capture some information items (for example, AbleToProject, and NetworkTime), instead of acquisition methods in SQL3.

In addition to the information about databases and query costs, the capacity of data sources to perform operations such as selections, joins, and projections can also be described in the Publishing File. If these operations are uninformed for a given data source, the DIG Collector assumes that this data source cannot process them.

```
<Site name=porto>
  <Collection name=Students>
    <SimpleAttribute name=adviser> <Reference>True</Reference>
      <Count>"select count(s.adviser) from s in Students"</Count>
    </SimpleAttribute>
  </Collection>

  <Collection name=Teachers>
    <Cardinality>"select count(t) from t in Teachers"</Cardinality>
  </Collection>

  <Method name=getStudent>
    <Execution>select s from s in Students</Execution> </Method>

  <Relationship name="advised by">
    <FirstCollection>Students</FirstCollection>
    <SecondCollection>Teachers</SecondCollection>
    <RelationAttribute>Adviser</RelationAttribute>
  </Relationship>

  <Type name=Student>
    <CollectionType>Student</CollectionType>
    <Extent>Students</Extent>
    <Schema>name;gpa;adviser</Schema>
  </Type>

  <AbleToProject>True</AbleToProject>
  <NetworkTime>10</NetworkTime>
  <PageSize>1024</PageSize>
</Site>
```

Fig. 2. An example of a publishing file in a DIG collector

The **Publishing Unit** (PU) represents tools that may help the local administrators to generate the Publishing Files for their data sources at the DIG system. The basic data input of this unit may be done by HTML forms, thereby activating scripts to generate the Publishing File in the XML format. For more sophisticated data sources, such as DBMSs, the Publishing File tends to be extensive, and the manual data input could be extenuating. In such cases, the Publishing Unit could automatically generate the description of the acquisition methods from the internal DMBS catalog. This task is not complex since, nowadays, many database systems offer tools to extract data in the XML format.

3.4 DIG Catalog

The DIG Catalog is maintained by the DIG Provider, and its design approaches two aspects: (i) which information is relevant to the query processing in a distributed environment; and (ii) how such information can be extracted from the data sources. This catalog supports the registry of both database statistics and costs parameters from diverse data sources. Moreover, the DIG Catalog is published through a standard interface, which encapsulates the heterogeneity of data sources.

The DIG Catalog may contain information on a basic set of common operators from many query languages. Therefore, since the DIG system is not limited to a specific query language, it can provide database statistics and costs parameters for many operators of several algebras.

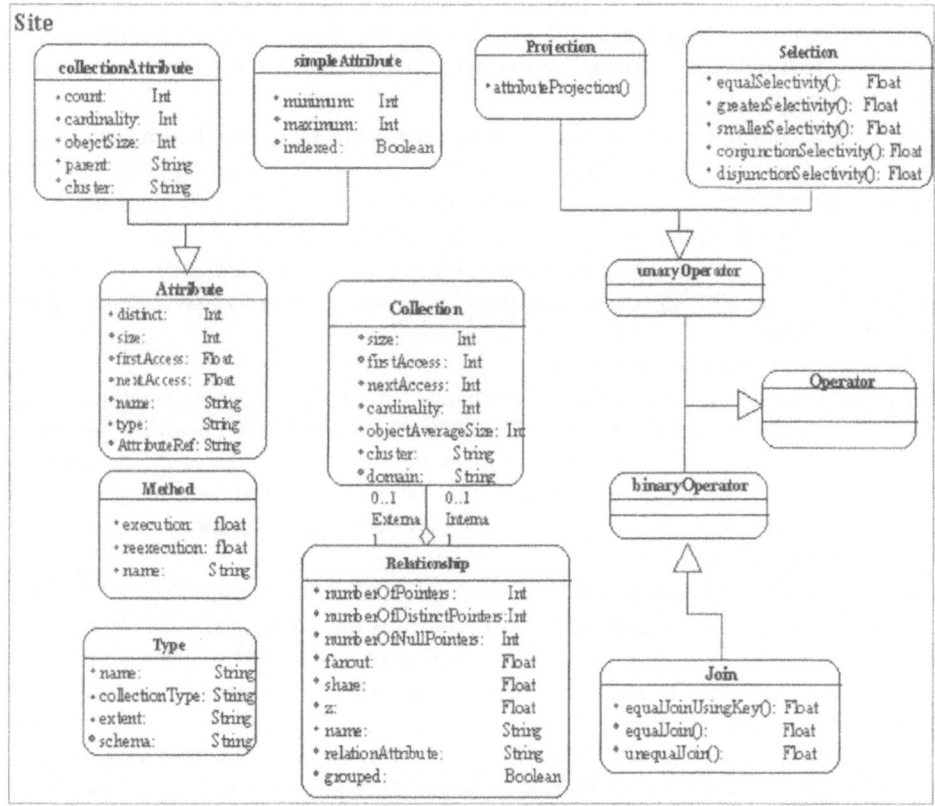

Fig. 3. UML class diagram of the DIG service catalog

To define which information is relevant to the distributed query optimization, in the specification of the DIG Catalog we considered that the query processor needs costs information related to the subqueries executed in each data source. It is important to mention that physical aspects are not focused on the DIG architecture because such characteristics usually are embedded in the data sources, and they may be hidden.

The information available in the DIG Catalog is described by the UML class diagram presented in Fig. 3. Notice that this model can be extended to support additional characteristics such as, for example, query aggregation operators. We assume that program executions are considered as special operators. The DIG Catalog classifies its information according to the following categories: site, collection, simple attribute, collection type attribute, method, types, relationship and operators. Each information may be acquired by data inspection or by mathematical estimation.

3.5 DIG Inter-peer Communication

Peer-to-peer architectures are interesting alternatives to approach the problems raised by data integration in the Web, particularly the large scale and the autonomy of data sources [4]. In cooperative information systems, the queries typically combine data located in multiple peers. There are two basic alternatives to evaluate the execution plan of such queries:

- The query optimizer of the peer where the query was submitted makes a "pre-plan", and resolves the parts requiring only local information. Then, it propagates this plan to the other peers, which recursively apply the same procedure until the query plan is completely evaluated;

- One peer is chosen to coordinate the query execution, and such peer requests to the other peers all the necessary information before sending them a complete query execution plan.

In both cases, the DIG service at each peer can help the query optimizer through a collaborative strategy for information exchange. In the first scenario, each peer may access its local information from its DIG Provider in order to transform the query execution plan. By local information we mean the information obtained from the data sources that are available for each peer. Thus, the query processor at each peer would not have to concern the heterogeneity of its data sources in order to transform the query execution plans.

For the second alternative, the coordinator peer (with the support of a DIG system) does not have to ask the necessary information to the other peers, but to the DIG Provider, which encapsulates the data distribution through the DIG Catalog, and then provides a transparent access to the remote information. To provide this, the DIG Catalog may contain information about remote sources that are captured by the communication among the DIG Providers. Since it is not interesting to replicate much information from other peers, the DIG Provider may keep a database cache of such information according to the queries frequencies.

4 The DIG Prototype

We have implemented a prototype of the DIG intra-query architecture using the C++ programming language and the CORBA communication platform. The DIG prototype was developed for two different data sources: the GOA system [12], an object DBMS prototype; and the LeSelect middleware [23]. The implementation of the DIG Collectors uses a wrapper that executes queries in the SQL3 language. Such query wrappers are based on the HIMPAR architecture presented in [19]. The canonical model of the HIMPAR architecture is the object-relational, thus we have assumed this one as the canonical model to represent the data sources, although the DIG supports others canonical models.

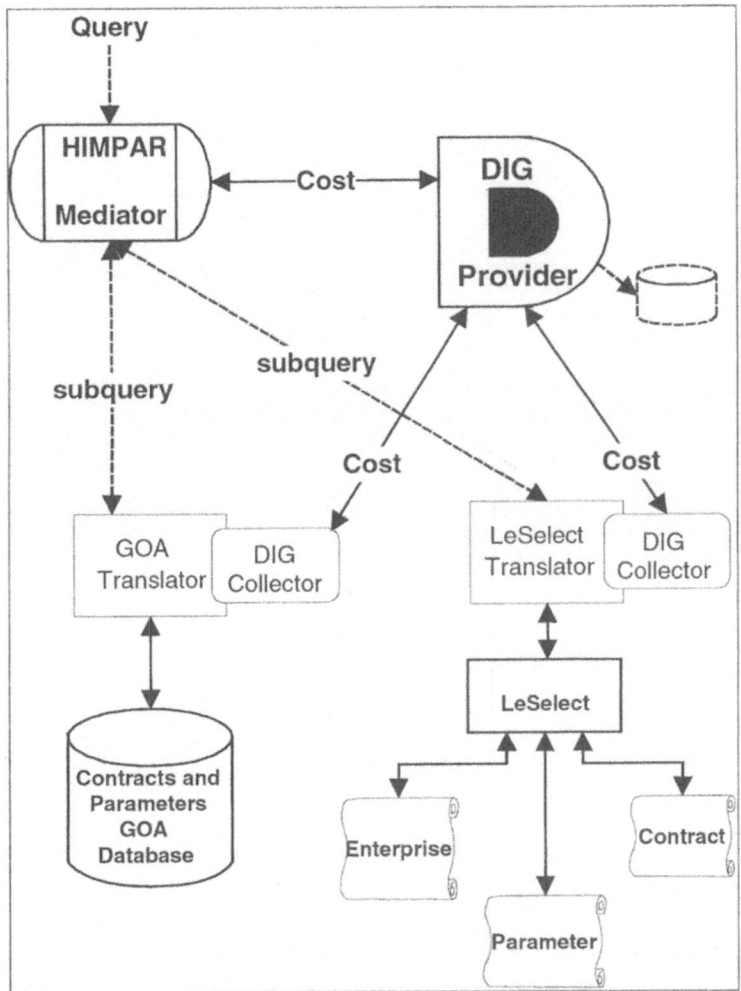

Fig. 4. Experimental scenario of DIG prototype

In order to evaluate the DIG prototype, an experimental setting was configured using databases of loans from a real financial institution. These information are distributed in GOA databases, and in text files with comma-separated fields. The text files are integrated by the LeSelect middleware. The entities found in these databases are "Enterprise", "Contract" and financial "Parameter". The configuration of the data sources is depicted in Fig. 4.

Figures 5 and 6 show, respectively, some data acquired from the databases stored at the GOA and middleware sources. In the last case, since the data sources are not provided with DBMS functionalities, there are no explicit relationships between the collections. It is also interesting to point out the average access time measured on the middleware sources. The time of the first access and the next access are identical, emphasizing the absence of a data caching techniques.

```
<Site name=porto>
<Collection name=Parameters>
    <SimpleAttribute name=periodicity>
        <Distinct>5</Distinct>
        <Minimum>0</Minimum>
        <Maximum>11</Maximum>
    </SimpleAttribute>
    <Cardinality>335</Cardinality>
    <Size>24792</Size>
    <AverageSize>74</AverageSize>
    <FirstAccess>24</FirstAccess>
    <NextAccess>20</NextAccess>
</Collection>

<Collection name=Contracts>
    <SimpleAttribute name=contract_type>
        <Distinct>6</Distinct>
        <Minimum>0</Minimum>
        <Maximum>9</Maximum>
    </SimpleAttribute>
    <Key>contract_number</Key>
    <Cardinality>572</Cardinality>
    <Size>62486</Size>
    <AverageSize>109</AverageSize>
    <FirstAccess>18</FirstAccess>
    <NextAccess>15</NextAccess>
</Collection>

<Relationship name="flow">
    <FirstCollection>Parameters</>
    <SecondCollection>Contracts</>
    <RelationAttribute>flow</>
    <Grouped>True</Grouped>
</Relationship>

<NetworkTime>10</NetworkTime>
<PageSize>1024</PageSize>
<AbleToProject>TRUE</AbleToProject>
</Site>
```

Fig. 5. Data Persistence Unit of GOA sources

Note that the DIG system does not perform tasks related to the integration of the information from the data sources, such as solving name conflicts for the data entities. Nevertheless, DIG can collect the structure of the stored databases, beyond the database statistics and costs parameters, which can ease the task of information integration.

The communication between the **DIG provider** and the data collectors was implemented in CORBA objects. Such objects have methods to perform the information acquisition in the data sources. Two main methods can be used by the **DIG provider** to start the acquisition process: `load()`, which loads the acquisition methods for the data sources; and **acquireCosts()**, that triggers the appropriate methods to acquire the costs and statistics in each *DIG Collector*.

```
<Site name=miami>
 <Collection name=Companies>
    <SimpleAttribute name=sequecial>
      <FirstAccess>8</FirstAccess>
      <NextAccess>8</NextAccess>
    </SimpleAttribute>
    <Cardinality>499</Cardinality>
    <Size>42826</Size>
    <AverageSize>85</AverageSize>
 </Collection>

 <Collection name=Contracts>
    <SimpleAttribute name=contract_type>
      <Distinct>6</Distinct>
      <Size>1</Size>
      <FirstAccess>10</FirstAccess>
      <NextAccess>10</NextAccess>
      <Minimum>0</Minimum>
      <Maximum>9</Maximum>
    </SimpleAttribute>
    <Cardinality>300</Cardinality>
    <Size>32772</Size>
 </Collection>

 <Collection name=Parameters>
    <Cardinality>335</Cardinality>
    <Size>24792</Size>
    <AverageSize>74</AverageSize>
    <FirstAccess>12</FirstAccess>
    <NextAccess>12</NextAccess>
 </Collection>

 <Type name=Parameter>
    <CollectionType>Parameter</ >
    <Extent>Parameters</>
 </Type>
  <NetworkTime>10</NetworkTime>
  <AbleToProject>FALSE</AbleToProject>
</Site>
```

Fig. 6. Data Persistence Unit of LeSelect sources

The DIG system has provided the HIMPAR mediator with information that helps the query optimizer to efficiently generate the query execution plans. For example, consider a query plan with a join operator between two data collections that are stored at distinct sites. If the HIMPAR query optimizer uses a heuristic optimization approach, it would need some basic information, such as the cardinality of each data collection, in order to decide how the query plan would be decomposed and sended to the data sources. Otherwise, unnecessary and high-cost operations may be executed. On the other hand, in a cost-based approach, database statistics and cost parameters consist of information *sine qua non* for the query optimization process.

Without the DIG services, the HIMPAR system would have to take care of how to capture each information required to the query optimization process. Hence, it would have to implement each acquisition method, and it would also have to keep a generic cost model in order to provide the uninformed parameters, according to the characteristics of each distinct data source. Obviously, such approach may compromise the system evolution. Moreover, once database statistics and costs parameters are acquired, they will be available only for the HIMPAR query optimizer, thus another distributed system that runs over the same data sources would also have to monitorate them.

Another important advantage of the DIG architecture consists of its adaptability to the system evolution, which is much frequent in a distributed, heterogeneous environment such as the Web. The system evolution often involves two kinds of changes:

(i) inclusion or removal of data sources; and
(ii) schema evolution and changes in the query processing capability of a given data source.

In the first case, it is only necessary to include or remove the data sources from the configuration file of the DIG Provider. Nevertheless, for each new data source, a Publishing File (PF) must be provided to its respective DIG Collector. In the second case, the changes in the schema or in query processing capability of the data source must be reflected in its PF. In both cases, it is worth to mention that the system evolution does not disturb the query optimizer due to the transparency of the DIG services.

5 Related Work

There are several works on estimating database statistics and query costs for specific database models, such as in [3], [7], [11], [21], [27], and [32]. These techniques are complementary to the DIG proposal, and they can be implemented in DIG collectors to improve their capabilities of information acquisition. Similarly, data mining and OLAP methods could be applied to refine the catalog database of the DIG providers.

We have analyzed different architectures for information integration according to the way database statistics and cost parameters are provided, and we have observed that they are mostly limited by a centralized catalog and a specific query processing strategy. In the CORDS multidatabase architecture [30], each CORDS server estimates database statistics and costs parameters by means of query sampling. The samples are special workloads of queries executed at the data sources. The CORDS servers keep in a global information catalog the average performance of traditional query algorithms, that is calculated from the collected query samples. In our setting, although we consider that DIG collectors may use similar sampling approaches in order to acquire database information, they are more flexible since they could also ask their data sources for more detailed information (when it is possible).

Another relevant work on information integration is the Garlic mediator architecture [12], whose query optimizer models execution plans as trees of "black-box" query operators named POPs (Plan Operators). These POPs can be grouped into high-level operators called PUSHDOWN POPs that represent subqueries executed at specific data sources, whose query costs are estimated by the respective wrappers based on the costs of the POPs involved. The Garlic architecture assumes that mediators do not need to know the costs of POPs in data sources, and they do not maintain detailed information about these operators. This approach restricts the query optimization alternatives at the Garlic mediator. Moreover, in contrast to CORDS and Garlic architectures, DIG services aims to support Web query systems that could not rely on a centralized catalog.

The DISCO (Distributed Information Search COmponent) [25] was one of the first systems that have pointed out the query translator as the supplier of database statistics and costs parameters for the query processing optimization. Nevertheless, the information provided by the DISCO translators is fairly simple, and it relays on the cost model used by the DISCO mediator, which might be insuficient for different scenarios. Concerning collection statistics, the DISCO translator publishes a triple with: number of objects; total size; and average size. Concerning attribute statistics, the triple contains: the maximum and minimum attribute values; and the number of distinct values. Moreover, the DISCO system mixes both the roles of query translation and information gathering at the DISCO translator, and it lets to the DISCO mediator both the roles of query processing and treatment of the collected information.

Recently, the database community has begun to adopt peer-to-peer architectures in order to solve problems such as scalability and availability in information integration systems [4]. In most P2P frameworks, such as the Active XML [1], the query optimizer of each peer has to ask for information at remote peers in order to support the query processing [2]. Another approach is exploited in [17], where query processors propagate "mutant" query plans that are modified with schema translations and costs annotations by the peers during distributed query evaluation. However, query optimization is fairly heuristic in this last case, since no distributed query plan can be assembled in advance, and each peer has no knowledge about the characteristics of data sources in the other peers. Besides that, to the best of our knowledge, the design of services for the acquisition of database statistics and cost parameters of heterogeneous, autonomous intra-peer data sources has never been addressed in P2P systems.

Notice that, in the aforementioned works, the query processor is responsible for the acquisition of information to support query optimization. The major problem of such approach consists of conciliating the query processor workload and the quality of the information acquired. The optimization time of query processing must be low, but the precision of database statistics and costs parameters is proportional to the effort in the acquisition of these data [18]. This problem is particularly present in the Web, where the cost acquisition process involves a large number of parameters, and requires specific methods to collect database information from diverse data sources. As a consequence of performing these tasks, the query optimizer has to deal with significant additional complexity. On the other hand, acquiring database statistics and costs parameters by an independent system component provides more flexibility to represent heterogeneity and autonomy in distributed query processing, and also leaves the query optimizer to better perform its proper roles. In addition, once the data is collected and organized in a catalog, virtually any query system could benefit from this information. This issue is relevant in scenarios such as the Web, and the Grid platforms [10], where the reuse of system components and services is a key requirement of cooperative information systems.

We found in the ObjectGlobe project [8] a system module for publishing a LDAP-based catalog of costs and statistics. Each data or service provider can register their descriptive information on this catalog, that is published by a Java-based lookup service. Nevertheless, there is no guarantee of data acquisition, since it completely depends on the data sources to register their information.

Going further, the DIG architecture presented in this paper consists of a specialized service that captures descriptive information, database statistics, and costs parameters from diverse autonomous data sources in cooperative information systems. The collected data are organized and published at a catalog that encapsulates data distribution and heterogeneity. Moreover, the DIG system may be implemented in an independent service accessible to several distributed query processors. The DIG intra-peer architecture simplifies the addition of new data collectors to the system, due to the distinction of the data acquisition and publishing processes, and thus it is suited for Web-scale frameworks. Finally, DIG inter-peer communication also contributes to the system scalability, as well as it helps to reduce the data replication.

6 Conclusion and Future Work

Providing distributed, cooperative database systems with information about data sources is extremely important to allow efficient query processing in the Web, since most techniques for query optimization rely on database statistics and costs parameters. However, acquiring this information is a complex task due to the distributed, heterogeneous and autonomous nature of Web data. Moreover, in Web-scale systems, publishing such information could not be done by centralized catalogs because of prohibitive drawbacks such as data replication and single-point access. Therefore, distributed query systems require decentralized, dynamic catalogs based on collaborative and scalable strategies for information exchange.

We considered in this paper the major issues raised in such scenario. Our main contribution lies in the proposal of DIG: a framework for distributed information gathering that allows to collect database statistics and costs parameters from diverse autonomous data sources. This proposal aims to support the optimization of query processing in cooperative information systems. Based on the DIG architecture, we have also presented a collaboration strategy for publishing a distributed catalog in peer-to-peer query systems.

In the first stage of the DIG project, we have implemented a prototype of DIG intra-peer components, and have experimented it in the context of the HIMPAR [19] mediated query system. Nowadays, the DIG prototype is being extended with inter-peer communication components, based on Web services standards such as XML, SOAP, and WSDL [29]. As future work, we intend to exploit DIG services to support XML query processing and the distributed optimization of XPath expressions.

Acknowledgement. This work was partially financed by CNPq, and BNDES. The author Gabriela Ruberg is on leave from the Central Bank of Brazil. The contents of this paper represent the viewpoint of their authors, and they do not necessarily represent the position of either the Central Bank of Brazil or its members.

References

[1] Abiteboul, S., Benjelloun, O., Manolescu, I., Milo, T., and Weber, R.: Active XML: Peer-to-Peer Data and Web Services Integration (demo). VLDB 2002, pp. 1087–1090.

[2] Abiteboul, S., Bonifati, A., Cobéna, G., Manolescu, I., and Milo, T.: Dynamic XML Documents with Distribution and Replication. SIGMOD Conference 2003, pp. 527–538.

[3] Aboulnaga, A., Alameldeen, and Naughton, J.: Estimating the Selectivity of XML Path Expressions for Internet Applications. VLDB 2001, pp. 591–600.

[4] Bernstein, P.A., Giunchiglia, F., Kementsietsidis, A., Mylopoulos, J., Serafini, L., and Zaihrayeu, I.: Data Management for Peer-to-Peer Computing: A Vision. WebDB 2002, pp. 89–94.

[5] Bouganim, L., Fabret, F., Porto, F., and Valduriez, P.: Processing Queries with Expensive Functions and Large Objects in Distributed Mediator Systems. ICDE 2001, pp. 91–98.

[6] Bouguettaya, A., Benatallah, B., and Elmagarmid, A.: An Overview of Multidatabase Systems: Past and Present. Management of Heterogeneous and Autonomous Database Systems, ISBN 1-55860-216-X, Morgan Kaufmann Eds. (1999), pp. 1–32.

[7] Boulos, J., and Ono, K.: Cost Estimation of User-Defined Methods in Object-Relational Database Systems. SIGMOD Record 28(3), pp. 22–28 (1999).

[8] Braumandl, R., Keidl, M., Kemper, A. *et al.*: ObjectGlobe: Ubiquitous query processing on the Internet. VLDB Journal 10(1), pp. 48–71 (2001).

[9] Domenig, R., and Dittrich, K.: An Overview and Classification of Mediated Query Systems. SIGMOD Record 28(3), pp. 63–72 (1999).

[10] Foster, I., Kesselman, C., and Tuecke, S.: The Anatomy of the Grid: Enabling Scalable Virtual Organizations. IJSA 15(3) (2001).

[11] Freire, J., Haritsa, J., Ramanath, M., Roy, P., and Simeon, J.: StatiX: Making XML count. SIGMOD Conference 2002, pp. 181–191.

[12] GOA Project, at http://www.cos.ufrj.br/~goa.

[13] Haas, L., Kossmann, D., Wimmers, E., and Yang, J.: Optimizing Queries Across Diverse Data Sources. VLDB 1997, pp. 276–285.

[14] Naacke, H., Gardarin, G., and Tomasic, A.: Leveraging Mediator Cost Models with Heterogeneous Data Sources. ICDE 1998, pp. 351–360.

[15] Ng, W.S., Ooi, B.C., Tan, K.-L., and Zhou, A.: PeerDB: A P2P-based System for Distributed Data Sharing. ICDE 2003.

[16] Özsu, M., and Valduriez, P.: Principles of Distributed Database Systems, 2nd ed. Prentice-Hall (1999).

[17] Papadimos, V., Maier, D., and Tufte, K.: Distributed Query Processing and Catalogs for Peer-to-Peer Systems. CIDR 2003, Online Proceedings at http://www.informatik.uni-trier.de/~ley/db/conf/cidr/cidr2003.html .

[18] Piatetsky-Shapiro, G., and Connel, C.: Accurate Estimation of the Number of Tuples Satisfying a Condition. SIGMOD Conference 1984, pp. 256–276.

[19] Pires, P.F., Mattoso, M.: A CORBA Based Architecture for Heterogeneous Information Source Interoperability. TOOLS 1997, IEEE Press, ISBN 0-8186-8485-2.

[20] Roth, M.T., Ozcan, F., and Haas, L.M.: Cost Models DO Matter: Providing Cost Information for Diverse Data Sources in a Federated System. VLDB 1999, pp. 599–610.

[21] Ruberg, G., Baião, F., and Mattoso, M.: Estimating Costs of Path Expression Processing in Distributed Databases, DEXA 2002, LNCS 2453, pp. 351–360.

[22] Sahuguet, A., and Azavant, F.: Building Light-Weight Wrappers for Legacy Web Data-Sources Using W4F. VLDB 1999, pp. 738–741.

[23] Simon, E.: LeSelect, a Middleware System that Eases the Publication of Scientific Data Sets and Programs. Workshop on Information Integration on the Web 2001, pp. 2.

[24] Sheth, A. P., and Larson, J. A.: Federated Database Systems for Managing Distributed, Heterogeneous, and Autonomous Databases. ACM Computing Surveys 22(3), pp. 183–236 (1990).

[25] Tomasic, A., Raschid, L., Valduriez, P.:Scalling Access to Heterogeneous Data Sources with Disco. IEEE Transactions on Knowledge and Data Engineering 10(5), pp. 808–823 (1998).

[26] Vaughan-Nichols, S. J.: Web Services: Beyond the Hype. IEEE Computer 35(2), pp. 18–21 (2002).

[27] Wang, Q.: Cost-Based Object Query Optimization. Ph.D. Thesis, Oregon Graduate Institute of Science and Technology, EUA (2001).

[28] Wiederhold, G.: Mediators in the Architecture of Future Information Systems. IEEE Computer 25(3), pp. 38–49 (1992).

[29] W3C, The World Wide Web Consortium, at http://www.w3c.org .

[30] Zhu, Q., and Larson, P.: Global Query Processing and Optimization in CORDS Multidatabase System. PDCS 1996, pp. 640–646.

[31] Zhu, Q., and Larson, P.: Solving Local Cost Estimation Problem for Global Query Optimization in Multidatabase Systems. Distributed and Parallel Databases 6(4), pp. 373–421 (1998).

[32] Zhu, Q., Sun, Y., and Motheramgari, S.: Developing Cost Models with Qualitative Variables for Dynamic Multidatabase Environments. ICDE 2000, pp. 413–424.

Forming Virtual Marketplaces with Knowledge Networks

Minsoo Lee

Dept of Computer Science and Engineering, Ewha Womans University,
11-1 Daehyun-Dong, Seodaemoon-Ku, Seoul, Korea 120-750
mlee@ewha.ac.kr.

Abstract. The current Web technology is not suitable for representing knowledge nor sharing it among organizations over the Web. There is a rapidly increasing need for exchanging and linking knowledge over the Web, especially when several sellers and buyers come together on the Web to form a virtual marketplace. This paper explains an infrastructure that enables sharing of knowledge over the Web and thus effectively supports the formation of virtual marketplaces on the Web. The concept of an active virtual marketplace can be realized using this infrastructure and such an application has been developed.

1 Introduction

Virtual Marketplaces enable buyers and suppliers of products to meet together in cyberspace and exchange information about products. Buyers look for product items that are wanted while suppliers provide information regarding their available products. The virtual marketplace is becoming increasingly popular on the Web. However, certain limitations still exist in the current technology that make the virtual marketplace a passive meeting place where buyers and suppliers have to perform many manual tasks to find each other or obtain information from each other. We find the necessity of an active virtual marketplace where such operations can be automated and more intelligence could be built into the virtual marketplace.

We have previously developed the concept of Knowledge Networks in order to build an infrastructure that can embed intelligence into the Web [1]. Knowledge Networks can link knowledge over the Web among publishers of knowledge and subscribers of knowledge. By linking knowledge it effectively enables real-time notification to subscribers of knowledge and also processing of knowledge.

Using the Knowledge Network, we have developed an application to demonstrate how an active virtual marketplace can be realized.

The organization of this paper is as follows. Section 2 provides a survey of related work regarding virtual marketplaces and also rule systems and event notification architectures. Section 3 discusses the requirements for an active virtual marketplace. Section 4 explains the knowledge network concept. Section 5 discusses how the knowledge network can be built and deployed. Section 6 describes an active virtual marketplace application developed with the Knowledge Network. Section 7 deals with the implementation of the Knowledge Network. Section 8 gives the summary and conclusion.

R. Meersman et al. (Eds.): CoopIS/DOA/ODBASE 2003, LNCS 2888, pp. 319–335, 2003.
© Springer-Verlag Berlin Heidelberg 2003

2   Related Research

Virtual marketplaces have become very popular with the rise of the Internet. Virtual marketplaces have intermediaries that can reduce the gap between suppliers and consumers of products [2]. These intermediaries are currently in the form of Web sites that bring suppliers and consumers together. There have been large and small virtual marketplaces being formed in several industries such as the food industry, automobile industry, and service professionals in addition to the popular general auction sites. Ford, DaimlerChrysler, and General Motors have developed a business exchange, Ebay is very well-known for its vast number of products available for auction, handshake.com and servicelane.com provide a site for professional services [3].

The benefits of virtual marketplaces are improved process efficiencies, improved supply chain efficiencies, better control over the process, convenience, access to additional suppliers/buyers.

There are several limitations to the current technology that prohibit the virtual marketplace from becoming an active meeting place. Suppliers of products have to actively monitor incoming buyers and try to contact the buyers to see if they have any matching interests to make a deal. On the other hand, buyers have to seek the right supplier that can satisfy its requirements. The suppliers and buyers could be wasting a significant amount of time during this process even though they are concentrating on this single task and not being able to take on any other tasks. Even when they have found each other many tasks can be automated.

We suggest that this process can be automated by inputting the right knowledge from both the supplier and buyer into the virtual marketplace. The knowledge is modeled as events, triggers, and rules and thus we have surveyed a few event and rule systems.

The concept of rules was originally introduced in the research areas of artificial intelligence and expert systems. The rules were soon incorporated into databases to create a new category of databases, namely, active databases [4,5]. Event-Condition-Action (ECA) rules have been used in many of these systems. They are composed of three parts: event, condition, and action. The semantics of an ECA rule is, "When an event occurs, check the condition. If the condition is true, then execute the action". The event provides a finer control as to when to evaluate the condition and gives more active capabilities to the database systems. Rules can automatically perform security and integrity constraint checking, alert people of important situations, enforce business policies and regulations, etc.

WebRules [6] is a framework to use rules to integrate servers on the Internet. The WebRules server has a set of built-in events that can notify remote systems, and has a library of system calls that can be used in a rule to connect Web servers. However, it does not include concepts such as event and rule publishing or event filtering. WebLogic [7] also includes a basic form of rules, which are called actions. These actions need to be provided to the WebLogic server at the time when an application is registering for an event. These actions are actually specified with program codes rather than a high-level specification facility.

Several content-based event notification architectures have been recently proposed to provide an abstraction of the communication infrastructure on the Internet. These architectures focus on providing a scalable architecture for event delivery, as well as a mechanism to selectively subscribe to information. Siena [8] proposes a mechanism to maximize the expressiveness of a language to specify filters and patterns while not degrading the scalability. NeoNet [9] provides a rule-based message routing, queueing and formatting system. Keryx [10] is a language and platform independent infrastructure to distribute events on the Internet and is based on the publish-subscribe model. JMS [11] provides reliable, asynchronous communication between components in a distributed computing environment. CORBA Notification Service [12] uses an event channel concept and extends the Event Service by providing event filtering and quality of service.

3 Requirements for an Active Virtual Marketplace

The currently implemented virtual marketplace configurations have significant limitations in terms of interactions among the participants of the marketplace. We identify the cause of such limitations as being manual operations that burden both the buyers, sellers, and coordinators of the marketplace. The following requirements need to be satisfied in order to make the marketplace more active.

(1) Automatic notification mechanisms need to be provided to alert buyers and sellers regarding new or changed information about their counter parties.

(2) Filtering mechanisms for accepting only the relevant information about their interested products and prices, or other specific purchase conditions need to be supported.

(3) An easy way to specify and establish business logic required by both the buyer and seller needs to be supported within the marketplace.

(4) A flexible way to connect notifications to various business logic pieces needs to be provided to encapsulate the complex transactions that occur between the buyers and sellers.

The active virtual marketplace can be realized by employing the Knowledge Network concept and adapt it to the requirements discussed above.

4 Knowledge Network

The main goal of the knowledge network is to share the knowledge available on the Internet among the users of the Internet. This would promote efficient exchange of knowledge and the development of more organized and interconnected knowledge among individual expertise that is currently isolated from other Web sites and users.

The knowledge network is composed not only of data elements but also knowledge elements which can be used to perform automatic reasoning and decision-making tasks. In this work, knowledge elements are presented by events, triggers, and rules. The events encapsulate timely information of what is happening on the Internet and makes the knowledge network actively responsive without human intervention. The rules express the decision-making factors allowing the intelligence of humans to be embedded into the knowledge network. The triggers model complex relationships among events and rules, checking histories of events and enabling various reasoning or activation sequences to reflect the complex decision making process. The knowledge network has a goal not just of sharing data but also sharing knowledge to make the Internet into a more active, collaborative, and intelligent infrastructure.

The knowledge network can enhance active collaboration of Web servers and users on the Internet by providing a framework to (1) publish data, applications, constraints, events, and rules, (2) register for subscription of events and deliver events to subscribers, (3) define rules on subscribed events.

The framework to accomplish these tasks is based on the idea of providing a component that can be plugged into any standard Web server. This should allow the Web servers that need to collaborate to have a symmetric architecture. Another technology that is needed to support this framework is event, trigger, and rule processing capability being built into the component. This is the major part that should be developed in order to provide any type of intelligent, distributed and collaborative infrastructure. The idea of using user profiles is also adopted to support a wide variety of users on the Internet who wish to have their own individually customized applications.

The architectural framework of the knowledge network shown in Figure 1 is used to explain the key features of the knowledge network: publishing events and rules, event filters, push-based event delivery, knowledge profile, and processing of triggers and rules. In Figure 1, several Web servers are interconnected through the Internet. Each server is extended with several components that form the basis of the knowledge network. Only the extensions to the Web server are shown in the figure for simplicity. We refer to a Web server with these extensions as a knowledge Web server (KWS). Assume that the knowledge Web server A takes the role of a data provider who is user A and knowledge Web servers B and C are maintained by two different users, namely, user B and user C, who need information from the knowledge Web server A. The active users A, B, and C are each residing on the sites for the KWS A, KWS B, and KWS C with a browser interface to the systems and the Internet.

Data providers can provide data and define events and rules, and publish them on web pages. Publishing of events will enable Web surfers to know what kind of data can be delivered to them in a timely manner. Interested Web surfers can register for the events and become subscribers of the event. Rules published by data providers can perform several operations on the knowledge Web server of the data provider. Subscribers of events can conveniently select these rules that will be executed remotely on the data provider's knowledge Web server when the subscribed event occurs. Figure 1 shows that the knowledge Web server A has published two events E1 and E2, and two rules R1 and R2. User B has subscribed to event E1 and linked it to rule R1, while user C has subscribed to event E2 and linked it to rule R2.

Event filter templates are provided by data providers to allow event subscribers to more precisely specify the subset of the event occurrences in which they are interested. The subscribers can give various conditions on the values that the event carries. Only those event instances that satisfy the condition will be delivered to the subscriber. By using event filters, only meaningful data will be provided to the subscribers. Thus, network traffic can be significantly reduced. Figure 1 shows that the event filter F1 is installed on event E1 by user B, while the event filter F2 is installed on event E2 by the user C.

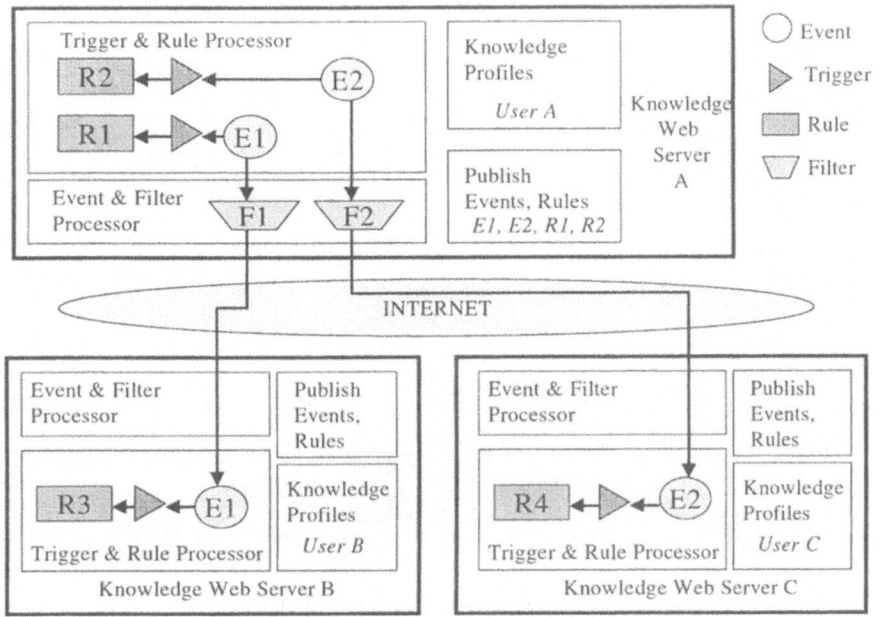

Fig. 1. Architectural framework of the knowledge network.

In a knowledge network, events are delivered via a push-based mechanism to subscribers' knowledge Web servers. When the event occurs, the push mechanism is activated in order to deliver the event to a large number of knowledge Web servers in a timely fashion. This push-based mechanism can radically change the paradigm of how interactions on the Internet are performed. Moreover, the combination of event pushing with the event filtering creates a more powerful communication infrastructure for the knowledge network. Figure 1 shows the extension related to the push-based event delivery combined with the event filtering in each knowledge Web server.

The providers and subscribers of knowledge can specify and store their knowledge (i.e., events, triggers, and rules) in knowledge profiles. Each knowledge Web server is extended with a component that can provide a web-based graphical user interface to the provider or subscriber of knowledge to edit their knowledge profile. The knowledge profile is persistently stored. The events, triggers, and rules stored in the knowledge profile are provided to other run-time components of the knowledge Web server. Figure 1 shows the knowledge profiles existing on different knowledge Web servers.

Triggers and rules are executed within the knowledge Web server when an event linked to it has occurred. Processing the triggers involves checking of complex relationships among event occurrences and also the scheduling of several rules. Rules can activate various operations on the Web server. The execution of a rule may again cause new events to occur, resulting in a chained execution of rules. Figure 1 shows the processing components for triggers and rules residing within each knowledge Web server. Knowledge Web server B will execute rule R3 upon receiving filtered event E1, and knowledge Web server C will execute rule R4 upon receiving filtered event E2.

324   M. Lee

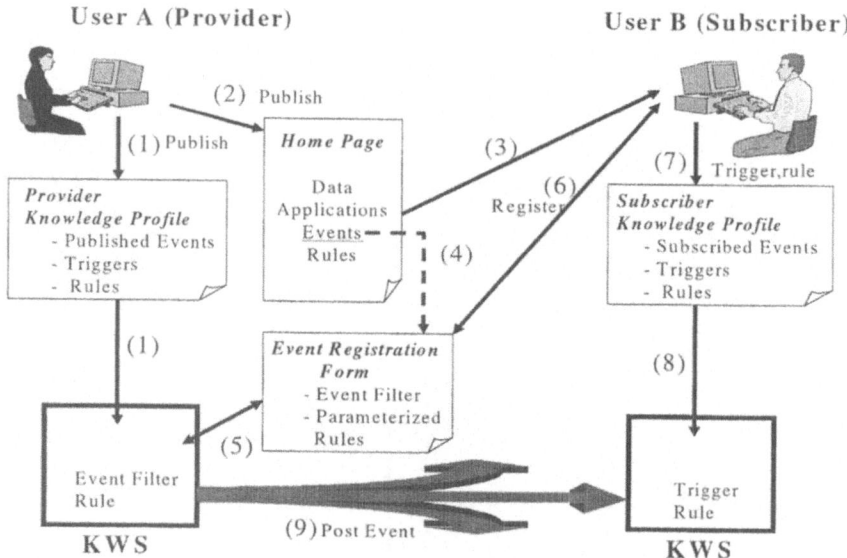

Fig. 2. Steps for constructing the knowledge network.

5   Building and Deploying the Knowledge Network

The knowledge network is constructed through a process involving a series of steps that need to be followed by the providers and subscribers participating in the knowledge network. This section explains each of the steps in the order they occur.

Figure 2 shows an example for a single provider and single subscriber participating in the construction of the knowledge network. This simplified view of the construction process is used as the example to be explained throughout this section.

5.1   Publishing Data, Applications, Events, and Rules

Currently, a user (or organization), say A, that has data and applications (i.e., methods that may be connected to a database in his/her home directory) can publish this data and application on his/her home page. Using the knowledge network concept, user A can also publish the events that can be raised from his/her own data and applications and allow other Web surfers to subscribe to those events. The definition of the events are input into the knowledge profile to enable the knowledge Web server to process the events. All other knowledge elements described in this section are also input into the knowledge profile. User A can easily hookup the event to his/her home page afterwards. An event filtering mechanism may also be provided by user A. Subscribers will later on give some value ranges for the filters during the event registration step (to be explained in Section 5.2), and when the event is being posted, the system checks if the event attribute values satisfy these given value ranges prior to sending out the event to the subscriber. Rules that are applied to user A's data can also be published for use by various applications that require meta-data (e.g., in e-commerce applications.) Several parameterized rules that can be triggered by user A's own events may also be published. The subscriber of user A's event can link the event to the parameterized rules during event registration so that automatic rule processing can be conducted on the provider site (i.e., user A's site) with the guarantee that these operations are authorized and safe for user A's own Web server. This is shown as steps (1) and (2) in Figure 2.

5.2 Event Registration

Another user, say B, is surfing on the web and discovers the homepage of user A and finds an event of interest. User B then accesses the event registration form and registers for an event that user A has published on his/her home page. User B may subscribe to the event to be sent out either as an e-mail notification or a pushed event to his/her knowledge Web server. At the time of registration, user B may also provide values that are to be used later on for filtering out irrelevant events. If some parameterized rules linked to the subscribed event are supported by the event provider, the user B may select some rules to be executed on the event provider's site. An example of such a rule could be changing user B's subscription information (i.e., discontinue subscription of an event after some specified number of postings) automatically after sending the event. The event registration steps are shown as steps (3) to (6) in Figure 2. After user B performs this registration, the event that occurs later on will be filtered and then either be sent out as an e-mail notification or be posted to the knowledge Web server on which the user B has his/her own knowledge profile. The knowledge profile should contain the events that the user B has subscribed to as well as the triggers and rules that are defined for the event. User B can also define additional triggers and rules that are to be processed at his/her own knowledge Web server when an event notification has reached the knowledge Web server. This is further described in the following subsection.

5.3 Trigger and Rule Specification

After subscribing to an event, user B may then access the Knowledge Profile Manager--a module which manages the user's knowledge profile (event subscription, trigger and rule definition information)--of his/her own knowledge Web server and specify the additional triggers and rules that should be executed upon the occurrences of the events he/she has subscribed to. Several events that user B has subscribed to may be linked to a set of rules, forming composite events and structures of rules. In Figure 2, these steps are shown as (7) and (8).

5.4 Event Posting, Filtering, and Rule Execution

Service providers will later generate events that first go through a filtering process to identify the relevant subscribers of the event. Once the subscribers are identified, rules on the provider's site can be executed. These rules are remote executable rules, which are intended to allow remote users to have a limited capability to execute units of code on the provider's site. The event is then posted either as an e-mail message to the subscriber or an event notification to the subscriber's knowledge Web server. If the subscriber has some triggers and rules defined on his/her own knowledge Web server linked to the event, the event will trigger the execution of these rules which may perform some operations within the subscriber's web server and/or generate another event that can be again posted to another site. This is step (9) in Figure 2.

6 Active Virtual Marketplace Implementation

The virtual marketplace is currently one of the most rapidly growing application areas on the Internet. The knowledge network concept can be used to further enhance the virtual marketplace and business-to-business e-commerce by adding active capabilities and intelligence to the Internet.

6.1 The IntelliBiz Company

The IntelliBiz company performs the Business-to-Business e-commerce service by connecting suppliers of products and/or services to buyers who are seeking these products and/or services. They publish a list of suppliers and buyers on their company's home pages categorized by the products and services. A new supplier can go through a supplier registration process and give information about the types of product or service the company provides along with the company contact information. New buyers go through a separate registration process and give information about the product or service for which they are seeking. IntelliBiz provides the services to allow businesses to easily find each other and forms a virtual marketplace of products and services at the business level.

The IntelliBiz company has several types of events to which the suppliers or buyers can subscribe. The description of these events and the supported filters are as follows:

- NewSupplier (String ID, String e-mail, String URL, String product, Range price): This event is posted when a new supplier registers with the IntelliBiz company. The information about the supplier is encapsulated in the event parameters. Buyers can subscribe to this event to obtain the information about the new suppliers. Filters on this event are supported for the product and price attributes.

- NewBuyer (String ID, String e-mail, String URL, String product, Range price): This event is posted when a new buyer registers with the IntelliBiz company. The event parameters encapsulate the buyer information. Suppliers can subscribe to this event to obtain this important information about newly registered buyers in a timely manner. Filters on this event are supported for the product and price attributes.

- RFQ (String ID, String BuyerURL, String product, String quantity, String delivery_date): This event represents an RFQ (Request For Quote) which is generated by a buyer who is looking for a specific product and wants to collect quotes from the suppliers registered with IntelliBiz. This event is originally generated and posted by a buyer to the IntelliBiz company. The IntelliBiz company will then post this event to any of the suppliers who have subscribed to this event through IntelliBiz. Filters on this event are supported for the product attribute.

The IntelliBiz company also has the following parameterized rules (provider-side rule) that the subscribers of the events can make use of while registering for the subscription of the event.

- NotifyBuyer(String SupplierID, String SupplierE-mail, String SupplierURL) : This rule will send an e-mail notification to a new buyer to introduce a new supplier. A supplier can select this rule to be installed when the supplier subscribes to the NewBuyer event. The parameter within this rule is the buyer's e-mail address to be used to send the e-mail notification. This rule is later invoked when a new buyer comes in and performs the registration task which posts the NewBuyer event.
- NotifySupplier(String BuyerID, String BuyerE-mail, String BuyerURL) : This rule does exactly the same thing as the NotifyBuyer rule except that the buyer and the supplier roles are reversed. This rule will send an e-mail notification to a new supplier to introduce a buyer. A buyer can select this rule to be installed when the buyer subscribes to the NewSupplier event. This rule is later invoked when a new supplier comes in and performs the registration task which posts the NewSupplier event.

The home page and the registration forms for the buyers and suppliers are shown in Figure 3. The event registration forms for the NewBuyer event and NewSupplier event are also shown.

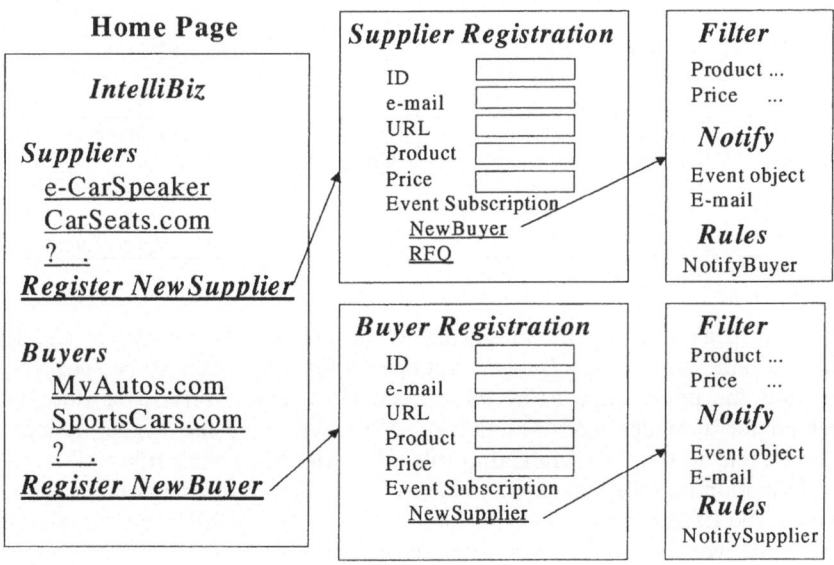

Fig. 3. The IntelliBiz home page and registration forms.

6.2 The Suppliers and Buyers

In our scenario, we assume that there are two suppliers, two buyers and the IntelliBiz company. All of these companies have their own web sites.

The suppliers are as follows:

- e-CarSpeakers : This Internet company specializes in selling audio speakers for cars.
- CarSeats.com : This company sells car seats over the Internet.
  The buyers are as follows:
- MyAutos.com : This company is a new manufacturer of economic class family sedans.
- SportsCars.com : This company is a sports car manufacturer.

The subscribed events and filters along with the triggers and rules that are defined for each of the suppliers are as follows:

Table 1. Subscription information of supplier e-CarSpeakers.

IntelliBiz Site (Publisher)			e-CarSpeakers Site (Subscriber)	
Subscribed Event	Event Filter	Provider Rule	Trigger [Event](Rule)	Rule
NewBuyer	(Product= Speaker) AND (Price. morethan (300))	Notify Buyer	[NewBuyer] (AlertMarketing)	AlertMarketing C: true; A: Store in DB; Alert Marketing dept.;
RFQ (also exist on other sites)	(Product= Speaker) AND (Quantity > 20)		[RFQ] (GenQuote)	GenQuote C: true A:GenerateQuote; Post QuoteEvent;

The e-CarSpeakers company subscribes to the two events NewBuyer and RFQ. The filter installed for the NewBuyer event checks for the product to be speakers and also restricts the price range to be more than $300. The NotifyBuyer rule is also selected on the provider side. On the e-CarSpeakers site, the trigger relates the NewBuyer event to the AlertMarketing rule. The AlertMarketing rule will store the buyer information into the database and also alert the marketing department about the new buyer. The RFQ event is not only subscribed on the IntelliBiz site but also from other potential web sites that can post the event to the e-CarSpeakers company. The company filters out all but the product being speakers and having a quantity constraint of more than 20 speakers. The RFQ event is tied to the GenQuote rule on the e-CarSpeakers web site. The GenQuote rule will generate the quote accordingly and

Table 2. Subscription information of supplier CarSeats.com.

IntelliBiz Site (Publisher)			CarSeats.com Site (Subscriber)	
Subscribed Event	Event Filter	Provider Rule	Trigger [Event](Rule)	Rule
NewBuyer	(Product= Seats) AND (Price. lessthan (300))	Notify Buyer		
RFQ (also exist on other sites)	(Product= Seats) AND (Quantity > 100)		[RFQ] (GenQuote)	GenQuote C: true A: Generate Quote; Post QuoteEvent;

post the QuoteEvent to whoever generated the RFQ event. The GenQuote rule will extract the buyer's URL from the RFQ event and use it to post the QuoteEvent back to the buyer. Explanations of the CarSeats.com events, triggers, and rules are similar to the e-CarSpeakers web site except that, for the NewBuyer event, it does not perform any operation on its web site. Using the knowledge network, the suppliers can effectively contact those buyers of interest with the events and filtering concepts and further initiate local operations such as alerting people and invoking applications within their companies via rules.

Table 3. Subscription information of buyer MyAutos.com.

IntelliBiz Site / any Site (Publisher)			MyAutos.com Site (Subscriber)	
Subscribed Event	Event Filter	Provider Rule	Trigger [Event](Rule)	Rule
New Supplier (IntelliBiz site)	(Product= Speaker) AND (Price. lessthan(500))	Notify Supplier	[NewSupplier] (EvalSupplier)	EvalSupplier C: Credibility = good; A: Save in DB; Post RFQ to Supplier;
Quote Event (any site)			[QuoteEvent] (ProcessQuote)	ProcessQuote C: [Count>10] Quote=best A: Post AcceptQuote;

The subscribed events and filters along with the triggers and rules that are defined for each of the buyers are as follows. The MyAutos.com company subscribes to the two events NewSupplier and QuoteEvent. The QuoteEvent can come from any website participating in a quote submission. When the NewSupplier event is posted, the MyAutos.com has put a filter that checks if the product is a speaker and also if the price is less than $500. If an event satisfying this filter is posted, the provider side rule NotifySupplier is invoked and then the event is delivered to the MyAutos.com web site. The MyAutos.com company is very cautious about posting its RFQs and only wants to post it individually to the suppliers that have good credit rather than posting its RFQ through the IntelliBiz web site and receiving many quotes from relatively small companies. Therefore, the NewSupplier event is linked to the EvalSupplier rule, which performs a credit check and then proceeds to send out an RFQ individually to the supplier. The capability of defining rules on each of the local web sites allows personal information or policies to be kept secure and undisclosed. The QuoteEvent is an event that is posted in response to the RFQ encapsulating a quote that is generated by a supplier. The QuoteEvent is linked to the ProcessQuote rule through a trigger. The ProcessQuote rule will check the number of quotes and see if it is the best quote received. If it is the best quote, then the quote accepting process is initiated.

Table 4. Subscription information of buyer SportsCars.com.

IntelliBiz Site / any Site (Publisher)			SportsCars.com Site (Subscriber)	
Subscribed Event	Event Filter	Provider Rule	Trigger [TriggerEvent] (EventHistory) <Rule>	Rule
New Supplier (IntelliBiz site)	(Product=Seats) AND (Price. lessthan(300))	Notify Supplier		
Quote Event (any site)			[QuoteEvent] (QE1 AND QE2) <ProcessQuote>	ProcessQuote C: true; A: Compare with QE1 and QE2;
			[QuoteEvent] ( ) <SaveRule>	SaveRule C: true; A: Save in DB;

The SportsCars.com web site has similar events, triggers and rules except that for the QuoteEvent it has two triggers. The first trigger also includes an event history expression - denoted as EH - and checks if two important quotes QE1 and QE2 have arrived. If they both have arrived, the quote comparison can be done by the ProcessQuote rule. Otherwise the quote is just saved in the database via the SaveRule.

6.3 The Big Picture

An overall diagram, which puts all of these knowledge elements together, is shown in Figure 4. The links in the figure show how the events are posted and the triggers and rules are executed on each of the supplier and buyer sites. The filters (which were described in detail in the previous section) are not shown in order to simplify the diagram. The figure shows how the IntelliBiz web site links the buyers and the suppliers through the knowledge network.

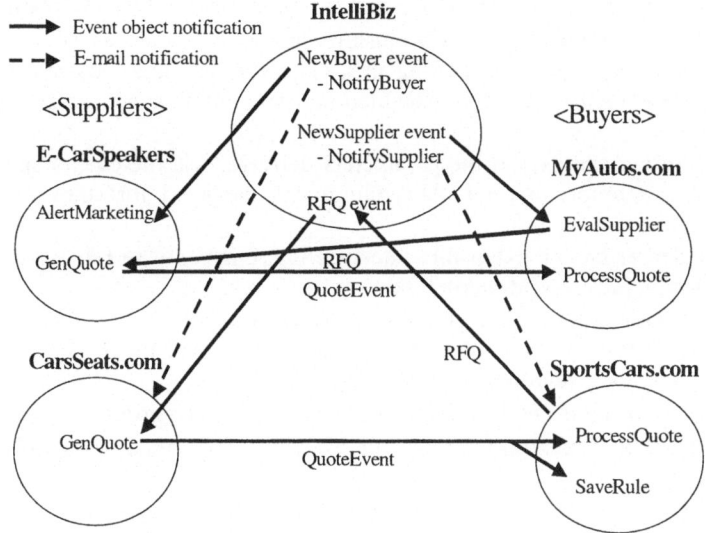

Fig. 4. The Business-to-Business e-commerce scenario.

As shown in the above scenario, the knowledge network provides an ideal infrastructure for collaboration and for adding knowledge into the web to make it more intelligent and applicable to the emerging areas of Internet applications such as virtual marketplaces and e-commerce applications.

7   Knowledge Network Modules

The Event Server, ETR Server, Knowledge Profile Manager components, which compose the knowledge Web Server were developed using Java (JDK 1.4). Applet, servlet and RMI technology were used to implement the components. The popular

Apache Web Server and Tomcat servlet engine were used as the basic existing infrastructure, which we extended with our newly developed components.

The core component is the ETR Server, which can process events, triggers and rules. The following subsections describe the implementation of the ETR Server, Event Server and Knowledge Profile Manager in detail.

7.1 ETR Server

The ETR Server has many key features that are not supported by other rule systems. They are:

- The ETR Server is developed in Java and is thus deployable on any platform.
- Processing of complex event relationships and rule sequences is possible. This includes checking events happening in a certain order, the occurrence of all (or any) of the events. Rules can be executed in a sequential, synchronized, or parallel fashion.
- The ETR Server can extract the parameters delivered via the events and distribute them to the appropriate rules. This eliminates the need for rules to be tightly coupled with event types.
- The ETR Server has an extensible interface that enables it to receive events from various communication infrastructures.
- The ETR Server supports run-time modifications of rules; i.e., rule instances in the previously defined form can be running while instances of the newly modified rule can be created and executed.
- Rules are grouped and can be activated or deactivated as a group.
- Events posted in synchronous mode or asynchronous mode is supported by the ETR Server.
- The ETR Server can process various built-in rule variable types that are useful for different applications. There are temporary type, persistent type, and existing type rule variables. Temporary type is a local variable of a rule. The persistent type will persist the value of the variable. The existing type references external servers modeled as objects. This makes the rules more powerful as they can act as the "glue" to several distributed systems.

Figure 5 illustrates the architecture of the ETR Server. The Java class name of the modules are shown. The classes on the left show the interfaces currently supported for the communication infrastructure. RMI, Orbix, and Vitria's Communicator are currently supported. The RuleObjectManager is the entry point to the core ETR Server classes. There exist two hash tables: event hash table and the trigger hash table to store the mappings to/from triggering events and triggers. Each trigger element in the trigger hash table also contains a complex structure called TriggerStruct, which contains the event history and rule sequence information. The event history is processed by the Event History Processor. TriggerStruct data structure stores information about predecessors and successors of each rule specified in the trigger. Scalability issues can be solved by the RuleScheduler which uses this data structure to schedule the multiple rules via threads. The RGCoordinator manages the rule group information.

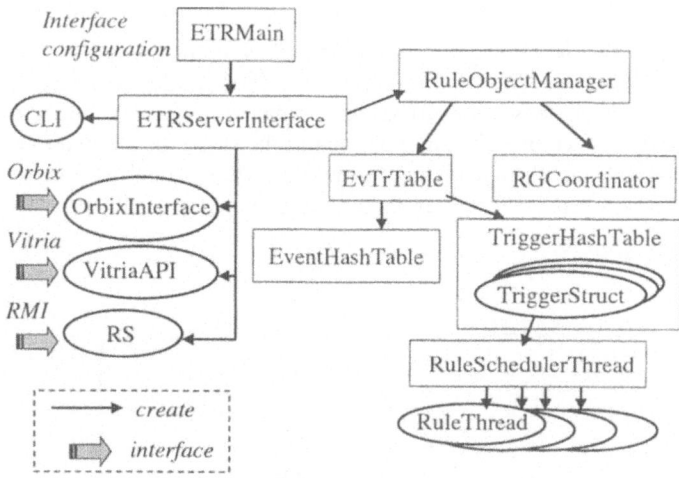

Fig. 5. Architecture of the ETR Server

7.2 Event Server

The Event Server consists of the following 4 key modules :
- A module to receive events : This module is implemented as a servlet or RMI server to receive events through HTTP or RMI. It then forwards the event to the ETR server through RMI.
- A module to deliver events : This module accepts requests to send events over the Internet through HTTP or RMI. Once a generated event goes through the event filtering module and identifies the appropriate subscribers, the delivering module will post the event to the destination.
- A module to filter events : This module keeps the event subscription information along with the event filters that have been defined. The event filters are kept in three kinds of data structures : inverted index, modified 2-3 tree, Range Table. This information is persistently stored.
- A module to process event registration : This module automatically generates event subscription forms that are shown to event subscribers during the event registration time. Events and their filters are stored in XML format and are processed with XSL to create the HTML forms. This module is implemented as a servlet.

Scalability of filtering are achieved by the efficient filtering data structures while the delivery mechanism can be improved by using an event multicasting scheme.

The above four key modules cooperatively form the basis of the communication infrastructure of the knowledge network.

7.3 Knowledge Profile Manager

The Knowledge Profile Manager is implemented as an applet, servlet and RMI server combination. The front end of the Knowledge Profile Manager is developed as an applet. The applet enables users to access menus for defining and viewing events, triggers, and rules. Two different menus such as the Provider menu and the Subscriber menu are available as shown in the following figure. The backend is formed as a servlet and talks to an RMI server that is used to persistently store the knowledge information.

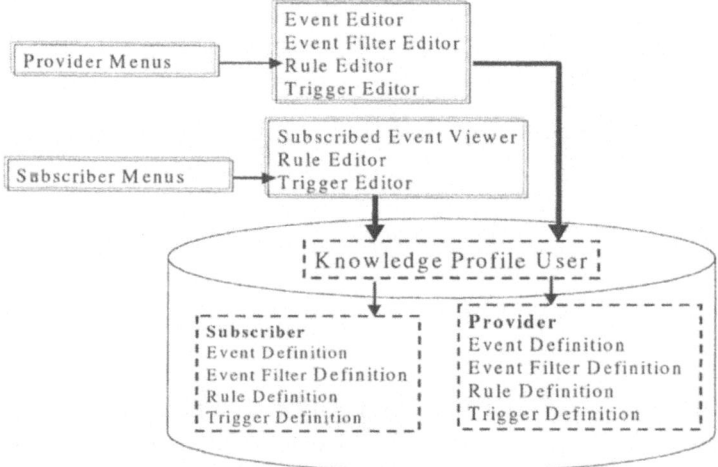

Fig. 6. The Knowledge Profile Manager GUI menus and storage

8 Conclusion

In this paper, we have discussed the concept and an implementation of an active virtual marketplace. The active virtual marketplace can be realized by adapting the knowledge network infrastructure. The knowledge network extends the existing Internet-Web infrastructure by adding event and rule services as a part of the information infrastructure. Events, rules, and triggers, which relate events to the evaluation of event history and the activation of rules, can be used to capture human and enterprise knowledge in the Internet, making the Internet an active knowledge network instead of a passive data network. The event, event filter, event history, and rule processing capabilities of the knowledge network offer very powerful and useful services to enable the timely delivery of relevant data and the activation of operations that are necessary for the realization of an active virtual marketplace application.

A few future research issues are identified as follows. First, security issues need to be further investigated due to the executable characteristics of rules on the provider (i.e., virtual marketplace coordinator) site. Rules can have potentially damaging effects if the proper authorization and security issues are not clearly specified. This is especially important when financial hazards could occur for virtual marketplaces.

Second, an event ontology is required to effectively make the infrastructure more scalable for a global marketplace. The event definitions may be controllable within a limited size group of nodes. However, when the target platform becomes the whole Internet, ontology issues need to be resolved. One way to practically solve this problem would be to provide an ontology server for specific business domains rather than supporting the entire business domain. Third, interconnecting rules in this way could have a potential to contradict each other or have infinitely looping effects among the buyers and sellers or coordinators in the virtual marketplace. Therefore, a validation mechanism for global rule chaining could be devised by adding distributed deadlock monitors into the infrastructure. Fourth, an enhancement on scalability is needed. Current scalability features are built into the rule scheduling and event filtering mechanisms. However, event notifications can also be very time-consuming. Therefore, rather than using point-to-point delivery as in our prototype, hierarchical broadcasting or multicasting techniques for event delivery need to be investigated.

References

1. M. Lee, S.Y.W. Su, and H. Lam. Event and Rule Services for Achieving a Web-based Knowledge Network. Technical Report, UF CISE TR00-002, University of Florida (2000).
2. Beat F. Schmid and Dorian Selz. Requirements for electronic markets architecture. *EM –* Electronic *Markets*, 7(1), 1997.
3. Lawrence J. Magid, Wednesday, March 22, 2000 Los Angeles Times, March 22, 2000, http://www.larrysworld.com/articles/sb_b2bvirtual.htm
4. U. Dayal, B.T. Blaustein, A.P. Buchmann, et al. The HiPAC Project: Combining Active Databases and Timing Constraints. In ACM SIGMOD Record, Vol. 17(1), March (1988) 51–70.
5. J. Widom, (ed.). Active Database Systems: Triggers and Rules for Advanced Database Processing. Morgan Kaufmann, San Francisco, California (1996).
6. I. Ben-Shaul and S. Ifergan. WebRule: An Event-based Framework for Active Collaboration among Web Servers. In Computer Networks and ISDN Systems, Vol. 29(8-13), October (1997) 1029–1040.
7. BEA, WebLogic Events, http://www4.weblogic.com/docs/techoverview/ em.html
8   A. Carzaniga, D.S. Rosenblum, and A.L. Wolf. Achieving Expressiveness and Scalability in an Internet-Scale Event Notification Service. In Proc. of the 19th ACM Symposium on Principles of Distributed Computing (PODC2000), Portland, OR, July (2000) 219–227.
9.   NEONet, http://www.neonsoft.com/products/NEONet.html
10. S. Brandt and A. Kristensen. Web Push as an Internet Notification Service. W3C Workshop on Push Technology. http://keryxsoft.hpl.hp.com/doc/ins.html, Boston, MA, September (1997).
11. Sun Microsystems. Java Message Service API, http://java.sun.com/products/jms/, January 22 (2001).
12. Object Management Group (OMG), CORBA Notification Service, specification version 1.0. June 20 (2000).

Providing a Progressive Access to Awareness Information

Manuele Kirsch Pinheiro[1], Marlène Villanova-Oliver[1], Jérôme Gensel[1],
José Valdeni de Lima[2], and Hervé Martin[1]

[1] Laboratoire LSR – IMAG
BP 72 – 38402 Saint Martin d'Hères Cedex, France
{Manuele.Kirsch-Pinheiro, Marlene.Villanova, Jerome.Gensel,
Herve.Martin }@imag.fr
[2] Instituto de Informática – UFRGS
CP 15064 – Av. Bento Gonçalves 9500, Campus do Vale, Bl. IV – Porto Alegre, Brazil
valdeni@inf.ufrgs.br

Abstract. Awareness has now become a widely accepted central feature in groupware systems. In this context, providing an awareness support consists in delivering to users involved in a collaborative task, information concerning their group, other users, their past, present or future roles or activities, etc. However, one of the potential underlying risks of such a support is to produce too much information. As a matter of fact, this amount of information may reveal itself cumbersome, leading to a cognitive overload for users which slows down the global activity of the group. In this paper, we propose to address this issue by stratifying the awareness information space into different levels of details. Such stratifications give users a progressive access to information: first, they can access to the most relevant information linked to their current activity and profile, and then, they can gradually access to the rest of awareness information. The proposed architecture relies on a generic Data Model for Awareness Information (DMAI) and on a Progressive Access Model (PAM), we have previously designed in the context of Web-based Information Systems. We show, on an example, how the coupling between the DMAI and the PAM allows groupware systems designers to describe a progressive access to awareness information. The defined stratifications can also be used as filters which save a given user, involved in a given role and performing a given activity, from useless, irrelevant or forbidden information.

Keywords: Awareness, groupware systems, progressive access, adaptability.

1 Introduction

When working cooperatively, users share a context of work in which their activities are "immersed". In fact, according to Schmidt [14], cooperating actors, even while doing their individual tasks, take heed of the context of their joint effort. Still according to this author, they try to align and integrate their activities with those of their colleagues without interrupting each other. This context, in Computer Supported Cooperative Work (CSCW) research area, refers to the notion of *awareness*. Awareness, according to Dourish [6], is "an understanding of the activities of others, which provides a context for your own activity. This context is used to ensure that

R. Meersman et al. (Eds.): CoopIS/DOA/ODBASE 2003, LNCS 2888, pp. 336–353, 2003.
© Springer-Verlag Berlin Heidelberg 2003

individual contributions are relevant to the group's activity as a whole and to evaluate individual actions with respect to the group goals and progress".

Awareness support appears to be a central feature in the design of collaborative work systems, since being aware of the other contributors and of their activities makes the work more natural and fluid [8]. This support intents to help the group to reach its goals and to increase the whole quality and efficiency of the collaborative work by providing a better understanding of the work context. By improving each individual contribution, awareness support also enhances the whole group contribution.

In groupware systems, users are implicitly or explicitly assigned a set of roles. Each role describes a set of activities and defines a group of users who are given rights to perform this set of activities. The efficiency of an awareness support depends also on its ability to deliver to users only the relevant information for the role they fulfill at a given moment. Nevertheless, even when information is targeted for a role, awareness support mechanisms often produce and manage large amounts of information, which may appear to be cumbersome in the achievement of the tasks.

In this paper, we propose to organize the information delivered by the awareness support into different levels of detail, in order to limit the amount of information presented. As a consequence, we expect to prevent groupware users from suffering from an information overload. The idea is to offer users a progressive access to information, by supplying them first, the most relevant information and by allowing them to access gradually to more information if needed.

This paper is organized as follows. In section 2, we advocate for the needs of a gradual delivery of awareness information in order to limit the risk of information overload, and present in section 3 an application scenario. Then, we present in section 4 a Progressive Access Model, called PAM, which enables to stratify any information space into different levels of detail [18]. In section 5, we show how to apply the PAM to a Data Model for Awareness Information, called DMAI, which describes users, roles and activities of a groupware system. In section 6, we illustrate our approach by applying the PAM to the application scenario introduced in section 3. Some related work are presented in section 7 before we conclude.

2   Towards Adaptability in Awareness

Awareness refers to an understanding of the group and its activities, which provides a context for individual activities [6]. The context of an action is what allows people to identify the meaning of this action [5]. Generally speaking, the term 'awareness' refers to actors taking heed of the context of their joint effort. In CSCW context, 'awareness' refers to actors who are or become aware of something, align and integrate their activities with the activities of others [14]. However, there is no single definition for awareness, and the term is used in very different situations [10]. In this paper, we decide to adopt the definition given by Dourish [6] and presented above in the introduction.

Awareness is widely accepted as a central feature in groupware systems. It deals with the delivery of information (about groups, users, activities, etc.) to each user involved in a collaborative task. However, when this information is not well-adapted to each particular individual needs, it turns out to be disturbing and prejudicial to each user's contributions, and as a consequence, to the group's ones.

When information is not appropriate, users are confronted to a cognitive overload due to a too massive and difficult to understand quantity of information [17]. Such a cognitive overload, even when it concerns just a few group's members, may have a negative impact on the whole group's work by penalizing other members in their work. In order to protect the group from these drawbacks, some adaptability in awareness support is required. Indeed, the execution of some activities can be disturbed, and the exchange of information about these activities can be slowed down.

Work dealing with adaptability in groupware systems mainly focus on the tailorability of the *functionalities* of the system. Tailorability refers to some extensions added to an application during its use in order to cover requirements that where not present in the original design [7][16]. In this paper, we propose to address the adaptation of the *information* delivered by the awareness support. Here, adaptability refers to the capacity the awareness support has to provide each user with awareness information which is useful and essential for her/him and the specific tasks she/he performs.

Obviously, collaborators do not need all the same information, neither do they need all the available information all the time [17]. Thus, one has to determine what information users actually need, when and how it should be delivered to them. Also, the relative importance of the information has to be determined, and exploited to choose a proper notification method [10].

When working cooperatively, users play, implicitly or explicitly, roles inside the group. Since each role encompasses a specific set of activities, all roles do not require the same information to be fulfilled. The content of awareness information delivered to a user has to be closely related to the role she/he plays. For instance, a user playing an author role in a cooperative authoring environment needs some information different from the one required by the team coordinator. Obviously, an author needs information related to the part of the document she/he writes, whilst a coordinator should be informed about the overall work progress. The former is interested in the text adjunctions or modifications made by other authors. The later needs a global view of the group activities, the defined tasks and deadlines, to take her/his decisions and guide the team efforts. Many research works (such as [4]) have emphasized the fact that coordinators need well-suited awareness information for this role to be better played.

Therefore, it is necessary to limit the awareness information presented to a user to the set of information which is relevant to the role she/he plays. Also, users whose role grants no right on a shared object in the workspace should not be notified about the operations that concern this object. Nevertheless, to limit the information to present to the user only considering what is relevant for her/his role may be not satisfactory for this user. It is important to consider that users, even when working cooperatively, have their own interests and personal goals, which affect their work inside the team. According to Schmidt [14], cooperative workers, in their "natural attitude", are not ignorant or disinterested spectators, they are engaged in and with the world in which they cooperate. As such, they have interests, things to do, things to achieve. Thus, we believe that personal interests of the users should be considered when selecting awareness information, and that groupware applications should identify the user's characteristics and interests. As Liechti [10] affirms, in some cases it is preferable to identify who is the user and what are the artifacts that are "interesting" for the user. When this is done, only a subset of the available information can be identified as critical and notified to the user.

However, even when reducing awareness information to the one related to user's interests and roles, the amount of available information may still be large. In this case, presenting the whole flow of information to the user decreases the time and attention she/he can spend on her/his work and finally submerges her/him.

Further, we strongly believe that the member's ability to assimilate information can be improved if the cognitive load is better controlled. One way of achieving this is to present to a user the most important information first and to offer her/him the possibility to progressively access information of lesser importance if needed.

Therefore, one can imagine that, ideally, a system should prioritize the information which is relevant to the role played by the user. Most of the time, this task is performed by the designer of the collaborative system or by the coordinator who assigns the roles to the different members. One can also imagine that an authorized user could be able to assign by herself/himself some priorities to information she/he wants to receive. In each case, one needs to describe the way information is structured in different levels of priority. In order to achieve such a structuration of information, we propose to apply and adapt to awareness in collaborative work the notion of *progressive access* [18] we have previously introduced in the field of Web-based Information Systems. We show in the example scenario described in the next section how this notion of progressive access can be relevant in the field of CSCW.

3   Application Scenario

Groupware systems, particularly web-based ones, have many similarities with Web-based Information Systems (WIS), which have inspired the proposition of the Progressive Access Model (cf. section 4). One of these similarities is the risk of cognitive overload, as discussed by Villanova-Oliver [18]. Based on these similarities, we think that coupling the notion of progressive access to the awareness support inside groupware systems can bring many advantages to these systems. The example below demonstrates some of these benefits.

Let us consider a web-based groupware system, for instance, a shared workspace, such as BSCW [2]. Such systems have often shared repositories, some awareness support, usually provided by subscription/notification methods, and some communication tools. In this example, we consider that this groupware offers such functions, and relies on a meeting tool (such as a Microsoft© NetMeeting) for communication purpose. Then, one can imagine that if a team member has missed the last group meeting, the awareness support may inform her/him about this meeting. The system may keep track of a lot of information about a meeting, but we consider that the system keeps only the following ones: the meeting goals, the decisions that have been taken, the discussions that have been raised (the chat register, for instance), and a multimedia resource associate to it, such as a video of the meeting or a slide presentation made during the meeting.

However, if the system presents to this user all the available information about the last meeting, together with all other events produced in the shared workspace, this team member may feel herself/himself overloaded by all this information, and she/he may miss some important one. For instance, she/he may not pay attention to the meeting decisions, which can seriously influence the group work. Then, how can the system prevent such an overload? One may suggest that the system could automatically resume the meeting content. Unfortunately, this solution usually involves complex algorithms to be integrated in the groupware. An alternative is to separate the information in levels of details, in order to present the most important one first. Thus, the meeting information can be divided into three levels: first, the user receives only the meeting goals and decisions. Only if user requests more information, she/he receives the discussions (second level), and at last, the multimedia resource associated (third level). This division will reduce the amount of information presented to the user and improve the assimilation of the most important information.

Let us carry on with this scenario, considering that the groupware has its own adaptation proxy, which is able to adapt web-oriented content to mobile devices. If the system stratifies the meeting information in levels of detail, the proxy will not be obliged to adapt all meeting content to such devices. If user does not request the third level, for instance, the proxy will not adapt the multimedia resource.

Thus, in order to organize the awareness information into these levels, we propose to adapt to awareness support the notion of progressive access. In the next section, we introduce this notion and a model that implements it, before showing how this Progressive Access Model can be exploited to adapt awareness information.

4   Progressive Access: Notions and Model

The central idea behind the notion of *progressive access* is that the user of an information system does *not* need to access *all* the information *all* the time. The goal is to make the system able to deliver *progressively* a personalized information to its users: first, information considered as essential for them is provided, and then, some complementary information, if needed, is available.

4.1 Notions Related to the Progressive Access

The notion of progressive access is related to the one of *Maskable Entity*. A *Maskable Entity (ME)* is a set of at least two elements (*i.e.* $|ME| \geq 2$) upon which a progressive access can be set up. The progressive access to a ME relies on the definition of *Representations of Maskable Entity (RoME)* for this ME. These RoME are subsets of the ME ordered by the set inclusion relation. Two kinds of RoME, *extensional* or *intensional*, are distinguished. *Extensional RoME* are built from the *extension* (*i.e.* the set of elements) of the ME. In the case where the ME is a set of structured data having the same type, *intensional RoME* can be built from the *intension* of the ME. The intension of a structured ME is here defined as the set of descriptions of variables (or slots, or fields) which constitute the structure of the ME. Whatever its nature – extensional or intensional –, each RoME of a ME is associated with a level of detail (or relevance, or priority, etc.). $RoME_i$ is defined as the RoME of a ME corresponding to the level of detail i, where $1 \leq i \leq max$, and *max* is the greatest level of detail available for this ME.

The Fig. 1 shows a ME with three associated RoME. Some rules impose that a $RoME_{i+1}$ – whether it is extensional or intensional – associated with the level of detail *i+1* (1≤i≤max-1) contains at least one more element than RoME$_i$. This way, extensional RoME can be seen as different ordered *masks* on the extension of a ME, while intensional RoME can be seen as different ordered *masks* on the intension of a ME.

A stratification for a ME is a sequence of RoME ordered by set inclusion as illustrated in the right part of the Fig. 1. Please note that several stratifications can be defined for a given ME.

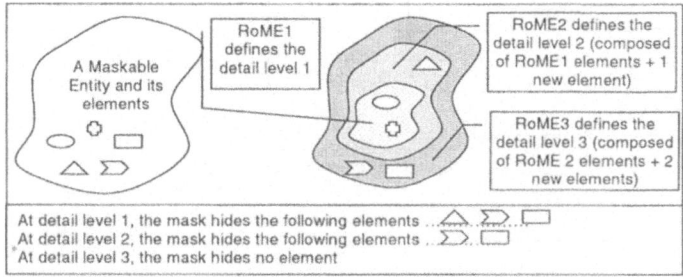

Fig. 1. A Maskable Entity with three RoME corresponding to three levels of detail.

The progressive access relies on two functions which allow to switch from a RoME to another within a given stratification:

–   from a RoME$_i$, at level of detail *i*, the *masking function* gives access to the RoME$_{i-1}$ at level of detail i-1:

$$masking(RoME_i)=RoME_{i-1}, \text{ where } 2≤i≤max.$$

–   from a RoME$_i$, at level of detail *i*, the *unmasking* function gives access to the RoME$_{i+1}$ at level of detail i+1:

$$unmasking(RoME_i)=RoME_{i+1}, \text{ where } 1≤i≤max-1.$$

4.2 The Progressive Access Model

The Progressive Access Model (PAM) is defined as a generic UML class diagram (see Fig. 2) which allows the description of well-formed stratifications for maskable entities.

Each notion presented in section 4.1 is implemented by a stereotyped class. An instance of the class "*Maskable Entity*" is, at least, composed of two instances of the class "*Element of Maskable Entity*". An instance of the class "*Stratification*" is represented as an aggregation of, at least, two *ordered* instances of the class "*Representation of Maskable Entity*". An instance of this class is linked by the association *adds* to one or more instance(s) of the class "*Element of Maskable Entity*" which are the elements of the ME added by the RoME$_i$ at the level of detail *i*. The dependency relation ({*subset*}) ensures that the added elements belong to the set of elements corresponding to the ME.

An important characteristic of the PAM is the ternary association called *definition* which links the classes "*Stratification*" (S), "*Maskable Entity*" (ME) and "*User Category*" (U). The class "User Category" is an abstract class which allows the connection with any user model so that each described user can benefit from a personalized progressive access to a given maskable entity.

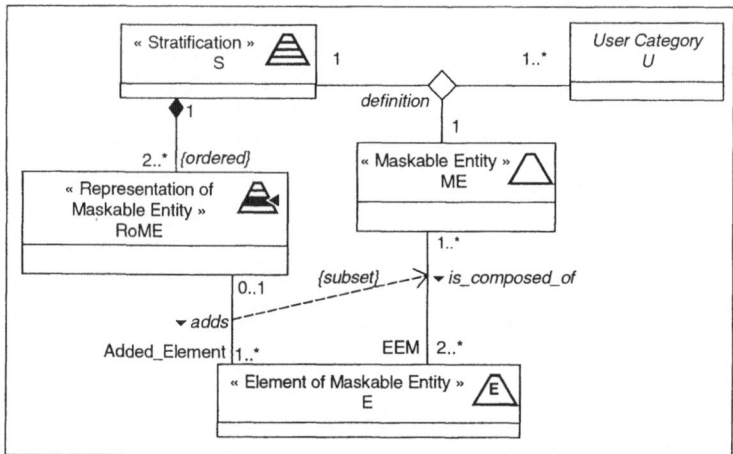

Fig. 2. The Progressive Access Model described using UML stereotypes

It is worth noting that maskable entities can be of several kinds. Basically, every data model (*e.g.* a class diagram) and every constituent (*e.g.* a class, an association...) of this model can be considered as maskable entities and, therefore, can be stratified (see [18] for a description). Also, the progressive access approach can apply to information represented by a non-structured data model, as well as to a semi-structured (XML) or to a structured (object or relational) one. For instance, in [17] the authors have shown how to couple the PAM with an object-based knowledge representation formalism in order to offer a progressive access to the objects of the knowledge base. In the next section, we explain how the PAM described above can be used to offer a progressive access to a data model supporting awareness information in collaborative systems.

5   Progressive Access to Awareness Information

In order to integrate the Progressive Access Model into the awareness support, we first define a data model dedicated to the awareness information. The different ways of stratifying this model are presented in section 5.2. Then, a stratification process which combines different kinds of stratifications is presented in section 5.3.

5.1 A Data Model for Awareness Information

The PAM presented in section 4 generally applies to a data model which describes the application domain. Using the PAM, stratifications can be defined for each user or group of users. These stratifications give them a progressive access to the information contained in the data model. Since our objective is to provide a progressive access to awareness information, we propose here a simplified data model, called Data Model for Awareness Information (DMAI), which describes the concepts related to awareness information and the relations between these concepts. Although this model is quite simple, we think it is sufficient enough for introducing our approach. It describes the basic concepts linked to the awareness definition given by Dourish [6], and it can be used or extended in order to be exploited by a groupware system. The different components of the DMAI (groups, roles, users, activities, and profiles) are represented in the UML description we give in Fig. 3.

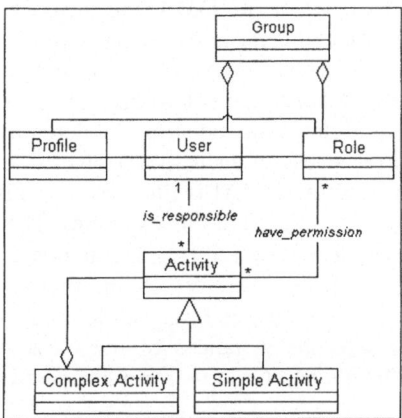

Fig. 3. Data Model for Awareness Information

As stated before, awareness information must help in understanding the group and the activities performed by its members. Then, we claim that the awareness information should be represented as the information about *groups, users, roles* and *activities*. A group is defined by a set of users and a set of roles. Users who are authorized to perform this set of roles are members of the group. A user can belong to one or more group(s) and a role can also be linked to one or more group(s). A user can fulfill one or more role(s). A role is possibly fulfilled by several users and defines the rights and responsibilities concerning a set of activities. An activity is an elementary task a user can perform when fulfilling a given role. Several users can perform the same activity, but only one of them is responsible for this activity. The activities can range from simple tasks to more complex ones which are composed of others tasks.

Another important characteristic when dealing with awareness information is the representation of both users and roles characteristics (cf. section 2). These features are represented through the notion of *profile*. A profile can be associated either with a user or with a role. In the former case, a profile represents the user's interest in terms of needs and preferences. In the later, a profile describes the requirements to meet in order to fulfill an associated role. A user's profile can be independent from or linked to the role fulfilled by the user. When linked, the profile represents the user's preferences associated to a specific role. Moreover, we consider that each profile gathers a set of activities that are important for the user or role, and also a time interval, which constrains this set of activities to take place during a certain period of time.

5.2 Possible Stratifications for the DMAI

In order to apply the principles of the PAM to the DMAI, one has to identify the possible Maskable Entities to be stratified. Three kinds of stratification are possible:

1. **Extensional stratification of the DMAI**. In this case, the DMAI as a whole is seen as a ME whose set of elements is the set of classes, associations and classes-associations which constitutes the DMAI. Then, an extensional stratification of the DMAI can be performed. It consists in defining subsets of the DMAI components (classes, associations and/or classes-associations) ordered by the set inclusion subsets, providing so a progressive access to each subset of this sequence. For instance, one extensional stratification S of the DMAI is illustrated by Fig. 4 (please note that only the components 'class' are considered in this example). The stratification is defined as S = {{User, Role}, {User, Role, Activity}}. S contains 2 RoME: $RoME_1$ = {User, Role}, and $RoME_2$ = {User, Role, Activity}. At the first level of detail, $RoME_1$ gives access to all the instances of the classes User and Role. At the second level of detail, $RoME_2$ gives also access to the instances of the class Activity. In this example, instances of the classes Profile and Group remain inaccessible.

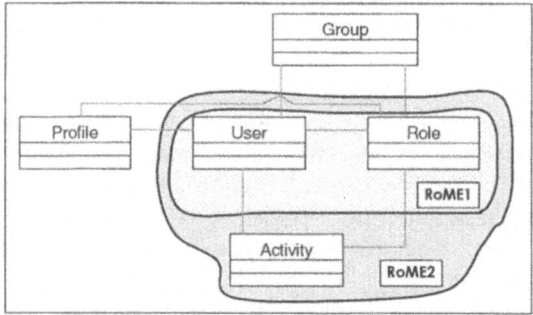

Fig. 4. Extensional stratification of the Data Model for Awareness Information.

2. **Extensional Stratification of a DMAI component**. In this case, components of the DMAI (classes, associations and classes-associations) are seen as ME whose set of elements is a set of instances. Then, an extensional stratification of a DMAI component can be performed. It consists in selecting some instances of the DMAI component and in ordering by the set inclusion subsets of this set of instances in order to provide a progressive access to each subset of this sequence. For instance (Fig. 5), one extensional stratification S of the class Activity for which ten instances {a_1, a_2, ..., a_{10}} exist can be defined as S = {{a_4, a_7, a_3}, {a_4, a_7, a_3, a_1, a_9}, {a_4, a_7, a_3, a_1, a_9, a_6}}. S contains 3 RoME. At first level of detail 3 activities are visible, at level two, two more activities are visible, at level three six activities are visible. In this example, activities a_2, a_5, a_8 and a_{10} are always masked and therefore can not be accessed when using the unmasking function (right part of Fig. 5)

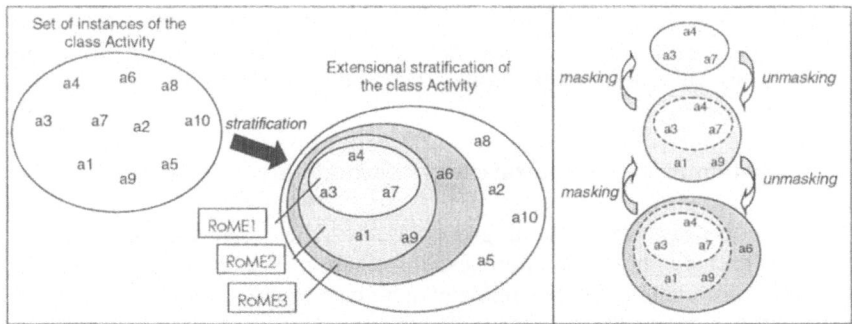

Fig. 5. Extensional Stratification for the class Activity.

3.   **Intensional Stratification of a DMAI component**. In this case, components of the DMAI (classes, associations and classes-associations) are seen as ME whose structure is made of a set of variables. Then, an intensional stratification of a DMAI component can be performed. It consists in selecting some (possibly all) variables of the DMAI component and in ordering by set inclusion subsets of this set of variables, providing a progressive access to each subset of this sequence. For instance, let us suppose that the class Activity contains the following variables: 'name', 'description', 'details', 'responsible' and 'time interval'. One intensional stratification S of the class Activity can be defined as S = {{'name', 'responsible', 'time interval'}, {'name', 'responsible', 'time interval', 'description'}, {'name', 'responsible', 'time interval', 'description', 'details'}. S contains 3 RoME. At the first level of detail 3 variables are visible and give some essential information about the activity, at level two, one more variable is visible ('description'), at level three the whole structure of the class is visible (see Fig. 6).

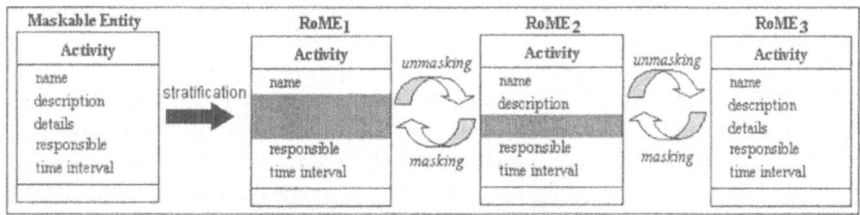

Fig. 6. Intensional Stratification of the class Activity.

We believe that applying only one of the stratification techniques is not enough to significantly reduce the overload risk. For instance, an extensional stratification of a component (e.g., a class) can be compared to a filtering process, since it selects instances of such component. However, we cannot ensure that such selection will sufficiently reduce the amount of instances presented to the user, since awareness mechanism often produces high amounts of it and a large proportion can be selected. Thus, we propose a process that combines some stratification techniques over the data model for awareness information. For instance, it is possible to apply an intensional stratification (selection of ordered subsets of variables), followed (or preceded) by an extensional stratification (selection of ordered subsets of instances) to a class which belongs itself to a RoME of an extensional stratification of the DMAI. Such a composition of stratifications is illustrated in the next section.

5.3 Stratification Process for Awareness Information

In this section, we show how a groupware designer can use the stratification techniques presented above for awareness information. We address here the delivery of awareness information which is relevant at a given time.

In order to determine this relevance, the awareness support needs to know *who* is performing activities as well as her/his *current role* and also the *tasks* associated with her/his activities. Groupware designer should then determine the target of the stratification, which can be, basically, *a given user, role or activity*. In the first case, stratification consists in providing a progressive access to information taking into account the general characteristics of the user (level of knowledge, presentation preferences, material configuration, etc.). In the second case (*given role*), stratification consists in providing a progressive access to some general awareness information related to this role (the associated activities, the users fulfilling the role, etc.), without considering who is assigned this role. In the last case (*a given activity*), stratification aims at giving a progressive access to the awareness information related to this activity, without considering who is performing this activity and her/his current role (e.g. stratifications given in Fig. 5 and Fig. 6). It is also possible to compose these possible targets, searching then stratifications for *a couple <user, role>*, *a couple <role, activity>*, or *<user, activity>*, or even *a triple <user, role, activity>*. In this last case, the stratification focuses on the awareness information dealing with one activity performed by a given user when she/he performs a given role.

As we discussed in section 2, we believe that awareness support should take into account the user's preferences as well as her/his role's needs. Thus, we suggest that groupware designer should target the triple *<user, role, activity>* when defining the stratifications of the DMAI.

Therefore, we propose to combine the stratification techniques (cf. section 5.2) by applying them in the following sequence: first, extensional stratifications of the DMAI, which organize the model itself in levels of details. Then, extensional stratifications of the DMAI components, which reduce and organize in levels the instances that will be presented to the user. Finally, intensional stratifications of these components, which define for each component levels of details. The Fig. 7 represents this process.

Thus, once defined the stratification target and its process, the groupware designer has to define the system's stratifications. To begin, the designer has to define an extensional stratification of the DMAI in order to serialize subsets of components (classes, association) of this model. For instance, she/he can assign the class Activity to the first level of detail in order to give an immediate access to the set of its instances. She/he can then define, in a similar way, the components of the DMAI that will appear at the other levels.

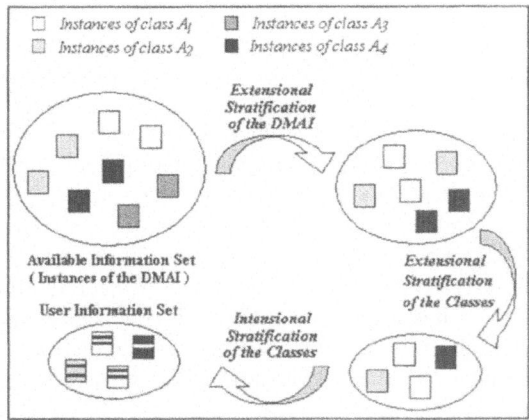

Fig. 7. The stratification process suggested for the awareness information

Then, the designer may apply an extensional stratification to each class (or just a subset) of the model in order to give a progressive access to this set of instances. For instance, she/he can consider that the most relevant is to inform the user about the last performed activities. This consists in associating the corresponding instances of the class Activity (*i.e.* the more recent ones) to the first RoME.

Considering that our target is the triple *<user, role, activity>* and since these extensional stratifications behave as a selection process in the set of available instances, groupware designer can use profiles to define (and allow users to define) these stratifications. A profile (cf. section 5.1) may include some conditions to perform an appropriate selection. Each profile can define information levels, each level being composed by DMAI classes that user/role wants/needs to be aware of and some special conditions (e.g. time intervals) that the instances of these classes should respect to be selected. In addition, by combining the three profile types suggested in section 5.1 (user profile, role profile and user profile linked to a specific role), these stratifications can perfectly match the target, by considering the activity, the role and the user.

For instance, a user may choose in her/his profile to receive at the first level the instances of the activities A_1 and A_2 (extensional stratification of the model) produced in the last week (extensional stratification of the components), while the same level of her/his role's profile includes only the activity A_3. The system could then combine these profiles and present to the user first the instances of the activities A_1, A_2 and A_3 produced in the last week.

Finally, the designer can take advantage of applying an intensional stratification to the structure of a component of the DMAI. This way, the user benefits from, according to her/his roles, more or less complete representations of the instances she/he can access progressively (cf. section 5.2). For instance, considering the Fig. 7, the designer may define that the role's profile determines the extensional stratification of the model and the user's profile, the extensional stratification of the classes, while the intensional stratification is linked to the role.

6 Example

In this section, we present an example of how a groupware designer can use the concepts presented in this paper during the development of a simple groupware tool.

Let us consider again the example presented in section 3 and let us suppose that the groupware system consists here of a simple meeting tool for such environment. Moreover, we suppose that this meeting tool integrates a DMAI in charge of representing awareness and user information. The unique activity handled by the tool is the meeting itself, represented by a Meeting class. Thus, the potential MEs are the model itself and the classes User, Role and Meeting. A meeting object is structured as suggested in section 3, it has a meeting title, goals, decisions, the discussion, and a related document. The discussion refers to the content of a chat session which is automatically registered by the tool. The rest (title, goals, etc.) is supplied by the meeting coordinator.

The Fig. 8 shows the meeting process adopted here: (1) first, the meeting coordinator demands to the meeting manager the creation of a new meeting. The coordinator also provides the manager with the meeting title, goals and the URL of the associated document. The meeting manager creates a new meeting object with such information and starts a new chat session for this meeting (2). Once the meeting has started, other users may join it (3-4), load the associated document (5) and contribute to the discussion (6). The end of the meeting is defined by the coordinator (7), who describes the decisions that have been taken (10). The system registers then the discussions (9) and notifies the awareness manager about it (11).

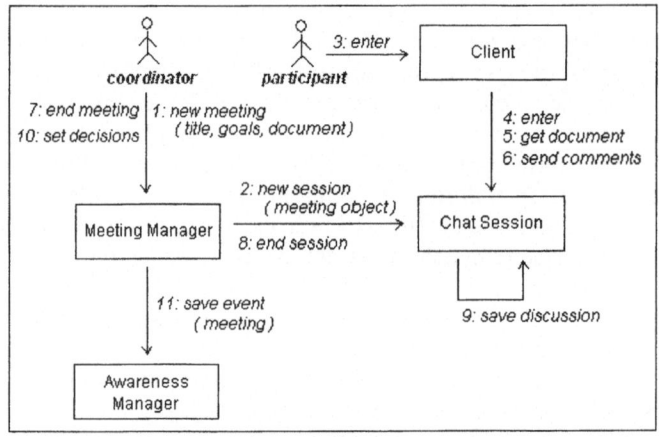

Fig. 8. Meeting process in the Simple Meeting Tool

The awareness support introduced in this tool is limited to inform the users about past (or missed) meetings. In order to facilitate the development of the awareness manager, we use a framework for awareness support called BW [9], we have designed for supplying awareness support about past activities (activities already concluded by the group) in groupware systems.

The BW Framework uses a data model that corresponds to the DMAI and which is stored in a package called Kernel. Beside the description of users, roles and activities (called "events" by this framework), the Kernel package also includes the definition of profiles for users (personal profiles), roles (role profiles) and users playing a specific role (personal role profiles). These profiles (cf. section 5.1) are composed by a set of relevant activities for the user or role, and an Allen's interval [1] during which they are relevant.

These profiles are used by the meeting tool to define the extensional stratification of the meeting class. This stratification is based on the time interval parameter associated to each object. Thus, each user (participant or the meeting coordinator) may define the time interval in which the information about the meetings is important for her/him.

This extensional stratification results from a filtering process performed by the BW framework. This process aims at reducing the amount of information delivered to the user by limiting the number of instances presented to those that match the profiles. It consists in selecting the available instances by merging the different profiles that concern the user (personal, role and personal role profiles). This merge creates a single set of activities (in our case, the meeting) and a resulting time interval, which is used to select the instances to be presented to the user. This resulting interval is the largest interval that encompasses all composing intervals. So, any instance whose interval is included in the interval of one of these profiles is also included in the resulting interval. Only instances whose time interval occurs during the resulting time interval are really presented to the user. As a result, the set of instances presented is reduced. It is over this resulting set of instances that other stratifications defined for the user and her/his active role apply. The Fig. 9 shows this filtering process, which combines personal and personal role profiles to select only the meeting instances $\{ a_3, a_4, a_5, a_6 \}$.

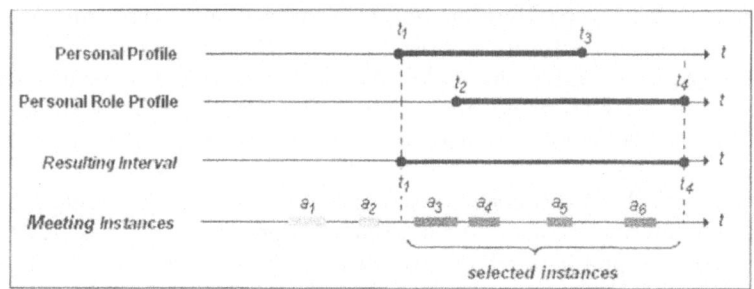

Fig. 9. The filtering process based on the time interval.

In order to define other stratifications (extensional stratification of the model and intensional stratification of the model components), we have designed a package, called PAM, which introduces the progressive access definitions (cf. section 4) and binds them with the BW Framework components, specially the Kernel package, which represents the data model used by the tool.

The PAM package implements the concept of stratification (class PAM_Stratification in Fig. 10), which represents the stratification of the awareness data model. This stratification is connected to the role representation (class BW_Role) through the association "defined_for". This association creates the relationship between stratifications and roles. Furthermore, this package integrates the concept of

RoME, which can be associated with a specific element of the data model to define an intensional stratification (PAM_ElementStratification) of this element.

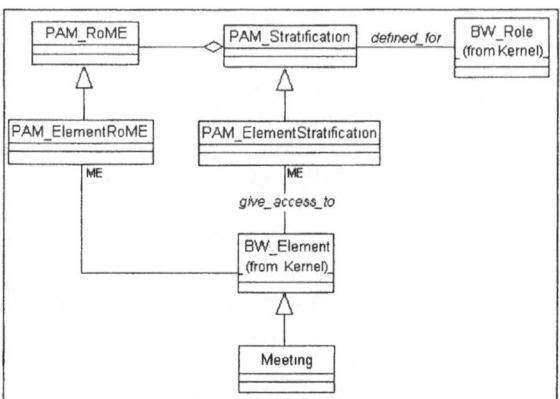

Fig. 10. The PAM package

Through this association between the stratification and the role, we can define, for instance, stratifications for one or more roles. For example, we can define, for the coordinator role, a stratification of the class Meeting, presented in Fig. 10, as $S_1 = \{\{\text{'title'}, \text{'time interval'}\}, \{\text{'goals'}, \text{'decisions'}\}, \{\text{'document'}\}, \{\text{'discussion'}\}\}$.

In order to better coordinate these stratifications with the presentation of the awareness information, the PAM package includes a manager which keeps track of all the defined stratifications. This manager is consulted by the user interface elements in order to know and respect the applicable stratifications. These interface elements receive the awareness information filtered by the BW framework. They consult the PAM manager and, based on the stratification definitions, control the behaviour of the presentation in order to respect these definitions. As a consequence, the awareness information can be supplied progressively to a user, following the stratifications defined for her/his roles.

Thus, through the BW framework and the PAM package, our meeting tool is able to collect the information about the meetings and present it progressively to the user according her/his profiles and the stratification definitions. These definitions are loaded by the tool during its start-up, and with the help of the PAM manager, users may define and load dynamically their own stratifications. A user can, for example, define for herself/himself the stratification S_1 defined above. Moreover, the developer may also define default stratifications. For instance, she/he may define an extensional stratification of the model, where in the first level only information about the meetings is presented, and the information about the users and roles is presented in the second level. We also associated the stratification S_1 to the coordinator role, thus any meeting coordinator will, by default, receive the awareness information through the 4 levels defined for this stratification. Accordingly to this loading policy, the responsibility of creating new stratifications, and then defining what information is relevant to a user or role, is shared between the system designer and the users themselves.

As one could observe, the complexity of our proposition concerns mainly the definition of the stratifications presented above. This definition requires some knowledge about the data model for the adopted awareness information, referring to the system designer. Then, some flexibility for modifying the stratification definition during the groupware execution is also needed. The expected flexibility must be directed towards system users, first of all towards the team coordinator. However, this flexibility has a cost: an overhead to the user interface design, since this interface should handle different and progressive information set. All this makes us believe that our proposition is better suited to large groupware systems, which generally handle huge and complex awareness information set. In such a system, we expect that the advantages of our proposition will exceed this design and definition complexity imposed by the proposition. Nevertheless, more tests are still needed to better evaluate the impact of this proposition in real-size applications.

7 Related Work

Awareness support is the target of many works that can be found in the CSCW literature. Some examples of groupware systems that are concerned with awareness support are the BSCW workspace [2] and the Alliance editor [12]. These systems try to present awareness information through icons and history windows. Although the Alliance editor proposes a "group awareness agent" to adapt the awareness mechanism to the user's needs by modifying the presentation of its information, none of these systems offers a mechanism for delivering this information gradually when huge amount of information is available.

Furthermore, considering toolkits and frameworks for groupware development, the situation is similar. There are in the literature toolkits and frameworks that can help groupware designers in the system development. We can name, for example, Groupkit [13], ANTS [11] and BW [9]. These tools allow the development of new groupware applications (as ANTS), or the development of awareness mechanism (as BW). Even if these frameworks offer some kind of awareness support (ANTS, for example, presents an awareness component integrated in its infrastructure), they are not really concerned with the adaptation of the system to a high amount of available information, and once again, no mechanism is proposed to gradually access this information, whenever it constitutes a large set.

Concerning the research about tailorability ([16] and [7], just to name a few), these works are mainly concerned with the adaptability of the functionalities of the system. Nevertheless, works that handle tailorability do not directly address the adaptability of the information content, which is our main concern. What we have presented here is a model that allows a gradual access to the awareness information available, adapting the information presented to the user's and role's interests and necessities, in order to prevent some overload in the delivery of information.

Finally, the research involving context-aware systems propose the use of the information about physical context, such as location, to adapt the information delivered to it (see [5] and [3]). An example is Rover [3], which tracks the location of the user dynamically to configure the content delivered to her/him. However, there are only a few studies concerning the context of the work in a cooperative environment, or awareness as defined in the section 2. An example is the AwareNex system [15], which allows a mobile user that is away from her/his desktop to maintain some awareness about her/his colleagues and their availability (know as "group awareness") and contact them. Unfortunately, AwareNex deals only with these group awareness functionalities, it does not present any other information concerning the context of the group's activities.

8   Conclusion

Awareness support in groupware systems is an important feature which aims at providing users with some knowledge essentially related to a group and to its activities (past, present or futures ones). Such a kind of knowledge constitutes an informational context which improves individual contributions and avoids contradictory interactions between members of the group. One of the well-known drawback of awareness information appears when the amount of delivered information is too large to be efficiently exploited by the user. In order to prevent groupware systems users from suffering from such a cognitive overload, we have proposed in this paper to give them a progressive access to awareness information. This progressive access relies on a stratification of the awareness information space into different levels of detail. We have shown how to link a Progressive Access Model to a Data Model for Awareness Information that we have described. After having defined the different ways of stratifying such a model, we have illustrated strategies the designer can adopt to define stratifications. These stratifications are adapted to a user performing activities when fulfilling a specific role in a groupware system. Finally, we have presented an example of the application of the progressive access in awareness support, by showing the development of a tool offering such a support.

By proposing this progressive access to the awareness information we expect to reduce significantly the risk of cognitive overload. The meeting tool that we have built, although simple, has demonstrated this reduction. We strongly believe that by reducing the cognitive overload it is possible to increase the efficiency of the awareness mechanism, and thus, to increase the performance of the whole group.

This work is just at its beginning. There are still many issues to be investigated concerning the application of the progressive access in awareness information delivery. We should consider, for example, the exploitation of the relationships and dependencies among the activities as a condition for stratification.

References

1. Allen, J.F.: Maintaining Knowledge about Temporal Intervals. Communications of the ACM, 26(11), ACM Press, 1983, p. 832–843.
2. Appelt, W.: What groupware functionality do users really use? Analysis of the usage of the BSCW system. 9th Euromicro Workshop on PDP, IEEE Computer Society, 2001. Available at: http://bscw.gmd.de/Papers/PDP2001/PDP2001.pdf. Access: February 2003.
3. Banerjee, S., Agarwal, S., Kamel, K., Kochut, A., Kommareddly, C., Nadeem, T., Thakkar, P., Trinh, B., Yossef, A., Larson, R.L., Shankar, A.U., Agrawala, A., Rover: scalable location-aware computing, Computer, 35(10), oct. 2002, IEEE Computer Society, p. 46–53.
4. Borges M.R.S., Pino, J.A.: Awareness Mechanisms for Coordination in Asynchronous CSCW. Proceedings of 9th Workshop on Information Technologies and Systems, 1999.

5. Dourish, P., Seeking a foundation for context-aware computing, Human Computer Interaction, 13(2–4), 2001, Hillsdale, p. 229–241.
6. Dourish, P., Bellotti, V.: Awareness and Coordination in Shared Workspaces. Proceedings of ACM Conference on Computer-Supported Cooperative Work, ACM Press, Toronto, Canada, 1992, p 107–114.
7. Fernández, A.; Haake, J.M.; Goldberg, A.: Tailoring group work. In: Haake, J.M, Pino, J.A. (eds.), CRIWG 2002, LNCS 2440, Springer-Verlag, 2002, p. 232–242.
8. Gutwin, C., Greenberg, S.:   Effects of awareness support on groupware usability. Proceedings of CHI'98 - Conference on Human Factors in Computing Systems, ACM Press, 1998, p. 511–518.
9. Kirsch-Pinheiro, M., Lima, J.V., Borges, M.R.S.: A Framework for Awareness Support in Groupware Systems. 7th International Conference on Computer Supported Cooperative Work in Design, 2002, p. 13–18.
10. Liechti, O.: Awareness and the WWW: an overview. CSCW'00 Workshop on Awareness and the WWW, ACM Press, 2000. Available at: http://www2.mic.atr.co.jp/dept2/awareness/fProgram.html Access: December 2002.
11. López, P.G, Skarneta, A.F.G.: ANTS framework for cooperative work environments. Computer, 36(3), IEEE Computer Society, 2003, p. 56–62.
12. Martínez-Enríquez, A.M., Decouchant, D., Morán, A.L., Favela, J. : An adaptive cooperative web authoring environment. 2nd International Conference on Adaptive Hypermedia and Adaptive Web-based Systems, Malaga, Spain, 2002.
13. Roseman, M., Greenberg, S.: Building real time groupware with GroupKit, a groupware toolkit. ACM Transactions on Computer Human Interactions, 1(3), 1996, p. 66–106. Available at: http://www.cpsc.ucalgary.ca/grouplab/papers. Access: January 2000.
14. Schmidt, K., The problem with 'awareness': introductory remarks on 'Awareness in CSCW', Computer Supported Cooperative Work, 11(3–4), 2002, Kluwer Academic Publishers, p. 285–298.
15. Tang, J.C., Yankelovich, N., Begole, J.B., Vankleike, M., ConNexus to Awarenex: extending awareness to mobile users, CHI Letters, 3(1), 2001, ACM Press, p. 221–229.
16. Teege, G.: Users as composers: Parts and features as a basis for tailorability in CSCW systems. Computer Supported Cooperative Work, vol. 9, Kluwer Academic Publishers, 2000, p. 101–122.
17. Villanova, M., Gensel, J., Martin, H.: Progressive Access: a Step towards Adaptability in Web-based Information Systems, 8th International Conference on Object-Oriented Information Systems (OOIS 2002), Montpellier, France, September 2–5, 2002, p. 422–433.
18. Villanova-Oliver, M.: Adaptabilité dans les systèmes d'Information sur le Web : Modélisation et mise en œuvre de l'accès progressif, Thèse de Doctorat, Institut National Polytechnique de Grenoble, décembre 2002 (in French). Available at: http://www-lsr.imag.fr/Les.Personnes/Marlene.Villanova/. Access: April 2003.

Trusting Data Quality in Cooperative Information Systems*

Luca De Santis[1], Monica Scannapieco[1,2], and Tiziana Catarci[1]

[1] Università di Roma "La Sapienza"
{lucadesantis,monscan,catarci}@dis.uniroma1.it
[2] Istituto di Analisi dei Sistemi ed Informatica
Consiglio Nazionale delle Ricerche (IASI-CNR)

Abstract. Managing the quality of exchanged data is a relevant problem in any cooperative information system. If the quality of exchanged data is not known, the cooperation itself is negatively affected; indeed, an organization can prefer not requiring data at all, rather than receiving bad quality data. Therefore, there is the need of providing mechanisms to certify organizations with respect to the quality of data that they spread in the cooperative system.
This paper describes a model for trusting cooperating organizations. In such a model, a trust value is assigned to each organization with respect to a specific data category. A set of experiments shows the effectiveness of the model. Moreover, the design of an architectural service that rates organizations on the basis of such model is also described.

Keywords: Cooperative systems, trust, peer-to-peer, data quality

1 Introduction

Peer-to-peer (P2P) systems are typically used in loosely coupled environments, like the Web, where peers interact each other without previously established mutual agreements and knowledge. Instead, in this paper we consider the problem of trusting P2P organizations that cooperate according to a *tight* interaction paradigm. These systems well-model real scenarios such as virtual districts in e-Business or public administrations in e-Gtovernment. We introduce a classification of P2P systems that takes into account the degree of coupling of the interacting peers, on the basis of which we place *Cooperative Information System (CIS)* [1] as a subclass of P2P systems. When organizations composing a CIS exchange data each other, a relevant problem is how to trust each organization with respect to the quality of provided data. This paper describes a model for trusting cooperating organizations, in which a trust value is assigned to each organization with respect to a specific data category. The trust level is assigned on the basis of a probabilistic model that considers the satisfaction

---

* This work is supported by MIUR, COFIN 2001 Project "DaQuinCIS -Methodologies and Tools for Data Quality inside Cooperative Information Systems",
http://www.dis.uniroma1.it/~dq/

R. Meersman et al. (Eds.): CoopIS/DOA/ODBASE 2003, LNCS 2888, pp. 354–369, 2003.
© Springer-Verlag Berlin Heidelberg 2003

of the receiving organization in a data exchange. We consider examples taken from the Italian e-Government scenario, where public administrations interact as peers in order to fulfill service requests from citizens and enterprises. In such a scenario, our method allows for assigning a trust level to administrations or private companies taking part to the cooperation. Therefore, for instance, in the Italian e-Government scenario the Department of Finance can have a high trust level with respect to Fiscal Codes of Citizens and a low trust level with respect to their Residence Addresses. The proposed model also allows to fix a threshold to discriminate between trusted and untrusted organizations.

For loosely coupled P2P environments, some examples of *reputation systems* have been introduced, in order to manage trust issues (see Section 6 for details). In this paper, we also describe the design of a reputation system that rates organizations on the basis of the proposed trust model, but it is targeted to tightly coupled P2P systems.

Different motivations can be provided for proposing a reputation system also for tightly coupled P2P systems, namely:

- In tightly coupled P2P systems, it is very difficult to individuate a subject that is responsible for a certain data category. In fact, data are typically replicated among the different participating organizations, and one does not know how to state that an organization has the primary responsibility for some specific data, i.e. it is the *Data Steward* [2] of that specific category. By proposing an evaluation of organizations's trust with respect to the quality of provided data, we give a mean for defining a data steward as the organization having the highest trust level with respect to a specific data category.
- For tightly coupled P2P systems of limited dimensions and bounded life-cycle, the use of trust techniques can be very useful as it dramatically reduces the typical start-up phase in which a peer needs to become confident versus other peers.

Many other significant benefits can derive from our proposal. First, as our model is thought for tightly coupled environments that are typically implemented by cooperative processes, such processes can be designed on the basis of the determined reputation on provided data. Second, the cooperation itself is strengthened by enabling to know organizations' reputation: data are more often asked to peer organizations if a trust value for them is available. As an example, in our e-Government scenario, administrations very often prefer asking citizens for data, rather than other administrations that have already stored the same data, because they do not know if trusting them or not. Third, a control mechanism on the quality of exchanged data prevents from a possible spread of low quality data all over the system.

We are presently experimenting our approach in the framework of the DaQuinCIS project [3]. The main objective of DaQuinCIS is to define an integrated framework that includes:

- a methodology for data quality enhancement in cooperative systems;
- a distributed architecture supporting data quality monitoring and improvement.

The paper is organized as follows. We provide a short introduction to the DaQuinCIS architecture in Section 2; a possible classification of P2P systems is described in Section 2.3. Then, we introduce a novel model for trust in Section 3 that is implemented by an architectural service detailed in Section 4. In Section 5, we illustrate some experimental results. Finally, after presenting the related work in Section 6, we draw some future research directions.

2   The DaQuinCIS Architecture

The trust model we propose in Section 3 is based on the assumption that organizations cooperate through tightly coupled processes. Basically, in such systems large-scale business processes are automated and workflows cross system and administrative boundaries. E-government initiatives are a notable example of this type of systems [4]. We also suppose that organizations agree on a common cooperative architecture providing the services necessary to manage the quality of exchanged data. These assumptions are also at the basis of the DaQuinCIS framework.

The architectural component that implements the trust model is called *Rating Service* and has been designed as a service provided by the DaQuinCIS framework.

In the following of this section, after a short introduction on what we mean for data quality in cooperative systems, we illustrate the DaQuinCIS architecture; we leave to Section 4 details on the Rating Service design.

2.1   Data Quality

Data Quality has been traditionally investigated in the context of single information systems: methodologies to manage data quality in such systems have been proposed both by researchers [5,6] and by industrial practitioners [7,2]. Instead, it is very recent the interest to data quality in cooperative systems [8,9,10].

In cooperative scenarios the main data quality issues regard: *(i)* assessment of the quality of the data owned by each organization; *(ii)* methods and techniques for exchanging quality information; *(iii)* improvement of quality within each cooperating organization; and *(iv)* heterogeneity, due to the presence of different organizations, in general with different data semantics.

Data quality dimensions characterize properties that are inherent to data. Examples of quality dimensions are accuracy, completeness, currency, consistency.

Some authors consider also *source reliability* as a quality dimension; it is defined as the credibility of a source with respect to provided data (e.g., [11]).

The trust model we propose in Section 3 considers source reliability as a characterization which is orthogonal to quality dimensions. Specifically, we propose a way to rate the reliability of sources in a CIS, and we distinguish trusted and untrusted sources on the basis of the quality of provided data.

2.2   The Architecture

The DaQuinCIS architecture allows the diffusion of data and related quality and exploits data replication to improve the overall quality of cooperative data. Each participating organization offers services to other organizations on its own cooperative gateway, and also specific services to its internal back-end systems. Therefore, cooperative gateways interface both internally and externally through services. Moreover, the communication infrastructure itself offers some specific services. The overall architecture is depicted in Figure 1.

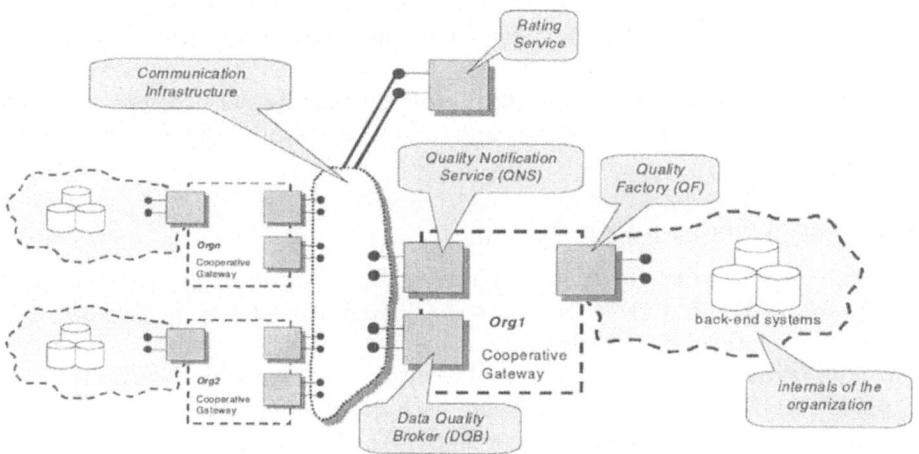

Fig. 1. The DaQuinCIS architecture

Organizations export data and quality data according to a common model. It includes the definition of *(i)* constructs to represent data, *(ii)* a common set of data quality properties, *(iii)* constructs to represent them and *(iv)* the association between data and quality data. Quality values are evaluated by the **Quality Factory**.

The **Data Quality Broker** (see Figure 1) poses, on behalf of a requesting user, a data request over other cooperating organizations, also specifying a set of quality requirements that the desired data have to satisfy; this is referred to as *quality brokering function*. Different copies of the same data received as responses to the request are reconciled and a best-quality value is selected and proposed to organizations, that can choose to discard their data and to adopt higher quality ones; this is referred to as *quality improvement function*. If the requirements specified in the request cannot be satisfied, then the broker initiates a negotiation with the user that can optionally weaken the constraints on the desired data. The Data Quality Broker is in essence a peer-to-peer data integration system [12] which allows to pose quality-enhanced query over a global schema and to select data satisfying such requirements.

The **Quality Notification Service** is a publish/subscribe engine used as a quality message bus between services and/or organizations. More specifically, it allows quality-based subscriptions for users to be notified on changes of the quality of data. For example, an organization may want to be notified if the quality of some data it uses degrades below a certain threshold, or when high quality data are available.

The **Rating Service** (top of Figure 1) associates trust values to each data source in the CIS. The Rating Service is a centralized service, to be provided by a third-party organization.

Notice that the DaQuinCIS architecture assumes a data quality driven redesign of inter-organizational processes, in which the Data Quality Broker is the principal architectural element used for all data exchanges implied by the new processes.

This paper concentrates specifically on the Rating Service. For a detailed description of the Quality Broker and the Quality Notification Service, please refer to [3].

2.3 DaQuinCIS as a P2P System

The interest for peer to peer systems has been considerably growing in the last years. Although P2P systems are considered a *revolution* in network based environments, they are actually only an evolution of the original internet model, enabling packet exchanges among nodes with interchangeable roles.

With the P2P acronym we indicate each distributed system in which nodes can be both clients and servers. In other words, all nodes provide access to some of the resources they own, enabling a basic form of interoperability. Many simple P2P applications are today widely spread, like file sharing and instant messaging. Moreover, more complex applications, such as distributed processing, begin to be available.

A large number of systems, having different objectives and functionalities, could be included in the basic definition given above. An interesting classification of P2P systems can be found in [13]. The following three models of P2P systems are introduced:

Decentralized Model. The applications belonging to this class can be considered as pure P2P systems. The architecture is completely decentralized, without common elements shared by peers. Each peer may have a knowledge of the system by exchanging information with other peers.

Centralized Model. P2P systems belonging to this class have at least one common element, such as a peer search index. This introduces a bottleneck, though allowing peers to look for information more accurately and quickly.

Hierarchical Model. This class could be consider as an intermediate class between the other two. There is a set of nodes, called super-peers, that assume particular functions such as peer address index or local control.

Such a classification is based upon the level of distribution of control and access functions, such as centralized or decentralized indexing. We extend this classification by adding another dimension, that is orthogonal to the other. This dimension takes into account how much *tight* can be a peer interaction. For example, with systems such as Kazaa [14], the interaction is not tight because users can only search for data and establish temporary connections. Indeed, with distributed workflow systems, each node can have more sophisticated and long interactions with the other nodes, thus originating a tight interaction. As an example, PARIDE [15], a framework that enables dynamic composition and orchestration of web services in peer to peer systems, allows complex, even transactional, process interactions between peers.

We classify P2P systems into the following two classes, on the basis of their interaction level:

– *Loosely* coupled systems, consisting of systems in which data exchanges are not pre-defined. Data exchanges simply imply a request/reply interaction between peers.
– *Tightly* coupled systems, based on pre-defined processes that cross organizational boundaries. Such processes can even be transactional thus originating a very tight interaction among the different organizations that participate to the system. All data exchanges are placed within a defined process.

Combining these categories with the ones described in [13], we can obtain a more complete description of P2P systems, based on behavioral characteristics. For examples, Self-Serv [16] belongs to the class of P2P decentralized models and has a tightly coupled interaction model; conversely, Gnutella [17] belongs to the decentralized class, and has a loosely coupled interaction model. In the matrix of Figure 2 we report the classification of some relevant proposals with respect to both illustrated dimensions. In this paper we concentrate on tightly coupled P2P systems (P2P-TCS's in the following) by providing a trust model for the DaQuinCIS architecture.

	Loosely Coupled	Tightly Coupled
Decentralized Model	Gnutella [17],Kazaa [14]	Self-Serv [16]
Hierarchical Model	FastTrack [18]	PARIDE [15]
Centralized Model	Napster [19]	DaQuinCIS [9]

Fig. 2. Examples of P2P systems classification

3   Trust Model

In defining a trust model for the DaQuinCIS architecture, we exploit some peculiarities of tightly coupled systems; instead, the techniques proposed by the current literature and described in Section 6 mainly concern loosely coupled peer to peer systems. In P2P-TCS's, a first important difference is the complete knowledge of the identity of peers involved in data exchanges. The possibility to maintain an anonymous identity is common in peer to peer applications. However, malicious agents can exploit this weakness to spread undesired contents or dangerous applications, like virus. The use of IP addresses to avoid these behaviors was proposed [20], but this solution is poorly efficient; for example, spoofing techniques or use of dynamic IP address and proxies servers can easily make the method unreliable. The organizations that take part to P2P-TCS's are instead known to each other and this reduces the probability of fraudulent behaviors. Nevertheless, we can't exclude that an organization has a dishonest behavior. For example, let us suppose that organizations Org_i and Org_j have the same kind of data $\mathcal{D}$. If $\mathcal{D}$ are somewhat crucial for Org_i's processes, Org_i could try to discredit Org_j to get a kind of data stewardship on $\mathcal{D}$ data.

Another important difference is the dynamism of the system, in terms of the number of participating organizations. In loosely coupled P2P systems, the number of peers changes frequently, due to the typical anonymous and transient nature of interactions. Conversely, P2P-TCS's organizations typically have a stable process-based interaction.

These differences have two main implications on the trust model, namely:

- a more specific trust model can be considered, based on the definition of trust with respect to a category of data;
- misbehavior may be involuntary, e.g. due to temporary problems. Therefore, once an organization is classified as untrusted, it cannot remain in this state indefinitely, but specific reinstatement methods need to be provided.

When deciding the *atomic* unit to trust, a first hypothesis could be to trust the organization as a whole, with respect to the totality of exchanged data or more generally to the transactions performed with other organizations. The method proposed in [13] is an example of this case.

We follow the approach of associating trust to an organization as a whole but we propose two major modifications, namely: *(i)* we consider a specific type of transaction, i.e. data exchanges; *(ii)* we evaluate trust of an organization with respect to a specific type of provided data.

More specifically, a trust value is associated to a couple $< Org_i, \mathcal{D} >$ where $\mathcal{D}$ is a data unit (see below). In this case we have a finest granularity level of trust on the sources. Organizations can choose different partners for data exchanges relying onto a wider range of possibilities in sources' selection. As an example, in the Italian e-Government scenario, it may happen that the Department of Finance is recognized as trusted with respect to Fiscal Codes, but untrusted with respect to Residence Addresses (of Italian citizens). Therefore, other administrations can ask mainly to the Department of Finance to obtain Fiscal Codes.

Before describing our trust model, we provide some basic definitions:

Organizations. They are considered with respect to the role of providing data each other and consuming data from each other. Notice that in such a way they are peers, i.e. they can have both roles of data consumer and data provider. Furthermore, we suppose that organizations are independent and have a competitive behavior.

Data Unit. A data unit can be a generic view on data provided by organizations. As an example, a class `Citizen`, or a single attribute, such as `Name` of `Citizen`.

Source Unit. A source unit is a couple $< Org_i, \mathcal{D} >$, where Org_i is the organization providing the data unit $\mathcal{D}$.

Complaint. Given Org_i sending a data unit $\mathcal{D}$ to Org_j, Org_j can raise a complaint $C_{i,\mathcal{D}}$ stating that $\mathcal{D}$ data are low (not satisfactory) quality data.

Complaints are used to calculate trust of source units.

In [13], a method to evaluate trust of sources in P2P systems is described. In this work, the authors introduce the following formula:

$$T(p) = | \{c(p,q) \mid q \epsilon P\} | \times | \{c(q,p) \mid q \epsilon P\} |$$

where P is the set of the agents and $c(p,q)$ represents a complaint raised by agent p if it believes agent q is cheating. The decision on the agent's trustworthiness is done on the basis of $T(\cdot)$ values. Low values indicate that the peer is trustworthy.

The method we propose to evaluate trust of source units is inspired by the one above, but with some major differences.

The first difference is related to the atomic unit of trust, that in our case is the couple $< Org_i, \mathcal{D} >$.

The second basic difference develops over an intuition described by the following example. Let us suppose that a set of organizations requires a typology of data $\mathcal{D}^k$ 100.000 times to Org_j and that 1000 complaints are fired by the same set. For the sake of simplicity, we suppose that only Org_j has $\mathcal{D}^k$ data. This should be interpreted as an indication that $\mathcal{D}^k$ are good quality data, because only a small fraction of it originated complaints. Notice that the function $T(\cdot)$ calculated on the couple $< Org_j, \mathcal{D}^k >$ is equal to 1000. Moreover, let us suppose that after 1000 accesses to data $\mathcal{D}^h$ provided by Org_i, 100 complaints are fired. The $T(\cdot)$ function of the couple $< Org_i, \mathcal{D}^h >$ is equal to 100. On the basis of $T(\cdot)$ values, we should consider $< Org_i, \mathcal{D}^h >$ as trusted and $< Org_j, \mathcal{D}^k >$ as untrusted. The decision algorithm proposed in [13] does not take into account the number of requests sent to a source unit, and run correctly only if each peer makes approximatively the same number of transactions; in this case, in fact, $T(\cdot)$ values are really comparable.

In the following section, we provide a method that considers the overall number of data exchanges with respect to which complaints are raised.

3.1   Definition of a Trust Parameter for Source Units

The trust level of a source unit is calculated on the basis of the number of complaints fired by other organizations. Let us assume that $\mathcal{O}$ is the set of peer organizations and that $C_{i,j,\mathcal{D}} = C(Org_i, < Org_j, \mathcal{D} >)$ is the complaint that Org_i fires with respect to the source unit $< Org_j, \mathcal{D} >$.

As previously discussed, the number of complaints is not sufficient by itself to evaluate source units' trust. Therefore, we need a mechanism to store the number of requests made to each source unit. We propose to associate such information to each complaint, thus defining the following structure for messages exchanged within the P2P system in order to guarantee trust management:

$$\mathcal{C} = < Org_i, < Org_j, \mathcal{D} >, n >$$

where Org_i is the organization which has fired the complaint and $< Org_j, \mathcal{D} >$ is the source unit the complaint is referred to. The integer n represents the number of requests of $\mathcal{D}$ issued by Org_i to Org_j, starting from the last complaint that Org_i fired against Org_j.

Furthermore, we assume that $n_{i,j,\mathcal{D}}$ is the number of complaints that Org_i sends to $< Org_j, \mathcal{D} >$. We introduce the following source unit's trust parameter:

$$R(< Org_j, \mathcal{D} >) = \frac{\sum_i \mathcal{C}_{i,j,\mathcal{D}}}{\sum_i n_{i,j,\mathcal{D}}} \quad \forall Org_i \in \mathcal{O}$$

The numerator represents the overall number of the complaints issued by organizations with reference to the data unit $< Org_i, \mathcal{D} >$. The denominator is the overall number of interactions in which the data unit $\mathcal{D}$ is sent by Org_j to other organizations.

High values of $R(\cdot)$ mean that the source unit is not trustworthy. We suppose that each interaction could be modelled as a random variable of a probabilistic process, that can have value 1 if a complaint is fired, 0 otherwise. Specifically, we introduce the random variable X such that:

$$X = \begin{cases} 1 \text{ if a complaint is fired} \\ 0 \text{ otherwise} \end{cases}$$

We suppose, without loss of generality, that variable X has a binomial probability distribution with $P(X = 0) = p$ and $P(X = 1) = 1 - p$. Moreover, we make the following basic assumption: $p \ll (1 - p)$. In fact it is reasonable to suppose that the number of unsuccessful interactions is low with respect to the number of successful ones.

Therefore, $R(\cdot)$ is a random variable, linear combination of a large number of independent random variables that have the same distribution of probability. Thus, due to the "Central Limit Theorem", we can suppose that $R(\cdot)$ has a normal probability distribution.

A Criterion for Trust. The calculation of $R(\cdot)$ values allows one to establish a sorting of source units on the basis of their trust values. This is a novel contribution with respect to the current literature, that simply allows for discriminating between trusted and untrusted sources, without establishing a rating within these two sets. Instead, such a rating can be very important because an organization can choose to request data from another organization which has not the best trust value (though being trusted) but for example has a higher response time.

Nevertheless, it is important to distinguish between trusted and untrusted organizations. Therefore, we need to introduce a *threshold*, such that one can easily identify which organizations can be trusted for data with a fixed probability. A threshold also allows for applying a policy for punishing untrusted organizations. When $R(< Org_j, \mathcal{D} >)$ exceeds the threshold value, the source unit is automatically excluded from the system.

We argued that $R(\cdot)$ is a normal distributed variable. Then, we can calculate the mean m and the standard deviation σ and, by exploiting properties of the normal distribution, we give the following trust criterion:

$$\text{IF } R(< Org_j, \mathcal{D} >) \leq m + 2 \cdot \sigma \text{ THEN } < Org_j, \mathcal{D} > \text{TRUSTED}$$
$$\text{ELSE } < Org_j, \mathcal{D} > \text{UNTRUSTED}$$

According to the properties of the normal distribution, such criterion ensures that the right number of samples is selected with a probability at least equal to 95%.

The hypothesis of the same distributions of X variables for the different organizations could be removed. In this case, the given criterion continues to be valid on the basis of the Tchebycheff inequality [21], i.e.:

$$P(|X - \mu| > K \cdot \sigma) < \frac{1}{K^2}$$

where μ is the mean and σ the variance of $R(\cdot)$ samples. In the case of a normal distribution, the inequality is exactly reduced to the given criterion for $K = 2$. In the general case, the Tchebycheff inequality simply guarantees a probability lower bound of 75%.

3.2   Managing Malicious Behaviors

Cheating for Data Stewardship. In the hypothesis of our system, it may happen that an organization sends a large number of complaints in order to discredit another organization on the same data it owns; in this way, it can conquer the stewardship on such data. In order to prevent from such a malicious behavior, we introduce an adjusting term in the trust parameter definition, as follows:

$$R(< Org_j, \mathcal{D} >) = \frac{\sum_i \mathcal{C}_{i,j,\mathcal{D}} + \sum_i \mathcal{C}_{j,i,\mathcal{D}}}{\sum_i n_{i,j,\mathcal{D}} + \sum_i n_{j,i,\mathcal{D}}} \quad \forall Org_i \in \mathcal{O}$$

The second term of the numerator penalizes organizations requiring data they already have to other organizations and firing a large number of complaints. The term at the denominator corresponds to the term introduced to take into account the number of interactions.

Bias Elimination. We adopted for the $R(\cdot)$ computation the following rule. If an organization has fired a very high percentage of complaints against a data unit then we do not consider them in $R(\cdot)$ calculation. In fact, this situation is due either to strict requirements on data quality or to malicious behavior. The fraction complaints-interactions, we call $F(c, i)$, is a normal random variable (see Section 3.1). If we focus on the $F(c, i)$ values of an organization, we first calculate the parameters (i.e. the mean and the standard deviation) of the normal distribution of the other organization $F(c, i)$ values. Then, if $F(c, i)$ is higher than the mean value plus two times the standard deviation, the organization's complaints are not included in the $R(\cdot)$ calculation.

4   Rating Service Design

In this section, we describe the design of the Rating Service module of the DaQuinCIS architecture, which implements the trust model described in the previous section. The Rating Service has a centralized architecture storing all complaints and is responsible for certifying the trust level of source units. The use of a centralized system does not give specific scalability problems, due to the low variability of the number of source units in P2P tightly coupled systems. Moreover, the presence of a trust service independent from each organization could be a disincentive to have a malicious behavior. The Rating Service provides a complete knowledge of organization's behaviors with respect to the quality of data they exchange. This is a further advantage with respect to the fully decentralized peer to peer systems, which have a limited knowledge of complaints on a single peer.

Calculation of $R(\cdot)$. We assume that each organization in the system tracks its interactions with other organizations. In such a way, the Rating Service can simply gather this information, and calculate the overall number of transactions on some specific data made by an organization, necessary for source units' trust evaluation.

The Rating Service works as follows. When an organization is not satisfied by a source unit, it sends a complaint to the Rating Service. The Rating Service stores such a complaint and updates the statistics about the source unit.

The Rating Service analyzes the source unit's complaints and interaction numbers and calculates the values of $R(\cdot)$ for each source unit. The frequency of trust values update is a parameter that the Rating Service administrator should fix. If the quality of the organization data changes frequently, the associated trust value should be often updated. Notice that malicious organizations could send complaints with false values in the interaction field, in order to make another organization untrustworthy. In this paper, we suppose that the values in the interaction field are correct, leaving to future work the treatment of fraudulent behaviors concerning this field.

Organizations can query the Rating Service in order to have the trust level of a source unit. Then, they can use such values to select a source unit, either in combination with other quality metrics, or simply by selecting the ones having the best (i.e, the smallest) values of $R(\cdot)$.

False Values of n. We briefly give some hints on a possible way to solve the problem of false values of n in the complaints. Organizations can query the

Rating Service to obtain source units' trust levels. However, they cannot see complete information about single organization exchanges. Let us assume that organizations track all received requests. This is easy to achieve; for example, current DBMS's maintain such a statistic information. When an organization supposes that its trust level does not conform to the value provided by the Rating Service, it can ask for a check procedure, sending the number of interactions it stored for each organization. Then, the Rating Service requests the last interaction number to organizations present in the source unit table. In such a way, the Rating Service interaction number values are directly comparable with data sent by the organization. The comparison of such values allows one to verify if an organization cheats on complaints.

5   Validation of the Model in the **DaQuinCIS** Architecture

We have verified the effectiveness of the trust model described in the previous section, by implementing the rating service within the DaQuinCIS architecture. We use the Colt distribution library [22] for the statistical functions and results analysis. The results obtained from the performed set of experiments confirm the reliability of our trust model. As a first set of experiments, we evaluate the ability of the Rating Service to identify those organizations having a malicious behavior or very strict requirements on data quality. We call this type of organizations *anomalous organizations*. We create one source unit and three sets of respectively 25, 50 and 75 organizations that require data from the source unit. Each organization poses a different number of data requests; the number of requests ranges from 150 to 600. We perform several simulation runs, varying the number of organizations that have an anomalous behavior. The experimental results are shown in Figure 3. Notice that when the number of anomalous organizations exceeds 15% of the total number of organizations, the performance of our Rating Service degrades rapidly. This result shows the importance of assuming the number of positive interactions much greater than the number of unsuccessful interactions.

In the second set of experiments, we prove the effectiveness of the trust decision criterion. We create 25 source units that export 14 different typologies of data units and 75 organizations requiring data. The number of requests varies between 150 e 600. We introduce an organization that cheats for data stewardship and one source unit that provides data generating an high number of complaints. The value of trust assigned by the Rating Service to each source unit is reported in the chart of Figure 4. The dashed line represents the mean of the trust values calculated by the Rating Service. Instead, the continuous line represents the threshold values of trustworthiness (see Section 3). Source unit 12 is a source unit providing poor quality data, and source unit 20 refers to an organization cheating for data stewardship. The results show that the Rating Service identifies correctly both untrusted source units.

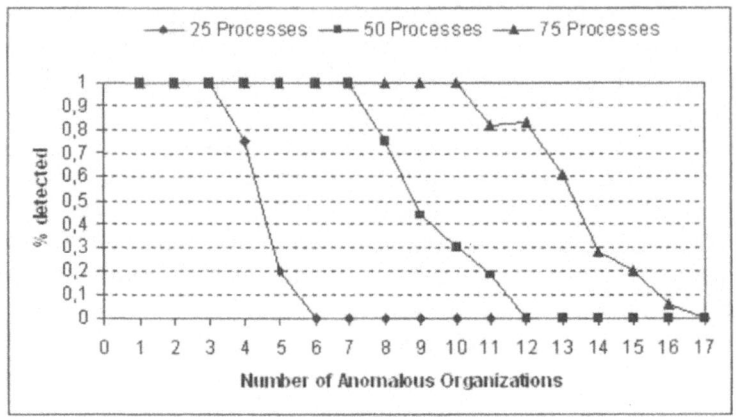

Fig. 3. Identified anomalous organizations vs actual number of anomalous organizations

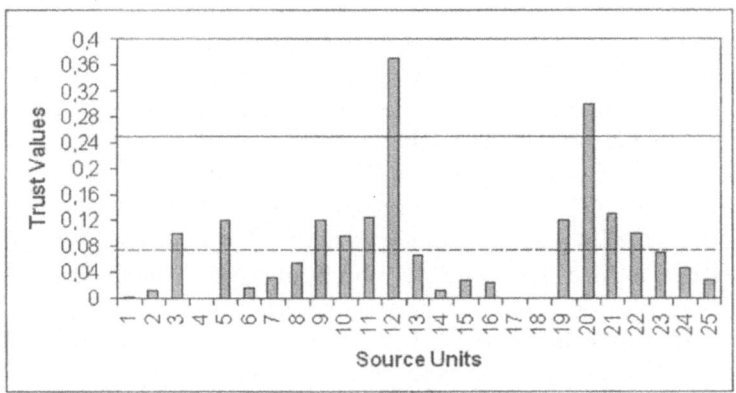

Fig. 4. Values of trust in a cooperative system simulation

6   Related Work

The problem of trusting agents is present in a wide number of different scientific areas, such as economics, sociology and computer science [23]. With respect to computer science, we note there are many applications that use simple techniques for agent reputation management. As an example, on-line auctions and trading systems frequently use methods for reputation calculations based on votes given by users. By means of this measures, users could be encouraged to make transactions. However, none of these simple mechanisms takes into account further possibilities of malicious uses. The diffusion of peer to peer architectures has shown the importance of managing trust of peers. Cheat agents use file sharing systems as Napster [19] or Kazaa [14] to spread dangerous programs or undesired contents. Therefore, many solutions have been proposed to enable trust management in P2P systems, as detailed in the following.

A model based on social properties of trust is illustrated in [24]. However, the complexity of its sociological foundation makes difficult its real implementation.

The method proposed in [25] allows to derive trust assessments on the basis of individual feedbacks about information sources. Users annotate the rationale of their opinion by means of a markup language for information analysis. An analysis tool then derives a rating for information sources.

A technique based on probabilistic models for reputation is described in [26]. The needed information are obtained by means of a propagation of the requests throughout the systems. The evaluations sent by peers are weighted with the reputation of the sender peer itself.

In [27], the authors propose an approach based on the definition of a semantic policy language and a distributed trust management system. Each peer can choose a personal policy on trustworthiness; a client peer is trusted on the basis of the policy of the server peer and on the basis of information gathered on its reputation.

The solution proposed in [28,20] exploits peer persistent identifiers built on IP addresses, by means of clustering techniques to eliminate malicious behaviors. The Gnutella [17] P2P infrastructure is the reference architecture. The trusting protocol is completely decentralized; peers maintain information about their past interactions and share it. When a peer wants to know the reputation of another peer, it makes a broadcast query, asking information about it. Furthermore, authors propose the use of public key encryption to detect tampered votes.

Another fully decentralized trust management system is proposed in [13]. It uses a distributed data management system to store reputation information in the P2P network. While the model of trust is global, the calculation of peer trustworthiness is done by a local algorithm. The authors propose a heuristic criterion to establish if a peer is trustworthy or not, based on a probabilistic analysis.

7   Conclusions

The paper describes a trust model valid for peer to peer tightly coupled systems. The main novel contributions of the model are: *(i)* the basic trust unit, consisting of the pair $< Org_j, \mathcal{D} >$, rather than simply a single peer; *(ii)* the criterion for rating source units with respect to trust, which takes into account the number of peers' interactions. Moreover, the criterion is targeted to tightly coupled systems by considering anomalies and malicious behaviors specific of such environments. We have implemented the proposed trust model as the Rating Service, a component of DaQuinCIS, a complete architecture for data quality diffusion and improvement in cooperative information systems. We have performed preliminary tests and experiments showing that the Rating Service works well when the number of malicious organizations are sufficiently less than the overall number of cooperating organizations.

The model needs to be refined in the following directions, which will be studied in future work. A more extensive simulation of the proposed model will be performed, in order to quantitatively evaluate the reliability of the trust model. Furthermore, we will apply our trust model to a real cooperative system.

We argued that organizations can not be left out from a cooperative system indefinitely. The problem of untrusted organizations reinstatement will be also investigated.

Finally, a method to verify the actual distribution of X for each organization could be introduced. The role of such a method would be to improve the probability lower bound used to identify untrusted organizations.

References

1. De Michelis, G., Dubois, E., Jarke, M., Matthes, F., Mylopoulos, J., Papazoglou, M., Pohl, K., Schmidt, J., Woo, C., Yu, E.: Cooperative Information Systems: A Manifesto. In Papazoglou, M., Schlageter, G., eds.: Cooperative Information Systems: Trends & Directions. Accademic-Press (1997)
2. Redman, T.: Data Quality for the Information Age. Artech House (1996)
3. Scannapieco, M., Virgillito, A., Marchetti, C., Mecella, M., Baldoni, R.: The daquincis architecture: a platform for exchanging and improving data quality in cooperative information systems. Accepted for publication on Information Systems (2003)
4. Batini, C., Mecella, M.: Enabling Italian e-Government Through a Cooperative Architecture. IEEE Computer 34 (2001)
5. Shankaranarayan, G., Wang, R., Ziad, M.: Modeling the Manufacture of an Information Product with IP-MAP. In: Proceedings of the 5th International Conference on Information Quality (IQ'00). (Boston, MA, USA, 2000)
6. Wang, R.: A Product Perspective on Total Data Quality Management. Communications of the ACM 41 (1998)
7. English, L.: Improving Data Warehouse and Business Information Quality. Wiley & Sons (1999)
8. Naumann, F.: Quality-Driven Query Answering for Integrated Information Systems. LNCS 2261 (2002)
9. Mecella, M., Scannapieco, M., Virgillito, A., Baldoni, R., Catarci, T., Batini, C.: Managing Data Quality in Cooperative Information Systems. In: Proceedings of the Tenth International Conference on Cooperative Information Systems. (Irvine, CA, 2002)
10. Catarci, T., ed.: Proceedings of the ICDT'03 International Workshop on Data Quality in Cooperative Information Systems (DaQuinCIS '03) . (Siena, Italy, 2003)
11. Jeusfeld, M., Quix, C., Jarke, M.: Design and Analysis of Quality Information for Data Warehouses. In: Proceedings of the 17th International Conference on Conceptual Modeling (ER'98). (Singapore, Singapore, 1998)
12. Lenzerini, M.: Data Integration: A Theoretical Perspective. In: Proceedings of the 21st ACM Symposium on Principles of Database Systems (PODS 2002). (Madison, Wisconsin, USA, 2002)
13. Aberer, K., Despotovic, Z.: Managing trust in a peer-2-peer information system. In: Proceedings of the tenth international conference on Information and knowledge management. (2001) 310–317

14. KaZaA. (http://www.kazaa.com)
15. Mecella, M.: Cooperative Processes and e-Services. Ph.D. Thesis in Computer Engineering, IV 2002, Università di Roma "La Sapienza", Dipartimento di Informatica e Sistemistica (2002)
16. Fauvet, M., Dumas, M., Benatallah, B., Paik, H.: Peer-to-Peer Traced Execution of Composite Services. In: Proceedings of the 2nd VLDB International Workshop on Technologies for e-Services (VLDB-TES 2001). (Rome, Italy, 2001)
17. Gnutella: The gnutella protocol specification v0.4. http://www9.limewire.com/developer/gnutella_protocol_0.4.pdf (2001)
18. FastTrack. (http://www.fasttrack.nu)
19. Napster. (http://www.napster.com)
20. Damiani, E., di Vimercati, D.C., Paraboschi, S., Samarati, P., Violante, F.: A reputation-based approach for choosing reliable resources in peer-to-peer networks. In: Proceedings of the 9th ACM conference on Computer and communications security. (2002) 207–216
21. Devore, J.L.: Probability and Statistics for Engineering and the Sciences. 5 edition edn. Duxbury Press (1999)
22. Colt: The colt distribution library. (http://hoschek.home.cern.ch/hoschek/colt/)
23. Mui, L., Mohtashemi, M., Halberstadt, A.: Notions of reputation in multi-agents systems: a review. In: Proceedings of the first international joint conference on Autonomous agents and multiagent systems. (2002) 280–287
24. S.Marsh: Formalising Trust as a Computational Concept. PhD thesis, University of Stirling (1994)
25. Gil, Y., Ratnaker, V.: Trusting information sources one citizen at a time. In: Proceedings of the first international Semantic Web conference (ISWC). (2002)
26. Mui, L., Mohtashemi, M., Ang, C., Szolovits, P., Halberstadt, A.: Ratings in distributed systems: A bayesian approach. 11th Workshop on Information Technologies and Systems (WITS'2001). (2001)
27. Finin, T., Joshi, A.: Agents, trust, and information access on the semantic web. ACM SIGMOD Record **31** (2002) 30–35
28. Cornelli, F., Damiani, E., di Vimercati, S.D.C., Paraboschi, S., Samarati, P.: Choosing reputable servents in a p2p network. In: Proceedings of the eleventh international conference on World Wide Web. (2002) 376–386

Static Type-Inference for Trust in Distributed Information Systems

Premkumar T. Devanbu, Michael Gertz, and Brian Toone

Department of Computer Science
University of California at Davis
Davis, CA 95616, U.S.A.
{devanbu,gertz,toone}@cs.ucdavis.edu

Abstract. Decision-makers in critical fields such as medicine and finance make use of a wide range of information available over the Internet. Mediation, a data integration technique for distributed, heterogeneous data sources, manages the complexity and diversity of the information schemas on behalf of clients. We raise here the issue of *trust*: is the information so obtained trustworthy? Each client can have different perspectives on the desired trustworthiness the information he or she needs. We consider here the *scaling problem* that arises from a very large number of users accessing information from many different sources. A mediator cannot be expected to manage the potentially quadratic scaling of trust relationships clients can have with information sources. Furthermore, the possibility of using untrustworthy data increases the risk that the resulting data will be unacceptable: a mediator might evaluate a complex query for a client, only to have the answer rejected because the client does not trust the sources of the information.

To help address these issues, we introduce a general *static trust-typing* model, which can infer the trust ratings of query plans, based on trust meta-data about the input data to the query, even before executing the query. We also define essential properties of such a trust-typing model, namely *correctness, precision and completeness*. We present an example of a trust-typing model and describe some algorithmic frameworks for the use of such trust-typing models in mediator-based query evaluation.

1 Introduction

In critical fields such as medicine, finance, environmental protection, and national defense, poorly-informed decisions can have unacceptable negative consequences. Thus, prompt access to the widest possible set of information sources is critical. A vast amount of information (e.g., drug interaction data, genomic data, ethnographic information, company financial histories, geophysical data) is becoming available over the Internet, and decision makers can benefit from unified access to this data. A unified schema, which supports querying over a diverse set of information sources can provide decision-makers with valuable access to a wide set of sources. A variety of mediator architectures (e.g., [4,8,10,20]) have evolved in response to this problem. Mediators shield data consumers from the

R. Meersman et al. (Eds.): CoopIS/DOA/ODBASE 2003, LNCS 2888, pp. 370–388, 2003.
© Springer-Verlag Berlin Heidelberg 2003

concerns of schema awareness and query planning. Clients issue queries on an integrated schema provided by the mediator. The mediator knows a wide set of information providers and their schema; it maps a client's query to distributed queries over the sources that provide data relevant to the client's query, and then integrates the returned data to construct the final answer to the client.

However, data consumers, specially in an inter-networked WAN context, need to worry about the *trustworthiness* of information sources. As described in, e.g., [11,12,13,14], data sources may have varying levels of quality. In this context, consumers would be well-advised to carefully consider the sources of the data when using data provided in response to a query. In addition, client applications may have different levels of trust. For example, when requesting a legal case-record for malpractice lawsuits against orthodontists living in Waco, Texas, a client may want a *complete* list; but when asking the locations of nearby Sri Lankan restaurants that are Glatt Kosher certified, clients might be satisfied with a partial list. Some sources may have complete data, and some sources might have incomplete or incorrect data. Current mediator architectures can process complex queries, and integrate data from multiple sources. However, they are not set up to handle the potentially quadratic scaling of possible trust relationships between clients and information sources.

In a WAN setting, mediators must also consider the possibility that the final result may have been computed using sources which may not satisfy the client's trust requirements. If the information providers and mediators charge for their services, the client might have to pay for data that she cannot use! It would therefore be desirable to determine *statically* during query plan generation and before query execution, if for a given query and a specific set of sources, the final answer would be acceptable to the client. Such a static typing scheme can be used by a mediator to prune query plans that, if executed, would result in answers to the query that do not satisfy the client's trust requirements.

In this paper, we first describe a mediator architecture that deals with the quadratic-scaling of trust relationships between clients and information sources (Sec. 2). In particular, we detail a generic model for *trust-type inference* in the style of programming languages type inference, which allows the static (or *partially static*) computation of the trust level of query results (Sec 3). Based on this general model, we provide an example of a static trust-typing algorithms in the context of a mediator architecture for relational databases as information sources (Sec. 4). After a discussion of related work (Sec. 5), we conclude the paper and outline our ongoing and future work (Sec. 6).

2   Trust Mediation

In our previous work [19], we described an architecture for trust mediation, which we briefly recapitulate here for completeness.

2.1   Mediated Query Systems

We build our trust mediation framework by extending the infrastructure typical of a mediated query system (MQS) (see, e.g., [4,10] for an overview). Multiple heterogeneous, distributed sources supply information to multiple clients. A mediator or collection of mediators connects clients to sources by integrating information from sources to satisfy client queries. Figure 1 shows the query/response interaction among components in a typical MQS. Dotted arrows indicate queries. Solid arrows indicate responses.

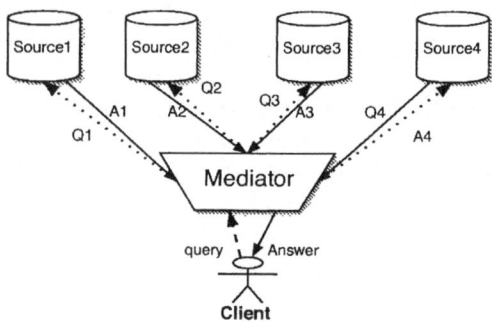

Fig. 1. Typical mediated query system. Note that the information sources used by the mediator must be trusted and acceptable to client.

With many clients and numerous information sources, mediators are in the untenable position of tracking a quadratically growing number of trust relationships in addition to their normal data integration tasks. Thus, in Fig. 1, clients must trust sources that are used to process queries. Clients must trust mediators to do correct data integration and query processing. Sources must trust clients and mediators to use the information provided in a proper way. It may be unnecessary to specify and account for every trust relationship in order to achieve the desired characteristics of a trustworthy distributed information system. For example, the trustworthiness of mediators can be assumed when the mediator exists within the same administrative and security domain as clients accessing the system. For simplicity, we will assume that the trustworthiness of mediators and access control over the information in the sources is either irrelevant or handled outside our trust mediation framework, e.g., using existing secure mediation techniques such as those proposed in [1,2,3,5].

2.2   Conceptual Architecture

Figure 2 shows a high level view of our approach. Trust authorities evaluate information sources and assign trust ratings based on precise, agreed-upon trust definitions. A trust authority may be an actual external entity such as the Better Business Bureau or a conceptual component consisting of a network of clients willing to share their expertise and experience interacting with a source in order to establish a trust rating for a source (see, e.g., [7,17,18]). Whatever the implementation, ratings assigned by trust authorities are used by the mediator while processing client queries. In [19], we use a *trust broker* to warehouse trust meta-data provided by trust authorities; for simplicity, we omit that here.

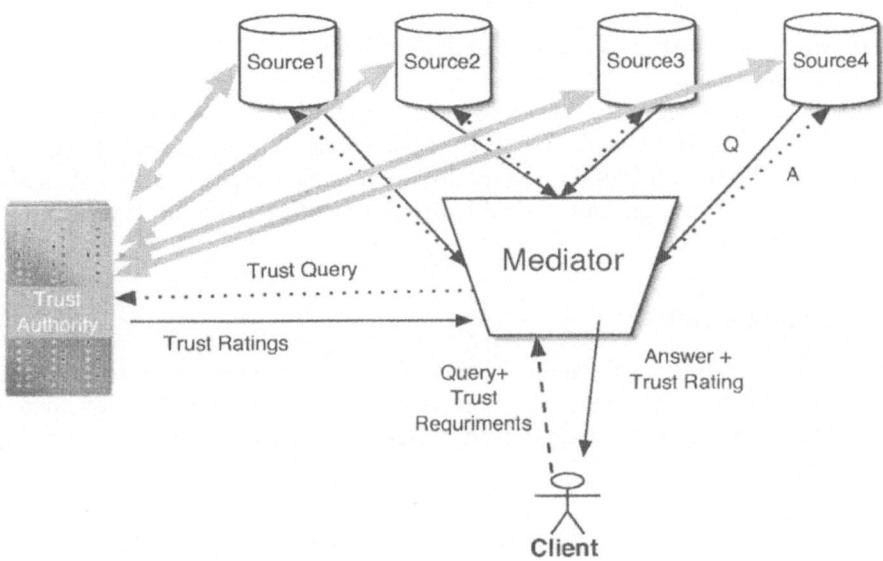

Fig. 2. Conceptual architecture for trust mediation. Gray arrows to Trust Authority represent assigning of trust meta-data. Dashed lines are query, and solid lines matching answers. Some labels are omitted for clarity.

The operation of our architecture begins when clients submit queries to a mediator. In particular, clients may attach *trust requirements* to the submitted queries. The mediator determines multiple query plans for the client query based on the global (mediated) schema. It is important to note here that multiple query plans exist because data may be duplicated in several sources. Recall that the trustworthiness of these sources may be different and thus the result of query plan execution may not be identical as is typical in a mediated query system. This is accounted for by the client through the specification of trust requirements. To select a query plan for execution, the mediator processes the trust ratings stored in the trust broker for the sources specified in each query plan. This processing step yields trust ratings for the integrated data that would be returned to the client for each executed query. The algorithmic framework for trust processing we present for performing this static analysis of query plans to determine trustworthiness of the integrated result is detailed in Sections 3 and 4. Operation of the framework continues as the mediator executes a query plan whose trust rating satisfies the client trust requirements. The retrieved data is then sent to the client. The mediator notifies the client if no query plan satisfies the client trust requirements.

The fundamental contribution of this paper is a static trust-typing model that can be used by the mediator for more efficient and effective query planning. In the next section, we formalize the model upon which the architecture described in this section is built.

3   General Static Trust-Typing Model

In this section, we begin first with a general, abstract data model (Sec. 3.1). We then present a general model (Sec. 3.2) of static trust-typing within this general data model. We then discuss a general notion of a trust-type inference algorithm (Sec. 3.3). Finally, we present desirable properties of such a trust-type inference algorithm (Sec. 3.4).

3.1   Preliminaries

We start with a very general data model, to avoid commitment to a specific data model such as the relational or an object-oriented model. Consider an *information domain*, consisting of a finite set of primitive types

$$T_p = \{t_1, t_2, \ldots, t_{|T_p|}\}.$$

These would evidently include strings, integers, floats and so on. We also assume a finite set of *type constructors*

$$C = \{c_1, c_2, \ldots, c_{|C|}\}.$$

Type constructors (e.g., products, sums, records, etc) have different arities and are applied to primitive types to create a potentially infinite set of possible derived types (which include primitive types)

$$T_d = \{t_1, t_2, \ldots\}.$$

Within this framework, we also allow *data sets* Δ_i, which *populate* these types, shown thus

$$\Delta_i : \tau, \ where \ \tau \in T_d.$$

Data sets are manipulated by a finite set of operators

$$O = \{o_1, o_2, \ldots, o_{|O|}\}$$

where each operator takes one or more inputs of specified types and then delivers an output of a specified type, thus:

$$o_i :: t_{i_1} \times t_{i_2} \times \ldots \times t_{i_m} \to t_{output}$$

We assume that operators have a well-defined computational semantics. That is, given input data items that instantiate the input types of an operator, there is a well-defined function to calculate the output, which will then instantiate the output type. Operators can be used to build complex (nested), well-formed *query expressions*, as allowed by the type signatures specified for the operators. Also, operators can have rewrite rules associated with them that specify typical properties such commutativity, associativity etc., which may allow for optimization of queries by a query processor.

A *schema* S is a collection of types

$$S = \{\tau_1, \tau_2, \ldots, \tau_{|S|}\}, \ where \ \tau_i \in T_d$$

An *instance* of a schema S is just a collection of sets $\{D_1, D_2, \ldots, D_{|S|}\}$ of data items that populate each type in the schema. Operationally, we assume that an information system (or database system) that manages the data items and to which clients submit well-formed queries. The information system then evaluates these queries and returns answers. The extension of this notion to a client who uses multiple information systems to process a single query (where the input datasets to the queries may originate from different sources) is self-evident.

So we capture here a broad set of data models, including relational, and object-oriented and even semi-structured models. In the following section, we develop a static typing model for trust.

3.2   Trust

Consider a collection of information sources, each instantiating a schema. The schemas may overlap, i.e., different source schemas may share types. For example, there may be two different databases which offer data about the set of antibiotics suitable for treating Anthrax. The client may have different levels of *trust* in each database, and may issue different queries, some of which are critical (and require high trust) and some that are not.

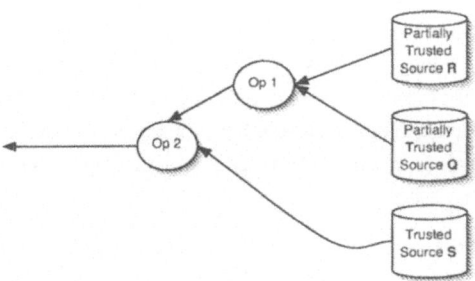

Fig. 3. Example of query answered using multiple sources, which are accorded differing levels of trust

Trust is a complex concept with many possible different meanings (see, e.g., [6,15]). Trust may refer to *aggregate* properties of an entire dataset, e.g, a user might believe that the set of anti-anthrax drugs identified by a database may be incomplete. Trust may be *content-based*, referring to detailed beliefs about specific members of a data set. For example, a client may believe that a dataset has incorrect information about anti-Anthrax drugs whose manufacturer is in Europe. Trust may also be at the level of individual data instances. How does the client assign these beliefs? The rational way to do so would be based on *experience*. In practice, for example, we assign trust to information sources based on how useful, accurate and/or valuable the information they provide is in the real world.

Evidently trust varies with the trustee (in this case, the information source). In a distributed/mediated environment we might have a situation as shown informally in Fig. 3, with a query of the form $op2(op1(R, Q), S)$, where different sources are needed to process the query. In this context, the sources for R and Q are only partially trusted, but the source for S is fully trusted. Evidently, the client cannot fully trust the final result; but what should the trust be? One can certainly use the result data and see how it works out; but clearly it is preferable to have good *a-priori knowledge* of the trustworthiness of data sets or information sources rather than having actually determine this post-facto, after using the data to make business-critical decisions (consider the implications of prescribing drugs using information of unknown trustworthiness). We can take this one step further: rather than evaluating the final answer set *after* the query has been processed, we would like to *statically* determine the trust level of the final answer before executing the query against the sources (and thus perhaps avoid paying for the processing of sub-queries that might result in untrustworthy answers).

Thus, there is strong motivation for a semantically well-founded *a-priori* calculation of the trust level that can be associated with answer datasets returned by incompletely trusted information sources. This can be considered a meta-data calculation based on trust meta-data that is available a-priori about those sources. In fact, we wish to calculate the trust meta-data *statically*, i.e., based on the structure of the query plan and available trust-meta on the data sources.

Consider the following setting of information sources $DB_1, \ldots, DB_n$, with schemas $S_1, \ldots, S_n$. Without loss of generality, assume that each database schema is a singleton type. We now assume a simple trust meta-data model, where we assume an aggregate trust-type associated with each source. Each aggregate type is drawn from a (potentially infinite) trust-type poset B, with ordering relation R_B :

$$B = \{b_1, \ldots, b_{|B|}\}, \quad R_B = \{(x, y) \mid x, y, \in B\}$$

We show the *assignment* of a trust-type b to a data set D_i of a particular type T thus:

$$TT(D_i : T) = b$$

In the ensuing discussion, the actual datatype is usually not of concern, so we just denote the trust-type, thus:

$$D_i :: b$$

The ordering relationship R_B is used to model the fact that some sources can be more trusted than others. In general, this relationship is not a total order: not all trust relationships are comparable, and different trust ratings may be preferred under different circumstances[1]. This trust-type assignment may be performed by the clients themselves, or (for better scalability) by a credible trust authority on behalf of the clients, e.g., the Better Business Bureau, or a government agency. We note that there may be multiple information source with the same schema, which have different trust types assigned to them. So, there may be several different ways of evaluating a given query, by sourcing information from one of several alternative sources.

Now consider that the clients need to evaluate results returned for queries against a mediator; how can they develop trust-type assignments for the results of the queries? Clearly, clients need this information. It would be impractical for third parties to develop trust ratings for all possible queries and all possible ways of evaluating respective query results. It is also possible that a client needs information at a trust level that is so high that it is impossible to get this information, given the trust assignment of input sources. It is also possible that some evaluations of a given query (using some specific information sources or combination of sources) will provide answers at the required trust levels, and some would not.

3.3   Trust-Type Inference

We propose an approach to processing *aggregate* trust meta-data or trust-types in the setting described above, which has a strong analogy to type systems in programming languages (see, e.g., [9]). Consider a query algebra $\mathcal{A}$ with operators

$$O = \{o_1, \ldots, o_{|O|}\}$$

as defined above. Consider a specific operator

$$o_i :: t_{i_1} \times t_{i_2} \times \ldots \times t_{i_m} \to t_{output}$$

A *trust typing system* associates with each such operator a *trust-type inference rule*

$$\frac{TT(D_{i_1} :: t_{i_1}) = b_{i_1} \ \& \ TT(D_{i_2} :: t_{i_2}) = b_{i_2} \ \& \ \ldots \ \& \ TT(D_{i_m} :: t_{i_m}) = b_{i_m}}{TT(o_i(D_{i_1}, \ldots, D_{i_m}) :: t_{output}) = f_{o_i}(b_{i_1}, \ldots, b_{i_m})}$$

where $b_{i_1} \ldots b_{i_m}, b_{output}$ are trust-type assignments. Given (1) an *a-priori* trust-type assignment for the input data sets to an operation o_i and (2) the inference rule, the associated trust computing function f_{o_i} allows the *static* (before query execution) derivation of a trust-type assignment for the result of evaluating the operation over those data sets. In general, the function f_{o_i} could return a set of

---

[1] We refer the reader to the earlier example of lawsuits and restaurants in Sec. 1, where different ratings are preferred.

trust-types rather than a single trust-type: in some situations (examples follow) more than one trust-type might be inferred.

Since query plans are nothing more than a nesting of query operators, this approach clearly can used for defining trust-type judgments for query plans as they are generated by a typical query processor in a mediator.

Definition 1. *A query plan Q_p in a query algebra is a well-formed expression using the operators defined in that algebra. The input data set to Q_p is the set of data sets $\{D_1, \ldots, D_n\}$ that form the inputs to the query plan. The input trust-type assignments for Q_p, $IT(Q_p)$ is the set of trust type assignments $\{D_1 :: T_1, \ldots, D_n :: T_n\}$ provided by some trust authority.*

Given a query plan generated by a mediator and a set of input trust-type assignments, one can use a trust typing system to produce, statically, a final trust-type rating for the result of the query. This provides several advantages:

1. Once the trust assignments of input data sets to a query are known, a mediator can compute the trust assignment of the result without any additional information.
2. Once trust ratings are known, the mediator does not have to actually execute a query to determine whether the query result will satisfy the trust requirements specified by the client.
3. Given a specific query and the required input data from several different alternate information sources, a mediator may be able to reformulate a query (plan) into a form that can be evaluated in order to satisfy the trust requirements.

However, in order to use a trust-typing system in this fashion, it must satisfy some important properties. We discuss these in the following section.

3.4   Soundness and Completeness

We define here two important properties of any static trust-type inferencing mechanism: soundness and completeness[2].

A Naive View of Soundness. By *soundness*, we mean that the judgments made by the trust typing system are accurate. This accuracy is established by comparison with a reliable "oracle" that can provide trust ratings; in our case, these ratings are provided by the trust authority. The trust authority provides ratings for the data available from the information sources. With the ratings on the data that constitute the inputs to a query plan, the trust typing system can now derive a static trust typing judgment for the final result of the query, if executed. The accuracy of this judgment can be evaluated empirically. First,

---

[2] In programming language type systems, completeness in any useful sense is typically an impossible goal, given a Turing-complete programming language. Since query languages are usually not as expressive, completeness is relevant here.

based on the determined query plan, the query is executed by the mediator, producing some final query result. The final result can then be subsequently considered by the trust authority, and given a rating. In this context, the trust typing system is considered *sound*, if the trusting rating judgment produced by the typing system for a given query plan and input data with a given rating *would be exactly the same rating* as what the trust authority would produce, were it given the query result. In general, we prove soundness of a typing system by considering each input rule in turn, and argue that its conclusions, given ratings on the input data, would be precisely the same as that of the trust authority.

However, in practice, this is not feasible. Imagine two information sources, each of which has partial data: one about the drugs to treat seasonal allergies, and the other drugs that are acceptable for patients with hypertension. The *intersection* of these two data sets would be drugs for seasonal allergies that can be used by hypertensive patients. Note here that even if two input data sets are rated partial, they may each have just those data items that would yield an *exactly correct* final result for their intersection; so, given the actual final result, a trust authority might in fact be able to rate it as exactly correct. However, a static typing system, without *a priori* access to this data, cannot make such a judgment. Given a rating, it has to take a pessimistic view on what the actual result data might be; so it must conclude that the result could be either exactly correct, or it could be missing some data. Thus, the notion of soundness has to be modified, to allow the static judgement to be pessimistically approximate.

A different view: Correct and Precise. Therefore, our notion of soundness has two aspects. First, we want our trust typing algorithm to be *correct*: given a final static typing judgement on a query (or query plan, to be more precise), there must be a particular configuration of data items on the input sources, consistent with the input type assignments given by the trust authority, that would lead to a final result that would be rated exactly the same way by *both* the typing judgement and the trust authority. Correctness guarantees that a derived typing judgment is never wrong. But this is not sufficient. We also need to be sure that the typing judgment does not miss any possibilities.

In general, several different configurations of input/output data may be possible for each operation, we do not want the type system to miss anything: we also want it to *precise*. That is, if it is possible that a particular configuration of inputs could lead to a result type rating by the trust authority, the static typing judgment should include that type. It is important here to note that *we assume that the trust authority behaves in some semantically consistent manner: viz.,* the authority does not capriciously confer trust ratings onto data sets, but does so in some well-defined manner. Only then can we hope to approximate the trust authority's behavior using a static typing model. We now present definitions for correctness, precision, and completeness.

Definition 2. *Consider a query plan Q_p, and input trust-type assignment $IT(Q_p)$, drawn from a trust-type poset (B, R_B), provided by a trust authority. Assume, without loss of generality, that Q_p is evaluated on some given set of* *inputs conforming to the input trust-type assignment, $IT(Q_p)$, and the result is evaluated by the trust authority and given the (empirical) trust-type $T_E(Q_p)$. Also assume that the trust-type algorithm derives the static trust type $T_S(Q_p)$.*

In this setting, a trust typing algorithm is correct, *if for each type $\mathcal{T} \in IT(Q_p)$, it is possible to construct an artificial input data set D_A for the query plan Q_p so that*

1. *The trust authority's ratings for the input data set D_A would be precisely $IT(Q_p)$, and*
2. *$T_E(Q_p) = \mathcal{T}$.*

Definition 3. *In the same setting, a trust typing algorithm is* precise, *if it is impossible to construct an artificial input data set D_A for the query plan Q_p so that*

1. *The trust authority's ratings for the input data set D_A would be precisely $IT(Q_p)$, and*
2. *the query result is given the trust rating $\mathcal{T}$ by the trust authority, where $\mathcal{T} \notin T_E(Q_p)$.*

Completeness. By this, we mean that the typing system is able to provide for judgments for every possible query expression. This is a measure of the expressiveness of the type system; can it provide ratings for any kind of query plan? Essentially the desired property is the following: given any given query plan, and ratings on the input data, a trust rating can be given to the final result. We show this by induction: for each operation, and each possible input trust-type rating, we show that a rating on the result can be produced by the trust typing system. Completeness then follows by structural induction.

Definition 4. *A trust-typing system for a query algebra $\mathcal{A}$ is* complete, *if for every operator o_i in the algebra, and for every possible input type assignment to the inputs to the operation, the trust-typing system includes an inference rule that infers a trust-type judgment for the result of the operation.*

4   An Example Trust-Type System

Consider a trust-type system such that every source rated using this system will match exactly one of five trust-types, C, I, E, O, W. The intuition behind this type system is based on a notion of *data coverage*. An information source is rated C if is complete, *i.e.*, if it has exactly the "correct" data set[3]. I refers to "incomplete", some data items are missing from what the source provides; E refers to "excessive", if all correct data items are present at the source, but some erroneous items are also present; O refers to "overlapping", meaning some

---

[3] We provide precise semantics for correctness later; first, we just provide an intuitive notion of this.

correct tuples are missing, and some erroneous ones are present; and finally W refers to the case where the source provides only wrong data items. As for ordering, we take C to be the most trusted, and W to be the least trusted; the other three trust-type are in between, and are mutually incommensurate, since they are each preferable under different circumstances.

Definition 5. *The* basic coverage trust-typing system *(CTS) is defined by* $B^b = \{C, I, E, O, W\}$, *and the poset on* B^b *is defined as* $R_B^b = \{ (W,E), (W,O), (W,I), (E,C), (I,C), (O,C) \}$; (X,Y) *means that* X *is a lower trust level than* Y.

As we will see below, when using our inference algorithms, it is possible that the result of a query plan may be given multiple ratings. For example, the result of the intersection of two data sets rated I might be rated I, C: both results are possible.

We can now provide a semantics for the trust-typing system, that is, we can precisely define the conditions under which we expect a trust authority TA to provide each of the above ratings to a source S. To do this, we assume that a trust authority has its own (presumably infallible) view of the set of data items that a source *should* have; this view of TA on S is denoted S_{TA}. The trust authority then compares its view of the source with the dataset actually provided by the source S and assigns ratings as defined below.

Definition 6. *A semantically consistent trust authority* TA *assigns trust-types in the basic coverage trust-typing system (CTS) for a source S as follows*

$$TT(S) = \begin{cases} C \text{ (complete)} & \text{, if } S = S_{TA} \\ I \text{ (incomplete)} & \text{, if } S \subset S_{TA} \wedge S_{TA} \neq \emptyset \\ E \text{ (excessive)} & \text{, if } S \supset S_{TA} \wedge S \neq \emptyset \\ O \text{ (overlapping)} & \text{, if } (S \cap S_{TA} \neq \emptyset) \wedge (S \not\subset S_{TA}) \wedge (S_{TA} \not\subset S) \\ W \text{ (wrong)} & \text{, if } (S \cap S_{TA} = \emptyset) \wedge (S \neq \emptyset) \wedge (S_{TA} \neq \emptyset) \end{cases}$$

For example, the trust authority TA rates S complete if S contains exactly all data items TA expects, i.e., $S = S_{TA}$. TA rates S wrong if there is no data item in S that is also in the trust authority's view S_{TA} and both sets of data items S_{TA} and S are non-empty. The definitions are a little tricky for the case where either S_{TA} or S_A might be empty: e.g., if $S_{TA} = \phi$, a non-empty source should be rated *excessive*, not *wrong*; and an empty source should be rated *complete*, not *wrong*. The above definition does work correctly, and in fact admits a correct, precise, and complete inference algorithm, as we shall see next.

4.1 Algorithm for CTS Trust-Type Inference

There are five possible trust-types in the basic coverage type system. Since the focus in this section is on relational databases as information sources a mediator operates on, we use the relational algebra to specify queries and assign trust-types to respective (intermediate) query results. We use the following six operators of the relational algebra, four binary operators and two unary operators: set union ($\cup$), set intersection ($\cap$), set difference ($-$), cross product ($\times$), selection

(σ), and projection (π). There is a total of 80 input trust-type combinations: for each commutative binary operator $(\cap, \cup, \times)$, there are 15 possible combinations of input trust-types $((I, I), (I, C), (I, O), (I, E), (I, O), (C, O), \ldots)$. For the non-commutative set difference, there are 25 possible input trust-type combinations, and for the two unary operators there is a total of 10 possible input trust-types. These 80 input trust-type configurations naturally lead to 80 trust inference rules. The basic 80-rule inference algorithm handles the basic type system, as presented in Def. 5, in practice, however, multiple type ratings, as envisioned in Def. 6, can occur when inferring types of query plans. Each of these types represent a possible trust rating of an intermediate result. If such a result is used in another operation, each possible trust-type rating must be considered in turn, with an appropriate inference rule, and the result trust-type rating will be union of all the resulting trust types. In case of a binary operation, each pair of trust-type ratings from the two inputs should be considered.

Our goal is to prove the following theorem for the basic coverage trust-typing algorithm:

Theorem 1. *The coverage trust-type system is correct, precise, and complete for the above six operators of the relational algebra and for trust authorities that assign semantically well-founded trust ratings.*

Proof. *Completeness* is demonstrated by listing all the 80 possible rules, which provide inference rules for all possible combinations of input types for all possible rules. We omit it here for brevity.

Correctness and *precision* can be demonstrated by considering each of the entire set of inference rules, and arguing correctness and precision. For brevity, we just provide proofs of correctness and precision for a few rules, for some of the combinations that illustrate the techniques.

Figure 4 shows some of the inference rules for projection operator (π), along with Venn diagrams that establish for each case a configuration that shows that the rule is correct, i.e, that there is a specific configuration of the input data set conforming to the input trust-type that leads to the output trust-type. For example, in row 3 on the rightmost column, the Venn diagram provides the correctness witness (existence proof) for the rule

$$\frac{S :: O}{\pi(S) :: E}$$

The actual dataset is shown with the dashed rectangle, and the dataset from the source is the solid ellipse. The actual, expected projection result is shown in the solid semi-ellipse, whereas projection applied to the data provided by the source yields the solid ellipse. Thus in this case, the output can be rated E, for excessive. This establishes that with an input conforming to an O (overlapping) rating from a trust authority, it is possible to have an output that would be rated E by the same authority. In this way, we can provide justification for each of the cases in the right column. This establishes *correctness* for the projection rule in the case where the input is rated O. Similarly, arguing by case, and providing

Inference Rule	Witness (for correctness)	Inference Rule	Witness (for correctness)
$\dfrac{S::C}{\pi(S)::C}$	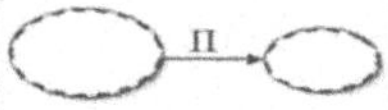	$\dfrac{O::C}{\pi(S)::C}$	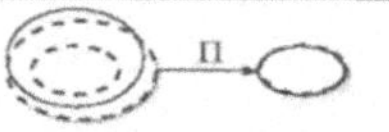
$\dfrac{S::I}{\pi(S)::C}$	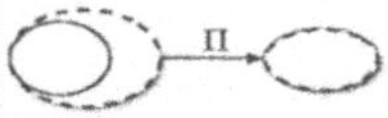	$\dfrac{S::O}{\pi(S)::I}$	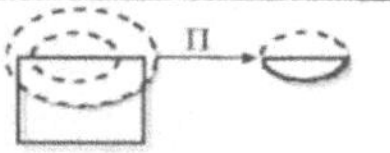
$\dfrac{S::I}{\pi(S)::I}$	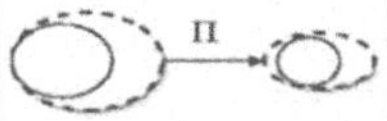	$\dfrac{S::O}{\pi(S)::E}$	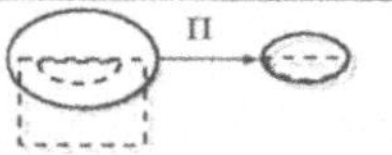
$\dfrac{S::E}{\pi(S)::C}$	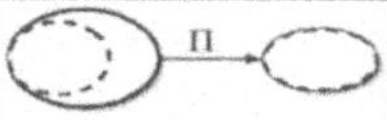	$\dfrac{S::O}{\pi(S):W}$	
$\dfrac{S::E}{\pi(S)::E}$	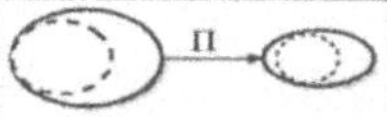	$\dfrac{S::O}{\pi(S)::O}$	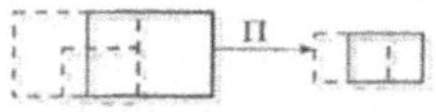

Fig. 4. Inference rules for projection operator; closed ellipses or rectangles represent sets. Sets with solid boundaries represent the actual dataset provided by the source S, and the dashed-line sets indicate the actual (or correct dataset, as assumed by the trust authority).

Venn diagrams, we can argue correctness for the entire rule-set for projection. Later we show some similar correctness arguments for the non-commutative binary operator, set-difference.

We also need to show that the static trust-typing inference rules for projection are *precise, viz.,* that a semantically consistent trust authority could never produce a rating other than what is provided by static inference. In the case of projection, we can see that an input rated *overlapping* leads to every possible rating for the output; so in this case, the inference rule is self-evidently precise. We now consider the other case

$$\frac{S :: I}{\pi(S) :: C, I}$$

The rule states that with an *incomplete* (I) input, projection yields an output that is either complete or incomplete. We now argue that no other output rating from a semantically consistent trust authority is possible, for *any* input that is rated I. If a trust authority provides such a rating, it does not conform to the semantics. In contradiction, suppose the result is rated W. This means that there is some result tuple t in it that should not be, as per the trust authority's view of the output. By the semantics of projection, this is only possible if there was at least one tuple τ in the input that gave rise to t, that the trust authority would not expect to see in the input; however, the input is rated I, so such a tuple cannot exist if the authority is semantically consistent. By a similar argument, we can show that the output cannot be rated E or O.

We now present a similar discussion for the asymmetric, binary set-difference operator. Figure 5 shows 4 of the 25 different rules for set difference for the case where one of the inputs is rated C and the other I. Note the asymmetry in the inferred output ratings (non-commutativity of set difference).

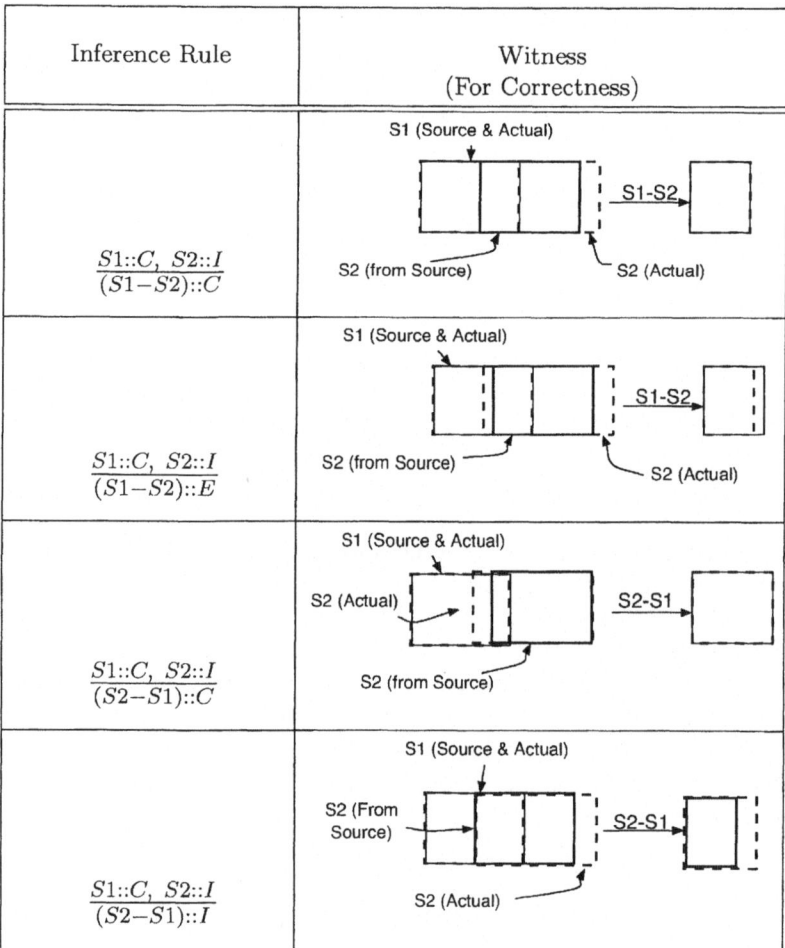

Inference Rule	Witness (For Correctness)
$\dfrac{S1::C,\ S2::I}{(S1-S2)::C}$	
$\dfrac{S1::C,\ S2::I}{(S1-S2)::E}$	
$\dfrac{S1::C,\ S2::I}{(S2-S1)::C}$	
$\dfrac{S1::C,\ S2::I}{(S2-S1)::I}$	

Fig. 5. Four out of twenty-five inference rules for the set-difference operator.

We can also argue precision. With the ratings { $S1::C,\ S2::I$ }, no other ratings are possible for $S1-S2$ besides C or E. In contradiction, suppose $S1-S2$ were rated I by a trust authority. This implies that some tuple t is missing in the output result of $S1-S2$ that the trust authority does not expect to be there. This implies that either this tuple is missing in $S1$ (not possible, since $S1$ is rated complete) or this is an incorrect extra tuple in $S2$ (also not possible, since $S2$ is rated incomplete). Thus, it is impossible find inputs $S1{::}C$ and $S2{::}I$ so that a semantically consistent trust authority would rate $S1 - S2$ as excessive. Similarly, we can argue that the ratings W and O are impossible. The precision of the entire rule-set for the set-difference operator is argued in the same way.

4.2   Query Processing and Trust-Type Inference

We conclude this section with an outline of how the above algorithmic framework for trust-type inference can be integrated into a mediated query system. For this, we assume a standard query processor as it can be found in proposed mediator architectures (e.g., [8,20]).

Initially, a client specifies a query Q against a mediated schema and also specifies a trust requirement for the query result, denoted $TR(Q)$. A trust requirement can be a singleton or a set of trust types, drawn from a basic coverage trust typing system (see Def. 5). The mediator processes the query in the standard way. That is, it generates a set of query plans $qp_1(Q), qp_2(Q), \ldots, qp_k(Q)$ for the query Q and chooses the most cost-effective plan for execution against the set of information sources referred to in the query plan.

Our trust-type inference algorithm can be plugged into the query plan generation component of the mediator's query processor as follows.

1. A query plan $qp(Q)$ for a query Q is generated bottom-up; leaf nodes of the plan (if considered as a hierarchical, bottom-up structure), are assigned input trust ratings. Leaf nodes refer to information sources and ratings are assigned to these sources by a trust authority.
2. After trust ratings have been assigned to leaf-nodes, the query processor builds the query plan as a nested expression tree, using the operators available in the data model used for the mediated schema. The root node designates the query result. For each operator o applied to one or two input data sets (which can be either the information sources or intermediate query results), the trust ratings for the input data sets are known. Assume two input data sets S_1, S_2 with trust ratings $\{t_1, t_2\}$ and $\{t_1\}$, respectively (note that intermediate results can have more than one trust rating, see Def. 6). The query processor now does a lookup of the inference rule for both possibilities of input ratings, $S_1 :: \{t_1\}, S_2 :: \{t_1\}$ and $S_1 :: \{t_2\}, S_2 :: \{t_1\}$ and thus obtains the output result type(s), which are assigned to the (intermediate) result node obtained by applying o to S_1, S_2. Eventually, by building the complete operator tree for Q, a trust rating is assigned to the final query result. If the final trust rating does not satisfy the trust requirements specified by the client, the query plan is pruned from the set of potential query plans. Finally, the most cost effective query plan that satisfies the client's trust requirements executed after the above static trust-type inferencing.

There are some important aspects to note regarding the usage of trust inference rules during query plan construction. First, the lookup of result trust-types

in the presence of rated input data sets and an operator can be done very efficiently, and intermediate result nodes are simply "annotated" by trust ratings.
Second, in general, the trust rating obtained for an intermediate query result
can be "better" (with respect the underlying trust-type lattice) than the trust
ratings of the input trust-types. That is, it is in general not possible to prune a
plan before it is completely constructed. However, there are several cases where
such a pruning can be done, i.e., when it is known that based on the rating of an
intermediate result, the final query result will never satisfy the client's trust requirements. We are currently investigating this aspect in the context of mediated
relational databases. Finally, it can happen that there is no query plan that satisfies the client's trust requirements. In this case, the mediator needs to provide
the client with respective feedback, e.g., by stating the trust levels that could
be assigned to the query result. Another interesting aspect is that the query
plan generation is not purely cost-driven anymore. That is, one can construct
scenarios where a query plan does not satisfy the client's trust requirements but
a more expensive plan does. This is typically the case if the information sources
referred to in a query plan contain non-disjoint data.

5   Related Work

The concept of trust in distributed, mediated information sources has mainly
been investigated in the context *secure mediation* [1,2,3,5]. These works address
the problem of managing client credentials to ensure that a mediator does not
violate information source security policies when integrating data to satisfy client
queries.

Our proposed static type inferencing framework provides an orthogonal aspect to these works and is most closely related to the management and handling
of data quality aspects in data integration and source mediation [11,12,13,14,16].
Our model can be considered as an abstract formal framework, which can incorporate a variety of data quality aspects as one or more aggregated trust-types.
However, while most works on managing data quality aspects in mediation deal
with the run-time aspects of data quality, our work leverages existing mediation
architectures and query processing strategies in particular by performing static
type-checking of potential query results. Thus, our framework in general provides the chance of avoiding expensive query execution in case no query result
will satisfy the (trust) requirements specified by clients. Finally, compared with
work in data quality management, our proposed framework provides a formal
framework for static typing and also an effective algorithmic infrastructure to
deal with ratings of information sources in the context of recommender systems
[7,17,18]. Currently, our results are limited to the basic completeness type system (CTS). In future work, we hope to extend it to other notions of data quality
and trust.

6   Conclusions and Future Work

In this paper, we address the problem of obtaining trustworthy information for clients in mediated architectures deployed in a WAN setting. In such settings, not all information sources may be trustworthy; mediators must be careful to use query plans that only take data from sources that clients would find acceptable. We describe a general model of *static trust-typing* to infer the trustworthiness of the results of query plans, even before executing these plans. Such a static trust-typing approach can be used by mediators to prune and thus avoid query plans that would compute query results that would be unacceptable to clients because they do not satisfy the trust requirements specified by clients. In the general model, we discuss desirable properties of static trust-typing systems, *viz.*, correctness, precision, and completeness. We then give an example of a trust-typing system in the context of relational databases that does show these properties.

In our ongoing work, we are currently developing a fine-grained trust-typing system in which trust authorities can assign trust-types to different components of a source (object sets, object attributes etc). In combination with such a framework, we are also studying how such fine-grained trust assignments can be used in query plan generation to annotate individual data items in query results with trust levels, eventually to provide clients with more detailed information regarding the trustworthiness of query results.

References

1. J. Biskup, U. Flegel, and Y. Karabulut: Secure mediation: Requirements and Design. In IFIP WG11.3 13th International Working Conference on Database Security (DBSec 98), Kluwer, 127–140, 1999.
2. J. Biskup, Y. Karabulut: A Hybrid PKI Model with an Application for Secure Mediation. In Proceedings of the 16th Annual IFIP WG11.3 Working Conference on Data and Application Security, Kluwer, 2002.
3. K. S. Candan, S. Jajodia, V. S. Subrahmanian: Secure Mediated Databases. In 12th International Conference on Data Engineering (ICDE 96), IEEE Computer Society 1996, 28–37.
4. R. Domenig, K. R. Dittrich: An Overview and Classification of Mediated Query Systems. SIGMOD Record 28(3): 63–72, 1999.
5. S. Dawson, S. Qian, P. Samarati: Secure Interoperation of Heterogeneous Systems: A Mediator-based Approach. In the 14th IFIP International Conference on Information Security, Kluwer, 1998.
6. R. Fagin, J. Y. Halpern: I'm OK if You're OK: On the Notion of Trusting Communication. In Proceedings of the Symposium on Logic in Computer Science (LICS '87), IEEE Computer Society, 280–292, 1987.
7. W. Hill, L. Stead, M. Rosenstein, and G. Furnas. Recommending and Evaluating Choices in a Virtual Community of Use. In Proceedings of the ACM Conference on Human Factors in Computing Systems, CHI'95, ACM/Addison-Wesley, 194–201.
8. V. Josifovski, and T. Risch: Query Decomposition for a Distributed Object-Oriented Mediator System. *Distributed and Parallel Databases* 11(3): 307–336 (2002)

9. J. C. Mitchell, Concepts in Programming Languages. *Cambridge University Press*, 2003.
10. I. Manolescu, L. Bouganim, F. Fabret, E. Simon: Efficient Querying of Distributed Resources in Mediator Systems. In *Confederated International Conferences DOA, CoopIS and ODBASE 2002*, LNCS 2519, Springer, 468–485, 2002.
11. G. A. Mihaila, L. Raschid, M.-E. Vidal: Using Quality of Data Metadata for Source Selection and Ranking. In Proceedings of the Third International Workshop on the Web and Databases, WebDB 2000 (Informal Proceedings), 93–98, 2000.
12. M. Mecella, M. Scannapieco, A. Virgillito, R. Baldoni, T. Catarci, C. Batini: Managing Data Quality in Cooperative Information Systems. In *Confederated International Conferences DOA, CoopIS and ODBASE 2002*, LNCS 2519, Springer, 486–502, 2002.
13. F. Naumann: Quality-Driven Query Answering for Integrated Information Systems. Lecture Notes in Computer Science 2261, Springer, 2002.
14. F. Naumann, U. Leser, J. C. Freytag: Quality-driven Integration of Heterogeneous Information Systems. In Proceedings of the 25th International Conference on Very Large Data Bases, 447–458, 1999.
15. NIST (National Institute of Standards and Technology). Glossary of Computer Security Terminology. NIST Technical Report, NISTIR 4659, September 1991.
16. L. Pipino, Y. W. Lee, R. Y. Wang: Data Quality Assessment. In Communications of the ACM 45(4): 211–218, 2002.
17. D. Pemberton, T. Rodden and R. Procter: GroupMark: A WWW Recommender System Combining Collaborative and Information Filtering. In the 6th ERCIM Workshop "User Interfaces for all", ui4all.ics.forth.gr/UI4ALL-2000/proceedings.html, 2000.
18. Recommender Systems. Special Section in Communications of the ACM, Vol. 40, No. 3; March 1997
19. B. Toone, M. Gertz, P. Devanbu: Trust Mediation for Distributed Information Systems. In Security and Privacy in the Age of Uncertainty, IFIP TC11 18th International Conference on Information Security (SEC2003), Kluwer, 1–12, 2003.
20. V. Zadorozhny, L. Raschid, M. Vidal, T. Urhan, L. Bright: Efficient Evaluation of Queries in a Mediator for WebSources. In ACM SIGMOD International Conference on Management of Data, ACM, 85-96, 2002.

Workflow Mining: Current Status and Future Directions

A.K.A. de Medeiros, W.M.P. van der Aalst, and A.J.M.M. Weijters

Department of Technology Management, Eindhoven University of Technology
P.O. Box 513, NL-5600 MB, Eindhoven, The Netherlands.
{a.k.medeiros, w.m.p.v.d.aalst, a.j.m.m.weijters}@tm.tue.nl

Abstract. Current workflow management systems require the explicit design of the workflows that express the business process of an organization. This process design is very time consuming and error prone. Considerable work has been done to develop heuristics to mine event-data logs to produce a process model that can support the workflow design process. However, all the existing heuristic-based mining algorithms have their limitations. To achieve more insight into these limitations the starting point in this paper is the α-algorithm [3] for which it is *proved* under which conditions and process constructs the algorithm works. After presentation of the α-algorithm, a classification is given of the process constructs that are difficult to handle for this type of algorithms. Then, for some constructs (i.e. short loops) it is illustrated in which way the α-algorithm can be extended so that it can correctly discover these constructs.

Keywords: Process mining, workflow mining, Petri nets, workflow Petri nets.

1   Introduction

Every company wants to produce more in less time. One way to accomplish this is having a well-defined business process model that reflects the dependencies among tasks and also tasks that can be processed in parallel. *Workflow management*(WFM) systems offer the functionality to design and enact operational processes.

In an ideal situation, well-defined business processes should be designed before enactment is possible and, redesigned whenever changes happen. However, in practice a lot of time is spent on modelling business process while the resulting workflow models are typically still error prone, because knowledge about the whole process is scattered among employees and paper procedures.

To avoid the above mentioned difficulties, instead of starting with a process design, our process mining starts by gathering information about the processes as they take place. We assume that it is possible to record events such that (i) each event refers to a task (i.e., a well-defined step in the process), (ii) each event refers to a case (i.e., a process instance), and (iii) events are totally ordered. Any information system using transactional systems such as ERP (Enterprise

R. Meersman et al. (Eds.): CoopIS/DOA/ODBASE 2003, LNCS 2888, pp. 389–406, 2003.
© Springer-Verlag Berlin Heidelberg 2003

Resource Planning), CRM (Customer Relationship Management), B2B (Business to Business), SCM (Supply Chain Management) and WFM systems will offer this information in some form. Note that we do not assume the presence of a WFM system. The only assumption we make, is that it is possible to collect a process log that records the order in which the events take place.

Table 1. A process log.

case identifier	task identifier
case 1	task A
case 2	task A
case 3	task A
case 3	task B
case 1	task B
case 1	task C
case 2	task C
case 4	task A
case 2	task B
case 2	task D
case 5	task E
case 4	task C
case 1	task D
case 3	task C
case 3	task D
case 4	task B
case 5	task F
case 4	task D

To illustrate the principle of process mining, we consider the process log shown in Table 1. This log contains information about five cases (i.e., process instances) and six tasks (A..F). Based on the information shown in Table 1 and by making some assumptions about the completeness of the log (i.e., assuming that the cases are representative and a sufficient large subset of possible behaviors is observed) we can deduce for example the process model shown in Figure 1. The model is represented in terms of a Petri net [17]. After executing A, tasks B and C are in parallel. Note that for this example we assume that two tasks are in parallel if they appear in any other. By distinguishing between start events and end events for tasks it is possible to explicitly detect parallelism. Instead of starting with A the process can also start with E. Task E is always followed by task F. Table 1 contains the minimal information we assume to be present.

For this simple example, it is quite easy to construct a process model that is able to regenerate the process log. For larger process models this is much more difficult. For example, if the model exhibits alternative and parallel routing, then the process log will typically not contain all possible combinations. Moreover, certain paths through the process model may have a low probability and therefore remain undetected. Noisy data (i.e., logs containing exceptions) can further

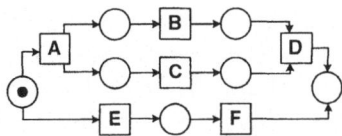

Fig. 1. A process model corresponding to the process log.

complicate matters. These are just some of the problems that we need to face in process mining research.

The focus of most research in the domain of process mining is on mining heuristics based on ordering relations of the events in the process log (cf. Section 5). Considerable work has been done on heuristics to mine event-data logs to produce a process model that can support the workflow design process. However, all the existing heuristic-based mining algorithms have their limitations. Typically, more advanced process constructs are difficult to handle for existing mining algorithms. Some of these problematic constructs are common in workflows and, therefore, need to be addressed to enable practical application. To achieve more insight into these limitations, the focus of this paper is a more analytical approach. The starting point of this paper is the α-algorithm [3]. Also the α-algorithm is primarily based on the ordening relations between events. However, the mining algorithm is not based on a heuristic, but on a formal algorithm for which it is *proved* under which conditions and process constructs the algorithm works. By discussing the weaknesses and strengths of the α-algorithm, we show how concepts in workflow mining could be improved in order to allow the correct mining of common constructs that appear in workflow system (loops, duplicate tasks, implicit places, non-free-choice constructs, etc.). Our final goal is to extend the α-algorithm so that the class of constructs for which we can *prove* that we can mine them correctly becomes larger. For some constructs (i.e. short loops) it is illustrated how the α-algorithm can be extended so that it can correctly handle these constructs.

The rest of the paper is organized as follows. In Section 2, the α-algorithm is explained. Problematic constructs that are not adequately tackled by α-algorithm are explained in Section 3. Possible ways to tackle these constructs are discussed in Section 4. Section 5 discusses related work on process mining. The final observations and comments are given in Section 6.

2   Workflow Mining: The α-Algorithm

The α-algorithm receives as input an event log and returns as output a Place/-Transition net (P/T-net) [17]. This section shows the main concepts required to understand the α-algorithm. A complete description and its properties is given in [3].

In the more theoretical approach, we do not focus on issues such as noise. We assume that there is no noise and that the workflow log contains "sufficient" information. Under these ideal circumstances we investigate whether the α algorithm is possible to *rediscover* the workflow process, i.e., for which class of workflow models is it possible to accurately construct the model by merely looking at their logs. The α algorithm is based on four ordering relations which can be derived from the log: $>_W$, $\to_W$, $\#_W$, and $\|_W$.

Definition 2.1. (Log-based ordering relations) Let W be a workflow log over T, i.e., $W \in \mathcal{P}(T^*)$. Let $a, b \in T$:

- $a >_W b$ if and only if there is a trace $\sigma = t_1 t_2 t_3 \ldots t_{n-1}$ and $i \in \{1, \ldots, n-2\}$ such that $\sigma \in W$ and $t_i = a$ and $t_{i+1} = b$,
- $a \to_W b$ if and only if $a >_W b$ and $b \not>_W a$,
- $a \#_W b$ if and only if $a \not>_W b$ and $b \not>_W a$, and
- $a \|_W b$ if and only if $a >_W b$ and $b >_W a$.

Relation $\to_W$ suggests causality and relations $\|_W$ and $\#_W$ are used to differentiate between parallelism and choice. Since all relations can be derived from $>_W$, we assume the log to be complete with respect to $>_W$ (i.e., if one task can follow another task directly, then the log should have registered this potential behavior). Structured Workflow Petri nets (SWF-nets) are a subclass of workflow nets (WF-nets) in which the net structure explicitly shows its behavior. Consequently, in SWF-nets (i) choice and synchronization are not mixed, and (ii) if there is a synchronization, all of its preceding transitions will have fired. These constraints are illustrated in Figure 2. Additionally, SWF-nets do not allow for implicit places in the net structure [3].

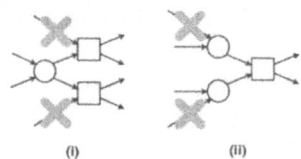

(i)   (ii)

Fig. 2. Constructs not allowed in SWF-nets.

To formally define the α algorithm we introduce some basic terminology.

Definition 2.2. ($\in$, *first*, *last*) Let T be a set of tasks. Let $\sigma = a_1 a_2 \ldots a_n \in T^*$ a sequence over T of length n. $\in$, *first*, and *last* are defined as follows:

1. $a \in \sigma$ if and only if $a \in \{a_1, a_2, \ldots a_n\}$,
2. if $n \geq 1$, then $first(\sigma) = a_1$ and $last(\sigma) = a_n$.

Now we can give the formal definition of the α algorithm followed by a more intuitive explanation.

Definition 2.3. (Mining algorithm α) Let W be a workflow log over T. $\alpha(W)$ is defined as follows.

1. $T_W = \{t \in T \mid \exists_{\sigma \in W} t \in \sigma\}$,
2. $T_I = \{t \in T \mid \exists_{\sigma \in W} t = first(\sigma)\}$,

3. $T_O = \{t \in T \mid \exists_{\sigma \in W} t = last(\sigma)\}$,

4. $X_W = \{(A,B) \mid A \subseteq T_W \ \wedge \ B \subseteq T_W \ \wedge \ \forall_{a \in A} \forall_{b \in B} a \ \rightarrow_W \ b \ \wedge$
   $\forall_{a_1,a_2 \in A} a_1 \#_W a_2 \ \wedge \ \forall_{b_1,b_2 \in B} b_1 \#_W b_2\}$,

5. $Y_W = \{(A,B) \in X_W \mid \forall_{(A',B') \in X_W} A \subseteq A' \wedge B \subseteq B' \Longrightarrow (A,B) = (A',B')\}$,

6. $P_W = \{p_{(A,B)} \mid (A,B) \in Y_W\} \cup \{i_W, o_W\}$,

7. $F_W = \{(a, p_{(A,B)}) \mid (A,B) \in Y_W \ \wedge \ a \in A\} \ \cup \ \{(p_{(A,B)}, b) \mid (A,B) \in Y_W \ \wedge \ b \in B\} \cup \{(i_W, t) \mid t \in T_I\} \cup \{(t, o_W) \mid t \in T_O\}$, and

8. $\alpha(W) = (P_W, T_W, F_W)$.

The α-algorithm works as follows. First, it examines the log traces and (Step 1) creates the set of transitions (T_W) in the workflow, (Step 2) the set of output transitions (T_I) of the source place , and (Step 3) the set of the input transitions (T_O) of the sink place[1]. In steps 4 and 5, the α-algorithm creates sets (X_W and Y_W, respectively) used to define the places of the mined workflow net. In Step 4, it discovers which transitions are causally related. Thus, for each tuple (A,B) in X_W, each transition in set A causally relates to *all* transitions in set B, and no transitions within A (or B) follow each other in some firing sequence. These constraints to the elements in sets A and B allow the correct mining of AND-split/join and OR-split/join constructs. Note that the OR-split/join requires the fusion of places. In Step 5, the α-algorithm refines set X_W by taking only the largest elements with respect to set inclusion. In fact, Step 5 establishes the exact amount of places the mined net has (excluding the source place i_W and the sink place o_W. The places are created in Step 6 and connected to their respective input/output transitions in Step 7. The mined workflow net is returned in Step 8.

Definition 2.4. (Ability to rediscover) Let $N = (P,T,F)$ be a sound WF-net and let the α be a mining algorithm which maps workflow logs of N onto sound WF-nets. If for any complete workflow log W of N the mining algorithm returns N (modulo renaming of places), then the α is able to *rediscover* N.

An algorithm/heuristic is said to rediscover a workflow net if this algorithm is able to regenerate the *exact net structure* of the original net, abstracting from the place labels (see Definition 2.4). The α-algorithm is proved to (re)discover all SWF-nets if the SWF-net does not contain short-loops. That means that short loops are a first limitation of the α-algorithm. However, if the notion of *ability to rediscover* is relaxed to *behaviorally equivalent* (i.e. both generate the same log traces), then the α-algorithm is able to mine other sound WF-nets, like the one in Figure 3. This net is not an SWF-net because transition G can be enabled without the firing of transitions E and F. However, even with this relaxed notion of *ability to rediscover* and the restriction on short-loops, the α-algorithm cannot be proved to correctly mine all sound WF-nets.

The next section classifies the situations to which the α-algorithm fails to mine sound WF-nets. Understanding the limitations of α-algorithm helps in developing new algorithms/heuristics to tackle these limitations.

---

[1] In a workflow net, the source place i has no input transitions and the sink place o has no output transitions.

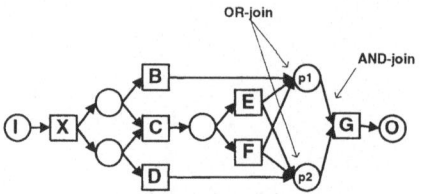

Fig. 3. A WF-net that can be rediscovered by the α-algorithm, although it is not an SWF-net.

3   Limitations of the α-Algorithm: Loops, Invisible Tasks, and Duplicate Tasks

As motivated in the previous section the α-algorithm can successfully mine SWF-nets that do not contain short-length loops. But, the α-algorithm has also serious limitations. Although it is possible to represent many real workflows using SWF-nets, these nets do not support other common constructs like *invisible tasks* and *duplicate tasks*. In this section we present a classification of possible common constructs the α-algorithm cannot mine correctly, and relations between these constructs. Some of the constructs are within the scope of SWF-nets (like *short loops*), but others are beyond the scope of SWF-nets (like *duplicate tasks*).

To find out the constructs the α-algorithm cannot mine correctly, it is necessary to understand how it works. Basically, the α-algorithm has the following behavior:

- A task *exists* in the resulting net if it *is in any* log trace;
- A task has *ingoing* arc(s) in the resulting net if (i) this task is the *first* task in a log trace, or (ii) this task *causally follows* another task.
- A task has *outgoing* arc(s) in the resulting net if (i) this task is the *last* task in a log trace, or (ii) this task *is causally followed* by another task.

If a task is not the first or last task in any trace log, *and* is not involved in any causal relation, the α-algorithm does not generate ingoing and outgoing arcs for this task. For instance, see net N_3 in Figure 4. Note that task B is not connected to any place in the resulting net. However, even if all the transitions are connected in the resulting net, this does not guarantee that the α-algorithm correctly mined the net. For instance, see the original and resulting nets in figures 5, 6, 7 and 8.

Places are created based on the *causal* ($\rightarrow_W$) and *exclusive* ($\#_W$) relations. However, in some situations the resulting net does not have the same number of places the original net has. For instance, consider the net in Figure 3 and net N_1 in Figure 5. Both nets are non-SWF-net and have similar net structures. In fact, these nets are not the same because each task E and F has only *one* outgoing arc in net N_1. This slight difference in the net structure leads to the inferring of different causal and exclusive relations to these two nets. Consequently, the α-algorithm cannot correctly mine N_1, but it can mine the net in Figure 3.

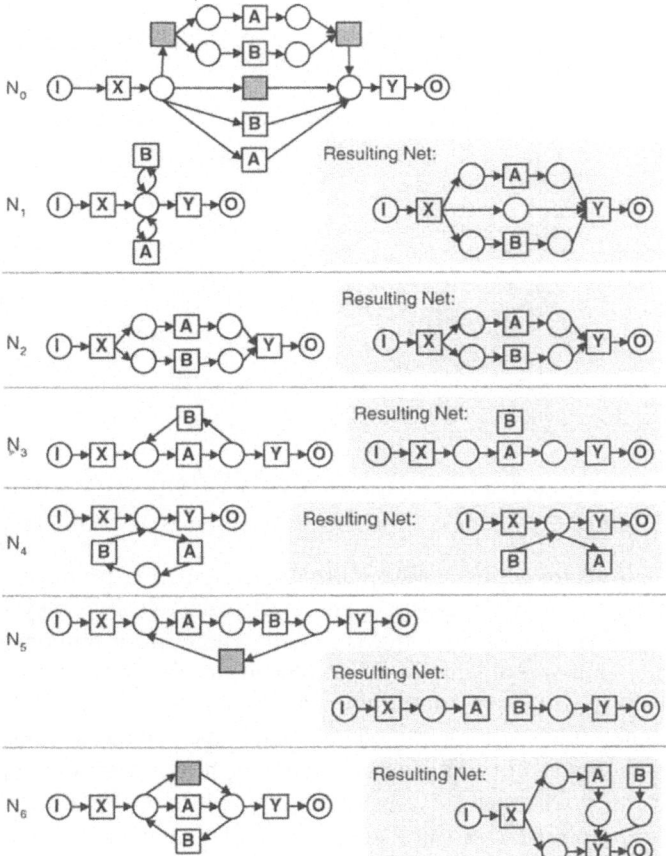

Fig. 4. Example of the existing relations between duplicate tasks, invisible tasks and one/two-length loops.

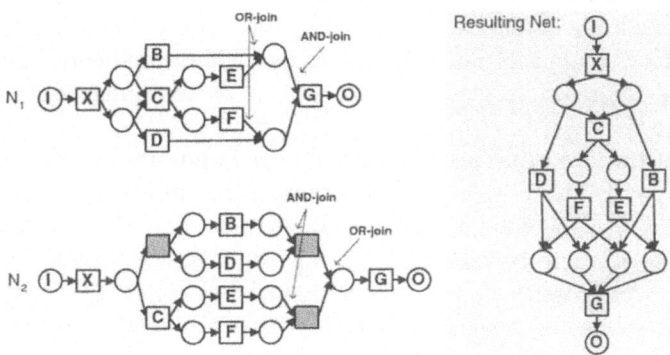

Fig. 5. Mined and original nets have different number of places.

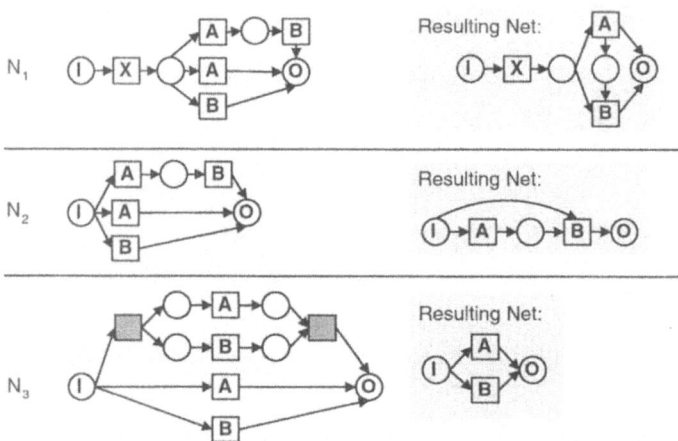

Fig. 6. Nets with duplicate tasks.

There are problems in the resulting net the α-algorithm produces when its *input* is incomplete and/or has noise (because different relations may be inferred). But even if the log is noise free and complete, there are a number of workflow constructs that causes problems for the α-algorithm. Below we will discuss them.
One-length loop. In a one-length loop, the same task can be executed multiple times in sequence. Thus, all ingoing places of this task are also its outgoing places in the WF-net. In fact, for SWF-nets, a one-length-loop task can only have one single place connected to it. As an example, see net N_5 in Figure 7, and also net N_1 in Figure 4. Note that in the resulting nets, the one-length-loop transitions do not have the same place as its ingoing and outgoing place. This happens because, to generate a place with a common ingoing and outgoing task, the α-algorithm requires the causal relation $task \rightarrow_W task$. But it is impossible to have $task >_W task$ and $task \not>_W task$ at the same time.
Two-length loop. In this case, the α-algorithm infers the two involved tasks are in parallel and, therefore, no place is created between them. For instance, see nets N_3 and N_4 in Figure 4. Note that there are no arcs between tasks A and B in the resulting net. However, the α-algorithm would correctly mine both N_3 and N_4 if the relations $A \rightarrow_W B$ and $B \rightarrow_W A$ were inferred, instead of the relation $A||_W B$.
Invisible Tasks. Invisible tasks do not appear in any log trace. Consequently, they do not belong to T_W (set of transitions in the mined net) and cannot be present in the net the α-algorithm generates. Two situations lead to invisible tasks: (i) a task is not registered in the log, for instance, because it may have only a routing purpose (e.g., see tasks without label in net N_2, Figure 5), or (ii) there is noise in the log generation and real tasks are missing in the log traces.
Duplicate Tasks. Sometimes a task appear more than once in the same workflow. In this case, the same label is given (and thus registered in the log) to more than one task. This can happen, for instance, when modelling the booking

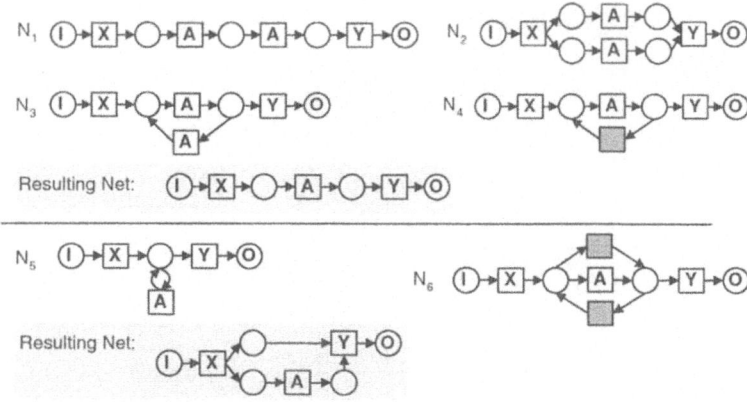

Fig. 7. Example of the existing relations between duplicate tasks, invisible tasks and one-length loops.

process in a travel agency. Clients can go there to *book a flight* only, *book a hotel* only, or *both*. Thus, a workflow model describing this booking situation could be like net N_3, in Figure 6 (assume A ="book flight" and B ="book hotel"). Note that the resulting net for net N_3 contains only one task with label A and one with B. The α-algorithm will never capture task duplication because it cannot distinguish different task with the same label (see also the other nets in Figure 6). In fact, in an SWF-net it is assumed that tasks are uniquely identifiable. Thus, a heuristic to capture duplicate tasks will have to generate WF-nets in which tasks can have identical labels.

Implicit Places. SWF-nets do not have implicit places. Places are implicit if their presence or absence does not affect the possible log traces of a workflow. For example, places $p3$ and $p4$ are implicit in net N_3 (see Figure 8). Note that the same causal relations are inferred when these implicit places are present or absent. However, the α-algorithm creates places according to the existing causal relations. Thus, implicit places cannot be captured because they do not influence causal relations between tasks. Note also that this same reason prevents the α-algorithm of generating *explicit* places between tasks that do not have a causal relation. As an example, see places $p1$ and $p2$ in net N_2 (also in Figure 8). Both places constrain the execution of tasks D and E because the choice between the execution of these tasks is made after the execution of A or B, respectively, and not after the execution of C. In fact, if the places $p1$ and $p2$ are removed from N_2, net N_4 is obtained (see Figure 8). However, in N_4, the choice between the execution of tasks D and E is made after the execution of task C. Consequently, a log trace like $XACEY$ can be generated by N_4, but cannot by N_2.

Non-free choice. The non-free choice construct combines synchronization and choice. Thus, it is not allowed in SWF-nets because it corresponds to construct (i) in Figure 2. Nets containing non-free choice constructs are not always mined correctly by the α-algorithm. For instance, consider the non-free-choice net N_2, Figure 8. The α-algorithm does not mine correctly N_2 because this net cannot

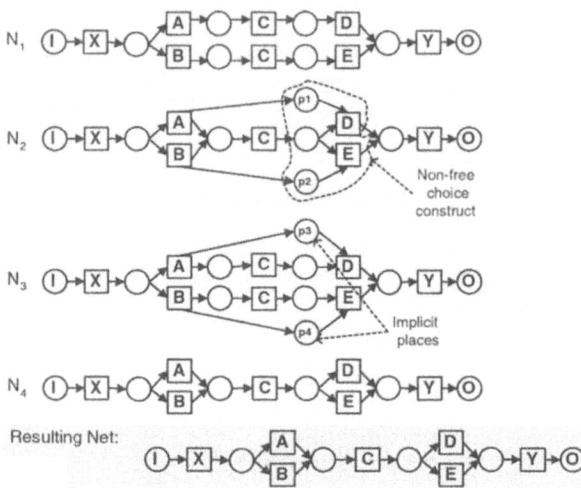

Fig. 8. Example of existing relations between duplicate tasks, non-free choice nets, implicit places and SWF-nets.

generate any log trace with the substring AD and/or BE. Consequently, there is no causal relation $A \rightarrow_W D$ and $B \rightarrow_W E$, and no creation of the respective places $p1$ and $p2$ in the resulting net. However, there are non-free choice constructs which the α-algorithm can mine correctly. As an example, consider net N_1 in Figure 9. This net is similar to net N_2 in Figure 8, but N_1 has two additional tasks F and G. The α-algorithm can correctly mine N_1 because there is a causal relation $F \rightarrow_W D$ (enabling the creation of place $p1$) and $G \rightarrow_W E$ (enabling the creation of $p2$). Thus, the α-algorithm can correctly mine non-free-choice constructs as far as the causal relations can be inferred.

Synchronization of OR-join places. The *synchronization of OR-join places* is a non-SWF-net construct because it correspond to construct (ii) in Figure 2. However, although this is a non-SWF-net construct, sometimes the α-algorithm can correctly mine it. For instance, see the WF-net in Figure 3. Places $p1$ and $p2$ are OR-join places. $p1$ is an OR-join place because it contains a token if task B *or* E *or* F is executed. Similarly, $p2$ if task D *or* E *or* F is executed. Besides, both $p1$ and $p2$ are synchronized at task G, since this task can happen only when there is a token in both $p1$ *and* $p2$. Note that this construct corresponds to a non-SWF-net because task G can be executed whenever *some* of the tasks that precede it have been executed. If the net in Figure 3 were an SWF-net, task G could be executed only after the execution of tasks B, D, E and F. However, although the net in Figure 3 is a non-SWF-net, the α-algorithm can correctly mine it because the necessary and sufficient *causal* ($\rightarrow_W$) and *exclusive*($\#_W$) relations are inferred. However, for some *synchronization of OR-join places* constructs, the inferred causal and exclusive relations are not enough to correctly mine the net. For instance, consider net N_1 in Figure 5. The resulting net the α-algorithm mines is not equal to N_1 because it contains two additional places among tasks B, D, E, F and task G. This net structure with extra places derives from the inferred relations. Note that because $B \parallel_W D$ and $E \parallel_W F$ in net N_1, but $B\#_W E$, $B\#_W F$, $D\#_W E$ and $D\#_W F$, the places $p_{(\{B,E\},\{G\})}$, $p_{(\{B,F\},\{G\})}$, $p_{(\{D,E\},\{G\})}$ and $p_{(\{D,F\},\{G\})}$ are created by the α-algorithm, when only places $p_{(\{B,E\},\{G\})}$ and $p_{(\{D,F\},\{G\})}$ would do. Thus, in this case, the inferred relations do not allow the α-algorithm to correctly mine the net. However, the resulting net is *behaviorally* equivalent to the original net, even if their structures are different because both nets generate exactly the same set of traces.

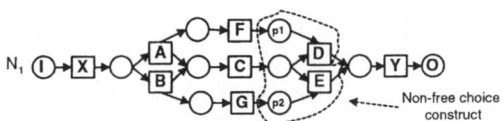

Fig. 9. Example of a non-free choice net which the α-algorithm can mine correctly.

There are relations among the problematic constructs that imply in trade-offs. The problematic constructs are related because (i) the same set of log traces can satisfy the current notion of log completeness, and/or (ii) the same set of ordering relations can be inferred when the original net contains one of the constructs. Therefore, no mining algorithm can detect which of the constructs are in the original net. In fact, any mining algorithm must choose which one of the related constructs is going to be used in the resulting net. Some examples demonstrating that the problematic constructs are related:

Duplicate Tasks (Sequence vs Parallel vs Choice). Duplicate tasks can be in *sequential*, *parallel*, or *choice* structures in the WF-net. These duplicate task structures are related because the same complete log can satisfy different WF-nets containing them. As an example, see the respective nets N_1, N_2 and N_3 in Figure 7. Note that a log containing *only* the trace $XAAY$ would be complete for the three nets N_1, N_2, and N_3. Thus, given this input trace, it is impossible for a mining algorithm to determine which duplicate task structure really exists in the original net.

Invisible Tasks vs Duplicate Tasks. WF-nets with the same ordering relations can be created either using invisible tasks or using duplicate tasks. For instance, consider nets N_3 and N_4 in Figure 7. Their ordering relations are the same whatever the workflow log. Additionally, note that a log containing *only* the trace $XAAY$ would be complete also for nets N_{1-3} and N_4.

Invisible Tasks vs Loops. Behaviorally equivalent WF-nets can be created either using invisible tasks or using loops. For instance, consider nets N_5 and N_6 in Figure 7. These nets generate exactly the same set of log traces.

Invisible Tasks vs Synchronization of OR-join places. See nets N_1 and N_2 in Figure 5. The α-algorithm generates the same resulting net for both N_1 and N_2 because these nets are behaviorally equivalent.

Non-Free Choice vs Duplicate Tasks. Nets N_1 and N_2 in Figure 8 are behaviorally equivalent.

Loops vs Invisible Tasks together with Duplicate Tasks. Nets with equal sets of ordering relations can be created if loops or invisible tasks in combination with duplicate tasks are used. For instance, see nets N_0 and N_1 in Figure 4. Net N_0 has duplicate tasks and invisible tasks in its structure. Net N_1 has two one-length loops, involving tasks A and B. These two nets lead to the same set of ordering relations because, whatever the complete log, the inferred causal and parallel ordering relations will always be $X \rightarrow_W A$, $X \rightarrow_W B$, $X \rightarrow_W Y$, $B \rightarrow_W Y$, $A \rightarrow_W Y$, and $A\|_W B$.

In fact, these relations raise questions like: Is it possible to develop heuristics that detect both loops and invisible tasks? Duplicate tasks and invisible tasks? If it is not, what problematic constructs should have priority in the mining? In what situations? These are the kind of questions our current research is trying to answer. In the following section we explain possible approaches to tackle the classes of structural constructs the α-algorithm cannot mine correctly. Additionally, we give examples on how to apply these approaches.

4   Approaches to Tackle Structural Problematic Constructs

Process mining can be viewed as a three-phase process: *pre-processing*, *processing* and *post-processing*. In the pre-processing phase, based on the assumption that the input log satisfies the required notion of log completeness, the ordering relations are inferred. The processing phase corresponds to the execution of the mining algorithm, given the log and the ordering relations as input. In our case, the mining algorithm is the α-algorithm. During post-processing, the mined Petri-net can be fine-tuned and a graphical representation can be build. Possible approaches to tackle structural problematic constructs focus on one or more of these phases.

In this section, we use the problematic constructs *one- and two-length loops* in SWF-nets to exemplify how approaches can be developed to tackle problematic constructs. We chose to tackle them first because in this way we can extend the α-algorithm to mine all SWF-nets (including short loops). Subsection 4.1 contains an approach to tackle one-length loops. This is a mixed approach that focusses both on the pre- and post-processing phases. Subsection 4.2 presents an approach to tackle two-length loops. This approach focusses on the pre-processing phase.

4.1   Example of a Mixed Approach Focusing on the Pre- and Post-processing Phases

To develop an approach to tackle one-length loops in SWF-nets, we first determine (i) how one-length loops can be identified in the input log and (ii) what kind of patterns can be used to build them in SWF-nets.

Identification. One-length loops can be identified by checking if there are log traces containing the substring t_1t_1. For instance, any complete log for N_5 in Figure 7 contains the trace $XAAY$.

WF-structure. For SWF-nets, it can be proven that one-length-loop tasks are connected to a single place. The WF-structure is illustrated in Figure 10.

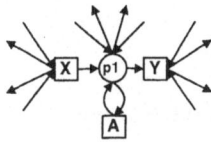

Fig. 10. Structure of one-length loops in SWF-nets.

The reasoning used to identify this single structure is as follows. Let task A be in a one-length loop. First, A can never be connected to source/sink places in an SWF-net because the source place i has no ingoing task and the sink place o has no outgoing task. Second, task A cannot have more than one ingoing place (see N_1 in Figure 11) because SWF-nets do not allow for synchronization and choice to mixed (recall construct (i) in Figure 2). Third, task A cannot be connected to places that are only its outgoing places (see N_2 in Figure 11) because these places can contain more than one token. All places in SWF-nets contain *at most* one token. Finally, at least two other tasks (X and Y) are necessary. The X task puts a token in the place connected to A (all tasks are live in SWF-nets). The Y removes a token from this place (in SWF-nets, no tasks can execute after the process termination).

Fig. 11. Illustration of the reasoning used to determine the single structure of one-length loops in SWF-nets.

The unique structure in which one-length loops appears in SWF-nets is represented in Figure 10. Three *distinct* tasks can be distinguished: the one-length-loop task (A), one *ingoing* task (X) and one *outgoing* task (Y). Consequently, for every one-length-loop pattern, there are *at least* the causal relations: $X \rightarrow_W Y$, $X \rightarrow_W A$ and $A \rightarrow_W Y$. Besides, every one-length-loop task A is connected to a single place ($p1$ in Figure 10) because we are working with SWF-nets. Thus, if we remove A from this pattern, it is still possible to mine $p1$ in this pattern because the causal relation $X \rightarrow_W Y$ still exists. In order words, it is possible to mine the basic SWF-net structure of the workflow process without considering the one-length-loop tasks when inferring the ordering relations. This reasoning is the base for the following mixed approach.

First, in a *pre-processing* phase the one-length-loop tasks and their respective neighbors are identified and recorded. Then, the one-length-loop tasks are eliminated from the log. Secondly, the α-algorithm is applied to the pre-processed log.

The result is a WF-net with the $X \to_W Y$ causal relation and the p_1 place. In the *post-processing* phase, based on the recorded data, the one-length loop tasks are connected to the right places in the WF-net generated by α-algorithm. Note that this approach does not modify the processing phase (i.e. the α algorithm) itself.

4.2   Example of an Approach Focusing on the Pre-processing Phase

To build an approach to tackle two-length loops in SWF-nets, we first need to set (i) how two-length loops can be identified and (ii) what kind of patterns can be used to build them in SWF-nets.

Identification. The current notion of log completeness does not allow the differentiation between tasks in parallel and tasks in a two-length loop. This happens because a log can be complete without having one trace in which the two-length-loop tasks follow one another in a row. In other words, if t_1 and t_2 belong to a two-length loop in an SWF-net, a log can be complete without having the pattern $t_1 t_2 t_1$. For instance, see net N_1 in Figure 12. The log containing the traces XAY, $XABW$, XW, ZBW, $ZBAY$ and ZY is complete. However, this log does not contain the pattern ABA. Thus, any approach to tackle two-length loops in SWF-nets requires a new notion of log completeness.

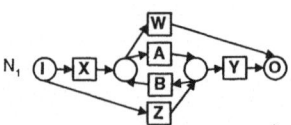

Fig. 12. Example of an SWF-net for which the new notion of log completeness is required to correctly capture 2-length loops.

WF-structure. Recall that the current definition of ordering relations infers that tasks in two-length loops are in parallel. In contrast to one-length-loops the possible structure for two-length loops is not completely clear. Our discoveries so far shows that two-length loops can be mined correctly if the causal relations of tasks involved in the two-length loop are correctly mined.

Our proposed solution for the two-length-loop problem is an adaptation of the original definition of log completeness and an adaptation of the definition of some the basic relations.

In the original definition of log completeness (Section 2), we assume the log to be complete with respect to $>_W$ (i.e., if one task can follow another task directly, then the log should have registered this potential behavior). In the adapted version not only the binary $>_W$ relation, but also triples are involved. If the pattern $t_1 t_2 t_1$ is possible, a complete log must contain this triple.

Using this insight, we redefine Definition 2.1, i.e., we provide new definitions for the four basic ordering relations $>_W$, $\to_W$, $\#_W$, and $\|_W$.

Definition 4.1. (Ordering relations capturing two-length loops) Let W be a loop-complete workflow log over T, i.e., $W \in \mathcal{P}(T^*)$. Let $a, b \in T$:

- $a >''_W b$ if and only if there is a trace $\sigma = t_1 t_2 t_3 \ldots t_{n-1}$ and $i \in \{1, \ldots, n-2\}$ such that $\sigma \in W$ and $t_i = a$ and $t_{i+1} = b$,
- $a \to''_W b$ if and only if $(a >_W b$ and $(b \not>_W a$ or $\exists_{\sigma \in W}[\sigma = t_1 t_2 t_3 \ldots t_n$ and $i \in \{1, \ldots, n-2\}$ and $t_i = t_{i+2} = a$ and $t_{i+1} = b]))$,
- $a \#''_W b$ if and only if $a \not>_W b$ and $b \not>_W a$, and
- $a \|''_W b$ if and only if $a >_W b$ and $b >_W a$ and $\neg \exists_{\sigma \in W}[\sigma = t_1 t_2 t_3 \ldots t_n$ and $i \in \{1, \ldots, n-2\}$ and $t_i = t_{i+2} = a$ and $t_{i+1} = b]))$.

Note that Definition 4.1 considers the new notion of log completeness. The main idea is that two tasks t_1 and t_2 (with $t_1 \neq t_2$), will be in parallel if, and only if, there is no log trace containing the substring $t_1 t_2 t_1$. If the α-algorithm is applied using the new Definition 4.1, an SWF-net containing two-length loops can be mined. Examples are the nets N_3 and N_4 in Figure 4, and net N_1 in Figure 12. Note that this approach enables the mining of SWF-nets with two-length-loops by modifying only the pre-processing phase (establishing the basic relations $\to_W$, $\#_W$, and $\|_W$).

5   Literature on Process Mining

The idea of process mining is not new [4,6,7,8,10,11,12,14,15,18,19,2,20,3]. Cook and Wolf have investigated similar issues in the context of software engineering processes. In [6] they describe three methods for process discovery: one using neural networks, one using a purely algorithmic approach, and one Markovian approach. The authors consider the latter two the most promising approaches. The purely algorithmic approach builds a finite state machine where states are fused if their futures (in terms of possible behavior in the next k steps) are identical. The Markovian approach uses a mixture of algorithmic and statistical methods and is able to deal with noise. Note that the results presented in [6] are limited to sequential behavior. Cook and Wolf extend their work to concurrent processes in [7]. They propose specific metrics (entropy, event type counts, periodicity, and causality) and use these metrics to discover models out of event streams. However, they do not provide an approach to generate explicit process models. Recall that the final goal of the approach presented in this paper is to find explicit representations for a broad range of process models, i.e., we want to be able to generate a concrete Petri net rather than a set of dependency relations between events. In [8] Cook and Wolf provide a measure to quantify discrepancies between a process model and the actual behavior as registered using event-based data. The idea of applying process mining in the context of workflow management was first introduced in [4]. This work is based on workflow graphs, which are inspired by workflow products such as IBM MQSeries workflow (formerly known as Flowmark) and InConcert. In this paper, two problems are defined. The first problem is to find a workflow graph generating events appearing in a given workflow log. The second problem is to find the definitions of edge conditions. A concrete algorithm is given for tackling the first problem. The approach is quite different from other approaches: Because the nature of workflow graphs there is no need to identify the nature (AND or OR) of joins and splits. As shown in [13], workflow graphs use true and false tokens which do not allow for cyclic graphs. Nevertheless, [4] partially deals with iteration by enumerating all occurrences of a given task and then folding the graph. However, the resulting conformal graph is not a complete model. In [15], a tool based on these algorithms is presented. Schimm [18,19] has developed a mining tool suitable for discovering hierarchically structured workflow processes. This requires all splits and joins to be balanced. Herbst and Karagiannis also address the issue of process mining in the context of workflow management [11,10,12] using an inductive approach. The work presented in [12] is limited to sequential models. The approach described in [11,10] also allows for concurrency. It uses stochastic task graphs as an intermediate representation and it generates a workflow model described in the ADONIS modeling language. In the induction step task nodes are merged and split in order to discover the underlying process. A notable difference with other approaches is that the same task can appear multiple times in the workflow model, i.e., the approach allows for duplicate tasks. The graph generation technique is similar to the approach of [4,15]. The nature of splits and joins (i.e., AND or OR) is discovered in the transformation step, where the stochastic task graph is transformed into an ADONIS workflow model with block-structured splits and joins. In contrast to the previous papers, our work [14,20] is characterized by the focus on workflow processes with concurrent behavior (rather than adding ad-hoc mechanisms to capture parallelism). In [20] a heuristic approach using rather simple metrics is used to construct so-called "dependency/frequency tables" and "dependency/frequency graphs". The preliminary results presented in [20] only provide heuristics and focus on issues such as noise. In [1] the EMiT tool is presented which uses an extended version of α-algorithm to incorporate timing information. For a detailed description of the α-algorithm and a proof of its correctness we refer to [3].

More from a theoretical point of view, the rediscovery problem discussed in this paper is related to the work discussed in [5,9,16]. In these papers the limits of inductive inference are explored. For example, in [9] it is shown that the computational problem of finding a minimum finite-state acceptor compatible with given data is NP-hard. Several of the more generic concepts discussed in these papers could be translated to the domain of process mining. It is possible to interpret the problem described in this paper as an inductive inference problem specified in terms of rules, a hypothesis space, examples, and criteria for successful inference. The comparison with literature in this domain raises interesting questions for process mining, e.g., how to deal with negative examples (i.e., suppose that besides log W there is a log V of traces that are not possible, e.g., added by a domain expert). However, despite the many relations with the work described in [5,9,16] there are also many differences, e.g., we are mining at the net level rather than sequential or lower level representations (e.g., Markov chains, finite state machines, or regular expressions). For a survey of existing research, we also refer to [2].

6   Discussion and Future Work

The focus of this paper has been on process mining algorithms and heuristics primarily based on binary ordering relations of the events in a process log. As an representative example of this type of algorithms we introduced the α-algorithm and we explained why it cannot correctly mine *short loops, invisible tasks, duplicate tasks, implicit places, non-free choice* and *synchronization of OR-join places*, which are all common constructs in workflows. It is important to note that these limitations are not specific for the α-algorithm but apply to most of the approaches described in literature.

Additionally, we have showed how two problematic constructs (i.e., loops of length one and length two) can be handled by adapting one or more process mining phases: *pre-processing, processing* or *post-processing.*

Our future research will be driven by the problems identified in this paper. First, we want to extend the class of WF-nets the α-algorithm can correctly mine. Secondly, we want to extend our mining algorithm in such a way that it can handle workflows beyond the scope of WF-nets (for instance workflows with duplicate or invisible tasks). Finally, we try to combine formal results with more practical approaches in which we try to develop mining heuristics so that we can handle more workflow logs (i.e., logs with noise and logs that are incomplete).

References

1. W.M.P. van der Aalst and B.F. van Dongen. Discovering Workflow Performance Models from Timed Logs. In Y. Han, S. Tai, and D. Wikarski, editors, *International Conference on Engineering and Deployment of Cooperative Information Systems (EDCIS 2002)*, volume 2480 of *Lecture Notes in Computer Science*, pages 45–63. Springer-Verlag, Berlin, 2002.
2. W.M.P. van der Aalst, B.F. van Dongen, J. Herbst, L. Maruster, G. Schimm, and A.J.M.M. Weijters. Workflow Mining: A Survey of Issues and Approaches. Data and Knowledge Engineering, Accepted for publication, 2003.
3. W.M.P. van der Aalst, A.J.M.M. Weijters, and L. Maruster. Workflow Mining: Discovering Process Models from Event Logs. IEEE Transactions on Knowledge and Data Engineering (TKDE), Accepted for publication, 2003.
4. R. Agrawal, D. Gunopulos, and F. Leymann. Mining Process Models from Workflow Logs. In *Sixth International Conference on Extending Database Technology*, pages 469–483, 1998.
5. D. Angluin and C.H. Smith. Inductive Inference: Theory and Methods. *Computing Surveys*, 15(3):237–269, 1983.
6. J.E. Cook and A.L. Wolf. Discovering Models of Software Processes from Event-Based Data. *ACM Transactions on Software Engineering and Methodology*, 7(3):215–249, 1998.
7. J.E. Cook and A.L. Wolf. Event-Based Detection of Concurrency. In *Proceedings of the Sixth International Symposium on the Foundations of Software Engineering (FSE-6)*, pages 35–45, 1998.
8. J.E. Cook and A.L. Wolf. Software Process Validation: Quantitatively Measuring the Correspondence of a Process to a Model. *ACM Transactions on Software Engineering and Methodology*, 8(2):147–176, 1999.

9. E.M. Gold. Complexity of Automaton Identification from Given Data. *Information and Control*, 37(3):302–320, 1978.

10. J. Herbst. Dealing with Concurrency in Workflow Induction. In U. Baake, R. Zobel, and M. Al-Akaidi, editors, *European Concurrent Engineering Conference*. SCS Europe, 2000.

11. J. Herbst. *Ein induktiver Ansatz zur Akquisition und Adaption von Workflow-Modellen*. PhD thesis, Universität Ulm, November 2001.

12. J. Herbst and D. Karagiannis. Integrating Machine Learning and Workflow Management to Support Acquisition and Adaptation of Workflow Models. *International Journal of Intelligent Systems in Accounting, Finance and Management*, 9:67–92, 2000.

13. B. Kiepuszewski. *Expressiveness and Suitability of Languages for Control Flow Modelling in Workflows (submitted)*. PhD thesis, Queensland University of Technology, Brisbane, Australia, 2002. Available via http://www.tm.tue.nl/it/research/patterns.

14. L. Maruster, A.J.M.M. Weijters, W.M.P. van der Aalst, and A. van den Bosch. Process Mining: Discovering Direct Successors in Process Logs. In *Proceedings of the 5th International Conference on Discovery Science (Discovery Science 2002)*, volume 2534 of *Lecture Notes in Artificial Intelligence*, pages 364–373. Springer-Verlag, Berlin, 2002.

15. M.K. Maxeiner, K. Küspert, and F. Leymann. Data Mining von Workflow-Protokollen zur teilautomatisierten Konstruktion von Prozeßmodellen. In *Proceedings of Datenbanksysteme in Büro, Technik und Wissenschaft*, pages 75–84. Informatik Aktuell Springer, Berlin, Germany, 2001.

16. L. Pitt. Inductive Inference, DFAs, and Computational Complexity. In K.P. Jantke, editor, *Proceedings of International Workshop on Analogical and Inductive Inference (AII)*, volume 397 of *Lecture Notes in Computer Science*, pages 18–44. Springer-Verlag, Berlin, 1889.

17. W. Reisig and G. Rozenberg, editors. *Lectures on Petri Nets I: Basic Models*, volume 1491 of *Lecture Notes in Computer Science*. Springer-Verlag, Berlin, 1998.

18. G. Schimm. Process Mining. http://www.processmining.de/.

19. G. Schimm. Process Miner – A Tool for Mining Process Schemes from Event-based Data. In S. Flesca and G. Ianni, editors, *Proceedings of the 8th European Conference on Artificial Intelligence (JELIA)*, volume 2424 of *Lecture Notes in Computer Science*, pages 525–528. Springer-Verlag, Berlin, 2002.

20. A.J.M.M. Weijters and W.M.P. van der Aalst. Rediscovering Workflow Models from Event-Based Data using Little Thumb. *Integrated Computer-Aided Engineering*, 10(2):151–162, 2003.

On the Common Support of Workflow Type and Instance Changes under Correctness Constraints

Manfred Reichert, Stefanie Rinderle, and Peter Dadam[*]

University of Ulm, Computer Science Faculty,
Dept. Databases and Information Systems
{reichert, rinderle, dadam}@informatik.uni-ulm.de

Abstract. The capability to rapidly adapt in-progress workflows (WF) is an essential requirement for any workflow system. Adaptations may concern single WF instances or a WF type as a whole. Especially for long-running business processes it is indispensable to propagate WF type changes to in-progress WF instances as well. Very challenging in this context is to correctly adapt a (potentially large) collection of WF instances, which may be in different states and to which various ad-hoc changes may have been previously applied. This paper presents a generic framework for the common support of both WF type and WF instance changes. We establish fundamental correctness principles, position formal theorems, and show how WF instances can be automatically and efficiently migrated to a modified WF schema. The adequate treatment of conflicting WF type and WF instance changes adds to the overall completeness of our approach. By offering more flexibility and adaptability the so promising WF technology will finally deliver.

1 Introduction

In real-world environments people are expected to flexibly deal with exceptions. Though they are trained to do so, this role is purely integrated with current WF technology [1]. Either ad-hoc deviations from the modeled WF schema are completely prohibited, thus requiring to bypass the WF system in exceptional situations, or they may cause severe problems [2]. Ad-hoc adaptations of single WF instances [2,3,4], however, represent only one kind of dynamic change. In order to support evolutionary changes, adaptations may have to be applied at the WF type level as well [3,5,6,7,8,9]. In principle, a WF type change can be accomplished by modifying the respective WF schema accordingly. In doing so, in-progress WF instances must not get into trouble due to the change. This could be achieved by finishing them according to the old schema whereas future instances are created from the new one. Obviously, this simple approach is only sufficient for workflows with short duration, but raises problems in conjunction with long-running processes. Therefore, very often it is desired to propagate a

---

[*] This work was done within the research project "Change management in adaptive workflow systems", which is funded by the German Research Community (DFG).

© Springer-Verlag Berlin Heidelberg 2003

type change Δ, which transforms the actual schema S into a new one, to in-progress WF instances as well. Very challenging in this context is to correctly adapt a (potentially large) collection of WF instances, which may be in different states and to which various ad-hoc changes may have been previously applied. In the latter case, we have to deal with the problem that Δ shall be propagated to WF instances whose current execution schema does not completely correspond to the original schema S. Nevertheless, such "biased" WF instances must not be needlessly excluded from change propagation.

In our previous work, we dealt with ad-hoc changes of single WF instances and related WF graph transformations [2]. The main emphasis was put on im-plementation and usability issues. The objective of this paper is to develop a for-mal framework for both the propagation of WF type changes to already running WF instances and ad-hoc changes of single WF instances. We present different change scenarios and have a look at fundamental principles concerning the de-sign of adaptive WF models. For this, we establish basic correctness principles and position formal theorems. Taking a simple, but powerful WF meta model, we exemplarily show how correctness can be efficiently checked and which in-formation is needed for this. In addition, we introduce well-defined rules and procedures for migrating WF instances to a modified schema.

Section 2 sketches the WF meta model, which we use in this paper to illus-trate fundamental principles of our approach. However, the presented approach is applicable in conjunction with comparable WF meta models as well. Section 3 develops our approach for dynamic WF changes, focusing on general correct-ness principles as well as on implementable rules for ensuring correctness when a change is applied. Section 4 deals with conflicting changes at the type and instance level, and it shows under which conditions WF type changes may be propagated to biased WF instances as well. We discuss related work in Section 5 and conclude with a summary in Section 6.

2   WF Modeling and Execution Basics

For each business process to be supported a *WF type* T has to be defined. It is represented by a *WF schema graph* S of which different versions V_1, ..., V_n may exist (reflecting the evolution of T). To simplify matters, we assume that there is only one version V_n from which new WF instances can be created. This is not really required. However, in the present paper we put the focus on formal considerations and do not deal with versioning issues in more detail.

2.1   Modeling and Execution of Workflows

A WF schema comprises a set of *activities* and defines the control and data flow between them. *Control flow* is modeled by linking activities with *control edges*, which may be optionally associated with *transition conditions*. The use of control edges must not lead to cyclic order relationships since this may cause deadlocks at runtime (see below). Depending on the defined control edges and the chosen

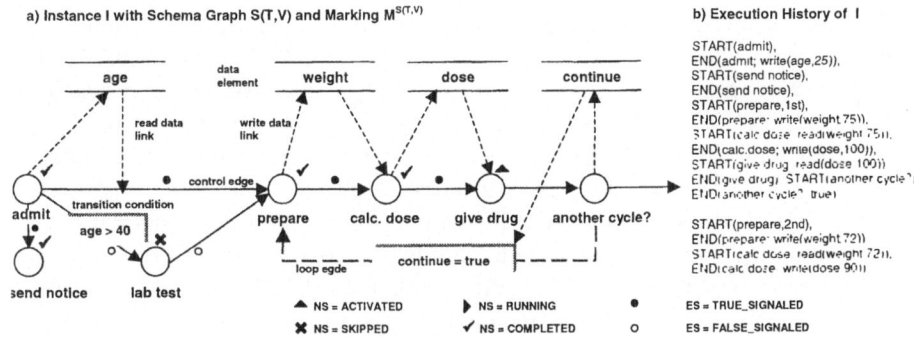

Fig. 1. WF Instance Example

transition conditions, sequences, parallel branchings, and conditional branchings can be described. For the modeling of loop backs, an additional edge type (*loop backward edge*) is provided, which allows us to distinguish between "undesired" and "desired" cycles. To simplify matters, we assume that an activity must not have more than one outgoing loop edge and that the activity nodes which constitute the loop body are well-defined (cf. Def. 1). Finally, *data flow* between activities is realized by connecting them with global *data elements*. For this, read and write *data edges* are provided. An example is depicted in Fig. 1. Formally:

Definition 1 (WF Schema Graph). *A tuple S with S = (N, D, CtrlEdges, LoopEdges, DataEdges, EC) is called a WF schema graph, if the following holds:*

- *N is a set of activities and D a set of data elements*
- *CtrlEdges ⊂ N × N is a precedence relation
  (notation: $n_{src} \to n_{dst} \equiv (n_{src}, n_{dst}) \in CtrlEdges$)*
- *LoopEdges ⊂ N × N is a set of loop backward edges*
- *DataEdges ⊆ N × D × {read, write} is a set of read/write data links between activities and data elements*
- *EC: CtrlEdges ∪ LoopEdges ↦ Conds(D) where Conds(D) denotes the set of all valid transition conditions on data elements from D.*

such that

1. *S_{fwd} = (N, CtrlEdges) is an acyclic graph*
2. *$\forall (n_1, n_2) \in LoopEdges$: $n_2 \in pred(S, n_1)$*
3. *$\forall (n_1, n_2) \in LoopEdges$: $succ(S, n_2) \subseteq L_{body}(n_1, n_2) \cup succ(S, n_1) \land$
   $pred(S, n_1) \subseteq L_{body}(n_1, n_2) \cup pred(S, n_2)$*
4. *$\forall (n_1, n_2), (m_1, m_2) \in LoopEdges$: $n_1 \neq m_1$*

The sets pred(S,n)/succ(S,n) comprise all direct and indirect predecessors/successors of n via control edges and $L_{body}(n_1, n_2) := succ(S, n_2) \cap pred(S, n_1) \cup \{n_1, n_2\}$.

The status of a single WF activity is initially set to NOT_ACTIVATED. When all pre-conditions for activity execution are met (see below), it changes to ACTIVATED. The activity is then either started automatically or corresponding work items are inserted into user worklists. When starting execution, activity status changes to RUNNING and the associated application component is invoked. Finally, at successful termination, status passes to COMPLETED.

Execution of a newly created WF instance starts with those activities that have no incoming control edge. When completing an activity, its outgoing edges are either evaluated to TRUE_SIGNALED or FALSE_SIGNALED, depending on their transition conditions. This, in turn, leads to re-evaluation of target activities. Generally, an activity may be activated as soon as all incoming edges have been signaled and at least of them is marked with TRUE_SIGNALED. Consequently, if all incoming edges are marked as FALSE_SIGNALED, the activity cannot be executed anymore. Its status is then set to SKIPPED, which may lead to cascaded skipping of subsequent activities. A loop edge is evaluated whenever its source activity terminates. If the associated loop condition evaluates to true, outgoing control edges will not be evaluated, the loop edge will be signalled, and all nodes contained within the loop body will be reset to their initial state. Finally, execution of a WF instance will terminate if all activities are in one of the states COMPLETED or SKIPPED.

Each WF instance I is associated with a schema $S = S(T,V)$, where T denotes the WF type of I and V the version of the WF schema graph to be taken for execution. (Note that other WF instances may be based on S as well). The control state of I is captured by a marking function $M^S =$(NS, ES). It assigns to each activity n its current status NS(n) and to each control and loop edge its marking ES(e) (cf. Fig. 1). These markings are determined according to the rules described above, whereas markings of already passed regions and skipped branches are preserved (except loop backs). Concerning data elements, different versions of a data object may be stored, which is important for the context-dependent reading of data elements and the handling of (partial) rollback operations.

Definition 2 (WF Instance). *A WF instance I is defined by a tuple $(T,\ V,\ M^{S(T,V)},\ Val^{S(T,V)},\ \mathcal{H})$ where*

- *T denotes the WF type of I and V the version of the schema graph $S :=$ $S(T,V) = (N,\ D,\ CtrlEdges,\ LoopEdges,\ ...)$ according to which I is executed.*
- *$M^S =$(NS^S, ES^S) reflects the current marking of nodes NS^S: $N \mapsto$ NodeStates and edges ES^S: CtrlEdges $\cup$ LoopEdges $\mapsto$ EdgeStates*
- *Val^S is a function on D. Val^S(d) reflects for each data element $d \in D$ either its current value or the value UNDEFINED (if d has not been written yet).*
- *$\mathcal{H} = <e_0,\ldots,e_k>$ is the execution history of I. It logs information about start / completion of activities. For each started activity X the values of the data elements read by X and for each completed activity Y the values of the data elements written by Y are logged (logical view).*

As described above, WF instances preserve their markings when proceeding in the flow of control. Thus M^S always reflects a consolidated view of the previous execution of I. As we will see later, this property is very useful in connection with dynamic WF instance changes. Formally:

Lemma 1 (Preserving Instance Markings). *Let I be a WF instance with schema graph $S = (N, D, ...)$ and marking $M^S = (NS, ES)$. Further, let $x \in N$ be an arbitrary activity node with $NS(x) \in \{\texttt{COMPLETED}, \texttt{SKIPPED}\}$. Then:*
$\forall\, n \in pred(S, x)\colon NS(n) \in \{\texttt{COMPLETED}, \texttt{SKIPPED}\}$.

2.2 Defining and Changing Schema Graphs

Table 1 contains some primitives that can be used to define and modify schema graphs. Each primitive has a well-defined semantics and is associated with formal pre-/post-conditions, necessary to preserve (structural) correctness of the respective schema (cf. Def. 1). In this paper, we exemplarily restrict our considerations to the avoidance of deadlocks that may be caused due to cyclic order relationships (via control edges). Generally, additional constraints exist. Concerning data flow, for example, no lost updates must occur during runtime and all data elements read by an activity must always have been written by preceding activities, independently of chosen execution branches. There are other primitives (e.g., to update edge conditions), which we do not consider in the following. Finally, change primitives serve as basis for defining high-level operations (e.g., to shift an activity from its current to another position) and for deriving formal conditions for them. However, this is outside the scope of this paper.

Table 1. Examples of Basic Change Primitives

addCtrlEdge(S, n_{src}, n_{dst})	Pre: $(n_{src} \notin succ(S, n_{dst}) \cup \{n_{dst}\}) \wedge (\forall\, (n_1, n_2) \in \text{LoopEdges}:$ $[n_{src} \in L_{body}(n_1, n_2) \Leftrightarrow n_{src} \in L_{body}(n_1, n_2)])$ Post: CtrlEdges' = CtrlEdges $\cup \{n_{src} \rightarrow n_{dst}\}$
addActivity(S, n_{ins}, Preds, Succs)	Pre: $(\forall\, p \in \text{Preds}, \forall\, s \in \text{Succs}: s \notin pred(S, p)) \wedge$ $\quad (\forall\, (n_1, n_2) \in \text{LoopEdges}:$ $\quad\quad (\text{Preds} \cup \text{Succs}) \subseteq L_{body}(n_1, n_2) \vee$ $\quad\quad (\text{Preds} \cup \text{Succs}) \cap L_{body}(n_1, n_2) = \emptyset)$ Post: N' = N $\cup \{n_{ins}\}$ $\quad$ CtrlEdges' = CtrlEdges $\cup \{p \rightarrow n_{ins} \mid p \in \text{Preds}\}$ $\quad\quad \cup \{n_{ins} \rightarrow s \mid s \in \text{Succs}\}$
deleteCtrlEdge(S, n_{src}, n_{dst})	Post: CtrlEdges' = CtrlEdges $\neg \{n_{src} \rightarrow n_{dst}\}$
deleteActivity(S, n_{del})	Post: N' = N $\neg \{n_{del}\}$ $\quad$ CtrlEdges' = CtrlEdges $\neg \{a \rightarrow b \mid n_{del} \in \{a, b\}\} \cup$ $\quad \{ p \rightarrow s$ with EC(p $\rightarrow$ s) = ec $\mid$ $\quad\quad p \rightarrow n_{del}, n_{del} \rightarrow s \in$ CtrlEdges $\wedge$ EC($n_{del} \rightarrow$ s) = ec$\}$

3 Dynamic Change Basics

In this section, we present issues related to dynamic change correctness in a formal and rigorous style. Due to lack of space, we restrict our considerations to changes definable by the primitives from Table 1. First of all, we do not make a difference between changes of single instances and adaptations of a collection of instances (e.g., due to a type change). Instead we focus on fundamental issues related to dynamic instance changes. In the following, let I be an instance with schema graph S and marking M^S. Assume that S is transformed into a correct schema graph S' by applying change Δ. Two challenging issues arise:

1. Can Δ be correctly *propagated* to I, i.e., without causing errors or inconsistencies? For this case, I is said to be *compliant* with S'.
2. Assuming I is compliant with S', how can we smoothly *migrate* it to S' such that its further execution can be based on S'? Which state (marking) adaptations become necessary in this context?

We will show that these two issues are fundamental for the design of any adaptive WF model. While the first one concerns pre-conditions on the state of I, the second issue is related to post-conditions that must be satisfied after the change has been applied. In any case, we have to find an efficient solution, which enables automatic and correct compliance checks as well as instance migrations. In Section 3.1 we introduce general correctness principles which address the above issues. Based on them, for the presented WF meta model (cf. Section 2) we develop formal pre-conditions for ensuring compliance of instances with a modified schema (cf. Section 3.2). Section 3.3 shows how to efficiently determine follow-up markings of compliant WF instances when migrating them to the new schema. Section 3.4 concludes with a discussion of different change scenarios.

3.1   Dynamic Change Correctness

To illustrate potential problems that may result from the uncontrolled migration of WF instances consider schema graph S from Fig. 2a. Let us assume that S is correctly transformed into S' by inserting two activities and a data dependency between them (cf. Fig. 2a, 2b). Assume that this change shall be applied to the instances from Fig. 2c) (currently based on S) but without performing any compliance check. Concerning I_1 no problem would occur, since its execution has not yet entered the change region. Uncontrolled migration of I_2, however, would cause malfunctions: Firstly, an inconsistent marking would result (cf. Lemma 1), thus leading to an undefined execution state. Secondly, activity give drug may be invoked though the data element allergyData read by this activity may not have been written. Concerning I_3 migration would be possible. However, when migrating I_3 to S', activation of activity prepare has to be undone and corresponding work items must be removed from worklists. Additionally, the newly inserted activity test must be activated. This example demonstrates that applicability of a dynamic change depends on current instance state as well as on applied change primitives. Furthermore, when migrating compliant instances, markings and worklist structures must be correctly adapted.

Comparable with serializability in DBMS, we need general principles which allow us to argue about the correctness of dynamic changes. In more detail, we require a formal criterion for deciding whether a given WF instance can be smoothly migrated to the modified schema or not. In addition, we must be able to determine correct new markings resulting from such a migration. One of our design goals is to define these correctness criteria independently of the operational semantics of the used WF meta model and the offered change operations. This allows us to apply them in different scope and to different WF meta models, thus providing a good basis for reasoning about the correctness of rules and methods for checking compliance and for migrating compliant instances.

Intuitively, instance I is compliant with the modified schema S' if I could have been executed according to S' as well and would have produced the same effects on data elements [3,10]. Trivially, this will be always the case if I has not yet entered the region affected by the change. Generally, we need information about previous execution to decide this property and to determine correct follow-up markings for compliant instances. To derive such a general compliance principle, at the logical level we make use of the execution history usually kept for each WF instance (cf. Fig. 1 and 2). We assume that this history logs events related to the start and termination of activity executions (cf. Def. 2).

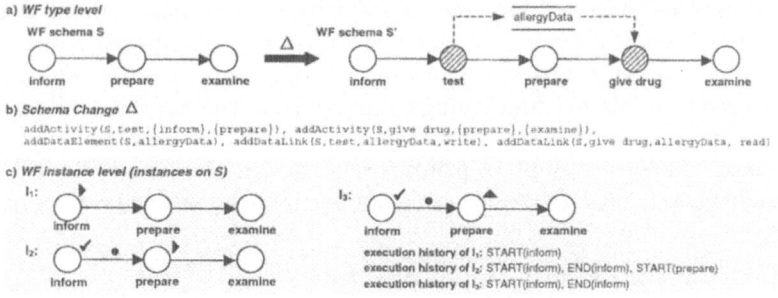

Fig. 2. Schema Graph and Related Instances

Obviously, instance I with history $\mathcal{H}$ is compliant with S' and can migrate to S' if $\mathcal{H}$ could have been produced on S' as well. We then obtain a correct new marking by "replaying" all events from $\mathcal{H}$ on S' in sequential order. Taking our example from Fig. 2 this property holds for I_1 and I_3 but does not apply to I_2. When replaying $\mathcal{H}_3$ on S' we obtain node markings as sketched above.

The described criterion is still too restrictive to serve as general correctness principle. Concerning loop changes it may needlessly exclude instances from migrations. As an example take instance I from Fig. 1 where the depicted loop is in its 2nd iteration. Assume that schema S is modified by applying change addActivity(S, perform test, {prepare}, {give drug}). Taking the above criterion this change would not be allowed since previous loop iteration of I is not compliant with the new schema; i.e., $\mathcal{H}$ cannot be produced based on the modified schema. However, excluding such instances from migrations very often is not in accordance with practice. To overcome this restrictiveness we relax the above criterion by (logically) discarding those history entries produced within another loop iteration than the last (completed loops) or the current one (running loops). We denote this reduced view $\mathcal{H}$ as red$_{\mathcal{H}}$. Based on this we now define a general correctness principle for dynamic WF changes:

Axiom 1 (Dynamic Change Correctness) *Let $I = (T, V, M^S, Val^S, \mathcal{H})$ be a WF instance with correct schema graph $S = S(T, V)$ and marking M^S. Assume that S is transformed into a correct schema graph S' by applying change Δ. Then:*

1. *Δ can be correctly propagated to I iff red$_{\mathcal{H}}$ can be produced on S' as well (For this case, I is said to be compliant with S').*
2. *Assume I is compliant with S'. When propagating Δ to I the correct marking $M^{S'}$ of I on S' can be obtained by replaying red$_{\mathcal{H}}$ on S'.*

These two basic properties satisfy our design goals since they do not depend on the operational semantics of the used WF meta model and the changes applied. Axiom 1 can therefore serve as fundamental correctness principle for adaptive workflow. Furthermore, it does not needlessly exclude instances from migrations on condition their execution will not get into trouble due to the change. Altogether Axiom 1 provides a good basis for arguing about dynamic change correctness. However, it would certainly be no good idea to guarantee compliance and to determine new markings of compliant instances by accessing the whole execution history and trying to replay it on the modified schema since this may cause a performance penalty. Note that histories comprise voluminous data and are usually not kept in primary storage. In the following we present optimized rules and procedures for ensuring correctness according to Axiom 1.

3.2   Rules for Checking Compliance

For the WF meta model from Section 2 and related change primitives we exemplarily show under which conditions compliance (cf. Axiom 1,1) can be guaranteed. Our basic design principles have been as follows:

1. We consider change semantics and context in order to derive precise compliance rules and to state which information is needed for checking them.
2. We make use of dynamic properties of the WF model. Particularly, the derivation of compliance rules benefits from activity markings which already provide a consolidated view on the (reduced) history of a WF instance.

We omit unnecessary details and focus on compliance rules for selected primitives from Table 1. Based on them, one can easily develop high-level change operations and related compliance rules. Since the latter can be derived by merging compliance conditions of the change primitives applied and by discarding unnecessary expressions (e.g., conditions on nodes not present in the original schema graph), we do not further consider complex change operations in this paper.

Let I be an instance with schema S, marking M^S, and history $\mathcal{H}$. Assume that S is transformed into correct schema S' by applying one of the primitives from Table 1. The challenge is to find conditions under which we can ensure compliance of I with S' (cf. Axiom 1,1). Table 2 summarizes some well-founded compliance conditions. Based on them we can state the following theorem:

Table 2. Examples of Compliance Rules

Change Operation Δ ...	... and Related Compliance Condition $Compliant(S, \Delta, NS. ES, Val^S, \mathcal{H})$
addActivity(S,n_{ins},Preds,Succs)	$(\forall\ n \in$ Preds: NS(n) = SKIPPED) $\vee$ $(\forall\ n \in$ Succs: NS(n) $\in$ {NOT_ACTIVATED, ACTIVATED} $\vee$ (NS(n) = SKIPPED $\wedge$ $\qquad\qquad\qquad\qquad\qquad\qquad\quad \forall\ m \in$ succ(S,n): NS(m) $\in$ {NOT_ACTIVATED, ACTIVATED, SKIPPED}))
addCtrlEdge(S, n_{src}, n_{dst}) (with EC($n_{src} \to n_{dst}$) = =True)	NS(n_{dst}) $\in$ {NOT_ACTIVATED, ACTIVATED} $\vee$ (NS(n_{dst}) $\in$ {RUNNING, COMPLETED} $\wedge$ NS(n_{src}) $\in$ {COMPLETED} $\wedge$ $(e_i = $ END(n_{src}), $e_j = $ START(n_{dst}) $\in \mathcal{H}, \Rightarrow i < j$)) $\vee$ (NS(n_{dst}) $\in$ {RUNNING, COMPLETED} $\wedge$ NS(n_{src}) = SKIPPED $\wedge$ $(\forall\ n \in N_1$ with NS(n) = COMPLETED. $e_j = $ END(n), $e_i = $ START(n_{dst}) $\in \mathcal{H}. \Rightarrow j < i$)) $\vee$ (NS(n_{dst}) = SKIPPED $\wedge$ NS(n_{src}) $\in$ {NOT_ACTIVATED, ACTIVATED, RUNNING, COMPLETED} $\wedge$ $(\forall\ n \in N_2$: NS(n) $\in$ {NOT_ACTIVATED, ACTIVATED, SKIPPED})) $\vee$ (NS(n_{dst}) = SKIPPED $\wedge$ NS(n_{src}) = COMPLETED $\wedge$ $(\forall\ n \in N_2$ with NS(n) $\in$ {RUNNING, COMPLETED}: $(e_j = $ START(n). $e_i = $ END(n_{src}) $\in \mathcal{H}. \Rightarrow j > i$) })) $\vee$ (NS(n_{dst}) = NS(n_{src}) = SKIPPED $\wedge$ $(\forall\ s \in N_2$ with NS(s) $\in$ {RUNNING, COMPLETED}, $\forall\ p \in N_1$ with NS(p) = COMPLETED: $e_i = $ END(p), $e_j = $ START(s) $\in \mathcal{H}, \Rightarrow j > i$)) where $N_1 := $ pred(S, n_{src})$\neg$ pred(S. n_{dst}) $\cup$ {n_{src}}, $\qquad N_2 := $ succ(S, n_{dst})$\neg$ succ(S, n_{src}) $\cup$ {n_{dst}}
deleteActivity(S,n_{del})	NS(n_{del})) $\in$ {NOT_ACTIVATED, ACTIVATED, SKIPPED}
deleteCtrlEdge(S,n_{src},n_{dst})	(NS(n_{dst}) $\in$ NOT_ACTIVATED, ACTIVATED) $\vee$ (ES($n_{src} \to n_{dst}$) = FALSE_SIGNALED $\wedge$ (($\exists\ n \to n_{dst} \in$ CtrlEdges, n $\neq n_{src}$) $\vee$ $\qquad\qquad (\forall\ n \in$ succ(S, n_{dst}): NS(n) $\notin$ {RUNNING, COMPLETED}))) $\vee$ (ES($n_{src} \to n_{dst}$) = TRUE_SIGNALED $\wedge$ ($\not\exists\ n \to n_{dst} \in$ CtrlEdges, n $\neq n_{src}$) $\vee$ $(\exists\ e = n \to n_{dst} \in$ CtrlEdges, n $\neq n_{src}$ with ES(e) $\neq$ FALSE_SIGNALED))
addDataElement(S,d)	no condition
deleteDataElement(S,d)	val(d) = UNDEFINED
addDataLink(S,n,d,read)	NS(n) $\in$ {NOT_ACTIVATED, ACTIVATED, SKIPPED}
addDataLink(S,n,d,write)	NS(n) $\neq$ COMPLETED

Theorem 1 (Compliance Rules). *Let I be a WF instance with schema graph S, marking $M^S = (NS, ES)$, data values Val^S, and execution history $\mathcal{H}$. Assume that S is transformed into a correct schema graph S' by applying change operation Δ to it. Then: I is compliant with S' (according to Axiom 1,1)* $\Leftrightarrow$
$Compliant(S, \Delta, NS, ES, Val^S, \mathcal{H}) = $ TRUE *(cf. Table 2).*

Due to lack of space we omit formal proofs. Instead we exemplarily describe compliance conditions for the primitives addActivity and addCtrlEdge. Regarding insertion of an activity n_{ins} between two node sets *Preds* and *Succs* compliance can be guaranteed if all nodes from *Succs* actually possess one of the markings ACTIVATED or NOT_ACTIVATED. In this case, none of the successors of n_{ins} has yet written any entry into $\mathcal{H}$. Furthermore, compliance can be ensured if all nodes from *Preds* are marked as SKIPPED. Then n_{ins} is skipped as well, i.e., its insertion has no effect on compliance. Finally, n_{ins} may be inserted as predecessor of a skipped node provided that none of the successors of this node has a marking other than ACTIVATED, NOT_ACTIVATED, or SKIPPED (see Fig. 3).

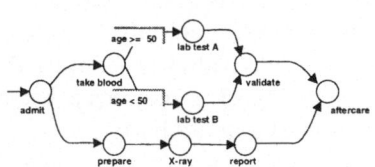

The addition of a control edge $n_{src} \to n_{dst}$ will always be possible if NS(n_{dst}) $\in$ {ACTIVATED, NOT_ACTIVATED} applies. In case n_{dst} is marked as SKIPPED compliance can be guaranteed if all successors of n_{dst} (less the successors of n_{src}) possess one of the markings ACTIVATED, NOT_ACTIVATED, or SKIPPED.

Under certain conditions dynamic insertion of a control edge $n_{src} \to n_{dst}$ is even allowed if n_{dst} has been already started or completed. As an example

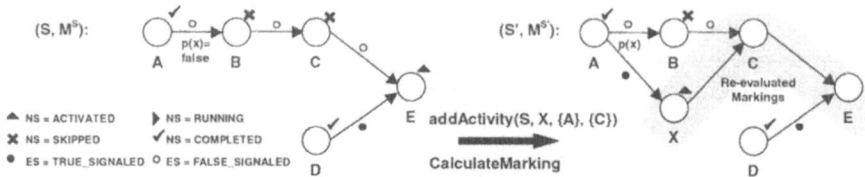

Fig. 3. Insertion before a Skipped Node

take the process schema (medical workflow) from the previous figure. Assume that an additional control edge is inserted between activities **test** B and X-ray. Concerning instances for which both activities are completed insertion is (only) allowed if **test** B had written its end entry into $\mathcal{H}$ before the start entry of X-ray was logged. As a second example, consider an instance I where **test** B is marked as SKIPPED and X-ray as COMPLETED. Taking this marking I would be only compliant with S' if **take blood** had been completed before X-ray started ($N_1 = \{$**take blood**$\}$).

Compliance conditions for the deletion of activities and control edges as well as for data flow changes are summarized in Table 2. In a similar way we can derive compliance rules for other primitives, e.g., insertion or deletion of loop edges or update of transition conditions. Altogether we can state that compliance – as postulated by Axiom 1,1 – can be checked on basis of current activity markings; i.e., we usually must not explicitly check the producibility of whole execution histories on the modified schema.

3.3   How to Correctly Adapt Workflow Instance Markings?

We have described how compliance can be ensured and which information is needed. Our main goal was to prevent access to the whole execution history. By holding this maxim we now show how compliant instances can be migrated to the changed schema. One problem to be solved is the efficient and correct adaptation of activity markings. According to Axiom 1,2 the marking of a migrated instance must be the same as it could be obtained when replaying the respective (reduced) history on the new schema. How extensive marking adaptations turn out for instance I depends on the kind and scope of the change. Except for initialization of newly inserted nodes and edges, no adaptations will become necessary if execution of I has not yet entered the change region. In other cases extensive marking adaptations may be required. An activity X, for example, may have to be deactivated if control edges are inserted with X as target activity. Conversely, a newly added activity will have to be immediately activated or skipped if all predecessors possess a final marking. As shown in Fig. 3 it may even become necessary to undo the skipping of nodes when inserting an activity.

We now describe how markings can be automatically and efficiently adapted when migrating compliant instances. Initially, we can restrict marking evaluations to those nodes and edges, which constitute the context of a change region. We sketch how these sets can be determined for selected change primitives as well as for complex changes. Based on this, we present an algorithm which correctly calculates new markings for compliant instances.

Table 3. Node and Edge Sets to be Evaluated

op = addActivity(S, n_{ins}, Preds, Succs)	$N_{check}(op) :=$ Succs ($\cup \{n_{ins}\}$ if Preds $= \emptyset$) $E_{check}(op) := \{p \to n_{ins} \in$ CtrlEdges' $\mid p \in$ Preds$\}$
op = deleteActivity(S, n_{del})	$N_{check}(op) := \{n \in N \mid n_{del} \to n \in$ CtrlEdges $\}$ $E_{check}(op) := \emptyset$
op = addCtrlEdge(S, n_{src}, n_{dst})	$N_{check}(op) := \{n_{dst}\}, E_{check}(op) := \{n_{src} \to n_{dst}\}$
op = deleteCtrlEdge(S, n_{src}, n_{dst})	$N_{check}(op) = \{n_{dst}\}$

Table 3 shows node and edge sets whose markings must be initially evaluated when the respective change operation op is applied – we denote these sets as $N_{check}(op)$ and $E_{check}(op)$ respectively. Depending on the evaluation result, inspection of additional nodes and edges may become necessary. As a first example, take the dynamic insertion of an activity n_{ins}. Firstly, all incoming control edges of n_{ins} must be evaluated. Depending on this, n_{ins} either has to be activated, skipped, or left in its initial state. (Note that an initial evaluation of n_{ins} only becomes necessary if $Preds = \emptyset$ holds.) Secondly, all successors of n_{ins} must be re-evaluated as well. Due to the insertion of n_{ins}, activation or skipping of these activities may have to be undone. Regarding the insertion of a control edge, the marking of both, the newly added edge and its target node n_{dst} have to be re-evaluated, i.e., we obtain $N_{check}(op) = \{n_{dst}\}$ and $E_{check}(op) := \{n_{src} \to n_{dst}\}$. The latter will be also required if the evaluation of the edge marking results in NOT_SIGNALED (for this case n_{dst} may have to be deactivated).

Concerning a complex change $\Delta = op_1, \ldots, op_n$ the total node and edge sets $N_{check}(\Delta)$ and $E_{check}(\Delta)$ to be (initially) evaluated can be determined with Algorithm 1. In principle, we obtain them by unifying the corresponding sets of the applied change operations. However, since these operations can be based on each other, there may be temporarily generated nodes or edges not present in the resulting schema graph anymore. This is considered by Algorithm 1.

Algorithm 1: CalcEvalSet(S, S', $\Delta = op_1, \ldots, op_n$) $\longrightarrow N_{check}(\Delta), E_{check}(\Delta)$

$E_{check}(\Delta) := \emptyset; N_{check}(\Delta) := \emptyset;$
for i:=1 to n **do**
     $E_{check}(\Delta) := E_{check}(\Delta) \cup E_{check}(op_i); N_{check}(\Delta) := N_{check}(\Delta) \cup N_{check}(op_i);$
done
$E_{check}(\Delta) := E_{check}(\Delta) \cap E'; N_{check}(\Delta) := N_{check}(\Delta) \cap N';$

Let I be an instance with schema S and marking M^S. Assume S is transformed into a correct schema S' by applying change $\Delta = op_1, \ldots, op_n$. Assume

---

Algorithm 2: CalcMarking(S, S', (NS, ES),$N_{check}(\Delta)$, $E_{check}(\Delta)$) $\longrightarrow$ (NS', ES')

```
N_check := N_check(Δ); E_check := E_check(Δ);
forall e ∈ E' ∩ E do ES'(e) = ES(e) done;
forall e ∈ E' ¬ E do ES'(e) = NOT_SIGNALED done
forall n ∈ N' ∩ N do NS'(n) = NS(n) done;
forall n ∈ N' ¬ N do NS'(n) = NOT_ACTIVATED done

repeat
    while E_check ≠ ∅ do
        fetch an edge e = n_src → n_dst from E_check;
        determine marking newES of e according to marking of n_src and transition cond. EC'(e)
        if ES'(e) ≠ newES then
            ES'(e) := newES , N_check := N_check ∪ {n_dst}
        endif
    done
    while N_check ≠ ∅ do
        fetch a node n from N_check;
        determine marking newNS of n according to markings of incoming control edges of n.
            if NS'(n) ≠ newNS then
                if newNS = SKIPPED or NS'(n) = SKIPPED then
                    E_check := E_check ∪ {e = n_src → n_dst ∈ E' | n_src = n }
            endif
            NS'(n) := newNS
        endif
    done
until E_check = ∅ and N_check = ∅;
```

---

further that I is compliant with S'. Algorithm 2 then correctly determines new marking $M^{S'}$ of I on S'. Basic to this are the marking and execution rules of our WF meta model. Algorithm 2 starts with sets $N_{check}(\Delta)$ and $E_{check}(\Delta)$ as input. If the markings of respective nodes or edges are adapted during execution of Algorithm 2, context nodes and edges will be re-evaluated as well, etc. By means of Algorithms 1 and 2, total expenditure for marking adaptations can be significantly reduced when compared to the re-evaluation of all node and edge markings or the complete replay of all history events on the new schema. Nevertheless, our approach guarantees correctness according to Axiom 1,2. Formally:

Theorem 2 (Optimized Marking Adaptations). *Let $I = (T, V, M^S, Val^S, \mathcal{H})$ be an instance with schema $S = S(T,V)$ and marking M^S. Assume that change Δ transforms S into a correct schema S' and I is compliant with S'. Then: With CalculateMarking(S, S', M^S, $N_{check}(\Delta)$, $E_{check}(\Delta)$) (cf. Alg. 2) we obtain the correct marking $M^{S'}$ of I (cf. Axiom 1,2) when migrating it to S'; i.e., we obtain the same marking as it would result when replaying $\mathcal{H}$ on S'.*

While Algorithm 1 has to be carried out only once at change definition time, Algorithm 2 must be applied for each instance to be migrated. The complexity of Algorithm 2 can be estimated by $O(n)$ (where n corresponds to the number of activities of schema S'). Additionally, for each WF instance complexity $O(n)$ arises from the described compliance checks.

As a first example, take the activity insertion from Fig. 3. As already shown, the depicted instance is compliant with the modified schema. With Algorithm 1 we obtain $N_{check} = \{C\}$ and $E_{check} = \{A \to X\}$. Furthermore, when running Algorithm 2 with these sets as input, the newly inserted activity X will be activated whereas skipping of C and activation of E will be undone. A second example, which shows a change at the type level (parallel ordering of activities that have been executed serially so far) and its propagation to compliant instances is depicted in Fig. 4. Note that both, necessary checks and marking adaptations can be completely automated in our approach. Thus the "dynamic change bug" as discussed in WF literature (e.g. [9,11]) is not present in our approach.

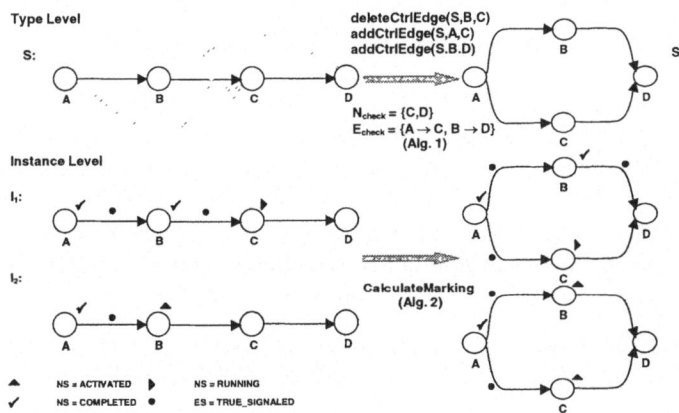

Fig. 4. Instance Migrations Due To Type Change

3.4   Realizing Workflow Type and Workflow Instance Changes

The presented correctness principles, compliance rules, and migration procedures are applicable for both WF schema evolution (incl. change propagation to running instances) and ad-hoc changes of single instances.

WF schema evolution: First of all, we allow designers to restrict the set of migratable instances by specifying appropriate selection predicates (based on WF attributes). For each selected instance I the WfMS checks whether it is compliant with the modified schema or not. In the former case I is re-linked to the new schema S' and its further execution is based on S' (cf. Fig. 5 b). Among other things this includes adaptation of markings and related data structures as described. Non-compliant instances may be finished according to the old schema version or be rolled back to a compliant state to enable their migration. In connection with loops such a compliant state may be reachable when a loop enters its next iteration. A discussion of this special case and the support of delayed instance migrations, however, is outside the scope of this paper.

(Ad-hoc) changes: An ad-hoc change of instance I may become necessary, for example, to deal with exceptional situations. For change definition, high-level operations are offered to users (e.g., to jump forward in the flow or to shift activities) which are based on the described primitives. All runtime deviations are

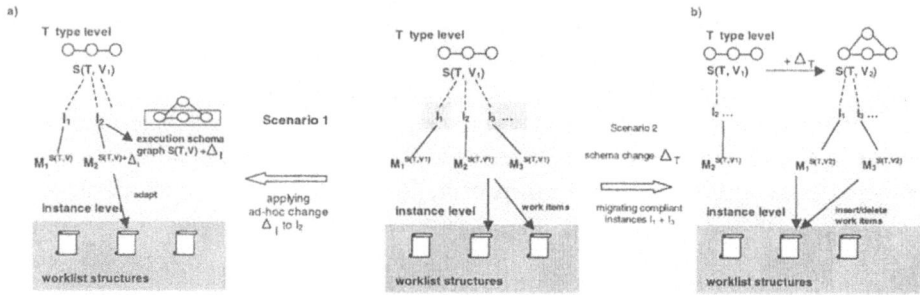

Fig. 5. Managing Type and Instance Changes

properly integrated with respect to authorization and are logged in the change history of I. Obviously, this results in an instance-specific execution schema S_I = S + Δ_I which differs from the original schema S (cf. Def. 3) – Δ_I is called the *bias* of I (with respect to S) and describes the set of instance-specific changes $op_I^1, \ldots, op_I^n$ that have been applied to I so far. Execution of I as well as future change definitions are logically based on S_I (cf. Fig. 5 a).

Definition 3 (Biased Instance). *A biased instance I is described by a tuple $(T, V, \Delta_I, M^{S+\Delta_I}, Val^{S+\Delta_I}, \mathcal{H})$, where $S = S(T,V)$ corresponds to the schema version from which I was created and Δ_I comprises instance-specific changes $op_I^1, \ldots, op_I^n$ that have been applied to I so far. Schema $S_I := S + \Delta_I$, which results from the application of Δ_I to S, is called the execution schema of I.*

Trivially, the execution schema S_I of an unbiased instance I (with $\Delta_I = \emptyset$) corresponds to its original schema S. A biased instance always keeps the reference to its original schema. As we will see in the next section, under certain conditions this allows us to propagate type changes to biased instances as well. How biased instances are "physically" represented, whether S_I is materialized or only Δ_I is stored and other implementation issues are outside the scope of this paper.

4   Conflicting Type and Instance Changes

Biased WF instances must not be needlessly excluded from adapting to a WF type change. As an example take a patient treatment process. Even though physicians may have deviated from the original WF schema S at the instance level (e.g., by inserting or skipping activities) this must not prohibit the propagation of future WF type changes to these instances on condition that they are not conflicting with current instance state and previously applied ad-hoc changes. In this section, we sketch what is needed and which issues arise in this context.

Let $I = (T, V_n, \Delta_I, ...)$ be a biased WF instance (cf. Def. 3) which was created from schema version S = S(T, V_n) and to which instance-specific changes op_I^1, $\ldots$, op_I^n – described by bias Δ_I – have been applied so far. Assume that a new schema version S' = S(T, V_{n+1}) is derived from S by applying WF type change Δ_T (= $op_T^1, \ldots, op_T^m$) to it (S' = S + Δ_T). Then the following issues arise:

1. May Δ_T be propagated to I as well though the current execution schema $S_I = S + \Delta_I$ of I differs from the original schema S?
2. If change propagation is possible how can it be efficiently and correctly accomplished? Which execution schema S_I' (and marking $M^{S_I'}$) must result?

4.1 Correctness Issues

Comparable to the migration of unbiased instances (cf. Section 3) we introduce a general criterion that allows us to argue about the two issues described above. Obviously, when propagating a WF type change Δ_T to a biased WF instance I we do not only have to consider its current marking M^{S_I} but must also deal with structural and semantical conflicts that may exist between the "concurrent" changes Δ_I and Δ_T (Note that Δ_I as well as Δ_T have been based on S). In this paper we restrict our considerations to structural conflicts. A comprehensive treatment of semantically conflicting changes is given in [12].

Axiom 2 (Propagating Type Changes To Biased Instances) *Let T be a WF type with actual schema version $S = S(T, V_n)$. Assume that a new schema version $S' = S(T, V_{n+1})$ is derived by applying type change Δ_T to S. Then: Δ_T may be propagated to WF instance $I = (T, V_n, \Delta_I, ...) :\Leftrightarrow$*

1. *$S^* = (S + \Delta_I) + \Delta_T$ is a correct schema graph, i.e., Δ_T can be correctly applied to the execution schema $S_I = (S + \Delta_I)$.*
2. *I is compliant with S^*; i.e., the reduced execution history red_H (cf. Section 3.1) can be produced on S^* as well. The marking M^{S^*} resulting from this is considered as a correct state.*

According to Axiom 2 type change Δ_T may be propagated to a biased instance I if Δ_T can be correctly applied to the execution schema of I and does not conflict with its current marking. The resulting schema $S^* = S_I + \Delta_T$ must therefore satisfy the correctness properties of the used WF meta model (cf. Section 2). In addition, I must be compliant with S^* according to Axiom 1. As an example take schema $S = S(T,V)$ from Fig. 6. Assume that type change $\Delta_T^1 = [\text{addCtrlEdge(S,E,D)}]$ is applied to S. Then condition 1 of Axiom 2 is not satisfied since the resulting schema $S_I + \Delta_T^1$ contains a deadlock-causing cycle. Δ_T^1 must therefore be not propagated to I. As opposed to this, type change $\Delta_T^2 = [\text{addActivity(S,Y,\{D\},\{E\})}]$ may be propagated to I since the conditions defined by Axiom 2 are met. As a last example take $\Delta_T^3 = [\text{deleteDataLink(S,C,d,write)}, \text{deleteActivity(S,C)}]$. It is quite evident that propagation of Δ_T^3 to I would result in an incorrect data flow schema since X (which was inserted by a previous instance change) would read data element d with undefined value.

4.2 Checking Correctness

The challenge is to efficiently verify the conditions from Axiom 2. A naive solution would be to first generate schema $S_I + \Delta_T$ and then to check whether

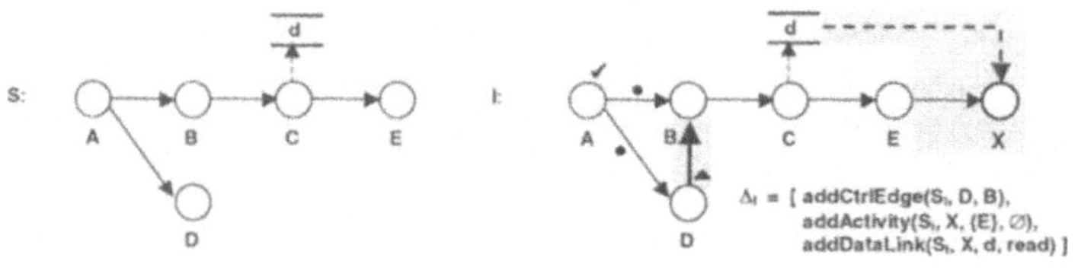

Fig. 6. Original Schema and Biased Instance

it satisfies the required structural and dynamic properties. Generally this would be too expensive, in particular if different WF aspects (control flow, data flow, etc.) are concerned or Δ_T shall be propagated to a large number of instances. Instead we must define appropriate rules for excluding conflicts between type and instance changes for as many cases as possible. Concerning the absence of deadlock-causing cycles, for example, the following conflict rule can be used:

Lemma 2 (Deadlock Prevention). *Let T be a WF type with actual schema version $S = S(T, V_n)$ and $I = (T, V_n, \Delta_I, ...)$ be a biased instance with execution schema $S_I = S + \Delta_I$. Assume that type change Δ_T transforms S into a correct schema $S' = S(T, V_{n+1})$. Then: $S^* = (S + \Delta_I) + \Delta_T$ does not contain deadlock-causing cycles if the following condition holds:*

$\forall\ s_1 \rightarrow d_1 \in AddedCtrlEdges_{\Delta_T},\ \forall\ s_2 \rightarrow d_2 \in AddedCtrlEdges_{\Delta_I}:$

$d_1 \notin pred(S, s_2) \vee d_2 \notin pred(S, s_1)$

(AddedCtrlEdges$_\Delta$ denotes the set of control edges inserted by change primitives addActivity and addCtrlEdge from Δ.)

Taking change Δ_T^1 from Section 4.1 the condition of this lemma is not satisfied. Concerning Δ_T^2, however, deadlocks can be excluded. Though the condition set out by Lemma 2 will not always be necessary, it is sufficient to exclude potential deadlocks. In particular, the related checks can be based on the original schema graph S and be accomplished by simple graph algorithms (with complexity O(n)). Generally, for each change operation we have to define corresponding conflict rules. Concerning data flow changes, for example, we can exclude potential conflicts by ensuring that the data element sets for which Δ_I and Δ_T have inserted or deleted data edges are disjoint. In our example from Section 4.1, Δ_I has inserted a read data link with source d and Δ_T^3 removed a write data link with target d. Thus a potential conflict exists, which requires additional checks.

4.3   Propagating Type Changes to Biased Instances

Assume that schema S is correctly transformed into a new schema S' by applying type change Δ_T to it. Assume further that $I = (T, V_n, \Delta_I, ...)$ is an instance to which Δ_T can be correctly propagated according to Axiom 2. Then the question arises how we can migrate this biased instance to the new schema version of type T. Due to lack of space we only consider changes based on the primitives from Table 1. For them the following theorem applies:

Theorem 3 (Commutativity of Type and Instance Changes). *Let T be a WF type with actual schema graph version $S = S(T, V_n)$ and $I = (T, V_n, \Delta_I, ...)$ be a biased instance (with type T). Assume that type change Δ_T transforms S into $S' = S(T, V_{n+1})$ and Δ_T can be correctly propagated to I (according to Axiom 2). Then: Δ_T and Δ_I are commutative, i.e., Δ_I can be correctly applied to S' as well and $(S + \Delta_I) + \Delta_T \equiv (S + \Delta_T) + \Delta_I$ ($= S' + \Delta_I$).*

According to this theorem, type and instance changes are commutative provided that the specified conditions are met. In particular, this property allows us to treat type changes and related change propagation similar to the unbiased case (cf. Section 3.4). More precisely, a type change can be propagated to a biased instance I by re-linking this instance to the new schema S' (cf. Fig. 7) and by re-calculating marking M^{S_I} for the resulting execution schema S_I'. Note that S_I' can be simply derived by applying bias Δ_I to S'. Though at first glance it seems to make no significant difference whether we apply Δ_T to S_I or Δ_I to S' the latter variant offers several advantages with respect to the management of schema versions and propagation of future type changes. Due to lack of space we abstain from further details.

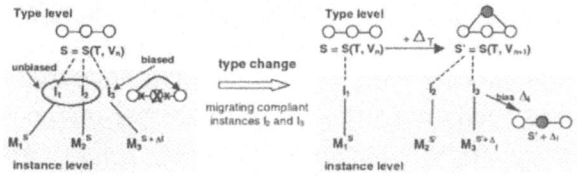

Fig. 7. WF Type Change and Propagation To Biased and Unbiased WF Instances

5   Related Work

One of the first approaches which has used a generic correctness criterion for dynamic WF changes was developed within the WIDE project [10]. WIDE applies a history-based compliance criterion to guarantee correctness when migrating instances to a modified schema. Concerning loops, however, this criterion is too restrictive. Furthermore, issues related to data flow changes, marking adaptations and conflicting changes are not considered. Similar correctness criteria have been applied in TRAMs and BREEZE. TRAMs [7] focuses on schema versioning concepts. To efficiently manage instance migrations the definition of migration conditions is proposed for every change operation. Based on them, it can be decided whether an instance can migrate to the new version or not. BREEZE [3] also uses formal compliance criteria but focuses on the handling of non-compliant WF instances. Furthermore it deals with the correct treatment of temporal constraints at the presence of dynamic changes.

Petri-Net based approaches for adaptive WF [9,11,13] must deal with the problem that actual state tokens of a net instance do not represent a view on previous instance execution as in our work. This, in turn, complicates compliance checking and marking adaptations in order to avoid the "dynamic change bug" [9]. [11] suggests the construction of a hybrid WF schema which reflects parts of both the old and the new WF schema. Additionally, the designer must explicitly specify rules for mapping tokens between old and new net versions. Actual results from the Petri Net field come from [9,14]. As correctness criterion *branching bisimularity* is proposed: An instance I can migrate to a modified schema if each action of I can be simulated on this schema as well. Unfortunately, branching bisimularity can be only ensured for special change operations and excludes, for example, order-changing operations. Apart from this, other issues addressed by our work (e.g., efficient compliance checks, treatment of loops, conflicting type and instance changes) have not been discussed in these papers.

In MOKASSIN [8] change primitives are encapsulated within WF instances. The compliance criterion is considered as being too restrictive. Instead, a more granular version concept is proposed. However, correctness issues are completely factored out by the authors. Another versioning approach has been offered by WASA$_2$ [4], which uses a correctness criterion based on the mapping of WF instances against WF schemes. In WASA$_2$, biased instances cannot be adapted to type changes anymore as opposed to our approach. Furthermore, changes in conjunction with loops have not been dealt with. Finally, ULTRAFlow [15] presents a rule-based approach. Changes are realized by modifying the implementation and meta data of activities. Special synchronization methods guaranteeing consistent access of instances on modified specifications are provided. However, ULTRAFlow totally factors out important change operations (e.g., deletion of activities) and does not consider data flow issues.

A formal treatment and comparison of correctness criteria of some of the above approaches has been given in [16].

6   Summary and Outlook

In many domains, like hospitals, engineering environments, or offices, process-centered applications will not be accepted whenever rigidity comes with them. Creating WF-based applications without a vision for adaptive WF is therefore shortsighted and expensive. Indeed, insufficient flexibility and adaptability have been primary reasons why WF technology failed in many process automation projects in the past. Both, the capability to quickly and correctly propagate WF type changes to in-progress WF instances and the support of ad-hoc adaptations will be key ingredients in the next generation of WfMS, ultimately resulting in highly adaptive process-oriented applications.

In this paper we have focused on the common support of WF type and WF instance changes and have discussed limitations of current approaches. The very important aspect of our work is its formal foundation. We have given general axioms and theorems which are fundamental for the correct handling of dynamic

WF changes. The treatment of conflicting type and instance changes adds to the completeness of our approach. Finally, there is already a powerful proof-of-concept prototype which demonstrates the feasibility of the presented concepts.

There are many other challenging issues related to adaptive workflow which must be better understood before we obtain a complete solution. First of all, we believe that usability issues constitute a field that would benefit by more intense study of the research community. Additionally, dynamic changes may also concern other components of the process-centered information system, like the organizational database, security constraints, temporal constraints [3], actor and resource assignments, or activity programs. Finally, we consider it as very important to incorporate more semantics into the dynamic change process [12].

References

1. van der Aalst, W., van Hee, K.: Workflow Management. MIT Press (2002)
2. Reichert, M., Dadam, P.: ADEPT$_{flex}$ - supporting dynamic changes of workflows without losing control. Int'l J Intelligent Information Systems **10** (1998) 93–129
3. Sadiq, S., Marjanovic, O., Orlowska, M.: Managing change and time in dynamic workflow processes. Int'l J Cooperative Information Systems **9** (2000)
4. Weske, M.: Formal foundation and conceptual design of dynamic adaptations in a workflow management system. In: Proc. HICSS-34, Maui, Hawaii (2001)
5. Edmond, D., ter Hofstede, A.: A reflective infrastructure for workflow adaptability. Data and Knowlege Engineering **34** (2000) 271–304
6. Kochut, K., Arnold, J., Sheth, A., Miller, J., Kraemer, E., Arpinar, B., Cardoso, J.: Intelligen: A distributed workflow system for discovering protein-protein interactions. Distributed and Parallel Databases **13** (2003) 43–72
7. Kradolfer, M., Geppert, A.: Dynamic workflow schema evolution based on workflow type versioning and workflow migration. In: Proc. CoopIS'99, Edinburgh (1999)
8. Joeris, G., Herzog, O.: Managing evolving workflow specifications. In: Proc. CoopIS '98, New York (1998) 310–321
9. van der Aalst, W.: Exterminating the dynamic change bug: A concrete approach to support worfklow change. Information Systems Frontiers **3** (2001) 297–317
10. Casati, F., Ceri, S., Pernici, B., Pozzi, G.: Workflow evolution. Data and Knowledge Engineering **24** (1998) 211–238
11. Ellis, C., Keddara, K., Rozenberg, G.: Dynamic change within workflow systems. In: Proc. Int'l Conf. on Org. Comp. Sys., Milpitas, CA (1995) 10–21
12. Rinderle, S., Reichert, M., Dadam, P.: On dealing with semantically conflicting business process changes. Technical Report UIB-2003-04, University of Ulm (2003)
13. Agostini, A., De Michelis, G.: Improving flexibility of workflow management systems. In: Proc. Int'l Conf. BPM'00, LNCS 1806. (2000) 218–234
14. van der Aalst, W., Basten, T.: Inheritance of workflows: An approach to tackling problems related to change. Theoretical Computer Science **270** (2002) 125–203
15. Fent, A., Reiter, H., Freitag, B.: Design for change: Evolving workflow specifications in ULTRAflow. In: Proc. CAISE '02. (2002) 516–534
16. Rinderle, S., Reichert, M., Dadam, P.: Evaluation of correctness criteria for dynamic workflow changes. In: Proc. Int'l Conf. BPM'03. (2003) 41–57

Animating ebXML Transactions with a Workflow Engine

Rik Eshuis, Pierre Brimont, Eric Dubois, Bertrand Grégoire, and Sophie Ramel

Centre de Recherche Public Henri Tudor
29, Avenue John F. Kennedy, L-1855 Luxembourg–Kirchberg, Luxembourg
{rik.eshuis,pierre.brimont,eric.dubois,bertrand.gregoire,
sophie.ramel}@tudor.lu

Abstract. ebXML is becoming the new international standard for the specification and deployment of complex B2B transactions over the internet. ebXML transactions are inherently distributed, involving many actors exchanging XML messages with each other according to complex flows and rules. This complexity hampers validation of the correctness of a modelled business transaction by business experts. To alleviate this problem, we have developed an animator to support the cooperative validation of ebXML transactions by business experts. The animator is internet-based, supporting distributed animation of an ebXML transaction. The animator automatically checks business rules on the messages exchanged during animation. Heart of the animator is a workflow engine that can read workflow descriptions in XPDL. In this paper, we show how the animator is automatically configured from the UML models describing the ebXML transaction. The main UML models used are class diagrams to model messages and an activity diagram to model the global flow of the messages that are exchanged by the actors. Class diagrams are annotated with business rules. The UML activity diagram maps into XPDL code for the workflow engine. The class diagrams map into XML Schemas that are used by the animator for receiving, checking and sending messages. The mapping algorithms have been implemented as plugins in a commercial UML-based CASE tool. Throughout the paper, we illustrate the whole approach on a real-life example.

1 Introduction

The world of B2B commerce is changing today. For more than 25 years, EDI standards, like UN/EDIFACT or ANSI X12, have been the dominant ways of interchanging data between geographically dispersed business applications. These standards are based upon a set of messages (like, e.g. an Order message), define the syntax of each message and give some recommendations of use. There are several problems with these actual standards. The grammar describing the syntax is often complex and in some cases ambiguous. Rules that constrain the message content and usage are expressed in natural language with the possibility of misinterpretations. As a consequence, the cost of introducing new messages and modifying existing messages is high in terms of software applications to be

R. Meersman et al. (Eds.): CoopIS/DOA/ODBASE 2003, LNCS 2888, pp. 426–443, 2003.
© Springer-Verlag Berlin Heidelberg 2003

changed: parsers and validators that check a complex syntax must be updated. This can be very costly, and is therefore only feasible for big companies, not for SME's. From a business perspective, the absence of precise rules also poses a problem as the validation of the content of a message can be subject to multiple interpretations, resulting in many exceptions that have to be manually handled. This poses a serious obstacle to the STP (straight-through-processing) principle which, at the Internet age, requires a complete automatic management of messages.

To overcome the problems described above, the international ebXML initiative [24] has been launched in 1999 by UN/CEFACT and OASIS, supported by several hundred participants. ebXML stands for 'Electronic Business using eXtensible Markup Language'. As a result of a first specification phase, ebXML has issued a number of recommendations regarding the future of B2B infrastructures. As the name already suggests, a major issue concerns the adoption of XML as standard language for messages. Besides the message syntax, ebXML has also considered the semantic aspects by recommending usage of a specific UML profile for specifying the message content as well as its business usage. Finally, ebXML has shifted from a message-oriented paradigm into a transaction-oriented paradigm through its associated UMM [11] methodology. This shift results in an end-to-end view of the business transaction where the purpose and the usage rules of each message can be make much more precise than with EDI.

To support the modelling and validation of new ebXML transactions, our research center has launched a project called Efficient (E-business Framework For an effIcient Capture and Implementation of ENd-to-end Transactions). The overall objective of Efficient is the development of an integrated tool set for supporting the modelling and validation of complex ebXML transactions. The tool set consists of an extension of a commercial UML-based CASE tool that supports the modelling of ebXML business transactions, and an animator tool that supports execution of the UML models. The animator allows business experts to cooperatively validate transactions models at the time they are built, before their implementation has started. Rather than simulation, we prefer to use the word 'animation' since the validation is done in an interactive way, each business expert playing the role of a business actor and participating in the execution of the transaction by receiving messages and sending answers. By doing this, business experts can validate the transaction by playing different possible scenarios that include different messages. Validating a specification by animating it has been proven a useful technique in different contexts [8,9,10,22]. Note that these other approaches also use the term 'animation' instead of simulation. More details on the animator can be found in Section 3.

In our project, we use a three layered approach (see Fig. 1):

– The business layer gives a general overview of the business transactions. At this layer, the global structure of each business transaction is depicted with a UML use case diagram and a UML class diagram. The use case diagram specifies the global structure of the business process underlying the business transaction. The global class diagram specifies the information manipulated

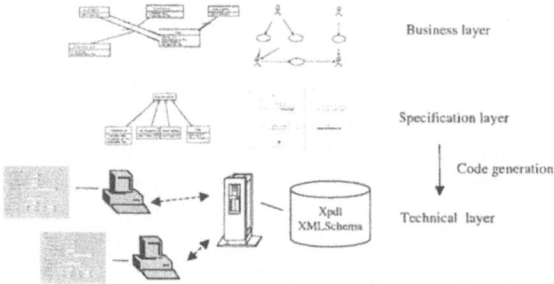

Fig. 1. Different levels within B2B project

in the business process. In addition, business rules can be specified in structured English. At this layer, there is no concept of message.

- The specification layer details a message-based structure of a business transaction. This detailed specification is needed to support the B2B automation of business transactions. The business process of the business transaction is specified with a UML activity diagram. Each message is specified with a class diagram. The activity diagram refines the use case diagram at the business layer. Each class diagram is a particular view of the global class diagram at the business layer. The message can have attached a business rule defined at the business layer in order to constrain the message's content.
- At the technical layer, the business transaction is executed using the animator. The infrastructure used at the technical layer is automatically configured from the models developed at the specification layer.

The goal of this paper is to explain how the animator is automatically configured by generating code from the UML specification models. UML activity diagrams are translated into XPDL [27], the XML variant of the WFMC's process definition language. UML class diagrams, modelling the messages, are translated into W3C XML Schemas [25]. The code generation algorithms have been implemented as Java plugins in MagicDraw [17], a commercial UML-based CASE tool. Since MagicDraw is a state of the art CASE tool, we expect that the developed plugins can be easily transferred to other UML-based CASE tools. In another paper [6], we have elaborated on the animator, but not upon its configuration from UML models.

As a running example, we consider Mercata, an online broker of standard products. (The example is adapted from an example of the MIT process handbook [15].) We focus here on one particular business transaction of Mercata: a business client creates an order by submitting to Mercata his demand for certain products. After Mercata provided some technical information on the delivery (e.g. delay, cost), the client can pay in four different ways. Either he buys on credit or using a credit card; these payment means are checked by a credit company. Or the client uses a bank transfer or post mail; these payment means are checked by Mercata's accountant. In Sect. 2 we discuss the specification layer of this business transaction in more detail. In Sect. 4 and 5 we give examples of code generated from the specification models.

The remainder of this paper is structured as follows. Section 2 discusses the models produced at the specification layer in more detail, including the business rules. Section 3 gives a general overview of the animator tool, which is based on a workflow engine. The remainder is about the automatic configuration of the animator from the specification models. Section 4 explains how to derive an XPDL model from a UML activity diagram. This XPDL model is the basis for the workflow engine execution. Section 5 explains how to derive a W3C XML Schema from a class diagram. From the W3C XML Schemas the web forms for manipulating messages are automatically generated. At run-time, the animator uses the schemas to check the structure of received message instances. Section 6 discusses related work. Section 7 winds up with conclusions and further work.

2   Specifying B2B Transactions

In this section we explain the models produced at the specification layer when modelling a business transaction (cf. Fig. 1).

2.1   Specifying Business Processes

At the specification layer, the business process of each business transaction is specified with a UML activity diagram. Figure 2 shows the activity diagram of our running example. The business partners involved in the transaction are modelled by swimlanes. Each business partner performs some activities, which are denoted by oval nodes. The input and output of these activities are typically messages (or business documents), which are denoted by rectangular nodes (object flow state nodes). Since messages do not have states, the corresponding object flow state nodes also do not have states. The structure of each message is specified with a class diagram; we show this in Sect. 5.

In ebXML, business process models have three levels. Swimlanes and object flow states only occur in the lowest level activity diagram, in which the behaviour of two parties that exchange business documents with each other is modelled. To make the specification more easy to comprehend, we decided to merge all these levels into one activity diagram. We can easily transform our activity diagrams into a layered ebXML model and vice versa, because we require that each object flow state has one input and one output activity, that belong to two different swimlanes.

The activity diagram specifies the global ordering of these activities and messages. The basic ordering construct is the arrow, which denotes sequence. If the source or target of an arrow is an object flow state node, the arrow is dotted. Otherwise, the arrow is solid. Next, there are some special ordering constructs. A diamond either denotes a XOR choice (one incoming arrow) or XOR merge (one outgoing arrow). Only one incoming arrow and one outgoing arrow of the decision node are taken at the same time. A bar either denotes an AND fork

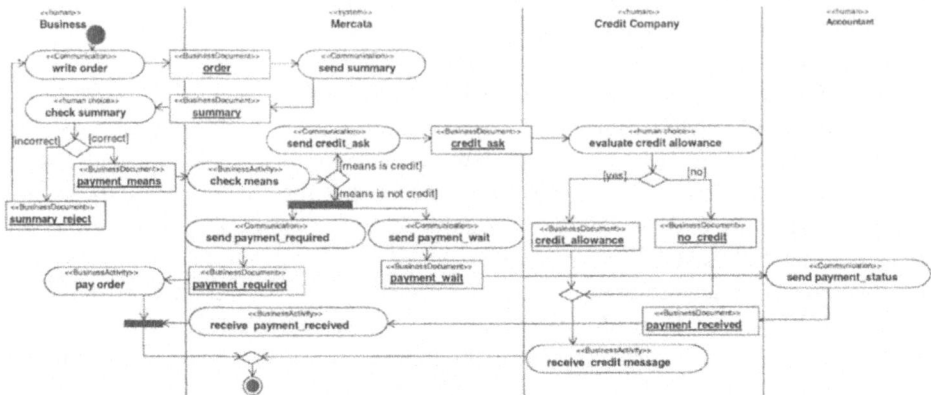

Fig. 2. Activity diagram of "create order"

(one incoming arrow) or AND join (one outgoing arrow). All incoming and all outgoing arrows of the bar are taken at the same time. The black dot denotes the initial state and a bull's eye a final state. For more details on the syntax of activity diagrams, see the UML specifications [18,20].

Unlike UML 1.4, we do not require that activity diagrams are translatable into statecharts. Thus, we allow activity diagrams that do not have balanced forks and joins. However, to rule out differences in behaviour w.r.t. the XPDL execution of the WF engine, in Section 4 we introduce the constraints that each activity diagram is safe, i.e., each node cannot be active more than once at the same time, and that there is one final node. Moreover, to ensure compliancy with ebXML, we require that each object flow state has one input activity and one output activity, that belong to two different swimlanes.

Activity nodes and object flow state nodes are stereotyped. Stereotype ≪BusinessDocument≫ is used for messages. In the future, we plan to add other stereotypes to represent non-message objects. Stereotype ≪CommunicationActivity≫ is used for activities that produce a single message as output. Stereotype ≪HumanChoice≫ is used for activities in which a user has to evaluate an input message, and stereotype ≪BusinessActivity≫for other activities. A human choice activity has two or more possible response messages. For example, in Fig. 2 message credit_ask is evaluated and there are two possible outcomes: message credit_allowance and message no_credit. A human choice activity is always modelled using a decision node as output node.

We do not use wait (statechart) nodes and events, including temporal events, because these constructs are not directly supported by MagicDraw and XPDL. In the future, we plan to add real-time constraints.

2.2   Specifying Business Messages

The structure of each message (≪BusinessDocument≫ object flow state in activity diagram) is specified using a UML class diagram (static structure dia-

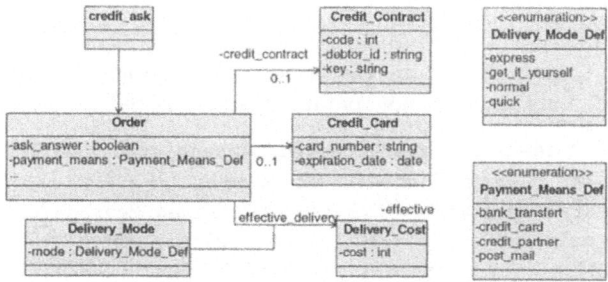

Fig. 3. Class diagram of message credit_ask

gram). One class represents the message, the other classes represent elements of the message. A class can have attributes, but no operations. Classes can be related to each other. Figure 3 shows an example class diagram modelling message credit_ask.

The CASE tool we use, MagicDraw [17], supports reuse of class diagrams by allowing hiding of elements of some common diagram. This way, different views of the same common diagram can be created for each message. For example, the class diagram in Fig. 3 is defined as a view of the class diagram of the business domain. This way, we guarantee the traceability between the business domain model and the message's content model. During generation, our mapping algorithm skips the elements of the diagrams that are hidden.

To enable the generation of a W3C XML Schema from a class diagram, we impose some constraints on the class diagram. The tool we use for generating a web form from an XML schema, Chiba [4], requires that schemas are hierarchical. To ensure that the generated schema is hierarchical, the class diagram must not contain loops. Consequently, only directed associations are allowed. Undirected associations are forbidden because they are navigable in both ways, and thus correspond to a loop between the two classes. Moreover, we only allow binary associations. However, we do allow association classes.

2.3 Specifying Business Rules

Class diagrams (messages) can have attached some business rules that constrain the content of the messages. Business rules are expressed in structured English. We did not choose OCL because of its poor readability for business experts. At run time, the rules are checked by xlinkit. xlinkit [16] is a tool that verifies consistency constraints that are defined on a set of XML documents, in this case XML messages. We are currently developing a tool that automatically transforms rules in structured English into xlinkit constraints.

Figure 4 shows an example of a business rule for message credit_ask. The xlinkit constraint has the following meaning. First, xlinkit finds the last credit_ask message, represented by variable a, by comparing the reception times of all received credit_ask messages. In theory, multiple instances of the same message

---

Rule name: "Consistent payment information"

Constraint in structured English: If the element payment_means of document credit_ask is credit_card, then credit_ask contains an element credit_card and credit_ask does not contain an element credit_contract.

xlinkit constraint:

```
<forall var="a" in="//messagesReceived/Message[credit_ask]">
  <implies> <!-- 'Current' credit_ask document -->
    <forall var="other_a" in="//messagesReceived/Message[credit_ask]">
      <equal op1="$a/WorkflowData/receptionTime/text() >
$other_a/WorkflowData/receptionTime/text()" op2="true"/>
    </forall>
    <implies>
      <equal op1="$a/Order/payment_means/text() eq "credit_card"
op2="true"/>
      <and>
        <exists var="e" in="$a/Order/credit_card">
          <equal op1="true" op2="true">
        </exists>
        <not>
          <exists var="e" in="$a/Order/credit_contract">
            <equal op1="true" op2="true">
          </exists>
        </not>
      </and>
    </implies>
  </implies>
</forall>
```

Fig. 4. Example of business rule for message credit_ask

can be generated due to a loop. However, for the activity diagram in Fig. 2 there is at most one credit_ask message. Operator / is a navigation operator on the XML tree, whereas [*pred*] selects those nodes of the XML tree satisfying *pred*. xlinkit returns diagnostic information in the form of consistent or inconsistent links after evaluating a constraint. To enable this, xlinkit has a special equal operator on XML elements. Next, for the last credit_ask message, the xlinkit constraint states that if the payment means is credit card, then there exists a link to credit card but not to credit contract. Both credit_card and credit_contract are XML elements modelling the link between Order on the one hand and Credit_Card and Credit_Contract on the other hand.

To facilitate the prefilling of messages by the animator, we have introduced the concept of building rules. A building rule specifies which different message parts of the business transaction are the same. Building rules are automatically generated by our CASE tool plugin. For each message *m* in the activity diagram, the building rule generation algorithm looks at previous messages and generates building rules for model elements (classes, attributes, associations) that have the same name as model elements of *m*. As many rules as possible are generated. After the generation, the user can delete or modify the rules that are incorrect, and add new rules, before applying the XML Schema generation. The

XML Schema generation algorithm translates these rules into annotations on the generated XML schema that are used by the animator to prefill messages (see Sect. 3). The generation algorithm also allows the translation of a rule into a corresponding xlinkit constraint; however, it is possible to skip this. At run-time, the animator checks the generated xlinkit constraints along with the ordinary business rules. If an xlinkit constraint is generated for some message fields, this means that during animation those prefilled fields are read only and cannot be changed.

3 The Animator Tool

The animator allows business experts to validate the models produced by inter-actively 'playing' with them. The animator is internet based, allowing business experts scattered over several places to cooperatively animate the specification through a simple web browser. Each of the experts is responsible for animating one or more of the actors involved in the transaction.

Heart of the animator is a workflow (WF) engine that has been developed before at our research center. The WF engine is based on the standard specifications of the WFMC. It runs on top of a commercial relational database system. The WF engine has been used in a number of projects at our research center.

In general, a WF engine coordinates the execution of automated business processes. In this case, it coordinates the execution of the business process modelled at the specification layer. The activities of the business process are executed by actors outside the workflow system (i.e. the business experts). In order to coordinate the business process, the WF engine needs to have a description of the process. Our WF engine reads process descriptions in XPDL format. XPDL [27] ('XML Process Definition Language') is a standard language developed by the Workflow Management Coalition (WFMC). The XPDL process description used during animation is derived automatically from the activity diagram at the specification layer; see Sect. 4.

Figure 5 shows the overall architecture of the animator. The animator exchanges XML messages with clients using the SOAP protocol. The GUI used at the client machines is derived automatically from the XML Schemas generated from the UML class diagrams (see Sect. 5 for an example). The animator works as follows. First, the XMLMessageHandler module receives XML messages from a client through a SOAP server. The module first stores the XML message in an XML database, eXist [14], and also stores some relevant information, i.e. the name of the recipient, initial sender and the reception time. This information is used in the subsequent checks. Next, XMLMessageHandler calls the WF engine using an API definition defined by the WFMC. Each message signals the end of some running activity: the XMLMessageHandler calls the WF engine to terminate this activity.

Next, the WF engine calls the XMLSchemaChecker module, which checks whether the message conforms to its defining W3C XML Schema. This XML Schema has been derived automatically from the class diagram of the message

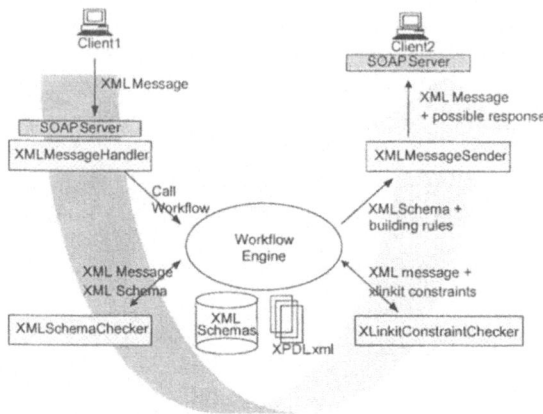

Fig. 5. Architecture of the animator

at the specification layer; see Sect. 5. In case of an error, an error message is generated and sent back to the initial sender, and the WF engine enables the sending activity again. Otherwise, the WF engine proceeds with the next activity.

If the message is error free, the WF engine calls module XlinkitConstraint-Checker. This module checks the business rules attached to the message, which are defined in the message class diagrams at the specification layer (see Sect. 2 for details). The constraints are checked by calling xlinkit [16], a tool that verifies consistency constraints that are defined on a set of XML documents, in this case XML messages. The current message is always part of the set. If a constraint refers to other (previous) messages, xlinkit retrieves these messages from the XML database. If the verification fails, an error message with feedback is sent to the message sender and the WF engine enables the sending activity again.

Finally, the workflow engine calls module XMLMessageSender. This module first retrieves the message that the recipient of the validated input message could send in response, in the next activity of the business transaction. The module prefills as many fields of the response message as possible with information already known from previous messages. This feature is helpful if the next message should include a lot of information items already included in the current message. However, the recipient can overwrite a prefilled field. The prefilling is governed by building rules, which identify which parts of the current message equal parts of previously sent messages. Building rules are generated automatically from the UML diagrams; see Sect. 2.3. XMLMessageSender attaches the next, prefilled message to the current message, and forwards the current message to the SOAP server at the recipient site. For example, if message order arrives, XMLMessageSender finds out that the next activity will output message summary, and it will therefore attach a prefilled summary message to order. If the activity started next is a ≪HumanChoice≫ activity, more than one response message is possible. For example, if message credit_ask arrives at the animator, there are two possible response messages for the evaluate credit_allowance ac-

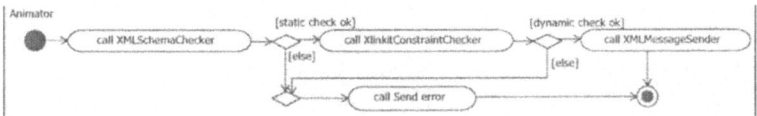

Fig. 6. Activity diagram of animator checks. Parameters and output variables are not shown

tivity started next, namely credit_allowance and no_credit. The module attaches responses to message credit_ask and forwards the message to the Credit Company. Note that the recipient, in the next activity, in most of the cases merely has to select the right answer. Hence, prefilling can reduce the workload of the message's recipient considerably.

4   Generating Code from Activity Diagrams

We generate code in two steps. First, we extend the activity diagram with some extra activities that do the message checks in the animator. Next, we generate from this extended activity diagram XPDL code that is input for the WF engine used by the animator.

4.1   Extending the Activity Diagram with Verification Support

During animation each message generated by a participant is sent to the recipient participants (corresponding to the recipient role) through the animator. Upon reception of a message, the animator first does a simple structural check of the message against its defining XML Schema, and then a checking of the xlinkit constraints. If one of these two checks fail, an error message, with feedback information, is sent to the original sender of the message. If the message checks succeed, the animator forwards the message to its designated recipients.

To allow the WF engine to automatically perform these activities, we extend the original activity diagram by inserting after every ≪CommunicationActivity≫ a compound subactivity, which decomposes into the activity diagram of Fig. 6. All the activities in this activity diagram are XPDL automatic activities: the activities are automatically completed when the module called has finished. After the subactivity completes, there are two possible continuations. If the check fails the ≪CommunicationActivity≫ is enabled again. Otherwise, the process continues as specified in the original activity diagram. Note that this insertion is allowed because a ≪CommunicationActivity≫ only has one outgoing edge.

Note that the module XMLMessageHandler is not called in the activity diagram of Fig. 6, i.e., XMLMessageHandler is not called by the WF engine, while the other modules are. Instead, XMLMessageHandler calls the WF engine (cf. Fig. 5). The reason for this is that the business activities, done by the business experts, are XPDL manual activities. The completion of XPDL manual activities is not done automatically by the WF engine, because no application has

Table 1. Mapping of activity diagram into XPDL

Activity Diagram Construct	XPDL Construct
ActivityGraph	Workflow Process Definition
B2B Activity state node	Activity, No Implementation, Manual end
Animator Activity state node	Activity, Tool Implementation, Automatic end
Object flow state node	Route activity (XOR join, XOR split)
Subactivity node	Sub-Process Definition (synchronous)
Pseudo state node	Route activity
- initial	XOR split
- final	XOR join
- fork	AND split
- join	AND join
- decision	XOR split
- merge	XOR join
Arrow	Transition
Non-animator swimlane	Resource with type ROLE
Animator swimlane	Resource with type SYSTEM

been called. Instead, completion has to be signalled explicitly to the WF engine, which in this case is done by XMLMessageHandler.

4.2   Mapping the Activity Diagram into XPDL

XPDL process models have a directed graph structure. A node represents the execution of some activity. Edges represent transitions between activities. Each XPDL activity node can have transition restrictions on the incoming and outgoing transitions. The restriction on the incoming transitions is called 'join', the restriction on the outgoing transitions is called 'split'. Restrictions can have type XOR or AND. A join restriction of type AND means that all incoming transitions must be taken before the activity is enabled. A join restriction of type XOR means that only one of the incoming transitions needs to be taken to enable the activity. Likewise, a XOR split means that one enabled outgoing transition is taken and an AND split means that all enabled outgoing transitions are taken. In order for a transition to be enabled, its condition must be true. Special activity nodes are the route activity nodes; these do not represent execution of activities but are merely used for routing the workflow instance to some other activity nodes. Non-route activity nodes may be implemented by a tool or a subflow; the tool or subflow is invoked when the activity node is entered. Finally, XPDL allows specification of resources that can execute the specified activities. Resource ROLE is generic for human persons, i.e. it specifies that any human can do the activity. Whereas resource SYSTEM denotes that the activity is executed by the system (computer) itself.

The main translation rules are shown in Table 1. (Due to space limitations, we cannot give full details.) Since both activity diagrams and XPDL have a graph structure, translating the control flow structure of activity diagrams into XPDL is straightforward. We just comment on the most interest-

```
...
  <Activity Id="A14" Name="send credit_ask"/>
    <Implementation><No/></Implementation>
  </Activity>
  <Activity Id="A14_check" Name="send credit_ask_check">
    <Implementation>
      <SubFlow Id="_checker">
        <ActualParameters>
          <ActualParameter>check_ok<ActualParameter>
        </ActualParameters>
      </SubFlow>
    </Implementation>
    <TransitionRestrictions>
      <TransitionRestriction>
        <Split Type="XOR">
          <TransitionRefs><TransitionRef Id="T12-1"/><TransitionRef
Id="T12-2"/></TransitionRefs>
        </Split>
      </TransitionRestriction>
    </TransitionRestrictions>
  </Activity>
  <Activity Id="A15" Name="credit_ask"><Route/></Activity>
...
  <Transition Id="T12" From="A14" To="A14_check"/>
  <Transition Id="T12-1" From="A14_check" To="A14">
    <Condition>NOT check_ok</Condition>
  </Transition>
  <Transition Id="T12-2" From="A14_check" To="A15">
    <Condition>check_ok</Condition>
  </Transition>
...
```

Fig. 7. Some parts of the generated XPDL code for the extended activity diagram of the "create order" transaction

ing features of the translation. The activities done by the users (business experts), so with stereotypes ≪CommunicationActivity≫, ≪BusinessActivity≫ and ≪HumanChoice≫, are manual. This means that the completion of these activities must be explicitly signalled to the WF engine by calling some method on the WF engine's API. This is done by module XMLMessageHandler. By contrast, an activity done by the animator is automatic: the WF engine waits for its completion and then automatically proceeds with the next activity. Note that object flow state nodes are not translated into datatypes, because the XML data is not stored by the WF engine. The animator modules shield the WF engine from the XML data. The XML data is stored in an XML database.

Figure 7 shows parts of the generated XPDL code for the extended activity diagram of the "create order" transaction. The code for activity send credit_ask to Credit Company and the subsequent compound animator check is shown. The decomposition of the animator check is not shown.

Fig. 8. Example UML activity diagram that is interpreted differently by the WF engine

Unfortunately, since neither UML activity diagrams nor XPDL come with a formal execution semantics, it is impossible to validate the correctness of our translation. However, two constructs of XPDL, as interpreted by our WF engine, differ clearly from the informal execution semantics of UML activity diagrams [18,20]. The first construct is the XOR merge. To explain the difference, suppose that in the activity diagram in Fig. 8 activities A and B are active and that A terminates. Then our WF engine will not only start C but also terminate B. However, according to UML 2.0, an instance of C is started while B continues executing. When B terminates, another instance of C is started. The work on workflow patterns [1] discusses other possible interpretations of the XOR merge. To rule out these differences, we impose the constraint that activity diagrams are safe. For safe activity diagrams, each XOR merge has at most one incoming branch at execution time, and all the different interpretations coincide.

The second construct is the final node. The WF engine supports two different workflow termination modes. A XOR termination mode means that if a final node is reached, the complete workflow stops. (A similar construct appears in UML 2.0 [20].) An AND termination mode means that the workflow stops as soon as all final nodes have been reached. But UML activity diagrams support implicit termination: the workflow is considered terminated if only final nodes are active, but not every final node has to be active. To resolve this difference, we impose the constraint that each activity diagram has one final node.

5   Generating Code from Class Diagrams

In this section we show how business messages, whose structure is defined by UML class diagrams, are mapped into W3C XML Schemas. The XML schema of a message defines the XML syntax of that message. To define the mapping rules between a class diagram and a W3C XML Schema, previous works on mapping class diagrams to DTD's were taken into account, in particular the design rules of SwiftML [23] and XMI [19]. We have chosen the W3C XML Schema language [25] instead of the DTD language because XML Schema is more expressive, and also because it is intended to describe object-oriented models, and is therefore closer to UML class diagrams than the DTD language.

Due to space limitations, we can only give a sketch of the mapping algorithm. We illustrate parts of the algorithm on the credit_ask message from the Mercata case study, whose class diagram is shown in Fig. 3. First, the algorithm retrieves the root class of the diagram, and creates an element declaration with the same name at the top layer of the document. This element declaration contains a

```
<xsd:element name="credit_ask">
  <xsd:complexType>
    <xsd:sequence>
      <xsd:element maxOccurs="1" minOccurs="1" name="role_Order"
type="Order"/>
    </xsd:sequence>
  </xsd:complexType>
</xsd:element>
...
<xsd:complexType name="Order">
  <xsd:sequence>
    <xsd:element name="ask_reference" type="xsd:integer"/>
    <xsd:element name="payment_means" type="Payment_Means_Def"/>
    <xsd:element maxOccurs="1" minOccurs="1" name="role_Credit_Card"
type="Credit_Card"/>
    <xsd:element maxOccurs="1" minOccurs="1" name="effective_delivery">
      <xsd:complexType>
        <xsd:sequence>
          <xsd:element name="effective_implication" type="Delivery_Cost"/>
          <xsd:element name="role_Delivery_Mode" type="Delivery_Mode"/>
        </xsd:sequence>
      </xsd:complexType>
    </xsd:element>
    <xsd:element maxOccurs="1" minOccurs="1" name="credit_contract"
type="Credit_Contract"/>
  </xsd:sequence>
</xsd:complexType>
...
```

Fig. 9. Part of the W3C XML Schema for credit_ask

complex type that is generated in the same way as for the other classes (see below). Figure 9 shows the XML code for the root of message credit_ask.

Next, each class C of the diagram is mapped into an XML Schema complex type definition with the same name, at the top layer of the document (in the schema declaration). The complex type comprises a sequence of element declarations. These element declarations correspond to the attributes and outgoing associations of class C. Each attribute and outgoing association of the class maps into an XML Schema element as follows.

Every attribute *name : type* of class C maps into element declaration with the same name and a similar type. (The mapping from basic UML data types to basic XML Schema datatypes is straightforward.) Multiplicity constraints on the attribute translate into minoccurs/maxoccurs constraints on the element. The father of the element is the sequence of the complex type to which class C is mapped. We do not map an attribute into an XML attribute declaration, because our attributes can have class types, i.e., complex types, whereas XML attributes cannot have complex types. The mapping is illustrated by the XML code generated for class Order in Fig. 9.

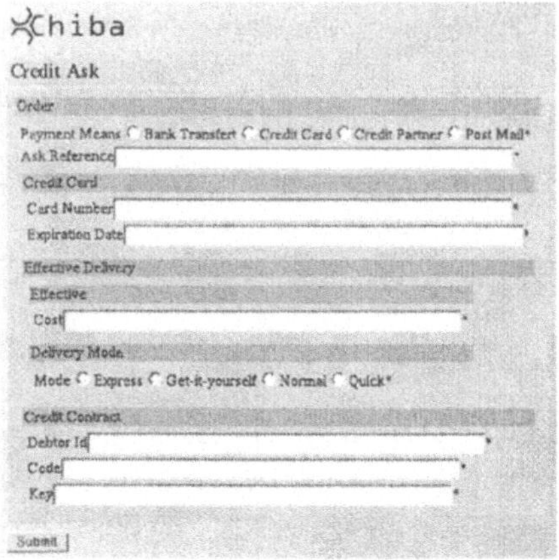

Fig. 10. Web form for message credit_ask

An association a from class C to D that has no association class maps into an element declaration. The element's name is the role name of D in a. The element's type is the complex type to which class D is mapped. Multiplicity constraints on D's association end translate into minoccurs/maxoccurs constraints on the element. The father of the element is the sequence of the complex type to which class C is mapped. This implements the navigation from C to D via a. The XLM code for classes credit_ask and Order in Fig. 9 illustrates this mapping.

An association a from class C to D with association class A maps into an element declaration, whose name is the name of the association, and whose type is a complex type. Multiplicity constraints on D's association end are translated into minoccurs/maxoccurs constraints on the element. The complex type of the element is a sequence containing an element declaration for the association class C and for the role end at D. The element's name is the role name of D in a. The element's type is the complex type to which class D is mapped. Multiplicity constraints on D's association end are translated into minoccurs/maxoccurs constraints on the element. The father of the element is the sequence of the complex type to which class C is mapped. This mapping ensures that each association instance (link) has its own distinct association object. The mapping is illustrated by the XML code for class Order in Fig. 9. This class has an outgoing association effective_delivery with a corresponding association class. Type Payment_Means_Def is a class defined elsewhere.

Single inheritance is supported by using XML `extension` definitions in the XML Schema code of the child class. Multiple inheritance is not supported by W3 XML Schema. Enumerations are mapped into XML Schema enumerations. xlinkit constraints on classes are mapped into annotations on the XML Schema document, using `appinfo` definitions that contain the text of the constraint. Our mapping supports more complex constructs on UML class diagrams, like aggregation, and composition, but we do not show these here due to space limitations.

From the obtained XML Schema, an XML based web form (based on XForms [26]) is generated by using Chiba [4]. Figure 10 shows the web form for message credit_ask, which is generated from the XML Schema that is partly shown in Fig. 9. During animation, the business experts use such web forms to send messages to each other via the animator.

6   Related Work

The concept of animating a specification is not new; several researchers have studied it, see e.g. [8,9,10,22], and some commercial CASE tools support animation of UML designs, e.g. Rhapsody by I-Logix [12] and Rose RT by Rational [21]. In contrast to our approach, most animation approaches, e.g. [8,9,22], including all commercial CASE tools, offer non-distributed, centralised animation facilities and are not internet based. Consequently, only a single actor is needed to animate the specification. In our approach, multiple actors can collaborate to cooperatively animate a business transaction. A notable exception to these animation approaches is the work by Heymans and Dubois [10], in which a distributed internet-based animator is presented that allows different actors to cooperatively animate a specification. However, that animator requires a human scheduler for coordinating the behaviour of the different actors, whereas our approach uses a workflow engine for this. Hence, we have automatic coordination whereas Heymans and Dubois have manual coordination. Another difference of our approach compared to the approaches mentioned above is that our animator is based on open XML-based standards and related technologies, and does not use a proprietary language.

The mapping from UML class diagrams to W3C XML Schemas is based on existing proposed mappings from UML class diagrams to DTD's, in particular swiftML [23] and XMI [19]. Independently Carlson [3] defined a mapping similar to ours. Our mapping ensures traceability from an XML schema to its defining UML class diagram.

As far as we know, there is no related work on the mapping of UML activity diagrams to XPDL or WPDL. Bastos and Ruiz [2] consider the reverse mapping, visualising WFMC-based workflow models with UML activity diagrams by introducing some annotations on activity diagrams. Next, there are approaches, e.g. [5,13], that use UML diagrams for modelling processes and that, in a fully automated way, derive from these process descriptions the input for some specific process support tools. Difference with our work is that these process support tools have a proprietary interface that is not based on XPDL. Casati et al. present a methodology for developing workflow applications, using UML activity diagrams as workflow modelling language. Among others, they discuss issues in mapping activity diagrams to workflow implementation languages, but they do not provide an actual mapping, nor do they consider XPDL or WPDL.

An important feature of both our mappings is that they require but few stereotypes, thus alleviating the work of the ebXML designer. Stereotypes are not needed that much because we use some specific domain knowledge (for example, for the animator communication activities are always manual). The price paid is that the mappings are not as flexible as they could be. However, it is not our purpose to define flexible mappings, but to use the mappings to automatically configure the animator.

7   Conclusion and Further Work

We have introduced a tool set that supports the development and validation of B2B transactions. The tool set consists of an extension of a CASE tool and an animator. The animator is automatically configured from the models specified in the CASE tool, thus enabling a fast animation. Moreover, the animator architecture is internet based, allowing business experts scattered over different places to cooperatively animate distributed business transactions using a simple web browser. Business rules defined in the UML models are checked automatically by the animator. The animator is tightly integrated with state of the art XML technology, showing the feasibility of our approach for ebXML. In the near future, we plan to validate the animator on some more examples, taken from industry.

Currently, we are developing a tool that automatically transforms business rules expressed in structured English into xlinkit constraints. We are also developing an algorithm to automatically transform a flat activity diagram into a layered ebXML activity diagram. In the near future, we plan to extend activity diagrams with the specification of real-time constraints, e.g. timeouts. At the tool level, we plan to interface the CASE tool with a model checker, building upon previous work [7]. This would allow an exhaustive verification of the dynamic behaviour of the business transaction. Error traces returned by the model checker can serve as input for the animator. Another topic of future work concerns the management of played scenario's, in particular to determine the coverage of a given set of scenario's, in order to find missing scenario's.

Acknowledgements. The research reported upon in this paper has been supported by the FNR under grant FNR/01/01/07 (Efficient). The work of Rik Eshuis has been supported by a grant from FNR and has been performed within the scope of the LIASIT (Luxembourg International Advanced Studies in Information Technologies) Institute.

References

1. W. Aalst, A. ter Hofstede, B. Kiepuszewksi, and A. Barros. Workflow patterns. *Distributed and Parallel Databases*, 14(3):5–51, 2003.
2. R. Bastos and D. Ruiz. Extending UML activity diagram for workflow modeling in production systems. In R. H. Sprague, Jr., editor, *Proc. 35th Annual Hawaii Intern. Conference on System Sciences (HICSS-35)*. IEEE Computer Society, 2002.
3. D. Carlson. *Modeling XML applications with UML*. Addison Wesley, 2001.
4. Chiba. URL: http://chiba.sourceforge.net.

5. E. Di Nitto, L. Lavazza, M. Schiavoni, E. Tracanella, and M. Trombetta. Deriving executable process descriptions from UML. In *Proc. 24th International Conference on Software Engineering (ICSE-02)*, pages 155–165. ACM Press, 2002.

6. R. Eshuis, P. Brimont, E. Dubois, B. Grégoire, and S. Ramel. Efficient: a tool set for supporting the modelling and validation of ebXML transactions (poster paper). In *Proc. ESEC/FSE 2003*, 2003.

7. R. Eshuis and R. Wieringa. Verification support for workflow design with UML activity graphs. In *Proc. 24th Intern. Conference on Software Engineering (ICSE-02)*, pages 166–176. ACM Press, 2002.

8. A. Grau and M. Kowsari. A validation system for object oriented specifications of information systems. In *Proc. of the First East-European Symposium on Advances in Databases and Information Systems (ADBIS'97) Vol. 1: Regular Papers*, pages 249–256. Nevsky Dialect, 1997.

9. D. Harel, H. Lachover, A. Naamad, A. Pnueli, M. Politi, R. Sherman, A. Shtull-Trauring, and M. Trakhtenbrot. STATEMATE: A working environment for the development of complex reactive systems. *IEEE Transactions on Software Engineering*, 16(4):403–414, Apr. 1990.

10. P. Heymans and E. Dubois. Scenario-based techniques for supporting the elaboration and the validation of formal requirements. *Requirements Engineering Journal*, 3(4):202–208, 1998.

11. C. Huemer. Defining electronic data interchange transactions with UML. In R. H. Sprague, Jr., editor, *Proc. 34th Annual Hawaii International Conference on System Sciences (HICSS-34)*. IEEE Computer Society, 2001.

12. I-Logix, Inc. Rhapsody. URL: http://www.ilogix.com.

13. D. Jäger, A. Schleicher, and B. Westfechtel. Using UML for software process modeling. In O. Nierstrasz and M. Lemoine, editors, *ESEC/FSE '99*, Lecture Notes in Computer Science 1687, pages 91–108. Springer-Verlag, 1999.

14. W. Meier. eXist: An open source native XML database. In A. B. Chaudhri, M. Jeckle, E. Rahm, and R. Unland, editors, *Web, Web-Services, and Database Systems*, Lecture Notes in Computer Science 2593. Springer, 2003.

15. MIT process handbook. URL: http://ccs.mit.edu/ph.

16. C. Nentwich, L. Capra, W. Emmerich, and A. Finkelstein. xlinkit: a Consistency Checking and Smart Link Generation Service. *ACM Transactions on Internet Technology*, 2(2):151–185, 2002. URL: http://www.xlinkit.com.

17. No Magic, Inc. MagicDraw. URL: http://www.magicdraw.com.

18. Object Management Group. OMG UML specification v. 1.4, 2001. formal/01-09-67. URL: http://www.omg.org.

19. Object Management Group. OMG-XML metadata interchange (XMI) specification, v1.2, 2002. formal/02-01-01. URL: http://www.omg.org/.

20. Object Management Group. UML 2.0 Superstructure Specification, 2003. ptc/03-08-02. URL: http://www.omg.org.

21. Rational. Rational Rose Real Time. URL: http://www.rational.com.

22. J. Siddiqi, I. Morrey, C. Roast, and M. Ozcan. Towards quality requirements via animated formal specifications. *Annals of Software Engineering*, 3:131–155, 1997.

23. SWIFT. swiftML design rules – technical specification, 2001.
    URL: http://xml.coverpages.org/swift-design-rules.pdf.

24. UN/CEFACT and OASIS. ebXML. URL: http://www.ebxml.org.

25. W3C. W3C XML Schema. URL: http://www.w3.org/XML/Schema.

26. W3C. XForms 1.0. URL: http://www.w3.org/TR/xforms/.

27. Workflow Management Coalition. Workflow process definition interface – XML process definition language, 2002. WFMC-TC-1025. URL: http://www.wfmc.org.

Dynamic Interconnection of Heterogeneous Workflow Processes through Services

Karim Baïna[1,2], Khalid Benali[1], and Claude Godart[1]

[1] LORIA – INRIA – CNRS (UMR 7503)
BP 239, F-54506 Vandœuvre-lès-Nancy Cedex, France
{benali,godart}@loria.fr
[2] School of Computer Science and Engineering,
The University of New South Wales, Sydney NSW 2052, Australia
kbaina@cse.unsw.edu.au

Abstract. Process interconnection mechanisms are necessary to co-ordinate geographically distributed business processes in order to strength awareness inside virtual enterprises, to facilitate multinational e-transactions, etc. Actually, existing business process modelling and enactment systems (workflow systems, project management tools, shared agendas, to do lists, etc.) have been mainly developed to suit enterprise internal needs. Thus, most of these systems are not adapted to inter-enterprise co-operation. As we are interested in workflow processes, we aim, through this paper, to provide a model supporting dynamic heterogeneous workflow process interconnection. We consider the interconnection of enterprise workflow processes as the management of a *"workflow of workflows"* in which several heterogeneous workflow systems coexist. This paper introduces our process interconnection model, its implementation, and its validation through an experimentation.

Keywords: Multi-workflow systems, business process mediators and wrappers, negotiation, matchmaking, and brokering, service based workflow integration, out-sourcing based workflow interconnection.

1 Introduction

Our aim is to provide a framework to support dynamic interconnection of enterprise workflow processes. By *interconnection of enterprise workflow processes*, we mean the management of a *"workflow of workflows"* in which several heterogeneous workflow management systems coexist. By *dynamics* of enterprise workflow process interconnection, we mean that process interconnection does not consider neither predetermined communication primitives, nor scheduled points of rendezvous. In other terms, an enterprise, aiming to interconnect its workflow process with another organisation workflow process has to discover and co-decide an interconnection contract at run-time. In fact, we have transformed the problem of interconnection of two workflow processes into the problem of dynamic out-sourcing between these processes. To be interconnected with other processes,

R. Meersman et al. (Eds.): CoopIS/DOA/ODBASE 2003, LNCS 2888, pp. 444–461, 2003.
© Springer-Verlag Berlin Heidelberg 2003

a workflow process out-sources dynamically parts of it to the other workflow processes. This enables interactions resulting from workflow *interconnection* to be limited in the time (*i.e.* to the out-sourcing period) and then to be well managed and controlled. Our process service interconnection model contribution consists of enriching SOA (Service Oriented Approach) with new paradigms and applying it to resolve heterogeneous workflow process interconnection problem. We propose a generic model for workflow process interconnection problem and validate this model on heterogeneous workflow management systems. Our paper is structured as follows: After a short introduction, section 2 presents the process interconnection problematics and state of the art, section 3 formalises our process service interconnection model, section 4 presents an implementation of our model, and gives some hints on our system experimentation. Finally, a short conclusion ends this paper.

2   Process Interconnection

Due to business process automation development, process interconnection becomes an important matter. Although a wide spectrum of tools for process modelling and enactment exists (workflow systems, project management tools, shared agendas, to do lists, etc.), they have been developed to suit the intern needs of enterprises, and thus, are not adapted to inter-enterprise interconnection. Compared to other enterprise process systems, workflow processes are the most mature and operational. Meanwhile, they still have many drawbacks when considering enterprise process interconnection. In spite of WFMS normalisation efforts achieved by the WfMC (*Workflow Management Coalition*), the OMG (*Object Management Group*) and the IETF (*Internet Engineering Task Force*), existing workflow management systems are: (1) *heterogeneous*: considering their definition and execution environments (disparate syntax and semantics of business process models and definition languages -BPDL-, ad-hoc process instance management), and their access means (non standard compliant API) ; (2) and *monolithic*: considering the absence or the poorness of their API, and the black box process instance encapsulation. Beside these problems related to workflow process entities, interconnection of these workflow processes implies several difficulties, among which, we can mention: (1) *process presentation* (how to present in a homogeneous manner workflow processes that have heterogeneous definition models ?), (2) *dynamic process interconnection* (which model to use for composing processes at run-time ?), and (3) *composed process enactment* (how to be able to execute a process interconnecting workflow processes that have heterogeneous execution models ?).

Because of heterogeneous and monolithic aspects of workflow management systems, developing generic models for enterprise workflow process interconnection is a big deal. Among several approaches for interconnecting enterprise processes we highlight the most important: (1) *Process message oriented communication* ([1], [2], and BizTalk describe several techniques for workflow process communication through asynchronous typed message passing, and adapt paradigms like subscribe-notify, push, pull to workflow processes ;) (2) *Process event synchronisation* ([3], ICN [4], OPERA [5], W*f*MC [6], and WF-nets [7] upgrade process message communication paradigms with event coordination languages and algebras for synchronising interleaving workflow processes ;) (3) *Process data and interface interoperability* (W*f*-XML, PIP, and e-speak establish interoperability frameworks for workflow data structures and interfaces ;) (4) *Process data concurrency and access control* ([3], [8], and IETF WebDAV & SWAP go beyond simple data interoperability to control access within shared workflow dataspaces ;) (5) *Process transactional exchange control* (COO [9], TRANSCOOP [10], WISE [11], and MQSeries [12] consider workflow processes as advanced transactions, and propose transactional models for workflow execution and data management ;) and (6) *Process service exchange* (Service concept has been defined in many research fields: Object Oriented research, Process Modelling research [1,13,14,15], Distributed System research [16,17], etc. In workflow research, CMI [1], OCoN [18], Crossflow [15,19], eFlow [14], define process service contracts for workflow process interconnection). To be more complete concerning process services, one may say that a process service can be seen as a software entity presenting process particularities and outcomes without totally revealing the process structure (*i.e.* its workflow implementation). A process service shows a functional abstraction of a process (or parts of a process) provided by an organisation. It specifies the amount of work that the organisation promises to carry out with a specific quality of service. It also specifies which parts of a workflow process it covers and how the requester could access to them. Proces service concept has been studied from several points of view: process service execution semantics abstraction [1], sub-workflow process service selection [19], dynamic process service activities configuration [14], process service control flow level abstraction [15], service methods and events wrapping [17], etc. Process service structure is to be seen as a co-operation pattern that relevantly supports dynamic workflow process interconnection and cooperation behaviours.

Compared to other approaches, *process service exchange approach* supports enterprise cooperation modelling in a very effective way. Actually, by it forces of abstracting enterprise workflow processes to be interconnected, process services are the *most adapted to build high level models for enterprise cooperation and generic models independent of workflow process particularities*. Moreover, process service exchange approach offers a high level paradigm which is very open to extensions dealing with other approaches basic paradigms (*e.g.* communication: message passing, data interoperability ; coordination: event synchronisation ; execution control: data access control, transaction management, etc.).

Hence, to build our dynamic enterprise workflow process model, we have chosen the process service exchange approach. For *process presentation problem*, we consider processes, beyond any process model, as services which are accessible object entities that possess object classification (*category*) and accept all object features (inheritance, overloading, etc.). Let call these specific services "process services". These process services possess application specific interface (*API*) and access rights to this API (*visibility contract*). A set of category specific typed values describe (*profiles*) of these process services. Our proposition for process presentation is in the same vain of workflow object vision of the OMG [20] even if this later do not take into account workflow *application specific properties*. We propose innovative service discovery concepts and algorithms which can improve OMG Trading Service. As far as *dynamic process interconnection problem* is concerned, we merge the W*f*MC *nested sub-process model* [6] with process service out-sourcing based interconnection [1,14,15]. Our constraint was to interconnect workflow processes without changing neither their classical definition nor execution manner. So, we improved W*f*MC *nested sub-process model* which was created for build-time process interconnection with new dynamic paradigms (*discovery, negotiation, and wrapping*) that will enable processes to be composed at run-time. By the fact, our proposition improves classical "publish-find-bind" service oriented approach with symmetric aspects and negotiation. Our process service interconnection model will enable co-operating enterprises to structure, classify, and compare process services, to select dynamically a provided process service among those matching a required process service, and finally to keep possible their business processes co-operating through process service wrapping. This process service wrapping will realize the out-sourcing based interconnection of each workflow process interconnected couples. A process service may concern either long e-transactions (e.g. out-sourcing the development of pieces of software, subscription to full e-learning sessions, etc.), or short e-transactions (e.g. online book commands, enactment of administrative processes, data exchange rendezvous in a virtual enterprise, etc.).

To illustrate our approach, let us consider the following example within an e-learning context (figure 1). This example context considers five enterprises: KManager (a knowledge management and e-learning enterprise), WAgency (a web agency enterprise), CoolHost (a site hosting enterprise), MediAgency (a multimedia agency enterprise), and e-Store (an e-learning content collection enterprise). Each of these enterprises possess several workflow systems to manage their everyday business processes. Let KManager be a service requester enterprise. Let WAgency, CoolHost, MediAgency, and e-Store be four (among other) service provider enterprises. Let notice, that each enterprise can be both a requester and a provider of process services. On the one hand, KManager requires three types of services: a portal development service (portalDevSrv), a portal hosting service (portalHostSrv), and an e-learning content collection service (moduleCollectorSrv). Such requested services can be implemented by several provided services. On the other hand, WAgency proposes an Internet site development process service (webBoosterSrv), CoolHost proposes an Internet site hosting process service (hostEasySrv), and e-Store proposes an e-learning content construction process service (e-robotSrv).

To the indeterminism problem of interconnecting couples of provided and requested services, we proposed a symmetric publishing-discovery-negotiation service approach. In fact, after discovery and negotiation sessions of published process services, KManager chooses WAgency process service webBoosterSrv which matches portalDevSrv, CoolHost process service hostEasySrv which matches portalHostSrv, and e-Store process service e-robotSrv which matches moduleCollectorSrv. The interconnection is instance-based (i.e. each process service provider can interconnect instances of their process services to different requesters).

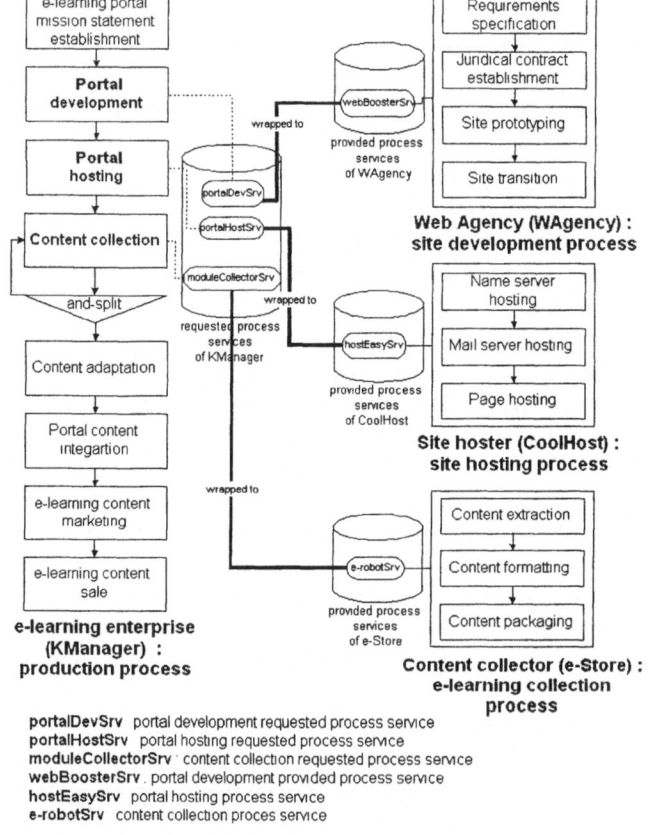

portalDevSrv   portal development requested process service
portalHostSrv   portal hosting requested process service
moduleCollectorSrv · content collection requested process service
webBoosterSrv . portal development provided process service
hostEasySrv   portal hosting process service
e-robotSrv   content collection proces service

Fig. 1. An e-learning interconnection example

3   Our Process Service Interconnection Model

The modelling of process service interconnection is based on a metamodel describing our service oriented approach, on structures participating to our enterprise process service interconnection model and on facilities presenting the dynamics of our model and its operational aspects.

3.1   Process Service Approach: Meta Model

To tackle enterprise process interconnection problems, our approach considers three abstraction levels and thus is structured in three layers: workflow layer (implementation level), process layer (object abstraction level), and process service layer (presentation and access level).

Figure 2 shows our oriented process service approach presenting enterprise workflow processes, evolving inside monolithic and heterogeneous workflow management systems, as processes able to be interconnected through process services.

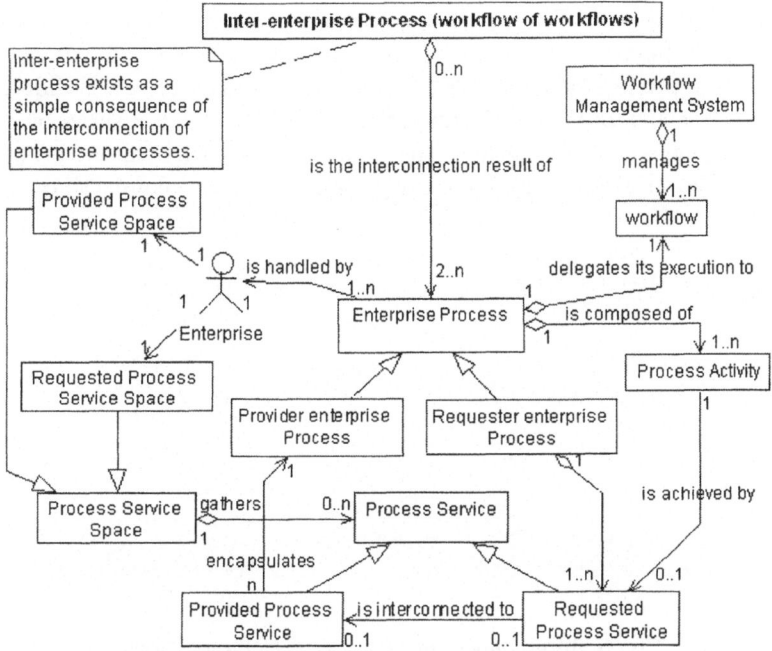

Fig. 2. Interconnection Approach: Meta Model

This interconnection yields an inter-enterprise process that represents *"a workflow of workflows"* whose management is distributed on all interconnected entreprises as follows:

- *processes:* Each enterprise possesses several processes. A process is composed of several process activities ;
- *workflows:* Each process delegates the execution of its activities to a workflow. The management of a workflow is specific to its WFMS engine (workflow management system) ;
- *process services:* An enterprise process activity can be achieved by the entreprise means or by an external service. We call a service achieving a process activity a process service. Each enterprise possesses a *requested process service space* and a *provided process service space*. A requested process service describes needs to accomplish a process activity. A provided process service encapsulates a process that represents an ability to achieve a process activity. Process interconnection is done through the wrapping of their requested and provided process services.

Figure 3 describes enterprise collaboration within our process service oriented approach. The operation <publish> represents the *publishing* (requesting and providing) of a process service, the operation <find> represents the *discovery* of a process service, while the operation <negotiate> represents a process service parameters *negotiation*. Finally, the operation <bind> represents the dynamic *interconnection* between an abstract process service (a requested process service) and a concrete process service offer (a provided process service). Beside the fact that our approach supports negotiation facility (which is not ensured by classical service approaches), its strengthens these approaches with symmetric aspects of process service publishing, discovery, negotiation and interconnection.

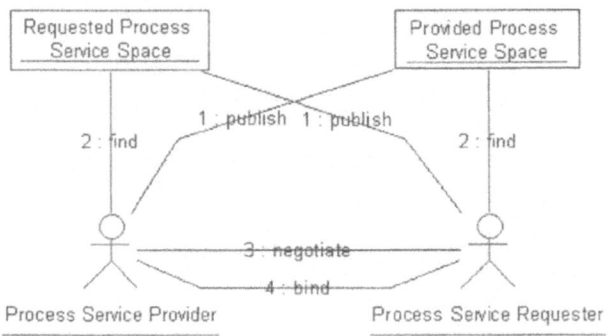

Fig. 3. Interconnection Approach: Collaborations

3.2   Process Service Interconnection Model: Structures

Process Structure. Our process interconnection model is initially based on the F. Leymann and D. Roller process definition model [12]. If this model can be applied very well for traditional workflows (within one enterprise), it does not consider explicitly process interconnection. Our objective is to enrich this model with new concepts and definitions in order to support some process interconnection aspects. Most of studied interconnection process models focus on process control flow and data flow definition without caring about two important process access points: process instance methods and process instance events.

The UML class diagram of figure 4 defines a process structure as follows:

- a process is defined by a process graph and a process interface ;
- a process graph describes the process control-flow structure [12]. It is the composition of nodes (process activities), edges (process activities transitions) and conditions (transition guards defined by business rules predicates);
- a process interface (or API) is the composition of methods (process instance reading and updating methods) and events (process event notification that are triggered off from a process instance during its execution). A process interface is specific to each process definition.

Figure 5 presents a process graph example and figure 6 a process interface example.

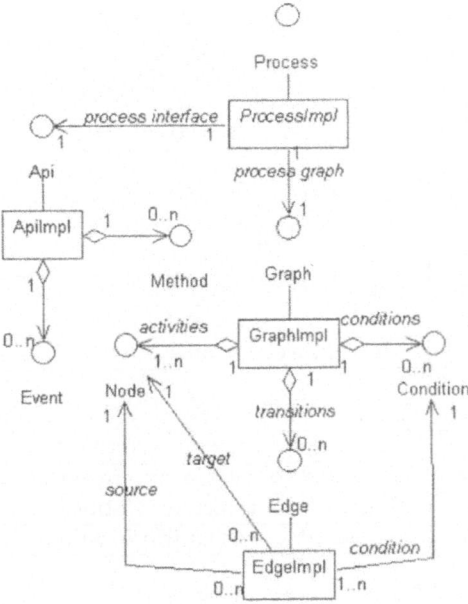

Fig. 4. Process Structure

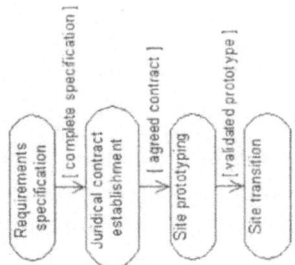

Fig. 5. WAgency Process Graph

Process Service Structure. The UML class diagram of the figure 7 defines the process service structure as follows:

- a process service is defined as a specific process wrapper that has a category, a profile and a visibility contract ;

- a process service category determines the process object type and its classification. Categories represent any enterprise agreed object ontologies ;

- a process service profile describes a relational structure defining a set of process named-typed-values attributes. Profile concept is in the same vein of OMG Trading Service properties ;

m_1	fetchProcessInstanceState(..)
m_2	fetchActivityInstanceState(..)
m_3	fetchWorkItem(..)
m_4	getProcessInstanceAttributeValue(..)
m_5	fetchWorkItemAttribute(..)
m_6	getWorkItem(..)
m_7	fetchActivityInstanceAttribute(..)
m_8	fetchActivityInstance(..)
m_9	getActivityInstance(..)
m_{10}	getWorkItemAttributeValue(..)
m_{11}	getActivityInstanceAttributeValue(..)
m_{12}	fetchProcessInstanceAttribute(..)

e_1	TerminatedProcessInstanceNotification
e_2	StartedProcessInstanceNotification
e_3	TerminatedActivityInstanceNotification
e_4	StartedActivityInstanceNotification
e_5	AvailableNewDataNotification

Fig. 6. WAgency process instance methods and events

- a process service visibility contract represents a subset of the wrapped process interface, "hiding" the complete process interface.

Figures 8 and 9 present a process service structure example.

Process Interconnection through Process Services. The WfMC has established a well known problem of *process interconnection by nested sub-process model*. The WfMC *nested sub-process model* expresses that an instance of an activity A_{i_j} belonging to a process P_i enacts remotely a known instance of an other process P_k and waits for its completion. Moreover, the WfMC has defined eight levels of process interoperability. The coexistence is the second lowest interoperability level (among these eight levels). Coexistent process interconnection are processes that do not possess any common interoperability standard. They meanwhile share, the same environment -machine or operating system or network- to be able to manage and achieve parts of the same process [6].

Process interconnection through process services aims to resolve the problem of *coexistent process interconnection through a dynamic variant of nested sub-process model*. That means that an instance of an activity A_{i_j} of a process P_i discovers dynamically a process P_k that suits its realisation profile, adapts it, wraps to it, instantiates it, enacts it dynamically, cooperates with it, and waits for its completion. Thus, a process service structure will be the glue keeping possible this dynamic coexistent process interconnection as shown in the UML class diagram of figure 10. Our complete approach is detailed in [21].

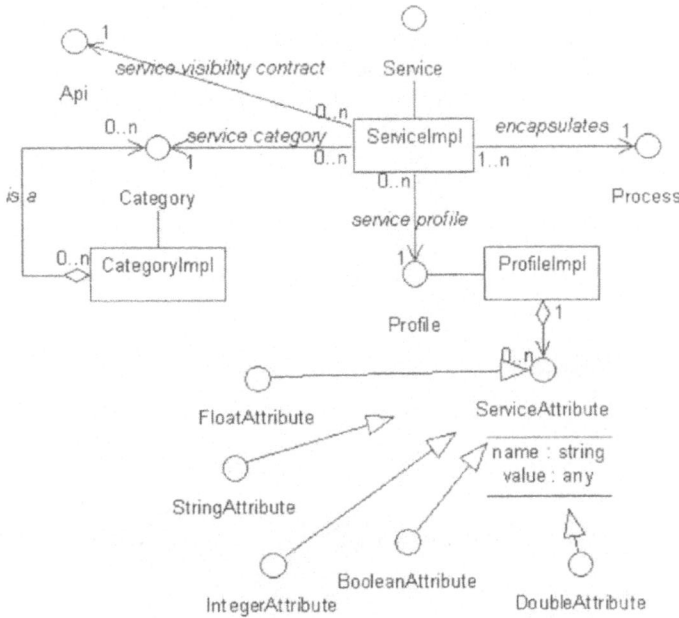

Fig. 7. Process Service Structure

m_1	fetchProcessInstanceState(..)
m_4	getProcessInstanceAttributeValue(..)
m_{11}	getActivityInstanceAttributeValue(..)
m_{12}	fetchProcessInstanceAttribute(..)

e_1	TerminatedProcessInstanceNotification
e_2	StartedProcessInstanceNotification
e_5	AvailableNewDataNotification

Fig. 8. WAgency.Provided.WebBoosterSrv methods visibility contract M_2 and events visibility contract EV_3

3.3 Process Service Interconnection Model: Dynamics

Process service structure is a wrapper that represents a functional and semantic abstraction of a process. It enables classification, indexing, comparison, and discovery of a certain type of process. This supposes that enterprises, within each business community, agreed about a common process service language (e.g. business key concept ontologies, business service taxonomies,...) to define and understand process services. Research and normalisation work are still emergent in this promising field. The dynamics of process service interconnection model will be presented through its publishing, discovering, negotiating and interconnecting process services facilities.

(*category* = e_learning_portal_development,
name   = "WAgency.WebBoosterSrv",
profile   = (duration=3 (month),
          price=100 (Keuro),
          dynamic_sites = true,
          dbms = "MySQL",
          XML_use = true,
          Java_use = true,
          JSP_use = true,
          flash_use = false),
process   = site_development_process)

Fig. 9. WAgency.Provided.WebBoosterSrv process service structure

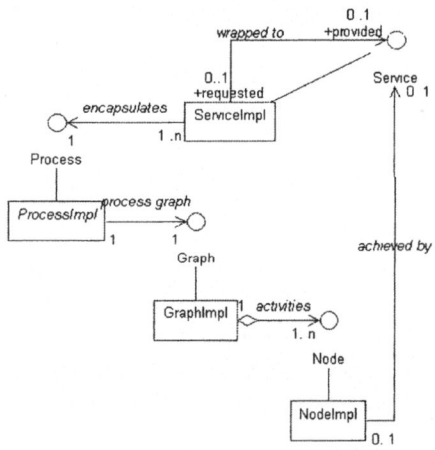

Fig. 10. Process Interconnection through Services

Process Service Spaces. The UML class diagram of figure 11 defines the process service spaces structure as follows:

– a process service space is a set composed of process services ;

– an enterprise possesses four types of process service spaces: (1) a private process service space (gathering all process services that the enterprise creates and keeps private to other enterprises before their publishing) ; (2) a requested process service space (public process service space gathering all process services that the enterprise requests (expressing the need of out-sourcing to an external enterprise). Each requested service knows its requester enterprise) ; (3) a provided process service space (public process service space gathering all process services the enterprise can achieve by her own means (expresses the capability to handle a requested process service of an external enterprise). Each provided service knows its provider) ; and (4) a wrapped process service space (public process service space gathering all process ser-

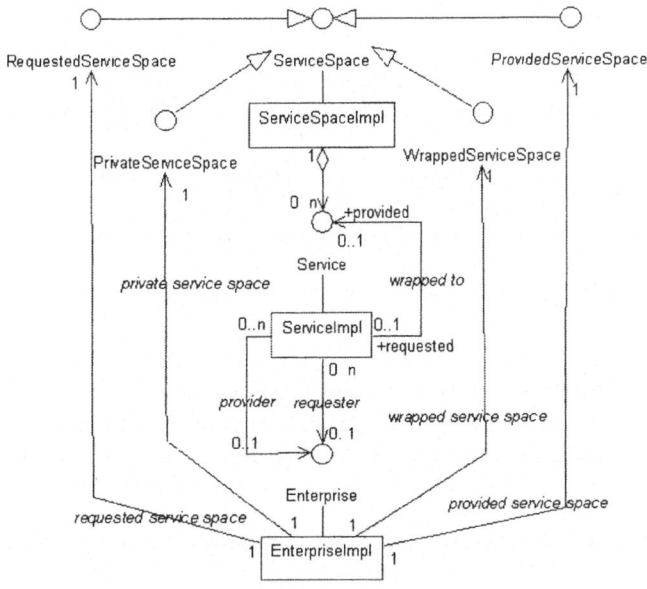

Fig. 11. Enterprise Process Service Spaces

vices that have been already wrapped -their requesting or providing need has been satisfied by an external process service-. Each wrapped service knows both its requester and its provider).

Process Service Publishing. Process service publishing deals with the communication of service description to other enterprises in order to find common agreement for enterprise process interconnections. Publishing of a process service is the result of the following steps:

1. The enterprise creates its process service within its private process space ;
2. the enterprise solicits its private process service space to publish (request of provide) its created process service ;
3. the private process service space constructs a clone of the process service and adds it to the requested process service space or to the provided process service space depending of the publishing type.

Actually, every subscribed enterprise possesses views on other enterprise requested and provided process service spaces. Every subscribed enterprise view is updated after each publishing event. These views enable enterprises to discover, to negotiate, and to be interconnected through other enterprise published process services. Figure 12 presents some process services among those defined and published by the five entreprises.

Process Service Discovery. Process service discovery deals with the application of algorithms that enable evaluation and comparison of process services

Enterprise	Process services (R = requested, P = provided)
KManager	R|portalDevSrv (handles the developpement of a portal), R|portalHostSrv (handles a portal hosting), R|moduleCollectorSrv (collects an e-learning module).
e-Store	P|e-robotSrv (collects e-learning content)
MediAgency	P|mediArtSrv (achieves multimedia content)
WAgency	P|webBoosterSrv (achieves a web site)
CoolHost	P|hostEasySrv (handles the hosting of a web site)

Fig. 12. Some defined and published process services

in order to help process service requesters (or providers) to find the process services that match their requested (or provided) process services in the best way. Discovery of a process service (for instance a requested one) is the result of the following steps:

1. The enterprise creates and provides a process service we will name "provided" ;

2. let $n + 1$ bet the current subscribed enterprise number,
   for ($set := \emptyset$, i := 1; i $\leq$ n; i++) loop
   a) the enterprise retrieves descriptions of process services published in the requested service space of the enterprise e_i :
      $services_i := \{rs_{i1}, rs_{i2}, ...\}$;
   b) $set := set \cup services_i$;
   end loop ;

3. the enterprise executes a neighbourhood algorithm on the process service provided among the set of possible requested process services set. This algorithm iterates on each element of set to find out the requested process services that suit the needs of the process service "provided". This neighbourhood algorithm is based on distances and matching measures that could be instantiated according to the application ;

4. The discovery finishes by building a set of requested process services $\{nrs_1, nrs_2, ...\}$ that are neighbour to the process service "provided".

Process service discovery is symmetric, it means that process service requesters can also discover provided process services that suit their needs. More details about matching and distance measures can be found in [22]. Actually, views on enterprise requested and provided process service spaces are organised using these matching measures. That enables enterprises to browse a restricted computed projection of the wide process service space.

Process Service Negotiation. Process service negotiation enables to decide dynamically and to adapt all interconnection parameters between processes to be interconnected (e.g. profile, visibility contract, process graph accessibility, etc.). Negotiation of a process service is the result of the following steps:

1. *solicitation phase:* the client contacts primarily the server and expresses its negotiation request (e.g. a new process service profile, a new process service visibility contract, etc.) ;

2. *effective negotiation phase:* both client and server exchange messages to build acceptable solutions set. An exchange protocol handles turn taking rules for expressing negotiation acts ;

3. *selection phase:* finally, the client or the server chooses a solution among those expressed during negotiation phase. The server takes its decisions according to the selected solution (e.g. allocating a solicited resource, tuning access rights for some service, etc.).

Actually, each subscribed enterprise is not only able to browse its views of other enterprise requested and provided process service spaces. It can also dynamically change these views by negotiating with process services publishers to customise their services for suiting its workflow process out-sourcing needs or offers. More details about generic negotiation component can be found in [23].

3.4   Process Service Interconnection Model: Protocol

Our process service interconnection protocol enables enterprise workflow processes to be interconnected and to cooperate through the following four steps:

1. *Workflow processes definition:* every workflow process is defined as a graph that manages process execution model within an enterprise chosen workflow management system.

2. *Workflow processes adaptation:* (a) *workflow process service provider adaptation:* each process service category is represented by an interface (ConcreteProcessInterface) that extends Process interface. A workflow process providing services of a certain category has to be associated to a program or a class that implements the category related interface. This adaptation has to be written in a language supported or inter-operable with the WFMS. (b) *workflow process service requester adaptation:* a workflow process requesting services has to express that its out-sourced activities (interface Node) are achieved by external process services. This adaptation has to program, in a language supported by the WFMS, the enactment of the requested process services and the cooperation protocol used to interact.

3. *Dynamic workflow processes interconnection by process services:* (a) *process service definition:* process services are created by requester and provider enterprises within their private process service spaces. Process services are defined by their name, textual description, category, profile, encapsulated process (if the process service is to be provided) and visibility contract that desires (if it is to be requested) or that permits (if it is to be provided). (b) *process service publishing:* process services are published by enterprises as provided or requested in their respective accessible requested or provided process service spaces. (c) *process service discovering:* process services publisher can look for process services suiting its process service definition needs.

(d) *process service negotiation:* process services publishers can negotiate with each others their process service requested and provided definitions (profile and visibility contract) to agree on common satisfying process service definition. (e) *process service wrapping:* process services wrapping deals with committing and dispatching, at run-time, agreed process service definitions (profile and visibility contract) on both process service views (requester and provider views).

4. *Workflow processes cooperation through process services:* workflow processes can cooperate through process services that adapt them. This cooperation between wrapped process services can vary from method invocation or event passing (according to agreed visibility contract), to data exchange or synchronisation on process execution states. Workflow processes cooperation through process services is to be considered as a generic paradigm that admits a wide panel of process cooperation modes.

4   Implementation and Experimentation

Our dynamic workflow process interconnection model has been implemented within our co-operative environment *DISCOBOLE* (DIStributed CO-operation and Business prOcess on LinE). *DISCOBOLE* integrates process and process service structures with their manipulation algorithms as innovative *CORBA application objects* within *process interconnection and cooperation facilities.* Through these facilities *DISCOBOLE* supplies mechanisms for process interconnection and cooperation applications. *DISCOBOLE* is implemented in Java on the CORBA broker architecture JacORB.

To experiment our enterprise workflow process interconnection model, we have deployed our e-learning enterprise context using *DISCOBOLE.* Each of the four enterprises KManager, e-Store, WAgency, and CoolHost uses a workflow management system to manage its business processes. *DISCOBOLE* is the environment that will enable them to interconnect dynamically these processes. In our experimentation, we selected and used three heterogeneous WFMS to model enterprise business processes: a lightweight component based WFMS *Breeze* [24], an object oriented PetriNets WFMS *Renew* [25], and a WfMC compliant WFMS *WorkCoordinator* (or WCO) [26]. These three WFMS are written in different languages and evolve in different environments. In order to keep possible the interconnection of their defined workflow processes, adaptation is achieved according to the WFMS supported language and environment (*Breeze* and *Renew* workflow processes adaptations have been programmed in Java on CORBA, while *WorkCoordinator* workflow processes adaptation has been programmed on a C++ CORBA bus). Thanks to this experimentation of our process service interconnection model, we effectively succeed to dynamically interconnect heterogeneous workflow processes. Moreover, another learned lesson from experimentation is that most of adaptation glue is redundant programming patterns that can be easily generated into WFMS supported languages to keep the enterprise focused on defining services and interconnecting processes through these services.

5   Conclusion and Perspectives

Our paper is a contribution in enterprise workflow interconnection domain which is a hot reseach topic as far as the current B2B (Business to Business) boom is concerned. In spite of normalisation efforts, WFMS are still presenting monolithic and heterogeneous drawbacks. Thanks to processes and process services frameworks, our model bypasses these drawbacks by enabling enterprise workflow processes interconnection within a *"workflow of workflows"* in which several workflow management systems coexist. Our model has been developed to support a wide panel of workflow management systems and experimented to prove the realisability of dynamic enterprise workflow processes. After dealing with process interconnection problems, we are tackling problems of *composed process service enactment and execution control* [27].

Acknowledgements. We would like to thank W. Gaaloul, S. Baïna, and A. Larhlimi for their development participation within the *DISCOBOLE* project, and Dr. B. Benatallah from UNSW, Sydney, Australia for this paper's review.

References

1. D. Baker, D. Georgakopoulos, H. Schuster, A. Cassandra, and A. Cichocki. Providing Customized Process and Situation Awarness in the Collaboration Management Infrastructure. In *4th IFCIS Int. Conf. on Cooperative Information Systems (CoopIS'99)*, pages 79–91, Edinburgh, Scotland, September 2–4, 1999. IEEE Computer Society Press.
2. F. Casati and A. Discenza. Supporting Workflow Cooperation Within and Across Organisations. In *15th ACM Symposium on Applied Computing (SAC'00)*, pages 19–21, Como, Italy, March 2000.
3. G. Alonso, D. Agrawal, and A. El Abbadi. Process Synchronisation in Workflow Management Systems. In *8th IEEE Symposium on Parallel and Distributed Processing (SPDS'97)*, New Orleans, Louisiana, October 1996.
4. C. A. Ellis. *Computer Supported Cooperative Work*, chapter Workflow Technology. John Wiley and Sons, 1999.
5. C. Hagen and G. Alonso. Beyond the Black Box: Event-based Inter-Process Communication in Process Support Systems. In *19th International Conference on Distributed Computing Systems (ICDCS'99)*, Austin, Texas, USA, May/June 1999.
6. L. Fischer, editor. *The Workflow Handbook 2001*. Published in association with the Workflow Management Coalition (WfMC), October 2000.
7. W. M. P. van der Aalst. Interorganizational workflows: An approach based on message sequence charts and Petri nets, System Analysis and Modeling, 34(3):335–367, 1999.
8. P. Dewan and H-H. Shen. Flexible meta access-control for collaborative applications. In *Proceedings of ACM Conference on Computer-Supported Cooperative Work (CSCW'98)*, Primitives for Building Flexibile Groupware Systems, pages 247–256. ACM Press, 1998.
9. C. Godart, O. Perrin, and H. Skaf. COO: a workflow operator to improve cooperative modelling in virtual processes. In *9th IEEE International Workshop on Research Issues on Data Engineering: Information Technology For Virtual Enterprises (RIDE-VE'99)*, Sydney, Australia, March 23–24, 1999.

10. J. Puustjärvi. *Transactional Workflows*. PhD thesis, Department of Computer Science, University of Helsinki, Finland, 1999.
11. G. Alonso, C. Hagen, and A. Lazcano. Process in Electronic Commerce. In *ICDS workshop on Electronic Commerce and Web-Based Applications*, Austin, Texas, USA, June 1999.
12. F. Leymann and D. Roller. *Production Workflow, Concepts and Techniques*. Prentice-Hall, Inc., 2000.
13. G. Piccinelli. Distributed Workflow Management: The TEAM Model. In *3rd IFCIS Int. Conf. on Cooperative Information Systems (CoopIS'98)*, pages 292–299, New York City, New York, USA, August 20–22, 1998. IEEE-CS Press.
14. F. Casati, S. Ilnicki, L. J. Jin, and M. C. Shan. eFlow: an Open, Flexible, and Configurable Approach to Service Composition. In *2nd International Workshop on Advance Issues of E-Commerce and Web-Based Information Systems (WECWIS'00)*, pages 125–132, Milpitas, California, June 8–9, 2000.
15. P. Grefen, K. Aberer, Y. Hoffner, and H. Ludwig. CrossFlow: cross-organisational workflow management in dynamic virtual enterprises. In *International Journal of Computer Systems, Science and Engineering (IJCSSE'00)*, pages 277–290, 2000.
16. L. Kutvonen. *Trading services in open distributed environments*. Th se en informatique, Department of Computer Science, University of Helsinki, Finland, 1998.
17. B. Benatallah, B. Medjahed, A. Boughettaya, A. Elmagarmid, and J. Beard. Composing and Maintaining Web-based Virtual Enterprises. In *1st Workshop on Technologies for E-Services, In Cooperation with VLDB'2000 (TES'00)*, Cairo, Egypt, September 14–15, 2000.
18. H. Giese and G. Wirtz. The OCoN Approach for Object-Oriented Distributed Software Systems Modeling. In *Software Engineering and Petri Nets, Workshop within the 21st International Conference on Application and Theory of Petri Nets, Aarhus, Denmark, June 26*, 2000.
19. J. Klingemann, J. Wasch, and K. Aberer. Deriving service models in cross organizational workflows. In *9th International Workshop on Research Issues on Data Engineering: Information Technology for Virtual Enterprises (ITVE'99)*, Sydney, Australia, 1999. IEEE Computer Society Press.
20. OMG. *Workflow Management Facility Specification, V 1.2*. OMG (Object Management Group), ww.omg.org, April 2000.
21. Karim Baïna. *Un Modèle Orienté Services Procédés pour l'Interconnexion et la Coopération des Procédés d'Entreprises*. Ph.D thesis in Computer Science, Université Henri Poincaré (Nancy 1), May 16, 2003.
22. K. Baïna, K. Benali, and C. Godart. A process service model for dynamic enterprise process interconnection. In C. Batini, F. Giunchiglia, P. Giorgini, and M. Mecella, editors, *9th Int. Conf. on Cooperative Information Systems, In Cooperation with IFCIS (CoopIS'01)*, number 2172 in LNCS, pages 239–254, Trento, Italy, September 5–7, 2001. Springer-Verlag.
23. M. Munier, K. Baïna, and K. Benali. A Negotiation Model for CSCW. In O. Etzion and P. Scheuermann, editors, *5th IFCIS Int. Conf. on Cooperative Information Systems, In Cooperation with VLDB'2000 (CoopIS'00)*, number 1901 in LNCS, pages 224–235, Eilat, Israel, September 6–8, 2000. Springer-Verlag.
24. DSTC. *Breeze: workflow with ease*. DSTC (Distributed Systems Technology Centre), Australia, www.dstc.edu.au/Downloads/, February 15, 2002.
25. O. Kummer, F. Wienberg, and M. Duvigneau. *Renew – User Guide*. University of Hamburg, Department for Informatics, Theoretical Foundations Group, Distributed Systems Group, Germany, www.renew.de, July 3, 2001.

26. Hitachi. *WorkCoordinator Workflow System.*
    Hitachi Ltd., www.hitachi.co.jp/Prod/comp/soft1/wco/, 2002.
27. K. Baïna, S. Tata, and K. Benali. A model for process service interaction. In
    W. van der Aalst, A. ter Hofstede, and M. Weske, editors, *Conference on Business
    Process Management, on the Application of Formal Methods to "Process-Aware"
    Information Systems (BPM'03)*, number 2678 in LNCS, pages 261–275, Eindhoven,
    The Netherlands, June 26–27, 2003. Springer-Verlag.

R-GMA: An Information Integration System for Grid Monitoring

Andy Cooke[1], Alasdair J.G. Gray[1], Lisha Ma[1], Werner Nutt[1],
James Magowan[2], Manfred Oevers[2], Paul Taylor[2], Rob Byrom[3],
Laurence Field[3], Steve Hicks[3], Jason Leake[3], Manish Soni[3], Antony Wilson[3],
Roney Cordenonsi[4], Linda Cornwall[5], Abdeslem Djaoui[5], Steve Fisher[5],
Norbert Podhorszki[6], Brian Coghlan[7], Stuart Kenny[7], and David O'Callaghan[7]

[1] Heriot-Watt University, Edinburgh, UK
[2] IBM-UK
[3] PPARC, UK
[4] Queen Mary, University of London, UK
[5] Rutherford Appleton Laboratory, UK
[6] SZTAKI, Hungary
[7] Trinity College Dublin, Ireland

Abstract. Computational Grids are distributed systems that provide access to computational resources in a transparent fashion. Collecting and providing information about the status of the Grid itself is called Grid monitoring.

We describe R-GMA (Relational Grid Monitoring Architecture) as a solution to the Grid monitoring problem. It uses a local as view approach to information integration and will be a component of the European Union's DataGrid.

The R-GMA architecture and mechanisms are general and could be used in other areas where there is a need for publishing and querying information in a distributed fashion.

1 Introduction

In this paper we discuss how to monitor the state of a dynamically changing computational Grid, and our approach to this—a data integration system called R-GMA (Relational Grid Monitoring Architecture). Grid monitoring requires the publication of static and dynamic data, a global view of this data, and a query mechanism capable of dealing with "latest-state", "continuous", and "history" queries. It also needs to be scalable to allow hundreds of nodes to publish and be resilient if any node fails. There are also issues of privacy of data that need to be addressed.

We have designed a data integration system that meets most of these requirements, within the European Union's DataGrid project [1]. It aims to develop a computational Grid to allow three major user groups to process and analyse the results of their scientific experiments: (1) high energy physics to allow them to distribute and analyse the vast amounts of data that will be produced by the

R. Meersman et al. (Eds.): CoopIS/DOA/ODBASE 2003, LNCS 2888, pp. 462–481, 2003.
© Springer-Verlag Berlin Heidelberg 2003

Large Hadron Collider at CERN, (2) biological and medical image processing as part of exploitation of genomes, and (3) the European Space Agency's Earth Observation project to analyse images of atmospheric ozone.

During the past two years, we have implemented a working R-GMA system within DataGrid. Our aim was to develop functionality that had a firm theoretical basis and that was flexible enough to quickly respond to requirements as they became clearer. We will describe the status of our implementation as DataGrid enters its final year. R-GMA has an open-source license, and can be downloaded from [2].

In section 2 we describe what a computational Grid is, and outline the requirements of a Grid monitoring system. In section 3 we describe possible approaches to Grid monitoring, including existing systems, and discuss why these do not meet the requirements identified. We then present our R-GMA architecture for a Grid monitoring system in section 4. Hierarchies of republishers will allow queries to be answered efficiently. We discuss the query planning needed to automatically maintain these hierarchies in section 5. The state of the current implementation is presented in section 6.

2   Grid Monitoring: Overview and Requirements

We shall introduce the idea of a computational Grid and describe the components of a Grid. We explain what is meant by Grid monitoring, and identify requirements for a Grid monitoring system.

2.1   Computational Grids

A *computational Grid* is a collection of connected, geographically distributed computing resources belonging to several different organisations. Typically the resources are a mix of computers, storage devices, network bandwidth and specialised equipment, e.g. supercomputers or databases. A computational Grid provides instantaneous access to files, remote computers, software and specialist equipment [10]. To a user, a Grid behaves like a single virtual supercomputer.

The concept of a computational Grid has existed since the mid 1990s and has grown out of the distributed and high performance computing communities. There have now been several projects to construct computational Grids to perform different tasks. These include: the Globus Toolkit [12], NASA's Information Power Grid [13], CrossGrid [9] and TeraGrid [6].

To make a computational Grid behave as a virtual computer requires various components that mimic the behaviour of a computer's operating system. The components of DataGrid, and their interactions, can be seen in Fig. 1 and are similar to those presented in [11].

User Interface: allows a human user to submit jobs, e.g. "analyse the data from a physics experiment, and store the result".

Resource Broker: controls the submission of jobs, finds suitable available resources and allocates them to the job.

464   A. Cooke et al.

Logging and Bookkeeping: tracks the progress of jobs, informs users when jobs are completed, which resources were used, and how much they will be charged for the job.

Storage Element (SE): provides physical storage for data files.

Replica Catalogue: tracks where data is stored and replicates data files as required.

Computing Element (CE): performs the processing of jobs, taking data from storage elements.

Monitoring System: monitors the state of the components of the Grid and makes this data available to other components.

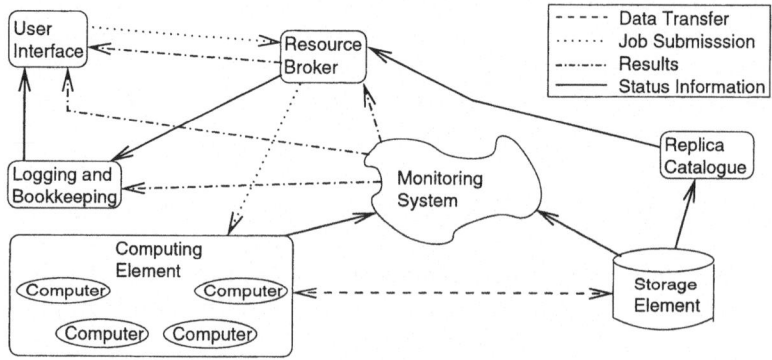

Fig. 1. The major components of DataGrid.

2.2   Grid Monitoring Requirements

The purpose of a Grid monitoring system is to make information about the status of a Grid available to users and to other components of the Grid. The following are typical use cases:

1. A resource broker needs to locate a computing element (CE), that has 5 CPUs available each with at least 200 MB of memory. The CE should have the right software installed, and the user must be authorised to use it. The throughput to an SE needs to be greater than 500 Mbps.
2. A visualisation tool is used by users to monitor the progress of their jobs needs to be updated whenever the status of a job changes.
3. Network administrators need to interrogate the past state of the network so that typical behaviour can be ascertained and anomalies identified.

Static and Stream Data. Information about a Grid comes from many different sources, e.g.

- Statistics from the resources on the Grid about themselves, e.g. the data about a machine delivered by a UNIX command such as w.
- Measurements of network throughput, e.g. made by sending a ping message across the network and publishing the runtime (use cases 1 and 3 above).
- Job progress statistics, either generated by annotated programs or by the resource broker (use case 2).
- Details about the topologies of the different networks connected (use cases 1 and 3).
- Details about the applications, licenses, etc., available at each resource (use case 1).

This monitoring data can be distinguished into two types based on the frequency with which it changes and depending on the way in which it is queried.

Static data (pools): This is data that does not change regularly or data that does not change for the duration of a query, e.g. data in a database with concurrency control. This is typically data about the operating system on a CE, or the total space on an SE (use case 1).

Dynamic data (streams): This is data that can be thought of as continually changing, e.g. the memory usage of a CE (use case 1), or data that leads to new query results as soon as it is available, for example the status of a job (use case 2).

A requirement, then, of a Grid monitoring system is that it should allow both static and streaming data to be published.

Locating Data. Monitoring data on a Grid will be published by the distributed components of the Grid. The monitoring system must provide mechanisms for users of the Grid to locate data sources. Users need a *global view* over these data sources, in order to understand how the data relates and to query it.

Queries with Different Temporal Characteristics. A monitoring system should support queries posed over data streams, over data pools, or over a mix of these (use case 1). It should be possible to ask one-time queries about the state of a stream right now (a *latest-state* query – use case 1), continuously from now on (a *continuous* query – use case 2) or in the past (a *history* query – use case 3). Up to date answers should be returned quickly—the resource broker needs information that is no more than 10 seconds old in use case 1. To be accepted by users, the query language should capture most of the common use cases, but should not force a user to learn too many new concepts.

Scalability and Performance. A Grid is potentially very large: DataGrid's testbed currently has hundreds of resources, and will scale up by the end of the project. The fabric of the Grid will be unreliable: network connections will fail, resources will become in-accessible.

It is important that the monitoring system can *scale* to handle the large amounts of data published and still return correct answers in a timely manner. It should not become a performance bottleneck for the entire Grid. It should be able to cope with large numbers of queries received at the same time.

The monitoring system itself should be resilient to failure of any of its components, otherwise the whole Grid could fail along with it. The monitoring system cannot have any sort of central control as resources will be contributed by organisations that are independent of each other.

Security. An information source must be able to control who can "see" its data and this must also be respected by the monitoring system. A user should be able to identify themselves so that they can make use of the resources that they are entitled to. Resources should be able to prevent access to users who are not authorised.

3   Possible Approaches to Grid Monitoring

Peer to Peer systems allow resources to be shared across the Internet. However, as such systems do not offer a global view over all the resources available, they could not be used for Grid monitoring. Another related technology are data stream management systems, for which several prototypes now exist. Here we will examine whether these could suitable for Grid monitoring. The Grid community have proposed the Grid Monitoring Architecture as a general architecture for a Grid monitoring system. We will discuss this architecture and existing systems such as the Monitoring and Discover Service which ships with Globus.

3.1   Data Stream Management Systems

Data streams show up in many different situations where dynamically changing data can be collected, e.g. stock market prices, sensor data, monitoring information. Recently, the idea of a centralised data stream management system (DSMS) has been developed, and some preliminary systems have been implemented, such as STREAM [5], Aurora [7], Tribeca [18] and AIMS [16]. They support querying and management of relations, akin to a relational database management system, only these relations may be either streaming or static.

The existing DSMS do not meet all the requirements of Grid monitoring (section 2.2). The centralised systems developed today would not cope dynamically with the creation and removal of geographically distributed streams nor coordinate the communication of data from sources to clients. This central point would become single point of failure as all information sources and clients of the systems would need to interact with it.

3.2   Grid Monitoring Architecture

The Grid Monitoring Architecture (GMA) was proposed by Tierney *et al.* [19] and has been accepted as a standard for Grid monitoring systems by the Global Grid Forum [3]. It is a simple architecture comprising of three main components:

Producers: A source of data on the Grid, e.g. a sensor, or a description of a network topology.

Consumers: A user of data available on the Grid, e.g. a resource broker, or a system administrator wanting to find out about the utilisation of a Grid resource.

Directory Service: Stores details of producers and consumers to allow consumers to locate relevant producers of data.

The interaction of these components can be seen in Fig. 2. A producer informs the directory service of the kind of data it has to offer. A consumer contacts the directory service to discover which producers have data relevant to its query. A communication link is then set up directly with each producer to acquire data. Consumers may also register with the directory service. This allows new producers to notify any consumers that have relevant queries.

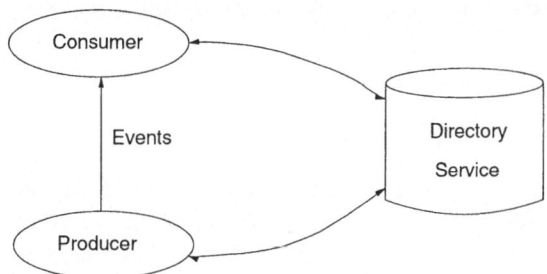

Fig. 2. The components of the GMA and their interactions

Intermediary components may be set up that consist of both a consumer and a producer. Intermediaries may be used to forward, broadcast, filter, aggregate or archive data from other producers. The intermediary then makes this data available for other consumers from a single point in the Grid.

By separating the tasks of information discovery, enquiry, and publication, the GMA is *scalable*. However, it does not define a data model, query language, or a protocol for data transmission. Nor does it say what information should be stored in the directory service. There are no details of how the directory service should perform the task of matching producers with consumers.

3.3   Existing Systems

There are several research systems implementing the GMA: AutoPilot [15], CODE [17], Monitoring and Discovery Service (MDS) [8], etc. However, only MDS is well known, because it is included in the widely-used Globus Toolkit [12].

Monitoring and Discovery Service. Although MDS[1] was designed and implemented before the GMA was proposed, it can still be seen to fit into the architecture. It consists of information providers (GMA producers) and aggregate directories (GMA directory service and intermediary). Data is organised in a hierarchical system based on the Lightweight Directory Access Protocol (LDAP); this provides the MDS system a name space, data model, wire protocol, and querying capabilities.

Although MDS is *scalable*, it does not meet other requirements outlined in section 2.2. Firstly, the LDAP query language has limitations. The hierarchy must be designed with popular queries in mind. Also, there is no support for users who want to relate data from different sections of the hierarchy—they must process these queries themselves.

To be able to offer a global view of the Grid to users, a hierarchy of intermediaries must be set up manually—providers and intermediary aggregate directories need to know which directory to register with. The system does not automate this, nor does it recover if any component in the hierarchy fails.

Lastly, MDS only supports latest-state queries with no assurance that the answers are up to date. It is claimed that you can create an archive of information by storing the latest-state values in a database and providing an LDAP interface to allow the system to access it. However, this would require considerable user effort.

4   The R-GMA Approach

R-GMA builds upon the GMA proposal (see section 3.2), but specifies a data model, a query language, and the functionality of the directory service. It also adds further components. Below, we introduce the main elements of the R-GMA architecture and explain the rationale of their design: consumers, producers, consumer and producer agents, schema, republishers, and registry.

We plan to finalise the implementation of the architecture presented by the end of this year. The current state of the implementation is discussed in section 6.

4.1   R-GMA as a Virtual Data Warehouse

The idea underlying R-GMA is to let the Grid monitoring data appear as being stored in or streaming through one large relational data warehouse.

Although it has occasionally been suggested to use a relational database management system for Grid monitoring [14], such an approach would not meet the requirements of section 2.2. For instance, the loading of data takes time; there may not be sufficient space to store all the data; connections to the database may fail so that the information will no longer be accessible; and finally, monitoring data often flow as data streams and queries ask for data streams as output, which is not supported by current database management systems.

---

[1] We discuss here the details of version 2, broadly similar to version 1 but the hierarchical LDAP structure has been decentralised.

In R-GMA, the warehouse is only virtual. Clients query the system via a global schema, but behind the scenes a data integration system directs data from the sources to the client.

4.2   Roles and Agents

R-GMA takes up the consumer and producer metaphors of the Grid Monitoring Architecture (see section 3.2) and refines them. An R-GMA installation allows clients, which may be Grid components or applications running on the Grid, to play the *roles* of information *producers* or *consumers*.

Producers. The producer role comes in two variants, the roles of *database producer* and of *stream producer,* depending on whether the data sets they make available are pools or streams. More specifically, a database producer publishes a collection of relations maintained in a relational database while a stream producer publishes several streams of tuples, each of which complies with the schema of a specific relation. We refer to these static or streamed relations as the *local relations* of a producer.

Consumers. A consumer is defined by a relational query. If the query is posed over a stream, the consumer has to declare whether it is to be interpreted as a continuous, a history, or a latest-state query (see section 2.2). Upon request, the consumer receives answers to its query.

Agents. R-GMA provides *agents* that support clients in their roles, for instance as consumer agents, or stream producer agents.

Currently, the role metaphor is implemented by an API that allows one to create objects for the various roles, like consumer or stream producer objects. Agents are realised as objects accessible via a Web server. Details are discussed in section 6.

4.3   The Global Schema

Producers and consumers can only interact with each other if there is a *language* and a *vocabulary* in which producers describe the information they supply and consumers the information for which they have a demand. In R-GMA, both the *language* for announcing supply and the one for specifying demand—that is, the query language—are essentially fragments of SQL.

The relations and attributes that make up the vocabulary are part of a global schema, which is stored in R-GMA's *schema* component.

The global schema distinguishes between two kinds of relations, *static* and *stream* relations. The two sets are disjoint. The global schema contains a collection of core relations that exist during the entire lifetime of an installation.

In addition, producers can introduce new relations to describe their data, and withdraw them again if they stop publishing.

Relations have attributes with types as in SQL. In addition to the attributes that are declared explicitly, stream relations have an additional attribute timestamp, which is of a type DateTime and records the point in time when a tuple was published.

For both kinds of relations, a subset of the attributes can be singled out as the *primary key*. We interpret primary keys as follows: any two tuples in the system that agree on the key attributes and the timestamp also agree on the remaining attributes. For the stream relations, the keys usually identify the parameters of a measurement. For instance, R-GMA's schema contains the core relation tp to publish measurements of the throughput of network links. The relation has the schema

$$tp(from, to, tool, psize, value, [timestamp]),$$

to record the time it took, according to measurements by a certain tool, to transport packets of a specific size from one node to another one. All attributes except value make up the primary key of tp. Intuitively, the key attributes of a stream relation identify a *channel* along which measurements are communicated.

Due to the distributed origin of information in R-GMA, the key constraints cannot be strictly enforced. However, R-GMA can check the views of producers to ensure that no two producers of a relation publish for the same keys. Consequently, key constraints hold globally if they hold locally.

Consumers pose queries over the global schema. Similarly, producers describe their local relations as views on the global schema. In Ullman's terminology [20], this means that R-GMA takes a "local as view" approach to data integration.

4.4 Producers and Consumers: Semantics

R-GMA requires that producers declare their content using views *without projections*. Thus, each producer contributes a set of tuples to each relation. This allows us to give an R-GMA installation an intuitive semantics: a static relation is interpreted as the union of the contributions published by the database producers; a stream relation is interpreted as a global stream obtained by merging the streams of all the stream producers.

Actually, the semantics of stream relations is not as well-defined as it may seem because it does not specify an order for the tuples in the global stream. We do not guarantee a specific order on the entire global stream. However, we require, that for a given channel the order of tuples in the global stream is the same as in the producer stream where they originated. We explain in section 5 how R-GMA enforces this constraint.

We are aware that our semantics of stream relations causes difficulties for some kinds of queries, for instance, aggregate queries over sliding windows where the set of grouping attributes is a strict subset of the keys. In such a case, different orderings of a stream can give rise to different query answers. We have not yet dealt with this issue.

Among the three temporal interpretation of stream queries, two are supported by stream producer agents, continuous and latest-state queries. For latest-state queries, the agent maintains a pool with the latest values of each channel for which its client produces values.

4.5   Republishers

Republishers in R-GMA correspond to the intermediaries in the GMA and resemble materialised views in database systems. Their main usage is to reduce the cost of certain query types, like continuous queries over streams, or to set up an infrastructure that enables queries of that type in the first place, like history queries.

A republisher is defined by one or more queries over the global schema and publishes the answers to those queries. The queries either have to be all continuous or all one-time queries.

A republisher combines the characteristics of a consumer and a producer. Due to the redundancy of information created by republishers, there are often several possibilities to answer a query. Section 5 describes how this is taken into account in the construction of query execution plans for simple stream queries.

Since R-GMA supports essentially two types of queries (one-time and continuous) and two types of producers (database and stream producers), in principle four main types of republishers are conceivable, depending on which query type is combined with which producer type. Currently, R-GMA supports two out of these four possible combinations: *stream republishers* and *archivers*.

Stream Republishers. Stream republishers output the query answers as they are generated, as a stream. In addition, similar to a stream producer agent, the stream republisher agent maintains a pool of latest-state values so that it can answer both continuous and latest-state queries.

Since both input and output are streams, one can build *hierarchies* of stream republishers over several levels. An important usage for such hierarchies is to bundle small flows of data into larger ones and thus reduce communication cost.

Stream producers often publish data obtained from sensors, such as the memory usage of computing elements, which are distributed all over the Grid. While such primary flows of data, to elaborate on the metaphor, tend to be trickles, with stream republishers they can be combined into streams proper. For instance, stream republishers may be used to collect first the memory usage of CEs at one site and, then at the next level up, of those belonging to an entire organisation participating in a Grid. Thus a consumer asking for the memory usage of the CEs at some site only needs to contact the republisher for that site instead of all the individual stream producers.

Archivers. An archiver stores the answers to a collection of continuous queries in a database. For each query, one can specify for how long query answers are stored. If a consumer poses a history query over one or more streams, it is answered using the data in archivers.

4.6   The Registry

We refer to producers and republishers together as *publishers*. Consumer agents need to find publishers that can contribute to answering their query. This is facilitated by R-GMA's *registry*, which records all publishers and consumers that exist at any given point in time. Publishers and consumers send a heartbeat to the registry at predefined intervals to maintain their registration.

When a new publisher is created, its agent contacts the registry to inform it about the type of that publisher. If the publisher is a producer, the agent registers its local relations together with the views on the global schema that describe their content. The registration is only accepted if the producer's view is disjoint from the view of all other producers. If it is a republisher, the agent registers its queries. Similarly, when a consumer is created, the consumer's agent contacts the registry with the consumer's query.

The registry cooperates with the consumer agent in constructing a query plan. It identifies publishers that can contribute to the answers of that query, called the *relevant* publishers. Due to the existence of republishers, there may be some redundancy among the relevant publishers. Therefore, the registry selects those which can contribute maximally, called *maximal* relevant publishers, and returns them to the consumer agent. Then the agent constructs the concrete plan.[2] For each consumer, the registry remembers the query and the list of maximal relevant publishers that it has returned.

When a consumer's query is registered, R-GMA ensures that during the entire lifetime of the consumer it can receive all the data the query asks for. To achieve this, whenever a new producer registers the registry identifies the consumers to which this producer is relevant. Then it inspects the the current list of maximal relevant publishers for the consumer to see whether the data from the new producer will be delivered by some republisher. If not, the new producer is added to the list and the consumer's agent is notified. Similarly, query plans need to be checked when a republisher goes offline because then a consumer may miss data that it has received via that republisher.

Finally, the registry informs consumer agents if a new relevant republisher is created and when a producer goes offline.

5   Republisher Hierarchies

Most queries in R-GMA require the latest values of several stream relations to be joined and aggregated. Consider for example the needs of the resource broker (section 2.2, use case 1). Such a query can be answered efficiently by setting up a hierarchy of republishers to collect the data needed. The complex query can then be answered by the top level republisher, with the help of a DBMS that holds a pool of latest-state values.

---

[2] In section 5 we discuss in detail how the registry selects those publishers for the case of continuous selection queries over streams and how the consumer agent creates the plan.

Each republisher poses a simple continuous query, which is a selection over a single relation. The currently deployed version of R-GMA supports only republishers defined by queries whose selection conditions are conjunctions of equalities of the form "*attr = val*". The next version will also allow comparisons such as "*attr ≤ val*" or tests of the form "*attr* in $(val_1, \ldots, val_n)$".

The creation and maintenance of such republisher hierarchies requires reasoning about the query conditions. We describe a mechanism that constructs and executes plans for the simple continuous queries defined above.

Consider a consumer that poses a continuous query Q over a stream relation r that selects all tuples satisfying a condition C where C involves comparisons and equalities between attributes of r and arbitrary values. Using relational algebra, we can write such a query as $Q = \sigma_C(r)$.

For such a consumer we discuss the query *planning* problem, which consists of locating relevant publishers, and planning how to query these and merge the results. Since republishers also play the role of consumers, the discussion applies to them as well.

Another important problem is the plan *adaptation* problem, which arises when a new publisher comes into existence or when a publisher from which the consumer is streaming ceases to exist. Our theory for query planning provides also a basis for adapting plans to a changed environment. However, due to space limitations we are unable to discuss this point in the present paper.

5.1   Properties of Streams and Stream Publishers

To design a suitable query processing mechanism, we first collect essential properties that all stream publishers in R-GMA are required to have.

Some of these are actually properties of the streams they publish. To ease our presentation, we assume that every stream publisher has only one local relation. This allows us to identify a publisher with its local relation and to denote both with the same letter, like P, R, S. The local relation is described by a view on the global schema, which has the form $\sigma_D(r)$.

We say that two streams are *disjoint* if they do not share any tuples. We say that two publishers are *disjoint* if their streams are disjoint. One can enforce that any two stream producers are disjoint by allowing a new stream producer S to register only if its descriptive view $\sigma_D(r)$ is disjoint from the view $\sigma_{D'}(r)$ of any existing stream producer S', i.e. if $D \wedge D'$ is unsatisfiable.

A publisher is *sound* w.r.t. its descriptive view $\sigma_D(r)$ if its output always consists of tuples that comply with the schema of relation r and satisfy the condition D. In R-GMA soundness of stream producers is enforced by the producer agents, which screen the tuples that are being published.

A publisher is *complete* w.r.t. its view if it outputs every tuple in the system that satisfies the view. Since stream producers are sound and their views are mutually disjoint, a stream producer S_1 can never output a tuple that satisfies the view of another producer S_2. Thus, stream producers are complete by design. For republishers, completeness has to be ensured via appropriate query planning.

A stream is *duplicate free* if it never outputs a tuple twice. This property is important when we compute aggregate values that are sensitive to multiplicities, like counts or sums. A stream is *weakly ordered* if for each channel, the tuples output in the order of their timestamps. We say that a publisher is duplicate free or weakly ordered if its stream has the corresponding property. Again, in R-GMA stream producers are duplicate free and weakly ordered by design because the producer agents attach a timestamp to a tuple when it is published, so that any two tuples are distinct. For republishers, these two properties have to be guaranteed by their query plans.

5.2   Query Plans and Their Properties

A query Q posed against the global schema is executed by querying suitable publishers and combining the results of those local queries. If the global query selects tuples from a single relation the execution is relatively easy: an agent poses selection queries over a collection of publishers and merge the answer streams. This process can be described by a simple kind of query plan. Note that the merging can produce duplicate tuples in the result stream.

Definition 1 (Query Plan). *A plan for a query* $Q = \sigma_C(r)$ *is an expression*

$$\sigma_{C_1}(P_1) \uplus \cdots \uplus \sigma_{C_m}(P_m) \tag{1}$$

where $P_1, \ldots, P_m$ *are stream publishers, each described by a view* $\sigma_{D_i}(r)$.

We say that a *plan* of the form (1) is *sound* or *complete* if the answer stream resulting from the plan is sound or complete w.r.t. query Q, provided the publishers $P_1, \ldots, P_n$ are sound or complete w.r.t. their views $D_1, \ldots, D_n$. Similarly, we say that a plan is *duplicate free* or *weakly orderered* if the answer stream inherits this property whenever the P_i have it. Our next goal is to identify sufficient or, if possible equivalent, formal criteria for each of the four properties.

Soundness. A plan is sound if its output always consists of tuples that answer the query. A *sufficient* criterion for this is that for each $i \in 1..m$, the condition on P_i in the query plan and the condition D_i in the view describing P_i together entail the query condition, i.e.

$$C_i \wedge D_i \models C. \tag{2}$$

Completeness. A plan is complete if every answer to the query can be obtained by executing the plan. More precisely, if t is a tuple satisfying the query condition and S is a stream producer that possibly outputs t, then there is publisher P_i in the plan such that t satisfies C_i and D_i, the view condition of P_i. Logically, this is *equivalent* to the fact that for every stream producer S with view $\sigma_E(r)$ we have

$$C \wedge E \models \bigvee_{i=1}^{m} C_i \wedge D_i. \tag{3}$$

Duplicate Free Plans. A plan as in Definition 1 is certainly duplicate free if two components cannot produce the same tuple, that is, if any two components are disjoint. This means that the conditions

$$(C_i \wedge D_i) \wedge (C_j \wedge D_j) \tag{4}$$

are unsatisfiable for all $i, j \in 1..m$ with $i \neq j$.

Weakly Ordered Plans. If two or more publishers in a plan contribute to the same channel then the order of tuples in a channel can be disturbed due to the merging of their streams. However, the resulting stream of a plan is weakly ordered if the publishers in a plan are weakly ordered and if tuples for a given channel come always from the same publisher.

The latter requirement can be formalised. We write the query condition C as $C(x, y)$, where x stands for the vector of key attributes of r, which identifies a channel, and y for the non-key attributes, including timestamp. Similarly, we write C_i and D_i as $C_i(x, y)$ and $D_i(x, y)$ and abbreviate the conjunction $C_i(x, y) \wedge D_i(x, y)$ as $F_i(x, y)$. Then publisher P_i contributes *all* values y on channel x to the plan, if it contributes *some* values y, provided the following entailment holds:

$$\exists y. \, (C(x, y) \wedge F_i(x, y)) \models \forall y. \, (C(x, y) \rightarrow F_i(x, y)) \tag{5}$$

A plan with this property is called *faithful*. Clearly, a faithful plan is weakly ordered.

Because of the universal quantifier, the entailment (5) is difficult to check in general. However, it can be simplified considerably if, as in R-GMA, conditions on key and on non-key attributes are decoupled, that is, if every condition $C(x, y)$ can be written equivalently as $C^k(x) \wedge C^v(y)$ (and C_i, D_i, F_i analogously). The following proposition can easily be verified using straightforward transformations of logical formulas.

Proposition 1. *Suppose $C(x, y) \equiv C^k(x) \wedge C^v(y)$ and $F_i(x, y) \equiv F_i^k(x) \wedge F_i^v(y)$. Then*

$$\exists y. \, (C(x, y) \wedge F_i(x, y)) \models \forall y. \, (C(x, y) \rightarrow F_i(x, y))$$

holds if and only if one of the following holds:

1. $C^k(x) \wedge F_i^k(x)$ *is unsatisfiable;*
2. $C^v(y) \wedge F_i^v(y)$ *is unsatisfiable;*
3. $C^v(y) \models F_i^v(y)$.

In summary, all plans run by R-GMA have to satisfy four *essential* properties: they have to be sound and complete with respect to the query, as well as duplicate free and weakly ordered. A plan is guaranteed to have these essential properties if it satisfies the properties specified in Formulas (2), (3), (4), and (5).

A plan without the essential four properties above would be outright useless. Other properties are less crucial, but make plans more useful. For instance, a plan should not have a disjunct $\sigma_{C_i}(r)$ that can never contribute an answer, i.e. a disjunct where $C_i \wedge D_i$ is unsatisfiable. More generally, a plan should be *irreducible*, in the sense that it is impossible to create a correct plan with a subset of the publishers involved.

5.3   Query Planning

To create a plan for a query, R-GMA goes through two phases. First, it retrieves a set of candidate publishers from the registry, each of which is maximally general w.r.t. the query. Then, it chooses a subset of the candidates and decides which local query to pose over each of them.

The registry is responsible for the first task, while the consumer (or republisher) agent takes over the second task. A reason why the second task is not left to the registry is that the agent actually contacts the publishers and it may need to modify its plan if some publishers cannot be reached.

Our algorithm works for selection queries and views where the conditions on key and non-key attributes are decoupled, that is, conditions have the form $C^k(x) \wedge C^v(y)$. The algorithm can be extended to the case of disjunctions $\bigvee_i C_i(x, y)$, where each disjunct $C_i(x, y)$ decouples the conditions on keys and non-keys. If no confusion can arise, we drop the arguments x, y of conditions.

Subsumption of Publishers. We want to define when one publisher is more general than another one with regard to a given query. If P and P' are publishers with views $\sigma_D(r)$ and $\sigma_{D'}(r)$, respectively, and $Q = \sigma_C(r)$ is a query, then we say that P is *subsumed* by P' w.r.t. Q and write $P \preceq_Q P'$ if every answer for Q that satisfies the view of P also satisfies the view of P'. Clearly, P is subsumed by P' w.r.t. to Q iff

$$C \wedge D \models D'. \tag{6}$$

We say that P is *strictly subsumed* by P' w.r.t. Q and write $P \prec_Q P'$ if P is subsumed by P' but not vice versa. We say that P is *subsumed* by P' and write $P \preceq P'$ if P is subsumed by P' w.r.t. the universal query $\sigma_{true}(r)$ over r.

Note that the definition of subsumption does not actually refer to the information currently available, since it is only based on the views describing the publishers. It may well be the case that a republisher R' strictly subsumes another republisher R, but in a given environment does not publish any more tuples than R because there are no stream producers generating tuples that R would publish but not R'.

Relevant Publishers. The first step in query planning is to identify publishers that can possibly contribute to a plan for Q. We consider a publisher P with view $\sigma_{D^k \wedge D^v}(r)$ and a query $\sigma_{C^k \wedge C^v}(r)$. Then P can potentially contribute to a plan for Q if its view condition satisfies the following two properties:

1. $C^k \wedge D^k$ is satisfiable   (Channel Consistency);
2. $C^v \models D^v$ (Value Entailment).

The first property states that P offers *at least one* channel that is requested by Q, while the second states that *all* values requested by Q are offered by P. We call a publisher with these two properties *relevant* to Q.

For a given query Q, the registry retrieves all relevant publishers. We note that for restricted classes of conditions relevance can be checked efficiently (see section 6).

Maximal Relevant Publishers. The second step is to single out those publishers among the relevant ones that, with regard to Q, are not strictly subsumed by another relevant publisher. We call such a publisher *maximal*.

We note that due to the value entailment property of relevant publishers, the subsumption test involves only the key attributes. More precisely, for any relevant publishers P_1, P_2 with conditions D_1, D_2 we have that $P_1 \preceq_Q P_2$ if and only if $C^k \wedge D_1^k \models D_2^k$. Again, for sufficiently simple conditions, this can be checked efficiently.

It may be that P_1, P_2 are both maximal and that $P_1 \preceq_Q P_2$. However, in this case we also have $P_2 \preceq_Q P_1$. Obviously, "$\preceq_Q$" is an equivalence relation on the set of maximal publishers. As far as answers to Q are concerned, there is no reason to prefer one of P_1, P_2 to the other for inclusion in a query plan.

To break the tie between equivalent maximal publishers, we apply a heuristic. It is possible that P_1, P_2 subsume each other w.r.t. Q, but P_2 publishes for a more general view than P_1, that is $P_1 \prec P_2$. In such a case, we prefer to contact P_1 rather than P_2, since it is more likely that P_2 will be relevant for another query than P_1.

In summary, when the registry is contacted by a consumer agent with a query Q, then it returns

- all maximal relevant publishers, grouped into equivalence classes w.r.t. "$\preceq_Q$",
- where each equivalence class is topologically sorted w.r.t. "$\preceq$", that is, if P_1 precedes P_2 then it is not the case that $P_2 \prec P_1$.

Constructing Query Plans. The consumer agent receives from the registry the maximal relevant publishers for its query and constructs a plan of the form (1). If among them there are equivalent publishers, then the agent has a choice as to which one to use in its plan. It chooses one publisher from each equivalence class, giving preference to those which are least general w.r.t. subsumption, thus obtaining a sequence of publishers $\langle P_1, \dots, P_m \rangle$.

We call a sequence of publishers $\langle P_1, \dots, P_m \rangle$, obtained by choosing one representative from each class of maximal relevant publishers a *supplier sequence*. Suppose $\langle P_1, \dots, P_m \rangle$ is a supplier sequence where each P_i is described by $\sigma_{D_i}(r)$. We define the *canonical plan* for the sequence as

$$\sigma_{C_1}(P_1) \uplus \cdots \uplus \sigma_{C_m}(P_m) \tag{7}$$

where $C_1 = C$ and $C_i = C \wedge \neg D_1 \wedge \cdots \wedge \neg D_{i-1}$.

Proposition 2 (Canonical Plans). *If $\langle P_1, \ldots, P_m \rangle$ is a supplier sequence for query Q, then the canonical plan for $\langle P_1, \ldots, P_m \rangle$ is sound and complete for Q, and it is duplicate free and weakly ordered.*

Proof. (Sketch) The plan (7) is sound because the condition C_i of each component contains the query condition C as a conjunct. The plan is complete because every stream producer that can contribute a channel is relevant and, due to the construction of a supplier sequence, for each relevant stream producer S the sequence contains a publisher P_i such that $S \preceq_Q P_i$. The plan is duplicate free because all components are disjoint. The plan is weakly ordered because it is faithful. It is faithful because all participating publishers satisfy the definition of relevant publishers.

The canonical plan (7) can often be simplified considerably. Firstly, the conjuncts $\neg D_j$ can be replaced with $\neg D_j^k$, the negated condition on the key attributes. Secondly, the conjunct $\neg D_j$ can be dropped altogether if $D_i \wedge D_j$ is unsatisfiable, which is often the case in practice, e.g. if both publishers are stream producers. For the limited types of conditions that are used in the current implementation of R-GMA (see section 6) this test can be performed efficiently.

Finally, we like to point out that the query planning algorithm can still be used for classes of conditions where entailment and unsatisfiability tests are intractable. In such a case it is sufficient to use checkers that are possibly incomplete, but sound, that is, checkers that recognise some cases of entailment and unsatisfiability, but not all of them. Proposition 2 would still hold in such a case because only the positive outcome of such a test allows us to replace a stream producer by a republisher in a query plan. If the outcome is negative, the stream producer will be used. Thus, incomplete checkers would only forgo opportunities for optimisation.

Irreducible Plans. In general, canonical plans are not irreducible. In fact, in a supplier sequence there is no publisher P_0 that is subsumed (w.r.t. the query) by another publisher P_1. However, it may be the case that P_1 together with another publisher P_2 can contribute the same tuples as P_0.

Example 1. Suppose R_0, R_1, R_2 are republishers for the throughput relation tp, where R_0 republishes measurements for traffic from Heriot-Watt University, R_1 republishes measurements for packets of size at most 10, and R_2 for packets of size at least 10. More formally, each R_i is described by a view $\sigma_{D_i}(\text{tp})$, where $D_0 = (\text{from} = '\text{hw}')$, $D_1 = (\text{psize} \leq 10)$, and $D_2 = (\text{psize} \geq 10)$.

Consider the query $Q = \sigma_{true}(\text{tp})$ and suppose R_0, R_1, R_2 are all the publishers available. Then all three republishers are maximal w.r.t. "$\preceq_Q$". But this set of republishers is not irreducible because R_1 and R_2 together "subsume" R_0.

We have proved that irreducibility of plans is already NP-hard if conditions are conjunctions of comparisons between attributes and values, i.e. comparisons of the form "attr $\{ \geq, \leq \}$ val", as in the example above. However, if the selection conditions can be expressed in Horn logic, one can show that a set of publishers is already irreducible provided no publisher subsumes another one. This is the case, for instance, if conditions are conjunctions of the form "*attr* $\{=, <\}$ *val*" or "*attr* $\{=, >\}$ *val*", where all comparisons have the same orientation.

It seems to us for this reason that in most practical cases an irreducibility test would not yield any improvement over the simpler subsumption check, which is the reason why R-GMA does not perform such a test.

6   R-GMA Implementation

We describe here the current implementation of R-GMA as the DataGrid project enters its final year. An implementation of the full system outlined in sections 4 and 5 is planned for the end of the project.

6.1   Overall Approach

R-GMA offers APIs in several programming languages: C, C++, Java, Perl, and Python. These support the roles described in section 4, e.g. a stream producer. A method invocation on an API object results in a request being sent to an agent object, running in a web server. This then acts on behalf of the component using the API.

The system presents the illusion of have a single registy and schema. However, these components are replicated to meet the resilience requirement (section 2.2). Registry replication is based on the gossip architecture: all copies of the registry swap messages periodically to keep each other up to date. A component can thus interact with any copy of the registry as if it were the only registry, and this ensures that the load is shared across registry instances.

The gossip architecture cannot be used for the schema because otherwise two users who simultaneously access the schema could introduce conflicting relations. Instead, a master-slave model is used: one of the schema instances is elected the leader and only the leader can allow the creation of a new relation. The other schema instances act as backups, but can also answer queries about relations.

6.2   R-GMA Components

Consumers. The consumer API allows users to pose continuous, latest-state and history queries in SQL. Generally, global queries may be posed over just one table of the schema, and are restricted to select-project queries. However, arbitrary one-time SQL queries can be answered if a republisher for all the relations of the query can be located. Results are *streamed* to the agent and merged so that quick partial answers can be returned, say, to a resource broker.

Producers. An ideal R-GMA system would offer two types of producer, stream and database producers. Our implementation only offers stream producers, and currently static information is published as streams. This was found to be the quickest and simplest way of providing minimal functionality for DataGrid.

Republishers. At present, our implementation only supports streams so it only offers two types of republisher: stream republishers and archivers. A hierarchy of stream republishers can be set up manually to merge streams together. Work is underway to automate this by implementing the algorithms presented in section 5.

Registry. Publishers may only register views over single relations with conditions that are conjunctions of equalities of the form "*attr* = *val*". With this simplification, the satisfiability and entailment tests of section 5 can be expressed as queries over the registry's database. So far, the entailment tests are trivial, as only republishers of entire relations are considered at the moment for query planning.

Schema. Built into R-GMA are a set of core relations known as the GLUE schema [4]. These relations were defined by a number of Grid projects, including DataGrid, and describe the components of a Grid, such as computing elements. However, publishers may also introduce new relations into the global schema.

Our implementation only supports a restricted set of types: Varchar, Real and Int. However, this simplifies the query planning task.

6.3   Performance of the Current R-GMA

Our limited implementation of R-GMA is currently undergoing resilience and performance testing on testbeds within DataGrid. An early result is that a consumer is able to merge data published every 30 seconds from up to 40 typical sites (one SE, three CEs). The performance is likely to benefit from republisher hierarchies.

7   Conclusions

We conclude with a brief discussion about how far R-GMA meets the requirements outlined at the beginning.

R-GMA allows for the publication of streaming and static data, although the current implementation only offers stream producers. The schema provides a global view of all the data available in the system. The registry can locate data sources that would be of interest to a user. It does so by matching a query that is posed against the global schema with suitable publishers. Scalability is provided through the replication of the registry and schema components, and the merging of small streams of data by hierarchies of stream republishers.

We have not yet addressed the issue of security. An approach using views describing which data a user is authorised to access may be appropriate.

Although R-GMA has been designed for monitoring the components of a computational Grid, it is a general architecture and could be used for other applications that require querying distributed pools and streams of data.

References

1. The DataGrid Project. http://www.eu-datagrid.org, June 2003.
2. DataGrid WP3 Information and Monitoring Services. http://hepunx.rl.ac.uk/ edg/wp3/, June 2003.
3. Global grid forum. http://www.ggf.org, June 2003.
4. High energy nuclear physics intergrid collaboration board. http://hicb.org/, June 2003.
5. B. Babcock, Sh. Babu, M. Datar, R. Motwani, and J. Widom. Models and issues in data stream systems. In *PODS-21*, pages 1–16, 2002.
6. F. Berman. From TeraGrid to Knowledge Grid. *Communications of the ACM*, 44(11):27–28, 2001.
7. D. Carney, U. Cetintemel, M. Cherniack, C. Convey, S. Lee, G. Seidman, M. Stonebraker, N. Tatbul, and S. Zdonik. Monitoring streams—a new class of data management applications. In *VLDB-28*, pages 215–226, 2002.
8. K. Czajkowski, S. Fitzgerald, I. Foster, and C. Kesselman. Grid information services for distributed resource sharing. In *HPDC-10*, 2001.
9. L. Dutka and J. Kitowski. Application of component-expert technology for selection of data-handlers in CrossGrid. In *Proc. 9th European PVM/MPI Users' Group Meeting*, volume 2474 of *LNCS*, pages 25–32. Springer, 2002.
10. I. Foster and C. Kesselman. *The Grid: Blueprint for a New Computing Infrastructure*, chapter 2: Computational Grids, pages 15–51. Morgan Kaufmann, 1999.
11. I. Foster, C. Kesselman, and S. Tuecke. The anatomy of the Grid: Enabling scalable virtual organization. *The International Journal of High Performance Computing Applications*, 15(3):200–222, 2001.
12. Globus Toolkit. http://www.globus.org, June 2003.
13. W.E. Johnston, D. Gannon, and B. Nitzberg. Grids as production computing environments: the engineering aspects of NASA's Information Power Grid. In *HPDC-11*, pages 197–204. IEEE, 1999.
14. B. Plale, P. Dinda, and G. von Laszewski. Key concepts and services of a Grid information service. In *ICSA PDCS-15*, 2002.
15. R.L. Ribler, J.S. Vetter, H. Simitci, and D.A. Reed. Autopilot: adaptive control of distributed applications. In *HPDC-7*, pages 172–179, 1998.
16. C. Shahabi. AIMS: an Immersidata management system. In *CIDR-2003*, 2003.
17. W. Smith. A system for monitoring and management of computational Grids. In *ICPP-31*, pages 55–, 2002.
18. M. Sullivan. Tribeca: A stream database manager for network traffic analysis. In *VLDB-22*, page 594, 1996.
19. B. Tierney, R. Aydt, D. Gunter, W. Smith, M. Swany, V. Taylor, and R. Wolski. A Grid monitoring architecture. Global Grid Forum Performance Working Group, March 2000. Revised January 2002.
20. J.D. Ullman. Information integration using logical views. In *ICDT-6*, volume 1186 of *LNCS*, pages 19–40. Springer, 1997.

CREAM: An Infrastructure for Distributed, Heterogeneous Event-Based Applications

M. Cilia*, C. Bornhövd**, and A.P. Buchmann

Databases and Distributed Systems Group, Department of Computer Science
Darmstadt University of Technology – Darmstadt, Germany
lastname@informatik.tu-darmstadt.de

Abstract. Applications ranging from event-based supply chain management to enterprise application integration and pervasive computing depend on the timely detection and notification of events. We present CREAM the event-based reactive component of the DREAM middleware platform. Here we address four key issues in distributed and heterogeneous environments: event detection and notification, event composition, an active functionality service, and ontology support. We show the need for ontology support at all levels in heterogeneous environments and present a distributed active functionality service that addresses the difficult issues of event composition in widely distributed environments. We illustrate the practicality of the proposed approach through two prototypes that are based on this infrastructure: a meta-auction service and a personalized service offering in Internet-enabled vehicles.

Keywords: Event-based applications; event handling; publish/subscribe; concept-based addressing; data integration; business rules.

1 Introduction

Application are moving away from tightly-coupled systems towards systems of loosely-coupled, dynamically bound components. This trend fits the event-based application paradigm which is well suited for integrating autonomous, heterogeneous components into complex systems by means of detecting and exchanging events. Since event-based systems do not require a-priori knowledge about the consumers of events they are easy to evolve and scale.

However, the exchanged events encapsulate data about a given happening of interest, which can only be properly interpreted and used when sufficient context information is known. In traditional, centralized systems this context information is typically known by the users and left implicit. It is normally lost when data and events are exchanged across component or institutional boundaries. To process events in a semantically meaningful way, explicit information about the semantics of events and data is required. Moreover, event-based systems use an event dissemination mechanism, such as a publish/subscribe mechanism, which

---

* also Faculty of Sciences, UNICEN, Tandil, Argentina
** IBM Almaden Research Center, USA. cborn@us.ibm.com

R. Meersman et al. (Eds.): CoopIS/DOA/ODBASE 2003, LNCS 2888, pp. 482–502, 2003.
© Springer-Verlag Berlin Heidelberg 2003

allows for asynchronous communication. Producers and consumers must share a common understanding in order to express their mutual interests.

The reaction to events on the application-side represents part of the business processes and, in general, is hard-coded. Since the domain knowledge is scattered and hard-wired into applications it has been difficult to adapt to new requirements quickly.

CREAM (Concept-based REActive Mechanism) is the reactive component of DREAM [1], a flexible middleware platform for developing open distributed and heterogeneous event-based applications. CREAM supports from the ground up ontologies that provide the base for correct data and event interpretation. Rather than requiring every producer or consumer to use the same homogeneous namespace (as is common in other pub/sub systems) we provide metadata and conversion functions to map from one context to another. On top of it a higher level addressing model for event dissemination is proposed. Event-triggered business rules can be explicitly defined and managed to adapt to new business requirements. For instance, modern large-scale applications, such as e-commerce, event-based supply chain management (ESCM), Internet or Intranet applications, enterprise application integration (EAI), and emerging pervasive systems, can effectively benefit from this infrastructure.

The power of CREAM is illustrated with the help of two case studies for which prototypes have been built: a meta-auction application and the personalization of car and driver portals in Internet-enabled vehicles. Examples presented throughout this paper are related to these scenarios.

The remainder of this paper is organized as follows. In Section 2 related work in the four main areas contributing to our event-based middleware platform is presented. Section 3 provides an overview of the proposed approach with additional detail presented in the corresponding subsections. An outline of the implementation of the infrastructure and two case studies built on top of it is given in Section 4. Conclusions and future work are presented in Section 5.

2   Related Work

The work presented in this paper involves the following areas: event dissemination, complex event detection, rule processing and data/event integration. Problems in individual areas have been solved for homogeneous and centralized environments but are much harder in heterogeneous, distributed environments where they have not been solved yet. Due to space limitations it is not possible to provide a more detailed discussion of related work. Therefore, the reader is pointed to [2,3] for additional discussion of related research.

2.1   Event Dissemination

In distributed environments events must be propagated to all interested consumers. For this purpose, event notification services, or notification services for short, are widely used. In CORBA an event service [4] was introduced to provide a mechanism for asynchronous interaction between CORBA objects. Here, an event channel acts as a mediator between suppliers and consumers of events. To overcome deficiencies of this service specification, the notification service [5] was proposed as a major extension with support for quality of service specifications and basic event filtering.

The Java Message Service (JMS) [6] provides the Java technology platform with the ability to process asynchronous messages. JMS was originally developed to provide a common Java interface (API) to legacy Message Oriented Middleware (MOM) products. This API brings portability of Java code which facilitates the replacement of the underlying messaging service without affecting existing code. JMS provides two models for messaging among clients: point-to-point (using a queue) and publish/subscribe (by means of topics). JMS was incorporated as an integral part of the Enterprise Java Beans (EJB) component model in the EJB 2.0 specification by defining a new bean type, known as message-driven bean (MDB). This new bean acts as a message consumer providing asynchrony to EJB-based applications.

In the past few years, publish/subscribe mechanisms have got more attention because they offer loosely coupled exchange of asynchronous notifications, facilitating extensibility and flexibility. The channel model has evolved to a more flexible subscription mechanism, known as subject-based, where a subject is attached to each notification [7]. Subject-based addressing features a set of rules that defines a uniform name space for messages and their destinations. This approach is inflexible if changes to the subject organization are required, implying fixes in all participating applications.

In order to improve expressiveness of subscriptions the content-based approach was proposed where predicates on the content of a notification can be used for subscriptions. This approach is more flexible but requires a more complex infrastructure [8]. Many projects in this category concentrate on scalability issues in wide-area networks and on efficient algorithms and techniques for matching and routing notifications to reduce network traffic [9,10,11]. Most of these approaches use simple Boolean expressions as subscription patterns and assume homogeneous name spaces.

2.2   Detecting Composite Events in Distributed Environments

The approaches mentioned in the previous section do not consider event composition. That means that they filter event notifications trying to deliver events of interest to consumers without considering any correlation with other event occurrences. Event composition involves the occurrence of two or more events. Composite events are expressed using an event algebra, such as those defined in HiPAC [12], or Snoop [13]. Such algebras require an order function between events to apply event operators (e.g. sequence), or to consume events. To determine which of these events should be consumed or selected, different consumption modes were defined [14]. Usually, events are timestamped to provide a time-based order with the purpose of facilitating event selection. However, in open distributed environments global time is not applicable.

An approximation for modeling the time imprecision in distributed systems has been proposed [15], which is known as the *2g-precedence* model. Since an upper bound to the precision is assumed, this model is not appropriated for wide area networks and open distributed systems. In [16] an approach for timestamping events in large-scale, loosely coupled distributed systems is proposed. This uses accuracy intervals with reliable error bounds for timestamping events that reflect the inherent inaccuracy in time measurements.

Schwiderski [17] adopted the 2g-precedence model to deal with distributed event ordering and composite event detection. She proposed a distributed event detector based on a global event tree and introduced 2g-precedence-based sequence and concurrency operators. However, event consumption is non-deterministic in the case of concurrent or unrelated events. Additionally, the violation of the granularity condition (2g) may lead to the detection of spurious events.

Many projects on event composition in distributed environments such as [18,19,20] either do not consider the possibility of partial event ordering or are based on the 2g-precedence model. Therefore, they suffer from one or more of the following drawbacks [16]: they do not scale to open systems, they provide the possibility of spurious events, or they present ambiguous event consumption.

Systems that support composite events must also address the semantic issues associated with processing composite events. For example, how timestamps are generated and the way in which events are selected and consumed.

2.3   Active Functionality

Once simple or composite events are detected a proper reaction must be performed. Reactive mechanisms were introduced in the late '80s in the form of Event-Condition-Action rules (ECA-rules) in active databases (aDBMS) [21]. The goal of active databases was to avoid unnecessary and resource intensive polling in monitoring applications where events are detected as changes to a database and the application reacts to the occurrence of these events.

Active functionality developed for a particular DBMS became part of a large monolithic piece of software (the DBMS). Active functionality tightly coupled to a concrete DBMS hinders its adaptation to today's Internet applications, such as e-commerce, where heterogeneity and distribution play a significant role but are not directly supported by traditional (active) database systems [22]. Another weakness of tightly coupled aDBMSs is that active functionality cannot be used on its own without the full data management functionality. However, active functionality is also needed in applications that require no database functionality at all, or that require only simple persistence support. Consequently, active functionality needs to be offered as a separate service that can be combined.

The unbundling of active databases consists of separating the active part from active DBMSs and breaking it up into components providing services like event detection, rule definition, rule management, and execution of ECA rules on the one hand, and persistence, transaction management and query processing services on the other [22]. Afterwards, only necessary components can be rebundled in order to provide the required functionality. A separation of active and conventional database functionality would allow the use of active capabilities depending on given application needs without the overhead of components that are not needed. Various projects like C^2offein [23], FRAMBOISE [24], and NODS [25] have followed this approach.

Unbundling in this context means to give up the "closed world" assumption that traditionally underlies a DBMS and therefore its applicability in an open distributed environment is questionable. This is because of the inherent characteristics of such environments that impose new requirements that were not considered in centralized environments, such as the lack of global time, independent failures of nodes or communication channels, message delays, etc. The consideration of these characteristics has an enormous impact on the event detector [16], which is the essential component of an aDBMS [26]. In [27] crosseffects and potential incompatibilities arising from the combination of selective features of active, real-time and distributed object systems are discussed.

2.4   Heterogeneity

The need for additional semantic metadata for the exchange of data or messages among independent applications or services has been clearly identified, not only in the context of B2B frameworks like ebXML [28], BizTalk [29], or RosettaNet [30] but also by the W3C in efforts like Semantic Web [31], or DAML+OIL [32].

In the first case, XML [33] and XML Schema [34] are used to define common vocabularies to describe data and business processes. XML tags may be explicitly defined in a XML Schema and can be used to give hints about the assumed meaning of the represented data. XML Namespaces [35] allow to contextualize XML tags in the sense of distinguishing different meanings of the same tag name.

In the context of W3C's Semantic Web initiative RDF [36] and RDF Schema [37] are used to provide additional semantic metadata to better enable computer and users to exchange and integrate data. RDF provides an infrastructure that supports the representation and exchange of structured metadata to describe Web resources, like (parts of) Web pages, or other RDF metadata. RDF allows the description of properties of and interrelationships among those resources in terms of ⟨resource, attribute, value⟩ triples. The attributes used can be declared in RDF Schemas which, similar to XML Schemas, give information about their intended meaning, and specify restrictions on their values. RDF Schemas and XML Schemas can play a role similar to ontologies as a common semantic basis for data and metadata representation.

In our framework we use the MIX model [2,38] for the representation of event content. Like XML/XML-Schema or RDF/RDF Schema MIX provides a flexible representation model for data plus additional metadata based on a common domain-specific vocabulary. However, in addition to the functionality provided by the data models discussed above, MIX directly supports data integration by making the concept of semantic context (i.e., the explicit description of implicit assumptions about the meaning of the data) and conversion functions (which allow the automatic conversion of data/events from different sources to a common context) first class citizens of the model itself. MIX should not be seen as an alternative to the models being developed in the context of the W3C but as a complementing approach that provides features that hopefully will find their way into the other XML-based models and standards.

3   Our Approach

CREAM provides a middleware platform for distributed, heterogeneous event-based applications. Such middleware requires event handling, support for integration of heterogeneous data and events, monitoring capabilities, reaction to events and of course an event dissemination service. Our approach is based on an ontology infrastructure which is the key to achieve our goal. Events are described with ontology concepts and are augmented with additional context information allowing in this way their correct interpretation outside the boundaries of an event source. On this basis, a concept-based notification service is proposed with the objective to provide event producers and consumers with a common level of abstraction to describe their interests.

More and more, event-based applications need to detect complex situations based on the event stream. For this purpose, a complex event detection mechanism that takes into consideration issues related to open distributed environments is proposed. ECA-rules are incorporated to avoid the definition of reactions to simple and complex events in the form of hard-wired code in the applications. Again, these high-level (business) rule definitions are based on the ontology providing the ability to define them using the most adequate domain specific language without affecting the active mechanism underneath. This active mechanism relies on a service-based architecture where elementary ECA-rule services are composed according to rule definitions. These elementary services are able to interact with external systems or services but always taking into account the data/event assumptions of the system they interact with.

3.1   Ontology Support

The event-based approach carries the potential for integrating autonomous, heterogeneous components into complex systems by means of exchanging events. These events encapsulate data about a given happening of interest, which can only be properly interpreted and used when sufficient context information about its intended meaning is known. In general, this context information (at least the larger part of it) is left implicit and as a consequence is lost when data/events are exchanged across institutional or system boundaries. For this reason, to exchange and process events from independent sources in a semantically meaningful way, explicit information about its semantics in the form of additional metadata is required. Our infrastructure is founded on the use of shared concepts expressed through common ontologies [39,40,41,42]. By *concept* we understand an abstraction of characteristics common to a set of real world phenomena. By associating a specific concept with a data object we describe the correspondence between the data and the respective real world phenomena.

Depending on the application domain at hand, ontologies as they are used in our infrastructure, can be obtained by negotiation between a small set of companies (like in the case of EDI), by a consortium responsible for providing standards for a given domain (e.g., the Unicorn standard [43] for travel data), or by formalizing existing commonly used vocabularies (e.g., for stock trading) by a service provider. It is important that ontologies, other than database schemas for example, are source-independent and need to be extensible to be useable in real-life situations.

We represent events, or to be more precise event content, using a self-describing data model called MIX [2,38]. MIX refers to concepts from a domain-specific ontology to enable the semantically correct interpretation of event content. Simple attributes of an event are represented as triplets of the form $\langle C, v, \$ \rangle$, with C referring to a concept from the underlying ontology, v representing the actual data value, and $\$$ providing a set of additional meta-attributes (also known as the *semantic context* of v) to make implicit modeling assumptions explicit. The semantic context specifies the interpretation context of a data value and is also represented as MIX data objects. For example, the fuel level of a gas tank can be represented as $\langle$ *FuelLevel, 20,* $\{\langle$ *VolumeUnit, "Liter"* $\rangle, \langle$ *ScalingFactor, 1* $\rangle\}\rangle$.

Complex data objects are represented in MIX as $\langle C, \mathbb{A} \rangle$ pairs, where C refers to a concept from the common ontology, and $\mathbb{A}$ provides the set of simple or complex sub-objects that represent its attributes. These attributes are divided into those that are mandatory, and additional attributes that are optional. Identifying attributes, which are used, similar to key attributes in the relational model, to identify an object of a given concept have to be mandatory attributes. For example[1], a PlaceBid event can be represented with a complex semantic object as follows:

```
CSO = <PlaceBid, {<ParticipantId, 412, {<IdentifierCode,"eBayCode">}>,
                  <ItemId, 5423, {<IdentifierCode, "eBayCode">}>,
                  <BidAmount, 99, {<Currency, "USD">, < Scale, 1>}>,
                  <ParticipantType, "Gold">,
                  ...} >
```

In the following, we refer to events represented in the MIX model, i.e., based on concepts from the common ontology and enhanced by additional context metadata as *semantic events*. Semantic events from different heterogeneous sources can be integrated by converting them to a common semantic context using conversion functions. Conversion functions can be specified in the underlying ontology if they are domain-specific and application-independent. Application- or service-specific conversion functions may be defined and stored in an application-specific conversion library [38].

As depicted in Fig. 1, we use ontologies at three different levels of abstraction:

---

[1] Mandatory attributes are underlined for presentation purposes.

- *Basic Representation Ontology*: defines concepts like Integer or String for the platform-independent representation of data. It is domain-independent and provides the basis for the higher levels of the ontology.
- *Infrastructure-specific Ontology*: contains the concepts needed for describing the infrastructure, i.e., event hierarchy, time notions, and notifications.
- *Domain-specific Ontology*: provides all the concepts needed for a particular domain. For example, PlaceBid, BidAmount, etc. for auctions and FuelLevel, VehicleStatus, GetInto, etc. for the Internet-enabled car.

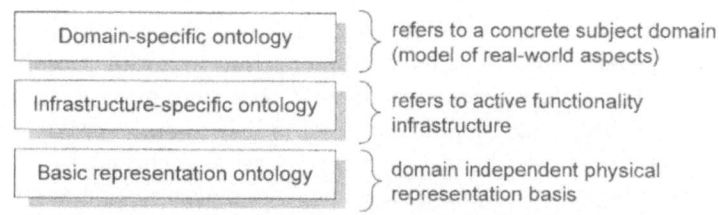

Fig. 1. Three abstraction levels of ontology concepts

Concept definitions from the last two levels are associated with a physical representation by inheriting from an appropriate concept of the basic representation ontology.

3.2   Events and Notifications

An *event* is a happening of interest. Events coming from diverse sources must be mapped to the common vocabulary. This is basically the task of *event adapters*. These components convert source-specific events into their corresponding concepts of the ontology augmented with semantic contexts. Event adapters deliver a semantic event. The association of context information with events serves as an explicit specification of the implicit assumptions made by the event source. Without this additional information the event content cannot be correctly interpreted once the event leaves the source boundaries. Based on the explicit description of the underlying context these semantic heterogeneities can be resolved by converting the data to a common context using appropriate conversion functions. As mentioned before, this common context is specified by the consumer of the semantic event. For instance, consider the placement of a bid that is generated at an American auction site. This happening is then mapped into the PlaceBid concept and the assumptions about the data involved are attached in the form of semantic context. Taking a closer look at one of its attributes, e.g. the bid amount, it is augmented with USD as currency in order to be correctly interpreted outside this particular auction site. PlaceBid consumers can specify the currency of interest, e.g. Euro, as the target context. This conversion is automatically done by the ontology support.

A *notification* is a message reporting a semantic event to interested consumers. A notification carries not only data about the event itself but also important operational data, such as detection time, event source, time-to-live, etc. Concepts related to notifications (e.g. Notification, OperationalData, Detection-Time, EventSource, TimeToLive) are specified as part of the infrastructure-specific ontology. On the other side, concepts related to the content of semantic events should be specified in the corresponding domain-specific ontology.

3.3   Event Dissemination

A *notification service* based on the publish/subscribe paradigm is responsible for delivering events to interested consumers. Here a notification flows from an event producer to one or more consumers. Consumers place a standing request for events by subscribing. A publisher makes information available for its subscribers. A publish/subscribe mechanism provides asynchronous communication, it naturally decouples producers and consumers, makes them anonymous to each other, allows a dynamic number of publishers and subscribers, and provides location transparency without requiring a name service.

In order to provide a higher level of abstraction to describe the interests of publishers and subscribers, *concept-based addressing* is proposed for our framework. Since semantic events are represented with concepts of the ontology, consumers can benefit from this situation and can specify their subscription patterns by also using the underlying ontology. In this way, consumers do not need to take care of proprietary representations and all participants use a common vocabulary not only for its physical and structural representation but also for expressing their interests. In addition, publishers do not require to specify additional information for event dissemination since the destination of notifications is determined by self-contained information.

The delivery of notifications to consumers is the responsibility of the delivery mechanism. Consequently, there is a correspondence between the concept-based approach and the addressing model (i.e. content-based, subject-based) of the underlying delivery mechanism. The latter is responsible for using efficiently the resources involved (network bandwidth, size of routing tables, etc.)[2] while the concept-based approach is responsible of providing a common level of abstraction for producers and consumers.

In our current implementation the concept-based addressing is built on top of a commercial delivery mechanism that uses the subject-based addressing model. Before getting into more details about the mapping between these two models, subject-based addressing needs to be introduced. Subjects define a uniform name space for messages and their destinations. A subject is associated with each notification. Subject names consist of one or more elements (usually a string) organized in a tree by means of a dot notation. Subjects are used to direct notifications to their destinations. Therefore, notifications need

---

[2] It is out of the scope of this paper to discuss routing algorithms and efficient use of the brokers' resources. For a detailed discussion see [44].

to have attached a specific subject which is a path on the subject tree e.g.
NEWS.SPORTS.BASKETBALL. Subscribers could also use wildcards for subscription purposes (e.g. NEWS.SPORTS.*).

In our prototype the subject name space is organized in two main parts. The
first one is to provide control of the destination of notifications (if needed). This
control part is used to concatenate services in the service chain (more details in
Section 3.6). The second part is used to capture the content of the semantic event
in question. For this purpose, the subject for a semantic event is derived from its
identifying attributes. This mapping is done by flattening the semantic event into
a subject structure. The first position of the subject is used for its concept name
and subsequent positions are used to locate the value of identifying attributes by
traversing the semantic event. Notice that both parts of the subject organization
are configurable. That is, the number of fields that form part of the control as
well as the depth of the traversing algorithm for mapping event content into a
subject can be configured. All this information and the name space organization
is maintained in a repository.

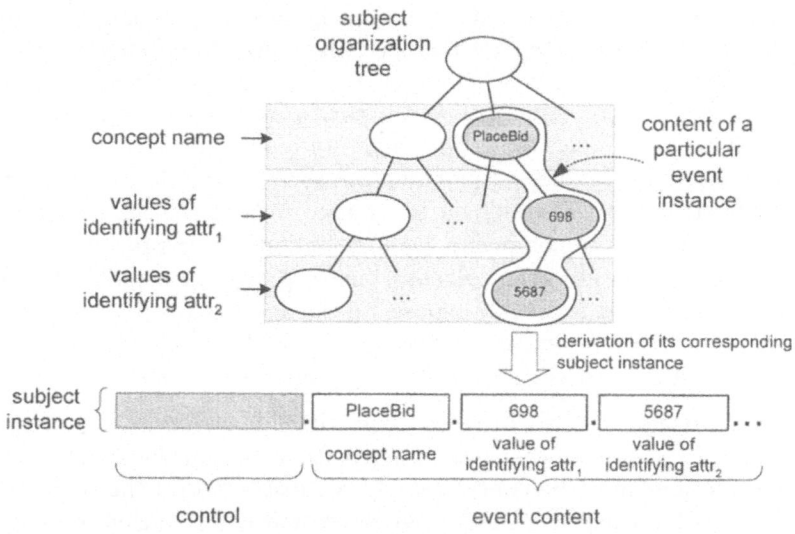

Fig. 2. Subject organization and subject instance derivation

Figure 2 shows how the content of a semantic event is mapped into the subject
model and how a particular subject instance is derived. The obtained subject
instance is attached to the notification that corresponds to the event in question
and then the notification is passed to the underlying delivery mechanism.

3.4   Composite Event Detection

Composite events involve the occurrence of two or more events. The component events can be simple events or may be composite events themselves. Composition is described through an event algebra. Event composition in its general form depends on the ability to determine the order of occurrence of events. The determination of this order is important not only for event operators such as sequence, but also for all other operators since the consumption of events directly depends on it[3]. Logical clocks can not be used for this purpose because they can not represent timed real world events. Therefore, event order is achieved by using timestamps that are attached to event occurrences.

In addition to defining an event algebra, middleware platforms that support event composition must also address the semantic issues associated with processing composite events. For example, the manner in which timestamps are generated and interpreted, and the way in which events are selected and consumed. Consequently, the adopted assumptions must be clearly exposed to the application developers and it must be possible for them to influence the service behavior by applying (predefined or user-defined) policies.

Inherent characteristics of distributed environments increase the difficulty of composite event detection and invalidate the use of approaches designed for centralized systems. Consider, for instance, the reuse of operators implemented for centralized environments where a total order of events was assumed and no transmission delays or failures were considered. Even though the intended meaning of the event operator is the same, its implementation may be invalid and demand a re-design due to the requirements of the distributed environment.

Our infrastructure was designed to be used in a variety of scenarios. This impacts the semantics of composite event detection. Therefore, the objective is not to define yet another event algebra but to provide a flexible platform for event composition that explicitly exposes to the application developer the decisions that must be taken and the policies that must be applied under particular circumstances. Three areas that received particular attention are:

- **Proper interpretation of time.** Since this infrastructure was designed to be used in a variety of scenarios different time assumptions and timestamp representations must be considered. At an abstract level the required functionality is basically the same in all cases: find a correlation among timestamps. Two main issues must be solved: i) how to represent timestamps in a flexible and open yet "understandable" way, and ii) how to correlate them. Timestamps and their related concepts are defined in the ontology. An abstract timestamp concept is defined and particular timestamp representations can be specialized for different scenarios and environments according to the adopted time model.
  To correlate events, the functionality of the abstract timestamp concept includes the methods **before** and **after** while the internal data representation

---

[3] Four consumption modes were defined in [14]. Recent and chronicle are of most common use. Recent selects the latest event occurrences of a given type, while chronicle selects the oldest event occurrences of a given type out of the event stream.

is maintained hidden. These methods must be specialized for each particular time model. Additionally, these methods throw exceptions when decisions cannot be taken transferring the decision control to a higher level, where application semantics can be used for resolution.

– **Consideration of transmission delays**. Incoming events are maintained in a temporary data structure (the EventList) before they are used for composition. Since it is the intermediary between event producers and the event composition, it is the appropriate place to tackle the problem of transmission delays, failures at event producers, network failures, and also the order and uncertainty issues when working with event streams. Specifically, our implemented approach combines a window scheme with a heartbeat protocol. When a producer node crashes or the network is partitioned an exception can be raised and treated by a failure handling policy. A *window mechanism* that works in tandem with the heartbeat protocol is used to separate the history of events (or event stream) into the *stable past* and the *unstable past and present* that still are subject to change. For composition purposes only events in the stable past are considered.

– **Adoption of partial order of events**. A partial order of events is adopted. With this in mind, correlation methods should include the possibility of throwing an exception (e.g. cannotDecide) in order to announce an uncertainty when comparing timestamps. That means that the underlying infrastructure is responsible for announcing an ambiguous situation to a higher level of decision, allowing the use of application semantics for the resolution. Events from the stable past are maintained (partially) ordered in the EventList according to the consumption mode criteria. EventList also implements the *event consumption interface* that is used for selecting and consuming events. With the provisions taken, it can be guaranteed in all cases that: i) situations of uncertain timestamp order are detected and the action taken is exposed and well defined, and ii) events are not erroneously ordered.

The composite event detector service is based on components and containers. Components are the event operators that are plugged into compositor containers. The container itself is the composite event detector kernel which controls the event detection process. As shown in Figure 3, the container has attached, in this case, two EventLists that play the role of event operands. Additionally, they are configured with appropriate policies according to the definition of the composite event that must be detected.

Components are responsible for the logic of the event operator. They implement the method evaluate. Components specialize the EventOperator class by re-writing the evaluate method according to the operator they represent. More details about the implementation can be found in [3].

The logic of operators detects the situation of interest. Other aspects are now under the responsibility of the EventList which implements the order in which events are accessed through the event consumption interface. The consideration of failures and transmission delays, as well as uncertainty issues are solved at the EventList by applying pre-configured policies.

Because of its uniform design, compositors can cooperate in the detection of other composite events. Compositors publish detected events in the same way primitive events are published. Thus, the output of a compositor can be used for subscription of other parties. Consequently, each compositor can be seen as an abstract tree where primitive events are injected at the leaves and compositors are located in the internal nodes. Detected events are pushed to the upper layer in the tree by using the publish mechanism. The whole composite event is detected once an event is published at the root of the tree.

3.5 ECA-Rule Definition

Rule representation is organized into three layers (see Figure 4):

- *external:* allows the tailoring of a rule's definition for each specific domain making the specification of rules convenient without the complexities imposed by a generic rule definition language. This is the layer seen by the *end-users.*
- *conceptual:* provides independence between the implementation of the underlying active mechanism and an end-user's rule definition. Concepts like Rule, Event, Condition, Action, etc. and their specialization are representatives of this layer. This is the layer of the *system developers.*
- *internal:* enables the use of a "generic" active functionality service where components or services that are involved can be implemented using different optimization criteria or different programming languages, but they all "understand" the conceptual layer while using an internal representation to process rules. This is the layer of the *service implementors.*

It must be borne in mind that domain-specific and infrastructure-specific terminology are represented here using ontologies as described previously. On this basis, developers can provide various "external" alternatives to end-users in order to define rules taking into account the domain in question, the target end-users, etc. Notice that details about event consumption, or coupling modes can

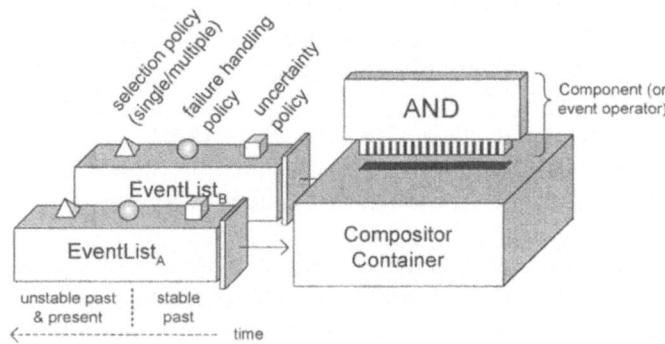

Fig. 3. Abstract view of an event compositor

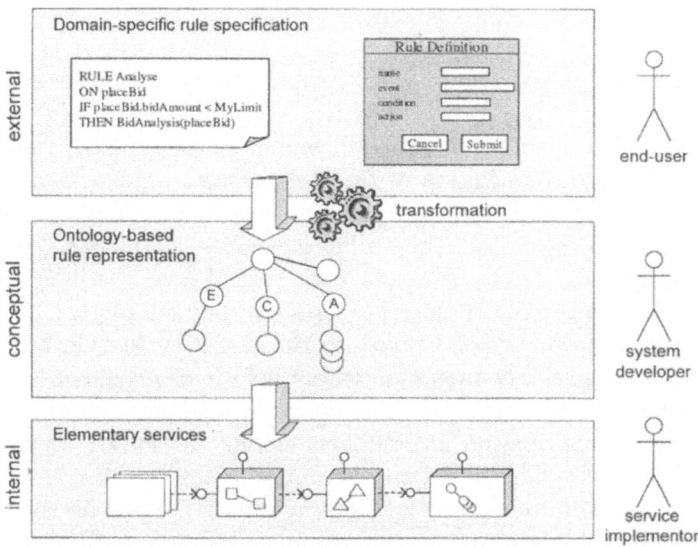

Fig. 4. Rule representation layers

be specified by the system developer hiding in this way such details from the end-user.

From the developer's point of view, all these alternatives rely on an *Ontology API* that facilitates the access and manipulation of the ontologies. In this way, all kinds of external rule definitions produce an ontology-based (conceptual) rule representation as output. As mentioned above, this conceptual rule representation provides independence between the underlying active mechanism and the end-users' rule definitions.

With the aid of ontologies as the foundation of our infrastructure, the definition of rules can benefit from the use of semantic contexts. Contexts can be associated with conditions and actions in order to evaluate them under the defined contextual information. For instance, a condition predicate that verifies distances can define "metric system" as its context. In this manner, incoming events from heterogeneous sources are first converted into the metric system (if necessary) before they are used for evaluation. Consequently, conditions and actions are always specified at a domain-specific level, and are independent of source-specific representations. This provides a very useful and powerful mechanism for interpreting events from heterogeneous sources by maintaining a high-level specification.

3.6   Service-Based ECA-Rule Processing

In CREAM, traditional ECA-rule processing is decomposed into its elementary parts (aka elementary services). These autonomous services are responsible for composite event detection, condition evaluation, and action execution. Elementary services expose two kinds of generic and very simple interfaces: i) a *service interface* with a single method that receives an event notification as an argument; ii) a *configuration interface* that is used for administration purposes, such as registration, activation, deactivation, deletion, etc. This service interface provides flexibility, enabling a simple interaction among services. ECA-rule processing is then realized as a composition of these elementary services according to the rule definition. Elementary services involved in its processing can interact with external services or systems (e.g. workflow engines, databases, Web Services) through *plug-ins* in order to complete their task. Plug-ins are also responsible for maintaining the target context of the system they interact with making possible the automatic conversion of data to the target system. From an abstract point of view, this service composition takes the form of a chain of services, where semantic event instances flow through the composed services to carry out the corresponding rule processing. Interactions among elementary services involved in the processing of a rule can be carried out by using traditional request/reply protocols. However, in our prototype interactions are based on the notification service described before providing several advantages as natural decoupling of services, asynchronous communication, location transparency to mention a few. Figure 5 shows the interaction among elementary services, where boxes denote services and lollipops their interfaces.

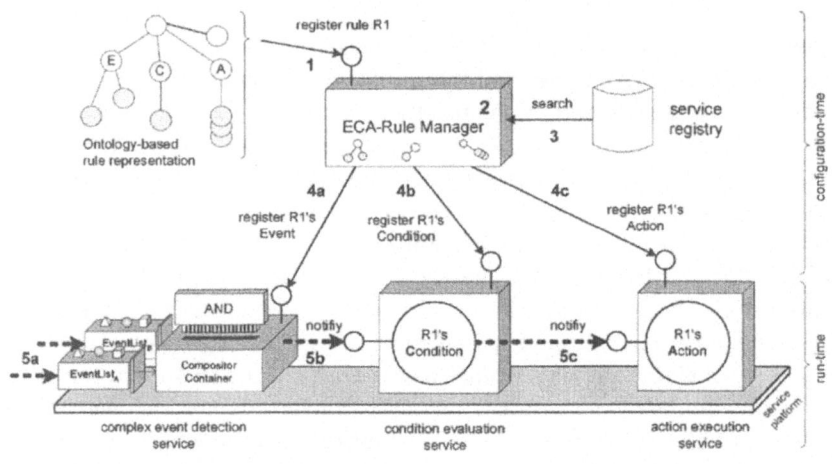

Fig. 5. Interaction among elementary services (ECA-rule processing chain)

Service composition is the responsibility of the *ECA-rule manager*. It exposes operations to register, remove, activate, and deactivate ECA-rules. The most complex of these operations is the registration of a rule, which involves the composition of elementary services. This composition consists of four steps: i) decomposing the rule, ii) finding, iii) contacting, and iv) configuring elementary services. The ECA-rule manager decomposes the rule definition passed for registration, and based on its parts it finds adequate elementary services in the service registry. The ECA-rule manager is responsible for building a chain of elementary services that will process the rule in question. Next, elementary services are contacted for configuration. The configuration of an elementary service itself comprises three steps: a) the subscription to the output of the preceding elementary service (this is achieved by using the control part of the subject as it was mentioned in Section 3.3), b) the configuration of the task under the responsibility of this service (e.g. a condition evaluation service is configured with the condition of the rule that must be evaluated) and c) the configuration of the publisher.

Interactions among elementary services rely on the notification service. Coupling modes (which specify the transactional relationship between elementary services involved) can be delegated to a notification service that supports them. For instance, the notification service implemented in the X^2TS Project [45] integrates notifications and transactions allowing the specification of coupling modes to be made on a per subscription basis [46].

Consider the registration of rule R1 which includes a composite event (Figure 5). Input for the registration is a rule definition represented using the ontology. The ECA-rule manager (1) breaks the incoming rule into elementary parts (2) and searches for proper services according to the parts obtained (3). Afterwards, the manager registers the rule parts of R1 with the services obtained (4a, 4b and 4c). As a consequence the composite event detector configures policies and consumption mode according to the rule definition to detect R1's event. Then the condition evaluation service instantiates a condition object which is responsible for subscribing to the event in question, for its evaluation and if satisfied for republishing the event. The action execution service instantiates an action object that is in charge of subscribing to the event passed by the ECA-rule manager and for the action execution. This completes the *service composition phase*.

At run-time, semantic events feed the EventLists (5a) and when R1's composite event is detected the compositor container publishes this happening (5b). In this particular case, the condition object is notified. If R1's condition is satisfied, the event is republished (5c) notifying in this case the action object in question.

Notice that more than one rule may be defined and they could share the same or similar event definitions. So, conflict resolution policies may be needed according to the execution model adopted (concurrent execution, sequential execution or based on a conflict resolution policy. See [3] for details.).

4   Case Studies and Implementation

This section presents two case studies where the proposed infrastructure was used. A short description of the implementation is provided.

4.1   Meta-auctions

A meta-auction broker [47] provides a unified view of different auction sites and services for category browsing, item search, auction participation, and auction tracking. To enable the brokering between different participating auction sites, the precise understanding of the terms used by each site is needed and is made explicit through a domain-specific common vocabulary. Notifications about events, such as the placement of a highest bid, and their timely delivery to the user represent valuable information. Propagation of events leads to an efficient non-polling realization of an auction tracking service. Events related to the auction process are disseminated using the concept-based notification service. This way, bidders and sellers use a semantic level of subscription which is common to all of them.

The auction process itself is defined using state charts. Because they are event-driven, they can be easily implemented with ECA-rules. In this way, different sets of rules can describe different types of auction processes (ascending, reverse, dutch, etc.) [48]. To track an item of interest during an auction process, e.g. to ascertain that another bidder has placed a highest bid, or that the deadline of an auction is approaching, an agent can be used. Here bidders benefit from an active functionality service to program their own agents. In contrast to current agent bidders that are owned, controlled, and implemented by the auction house, these agents can react to happenings of the auction process according to the bidders' strategy.

4.2   Internet-Enabled Car

Automotive systems will no longer be limited to information located on-board, but can benefit from a remote network and service infrastructure. Consider the scenario where vehicles, persons and devices have a web presence (or portal). Within this scenario new possibilities emerge, e.g. the adjustment of instruments according to personal preferences, favorite news channels, sports, music or access to one's e-mail and calendar through the portals. Through the portals this can be made independent of a particular car and could be applied to other vehicles (rental cars, company cars, etc). But not only instruments can be adjusted, services can be personalized too. For instance, services such as, "find the route to the next gas station", or "book an appointment to change oil" can take into account car manufacturer's, company's, and/or driver's preferences.

The content of portals is kept up-to-date by means of events. Events are disseminated to interested consumers (e.g. other portals) through of the concept-based publish/subscribe mechanism. For instance, vehicle manufacturers are interested in subscribing to vehicle failures obtaining in this way an "on-line" statistic which can provide valuable data that could be fed back into the design.

Portal managers are enhanced with the active functionality service in order to provide the possibility to specify reactions according to happenings of interest. These reactions can also take into consideration user preferences. For instance, when the driver gets into the car, it is a workday and between 8:00 am and 9:00 am the vehicle can react by loading the best route to the office, and by reading out her company news, her e-mail and by checking her calendar.

Based on CREAM, our prototype [49] shows the reaction of vehicles to different situations according to a set of user-defined rules. External services are implemented using Web Services technologies.

4.3 Implementation

A prototype of CREAM has been developed. Java is used to specify and implement ontology concepts and their relationships. Ontology support and the necessary ontology concepts of the infrastructure are completely implemented. Event adapters are manually configured. The concept-based notification service was implemented on top of TIB/Rendezvous (for historical reasons). The active functionality service and its elementary services were developed using Java and run on top of HP's Core Service Framework (CSF). Event adapters (for Java applications and for XML) and plug-ins (for workflow engines and for Web Services) were also implemented.

For the meta-auction scenario event adapters were built to integrate data and events from different auction sites. An auction service on the basis of ECA-rules was also defined. For the Internet-enabled car scenario an adapted version of the CoolTown Web Presence Manager was used to manage portals and it was extended to collaborate with CREAM. Complex rule reactions which involve several services are carried out using a workflow engine. The domain-specific ontologies for both scenarios were defined.

5 Conclusions

Event-based applications require a middleware layer that includes event handling, support for integration of heterogeneous data, monitoring capabilities, reaction to events, and notification mechanisms.

Approaches found today in the literature focus on specific issues (i.e. event dissemination, active functionality) providing isolated solutions. CREAM presents a uniform and integrated approach based on ontologies. Our ontology-based infrastructure applies homogeneously the ontology approach not only to integrate events from different sources but also to support a higher level subscription abstraction. Therefore, consumers do not deal with proprietary representations. Moreover, a conceptual representation of business rules makes a high-level and domain-specific rule definition language possible providing independence between specification of rules and the active functionality mechanism.

ECA-rule processing in CREAM is decomposed into elementary services. These services provide a very simple and generic interface, where parameters of methods are represented using the common ontology. Therefore, the flow of work through services can be easily configured – inclusion or conscious exclusion of services like condition evaluation, event filtering or complex event detection is made easy. Services interact through notifications. For this purpose, a notification service, based on a publish/subscribe mechanism using concept-based addressing, is employed. The use of this mechanism is appropriate for loosely-coupled distributed systems. Because of this conceptual foundation, our architecture promotes flexibility, extensibility and integration for large-scale, event-based distributed applications.

We are currently moving our implementation from a proprietary to an open platform for the service-based architecture. The notification service is being migrated to JMS. We are also studying how to integrate Web Services with the conversion function mechanism supported by our ontology.

References

1. Buchmann, A., Bornhövd, C., Cilia, M., Fiege, L., Gärtner, F., Liebig, C., Meixner, M., Mühl, G.: DREAM: Distributed Reliable Event-based Applcation Management. In: Web Dynamics (to appear). Springer (2003)
2. Bornhövd, C.: Semantic Metadata for the Integration of Heterogeneous Internet Data (in German). Ph.D. Thesis, Department of Computer Science, Darmstadt University of Technology, ISBN: 8265-8390-6, Shaker-Verlag, Germany (2000)
3. Cilia, M.: An Active Functionality Service for Open Distributed Heterogeneous Environments. Ph.D. Thesis, Department of Computer Science, Darmstadt University of Technology, ISBN:3-8322-0790-2, Shaker-Verlag, Germany (2002)
4. Object Management Group: Event Service Specification. Technical Report formal/97-12-11, Object Management Group (OMG) (1997)
5. Object Management Group: CORBA Notification Service Specification. Technical Report telecom/98-06-15, Object Management Group (OMG) (1998)
6. Hapner, M., Burridge, R., Sharma, R.: Java Message Service. Specification Version 1.0.2, Sun Microsystems, JavaSoftware (1999)
7. Oki, B., Pfluegl, M., Siegel, A., Skeen, D.: The Information Bus – An Architecture for Extensible Distributed Systems. In: Proceedings of SIGOPS, USA (1993) 58–68
8. Carzaniga, A., Rosenblum, D.R., Wolf, A.L.: Challenges for Distributed Event Services: Scalability vs. Expressiveness. In: Proc. of EDO. (1999)
9. Opyrchal, L., Astley, M., Auerbach, J., Banavar, G., Strom, R., Sturman, D.: Exploiting IP Multicast in Content-based Publish-Subscribe Systems. In: Proceedings of Middleware. Volume 1795 of LNCS., Springer (2000) 185–207
10. Mühl, G., Fiege, L., Buchmann, A.: Filter Similarities in Content-Based Pub/Sub Systems. In: Proc of ARCS. Volume 2299 of LNCS., Springer (2002) 224–238
11. Fabret, F., Llirbat, F., Pereira, J., Jacobsen, A., Ross, K., Shasha, D.: Filtering Algorithms and Implementation for Very Fast Publish/Subscribe. In: Proceedings of ACM SIGMOD. (2001) 115–126
12. Dayal, U., et al.: The HiPAC Project: Combining Active Databases and Timing Constraints. ACM SIGMOD Record **17** (1988)
13. Chakravarthy, S., Mishra, D.: Snoop: An Expressive Event Specification Language for Active Databases. Data and Knowledge Engineering **14** (1994) 1–26
14. Charkravarthy, S., Krishnaprasad, V., Anwar, E., Kim, S.: Composite Events for Active Databases: Semantics, Contexts and Detection. In: Proc. of VLDB. (1994) 606–617
15. Kopetz, H.: Sparse Time versus Dense Time in Distributed Real-Time Systems. In: Proc. ICDCS, Yakohama, Japan (1992) 460–467
16. Liebig, C., Cilia, M., Buchmann, A.: Event Composition in Time-dependent Distributed Systems. In: Proceedings of CoopIS. (1999) 70–78

17. Schwiderski, S.: Monitoring the Behaviour of Distributed Systems. PhD thesis, Selwyn College, Computer Lab, University of Cambridge, United Kingdom (1996)
18. Ma, C., Bacon, J.: COBEA: A CORBA-based Event Architecture. In: Proceedings of COOTS'98, New Mexico, USA, USENIX (1998) 117–131
19. Geppert, A., Tombros, D.: Event-based Distributed Workflow Execution with EVE. In: Proceedings of Middleware, The Lake District (1998)
20. Yang, S., Chakravarthy, S.: Formal Semantics of Composite Events for Distributed Environments. In: Proceedings of ICDE, Sydney, Australia (1999) 400–407
21. Paton, N., ed.: Active Rules in Database Systems. Springer (1999)
22. Gatziu, S., Koschel, A., v. Buetzingsloewen, G., Fritschi, H.: Unbundling Active Functionality. ACM SIGMOD Record 27 (1998) 35–40
23. Koschel, A., Lockemann, P.: Distributed Events in Active Database Systems - Letting the Genie out of the Bottle. Data & Knowledge Engineering 25 (1998) 29–53
24. Fritschi, H., Gatziu, S., Dittrich, K.: FRAMBOISE - an Approach to Framework-based Active Data Management System Construction. In: Proc. of CIKM. (1998)
25. Collet, C.: The NODS Project: Networked Open Database Services. In et.al., K.D., ed.: Object and Databases 2000. Number 1944 in LNCS, Springer (2000) 153–169
26. Buchmann, A.: Architecture of Active Database Systems. In: Active Rules in Database Systems. Springer (1999) 29–48
27. Buchmann, A., Liebig, C.: Distributed, Object-Oriented, Active, Real-Time DBMSs: We Want It All – Do We Need Them (At) All? Annual Reviews in Control 25 (2001)
28. Eisenberg, B., Nickull, D.: ebXML Technical Architecture Specification v1.04. Technical report (2001) http://www.ebxml.org.
29. Microsoft Corp.: BizTalk Framework 2.0: Document and Message Specification. Microsoft Technical Specification (2000)
30. RosettaNet: RosettaNet Implementation Framework: Core Specification v2.00.01. RosettaNet Technical Specification (2002)
31. Berners-Lee, T., Hendler, J., Lassila, O.: The semantic web. In: Scientific American. (2001)
32. Conolly, D., van Harmelen, F., Horrocks, I., at al.: Daml+oil (march 2001) reference desciption. W3C Note, W3C (2001)
33. Bray, T., Paoli, J., Sperberg-McQueen, C.: Extensible markup language (xml) 1.0. W3C Recommendation, W3C (1998)
34. Fallside, D.: XML Schema Part 0: Primer. W3c recommendation, W3C (2001)
35. Bray, T., Hollander, D., Layman, A.: Namespaces in XML. W3C Recommendation, W3C (1999) http://www.w3.org/TR/REC-xml-names.
36. Lassila, O., Swick, R.: Resource Description Framework (RDF) Model and Syntax Specification. W3c recommendation, W3C (1999)
37. Brickley, D., Guha, R.: RDF Vocabulary Description Language 1.0: RDF Schema. W3c working draft, W3C (2002) http://www.w3.org/TR/rdf-schema.
38. Bornhövd, C., Buchmann, A.: A Prototype for Metadata-Based Integration of Internet Sources. In: Proc. of CAiSE. Volume 1626 of LNCS. (1999) 439–445
39. Gruber, T.R.: Towards Principles for the Design of Ontologies Used for Knowledge Sharing. Int. Journal of Human-Computer Studies (IJHCS) 43 (1995) 907–928
40. Guarino, N.: Understanding, Building and using Ontologies. Int. Journal of Human-Computer Studies (IJHCS) 46 (1997) 293–310
41. Mena, E., Kashyap, V., Illarramendi, A., Sheth, A.: Domain specific ontologies for semantic information brokering on the global information infrastructure. In: Intl. Conf. on Formal Ontology in Information Systems, Trento, Italy (1998)

42. Heflin, J., Volz, R., Dale, J.: Requirements for a web ontology language. W3C Working Draft, W3C (2002) http://www.w3.org/TR/webont-req/.
43. UNICORN Maintenance Authority: UNICORN Application Standard. Technical Report TTIP03 V4.0, Travel Technology Initiative Ldt. (1994)
44. Mühl, G.: Large-Scale Content-Based Publish/Subscribe Systems. PhD thesis, Darmstadt University of Technology, Germany (2002)
45. Liebig, C., Malva, M., Buchmann, A.: X^2TS: Unbundling Active Object Systems (Short Paper). In: Proceedings of Middleware. Volume 1795 of LNCS. (2000)
46. Liebig, C., Tai, S.: Middleware Mediated Transactions. In: Proc. of DOA'00. (2001)
47. Bornhövd, C., Cilia, M., Liebig, C., Buchmann, A.: An Infrastructure for Meta-Auctions. In: Proceedings of WECWIS, IEEE Computer Society (2000) 21–30
48. Cilia, M., Buchmann, A.: An Active Functionality Service for E-Business Applications. ACM SIGMOD Record **31** (2002) 24–30
49. Cilia, M., Hasselmeyer, P., Buchmann, A.: Profiling and Internet Connectivity in Automotive Environments. In: Proc. of VLDB. (2002) 1071–1074

Versions for Context Dependent Information Services

Moira C. Norrie and Alexios Palinginis

Institute for Information Systems
ETH Zurich, CH-8092 Zurich, Switzerland
{norrie,palinginis}@inf.ethz.ch

Abstract. Context dependent information delivery is an important requirement of cooperative information systems supporting global and mobile access. These systems must be able to adapt the content, structure and presentation of information according to various factors such as the user, the access device and the task at hand. We present a versioning model designed to manage context-varying versions of content, structure and presentation database objects. Further, we describe how this has been integrated into a general web publishing platform to dynamically compose web documents according to the current context state.

1 Introduction

The increasing desire for global and mobile access to information by communities of users places additional demands on systems to provide multi-channel, adaptive information delivery. A new generation of information infrastructures is therefore required that can easily adapt both the content and presentation of information according to various factors related to the user, the access device and the task at hand. It is a matter of *delivering the right information, to the right person, at the right time.*

Our overall goal is to develop such an information infrastructure capable of supporting highly-interactive, cooperative information environments. Our approach was to investigate what key concepts need to be integrated into an object-oriented database management system to provide full web publishing support. This resulted in the development of OMSwe, a very flexible web publishing framework that can dynamically compose information presentations from database objects that represent, not only application entities, but also document structures and presentation templates. Central to the framework is a notion of *state* that was integrated into the database management system to keep track of both interaction and context states. Context-dependent information delivery is then controlled by matching the current context state of a request to context-specific versions of the objects involved.

In this paper, we present a general model and mechanisms for supporting context-dependent delivery and describe how these were implemented in the OMSwe system through an extension of existing versioning mechanisms.

R. Meersman et al. (Eds.): CoopIS/DOA/ODBASE 2003, LNCS 2888, pp. 503–515, 2003.
© Springer-Verlag Berlin Heidelberg 2003

We start in Section 2 with a discussion of context-dependent information delivery and introduce an example used throughout the paper. Section 3 then presents a general model of context suitable for web publishing and describes how this is used to match object versions to context states. In Section 4, we provide an overview of the OMSwe system, its representation of interface components as *web elements* and its use of XML and XSLT technologies. Section 5 then presents the versioning model and mechanisms of OMSwe and how they are used to support context-dependent delivery. Concluding remarks are give in Section 6.

2   Context-Dependent Information Delivery

Nowadays a web publishing framework has to support access through, not only desktop browsers, but also a range of mobile devices such as mobile phones and PDAs. Both the content and presentation of data may have to be adapted to cater for both the variation in formats supported by client browsers and also physical attributes of the client device such as the screen size and means of navigation and selection. The fact that users are mobile may also require changes to the interface in terms of both the information to be delivered and also the means used to present that information. For example, mobility may involve physical activities such as driving a car or carrying goods and hence the use of non-visual channels, such as voice channels, may be appropriate. In such cases, the information really needs to be concise and specific to the task at hand. This contrasts with a desktop browser where the user is able to consume more information and browse at leisure. Multi-channel access may therefore involve adaptation of, not only the format of the information delivered, but also its content and structure to ensure that only the essential information is delivered for the task at hand.

As an example, consider a multi-lingual and multi-channel news service that supports both browsing by anonymous users and entry of articles by journalists. We can assume a workflow that new articles entered by journalists have to be approved by an editor before being released onto the public new browsing service. We illustrate the service in figure 1 with some interface snapshots. On the right of the figure, we show the news browsing service as accessed through a desktop browser and through a WAP-enabled phone. The desktop browser shows a general document layout of a header, a navigation menu of news categories on the left, a news article in the centre and links to related news articles on the right. Note that there is also an Edit link showing that the current user is either the journalist or an editor with rights to update the news article.

Clearly, this layout is not suited to a mobile phone and hence the content, structure and presentation are different. Only the leader (i.e. summary text) of the news article is given rather than the full text. The menu of news categories is accessible through one of the phone selection buttons and editing of news articles is not available due to the inconvenience of data entry on mobile phones.

On the left of figure 1, we show a desktop browser interface for the editing of an Italian version of the same news article. Language selection is performed

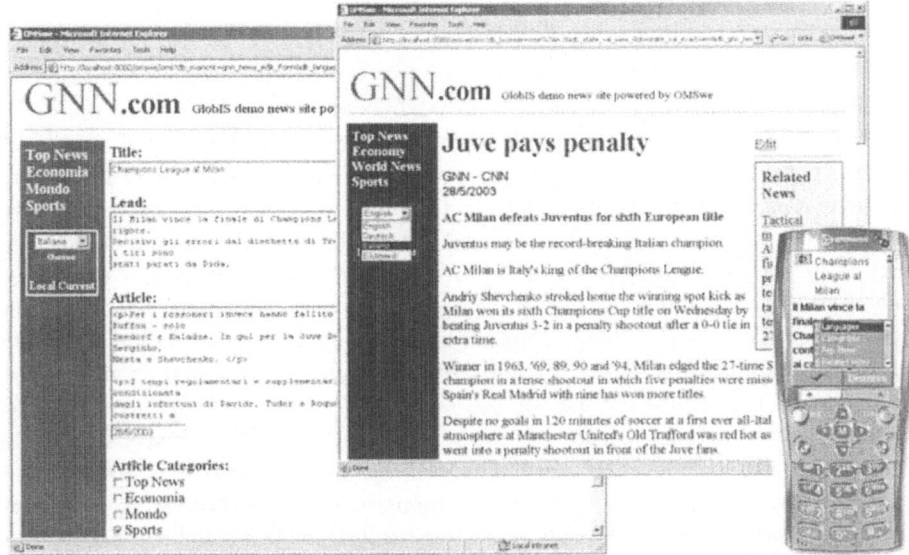

Updating News in Italian   Browsing News in English

Fig. 1. Context-Dependent News Service Delivery

through a menu situated in the left section of the page under the menu of news categories. Note that the change from English to Italian will cause, not only the content of the news article to change, but also the presentation of web site in that we change the colour of the menu bar from blue to green. While this is a simple example, it is important to emphasise that change of context — in this case language context — may change content, structure and presentation just as we saw with the case of the device context in the case of the WAP-enabled phone.

A number of systems and tools tackle the problem of working with existing documents and automatically adapting them for display on different client devices based on an analysis of their structure. For example, the Content Repurposing Suite (CRS) [CRS] of TextWise Labs uses natural language processing techniques to analyse entire text documents and generate summaries for content delivery to desktop or mobile devices. SmartView [MFS02] is an example of a system that enables existing HTML documents to be viewed from mobile devices by analysing the structure of the HTML page and using this structure and heuristics to generate an alternative representation suited to a small screen. These approaches can be categorised as *content repurposing*. We instead want to perform *information repurposing*, where the adaptation of interfaces in a given context is performed at the information level rather than the document content level. This has advantages in terms of the development, maintenance and evolution of web sites.

3   Context Model

The notion of context-aware computing has become very popular and many different models have been proposed. It is important to recognise the different levels of these models since they may cover everything from the physical infrastructure level dealing with sensors and embedded systems to the organisational level dealing with semantic roles and tasks. At the information infrastructure level, what is important is that we can achieve a simple characterisation of context that enables a matching of state to appropriate content, structure and presentation objects of the database. Applications should be able to define their own definition of context, possibly mapping from a higher-level semantic model.

The model of context that we use is in fact similar to that proposed for semi-structured data in [SG02] where they present MOEM, an extension of the semi-structured data model OEM [CGMH+94] to represent multidimensional data, and describe how an MOEM document can be transformed to an OEM document under a specific context state. Similar ideas have been introduced into both HTML [WBSY98] and XML [GSK01] to support context-dependent variants of documents.

Context is defined in terms of a set of *characteristics* which specify the various factors to be taken into account in deciding on the content and presentation of a document to be returned to the client in response to a request. These characteristics can include anything from system-related factors such as the request protocol and the user agent specified in a request header to user-related factors such as language preference.

For a given application A, we define its context domain C_A as a set of n characteristic variables $\{c_1, c_2, ...c_n\}$ for some $n \geq 0$. Each characteristic variable c_i will have an associated domain of values V_i. Then a characteristic is any given pair (c_i, v_i) for $c_i \in C_A$ and $v_i \in V_i$. A valid *context state* CS_A is any set $\{(c_i, v_i) | c_i \in C_A \text{ and } v_i \in V_i \text{ for } 1 \geq i \geq n\}$.

For a given object O of the database, we use versions of the object to represent the set of possible instances and a best match of the current context state and the versions is used to determine which version to use in the given context.

If $O^V = \{O_1, O_2, ...O_k\}$ is the version set of O, then for any $O_i \in O^V$, O_i will have a set of characteristics $CS(O_i)$. We refer to $CS(O_i)$ as the *version context* of O_i. To avoid having to create versions for each meaningful combination of characteristics, defaults are used. For example, the default value of the language characteristic variable could be set to english. However, for some characteristics, it makes no sense to use default and we may specify that they are *necessary* meaning that a value must be specified. For example, this could be the case in terms of a characteristic that specifies the request protocol.

We introduce a characteristic function ϕ which specifies whether or not a characteristic variable is necessary, i.e. for any $c_i \in C_A$, $\phi(c_i) = $ true indicates that c_i is necessary. Further, we introduce a priority scheme over characteristics by imposing a total ordering over C_A. Thus, we use $|C_A|$ to denote the resulting sequence of characteristic variables where $P(c_i)$ gives the priority of c_i as an index of its position in the sequence, i.e. $1 \geq P(c_i) \geq n$ and for any $c_j \in C_A$ where $i \neq j$, $P(c_i) \neq P(c_j)$.

Two further refinements of our characteristic model are required before we can detail how the matching of context state to version contexts is performed. These are concerned with the characteristic values of either the context state or the version states. The first of these deals with the multiplicity of values and the second with value refinement.

Instead of being restricted to atomic values of the domain, a context or version state may specify multiple possible values for a given characteristic. Multiple values can take the form of ranges, sets or priority lists. For example, we might use a range of numeric values to specify that a version of an object is appropriate for a version range of a client browser. Sets can be used to specify alternatives such as the set of languages that a browser can accept. In the case of user language preferences, the languages may instead be specified as a priority list indicating the order of language preference. Thus, the context state could specify the language characteristic as (language, [en,de,it]) indicating that a user could accept English, German or Italian versions, but their first preference would be English.

Value refinement occurs when a characteristic may have a sub-dimension. For example, a web site in German might have regional variants for Germany, Austria and Switzerland. Therefore in addition to having the language characteristic with the value de, we allow refinements to be introduced by appending sub-dimension values to give de-de, de-au and de-ch. In such values, we refer to de as the major characteristic and the sub-dimension value as the minor characteristic. The minor characteristic is only considered when the major characteristic value matches and when no minor characteristic is present then the match will be over the major characteristic. For example, when the context state defines the language as de (without specifying region), all versions defined for de or de-ch are considered as candidates.

There are cases when a stronger relationship between the major and minor characteristic exists and matching must be over both values. For example, consider the browser/browser_version pair as major/minor characteristics. Since we cannot assume compatibility between all version of Microsoft Internet Explorer, it would not be appropriate to match a version that specifies a particular browser/browser_version pair to a request that simply specifies the browser or even another version of the browser. We therefore introduce a second form of refinement represented using a ":" instead of a "-" to connect the major and minor values. We could therefore represent use a characteristic of the form (browser,msie:5.0) to represent Microsoft Internet Explorer version 5.0.

The concept of major/minor characteristics can be combined with range and list characteristics. For example, a range definition could be used to specify that one template is compatible with browsers of version msie:(3.0,5.0), while another can be used only for msie:5.0.

Matching of context states to versions is therefore performed based on various factors such as whether or not a characteristic is optional and the format of the values specified. To deal with multiple candidate matches, we use a simple weighting algorithm to perform the matching. The following table summarises the weights:

Table 1.

Class	State	Contend	Ranking
mandatory	X	Y	not considered
any	major	major	1
weak	major-X	major-X	1
weak	major-X	major	2
weak	major	major-X	2
weak	major-X	major-Y	2
strong	major:X	major:X	1
strong	major:X	major:(A,B)	1 if X in [A,B]
strong	major:X	major	2
any	X	(A,B)	1 if X in [A,B]
any	[A,..,X,..,B]	X	$P = pos(X)^3$

The matching algorithm will sum the rankings results for all characteristics defined for each version for the current context. The one with the highest ranking (lowest number) will be chosen. In the case that no `webElement` could be chosen, the default will be used. The current algorithm gives lower ranking when matching values defined deeper in a list construct as indicated in the last row of the table. In this way, we assign the list a priority semantic. Furthermore, the weight of priority is much less than the weight from matching first choice characteristics. In this way, versions that match some first choice characteristics will be preferred over versions that match even more characteristics but are defined lower in the priority list. The priority weight can be defined differently for each characteristic giving the possibility to even consider the list values as equal to each other.

The number of optional matched characteristics and the matching position in the case of list definitions influence the ranking. In the rare case of equal total weights for two or more candidates, a random or default version can be used.

With this approach it is possible to have a very rich model of context that takes into account all sorts of factors, without having to define a unique version for each possible combination. This not only reduces the development time, but also unnecessary replication.

The basic model could be generalised to introduce other value formats and additional levels of sub-dimensions. While our empirical studies have shown that the current range of value formats along with the weighting algorithm works well for typical web site requirements, we are investigating possible generalisations and extensions to cater for new forms of cooperative information environments.

4   OMSwe Web Publishing Platform

OMSwe is a general web publishing platform based on the the OMS object data management system. Our overall aim was to demonstrate the suitability of the underlying OM data model and OMS system for web site engineering, while investigating the key constructs that need to be integrated into a database management system to support web publishing. In contrast to a number of existing model-based approaches to web site development such as WebML [CFB+03], our focus is system-based rather than tool-based. By this, we mean that we wanted to extend the database technologies to support web engineering, rather than developing tools to assist in the generation of solutions based on existing database technologies.

At the same time, we wanted to integrate the web database and content management perspectives and manage not only content and the web development process, but also representations of application entities. This means that semantic concepts such as news articles and news categories are the focus of attention, rather than the basic publishing concepts of text, image, link etc. This in turn makes it much easier to separate the concerns of the designers and developers and also to maintain consistency.

In addition to providing support for the operation of dynamic web sites, we wanted to support the development process itself in terms of rapid prototyping, system evolution, reusability and both static and dynamic web site generation. Further, we wanted to cater for both the publishing of existing databases on the web, as well as the development of web sites from scratch. All of these requirements were coupled with those discussed in earlier sections of supporting multi-channel and context-dependent access.

To achieve maximum flexibility, we therefore decided that all of the information that defines a web site be managed by a publishing database. This means not only the application data such as news items and their categories, but also the definition of document structures and their presentations. Note that this does not mean that all information, inclusive of multimedia materials, actually has to be stored in that database. It may be the case that application data is stored in one or more external databases and multimedia stored in external files. However, the publishing database manages references to all external data and also includes mechanisms to support the synchronisation of these sources with published information. In the case of external files, this involves the automatic copying of updated files to the relevant web server directories at pre-determined or manually invoked synchronisation points.

In figure 2, we show the GNN web site displayed under a debugging option of OMSwe that reveals the structure of the page in terms its logical components such as the header, menu bar and main content component. Components can be nested arbitrarily and often have deeply nested structures due to ensure maximum flexibility.

A component is specified in terms of its *content* and *presentation*. The content defines the dynamic information contained within the component, and this can be a combination of information retrieved or generated from objects of the database and references to subcomponents. In this way, the content is defined in terms of a content hierarchy where each node is bound to a database operation (macro) that generates data. The content generated data is represented in XML.

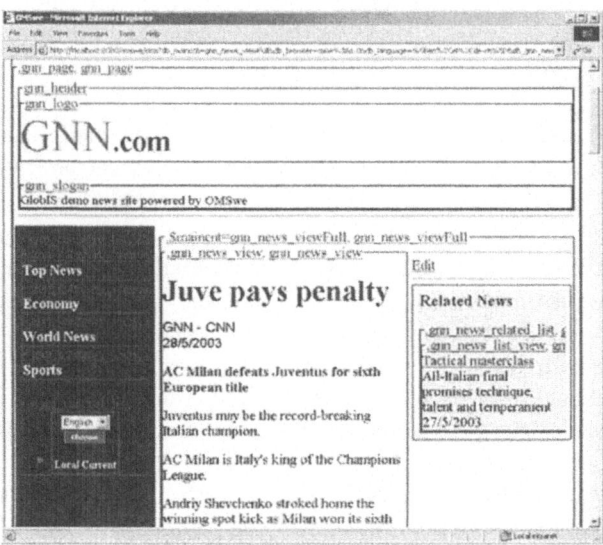

Fig. 2. News Service Components

The presentation of a component is defined using XSLT templates which determine how the content data is top be presented, specifying static content (text, images etc.) to be included as well as appropriate markup. It is at this level that the developer specifies whether XHTML, WML, Voice XML or some other markup should be included.

Both the content and presentation of a component may vary according to context. We achieve context-dependent web pages by selecting content and templates according to the context state of the current request. Contents and templates are actually represented by a set of object versions with different *activation contexts*. In the next section, we describe in detail how versions are used in OMSwe by using context as version descriptions.

It is beyond the scope of this paper to describe all aspects of the OMSwe system in detail. Further details of the general operation of the system, inclusive of an outline of caching strategies, are given in [NP03] and documentation can be found at http://www.omspro.ethz.ch/omspro/api.html.

5   Versioning in OMSwe

In this section, we will discuss the version model that we introduced into the OO database management system and used to support the context facility. Our aim was to introduce a general concept that would allow us to create different flavours of the same conceptual object. Imagine, for instance, a news article in our example that we would like to provide for different languages. We could enrich our model by introducing into the database schema a new concept of `news_instance` associated with the abstract concept of a news article. This is a common modelling issue when trying to map some real world abstraction and real instance objects of the given abstraction, e.g. books and physical copies of books.

During our work, we encountered many such cases either on the data level, as described before, or on the presentation level were it is necessary to provide different views for the same concept. For example, the presentation element of an article may vary according to the browser that it is intended for or the decision made to use frames versus table-oriented implementations. It is obvious that, also in this case, we need a notion of versions on the article view presentation object.

Versioning is discussed extensively in earlier works from researchers mainly from temporal databases [Ste98], software configuration management (SCM) [Sci94,CW98] and product management [KR88,Kat90]. The work done in the temporal database area focuses mainly on the time dimension. Although time is of great importance for the applications in which we are interested, other dimensions such as media and device properties must also be incorporated into the model. In the area of SCM, versions are strongly organised into branches and hierarchies. They are intended either for multi-user management or distinct file management over changes. In our application scenario, an object should be versioned according to multiple dimensions such as the language and workflow status or the browser and protocol used etc., which makes a hierarchical versioning system inappropriate. Finally, the work done in the product engineering area concerns versions across multiple representations and over time. The concepts of refinements, alternatives, and variants seems closer to our domain. Nevertheless, for those systems, the model of version descriptors is aimed at product management applications and they are also organised in hierarchies. The model that we describe is influenced by the above-mentioned work and adapted to the requirement posed by a publishing system. The notion of context is introduced as general version descriptor and, instead of introducing a "current" or "design object", we deal with a context default object.

We extended our system by introducing a new system type `context_obj` which defines the version descriptor. Objects that are inherited from this type are eligible for version operations. While extending our system to support versions, we were concerned to keep applications not using versioning unaffected in terms of definitions and efficiency. By applying versioning only to objects inherited from `context_obj`, we obtained a natural approach that is also well suited to storage management, since all version objects could be partitioned according to the existence of a specialisation of the `context_obj` type. Please note that our system and model supports multiple-inheritance and mechanisms for schema evolution which make feasible the inheritance of objects from `context_obj` while keeping any application specific type hierarchy. This allows us to evolve a non-versioning application to a version-aware application.

The first operation that can be applied on object instances of the `context_obj` type is the `create_version` operation. Given a current existing object, the system will create the new version by using a unique version number attached to the original object id. A major concern when designing a versioning system is to avoid storage redundancy. Rather than copying the whole object for each version, we use the granularity of a stored unit.

A stored unit is the object information for a specific type. For the type hierarchy of figure3, an object is built from three storage units, one for each type: the `context_obj` unit, the **news** unit and the **sponsored_news** unit. If needed, the object is composed at runtime from those units to form a unified object view. In the past, we have also used this unit storage granularity to successfully support schema evolution and also multiple inheritance and instantiation [NP02]. In the current system with version support, the choice of type units for storage granularity seems appropriate to reduce data redundancy. We could have taken the more extreme approach of storing objects in the smallest granularity, namely attributes, which is very flexible on updates and actually a redundant free representation for versioning. Nevertheless, this choice dramatically increases the access times due to the recomposition of an object from its attribute values.

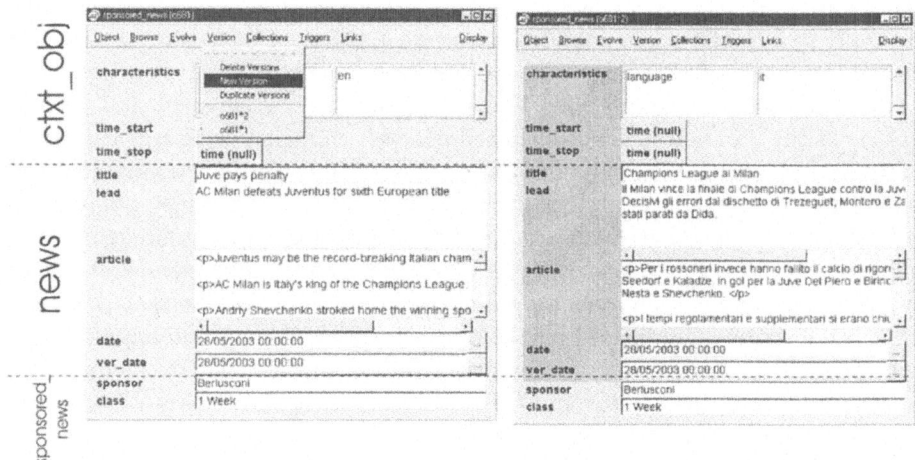

Fig. 3. Creating an article version

When creating a new version, only the `context_obj` unit is created. The type units from the original object will be used to compose the version information on access. Only when the user explicitly makes an update on the version, will a unit be copied. In figure 3, the **news** object o681 is shown. The new version gets the id o681*2 and the `context_obj` unit is created. Upon update of some news fields (title, lead, article), a version unit for news is created (all version units are marked with dark grey). The information from the **sponsored_news** is shared from the original object.

In the case where some unit attributes should shared among version units, a mechanism exists to synchronise their value with the original object upon update.

For example, the date of a new article should be shared by all versions of that article. By using the unit granularity together with the attribute synchronisation mechanism, we achieve a good compromise between flexibility, efficiency and redundancy.

We already mentioned that the context_obj type holds the version description. This description is the context state definition for which the instance is valid. In figure3, the original object shown on the left is defined for the simple state where the variable language is set to english. On the right, we show a version of the same news article that exists for the italian language. The english object is defined as the original object which means that it acts as the default representative of the version family.

Apart from the version creation operation, two more flavours exist. The duplicate_versions will duplicate the whole version family, providing an easy way to create a new object versioned according to the given source object family. This operation is very useful to duplicate already existing object versions and their version descriptors and leave the user responsible for editing the application relevant attributes.

For applications unaware of the versioning mechanism, we kept all system operations intact and operational on the original object representatives. For version-aware applications, access selector operations exist to incorporate the version objects in the searching process. For point queries, when the object id is given, the old operations can retrieve version objects only if referenced explicitly.

As explained in the previous sections, the system is aware of the current state which is composed of a set of characteristics. A new operator choose_ver exists to choose the best matching object from the given object family. The algorithm used is the one discussed in Section 3. After a select operator, the user can call the choose_ver operator to get the best matching object. An exact match operator exists to retrieve versions that match exactly the given context. Imagine, for instance, the case where we are searching to see whether an Italian version of our news article exists. The choose version operator will return the best matching object which will be the English language version, if no Italian version is available. On the other hand, the exact matching predicate will fail if no Italian version exist.

Finally, an operator version_original exists that retrieves the original object of the given version object. This serves as the inverse operation to choose_version and is used when we want to reference the whole version family. Most of the applications that we have migrated into the version-aware system use references between the original objects and, only before delivering the objects, are they matched for the given context. For example, to associate related articles, it is sufficient to use a related_news association on the original representative article objects. In essence, any and all language versions belonging to the same article family are related to the articles to which their original object is related.

Although the operations explained are sufficient at the object level, we wanted to provide improved handling when working with collections of objects. Our original information model and system heavily uses the notion of collection as a means for classification. Furthermore, the construct of object association is also based on collections. The question that arises is how to handle object references. Should all references use the original object representative or is it of any use to reference version objects directly? Depending on how we use the notion of version, it is easy to notice that referencing versions could be desirable. Consider, for example, extending our application to hold the author of each article. In this case, the association between authors and articles should incorporate the detailed article version since different language versions of the same article are normally authored by different persons. In this case, the association between collections Authors and Articles must be version-aware.

To facilitate this dual reference scheme, we introduce the notion of version-aware collections. These are collection that accept references of version objects. Notice here that, while associations are also based on collections of binary references, we also distinguish between version-aware and unaware associations. Version unaware collections are the default collection type allowing older applications to be smoothly migrated into the extended system. Each time an object is inserted into a collection, the system chooses the original representative object and inserts this in the given collection.

On the other hand, insertion of a version of an object in a version-aware collection will reference exactly the given version. All collection constraints will be applied on a version-aware process. If, for instance, a cardinality constraint over the articles' authors is applied, the system will also take into account the existing versions.

6   Concluding Remarks

We have presented a general context model that can be used to support context-dependent delivery in web applications. We briefly explained how the notion of context can influence all three aspects of a web application — the data, the structure and the presentation. An application is represented by a set of data, structure and presentation objects defined to be valid for a certain context. The system then uses a best match algorithm to provide the best possible result for the given context. We believe that a best match approach supports cooperation by making available the information between context discrepant sites rather than not responding.

We also outlined the implementation scheme that we used to extend our system to support context-dependent delivery. The implementation is based on extending an object-oriented database system with the notion of versions. To our best knowledge, this approach of using versions to support context issues in the domain of web application development is unique. Our experiences of developing some prototype applications using the system, show it to be extremely useful and simple to implement.

Currently, we are testing how the system can support workflow and history scenarios based on the two notions of context and versioning.

References

[CFB⁺03]   S. Ceri, P. Fraternali, A. Bongio, M. Brambilla, S. Comai, and M. Matera. *Designing Data-Intensive Web Applications*. Morgan Kaufmann, 2003.

[CGMH⁺94]   S. Chawathe, H. Garcia-Molina, J. Hammer, K. Ireland, Y. Papakonstantinou, J. Ullman, and J. Widom. The TSIMMIS Project: Integration of Heterogeneous Information Sources. In *16th Meeting of the Information Processing Society of Japan*, 1994.

[CRS]   Content Repurposing Suite, http://www.textwise.com/technology/crs/.

[CW98]   R. Conradi and B. Westfechtel. Version models for software conguration management, 1998.

[GSK01]   M. Gergatsoulis, Y. Stavrakas, and D. Karteris. Incorportaing Dimensions to XML and DTD. In *In Database and Expert Systems Applications (DEXA'01)*, Munich, Germany, September 2001.

[Kat90]   Randy H. Katz. Towards a unified framework for version modeling in engineering databases. *ACM Computing Surveys*, 22(4):375–408, 1990.

[KR88]   Dittrich K. and Lorie R. Version support for engineering database systems. *IEEE Transactions on Software Engineering*, 14(4):429–437, 1988.

[MFS02]   N. Milic-Frayling and R. Sommerer. Smartview: Enhanced document viewer for mobile devices. Technical Report MSR-TR-2002-114, Microsoft Research, Cambridge, UK, November 2002.

[NP02]   M. C. Norrie and A. Palinginis. A Modelling Approach to the Realisation of Modular Information Spaces. In *Proc. 14th Conference on Advanced Information Systems Engineering (CAiSE 2002)*, June 2002.

[NP03]   M. C. Norrie and A. Palinginis. Empowering Databases for Context-Dependent Information Delivery. In *Ubiquitous Mobile Information and Collaboration Systems (UMICS), CAiSE Workshop Proceedings*, June 2003.

[Sci94]   Edward Sciore. Versioning and configuration management in an object-oriented data model. *VLDB Journal*, 3(1):77–106, 1994.

[SG02]   Y. Stavrakas and M. Gergatsoulis. Multidimensional Semistructured Data: Representing Context-Dependent Information on the Web. In *Proc. 14th Conference on Advanced Information Systems Engineering (CAiSE 2002)*, Toronto, Canada, June 2002.

[Ste98]   A. Steiner. *A Generalisation Approach to Temporal Data Models and their Implementations*. Phd thesis, Department of Computer Science, ETH, CH-8092 Zurich, Switzerland, 1998.

[WBSY98]   W.W. Wadge, G.D. Brown, M.C. Schraefel, and T. Yildirim. Intensional HTML. In *Proc. 4th Intl. Workshop on Principles of Digital Document Processing (PODDP'98)*, March 1998.

Cache Invalidation for Updated Data in Ad Hoc Networks

Hideki Hayashi, Takahiro Hara, and Shojiro Nishio

Dept. of Multimedia Engineering, Graduate School of Information Science and
Technology Osaka University 2-1 Yamadaoka, Suita, Osaka 565-0871, Japan
{hideki, hara, nishio}@ist.osaka-u.ac.jp
http://www-nishio.ist.osaka-u.ac.jp/index-e.html

Abstract. Recent advances in computer and wireless communication
technologies have led to an increasing interest in ad hoc networks which
are constructed of only mobile hosts. In this paper, we propose two cache
invalidation methods in ad hoc networks where each data item is updated
at inconstant intervals. In the first method, when a mobile host holding
an original data item updates the data item, it broadcasts an invalidation report to all connected mobile hosts. In the other method, when
two mobile hosts are connected, they rebroadcast invalidation reports
received before to newly connected mobile hosts. Our proposed methods
reduce the number of accesses to invalid cached data items which have
been updated and the number of roll backs caused by such invalid accesses. We also show the results of simulation experiments regarding the
performance evaluation of our proposed methods.

1   Introduction

Recent advances in computer and wireless communication technologies have led
to an increasing interest in *ad hoc networks* which are constructed of only mobile hosts [3,12,13]. In ad hoc networks, every mobile host plays the role of a
router, and communicates with the other mobile hosts. Even if the source and
the destination mobile hosts are not in communication range of each other, data
packets are forwarded to the destination mobile host by relaying transmission
through other mobile hosts which exist between the two mobile hosts. Since no
special infrastructure is required, in various fields such as military affairs and
commerce, many applications are expected to be developed in ad hoc networks.

In ad hoc networks, since mobile hosts move freely, disconnections occur
frequently, and this causes frequent network division. If network division occurs
due to the migrations of mobile hosts, mobile hosts in one of the divided two
networks cannot access data items held by mobile hosts in the other network.
In Figure 1, if the radio link between two mobile hosts is disconnected at the
central part, the mobile hosts on the left-hand side and those on the right-hand
side cannot access data items D_1 and D_2, respectively. Thus, data accessibility
in ad hoc networks is lower than that in conventional fixed networks. A key
solution to this problem is to replicate data items on mobile hosts that are not
the owners of the original data item.

R. Meersman et al. (Eds.): CoopIS/DOA/ODBASE 2003, LNCS 2888, pp. 516–535, 2003.
© Springer-Verlag Berlin Heidelberg 2003

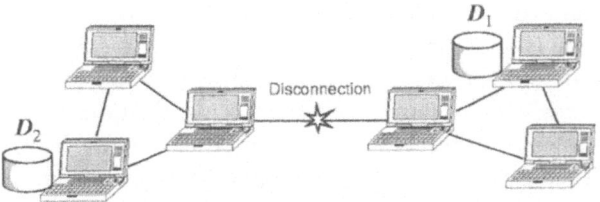

Fig. 1. Network division and data access.

Most conventional works on ad hoc networks, which have been done in various research projects such as IETF (Internet Engineering Task Force), have proposed routing protocols to support communications among mobile hosts connected to each other by one-hop/multihop links [9,11,16,17,18]. In this paper, mobile hosts connected to each other by one-hop/multihop links are simply called *connected mobile hosts*. Such routing protocols are useful for applications in which mobile hosts directly communicate with each other, e.g., video conference systems. However, in ad hoc networks, there also be many applications in which mobile hosts access data held by other mobile hosts. A good example is when a research project team constructs an ad hoc network and the team members refer to data obtained by other members for efficiency. Recently, ad hoc networks have attracted much attention as one of typical infrastructures of next generation computer environments, e.g., wearable computing environments and sensor networks. Therefore, it will be more and more important to improve data accessibility in ad hoc networks. To the best of our knowledge, no study was made to improve data accessibility in ad hoc networks before our previous work [6]. Recently, several studies [15,20] were made for the same purpose. We show these related works in next section.

In [6], we assumed that each mobile host has limited memory space for creating replicas in ad hoc networks where data item is not updated and proposed three replica allocation methods for improving data accessibility. These methods heuristically determine replica allocation based on the access frequency from each mobile host to each data item and the network topology at that moment. In [7], we extended the three methods proposed in [6] to adapt to an environment where each data item is periodically updated. These extended methods replicate data items on mobile hosts based on the access frequency, the time remaining until each item is updated next, and the network topology.

In a real environment, it is more likely that data items are updated at inconstant intervals. In such a case, mobile hosts may access invalid cached data items which have been updated. If a mobile host accesses an invalid cached data item, a roll back occurs when it connects with the mobile host holding the original. Such invalid accesses consume the power of mobile hosts and this is a serious problem for mobile hosts that usually have poor resources. In this paper, we propose two cache invalidation methods in ad hoc networks where each data item is updated at inconstant intervals. These methods broadcast invalidation reports for invalidating old cached items effectively and reducing the number of accesses to invalid cached items. We also verify the effectiveness of the proposed methods by simulation experiments.

The remainder of the paper is organized as follows. In Section 2, we show some conventional works related to our work. In Section 3, we present our assuming environment. In Section 4, we propose two cache invalidation methods for reducing the number of accessing invalid cached data items. In Section 5, we explain data access manners which are specialized for our proposed methods. In Section 6, we show the results of simulation experiments. Finally, in Section 7, we summarize this paper.

2   Related Works

In [7], we proposed three replica allocation methods for improving data availability in ad hoc networks where each data item is updated periodically. Our proposed methods periodically relocate replicas of data items based on the access frequency from each mobile host to each data item, the time remaining until each data item is updated next, and the network topology at the time. Furthermore, we extended these methods to adapt to environments where each data item is updated at inconstant intervals. These extended methods calculate the time remaining until each data item is updated next by probabilistic analysis, and relocate replicas effectively based on the calculation. This approach is considered to be similar to the approach in this paper because both approaches deal with data update in ad hoc networks. However, while the methods proposed in [7] aim to improve data availability, the methods proposed in this paper aim to reduce the number of accesses to invalid cached data items which have been updated.

In [15], a method based on the principle of probabilistic quorum system has been proposed to improve data accessibility and manage cache consistency in ad hoc networks. This is considered similar to our assumption, because each data item is owned by a particular mobile host and only this can update the data item. However, in [15] it is assumed that network division due to migration of mobile hosts does not frequently occur and thus this method is different from our methods.

In [20], the authors have proposed a method that predicts time when a network division occurs in ad hoc networks and creates replicas at each mobile host before the network division occurs. This is similar to our proposed methods, because the authors consider frequent network division. However, this method differs from our methods with the point that the authors assume a specific mobility model, in which mobile hosts with the same characteristic in terms of the velocity create a group. On the other hand, our methods work for any mobility model.

In the research field of database systems in mobile computing environments, several strategies for invalidating cached data items have been proposed. In [2], it is assumed that mobile hosts cache data items held by database servers in the fixed network and each database is updated only by the database server that holds the database. In this environment, if a mobile host asks the database server whether the target data item has been updated every time when the host accesses the item, communication contentions frequently occur because the bandwidth of radio communication is usually narrow. Therefore, the authors of [2] proposed cache invalidation strategies in which the server periodically broadcasts invalidation reports to mobile hosts and invalidates cached data items held by the mobile hosts efficiently. In [4], cache consistency management methods were classified into several categories and detailed simulation experiments were performed in both cases in which the server broadcasts invalidation reports and *update information* that includes new values of the updated data items. In [14], the authors pointed out that conventional approaches which do not allow mobile hosts to commit read transactions until they receive new invalidation reports degrades the transaction throughput. Then, they proposed an optimistic method which allow mobile hosts to tentatively commit their read transactions before receiving new invalidation reports. In this method, when a write-read conflict occurs, the tentative transaction that has caused the conflict is aborted. In [5, 8,10,19,21], several methods which reduces the size of invalidation reports efficiently were proposed to reduce the power consumption of mobile hosts and the radio communication overhead. Although all these approaches are similar to our approach because they invalidate cached data items held by mobile hosts, they assume that the database servers in the fixed network update data items and broadcast the invalidation reports to mobile hosts that connect to the servers by one-hop radio links. Our approach differs from these approaches because mobile hosts effectively broadcast invalidation reports considering the changes of network topology and the reports are sent to mobile hosts that are connected by multi-hop links in ad hoc networks.

3   Assumptions and Approach

The system environment is assumed to be an ad hoc network where mobile hosts access data items held as originals by other mobile hosts. Data items are updated at inconstant intervals. Each mobile host creates replicas of data items held by other mobile hosts in its cache space. Replicas (cached items) are relocated in a specific period called *relocation period* by using the following three replica allocation methods proposed in [6]:

1. *SAF (Static Access Frequency)* method:
   Each mobile host allocates replicas of data items in descending order of the access frequencies within the limit of its own memory space. If a mobile host issues an access request for a data item where the replica at the host has become invalid and the request is satisfied because some other connected mobile hosts have the original or its valid replicas, the request issuing host again allocates the valid replica, i.e., refreshes the replica. This operation is also done in the other two methods, the DAFN method and the DCG method, explained below.

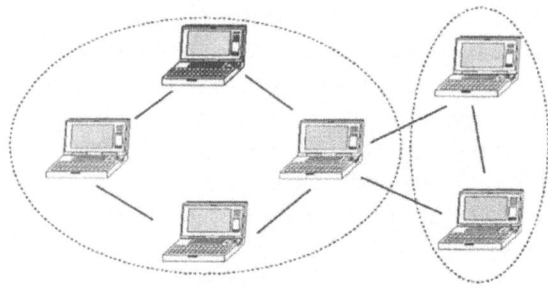

Fig. 2. Groups in DCG method.

2. *DAFN (Dynamic Access Frequency and Neighborhood)* method:
   In the SAF method, since mobile hosts with the same access characteristic allocate the same replicas and there are many replica duplications, the data accessibility in the entire network is low. To solve this problem, the DAFN method preliminary determines the replica allocation in the same way as the SAF method. Then, if there is replica duplication of a data item between two neighboring mobile hosts, the mobile host with the lower access frequency relative to the data item replaces the replica with another replica. Since many kinds of replicas can be shared among the neighboring mobile host, the data accessibility is higher than that in the SAF method.

3. *DCG (Dynamic Connectivity based Grouping)* method:
   The DCG method shares replicas in larger groups of mobile hosts than the DAFN method, which shares replicas among neighboring hosts. This method creates stable groups of mobile hosts at every relocation period and shares replicas in the groups. More specifically, this method creates groups of mobile hosts as *biconnected components* [1] in the network as shown in Figure 2 and then allocates replicas of data items on mobile hosts in each group in descending order of the access frequencies in the group. If a mobile host belongs to more than one biconnected component, i.e., the host is an *articulation point*, it belongs to only one group in which the corresponding biconnected component is first found. By grouping mobile hosts as a biconnected component, the group is not divided even if one mobile host disappears from the network or one link is disconnected in the groups. Thus, it is assumed that the group has high stability.

In this system environment, a request for a data item is successful only when the request issuing host accesses the original target data item or its replica with the same time stamp (version) as the original. That is, replicas of a data item become invalid after the original is updated. The request succeeds immediately if the request issuing host holds the original target data item or connects to the mobile host holding the original. Otherwise, if the request issuing host or at least one connected mobile host holds the replica of the target data item, the request issuing host tentatively accesses the replica. After the tentative access, when the request issuing host connects to the mobile host holding the original of the target data item, the tentative access is determined as having either succeeded or failed. This can be achieved by comparing the update logs recorded at the host holding the original with the information on the version (time stamp) of the accessed replica and the access time that are sent by the request issuing host. If the tentative access fails, the roll back occurs so that the request issuing mobile host recovers its state before accessing the replica. If the request issuing host and connected mobile hosts do not hold the original/replicas of the target data item, the request fails immediately.

In addition, we also make the following assumptions:

- We assign a unique *host identifier* to each mobile host in the system. The set of all mobile hosts in the system is denoted by $M = \{M_1, M_2, \cdots, M_m\}$, where m is the total number of mobile hosts and M_j $(1 \leq j \leq m)$ is a host identifier. Each mobile host moves freely.
- Data are handled as a data item which is a collection of data. We assign a unique *data identifier* to each data item located in the system. The set of all data items is denoted by $D = \{D_1, D_2, \cdots, D_n\}$, where n is the total number of data items and D_j $(1 \leq j \leq n)$ is a data identifier. All data items are of the same size, and the original of each data item is held by a particular mobile host.
- Each mobile host has memory space of C data items for creating replicas excluding the space for the original data item that the host holds.
- The access frequencies to data items from each mobile host are known and do not change. In a real environment, the access frequencies can usually be known by recording the log of access requests at each host and periodically calculating the values.
- Each data item is updated at inconstant intervals. This is done only by the mobile host which holds the original. After a data item is updated, its replicas become invalid.
- Each mobile host holds a table in which the information on time stamps of all data items in the entire network is recorded. A time stamp is the latest update time of the corresponding data item which the mobile host knows. This might be different from the actual latest update time. This information table is called the *time stamp table*.

4   Cache Invalidation Methods

In the assumed environment, we propose two new cache invalidation methods, which reduce the number of accessing invalid cached data items that have been updated. We call the methods, the *update broadcast* method and the *connection rebroadcast* method, respectively. In the following, we describe the details of the two methods.

4.1   Update Broadcast Method

In the update broadcast method, a mobile host holding an original data item broadcasts the invalidation report to connected mobile hosts every time when it updates the data item. Figure 3 shows an example of executing the update broadcast method.

The invalidation report includes the following information:

- The data identifier.
- The update time (time stamp).

When a mobile host receives the invalidation report, it refers to its own time stamp table and checks whether the replica held by the host is valid.

More specifically, first, the mobile host compares the time stamp in the received invalidation report with that of the corresponding data item in its own time stamp table. If the former is larger, the host updates the time stamp in its own time stamp table to that in the received invalidation report. At the same time, the host transmits the received invalidation report to its neighboring mobile hosts. Furthermore, if the host holds the invalid replica of the corresponding data item, the host discards the replica from its own cache. The memory space for the discarded replica is kept free, and the new replica of the data item is allocated again on the free memory space when it accesses the original/replica of the data item with the same or larger time stamp than that in its own time stamp table.

On the other hand, if the time stamp in the received invalidation report is same as that in the time stamp table, i.e., the host receives the same invalidation report once again, it does not transmit the received invalidation report to its neighboring mobile hosts and discards the report.

In this method, the traffic caused by broadcasting invalidation reports is small since mobile hosts broadcast only when they update the original data items. Mobile hosts connected to the host holding the original data item can keep the time stamp of the corresponding data item latest. However, since the network topology frequently changes due to the movement of mobile hosts, connected mobile hosts may hold different time stamps and different versions of the replicas for the same data item. Therefore, a special technique for data access is required which takes this fact into account.

4.2   Connection Rebroadcast Method

In the connection rebroadcast method, similar to the update broadcast method, a mobile host holding an original data item broadcasts the invalidation report every time when it updates the data item. In addition, every time when two mobile hosts are newly connected with each other, they rebroadcast invalidation reports that they have received before. Figure 4 shows an example of executing the connection rebroadcast method. Details of this method are as follows:

1. When two mobile hosts M_i and M_j ($i < j$) are newly connected with each other, the mobile host with larger suffix (j) of host identifier (M_j) transmits its own time stamp table to the other one.

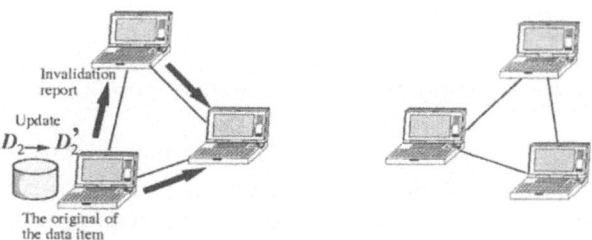

Fig. 3. Update broadcast method.

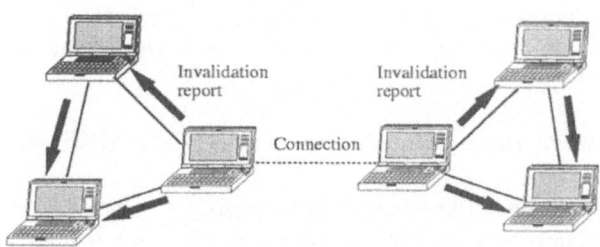

Fig. 4. Connection rebroadcast method.

2. Mobile host M_i compares the entry for each data item in its own time stamp table with that in the time stamp table received from mobile host M_j and updates its own time stamp table. Then, the following processes are executed:

   - M_i broadcasts the invalidation reports for data items whose time stamps held by M_i are smaller than that held by M_j to its connected mobile hosts except for M_j.
   - M_i sends the information on the updated time stamps for data items whose time stamps held by M_j are smaller than that held by M_i to M_j. Then, M_j broadcasts the invalidation reports for these items to its connected mobile hosts except for M_i.

Mobile hosts that receive the invalidation reports invalidate their replicas in the same way as the update broadcast method.

In this method, connected mobile hosts hold the same time stamp table because invalidation reports are rebroadcast whenever two mobile hosts are newly connected. Moreover, invalidation reports spread among a large number of mobile hosts and the cache invalidation is performed at these mobile hosts even if they are not connected to the mobile hosts holding the original data items. Thus, this method can further reduce the number of accesses to invalid cached data items than the update broadcast method. However, when the network topology frequently changes, the traffic caused by broadcasting invalidation reports is much higher than that in the update broadcast method due to the frequent rebroadcast of the reports.

5   Data Access

In this section, we explain data access techniques specialized for our proposed methods.

As mentioned in Section 3, when a request issuing host does not hold the original target data item, it broadcasts the access request in the network. Then, if one of the connected mobile hosts holds the original, the request issuing host accesses the original. Otherwise, if connected mobile hosts including the request issuing host hold the replicas, the request issuing host tentatively accesses the latest replica among them. When it connects with the mobile host holding the original afterward, the tentative data access is determined whether it has succeeded or failed. To do so, the request issuing host records the following information as the access log:

- The time when the request issuing host accessed the replica of the target data item.
- The data identifier of the target data items.
- The time stamp (version) of the replica at the time it was accessed.

Since the techniques for maintaining time stamp tables differ between the update broadcast method and the connect rebroadcast method, the data access technique specialized for each of the cache invalidation methods is needed. In the following, we explain the details of these data access techniques.

5.1   Data Access Manner for the Update Broadcast Method

In order to find out whether connected mobile hosts hold the original or replicas of the target data item, the request issuing host broadcasts a *data query packet*. The data query packet includes the following information:

- The host identifier of the mobile host that broadcasts the data query packet.
- The data identifier of the target data item.

If a mobile host that received the data query packet holds the original or a replica of the target data item, it sends a *data query reply packet* to the request issuing host. In the update broadcast method, since connected mobile hosts may have different time stamp tables, i.e., they may hold replicas of different versions, the data query reply packet includes the information on the time stamp of the target item. Specifically, it includes the following information:

- The host identifier of the mobile host that sends the data query reply packet.
- The data identifier of the target data item.
- The flag which shows whether the host holds the original target data item a replica.
- The time stamp of the original/replica of the target data item held by the mobile host.

If the request issuing host receives the data query reply packet from the mobile host holding the original target data item, it sends a *data request packet* to the mobile host holding the original immediately and accesses the original. Otherwise, it waits for a predetermined fixed time, e.g., one second in a mesoscale ad hoc network consisting of dozens of mobile hosts. After the time, if it receives the data query reply packets from mobile hosts holding replicas of the target item during the time, it sends a data request packet to the mobile host holding the latest replica among the hosts that sent the reply packet. Then, it tentatively accesses the latest replica.

5.2   Data Access Manner for the Connection Rebroadcast Method

In the connection rebroadcast method, a request issuing mobile host broadcasts a data query packet similar to the update broadcast method. If a mobile host that received the data query packet holds the original or a replica of the target data item, it sends a data query reply packet to the request issuing host. The data query reply packet includes the following information:

- The host identifier of the mobile host that sends the data query reply packet.
- The data identifier of the target data item.
- The flag which shows whether the host holds the original target data item or a replica.

In this method, connected mobile hosts have the same time stamp table, and thus, the hosts that send the data query reply packet hold replicas of the same version. Therefore, it is not necessary to add the information on the time stamp of the replica in the data query reply packet. Without waiting during fixed time, if the request issuing host receives the data query reply packet from mobile hosts holding the original or replicas of the target item, it sends a data request packet to the mobile host that sent the reply packet immediately.

6   Simulation Experiments

In this section, we present simulation results from our performance evaluation of the proposed methods.

6.1   Simulation Model

The number of mobile hosts in the entire network is 40 ($M = M_1, \cdots, M_{40}$), and they exist in a size 50×50 flatland. Each host randomly moves in all directions, and the movement speed is randomly determined from 0 to 1. The radio communication range of each mobile host is a circle with the radius of R. The number of kinds of data items in the entire network is 40, and M_i holds D_i ($i = 1, \cdots, 40$) as the original. Each mobile host creates up to C replicas. We adopt the three replica allocation methods proposed in [6]. Replicas are periodically relocated based on the relocation period T. The access frequency of each

Table 1. Parameter configuration.

Parameter	value
R	7 (1~19)
C	10 (1~39)
T	100
U_{avg}	100 (1~300)

Table 2. Packet size.

Packet name	size
Invalidation report	2
Data query packet	2
Data query reply packet (update broadcast method)	4
Data query reply packet (connection rebroadcast method)	3

mobile host, M_i, to D_j is $p_{ij} = 0.5 \times (1 + 0.001j)$. Each mobile host issues access requests for data items based on their access frequencies at every unit of time. Updates of data item D_i occur with intervals based on the exponential distribution with mean U_{avg}. Table 1 shows parameters and their values used in the simulation experiments. The parameters are basically fixed to constant values, but some parameters are changed within values in parentheses shown in Table 1. We define the size of each packet used in our proposed methods as the number of attributes in the packet. Table 2 shows the size of an invalidation report, a data query packet, and a data query reply packet.

In the simulation experiments, we randomly determine the initial position of each mobile host in the 50×50 flatland and evaluate the following four criteria of each of the two proposed methods during 50,000 units of time.

- *Data accessibility*:
  The ratio of the number of successful access requests to the number of all access requests issued during 50,000 units of time.
- *Number of accessing invalid replicas*:
  The number of tentative data accesses that resulted in failure during 50,000 units of time.
- *Invalidation report traffic*:
  The total traffic caused by broadcasting invalidation reports during 50,000 units of time. Here, the traffic for broadcasting an invalidation report is defined as the product of the total hop count for broadcasting it and its packet size.
- *Access traffic*:
  The total traffic caused by data accesses during 50,000 units of time. Here, the traffic for accessing a data item is defined as the product of the total hop count for broadcasting a data query packet and for sending the data query reply packets and the size of each packet.

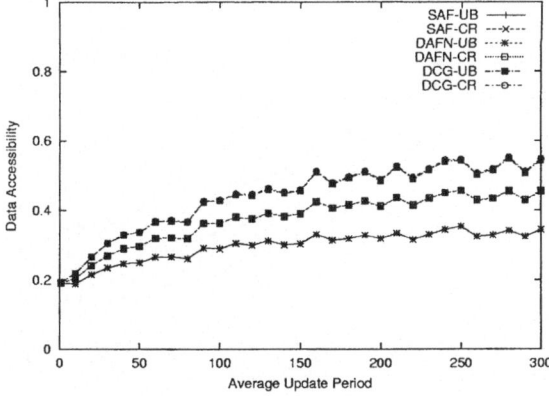

Fig. 5. Average update period and data accessibility.

6.2   Effects of Average Update Period

First, we examine the effects of the average update period of data items on each of the proposed methods. Figures 5, 6, 7, and 8 show the simulation results. In all graphs, the horizontal axis indicates the average update period, U_{avg}. The vertical axes indicate the data accessibility, the number of accessing invalid replicas, the invalidation report traffic, and the data access traffic, respectively. In all graphs, 'UB' denotes the update broadcast method and 'CR' denotes the connection rebroadcast method. Therefore, for example, 'SAF–UB' denotes the case where the SAF method is used as a replica relocation method and the update broadcast method is used as a cache invalidation method.

In Figure 5, two lines for the update broadcast method and the connection rebroadcast method overlap for each of the three replica allocation methods. The DCG method gives the highest data accessibility and the DAFN method gives the next highest. This result shows that the two cash invalidation methods give the same data accessibility when employing the same replica allocation method. This is because cache invalidation methods reduce the number of accessing invalid cached data items, but do not increase the number of accessing valid data items. Moreover, as the average update period gets longer, cached data items are valid for longer time, and thus the data accessibility of every replica allocation method gets higher.

Figure 6 shows that the connection rebroadcast method drastically reduces the number of accessing invalid replicas compared with the update broadcast method when employing the same replica allocation method. Of the replica allocation methods, the DCG method gives the largest number of accessing invalid cached data items, while it also gives the largest number of successful accesses as shown in Figure 5. This is because the DCG method has the highest possibility that connected mobile hosts hold replicas of the target data items.

In Figure 7, three lines for the three replica allocation methods overlap for each of the two cache invalidation methods. The connection rebroadcast method

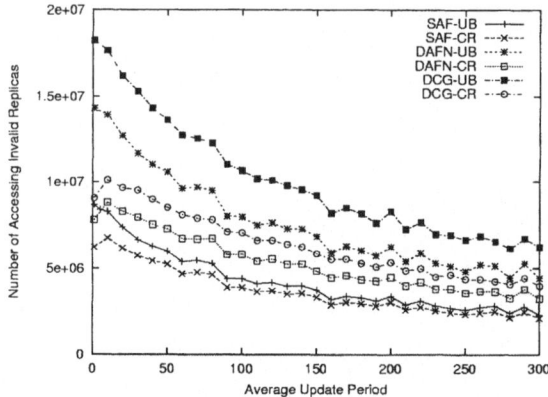

Fig. 6. Average update period and number of accessing invalid replicas.

produces higher amount of invalidation report traffic than the update broadcast method when employing the same replica allocation method. This result shows that the connection rebroadcast method produces much larger number of invalidation reports than the update broadcast method. As the average update period gets shorter, in both cache invalidation methods, the invalidation report traffic gets higher due to frequent broadcast of invalidation reports. As the average update period gets longer, in the update broadcast method, the invalidation report traffic gets closer to zero since invalidation reports are rarely broadcast. On the other hand, in the connection rebroadcast method, as the average update period gets longer, the invalidation report traffic gets closer to a certain value but not to zero. This is due to the impact of rebroadcasting invalidation reports when two hosts are newly connected. Since the invalidation report traffic greatly depends on the network topology but not replica allocation methods, every replica allocation method produces almost the same amount of invalidation report traffic.

In Figure 8, three lines for the three replica allocation methods almost overlap for each of the two cache invalidation methods. The update broadcast method gives higher amount of data access traffic when employing the same replica allocation method. This is because the size of a data query reply packet used in the connection rebroadcast method is smaller than that in the update broadcast method and the connection rebroadcast method can reduce useless data query reply packets by means of effective cache invalidation. As the average update period gets longer, in both cache invalidation methods, the data access traffic changes unstably. This is because depending on the network topology and the average update period, the number of replicas held by each mobile host changes unstably.

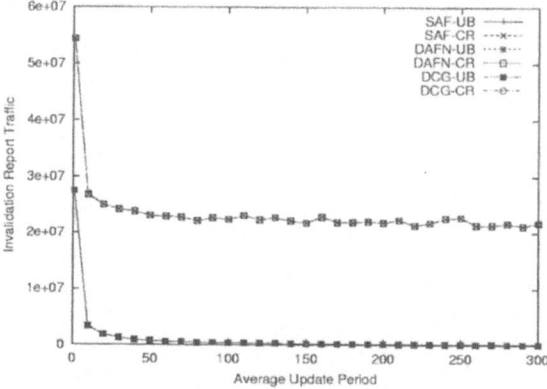

Fig. 7. Average update period and invalidation report traffic.

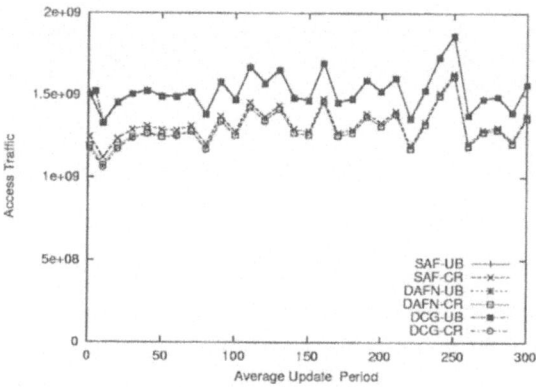

Fig. 8. Average update period and data access traffic.

6.3   Effects of Radio Communication Range

Next, we examine the effects of the radio communication range of mobile hosts on each of the proposed methods. Figures 9, 10, 11, and 12 show the simulation results. In all graphs, the horizontal axis indicates the radio communication range. The vertical axes indicate the data accessibility, the number of accessing invalid replicas, the invalidation report traffic, and the data access traffic, respectively.

In Figure 9, two lines for the update broadcast method and the connection rebroadcast method overlap for each of the three replica allocation methods similar to the case in Figure 5. The DCG method gives the highest data accessibility and the DAFN method gives the next highest. As the radio communication range gets longer, the data accessibility of each replica allocation method gets higher. This is because the possibility that the request issuing host connects with the mobile host holding the original of the target data item gets higher.

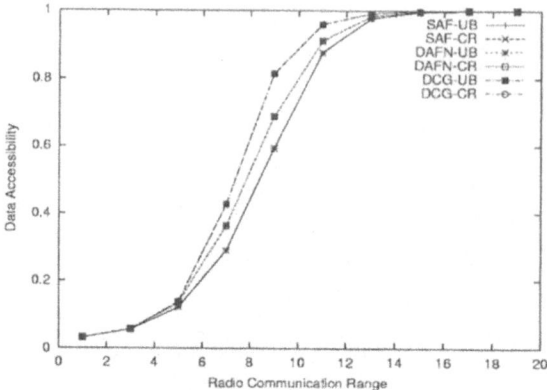

Fig. 9. Radio communication range and data accessibility.

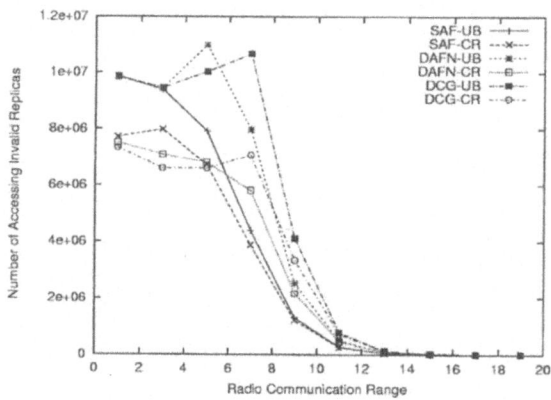

Fig. 10. Radio communication range and number of accessing invalid replicas.

Figure 10 shows that the connection rebroadcast method reduces the number of accessing invalid replicas compared with the update broadcast method when employing the same replica allocation method. In most cases, as the radio communication range gets longer, the number of accessing invalid replicas gets smaller. This is because the possibility that the request issuing host connects with the mobile host holding the original of the target data item gets higher, and thus, the request issuing host can access the original data item with high probability. However, in 'DAFN–UB'/'DCG–UB', the number of accessing invalid replicas gets larger when the radio communication range is between 4 and 6/8. In this range, as the radio communication range gets longer, the number of connected mobile hosts gets larger, and thus, the number of replicas held by them gets larger. Therefore, in the update broadcast method, the number of accessing invalid replicas also gets larger since invalidation reports are broadcast only when updates occur.

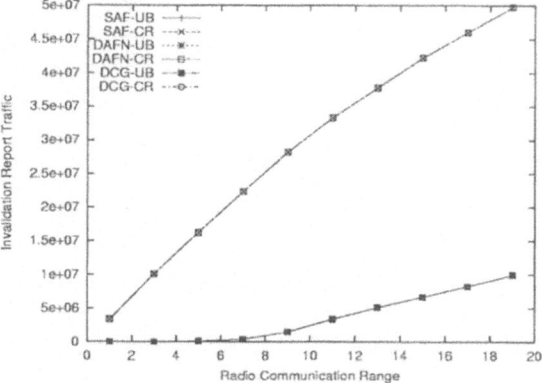

Fig. 11. Radio communication range and invalidation report traffic.

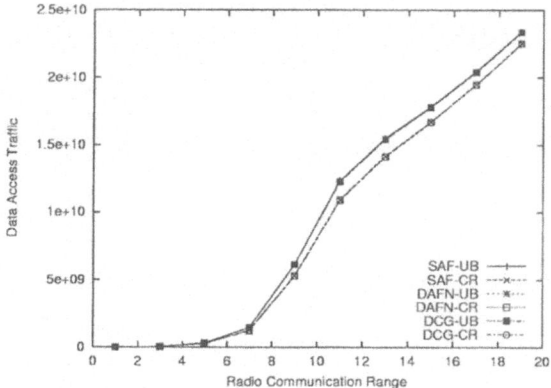

Fig. 12. Radio communication range and data access traffic.

In Figure 11, three lines for the three replica allocation methods overlap for each of the two cache invalidation methods. The connection rebroadcast method produces higher amount of invalidation report traffic than the update broadcast method when employing the same replica allocation method, similar to the result in Figure 7. As the radio communication range gets longer, the amount of invalidation report traffic gets higher because the number of connected mobile hosts gets larger.

In Figure 12, three lines for the three replica allocation methods overlap for each of the two cache invalidation methods. The update broadcast method gives higher amount of data access traffic when employing the same replica allocation method. This is due to the same reason in the case of Figure 8. As the radio communication range gets longer, in both cache invalidation methods, the amount of the data access traffic drastically gets higher. This is because the number of mobile hosts that send back the data query reply packets after

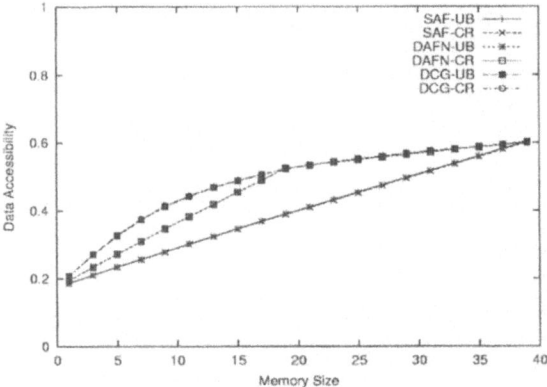

Fig. 13. Memory size and data accessibility.

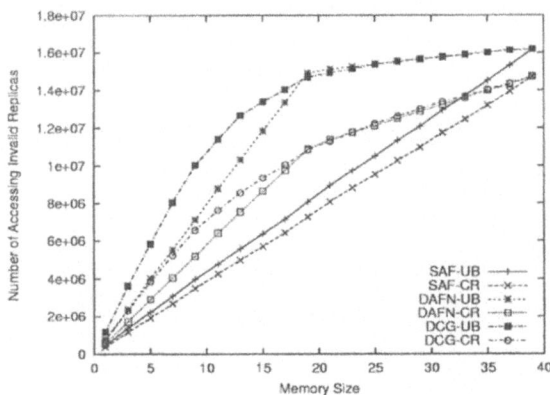

Fig. 14. Memory size period and number of accessing invalid replicas.

receiving the data query packet is large when the number of connected mobile hosts is large.

6.4 Effects of Memory Size

Finally, we examine the effects of the memory size of mobile hosts on each of the proposed methods. Figures 13, 14, 15, and 16 show the simulation results. In all graphs, the horizontal axis indicates the memory size. The vertical axes indicate the data accessibility, the number of accessing invalid replicas, the invalidation report traffic, and the data access traffic, respectively.

Figure 13 shows that cache invalidation methods do not affect the data accessibility similar to the cases in Figures 5 and 9. When the memory size is quite small or large, every replica allocation method gives almost the same data accessibility. This is because replica allocation method do not affect the data

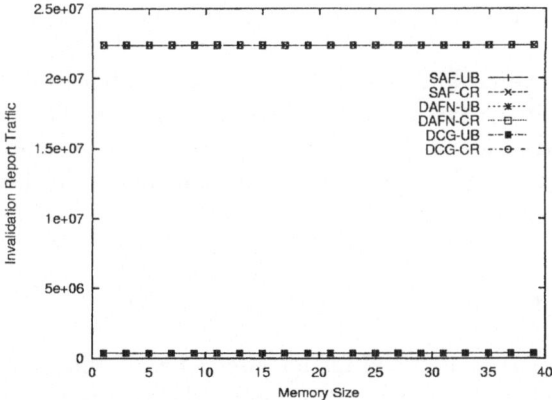

Fig. 15. Memory size and invalidation report traffic.

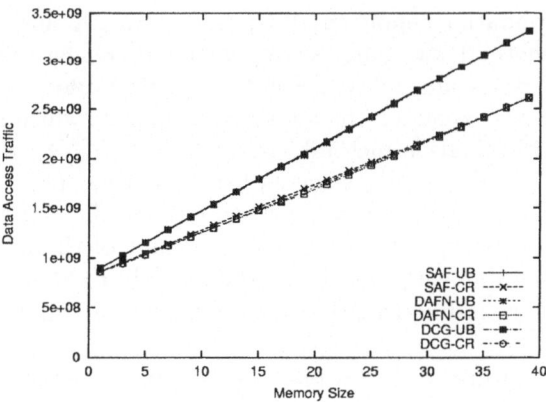

Fig. 16. Memory size and data access traffic.

accessibility because mobile hosts can hold very few replicas in the former case and because they can hold most replicas in the latter case.

Figure 14 shows that the connection rebroadcast method reduces the number of accessing invalid replicas compared with the update broadcast method similar to the cases in Figures 6 and 10. As the memory size gets larger, the number of accessing invalid replicas gets larger in all cases. This is because a large cache allows connected mobile hosts to share many kinds of replicas but also produces many invalid replicas.

In Figure 15, three lines for the three replica allocation methods overlap for each of the two cache invalidation methods. The connection rebroadcast method produces higher amount of invalidation report traffic than the update broadcast method when employing the same replica allocation method, similar to the results in Figures 7 and 11. In both methods, the cache size dose not affect the amount of invalidation report traffic. This is because the invalidation report traffic depends on the update period and the number of connected mobile hosts but not the memory size.

In Figure 16, three lines for the three replica allocation methods almost overlap for each of the two cache invalidation methods. The update broadcast method gives higher amount of data access traffic when employing the same replica allocation method. This is due to the same reason in the cases in Figures 8 and 12.

7   Conclusions

In this paper, we have assumed an ad hoc network where each data item is updated at inconstant intervals and proposed the two cache invalidation methods, the update broadcast method and the connection rebroadcast method, to invalidate cached data items that have been updated. In the update broadcast method, when a mobile host holding an original data item updates the item, it broadcasts an invalidation report to all connected mobile hosts. In the connection rebroadcast method, two mobile hosts which are connected newly compare their time stamp tables and rebroadcast the updated information on the time stamps. Moreover, we explained the data access manner which is specialized for each of the cache invalidation method.

The results of simulation experiments for evaluating the proposed methods show that the connection rebroadcast method reduces the number of accesses to invalid cached data items, but increases the amount of the invalidation report traffic. In a real environment, a proper method should be chosen among the two proposed methods according to the system characteristic and the performance requirement.

As part of our future work, we plan to consider a method which does not broadcast invalidation reports but broadcasts update information itself to keep replicas up-to-date efficiently and reduce the amount of data access traffic.

Acknowledgments. This research was supported in part by Special Coordination Funds for promoting Science and Technology of the Ministry of Education, Culture, Sports, Science and Technology of Japan and by "The 21st Century Center of Excellence Program" of the Ministry of Education, Culture, Sports, Science and Technology, Japan.

References

1. Aho, A.V., Hopcroft, J.E., and Ullman, J.D.: The design and analysis of computer algorithms, *Addison-Wesley*, 1974.
2. Barbara, D., and Imielinski, T.: Sleepers and workaholics: caching strategies in mobile environments, *Proc. ACM SIGMOD'94*, pp. 1–12, 1994.
3. Broch, J., Maltz, D.A., Johnson, D.B., Hu Y.C., and Jetcheva, J.: A performance comparison of multi-hop wireless ad hoc network routing protocols, *Proc. ACM MobiCom'98*, pp. 85–97, 1998.

4. Cai, J., Tan K.L., and Ooi, B.C.: On incremental cache coherency schemes in mobile computing environments, *Proc. IEEE ICDE'97*, pp. 114–123, 1997.
5. Cao, G.: A scalable low-latency cache invalidation strategy for mobile environments, *Proc. ACM MobiCom'00*, pp. 200–209, 2000.
6. Hara, T.: Effective replica allocation in ad hoc networks for improving data accessibility, *Proc. IEEE Infocom'01*, pp. 1568–1576, 2001.
7. Hara, T.: Replica allocation methods in ad hoc networks with data update, *ACM–Kluwer Journal on Mobile Networks and Applications*, to appear 2003.
8. Hu, Q., and Lee, D.: Cache algorithms based on adaptive invalidation reports for mobile environments, *Cluster Computing*, vol. 1, no. 1, pp. 39–48, 1998.
9. Jiang, M., Li, J., and Tay, Y.C.: Cluster based routing protocol(CBRP)," *Internet Draft, draft–ietf–manet–cbrp–spec–01.txt*, 1999.
10. Jing, J., Elmagarmid, A., Helal, A., and Alonso, R.: Bit-sequences: An adaptive cache invalidation method in mobile client/server environments, *ACM–Kluwer Journal on Mobile Networks and Applications* vol. 2, no. 2, pp. 115–127, 1997.
11. Johnson, D.B.: Routing in ad hoc networks of mobile hosts, *Proc. IEEE Workshop on Mobile Computing Systems and Applications*, pp. 158–163, 1994.
12. Lee, S., and Kim, C.: Neighbor supporting ad hoc multicast routing protocol, *Proc. ACM MobiHoc'00*, pp. 37–44, 2000.
13. Lee, S., Su, W., Hsu, J., Gerla, M., and Bagrodia, R.: A performance comparison study of ad hoc wireless multicast protocols, *Proc. IEEE Infocom'00*, pp. 565–574, 2000.
14. Lee, S.K., Hwang, C.S., and Yu, H.C.: Supporting transactional cache consistency in mobile database systems, *Proc. ACM MobiDE'99*, pp. 6–13, 1999.
15. Luo, J., Hubaux, J.P., and Eugster, P.: PAN: Providing reliable storage in mobile ad hoc networks with probabilistic quorum systems, *Proc. ACM MobiHoc'03*, pp. 1–12, 2003.
16. Pearlman, M.R. and Haas, Z.J.: Determining the optimal configuration for the zone routing protocol, *IEEE Journal on Selected Areas in Communications*, vol. 17, no. 8, pp. 1395–1414, 1999.
17. Perkins, C.E., and Bhagwat, P.: Highly dynamic destination–sequenced distance–vector routing (DSDV) for mobile computers, *Proc. ACM SIGCOMM'94*, pp. 234–244, 1994.
18. Perkins, C.E., and Royer, E.M.: Ad hoc on demand distance vector routing, *Proc. IEEE Workshop on Mobile Computing Systems and Applications (WMCSA'99)*, pp. 90–100, 1999.
19. Tan, K.L.: Organization of invalidation reports for energy-efficient cache invalidation in mobile environments, *ACM–Kluwer Journal on Mobile Networks and Applications*, vol. 6, no. 3, pp. 279–290, 2001.
20. Wang, K., and Li, B.: Efficient and guaranteed service coverage in partitionable mobile ad-hoc networks, *Proc. IEEE Infocom'02*, vol. 2, pp. 1089–1098, 2002.
21. Wu, K.L., Yu, P.S., and Chen, M.S.: Energy-efficient caching for wireless mobile computing," *Proc. IEEE ICDE'96*, pp. 336–343, 1996.

Taxonomy-Based Context Conveyance for Web Search

Said Mirza Pahlevi[1] and Hiroyuki Kitagawa[2]

[1] National Institute of Advanced Industrial Science and Technology (AIST),
Tsukuba, Ibaraki 305-8568, Japan
[2] University of Tsukuba,Tsukuba, Ibaraki 305-8573, Japan

Abstract. Taxonomy-based search services such as web directories are good starting points for users to search information needed from the web. In this paper we propose a method employing the search services to facilitate searches in any web search interfaces that support Boolean queries. The proposed method enables one to convey his current search context on taxonomy of a taxonomy-based search service to the searches conducted with the web search interfaces. The basic idea is to learn the search context in the form of a Boolean condition that is commonly accepted by many web search interfaces, and use the condition to modify the user query before forwarding it to the web search interfaces. To guarantee that the modified query can always be processed by the web search interfaces and to make the method adaptive to different user requirements on search result effectiveness, we have developed a new fast classification rule learning algorithm. Extensive experiments show that the proposed method can significantly improve the search result effectiveness of the web search interfaces.

1 Introduction

Taxonomy, which is a hierarchical arrangement of topics, has been used to facilitate web search and proved to be useful to improve the search precision. *Web directories* such as Yahoo [1] and ODP [2] are examples of the taxonomy-based search services. These search services are useful when we only have general topics or we are not sure how to narrow our search from a general topic. They can also help users understand how topics within a specific area are related and may suggest useful terms in conducting a search. As a result, they seem good starting points for novice users or for those who lack background and domain knowledge to find useful information on the web.

As a motivating example, imagine that a user wants to buy *salsa sauce* and its related products. The user starts to search the information from ODP. He goes to directory "/Shopping/Food/Condiments/" and finds dozens of relevant website entries there. After browsing the directory, suppose now he wants to search another type of information such as web pages, images or news that is also related to the salsa products but by using other web search interfaces/services that are not based on the taxonomy. He then puts keyword "salsa" in the search

R. Meersman et al. (Eds.): CoopIS/DOA/ODBASE 2003, LNCS 2888, pp. 536–553, 2003.
© Springer-Verlag Berlin Heidelberg 2003

field of the search services and gets many irrelevant matches such as web pages describing salsa dance and music. He then tries to refine his search by adding keyword "sauce" but still gets many irrelevant matches, for example pages related to salsa recipe and cooking. He can inspect the website entries in the "/Shopping/Food/Condiments/" directory to refine his query. But it is a rather hard and time-consuming task. The idea here is that we can automatically convey the current context on the directory to the search conducted with the other web search services so that the user can easily get many relevant matches from them.

The conveyance of taxonomy context becomes more important in the current situation where many search sites have started to integrate different search services including the taxonomy-based search services to enrich and improve their search functionalities. For example, Google [3] and Altavista [4] provide images, news and other types of search services besides the ordinary web and taxonomy-based search services. Lycos [5] also provides news search service but with an additional shopping search service.

In this paper, we propose a *taxonomy-based context conveyance method* (TACC) for integration of multiple web search services. A user starts a search from a taxonomy-based search service such as a web directory by specifying search keywords and a category. The system then probes the taxonomy-based search service using the given information and learns the user's current context in the form of a classification rule from the probe result. Finally, a query modifier is extracted from the rule, which in turn is used to modify the user query which is sent to target web search services.

To adapt TACC to different user requirements on search result effectiveness and properties of the target web search services, we have developed a *new fast classification rule learning algorithm*. The algorithm is aware of the precision/recall measures and query processing constraints of the target web search services.

The rest of the paper is organized as follows. Section 2 presents the architecture of TACC. Section 3 explains the proposed classification rule learning algorithm. Section 4 presents the experiments to evaluate the TACC and rule learning algorithm. Section 5 reviews related work. In the final section, we conclude the paper and mention future work.

2 Proposed Method

2.1 Taxonomy-Based Search Service

In this paper, we consider a taxonomy-based search service satisfying the following conditions. Note that most of the major web directories satisfy the conditions.

1. It maintains information pre-classified according to a hierarchy in a taxonomy. We call searchable units of information in the taxonomy *t-entries*. In the case of web directories, a t-entry is a combination of URL and short description of a web site.

2. Accepting a Boolean query and a category in the taxonomy, it executes search of t-entries located under the specified category. In addition, with just a Boolean query, it executes search of t-entries from the entire taxonomy hierarchy. We assume the Boolean query can be a conjunction of terms.
3. Information on the category of each matched t-entry is given in the returned result. Furthermore, we assume that information on the number of matched t-entries is also provided and it is placed at the first page of the returned result.

2.2   Web Search Service

TACC modifies a user query and sends the query to web search services. Most of the web search services accept Boolean queries, but they have differing acceptable query formats. Generally, there are two Boolean query formats accepted by the search services: *ordinary Boolean query format* and *template-based Boolean query format*. The former allows nested expressions with parentheses, while the latter does not. Examples of search services supporting the ordinary Boolean query format are Altavista and MSN [6]. Usually, a query is directly formulated and put into a search field provided by the search services.

Some search engines such as Google and Lycos support queries expressed in the template-based Boolean query format. In their advanced search facilities, a query is formulated indirectly using a *query template/form* consisting of fields associated with Boolean operators. For example, the advanced search of Google provides a template consisting of fields labeled by "with all of the words" corresponding to the AND operator, "without the words" corresponding to the NOT operator and "with one of the words" corresponding to the OR operator. Hence, the expressive power of the Boolean query expression supported by the template-based Boolean query format is very limited compared to that of the ordinary Boolean query format. Some search services such as Google and Lycos only support query expression of this type, and cannot accept queries in the form of the ordinary Boolean query format.

More precisely, queries in the template-based Boolean query format can be expressed as follows:

$$C = (w_{1,1} \wedge \ldots \wedge w_{1,i}) \wedge (\neg w_{2,1} \wedge \ldots \wedge \neg w_{2,j}) \wedge (w_{3,1} \vee \ldots \vee w_{3,k}) \qquad (1)$$

where $w_{m,n}$ corresponds to a search term/keyword, $i, j \geq 0$ and $k = 0$ or $k \geq 2$. For easy reference, we denote the first, second and third subexpression of Eq. 1 as $Conj_p$, $Conj_n$ and $Disj_p$, respectively.

Beyond the above format constraint, web search services also impose query size and units constraint. For example, Google accepts Boolean queries with a maximum of 10 keywords, while MSN with a maximum of 150 characters.

As a consequence, to guarantee that the modified queries are always acceptable by commonly used web search services, we must modify the user query such that its form conforms to the format supported by target web search services and its size is within the maximum allowable size. Since queries in the

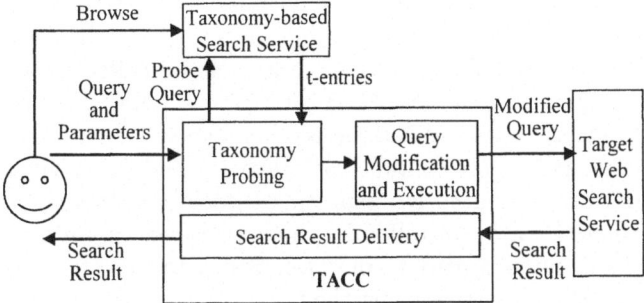

Fig. 1. System architecture of TACC.

template-based Boolean query format can also be processed by web search services accepting queries in the ordinary Boolean query format, we focus on queries in the format shown by Eq. 1[1]. Note that there are some web search services supporting only Boolean queries with $Disj_p = null$. The algorithm proposed here can cope with this case by imposing an addition constraint $k = 0$.

2.3 System Architecture and Query Modification Procedure

Fig.1 shows the system architecture of the TACC system we propose. The following are the processing steps involved in the system.

1. **Taxonomy Browsing Step.** In this step the user selects a *context category* G that matches his search intent by interactively browsing the taxonomy. He then defines a *query condition* Q which is a conjunction of terms. In this paper we call the pair of Q and G a *query* (Q, G). The user may also specify some search parameters that affect the search and modification process as explained below.

2. **Taxonomy Probing Step.** In this step, the system uses query (Q, G) given by the user to fetch the matched t-entries from the taxonomy-based search service. Since the matched t-entries are usually arranged in multiple result pages, fetching all of them will need many HTTP requests and take a lot of time. Hence, the system does not fetch all of the t-entries, rather it samples them as follows. Note that, we call the matched t-entries (not) under the specified context category G (including its subcategories) *relevant t-entries* (*irrelevant t-entries*).

   a) Get the number of all the relevant t-entries N_1 and the irrelevant t-entries N_2 by sending queries (Q, G) and $(Q, null)$ to the taxonomy-based search service. Note that $(Q, null)$ means that no context category is specified.

   b) Fetch $p + q \cdot N_1 / (N_1 + N_2)$ relevant t-entries, called *relevant samples*, from the context category. This step may need multiple HTTP requests to be

---

[1] In the preliminary work [7], we dealt with search services accepting the ordinary Boolean query format. This works deals with a broader scope of web search services.

issued to the search service. The purpose is to get t-entries contained in the search result for (Q, G) in addition to those returned in step (a)[2].

c) Fetch $p + q \cdot N_2/(N_1 + N_2)$ irrelevant t-entries called *irrelevant samples*, from categories other than G. It is done by sending queries (Q, g_i) to the search service, where g_i is a top-level category. When G is a subcategory of g_i, the result may contain both relevant and irrelevant t-entries. The t-entries are separated by inspecting associated category information.

Note that p and q are controlled by the user as search parameters.

3. **Query Modification and Execution Step.** In this step, first the system creates a classification rule using the t-entries sampled in the previous step. The rule is used to distinguish the *relevant class* from the *irrelevant class*. The relevant class is a class for the relevant t-entries while the irrelevant class is for the irrelevant t-entries. The rule takes the form of "$H \mapsto class$", where H conforms to Eq. 1. The system then extracts H from the rule and makes it a *query modifier*, which in turn is used to modify Q. Q is modified by AND-ing it with H (i.e., $Q \wedge H$). The modified query is then sent to the target web search service and the returned result is presented to the user.

3   Rule Learning Algorithm

3.1   Preliminaries

Constructing classification rules from a training set has been intensively studied in the area of machine learning [8,9]. Usually, the existing algorithms induce a set of rules. Each rule takes the form of "$H \mapsto class$", where H is a conjunction of positive and negative literals and class is the target class name.

Three points differentiate the learning algorithm proposed here from the existing ones. First, it constructs a rule "$H \mapsto Relevant$" with H conforming to Eq. 1. Second, it induces a rule by explicitly constraining its size. Third, it selects the most promising rule based on the estimated *G-measure* of the modified query. Specifically, it selects a rule which would lead to the maximum *generalized effectiveness measure* (*G-measure*) given as follows [10]:

$$G - measure = \frac{1}{\alpha \cdot (1/recall) + (1 - \alpha) \cdot (1/precision)} \tag{2}$$

where we can trade off *precision* and *recall* by adjusting α ($0 \leq \alpha \leq 1$).

These three points are crucial in the context of web search. First, most of target web search services accept queries in the form of Eq. 1. Second, target web search services have different constraints on the acceptable query sizes as explained before. Third, the rule constructed here is used to modify the initial query condition Q. Therefore, the most promising rule should be chosen on the basis of how well it can improve search result effectiveness (*G-measure*) of the modified query.

---

[2] Query (Q, G) in step (a) fetches only the first page of the returned result that contains N_1.

3.2   Algorithm

A t-entry is regarded as a tuple and each attribute represents the presence or absence of a term in the t-entry as a binary feature. We use the set of t-entries fetched in the taxonomy probing step as the training set $(TSet)$. We label relevant t-entries as *relevant* and irrelevant ones as *irrelevant*.

The algorithm is summarized in Fig. 2. It accepts a training set $TSet$, rule size $mSize$ and α of *G-measure* as parameters. $TSet$ is randomly split into two disjointed subsets $GSet$ and $VSet$ with ratio 1:1. $GSet$ is used to construct candidate rules, while $VSet$ is used to select the best rule. The algorithm induces rule "$H \mapsto relevant$," which covers as many relevant t-entries and as few irrelevant t-entries in $GSet$. The rule also has the best estimated *G-measure* calculated with $VSet$ under a given α. H is created by first greedily constructing conjunct $Conj$ ($=Conj_p \wedge Conj_n$), and then disjunct $Disj_p$. The size of condition x, denoted as $size(x)$, is the number of literals included in it.

First, the algorithm splits $TSet$ into $GSet$ and $VSet$, and then extracts literal set $litSet$ from $GSet$ (line 2). This is done by first extracting terms from $GSet$, constructing positive and negative literals for each extracted term and then selecting the best literals. The best literals are selected by calculating the *weighted information gain* (WIG) of each literal when it is used to expand an empty/true condition and by picking literals with the k largest WIG values. The WIG [11] is given below.

$$WIG(c_{i+1}, c_i) = rel_{i+1} \cdot \left(log_2 \frac{rel_{i+1}}{rel_{i+1} + irrel_{i+1}} - log_2 \frac{rel_i}{rel_i + irrel_i} \right) \quad (3)$$

where rel_i $(irrel_i)$ is the number of relevant (irrelevant) t-entries in $GSet$ covered by condition c_i. c_i and c_{i+1} are conditions before and after the expansion. This measure rewards condition c_{i+1} which increases the density of relevant t-entries covered without greatly reducing the total number of covered relevant t-entries relative to c_i.

Next, the algorithm creates conjunct $Conj$ by calling function CRCONJ (line 3). CRCONJ creates $Conj$ by repeatedly AND-ing literals starting from an empty/true condition. At each iteration i, condition c_i is AND-ed with literal $l_i \in litSet$ producing a more restricted condition c_{i+1} (line 16). l_i is the one that yields the largest WIG for c_{i+1} relative to c_i. The literal selection is done by function BESTLITERAL at line 14. After c_{i+1} is produced, its *G-measure* for the given α is calculated with $VSet$ (line 17). If the *G-measure* value is greater than the maximum one obtained so far, then c_{i+1} is put into c_{best} (line 18). The loop stops if there is no literal with positive gain (line 15), no unused literal in $litSet$ (line 20), or the size of c_{i+1} is already equal to a given $mSize$ (i.e., the loop has completed). Finally, the best conjunct c_{best} is returned at line 22.

The algorithm then invokes CRDISJ (line 8) to construct $Disj_p$. The invocation is done, if the (current) sizes of $litSet$ and $mSize$ are greater than 1 (line 7). Similar to $Conj$, $Disj_p$ is created by repeatedly OR-ing positive literals. At each iteration i, condition c_i is OR-ed with (positive) literal $l_i \in litSet$ producing a longer condition c_{i+1}. l_i is selected such that it yields the largest weighted

CREATERULE($TSet, mSize, \alpha$)
1:   Split $TSet$ into $GSet$ and $VSet$;
2:   Determine literal set $litSet$;
3:   $Conj \leftarrow$ CRCONJ($GSet, VSet,$
       $litSet, mSize, \alpha$);
4:   $mSize \leftarrow mSize - size(Conj)$;
5:   $Disj_p \leftarrow true$;
6:   Remove negative literals
       from $litSet$;
7:   If $|litSet| > 1$ and $mSize > 1$
8:       $Disj_p \leftarrow$ CRDISJ($GSet, VSet,$
         $litSet, Conj, mSize, \alpha$);
9:   $H \leftarrow Conj \wedge Disj_p$;
10: Return rule "$H \mapsto relevant$";

CRCONJ($GSet, VSet, litSet, mSize, \alpha$)
11: $c_0 \leftarrow true$;
12: $c_{best} \leftarrow true$;
13: Loop ($i = 0$ to $mSize - 1$) {
14:      $l_i \leftarrow$ BESTLITERAL($GSet, litSet, c_i$);
15:      If no best literal, exit the loop;
16:      $c_{i+1} \leftarrow c_i \wedge l_i$;
17:      If $G\text{-}measure(c_{i+1}) >$
             $G\text{-}measure(c_{best})$
18:          $c_{best} \leftarrow c_{i+1}$;
19:      $litSet \leftarrow litSet \setminus \{l_i\}$;
20:      if $|litSet| = 0$, exit the loop;
21: }
22: return c_{best};

Fig. 2. Rule learning algorithm

information gain for c_{i+1} relative to $Conj$. This is done to ensure that we always create a disjunct that can further improve the weighted information gain of the previously created $Conj$. The remaining procedure is similar to CRCONJ, where CRDISJ returns the best disjunct obtained so far based on its $G\text{-}measure$. Finally, at the end of the algorithm (lines 9 and 10), $Conj$ is AND-ed with $Disj_p$ yielding H, and rule "$H \mapsto relevant$" is returned.

4   Experimental Evaluation

This section evaluates the effectiveness of TACC and the rule learning algorithm. The evaluation is done as follows.

1. To see the effect of the change of sample size, we calculate the *search result effectiveness* (*G-measure*) and *query modification time* of TACC with respect to different number of t-entries fetched in the taxonomy probing step. The query modification time is the time to sample the matched t-entries from the taxonomy-based search service and to construct a rule. For clarity, let us call taxonomy probing that samples t-entries based on parameters p and q as *p_q partial probing* and the one that fetches all the matched t-entries as *full probing*. This experiment is explained in Section 4.2.
2. To see the *effectiveness of the proposed algorithms*, we compare *G-measure* of the queries modified by TACC with that obtained by a method using an alternative rule learning algorithm that does not consider *G-measure*. This experiment is explained in Section 4.3.
3. To see the *dynamic behavior* of TACC, we compare *G-measure* of the queries modified by TACC with that obtained by a static query modification method. The static query modification method constructs a modification rule for each category in a taxonomy before running. To modify queries, it uses the same

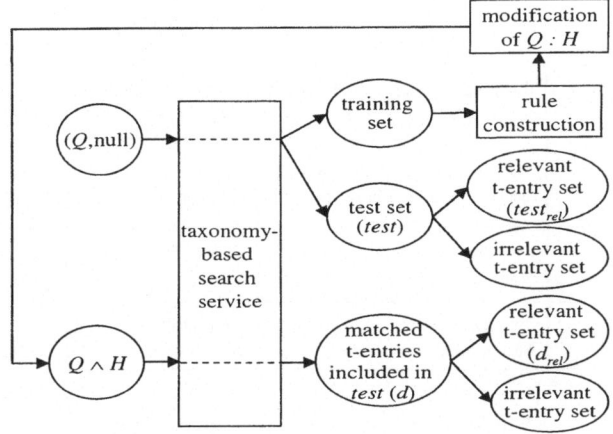

Fig. 3. G-measure calculation.

rule for a given context category, regardless of the query conditions given by the user. This experiment is explained in Section 4.4.

4. To see the precision of TACC with a real web search service, we measure the *document level precision* of queries modified by TACC using the Google search engine. This experiment is explained in Section 4.5.

4.1   G-Measure Calculation

This section explains the G-measure calculation in the first, second and third experiments. To calculate the *G-measure* of a modified query we need to know the "true answer" of the query. To easy relevance judgement, instead of sending the modified query to the target web search service, we send it "back" to the taxonomy-based search service. Since each t-entry in the result returned by the taxonomy-based search service is associated with the category information, we can easily identify the "true answer" of the query. Of course, to get an unbiased evaluation, we should not use the same data for rule construction and performance evaluation.

More specifically, the following steps are taken to calculate the G-measure in the experiments (Fig. 3).

1. We define a query (Q, G) and send $(Q, null)$ to the taxonomy-based search service.
2. Training and test sets are constructed using query result returned by the taxonomy-based search service. The construction is done as follows.
   a) For full probing, 2/3 of the matched t-entries are fetched and used as the training set; the remaining 1/3 is used as the test set[3].

---

[3] In the experiments, we send $(Q, null)$ to the taxonomy-based search service, get all the matched t-entries, and divide them into the training and test sets randomly using the ratio 2:1.

Query condition	Broad context category	Meaning	Narrow context category	Meaning
oil ∧ product	/Shopping/ Health/	Pages related to oil products for health (including beauty products)	/Shopping/Health/ Beauty/	Pages related to beauty oil products only
diet	/Shopping/ Health/	Pages selling diet products such as diet nutrition and weight loss products	/Shopping/Health/ Nutrition/	Pages especially selling diet nutrition products
solar	/Science/ Technology/	Pages about solar engineering and related applied sciences	/Science/Technology/ Energy/	Pages about solar energy sciences and technologies
Nepal	/Recreation/ Travel/	Pages about travel information of Nepal including travel business	/Recreation/Travel/ Travelogue/	Pages about personal travelogues of Nepal

Fig. 4. Some queries and their meanings.

b) For p_q partial probing, $(2p+q)$ matched t-entries are sampled and used for the training set. The test set is formed to include the same number of t-entries as the full probing case[4].

3. The training set is used to construct a rule, which in turn is used to modify the query condition Q.

4. The *modified query (condition)* $Q \wedge H$ is then sent "back" to the taxonomy-based search service and the *precision* and *recall* of the returned result are calculated based on the test set (*test*).

The *precision* and *recall* calculation is done as follows. Let d be a set of t-entries that are included both in the returned result set and *test*, and d_{rel} be a set of relevant t-entries in d. Recall that relevant t-entries are the ones under the context category G. Similarly, let $test_{rel}$ be a set of relevant t-entries in *test*. In the experiments, $test_{rel}$ is the "true answer" of the query because it is a relevant t-entry set that is not involved in constructing the rule. The *precision* and *recall* of the modified query $Q \wedge H$ and the *precision* of the initial query condition Q are given below. (Note that *recall* of Q is always 1.)

$$prec(Q \wedge H) = \frac{|d_{rel}|}{|d|} \quad recall(Q \wedge H) = \frac{|d_{rel}|}{|test_{rel}|} \quad prec(Q) = \frac{|test_{rel}|}{|test|}$$

We conduct the evaluation process with 3-fold cross validation and present the average of the three evaluation results. In the experiment we use ODP [2] as the taxonomy-based search service. We define 50 queries, which are divided into two types: 25 queries with *broad context categories* and 25 queries with *narrow context categories*. We say a context category as a broad one, if it is a direct subcategory of a top-category of the taxonomy and as a narrow one if it is a subcategory of a broad context category.

---

[4] In the experiments, we construct the test set by randomly taking t-entries fetched in the full probing that are not included in the training set of the p_q partial probing.

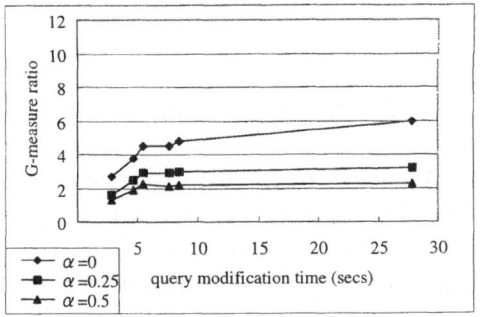

Fig. 5. Query modification time and *G-measure* ratio (broad context).

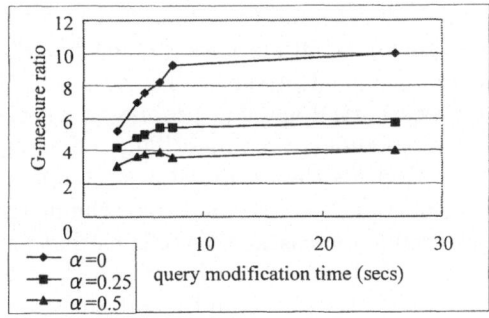

Fig. 6. Query modification time and *G-measure* ratio (narrow context).

Fig. 4 shows some queries and their meanings. The meanings are derived from the category description of the context categories provided by ODP. As shown in the figure, the meanings of queries with narrow context are more specific than those with broad context. The derived rules also have the same characteristic. That is, a rule for a query with a broad context has a broader scope than a rule for a query with a narrow context. For example, a derived rule for query ("diet", "/Shopping/Health/") is "offers ∧ products", while for query ("diet", "/Shopping/Health/Nutrition/") is "vitamins ∧ (supplements ∨ herbs)". We define the queries in this manner because we want to see the dynamic behavior of TACC. Terms in the query conditions are taken from the popular terms used in Google (http://www.google.com/press/zeitgeist.html) and Yahoo (http://buzz.yahoo.com).

4.2 Query Modification Time and Search Result Effectiveness

In this section we reveal the relationship between the query modification time and search result effectiveness (*G-measure*) for different number of fetched t-entries. For the p_q partial probing, we set $p = 20$ and $q = \{0, 80, 160, 240,$

320$\}^5$. The cardinality of the literal set ($|litSet|$) is set equal to the maximum query size $mSize$. The value of $mSize$ is set to 10 and α of *G-measure* is set to $\{0, 0.25, 0.5\}$.

Figs. 5 and 6 plot the query modification time versus the *G-measure* ratio for queries with broad and narrow context categories, respectively. The points in each line represent the 20_0, 20_80, 20_160, 20_240, 20_320 and full probing cases from left to right. The *G-measure* ratio is the relative *G-measure* value taking *G-measure* of the initial query condition Q as the base. It is obtained by dividing the *G-measure* value of the modified query ($Q \wedge H$) by that of Q, then taking the average over 25 queries.

The figures show that all probing types can significantly increase search result effectiveness of the modified queries. The query modification time of the p_q partial probing is much smaller than that of full probing. The reason is that the partial probing gets only a fixed number of matched t-entries, which is usually much smaller than the number of all matches. Longer modification time usually results in a higher search result effectiveness. However, the difference in search result effectiveness between partial and full probing is not significant compared to the differences in their modification times. This indicates that choosing appropriate parameters (p, q) yields the results almost comparable to full probing, but with much less modification time. Beyond that, the increase in search result effectiveness lessens as α value increases. This tells us that for α of 0.25 or more, full probing search result effectiveness can be obtained with a relatively small sample size. Since the modification time and result effectiveness depend on the sample size, a user may control the trade off between them by adjusting the parameters.

4.3   Use of G-Measure in Rule Construction

This section evaluates the effectiveness of selecting the best rule condition (H) based on *G-measure*. We do this by comparing *G-measure* of queries modified using TACC and those modified using a method employing an alternative algorithm (denoted as an *alternative method*). The alternative algorithm is the one that constructs *Conj* and *Disj$_p$* without considering *G-measure* value of the condition. That is, the condition is repeatedly expanded until one of the stop conditions is satisfied and the finally constructed condition is returned[6].

Figs. 7 and 8 show the result for 20_320 partial probing for queries with broad and narrow context categories, respectively. The result for full probing is similar so we omit it. The *G-measure* ratio here is the relative *G-measure* value taking that of the TACC as the base. Thus, it is obtained by dividing the *G-measure* value of the alternative method by that of the TACC. The *precision* and *recall* ratio are obtained in the same way. An asterisk above the bar indicates that

---

[5] We set p and q in this manner because ODP provides 20 t-entries in each result page.

[6] For CRCONJ in Fig. 2, it is without lines 17 and 18, and line 22 returns the finally created condition.

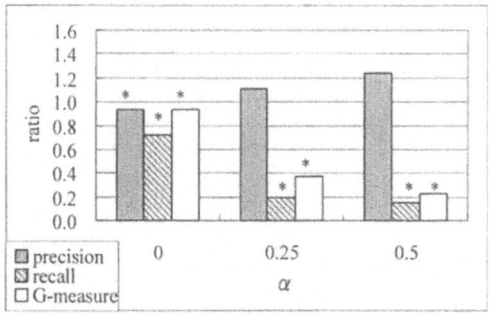

Fig. 7. Comparison with an alternative method (broad context).

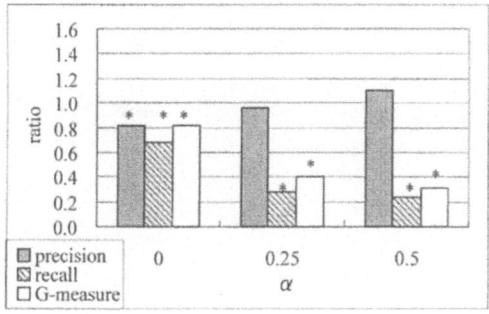

Fig. 8. Comparison with an alternative method (narrow context).

the difference between the TACC and the alternative method is statistically significant according to a paired one-sided t-test.

As can be seen, the *G-measure* of TACC always outperforms that of the alternative method for all α. The reason is that the rule learning algorithm used in TACC always selects the best rule condition having the maximum *G-measure* value. For $\alpha = 0$, precision of TACC outperforms that of the alternative method. As α increases, the precision ratio also increases but with a decrease in recall ratio. This indicates that the α is reflected in the search result of modified queries from TACC. (Note that the *precision* and *recall* of the alternative method do not change with the α value.)

4.4   Comparison with a Static Method

In this section, we reveal the dynamic characteristic of TACC. To do this, we compare TACC with a *static method*. The static method is a method that modifies a query with a pre-computed fixed classification rule. That is, different queries with the same context category are modified by the same rule associated with the category.

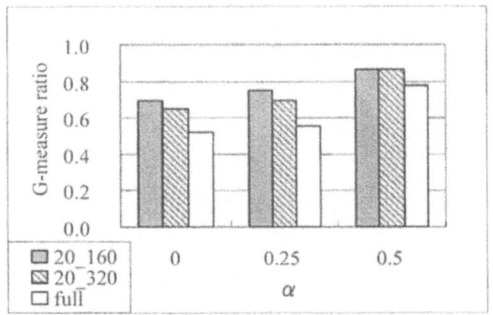

Fig. 9. Comparison with a static method (broad context).

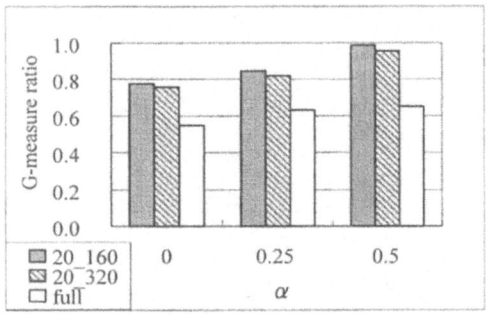

Fig. 10. Comparison with a static method (narrow context).

In the static method, a classification rule is created for each category of a taxonomy prior to query processing. It is done by treating t-entries in the category as relevant ones and those in the other categories as irrelevant ones. Note that the relevant/irrelevant t-entries do not necessarily meet the query condition Q. The rules are created by the proposed rule learning algorithm described in Section 3.2. We sample relevant t-entries of a category by taking randomly 30 percent of t-entries from the category, but limiting the maximum number to 6000 t-entries. For irrelevant t-entries, we sample them from the other categories, such that the number of irrelevant t-entries is three times larger than that of the relevant t-entries.

Figs. 9 and 10 show the result for queries with broad and narrow context categories, respectively. The *G-measure* ratio here is the relative *G-measure* value taking that of TACC as the base. As shown in the figure, TACC always outperforms the static method. The reason why the performance of the static method is poor is that the fixed rules associated with the context categories are forced to cover many topics that may exist in the categories. As a result, the query modifier derived from the rules cannot "fit" well to the queries. In contrast, rules derived in TACC need to cover specific topics implied by given queries.

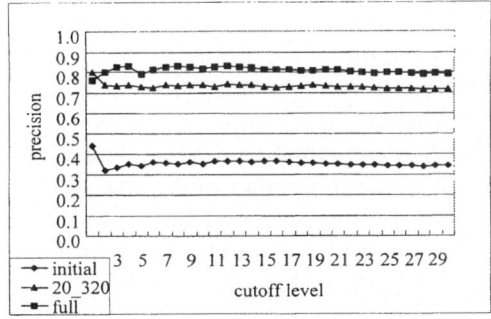

Fig. 11. Document level precision with Google (broad context).

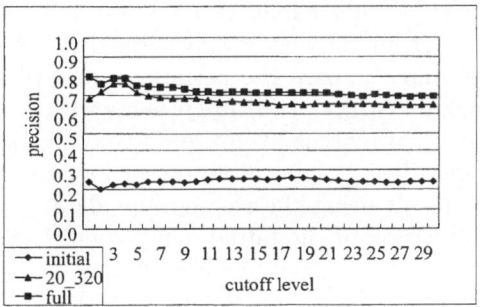

Fig. 12. Document level precision with Google (narrow context).

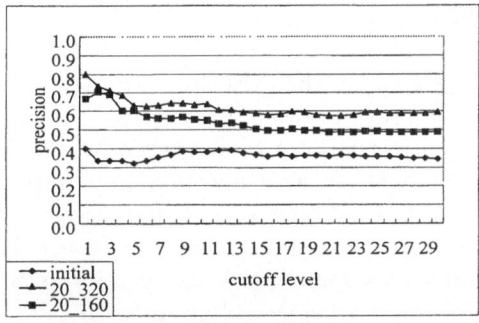

Fig. 13. Document level precision with Google (using newsgroups data).

4.5   Evaluation with Google

In this experiment, we evaluate the performance of TACC with a real web search service. We use Google as the target web search service and the *document level precision* as a performance measure. The document level precision is precision computed after a given number of documents/matches in the ranked query result have been fetched. We calculate the precision until cutoff 30. Relevance judgment is done manually by directly checking whether cited pages conform to the combination of the given query condition (Q) and context category (G). We use ODP as the taxonomy-based search service again and take the 25 queries from the previous experiment. The comparison is done for 20_320 partial and full probing. The $|litSet|$ is set equal to $mSize$. The value of $mSize$ is set to $10 - initSize$, where 10 is the maximum query size of Google and $initSize$ is the size of the initial query condition. In addition, α is set to 0.

Figs. 11 and 12 show the result. As can be seen, the document level precision with the 20_320 partial and full probing is much better than that of the initial query condition. Beyond that, the precision of the 20_320 partial and full probing is comparable.

In order to see the behavior of TACC for different taxonomy data, we use the Newsgroups search service provided by Google as the taxonomy-based search service. Similar to the ODP, this search service allows a user to search for articles in a particular newsgroup in the newsgroup hierarchy. For the experiment, we define new 15 queries and compare the performance of the 20_320 and 20_160 partial probing. We cannot carry out the full probing with the Newsgroups search service since the number of matched t-entries is too large and Google terms of service (TOS) does not allow us to send automated queries[7].

Fig. 13 shows the result using the Newsgroups data. As before, TACC can greatly increase the precision of the initial query condition, especially with the 20_320 partial probing. However, the precision increase is smaller compared to the ODP case because the quality of document collection in Newsgroups is lower compared to that of ODP[8].

5   Related Work

Inquirus 2 [12,13] developed at the NEC research institute also conveys the context information to improve the web search result. The system takes a query with context information in the form of a category of information desired and modifies the query based on the context information to improve the search result quality. The query is modified by using a set of modification terms extracted from the document collection of the category using the expected entropy loss. They have extended the work by extracting the modification terms using SVMs [14]. Another related work is keyword-spice [15]. Similar to the Inquirus, the system also modifies a user query based on a specific category, but it uses a decision tree learning algorithm to construct the modification terms instead. Both methods do not utilize existing taxonomy, rather they require the system administrators to construct (flat) context categories and extract the modification terms from them prior to the running time. In this sense, these methods are similar with the static method described in Section 4.4.

---

[7] For the partial probing, we send queries using an ordinary web browser, fetch some returned pages and process them offline.

[8] The quality is low because most context categories selected from the Newsgroup hierarchy are unmoderated groups.

Another related work is to automatically infer context information from the everyday productivity application such as word processor to guide the web and database searching. The Watson project [16,17,18,19] and IntelliZap project [20] analize the web pages/documents that are currently opened by the user to extract important terms from the pages/documents. The extracted terms are then used to construct/modify a query sent to the search services. The Remembrance Agent [21,22,23] is an Emacs plug-in that suggests information relevant to what the user is reading or writing. This system continually looks for documents (such as e-mail archives and notes files) on the web related to documents that users are reading or writing. Adaptive web page recommendation services such as Fab [24], Webmate [25], Letizia [26], WebWatcher [27,28], HotList and ColdList [29] and Syskill & Webert [30] are also related to this work. Again, the above systems do not utilize taxonomy. Some of them use a vector space model to infer the context while the others use a clustering algorithm.

6   Conclusions and Future Work

Taxonomy-based search services such as web directories maintain web site information using taxonomy and provide users a category-based search. TACC ulitizes the characteristics of the taxonomy-based search services to facilitate searches in other Boolean web search services such as search engines. With TACC a user can convey his current search context in taxonomy of taxonomy-based search services to the next searches conducted with the other web search services.

The experiments indicate that by sampling only a small amount of data from the taxonomy-based search service, we can get a reasonably high retrieval effectiveness performance with fast query modification time. Beyond that, TACC is dynamic in that the classification rule constructed to modify a query is different depending on both the selected context category and the query condition given by the user. This dynamic nature leads to high retrieval effectiveness performance comparing to the static method. Another important characteristics is that TACC can effectively modify a query regardless of the position of its context category in the taxonomy. This enables the user to freely shift the broadness of his intent topics just by selecting an appropriate category from the taxonomy.

Another contribution is the new classification rule learning algorithm which is aware of the *G-measure* and query processing constraints imposed by the target web search services. This makes TACC adaptable to the variety of search effectiveness requirements and the query processing constraints.

TACC can be implemented in an interactive fashion. That is, a user may interactively modify his query if he does not satisfy with results from a current (modified) query. This can be done by allowing the user to change query modification parameters α, p and q, and resubmit his queries. For example, if a user gets a very small number of matches but most of them are relevant, and the user wants more matches probably with some noises, then he can increase the recall by increasing the α value. The system can also allow a user to select a rule to modify his query. Classification rule induction is an unstable/nondeterministic process: slightly changing the training data may result in a different rule. The system may repeat the rule construction n times, where each time it divides the training set randomly into $GSet$ and $VSet$. In this manner, the resulting $GSet$ and $VSet$ in each division are different and might result in different rules. The resulting rules are then presented to the user after ordering them in descending order according to their occurence number .

We are now investigating the t-entry fetching procedure to decrease the probing time. One alternative is to provide the irrelevant samples locally before running and fetch only the relevant ones from the taxonomy-based search services.

Acknowledgement. This research has been supported in part by the Grant-in-Aid for Scientific Research (#15017207, #15650011, #15300027) from MEXT and JSPS, Japan.

References

1. Yahoo. http://www.yahoo.com/.
2. ODP. http://dmoz.org/.
3. Google. http://www.google.com/.
4. Altavista. http://www.altavista.com/.
5. Lycos. http://dir.lycos.com/.
6. MSN. http://www.msn.com/.
7. Pahlevi, S.M., Kitagawa, H.: TAX-PQ: Dynamic taxonomy probing and query modification for topic-focused web search. In: 8th International Conference on Database Systems for Advanced Applications (DASFAA 2003). (2003) 91–100
8. Cohen, W.W.: Fast effective rule induction. In: International Conference on Machine Learning. (1995) 115–123
9. Clark, P., Niblett, T.: The CN2 induction algorithm. Machine Learning **3** (1989) 261–283
10. Ding, J., Berleant, D., Nettleton, D., Wurtele, E.: Mining medline: Abstracts, sentences, or phrases? In: Pacific Symposium on Biocomputing (PSB 2002). (2002) 326–337
11. Quinlan, J.: Learning logical definitions from relations. Machine Learning **5** (1990)
12. Glover, E., et al.: Improving category specific web search by learning query modifications. In: Symposium on Applications and the Internet, SAINT, San Diego, CA (2001)
13. Glover, E.J., Lawrence, S., Gordon, M.D., Birmingham, W.P., Giles, C.L.: Web search – your way. Communications of the ACM (1999) accepted for publication.
14. Flake, G., Glover, E., Lawrence, S., Giles, C.L.: Extracting query modifications from nonlinear SVMs. In: International World Wide Web Conference, Honolulu, Hawaii (2002)
15. Oyama, S., Kokubo, T., Ishida, T., Yamada, T., Kitamura, Y.: Keyword spices: A new method for building domain-specific web search engines. In: IJCAI. (2001) 1457–1466
16. Budzik, J., Hammond, K.: Watson: Anticipating and contextualizing information needs. In: 62nd Annual Meeting of the American Society for Information Science, Medford, NJ (1999)

17. Leake, D.B., Scherle, R., Budzik, J., Hammond, K.: Selecting task-relevant sources for just-in-time retrieval. In: AAAI-99 Workshop on Intelligent Information Systems), Menlo Park, CA, AAAI Press (1999)

18. Budzik, J., Hammond, K.: User interactions with everyday applications as context for just-in-time information access. In: Proceedings of the 2000 International Conference on Intelligent User Interfaces, New Orleans, Louisiana, ACM Press (2000)

19. Budzik, J., Hammond, K.J., Birnbaum, L., Krema, M.: Beyond similarity. In: Proceedings of the 2000 Workshop on Artificial Intelligence and Web Search, AAAI Press (2000)

20. Finkelstein, L., Gabrilovich, E., Matias, Y., Rivlin, E., Solan, Z., Wolfman, G., Ruppin, E.: Placing search in context: the concept revisited. In: World Wide Web. (2001) 406–414

21. Rhodes, J., Maes, P.: Just-in-time information retrieval agents. IBM Systems Journal special issue on the MIT Media Laboratory **39** (2000) 685–704

22. Rhodes, B., Starner, T.: The remembrance agent: A continuously running automated information retrieval system. In: The Proceedings of The First International Conference on The Practical Application of Intelligent Agents and Multi Agent Technology (PAAM '96). (1996) 487–495

23. Rhodes, B.: Margin notes: Building a contextually aware associative memory. In: Proceedings of the International Conference on Intelligent User Interfaces (IUI '00). (2000)

24. Balabanovic, M.: An adaptive web page recommendation service. In Johnson, W.L., Hayes-Roth, B., eds.: Proceedings of the First International Conference on Autonomous Agents (Agents'97), New York, ACM Press (1997) 378–385

25. Chen, L., Sycara, K.: WebMate: A personal agent for browsing and searching. In Sycara, K.P., Wooldridge, M., eds.: Proceedings of the 2nd International Conference on Autonomous Agents (Agents'98), New York, ACM Press (1998) 132–139

26. Lieberman, H.: Letizia: An agent that assists web browsing. In Mellish, C.S., ed.: Proceedings of the Fourteenth International Joint Conference on Artificial Intelligence (IJCAI-95), Montreal, Quebec, Canada, Morgan Kaufmann publishers Inc.: San Mateo, CA, USA (1995) 924–929

27. Armstrong, R., Freitag, D., Joachims, T., Mitchell, T.: Webwatcher: A learning apprentice for the world wide web. In: AAAI Spring Symposium on Information Gathering. (1995) 6–12

28. Joachims, T., Freitag, D., Mitchell, T.M.: Web watcher: A tour guide for the world wide web. In: IJCAI (1). (1997) 770–777

29. Pazzani, M., Nguyen, L., Mantik, S.: Learning from hotlists and coldlists: towards a www information filtering and seeking agent (1995)

30. Pazzani, M.J., Muramatsu, J., Billsus, D.: Syskill webert: Identifying interesting web sites. In: AAAI/IAAI, Vol. 1. (1996) 54–61

An Analytical Study of Broadcast Based Cache Invalidation in Mobile Computing Networks

Kwong Yuen Lai, Zahir Tari, and Peter Bertok

RMIT University, School of Computer Science and Information Technology
GPO Box 3476V, Melbourne VIC 3001, Australia
{kwonlai,zahirt,pbertok}@cs.rmit.edu.au

Abstract. Maintaining client cache consistency is a difficult problem in large scale mobile computing systems due to limitations in bandwidth and client resources. Broadcast-based cache invalidation techniques can help coordinate clients and servers in such systems to ensure cache consistency. However, most performance analysis of existing invalidation techniques were carried out through simulation. In this paper we present analytical models of a number of existing cache invalidation schemes to facilitate comparison and provide a basis for future investigation into broadcast based cache invalidation techniques. In addition, we propose two new techniques to reduce the overhead of cache invalidation. The first technique improves downlink channel utilisation by reducing the size of invalidation reports. The second technique lowers uplink transmission by eliminating duplicate uplink requests. Test results show that the proposed methods significantly reduce the overhead of maintaining client cache consistency in mobile computing systems.

1 Introduction

Due to the limitation of wireless transmission mediums and handheld technologies, mobile computing networks are limited in bandwidth. Furthermore, in this environment, mobile clients are limited in transmission power and often experience disconnection. One technique commonly used to overcome these problems is *caching*. By storing data items in the caches of mobile clients, performance could be improved as clients can fetch data much more quickly from cache compared to fetching them over the wireless channel. Bandwidth and battery power are saved, as no transmission is required for clients to access data from their caches. Furthermore, the availability of data is improved because even when a mobile client is disconnected from the network, data stored in their local cache are still accessible, making disconnected operations a possibility.

In order to assist mobile clients in maintaining the consistency of their caches, a number of broadcast based cache invalidation techniques (e.g. [2], [9], [7], [10]) have been proposed. In these approaches, the server assist mobile clients in maintaining cache consistency by periodically broadcasting invalidation reports to the clients. An invalidation report contains information about data items that have been updated. When a mobile client receives an invalidation report, it can

R. Meersman et al. (Eds.): CoopIS/DOA/ODBASE 2003, LNCS 2888, pp. 554–572, 2003.
© Springer-Verlag Berlin Heidelberg 2003

use the report to identify out-dated data items in its cache and discard them before using the cache to answer queries.

Existing work on broadcast based cache invalidation (e.g. [2], [5], [6]) have focused on providing support for clients with different disconnection times, reducing access delay and improving energy efficiency. In these approaches, the size of an invalidation report is either static or determined by the' number of data items to be invalidated. Static size invalidation reports are expensive when only a few data items need to be invalidated, while schemes that depend on the number of data items updated are inefficient when the update rate of data items is high. For example, in the Broadcast Timestamp scheme [2], the size of each invalidation report is $g\times$(size of data item ID + size of timestamp), where g is the number of items updated. When few items are updated, the invalidation reports are small, however, when the update rate is high, the size of invalidation reports will increase proportionally. Similarly, other approaches such as the Update Invalidation Reports (UIR) scheme [7], Bit-Sequence invalidation (BS) scheme [9] and Broadcast-Based Group Invalidation (BGI) [13], do not address the issue of invalidation report size. The second problem with existing broadcast based cache invalidation schemes is that when a data item cached by many clients is invalidated, each client would send an uplink request to the server to ask for a new copy of it. This duplication of uplink requests results in a waste of bandwidth and client transmission power.

In this paper, we propose two techniques Validation-Invalidation Reports (VIR) and Delayed Requests Scheme (DRS) to solve the problem of large invalidation reports and duplicate uplink requests. Results from our analytical study of VIR and DRS are also presented. Existing work on broadcast based cache invalidation have rely on simulation in their analysis. We have developed analytical models of a number of existing representative broadcast-based cache invalidation schemes to provide a basis for evaluation and comparison. The rest of this paper is organised as follows. In section 2, a number of broadcast based cache invalidation schemes are described. This is followed by a description of VIR and DRS in section 3 and section 4. Detailed analytical models of the different schemes are presented in section 5. Lastly, our simulation results and conclusion are discussed in section 6 and section 7 respectively.

2 Related Work

This section describes four representative cache invalidation schemes, namely Broadcast Timestamp (TS)[2], Hierarchical Bit Sequences (BS) [9], Broadcast Based Group Invalidation (BGI) [13] and Update Invalidation Reports (UIR) [6]. We have studied these schemes in detail and identified their strengths and weaknesses to provide a basis for describing our contribution. The TS and BS scheme have been chosen in our study because these two schemes represent some of the earliest work in addressing cache invalidation issues in mobile environments. Much existing research on this topic have used the TS and BS schemes as benchmarks. The BGI and UIR schemes represent more recent work on broadcast based cache invalidation.

In the Broadcast Timestamp scheme (TS) [2], the server broadcasts invalidation reports periodically at intervals of L time units. Each invalidation report consists of the IDs and timestamps of all data items that have been updated during the last w broadcast intervals, where wL is referred to as the broadcast window.

Definition 1 *The invalidation reports used in TS is defined as:*

$$IR_i = \{[ID_j, t_j] \mid j \in D \text{ and } t_j \text{ is the timestamp of}$$
$$\text{the last update of } d_j \text{ such that } T_i - wL \leq t_j \leq T_i\},$$

where D is the set of all data items on the server, ID_j is the ID of a data item d_j and T_i is the time the validation report is broadcast. In the TS scheme, a client keeps all its queries in a list until an invalidation report is received. When the invalidation report is received, the client checks for any data items in its cache that has a timestamp earlier than that specified in the invalidation report. These data items are outdated, and are dropped from the cache. Once the cache has been validated, the client can use it to answer the queries stored. Uplink requests are sent to the server for any data items queried but not found in cache.

The Bit Sequences approach (BS) [9] attempts to optimise the size of invalidation reports by using a technique called bit-sequence naming. A bit sequence consists of N bits, each representing a data item on the server. Any bit set to 1 indicates the corresponding data item has been updated since the time of the time stamp attached to the bit sequence. Since mobile clients are subjected to frequent disconnections, the BS approach is further extended to cater for clients with different disconnection time by using a hierarchy of bit sequences each with a different time stamp instead of just one single bit sequence. Unlike the invalidation reports used in the TS scheme, the hierarchical bit sequence structure has a static size that is dependent on the number of data items on the server, and independent of the number of data items updated.

The Broadcast-based Group Invalidation scheme (BGI) [13] takes advantage of group level invalidation to salvage as much of client's cache as possible after disconnections. Data items on the server are divided into groups based on their update frequencies. The server periodically broadcasts invalidation reports consisting of two parts, called Object Invalidation Report (OIR) and Group Invalidation Report (GIR). Each OIR records any updates that have occurred in the last w broadcast intervals, while each GIR contains the latest update timestamps for each group in the last W broadcast intervals where $W > w > 0$. If a client was disconnected for a short period of time (i.e. less than wL time units), it makes use of the OIR to validate its cache. If it was disconnected for longer than wL but less than WL, then it can use the GIR to validate groups of objects in its cache. Because $W > w$, the GIR can help clients who were disconnected for a long period to validate their caches at a low cost.

In TS, BS and BGI, invalidation reports are broadcast every L time units. As a result, mobile clients must wait on average $\frac{L}{2}$ time units before receiving an invalidation report. To deal with this problem, the UIR scheme [7] was proposed. The UIR scheme is similar to TS, but instead of only broadcasting invalidation reports every L time units, the server also broadcasts a smaller version of the invalidation report every $\frac{L}{m}$ time units, where $m - 1$ is the number of times the smaller report is replicated during each broadcast interval. This smaller report is called the Update Invalidation Report (UIR). It contains the IDs of all data items updated since the last invalidation report was broadcast and the timestamp of the most recent update. It is therefore smaller in size compared to a normal invalidation report which covers updates that have occurred during the past w broadcast intervals. The advantage of this approach is that since UIRs are broadcast more frequently, clients can validate their caches and answer queries more quickly, however, this is at the expense of higher transmission overhead.

3   Dealing with Large Invalidation Reports

The approaches described in the previous section all suffer from the same problem which is related to the fact that the size of the invalidation reports grow proportionally to the update rate. At high update rates, very large reports are broadcast. The VIR (Validation-Invalidation Reports) scheme was proposed to deal with this problem.

In the VIR scheme, invalidation information are communicated to mobile clients using a combination of validation reports and invalidation reports. The invalidation reports used in VIR are similar to those used in the TS scheme and they take the form as described in Definition 1. To deal with the inefficiency of large invalidation reports, "Validation reports" are introduced. Validation reports are the opposite to invalidation reports. They contain information about data items that were *not* updated during the last broadcast interval. The reason validation reports are needed is so that when the size of invalidation reports becomes large due to large number of items being updated, validation reports can be used instead.

Definition 2 *The structure of the Validation Report at time T_i is in the form of:*

$$VR_i = \{[ID_j, t_j] \mid j \in D \text{ and } t_j \text{ is the timestamp of}$$
$$\text{the last update of } d_j \text{ such that } t_j \leq T_i - L\},$$

where D is the set of all data items on the server, ID_j is the ID of a data item d_j and T_i is the time the invalidation report is broadcast.

To take advantage of both validation reports and invalidation reports, in the VIR scheme, data items are divided into k clusters. The purpose of clustering is to separate those data items that are likely to be updated from those that are not. This results in clusters where either most items will be updated or most items will remain valid. At the end of each broadcast interval, the server constructs a report called a VIR and broadcasts it to help clients validate their caches. To inform clients about the clustering, the server attaches a cluster ID with each item it broadcasts.

A VIR consists of k subsections, called "swap vectors". Each swap vector contains information that will help clients validate data items belonging to the corresponding cluster. That is, clients can use swap vector x to validate data items belonging to Cluster x. Each swap vector takes the form of either a validation report or an invalidation report. When constructing VIRs, the server determines for each cluster whether a validation report or an invalidation report is smaller. The smaller of the two will be used as the corresponding swap vector in the VIR.

Definition 3 *Given a Cluster x, the swap vector for x at time i is defined as:*

$$SwapVector_{i,x} = \begin{cases} IR_{i,x} & if\ size(IR_{i,x}) \le size(VR_{i,x}) \\ VR_{i,x} & if\ size(VR_{i,x}) < size(IR_{i,x}), \end{cases}$$

where $IR_{i,x}$ is an invalidation report constructed for Cluster x at time i, $VR_{i,x}$ is a validation report constructed for Cluster x at time T_i.

Definition 4 *$size(IR_{i,x})$ and $size(VR_{i,x})$ in Definition 3 are calculated as follows:*

$$size(IR_{i,x}) = g_x \times (size_{ID} + size_{ts})$$
$$size(VR_{i,x}) = (n_x - p_x) \times (size_{ID} + size_{ts}),$$

where g_x is the number of items from Cluster x updated in the last w intervals, p_x is the number of items from Cluster x updated since the last report was broadcast, n_x is the number of items in Cluster x, $size_{ID}$ is the size of a data item ID and $size_{ts}$ is the size of a time stamp.

Definition 5 *The VIR broadcast at time T_i consists of k swap-vectors and is in the following form:*

$$VIR_i = \{[flag_x, SwapVector_{i,x}] \mid x \in 1..k\},$$

where k is the number of clusters and $flag_x$ is a single bit that indicates if a validation report or an invalidation report is used for the x-th cluster. $flag_x = 0$ indicates an invalidation report and $flag_x = 1$ is used for a validation report.

As suggested in definition 5, a VIR consists of a set of $(flag_x, SwapVector_{i,x})$ pairs, one for each cluster of data items. As each Swap Vector is the smaller of the validation report or invalidation report for the corresponding cluster, the overall size of the VIR will be smaller compared to using only invalidation reports or just validation reports. As demonstrated in our test results and analysis later in this paper, VIR effectively improves the utilisation of the downlink channel by reducing the amount of transmission used for transmitting cache validation information.

The size of a VIR is dependent on the difference between the number of valid data items and the number of invalid data items in each cluster. To minimise the size of a VIR, we need to create clusters where either most items will be updated, or most will remain valid. To do this, clustering is performed on the basis of update probability of each data item, $\Pr(d_i\ updated)$, which can be obtained from update history.

Definition 6 *The x-th cluster is defined as:*

$$Cluster_x = \left\{ [d_i] \mid \frac{x-1}{k} < Pr(d_i\ updated) \leq \frac{x}{k} \right\} \qquad where\ 1 \leq x \leq k.$$

That is, the x-th cluster consists of all data items that has an update probability between $\frac{x-1}{k}$ and $\frac{x}{k}$.

Using this clustering scheme, data items that are likely to be updated will be placed into the same cluster, while data items with low probability of update will be placed into other clusters. The optimal value for k depends on the distribution of update rates. In our testing (where the update rate is modelled using a Zipf distribution) we found that large k values are suitable when the mean update rate is high, while smaller k performs better when mean update rate is low.

4 Eliminating Duplicate Requests

In the VIR scheme, as well as in other existing invalidation schemes, when a data item cached by many clients is invalidated, a large number of uplink requests are sent to the server to request for the same item. This is a waste of bandwidth and transmission power because only one request is necessary to inform the server that the data item is needed by many clients. To improve the efficiency of the uplink channel, a second technique called the Delayed Requests Scheme (DRS) was proposed.

In DRS, when a data item d needed by client x is invalidated, the client does not send an uplink request to the server straight away. Instead, it waits for a period t_{wait}. The values of t_{wait} are uniformly distributed within the range 0 to t_{max}, where t_{max} is a system parameter that defines the maximum time a client would wait after receiving an invalidation report before sending an uplink request for the data item it needs. During the waiting period, clients would listen to the downlink channel to see if the server has planned to broadcast the item needed. If the item is going to be broadcast, the client does not need to send an uplink request. If the period t_{wait} expires and the client has not heard from the server about the scheduled broadcast of the item, then it will send an uplink request to ask for it. Because t_{wait} is distributed over the range 0 to t_{max}, different clients needing the same data item will wait different amount of time before sending uplink requests to the server. When the server receives a request, it sends out a notification message to inform all clients the data item has been requested. As a result of this, any clients still waiting (i.e., their t_{wait} have not yet expired) will stop the count down of t_{wait} and wait for the broadcast of the item.

When comparing DRS to existing invalidation schemes, the advantages become very clear. For example in the TS scheme, if c clients have cached data item d_i, and later on, d_i is invalidated, then c uplink requests will be sent to the server to ask for d_i. Using DRS, when a client x finishes waiting its waiting period, $t_{wait}(x, d_i)$, it will send an uplink request to the server. The server then informs all other clients that d_i has been requested, and there is no need to send any more requests for it. In this case, the number of uplink requests is reduced by c - 1. Although the waiting period increases access latency, the increase is bounded, and is generally small for cases where multiple clients need the same data item. The maximum waiting time for a client needing item d_i is equal to $min(t_{wait}(x, d_i)|x \in X)$ where X is the set of clients waiting for item d_i.

Although t_{wait} can be generated using a uniformly distributed random variable, this does not take in to consideration how long clients have already been waiting for their queries to be answered. To compute better values for t_{wait}, it would be reasonable to assume that clients who have been waiting longer are more eager to have their queries answered. With this in mind, we propose an alternative method to generate values for t_{wait}. Assume client x queries data item d_i at time t_{query} and the last invalidation report was broadcast at time t_{IR}. The value of $t_{wait}(x, d_i)$ can be calculated as :

$$t_{wait}(x, d_i) = \frac{(t_{query} - t_{IR})}{L} \times t_{max}, \tag{1}$$

where L is the length of the broadcast period.

By calculating t_{wait} based on t_{query} and t_{IR} as shown in Equation 1, clients who have submitted queries earlier in the broadcast interval will finish their t_{wait} sooner than clients who have submitted their queries late in the broadcast interval. Since clients query data items independently of each other, queries from all clients are distributed uniformly throughout each broadcast interval. As a result, using Eq. 1 to generate t_{wait} allows clients who have been waiting longer to send uplink requests sooner, while other clients can benefit from not having to send uplink requests once notification is received.

5   Analytical Comparison

As far as we are aware, none of the existing work on broadcast based cache invalidation has provided formalisation of their models. The performance evaluation in these papers are all simulation-based. In order to verify the accuracy of simulation results, and provide an easy comparison of the different schemes, we have developed formal models of a number of existing schemes, including Broadcast Time Stamp(TS), Bit Sequences(BS), Update Invalidation Reports Scheme (UIR), the Broadcast Group Invalidation scheme (BGI) and also our proposed schemes, VIR and DRS. In this section, we compare the performance of these schemes with regards to the mean report size, mean query delay and the mean number of uplink requests sent by each client during a broadcast interval.

5.1   System Model

In this section, we outline the basic system model and the assumptions made in our analysis. We consider a large number of C mobile clients located within a cell serviced by a single information server. Stored at the information server are N data items with a mean item size of $size_{item}$ bits. Each data item is labelled with a unique ID, starting from 1 to N. i.e., data item one is referred to as d_1, data item two as d_2 and the i-th data item is referred to as d_i. Furthermore, we assume data items are sorted based on their access rate, such that d_1 is the most frequently accessed data item, while d_N is the least frequently accessed.

Each mobile client is equipped with a wireless interface, allowing it to transmit requests to the server via an uplink channel with bandwidth BW_{uplink}, and receive data from the server via a downlink broadcast channel with bandwidth $BW_{downlink}$. Clients are also equipped with a cache of size $size_{cache}$, which can be used to store copies of data items. The Least Frequently Used (LFU) scheme is used to make cache replacement decisions when a client's cache becomes full.

Clients generate queries to access data items. If the latest copy of a queried data item can be found in cache, the client can answer the query using the cached copy. Otherwise, the client sends an uplink request with a size of $size_{request}$ to the server to request for the item it needs. Every client generates queries at a rate of λ_{query} queries per time unit following a Poisson process. To model access locality, we assume queries are distributed among data items following a Zipf distribution with parameter α [3] [4].

We also assume data items are only updated at the server. Updates arrive at a rate of μ updates per time unit and the inter-arrival times between updates are exponentially distributed. Updates are distributed among data items following a Zipf distribution. Similar to the model used in [1], the parameter $Offset_{update}$ is used to simulate an offset between the query and update distributions. The server keeps track of the list of data items that have been updated during each broadcast interval, and broadcasts invalidation reports every L time units to help clients validate their caches.

Given queries are distributed among data items following a Zipf distribution and data items are sorted according to their access frequency, the probability that a data item d_i is chosen for a query Q_j can be calculated by substituting the number of items, say N, and the data item ID, i, into the Zipf distribution [4]:

$$\Pr(d_i \in Q_j) = \frac{1}{i^\alpha} \frac{1}{\sum\limits_{b=1}^{N} \frac{1}{b^\alpha}} \qquad i \in 1..N \qquad (2)$$

Based on Eq. 2, the rate at which each client queries data item d_i is:

$$\lambda_i = \lambda_{query} \Pr(d_i \in Q_j) \qquad (3)$$

To calculate the probability that a data item is chosen for an update, we note that since the update distribution is shifted by $Offset_{update}$, this offset must be added to i in the equation. A modulus operator is also used to fold the value of the denominator $(i + Offset_{update} - 1)$ back to the range between $1..N$. The result is shown in Eq. 4, which expresses the probability of d_i being chosen for an update U_j.

$$\Pr(d_i \in U_j) = \frac{1}{((i + Offset_{update} - 1) \bmod N + 1)^\alpha} \frac{1}{\sum\limits_{b=1}^{N} \frac{1}{b^\alpha}} \qquad i \in 1..N \qquad (4)$$

Table 1. Legend of symbols used in theoretical model

Symbol	Meaning
C	The number of mobile clients
N	The number of data items on the server
D	The set of all data items on the server
$size_{item}$	The mean data item size (bits)
d_i	The i-th most frequently accessed data item
$size_{cache}$	Size of client cache (number of items)
$size_{request}$	Size of uplink request
$size_{ts}$	Size of a timestamp
$size_{ID}$	Size of a data item ID
λ_{query}	Query rate of a single client
λ_i	Query rate of d_i by a single client
μ	Server update rate
μ_i	Update rate of d_i
L	Broadcast interval (s)
w	Broadcast window (number of intervals)
$Offset_{update}$	Offset of update distribution
Q_j	A query at time t_j
U_j	An update at time t_j
k	Number of clusters used in the VIR scheme
m	Number of times UIRs are broadcast per interval in the UIR scheme
G	Number of groups used in the BGI scheme
t_{max}	Maximum waiting period in the DRS scheme
α	The Zipf parameter
MRS	Mean report size
MUR	Mean number of uplink requests per interval

Since the server generates updates at a rate of μ updates per time unit, the update rate of d_i is in the following form:

$$\mu_i = \mu \Pr(d_i \in U_j) \tag{5}$$

5.2   Mean Report Size

With the basics defined, we now compare the various schemes in terms of mean broadcast report size. Table 1 shows the different symbols used in our analysis.

Broadcast Timestamp (TS). In the TS scheme, the server broadcasts invalidation reports every L time units. These invalidation reports contain a list of IDs and update timestamps of data items that have been updated during the last wL time units (where wL is the broadcast window size). Since the server generate updates at a rate of μ updates per time unit, μwL updates are generated during each broadcast window. The number of data items included in each invalidation report (denoted as Y_{IR}) is therefore approximately equal to the sum of the probability of each data item being updated at least once in μwL updates.

$$Y_{IR} = \sum_{i=1}^{N} \left(1 - (1 - \Pr(d_i \in U_j))^{\mu w L}\right) \qquad (6)$$

For each data item that has been updated, their timestamp and ID are included in the invalidation report. The mean report size of the TS scheme (denoted by MRS_{TS}) is therefore:

$$MRS_{TS} = Y_{IR} \times (size_{ts} + size_{ID}) \qquad (7)$$

Bit Sequences (BS). The invalidation reports in the hierarchical bit sequences scheme is constructed from $log(N)$ bit sequences, where N is the number of items on the server. A timestamp is associated with each bit-sequence to support clients with different disconnection times. Since each bit sequence, b_i is twice the size of the bit sequence following it, $b_i - 1$, and the highest bit sequence use 1 bit to represent each data item on the server, the size of the invalidation reports used in BS is [9]:

$$MRS_{BS} = 2N + size_{ts} \times log(N) \qquad (8)$$

Note that unlike the other schemes investigated, the report size in the BS scheme is dependent only on the number of data items on the server, N, and independent of the update rate.

Update Invalidation Report (UIR). The UIR scheme is similar to TS in broadcasting a periodical invalidation report every L time units, but in this approach, the server also broadcasts Update Invalidation Reports every $\frac{L}{m}$ time units, where m is the number of update invalidation reports per interval. Update Invalidation Reports contain the IDs of data items updated since the last invalidation report or update invalidation report was broadcast, plus a single timestamp denoting the most recent update. The number of data items included in the p-th UIR broadcast during a period can be expressed as:

$$Y_{UIR,p} = \sum_{i=1}^{N} \left(1 - (1 - \Pr(d_i \in U_j))^{\mu \frac{L}{m} p}\right) \qquad p = \{1..m\} \qquad (9)$$

During each broadcast interval, one invalidation report, and m update invalidation reports are broadcast. In order to compare the UIR scheme to the other schemes, we calculate the mean report size for the UIR scheme as the sum of the sizes of all reports the server broadcast during a broadcast interval, that is:

$$MRS_{UIR} = Y_{IR} \times (size_{ts} + size_{ID}) + \sum_{p=1}^{m} [(Y_{UIR,p} \times size_{ID}) + size_{ts}] \qquad (10)$$

Broadcast based Group Invalidation(BGI). In the BGI scheme, the server broadcast a pair of invalidation reports during each broadcast interval. The first report is called the object invalidation report (OIR), which is similar to the invalidation reports used in the TS scheme. The second report is a group invalidation report (GIR) containing a set of group IDs and timestamps for each group. Assuming data items on the server have been divided in to G groups and the size of a group ID is $size_{groupID}$, the size of the group invalidation report is:

$$G \times (size_{ts} + size_{groupID}) \tag{11}$$

Since one OIR-GIR pair is broadcast in each broadcast interval, the mean report size for the BGI scheme is the sum of the mean OIR size and mean GIR size:

$$MRS_{BGI} = Y_{IR} \times (size_{ts} + size_{ID}) + G \times (size_{ts} + size_{groupID}) \tag{12}$$

Validation Invalidation Report(VIR). In the VIR scheme, data items are grouped into k different clusters based on their update probability. We define the j-th cluster as follows:

$$C_j = \left\{ d_i \in D : \frac{j-1}{k} < \left(1 - (1 - \Pr(d_i \in U_j))^{\mu w L}\right) \leq \frac{j}{k} \right\} \qquad k > 0, j \in 1..k, \tag{13}$$

where D is the set of all data items on the server. Based on this definition, the mean number of data items updated in the j-th cluster during a broadcast window is equal to:

$$Y_{VIR}(j) = \sum \left(1 - (1 - \Pr(d_i \in U_j))^{\mu w L}\right) \qquad \forall d_i \in C_j, j \in 1..k \tag{14}$$

The size of a validation-invalidation report is equal to the sum of all of its swap vectors. A swap vector contains the ID and timestamp of either all valid items or all updated items from a cluster depending on which list is smaller. It also has a single bit flag indicating if validation or invalidation is used for the cluster and a delimiter used to separate it from other swap vectors. Assuming the size of a delimiter is $size_{delim}$, the mean report size of the VIR scheme can be expressed as:

$$MRS_{VIR} = \sum_{j=1}^{k} \left((\min[Y_{VIR}(j), |C_j| - Y_{VIR}(j)]) \times (size_{ts} + size_{ID}) + 1 + size_{delim}\right) \tag{15}$$

Delayed Requests Scheme. The Delayed Requests scheme does not deal with optimising the mean broadcast report size, therefore the mean report size analysis is not applicable for DRS.

5.3   Mean Uplink Requests per Broadcast Interval

The number of uplink requests determines the amount of power clients spend on transmitting to the server. It is an important measure of how efficient a cache invalidation scheme is. Since uplink requests are only generated when a cache miss occurs, we must first calculate the cache miss ratio in order to find the mean uplink requests per broadcast interval.

In our model, the LFU cache replacement scheme is used, as a result the top $size_{cache}$ most frequently queried data items are cached by each client. A cache miss occurs if a client queries a data item d_i that is not in the most frequently queried list, i.e. a data item from the set $\{d_i : i \in (size_{cache} + 1)..N\}$. A cache miss also occurs if the queried item is updated before the arrival of the next invalidation report or if the queried item has been updated since it was last queried. The probability of a cache miss, $\Pr(cache\ miss)$ is therefore the sum of the probability of the following three conditions:

Pr(queried item not in most frequently queried list) $+$

Pr(queried item in frequently queried list)$\times$ Pr(queried item updated since last query) $+$

Pr(queried item in frequently queried list)$\times$ Pr(queried item not updated since last query) $\times$

Pr(queried item updated before next report is received)

$= \Pr(d_i \in Q_q : i \in (size_{cache} + 1)..N) +$

$\Pr(d_i \in Q_q : i \in 1..size_{cache}) \times \Pr(d_i \in U_u : t_u > t_{q-1}) +$

$\Pr(d_i \in Q_q : i \in 1..size_{cache}) \times \Pr(d_i \in U_u : t_u \leq t_{q-1}) \times \Pr(d_i \in U_u : t_u < t_{IR+1})$

$$(16)$$

The probability of the first condition can be calculated by summing the access probability of data items in the set $\{d_i : i \in (size_{cache} + 1)..N\}$:

$$\Pr(d_i \in Q_q : i \in (size_{cache} + 1)..N) = \sum_{i=size_{cache}+1}^{N} \Pr(d_i \in Q_j) \qquad (17)$$

To calculate the probability of the second condition, we denote the time since the client last queried d_i as t (where $t = t_q - t_{q-1}$). Since updates are distributed following a Poisson distribution, the probability that d_i has been updated during t is equal to:

$$\Pr(d_i \in U_u : t_{q-1} < t_u \leq t_q) = 1 - e^{-\mu_i t} \qquad (18)$$

Queries are distributed following a Poisson distribution, the probability density function of the time between two queries for d_i is therefore:

$$\Pr(t_q - t_{q-1} = t) = \lambda_i e^{-\lambda_i t} \qquad (19)$$

Integrating the product of Eq 18 and Eq 19 over t and then multiplying by the probability that d_i is in the set $\{d_i : i \in 1..size_{cache}\}$, we arrive at the expression for the probability of the second condition:

$$\Pr(d_i \in Q_q : i \in 1..size_{cache}) \times \Pr(d_i \in U_u : t_u > t_{q-1}) =$$

$$\sum_{i=1}^{size_{cache}} \left(\Pr(d_i \in Q_q) \times \int_0^{\infty} (\lambda_i e^{-\lambda_i t})(1 - e^{-\mu_i t}) dt \right) \qquad (20)$$

Lastly, for the third condition, we calculate the probability that the queried item is in the most frequently queried list, and have not been updated since it was last queried, but is updated before the arrival of the next invalidation report. Since the mean time between the arrival of invalidation reports is equal to $\frac{L}{2}$, the probability of the third condition is:

$$Pr(d_i \in Q_q : i \in 1..size_{cache}) \times Pr(d_i \in U_u : t_u \leq t_{q-1}) \times Pr(d_i \in U_u : t_u < t_{IR+1}) =$$

$$\sum_{i=1}^{size_{cache}} \left(Pr(d_i \in Q_q) \times \left(1 - \int_0^\infty (\lambda_i e^{-\lambda_i t})(1 - e^{-\mu_i t}) dt\right) \times \left(1 - (1 - Pr(d_i \in U_u))^{\frac{\mu L}{2}}\right)\right)$$

$$(21)$$

Based on the Eq 17, Eq 20 and Eq 21, the probability of cache miss for a mobile client, $Pr(cache\ miss)$, is equal to:

$$\sum_{i=size_{cache}+1}^{N} Pr(d_i \in Q_j) + \sum_{i=1}^{size_{cache}} \left(Pr(d_i \in Q_q) \int_0^\infty (\lambda_i e^{-\lambda_i t})(1 - e^{-\mu_i t}) dt \right) +$$

$$\sum_{i=1}^{size_{cache}} \left(Pr(d_i \in Q_q) \times \left(1 - \int_0^\infty (\lambda_i e^{-\lambda_i t})(1 - e^{-\mu_i t}) dt\right) \times \left(1 - (1 - Pr(d_i \in U_u))^{\frac{\mu L}{2}}\right)\right)$$

$$(22)$$

Simplifying the integration gives:

$$Pr(cache\ miss) = \sum_{i=size_{cache}+1}^{N} Pr(d_i \in Q_j) + \sum_{i=1}^{size_{cache}} \left(Pr(d_i \in Q_q) \left(\frac{\mu_i}{\lambda_i + \mu_i}\right)\right) +$$

$$\sum_{i=1}^{size_{cache}} \left(Pr(d_i \in Q_q) \times \left(\frac{\lambda_i}{\lambda_i + \mu_i}\right) \times \left(1 - (1 - Pr(d_i \in U_u))^{\frac{\mu L}{2}}\right)\right)$$

$$(23)$$

Given the cache miss ratio, the cache-hit ratio can be easily obtained:

$$Pr(cache\ hit) = 1 - Pr(cache\ miss) \tag{24}$$

Broadcast Timestamp (TS). Given the cache hit/miss ratio, we can now calculate the mean uplink requests per interval for the different schemes. In the TS scheme, the probability the i-item is queried by a client during a period is:

$$1 - (1 - Pr(d_i \in Q_j))^{\lambda_i L} \tag{25}$$

A client sends an uplink request if the item queried cannot be found in its cache. The probability a client would send an uplink request R_j for a data item d_i is therefore:

$$Pr(d_i \in R_j) = \left(1 - (1 - Pr(d_i \in Q_j))^{\lambda_i L}\right) \times Pr(cache\ miss) \tag{26}$$

The total number of uplink requests sent by a client for all data items is:

$$\sum_{i=1}^{N} \left(1 - (1 - Pr(d_i \in Q_j))^{\lambda_i L}\right) \times Pr(cache\ miss) \tag{27}$$

Lastly, the mean number of uplink requests sent by all clients during a broadcast interval in the TS is equal to:

$$MUR_{TS} = C. \sum_{i=1}^{N} \left(1 - (1 - \Pr(d_i \in Q_j))^{\lambda_i L}\right) \times \Pr(cache \; miss) \qquad (28)$$

Bit Sequences, Update Invalidation Reports, BGI, and VIR. Clients in the BS, UIR, BGI and VIR schemes respond to cache misses in the same manner as in the TS scheme, therefore the mean number of uplink requests sent by clients during each interval is the same as TS:

$$MUR = C \times \sum_{i=1}^{N} \left(1 - (1 - \Pr(d_i \in Q_j))^{\lambda_i L}\right) \times \Pr(cache \; miss) \qquad (29)$$

Delayed Requests Scheme (DRS). In the Delay Request Scheme, a request is sent only if no other client has already sent a request for the data item needed. As a result, we can approximate the DRS scheme by treating all clients in the system as one client, and all requests are coming from this same client. Only one unique request is sent for a data item needed from a cache miss. From this, we can calculate the mean number of uplink requests sent by clients during a period in the DRS scheme as:

$$MUR_{DRS} = \sum_{i=1}^{N} \left(1 - (1 - \Pr(d_i \in Q_j))^{\lambda_i LC}\right) \times \Pr(cache \; miss) \qquad (30)$$

6 Performance Testing

6.1 The Simulation Model

To ensure the accuracy of the analytical model developed, we performed simulation of the various schemes. The simulation was built using a discrete event simulation package called OMNET++ [14]. Different modules were written using C++, and these modules were then linked together using a proprietary language called "ned" provided by OMNET++.

The simulation model consists of a single server servicing multiple mobile clients. An update generator and a broadcast timer are connected to the server to simulate updates to data items, and periodical broadcasts. Updates are distributed among data items following a Zipf distribution, with exponentially distributed interarrival time. Attached to each client is a query generator, which generates queries following the Zipf distribution. Clients can send requests to the server via dedicated uplink channels, while the server communicates with the clients using a high bandwidth downlink channel.

In our simulation, clients manage their cache following the Least Frequently Used (LFU) scheme. At the start of the simulation, client caches are initialised

Table 2. Simulation Parameters

Parameter	Value
Simulation Duration	5000s
Number of Data Items on Server (N)	1000
Number of mobile clients (C)	100
Length of broadcast period (L)	20s
Broadcast windows size (w)	10
Client cache size ($size_{cache}$)	50 items
Client query rate (λ)	0.2/s
Update rate (μ)	0.2/s
Mean size of data item ($size_{cache}$)	4096 bits
Size of data item ID($size_{ID}$)	32 bits
Size of uplink request message ($size_{request}$)	64 bits
Size of data item timestamp ($size_{ts}$)	64 bits
Downlink channel bandwidth ($BW_{downlink}$)	200 kbps
Uplink channel bandwidth (BW_{up})	20 kbps
Zipf distribution parameter (α)	1.0

with the most frequently accessed data items. Each simulation run lasts for a duration of 5000 seconds (simulation time). Collection of all statistics starts only after the first 200 seconds to eliminate any effect of the initialisation on the measurements.

Table 2 shows the parameters used in our simulation; They are similar to those used in other studies of cache invalidation schemes for mobile environments [8] [10].

6.2   Simulation and Analytical Results – Mean Report Size

Figure 1 shows the mean report size of the TS, UIR and VIR schemes at different update rates. When update rate is low, the VIR scheme performance is similar to that of existing schemes. At higher update rates however, the VIR scheme reduces the size of the reports broadcast, and provides better performance than other schemes. The reason for this is that at high update rates, some clusters are likely to have more invalid items than valid items, which allows the VIR scheme to reduce report size by using a mix of validation and invalidation reports. From our test results, we can see that VIR can reduce mean report size by 5 to 15% across a range of different update rates. At very high update rate (20 updates/sec), VIR can provide a saving of 25% over existing schemes.

The number of data items on the server also has an effect on the size of broadcast reports as can be seen from Figure 2. The Bit-Sequences scheme performs much better than other schemes when the number of data items on the server is low. However, for servers with larger number of data items, the BS scheme is unsuitable because the report size in BS grows linearly to the number of data items. In our simulation, the BS scheme becomes more expensive when the number of items on the server reaches about 25000. When the number of items reaches 50000, report size in BS double that of other schemes. On the

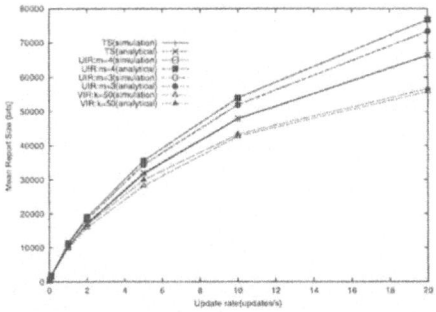

Fig. 1. Mean Report Size vs. Mean Update Rate

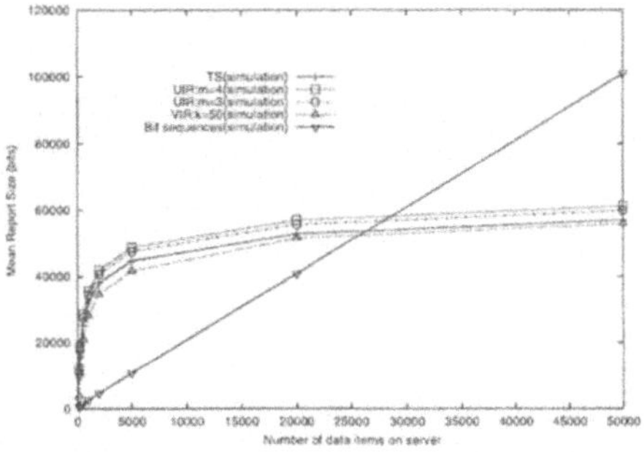

Fig. 2. Mean Report Size vs. Number of data items on server

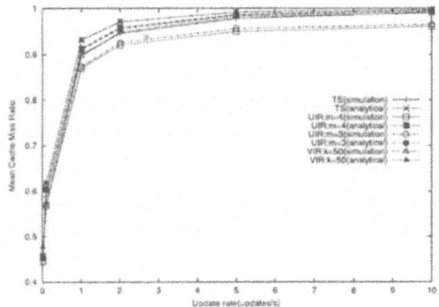

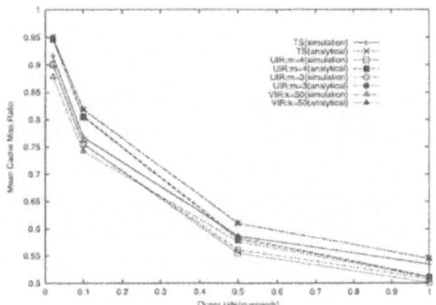

Fig. 3. Cache Miss Ratio vs. Update Rate

Fig. 4. Cache Miss Ratio vs. Query Rate

other hand, due to the effect of access locality, the TS, UIR and VIR schemes are much more scalable compared to BS.

6.3 Simulation and Analytical Results – Mean Cache Miss Ratio

The mean cache miss ratio at different update rates for different schemes is presented in Figure 3. In this simulation, the client query generation rate is 0.2 queries/second. We can see that when the query rate is higher compared to the update rate, the cache miss ratio drops significantly. The simulation results obtained differs slightly from the analytical models due to simplifications made in the analytical model. Similar results can be seen in Figure 4 where the cache miss ratio is graphed against the client query rate, with the update rate set at 0.2 updates/second. The cache miss ratio continues to drop as the query rate becomes higher in comparison to the update rate. This result shows that the query vs update rate ratio has great impact on the performance of cache invalidation schemes. When the query vs. update rate ratio is high, cache miss ratio becomes low, resulting in fewer uplink requests from clients, as clients can answer most queries through their caches. On the other hand, when the query vs update ratio is low, data items are updated more frequently than they are queried, resulting in high cache miss ratio, and more uplink requests.

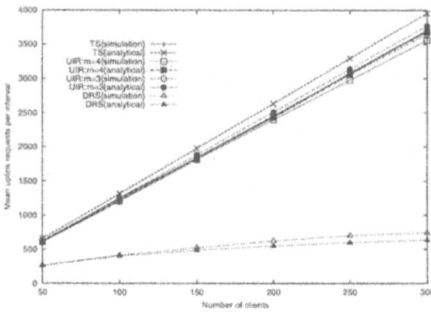

Fig. 5. Number of uplink request per period vs. Number of clients

6.4   Simulation and Analytical Results – Mean Uplink Requests per Broadcast Period

The effect of having different number of mobile clients on the number of uplink requests per period is presented in Figure 5. From the graphs we can see that in existing schemes, the number of uplink requests sent by clients during each period increases in a linear fashion as the number of clients grows. Therefore, if the number of mobile clients is doubled, twice as many uplink requests can be expected. The results obtained for DRS shows that by using delayed requests, the number of uplink requests sent by clients is reduced significantly. The benefit of using DRS is greatest when there is a large number of clients in the system as this has highest probability of duplicate uplink requests.

Figure 6 shows the number of uplink requests sent by clients per period for different update rates. The results shows that in both TS and UIR, the number of uplink requests increases very quickly as update rate increases. When update rate is high, the number of data items invalidated by clients will also be high. This results in higher cache miss ratio, thus in more uplink requests. On the other hand, for the DRS scheme, the number of uplink requests sent by clients per period grows much more slowly with increased update rate as compared to the other schemes. Our test results shows that the DRS scheme can reduce the number of uplink requests sent by mobile clients significantly. Note that there is a discrepancy between the DRS simulation and DRS analytical graph. The difference is due to some clients sending uplink requests before they receive notification messages from the server. Since the time from the first client finishing waiting and sending an uplink request until the time when all clients receive notification about the uplink request is small, we assumed in our analytical model that for each data item queried, there can be at most one uplink request. However, from our simulation result it can be seen that occasionally a client would finish its waiting period before server notification arrives. As a result, the number of uplink requests in the simulation for DRS is slightly higher when compared to our analytical model.

The mean number of uplink requests sent by clients per period is shown against different query rates in Figure 7. As the query rate increases, the number of uplink requests sent by clients in the TS and UIR scheme also increases

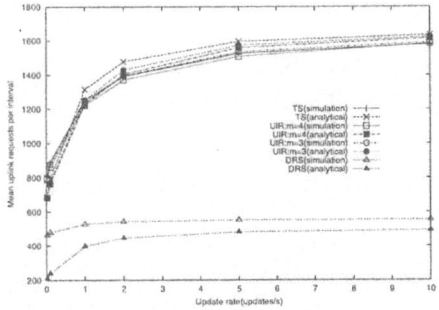

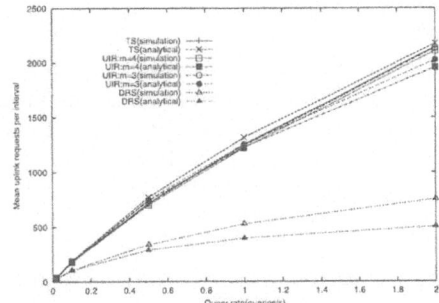

Fig. 6. Number of uplink request per period vs. Update rate

Fig. 7. Number of uplink request per period vs. Query rate

quickly. On the other hand, under DRS, the number of uplink requests remains very low, even at high query rates. In fact, our results show that using the DRS scheme reduces the total uplink requests per broadcast period by over 50%. The discrepancy between the simulation result and the analytical model is due to some clients finishing their waiting period before the arrival of the notifications as explained in the discussion of the previous figure.

7 Summary

In this paper, we have developed detailed analytical models to evaluate the performance of a number of existing schemes as well as VIR and DRS. We verified the accuracy of our simulation and found that the simulation results match closely with the models. We showed that VIR and DRS provide significant improvement in terms of bandwidth utilisation and energy efficiency over existing cache invalidation schemes. The VIR scheme reduces the size of the broadcast reports by clustering data items based on their update rate and providing validation information of each cluster using either validation or invalidation reports. The reduction in report size results in a saving in downlink bandwidth. DRS addresses the problem of duplicate uplink requests by using co-ordination messages sent by the server and delay timers at the clients.

Lastly, similar to other broadcast based invalidation schemes, VIR and DRS are only suitable in environments where a large population of clients share similar interest in the information they need to access. This is because the nature of broadcasting is a one-to-many relationship. If different clients have very different needs, then it becomes necessary for clients to set up one-to-one relationships with the server to access the information they need. In this case, pull based techniques are more suitable. As part of our future work, we intend to investigate the effect changing update and query patterns have on the different schemes.

Acknowledgement. This research is funded by the ARC Linkage Grant, project no. LP0218853 awarded by the Australian Research Council (ARC) 2002-2004 and partially funded SUN Microsystems grant no. 7832-030217-AUS.

References

[1]   S.A. Charya, R. Alonso, M. Franklin, and S. Zdonik: Broadcast Disks: Data Management for Asymmetric Communication Environments. In Proc. *ACM SIGMOD Conference on Management of Data*, pp. 199–210, May 1995.

[2]   D. Barbara and T. Imielinski: Sleepers and workaholics: caching strategies for mobile environments. In Proc. *ACM SIGMOD Conference on Management of Data*, pp. 1–12, 1994.

[3]   P. Barford, A. Bestavros, A. Bradley, and M. Crovella: Changes in Web client access patterns: Characteristics and caching implications. *World Wide Web, Special issue on Characterisation and Performance Evaluation*, Volume 2 Issue 1–2, 1999.

[4]   L. Breslau, P. Cao, L. Fan, G. Phillips, and S. Shenker: Web caching and Zipf-like distributions: Evidence and Implications. In Proc. *INFOCOM*, pp. 126–134, 1999.

[5]   J. Cai and K. Tan: Energy-efficient selective cache invalidation. *Wireless Networks* (5), pp. 489–502, 1999.

[6]   G. Cao: Proactive power-aware cache management for mobile computing systems. *IEEE Transactions on Computers*, 51(6),pp. 608–621, June 2002.

[7]   G. Cao: A scalable low-latency cache invalidation strategy for mobile environments. In Proc. *International Conference on Mobile Computing and Networking*, pp. 200–209, 2000.

[8]   Q. Hu and D.L. Lee: Adaptive cache invalidation methods in mobile environments. In Proc. *International Symposium on High Performance Distributed Computing*, pp. 264–273,1997.

[9]   J. Jing and A. Elmagarmid: Bit-sequences: an adaptive cache invalidation method in mobile client/server environments. *ACM Mobile Networks and Applications*, 2 (2),pp. 115–127, 1997.

[10] A. Kahol, S.K Hurana, and S. Gupta: A strategy to manage cache consistency in a disconnected distributed environment. *IEEE Transactions on Parallel and Distributed Systems*, 12(7),pp. 686–700, July 2001.

[11] K.Y. Lai, Z. Tari, and P. Bertok: Cost efficient broadcast based cache invalidation for mobile environments. In Proc. *ACM Symposium on Applied Computing*, pp. 871–877, 2003.

[12] K. Tan, J. Cai, and B.C. Ooi: An evaluation of cache invalidation strategies in wireless environments. *IEEE Transactions on Parallel and Distributed Systems*, 12(8),pp. 789–807, August 2001.

[13] K. Tan and J. Cai: Broadcast based group invalidation: An energy-efficient cache invalidation strategy. *Information Sciences* (100), pp. 229–254, 1997.

[14] A. Varga: OMNET+ Discrete Event Simulation System Manual.
      http://whale.hit.bme.hu/omnetpp/manual/usman.htm

Fine-Grained Parallelism in Dynamic Web Content Generation: The Parse and Dispatch Approach

Stavros Papastavrou[1], George Samaras[1], Paraskevas Evripidou[1], and Panos K. Chrysanthis[2]

[1] Computer Science Department, University of Cyprus,
75 Kallipoleos St. P.O.Box 20537, Nicosia, Cyprus
{stavrosp,cssamara,skevos}@ucy.ac.cy
[2] Computer Science Department, University of Pittsburgh,
Sennott Square, Pittsburgh PA 15260, USA
panos@cs.pitt.edu

Abstract. Dynamic Web content is gaining in popularity over traditional static HTML as the means of providing Web users with personalized and dynamic information. To enable dynamic content, various technologies have been developed for embedding of script code blocks into static HTML files in order to perform various forms of tasks such as session tracking, bank transactions, financial calculations, products catalog generation, dynamic image generation, or even fetching information from remote servers. In this way, static HTML pages are transformed into dynamic web pages. Typically, dynamic Web pages include a number of tasks that are executed in a serial manner by current Web servers. In this paper, we propose a back-end, finer-grained parallel approach for dynamic content generation, and elaborate on how it affects the design and performance of Web servers. We have developed a prototype Web server that supports the parallel processing of tasks involved in the dynamic content generation with improved throughput as compared to the serial approach.

1 Introduction

Web servers are the basic component of the World Wide Web [4] in terms of content delivery. Early Web servers, such as the NSCA HTTPd Web server [15], were used for dissemination of static documents (files) based on a specification called the Hypertext Markup Language [13], a standard for publishing documents on the Internet. The need, however, for the delivery of non-static content, such as documents customized on the fly based on information provided by a single user, led to the specification of the Common Gateway Interface (CGI) [8, 24]. Web servers supporting the CGI generate dynamic content by running external programs (executables or scripts) that typically access an application specific database. According to CGI, each client request requires the separate execution of an external program.

With the great expansion of the Web, the need for a more scalable, persistent, and faster alternative to CGI revolutionized the design of Web servers. Modern Web servers [14] support multiple runtime environments in which various augmented

R. Meersman et al. (Eds.): CoopIS/DOA/ODBASE 2003, LNCS 2888, pp. 573–588, 2003.
© Springer-Verlag Berlin Heidelberg 2003

versions of HTML code execute in a scripting mode in order to generate dynamic content. Such a runtime environment executes either as library code within the Web server process, or as a separate process communicating via a standard application interface. Microsoft's Active Server Pages [1], Macromedia's Cold Fusion [12], and PHP [22] are examples of such a runtime technology that support augmented versions of HTML.

A typical augmented HTML script file that is executed in order to generate a dynamic Web page consists of both standard HTML code and multiple insertions of vendor-specific script code. A piece of script code (code block) may map to a simple task, such as an animated counter or a personal menu bar generation, to complex tasks, such as lengthy distributed database transactions. As we explain later on, there can be notable delays in generating a dynamic Web page due to (a) the serial manner in which traditional Web servers execute those tasks, and (b) the long duration of executing a particular task.

In order to boost performance, recent studies propose a number of content-aware and link-aware dispatching and load balancing algorithms to be used over a cluster of Web servers [3, 5, 10, 11, 23]. According to *content-aware dispatching*, HTTP requests are routed to specialized Web servers based on their content type whereas *link-aware dispatching* routes HTTP request by mapping their URL using a hash table. Both approaches can boost the total throughput of a Web site's hosting environment by independently executing entire HTML scripts in parallel, however, they do not improve the throughput of a single Web server per se.

In this paper, we focus on improving a Web server's performance in producing dynamic Web content by introducing parallelism at finer granularities. In nutshell, the underline idea of our proposed in this paper *Parse & Dispatch* approach is to execute the tasks included in a dynamic Web page in parallel or concurrently. Our goal is not limited only in accelerating Web server performance, but also in identifying the design principles and limitations of such an approach. We study a novel Web server design and compare its performance to that of a traditional Web server that executes those tasks in a serial manner. Furthermore, we study the design and performance challenges for our approach in the presence of dependencies between tasks included in a dynamic Web page. To the best of our knowledge, there is neither related literature nor a Web server product that employs such a design.

As opposed to *Proxy-based* [7] and server-side caching [6] approaches, *Parse & Dispatch* is introduced in this paper as a *back-end* Web server *acceleration* technique as asynchronous caches [16, 17], in the sense that it is employed at the opposite side from the Web client, i.e., at the other end of the client/server communication path. The path may also include a client cache, a proxy server caching system(s), and a Web server cache plug-in mechanism.

The rest of this paper is organized as follows: In Section 2, we discuss some necessary background information on dynamic content and how Web servers generate and deliver it. In Section 3, we introduce and analyze our methodology for dynamic content generation, while in Section 4 we put our methodology to the test assuming no dependencies among tasks. However, in some cases, dependencies may exist between two (or more) tasks included in an HTML script file. For example, the total amount owed by a visitor in a retail Web site cannot be generated unless her shopping cart has been validated. In Section 5, we present one way to handle dependencies using our approach. We conclude and discuss future work in Section 6.

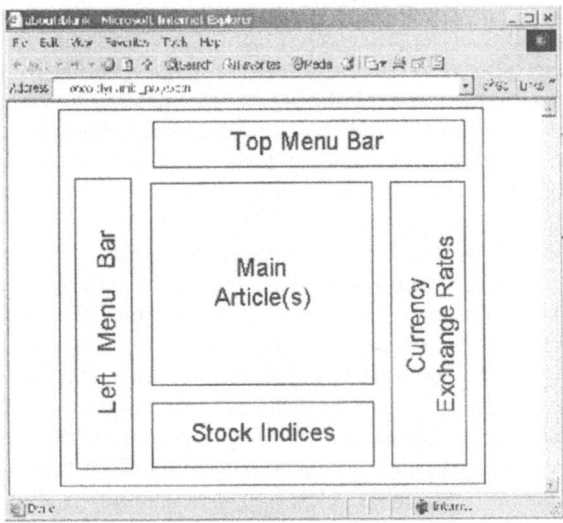

Fig. 1. The layout of a typical stock-related dynamic Web page

2 Background Information

2.1 Dynamic Content

Modern Web sites utilize dynamic content technology in order to respond with dynamic and personalized content to clients/visitors without having to construct and store it a-priori. Thus, it is possible to tailor the content served to a client according to her most recent needs and expectations, while saving huge amounts of disk space. Web applications that are benefited by dynamic content technology include e-commerce, online financial brokers, portals and news related sites.

A typical dynamic Web page includes tasks that are processed at the Web server site in order to produce the dynamic fragments of the Web page. Although the number of tasks may vary across Web pages of different applications, we assume that this number lies between four and eight. For instance, consider a typical stock-related dynamic page (Fig. 1) with the following tasks:

- Session handling (not seen in Fig. 1).
- Left menu bar generation. Links are dynamically generated from the local content database.
- Top menu bar generation. Links are customized to a particular client's preferences stored in the local content database.
- One or more main articles/stories retrieval. Articles are extracted from a corporate news database.
- Current stock market indices retrieval. Indices are pulled from a remote financial provider via XML, and they can be presented either graphically or in text.
- Currency exchange rates retrieval (Similar to stock market indices).

In addition, e-commerce dynamic Web pages include tasks such as catalog generation code, user cart handling code, credit card verification, banner advertisements rotation, counter update and more. Product customization pages (i.e., from a computer retailer site) include tasks that consist of thousands of lines of script code and multiple database queries in order to generate dynamic Web forms for product customization.

Dynamic Web pages are generated with the parsing of static files (HTML script files) normally located in the file system of the Web server but not necessarily under a public directory. Such files may have extensions such as ".asp", ".cfm", or ".php" that denote different scripting languages from various vendors. The asp extension stands for Active Server Pages, a technology developed by Microsoft Corp. to support the insertion of Visual Basic code (vbscript) blocks that may generate dynamic content. Cold Fusion, a product of Macromedia Inc., uses a tagged-based script code while PHP, o project of Apache Software Foundation, supports a Unix-like script code.

In any case, we can safely assume that the static content (HTML) and dynamic content (blocks of script code) are both arranged in HTML script files in an interleaved manner. Static content is transmitted to the Web user as is. The blocks of script code that perform the tasks related to the dynamic Web page, however, are substituted by their execution output which is then transmitted to the Web user.

This interleaved usage of static and dynamic content is a popular way of defining the layout/arrangement of the dynamic parts in a dynamic Web page. For example, the <table> tag, and the <tr> and <td> sub tags, are used to define the placement of the dynamic content under the assumption that a Web page's layout can be simply overviewed as a grid. Consequently, HTML script files are often called "HTML templates" and are widely employed in Content Management Tools.

In past few years, Content Management Systems (CMS) have been gaining in popularity as the means for serving and managing dynamic Web content. Such tools provide a secured graphical user interface for the Web site administrator to update the contents of the Web site by updating the site's database. To materialize a dynamic Web page, the CMS parses an HTML template given that page's name or unique identifier. The http://host.com/generatepage.asp?pagename=home URL, for example, will generate on the fly the home page of the host.com site.

2.2 Dynamic Content Generation

In this subsection, we illustrate in brief the traditional processing steps taken by a Web server in order to generate dynamic content. We assume the usage of a Multi-Threaded Web server over Event-Driven or Single-Process Web servers (for a descriptive comparison between Web server architectures, please see [21] and [25]). This assumption is based on the fact that popular multi-threaded Web servers, such as Microsoft's Internet Information Server [19] and Apache's HTTP Server [9], generate the substantial majority of dynamic Web content today. For a detailed report on Web server usage, please see [20].

Figure 2 highlights the structure and functionality of a multi-threaded Web server. A single parent process accepts incoming HTTP requests from Web clients in a sequential manner through a server socket. Upon arrival of a new request, an available worker thread is selected out of a pool of suspended pre-dispatched threads in order to serve that request. Meanwhile, the parent process continues execution free to accept

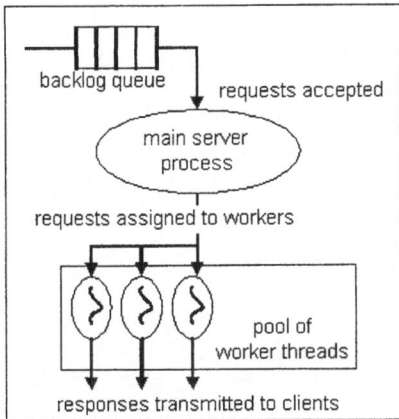

Fig. 2. A multi-threaded Web server

more requests, enabling in this way the concurrent processing of multiple clients. Once a worker thread has served its assigned request, it places itself back to the thread pool.

An upper limit on the number of worker threads allowed to execute in parallel is set in order to ensure the proper (non-thrashing) execution of the Web server. In popular Web servers, the pre-configured size of the thread pool ranges from five to twenty. In the case that all worker threads are busy, excessive client requests are not accepted, however, they are queued in the special buffer called *backlog* for upcoming admission. With the backlog buffer full, additional client requests are refused.

Client requests for static content refer to files located in the file system of the Web server under a pubic html directory. Static HTML files usually have an ".html" or "htm" extension and contain only standard HTML code. Following a client request for a static content, a worker thread extracts the file name from the client's HTTP request header, and searches for that file, first, in the Web server's cache, and then in the file system. Once the file is found, an HTTP response header is sent to the client followed by the contents of the requested file. The contents of a static HTML file are not always sent in one chunk. A repeat-until loop loads and transmits successive fragments of the file until the end of the file is reached.

As mentioned above, client requests for dynamic content refer to HTML script files (usually having an asp, cfm, or php extension). Following a client request, the worker thread assigned to the particular client must locate the appropriate file and, according to the file's extension, invoke a handler method from the appropriate library provided by the corresponding vendor.

Running within the worker thread's resources, the handler method opens and parses the script file. Static HTML content is appended in a temporary buffer while script code forces the handler method to *pause parsing*, for as long as it takes, in order to execute the task. The script code output (in HTML) is appended in the buffer (buffered mode) and the handler method continues parsing. With the end of file reached, the entire contents of the buffer are transmitted to the client following an HTTP response header. Some scripting languages explicitly allow the transmission of content as soon as this becomes available (unbuffered mode), however, a comparison

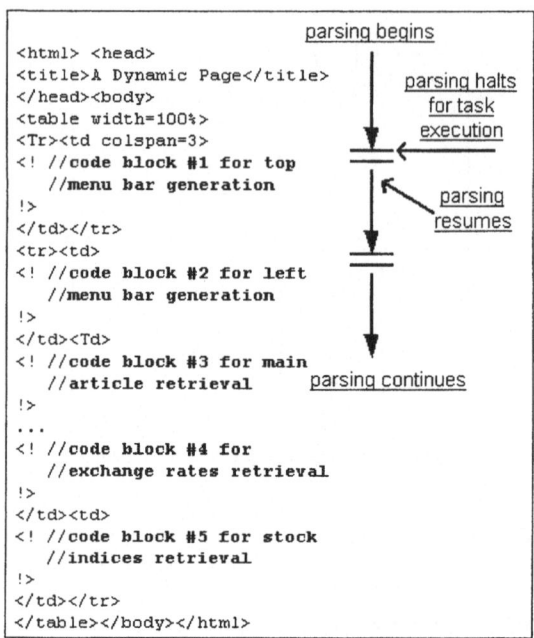

```
<html> <head>                          parsing begins
<title>A Dynamic Page</title>
</head><body>                           parsing halts
<table width=100%>                        for task
<Tr><td colspan=3>                        execution
<! //code block #1 for top
    //menu bar generation
!>
</td></tr>                                 parsing
<tr><td>                                   resumes
<! //code block #2 for left
    //menu bar generation
!>
</td><Td>
<! //code block #3 for main
    //article retrieval          parsing continues
!>
...
<! //code block #4 for
    //exchange rates retrieval
!>
</td><td>
<! //code block #5 for stock
    //indices retrieval
!>
</td></tr>
</table></body></html>
```

Fig. 3. Contents and parsing of file MainPage.dyn

in performance and network utilization between buffered and unbuffered content transmissions on Web servers remains an open topic for research. In either case, blocking the parsing of the HTML script file for task execution directly hurts performance since it creates an unnecessary processing bottleneck.

Figure 3 demonstrates the processing steps required to generate a sample home page by executing the MainPage.dyn[1] HTML script file that includes five tasks. The vertical arrows, pointing downward, represent the parsing steps and the horizontal lines the temporal halting of the parsing in order to execute the encountered script code. The generated content is rendered by the client's browser to display a top menu bar, a left menu bar, the main article of the day followed the current exchange rates, and finally the current stock marker indices. The two menu bars are generated by running queries on a local (to the Web server) database provided the personal preferences of the user. The main article is loaded from a news database, while the current exchange rates and stock indices are acquired from a remote financial provider via XML.

In order to generate the dynamic content of MainPage.dyn, the parsing of the file was suspended for five times. Table 1 contains an approximation of the execution time for various tasks that scripting code might refer to. The execution time of tasks depends on various parameters such as computational complexity, hardware power and network speed.

---

[1] We use our own file extension (.dyn), which stands for "dynamic," for HTML script files in favor of no particular vendor.

Table 1. Approximate execution time for various tasks

Task	Execution Time
Counter Update	~ 10 ms
Session Handling	~ 10 ms
SQL execution	10 to 100 ms (depending on complexity)
Image Generation	Multiples of 10 ms (depending or resolution and contents)
Remote data retrieval	Multiples of 100 ms (depending on connectivity)

3   A New Model for Dynamic Content Generation

With both the popularity of dynamic content and number of Web users growing, a more efficient processing methodology is needed for materializing dynamic Web pages. The current serial processing manner in which the tasks of a dynamic Web page are executed by traditional Web servers is computationally and implementation-wise simple, yet it is not efficient. We realize efficiency in terms of computational resources utilization that is translated into improved Web server throughput.

Our suggested methodology puts more parallelism in dynamic content generation by processing the tasks, embedded in a dynamic HTML file, in a concurrent fashion based on the proposed *Parse & Dispatch* approach. Our methodology provides an additional level of parallelism under the one obtained by using clustered Web servers. We next present our approach that assumes no dependencies between tasks.

3.1   The Parse and Dispatch Approach without Dependencies

The intuition behind the Parse & Dispatch approach is to enable the uninterrupted/non-blocking parsing of an HTML script file by assigning the execution of the script code blocks (tasks) to auxiliary threads that run in parallel. Our approach consists of two phases: (a) the *Content Expansion Phase*, and (b) the *Content Serialization Phase*.

The Content Expansion Phase. Following a client request, the Web server selects an available worker thread out of the thread pool that will carry out the request. The worker thread initializes an indexed buffer (a variable-length array with variable-length strings as elements) that will be used as a temporary content storage. With the current index at the buffer set to 1, the worker thread locates the requested HTML script file and opens it for parsing.

The first consecutive block of static content (see Fig. 4) is stored as a character string at buffer index 1 and the current index is increased by one. Then, the thread worker detects the first block of script code and initializes an auxiliary thread that will execute the code. Reserving the current index on the buffer for the auxiliary thread, the worker thread increases the current index by one and continues parsing.

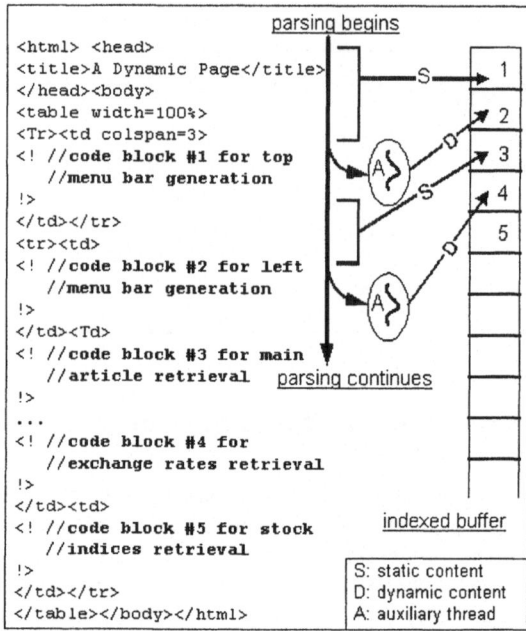

Fig. 4. Contents and parsing of file MainPage.dyn using the Parse & Dispatch approach

The same tactic is followed for the rest of the file contents. In case of having two consecutive blocks of script code (with no static content separating them), two successive buffer indices will be reserved. A block of uninterrupted static content is never split. The content expansion phase ends when all tasks are under processing.

The Content Serialization Phase. An auxiliary thread that finishes its script code execution, stores the generated content in the buffer position that was reserved for it during the content expansion phase and terminates. The worker thread waits for all the dynamic content to become available. (In our current implementation, the worker thread detects the termination of all the auxiliary threads by periodically checking the reserved buffer indices.) With all the auxiliary threads terminated and the dynamic content available, the worker thread scans the buffer and transmits both static and dynamic content to the client. Scanning the buffer from index 1 and up ensures that the content parts are delivered to the client in the right order.

Figure 4 illustrates both the expansion phase and the usage the indexed buffer. The vertical arrow, pointing downward, represents the file parsing, while a curved arrow represents the concurrent execution of the encountered script code by an auxiliary thread. The "S" arrows denote the placement of static content in the buffer, and the "D" arrows the placement of the dynamic content in the buffer. Figure 5 displays the processing timeline of the approach.

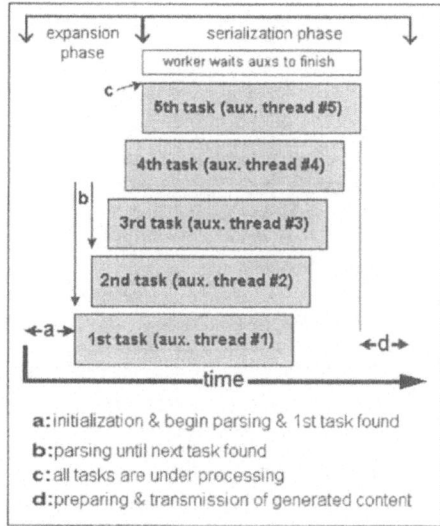

Fig. 5. Processing timeline of file MainPage.dyn using the Parse & Dispatch approach

3.2 Improving the Content Serialization Phase

During the content serialization phase, the worker thread makes sure that all the auxiliary threads have stopped executing by periodically checking whether they have placed their generated content in their reserved buffer index. In order to minimize the overhead of such a procedure, the ideal scenario would be that all the auxiliary threads terminate as soon as the worker thread finishes parsing and enters the content serialization phase.

The worker thread, however, enters the content serialization phase before all of the auxiliary threads have terminated and wastes valuable computational resources waiting for them (point c in Fig. 5). We can exploit those wasted resources, by assigning to the worker thread itself the execution of the last script code block of the HTML script file. The benefits of such an optimization are twofold. First, we shorten the period that the worker thread spends waiting for the auxiliary threads to terminate. Second, we decrease by one the number of auxiliary threads initialized during the expansion phase. Thread initialization may not be as expensive as process forking, nevertheless, it poses a significant overhead in a computationally intensive, multithreaded application such as a Web server. Figure 6 displays the processing timeline with the above improvement.

The challenge is how the worker thread detects the final script code block in order to hold back from initializing the last auxiliary thread. An apparent solution would be to delay an auxiliary thread initialization and parse ahead to detect the next script code block occurrence or detect the end of file. Nonetheless, such a tactic would harm performance since it widens the time gap between the initialization of auxiliary threads and thus reducing parallelism. A more efficient solution requires from the worker thread to know, prior to the expansion phase, the exact number of script code blocks in an HTML script file. For that reason, an additional piece of code is inserted

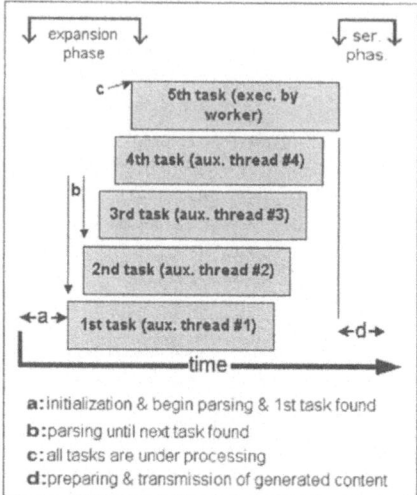

Fig. 6. Processing timeline of MainPage.dyn using the improved Parse & Dispatch approach

in the beginning of a file in the form of a pre-processor directive. Such a directive may look like "<script_blocks count=5/>", or "<tasks count=5/>" and it is the first code that the worker thread parses during the Content Expansion phase.

The challenge is how the worker thread detects the final script code block in order to hold back from initializing the last auxiliary thread. An apparent solution would be to delay an auxiliary thread initialization and parse ahead to detect the next script code block occurrence or detect the end of file. Nonetheless, such a tactic would harm performance since it widens the time gap between the initialization of auxiliary threads and thus reducing parallelism. A more efficient solution requires from the worker thread to know, prior to the expansion phase, the exact number of script code blocks in an HTML script file. For that reason, an additional piece of code is inserted in the beginning of a file in the form of a pre-processor directive. Such a directive may look like "<script_blocks count=5/>", or "<tasks count=5/>" and it is the first code that the worker thread parses during the Content Expansion phase.

4   Performance Evaluation of the Parse and Dispatch Approach without Dependencies

In our experiments, we compare the performance between (a) a traditional multi-threaded Web server that executes the tasks of dynamic Web page in serial (as described in Section 2.1), and (b) an experimental multi-threaded Web server that executes the tasks of a dynamic Web page in parallel according to the Parse & Dispatch approach assuming no dependencies between two tasks. Next, we describe our experimental setup in terms of hardware, software and topology. We then discuss the experiments and our findings.

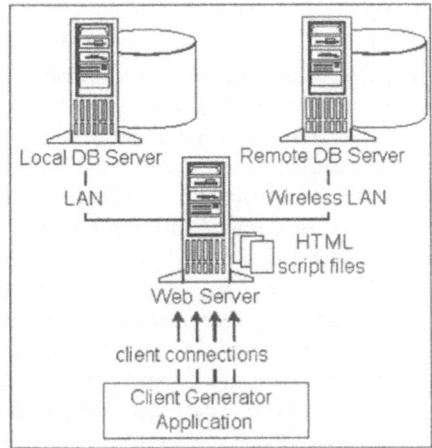

Fig. 7. Topology of the experiments

4.1 Experimental Setup

For the development of the traditional Web server, we adopted the thread management and client admittance routines from the Java-based Apache Web server (Jserv). We then developed the proposed experimental Web server by (a) modifying the code of the worker threads and, (b) adding support for the auxiliary threads and the indexed buffer. We chose to derive the experimental Web server from the traditional one to ensure maximum compatibility between the performance results of the two approaches. The decision for using Java was based on the language's rich, easy-to-use APIs that speed-up the programming of experimental multi-threaded, and network applications [2].

For both the traditional and the experimental Web servers, we assume a worker thread pool of size 21, meaning that both Web servers do not admit more than 21 concurrent clients. We base our assumption on the fact that popular Web servers recommend a size between 5 and 20 to avoid thrashing. It will be made clear by the performance results that this assumption does provide a complete scope of results for evaluating the two approaches.

Our next consideration is the formation of the HTML script files that the Web servers will process in the experiments, given that dynamic Web pages from various applications differ on the blend and number of tasks that they include. For example, a financial-related Web page may include more tasks that generate dynamic content with data obtained by remote financial providers. On the other hand, an e-commerce Web page may include more tasks for dynamic catalog generation by querying local databases.

For the structure of the tasks, we assume a typical task with an approximate execution time of 50 milliseconds that favors no particular type of application. The typical task consists of the following: (a) script code for two queries performed randomly either on a local or a distant database to emulate local or remote database access, (b) script code for string manipulation that executes in long loops to emulate dynamic HTML generation. The decision on forming the typical task is based on certain experience gained in working with commercial Web sites.

The topology of the experimental setup is shown in Fig. 7 and attempts to emulate a real-world commercial environment. The Web server (either the traditional or the experimental one) runs on our main server machine in our local area network. The HTML script files to be processed are copied under the Web server's public directory. The first content database server is installed locally to the Web server while the second one is installed on a remote machine through a WAN.

The last piece of our setup is the application program that implements the client requests called the Client Generator. This application is capable of instantiating a predefined number of individual client programs each one capable of independently submitting consecutive HTTP requests to a Web server. Client programs are implemented by threads and are arbitrated, similar to a Web server, by the Client Generator program using a thread pool. The Client Generator program can emulate a number of concurrent clients that submit requests on a Web server for a given period. To avoid interfering with the Web server's computational resources, the Client Generator resides locally on a different machine.

All the machines used in the experiments were Pentium 4 class computers with 1GB of main memory and SCSI-based secondary storage. The local network was a 100Mps Ethernet, and the remote network a 1Mbps WAN. The database servers used were both Microsoft SQL Server 2000 and the Java Virtual Machine for both the Web servers was version 1.3.1.

4.2 Experiments and Performance Results

We measure the performance of a Web server in terms of (a) average throughput, and (b) client response time under different (stable) workloads. Formally, we define throughput to be the average number of client HTTP requests that are completely processed by a Web server in a period of one second and it is computed at the Web server site. We define client response time to be the client perceived latency from the moment the client issues an HTTP request to the Web server, until the client receives the complete HTTP response.

In our experiments, Web server workload depends on the number of client requests that are simultaneously admitted by the Web server for processing. We also refer to this as 'Concurrent Clients'. For our experiments, workload varies from 1 to 21 since a Web server with a worker thread pool of size 21 does not admit more than 21 concurrent clients. Due to space shortage, in this paper we present our findings for 2 and 5 embedded tasks in an HTML script file.

The results shown in Fig. 8 indicate that, for five embedded tasks in an HTML file, the suggested Parse & Dispatch approach outperforms the traditional approach in both response time and throughput. However, the performance gains for the Parse & Dispatch approach are less obvious for two included tasks (Fig. 9). This is because by having only two tasks in an HTML file, we reduce the amount of parallelism that the Parse & Dispatch approach can benefit from.

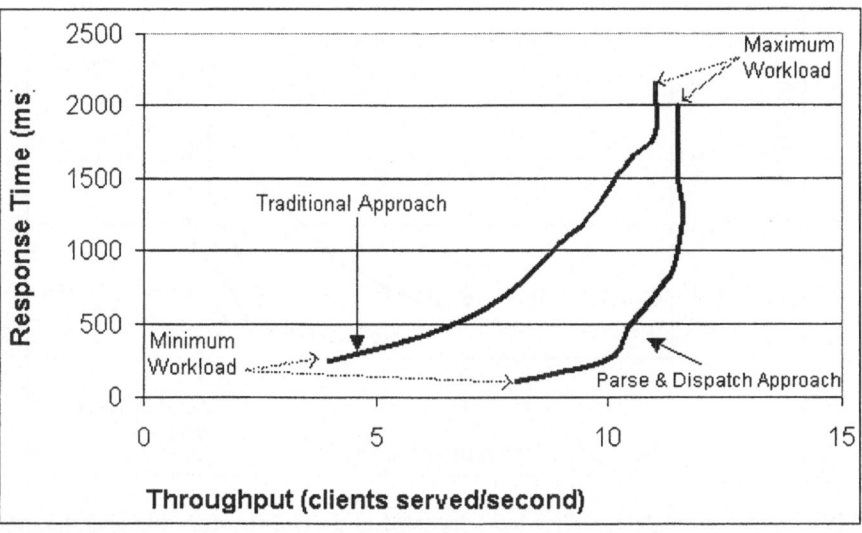

Fig. 8. Performance Comparison with 5 tasks included in an HTML script file with no dependencies between tasks

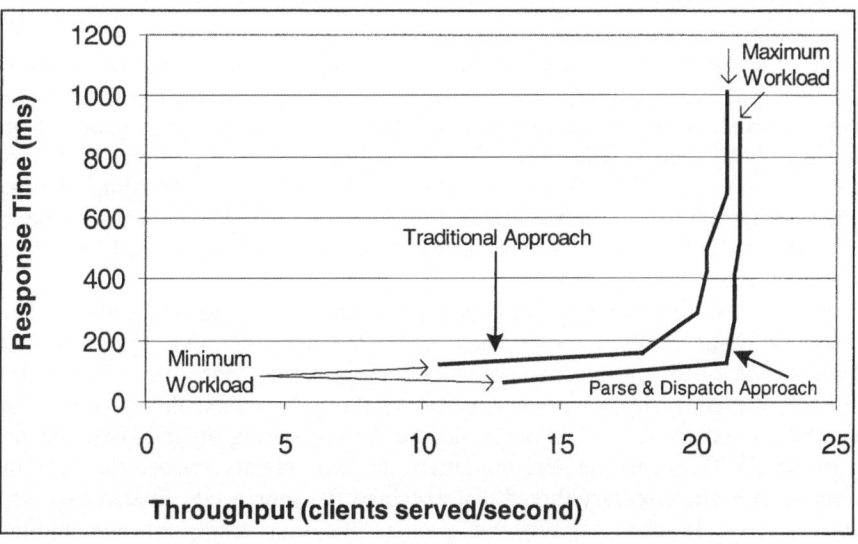

Fig. 9. Performance Comparison with 2 tasks included in an HTML script file with no dependencies between tasks

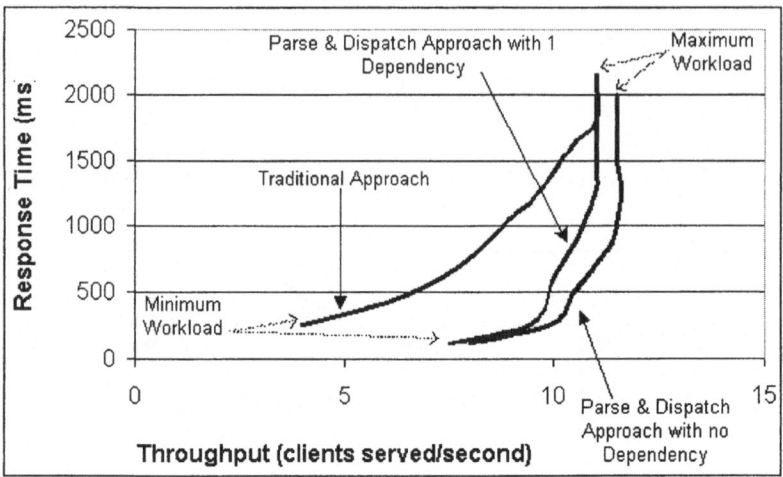

Fig. 10. Average throughput with 5 tasks included in an HTML script file plus the average throughput of the Parse & Dispatch approach having 2 dependent tasks (1 dependency)

5 Parse and Dispatch Approach with Dependent Tasks

In some Web applications, dependencies may exist between two or more tasks included in the some HMTL script file. For example, a graph (jpeg image) that compares two stock quotes cannot be generated unless the two user-supplied quote names have been successfully retrieved, and analyzed. Since traditional Web servers execute the tasks of an HTML page in serial, additional special handling of tasks is not required (given that the developer of the Web page has put the tasks in the right order!). In the case of our approach, we had to enhance our task dispatching algorithms.

In doing so, we came across two challenges. First, we had to find a way of letting the Parse & Dispatch Web server know about the dependencies. Then, we had to implement a cost-efficient mechanism of executing the dependent tasks in serial. For the former, we use a pre-processor directive of the form <dependency source=task1 target=task3>, where *source* and *target* denote the numbering order of two dependent tasks in the HMTL script file. For the latter, our experiments showed that it is more efficient to have the auxiliary thread that executed the source task to also execute the destination task. In this way, (a) we prevent the dispatching of one additional auxiliary thread, and (b) we minimize the time gap between the successive executions of the dependent tasks.

Figure 10 shows the performance results of the Parse & Dispatch approach with five included tasks and having two dependent tasks (1 dependency) next to our earlier results reported in Fig. 8 with five included tasks but with no dependencies. For this experiment, we have used various orderings for the dependent tasks and calculated their average performance. The results indicate that the performance gains still hold even at the existence of one dependency between two tasks which reduces the opportunity for parallelism.

6   Conclusions and Future Work

In this paper, we introduced a new approach for dynamic Web content generation, called Parse & Dispatch. Our approach suggests parallelism at the granularity of dynamic Web page fragments, in addition to that of a whole Web page obtained by using clustered Web servers. The proposed approach was used to build an experimental Web server and its performance was compared to that of a traditional Web server. The experimental results yielded significant performance gains in favor of our approach in terms of Web server throughput and client response time.

We believe that our approach is not only applicable in simple multithreading Web server architectures but it is compatible with the recently proposed staged-based Web Servers which replace threads and introduce a more sophisticated task scheduling aiming at enhancing server throughout [18, 23]. As part of our future work, we will investigate Parse & Dispatch with staged computation that will enable the group execution of dispatched tasks belonging to different web requests.

Besides staged-based Web servers, we will also continue our investigation on alternative, more efficient multithreaded Web server architecture that support dynamic content, particularly paying attention on exploring parallel processing techniques in handling dependencies between tasks included in a HTML script file.

Acknowledgements. This work is partially funded by the IST-2001-32645 DBGlobe project and by the NSF award ANI-0123705 focusing on scalable web servers.

References

1. Active Server Pages. Available at http://www.microsoft.com/.
2. K. Arnold, J. Gosling: The Java Programming Language. Addison-Wesley 1996.
3. J. Aweya, L M. Ouellette, D. Y. Montuno, B. Doray, K. Felske. An adaptive load balancing scheme for web servers. Int. J. Network Mgmt 2002; 12: 3–39.
4. T. Berners-Lee, R. Cailliau, A. Luotonen, H. F. Nielsen, A. Secret: The World-Wide Web. CACM 37(8): 76–82(1994).
5. V. Cardellini, E. Casalicchio, M. Colajanni, P. S. Yu: The state of the art in locally distributed Web-server systems. ACM Computing Surveys 34(2): 263–311 (2002).
6. A. Datta, K. Dutta, K. Ramamritham, H. M. Thomas, D. E. VanderMeer: Dynamic Content Acceleration: A Caching Solution to Enable Scalable Dynamic Web Page Generation. SIGMOD Conference 2001.
7. A. Datta, K. Dutta, H. M. Thomas, D. E. VanderMeer, Suresha, K. Ramamritham: Proxy-based acceleration of dynamically generated content on the world wide web: an approach and implementation. SIGMOD Conference 2002: 97–108.
8. G. Ehmayer, G. Kappel, S. Reich: Connecting Databases to the Web: A Taxonomy of Gateways. DEXA 1997: 1–15.
9. R. T. Fielding, G. E. Kaiser: The Apache HTTP Server Project. IEEE Internet Computing 1(4): 88–90 (1997).
10. X Gan, T. Schroeder, S. Goddard, B. Ramamurthy: LSMAC and LSNAT: Two Approaches for Cluster-Based Scalable Web Servers. ICC (2) 2000: 1164–1168
11. S. Goddard, T. Schroeder: The SASHA Architecture for Network-Clustered Web Servers. HASE 2001: 163–172

12. G. Hutchinson, G. Baur, D. Pigford: Implementation of a Dynamic Web Database: Interface Using Cold Fusion. SIGUCCS 1998: 131–135
13. HyperText Markup Language (HTML). Overview available at http://www.w3.org/MarkUp.
14. K. Kant, P. Mohapatra: Workshop on Performance and Architecture of Web Servers (PAWS-2000, held in conjunction with SIGMETRICS-2000). SIGMOD Record 29(3): 12–14 (2000).
15. E. D. Katz, M. Butler, R. McGrath: A Scalable HTTP Server: The NCSA Prototype. Computer Networks and ISDN Systems 27(2): 155–164 (1994).
16. A. Labrinidis, N. Roussopoulos: WebView Materialization. In Proc. of the ACM SIGMOD International Conference on Management of Data,, May 2000.
17. A. Labrinidis, N. Roussopoulos: WebView Balancing Performance and Data Freshness in Web Database Servers. In proc. of VLDB 2003.
18. J. R. Larus, M. Parkes: Using Cohort-Scheduling to Enhance Server Performance. USENIX Annual Technical Conference, General Track 2002: 103–114.
19. Microsoft Internet Information Server. Available at http://www.microsoft.com.
20. Netcraft Web Server Survey. Available at http://www.netcraft.com/survey/.
21. V. Pai, P. Druschel, W. Zwaenepoel: Flash: An Efficient and Portable Web Server. Proceedings of the 1999 USENIX Annual Technical Conference, Monterey, CA, USA, June 1999.
22. PHP. Available at http://www.php.net/.
23. M. Di Santo, F. Frattolillo, W. Russo, E. Zimeo: Efficient Content-aware Connections Dispatching in Clustered Web Servers. PDPTA 2002: 843–849.
24. The Common Gateway Interface. Overview available at http://hoohoo.ncsa.uiuc.edu/cgi/overview.html.
25. M. Welsh, D. E. Culler, E. A. Brewer: SEDA: An Architecture for Well-Conditioned, Scalable Internet Services. SOSP 2001: 230–243.

The Grid Needs You! Enlist Now.

Carole Goble

Information Management Group, Department of Computer Science,
University of Manchester, Oxford Road, Manchester, M13 9PL.
carole@cs.man.ac.uk,
http://www.cs.man.ac.uk/~carole

Abstract. "the next big thing will be grid computing" – John Patrick, IBM's vice-president for Internet strategies. Are you involved with Grid applications or infrastructure? If not, why not? Not sure what Grid is? Think it isn't relevant to you or you aren't relevant to it? Think its just high performance computing for high energy physicists? Think that it's a semantic-free or data-free zone? Think it isn't important? In this talk I'll give an introduction to the state of play of Grid today and the applications using it. I'll give a summary of its evolution, paying particular attention to three significant initiatives that impact the OTM community: the emergence of the Open Grid Service Architecture, the prominence of Data/Information Grids and the appearance of Semantic Grids. I'll give a few examples of early Semantic Grid projects, and show why distributed information and knowledge management are key-enablers of Grid Services and their applications. The Grid is a terrific use case for the research described in this conference. Moreover, I do not believe that the Grid vision cannot be achieved without knowing about and using your past experiences, current technologies and future research. If this community and the Grid community fail to communicate we will all be the poorer for it. However, although inter-community technology exchange and inter-disciplinary research can generate inspirational innovations, it doesn't just happen. It takes work and it takes people prepared to reach out and engage. In this talk I hope to inform you, interest you and may be even enlist you to the cause. . . .

1 The Grid

The Grid was originally conceived as a means of securely and transparently sharing (super)computing resources on demand. The name comes from an analogy with an electricity power grid – computing, storage, data sets, expensive scientific instruments and so on are utilities to be delivered over the Internet seamlessly, transparently and dynamically as and when needed by virtualizing these resources [1]. The original, and still main, driver is to support global large-scale scientific collaborations that transcended organisational and geographic boundaries, and made the best use of expensive or scarce resources as and when they were required. The first production grid was probably NASA's Information Power Grid (http://www.ipg.nasa.gov/)[2], developed to simulate the US

R. Meersman et al. (Eds.): CoopIS/DOA/ODBASE 2003, LNCS 2888, pp. 589–600, 2003.
© Springer-Verlag Berlin Heidelberg 2003

national air space. The application involves the integration of many existing computational resources, and the provision of a large collection of inter-related services – security services, uniform data access services, global event services, co-scheduling, accounting etc. – to help in the management of the resources. At its heart lay high-speed networked communications, dynamic machine processor sharing and vast data handling.

Grid computing has harnessed compute cycles on thousands of machines to enable high throughput screening of 10,000's of drug compounds in an hour instead of a year, as in the SmallPox Grid. It can allow civil engineers to test an earthquake-resistant bridge design in minutes rather than months such as on the NESSGrid, a national virtual laboratory for earthquake engineering that is part of NSF's Network for Earthquake Engineering Simulation (NEES) project. Brain neuroscientists in NCMIR in San Diego, USA can remotely control and collect data from the world's largest ultra high voltage electron microscopy in Osaka University, Japan [3]. Similarly, astronomers can steer telescopes from their offices, collect the data using remote archive repositories, and process it by exploiting the availability of machines of other institutions, for example, the Sloan Sky Observatory (http://www.sdss.org/) and AstroGrid (http://www.astrogrid.org/) make available vast digital sky surveys to all astronomers not just a lucky few, and provide the computing, storage and software resources needed to analyse the data. Grid middleware such as myGrid (http://www.mygrid.org.uk) [4,5] allows biologists to assemble personalised exploratory in-silico experiments that interoperate between remotely and locally available applications, code-bases and databases. Other Grids monitor thousands of sensors in flying aircraft to analyse and diagnose in real time operational faults (http://www.cs.york.ac.uk/dame/).

Scientists cluster together "virtually" to solve problems. To collaborate they need to share data sets, software, computational resources, and specialist instruments such as telescopes and microscopes in a controlled way, despite the heterogeneity of their respective policies, platforms and technologies. So, since the mid-1990s, the Grid's vision and reach has evolved rapidly to now mean intelligent middleware for "flexible, secure, coordinated resource sharing among dynamic collections of individuals, institutions, and resources – what we refer to as virtual organizations (VO)" [1]. These resource configurations are dynamic and volatile as a consortium of services (databases, sensors, compute servers) participating in a complex analysis may be switched in and out as they become, or cease to be, available. They are anticipated to be ad-hoc as service consortia have no central location, no central control, and no existing trust relationships. The configurations and the services that make them up may be large, with potentially hundreds of services orchestrated at any time, and long-lived, for example a protein folding simulation or a computational fluid dynamics optimization function could take weeks.

The platform must be scalable, be able to evolve to be future proof and be fault-tolerant, robust, persistent and reliable. It should work seamlessly, and transparently – the user won't care where their calculation is done using how many machines, or where data is actually held, it will just happen. Of course metadata is ubiquitous; describing the environment, *the services available and* the ways they can be combined and exploited, keeping audit trails of resource use and configurations and so on.

2   Grid Vision Buy-In

Today, the Grid is recognised as a major initiative, with buy-in from nations, funding agencies, scientists and industry. The UK government has invested £240 million into Grid-related research. The European Union has a major Grid computing programme. The Japanese have invested in a national Grid infrastructure. The Biomedical Informatics Research Network (BIRN) in the USA (http://www.nbirn.net/) and e-Diamond in the UK are building national Grids for healthcare: both are designed to handle large scale digital image processing and analysis for brain scans and mammograms respectively. GridPP (http://www.gridpp.ac.uk/), a particle physics Grid, is being built to deal with the processing of terabytes data that will emerge from the Large Hadron Collider (LHC) at CERN in burst of just a few seconds. Commercial deployments are offered from Avaki, Data Synapse, Fujitsu, Hitachi, HP, IBM, NEC, Oracle, Platform, Sun, and United Devices. Although begun as a technology for scientific collaboration, similar requirements for sharing resources between cross-organizational collaborations arise within commercial environments, enterprise-wide integration, business data analysis and forecasting and e-business. Butterfly.net, for example, is using the Grid for online gaming (http://www.butterfly.net/).

Practically every European country is building a national Grid facility, and practically every scientific discipline has a project or plans to either: build a Grid, to Grid-enable their resources, to develop applications for a Grid; to research and develop the Grid middleware itself or to do all of these things. The Grid community's standards body Global Grid Forum (http://www.ggf.org) routinely attracts over 800 people to its meetings three times a year.

3   "Grid" Means What I Say It Means

Despite the relative youth of the Grid it already has legacies and myths that sow confusion and prevent essential and relevant fields from getting involved.

Part of the confusion is that the term "the Grid" or Grid computing is used rather loosely. "Grid" has been used to denote middleware infrastructure, tools, and applications concerned with integrating geographically distributed computational resources. Extra confusion is caused by obvious overlaps with the established fields of traditional networking and distributed computing. Here are my definitions.

"The" Grid refers to the concept and vision. "A" Grid is a virtual organisation of a set of heterogeneous distributed resources and the high performance networks used to link them. A VO of machines is one particular manifestation of a Computational Grid, and the most well known. Other VOs reflect geography (a UK Grid), a specific field (a Mouse Genome Grid), a scientific discipline (a BioGrid), or even a specific problem for a short space of time (for a protein folding simulation). In this sense there is no one Grid but lots of Grids that may interoperate between themselves. Grid middleware infrastructure is the specification of the software services stack, policies, protocols, standards and APIs that make this all possible. Particular reference software implementations of Grid middleware include Condor (http://www.cs.wisc.edu/condor/), Globus (http://www.globus.org/) [7] and Unicore (http://www.unicore.org/). Grid tools such as resource heartbeat monitors and portals enable developers and users to manage the infrastructure and use the Grid. Grid applications assemble and use a Grid by means of its middleware to solve a problem. Finally, e-Science (often used synonymously with the Grid, especially in the UK) is a particular general application of Grids to benefit Scientific Endeavours. e-Science also makes use of the Web, Web Services, The Semantic Web or any other software infrastructure that it can benefit from.

4   Grid Middleware on the Move

Grid middleware is evolving as rapidly as the Grid vision is. Right now we are at a particularly busy, and perhaps even unsettling, time in the Grid's evolution. Although things are changing, old perceptions still persist. Three of these perceptions are particularly relevant to the OTM community: (a) the Grid is just about low-level protocols, (b) The Grid is just to do with compute cycle stealing sharing, and (c) the Grid has nothing to do with semantics. These issues match three major evolutionary steps that the Grid is undergoing: Grid service architecture, Information Grids and the Semantic Grid.

Open Service Architecture. As recently as 2002 Grid middleware suffered from: no standards (Globus was a de facto standard rather than de jure standard); monolithic design making it difficult to integrate existing components and little or no synergy with existing middleware standards and tools. The second generation Grid middleware moves on from a collection of disparate protocols to a service-oriented one, converging with and extending Web Services [8]. The Open Grid Service Architecture makes the middleware more open and extensible, as well as more palatable to commercial concerns. It forms the basis of open-source and commercial products. The OGSA Grid Service specification defines abstract descriptions of existing grid capabilities and collections of standard interfaces that characterise grid services such as creation, lifetime management, introspection, and grouping of services. When it comes down to it, this is a distributed object architecture. So although its true that most of the past work focused on essential low level "plumbing" such as GridFTP, and will continue to do so, a whole middleware stack of higher-level services are currently being specified and built such as security, registries, policy management, data access and integration, service management, and workflow.

Data and Information Grids. Scientific applications are awash with vast amounts of difficult data of different kinds to be integrated, aggregated, analysed and archived. Data grids have become more prominent as many commentators see data-intensive, not compute-intensive problem solving as the "killer application" of Grid computing [22]. Data Grids such as the EU Data-Grid (http://eu-datagrid. web. cern. ch /eu-datagrid/) or Chimera (http:// www. griphyn. org/ chimera/) [10] provide storage system and transport protocol neutral ways of storing and conveying uninterpreted data. Information Grids are more semantically aware, providing data access and manipulation mechanisms that can take account of the structure or content of the data being processed. OGSA-Data Access and Integration (http://www.ogsa-dai.org/) [22], OGSA-Distributed Query Processing [6] and Spitfire are information grid services. The scale, behavioural characteristics and complexity of the Grid and its user applications present significant challenges for databases. For example, multi-database query processing, schema integration and evolution, data transport, distributed transaction management, data mining and hybrid processing of semi-structured and structured data, change notification, archiving and security are major issues. Although some Information Grids use virtual databases implemented using wrappers and mediators to integrate data-generating resources [12,14], many orchestrate services using scientific workflows [4, 24,13]. These workflows represent in silico scientific experiments or data collection and archiving pipelines. Workflow discovery, composition, data streaming for large volumes of data, suspension and resumption of workflows and failure compensation is becoming a ubiquitous topic within the Global Grid Forum and is perceived as one of the high level services in OGSA. Another, driven by its scientific client-base, is the accurate logging and exploitation of provenance (who, what, when, how, why) metadata [19].

Semantics in Grids. The operation of the Grid middleware itself is dependent on the capturing and harnessing of metadata, as well as the metadata required of the Grid applications themselves. To manage a Grid beyond bespoke "hackery" requires "Grid intelligence" to interpret extensive quantities of knowledge about the state and properties of Grid components and their configurations for solving problems [11]. For example, the dynamic discovery, formation, and disbanding of ad hoc virtual organizations of (third-party) resources requires that Grid middleware be able to use and process knowledge about the availability of services; their purpose; the way they can be combined and configured or substituted; and how they are discovered, are invoked, and evolve. Work in Semantic Web Services is just as relevant to Semantic Grid Services. Advocates of Semantic Grids (Grids that explicitly represent and explicitly use semantics) argue that there is a gap between current grid endeavours and the vision of a grid future in which there is a high degree of easy-to-use and seamless automation and in which there are flexible collaborations and computations on a global scale. The Grid stands to benefit from Semantic Web techniques such as semantic annotations, ontologies, and reasoning for its metadata, text and multimedia, with

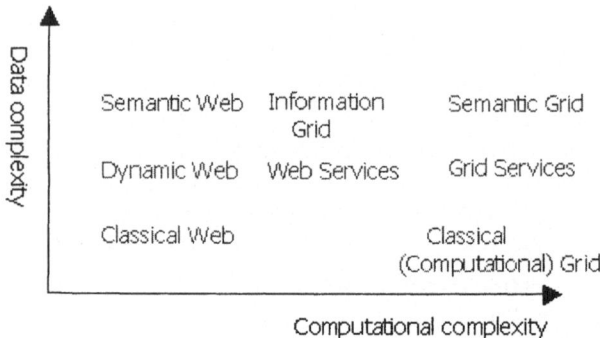

Fig. 1. Grid Services in relation to other technologies

their accompanying languages (RDF, DAML+OIL, OWL), tools and technologies (content analysis, semantic information extraction and integration, ontology engineering etc) [11, 25, 26].

The Open Grid Service Architecture and Information Grids are not yet mature but are at least in their adolescence; early reference implementations are just available at the Global Grid Forum portal. Semantic Grids are still in their infanthood. Both the Semantic Web and the Grid lean on the loose coupled, open and distributed platform provided by Web Services (Figure 1).

5   Change Brings Opportunities

Standards are in a state of flux. OGSA and OGSI (Open Grid Service Infrastructure) are still in their beta stages and remain untried. But times of instability provide the best opportunities for new possibilities. These shifts in paradigms and perspectives open up Grid middleware and the Grid community to contributions from other fields. Old ideas (schema integration, query optimisation, transaction management, knowledge discovery) urgently need to be disseminated and applied if we are to avoid reinventing the wheel. New ideas (semantic-based service discovery, ontology-based integration) acquire a challenging and vibrant application area. In return the Grid contributes with a universal computing platform for bridging heterogeneous and dynamic systems for building and managing multi-database federations or even, perhaps, the Semantic Web.

6   Semantics Wanted, Apply within

A scan through the working groups of Global Grid Forum identifies working groups (WG) and research groups (RG) working on schemas and semantics: the Common Information Model Grid schema WG; the Scheduling Ontology WG; the Persistent Data Archives RG, the Grid Information Retrieval WG, and, of course, the Semantic Grid RG.

The application of ontologies, annotations, and all manner of knowledge technologies arising from the Semantic Web, are getting their first tentative try-outs by early adopters. The Grid Interoperability Project (GRIP) used ontologies deep in the heart of low-level Grid middleware to support mediation between different resource brokers. Others use ontologies and reasoning to improve resource matchmaking [21]. myGrid, Geodise, GEON, SEEK, SCEC/IT, BIRN, and so on all, to varying degrees, adopt scientific workflows to interoperate Grid resources; support grid-enabled data integration and mediation using semantics; and manage the metadata by means of advanced knowledge techniques exploiting ontologies and reasoning [11, 12, 13, 14, 15, 16].

As a taster, open research questions include:

- "Semantic registration" of data sets: How to describe (beyond conventional, descriptive, plain text metadata) the semantics and integrity constraints of data objects, measurements, protocols used for an experiment, etc;
- How to employ semantic information in data discovery, workflow discovery, service discovery, data binding, query and workflow planning and execution;
- Semantic matchmaking of grid resources to satisfy requirements of application components in workflows, and indeed substituting whole workflows;
- Intelligent reasoners for grid computing (semantic matchmakers, planners, resource brokers, etc.) that exploit knowledge of scientific applications as well as grid resources;
- Scientific workflow design and execution: Can there be a common standard language for describing, executing and exchanging scientific workflows or do the various dimensions of the problem space (data-intensive vs. compute-intensive, large and regular data vs. (small) and complex data, simple control flows (pipelines) vs. complex control flows (visual programming)) and the different requirements resulting from them, force us to consider different standards?
- Scientific workflow lifecycle & methodology. Workflow lifecycle means the authoring, publishing, discovering, personalising, enacting, validating, modifying of workflows. In myGrid [4] this is an iterative, interactive and potentially collaborative process involving people and a set of decision support tools, e.g. for workflow and service discovery, workflow editing, interactive workflow execution etc. This contrasts with BIRN& SCEC/IT's 'automated agent-based' approach [13,16]. Is there an overarching process/lifecycle that we share, or are the differences irreconcilable? Key areas include (collaborative) authoring and versioning, provenance, and scientific validation.

7   All Hands to the Deck

The Grid is an ambitious and encompassing vision only possible if the community can build on the past successes of distributed computing, information management and computing architecture, and harness current and future research. I've painted a pretty picture, but reality is uglier. Few production grids currently exist. Current middleware is hard to use and incomplete. The ideas and technologies sketched here are in varying degrees of maturity. Deployment, research, development, applications and standardisation efforts are all co-occurring and yet are interdependent. This makes it hard to find a stable berth in a maelstrom of activities. The gap between reality and vision is wide. Early adoption of partially baked infrastructure may lead to disillusionment and a back lash. A particular worry is premature standardisation, yet standards are the key to successful interoperation. Already a number of incompatible grid infrastructure have arisen, needing interoperability programs themselves. Sometimes Forum meetings feel like town meetings at the frontier of the Wild West.

This all makes for challenging and exciting opportunities for all disciplines of computing, but especially those of the "On The Move" federated conference. I was gladdened to see that there is at least one self-proclaimed grid paper in each of the component conferences, though many more are directly relevant. There are signs of increasing engagement by researchers in other fields- networking, distributed systems, databases, algorithms, system management, security, human factors, artificial intelligence, agents, computer-assisted collaborative work, the semantic web. Keynotes, workshops and tutorials about the grid have started to accompany many conferences of more established disciplines such as the WWW2003 and VLDB2003. This is hopeful but still kind of slow. Participants developing the grid are still largely from "the Grid community". We have seen that grid middleware is currently undergoing a major step in its evolution and needs to draw collaborators from other fields if it is to avoid reinvention or adopt inappropriate or outdated concepts or technologies.

For example, those working in grid applications have long understood the necessity of data archiving and secure and efficient data transport at least [9]. Scientific metadata standards and resource catalogues and directories such the Grid Information Service are schema issues. Yet the database community has taken a surprisingly long time to actively engage with the Grid (with some honourable exceptions such as SRB [17]). This inevitably led to examples of unnecessary and wasteful reinvention and sometimes downright muddle. For a long time the main grid-enabled data storage mechanism was a file and the chief query mechanism was LDAP. Only recently (2003) has access to conventional (relational) databases been incorporated into grid middleware, OGSA-DAI [28].

Intriguingly, the database community is perceived as not only coming late to the Grid but also coming late to the Semantic Web [27]. Although the Semantic Web has been thought of by many to be an opportunity for distributed A.I., at its heart it is about data integration and aggregation [18]. Despite being the two great distributed computing movements of the current age, the Semantic Web and the Grid have had little interaction until comparatively recently. This is perhaps understandable. The Semantic Web is itself a new area still finding its feet and yet to produce convincing demonstrators. However, the paradigm of Grid computing complements the current approach of Semantic Web and Web Services by providing an infrastructure to handle large-scale distributed enterprise information systems. Where the Semantic Web is primarily concerned with large scale information discovery and integration, the Grid provides a large scale and extensible programmatic infrastructure; the Grid infrastructure itself and its applications are driven by extensive quantities of metadata and the Semantic Web provides a distributed and flexible means to manage this. Pretty well all the opportunities identified for the Semantic Web in [27] apply equally to the Grid, with the added bonus of on-tap application pull and large projects such as the LHC and BIRN generating large amounts of metadata and data.

8   The Grid Community

The Grid community is a vibrant international community of researchers, developers, and users. It is quite easy to please in some ways; if the technology works reliably and scales sensibly they will use it. A valued measure in Global Grid Forum is that there are reference implementations for proposals. Code counts. The Forum gives open and direct access to the community and standardisation efforts and is committed to open source and open process. Anyone can join in and rapidly make a mark so long as they put in the hours (and the commitment is heavy). Of course there are still politics, and the "moving target" that is grid middleware makes for real headaches for those trying to deploy Grids.

Forty four research and working groups are currently active. Participants include application scientists, industrial researchers, and academic computer scientists. The working groups associated with data management, including the influential OGSA-Data Access and Integration Services Working Group, are respected and embraced as it is widely acknowledged that data and its management is the main driver of most (scientific) Grid applications [23, 22, 9]. It is less clear whether the database research community embraces the Grid, seeing it as the opportunity it is.

This is a genuinely application driven community. Early adopters with challenging scientific application problems are prepared to try out new approaches and are remarkably tolerant of untidiness and instability. The active and vocal participation of application communities is important. Their range of engagement reflects the maturity of the Grid: some such as the Particle Physics needs robust and sophisticated operational deployments to support ambitious application scenarios. Others such as the Life Sciences look to using at least some grid technologies to handle overwhelming quantities of data.

9   What's in It for You?

Established communities often don't take new initiatives seriously, wearily dismissing them as another re-run of old news; patronising them if they fly in the face of orthodoxy (the dismissal of the Web by the Hypertext community is a famous case in point); or fearing them as a diversion or a potential threat to the "purity" of their core subject. It is easy to get into a rut.

The new community may not recognise their problems as having old solutions, albeit in disguised clothes, or may not want to believe that approaches already exist. Research findings (in particular failures) of ten years previous, particularly from outside the immediate field of expertise, are those that are doomed to be rediscovered over and over again. Established communities hold a corporate memory of what doesn't work as much as what does.

For researchers with interests in databases, ontologies, the large scale application of semantics, and cooperative information systems, the Grid evolution (revolution?) provides an exciting opportunity for research. It's a challenging application that can immediately benefit from past experience and current expertise. It's a sand-box with real users for large scale experimentation on extensive grid deployments. The Semantic Grid is a particularly exciting prospect. The Grid community is (understandably?) a little suspicious of the "crazy A.I. people" of the Semantic Web, airing concerns regarding performance, pragmatism and effectiveness, but prepared to be convinced. The A.I. and knowledge communities embraced the Semantic Web with zeal; many of these same pioneers see the Grid as an application of Semantic Web approaches.

To get intercommunity activities going we need (a) between-community travelers who behave like professional gossips: spreading news, transferring technologies and techniques, and brokering partnerships; and (b) early pioneers open to new opportunities and different ways of doing things. I'm a traveler between Grid, the Semantic Web and Bioinformatics. We need more travelers and more pioneers. **The Grid needs you! Enlist now.**

Acknowledgements. I should like to acknowledge my colleagues David De Roure, Nigel Shadbolt, Norman Paton, Bertram Ludaescher, Yolanda Gil, and Simon Harper for the many hours of insightful discussion on Semantics and Grids.

References

1. I. Foster and C Kesselman, The Grid: Blueprint for a New Computing Infrastructure, Morgan Kaufmann, 1999.
2. W.E. Johnston, D. Gannon and Bill Nitzberg, Grids as Production Computing Environments: The Engineering Aspects of NASA's Information Power Grid, Proc. 8th IEEE International Symposium on High Performance Distributed Computing (HPDC), IEEE Press, 1999.
3. http://www.startap.net/starlight/igrid2002/globalTelesci02.html
4. CA Goble, S. Pettifer and R. Stevens Knowledge Integration: In silico Experiments in Bioinformatics in The Grid: Blueprint for a New Computing Infrastructure Second Edition (eds. I Foster and C Kesselman), 2003, Morgan Kaufman, in press.
5. R Stevens, A Robinson, and CA. Goble myGrid: Personalised Bioinformatics on the Information Grid in proceedings of 11th International Conference on Intelligent Systems in Molecular Biology, 29th June–3rd July 2003.
6. N Alpdemir, J Smith, NW Paton, P Watson, Service-Based Distributed Query Processing on the Grid to appear in Proc UK e-Science programme All Hands Conference, 2–4 Sept 2003, Nottingham, UK.
7. I. Foster, C. Kesselman, Globus: A Metacomputing Infrastructure Toolkit. Intl J. Supercomputer Applications, 11(2):115–128, 1997.

8. I. Foster, C. Kesselman, J. Nick, S. Tuecke. Grid Services for Distributed System Integration. Computer, 35(6), 2002.
9. R.W. Moore, C. Baru, R. Mrciano, A. Rajasekar and M. Wan, Data-Intensive Computing, in The Grid: Blueprint for a New Computing Infrastructure, I. Foster and C Kesselman (eds), Morgan Kaufmann, 105–129, 1999.
10. I. Foster, J. Vöckler, M.Wilde, Y Zhao Chimera: A Virtual Data System for Representing, Querying, and Automating Data Derivation, in 14th International Conference on Scientific and Statistical Database Management (SSDBM 2002).
11. CA. Goble, D De Roure, N.R. Shadbolt and A.A.A. Fernandes Enhancing Services and Applications with Knowledge and Semantics in The Grid: Blueprint for a New Computing Infrastructure Second Edition eds. Ian Foster and Carl Kesselman, Morgan Kaufman, in press.
12. B. Ludaescher, A. Gupta, and M. E. Martone. A Model-Based Mediator System for Scientific Data Management. In Bioinformatics: Managing Scientific Data. Data (ed Zoe Lacroix and Terence Critchlow), Morgan Kaufmann, May, 2003, 1-55860-829-X.
13. B. Ludaescher, I. Altintas, and A. Gupta. Compiling Abstract Scientific Workflows into Web Service Workflows. In 15th Intl. Conference on Scientific and Statistical Database Management (SSDBM), Boston, Massachussets, 2003.
14. A. Gupta, B. Ludaescher, and M. Martone. BIRN-M: A Semantic Mediator for Solving Real-World Neuroscience Problems. In ACM Intl. Conference on Management of Data (SIGMOD), 2003, system demonstration.
15. J. Blythe, E. Deelman, Y. Gil, C. Kesselman, A. Agarwal, G. Mehta, K. Vahi. The Role of Planning in Grid Computing, In Proceedings of the 13th International Conference on Automated Planning and Scheduling (ICAPS), to appear, June 9–13, 2003, Trento, Italy.
16. J. Blythe, E. Deelman, Y. Gil, C. Kesselman. Transparent Grid Computing: A Knowledge-Based Approach, In Proceedings of the 15th Conference on Innovative Applications of Artificial Intelligence (IAAI), August 12–15, 2003, Acapulco, Mexico.
17. A. Rajasekar, M. Wan and R. Moore, MySRB & SRB – Components of a Data Grid, The 11th International Symposium on High Performance Distributed Computing (HPDC-11) Edinburgh, Scotland, July 24–26, 2002.
18. B. McBride, Four Steps Towards the Widespread Adoption of a Semantic Web, in Proceedings of the First International Semantic Web Conference (ISWC 2002), Sardinia, Italy, June 9–12, 2002. LNCS 2342, pp. 419–422.
19. M. Szomszor, L. Moreau Recording and Reasoning over Data Provenance in Web and Grid Services in Proceedings of 2nd International Conference on Ontologies, Databases and Applications of Semantics ODBASE, Sicily, Italy, November 2003.
20. A. Cooke, A. Gray, L. Ma, W. Nutt RGMA – An Information Integration System for Grid Monitoring in Tenth International Conference on Cooperative Information Systems (CoopIS 2003), Sicily, Italy, November 2003.
21. H. Tangmunarunkit, S. Decker and C. Kesselman, Ontology-based Resource Matching in Proceedings 2nd International Semantic Web Conference (ISWC2003), Florida, USA, Oct, 2003.
22. M. Atkinson, A.L. Chervenak, P. Kunszt, I. Narang, N.W. Paton, D. Pearson, A. Shoshani, and P. Watson, Data Access, Integration, and Management, in The Grid: Blueprint for a New Computing Infrastructure Second Edition (eds. I Foster and C Kesselman), Morgan Kaufman, in press.
23. P. Watson, Databases and The Grid, in Grid Computing: Making The Global Infrastructure a Reality, Wiley 2003.

24. L. Chen, N.R. Shadbolt, C.A. Goble, F. Tao, S.J. Cox, C. Puleston, P.R. Smart Towards a Knowledge-based Approach to Semantic Service Composition in 2nd International Semantic Web Conference, 2003 (ISWC2003), Florida, USA, October 2003.
25. Goble C.A. and De Roure D. Grid: An Application of the Semantic Web in ACM SIGMOD Record, Volume 31, Number 4, December 2002.
26. Goble C.A. and De Roure D. The Semantic Web and Grid Computing in Real World Semantic Web Applications (ed Vipul Kashyap). IOS Press Dec, 2002.
27. R. Meersman and A. Sheth Special Section on Semantic Web and Data Management, SIGMOD Record, Vol 31 No. 4 December 2002.
28. S. Malaika, A. Eisenberg, J. Melton Standards for Databases on the Grid Vol. 32 No. 3 September 2003.

From the "Eyeball" Web to the Transaction Web

Katia P. Sycara

School of Computer Science
Carnegie Mellon University
katia@cs.cmu.edu
www.cs.cmu.edu/~softagents

Abstract. The Web, as we know it, is a collection of human readable pages that are virtually unintelligible to computer programs. For that reason, it has been called the "eyeball" Web. While the Web emerged as a World Wide repository of digitized information, by and large, the very same information is not available for automatic computation. In recent years two parallel efforts emerged that have the potential of overcoming this paradox: the first effort is the Semantic Web which provides the tools for the explicit markup of the content of Web pages; the second effort is the development of Web Services which results in a Web where programs act as independent agents to become the producers and consumers of information and enable automation of business transactions.

In this talk I will focus on research that attempts to bridge the gap between the Web as we know it, the Semantic Web and Web services. Under this approach, I propose the vision of Web services as autonomous goal-directed agents which select other agents to interact with, and flexibly negotiate their interaction model, acting at times in client server mode, or at other times in peer to peer mode. The resulting Web services, that I call Autonomous Semantic Web services, utilize ontologies and semantically annotated Web pages to automate the fulfillment of tasks and transactions with other Web agents. In particular, Autonomous Semantic Web services use the Semantic Web to support capability based discovery and interoperation at run time. A first step towards this vision is the development of formal languages and inference mechanisms for representing and reasoning with core concepts of Web services. DAML-S (the Darpa Agent Markup Language for Services) is the first attempt to define such a language. I will give a brief overview of DAML-S and its relations with the Semantic Web and Web services. In addition, I will provide concrete examples of computational models of how DAML-S can be viewed as the first step in bridging the gap between the Semantic Web and current proposed industry standards for Web services. I will provide concrete examples of DAML-S in action, discuss challenges still open in the bridging between the Semantic Web and Web services and provide a roadmap to get us from today's Web to the Web of autonomous Semantic Web services.

R. Meersman et al. (Eds.): CoopIS/DOA/ODBASE 2003, LNCS 2888, p. 601, 2003.
© Springer-Verlag Berlin Heidelberg 2003

ODBASE 2003 PC Co-chairs' Message

This volume contains the proceedings of the 2nd International Conference on Ontologies, Databases, and Applications of Semantics for Large Scale Information Systems (ODBASE'03), held in Sicily from November 3 to November 7, 2003.

ODBASE holds a critical position in computer science as a primary meeting place for researchers interested in the interplay between Web research and information management technologies. In particular, ODBASE'03 presents papers addressing "Semantic" Web tools, data mining, data semantics, as well as advanced information system requirements, such as temporal and spatial capabilities.

In response to the call for papers 116 papers were submitted. Each paper was assigned to at least three reviewers chosen from the program committee. 27 were accepted as regular papers for presentation at the conference, and an additional 9 papers were accepted for presentation in the form of posters. This gives an acceptance rate of a little over 30%.

Given the high submission rate, the program committee members were asked to review about eight papers each, with some members volunteering to provide extra reviews at the last minute in order to ensure a fair evaluation of every paper. We would like to thank the program committee members for their prompt and thoughtful work.

The program chairs would like to thank Robert Meersman, Zahir Tari, and especially Kwong Yuen Lai for guiding us through the process of creating a program and for keeping us on track.

We would also like to thank Carole Goble for agreeing to serve as the conference keynote speaker, and thus helping to ensure a successful conference.

August 2003

Roger (Buzz) King, University of Colorado, U.S.A.
Maria E. Orlowska, University of Queensland, Australia
Rudi Studer, University of Karlsruhe, Germany
(ODBASE 2003 Program Committee Co-chairs)

R. Meersman et al. (Eds.): CoopIS/DOA/ODBASE 2003, LNCS 2888, p. 602, 2003.
© Springer-Verlag Berlin Heidelberg 2003

Recording and Reasoning over Data Provenance in Web and Grid Services

Martin Szomszor and Luc Moreau

School of Electronics and Computer Science
University of Southampton
Southampton SO17 1BJ UK
martinszomszor@yahoo.co.uk
L.Moreau@ecs.soton.ac.uk

Abstract. Large-scale, dynamic and open environments such as the Grid and Web Services build upon existing computing infrastructures to supply dependable and consistent large-scale computational systems. This kind of architecture has been adopted by the business and scientific communities allowing them to exploit extensive and diverse computing resources to perform complex data processing tasks. In such systems, results are often derived by composing multiple, geographically distributed, heterogeneous services as specified by intricate workflow management. This leads to the undesirable situation where the results are known, but the means by which they were achieved is not. With both scientific experiments and business transactions, the notion of lineage and dataset derivation is of paramount importance since without it, information is potentially worthless. We address the issue of *data provenance*, the description of the origin of a piece of data, in these environments showing the requirements, uses and implementation difficulties. We propose an infrastructure level support for a provenance recording capability for service-oriented architectures such as the Grid and Web Services. We also offer services to view and retrieve provenance and we provide a mechanism by which provenance is used to determine whether previous computed results are still up to date.

1 Introduction

Grids and Web Services are evolving into large-scale dynamic and open environments providing services owned and managed by multiple stakeholders [5]. The concept of virtual organisation (VO) is being anticipated by many [8,5] as the computational model for coordinating the complex interactions of such services. A typical VO's lifecycle consists of the following steps: VO participants are discovered, the purpose and the terms of the VO are negotiated, the VO is created and then executed to deliver some result, before it is disbanded. At the end of a VO's lifetime, users potentially find themselves in the awkward situation in which they have access to the result of the computation without any information on why and how such a result has been obtained. The lack of information about

R. Meersman et al. (Eds.): CoopIS/DOA/ODBASE 2003, LNCS 2888, pp. 603–620, 2003.
© Springer-Verlag Berlin Heidelberg 2003

the origin of results does not help users to trust such open environments, and therefore may hamper the deployment of advanced services [15].

Workflow enactment has become popular in the Web Services [14,4] and Grid communities [11]. Workflow enactment can be seen as a mechanism offering a simpler form of virtual organisation: it is capable of composing Web Services, potentially discovered dynamically, according to data and control flows specified in a workflow language, such as WSFL [14] or BPEL4WS [4]. Similarly, users are confronted with the problem of determining the origin of a result produced by such enactment. Furthermore, deciding when results of computation, whether a scientific analysis or a business transaction, are no longer valid becomes an important concern.

Against this background, *provenance* is an annotation able to explain how a particular result has been derived; such a provenance information can be used to better identify the process that was used to reach a particular conclusion. Specifically, in a service-oriented architecture, provenance identifies what data is passed between services, what services are available, and what results are generated for particular sets of input values, etc. Using provenance, a user can trace the "process" that led to the aggregation of services producing a particular output.

It is our belief that provenance recording should be part of the infrastructure, so that users can elect to enable it when they execute their complex tasks over the Grid or in Web Services environments. Currently, the Web Services protocol stack and the Open Grid Services Architecture [7] do not provide any support for recording provenance, though the need has been acknowledged by that community, as illustrated by a recent workshop on provenance [18], and some Grid projects such as myGrid (`www.mygrid.org.uk`). Additionally, producing provenance data is of no use, if we do not provide the means of exploiting it — an activity referred to as *provenance reasoning* in this paper.

The purpose of this paper is to investigate the notion of provenance in services-oriented architecture, such as Grids and Web Services, and more specifically when computations are the result of workflow enactment. Our specific contributions are:

1. A service-oriented architecture for provenance support in Grid and Web Services environments, based on the idea of a provenance service;
2. A client-side API for recording provenance data for Web Service invocation;
3. A data model for storing provenance data;
4. A server-side interface for querying provenance data;
5. Two components making use of provenance: provenance browsing and provenance validation.

This paper is organised as follows. In Section 2, we discuss the notion of provenance and identify some of its requirements. In Section 3, we present the architecture for provenance support in a service-oriented environment. We then discuss some implementation aspects of our provenance system in Section 4. Finally, in Section 5, we analyse our design and conclude the paper by identifying issues that need further investigation.

2   Background

Provenance is primarily concerned with data derivation. It provides a proof of origin for a segment of data and a record of its history. This section looks at what provenance is, why it is useful and how it might be provided in a dynamic and open environment such as the Grid and Web Services.

2.1   Provenance

Provenance allows us to take a quantity of data and examine its lineage. Lineage shows each of the steps involved in sourcing, moving and processing the data [17]. In many of today's modern information systems, particularly those concerned with business and scientific data handling, data can be collated from a variety of distributed and diverse resources and processed to form new data. We can consider the sequence of taking a dataset, processing it and producing a dataset product as a dataset *transformation*. In order to provide provenance, all datasets and their transformations must be recorded. Saltz [19] suggests that we can achieve a sound lineage record by recording enough information to ensure that any dataset transformation is reproducible.

The storage and maintenance of provenance records is an important consideration. Frew and Bose [10] propose the following requirements for provenance collection:

1. A standard lineage representation is required so data lineage can be communicated reliably between systems (currently there is no standard lineage format).
2. Automated lineage recording is essential since humans are unlikely to record all the necessary information manually.
3. Unobtrusive information collecting is desirable so that current working practices are not disrupted.

The concept of providing provenance is relatively new and unexplored. It has attracted interest from both the academic and business communities where speculation about its benefits is widespread. Scientists are often interested in provenance because it allows them to view data in a derived view and make observations about its quality and reliability [3]. Goble [12] presents some notable uses for provenance:

- *Reliability and quality*
  Given a derived dataset we are able to cite its lineage and therefore measure its credibility. This is particularly important for data produced in scientific information systems.
- *Justification and audit*
  Provenance can be used to give a historical account of when and how data has been produced. In some situations, it will also show why certain derivations have been made.

- *Re-usability, reproducibility and repeatability*
  A provenance record not only shows how data has been produced, it provides all the necessary information to reproduce the results. In some cases the distinction between repeatability and reproducibility must be made. In scientific experiments results may be different due to observational error or processing may rely on external and volatile resources.
- *Change and evolution*
  Audit trails support the implementation of change management.
- *Ownership, security, credit and copyright*
  Provenance provides a trusted source from which we can procure who the information belongs to and precisely when and how it was created.

It could also be said that provenance significantly increases productivity by facilitating the discovery of existing derivations, which can save time, computational effort and storage. With a standard lineage representation, collaboration of resources is also made considerably easier [9,6].

2.2   Workflow Enactment and Provenance

The Grid [11] and Web Services communities [14,21,4] have identified workflow enactment as a key concept, essentially offering a scripted form of virtual organisation [8]. Workflow enactement is the automation of a process during which documents, information or tasks are passed from one participant to another for action, according to a set of declarative or procedural rules. In Grid applications, this task is often performed by a "workflow enactment engine". The enactment engine uses a workflow script, such as WSFL or BPEL4WS, to determine which services to call, the order to execute them in and how to pass datasets between them. Each of these services can be invoked by using their respective WSDL interface documents. This concept can be seen in Fig. 1. This diagram shows a workflow enactment engine using a workflow script to control the flow of data between two Web Services. Each Web Service is passed an input and returns an output.

In terms of provenance, we can consider the input for a Web Service as a dataset, the Web Service itself as the transformation and the result as the data product. Therefore, provenance for a service-oriented architecture can be provided by logging all of the Web Services invoked by the enactment engine, the inputs given and the outputs returned. In order to meet the requirement that the provenance records must enable the re-creation of any dataset transformations, the WSDL documents for the services invoked must be recorded along with the workflow script describing their invocation context.

2.3   Accessing Provenance Records

Assuming that a system is capable of recording provenance, we should consider how these records are accessed and what they might be used for. A standard lineage representation should be formulated that is capable of recording the diverse

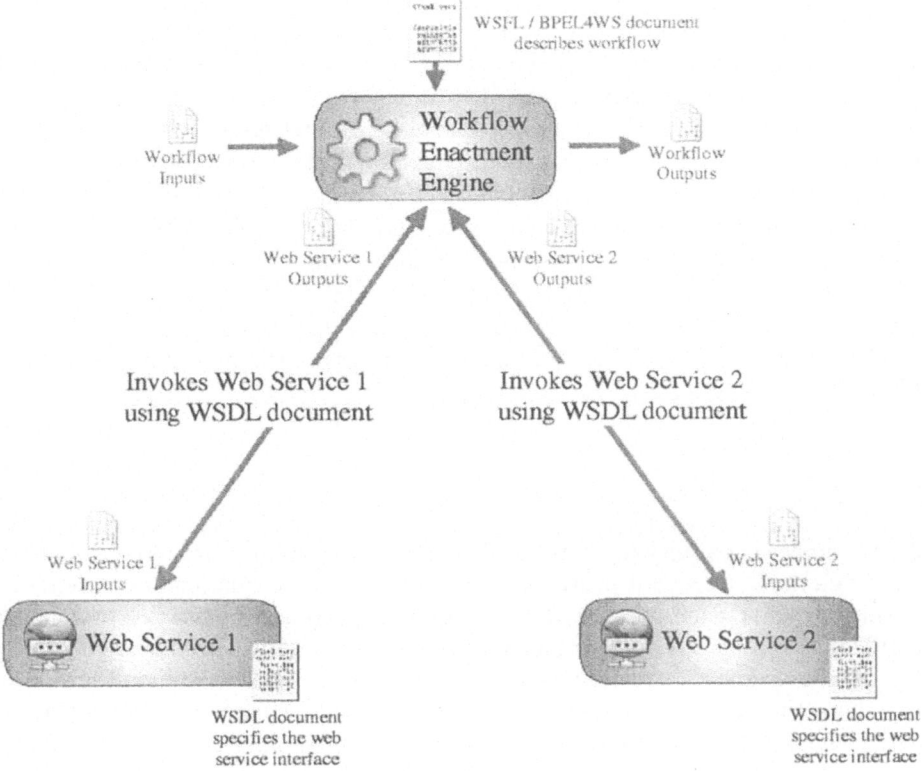

Fig. 1. Workflow Enactment

range of services possible and the multifarious data structures used. Since the current workflow languages and service descriptions are represented using XML, the obvious syntactic framework for a provenance record is also XML. Some form of querying interface should be supplied that enables the retrieval of provenance records by both content and type. For example, it would be useful to query a provenance repository for records about a particular invoked Web Service, a specific workflow script used for enactment, or an exact observed output. It would also be desirable to provide an automated service to reproduce datasets and re-run dataset derivations.

2.4   Related Work

Other work [2] on provenance has concentrated on models grounded on database architectures in which queries are used to extract information. In general, if a query Q is applied to some database D, we can obtain the view V such that $V = Q(D)$. In this scenario, the provenance of a specific piece of data d in the output V shows which parts of the database D contributed to it. In [2], the important distinction between 'why' provenance (the set of tuples that contribute to the result) and 'where' provenance (the location(s) in the source database from which the result was extracted) is made. Using the explicit notions of location defined in the deterministic model [1] and a formal query language, a precise definition of provenance is formulated using a general data model that applies to both relational databases and hierarchical data structures such as XML.

MyGrid (www.mygrid.org.uk) aims at providing a personalised environment for bioinformaticians to perform *in silico* experiments [16]. In myGrid, provenance is stored in a user's personal repository and provenance generation is tightly integrated with the enactment engine [13]. In that context, the focus is not on the architecture and protocols required for supporting provenance in service-oriented architectures, but on personalising provenance information when presented to the scientist.

3   Architecture

A provenance capability in a Grid or Web Services environment has has two principal functions: to record provenance on dataset transformations executed, e.g. during workflow enactment, and to expose this provenance data in a consistent and logical format via a query interface. In this section, we discuss the design of a provenance architecture for Grid and Web Services, which is dictated primarily by where the data provenance is held, how this provenance is collected, what exactly constitutes a provenance record, and how provenance can be queried and reasoned over.

Provenance needs to be stored, and two possible solutions can be envisaged for storage. On the one hand, the data provenance is held alongside the data as metadata, whereas on the other hand, the data provenance can be stored in a dedicated repository, made accessible as a Grid or Web Service. The first solution requires the holders of any such data to maintain the integrity of the provenance records as transformations take place, and it imposes significant changes to any existing data storage structures. Such a kind of provenance can be useful for a user to remember how a result was derived, and what steps were involved. It is unclear that such provenance can be trusted by any third party, since the data and provenance owner has to be trusted to have recorded provenance properly.

Alternatively, the provenance service solution requires any party performing a dataset transformation to update the provenance service, with any new derivations and how they were performed. Many provenance services may exist over the Grid, some more trusted than others, and users may select which one to adopt when executing their workflows. By adopting a suitable protocol to submit provenance, some desirable properties can be enforced by the provenance service, such as non-repudiation (to be discussed in Section 5); the provenance service could therefore be used as a generalised auditing mechanisms, which can be trusted by any third party. While such protocols are interesting, they are beyond the scope of the current paper; and we will only focus on provenance being submitted by a workflow enactor.

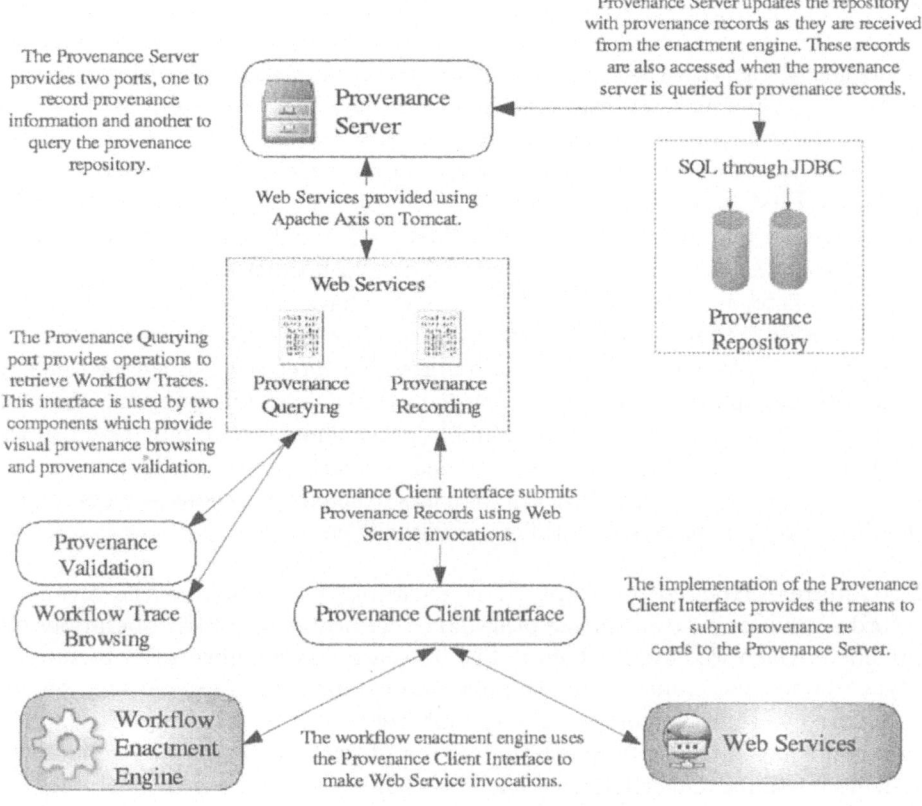

Fig. 2. Provenance Architecture

Architecture Overview. Our service-oriented provenance architecture is shown in Fig. 2. As far as *provenance creation* is concerned, the architecture is composed of a server side and a client side. The Provenance Server holds the provenance records and provides methods to access and update them via a Web Service. The records themselves are held in a relational database. The Provenance Client Interface is responsible for submitting to the Provenance Server provenance records about any Web Service invocation executed by a client such as a workflow enactment engine. To this end, the Client Side Interface uses the Provenance Recording port provided by the Provenance Server.

In order to provide data provenance on workflows, our approach is to record enough information to be able to re-create any dataset transformation (cf. Section 2.2). We are making here a simplifying assumption: we assume that all dataset transformations are carried out by invoking Web Services or workflows. The order in which these services are invoked, the control flow and the data flow between services are governed by a workflow script, expressed in a workflow language such as WSFL or BPEL4WS. For any workflow execution, we store records in the provenance repository defining the workflow details, with precise information on each activity carried out. Any datasets passed to an activity will be logged along with the outputs that are received. We define a *workflow trace* as the conglomeration of provenance records for both the workflow itself and each of the activities it executed.

As far as *provenance retrieval and reasoning* is concerned, two facilities are provided. First, a browsing interface is offered so that users can navigate provenance traces. Second, a provenance validation capability is provided in order to decide if the results logged in a workflow trace are still up to date; such a capability is for instance beneficial to users who have run a workflow, but would like to decide if they need to re-enact the workflow because some of its services now produce different results. Both the browsing interface and the provenance validation capability make use of a common Provenance Querying Interface.

From a practical viewpoint, although a provenance service may result in the redundant storage of data, it does not demand any alterations to the services invoked by workflows; only those components which invoke these services require modification — namely the workflow enactment engine.

Provenance Recording Port. The recording port provides the means to record a provenance trace in the provenance service. A set of key operations are provided, which we describe below. The interface was designed so as to support asynchronous and transactional submission of provenance data. Asynchronicity is required so that the performance of Web Services intensive workflow application is not penalised by frequent submission of data. Transactional capabilities provide for simple cancellation of trace recording.

The `beginTrace` operation is called by the Provenance Client Interface (PCI) when a new workflow is started. It requires the workflow script, its description, and workflow inputs as arguments. These are used to create a new trace in the provenance database, for which a unique workflow Trace ID is returned. This ID must be used by the PCI in subsequent activity registrations.

The `registerWSActivity` operation is called by the PCI whenever a Web Service invocation is about to be made. It requires the trace ID (returned by the previous method), the workflow activity name corresponding to this Web Service invocation, the URL of the WSDL interface specifying the Web Service, the operation that is going to be called and further information needed to invoke the Web Service (the service namespace, the service name, the port type namespace and the port type name). A unique activity ID is returned which is used later to register the activity inputs and outputs.

The `registerSubWorklowActivity` operation is called by the PCI whenever a sub-workflow activity is executed. The trace ID and activity name are passed as arguments along with the sub-Workflow Trace ID. A unique activity ID is returned.

The `registerWSInput` operation is called by the PCI just before a Web Service invocation is made. It takes as argument the activity ID (allocated when the Web Service is registered) the message parts and the operation increment. All message parts are supposed to be encoded in XML, like they would be for the message invocation, which allows the provenance service to be able to store any complex data type.

The `registerWSOutput` operation is called by the PCI just after the results of the Web Service invocation have been received. The arguments are the same as the `registerWSInput` operation.

The `commitTrace` operation is called by the PCI when the workflow enactment has been completed. Once this operation is called, the workflow status is changed from 'active' to 'committed'. It takes the workflow outputs in XML format in the arguments along with the trace ID for the trace which is to be committed.

The `abandonTrace` operation may be called when a workflow status is 'active' after which it will be changed to 'abandoned'. Once this operation has been called, the trace is abandoned and no further logging can take place.

The interaction between the Provenance Server and the Provenance Client Interface during workflow execution is best shown using the sequence diagram in Fig. 3. The interaction can be divided into three major phases: the first initialises the provenance recording, the second registers workflow activities and the third commits the workflow trace. From the perspective of the enactment engine, the interaction is simple. When a new workflow is started, the 'Begin Trace' method is called on the Provenance Client Interface. For every unique Web Service invocation, a new client-side stub is requested from the PCI by calling the 'Get New Port Invoker' method, passing the WSDL document location and desired operation as arguments. The input message can then be created in the usual way with the message parts being set using the 'Set Message Parts' method on the client-side stub. Consequently, the operation is executed using the 'Execute Operation' method and the result message is returned. On completion of the workflow, the enactment engine must notify the PCI that the provenance trace has to be committed by calling the 'Commit' method.

The Provenance Client Interface interacts with the Provenance Server by making Web Service invocations on the Provenance Recording Port. When the workflow is started, it calls the 'Begin Trace' operation and stores the unique trace ID allocated. When a new client-side stub is created, the PCI registers the new activity with the Provenance Server by using the 'Register WS Activity' operation, storing the unique activity ID alloted. When asked by the enactment engine to invoke a Web Service, the PCI first registers the inputs with the Provenance Server using the 'Register WS Input' operation. It then invokes the desired Web Service and registers the results using the 'Register WS Output' operation before passing them back to the enactment engine.

Provenance Query Port. The Query port supplies a set of operations by which a client can retrieve workflow trace information. The operation `getTraceListXML` can be used to query the workflow repository for a list of trace ID numbers. These numbers identify traces that must satisfy some properties specified in the query interface, such as start and end time, etc.

It is possible to retrieve workflow trace information in two ways. The operation `getFullTraceXML` takes a trace ID as input and returns a complete XML representation of the workflow trace. For a complex workflow, this XML docu-

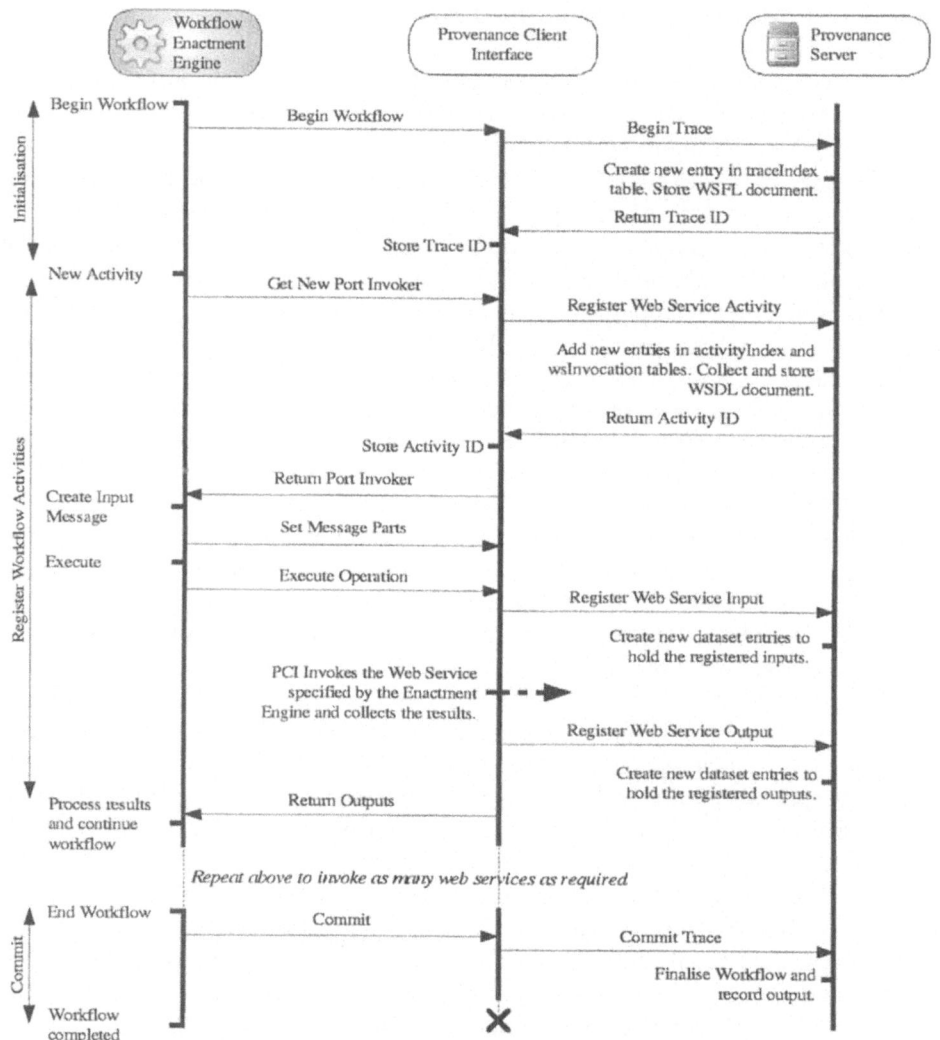

Fig. 3. A Sequence Diagram showing the interaction between the Enactment Engine, the Provenance Client Interface, and the Provenance Server

ment could be very large, so a set of operations are also provided to request parts of a workflow trace. With these operations, it is possible to extract a list of activities composing a trace, details for each activies, including inputs and outputs. To this end, the ProvenanceQuery Port offers a querying API which we use in the deployment of the provenance reasoning components.

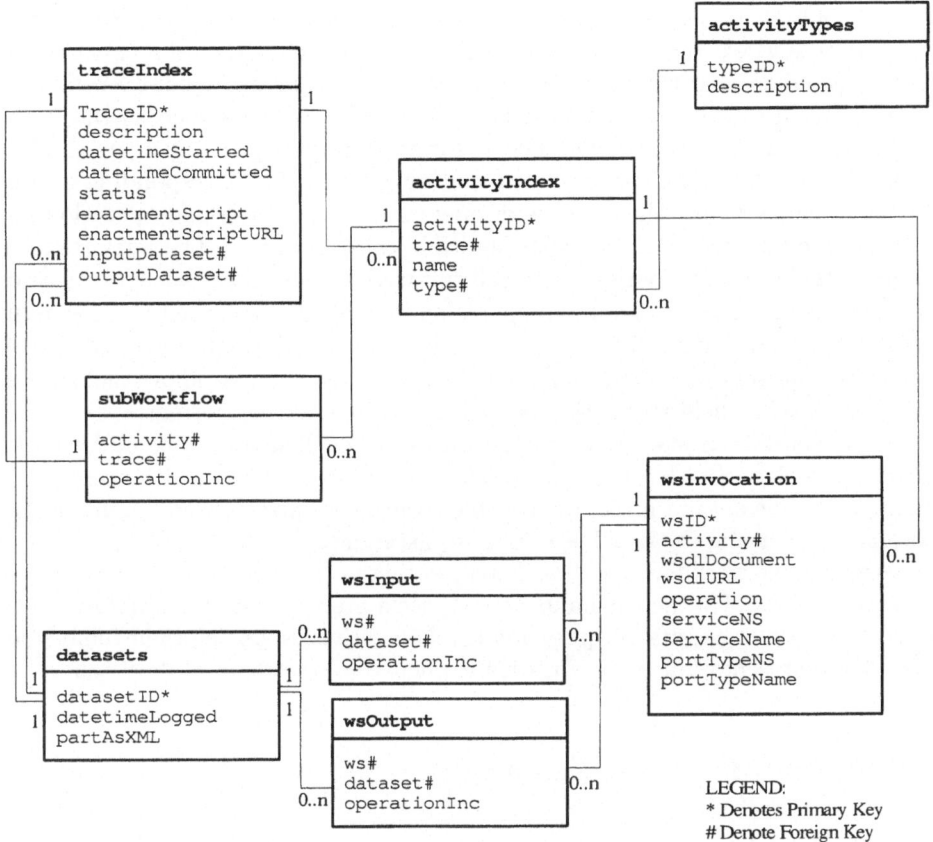

Fig. 4. Provenance Database

4   Implementation

The Provenance Server receives provenance data via the Provenance Recording port and stores it in the Provenance Repository. The repository is a relational database that uses the tables and relationships shown in Fig. 4.

It is designed to store all the information necessary to provide provenance data on workflows, activities and all datasets passed between them. There follows a brief overview of the role of each table. The `traceIndex` table holds the workflow trace information for every workflow enacted. The trace ID is automatically allocated by the database incrementally and provides a unique handle to each workflow trace. The inputDataset and outputDataset fields are references to entries in the datasets table. The status field can take one of three values - active, committed or abandoned. The `activityIndex` table links activities executed to their given workflow by the trace field. The type field references an entry in the activityTypes table to specify the activity type. The `activityTypes` table holds descriptions of the possible activity types. In this implementation, there is only two types: Web Service invocations and sub-workflows. It would be feasible to add extra activity types such as JMS or RMI providing extra tables were created to hold the relevant provenance data. The wsInvocation table is used to store details on activities that invoke Web Services such as the WSDL document and operation name. The wsInput and wsOutput tables are used to link a Web Service invocation inputs and outputs to the corresponding entries in the datasets table. The purpose of operation increments (field operationInc) is to accommodate activities where multiple calls are made. The subWorkflow table is used to link activities which call sub-workflows to their respective entries in the traceIndex table. Again, an operation increment is recorded to allow multiple sub-workflow calls. The dataset table holds any datasets recorded. These might be datasets passed to and from Web Services or to workflow themselves. The partAsXML field stores the dataset in a serialised XML format.

As a workflow is executed and the Provenance Client Interface updates the Provenance Server with invocation details, the database is filled with provenance data. With this data in place, we are able to generate workflow traces in an XML format by querying the database using SQL statements.

An example workflow trace, as displayed by the trace browsing interface, can be seen in Fig. 5. On the left-hand side, we see a pretty-printed hierarchical view of a trace with its inputs, outputs and invoked activities; on the right hand-side, the XML representation is shown, with explicit representation of data types.

4.1   Client Side Dataset Encoding

A challenging task was finding an appropriate way to submit the recorded datasets in a structured manner. In simple cases, the inputs and outputs to a Web Service are primitive data types such as integers and strings. However, WSDL also provides the ability to define and use complex types, which are formed of primitive or other complex types. As far as the client side library was concerned, we needed a mechanism to convert arbitrary data types into a serialized format that enabled easy re-creation and re-use. To this end, we adopted Java Record Object Model (JROM) from IBM's Alphaworks. This provides methods to serialize Java Objects used in Web Service invocations into XML format.

A typical Grid or Web Service client relies on a communication layer, such as WSIF or JAX-RPC, to invoke Web Services using using their respective WSDL documents. We have provided a wrapper class, making use of WSIF for invocation of Web Services, and at the same time implementing the PCI for submitting provenance data.

Using JROM to construct the XML representations of Java objects also has an added advantage: The JROM API also provides methods to convert XML representation back into JROMValues. This allows the datasets recorded to be easily re-used for other tasks such as provenance validation.

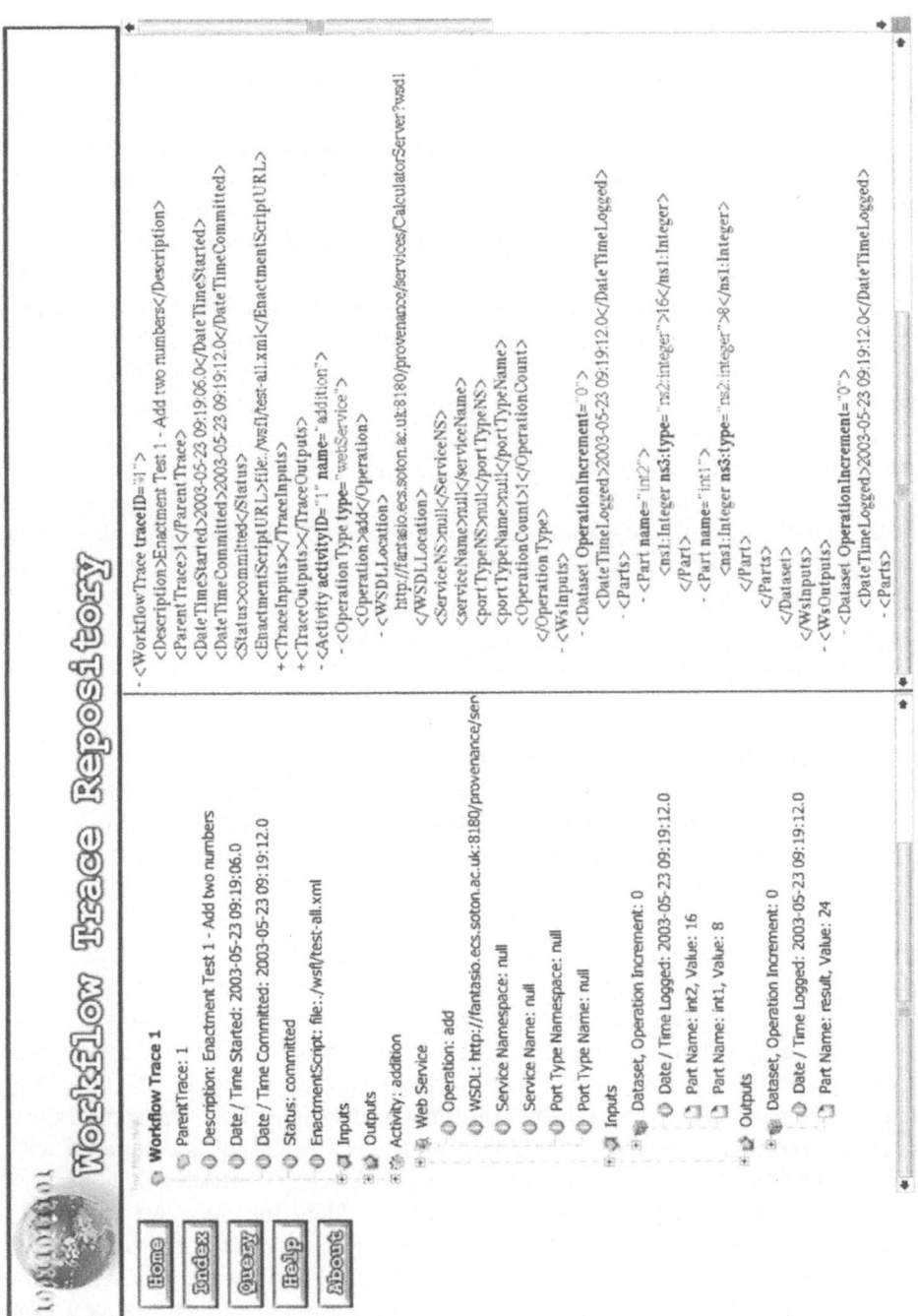

Fig. 5. A screen shot of the web interface showing a tree-view of a workflow trace

4.2   Logging Mechanism

There are two possible ways in which the Provenance Client Interface can submit provenance trace to the the Provenance Server.   *(i)* In a *synchronous* submission, the Provenance Client blocks workflow enactment, while updating the Provenance Server. This is the submission mode that underlies the sequence diagram of Fig. 3.   *(ii)* Alternatively, using an *asynchronous* submission mode, the enactment can continue in parallel with submission of data to the Provenance Server, which takes place in another execution thread.

Synchronous recording can have significant detrimental effect on the performance of the enactment engine, but it provides timeliness as the provenance information is recorded as enactment proceeds, and therefore can be seen as a detailed progress log. On the other hand, with the asynchronous mode, an extremely lazy manner of submitting provenance data would be only to schedule the transfer of such provenance data at enactment time. The provenance data to be submitted could be stored temporarily in a local database; when network traffic is reduced, the data could then be transferred, possibly well after completion of the workflow. Such an asynchronous mode of submission is particular appealing for large data sets.

4.3   Retrieving and Reasoning over Data Provenance

As an experiment into the uses of Data Provenance, we designed and implemented two additional system components; a set of web pages to provide a browse-able workflow trace interface and a provenance validation mechanism which checks each of the Web Service invocations still provides the same results. A screenshot of the web page interface is supplied in Fig. 5, it shows the workflow trace for a simple workflow with only one activity that invokes a Web Service to add two integers together. The left frame shows the workflow trace in a familiar tree-view format, while the right frame shows the raw XML for the trace. It is possible to use this interface to browse workflows that are still in progress and therefore it also provides a way to monitor long and complex workflows.

Provenance Validation allows a user to check that each Web Service invocation made during a workflow still produces the same results. It iteratively re-executes each Web Service invocation made, using precisely the same inputs as those recorded. The output produced by the re-invocation is compared with the output stored in the provenance trace. A difference in the result is notified to the user. By re-using the existing Provenance Client Interface, we are able to record provenance on this re-execution and hence compare it with the original.

A typical example of the use of this facility is the following. A user having been informed that new data are available in a database (accessible as a Web Service), or that a new version of a service has been deployed, may decide to use the provenance validation facility to verify if the results produced by a previous execution of a workflow are still up to date. The workflow activities that produce results that differ from those stored in the provenance database indicate points in the workflow at which re-enactment should occur.

It is important to distinguish provenance validation from workflow re-enactment. The former only uses the information recorded in a provenance trace to detect which Web Service produces outputs that do not match the ones in the trace for the same inputs. Web Services can be invoked in any order, and this activity does not require knowledge of the workflow script and service dependencies. On the contrary, workflow re-enactment requires the understanding of a workflow script: it typically requires the enactment engine to be provided with a runtime state (i.e. its continuation) to resume the execution at a specific point of the workflow.

5   Discussion and Conclusion

In this section, we study how the proposed architecture meets the requirements identified in Section 2; we then summarise our contributions, and discuss how our work can be extended.

The principal requirement for a provenance recording facility is that data lineage must be recorded and stored. We adopted the position that a sound lineage record can be achieved by logging enough information to enable the re-creation any dataset transformation. For a service-oriented architecture, in which Web Service invocations are used to perform these transformations, this means collecting all the invocation details. Our Provenance Client Interface does this autonomously, supplying the user with the option to turn provenance recording on or off as desired. The data model put forward in Section 4 provides a means to store this provenance, accommodating complex workflow activities and arbitrary data types. With the client-server interaction described in Section 3, we are able to reliably record and store all Web Service invocations carried out by a client and hence describe all dataset transformations. We also designed our system so that it could be integrated with any existing components simply and unobtrusively.

The second major requirement is that the data provenance is made available through a query interface. This is provided through the Provenance Query Port; an API that allows a user to extract data provenance according to content and type via Web Services. The provenance records are made available in the form of a workflow trace, an XML formated data structure that shows precise details of all aspects of a complex data processing task such as workflow enactment. Although our workflow trace definition is by no means an attempt at a standard lineage representation, it does uphold the requirement that it allows data provenance to be communicated reliably and consistently between platforms.

The greatest testament that our architecture meets the requirements is demonstrated through the Provenance Validation component. By enabling the validation of any dataset transformation, we show that the records have been recorded correctly, stored in a reliable format that facilitates re-use, and exposed via a user friendly query interface.

In this paper, we have defined a notion of provenance for service-oriented architectures such as Web Services and the Open Grid Services Architecture.

Based on this definition, we have proposed a provenance architecture, composed of two key components: *(i)* a provenance server capable of recording provenance information and offering a querying interface over the provenance information it stores; *(ii)* a client-side API that allows clients invoking Web Services to submit provenance records to the provenance server. We demonstrated the use of provenance data by providing two further components making use of the querying interface: *(i)* A browsing interface allows users to navigate provenance records as they are submitted; *(ii)* a provenance validation capability is able to decide if the results produced by previous workflow enactments are still up to date by re-executing all invoked services and comparing their outputs with the ones stored in the provenance trace.

Provenance is a rather new topic in service-oriented architectures, and a number of issues still need to be addressed. In our implementation, the provenance service is acting as a single point of contact, and therefore may become a bottleneck and a single point of failure. Provenance information need not be stored at a single location, and could be distributed. It makes however life easier for the implementor of the querying of interface if all provenance records are stored at a single location.

In Section 3, we motivated the existence of a provenance service by the possibility of auditing provenance information by third parties. The architecture includes a Provenance Client Interface, which allows a client, such as a workflow enactment engine, to submit provenance records. In such a context, provenance can only be trusted if the provenance service and the enactment engine are trusted. It is desirable to reduce the trust assumptions so that the provenance service can be accepted as properly auditable by third parties. In particular, not having to trust the enactment engine to conformly execute a workflow will make the system more attractive. To this end, we could request from the invoked services to contribute to the provenance record submission process, in order to certify the records submitted by the enactment engine. There is here an interesting similarity with Mobile Agents having to run on non-trusted platforms [20]: provenance protocols could be inspired by protocols designed to verify that the results returned by a mobile agent have not been corrupted by the environments in which it operated. Distributed systems properties are sought such as mutual authentication of all parties involved in the computation, and non-repudiation, by which we can retain evidence of the fact that a service has committed to executing a particular invocation and has produced a given result.

Section 4.2 evoked the problem of large data sets, for which the transfer of data could be performed asynchronously. In some cases, it may not be desirable to duplicate the data either because it is too large, or because of copyright or intellectual property reasons. The data owner would have to commit to archive such data, and a unforgeable digest could be submitted instead. The protocol should be extended to accomodate such cases, and incorporate data owners in a network of trust.

We propose a provenance validation component capable of re-invoking Web Services and compare their results with the results stored in the provenance server. Currently, our comparison relies on a strict syntactic equality check, but this has some restrictions. Some services can be based on stochastic processes (e.g. Monte-Carlo simulation), and therefore generated results may not be syntactically equal, though they could be considered equivalent. To be generic, a provenance architecture must be able to support domain specific comparisons, so that from a domain's viewpoint, one can decide whether two results are similar.

Acknowledgments. Thanks to colleagues for discussions on provenance including Syd Chapman, Omer Rana, Carole Goble, Matthew Addis and Mark Greenwood. This research is funded in part by EPSRC myGrid project (reference GR/R67743/01).

References

[1] Peter Buneman, Alin Deutsch, and Wang-Chiew Tan. A deterministic model for semistructured data. In *Workshop on Query Processing for Semistructured Data and Non-Standard Data Formats*, 1998.

[2] Peter Buneman, Sanjeev Khanna, and Wang-Chiew Tan. Why and Where: A Characterization of Data Provenance. In *International Conference on Database Theory (ICDT)*, 2001.

[3] Peter Buneman, Sanjeev Khanna, and Wang-Chiew Tan. Computing provenance and annotations for views, October 2002. Published at [18].

[4] Francisco Curbera, Yaron Goland, Johannes Klein, Frank Leymann, Dieter Roller, Satish Thatte, and Sanjiva Weerawarana. Business process execution language for web services (bpel4ws). http://www.ibm.com/developerworks/library/ws-bpel/, 2002.

[5] David de Roure, Nicholas R. Jennings, and Nigel Shadbolt. The semantic grid: A future e-science infrastructure. *International Journal of Concurrency and Computation: Practice and Experience*, 2003.

[6] I. Foster, J. Voeckler, M. Wilde, and Y. Zhao. Chimera: A virtual data system for representing, querying and automating data derivation. In *Proceedings of the 14th Conference on Scientific and Statistical Database Management*, Edinburgh, Scotland, July 2002.

[7] Ian Foster, Carl Kesselman, Jeffrey M. Nick, and Steven Tuecke. The Physiology of the Grid – An Open Grid Services Architecture for Distributed Systems Integration. Technical report, Argonne National Laboratory, 2002.

[8] Ian Foster, Carl Kesselman, and Steve Tuecke. The Anatomy of the Grid. Enabling Scalable Virtual Organizations. *International Journal of Supercomputer Applications*, 2001.

[9] Ian Foster, Jens Vockler, Michael Wilde, and Yong Zhao. The virtual data grid: A new model and architecture for data-intensive collaboration, October 2002. Published at [18].

[10] James Frew and Rajendra Bose. Lineage issues for scientific data and information, October 2002. Published at [18].

[11] Grid computing environments working group at the global grid forum. http://www.computingportals.org/, November 2002.

[12] Carole Goble. Position statement: Musings on provenance, workflow and (semantic web) annotations for bioinformatics, October 2002. Published at [18].

[13] Mark Greenwood, Carole Goble, Robert Stevens, Jun Zhao, Matthew Addis, Darren Marvin, Luc Moreau, and Tom Oinn. Provenance of e-science experiments – experience from bioinformatics. In *Proceedings of the UK OST e-Science second All Hands Meeting 2003 (AHM'03)*, 4 pages, Nottingham, UK, September 2003.

[14] Frank Leyman. Web Services Flow Language (WSFL). Technical report, IBM, May 2001.

[15] Michael Luck, Peter McBurney, and Chris Preist. *Agent Technolgy: Enabling Next Generation Computing*. AgentLink, 2003.

[16] Luc Moreau, Simon Miles, Carole Goble, Mark Greenwood, Vijay Dialani, Matthew Addis, Nedim Alpdemir, Rich Cawley, David De Roure, Justin Ferris, Rob Gaizauskas, Kevin Glover, Chris Greenhalgh, Peter Li, Xiaojian Liu, Phillip Lord, Michael Luck, Darren Marvin, Tom Oinn, Norman Paton, Stephen Pettifer, Milena V Radenkovic, Angus Roberts, Alan Robinson, Tom Rodden, Martin Senger, Nick Sharman, Robert Stevens, Brian Warboys, Anil Wipat, and Chris Wroe. On the Use of Agents in a BioInformatics Grid. In Sangsan Lee, Satoshi Sekguchi, Satoshi Matsuoka, and Mitsuhisa Sato, editors, *Proceedings of the Third IEEE/ACM CCGRID'2003 Workshop on Agent Based Cluster and Grid Computing*, pages 653–661, Tokyo, Japan, May 2003.

[17] Dave Pearson. Data requirements for the grid – scoping study report, February 2002. Status Draft.

[18] Data provenance/derivation workshop. http://people.cs.uchicago.edu/ yongzh/position_papers.html, October 2002.

[19] Joel Saltz. Data provenance, October 2002. Published at [18].

[20] Hock Kim Tan and Luc Moreau. Extending Execution Tracing for Mobile Code Security. In Klaus Fischer and Dieter Hutter, editors, *Second International Workshop on Security of Mobile MultiAgent Systems (SEMAS'2002)*, DFKI Research Report, RR-02-03, pages 51–59, Bologna, Italy, June 2002. DFKI Saarbrucken.

[21] Satish Thatte. Xlang, web services for business process design, 2001.

Preparing SCORM for the Semantic Web

Lora Aroyo[1,2], Stanislav Pokraev[3], and Rogier Brussee[3]

[1] Department of Computer Science, University of Twente
P.O. BOX 217, 7500 AE Enschede, The Netherlands
[2] Department of Mathematics and Computer Science,
Eindhoven University of Technology
P.O. Box 513, 5600 MB Eindhoven, The Netherlands
l.m.aroyo@tue.nl
[3] Telematica Institute,
P.O. BOX 589, 7500 AN Enschede, The Netherlands
{stanislav.pokraev,rogier.brussee}@telin.nl

Abstract. In this paper we argue that the effort within the context of Semantic Web research, such as RDF and DAML-S. will allow for better knowledge representation and engineering of educational systems and easier integration of e-learning with other business processes. We also argue that existing educational standards, such as SCORM and LOM could be mapped to those technologies, providing for more efficient automation of processes like educational resource annotation, and intelligent accessibility management. In this way we can use a successful combination of the technical advances outside of educational context and the existing educational standards, and allow for easier interoperability. To illustrate these issues and a solution approach we present the OntoAIMS educational environment.

1 Introduction

The learning technology community is quickly adopting many of the Web technologies (XML, RDF(S), streaming video, etc.) [Dev01]. Simultaneously, the educational technology standardisation is moving forward at rapid pace, with the IMS [IMS] and the ADL [ADL] having become the specification consortia that are tracked by vendors, implementers and academia. Both bring important contributions with respect to management of educational resources. The emerging educational specification for learning content SCORM addresses semantic annotations, content aggregation and sequencing. However, SCORM [Dod02] has chosen its own XML formats and methodologies, thereby limiting the educational community to a restricted universe, and making it much more difficult to integrate e-learning with other business processes. For example, although SCORM was designed for the military, without special interfacing code, e-learning systems will not be able to tell military planners which soldiers have absolved a course for safe operation of a particular weapon system because the SCORM specific XML schema used to track course results, is almost certainly not used by the (many) military planning systems. It is thus recognised by some, including leaders of the SCORM development community, that there is a benefit in opening up to the larger (semantic) web

R. Meersman et al. (Eds.): CoopIS/DOA/ODBASE 2003, LNCS 2888, pp. 621–634, 2003.
© Springer-Verlag Berlin Heidelberg 2003

community. By design, these technologies make it easier to integrate learning material with other material by avoiding cumbersome translations of existing vocabulary and semantic descriptions. Moreover, there is the hope of getting better tool support and using a more widely deployed infrastructure by tapping in the resources of a larger community.

Current web-based courseware (both static material and dynamic activities) is usually decomposed into independent modules, which are further combined in complete courses [Che98, Mur99]. This approach stimulates reuse and makes it easier to create variants of courses adapted to different purposes or audiences, up to the level of individual students. This also leads to the possibility that different students can take different learning paths through the content based on navigation requests and guided by their learning goals and current capabilities. Often various limitations are set, such as being given a fixed amount of time or being able to see the material only once e.g. for the answers to quizzes, or expensive commercial material. Therefore, in this area it has become an important technological problem to specify how individual learning units should be found and sequenced based on different conditions. Conditions can come from interaction of students such as queries, navigation requests, test results, or predefined conditions such as learning goals, previous experiences of students, and externally imposed limits. Such (semi-) automatic choices of learning material are at heart didactic choices, and a lot of effort has been put into finding didactic templates that formalise and encapsulate the underlying didactic choices in a simple model [IMS LD]. However, here, we will only consider effective specification of sequencing and annotation of material on a semantic level.

In this paper, we will discuss how the sequencing of the current SCORM standards can be mapped onto OWL [OWL] and DAML-S [DAM02]. Such a DAML-S translation can then be used to integrate SCORM based learning environments with other business processes or webservices that have a DAML-S description. We also refer to existing work on integrating the annotation part of SCORM in the larger Semantic Web framework. In order to exemplify some of the issues related to the use and the authoring of intelligent web-based courseware we have developed the system OntoAIMS [Aro01], which provides intelligent (adaptive) information support to both students and authors. Its instructional goal is to act as an adaptive educational portal for instructional material, services, learning activities and teaching content. We will illustrate the sequencing model of AIMS and it options for reuse and interoperability of content.

2   State-of-the-Art and Related Work

In this section we present a brief description of the current state-of-the-art within educational and relevant semantic web standards and technologies. We will point out the role of ontologies for the improvement of educational content management. We will base our discussion on the ADL SCORM, which incorporates many specifications of the IMS and the IEEE LOM [Nil02] educational metadata scheme. We also describe the DAML-S process specification language, which we propose to use for sequencing to improve interoperability and interchangeability of the educational services with other services.

2.1   Ontology Research, DAML, and DAML-S

Ontologies will play a crucial part in facilitating the sharing of information between communities, both of people and software agents. A number of representational formats have been proposed, e.g. RDF Schema [RDF], the Ontology Interchange Language [OIL], the DARPA Agent Markup Language [DAML], later in the form of DAML+OIL [DAM01]. The latter provides the basis for the ontology web language [OWL], currently proposed as a W3C standard for ontology and metadata representation. DAML+OIL exploits existing web standards such as XML, RDF and RDFS and adds the primitives of the object-oriented and frame-based systems, as well as the formal thoroughness of description logic. Its formal and rational basis provides powerful means for reasoning services.

The DAML-S coalition [DAM02] has developed the DAML+OIL ontology for Web Services, DAML-S, aiming at making web services computer-interpretable, to enable discovery of services, invocation of an identified service by an agent or other service and interoperation, i.e. breaking down interoperability barriers through semantics, composition of new services through automatic selection, composition and interoperation of existing services, verification of service properties and execution monitoring. In DAML+OIL, abstract categories of entities, events, etc. are defined in terms of classes and properties. DAML-S defines a set of classes and properties, specific to the description of services, within DAML+OIL.

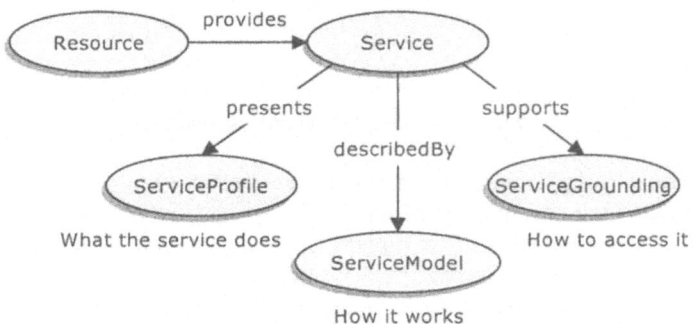

Fig. 1. Top level of the service ontology

Figure 1 resents the top-level service ontology of DAML-S. At the top level is the class *Service*, where all defined properties are very general. The idea is to provide a conceptual basis for structuring the services taxonomy, but it is expected that the taxonomy itself will be created according to functional and domain-specific needs. A service *presents* a *ServiceProfile*. This is a high level description of the service and its provider. A *ServiceProfile* describes the service in a human readable way, specifies the functionalities provided by the service and its functional attributes (e.g. requirements and capabilities). A *Service* is formally described by a *ServiceModel*. It facilitates automated services invocation, composition, interoperation and execution monitoring. The *ServiceModel* provides means for describing the data flow and the control flow in case of a composite service. Finally, a Service supports a *ServiceGrounding*, which is a specification of service access information. The

ServiceGrounding specifies the communication protocols, transport mechanisms, etc. Web services are web-accessible programs or devices. Their operation is described in terms of a process model, e.g. by means of control and data flows. The service model shows the possible steps (typically initiated by messages sent by the client) required to execute a service.

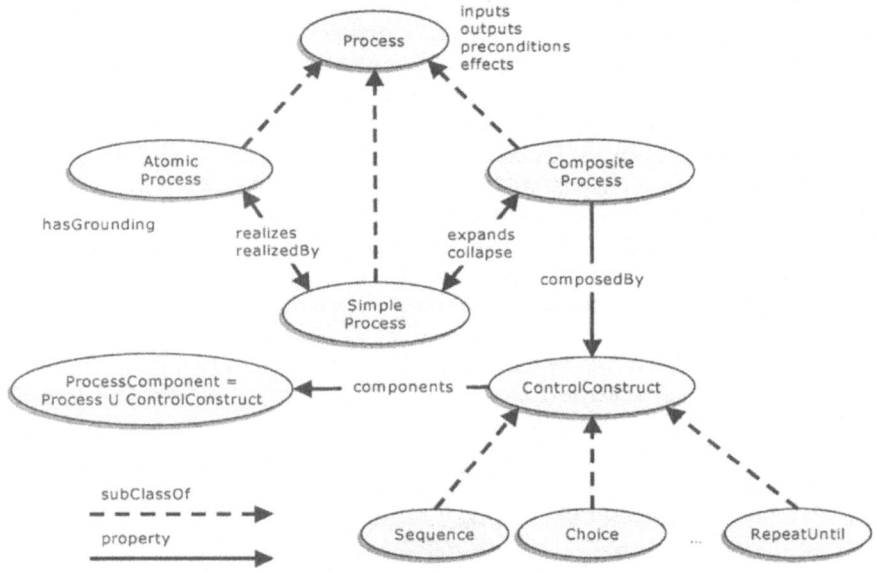

Fig. 2. Top level of the process ontology

The process model comprises of subclasses and properties of the *ProcessModel* class. The two chief components of the process model are the *Process Ontology* that describes a service in terms of its *inputs, outputs, preconditions, effects*, and, where appropriate, its *component subprocesses*; and the *Process Control Ontology* which describes each process in terms of its state, including initial activation, execution, and completion. The DAML-S process model is presented in Fig. 2.

2.2   Sharable Content Object Reference Model (SCORM)

The SCORM or Sharable Content Object Reference model is a collection of existing or further and newly developed specifications driven by the Advanced Distributed Learning (ADL) Initiative [ADL]. The ADL initiative is sponsored by the department of defence (DoD) and works in close cooperation with the industry forum IMS [IMS] and academia. The goal is to establish a new distributed learning environment that permits the interoperability of learning tools and course content on a global scale. Its roots in the DoD have produced specifications that work [SCO1.2] but which have been criticised for the rigid model they enforce on the creators and users of educational content. The main parts of the SCORM specification are the metadata model borrowed from the IEEE-LOM [LOM] the IMS content packaging model developed further together with the IMS [IMS CP], the IMS simple sequencing model co-developed with the IMS for SCORM 1.3 [SCO1.3] and a SCORM specific runtime and data model. The SCORM model assumes that content is build up out of small learning units, the SCO's (Sharable Content Objects)[1]. A SCO is intended to be a self-contained unit of learning. Courses are designed by creating a IMS packaging manifest document describing *organisations*. An organisation is comparable to a document tree structure, whose leaves consist of SCO's and whose nodes (items) represent the course internal structure. Each structuring level (manifest, organisation, item and SCO) can be annotated with metadata. The separation of content and organisation means that the same SCO can be reused in different organisation documents.

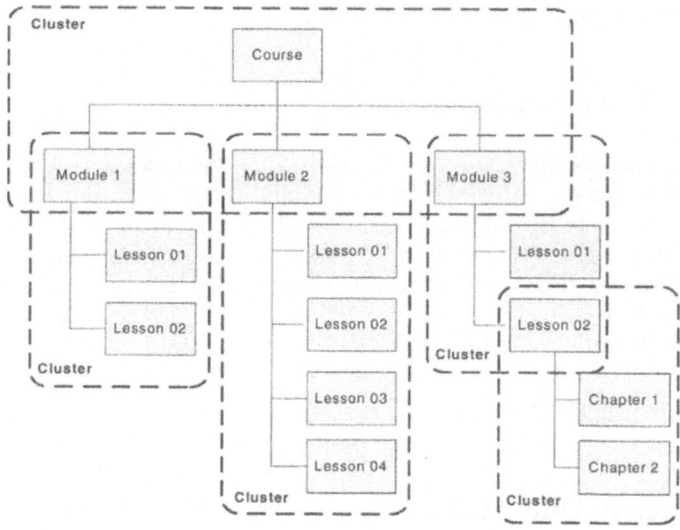

Fig. 3. An organisation document with clusters of activities © ADL

The other assumption of the SCORM model is that the only communication to the outside world is with a so-called earning management system (LMS) through a well-defined interface. In particular, it is the sole responsibility of the LMS to launch SCO's for presentation to the user, which means that the LMS is aware of the material the user has seen and of his or her responses. It also means that SCO's cannot by them selves launch other "related" SCO's which make then independent and therefore more reusable.

The IMS simple sequencing specification provides the model of learning activities organised as tree of clusters of more primitive activities. This tree of activities is mapped directly onto the items in the "document tree" of the organisation document (Fig. 3) but with a separate specification what the learning path through the tree is. By default, the learning path is a depth first walk through the tree, but one can specify an

---

[1] There also exist SCA's (Sharable Content Assets) as learning unit. The difference between SCO's and SCA's is that SCO's register themselves as being launched, but this will not be relevant on this level of detail.

action for each item depending on conditions. The actions allowed are either a move to a different leaning activity or a change of state of the learning management system. Conditions can either refer to the state of the learning management system or to a navigation request of the user. Only the simplest of sequencing controls are available: "choice" (with a variant called "choice exit") and "if condition then action" with various conditions and actions being hardwired in the specification.

The possible action of changing the state of the learning management system is used for the specification of the progress of *objectives*. Conditioning on objectives is the primary mechanism to define more subtle behavior linking activities in different clusters. Objectives can be specified separately from the learning activity and can be either local to specific activities or global and involving several activities. The specification does not specify which objectives exist, but only standardizes on a scoring scheme, a syntax and a run time model.

2.3   Learning Objects Metadata (LOM)

The Learning Objects Metadata [LOM] standard has been developed specifically for the educational domain. It focuses on the minimal set of properties needed to allow learning objects to be found, evaluated, acquired, and used. LOM only provides metadata fields for specifying descriptive tokens related to areas such as security and commerce. The standard supports security, privacy, commerce, and evaluation, but does not concern itself with the implementation of these features. The LOM has been given an RDFS binding [Nil02] which makes the (IEEE specified) interoperability with the Dublin Core more apparent by simply using the Dublin Core RDFS vocabulary where appropriate.

3   Authoring in OntoAIMS

OntoAIMS (its processor AIMS [Aro01]) is designed on the one hand to support students in such as discovery-based learning and task-based search, browsing and retrieving of educational information. On the other hand OntoAIMS is also designed to support authors (instructors, experts, courseware designers) in the construction, description and conceptualisation of content items and in the generation and composition of the course sequence (structure) [Aro03]. In the context of the latter, the main goal of OntoAIMS is to facilitate the creation, editing, maintenance and reusability of teaching material and its efficient application within various courseware. This is achieved by applying ontology-driven course decomposition process within a web-based learning architecture building upon existing instructional models. OntoAIMS is based on the AIMS reference model specifying the strict separation between content, data and their application and defines three main application modules (e.g. domain, course and resources) and in this way allows authoring within three main system modules – *Domain Editor*, *Course Composition* and *Resources Management*, where the main goal is to construct a course sequence structure on the basis of already defined conceptual model of the subject domain and semantically annotated resources. The course composition offers a. wizard-like tool to support the author through the entire process of defining course sequence structure and to associate the related teaching material. OntoAIMS sequence model (based on SCORM) allows the author define the learning process and to organise all the course relevant metadata. In order to create the course structure the author should (1) select concepts from the domain model and assign them to course topics (components); (2) select a specific sequence of course topics realising the specified learning goals; (3) assign course activities for each topic; and (4) link educational resources to each course topic. Some concepts can already be linked to resources in the domain. The author is therefore guided by OntoAIMS to organise and annotate his educational materials and his intentions to create a specific course.

We will illustrate how these three modules are implemented within OntoAIMS architecture and how they are mapped to semantic web technologies. We will also illustrate how to use SCORM and DAML-S in order to facilitate the course sequencing process.

3.1   OntoAIMS Architectural Description

To describe the OntoAIMS architecture (Fig. 4) we introduce five roles to interact with the system: the authoring roles of the domain, resource and course authors, and the user roles of instructor and learner. Every user (designer, content expert, author, instructor or student) can play each of the roles in different stages in the process. One and the same user can also perform in all of the roles alone. Each role is defined with a set of authoring or learning activities.

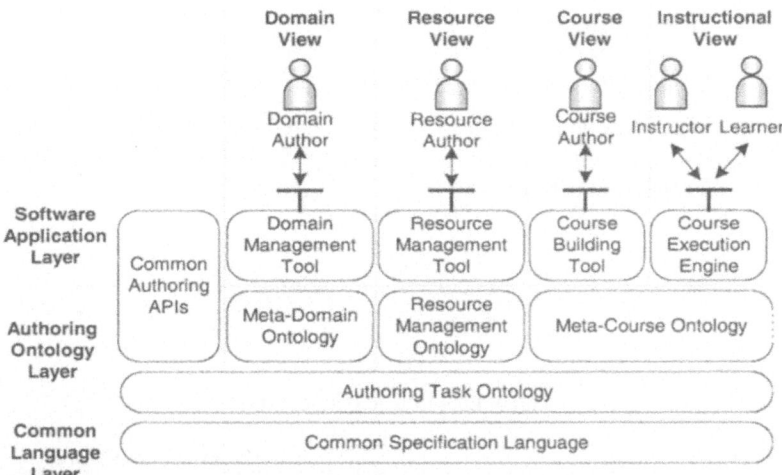

Fig. 4. Enterprise view on OntoAIMS

For the realisation of the *Common Specification Language* we choose OWL because of its openness and because it provides a large amount of flexibility for reasoning. This allows us to use semantic web tools and methodologies within the context of OntoAIMS. It also allows for the modularisation and semantic organisation of courseware authoring process and offers openness and interoperability of the authoring tools. Based on the results of organising functional knowledge in a task ontology [Fuk95, Miz96], we define the concepts and the semantics of the authoring process within the upper *Authoring Task Ontology* (*ATO*), where each of the phases (domain, course and resource views) define sub-sets of specific authoring concepts (e.g. meta-domain ontology, meta-course ontology and resource management ontology).

3.2   OntoAIMS Course Composition

A course in OntoAIMS is defined as a set of course components (*activities*) interconnected by composition (instructional) operators in order to achieve a coherent didactic sequence of learning activities and educational resources. In the following sections we will present the definitions of the composite operators, the learning activities and their mapping to DAML-S concepts.

3.3   Learning Activities

The learning activities (Fig. 5) capture learning-specific tasks within the context of a selected course and the formal definitions of these activities are presumed to support their interpretation. In analogy with the DAML-S process ontology (Fig. 2), we view the learning activity as an *atomic* or *composite* process, where the composite process is constructed from atomic or other composite processes by applying the composition operators, based on the DAML-S control constructs (Table 1). Each primitive learning activity $\mathcal{LA}$ is determined by a tuple

<Activity_ID, Input, Output, PreCond, Effect, Composite_Components>.

Thus it specifies some prerequisites (pre-conditions) and some input and produces some effect (post-conditions) and some output (Fig. 5), which are further used for the selection of the following activity, and it may have an internal structure.

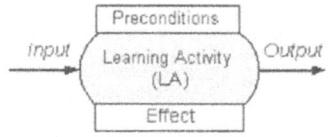

Fig. 5. Learning activity definition

Chains of atomic and composite learning activities (Fig. 6) are realised by applying the same composition operators. Figure 6 describes the sequencing process corresponding to the course clustering shown in Fig. 3.

The *primitive* (atomic activities) functional concepts are basic for the learning sequence process, and build OntoAIMS instructional vocabulary. They are generic for every educational process and are used to form *composite* semantic rich learning activities. This way we modularise all the learning activities within their specific context of use. They are also independent of the system's domain, the educational strategy and the educational goal. Examples of learning activities include: 'read', 'write', 'compute', 'exercise', 'proceed', etc.

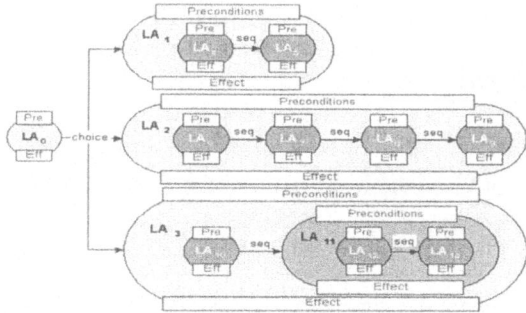

Fig. 6. Sequencing process of atomic and composite learning activities

3.4   Composition Operators

We define composition operators based on the DAML-S process ontology definition of control constructs. This will allow us to build composite activities and course components as sequences of both primitive and composite activities.

In Figure 6 we illustrate the composition process of learning activities by applying the composition operators. For example the learning activity $\mathcal{L}\mathcal{A}_3$ is expressed as a sequence of two learning activities $\mathcal{L}\mathcal{A}_{10}$ seq $\mathcal{L}\mathcal{A}_{11}$, where $\mathcal{L}\mathcal{A}_{11}$ is also a composite activity of two other learning activities also organized in a sequence $\mathcal{L}\mathcal{A}_{12}$ seq $\mathcal{L}\mathcal{A}_{13}$ On the other hand the main course activity in this example $\mathcal{L}\mathcal{A}_0$ allows for applying the *choice* operator by offering a choice of three other activities $\mathcal{L}\mathcal{A}_1$ or $\mathcal{L}\mathcal{A}_2$ or $\mathcal{L}\mathcal{A}_3$.

Table 1. Composition operators

DAML-S Control Constructs	Description
Sequence	Sequence defines a set of learning activities (processes) to be executed in order one after each other. The learning activities in this sequence can be either *atomic* (primitive), *simple* (clustered) or *composite* with the same or other *composition operators*
Choice	Choice is a composition operator defining a set of activities with two property states: (1) *chosen* and (2) *chooseFrom*. It allows a choice between alternative activities and afterwards executes the 'chosen' one(s). By this operator the following constructs are also allowed 'choose at least n activities from total m', 'choose exactly n activities from total m', 'choose at most n activities from total m'.
Conditional (*If Then Else*)	The conditional construct is an operator with *if Condition*, *then* and *else* properties. Its semantics is intended as 'Test If-condition; if True do Then, if False do Else' (class CONDITION is defined as a class of logical expressions.)

In the following section we illustrate the application of DAML-S for learning activities sequencing, based on the same sequencing example of Figure 6 and the course clustering of Figure 3.

4 Mapping SCORM Simple Sequencing onto DAML-S

Mapping the simple sequencing specification onto DAML-S is based on a separation between the processes corresponding to learning activities and the processes corresponding to actions performed by the learning management system to support the sequencing model. This separation is inherent to the SCORM model in that the flow of learning activities can only be changed by the state of the LMS and navigation requests of the user. Written in N3 notation [BL03] we have

```
scorm:LearningActivity rdfs:subClassOf daml-s:Process
scorm:LMSActivity      rdfs:subClassOf daml-s:Process
```

Learning activities can be either `daml-s:AtomicProcess` es or `daml-s:CompositeProcess` es. The DAML-S specification requires that an atomic process has a grounding in a web service specified in a WSDL document. However in this context, a grounding would be a specific learning object (SCO or SCA). Although a SCO is not (currently) a web service it has a well-defined interface, and is conceptually close to a realisation of a service. Note that it is easy to imagine "atomic" learning activities that are not grounded in this sense but that may still rightfully be called leaning activities e.g. discussions or traditional courses, and may result in some grading and a corresponding change of state of the LMS.

The internal structure of learning activities as clusters can be modelled by the DAML-S vocabularies. In addition, the simple sequencing specification implicitly contains standard conditions and state changes of the LMS like timeouts that can be given an owl/DAML-S binding. These can then be used in the specification of the learning process flow. The cluster structure of Fig.3 together with some imaginary expression of the way the different modules are sequenced is illustrated in Sec. 4.1

Given the distinction between learning and LMS activities, a mapping of the sequencing model to DAML-S is further a matter of identifying the relevant pre- and post conditions, input output and effect. For the purpose of the sequencing model a `scorm:LearningActivity` can have three sorts of input: a user navigation request, state from the learning management system, and parameters specified in the organisations document. Pre and post conditions are determined by the state of the LMS and by input parameters in the organisation document. The sequencing specification defines several such pre and post conditions. Of all the inputs, the navigation requests are the most problematic because they arrive asynchronously and the sequencing model takes timeouts into account. It is probably desirable to not consider the learner part of this process, because due to its inherent human complexity, and only consider input to the learning activity object. However it seems to be worthwhile to have the notion of a `scorm:theLearner` so that statements about the behaviour of "the learner" like passing or failing course modules can be made. Due to its special role in the SCORM specification we also propose to define an instance scorm:LMS of a daml-s:process. This process can then be used for low level specification of the SCORM run time model and in higher level constructs that can be used in course specifications For example in this way the navigation requests can be considered as a time stamped message that a learning activity can direct to the LMS process. Likewise the precise effect of a higher level scorm:LMSActivity can be specified in terms of this process.

4.1   Example of DAML-S Specification of a Complex Learning Path

Here we give an example of how the SCORM-based course clustering presented in Fig. 3 and the corresponding course sequencing in Fig. 6 can be translated into DAML-S specification of a complex learning path (we view clustering as DAML-S simple process, modules as composite and chapters as atomic). We use the N3 notation for the specification with daml-s denoting the DAML-S, and scorm denoting the SCORM namespace. A partial binding of SCORM concepts expressed in an OWL ontology used in the example is also included.

```
:Course a scorm:LearningActivity;
       daml-s:consistsOf      [a daml-s:Sequence;
                              daml-s: components
                                     (:Module1 :Module2 :Module3)
                              ].
:Module1 a scorm:LearningActivity;
       daml-s:consistsOf      [a daml-s:Choice;
                              daml-s:components
                                     (:Lesson01 :Lesson02)
                              ] .
:Module2 a scorm:LearningActivity;
       daml-s:consistsOf      [a daml-s:Unordered;
                              daml-s:components
                              (:Lesson01 :Lesson02 :Lesson03: Lesson04)
                              ].
:Module3 a scorm:LearningActivity
       daml-s:consistsOf   [a daml-s: If-Then-Else;
                           daml-s:ifCondition
                     {:Lesson02 scorm:objectiveMeasureGreater "0.75"};
                           daml-s:then
                                :Lesson01;
                           daml-s:else
                                :Lesson02
                           ].
:Lesson02 a scorm:LearningActivity
       daml-s:consistsOf [a daml:Sequence;
                         daml-s:components
                         ([a scorm:BeginTimelimit scorm:timeLimit "10M"]
                   :Chapter1
                   :Chapter2
                   [a scorm:EndTimeLimit]
                   [a scorm:RollUp;
                    daml-s:ifCondition
                           {scorm:theLearner scorm:satisfied
                   [scorm:activityObjective :Chapter1]};
                       daml-s:then {
                               scorm:theLearner scorm:satisfied
                                   [scorm:activityObjective :Lesson02;
```

```
                              scorm:objectiveMeasure "0.5"]
                     }
                  ]
              [a scorm:RollUp;
               daml-s:ifCondition
                  {scorm:theLearner scorm:satisfied :Chapter2}
               daml-s:then {
                      scorm:theLearner scorm:satisfied
                      [scorm:activityObjective :Lesson02;
                       scorm:objectiveMeasure "1.0"]
              }
              )
              ].
    :Chapter1 a scorm:LearningActivity.
    :Chapter2 a scorm:LearningActivity.
```

The following would be the start of a SCORM ontology that formalises and binds
the SCORM spec. Namespaces left out for conciseness

In this ontology Learners are not processes.

```
    scorm:Learner a owl:Class.
    scorm:theLearner a scorm:Learner.
```

Normalised scorings cf. SCORM v1.3, 7.1.1.3, maybe this is better done with a new
XML schema datatype.

```
    scorm:ObjectiveNormalisedMeasure rdfs:subClassOf xsd:double,
                 [a owl:Restriction;
                  owl:onProperty xsd:maxInclusive;
                     owl:toValue "1.0"],
                 [a owl:Restriction;
                  owl:onProperty xsd:minInclusive;
                  owl:toValue "-1.0"].

    scorm:objectiveMeasure a owl:DataTypeProperty;
         rdfs:range scorm:ObjectiveNormalisedMeasure.
    scorm:objectiveMeasureGreater a owl:DataTypeProperty;
         rdfs:range scorm:ObjectiveNormalisedMeasure.
```

Many things can be objectives so objectives are orthogonal to learning activities

```
    scorm:Objective a owl:Class.
    scorm:activityObjective a rdf:Property;
         rdfs:domain scorm:Objective.
    scorm:satisfied a rdf:Property;
         rdf:domain scorm:Learner;
         rdf:range scorm:Objective.

    scorm:timeLimit a owl:DataTypeProperty;
         rdfs:range xsd:duration.
```

Learning activities are considered processes and can be handled as such

```
    scorm:LearningActivity rdfs:subClassOf daml-s:Process.
    scorm:LMSActivity rdfs:subClassOf daml-s:Process.

    scorm:theLMS a daml-s:Process.
```

Starting and stopping "the stopwatch" is a very explicit LMSactivity
a process ontology could specify the precise description of

scorm:BeginTimeLimit in terms of interaction with the scorm:theLMS
process

```
scorm:BeginTimeLimit a scorm:LMSActivty, daml-s:AtomicProperty.
scorm:EndTimeLimit a scorm:LMSActivity, daml-s:AtomicProperty
```

The RollUp process gathers the "conclusion" of the learning activity, cf. SCORM v.
1.3 7.1.2. Many other rollup actions can be defined besides the ones used in the
example

```
scorm:RollUp a scorm:LMSActivity, daml-s:If-Then-Else.
```

5 Conclusions

We argued that the adoption of semantic web technologies is useful for learning technologies due to the expected broader adoption and easier interoperability with infrastructure, tools and business processes outside the educational area. We focussed on the specification of the sequencing of learning activities, and attempted to map these on the general purpose process and service specification language DAML-S. We found that that the concepts used in the IMS simple sequencing specification and the SCORM run time model, leading specifications in the educational area, as well as the model used in the experimental OntoAIMS platform seem to map readily onto the concepts and vocabulary in the DAML-S specification. The added value of using the DAML-S based specification is that it will allow for integration of e-learning in larger business processes (e.g. to facilitate the interoperability and information exchange information with a human resource management system).

Acknowledgements. The research work for this paper is realized within the scope of Topia project funded by the Telematica Instituut, the Netherlands. We want to tank Christian Tzolov for his valuable comments on the AIMS architecture.

References

[ADL]   Advanced Distributed Learning Network. http://www.adlnet.org/ (visited 19-6-2003)
[Aro01]   Aroyo, L. and Dicheva, D. (2001). AIMS: Learning and Teaching Support for WWW-based Education. IJCEELL, 11(1/2), 152–164.
[Aro03]   Aroyo, L, and Mizoguchi, R. (2003). Authoring Support Framework for Intelligent Educational Systems. In Proc. AIED'03 Conference (in print).
[BL03]   Berners Lee, T. Semantic Web Tutorial using N3 , tutorial at WWW 2003 Budapest April 2003 available at http://www.w3.org/2000/10/swap/doc/ (Visited 29-8-2003)
[Che98]   Chen, W. Hayashi, Y., Kin, L. Ikeda, M. and Mizoguchi, R. (1998) Ontological Issues in an Intelligent Authoring Tool, in Chan T-W., Collins A. & Lin J. (Eds.), In Proc. of ICCE'98, 1, 41–50.
[DAM01] DAML+OIL Reference Description, http://www.w3.org/TR/daml+oil-reference
[DAM02] DAML-S: Web Service Description for the Semantic Web, DAML-S coalition, ICSW 2002, Sardinia, Italy, http://www.daml.org/services/ISWC2002-DAMLS.pdf
[DAML]   DARPA Agent Markup Language (DAML), http://www.daml.org/

[Dev01]   Devedzic, V. (2001). The Semantic Web – Implications for Teaching and Learning, In Proc. of ICCE 2001Conference, Seoul, Korea. [OIL] Ontology Inference Layer (OIL), http://www.ontoknowledge.org/oil/

[Dod02]   Dodds, P., Hoberny, A., Blackmon, B. SCORM Next Generation, available at http://www.lsal.cmu.edu/lsal/expertise/papers/presentations/plugfest703122002joint/ plugfest703122002joint.pdf (visited 19-6-2003)

[Fuk95]   Fukuhara, Y., Kimura, F., Kohama, C., and Nakamura, Y. (1995). A Knowledge-based Educational Environment Integrating Conceptual Knowledge and Procedural Knowledge in Telecommunication Service Field. In Proc.ED-MEDIA'95, 229-234.

[IMS]   IMS Global Leaning Consortium Inc. http://www.imsproject.org/ (visited 19-6-2003)

[IMS LD]   IMS Learning design. http://www.imsproject.org/learningdesign/index.cfm (visited 19-6-2003)

[LOM]   IEEE P1484.12 Learning Object Metadata Working Group, http://ltsc.ieee.org/wg12/

[Miz96]   Mizoguchi, R., Sinitsa, K., and Ikeda, M. (1996). Task ontology design for intelligent educational/training systems. In Proc. of Architectures and Methods for designing Cost-Effective and Reusable ITSs Workshop, at ITS'96 Conference.

[Mur99]   Murray, T. (1999). Authoring Intelligent Tutoring Systems: An analysis of the state of the art. International Journal of Artificial Intelligence in Education, 10, 98–129.

[Nil02]   Mikael Nilsson (ed.). IEEE LOM RDF binding, http://kmr.nada.kth.se/el/ims/md-lomrdf.html

[OWL]   Web Ontology Language (OWL), http://www.w3.org/TR/owl-ref/

[RDF]   RDF Vocabulary Description Language: RDF Schema, http://www.w3.org/TR/rdf-schema/

[SCO1.2]   ADL Initiative, SCORM 1.2 specification, (visited 19-6-2003) http://www.adlnet.org/screens/shares/dsp_displayfile.cfm?fileid=840

[SCO1.3]   ADL Initiative SCORM 1.3 specification, (visited 19-6-2003) http://www.adlnet.org/screens/shares/dsp_displayfile.cfm?fileid=836

Ontology-Driven Knowledge Logistics Approach as Constraint Satisfaction Problem

Alexander Smirnov, Mikhail Pashkin, Nikolai Chilov, Tatiana Levashova,
and Andrew Krizhanovsky

St.Petersburg Institute for Informatics and Automation of the Russian Academy of Sciences
39, 14th Line, St Petersburg, 199178, Russia
{smir,michael,nick,oleg,aka}@mail.iias.spb.su

Abstract. The paper is devoted to knowledge logistics problems. Knowledge logistics with regard to individual user requirements, available knowledge sources, and current situation analysis in an open information environment addresses problems of intelligent support of user activities. Knowledge logistics is guided by the principles underlying both Web services and Semantic Web as understandability of knowledge representation both to humans and machines, enabling knowledge sharing and reuse, ensuring intellectual support, etc. The paper describes an approach to knowledge logistics problem based on ontology-driven methodology and constraint satisfaction / propagation technology. Compatibility of object-oriented constraint network notation with DAML+OIL formalism is considered. Applicability of the approach to actual content is illustrated through a case study based on Binni scenario of humanitarian coalition-based operation.

1 Introduction

The World Wide Web (WWW) has dramatically changed the accessibility of electronically available information. Regardless of the fact that WWW is a valuable repository of knowledge as volumes of information continue to increase rapidly, the task of turning them into useful knowledge has become a major problem [Fensel *et. al.*, 2003]. Web services providing standardized interfaces coupled with the Semantic Web activity trying to represent information in the WWW such that it can be used by machines not just for display purposes, but also for automation, integration, and reuse across applications are the key technologies promising a new era of the Internet.

Knowledge logistics (KL) is a new direction in the knowledge management dealing with activities on acquisition, integration, and transfer of the right knowledge from distributed sources in the right context to the right person in the right time for the right purpose [Smirnov *et al.*, 2003a]. KL with regard to individual user requirements, available knowledge sources, and current situation analysis in an open information environment addresses problems of intelligent support of user activities. KL is guided by the principles underlying both Web services and Semantic Web as understandability of knowledge representation both to humans and machines, enabling knowledge sharing and reuse, ensuring intellectual support, etc. It focuses on

R. Meersman et al. (Eds.): CoopIS/DOA/ODBASE 2003, LNCS 2888, pp. 635–652, 2003.
© Springer-Verlag Berlin Heidelberg 2003

development of methods and tools allowing to turn distributed information into useful knowledge.

The paper describes an approach to KL problem based on ontology-driven methodology and constraint satisfaction / propagation technology. The proposed approach considers the knowledge logistics problem as a problem of a Knowledge Source Network (KSNet) configuration. Knowledge sources are to be configured include end-users / customers, loosely coupled knowledge sources / resources, and a set of tools and methods for information / knowledge processing. The approach is referred to as KSNet-approach and a system implementing the approach is referred to as the system "KSNet".

The paper is organized as follows. Section 2 describes a framework of the KSNet-approach. Section 3 depicts a knowledge representation formalism of object-oriented constraint networks and shows its compatibility with DAML+OIL representation language. Applicability of the approach to actual content is illustrated by an example of a user request processing through a case study (section 4) based on Binni scenario of humanitarian coalition-based operation.

2 KSNet-Approach

Since KL deals with distributed and heterogeneous knowledge sources the approach is oriented to ontological model providing a common way of knowledge representation. KSNet-approach proposes ontology-driven methodology to knowledge source network configuration (Fig. 1). The methodology addresses user needs (problems) identification and solving these problems. As it is mentioned above main components of knowledge source network are user and knowledge sources (KSs) representing various kind of knowledge. User needs are introduced by a user request. The aim of user request processing consists in the configuration of a network of KSs containing information relevant to the user request, generation of an appropriate solution relying on this information, and presenting the solution to the user.

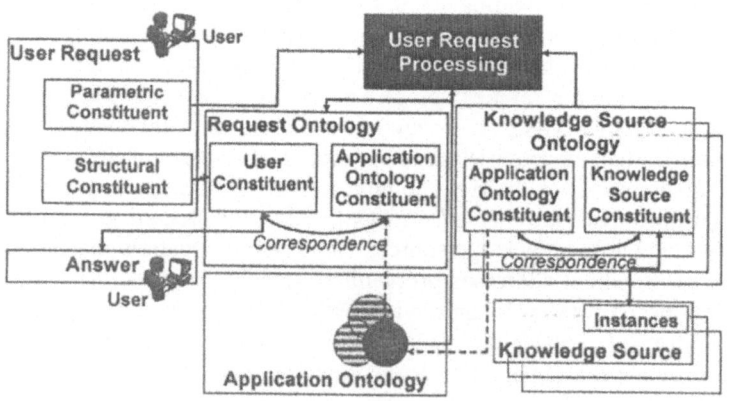

Fig. 1. Framework of ontology-driven methodology

At the heart of the framework a fundamental ontology providing a common notation lies. This is implemented through an ontology library. It is a central knowledge storage assigning a common notation and providing a common vocabulary to ontologies that it stores. These common representative aids enable the performance of operations on ontology integrations as alignment and merging.

Main components of the ontology library are domain, tasks & methods, and application ontologies. All these ontologies are interrelated according to N. Guarino proposal [Guarino, 1998] in such a way that an application ontology (AO) is a specialization of both domain and tasks & methods ontologies. Since ontologies of different domains are stored in the ontology library (every domain is represented by its domain ontology) AO can specialize knowledge of several domains. Therefore it serves as a cross-domain ontology.

AO plays a central role in the user request processing. It describes both knowledge related to the user request (user constituent in Fig. 1) and knowledge representing requested information containing in KSs (knowledge source constituent in Fig. 1). AO is formed through merging parts of domain and tasks & methods ontologies relevant to the user request into a single ontology. If AO describing user needs exists in the ontology library then this AO is reused. Requested information from KSs is associated with the same AO that is formed for the user request processing [Smirnov *et al.*, 2003b]. Thereby AO represents a shared knowledge of a user and knowledge sources. The KSNet-approach is based on the idea that knowledge corresponding to individual user requirements and knowledge peculiar to knowledge sources are represented by restrictions on the shared knowledge described by AO. That was the main reason to use a constraint-based approach to the problem description.

3 Knowledge Representation Formalism

Object-oriented constraint networks technique has been chosen as a way of user request processing [Smirnov *et al.*, 2003a]. Object-oriented constraint networks (OOCN) is described by sets of objects, variables, variable domains, and constraints $OOCN = (\{\text{Object}\}\{\text{Variable}\}\{\text{Domain}\}\{\text{Constraints}\})$. As a constraint-based tool ILOG tool has been chosen [ILOG, 2003]. A constraint satisfaction model supported by ILOG is presented in Fig. 2.

The approach is oriented on the use of a common notation for knowledge description (ontology) and for representation of the knowledge in ILOG. This is achieved by union of the notations of object-oriented constraint networks and ILOG's constraint satisfaction model. In the accepted notation an ontology (A) is defined as: $A = (O, Q, D, C)$ where: O – a set of *object classes* ("*classes*"); each of the entities in a class is considered as an *instance* of the class; Q – a set of class attributes ("*attributes*"); D – a set of attribute domains ("*domains*"); and C – a set of *constraints*.

For the chosen notation the following six types of constraints have been defined $C = C^I \cup C^{II} \cup C^{III} \cup C^{IV} \cup C^V \cup C^{VI}$: $C^I = \{c^I\}$, $c^I = (o, q)$, $o \in O$, $q \in Q$ – accessory of attributes to classes; $C^{II} = \{c^{II}\}$, $c^{II} = (o, q, d)$, $o \in O$, $q \in Q$, $d \in D$ – accessory of domains to attributes; $C^{III} = \{c^{III}\}$, $c^{III} = (\{o\}, True \vee False)$, $|\{o\}| \geq 2$, $o \in O$ – classes

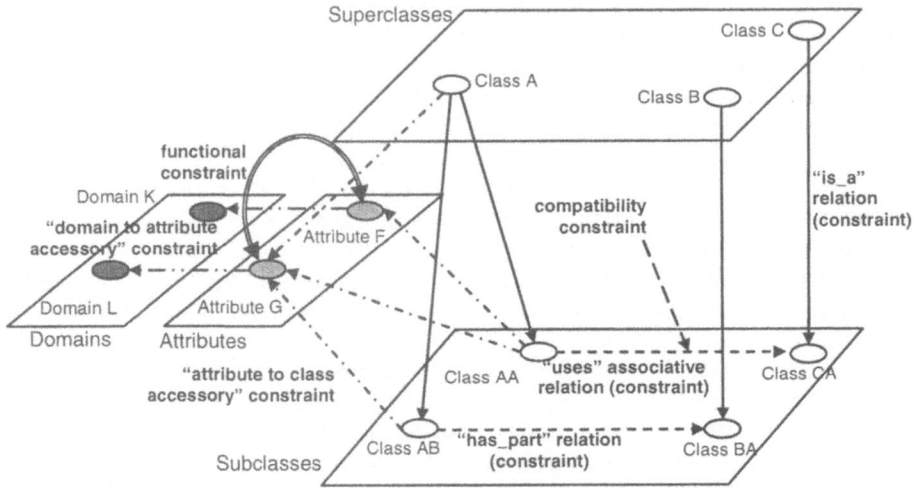

Fig. 2. ILOG Constraint Satisfaction Model

compatibility (compatibility structural constraints); $C^{IV} = \{c^{IV}\}$, $c^{IV} = \langle o', o'', type \rangle$, $o' \in O$, $o'' \in O$, $o' \neq o''$ – hierarchical relationships (hierarchical structural constraints) "is a" defining class taxonomy (*type*=0), and "has part"/"part of" defining class hierarchy (*type*=1); $C^{V} = \{c^{V}\}$, $c^{V} = (\{o\})$, $|\{o\}| \geq 2$, $o \in O$ – associative relationships ("one-level" structural constraints); $C^{VI} = \{c^{VI}\}$, $c^{VI} = f(\{o\}, \{o, q\}) = True \lor False$, $|\{o\}| \geq 0$, $|\{q\}| \geq 0$, $o \in O$, $q \in Q$ – functional constraints referring to the names of classes and attributes.

Below, as an example some sample constraints used in the case study are given:

- the attribute *costs* (q_1) belongs to the class *hospital* (o_1): $c^{I}_1 = (o_1, q_1)$;
- the attribute *costs* (q_1) belonging to the class *hospital* (o_1) takes positive values: $c^{II}_1 = (o_1, q_1, R^+)$;
- *mobile hospital* (o_5) is a *hospital* (o_1): $c^{IV}_1 = \langle o_1, o_5, 0 \rangle$;
- the class *medical equipment* (o_4) is a part of the class *hospital* (o_1): $c^{IV}_1 = \langle o_1, o_4, 1 \rangle$;
- the class *furniture* (o_2) is compatible with the class *furniture supplier* (o_3): $c^{III}_1 = (\{o_2, o_3\}, True)$;
- the attribute *capacity* of the class *mobile hospital* (o_5) serves as an input parameter in the class *components definition* (o_6): $c^{V}_1 = (o_5, o_6)$;
- the value of the attribute *cost* (q_1) of an instance of the class *furniture* (o_2) depends on the values of the attribute *price* (q_2) of instances of the class *suppliers* (o_6) and on the number of such instances (the attribute *quantity* (q_3) of the class *furniture*): $c^{VI}_1 = f(\{o_2, q_1\}, \{(o_6, q_2), (o_2, q_3)\})$;

The quadruple $A = (O, Q, D, C)$ defines the common notation for internal knowledge representation supported by the ontology library. This notation has much in common with both frame-based (KIF) [KIF, 1992] and object oriented (DAML+OIL) [DAML+OIL, 2001] approaches to knowledge representations.

3.1 Internal Knowledge Representation

Internal knowledge representation of object-oriented constraint networks is governed by the ILOG constraint satisfaction model. Additionally to the compatibility of the common notations a compatibility with the model is needed at the level of *goal* identification and at the level of *functional constraints* description. The goal is responsible for optimal solutions generation by ILOG. The search of the optimal solutions is considered as constraint satisfaction problem. Referring to the framework (section 2) this means obtaining of a knowledge source network configuration the closest to the user needs defined by the user request. In this connection before processing the request by ILOG (i) a goal is to be identified in accordance with the user request and (ii) functional constraints describing functional relations between attributes are to be represented in a way supported by ILOG functions.

Features of KL concerned with its distributed and heterogeneous units demand appealing to such technologies as intelligent agents offering an efficient way to understand, manage, and use the distributed, large-scale, dynamic, open, and heterogeneous computing and information systems [Weiss, 2000]. As the technological kernel the system uses agents proposed by FIPA specification [FIPA, 2000 – 2001]: *wrapper* (interaction with knowledge sources), *facilitator* ("yellow pages" directory service for the agents), *mediator* (task execution control), and *user agent* (interaction with the users). Additionally a set of problem-oriented agents specific for KL tasks and scenarios for their collaboration were developed: *translation agent* (terms translation between different vocabularies), *knowledge fusion agent* (knowledge fusion operation performance), *configuration agent* (efficient use of the knowledge source network), *ontology management agent* (ontology operations performance), *expert assistant agent* (interactions with experts), and *monitoring agent* (knowledge sources verifications). The multi-agent architecture is given in Fig. 3 and mainly described in [Smirnov *et al.*, 2002]. Below, only services supporting compatibilities between the internal representation and the ILOG constraint satisfaction model are described.

Goal Identification
Services for goal identification are provided by *translation agent*. It parses the user request and decomposes it into the parametric and structural request constituents (Fig. 1). The user request parsing is performed by mapping the request terms into WordNet thesaurus [WordNet, 2003] terms. User terms found in the thesaurus are supposed to correspond to ontology elements (O, Q, D, C); these terms are referred to the structural constituent. User terms not included in the structural constituent are considered as the parametric request constituent. This constituent is equal to user constraints on the ontology elements. As a rule, the parametric constituent is made up of user constraints on attribute domains or on attribute values.

A goal describes traditional optimization problems concerning minimization and maximization tasks. In the user request these tasks usually are represented by terms having the same meaning as minimum and maximum. *Translation agent* recognizes such the terms and terms being objectives of the optimization and formulates a goal. If the user request does not concern any optimization problems ILOG generates a feasible solution.

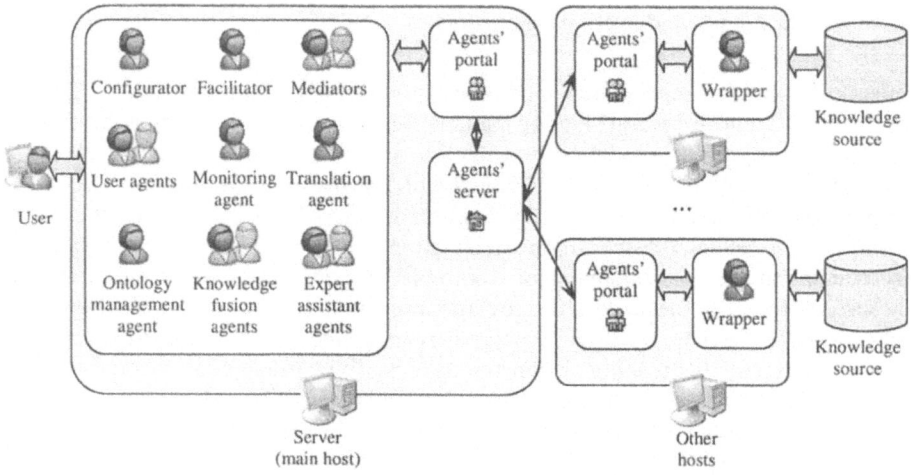

Fig. 3. Multi-agent community of the system "KSNet"

Functional Constraints and ILOG Functions Compatibility

Services providing compatibility of the functional constraints with ILOG notations are supported by *ontology management agent*. ILOG Configurator functions are used as a basis for functional constraints in the system "KSNet". Applied to an object the functions have the following meanings:

- *IloNumVar getCardOf(IloComponentType t)*: the number of components connected to the given object and specialized as the type *t*.
- *IloNumVar getMax(const char* name)*: maximum value of the numeric attribute *"name"* on the components connected to the given object.
- *IloNumVar getMaxCard(const char* name)*: maximum value of the cardinality of the constraint *"name"* on the components connected to the given object.
- *IloNumVar getMin(const char* name)*: minimum value of the numeric attribute *"name"* on the components connected to the given object.
- *IloNumVar getMinCard(const char* name)*: minimum value of the cardinality of the constraint *"name"* on the components connected to the given object.
- *IloNumVar getSum(const char* name)*: the sum of the values of the integer attribute *"name"* on the components connected to the given object.
- *IloNumVar getSumCard(const char* name)*: the total value of the cardinality of the constraint *"name"* on the components connected to the given object.

Due to the specific syntax two different representations for functional constraints are used: a human-readable view and the internal ILOG representation. The functional constraints are entered by an ontology engineer. For this purpose "Web-DESO" (Web-DEsign of Structured Objects) tool developed in the framework of the research is applied. The tool is intended for the ontology library management. It enables shared access to the ontologies stored there, their collaborative browsing and editing.

The constraints are entered as follows: the ontology engineer selects a function from the list of available functions and assigns values of which attributes serve as input or output parameters of the function. An *expert assistant agent* sends a message to the *ontology management agent* to validate the syntax and to prepare the internal representation. The *ontology management agent* parses the constraint, checks the function's name, attribute names and attribute domains. If the constraint is correct, it prepares the internal ILOG representation of the constraint. If the constraint is incorrect, it returns an error message to the *expert assistant agent*. The process of creating functional constraints in the system "KSNet" is illustrated by an UML sequence diagram (Fig. 4).

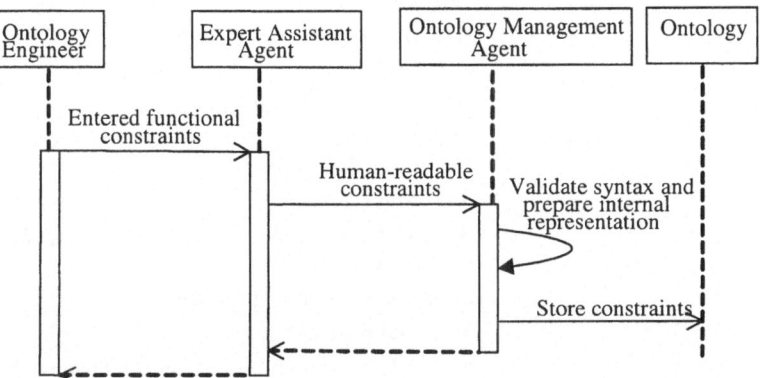

Fig. 4. Scenario of functional constraints creation, conversion and storage

As the approach assumes processing the information containing in distributed and heterogeneous KSs a compatibility of the internal knowledge representation with external knowledge representations is needed. The next section describes compatibility of the internal knowledge representation with knowledge representation capabilities of DAML+OIL representation format.

3.2   Compatibility with External Knowledge Representations

To the system can process information containing in heterogeneous KSs a mechanism supporting import of source knowledge representation is provided for. At present the import from DAML+OIL representation language into the internal representation is available.

The main constructions mapped from DAML+OIL ontologies to the system "KSNet" notation are:
1. DAML: Class
2. DAML: ObjectProperty
3. DAML: DatatypeProperty

A correspondence between DAML+OIL and the system "KSNet" notations is presented in Table 1. The table does not pretend to be complete but at present it is enough for processing most of accessible DAML+OIL ontologies.

Table 1. Import of DAML+OIL representation into the system "KSNet" representation

DAML+OIL elements	Mapping type*	Implementation
cardinality	+/-	If the value of cardinality is equal "1", no special actions are performed. If the value of cardinality is more than "1", the further actions depend on an ontology engineer's decision.
cardinalityQ	+/-	The same as *daml: cardinality*
Class	+	For class *O*: • Check number of parents. If the class does not have parents (does not contain *daml: subClassOf* tag): • Add class O; • Add a taxonomy constraint from class *Thing* to class *O*. If the class has only one parent: • Add class O; • Add a taxonomy constraint from parent class (denoted by *daml: subClassOf*) to class *O*. If the class has more than one parent the further scenario depends on an ontology engineer's opinion.
complementOf	+	For class *O*: Add new class *O1* with description *complement of class O*; Add a taxonomy constraint between new classes *O1* and parent of class of *O*; Add a compatibility constraint between classes *O* and *O1*.
DatatypeProperty	+/-	For DatatypeProperty *DP*: • Add an attribute name; • Add an attribute domain (if necessary); • Add one or more structural constraints: class + attribute (C'), and class + attribute + domain (C'')
DatatypeRestriction	+	The same as *daml: Restriction* element
differentIndividualFrom	TBI	At present, the system "KSNet" does not support ontologies with individuals

---

* "+" in the current version the ontology element can be mapped;

"+/-"in the current version the ontology element can be mapped, but only a restricted syntax is supported or a scenario of mapping process depends on an ontology engineer's opinion;

"TBD" (to be developed) - in the current version the ontology element can not be mapped, but in the future it will be possible;

"TBI" (to be investigated) – in the current version the ontology element can not be mapped and a necessity to use them in the future requires an additional research. At present, an ontology engineer may create additional constraints to map such elements.

DAML+OIL elements	Mapping type*	Implementation
Disjoint	+	For a set of classes – members of *daml: collection* tag: Add a set of compatibility constraint – for each pair of classes between *daml: Disjoint* and */daml: Disjoint* tags.
disjointUnionOf	TBI	Depends on ontology engineer's opinion
disjointWith	+	For class *O*: Add a compatibility constraint with class *O1* located inside *daml: Disjoint* tag.
domain	+/-	Inside *daml: ObjectProperty* tag: Build associative constraint (together with *daml: range* element) Inside *daml: DatatypeProperty* tag: Build structural constraint class + attribute (*C'*)
equivalentTo	TBI	Used inside *daml: Class, daml: ObjectProperty, daml: DatatypeProperty* tags, and tags of instances description. May be used for additional validation of the DAML+OIL ontology content.
hasClass	TBD	This tag locates inside *daml: Restriction* tag, relates to *daml: onProperty* tag element, and contains a name of *daml: ObjecttypeProperty* or *daml: DatatypeProperty* tags element. May be mapped as functional constraint for attribute value or class property.
hasClassQ	TBD	The same as *daml: hasClass* element
hasValue	TBD	Functional constraint for attribute value
imports	TBD	Reference to other ontology. Used to find external ontology elements.
intersectionOf	TBI	Depends on ontology engineer's opinion
inverseOf	TBD	For *daml: ObjectProperty*: • Find accusative constraint for object property • Add new inverse associative constraint
maxCardinality	+	The same as *daml: cardinality* element
maxCardinalityQ	+	The same as *daml: cardinalityQ* element
minCardinality	+	The same as *daml: cardinality* element
minCardinalityQ	+	The same as *daml: cardinalityQ* element
ObjectProperty	TBD	Adds associative relation from class located in the daml: domain tag to class located in the daml: range
ObjectRestriction	+	The same as *daml: Restriction* element
oneof	TBI	Depends on ontology engineer's opinion
onProperty	TBD	Used in complex with content located between *daml: Restriction* and */daml: Restriction* tags (see *daml: Restriction*).
Ontology	+	Analyze content between *daml: Ontology* and */daml: Ontology* tags. Add new domain ontology into the ontology library.

DAML+OIL elements	Mapping type*	Implementation
range	+/-	Inside *daml: ObjectProperty* tag: Build an associative constraint (together with *daml: domain* tag element) Inside *daml: DatatypeProperty* tag: Build a structural constraint class + attribute + domain(C''); • Add a new domain (if necessary).
Restriction	+	Used in complex with content located between daml: Restriction and /daml: Restriction tags: daml: toClass, daml: hasValue, daml: hasClass, daml: hasClass, and different cardinality tags.
sameClassAs	TBD	For class O: Find the pattern class *O1* (the same as *daml: equivalentTo*) Change all occurrences of class name *O* to class name *O1* in the ontology (where necessary) Remove all unused occurrences of class name *O* from the ontology.
sameIndividualAs	TBI	At present, the system "KSNet" does not support ontologies with individuals
samePropertyAs	TBD	For property *P*: Find the pattern property *P1*; Change all occurrences of property name *P* to property name *P1* in the ontology (where necessary) Remove all unused occurrence of property name *P* from the ontology.
subClassOf	+/-	For class *O*: If the *daml: subClassOf* tag contains only class name *O1* Add taxonomy constraint from class *O1* to class *O* Other cases (like *daml: Restrictions*) are to be developed
subPropertyOf	TBI	Depends on ontology engineer's opinion
toClass	TBD	Used inside *daml: Restriction* and */daml: Restriction* tags together with *daml: onProperty* tags element. Can be used for associative constraint.
TransitiveProperty	TBI	Depends on ontology engineer's opinion
UnambigousProperty	TBI	Depends on ontology engineer's opinion
unionOf	+/-	For a set of classes – members of *daml: collection* tag: • Checks for number of subclasses elements
UniqueProperty	TBI	Depends on ontology engineer's opinion
versionInfo	+	Ontology description

The implementation of the methodology proposed by the KSNet-approach is illustrated by the example of user request processing scenario served as a case study.

4 Case Study

As an application domain to verification and validation of the approach the coalition formation problem oriented to war avoidance operations was chosen. The war avoidance operations are based on cooperation of a number of different, quasivolunteered, vaguely organized groups of people, non-governmental organizations, and institutions providing humanitarian aid [Marik, Pechoucek, and Bárta, 2002]. Such the cooperation is close to various formations of people and organizations supported by the Web services. Moreover, the cooperation scenario includes problems similar to ones of such application domain models as e-business, logistics, supply chain management, configuration management, etc. and thereby this case study can be reapplied to different domains.

The aim of Binni scenario [Rathmell, 1999] is to provide a rich environment, focusing on new aspects of coalition problems and new technologies demonstrating the ability of distributed intelligent support service in an increasingly dynamic environment. This was a main reason of using this scenario as a case study for the system KSNet in regard to the providing services. The considered task is a mobile hospital configuration in the Binni region.

Based on results of the parsing several user requests concerning the mobile hospital configuration task a template for the entering a request and a case study scenario were developed. Below, a general request is considered. Request terms defined in the template are italicized.

Define *suppliers, transportation routes* and *schedules* for *building*
a *mobile hospital* of *given capacity* at *given location* by *given time*.

The term *given* generalizes values for the assumed number of patients, desirable hospital sites, and deadlines of the hospital formation used in the parsed requests. This term corresponds to the input fields of the template.

Request terms corresponding to the structural request constituent are: *suppliers, transportation routes, schedules, building, mobile hospital, capacity, location, time*. A parametric request constituent consists of the values represented by the term "*given*". A general task supposes that the input fields may be not filled. In this case the request does not have a parametric constituent in an explicit form. According to the scenario this constituent is to be discovering through an interactive dialogue with the user.

Parts of ontologies corresponding to the described task were found in Internet's ontology libraries [Clin-Act, 2000; Cyc, 1998; Loom, 1997; NAICS, 2001; UNSPSC, 2001; WebOnto, 2002] by an expert. These ontologies represent a hospital in different manners using different representation formats. Firstly, the ontologies were imported from the source formats into the system notation. After that, they were included into the ontology library, henceforth they can be reused for the solution of similar problems. Some results of the import are shown by example of importing ontology parts corresponding to the hospital representation of the North American Industry Classification System (NAICS) code and United Nations Standard Products and Services Code (UNSPSC). Figure 5 presents hospital position in the NAICS code [NAICS, 2001] in DAML+OIL source format. Fig. 6 and Fig. 7 show representation of the imported parts of NAICS code and UNSPSC [UNSPSC, 2001] by "Web-DESO" tool.

```
<?xml version='1.0' encoding='ISO-8859-1'?>
<!DOCTYPE rdf:RDF [
      <!ENTITY a 'http://www.daml.org/2001/03/daml+oil#'>
      <!ENTITY rdf 'http://www.w3.org/1999/02/22-rdf-syntax-ns#'>
      <!ENTITY b 'http://www.w3.org/2000/01/rdf-schema#'>
      <!ENTITY c 'http://opencyc.sourceforge.net/daml/naics#'>
]>
<rdf:RDF xmlns:rdf="&rdf;"
      xmlns:a="&a;"
      xmlns:c="&c;"
      xmlns:b="&b;">

<b:Class rdf:about="Health-Care-and-Social-Assistance;62"
      c:naics-code="62"
      b:label="Health Care and Social Assistance"/>
</b:Class>
<b:Class rdf:about="Ambulatory-Health-Care-Services;621"
      c:naics-code="621"
      b:label="Ambulatory Health Care Services">
      <b:subClassOf                 rdf:resource="Health-Care-and-Social-
      Assistance;62"/>
</b:Class>
<b:Class rdf:about="Hospitals;622"
      c:naics-code="622"
      b:label="Hospitals">
      <b:subClassOf                 rdf:resource="Health-Care-and-Social-
      Assistance;62"/>
</b:Class>
<b:Class rdf:about="General-Medical-and-Surgical-Hospitals;6221"
      c:naics-code="6221"
      b:label="General Medical and Surgical Hospitals">
      <b:subClassOf rdf:resource="Hospitals;622"/>
</b:Class>
<b:Class rdf:about="Psychiatric-and-Substance-Abuse-Hospitals;6222"
      c:naics-code="6222"
      b:label="Psychiatric and Substance Abuse Hospitals">
      <b:subClassOf rdf:resource="Hospitals;622"/>
</b:Class>
<b:Class         rdf:about="Specialty-(except-Psychiatric-and-Substance-
Abuse)-Hospitals;6223"
      c:naics-code="6223"
       b:label="Specialty (except Psychiatric and Substance Abuse)
      Hospitals">
      <b:subClassOf rdf:resource="Hospitals;622"/>
</b:Class>

<a:UniqueProperty rdf:about="naics-code"
      b:comment="North American Industry Classification System code"
      b:label="naics code">
      <b:domain rdf:resource="&a;Thing"/>
      <b:range rdf:resource="&b;Literal"/>
</a:UniqueProperty>
</rdf:RDF>
```

Fig. 5. Hospital as 'Health-Care-and-Social-Assistance' in North American Industry Classification System code [NAICS, 2001]

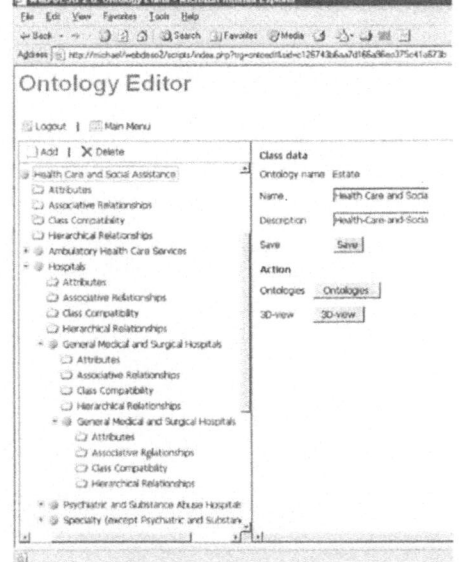
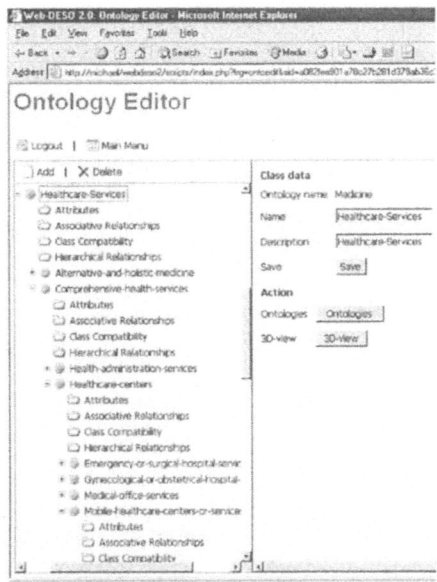

Fig. 6. Hospitals as 'Health-Care-and-Social-Assistance': "Web-DESO" view

Fig. 7. Mobile-healthcare-centers-or-services as Healthcare-Services: "Web-DESO" view

Next, ontology parts relevant to the request were combined into a single ontology. So, the parts presented in Fig. 6 and Fig. 7 were merged and modified by an ontology engineer using "Web-DESO" tool as it is shown in Fig. 8. The resulting AO is shown in Fig. 9. Regarding to the ontology part shown in Fig. 8 the following modifications were introduced:

- classes "General-building-construction", "Public-use-buildings", "Specialized-public-use-building-construction", "Healthcare-centers", "Hospitals" were removed so that class "Mobile-healthcare-centers-or-services" became a subclass of class "Construction";
- class "Mobile-healthcare-centers-or-services" was renamed to "Mobile hospital";
- attributes "capacity", "costs", "location", "time" were added;
- class "Hospital configuration" was added.

Fig. 9 has the following notation. Reused ontology classes (the classes adopted from the Internet's ontology libraries) are shown by firm lines, reused classes that were renamed are shown by dotted lines, new ontology classes (the classes included by experts) are outlined by thick lines, firm unidirectional arrows represent hierarchical relationships "is-a", dotted unidirectional arrows represent hierarchical relationships "part-of", double-headed arrows show associative relationships. Ontology part corresponding to AO included into the case study is represented by the shaded area.

Any ontologies corresponding to configuration tasks were not found out at the known ontology libraries and servers. An ontology for the hospital configuration task (the class "hospital configuration" in Fig. 9) was elaborated by knowledge and

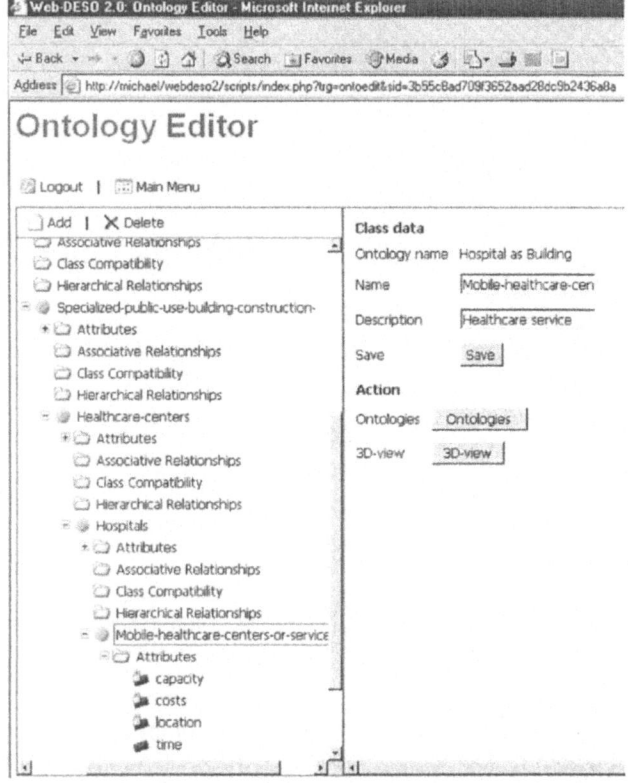

Fig. 8. Merged slices of NAICS.daml and UNSPSC.daml ontologies: "Web-DESO" view

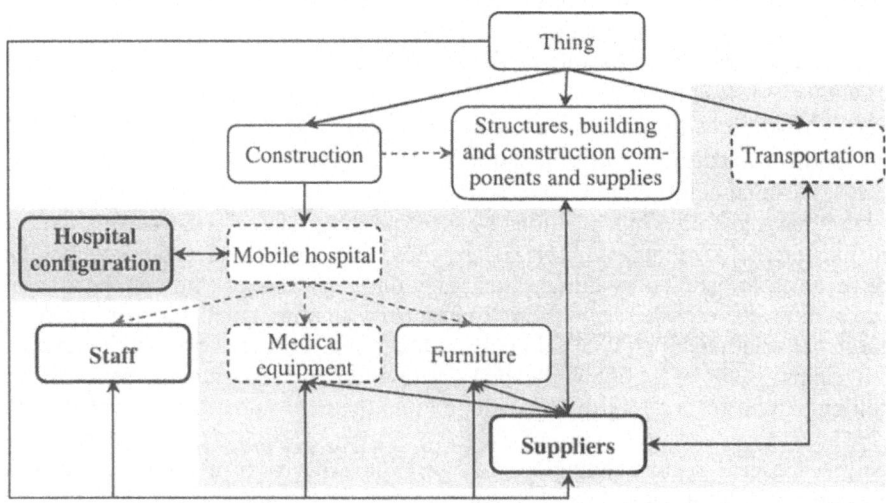

Fig. 9. "Mobile hospital" application ontology

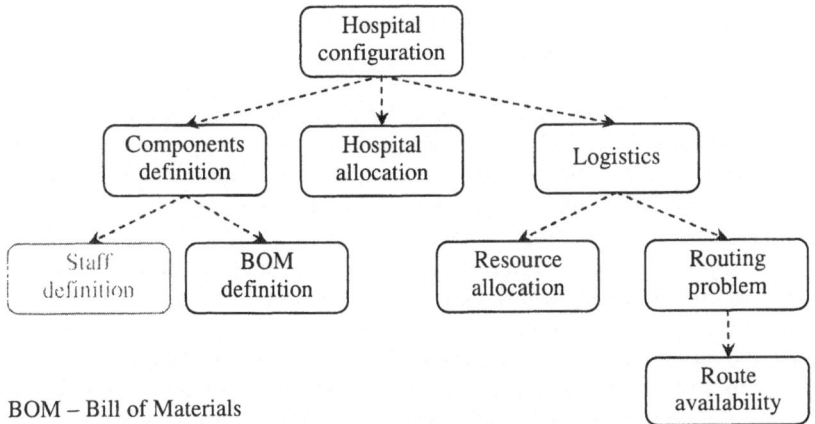

BOM – Bill of Materials

Fig. 10. Task ontology "Hospital configuration"

ontology engineers. The ontology is expanded in Fig. 10. In the figure "part-of" relationships between the classes are represented. In the considered example the method for staff definition is not taken into account as class "Staff" related to it is not included in the part of the case study being under consideration.

As the parametric request constituent was not shown explicitly the next step according to the scenario consists in its definition through an interactive dialogue with the user. Initially a user sees the screen presenting a map of the Binni region with cities and roads shown. Then he/she points on the map a desirable location of the hospital to be built. The map is updated and possible locations closest to one pointed by the user are displayed. These locations were entered into the system by experts taking into account such facts as availability of water resources, roads, surrounding areas and cities. The user selects a desirable destination from ones suggested by the system. Besides a hospital destination the system requests additional hospital characteristics such as hospital capacity or furniture and medical equipment volume. The characteristics are the result of the ontologies analyses and, as a rule, correspond to attribute values needed to the task solution. After the entering information by the user a set of KSs containing information relevant to the user request is formed.

An analysis of AO shows a necessity of finding and utilizing KSs containing the following information/knowledge: hospital related information (constraints on its structure, required quantities of components, required times of delivery); available suppliers (constraints on suppliers' capabilities, capacities, locations); available providers of transportation services (constraints on available types, routes, and time of delivery); factors influencing on route availabilities as geography and weather of the Binni region (constraints on types, routes, and time of delivery, e.g. by air, by trucks, by off-road vehicles) and current situation in the region, e.g. who occupies the territory used for transportation, existence of military actions on the routes, etc. (additional constraints on routes of delivery).

The problem of an automatic knowledge seeking is a future research. For the case study a list of KSs containing information for the user request processing was prepared by an expert team. The list includes an index of the Internet sites containing information about suppliers and their products, a specification of dependencies between the weather and delivery types (routes), a specification of the route availabilities depending on the current situation in the region, and analysis of charges for delivery of the hospital supplies. Information about the KS locations is included in the knowledge map for its future reuse.

To solve the case study task the *knowledge fusion agent* based on AO gathers required information from distributed KSs the knowledge map refers to with help of *wrappers*. In the paper as an example such supplier products which are the hospital components as operating tables, hospital beds, and tool sets are chosen. The products are described by classes (not represented in Fig. 9) which are instances of the classes "Medical equipment" and "Furniture" of AO. The supplier information includes availability of commodities, lead time, price per item, etc.; these values correspond to the parametric constituent entered by the user at the previous step.

As all the components ILOG needs to the user request processing (see the framework in Fig. 1) are specified the parametric constituent, AO (Fig. 9), and information containing in a set of knowledge related to this AO are processed by ILOG. The result (for target values of hospital location, hospital component volume, and suppliers of the components) of processing the considered request is presented in Fig. 11.

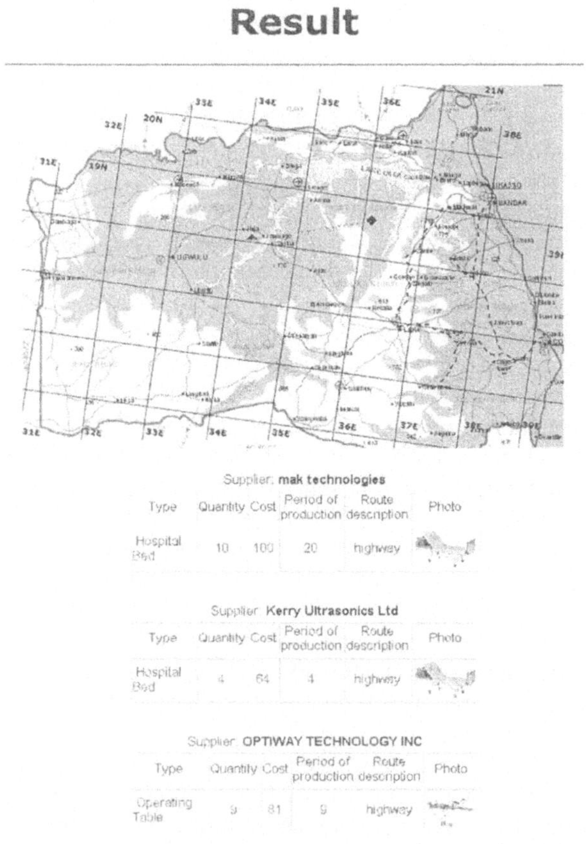

Fig. 11. Example results of user request processing

Conclusion

The paper describes a user-oriented approach to knowledge logistics. The approach addresses the ontology-driven methodology for user's problem solving through a knowledge source network configuration. It is based on object-oriented constraint networks theory as a fundamental / representation ontology and technology of constraint satisfaction / propagation.

Main advantages of the approach are related to ontology library features. The ontology library provides common vocabulary and notation to ontologies it stores. It is also a central ontology storage collecting knowledge describing different domains. Due to common vocabulary and notation the ontology library allows performing operations on ontology integration and thus enabling ontology sharing and reuse and ensuing cross-domain ontologies. Other advantages concern application ontology aspects. The application ontology is a context-dependent conceptual model that describes a real-world application domain depending on a specific user request and relevant to it particular domains and problems (tasks). Reuse of application ontologies increases rapidity of the user request processing. Being a specialization of domain and tasks & methods ontologies the application ontology enables cross-domain problem solving. A compatibility of object-oriented constraint networks notation with KIF and DAML+OIL knowledge representation formats enables processing information represented in these formats. Binni scenario as the application domain of the case study includes problems similar to ones of such application domain models as e-business, logistics, supply chain management, configuration management, etc. and thereby this case study can be reapplied to different domains.

Acknowledgements. Some parts of the research were done as parts of the ISTC partner project # 1993P funded by Air Force Research Laboratory at Rome, NY, the project # 16.2.44 of the research program "Mathematical Modelling, Intelligent Systems and Nonlinear Mechanical Systems Control" & the project # 1.9 of the research program "Fundamental Basics of Information Technologies and Computer Systems" of the Russian Academy of Sciences, and the grant # 02-01-00284 of the Russian Foundation for Basic Research. Some prototypes were developed using software granted by ILOG Inc. and Intelligent Systems Laboratory of St.Petersburg Institute for Informatics and Automation.

References

(Clin-Act, 2000) Clin-Act (Clinical Activity), The ON9.3 Library of Ontologies: Ontology Group of IP-CNR (a part of the Institute of Psychology of the Italian National Research Council (CNR)), December, 2000. http://saussure.irmkant.rm.cnr.it/onto/.
(Cyc, 1998) Hpkb-Upper-Level-Kernel-Latest: Upper Cyc / HPKB IKB Ontology with links to SENSUS, Version 1.4, February 1998. Ontolingua Ontology Server. http://www-ksl-svc.stanford.edu:5915.
(DAML+OIL, 2001) Reference description of the ontology markup language, eds. by van Harmelen F., Horrocks I., 2001. URL: http://www.daml.org/2001/03/reference

(Fensel *et. al.*, 2003) Fensel D. *et. al*, On-To-Knowledge: Semantic Web Enabled Knowledge Management. Submitted to: *Special Issue of Computer on Web Intelligence (WI)*. URL: http://www.aifb.uni-karlsruhe.de/WBS/ysu/publications/2002_otk_ieee.pdf.

(FIPA, 2000 – 2001) FIPA Agent Software Integration Specification. Foundation for Intelligent Physical Agents, 00079, 2000–2001. URL: http://www.fipa.org/specs/fipa00079/.

(Guarino, 1998) Guarino N. Formal Ontology and Information Systems. *Proceedings of FOIS'98*. Trento, Italy. Amsterdam: IOS Press, 1998. 3–15.

(ILOG, 2003) ILOG Corporate Web-site, 2003. URL: http://www.ilog.com.

(KIF, 1992) Knowledge Interchange Format (ed. by M.R. Genesereth and R.E. Fikes). Version 3.0. Reference Manual, 1992. URL: http://logic.stanford.edu/kif/Hypertext/kif-manual.html.

(Loom, 1997) Weather Theory. Loom ontology browser, Information sciences Institute, The University of Southern California, 1997. http://sevak.isi.edu:4676/loom/shuttle.html.

(Marik, Pechoucek, and Bárta, 2002) Marik V., Pechoucek M., and Bárta J. Reduction of Task Complexity in Coalition Planning. *Proceedings of the International Symposium "From Agent Theory to Agent Implementation" (AT2AI-3)*. Vienna, Austria (EU), April 3–5, 2002. URL: http://www.ai.univie.ac.at/%7Epaolo/conf/at2ai3/final/at2ai3Marik.pdf.

(NAICS, 2001) North American Industry Classification System code, DAML Ontology Library, Stanford University, July 2001. http://opencyc.sourceforge.net/daml/naics.daml.

(Rathmell, 1999) Rathmell R.A. A Coalition Force Scenario "Binni – Gateway to the Golden Bowl of Africa. *Proceedings on the International Workshop on Knowledge-Based Planning for Coalition Forces* (ed. by A. Tate). Edinburgh, Scotland, 1999. 115–125.

(Smirnov *et al.*, 2002) Smirnov A. Pashkin M. Chilov N., Levashova T. Multi-agent Architecture for Knowledge Fusion from Distributed Sources. *Lecture Notes in Artificial Intelligence*. Springer, 2296, 2002. 293–302.

(Smirnov *et al.*, 2003a) Smirnov A., Pashkin M., Chilov N., Levashova T. Haritatos F. Knowledge Source Network Configuration Approach to Knowledge Logistics. *International Journal of General Systems*. Taylor & Francis Group, 32 (3), 2003. 251–269.

(Smirnov *et al.*, 2003b) Smirnov A., Pashkin M., Chilov N., Levashova T. Knowledge Logistics in Information Grid. *Special Issue of Future Generation Computer Systems* (ed. H. Zhuge) (accepted in April 2003).

(UNSPSC, 2001) The UNSPSC Code (Universal Standard Products and Services Classification Code), DAML Ontology Library, Stanford University, January 2001. http://www.ksl.stanford.edu/projects/DAML/UNSPSC.daml.

(WebOnto, 2002) WebOnto: Knowledge Media Institute (KMI), The Open University, UK, 2002. http://eldora.open.ac.uk:3000/webonto.

(Weiss, 2000) Weiss G. (ed.): Multiagent Systems: a Modern Approach to Distributed Artificial Intelligence (ed. Weiss). The MIT Press, Cambridge, Massachusetts, London, 2000. 622 p.

(WordNet, 2003) WordNet Homepage, 2003. URL: http://www.cogsci.princeton.edu/~wn/.

Dynamic Topic Mining from News Stream Data

Seokkyung Chung and Dennis McLeod

Department of Computer Science
and Integrated Media System Center
University of Southern California
Los Angeles, California 90089-0781
{seokkyuc,mcleod}@usc.edu

Abstract. Given the popularity of Web news services, we propose a topic mining framework that supports the identification of meaningful topics (themes) from news stream data. News articles are retrieved from Web news services and processed by data mining tools to produce useful higher-level knowledge, which is stored in a content description database. Instead of interacting with a Web news service directly, by exploiting the knowledge in the database, an information delivery agent can present an answer in response to a user request. A key challenging issue within news repository management is the high rate of documents update. That is, since several hundred news articles are published everyday by a single Web news service, it is essential to develop incremental data mining tools to cope with such dynamic environments. To this end, we present a sophisticated incremental hierarchical document clustering algorithm using a neighborhood search. The novelty of our proposed algorithm lies in exploiting locality information to reduce the amount of computation while producing high-quality clusters. Other components of topic mining (e.g., learning topic ontologies) can be performed based on the obtained document hierarchy. Experimental results show that our proposed incremental clustering produces high-quality clusters, and topic ontology provides an interpretation of the data at different levels of abstraction.

1   Introduction

As every news organization provides Web news service, Internet users are experiencing overwhelming quantities of online news information. In these circumstances, the users have no time to read every news story. Instead, the navigation of news repository should be aided by data mining tools that allow the users to quickly locate their information needs from a news stream.

Web news articles are composed of hyperlinks, audio, video, images, and text. However, since not all news stories have corresponding multimedia data, text carries the most important information about the news. Since text is unstructured data, efficient text mining and access methods are required to obtain valuable knowledge embedded into the text document.

The simplest document access method is to employ keyword-based retrieval. Although this method seems to be effective, it suffers from serious drawbacks. For

R. Meersman et al. (Eds.): CoopIS/DOA/ODBASE 2003, LNCS 2888, pp. 653–670, 2003.
© Springer-Verlag Berlin Heidelberg 2003

example, if a user chooses irrelevant keywords (due to his/her vague information needs or unfamiliarity with the domain of interest), retrieval accuracy will be degraded. In addition, since keyword-based retrieval is based on simple keyword counting, it cannot address language semantics (e.g., synonym).

The problems stated above have been tackled by query expansion based on domain-independent (general) ontologies like WordNet [14]. However, it is well known that this approach leads to a degradation of precision. That is, since the words introduced by term expansion may have more than one meaning, using additional terms can improve recall, but decrease precision. Manually building ontology with controlled vocabulary is helpful in this situation [10]. However, though ontology authoring tools have been developed in the past decades, constructing ontology by hand whenever we encounter new domains is error-prone and time-consuming work. When developing information retrieval applications based on ontologies, this knowledge acquisition bottleneck problem is always faced. Therefore, integration of knowledge acquisition with data mining, which is referred to as ontology learning, becomes a must [12].

To illustrate our sample application within news stream data management, consider the following two issues. First, most of the news articles are related to previously published stories or future ones. Hence, this strong temporal dependency between the documents should not be ignored when navigating the news collection. In some Web news services (e.g., Washington Post), in order to present comfortable navigation interfaces to the user, editors manually add hyperlinks to the related stories when publishing news articles. Thus, a story about the safe return of a kidnapped child can be linked to the earlier stories reporting the police's search for the abducted child, investigation of the suspect, etc. Since those hyperlinks are added at the time of publication, they always point backwards in time. However, to read subsequent stories, a news service system should provide hyperlinks which allow a user to navigate forward in time. Next, search engines in current Web news services can only find the users' expected information. This is because the specified keywords are generated from their knowledge space. Note that the information the users cannot specify may be valuable to them. For example, if the users do not know about an airplane crash that occurred yesterday, then they cannot issue a query about that accident though they might be interested in that topic.

The first issue can be addressed by considering the nearest neighbors. A simple distance metric between two document feature vectors will show how much two documents are related to each other. Hence, this nearest neighbor analysis allows us to automatically identify related stories. Moreover, it can be used to find near-duplicate articles. This especially holds true for news feeds that tend to repeat stories with minor changes from hour to hour. In this situation, presenting the only most recent article is probably sufficient.

In addition, if the documents are clustered according to their topics and the meaningful labels are assigned to each cluster, then those labels can be used to understand the main themes of the clusters. Hence, if a user found an interesting story about a famous actor's court trial, and wants to know about

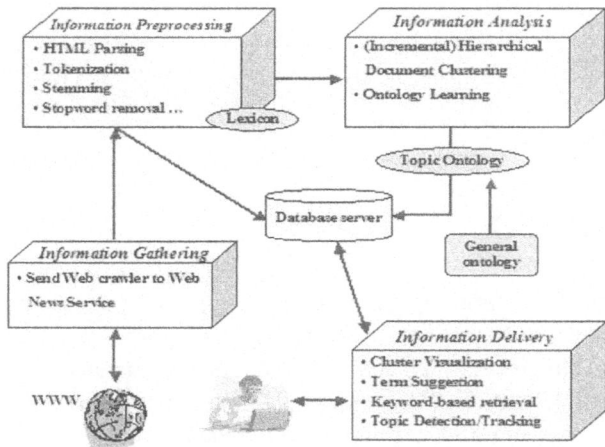

Fig. 1. Overview of a proposed model

the movies he stars in, then the user can jump from the "court trial" cluster to the "entertainment" cluster based on the cluster labels. Moreover, if a user has vague information needs, document cluster hierarchy can be a reasonable starting point.

To address the above issues, we propose a topic mining framework that supports the identification of meaningful topics (themes) from news stream data. News articles are retrieved[1] from Web news services and processed by data mining tools to produce useful higher-level knowledge, which is stored in a content description database. Instead of interacting with a Web news service directly, by exploiting the knowledge in the database, an information delivery agent can present an answer in response to a user request[2]. Figure 1 illustrates main parts of topic mining.

The challenging issue within news repository management is the high rate of documents insertion. That is, since several hundred news stories are published everyday by a single Web news service, it is essential to develop incremental data mining tools to cope with such dynamic environments. To this end, we present a sophisticated incremental hierarchical document clustering algorithm using a neighborhood search. The novelty of our proposed algorithm lies in exploiting locality information to reduce the amount of computation while producing high-quality clusters. Other components of topic mining can be performed based on the obtained document hierarchy.

---

[1] In the information gathering stage, a Web crawler retrieves a set of news stories from a news Web site (e.g., CNN). Developing an intelligent Web crawler is another research area, and it is not our main focus. Hence, we implement a simple Web spider which downloads news articles from news Web site on a daily basis.

[2] Due to the space limitation, we skip the detailed discussion about information delivery.

The remainder of this paper is organized as follows. Section 2 presents the related work on document clustering. Section 3 provides the discussion about the information preprocessing step, and Section 4 explains information analysis, which is a key focus of this paper. Finally, we conclude the paper and provide our future plans in Section 5.

2   Related Work

Utilizing document clustering for intelligent information retrieval is not a new idea. In this section we provide a brief survey on previous text clustering work.

Document clustering has received significant attention during the past decades [6,7,9,11,1,22,15]. This work is broadly classified into two categories: center-based clustering and hierarchical clustering.

Center-based algorithms find the clusters by partitioning the entire dataset into either a pre-determined (e.g., k-means clustering) or an automatically derived number of clusters (e.g., X-means clustering) [6,11,15]. A key characteristic of many center-based clustering algorithms is that they use a global criterion function whose optimization produces the entire clustering process. The main disadvantage of this approach is that it is susceptible to a local optimum.

In contrast, hierarchical agglomerative clustering (HAC) finds the clusters by initially assigning each document to its own cluster and then repeatedly merging pairs of clusters until a certain stopping condition is met [6,22]. Thus, its result is in the form of tree, which is referred to as a *dendrogram*. The main advantage of HAC lies in its ability to provide a view of data at multiple levels of abstraction. However, we should determine where to cut the dendrogram to produce clusters. This step is usually performed by human visual inspection, which is a time-consuming and subjective process.

To cope with frequent document insertion into the database, incremental clustering algorithm should be applied to news repository management [21,2]. However, previously proposed algorithms on incremental clustering are not applicable to our topic mining framework in that (1) they are sensitive to the input order (i.e., it produces different clusters for different order of the same input data); or (2) they are not relevant for high-dimensional data like documents.

3   Information Preprocessing

The information preprocessing step extracts meaningful information from the collected data using NLP tool, and transform unstructured text data into structured knowledge. Toward this end we employ natural language processing tools as follows:

- *HTML preprocessing.* Since downloaded news articles are in HTML format, we remove irrelevant HTML tags, and extract meaningful information.
- *Tokenization.* Its main task is to identify the boundaries of the words.

- *Stemming.* There can be different forms for the same words (e.g., *students* and *student*, *go* and *went*). We need to convert these different forms of the same word to their root. Toward this end, instead of solely relying on Porter stemmer [16], in order to deal with irregular plural/tense, we combine Porter stemmer with the lexical database [13].
- *Stopwords removal.* Stopwords are the words that occur frequently in text but do not carry useful information. For example, *have*, *did*, and *get* are not meaningful. Removing such stopwords provides us with a dimensionality reduction effect. We employ stopword list used in Smart project [18].

After preprocessing, a document is represented as a vector in an n-dimensional vector space [18]. The simple way to do this is to employ *bag-of-words* approach. That is, all content-bearing words in the document are taken and any structure of text or the word sequence is ignored. We treat each term as a feature, and represent each document as a vector of certain weighted word frequencies in this feature space. There are several ways to determine the weight of a term in a document. However, most methods are based on following two heuristics.

- Important terms occur more frequently within a document than unimportant terms do.
- The more times a term occur throughout all documents, the weaker its discriminating power becomes.

The term frequency (TF) is based on the first heuristic. In addition TF can be normalized to reflect different document length. Let $freq_{ij}$ be the number of w_i's occurrence in a document j, and l be the length of the document j. Then, term frequency (tf_{ij}) of w_i in the document j is defined as follows:

$$tf_{ij} = \frac{freq_{ij}}{l} \tag{1}$$

The document frequency (DF) of the term (the percentage of the documents that contains this term) is based on the second heuristic. A combination of TF and DF introduces TF-IDF ranking scheme, which is defined as follows:

$$w_{ij} = tf_{ij} \times log\frac{N}{n} \tag{2}$$

where w_{ij} is the weight of w_i in a document j, N is the total number of documents in the collection, and n is the number of documents where w_i occurs at least once.

We refer to the above ranking scheme as a static TF-IDF since it is based on static document collection. However, since our data is incrementally updated, we learn *idf* from certain amount of documents (i.e., the document frequency is generated from training corpus), and incrementally update *idf* as we process subsequent documents. In particular, we employ an incremental update of the *idf* value proposed by Yang et al. [19].

Table 1. Document × term matrix

	kidnap	abduct	child	boy	police	search	missing	investigate	suspect	return	home
D_1	1	0	1	0	1	1	0	1	0	0	0
D_2	1	1	1	1	1	0	1	1	1	0	0
D_3	0	1	0	1	0	0	1	0	0	1	1

Finally, to measure closeness between two documents, we employ Cosine metric which has been widely used in much information retrieval literature [18]. It measures similarity of two items according to the angle between them. Thus, vectors pointing to similar directions are considered as representing similar concepts. The cosine of the angles between two n-dimensional vectors x and y is defined by

$$Similarity(x, y) = Cosine(x, y) = \frac{\sum_{i=1}^{n} x_i \cdot y_i}{||x||_2 \cdot ||y||_2} \tag{3}$$

4   Information Analysis

In the information analysis step, we perform incremental hierarchical document clustering to build dynamic document cluster hierarchy. In addition, an algorithm for dynamic topic ontology learning is provided. In this step, we can also incorporate background knowledge (e.g., WordNet) in order to reinforce our automatically obtained topic ontology.

Section 4.1 explains the motivation of our proposed clustering algorithm. Section 4.2 provides a non-hierarchical incremental clustering algorithm using a neighborhood search. In Section 4.3, we show how to extend it into hierarchical version. Finally, in Section 4.4, we discuss how to build a dynamic topic ontology.

4.1   A Motivating Example

In this section, we provide the basic motivations for the proposed clustering algorithm. In particular we explain why neighborhood-based approach is useful in incremental document clustering.

To illustrate a simple example, consider following three documents (whose document × term matrix is shown in Table 1).

- D_1: A child is kidnapped so police starts searching.
- D_2: Police found the suspect of child kidnapping.
- D_3: An abducted boy safely returned home.

In the above three documents, though D_1 and D_2 is similar, and D_2 and D_3 is similar, D_1 and D_3 share no terms, consequently, transitivity relation does not hold. Why does this happen? We provide explanations to this question in terms of three different perspectives.

- *Fuzzy similarity relation.* As discussed in the fuzzy theory [20], the similarity relation does not satisfy transitivity. To make it satisfy transitivity, fuzzy transitivity closure can be used. However, this is not scalable with the number of data points.
- *Inherent characteristic of news.* As discussed in Allan et al. [2], *event* is defined as "some unique thing that happens at some point in time". Thus, event is considered as an evolving object through some time interval. Hence, though the documents belong to the same event, if they discuss different aspects of the event, the words they use should be different.
- *Language semantics.* We need to consider the diversity of word usage for the same meaning. Using only keyword counting aggravates the problem.

The transitivity is important in the incremental clustering algorithm. Consider the following incremental clustering algorithm which has been widely used in Topic Detection and Tracking research [2].

1. Initially, there is only one news story, and it forms a singleton cluster.
2. For an incoming story (d_i), we compute the similarity between d_i and pre-generated clusters. The similarity is computed by the distance between d_i and the representative (e.g., center) of the cluster.
3. Selects the cluster (C_i) which has the maximum proximity with d_i.
4. If the similarity between d_i and C_i exceeds a pre-defined threshold, then all documents in C_i are considered as related stories to d_i (topic tracking), and d_i is assigned to C_i. Otherwise, d_i is considered as a novel story (first story detection), and creates a new cluster for d_i.
5. Repeat 2-4 whenever a story comes out.

The above algorithm implies that the order of document insertion is critical. For example, in Table 1, if the order of document insertion is "$D_1 D_2 D_3$", then we may obtain one cluster $\{\{D_1, D_2, D_3\}\}$. However, if the order is "$D_1 D_3 D_2$", then two clusters will be obtained: $\{\{D_1, D_2\}, \{D_3\}\}$. Though the order of document insertion is fixed (because the document is inserted into a database whenever they are published), it is undesirable if the clustering result heavily depends on the insertion order.

In what follows, we identify two key requirements that the incremental document clustering should satisfy:

1. *Insensitivity to the input order.* Given different ordering of same dataset, many incremental clustering algorithms produce different clusters, which is an unreliable phenomenon. Hence, the incremental clustering should be robust to the input sequence. Thus, for the example above, regardless of the input order, the successful algorithm should produce a single cluster, $\{\{D_1, D_2, D_3\}\}$.
2. *Fast incremental processing of a new document.* Due to the frequent document insertion into the database, triggering the whole clustering process is computationally infeasible. Hence, to cope with such dynamic nature of the problem, the placement of a new document should not be decided by

Table 2. Notations for incremental non-hierarchical document clustering

Notation	Meaning
n	The total number of documents in a database
d_i	A new document
ϵ	Threshold for determining the neighborhood
$N_\epsilon(p)$	ϵ-neighborhood for p
D_d	The set of documents which contain any term of d
C_d	The set of clusters which contain any neighbor of d
$|A|$	The size of a set A
S_j	Signature vector for a set A_j
df_i^j	Document frequency of w_i within a set A_j
s_i^j	j-th component of S_i

a metric that requires all the documents that have been processed in the past. Whenever a new document is inserted, it should perform fast update of existing cluster structure.

4.2   Incremental Non-hierarchical Document Clustering

In this section, we propose incremental non-hierarchical document clustering algorithm based on a neighborhood search. Before going into detailed discussions, we present definitions for necessary terminologies. Table 2 also outlines the symbols with the meaning, which will be used throughout this paper.

Definition 1. [similar] *If similarity$(p, q) \geq \epsilon$, then a point p is referred to as similar to a point q.*

Definition 2. $[N_\epsilon(p)]$ *ϵ-neighborhood for a point p is $\{x : similarity(x, p) \geq \epsilon\}$.*

That is, ϵ-neighborhood for a document d is defined as a set of documents which are similar to d. In this paper we use ϵ-neighborhood and neighborhood, interchangeably.

Our proposed clustering algorithm exploits characteristic of a neighborhood. The idea is that label of an object is influenced by the features of its neighbors. Examples of such features are the labels of its neighbors, or the percentage of the neighbors which satisfy the certain constraint. Based on this idea, we define *Cluster Membership Hypothesis* as follows:

Definition 3. [Cluster Membership Hypothesis] *A point p is referred to as belonging to a cluster C_i if and only if 1 - δ fraction of $N_\epsilon(p)$ belong to C_i.*

Figure 2 illustrates the proposed incremental clustering algorithm. The overall algorithm proceeds in four phases: initialization, neighborhood search, identifying an appropriate cluster for a new document, and re-clustering based on local information.

Step 1. Initialization:
    Document d_0 forms a singleton cluster c_0;

Step 2. Neighborhood search:
    Given a new incoming document d_i, obtain $N_\epsilon(d_i)$ by performing
    neighborhood search;

Step 3. Identifying a cluster which can host a new document:
    Let C_{d_i} be the the set of clusters containing
    any document belonging to $N_\epsilon(d_i)$;
    Compute similarity between d_i and a cluster $c \in C_{d_i}$

    Based on the value obtained from above,
    if there exists a cluster which can absorb d_i, then
        add d_i to the cluster and update DCF vector for the cluster;
    otherwise,
        create a new cluster for d_i and
        create a corresponding DCF vector for this new cluster;

Step 4. Re-clustering:
    Let C_i be the cluster which hosts d_i;
    If C_i is not a singleton cluster, then trigger merge operation;

Fig. 2. The incremental non-hierarchical document clustering algorithm

Step 1: Initialization. Initially, we assume that only one document is available. Hence this document itself forms a singleton cluster.

Step 2: Neighborhood search. Achieving an efficient neighborhood search is a key issue in our proposed clustering algorithm. If the dimensions of the data are low (e.g., 5-20), then the multi-dimensional index structure can be employed to support fast search [3,8,4]. However, since our data set has extremely high dimensions, though we conduct dimensionality reduction using Singular Value Decomposition [5], the reduced dimensions (which are more than 100) are still beyond the capacity of the current spatial indexing structure.

Instead we employ an inverted index for the purpose of the neighborhood search. In the inverted index [18], the index associates a set of documents with words. That is, for each word w, we build a document list which contains all documents containing w. Let a document d be composed of $w_1, \dots, w_n$. In order to find similar documents to d, instead of looking into whole document collections, it is sufficient to examine the documents which contain any w_i. Hence, given document d, finding the neighborhood can be accomplished in $O(|D_d|)$ where D_d is the set of documents containing any w which appear in d[3].

---

[3] Note that $|D_d|$ is much smaller than n thanks to Zipf's law [17].

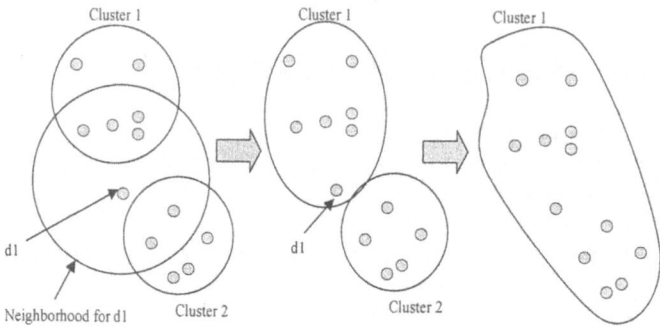

Step 1: Check whether d1 can be added to cluster 1

Step 2: Add d1 to cluster 1

Step 3: Merge cluster 1 and cluster 2 if they satisfy the merge constraint

Fig. 3. Illustration of re-clustering phase

Step 3: Identifying an appropriate cluster. To assign an incoming document (d_i) to the existing cluster, we need to compute the similarity between each candidate cluster and a document. Using the neighborhood of the new document, we determine the cluster which can host a new document.

One possible approach is to select the cluster that has the biggest number of its members in the ϵ-neighborhood. This approach only considers the number of documents in the overlapped region, and ignores the proximity between neighbors and the d_i.

Instead, we can exploit the similarity between the candidate cluster and its neighbors when determining the assignment. That is, each neighbor can vote for its class with a weight proportional to its proximity to the new document. Let w_j be a weight for representing the proximity of n_j to the new document. Then, we select a cluster for the new document which has the maximum value for the following formula:

$$\sum_{n_j \in N_\epsilon(d_i)} w_j \cdot Similarity(n_j, S_k) \text{ where } S_k \in C_d \tag{4}$$

In addition, we can simply measure the similarity between the signature vector of the neighborhood and that of the cluster.

Then, how can we define a signature vector? The signature vector should be composed of words which reflect the main characteristics of the documents in the set. For each word w_i in the set A_j (e.g., a cluster/neighborhood), we compute the weight for the word using a following formula:

$$s_i^j = \frac{df_i^j}{|A_j|} \cdot \frac{\sum_{d_k \in A_j} w_{ik}}{|A_j|} \tag{5}$$

In Equation (5) the first factor measures document frequency within a set, and the second factor measures the sum of the weight for the word over the whole documents within a set.

When computing similarity between a document and a cluster, we only need signature vectors of a cluster and a document. This is a computationally efficient scheme if the signature vector can be incrementally updated as a new document is added to the cluster. The notion of Document Cluster Feature (DCF) vector is defined for this purpose.

Definition 4. [DCF] *Document Cluster Feature (DCF) vector for a cluster C_i is defined as a triple $DCF_i = (N_i, DF_i, W_i)$ where N_i is the number of documents in C_i, DF_i is a document frequency vector for C_i, and W_i is a weight sum vector for C_i, respectively.*

Theorem 5. [**Additivity of DCF**] *Let $DCF_i = (N_i, DF_i, W_i)$ and $DCF_j = (N_j, DF_j, W_j)$ be the document cluster vectors for C_i and C_j, respectively. Then, DCF for a new cluster (by merging C_i and C_j) is defined by $(N_i + N_j, DF_i + DF_j, W_i + W_j)$.*

Proof. It is straightforward by simple linear algebra.

Based on the definition of DCF and above theorem, we can incrementally update the signature vector of a cluster whenever a new document is inserted. Therefore, if there exists a cluster (say, C_i) which can absorb d_i (i.e., the similarity is greater than pre-defined threshold), then assign it to C_i, and update the DCF_i. Otherwise, create a new cluster for d_i and DCF vector for this cluster.

Step 4: Re-clustering. If we assign d_i to C_i, then we need to trigger the merge operation. This is based on local approach. Instead of re-clustering the whole data set, we only need to focus on the clusters which are affected by the new document. That is, a new document is placed in the cluster, and a sequence of cluster re-structuring process is performed only in regions that have been affected by the new document. Figure 3 illustrates this idea. As shown, we only consider clusters which contain any document belonging to the neighborhood of a new document.

Recent data mining literature have proposed Shared Nearest Neighbors (SNN) clustering approach [7,9]. In this method, the k-nearest neighbors of each point are identified, and similarity between two points is defined as the number of neighbors they share. Thus, basic motivation of SNN clustering is similar to ours, however, the detailed approach is completely different. The key difference between SNN and ours is how to define a neighborhood. In SNN, a neighborhood is defined as a set of k-nearest neighbors while we employ an ϵ-neighborhood concept. Thus, the neighborhood constructed from k-nearest neighbors is local in that it is defined narrowly in dense region, and more widely in sparse region. However, for document clustering, a global neighborhood approach produces more meaningful clusters. Next, SNN is defined in the static dataset while ours is working on incremental dataset. Finally, our algorithm can easily identify the singleton clusters. This is especially important in our application since unique documents in a news stream may imply new events that have not been mentioned in previous articles. In contrast, SNN considers singleton clusters as noise, and remove them, hence it does not cluster all the points.

4.3   How to Extend Non-hierarchical Clustering into Hierarchical Version?

When we apply the algorithm in Fig. 2 to the news story collection, we can obtain different types of event clusters. These clusters are defined at level 1. Note that level 0 corresponds to the lowest level in a cluster tree (i.e., each document itself is a cluster at level 0). Now, since our goal is to generate document hierarchy, all trial clusters at level 1 should be combined as a single cluster at level 2 to reflect the court trial topic. However, due to the named entity (NE)[4], this becomes a difficult task since NE has very high term-frequency within a document. Consequently, similarity between different event clusters which belong to same topic becomes extremely low. In this section, we provide a hierarchical clustering algorithm, and show some preliminary experimental results. Before presenting our algorithm, we first define necessary terminologies in the following.

Definition 6. [**Specific features (SF)**] *Specific features for a cluster C_i is the collection of terms which frequently occur within a cluster C_i, but rarely occur outside of C_i. We denote it by SF_{C_i}.*

Definition 7. [**Actual time (T)**] *Actual time is obtained from the time stamp of each news article. For example, T corresponds to the date of the publication for a news article.*

Definition 8. [**Virtual time (t)**] *Virtual time t is initialized by 0. At any time t, only one operation (e.g., document add, cluster merge, etc) can be performed. In addition, time is increased by one when we perform an operation and remains unchanged if there is no operation.*

Let $df^i(t)$ be the document frequency of a word w_i in whole documents at time t. Then, document frequency of w_i at time $t+1$ is defined as follows:

$$df^i(t+1) = \begin{cases} df^i(t) + 1, & \text{if } d \text{ is added at } t \text{ and it contains } w_i \\ df^i(t), & \text{otherwise} \end{cases} \quad (6)$$

Let $df_{in}^{ij}(t)$ be the document frequency of a word w_i within a C_j at time t. Then $df_{in}^{ij}(t+1)$ is recursively defined as follows:

$$df_{in}^{ij}(t+1) = \begin{cases} df_{in}^{ij}(t) + 1, & \text{if } d \text{ is added to } C_j \text{ at } t \text{ and } d \text{ contains } w_i \\ df_{in}^{ij}(t), & \text{otherwise} \end{cases} \quad (7)$$

---

[4] Named entities are people/organization, time/date and location, which play a key role in defining "who", "when", and "where" of an event.

We denote $k(t)$ as a number of clusters at level 1 at time t. Then, $k(t+1)$ is defined as follows:

$$k(t+1) = \begin{cases} k(t), & \text{if } d \text{ is added to an existing cluster at } t \\ k(t)+1, & \text{if } d \text{ itself forms a new cluster at } t \\ k(t)-1, & \text{if two clusters are merged at } t \end{cases} \quad (8)$$

Let $df_{out}^{ij}(t+1)$ represent how much w_i occurs outside the cluster C_j at time $t+1$.

$$df_{out}^{ij}(t+1) = \frac{df^i(t+1) - df_{in}^{ij}(t+1)}{k(t+1)} \quad (9)$$

Then, predictive strength of a word w_i for the cluster C_j at time $t+1$ is defined as follows:

$$pred_j^i(t+1) = log\frac{df_{in}^{ij}(t+1)}{df_{out}^{ij}(t+1)} \quad (10)$$

In sum, Equation (10) gives more weight to the words occurring frequently within C_j and less weight to those occurring rarely outside of C_j. Thus, a highly predictive word can select the most specific feature for the cluster.

We informally describe our hierarchical algorithm as follows. We generate clusters at level 1 based on the algorithm in Fig. 2. During some pre-defined time interval, if no more documents are added to certain cluster at level 1, then we assume that the event for the cluster ends[5], and associate SF with this cluster at level 1. We then perform neighborhood search for this cluster to generate cluster at level 2. Since SF reflects the most specific characteristics for the cluster, it is not helpful to merge two topically similar clusters. Hence, when we build a vector for C_i^j, terms in SF (for C_i^j) are not included for building cluster vector.

Our clustering algorithm exploits multi-resolution inverted index for the efficient discovery of neighborhood at different levels of the hierarchy. That is, in the inverted index at level i, the index associates a set of clusters (at level i) with words. For each word w, we build a cluster list which is composed of all clusters containing w. Note that the cluster is referred to as containing a word w if the second factor of Equation (5) exceeds the pre-defined threshold.

For the empirical evaluation of the proposed clustering algorithm, we manually labeled approximately 2,000 stories downloaded from CNN news Web site. The total number of topics and events used in this research is 15 and 150, respectively. Thus, the maximum possible number of clusters we can obtain (at level 1) is 150. Note that the number of stories for the events ranges from 1 to 142. The quality of clustering solution was determined by two metrics, precision and recall. Let T_r be a class on topic r. Then, cluster C_r is referred to as a topic r cluster if and only if the majority of subclusters for C_r belong to T_r. The precision and recall of the clustering at level i (where k_i is the number of clusters at level i) then can be defined as follows:

---

[5] This assumption is based on the temporal proximity of the event [19].

	Precision	Recall		Precision	Recall
Level 1	91.5%	90.3%	Level 1	83.1%	86.7%
Level 2	100%	81.4%			

(a) Proposed algorithm   (b) Modified K-means

Fig. 4. Comparison of the clustering algorithms

$$P_i = \frac{1}{k_i} \sum_{j=1}^{k_i} \frac{|C_j \cap T_j|}{|C_j|} \qquad (11)$$

$$R_i = \frac{1}{k_i} \sum_{j=1}^{k_i} \frac{|C_j \cap T_j|}{|T_j|} \qquad (12)$$

Figure 4 compares the accuracy of our clustering algorithm with the modified k-means algorithm. Since k-means is not suitable for incremental clustering, we performed k-means clustering retrospectively on the dataset while our proposed algorithm was tested on incremental data set after learning idf. Since we already know the number of clusters at level 1 (based on the ground-truth data), for k-means, we fixed k in advance. In addition, to overcome the k-mean's sensitivity to the initial seed selections, we select the seed p with the condition that the chosen seed should not belong to the neighborhoods of the pre-selected seeds. Each seed selected by the above process is far from each other since they are approximately mutually orthogonal. As shown in Fig. 4, the proposed algorithm outperforms the modified k-means in terms of precision and recall[6]. As illustrated, the recall of our algorithm decreases as the level increases. The main reason for this poor recall at level 2 is related with the characteristics of the news articles. As discussed, named entity plays a key role in defining who/when/where of an event. Thus, at level 1, NE contributes to high quality clustering. However, at level 2, since the strength of topical terms are not so strong like named entity, it is not easy to merge different event clusters (belong to the same topic) into same topical cluster. There are some events we could not correctly separate. For example, on the wildfire topic, there exist different events such as "Oregon wildfire", "Arizona wildfire", etc. However, at level 1, we failed to separate those events into different clusters.

4.4 Building Topic Ontology

One of the main problems with domain-independent ontologies is that topically related concepts/terms are not explicitly linked. That is, there is no relationship between *court-attorney, kidnap-police*, etc.

Topic ontology is a collection of concepts and relations. One view of a concept is as a set of terms which characterize a topic. We employ two generic kinds of

---

[6] Note that we did not compare modified k-means with ours at level 2. To do this, we also need to develop feature selection algorithm to extend modified k-means into hierarchical version.

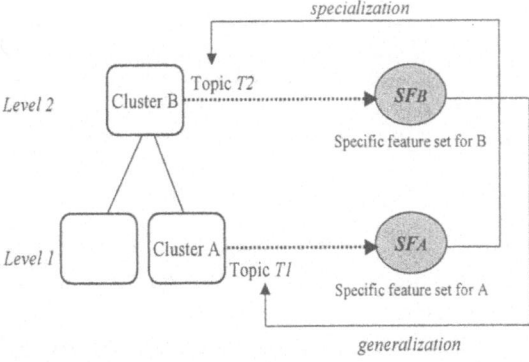

Fig. 5. Illustration of relationship in topic ontology

Table 3. Examples of specific features for the clusters at level 1

Event	Specific features
Court trial 1	winona ryder actress shoplift beverly
Court trial 2	andrea yates drown insanity
Court trial 3	blake bakley actor
Kidnapping 1	elizabeth smart utah salt lake
Kidnapping 2	jessica holly soham cambridgeshire england
Kidnapping 3	weaver ashlei miranda gaddis
Wildfire	wildfire firefighter colorado forest blaze acre

Table 4. Examples of specific features for the clusters at level 2

Topic	Specific features
Earthquake	quake earthquake magnitude collapse building
Court trial	court trial law murder defense legal prosecutor attorney testify jury evidence kill
Kidnapping	girl miss parent disappear abduct enforce police family kidnap
Airplane crash	crash air airline safety dead boeing accident traffic passenger flight pilot collision aircraft warn aviat
West nile virus	disease blood organ louisiana symptom spread
Wildfire	arizona burn evacuate hayman rodeo residence wind denver force size danger flame national line

Table 5. Examples of general features for the court trial cluster 1

Event	General features
Trial 1	hear hill gerago women delay injury guilty camera store stand charge court target trial drug arm count law legal attorney evidence victim arrest order

relations, specialization and generalization. The former is useful when refining a query while the latter can be used when we generalize the query to increase recall or broaden the search.

A topic ontology is built on top of the document hierarchy. We associate each node of hierarchy with specific features. Specific features of a parent node are more topically abstract than those of a child node. That is, as shown in Table 3 and Table 4, with respect to the topic, we observed that the specific details are captured by the lower levels (e.g., level 1), while higher levels (e.g., level 2) are abstract. Hence, SF at lower level is a specialization of a higher level node while SF at upper level is a generalization of a lower level node. Figure 5 illustrates this idea. SF_A is a specialization with respect to the topic T_2 while SF_B is a generalization of the topic T_1. Thus, SF_B is a super concept of SF_A with respect to topic T_1.

We can also generate general features (GF) for the node which is defined as follows:

Definition 9. [General features (GF)] *General features for a cluster C_i is the collection of terms which frequently occur within a cluster C_i, and also occur outside of C_i. We denote it by GF_{C_i}.*

In comparison with SF, the predictive power of GF is weaker than that of SF. Table 5 shows GF for a cluster for "court trial 1" in Table 3. In sum, those SF and GF constitute the concepts of topic ontology.

5   Conclusion and Future Works

This paper presented a topic mining framework that is vital to intelligent information retrieval. In order to accommodate dynamically changing topics, the incremental document clustering based on neighborhood search is employed. We also presented topic ontology learning scheme based on the obtained document hierarchy.

We intend to extend this work in the following directions. Though we can obtain document hierarchy based on unsupervised clustering, as shown in Aggarwal et al. [1], we can enhance the cluster quality if we exploit the pre-existing knowledge base. In addition, we can augment topic ontology using WordNet to obtain rich semantics.

Acknowledgement. This research has been funded in part by the Integrated Media Systems Center, a National Science Foundation Engineering Research Center, Cooperative Agreement No. EEC-9529152.

References

1. C.C. Aggarwal, S.C. Gates, and P.S. Yu. On the merits of using supervised clustering for building categorization systems. In *Proceedings of the 5th ACM SIGKDD International Conference on Knowledge Discovery and Data Mining*, 1999.
2. J. Allan, J. Carbonell, G. Doddington, J. Yamron, and Y. Yang. Topic detection and tracking pilot study final report. In *Proceedings of the DARPA Broadcast News Transcription and Understanding Workshop*, 1998.
3. N. Beckmann, H.P. Kriegel, R. Schneider, and B. Seeger. The R*-tree: an efficient and robust access method for points and rectangles. *ACM SIGMOD Record*, 19:(2):322–331, 1990.
4. S. Berchtold, D.A. Keim, and H.P. Kreigel. The X-tree: An index structure for high dimensional data. In *Proceedings of the 22nd International Conference on Very Large Data Bases*, 1996.
5. M.W. Berry, S.T. Dumais, and G.W. O'Brien. Using linear algebra for intelligent information retrieval. *SIAM Review*, 37(4):573–595, 1995.
6. R. O. Duda, P. E. Hart, and D. G. Stork. *Pattern Classification (2nd Ed.)*. Wiley, New York, 2001.
7. L. Ertöz, M. Steinbach, and V. Kumar. Finding clusters of different sizes, shapes, and densities in noisy, high dimensional data. In *Proceedings of the 3rd SIAM International Conference on Data Mining*, 2003.
8. A. Guttman. R-Trees: A dynamic index structure for spatial searching. In *Proceedings of the ACM SIGMOD International Conference on Management of Data*, 1985.
9. R.A. Jarvis, and E.A. Patrick. Clustering using a similarity measure based on shared near neighbors. *IEEE Transactions on Computers*, C22, 1025–1034, 1973.
10. L. Khan. Ontology-based information selection. *Ph.D. Thesis, University of Southern California*, 2000.
11. B. Larsen and C. Aone. Fast and effective text mining using linear-time document clustering. In *Proceedings of the 5th ACM SIGKDD International Conference on Knowledge Discovery and Data Mining*, 1999.
12. A. Maedche, and S. Staab. Ontology learning for the Semantic Web. *IEEE Intelligent Systems*, 16(2), 2001.
13. I.D. Melamed. Automatic evaluation and uniform filter cascades for inducing n-best translation lexicons. In *Proceedings of the 3rd Workshop on Very Large Corpora*, 1995.
14. G. Miller. Wordnet: An on-line lexical database. *International Journal of Lexicography*, 3(4):235–312, 1990.
15. D. Pelleg, and A. Moore. X-means: Extending K-means with efficient estimation of the number of clusters. In *Proceedings of the 17th International Conference on Machine Learning*.
16. M.F. Porter. An algorithm for suffix stripping. *Program*, 14(3):130–137, 1980.
17. M. Sahami. Using machine learning to improve information access. *Ph.D. Thesis, Stanford University*, 1999.

18. G. Salton and M.J. McGill. *Introduction to modern information retrieval.* McGraw-Hill, 1983.
19. Y. Yang, J. Carbonell, R. Brown, T. Pierce, B.T. Archibald, and X. Liu. Learning approaches for detecting and tracking news events. *IEEE Intelligent Systems: Special Issue on Applications of Intelligent Information Retrieval, 14(4):32–43,* 1999.
20. L.A. Zadeh. Similarity relations and fuzzy orderings. *Information Sciences,* 3:177–200, 1971.
21. T. Zhang, R. Ramakrishnan, and M. Livny. BIRCH: an efficient data clustering method for very large databases. In *Proceedings of the ACM SIGMOD International Conference on Management of Data,* 1996.
22. Y. Zhao, and G. Karypis. Evaluations of hierarchical clustering algorithms for document datasets. In *Proceedings of the 11th ACM International Conference on Information and Knowledge Management,* 2002.

$\mathcal{F}$LORA-2: A Rule-Based Knowledge Representation and Inference Infrastructure for the Semantic Web[*]

Guizhen Yang[1], Michael Kifer[2], and Chang Zhao[2]

[1] Department of Computer Science and Engineering
University at Buffalo, Buffalo, NY 14260-2000, USA
gzyang@CSE.Buffalo.EDU
[2] Department of Computer Science
Stony Brook University, Stony Brook, NY 11794-4400, USA
{kifer,changz}@CS.StonyBrook.EDU

Abstract. $\mathcal{F}$LORA-2 is a rule-based object-oriented knowledge base system designed for a variety of automated tasks on the Semantic Web, ranging from meta-data management to information integration to intelligent agents. The $\mathcal{F}$LORA-2 system integrates F-logic, HiLog, and Transaction Logic into a coherent knowledge representation and inference language. The result is a flexible and natural framework that combines rule-based and object-oriented paradigms. This paper discusses the principles underlying the design of the $\mathcal{F}$LORA-2 system and describes its salient features, including meta-programming, reification, logical database updates, encapsulation, and support for dynamic modules.

1 Introduction

$\mathcal{F}$LORA-2 [42] is a rule-based knowledge representation and inference system, which seeks to provide a rich infrastructure for reasoning with semantic information on the Web. The logical foundations of $\mathcal{F}$LORA-2 are deeply rooted in F-logic [20], HiLog [9], and Transaction Logic [5]. Firstly, F-logic brings many important object-oriented features such as complex objects, class hierarchies, and inheritance. Secondly, HiLog provides a basis for reification and enhances F-logic with meta-information processing capabilities. Finally, Transaction Logic supports declarative programming of "procedural knowledge" that is often embedded in intelligent agents or Semantic Web services. In $\mathcal{F}$LORA-2 these three formalisms are seamlessly pieced together, thus providing a coherent framework for specifying and manipulating knowledge as well as meta-knowledge in a logically clean fashion.

In this paper we discuss the design principles underlying the $\mathcal{F}$LORA-2 system and present the main features of its language. In particular, we point out how these principles relate to the rule-based reasoning infrastructure for the Semantic Web and to the various features of the $\mathcal{F}$LORA-2 system. Of special interest are

[*] This work was supported in part by NSF grants IIS-0072927 and CCR-0311512.

R. Meersman et al. (Eds.): CoopIS/DOA/ODBASE 2003, LNCS 2888, pp. 671–688, 2003.
© Springer-Verlag Berlin Heidelberg 2003

many different extensions to F-logic, which have been developed in order to meet the specific requirements of the Semantic Web. These include a logical theory for nonmonotonic multiple inheritance [37]; reification [41], which extends the basic theory provided by HiLog; and support for anonymous resources [41].

Another important extension is the novel module system of $\mathcal{F}$LORA-2, which was designed explicitly with the goal of supporting intelligent agents and knowledge integration. Unlike other module systems, which are tied to specific program code, $\mathcal{F}$LORA-2 modules are abstractions that represent structural components of a running system. Program code can be loaded into any module on-the-fly, and the already loaded code can be replaced by other code while the system runs. New modules can also be created and loaded at run time. Finally, to accommodate a wide variety of semantic components in knowledge integration, different modules can have different (even customized) semantics.

This paper is organized as follows. Section 2 introduces the principles underlying the design of $\mathcal{F}$LORA-2. Section 3 provides an overview of the three logics underlying $\mathcal{F}$LORA-2 and presents the extensions that have been developed specifically to support the Semantic Web infrastructure. In Section 4, we introduce the module system of $\mathcal{F}$LORA-2. Section 5 concludes the paper with a discussion of future work.

2   Design Principles

In this section we discuss and motivate the main principles underlying the design of $\mathcal{F}$LORA-2. Some of the design decisions were adopted directly from the three logics: F-logic, HiLog, and Transaction Logic. Other principles stem from the high-level goal that motivated our effort — the development of a powerful rule-based language that is suitable for the Semantic Web.

2.1   Choice of Semantics

Asserted versus Inferred Knowledge. While current standardization efforts, such as OWL [35], are focusing on first-order logic, new, forward-looking research is arguing that nonmonotonic extensions are needed for more sophisticated uses of the Semantic Web (*e.g.*, [1,23]). In ontologies, nonmonotonicity arises in advanced applications, such as Semantic Web services; in agent-based systems, it arises in the form of common-sense reasoning.

In the past, claims has been made in various discussion forums that nonmonotonic closed-world assumption is inherently inappropriate for reasoning about the Web because the totality of all the information is not known in advance to the reasoner. We believe that this point of view stems from insufficient attention given to the view that knowledge on the Web comes in two main varieties: *asserted knowledge*, which is specified mostly as sets of facts, and *inferred knowledge*, which is derived using rules.

While the distinction between closed-world assumption and open-world assumption may seem insignificant for asserted knowledge, it makes a world of difference in the interpretation of rules. To date, the best studied and the most successful applications of rules in intelligent systems are based on a form of nonmonotonic closed-world assumption.

The misconception about the inapplicability of semantic closure originates, in part, in the tradition of logic programming, where data and rules are part of the same program. In contrast, the tradition of databases has always made a distinction between data and rules, and referred to these two kinds of knowledge as *extensional* and *intentional* database, respectively. The extensional database has been viewed as a variable part of the knowledge base, and closed-world inferences were always subject to change when the extensional part changes.

It is not hard to see that this point of view is very similar to the Web environment, where data sources can be viewed as sets of facts asserted into the extensional database. When data at the sources changes or the sources are added or deleted, the old nonmonotonic inferences are revised. For instance, an intelligent travel agent service can be defined by a set of $\mathcal{F}$LORA-2 rules, which are interpreted using the closed-world assumption. However, the concrete inferences made by the agent would depend on the specific data sources that the agent is aware of. Adding or removing these sources will change the recommendations made by the agent.

Comprehensive Semantics. An important principle underlying $\mathcal{F}$LORA-2 is that the language should be comprehensive and every syntactically correct specification should have a natural semantics. Since $\mathcal{F}$LORA-2 is as general as Prolog and thus is Turing-complete, it is possible to write non-terminating programs. In fact, since Transaction Logic is part of the language and thus $\mathcal{F}$LORA-2 programs can modify the underlying database, the language is Turing-complete even if we do not use function symbols in queries and rules [3]. However, it was always our intention to design a complete language that has tractable subsets suitable for query answering. For instance, [37] shows that query answering is polynomial in function-free $\mathcal{F}$LORA-2 programs even in the presence of nonmonotonic multiple inheritance, and [3] describes subsets of Transaction Logic with various degrees of computational complexity.

The semantics of a rule-based object-oriented language that supports multiple inheritance with overriding was known to be a hard issue. The original proposal [20], as well as a number of subsequent semantics [7,17,18,29,30], had suffered from a number of anomalies (see [39] for more details). A comprehensive solution was recently proposed in [39] and [40].

2.2 Lazy Assimilation of Knowledge

Due to the dynamic nature of data sources on the Web and general incompleteness of information in this medium, a Semantic Web language must be as impervious to changes in the asserted knowledge as possible.

Thus, Semantic Web applications need to be able to assimilate knowledge *lazily*, without having to *revise* existing knowledge substantially when new knowledge is added. This is especially important for data sources that are not under the control of client applications. When such sources change, they normally do not send notification to the client applications, and exhaustive querying of these sources (to determine what the changes are) is expensive and often impossible.

Partial Knowledge about Class Hierarchies and Objects. F-logic and $\mathcal{F}$LORA-2 address the above problems in several ways. First, subclass relationship, sub :: super, is not immediate, *i.e.*, it is not invalidated if a new intermediate class is discovered later on. Thus, sub :: intermediate and intermediate :: super do not contradict sub :: super. Likewise, class membership, object : class, is not immediate; it does not rule out the possibility that there may exist an intermediate class between object and class, *i.e.*, object : intermediate and intermediate :: class. This reflects the view that knowledge about class hierarchies is *incomplete*. Likewise, any assertion about an object is assumed to be incomplete. For instance, asserting that an object, say, john, has a set-valued attribute siblings with a known set of values, *e.g.*, {bill, mary}, does not imply that these are the only values. It will not be a contradiction if later we learn that anne is also a sibling. Moreover, the available knowledge of an object schema is also assumed to be incomplete (unless the user imposes a strict type constraint on the object). Thus, if john is said to be an object with the attributes name, parents, and siblings, adding information about a new attribute, say, address will remain consistent with the old knowledge about the schema. Note that traditional object-oriented programming and database languages take exactly the opposite view on each of the above four points.

Incomplete Knowledge about Identity. Logic-based languages do not normally support equality between terms and assume that distinct variable-free terms represent different entities. However, this assumption is not appropriate when applied to resources on the Semantic Web. For instance, different URIs might, in fact, represent the same resource. $\mathcal{F}$LORA-2 addresses this problem by offering an explicit equality operator, :=:, which has all the normal properties of equality: commutativity, transitivity, congruence, etc. Another source of incomplete identity comes from the so-called *anonymous resources* (or *blank nodes*) in RDF [26]. We discuss equality and anonymous resources in Section 3.

2.3 Integrated Meta-knowledge Handling

Meta-Information. Most of Web data is semistructured in the sense that it has object-like structure with complex relationships among the objects, but the schema of these objects is not known to the application in advance. Two scenarios are possible here: (1) Data is shipped together with the schema. In this case the application must be able to query and explore the schema before processing the data. We call this scenario *schema-level meta-querying*; (2) Data is shipped without the schema, but it is self-describing (*i.e.*, some attribute information is embedded in the data). In this case, the application should be able to query whatever structural information is available as part of the data.

We call this situation *instance-level meta-querying*. We claim that querying meta-information should be as natural as querying instance data, and this capability should be integrated into the language *without* any extra machinery. The next section discusses how this is achieved in $\mathcal{F}$LORA-2 through its integration of F-logic and HiLog.

Reification. Since the advent of RDF [26], the ability to reify statements about Web resources has been viewed as one of the fundamental requirements for a Semantic Web language. Here, again, we claim that reification should be integrated into the language naturally, without extra machinery, and in a paradox-free way. Section 3.6 discusses how this is achieved in $\mathcal{F}$LORA-2 by building on the ideas underlying HiLog.

3   The $\mathcal{F}$LORA-2 Language

In this section we review the technical foundations of $\mathcal{F}$LORA-2 — F-logic [20], HiLog [9], and Transaction Logic [5] — and discuss various extensions to F-logic which were developed to meet the specific requirements of the Semantic Web.

3.1   F-Logic

F-logic subsumes predicate calculus both syntactically and semantically by explicitly introducing the concepts adapted from object-oriented programming. At the same time, much of F-logic can be viewed as a syntactic variant of classical logic, which makes implementation through source-level translation possible. However, we will not discuss implementation issues here for want of space.

Basic Syntax. F-logic uses first-order variable-free terms to represent *object identity* (abbr., OID), *e.g.*, john and father(mary). Objects can have single-valued, set-valued or Boolean attributes, for instance,

   mary[spouse → john, children →→ {alice,nancy}].
   mary[children →→ {jack}, married].

These formulas are called F-logic *molecules*. Note that each formula above asserts several facts *simultaneously*. In the first formula spouse → john says that object mary has a single-valued attribute spouse, whose value is OID john, while children →→ {alice, nancy} in the same object description says that the value of the set-valued attribute children is a set that *contains* two OIDs: alice and nancy. We emphasize "contains" because sets do not need to be specified all at once. For instance, the second formula above says that mary has another child jack. The attribute married in the second formula is Boolean: its value is *true* in the above example. This is one of the manifestations of the lazy knowledge assimilation principle of Section 2.

While some attributes of an object are specified explicitly, as facts, other attributes can be defined using inference rules. For instance, we can derive john[children →→ {alice, nancy, jack}] using the following rule:

X[children →» {C}] : − Y[spouse → X, children →» {C}].

Here we adopt the standard convention that uppercase symbols denote variables while symbols beginning with a lowercase letter denote constants.

F-logic objects can also have *methods*, which are functions that take arguments. For instance,

john[grade(cs305,f99) → 100, courses(f99) →» {cs305,cs306}].

says that john has a single-valued method, grade, whose value on the arguments cs305 and f99 is 100; it also has a set-valued method courses, whose value on the argument f99 is a set of OIDs that contains cs305 and cs306. Like attributes, methods can be defined using inference rules.

The F-logic syntax for *class membership* is john : student and for *subclass relationship* it is student :: person. In addition, F-logic supports specification of schema information. For instance, person[name ⇒ string, child ⇒» person] says that the signature of class person has two attributes, a single-valued attribute name and a set-valued attribute child. Moreover, the first attribute returns objects of type string and the second returns sets of objects such that each object in the set is of type person. F-logic also supports first-order predicate syntax and thus it integrates relational and object-oriented paradigms.

Querying Meta-Information. F-logic provides simple and natural facilities for exploring the structure of object data. Both schema information associated with classes and structures of individual objects can be queried by simply putting variables in the appropriate syntactic positions. For instance, to find out which set-valued methods defined in the *schema* of class student return objects of type person one can pose the following simple query:

?-   student[M ⇒» person].

The following query returns the type of the attribute name in class student and all student's superclasses:

?-   student::C, student[name ⇒ T].

The above two queries involve subclass relationship and type information (as indicated by the operators ::, ⇒, and ⇒»); they are called *schema-level meta-queries*. In contrast the following two queries return all methods that are defined for the object with OID john[1]:

?-   john[SingleM → _].
?-   john[SetM →» _].

Note that these queries check what is defined for the object itself rather than what is defined in the schema; they are thus called *instance-level meta-queries*. The two kinds of meta-queries can return different results for several reasons. First, in case of semistructured data, schema information might be incomplete

---

[1] Every occurrence of "_" stands for a don't-care variable.

and additional attributes can be defined for individual objects than what the schema reveals. Second, even if the schema is complete, the values of some attributes can be undefined for some of the objects in the class. In this latter case, the undefined attributes will not be returned by instance-level meta-queries, while they would be returned by schema-level meta-queries.

In Section 3.2, we will see more examples of meta-queries, which are enhanced by the facilities of HiLog.

Path Expressions. In addition to the basic syntax, F-logic supports *path expressions* to simplify navigation along single-valued and set-valued attribute and method invocations, and to avoid explicit join conditions [15]. The basic idea is to allow path expressions like O.M and O..M wherever OIDs are allowed.

A *single-valued* path expression, O.M, refers to the *unique* object R for which $O[M \rightarrow R]$ holds; a *set-valued* path expression, O..M, refers to some object, R, such that $O[M \twoheadrightarrow \{R\}]$ holds. Here the symbols O and M can be either an OID or a path expression. Furthermore, M can be a method with arguments, *e.g.*, $O.M(P_1,\ldots,P_k)$ is a valid path expression that refers to the object R that satisfies $O[M(P_1,\ldots,P_k) \rightarrow R]$.

Path expressions and F-logic formulas can be arbitrarily nested. This leads to a very concise and flexible query language for specifying object properties. For instance, the following path expression:

Paper[authors $\twoheadrightarrow$ {Author[name $\rightarrow$ john]}].publication..editors

refers to all editors of those papers in which john is the name of a co-author. The reader has probably noticed the conceptual similarity of such extended path expressions with XPath, which was developed after the extended path expressions were introduced to F-logic in [15].

Equality. Unlike regular logic programming languages, such as Prolog, in F-logic variable-free terms can become *equal* because of single-valued attributes and methods. For instance, consider the following facts:

mary[spouse $\rightarrow$ joseph].   mary[spouse $\rightarrow$ joe].   joseph[son $\twoheadrightarrow$ frank].

Since spouse is a single-valued attribute, it can have at most one value for any given object. Therefore, the OIDs joseph and joe must refer to the same object and whatever is true about joseph should also be true about joe. In particular, we should be able to derive that joe[son $\twoheadrightarrow$ frank].

On the Web, equality is also sometimes required to represent the fact that two different URIs represent the same resource. To accommodate this requirement, $\mathcal{F}$LORA-2 provides inference infrastructure for user-defined equality theories. This is made possible through the explicit equality predicate, :=:. Equality can be asserted as a fact or derived via rules, such as this:

U1 :=: U2 :− sameURL(U1,U2).

$\mathcal{F}$LORA-2 supports two built-in equality theories: one where :=: is the usual congruent equivalence relationship and the other where the functional constraints imposed by single-valued methods are enforced, *i.e.*, a[b → c] and a[b → d] implies c:=:d. The user can specify the desired default equality theory to use for each program module separately (see Section 4). The interested reader is referred to [42] for more information about equality maintenance in $\mathcal{F}$LORA-2.

3.2   HiLog

HiLog was introduced in [9] in order to extend logic programming with higher-order syntax, yet tractable and first-order semantics. In particular, the goal was to extend classical predicate calculus to enable flexible and natural querying of term structures and to support reification of atomic formulas. The simplest and yet most unusual illustration of HiLog is the following definition of the standard Prolog meta-predicate call:

$$call(X) : - X.$$

This means that HiLog does not distinguish between function terms and atomic formulas: The same variable can range over both and thus *atomic formulas are reified*. Variables can also range over function and predicate symbols, as in X(Y,a), and queries of the form ?- p(X), X, X(Y,X) are well within the boundaries of HiLog. The syntax for HiLog terms also extends that of classical logic. For instance, g(X)(f(a,X),Y)(b,Y) is perfectly fine, and there are several important uses for this multi-level syntax (see [9] for some).

Variables in the position of function and predicate symbols eliminate the need for many uses of non-logical meta-operators of Prolog and serve as a much more natural replacement for such uses. Combined with F-logic, HiLog enhances the already powerful meta-features of the language. For instance, in the combined language, one can write:

$$X[methods \twoheadrightarrow \{M\}] : - X[M(\_,\_) \to \_].$$

Thus, a query of the form

$$?- john[methods \twoheadrightarrow \{M\}].$$

will return the set of all 2-argument set-valued methods defined for the object john, while the query

$$X[methods \twoheadrightarrow \{M\}] : - X[M(\_) \Rightarrow \_].$$
$$?- student[methods \twoheadrightarrow \{M\}].$$

returns the set of all single-valued methods defined in the schema (signature) of class student.

3.3   Transaction Logic

A programming language, especially an object-oriented programming language, needs primitives for modifying the underlying state of the system. In a logic-based language, modifying the underlying state means updating the database part of the program. This need was recognized by the designers of Prolog who introduced the well-known assert and retract operators. From the very beginning, assert and retract were perceived as the necessary evil in the absence of a truly logical solution. Various attempts at formalizing updates in a logic programming language met with limited success (*e.g.*, [24,33,27]). A detailed discussion of this subject appears in [5]. One of the most serious drawbacks of these approaches is that they impose special programming styles (which require significant programming effort) and that they do not support subroutines — one of the most fundamental aspects of any programming language.

Transaction Logic [4,5] provides a comprehensive theory of logical updates in logic programming, which does not suffer from any of the above drawbacks, and its programming style is very much in the spirit of Prolog. The utility of Transaction Logic has been demonstrated on a vast range of applications: from databases to robot action planning to reasoning about actions to workflow analysis [6,10].

One of the implications of the update semantics provided by Transaction Logic is that update transactions are *atomic*. For instance, in Prolog, if a post-condition of a state-changing operator is false, the entire execution fails, returning the answer "No". Despite that, all the changes made by assert and retract would stay and the database may be left in a inconsistent state. This non-logical property is responsible for many complications in Prolog programming. Transaction Logic rectifies this and similar problems with updates in logic programming.

$\mathcal{F}$LORA-2 integrates F-logic and Transaction Logic along the lines of [19] with new extensions, which distinguishes queries from transactions and thus enables a number of compile-time checks. In Transaction Logic, both actions (transactions) and queries are represented as predicates. In $\mathcal{F}$LORA-2, transactions are expressed as object methods that are prefixed with the special symbol "#".

The following program is an implementation of a block-stacking robot in $\mathcal{F}$LORA-2. Here, the action stack is defined as a Boolean method of the robot.

```
R[#stack(0,X)]  : —  R : robot.
R[#stack(N,X)]  : —  R : robot, N > 0,
                     Y[#move(X)], R[#stack(N-1,Y)].
Y[#move(X)]     : —  Y : block, Y[clear], X[clear], X[widerThen(Y)],
                     delete{Y[on → Z]}, insert{Z[clear]},
                     insert{Y[on → X]}, delete{X[clear]}.
```

Informally, the program says that to stack a pyramid of N blocks on top of block X, the robot must find a block Y, move it onto X, and then stack N-1 blocks on top of Y. To move Y onto X, both blocks must be "clear" (*i.e.*, with no other block sitting on top of them), and X must be wider than Y. If these conditions are satisfied, the database will be updated accordingly. If any of the conditions fails, it means that the current attempted execution is not a valid try and another attempt will be made. If no valid execution is found, the transaction fails and no changes will be made to the database. Again, we would like to point out that in a similar situation an analogous Prolog program can leave the database in an inconsistent state.

3.4   Value and Code Inheritance

Object-oriented languages normally distinguish between *instance methods* and *class methods*. The former characterize all instances of a class while the latter characterize classes as objects [32]. Class methods are analogous to "static" methods in Java and instance methods correspond to nonstatic methods (which are sometimes also called "instance methods" in Java). In object-oriented data modeling, especially in dealing with semistructured objects on the Web, it is also useful to consider *object methods* that are defined explicitly for individual objects and override inheritance from superclasses. Object methods are similar to class methods except that they cannot be inherited. All three kinds of methods are specified using rules; the differences among them are illustrated with the following examples.

Example 1. Suppose we want to compute bonus for employees in the software department. Our policy is to award bonus based on the overall sales of the entire department. For example, every employee gets a bonus of 1% of the total amount of sales. This policy can be represented as follows:

```
softDept[bonus ⟶ N]   : − softDept[salesTotal ⟶ S], N is S * 1%.
softDept[salesTotal ⟶ 1000].
john : softDept.
mary : softDept.
```

The first two clauses in the above program are class method definitions for the methods bonus and salesTotal, respectively. The first rule defines the method bonus, whose value depends on the class method salesTotal, whose value is specified in the second clause. Both methods are class methods in the class salesTotal. With these rules, we can infer softDept[bonus ⟶ 10].

The last two facts simply state that john and mary are members of the class softDept. Although the program does not explicitly define the method bonus for john, since john is a member of the class softDept, it will inherit the method bonus together with its value (*i.e.*, 10). Similarly, we can derive mary[bonus ⟶ 10].

Example 2. Rather than giving the same bonus to every employee, suppose that the hardware department has a policy that rewards individual performance, where an employee gets a bonus of 10% of the amount of his/her sales. This idea can be illustrated using the following program:

```
code hardDept[bonus ⟶ N]   : − hardDept[sales ⟶ S], N is S * 10%.
      mike : hardDept.
      lucy : hardDept.
      mike[sales ⟶ 300].
      lucy[sales ⟶ 200].
```

Note that the first rule is preceded with a special keyword, code, which marks the definition of an *instance method*, bonus, for class hardDept. Recall that instance methods, as part of class specifications, apply to every member of the class. Intuitively, the symbol hardDept in the above rule is treated as a "placeholder" that stands for every member of the class hardDept. The remaining clauses state that mike and lucy are members of hardDept, and provide sales figures for mike and lucy, respectively.

Let us examine how the method bonus is computed for mike. Since mike is a member of hardDept and the first rule in the last program defines the method bonus for all instances of hardDept, mike inherits the following instantiated rule:

mike[bonus $\twoheadrightarrow$ N]   : $-$ mike[sales $\twoheadrightarrow$ S], N is S $*$ 10%.

where mike is substituted for hardDept. This instantiation corresponds to the so called *late binding* in traditional object-oriented languages like Java. From this rule and the facts, we can derive mike[bonus $\twoheadrightarrow$ 30] and lucy[bonus $\twoheadrightarrow$ 20].

Inheritance via instance method definitions, as illustrated in Example 2, is called *code inheritance*, because what is inherited is the code rather than the result returned by the method (as in Example 1). Code inheritance is commonly used in imperative object-oriented languages such as C^{++} and Java. Inheritance via class method definitions, as illustrated in Example 1, is called *value inheritance*, because what is inherited is the result returned by the method. This kind of inheritance is commonly used in AI [36,25].

The original F-logic [20] supports value inheritance only (and not satisfactorily at that — see [39]). Since $\mathcal{F}$LORA-2 is a practical knowledge engineering environment, it requires a theory of code inheritance as well. The interaction of the two kinds of inheritance introduces a number of interesting semantic and algorithmic problems, which were solved in [37].

3.5   Anonymous Identity

It has been argued in [11] that F-logic is a natural formalism to provide inference service for RDF(S) [26]. Representation of RDF statements with named resources in F-logic is rather straightforward. For instance, the statement *"Thomas Edison is the inventor of the bulb (denoted by URI http://foo.org/TheBulb)"* directly corresponds to the following F-logic statement

'http : //foo.org/TheBulb'[inventor $\twoheadrightarrow$ 'Thomas Edison'].

However, one difficulty arises in representing RDF statements with *anonymous resources*. Consider the following statement: *"Someone, named Thomas Edison, born in 1847, is the inventor of the resource http://foo.org/TheBulb."* The intent here is to make a structured resource *without a known object ID* and assert that it has two properties, name and born.

Anonymous resources were not envisioned in the original work on F-logic [20], but appropriate extensions were introduced in $\mathcal{F}$LORA-2 [42,38]. To represent anonymous objects, $\mathcal{F}$LORA-2 uses a special symbol, _#, called an *unnumbered anonymous ID symbol*, and a countable set of *numbered anonymous ID symbols*: _#1, _#2, ..., etc. The intended meaning is that each occurrence of _# denotes a distinct object ID that does not occur anywhere else in the program. All occurrences of the same numbered anonymous ID symbol, *e.g.*, _#1, within the same clause are treated as representing the same object ID, but this ID is distinct from any other ID used elsewhere in the program (including the occurrences of _#1 in a different clause). The reader is referred to [41] for a formal treatment of anonymous ID symbols in $\mathcal{F}$LORA-2.

Thus, in $\mathcal{F}$LORA-2, the above statement can be represented as follows:

'http://foo.org/TheBulb'[inventor ⟶ _#1],
_#1[name ⟶ 'Thomas Edison', born ⟶ 1847].

Note that here the two occurrences of _#1 are within the same clause (here "," means conjunction) and thus refer to the same object. If we want to state that "*Someone invented the bulb and someone called Thomas Edison was born in 1847*", then we could write

'http://foo.org/TheBulb'[inventor ⟶ _#],
_#[name ⟶ 'Thomas Edison', born ⟶ 1847].

Here we use unnumbered anonymous ID symbols. Even though they occur within the same clause, they refer to distinct objects.

The semantics of anonymous ID symbols in $\mathcal{F}$LORA-2 as well as other uses of this extension (*e.g.*, to represent RDF *containers*) are described in [41].

3.6   Reification

Reification is needed to make statements about statements and is considered an important part of RDF. Since statements are formulas, making statements about them implies that formulas must be somehow treated as objects.

In $\mathcal{F}$LORA-2, reification is specified using a new language construct, ${...}. The statement inside ${...} is reified and this reified formula itself is treated as an object identity. For instance, the statement "*Someone named John Doe believes that a person, called Thomas Edison, invented the bulb (represented by the resource http://foo.org/TheBulb)*" is expressed in $\mathcal{F}$LORA-2 as follows:

_#[
  name ⟶ 'John Doe',
  believes ⟶
      ${'http://foo.org/TheBulb'[inventor ⟶ {_#[name ⟶ 'Thomas Edison]}]}
].

In $\mathcal{F}$LORA-2, one can reason about reified statements in many interesting ways. For example, conjunctions, disjunctions, and even negations of formulas can be reified. Because reification can lead to logical paradoxes, especially in an expressive language like $\mathcal{F}$LORA-2, restrictions must be imposed on the language to prevent paradoxes. It turns out that it is enough to prohibit rules of the form X : — body, where X is a variable. A detailed account of the semantics of reification and of how paradoxes are avoided in $\mathcal{F}$LORA-2 can be found in [41].

4 Modules and Knowledge Integration

One of the most interesting and novel aspects of $\mathcal{F}$LORA-2 is its module system. It was designed with the intent to support autonomous agents and knowledge integration.

A $\mathcal{F}$LORA-2 module is an abstract container for a collection of data (which can be in main memory, a file, or a database), a chunk of program code, or an external procedure written in a different language. Modules can be created on the fly, and code or data can be loaded into the modules at runtime. Modules can be encapsulated, and the user can even specify the semantics for making inferences inside any module.

This section provides further details of the $\mathcal{F}$LORA-2 module system and discusses some applications.

Dynamic Module System. A $\mathcal{F}$LORA-2 program may consist of multiple modules. A *module* has a *name*, which other modules use to refer to information in that module, and the *content*. The content can be defined when the module is created, or it can be loaded (and, in fact, replaced) at any moment during runtime. The content of a module normally contains definitions of several classes, predicates, objects, and rules. Rules and data loaded into different modules do not interfere with each other, but they can interact: rule bodies can contain queries and even update operators that refer to other modules. This interaction is governed by encapsulation policies to be discussed later.

Suppose our program includes module people, which defines classes person, student, etc. Assume that student-objects expose a single-valued attribute name and a set-valued attribute major. Let us further assume that these definitions and rules are stored in a file named foo.flr. We can load this file into module people, and other modules will be able to query student-objects in it as follows:

```
?- load(foo >> people).
?- S:student[name → Name, major ↠ 'Computer Science']@people.
```

One can load a different file, say, bar.flr, into the same module at any time during execution with the command load(bar >> people). Since other modules have to know how to query the objects in module people, the code in file bar.flr would normally export the same interface to other modules. However, this is not always necessary, due to the flexible meta-programming features of $\mathcal{F}$LORA-2. A client module can *discover* the methods exported by the new content of people through a series of simple queries, such as

```
?- _[SingValMeth → _]@people, _[SetValMeth ↠ _]@people.
```

where "_" is an anonymous variable. It is even possible to find out which modules define, say, attribute major, by placing a variable in the module position:

?- _[major —↠ _]@Module.

This type of flexibility is important in knowledge integration systems where the mediators can formulate the right queries to the various data sources based on the results of previously posed meta-queries.

A module can also be created empty and then filled in with rules and data. For instance, the statement

?- newmodule{stuff}.

creates a module named stuff; it can be filled with content either by loading it from a file (using the load statement) or through insertion of facts and rules at runtime:

?- insert{p(a)@stuff, john[major —↠ cs]@stuff}.
?- insertrule{(q(X):-p(X))@stuff, (X[Y → Z] :- p(X,Z),q(Y))@stuff}.

The content of a module, say stuff, can be manipulated freely by the *owner* module — the module that created module stuff (*i.e.*, the one that executed the newmodule command). Previously inserted facts and rules can also be deleted.

?- delete{p(a)@stuff}.
?- deleterule{(q(X):-p(X))@stuff}.

Such ability to create the content of a module on-the-fly is very useful for systems of autonomous intelligent agents. An agent may need to create a new module dynamically for several reasons. One is to store acquired data or rules, which constitute a separate corpus of knowledge. Storing this corpus in a separate module can prevent unforeseen interaction with the agent's main code or other acquired knowledge. Second, an agent may need to create another module in order to spawn off a "child" agent, similarly to how processes create child processes in operating systems.[2]

Encapsulation. Encapsulation is a generally accepted software engineering device, which helps prevent erroneous interactions among software components. $\mathcal{F}$LORA-2 supports encapsulation at the level of modules, and each module can encapsulate several classes. To limit the ways in which other modules can interact with a given module, the latter exports the methods and predicates that other modules can query or update. This is accomplished using the export directive. When it is used as a compile-time directive, the exported interfaces become available when the program is loaded into a module. An export instruction can also be executed at runtime. A method or a predicate can be exported as either readable or updatable. The latter allows the corresponding facts to be both queried and modified. Finally, interfaces can be exported to all modules or only to a specific list of modules.

The following directive, if executed in a module, people, will allow every other module to query the membership of class student and the membership of each of its subclasses.

---

[2] A module designer or owner can also protect the content from being owned (and thus modified) by other modules through the noowner directive.

?- export _: student readable.

In contrast, the following directive

?- export _[major $\twoheadrightarrow$ _] updatable to administrator.

will allow the administrator module (but no other modules) to not only query, but also change the majors of student-objects in module person. If module root is the owner of module people then it can also control what is exported by module person by executing an appropriate export directive in the latter module. For instance, executing

?- (export _: major readable)@person.

will give the right to query student majors, but the update privilege stays with the administrator module only (and the owner module).

Customized Semantics of Modules. A system that integrates different information sources or agents should be prepared to deal with modules that are implemented using different semantics. The module system of $\mathcal{F}$LORA-2 has been specially designed so as to allow each module to have its own semantics, which can vary according to three parameters: equality maintenance, inheritance semantics, and customized semantics.

- *Equality Maintenance.* As discussed in Sections 2 and 3.1, it is important to be able to equate OIDs that denote the same resource. However, $\mathcal{F}$LORA-2 recognizes that different equality theories are possible. First, there is a standard theory, where equality is a congruent equivalence relationship. F-logic [20] introduces one additional axiom that allows to infer new equalities from single-valued methods. Finally, for efficiency reasons, it is important to be able to tell the system that no equality maintenance is required if a certain module is known to not need this feature. Thus, at present, $\mathcal{F}$LORA-2 supports three equality options: basic, flogic, and none.
- *Inheritance Semantics.* This is the second parameter that a knowledge engineer can vary to tune the semantics of a module. At present, the user can request either the default inheritance semantics, as described in [39] (using the flogic option), or inheritance can be turned off (which can speed up queries, if inheritance is not needed).
- *Customized Semantics.* $\mathcal{F}$LORA-2 provides APIs, which allow the user to specify the semantics of a module through a set of axioms, which will be loaded into the module when it is created. The set of the axioms is placed in a file, which is communicated to the module loader using the custom option.

For instance, the following directive says that the module should be created with no support for equality, with F-logic style inheritance, and additional axioms that are defined in a file:

: − setsemantics equality(none), inheritance(flogic), custom('myaxioms.P').

The system also provides a primitive to query the semantic parameters used by any of the currently loaded modules. Thus, the architecture of $\mathcal{F}$LORA-2 supports integration of heterogeneous resources with different semantics.

5   Discussion and Conclusion

$\mathcal{F}$LORA-2 provides a large number of fundamental features that are essential for modeling semantic information on the Web. These include rules, classification, and frame-based syntax, powerful ways of processing meta-information, reification, transactional updates, and so on. All this is achieved using a natural and coherent syntax, which is supported by a comprehensive model-theoretic semantics for the unified language. In this way, $\mathcal{F}$LORA-2 is an embodiment of the principles outlined in Section 2.

We should note that other Semantic Web languages, such as OWL [35] and RDF [26], do follow some of the principles discussed in Section 2. However, these languages are rather limited in their features compared with $\mathcal{F}$LORA-2. In particular, they do not support general rules (including recursive rules and rules with negation in the rule body), common-sense reasoning, multiple inheritance, or logical updates. As a result, designing such languages and defining their semantics is in many ways a simpler task.

$\mathcal{F}$LORA-2 was inspired by and has inspired a number of other F-logic based systems, such as FLORID [14], TFL [8], FLIP [28], Ontobroker [12], and TRIPLE [34]. None of these systems supports HiLog, none (except TFL) supports Transaction Logic, none (except FLORID) supports inheritance, and none (except TRIPLE) supports reification.

The module systems of $\mathcal{F}$LORA-2 has some similarity with TRIPLE. However, in TRIPLE modules cannot be created and reloaded at run time — they have to be defined before the system starts running. Likewise, TRIPLE does not support encapsulation and, although one of its design goals is to enable integration of modules with different semantics, the system does not provide infrastructural support for this goal.

We have presented an overview of the $\mathcal{F}$LORA-2 system, its underlying design principles, logical foundations, language features, as well as its novel module system. Although $\mathcal{F}$LORA-2 already provides a wealth of features in support of semantic reasoning on the Web, a number of important issues still need to be addressed. For instance, we believe that the ability to handle inconsistent information should be part of the infrastructure. Handling imprecise and probabilistic information is another important missing piece. These issues can possibly be addressed with the help of paraconsistent and probabilistic logics such as [2,21, 22,31]. Another possible extension could be in the direction of prioritized rules, such as those described in [16].

References

1. A. Bernstein and B. N. Grosof. Beyond monotonic inheritance: Towards semantic web process ontologies. unpublished manuscript, 2003.
2. H. Blair and V. Subrahmanian. Paraconsistent logic programming. *Theoretical Computer Science*, 68:135–154, 1989.
3. A. J. Bonner. Workflow, transactions, and datalog. In *ACM International Symposium on Principles of Database Systems (PODS)*, 1999.

4. A. J. Bonner and M. Kifer. An overview of transaction logic. *Theoretical Computer Science*, 133:205–265, October 1994.
5. A. J. Bonner and M. Kifer. A logic for programming database transactions. In J. Chomicki and G. Saake, editors, *Logics for Databases and Information Systems*, chapter 5, pages 117–166. Kluwer Academic Publishers, March 1998.
6. A. J. Bonner and M. Kifer. Results on reasoning about action in transaction logic. In [13]. Springer-Verlag, 1998.
7. M. Bugliesi and H. M. Jamil. A stable model semantics for behavioral inheritance in deductive object oriented languages. In *International Conference on Database Theory (ICDT)*, 1995.
8. J. Carsi, P. Letelier, and P. Palma. A dood system for treating the schema evolution problem, 1998.
9. W. Chen, M. Kifer, and D. S. Warren. HiLog: A foundation for higher-order logic programming. *Journal of Logic Programming*, 15(3):187–230, February 1993.
10. H. Davulcu, M. Kifer, C. Ramakrishnan, and I. Ramakrishnan. Logic based modeling and analysis of workflows. In *ACM International Symposium on Principles of Database Systems (PODS)*, 1998.
11. S. Decker, D. Brickley, J. Saarela, and J. Angele. A query and inference service for RDF. In *QL'98 – The Query Languages Workshop*, December 1998.
12. S. Decker, M. Erdmann, D. Fensel, and R. Studer. Ontobroker: Ontology based access to distributed and semi-structured information. In R. M. et al., editor, *Database Semantics, Semantic Issues in Multimedia Systems*, pages 351–369. Kluwer Academic Publisher, Boston, 1999.
13. B. Freitag, H. Decker, M. Kifer, and A. Voronkov, editors. *Transactions and Change in Logic Databases*, volume 1472 of *LNCS*. Springer-Verlag, Berlin, 1998.
14. J. Frohn, R. Himmeröder, G. Lausen, W. May, and C. Schlepphorst. Managing semistructured data with FLORID: A deductive object-oriented perspective. *Information Systems*, 23(8):589–613, 1998.
15. J. Frohn, G. Lausen, and H. Uphoff. Access to objects by path expressions and rules. In *International Conference on Very Large Data Bases (VLDB)*, 1994.
16. B. N. Grosof. Prioritized conflict handling for logic programs. In *International Logic Programming Symposium*, 1997.
17. H. M. Jamil. Implementing abstract objects with inheritance in Datalog[neg]. In *International Conference on Very Large Data Bases (VLDB)*, 1997.
18. H. M. Jamil. A logic-based language for parametric inheritance. In A. G. Cohn, F. Giunchiglia, and B. Selman, editors, *KR2000: Principles of Knowledge Representation and Reasoning*, San Francisco, 2000. Morgan Kaufmann.
19. M. Kifer. Deductive and object-oriented data languages: A quest for integration. In *International Conference on Deductive and Object-Oriented Databases (DOOD)*, volume 1013 of *Lecture Notes in Computer Science*, Singapore, 1995. Springer-Verlag. Keynote Address at the 3rd International Conference on Deductive and Object-Oriented databases.
20. M. Kifer, G. Lausen, and J. Wu. Logical foundations of object-oriented and frame-based languages. *Journal of ACM (JACM)*, 42:741–843, July 1995.
21. M. Kifer and E. Lozinskii. A logic for reasoning with inconsistency. *Journal of Automated Reasoning*, 9(2):179–215, November 1992.
22. M. Kifer and V. Subrahmanian. Theory of generalized annotated logic programming and its applications. *Journal of Logic Programming*, 12(4):335–368, April 1992.
23. H.-G. Kim. Pragmatics of the semantic web. In *Semantic Web Workshop at WWW-2002*, 2002.

24. R. A. Kowalski. Database updates in event calculus. *Journal of Logic Programming*, 12(1&2):121–146, January 1992.
25. L. V. S. Lakshmanan and K. Thirunarayan. Declarative frameworks for inheritance. In J. Chomicki and G. Saake, editors, *Logics for Databases and Information Systems*, pages 357–388. Kluwer Academic Publishers, 1998.
26. O. Lasilla and R. S. (editors). Resource description framework (RDF) model and syntax specification. Technical report, W3C, February 1999. http://www.w3.org/TR/1999/REC-rdf-syntax-19990222/.
27. G. Lausen and B. Ludäscher. Updates by reasoning about states. In *Second International East/West Database Workshop*, Klagenfurt, Austria, September 1994.
28. B. Ludäscher. The FLIP system (F-logic to XSB-Prolog compiler). http://www.informatik.uni-freiburg.de/~ludaesch/flip/, 1994.
29. W. May and P. Kandzia. Nonmonotonic inheritance in object-oriented deductive database languages. *Journal of Logic and Computation*, 11(4), 2001.
30. W. May, B. Ludäscher, and G. Lausen. Well-founded semantics for deductive object-oriented database languages. In *International Conference on Deductive and Object-Oriented Databases (DOOD)*, 1997.
31. R. Ng and V. Subrahmanian. Probabilistic logic programming. *Information and Computation*, 101(2):150–201, December 1992.
32. F. Rabitti, E. Bertino, W. Kim, and D. Woelk. A model of authorization for next-generation database systems. *ACM Transactions on Database Systems*, 16(1):88–131, March 1991.
33. R. Reiter. Formalizing database evolution in the situation calculus. In *Conference on Fifth Generation Computer Systems*, 1992.
34. M. Sintek and S. Decker. TRIPLE – a query, inference, and transformation language for the semantic web. In *International Semantic Web Conference*, 2002.
35. M. K. Smith, C. Welty, and D. L. McGuinness. OWL web ontology language guide. http://www.w3.org/TR/owl-guide/, 2003.
36. D. S. Touretzky. *The Mathematics of Inheritance*. Morgan-Kaufmann, Los Altos, CA, 1986.
37. G. Yang. *A Model Theory for Nonmonotonic Multiple Value and Code Inheritance in Object-Oriented Knowledge Bases*. PhD thesis, SUNY at Stony Brook, December 2002.
38. G. Yang and M. Kifer. Implementing an efficient DOOD system using a tabling logic engine. In *First International Conference on Computational Logic, DOOD'2000 Stream*, July 2000.
39. G. Yang and M. Kifer. Well-founded optimism: Inheritance in frame-based knowledge bases. In *International Conference on Ontologies, DataBases, and Applications of Semantics (ODBASE)*, October 2002.
40. G. Yang and M. Kifer. Inheritance and rules in object-oriented semantic web languages. In *International Workshop on Rules and Rule Markup Languages for the Semantic Web (RuleML)*, 2003.
41. G. Yang and M. Kifer. Reasoning about anonymous resources and meta statements on the semantic web. *Journal of Data Semantics*, 2004. To appear.
42. G. Yang, M. Kifer, and C. Zhao. $\mathcal{F}$LORA-2: User's Manual. http://flora.sourceforge.net/, June 2002.

Understanding the Semantic Web through Descriptions and Situations

Aldo Gangemi[1] and Peter Mika[2]

[1] Laboratory for Applied Ontology,
Institute for Cognitive Sciences and Technology,
National Research Council, I-00137 Rome, Italy
gangemi@ip.rm.cnr.it
[2] Vrije Universiteit Amsterdam,
1081HV Amsterdam, The Netherlands
pmika@cs.vu.nl

Abstract. The Semantic Web is a powerful vision that is getting to grips with the challenge of providing more human-oriented web services. Hence, reasoning with and across distributed, partially implicit assumptions (contextual knowledge), is a milestone.
Ontologies are a primary means to deploy the Semantic Web vision, but few work has been done on them to manage the context-dependency of Web knowledge. In this paper we introduce an ontology for representing a variety of reified contexts and states of affairs, called D&S, currently implemented as a plug-in to the DOLCE foundational ontology, and its application to two cases: an ontology for communication situations and roles, and an ontology for peer-to-peer communication. The reified contexts represented in D&S have a rich structure, and are a middleware between full-fledged formal contexts and theories, and the often poor vocabularies implemented in Web ontologies...

1 Introduction

Ontologies, as discussed in Artificial Intelligence, are formal, partial specifications of an agreement over the description of a domain [1]. Ontology-based communication and the integration of passive knowledge sources, dynamic agents and services on a global scale is also known as the vision of the Semantic Web. However, the difficulty of reaching agreements in large and diverse communities and the decentralized, uncontrolled nature of the current web suggests that the Semantic Web will be likely to propose new challenges unknown to current centralized, single authority ontology applications.

Due to its decentralized nature, the Semantic Web will be dominated by multiple domain ontologies used in various systems by the different communities. Once the consensus surrounding the ontology of a domain breaks down, merely the constructs of the ontology language remain to aid interpretation. A solution could come from the adoption of a universal upper ontology; such attempts however seem to fail as upper ontologies are broken apart into hundreds of contexts

R. Meersman et al. (Eds.): CoopIS/DOA/ODBASE 2003, LNCS 2888, pp. 689–706, 2003.
© Springer-Verlag Berlin Heidelberg 2003

or microtheories. A monolithic ontology that is adopted as a standard is not convincing either under many respects (see [2]).

Adds to the challenge that scalability requirements will push towards the use of automated methods to acquire, translate or merge ontologies. Such methods are known to degrade the level of formality of ontologies, resulting in the prevalence of lightweight ontologies [3]. We believe that such limitation is fundamental rather than technical; we refer the reader to the paper of Elst and Abecker for a detailed treatment of the contradiction of sharing scope, stability and formality of knowledge in information systems [4].

A possible direction might be adopting a complex workflow for ontology maintenance that allows a periodical maintenance of lightweight ontologies by means of well-crafted, expressive reference ontologies [2], and according to reconciliation, integration, and merging procedures [5]. But the massively distributed and unpredictable nature of Semantic Web ontologies does not easily yield to such a treatment for the level of detail required by the workflow.

The breakdown of consensus and the weakening of formality means a loss of both defining aspects of an ontology meant for communication. Ontologies transferred through the Semantic Web will be reduced to scanty structures, due to the lack of commitment and the low expressivity of the standard constructs that are used. We argue that such black-box ontologies will be a fact of life; which means we have to look elsewhere for meaning to be recreated.

We propose a mechanism to mime the human cognitive ability to contextualize our ontological commitments, even when we have scanty evidence of them. This ability originates from extensive reification, and from the representation of other cognitive processes described e.g. by Gestalt psychology [6], which allow us to refer synthetically to some commonly agreed context labels.

From the Semantic Web perspective, we propose that –when a complete theory is lacking– we may still recurse to contextual evidence to help interpretation. An ontological context can be preliminarily defined here as a first-order entity, usually quite complex, which is defined by certain typical elements that result from the reification of the elements of a theory.

In this paper we describe two advances along the road towards representing communication contexts for the Semantic Web. We have developed and are exploiting an ontology of contexts, called Descriptions and Situations (D&S), which provides a principled approach to context reification through a clear separation of states-of-affairs and their interpretation based on a non-physical context, called a description. The ontology of descriptions also offers a situation-description template and reification rules for the principal categories of the DOLCE foundational ontology. Both DOLCE and the D&S extension to DOLCE are being developed in the EU WonderWeb project[1].

Our second contribution is a preliminary attempt to an ontology of communication. This ontology is modelled using D&S as this framework allows us to separate our theories of communication and interpretation (descriptions) from the level of a Semantic Web model (a setting where communication situations

---

[1] http://wonderweb.semanticweb.org

take place). Integrating theories of communication (linguistic theories) with theories of interpretation (computational semiotics), such an ontology is in fact an attempt to describe ontology-based communication on the Semantic Web. The inclusion of a theory of interpretation in this ontology is crucial in relating the contexts of ontology use to the communication system.

Although the Semantic Web is largely a vision, we demonstrate the validity of this ontology by extending it to model a peer-to-peer ontology-based knowledge sharing environment under development within the European SWAP (Semantic Web And Peer-to-Peer) project[2]. The SWAP system is a forerunner of Semantic Web technology and implements several important aspects of the vision, namely the use of ontologies for organizing domain knowledge and a distributed architecture without centralized control.

The remaining of the paper is organized as follows. In Sect. 2, we introduce the Descriptions and Situations framework and discuss its implementation in DOLCE. Next, in Sect. 3 we describe the development of the ontology of communication and show how it may applied and adapted for the SWAP system. Lastly, we conclude with a discussion of related and future work in Sect. 4.

2 Descriptions and Situations

This Section presents the motivation and development of our ontology of descriptions, called Descriptions and Situations (D&S). The D&S ontology is designed as a plug-in to the DOLCE foundational ontology [2], which is the first module of a future Foundational Ontology Library being developed within the European WonderWeb project. The WonderWeb architecture envisages a tight integration among web languages, ontology learning and manipulation tools, foundational ontologies and ontology building methodologies. With additional effort, however, the D&S ontology may be adapted to other foundational ontologies.

2.1 Motivation

Foundational ontologies in WonderWeb are ontologies that contain a specification of domain-independent concepts and relations based on formal principles derived from linguistics, philosophy, and mathematics. Formal principles are needed to allow an explicit comparison between alternative ontologies. Examples of formal principles are spatio-temporal localization, topological closure, heterogeneity of parts, dependency on the intention of agents, etc. We refer to [2] to a detailed explanation.

While formalizing the principles governing physical objects or events is (quite) straightforward, intuition comes to odds when an ontology needs to be extended with *non-physical objects*, such as social institutions, organizations, plans, regulations, narratives, mental contents, schedules, parameters, diagnoses, etc. In fact, important fields of investigation have negated an ontological primitiveness to non-physical objects [7], because they are taken to have meaning only in

---

[2] http://swap.semanticweb.org

combination with some other entity, i.e. their intended meaning results from a statement. For example, a norm, a plan, or a social role are to be represented as a (set of) statement(s), not as concepts. This position is documented by the almost exclusive attention dedicated by many important theoretical frameworks (BDI agent model, theory of trust, situation calculus, formal context analysis), to states of affairs, facts, beliefs, viewpoints, contexts, whose logical representation is set at the level of theories or models, not at the level of concepts or relations.

On the other hand, recent work (e.g. [7]) addresses non-physical objects as first-order entities that can change, or that can be manipulated similarly to physical entities. This means that many relations and axioms that are valid for physical entities can be used for non-physical ones as well.

Here we support the position by which non-physical entities can be represented both as theories/models and as concepts with explicit reification rules, and we share the following motivations:

- Technology and society are full of reifications, for example when we divide human experience into social, cultural, educational, political, religious, legal, economic, industrial, scientific or technological experiences
- In realistic domains, specially in socially-intensive applications (e.g. law, finance, business, politics), a significant amount of terms convey concepts related to non-physical entities, and such concepts seem to be tightly interrelated
- Interrelations between theories are notoriously difficult to be manipulated, then it would be an advantage to represent non-physical objects as instances of concepts instead of models satisfying some theory
- For many domains of application, we are faced with partial theories and partial models that are explicated and/or used at various detail levels. Partiality and granularity are two more reasons to have some theories and models manipulated as first-order entities
- Natural languages are able to reify whatever fragment of (usually informal) theories and models by simply creating or reusing a noun. Once linguistically reified, a theory or a model (either formal or informal) enters a life-cycle that allows agents to communicate even in presence of partial (or even no) information about the reified theory or model. The Web contains plenty of examples of such creatures: catalog subjects or topics, references to distributed resources, unstructured or semi-structured (but explicitly referenced) contents, such as plans, methods, regulations, formats, profiles, etc., and even linguistic elements and texts (taken independently from a particular physical encoding) can be considered a further example
- Recent unpublished work by one of the authors reports that more than 25% of WordNet (v1.6) noun synsets [8] can be formalised as non-physical object classes

In general, we feel entitled to say that representing ontological (reified) contexts is a difficult alternative to avoid, when so much domain-oriented and linguistic categorisations involve reification. However, we also want to provide an explicit account of the contextual nature of non-physical entities and thus aim for a reification that accounts to some extent for the partial and hybrid structure of such entities.

From the logical viewpoint, any reification of theories and models provides a first order representation. From the ontological engineering viewpoint, a straightforward reification is not enough, since the elements resulting from reification must be framed within an ontology, possibly built according to a foundational ontology.

We also need specific reification rules for at least some distinct elements of a theory or a model. Moreover, from a practical viewpoint, the actual import of theories and models (when they are used as concepts) into an ontology requires not only reification rules, but also mapping and inheritance rules. This partial and hybrid transformation allows an easy grasp and manipulation of reified theories and models.

2.2   An Ontology of Descriptions and Situations

D&S is intended to provide a framework for representing contexts, methods, norms, theories, situations, and models at first-order, thus allowing a partial specification of those entities.

Partial specification[3] is the usual assumption for cognitive artifacts used in many rational activities: planning, viewpoints, perspectival thinking, modular conceptualizations, naïve theories, granularities, problem solving methods, etc.

D&S axioms try to capture the notion of "situation" as a *unitarian* entity out of a "state of affairs" [2]. The *unity* criterion is provided by a "description".

A *state of affairs* is any non-empty set SoA of assertions $a_{1..n}$ that are individually coherent with the axioms in a first-order theory O, called a "ground ontology". A SoA is a second-order entity, therefore it cannot be represented (as such) as an individual in O. Examples: a clinical data set, a set of temperatures with spatio-temporal coordinates, etc.

A *description* is an entity that *partly represents* a (possibly formalized) theory T (or one of its elements) that can be "conceived" by an agent: either human, collective, social, or artificial. A description can be an individual in O. Examples: a diagnosis, a climate change theory, etc.

A *situation* is *constituted by* the entities and the relations among them that are mentioned in assertions $a_{1..n}$ from a SoA, and it is an entity in O that *partly represents* a (possibly formalized) model M for T, according to the axioms in O. A situation can be an individual in O. $a_{1..n}$ must be systematically related to

---

[3] Any axiomatic theory and its models are partial, since they usually formalize only part of the assumptions or facts in a domain of interest. This can be called external incompleteness, and should be taken for granted, at least for the well known logical reasons. On the other hand, internal incompleteness can be considered for entities that represent only some of the elements of a theory or a model. Internal incompleteness is assumed for D&S descriptions and situations.

the components of a description in order to constitute a situation.[4] Example: a clinical condition, a climate change history, etc.

Intuitively, when a description is applied to a state of affairs, some *structure* (a "situation") emerges (this reflects the cognitive structuring cognitive process [6]). The emerging structure is not necessarily equivalent to the actual structure.

Due to its neutrality with respect to realism, D&S can generalize the distinction between state of affairs and description, in order to obtain an epistemological layering. Epistemological layering consists of assuming that any logical structure L_i (either formal or capable of being at least partly formalised) is built upon a structure SoA that it describes according to a theory T_i (either formal or capable of being at least partly formalised). In other words, T_i describes what kind of ontological commitment L_i is supposed to have within the epistemological layer that is shared by the encoder of an ontology.

Epistemological layering reflects the so-called *figure-ground* shifting cognitive process [6]. For example, a functional biological theory can assume a molecular biological theory as "data" in a SoA, instead of including it, or a legal norm can overrule a social practice without including it.

A ground ontology O is here restricted to be a foundational ontology that in its signature contains at least one unary predicate P and one n-ary predicate R whose universe is restricted to P. D&S adds to O by inserting two unary predicates: D (Description) and S (Situation), and a binary predicate *satisfies*, holding between S and a subset of D, called SD (Situation Description):

$$SD(x) \rightarrow D(x) \tag{1}$$

$$satisfies(x, y) \rightarrow S(x) \land SD(y) \tag{2}$$

$$satisfiedBy(y, x) \leftrightarrow satisfies(x, y) \tag{3}$$

$$\forall x. S(x) \rightarrow \exists y. SD(y) \land satisfies(x, y) \tag{4}$$

D is inserted under one of the predicates P_i in O, provided that D instances are unitarian, non-physical entities depending on the intentionality of an agent. *Unitarian* entities, *non-physicality* and *intentionality* are introduced in [2]. For example, in DOLCE D is inserted under the predicate "Non-physical Endurant". If no P_i can subsume D, D is inserted as a new most general predicate. O enriched with D&S is called $O+$.

A further transformation induced by D&S on O is the so-called *functional* (or "selectional") *structure*. For each most general predicate P_i in $O+$, there exists a predicate P_i^D subsumed by D (but disjoint from SD), and between each pair P_i, P_i^D the *selects* binary predicate may hold when an instance of P_i is a constituent of a situation:

---

[4] Other names have been proposed for these concepts, for example flux, unstructured world, or data for "state of affairs", conceptualization, representation, schema, or function for "description", setting, Gestalt, configuration, or structure for "situation". Context is a word used for all three concepts, thus reaching a very high ambiguity score. "Situation" in D&S is not related to "situations" in situation calculus: these are independent punctual entities used to assemble fluents, while in D&S situations are not bound to temporal instants, and depend on an s-description.

$$P_i^D(y) \rightarrow D(y) \tag{5}$$

$$\neg(P_i^D(y) \wedge SD(y)) \tag{6}$$

$$selects(x, y) \rightarrow P_i^D(x) \wedge P_i(y) \tag{7}$$

For example, in DOLCE a "Perdurant" can be "selected by" a "Course", an "Endurant" can be selected by a "Functional Role", and a "Region" can be selected by a "Parameter".

The functional structure in $O+$ requires that a P_i^D is a *(temporary) component of* an SD_i, and for each P_i in the *setting* of an S_i that *satisfies* an SD_i, a P_i is *selected by* a P_i^D.

$$\forall x.P_i^D(x) \rightarrow \exists y.SD(y) \wedge t\_component(y, x) \tag{8}$$

$$\forall x.SD(x) \rightarrow \exists y.P_i^D(y) \wedge t\_component(x, y) \tag{9}$$

$$\forall x.S(x) \rightarrow \forall y.part(x, y) \rightarrow S(y) \tag{10}$$

$$settingFor(x, y) \rightarrow constituent(x, y) \wedge S(x) \wedge P_i(y) \tag{11}$$

$$\forall x.S(x) \rightarrow \exists y.P_i(y) \wedge settingFor(x, y) \tag{12}$$

$$settingFor(x, y) \rightarrow \exists zw.P_i^D(z) \wedge SD(w) \wedge \tag{13}$$
$$t\_component(w, z) \wedge satisfies(x, w) \wedge selectedBy(y, z)$$

"Component" and "setting for" binary predicates can have various names. These ones are used in the extension of DOLCE (DOLCE+). *T_component* is the non-transitive, systemic restriction of "(temporary) part", while *setting for* is a "constitution" relation holding between a situation and its constitutive elements. "Part" and "constitution" are defined in [2].

Functional structure in $O+$ allows to maintain a dependency of the constituents of a situation, on the components of an s-description (cf. Ax.13). Such dependency is the analytic motivation for a situation to "satisfy" an s-description. Since situations and s-descriptions are partial representations of models and theories respectively, this notion of satisfaction "mirrors" the satisfiability relation between models and theories.

Realistic uses of D&S that empower ground ontologies have richer structures. For example, extending DOLCE with D&S requires finding a component of SD for each most general concept in DOLCE. DOLCE features four such categories: Endurant, Perdurant, Quality, and Abstract. Abstract includes one major subconcept: Region. Qualities in most applications are mediated by a position in some (dimensional) region. DOLCE+ currently simplifies DOLCE's ontological commitment by considering only regions within abstracts, and ignoring qualities.

Figure 1 shows a UML class diagram of the full ontology, with the following semantics: generalization is interpreted as subsumption, tagged associations are interpreted as binary predicates, classes as unary predicates, and cardinalities as generalized quantifications on axioms that use binary predicates and their inverses.

DOLCE+ s-description components have the following types: "Course (of events)" for Perdurant, "Function(al role)" for Endurant, and "Parameter" for Region. The relation "selects" is specialized for c-descriptions accordingly:

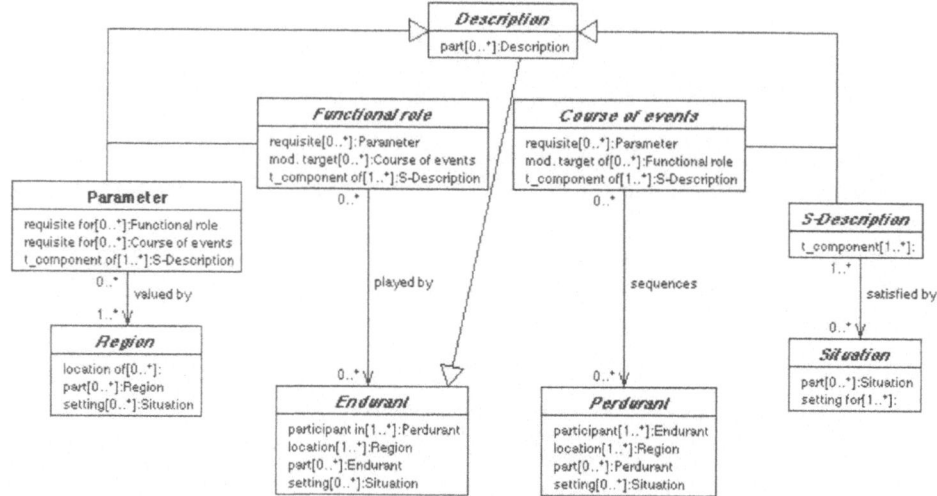

Fig. 1. UML model of the D&S ontology and its relations to the top-level of DOLCE

$$SD(x) \rightarrow \exists y.COU(y) \vee FR(y) \vee PAR(y) \wedge t\_component(x,y) \qquad (14)$$

$$COU(x) \rightarrow \exists y.SD(y) \wedge t\_component(y,x) \qquad (15)$$

$$FR(x) \rightarrow \exists y.SD(y) \wedge t\_component(y,x) \qquad (16)$$

$$PAR(x) \rightarrow \exists y.SD(y) \wedge t\_component(y,x) \qquad (17)$$

$$sequences(x,y) \rightarrow selects(x,y) \wedge COU(x) \wedge Perdurant(y) \qquad (18)$$

$$playedBy(x,y) \rightarrow selects(x,y) \wedge FR(x) \wedge Endurant(y) \qquad (19)$$

$$valuedBy(x,y) \rightarrow selects(x,y) \wedge PAR(x) \wedge Region(y) \qquad (20)$$

$$PAR(x) \rightarrow \exists y.Region(y) \wedge valuedBy(x,y) \qquad (21)$$

It is easy to notice that, while in general s-descriptions require at least one component (a c-description, cf. Ax.9), no further specification can be given of what c-description is required. For example, in DOLCE+, an s-description can be composed of functions only, of courses only, of parameters only, or of a mixture of them (cf. Ax.14). This is quite natural, since the requirement comes from D&S functional structure, but further distinctions derive from the categories in the ground ontology.

C-description types can be related one to another in peculiar ways. For example, *inter-categorial* relations (holding within different kinds of c-description) have the following argument restrictions:

$$modalityFor(x,y) \rightarrow FR(x) \wedge COU(y) \qquad (22)$$

$$requisiteFor(x,y) \rightarrow PAR(x) \wedge (COU(y) \vee FR(y)) \qquad (23)$$

"Modality for" is the functional counterpart of the "participation" relation from DOLCE ground ontology: in analogy with endurants participating in perdurants, functions have a way of participating to courses (according to a certain s-description). For example if a person p participates in an event e according to a mental plan, a social habit, a legal norm, etc., then *the function f played by p* can respectively be "willing", "hopeful", "cautious", "obliged", "allowed", etc. with reference to a course c that sequences e. Modalities and functions can be also used to characterize special participation relations, e.g. so-called "thematic roles".

"Requisite for" is the functional counterpart of the "localization" relation from DOLCE: in analogy with regions being the localizations of endurants or perdurants, parameters give requisites to functions and courses for endurants or perdurants to be localized (according to a certain s-description).

Examples of descriptions and situations in DOLCE+ include: a clinical condition (situation) with a diagnosis (s-description) made by some agent (functional-role), a case in point (situation) constrained by a certain norm (s-description), a murder (situation) reported by a witness (functional role) in a testimony (s-description), a 40kmph (region) as the value for a speed limit (parameter) in the context of an accident (state of affairs) described as a speed excess case (situation) in an area covered by traffic code (s-description) etc.

D&S is currently employed in various academic and industrial domains, including legal norm dynamics, services, financial risk, biological pathways, fishery information, etc. In the following, we will demonstrate the use of D&S through the development of an ontology of communication. While this is an instantiation of the D&S schema, the observant reader may note that the ties between the two ontologies run deeper: interpretation logically depends on the notion of a description, which on its turn depends on an intuitive notion of referencing to (having an intention towards) some configuration. Such referencing requires a communication setting including information objects. A communication setting can be understood only within a semiotic framework, and the circle is complete.

3 Modelling Ontology-Based Communication with D&S

In the previous work of a survey of ontology-based systems, we have shown that all proposed application scenarios of ontologies in information systems build upon the primitive notion of ontology-based communication [10]. To our knowledge, no formal descriptions of this process has been given so far; even though such formalization would allow us to reason about the workings of our systems.

In the following, we describe the creation of an ontology of communication using the D&S framework. Theories of communication and interpretation lend naturally to be modelled as descriptions. While disjoint from the actual setting of interaction, they have the power to bring structure to a state of affairs consisting of primitives such as the rise and fall of electrical signals over a wire. The contextual nature of these theories is also reflected by the fact that multiple descriptions of communication may be mapped to a given state of affairs. Multiple situations present in the same state of affairs, however, do not necessarily constitute a contradiction and in fact, are a natural phenomenon in scientific work.

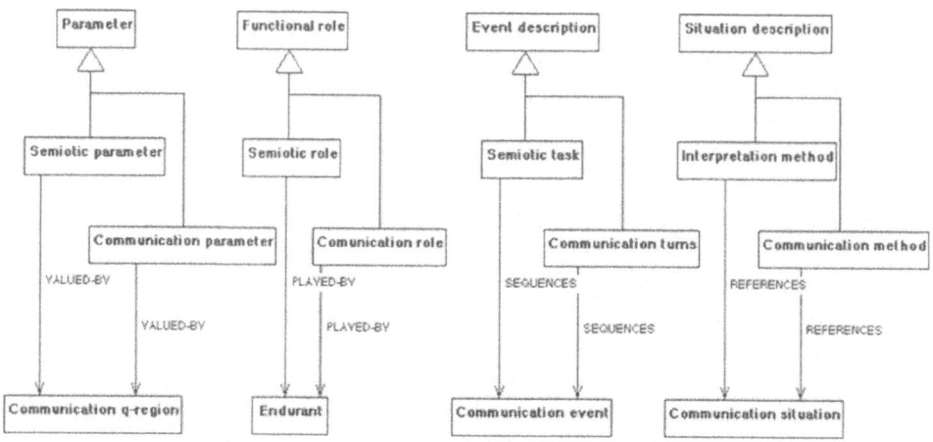

Fig. 2. The schema for communication and interpretation descriptions

The generic schema for our communication ontology combines two skeletal descriptions as shown in Fig. 2. The description for communication consists of communication parameters valued by communication regions, communication roles played by endurants and communication turns that sequence a communication event according to some method of communication. The description for interpretation concerns semiotic parameters, roles and semiotic tasks according to some interpretation method.

Beyond the fact that the two descriptions reference the same situation (albeit from different perspectives), we will see that they are also interrelated in more intricate ways. We consider these connections particularly important, as there is a tendency in the Semantic Web community to dismiss questions of interpretation as external to the system. In this respect the community follows the tradition of symbolic AI, ignoring the fact that ontologies are social artifacts.

While tenable in closed environment, this attitude quickly leads to practical problems in heterogeneous contexts, such as the one known as the Web's identity crisis [11]. This crisis resulted from the vague definition of Universal Resource Identifiers (URI). In practice, symbols of Semantic Web ontologies are often used to denote documents, in other cases documents containing definitions of concepts or the concepts themselves. A further difficulty with the URIs of the last type is that they cannot be denoted (resolved) by machines. As there is no authority provisioning such identifiers, individuals or communities may take the authority upon them to use the same URIs to denote different real world entities (not to mention fictitious ones). Without accessing and processing the interpretation context, such cases may not be disambiguated by a machine.

In the words of John Sowa, "... meaningless data cannot acquire meaning by being tagged with meaningless metadata. The ultimate source of meaning is the physical world and the agents who use signs to represent entities in the world and their intentions concerning them." [12]. Coupling our theories of communication with theories of interpretation will allow us to map the connections between elements of the communication system and those external to it, such as the agents who (re)create meaning.

To demonstrate the use of this template, we will fill our schema by modelling a communication theory developed by Roman Jakobson and a theory of semiotics originating from the work of Ferdinand de Saussure. This combination results in a simple, but generic model that can provide systematic account of communication acts regardless whether direct (oral) or mediated (as in the case of an information system), independently from a particular encoding.

The ontology of communication may be used in two ways. By mapping it to elements of a model of an information system such as the SWAP environment, it allows us to understand states of affairs as a communication situation, i.e. to check whether our respective theories of communication are upheld by the system.

While the descriptions obtained by instantiating the ontology are very fine grained (and therefore of low expressivity), they may be collected in the form of a knowledge base and interpreted later on according to additional heuristics (e.g. by detecting that communications are part of the same dialogue or broadcast). These heuristics may also be captured in an extended description which is able to express more complex patterns of interaction, such as communications involving multiple peers. We will demonstrate this method by modelling the resolution of queries in the peer-to-peer network. This description is naturally related to the previous one in that activities may be translated to the message exchanges of the previous example.

3.1   Theories of Communication and Interpretation

Jakobson's model of communication and the functions of language had a decisive impact on linguistic theory ever since its original publication over 40 years ago. As he writes in "Linguistics and Poetics: Closing Statement" all acts of communication are contingent on six constituent elements [13]: the addresser or encoder [speaker, author], a message [the verbal act, the signifier), the addressee or decoder (the hearer or reader), a context[5] (a referent, the signified), a code (shared mode of discourse, shared language) and a contact or channel.

Using the ontology of descriptions, all six constituents are modelled as functional roles: the encoder and decoder are agentive roles, while the other elements of theory are non-agentive functional roles. The method of communication is represented as a course.

Missing from Jakobson's model is a theory of interpretation: his model gives no indication as to how meaning is constructed from messages. To find such a theory and fill the missing gap one may turn to the models of semiotics.

Semiotics is the science of signs. While deriving from linguistics, semiotics is an application of linguistic methods to objects other than natural language; it is a way of viewing any system as constructed and functioning similarly to language.

---

[5] One should note that by "context" Jakobson means referent, i.e. what the message is about and not the circumstances of utterance.

Semiotics was independently developed by the logician and philosopher Charles Sanders Peirce and the linguist Ferdinand de Saussure in the second half of the 19th century. For our purposes of extending our communication description with an interpretation theory, we will commit to the Saussurean idea of interpretation, shared by Jakobson himself.

Ferdinand de Saussure was the first to describe scientifically the interaction between the two distinct but interoperating structures of language (at the level of meaning: the lexical structure, and at the level of expression: the phonologic structure), and the interaction between the emergent linguistic structure (morpho-syntactic), and the underlying linguistic structure (conceptual or paradigmatic) [14]. Meaning in Saussurean terms is created by (morphosyntactic, lexical) Expressions in (a conceptual) Context, i.e. by the interpretation function $I : (e, c) \rightarrow m$. Thus the semiotic roles of this theory are the expressions, contexts and meanings used to fill the domains and the range of the interpretation function.

Again using our ontology of descriptions, expressions are modelled as functional roles played by information objects and are equivalent to the message communication function.

S-Contexts are played by S-Descriptions. These descriptions are reifications of the various contexts affecting communication and interpretation of knowledge.

While the ontology is open at this point to further modelling, we note that related work exists in several communities. For example, the so called organizational context of knowledge (agents and their groups or communities, and the task and processes they perform) have been extensively studied in Knowledge Engineering [15]. Context modelling is also relevant to the effort of ontology mapping. Here, the most widely used contexts are the instance context and the natural language context. Algorithms using the first type of context build on the ability to compare concrete instances of classes even if the classes themselves represent external or abstract concepts. Algorithms of the second kind attempt to interpret symbols of the ontology as (particular senses of) natural language terms and map them to standard linguistic dictionaries. (Better mappings can be established by using 'ontologised' dictionaries such as the DOLCE-enhanced version of WordNet [9]).

Meanings are played by descriptions whatsoever and are not equivalent to any communication function. Descriptions playing the role of meaning have different natures according to the situation referenced by S-Contexts: legal cases, narrative worlds, planned procedures, clinical conditions, telephone calls, etc.

Our description for ontology-based communication, based on Jakobson's model of communication combined with a Saussurean interpretation theory is shown in the upper half of Fig. 3.

3.2   Communication in a Semantic Web Environment

The European SWAP project aims to develop a distributed knowledge sharing solution using ontology-based methods in a peer-to-peer environment. The

SWAP system is an extension of centralized ontology-based Knowledge Management solutions to decentralized scenarios.

The knowledge of peers is maintained and managed locally in the form of knowledge sources (e.g. documents, emails etc.) and an ontology used to organize those sources. Autonomy on the local level is complemented by coordination in the form of mappings between the ontologies of individual peers. Organizational knowledge networks subsequently emerge through the bottom-up process of making the connections between the ontologies of single nodes. An advantage of this network construction is that it is dynamically reconfigures itself as the underlying ontologies evolve. Furthermore, since the network is invoked on the basis of need for cooperation, its structure reflects the goals and interests of the various groups in the network. For more information on the SWAP system, we refer the reader to the project website[6].

The lower half of Fig. 3 shows a simple ontology of the SWAP system developed using DOLCE. In applying our description of communication and interpretation to the SWAP environment, we have to map the elements of the theories to the elements of this setting through the predicates *valued-by*, *played-by* and *sequences* as shown in Fig. 1.

In this case, the abstract Channel role is realized by a physical connection between the parties involved. Messages are played by information objects, which are realized by a physical stream of bytes going through the network. The encoder and decoder roles are played by SWAP peers, which stand in a direct relation with the human agents controlling them.[7] The encoding and decoding agents, the physical channel and the message are all *participant-in* the message transfer activity, which is sequenced by the communication method.[8]

The semiotic role of expressions are also played by the information objects. Interpretation is carried out by an element external to the information system, namely the human agent who manages his knowledge in the form of an ontology. She is the one who evaluates her personal interpretation function, which takes into account the expressions (along with axiomatization of the ontology as constraints on the possible models) and the contexts in which the communication takes place. In the end, an interpretation of the expressions results in meaning, which may or may not cover the intended meaning for the expression. In case a software agent has reasoning capabilities, it can use ontologies as the interpretive context, and the meaning will be the axioms for a given term e.g. in a query an agent tries to expand or to satisfy.

This modelling also shows how the previously mentioned dependency on interpretation translates into the system design of SWAP. Specifically, our theory

---

[6] http://swap.semanticweb.org

[7] For the purposes of this example (and without entering the debate whether intentionality can be attributed to software agents) we suppose that peers are agentive, but receive their intentionality from a natural person.

[8] Omitted from the figure are participation relations (between endurants and perdurants) and setting relations (between the elements of the model and the situation object).

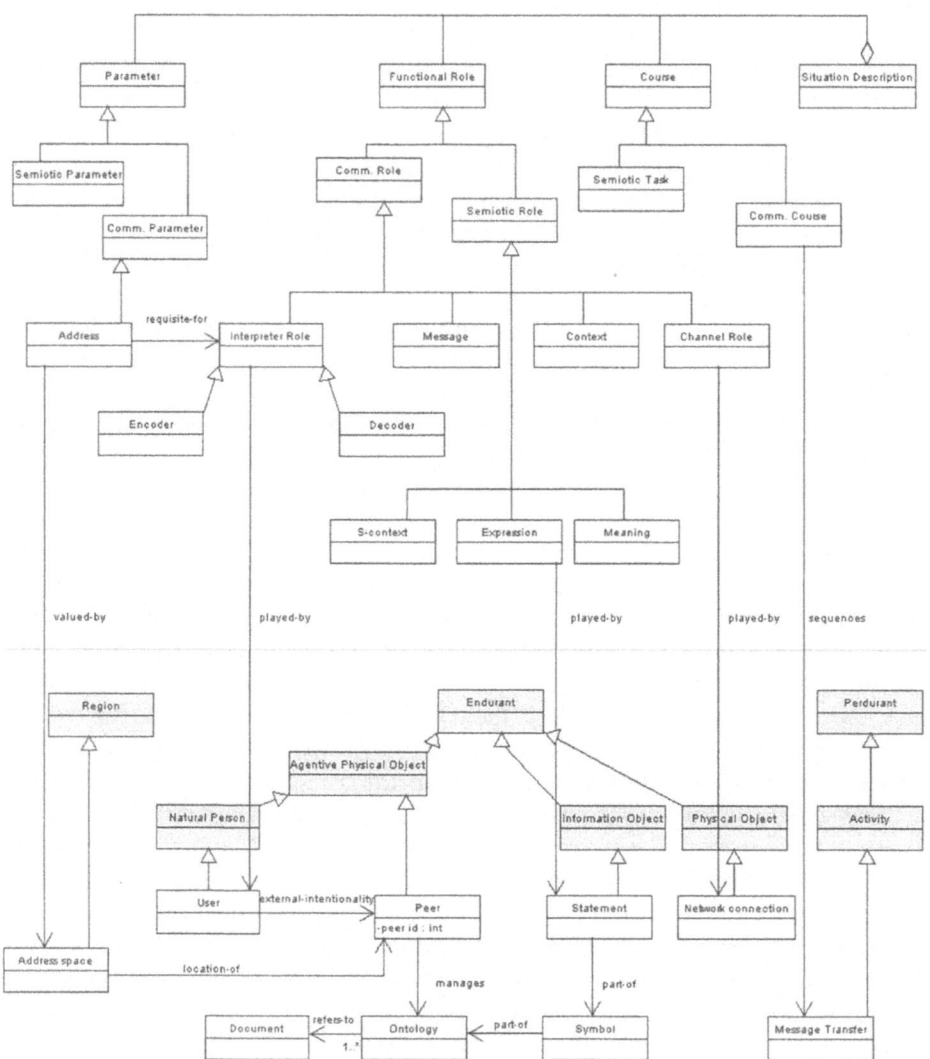

Fig. 3. The description of communication and interpretation (upper half of the picture) and its mapping to elements of the SWAP system (lower half). Shaded classes are defined in basic DOLCE.

suggests that the system should retain as much contextual information regarding its users as possible. In fact, there is no shared interpretation outside of local groups without an inherent community, i.e. a shared background of the users regarding the interest or task at hand. Matching the social contexts of the communicating parties, for example, may significantly increase the chance of successful interactions.

In our second example we provide a description for the query resolution process of the SWAP system as shown in Fig. 4.

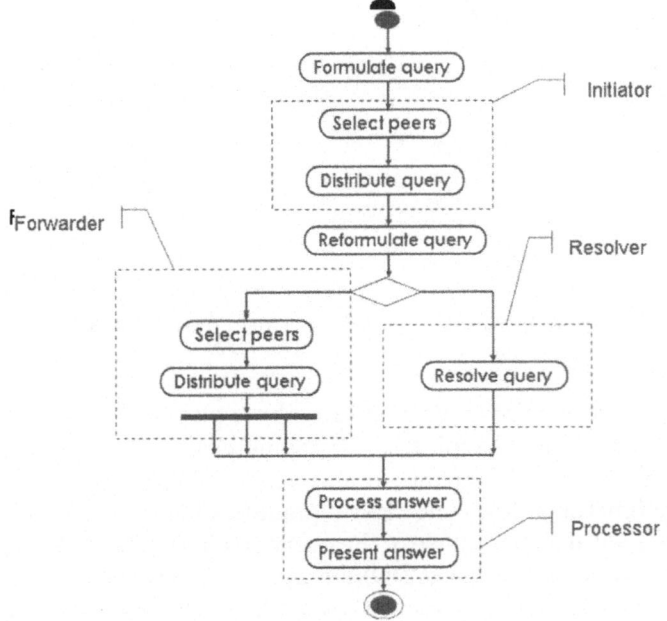

Fig. 4. The query resolution process of SWAP

This process is started by a user creating a query using the interface of the system [16]. This query is handed to the Peer Selector which decides which peers to contact among those known locally. The Peer Selector takes into consideration the content of the query and tries to select those peers that are rated highly as expert on the subject and are also trusted. Then the query is wrapped in a message (which also contains relevant parts of the local ontology) and distributed over the peer network.

When the message arrives to a peer, the query is reformulated in terms of the local ontology of the receiving peer. Subsequently, a decision is made whether the query can be resolved based on local knowledge or it needs to be forwarded to other known experts. In the latter case, the query is carried out iteratively, i.e. a new query process is initiated whose results provide feedback to the original query.

In the meantime, the initiating peer waits for the incoming results and processes them asynchronously until a certain timeout is reached. Processing entails maintaining the rating system used for peer selection and carrying out updates to the local ontology.

Creating a formal description from this process model starts with attributing a number of the activities depicted to certain functional roles. In this case, the informal description suggests the three roles of Initiator, Resolver, Forwarder and Processor as shown in Fig. 4. Functional roles in query resolution are also systematically related to the simpler roles identified in the communication description (see Fig. 5). Initiators play the role of encoders, Processors play the

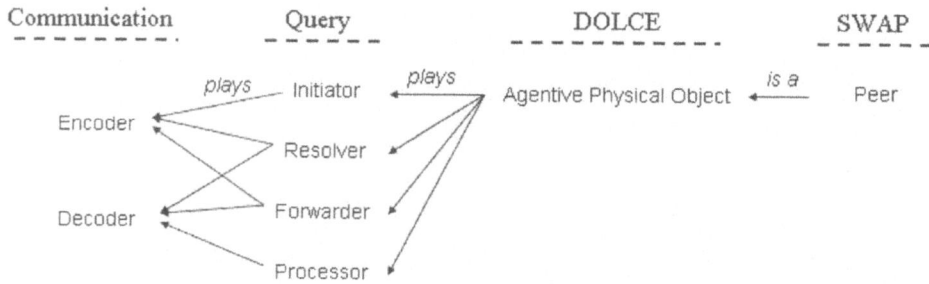

Fig. 5. Mapping of roles between descriptions.

role of decoders, while Forwarders and Resolvers play both roles with respect to different messages. This mapping to the communication description also results in the constraint that all four roles are played by SWAP peers in the system.

Once the functional roles and their parameters have been found, the process diagram is modelled as the course of the query resolution. (For the representation of processes another extension of DOLCE is used.) The course, as mentioned before, defines the succession relations that prefigure the temporal relations which may exist between activities in the situation. Elements of the course are said to sequence the communication activities.

The refined description (omitted for brevity) may be mapped to actual settings as before. However, the expressive power of this mapping is greater than in the previous case as we are now able to understand patterns at a larger granularity. This process of refinement may be continued in a similar way and its gradual, cumulative nature makes sure that agents who do not commit to more refined descriptions of the system may still use less expressive theories.

4   Related and Future Work

In the previous sections we described the Descriptions and Situations framework and applied D&S to create an ontology of communication based on Jakobson's theory and Saussurean semiotics. We also showed how this ontology may be used as a basis for a more expressive description which models the query process in the peer-to-peer ontology-based system developed within the European SWAP project.

Our contribution is thus twofold:

Descriptions and Situations. The D&S framework is an ontology of descriptions based on the fundamental distinction between the flux (an unstructured world) and logos (an intentionality). D&S provides a number of reification rules for various kinds of non-physical contexts and offers a template for complex descriptions based on theories such as laws, plans, norms etc.

Descriptions as contexts are first-order entities, but themselves may have a structure consisting of other referenced descriptions. D&S thus provides a middle ground between the formal, analytic treatment of context [17,18] and practical applications based on the structural investigation of particular contexts (such as the social context or workflow setting) and their effect on information systems.

The D&S ontology will be further developed and maintained within Wonder-Web. In particular, D&S forms the backbone of an ontology of services, which takes into account the multitude of views on a service: the offering of the provider, the expectations of the requestor, the contract agreed, the service norms etc.

An ontology of ontology-based communication. The description of communication is an application of the D&S framework. This ontology is of particular interest to the Semantic Web community as it makes an attempt to formalize the first time the workings of communication using ontologies. The community is expected to gain from this formalization by reaching a shared understanding over the workings of its models and in particular the dependence of communication on interpretation. In short, this ontology should serve as a reference point in arguments both within the community and externally.

We also demonstrated how this ontology may be specialized to provide useful descriptions of specific ontology-based communication methods, by encoding additional knowledge about tasks or control mechanisms. The ground level of this ontology, namely the elements of the communication context could be modelled in more detail. This amounts to developing a formal description of the Semantic Web, which might be challenging at times when so many contrasting visions exist side-by-side. Nevertheless, the rewards would outweigh the benefits: even if ontologies will become a black box similarly to content today, information on the broader context of an ontology may be used to help answer questions of relevancy and legitimacy and thus might be a factor in partitioning the web in communities of practice or interest.

References

1. Guarino, N.: Formal Ontology in Information Systems. In Guarino, N., ed.: Proceedings of the International Conference on Formal Ontology in Information Systems (FOIS'98), Trento, Italy, IOS Press, Amsterdam (1998) 3–15
2. Masolo, C., Borgo, S., Gangemi, A., Guarino, N., Oltramari, A., Schneider, L.: The WonderWeb Library of Foundational Ontologies. WonderWeb Deliverable 17 (2002)
3. Fensel, D., van Harmelen, F., Ding, Y., Klein, M., Mika, P., Akkermans, H., Broekstra, J., Kampman, A., van der Meer, J., Studer, R., Sure, Y., Davies, J., Duke, A., Engels, R., Iosif, V., Kiryakov, A., Lau, T., Reimer, U., Horrocks, I.: Final Report. On-To-Knowledge Deliverable 43 (2002)
4. van Elst, L., Abecker, A.: Ontologies for information management: balancing formality, stability, and sharing scope. Expert Systems with Applications **23** (2002) 357–366
5. Gangemi, A., Pisanelli, D.M., Steve, G.: An overview of the ONIONS project: Applying ontologies to the integration of medical terminologies. Data Knowledge Engineering **31** (1999) 183–220
6. Köhler, W.: Gestalt Psychology. Liveright, New York (1947/1929)
7. Moore, M.S.: Legal Reality: A Naturalist Approach to Legal Ontology. Law and Philosophy **21** (2002) 619–705

8. Fellbaum, C., ed.: WordNet – An electronic lexical database. MIT Press (1998)
9. Gangemi, A., Guarino, N., Masolo, C., Oltramari, A., Schneider, L.: Sweetening Ontologies with DOLCE. In: Proceedings of the 13th European Conference on Knowledge Engineering and Knowledge Management (EKAW2002), Siguenza, Spain. (2002)
10. Mika, P., Akkermans, H.: Analysis of Ontology-based Knowledge Management. SWAP (Semantic Web and Peer-to-Peer) Deliverable 1.2 (2002)
11. Pepper, S., Schwab, S.: Curing the Web's Identity Crisis. Technical report, Ontopia (http://www.ontopia.net) (2003)
12. Sowa, J.F.: Ontology, Metadata, and Semiotics. Number 1867 in Lecture Notes in AI. In: Conceptual Structures: Logical, Linguistic, and Computational Issues. Springer Verlag, Berlin (2000) 55–81
13. Jakobson, R.: Linguistics and Poetics: Closing Statement. In: Style in Language. MIT Press, Cambridge, MA (1960)
14. de Saussure, F.: Cours de linguistique générale. Payot, Lausanne (1906/1911)
15. Schreiber, G., Akkermans, H., Anjewierden, A., de Hoog, R., Shadbolt, N., van de Velde, W., Wielinga, B.: Knowledge engineering and management. The CommonKADS Methodology. MIT Press (1999)
16. Ehrig, M., Haase, P., Tempich, C.: Method Design. SWAP (Semantic Web and Peer-to-Peer) Deliverable 3.2 (2003)
17. Giunchiglia, F., Ghidini, C.: Local Models Semantics, or Contextual Reasoning = Locality + Compatibility. Artificial Intelligence **127** (2001) 221–259
18. Guha, R.V.: Contexts: A Formalization and Some Applications. PhD thesis, Stanford University (1991)

Incremental Maintenance of Materialized Ontologies

Raphael Volz[1,2], Steffen Staab[1], and Boris Motik[2]

[1] Institute AIFB, University of Karlsruhe
76128 Karlsruhe, Germany
{volz,staab}@aifb.uni-karlsruhe.de
http://www.aifb.uni-karlsruhe.de/WBS/
[2] WIM, Forschungszentrum Informatik (FZI)
76131 Karlsruhe, Germany
{volz,motik}@fzi.de
http://www.fzi.de/wim/

Abstract. This paper discusses the incremental maintenance of materialized ontologies in a rule-enabled Semantic Web. Materialization allows to speed up query processing by explicating the implicit entailments which are sanctioned by the semantics of an ontology. The complexity of reasoning with the ontology is thereby shifted from query time to update time. We assume that materialization techniques will frequently be important to achieve a scalable Semantic Web, since read access to ontologies is predominant. Central to materialization are maintenance techniques that allow to incrementally update a materialization when changes occur.

We present a novel solution that allows to cope with changes in rules and facts. To achieve this we extend a known approach for the incremental maintenance of views in deductive databases. We show how our technique can be employed for a broad range of existing Web ontology languages, such as RDF/S and subsets of OWL and present a first evaluation.

1 Introduction

Germane to the idea of the Semantic Web are the capabilities to assert facts and to derive new *implicit* facts from the asserted facts using the semantics specified by an ontology. The current building blocks of the Semantic Web, Resource Description Framework (RDF) [10] and Web Ontology Language (OWL) [15], define how to assert facts and specify how implicit facts should be derived from stated facts.

The derivation of implicit information is usually achieved at the time clients issue queries to inference engines. Situations where the query rate is high or the procedure to derive implicit information is time consuming and complex lead to slow performance. Materialization can be used to increase the performance at query time and to make implicit information explicit. This avoids to recompute derived information for every query.

Materialization has been applied successfully in many applications where reading access to data is predominant. For example, data warehouses usually apply materialization techniques to make *online* analytical processing possible. In the traditional web,

R. Meersman et al. (Eds.): CoopIS/DOA/ODBASE 2003, LNCS 2888, pp. 707–724, 2003.
© Springer-Verlag Berlin Heidelberg 2003

portals maintain cached web pages to offer fast access to dynamically generated web pages.

We assume that reading access to ontologies is predominant in the Semantic Web and other ontology based applications, hence materialization seems to be a promising technique for fast query processing.

Central to materialization approaches is the issue of maintaining a materialization when changes occur. This issue can be handled by simply recomputing the whole materialization. However, as the computation of the materialization is often complex and time consuming, more efficient techniques need to be applied in practise.

Contribution. We present a technique for the incremental maintenance of materialized ontologies. Our technique can be applied to a wide range of ontology languages, namely those that can be axiomatized by a set of rules[1].

The challenge that has not been tackled before comes from the fact that updates of ontology definitions are equivalent to the update and new definitions of rules, whereas existing maintenance techniques only address the update of ground facts.

To cope with changing rules, our solution extends a declarative algorithm for the incremental maintenance of views [19] that was developed in the deductive database context. We show the feasibility of our solution in a first performance evaluation.

Paper structure. The remainder of the paper will consist of a review of how Web ontology languages and rules interplay (Section 2), presentation of the algorithm for maintenance for changing facts (Section 3), extension of the algorithm for maintenance with changing rules (Section 4), a first performance evaluation (Section 5), a review of related work (Section 6) followed by general conclusions (Section 7).

2   Web Ontology Languages and Rules

2.1   Axiomatization of the Language

Since the early days of the Semantic Web, many systems have tried to reason with Web ontology languages using rule-based systems, e.g. SiLRi [4], CWM[2], Euler [16], JTP[3] or Triple [17]. To do so, a particular Web ontology language is axiomatized via a static set of rules which capture the semantics specified for a particular ontology language.

For example, Fig. 1 presents the Datalog axiomatization of RDF/S. This axiomatization implements the semantics of RDF specified by the RDF model theory [10] (without datatype entailments and support for stronger iff semantics of domain and ranges). The ontology and associated data is stored in a single ternary predicate t, i.e. the extension of t stores all triples that constitute a particular RDF graph.

In many applications, e.g. editors, it is necessary to distinguish between asserted information and entailed information [2]. This can be achieved by turning the predicate t into a completely intensional predicate (view) that is derived from the explicitly asserted

---

[1] The underlying rule language used for our approach is Datalog with stratified negation.

[2] http://www.w3.org/2000/10/swap/doc/cwm

[3] http://ksl.stanford.edu/software/jtp/

t(P,a,rdf:Property)	:-	t(S,P,O).	*rdf1*
t(S,a,C)	:-	t(P,domain,C), t(S,P,O).	*rdfs2*
t(O,a,C)	:-	t(P,range,C), t(S,P,O).	*rdfs3*
t(S,a,Resource)	:-	t(S,P,O).	*rdfs4a*
t(O,a,Resource)	:-	t(S,P,O).	*rdfs4b*
t(P,subPropertyOf,R)	:-	t(Q,subPropertyOf,R), t(P,subPropertyOf,Q).	*rdfs5a*
t(S,R,0)	:-	t(P,subPropertyOf,R), t(S,P,O).	*rdfs6*
t(C,a,Class)	:-	t(C,subClassOf,Resource).	*rdfs7*
t(A,subClassOf,C)	:-	t(B,subClassOf,C), t(A,subClassOf,B).	*rdfs8*
t(S,a;B)	:-	t(S,a,A), t(A,subClassOf,B).	*rdfs9*
t(X,subPropertyOf,member)	:-	t(X,a,ContainerMembershipProperty).	*rdfs10*
t(X,subClassOf,Literal)	:-	t(X,a,Datatype).	*rdfs11*
t(Resource,subClassOf,Y)	:-	t(X,domain,Y), t(rdf:type,subPropertyOf,X).	*rdfs12*

Fig. 1. Static Datalog rules for implementing RDF(S)

information. Hence, asserted RDF triples constitute a separate extensional predicate, say t_{Ext}, and t is derived from t_{Ext} via a rule:

$$t(X, Y, Z) :\text{-} t_{Ext}(X, Y, Z).$$

Such view definitions allow not only to distinguish between asserted and entailed information in queries but also to re-use results established for the incremental maintenance of views (intensional predicates) in the deductive database context for the purpose of materialization.

2.2 Dynamic Rule Sets

The set of rules is typically not immutable. With the advent of higher layers of the Semantic Web stack, i.e. the rule layer, users can create their own rules. Hence, we are facing a scenario where not only base facts can change but also the set of rules. This requires the ability to maintain a materialization in this situation. Besides support for a rule layer, the ability to maintain a materialization under changing rule sets is also required for approaches where the semantics of the ontology language is not captured via a static set of rules but instead compiled into a set of rules. Such an approach is for example required by Description Logic Programs (DLP) [6], where OWL ontologies are translated to logic programs. Other implementations of knowledge representation languages, e.g. O-Telos [11] and F-Logic [20], have also been achieved via such a compilation.

Semantic Web Rule Layer. We now briefly present some languages for the specification of Semantic Web rules that may be compiled into the paradigm we use. The Rule Markup Initiative aims to develop a canonical Web language for rules called RuleML. RuleML covers the entire rule spectrum and spans from derivation rules to transformation rules to reaction rules. It has a well-defined Datalog subset, which can be enforced using XML schemas, and for which we can employ the materialization techniques developed within this paper. The reader may note, that materialization is not an issue for many other aspects found in RuleML, e.g. transformation rules or reaction rules.

In parallel to the RuleML iniative, Notation3 (N3) has emerged as a human-readable language for RDF/XML. Its aim is to optimize expression of data and logic in the same language and has become a serious alternative since many systems that support inference on RDF data (e.g. cwm, Euler, Jena2) support it. The rule language supported by N3 is an extension of Datalog with existential quantifiers in rule heads Hence, the materialization techniques developed within this paper can be applied to the subset of all N3 programs which do not make use of existential quantification in the head.

Description Logic Programs. Both of the above mentioned approaches allow the definition of rules but are not integrated with the ontology layer in the Semantic Web architecture. Description Logic Programs [6] aim to integrate rules with the ontology layer by compiling ontology definitions into a logic program which can later be extended with additional rules. This approach can deal with a very expressive subset of the standardized Web ontology language OWL (i.e. OWL without existential quantification, negation and disjunction in rule heads).

The following example OWL fragment declares Wine to be potable liquids who are made by Wineries:

$$\text{Wine} \sqsubseteq \text{PotableLiquid} \sqcap \forall \text{hasMaker.Winery}$$

This will be translated in DLP to the following set of rules:
PotableLiquid(X) :- Wine(X).
Winery(Y) :- Wine(X), hasMaker(X, Y).

Hence, a change to the ontologies class and property structure will result in a change of the compiled rules. Again, it is necessary to be able to maintain a materialization in case of such a change.

3   Changing Facts

This section presents the maintenance of a materialization when facts change, viz. new tuples are added or removed from the extension of a predicate. We first demonstrate how changes can effect a materialization in an example and then recapitulate the incremental maintenance approach [19] upon which we build our approach.

3.1   An Example

Let's consider the effects of adding and removing a subClassOf relationship in RDF/S with respect to some of the relevant rules that axiomatize RDF Schema. The first rule links the intensional predicate t with ground facts. The second rule implements the transitive closure of the subClassOf relationship:

R_1 : $t(X, Y, Z)$:- $t_{ext}(X, Y, Z)$.
R_2 :   t(A,subClassOf,C) :- t(B,subClassOf,C), t(A,subClassOf,B).

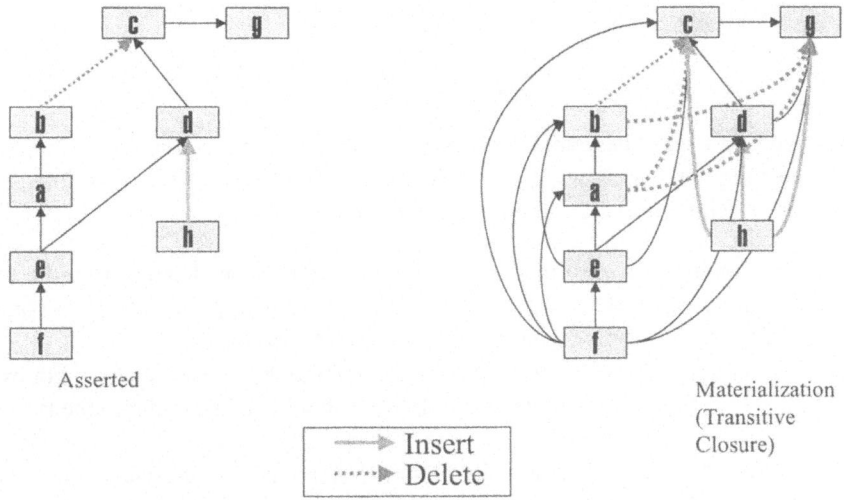

Asserted

Materialization (Transitive Closure)

⟶ Insert
┈┈▶ Delete

Fig. 2. Changes to a RDF/S taxonomy and its materialization

Let us consider the effects of updates on the taxonomy depicted in Fig. 2:

– b is no longer a subclass of c, viz. the $t_{ext}(b, \text{subClassOf}, c)$ fact is deleted.
– h is asserted to be a subclass of d, hence a $t_{ext}(h, \text{subClassOf}, d)$ fact is inserted.

The deletion has the following consequences to t: It eliminates the links between (a,c), (a,g), (b,c) and (b,g). Since the facts $t_{ext}(d, \text{subClassOf}, c)$ and $t_{ext}(e, \text{subClassOf}, d)$ exist, alternative derivations also exist for the links (e,c), (e,g), (f,c) and (f,g). These alternative derivations have to be taken into account in our approach. The insertion yields three new derivations namely links between (h,c), (h,d) and (h,g).

3.2   Generating Maintenance Rules

Several algorithms (e.g. [9,12,7]) have been presented for the incremental maintenance of views (or intensional predicates) in the deductive database context. The most common procedure is to compute the changes (differentials) to views in three steps:

– Firstly, to overestimate the consequences of deletions, so a super set of the facts that are eventually deleted is computed for deletion.
– Secondly, a rederivation step prunes those computed deletions from the set of deletions for which alternative derivations (via some other rules defining the view) exist.
– Thirdly, the consequences of insertions to extensional predicates are added to the view, if applicable.

Our approach is based on the results established in [19], which realize the DRed (delete and rederive) algorithm presented in [7] in a purely declarative way. The approach is based on rewriting the original program into a maintenance program, which is evaluated instead of the old program.

Hence, an original Datalog rule:

$$p :\text{-} r_1, \ldots, r_n.$$

is rewritten into a set of new predicates and several maintenance rules that calculate the differentials required to maintain a materialization. The maintenance of an intensional predicate p is achieved via six additional predicates:

1. p^{Del} computes an overestimation of facts that ought to be deleted from the materialization so-called deletion candidates. For extensional predicates p^{Del} contains explicitly what should be removed from the materialization.
2. p^{Ins} contains the facts that ought to be inserted into the materialization. For extensional predicates p^{Ins} contains explicitly what should be inserted into the materialization.
3. p^{Red} stores those facts that are marked for deletion but have alternative derivations.
4. p^{New} describes the new state of the materialization after updates.
5. p^{Plus} computes the net insertions required to maintain the materialization.
6. p^{Minus} computes the net deletions required to maintain the materializaion.

The extension of p itself contains the materialization. The reader may note that the evaluation of the set of maintenance rules computes the set of implicit insertions and deletions that have to be propagated to the materialization of the predicate and to other predicates, which depend on the predicate through some rules.

Deletion Candidates. The first subset of maintenance rules derive all possible deletion candidates for a predicate p. Deletion candidates are constituted by deleted facts in the body predicates. For all rules and all body predicates r_i in these rules, we define a rule

$$D_i: \qquad p^{Del} :\text{-} r_1, \ldots, r_{i-1}, r_i^{Del}, r_{i+1}, \ldots, r_n.$$

If r_i is a extensional predicate, r_i^{Del} contains either the explicitly deleted facts in r_i or it contains a superset of the derived facts to be deleted in r_i due to deletions caused by other rules.

With respect to our example we would have to generate three deletion rules. The transformation of $R1$ yields one deletion rule, while the transformation of $R2$ results in two deletion rules.

$R_1 D_1:$ $t^{Del}(X, Y, Z)$ $:\text{-} t_{ext}^{Del}(X, Y, Z).$

$R_2 D_1:$ $t^{Del}(A, \text{subClassOf}, C) :\text{-} t^{Del}(B, \text{subClassOf}, C), t(A, \text{subClassOf}, B).$

$R_2 D_2:$ $t^{Del}(A, \text{subClassOf}, C) :\text{-} t(B, \text{subClassOf}, C), t^{Del}(A, \text{subClassOf}, B).$

If b is no longer a subclass of c (viz. $t_{ext}^{Del}(b, \text{subClassOf}, c)$ exists), the extension of the t^{Del} predicate would be constituted by the following derived subclass relationships:

$$(b, c), (b, g), (a, c), (a, g), (e, c), (e, g), (f, c), (f, g)$$

Rederivation. We now have to check which tuples in p^{Del} have alternative derivations in the new database state. This is achieved using the following rule:

$$R: \qquad p^{Red} \text{ :- } p^{Del}, r_1^{New}, \dots, r_n^{New}.$$

With respect to our example, t^{Red} is axiomatized by two rules:

$$R_1 R: \qquad t^{Red}(X, Y, Z) \qquad \text{ :- } t^{Del}(X, Y, Z), t_{ext}^{New}(X, Y, Z).$$
$$R_2 R: \qquad t^{Red}(A, \text{subClassOf}, C) \text{ :- } t^{Del}(A, \text{subClassOf}, C),$$
$$t^{New}(B, \text{subClassOf}, C), t^{New}(A, \text{subClassOf}, B).$$

t^{Red} has the following subClassOf relationships as its extension:

$$(e, c), (e, g), (f, c), (f, g)$$

This is due to the facts $t(d, \text{subClassOf}, c)$ and $t(e, \text{subClassOf}, d)$, which generate these alternative derivations.

Insertion. The next rules propagate insertions of extensional facts to the intensional predicates. This is done by ordinary semi-naive rewriting, i.e. by constructing rules (I_i) that join new facts inserted into one body relation with full extensions of all others:

$$I_i: \qquad p^{Ins} \text{ :- } r_1^{New}, \dots, r_{i-1}^{New}, r_i^{Ins}, r_{i+1}^{New}, \dots, r_n^{New}.$$

With respect to our example we have to generate three insertion rules (one for R_1 and two for R_2):

$$R_1 I_1: \qquad t^{Ins}(X, Y, Z) \qquad \text{ :- } t_{ext}^{Ins}(X, Y, Z).$$
$$R_2 I_1: \qquad t^{Ins}(A, \text{subClassOf}, C) \text{ :- } t^{Ins}(B, \text{subClassOf}, C), t^{New}(A, \text{subClassOf}, B).$$
$$R_2 I_2: \qquad t^{Ins}(A, \text{subClassOf}, C) \text{ :- } t^{New}(B, \text{subClassOf}, C), t^{Ins}(A, \text{subClassOf}, B).$$

If we assert h to be a subclass of d (viz. $t_{ext}^{Ins}(h, \text{subClassOf}, d)$ exists), we can derive the following new subclass relationships in the extension of t^{Ins}:

$$(h, d), (h, c), (h, g)$$

Description of the New State. The new state of a predicate p after updates is captured in a new predicate p^{New}. A set of rules captures the changes:

$$N_1: \qquad p^{New} \text{ :- } p, \neg p^{Del}.$$
$$N_2: \qquad p^{New} \text{ :- } p^{Red}.$$
$$N_3: \qquad p^{New} \text{ :- } p^{Ins}.$$

Rule N_1 ensures that the new state of a predicate p does not contain the deleted information. Rule N_2 ensures that rederived facts are part of the new state of the predicate. Finally, rule N_3 pushes insertions into the new state of the predicate.

Computation of Differentials. We can compute the deletions and insertions that have to be performed to maintain the materialization of a predicate p via two predicates p^{Plus} and p^{Minus}, which compute the net insertions and deletions to a predicate p.

p^{Plus} contains those facts, which were not present before and are derived for insertion. p^{Minus} contains those facts, which are deletion candidates and are neither inserted nor re-derived.

$$P: \quad p^{Plus} \quad :\text{-} \quad p^{Ins}, \neg p.$$
$$M: \quad p^{Minus} \quad :\text{-} \quad p^{Del}, \neg p^{Ins}, \neg p^{Red}.$$

In our example the extension of t^{Plus} is made up by the following subclassOf assertions:

$$(h, d), (h, c), (h, g)$$

The extension of t^{Minus} is:

$$(a, c), (a, g), (b, c), (b, g)$$

3.3   Static RDF/S Rules Revisited

The 15 static Datalog rules for the axiomatization of RDF/S (cf. Fig. 1) contain 21 body predicates. This leads to the generation of 21 insertion rules and 21 deletion rules. Additionally 15 rederivation rules are generated. 5 predicates are generated to capture the new state of the predicate t and the differentials. The total number of 62 generated rules can be found online[4].

3.4   Evaluation of Maintenance Rules

[18] shows that the evaluation of the maintenance rules is a sound and complete procedure for computing the differentials between two database states when extensional update operations occur.

During the evaluation it is necessary to access the old state of a predicate. Bottom-up evaluation approaches therefore require that all intensional relations involved in the computation are completely materialized, viz. the initial rules defining the predicates are not considered during the evaluation of the maintenance rules.

The rewriting contain negated predicates to express the algebraic set difference operation. Hence, even though the original rules may be pure Datalog (without negation), a program with negation is generated. The rewriting transformation keeps the property of stratifiability, since newly introduced predicates do not occur in cycles with other negations. Hence, the evaluation can partition predicates into strata such that no two predicates in one stratum depend negatively on each other. Predicates may only occur negatively in rules that define predicates of a higher stratum. The evaluation can then proceed as usual stratum-by-stratum starting with the extensional predicates themselves.

Not only changed predicates have to be maintained but also all predicates that depend on predicates whose extension changes. An axiomatization of RDF/S based on a single

---

[4] http://kaon.semanticweb.org/research/materialization

Table 1. Versions of the example ontology: (a) DL-based (b) DLP translation

DL-Style	DLP Translation	explanation
1. hasChild $\sqsubseteq$ inDynasty	inDynasty(X,Y) :- hasChild(X,Y).	*hasChild constitutes in-Dynasty*
2. inDynasty$^+$ $\sqsubseteq$ inDynasty	inDynasty(X,Y) :- inDynasty(X,Z), inDynasty(Z,Y).	*the inDynasty relation is transitive*
3. inDynasty$^-$ $\equiv$ inDynasty	inDynasty(X,Y) :- inDynasty(Y,X).	*the inDynasty relation is symmetric*

ternary predicate (cf. Fig. 1) therefore leads to complete re-materialization in case of updates. We present an optimization for this case in Section 4.3 which results in more efficient results.

4   Changing Rules

This section presents the maintenance of a materialization if the definition of views (intensional predicates) changes, viz. rules that define the predicate are added or removed. Our solution has two main components. Firstly, the materialization itself has to be maintained. Secondly, the materialization rules for a predicate p themselves have to be maintained.

4.1   An Example

Table 1 depicts a small sample ontology that describes the relationships in a family dynasty. The OWL rules stated in DL-style syntax are compiled into appropriate Datalog rules using the DLP approach. Let's assume that DLP has been used to implement the semantics and that the extension of hasChild is constituted by the tuples $\{(1,2),(2,3),(4,3)\}$. If the ontology only contains the first and second axiom then the extension of inDynasty corresponds to hasChild $\cup \{(1,3)\}$

If the first axiom is deleted, inDynasty has an empty extension. Similarly the extension of inDynasty would be equivalent to hasChild, if the second axiom were deleted.

Now assume that the third rule is inserted. Apparently the new extension will contain the tuple $(1,4)$ (among others), which is derived by one of the existing rules, i.e. rule 2 which operated on tuples derived by rule 3.

4.2   Maintaining the Materialization

Every change in the rule set causes changes in the extension of a predicate p. Hence, the materialization has to be updated as well. However, unlike in the case of changing extensions, the existing maintenance rules cannot capture this situation.

As we can see in the above examples, adding and removing rules requires the reevaluation of all other rules defining a predicate. The reader may note, that it does not suffice to simply change the maintenance rules. Since there is no change to hasChild, both predicates which capture the difference hasChild^{Plus} and hasChild^{Minus} are empty. In consequence inDynasty^{Ins}, inDynasty^{Del}, inDynasty^{Red} and thereby inDynasty^{Plus} and inDynasty^{Minus} are empty.

Our solution is based on the creation of a temporary predicate p^{Temp}, which is used to calculate the extension of p using the changed set of rules. Hence, p^{Temp} is axiomatized using the updated rule set for a predicate p. Self-references of the predicate have to be substituted by the temporary predicate:

$$\text{inDynasty}^{Temp}(x,y) \ :\text{-}\ \text{hasChild}(x,y).$$
$$\text{inDynasty}^{Temp}(x,y) \ :\text{-}\ \text{inDynasty}^{Temp}(x,z), \text{inDynasty}^{Temp}(z,y).$$
$$\text{inDynasty}^{Temp}(x,y) \ :\text{-}\ \text{inDynasty}^{Temp}(y,x).$$

Then, p^{Temp} is used for the calculation of p^{Plus} and p^{Minus} by augmenting the definition of p^{Ins} and p^{Del} with the following rules:

$$p^{Ins} \ :\text{-}\ p^{Temp}, \neg p.$$
$$p^{Del} \ :\text{-}\ p, \neg p^{Temp}.$$

The view maintenance process is carried out by evaluating the maintenance rules without the initial rules that define p. All predicates, which depend on p can be updated using p^{Ins} and p^{Del}. The reader may note, that our solution allows the simultaneous modification of both rules and facts. However, the new facts can already be taken into account when p^{Temp} is computed.

4.3   Selection-Based Optimization

Alternatively to DLP, the semantics of the ontology stated in Table 1 could have been given by specifying several rules that axiomatize a single triple predicate. For example the symmetry of the dynastic relationship could be axiomatized as follows:

$$t(X, \text{inDynasty}, Y) :\text{-} t(Y, \text{inDynasty}, X).$$

In this case our approach requires to access the whole database, since only one predicate is materialized and all rules defining this predicate have to be reevaluated. Naturally, this situation corresponds to the simple strategy of recomputing a materialization from scratch.

We therefore introduce an optimization, which improves the recomputation by limiting the part of the database which takes part in the evaluation. Selection-based optimization assumes that the extension of the database is split depending on split points. Split points are given by constants that occur at a certain argument position of a predicate.

The optimization transforms a Datalog program into an equivalent program, such that all references to p where a split point occurs are replaced by split predicates. This is the case, if a constant c was used as the i-th argument in the predicate p.

To generate split predicates, we split the extension of a predicate p_{Ext} into several edb predicates of the form $p_{Ext}^{c_i}(Var_1, Var_2, \ldots, Var_{i-1}, c, Var_{i+1}, Var_n)$ to store tuples based on equal constant values c in their i-th component.

Hence, instead of using a single predicate p_{Ext} for representing the direct RDF assertion, the database is split into several $p_{Ext}^{c_i}$. Again, we want to distinguish between asserted and derived information and consequently introduce intensional predicates (views) for each component of the extension (i.e. rules of the form $p^{c_i} :- p_{Ext}^{c_i}$).The complete predicate p is represented by n rules that unify the used split predicates: $p :- p^{c_i}$

Returning to the triple based axiomatization of the example, we can transform the program by introducing a split point $t^{inDynasty_2}$ for the inDynasty constant (when used as second argument in the ternary predicate t):

- We use two extensional predicates: $t_{Ext}^{Rest}, t_{Ext}^{inDynasty_2}$ to store the extension in two disjoint sets.
- We capture the intensional predicates and integrate the splits into a complete extension of t and rewrite the example rule 2 such that split predicates are used instead of the full predicate:

$$
\begin{aligned}
t^{Rest}(X,Y,Z) &:- t_{Ext}^{Rest}(X,Y,Z).\\
t^{inDynasty_2} &:- t_{Ext}^{inDynasty_2}(X,Y,Z).\\
t(X,Y,Z) &:- t^{Rest}(X,Y,Z).\\
t(X,Y,Z) &:- t^{inDynasty_2}(X,Y,Z).\\
t^{inDynasty_2}(X, \text{inDynasty}, Y) &:- t^{inDynasty_2}(Z, \text{inDynasty}, Y),\\
&\quad\ t^{inDynasty_2}(X, \text{inDynasty}, Y).
\end{aligned}
$$

Assume now that the third rule of Table 1 is inserted. We can again transform this rule into a rule, which uses the split predicate $t^{inDynasty_2}$. However, the maintenance of $t^{inDynasty_2}$ can now be carried out by ignoring all non-relevant rules for t. Hence, the whole extension of t can be updated via the insert and delete maintenance rules that are created for $t^{inDynasty_2}$ only, viz. without using the complete database.

4.4 Maintaining Maintenance Rules

Additionally to the maintenance of the materialization itself, the maintenance rules have to be altered when changes occur. In case of insertion of a rule r new maintenance rules are generated. In case of deletion of a rule r, all maintenance rules generated from the rule are deleted as well. If the predicate p itself is deleted, i.e. the last rule r defining p is deleted, all maintenance predicates, e.g. p^{New}, p^{Red} etc. are removed from the database by removing the rules that define those predicates.

The maintenance algorithms operate on the following data structures:

- R set of rules
- MR set of maintenance rules,
- P set of predicates,
- MP set of maintenance predicates,
- $ruleMaintenance : R \rightarrow MR$ function that maps rule to its maintenance rules
- $head : R \rightarrow P$ function maps a rule to the rule head
- $rules : P \rightarrow R$ function that maps a predicate to defining rules

---

Algorithm 1 Changing Rules

Require: New rules *Changes* that are changed, operator $\circ = \{\cup, \backslash\}$ specifying insert or delete

$R = R \circ$ Changes

for all $r \in Changes$ **do**

    maintenanceRules $= \emptyset$

    p = head(r)

    if $((\{p\} \cap P = \emptyset) \wedge (\circ = \cup)) \vee ((\text{rules}(p)\backslash\{r\} = \emptyset) \wedge (\circ = \backslash))$ **then**

        $P = P \circ \{p\}$

        $MP = MP \circ \{p^{New}, p^{Temp}, p^{Red}, p^{Minus}, p^{Plus}, p^{Del}, p^{Red}, p^{Ins}\}$

        maintenanceRules = staticMaintenanceRules(p)

    end if

    rules(p) = rules(p) $\circ$ r

    maintenanceRules = maintenanceRules $\cup$ dynamicMaintenanceRules(r)

    ruleMaintenance(r) = ruleMaintenance(r) $\circ$ maintenanceRules

    $MR = MR \circ$ maintenanceRules

end for

Ensure: Updated sets MR, MP, R, P and maps $ruleMaintenance\ldots$

Two procedures generate the maintenance rules for a given rule r and its head p:

- $staticMaintenanceRules$ generates the rules defining p^{New}, p^{Plus} and p^{Minus},
- $dynamicMaintenanceRules$ generates the rules defining p^{Del}, p^{Red} and p^{Ins}

Maintaining maintenance rules is achieved by algorithm 1. The if branch checks whether a rule is the first (respectively last) rule defining a predicate p and generate (respectively delete) the static maintenance predicates and rules.

5 Evaluation

This section reports on our prototypical implementation and a first evaluation of our approach.

5.1 Implementation

We implemented our approach to materialization as an extension to the KAON Datalog engine. The implementation is freely available via the KAON web site[5]. In case of the materialization of a predicate all changes to facts relevant for the predicate and the rule set defining a predicate are monitored. The materialization and corresponding maintenance rules are updated as described in the previous sections.

The maintenance process is carried out as follows. When a program is designated for materialization, all maintenance rules are generated, the program itself is evaluated and the extension of all predicates designated for materialization is stored explicitly. The maintenance program is used for future evaluation instead of the original program. Therefore, all rules defining non-materialized predicates are added to the maintenance program.

---

[5] http://kaon.semanticweb.org/

Changes in facts are stored in the appropriate p^{Ins} and p^{Del} predicates. The change triggers the evaluation of the maintenance rules and consequently updates the extensions of all materialized predicates is updated by adding p^{Plus} and removing p^{Minus}. Afterwards the extension of extensional predicates is updated by adding p^{Ins} and removing p^{Del}. As a last step, the extension of p^{Ins} and all other auxiliary predicates is cleared.

Changes in rules are carried out by retrieving all rules defining the same predicates as the changed rules from the original program. These rules are then rewritten to refer to p^{Temp} only. Then the maintenance rules are evaluated and extensions are updated as described for facts. As a last step the auxiliary rules defining p^{Temp} are deleted.

5.2   Evaluation Setting

Test Assumptions. The evaluation has been carried out with changing OWL ontologies that are compiled into logic programs via the DLP translation [6]. It is assumed that all predicates are materialized. We assume that an inference engine builds its knowledge base by aggregating data from several web sources. Therefore bulk updates will be predominant.

Test Procedure. Each test is characterized by a certain ontology structure and a class whose extension is to be read. The ontology structure has been generated for different input parameters, resulting in ontologies of different sizes. The average of five such invocations has been taken as the performance measure for each test.

We obtain six measures: *(a)* the time of query processing without materialization, *(b)* the time required to set up the materialization and the maintenance program, *(c)* the time required to perform maintenance when rules are added, *(d)* rules are removed, *(e)* facts are added, and *(f)* facts are removed. Finally, *(g)* assesses the time of query processing with materialization.

Test Platform. We performed the tests on a laptop with Pentium IV Mobile processor running at 2 GHz, 512 MB of RAM using the Windows XP operating system. The implementation itself is written in Java and executed using Sun's JDK version 1.4.1_01.

5.3   Evaluation Scenarios

First we give an overview of the types of tests we conducted. In the following we use D to denote the depth of the class hierarchy, NS to denote the number of sub classes at each level in the hierarchy, NI to denote the number of instances per class and P to denote the number of properties.

To test changes in facts, we add and remove a random percentage *Change* of the facts. For rules, we add and remove a random rule. This is due to the limitation of the underlying engine, which currently does not allow to alter rules in a bulk manner. The test was performed for different depths of the taxonomy $D = 3, 4, 5$ while the number of sub classes and the number of instances was not altered ($NS = 5$; $NI = 5$). Test 2 and 3 made use of properties. Here, every class had five properties, which are instantiated for every third instance of the class ($NI = 5$). We carried out each test using varying *Change* ratios of 10% and 15% of the facts.

Evaluation Results

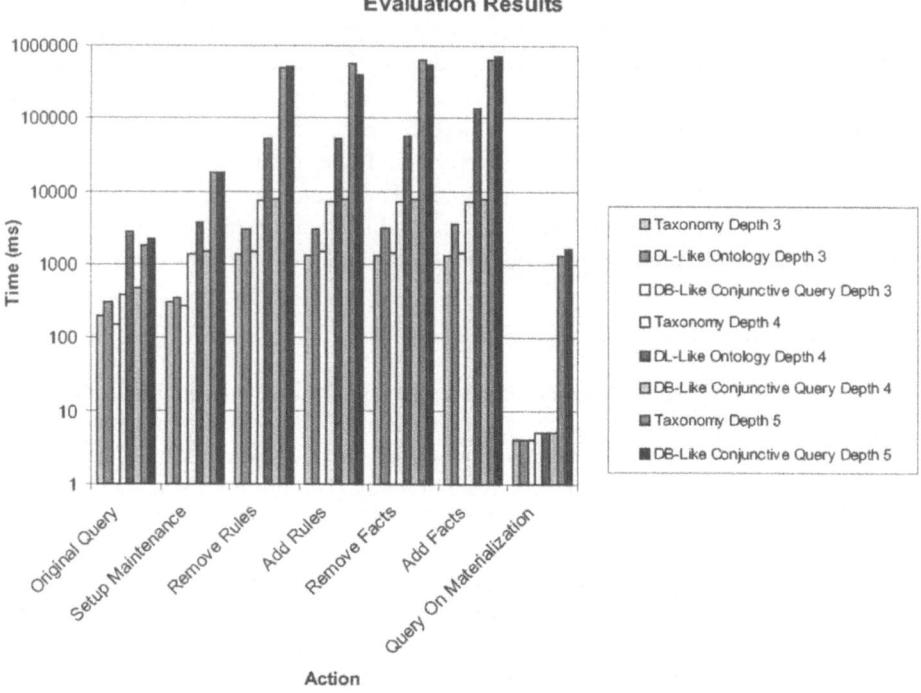

Fig. 3. Evaluation Results (Average Values)

Test 1: Taxonomy. Extended taxonomies, e.g. WordNet, currently constitute a large portion of the ontologies that are in use. Our goal with this test is to see how the very basic task of taking the taxonomy into account when retrieving the extension of a class is improved. The taxonomy is constituted by a symmetric tree of classes. We did not make use of properties, hence $P = 0$. The test query involved computing the extension of one of the concepts on the first level of the class hierarchy. This is a realistic query in systems where taxonomies are used for navigation in document collections. Here, navigation typically starts with top-level classes and the set of documents is displayed as the class extension.

Test 2: Database-like. The goal of this test was to see how ontologies with larger number of properties are handled. Our goal was to answer a simple conjunctive query on top of this ontology. The DL-like query is c1 ⊓ ∃p0.c12.

Test 3: DL-like. This test shows how materialization performs in DL-like ontologies, which contain simple class definitions. Each class in the class tree is defined using the following axiom: $c_i \sqcup \exists p_k.c_{i-1} \sqsubseteq c$ (where c_i denotes i-th child of concept c). The query retrieves the extension of some random class in the first-level of the taxonomy.

5.4   Results

Figure 3 depicts the average time[6] for querying an ontology without using materialization, setting up the materialization and cost of maintenance for different types of changes (adding and removing rules and facts). Finally, the time for answering the same query using the materialization is depicted. The exact results of the evaluation can be online[7].

As we can see in the figure, maintenance costs do not vary significantly with the quantity of updates. All costs are directly related to the size of the ontologies. The performance behavior between the taxonomy and DB-like ontologies do also not alter significantly. However, more complex rules as they are constituted by DL-like ontologies are always more expensive to evaluate, therefore setup costs and the cost of evaluating the maintenance rules is also higher.

We want to stress that we measured the performance of concrete tools. Although algorithms implemented by a system are certainly important, the overall performance of a system is influenced by many other factors as well, such the quality of the implementation or the language. It is virtually impossible to exclude these factors from the performance measurement. For example, our Datalog engine ran out of memory with the DL-like ontology where the taxonomic depth was five, viz. the set of rules was generated from 3950 class and 19750 property definitions, while the underlying knowledge base contained 19750 class instantiations and 32915 property instantiations.

5.5   Discussion

The different costs of each step in the maintenance procedure are always higher than the costs of evaluating a single query. The question whether or not to materialize is therefore determined by the application and the issue whether the system can handle its typical workload, e.g. can it handle the intended number of users if answering a single query takes almost 3 seconds ?

With materialization the cost of accessing the materialized predicates is can be neglected. However, the time for the evaluation of the maintenance rules can be a significant bottleneck for a system especially for large knowledge-bases. For example, in one of our test runs it took almost 16 minutes to recompute the materialization after fact changes for the DB-like test with taxonomic depth 5. Fortunately, materialization can be carried out in parallel to answering queries on top of the existing materialization.

In consequence, users will have to operate on stale copies of data. Staleness of data cannot be avoided in distributed scenarios like the Web in the first place, and existing experiences, e.g. with outdated page ranks of a web pages in Google, show that the quality of query answering is still good enough, if data is updated occasionally.

6   Related Work

We can find related work in two areas: Firstly, incremental maintenance of materialized views in deductive databases. Secondly, truth maintenance systems in the Artificial Intelligence context.

---

[6] in milliseconds on a logarithmic scale

[7] http://kaon.semanticweb.org/research/materialization

Incremental Maintenance of Materialized Views. Several algorithms have been devised for the incremental maintenance of views. All of these approaches do not consider changes in the set of rules and differ in the techniques used to cope with changes in facts. In order to cope with changing facts [1,12] efficiently compute the standard model of a stratified database after a database is updated. The proposed solution of [1] uses sets of positive and negative dependencies that are maintained for all derived facts. This leads to low space efficiency and high cost for maintaining the dependencies. Another drawback of the approach is the granularity of the materialization which is the whole database.

[12] also derives rules (so-called meta-programs) to compute the difference between consecutive database states for a stratified Datalog program. The rules do not follow our three step principle and some of the generated rules are not safe making it impossible to implement the rules in typical Datalog engines. Additionally duplicate derivations are not discarded in the algorithm.

[7] present the DRed algorithm, which is a procedural approach to view maintenance in Datalog with stratified negation. We follow their principal approach in the for the computation of changes, in fact their procedural algorithm has been rewritten into the declarative version we use by [19].

The Progragation Filtration algorithm of [9] is similar to the DRed algorithm, except that changes are propagated on a predicate by predicate basis. Hence, it computes changes in one intensional predicate due to changes in one extensional predicate, looping over all derived and extensional predicate to complete the maintenance procedure. In each step of the loop the delete, re-derive and insert steps are executed. The algorithm ends up fragmenting computation and rederiving changed and deleted facts over and over again.

Truth Maintenance Systems. Truth maintenance (also called belief revision or reason maintenance) is an area of AI concerned with revising sets of beliefs and maintaining the truth in the system when new information alters existing information. To this extent a representation of beliefs and their dependencies is necessary to achieve the retraction of believes and to identify contradictions. For example, justification-based TMS [5] uses a graph data structure where nodes are augmented with two fields indicating their belief status and supporting justification. When the belief status is changed, dependencies are propagated through the graph. Making TMSs more efficient was a cottage industry in the late 1980s, with most of the attention focused on the Assumption-based TMS [3]. The primary advantage of the ATMS is its ability to rapidly switch among many different contexts, e.g. it is simpler to propagate the withdrawal of facts, but this comes at the cost of an exponential node-label updating process. Disadvantages of TMS is that the set of justifications (and nodes) grows monotonically as it is not allowed to retract a justification, but only disable information. The fact that the set of assumption is always in flux introduces most of the complexity in the TMS algorithms. More recent work (e.g. [14]) primarily tried to reduce the cost for incremental updates. However, the underlying principle of labelling does not change. To the best of our knowledge, there is no TMS, where the aggregation of all historic information is avoided, viz. facts are permanently removed from the system. Additionally the primary technique deployed in TMS (backtracking) does not fit well with the bottom-up computation that is usually applied in deductive databases.

7 Conclusion

We have presented an incremental maintenance technique for the materialization of intentional predicates (views). Unlike previous approaches, our approach allows to change the set of rules in a stratified Datalog program. We have presented a preliminary performance evaluation which underlines the feasibility of our solution. We regard our results to be central to achieve scalability in large-scale Semantic systems such as presented by the Semantic Web. We have shown how our approach can be used with current means for specifying semantics in the Semantic Web. As we present a generic solution, future developments, e.g. for the rule layer of the Semantic Web, are likely to benefit from our technique as well. Materialization is certainly not a panacea to all tractability problems. One drawback is that it trades off required inferencing time against storage space and access time.

In spite of such restrictions, we conjecture that materialization as explained in this paper will help to progress the Semantic Web and to build the large Semantic Web engines of tomorrow — the Semantic Web analogon to a syntactic Google.

Future work will address the maintenance when existential quantification is available in the rule language, such as in N3. This will involve maintaining skolem constants, which are used in the implementation of existential quantification. Additionally, we will investigate the obvious space-time trade-off between the solutions presented in sections 3 and 4 and non-materialized evaluation. This needs to be investigated quantitatively, including different options how to materialize: fully, by view indexes, with or without intermediate results, etc. Further, one might integrate algorithms that determine when modifications leave a predicate unchanged. This could be done for facts in style of [13] and for rules in style of [8].

References

1. K. Apt and J.-M. Pugin. Maintenance of stratified databases viewed as belief revision system. In *Proc. of the 6th Symposium on Principles of Database Systems (PODS)*, pages 136–145, San Diego, CA, USA, March 1987.
2. S. Bechhofer, C. Goble, and I. Horrocks. DAML+OIL is not enough. In *SWWS-1, Semantic Web working symposium*, Jul/Aug 2001.
3. J. de Kleer. An assumption-based truth maintenance system. *Artificial Intelligence*, 28(1986), 127–162.
4. S. Decker, D. Brickley, J. Saarela, and J. Angele. A query and inference service for RDF. In *QL98 – Query Languages Workshop*, December 1998.
5. J. Doyle. A truth maintenance system. In B. Webber and N. J. Nilsson, editors, *Readings in Artifcial Intelligence*, pages 496–516. SMorgan Kaufmann, Los Altos, California, 1981.
6. B. Grossof, I. Horrocks, R. Volz, and S. Decker. Description Logic Programs: Combining Logic Programs with Description Logic. In *Proceedings of WWW 2003*, Budapest, Hungary, May 2003.
7. A. Gupta, I.S. Mumick, and V.S. Subrahmanian. Maintaining views incrementally. In *ACM SIGMOD Conference on Management of Data*, 1993.
8. Ashish Gupta, Inderpal Singh Mumick, and Kenneth A. Ross. Adapting materialized views after redefinitions. In Michael J. Carey and Donovan A. Schneider, editors, *Proceedings of the 1995 ACM SIGMOD International Conference on Management of Data, San Jose, California, May 22–25, 1995*, pages 211–222. ACM Press, 1995.

9. John Harrison and Suzanne Dietrich. Maintenance of materialized views in a deductive database: An update propagation approach. In *Workshop on Deductive Databases, JICSLP*, 1992.
10. Patrick Hayes. RDF Semantics. W3C Working Draft, World-Wide Web Consortium (W3C), http://www.w3.org/TR/rdf-mt/, January 2003.
11. Matthias Jarke, Rainer Gallersdoerfer, Manfred A. Jeusfeld, and Martin Staudt. ConceptBase – A Deductive Object Base for Meta Data Management. *JIIS*, 4(2):167–192, 1995.
12. V. Kuchenhoff. On the efficient computation of the difference betwen consecutive database states. In Claude Delobel, Michael Kifer, and Yoshifumi Masunaga, editors, *Proc. of 2nd Int. Conf. on Deductive and Object-Oriented Databases*, volume 566 of *Lecture Notes in Computer Science (LNCS)*, pages 478–502, Munich, Germany, December 1991. Springer.
13. A. Y. Levy and Y. Sagiv. Queries independent of updates. In *Proc. of 19th VLDB*, pages 171–181, 1993.
14. P. Pandurang Nayak and Brian C. Williams. Fast Context Switching in Real-time Propositional Reasoning. In *Proceedings of AAAI-97*, 1997.
15. P. F. Patel-Schneider, P. Hayes, I. Horrocks, and F. van Harmelen. Web Ontology Language (OWL) Abstract Syntax and Semantics. http://www.w3.org/TR/owl-semantics/, 2002.
16. Jos De Roo. Euler proof mechanism. Internet: http://www.agfa.com/w3c/euler/, 2002.
17. Michael Sintek and Stefan Decker. TRIPLE – A Query, Inference, and Transformation Language for the Semantic Web. In *International Semantic Web Conference (ISWC)*, June 2002.
18. M. Staudt and M. Jarke. Incremental maintenance of externally materialized views. Technical Report AIB-95-13, RWTH Aachen, 1995.
19. Martin Staudt and Matthias Jarke. Incremental maintenance of externally materialized views. In T. M. Vijayaraman, Alejandro P. Buchmann, C. Mohan, and Nandlal L. Sarda, editors, *VLDB'96, Proceedings of 22th International Conference on Very Large Data Bases, September 3–6, 1996, Mumbai (Bombay), India*, pages 75–86. Morgan Kaufmann, 1996.
20. Guizhen Yang and Michael Kifer. FLORA: Implementing an Efficient DOOD System Using a Tabling Logic Engine. In *Computational Logic 2000*, pages 1078–1093, 2000.

Scalable and Reliable Semantic Portals (SEAL) in Practice

Jens Hartmann and York Sure

Institute AIFB, University of Karlsruhe,
76128 Karlsruhe, Germany
{hartmann,sure}@aifb.uni-karlsruhe.de
http://www.aifb.uni-karlsruhe.de/WBS/

Abstract. We present a scalable and reliable framework for Semantic Portals which is an extension of our existing SEAL approach. We illustrate the instantiation of our framework by the real-world example of a heterogeneous and distributed infrastructure of Semantic Portals, viz. the portal of our institute AIFB, the OntoWeb.org portals and the KM-Vision.org portal. The approach relies on the application of current semantic technologies whereby we still keep practical usability. Generally, we show that our approach can be used to build up Semantic Portals from scratch or to build up on existing portal infrastructures as a layered Semantic Portal on top. We present several modi for integration of multiple portals and show how we address practical issues like scalability and robustness of Semantic Portals.

1 Introduction

Identifying and presenting useful information for a given context is an important challenge for current research activities and developments of web technologies (cf., e.g., [Cha03,HRGMP00]). Providing access to information for humans and machines is one of the main motivations for the Semantic Web (cf. [BL99]) which is constantly moving from being a vision to becoming reality.

We present an approach which realizes semantic-based search and access facilities to information represented by Semantic Portals. Semantic Portals rely on domain ontologies to structure and exchange knowledge. Ontologies were exploited in Computer Science to enhance knowledge sharing and re-use (cf., e.g., [Gru95,Fen01]). Firstly, they provide a shared and common understanding of knowledge in a domain of interest. Secondly, they capture and formalize knowledge by connecting human understanding of symbols with their machine processability. As such, ontologies act as common language between agents and play a key role for realizing the Semantic Web.

Our approach relies on the SEAL conceptual architecture (cf. [MSS+02]) for building Semantic Portals. This paper presents the extension of SEAL to provide scalable and reliable infrastructure for Semantic Portals. In particular we show how multiple Semantic Portals can interact with each other to exchange knowledge, thus re-using it. The building blocks of our extension consist of knowledge integration, processing, representation, organization and access.

R. Meersman et al. (Eds.): CoopIS/DOA/ODBASE 2003, LNCS 2888, pp. 725–738, 2003.
© Springer-Verlag Berlin Heidelberg 2003

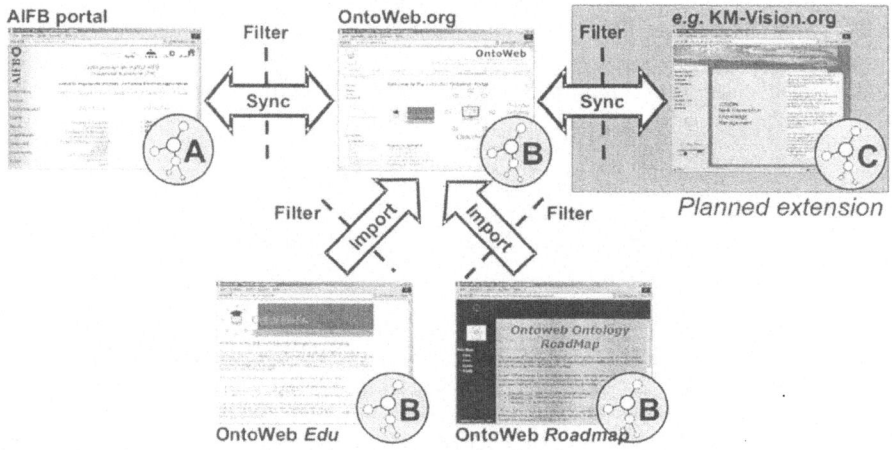

Fig. 1. Semantic Portal infrastructure

The paper is structured as follows: in section 2 we illustrate a real-world Semantic Portal infrastructure which currently consists of the portal of our institute AIFB and the OntoWeb.org portals. We plan to extend the infrastructure by the KM-Vision.org portal. Common to all these portals is their usage of domain ontologies as backbone, but they differ in their underlying technologies and their represented knowledge. We use this example to illustrate one of the key benefits of Semantic Portals, viz. to exchange knowledge automatically. In section 3 we describe the core SEAL approach, i.e. the AIFB conceptual architecture for building Semantic Portals. In section 4 we describe in detail how we extended SEAL to a scalable and reliable framework for portals in practice, e.g. instantiated by the infrastructure presented in section 2. Before concluding in section 6 we present related work in section 5.

2   Semantic Portals in Practice

We now introduce an up-and-running infrastructure of Semantic Portals as showcase of our underlying extended SEAL framework. Currently the following portals are part of the infrastructure which is depicted in figure 1:

- AIFB portal
- OntoWeb portals
    - OntoWeb.org
    - OntoWeb *Edu*
    - OntoWeb *Roadmap*
- planned: KM-Vision.org

The AIFB portal, OntoWeb.org and KM-Vision.org are relying on different ontologies (named A, B and C) since they cover different domains and are targeted to a different audience. The three portals related to OntoWeb rely on the same ontology (named B). In fact, the initial ontology for the OntoWeb.org portal (cf. [SSV⁺01]) has been meanwhile extended to cover also the contents of the other two OntoWeb portals.

From a technical point of view, the upper three portals rely more or less on the same technology as a baseline, viz. the Open Source ZOPE[1] web application server framework and its extensions. This baseline technology enables us to automatically synchronize content between these portals. The three OntoWeb related portals rely on different baseline technologies. Since there are currently few changes in OntoWeb *Edu* and OntoWeb *Roadmap* no synchronization is actually needed. Filters allow to specify on a rather detailed level what kind of content will be exchanged. If needed, a publication workflow which involves human reviewers in the loop ensures the quality of the provided content (cf. [SSV02]). More technical details will be presented in section 4.

We now describe briefly each portal, thereby introducing main rationales and targeted audiences. Then we give examples for content exchange to illustrate how it works in practice.

2.1   AIFB Portal

The portal of the institute AIFB[2] is dedicated mainly to students and researchers. It provides information about teaching, exams, people, research groups, projects, events, jobs etc., thus acting as a single entry point for all teaching and research actions of the research groups hosted by the institute. Details on the modelling of the ontology for the AIFB portal can be found in [SEA⁺02].

2.2   OntoWeb Portals

The EU IST-2000-29243 "OntoWeb: Ontology-based Information Exchange for Knowledge Management and Electronic Commerce" thematic network is a part of the Information Societies Technologies (IST) Programme of the European Union (EU). The thematic network has currently over 100 partners coming from academia and industry. Most of them are located in Europe, but there exist also strong links to communities in the United States of America and Asia. The goal of OntoWeb Network is to bring researcher and industrials together enabling the full power ontologies may have to improve information exchange in areas such as: information retrieval, knowledge management, electronic commerce, and bioinformatics.

As part of the work, three portals have been built up: OntoWeb.org[3], OntoWeb *Edu*[4] and OntoWeb *Roadmap*[5]. OntoWeb.org represents the OntoWeb

---

[1] http://www.zope.org/

[2] http://www.aifb.uni-karlsruhe.de/

[3] http://www.ontoweb.org/

[4] http://qmir.dcs.qmul.ac.uk/ontoweb/

[5] http://babage.dia.fi.upm.es/ontoweb/wp1/OntoRoadMap/index.html

community and serves as a main community platform to exchange information (cf., e.g., [SOV+02]) between partners of the network and to distribute information to "the rest of the world". OntoWeb *Edu* provides a large collection of course materials dedicated to Semantic Web and ontologies. Last, but not least, OntoWeb *Roadmap* provides a state-of-the-art overview of existing tools, applications, methodologies related to Semantic Web and ontologies, including a list of available ontologies.

2.3   KM-Vision.org

KM-Vision.org[6] is a widely known information source for the Knowledge Management community and interested parties. It represents the EU IST-2002-38513 Vision roadmap project and provides information about current events, projects and the KM roadmap for Europe.

2.4   Examples for Knowledge Exchange

Before we describe the underlying SEAL conceptual architecture in the next section, we will now illustrate knowledge exchange by two examples. Common concepts in the ontologies of the AIFB portal, OntoWeb.org and KM-Vision.org are events and publications. In a traditional setting one would maintain these items separately in each portal. But, since there are overlapping interests, several chances for re-using of provided knowledge occur to reduce the manual maintenance burden, e.g.:

- OntoWeb.org and KM-Vision.org are very closely related, therefore the same kinds of events are published at the two portals.
- These events are also related to our working group at the AIFB, but they are typically not related the other working groups.
- All publications of our working group at the AIFB should also be findable through the OntoWeb.org portal.

In a first step we mapped the parts of the three ontologies A, B, and C which relate to events and of A and B which relate to publications. We followed a rather pragmatic approach for mapping and engineered the ontologies so that the mappings are one-to-one mappings, e.g. one concept in A is mapped directly to a corresponding concept in B etc. By using further filters we then were able to put further constraints, e.g. only to synchronize between the AIFB portal and OntoWeb.org the events related to our working group (not the other ones).

Currently we are working on the support for more advanced ontology mapping features. A first version of an full-fledged ontology mapping tool already exists for our ontology editor OntoEdit, called OntoMap, which supports the graphically oriented creation of mappings between ontologies. These mappings are stored as F-Logic (cf. [KLW95]) axioms and can be processed by Ontobroker (cf. [DEFS99]).

---

[6] http://www.km-vision.org/

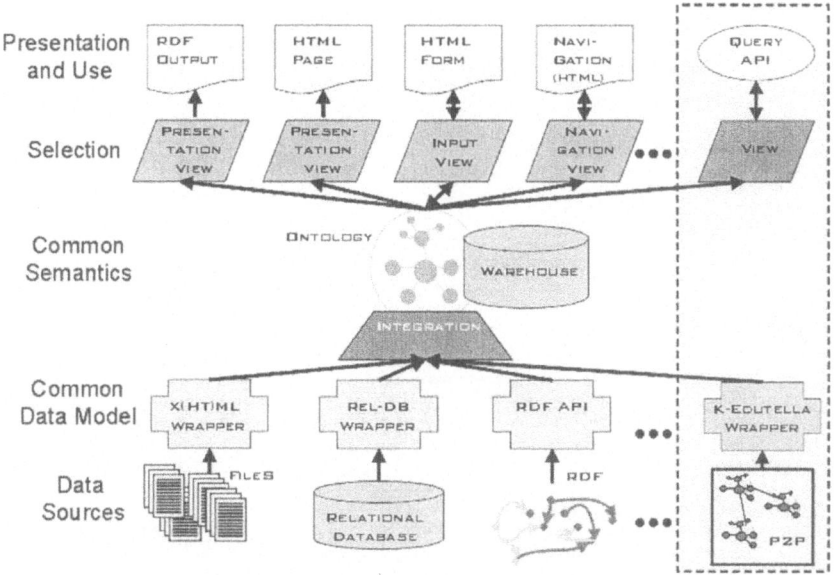

Fig. 2. SEAL conceptual architecture

3   The Core SEAL Approach

SEAL (cf. [MSS+02]), the AIFB conceptual architecture for building Semantic Portals, has been developed to use ontologies as key elements for managing community web sites and web portals. The ontology supports queries to multiple sources, but beyond that it also includes the intensive use of the schema information itself allowing for automatic generation of navigational views[7] and mixed ontology and content-based presentation. The core idea of SEAL is that Semantic Portals for a community of users that contribute *and* consume information [SAD+00] require web site management *and* web information integration. In order to reduce engineering and maintenance efforts SEAL uses an ontology for semantic integration of existing data sources as well as for web site management and presentation to the outside world. SEAL exploits the ontology to offer mechanisms for acquiring, structuring and sharing information by means of semantic annotations [HS02] between human and/or machine agents. Thus, SEAL combines the advantages of the two worlds briefly sketched above.

The SEAL conceptual architecture (cf. Figure 2) depicts the general scheme. Approaches for web site management emphasize on the upper part of the figure and approaches for web information integration focus on the lower part while SEAL combines both with an ontology as the knot in the middle.

---

[7] Examples are navigation hierarchies that appear as `has-part`-trees or `has-subtopic` trees in the ontology.

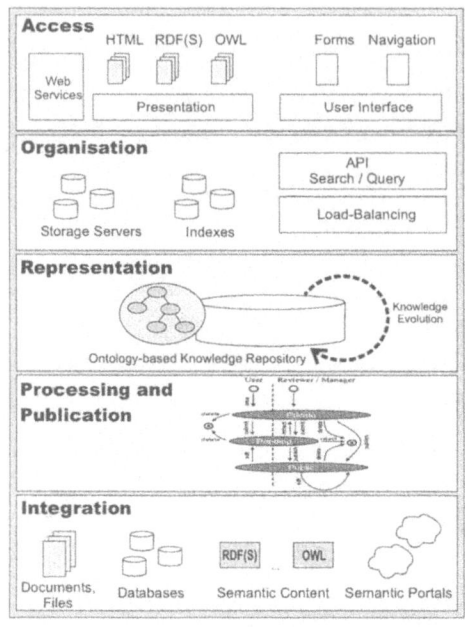

Fig. 3. Building blocks of our Semantic Portal Framework

4   Scalable and Reliable SEAL Extension

Our approach enhances the core SEAL approach with a sophisticated framework for **integrating knowledge** and shows how this approach can be applied on **existing knowledge bases** respectively existing information portals. Besides, it provides the ability to set up a very *scalable infrastructure* which can be *distributed and interconnected* across the web with other participants towards the Semantic Web vision.

We argue that, often some kind of information sources already exists and these sources and their appendant infrastructure should be re-used. Therefore our approach can be set up on top of existing technologies and act as a kind of Semantic Layer for them using the developed integration mechanisms.

Generally, the approach consists of several conceptual layers which are presented in figure 3.

These layers can be seen as Knowledge workflows from the integration towards the final visualisation of stored knowledge in the users browser. The basis is the *Knowledge Integration* layer which holds a set of modules whereby each module can handle a specific information source. For instance, the database module handles in- and output requests to specific databases. Further, the *Knowledge Processing* layer, creates content instances and provides a set of knowledge processing methods, e.g. publishing workflows. The representation of knowledge, is handled by the *Knowledge Representation* layer whereby we use Ontologies for a formal knowledge representation method. The next layer, going upwards, is the *Knowledge Organisation* layer which provides methods for indexing and search functionalities. The layer *Knowledge Access* defines methods for presenting content in different output formats and defines interaction interfaces.

In the next sections we will describe each layer in detail.

4.1 Knowledge Integration

In general, information sources may appear *distributed, heterogenous* and tend to be *impermanent* while the semantic interrelation aggravating the task of integrating information into one common knowledge repository.

The Knowledge Integration mechanism is divided up into three main parts. We speak of *Interconnected Integration* of knowledge when the data sources are closely **technically and semantically interconnected**. Mainly, we use this method to integrate other portals or metadata from them. As a result, this set of portals can build one large common portal like the OntoWeb.org portal[8]. On the other hand, we use the term of *Bounded Integration* when the information sources (as the case may be: other portals) are **semantically bounded** and may technically diverge. For instance the KM-Vision.org and OntoWeb.org portal are semantically bounded portals. Nevertheless, to share and integrate knowledge from previously unknown information sources or single (small) sources, we use the generic *Knowledge Integration* module providing integration facilities for several formats like the widely accepted RDF(S) [LS99,W3C99] and the upcoming Semantic Web language OWL [MvHe03].

As a result, the integration mechanisms makes the approach scalable and powerful, since it is possible to build up on information sources. On one hand, one can keep using existing information sources and its infrastructure and, on the other hand, easily setting up a Semantic Portal without a time and cost consuming transformation progress. The Semantic Portal remains flexible and adaptable to different information sources.

Further, the investment in such a Semantic Portal can become more straightforward and more transparent already in the planning phase as also in the execution period.

Generic Knowledge Integration. Our approach basically supports a set of standard data formats which can be integrated, ad-hoc. In particular, these consist of a set of several database-connectors, interpreters for standard file formats and RDF(S) and OWL parsers.

Interconnected Integration. The *Interconnected Integration* is used for integrating large, complex information sources which have a similar technical architecture. Therefore the integrated knowledge is kept as it is and the mediation

---

[8] Which consist physically of three portals. The main AIFB+VUB OntoWeb.org portal, the OntoWeb Edu portal and the Ontology Roadmap portal.

between the information source and the Semantic Portal has to be defined. This method can be applied to complete information portals acting as one large information source. However, since there is no knowledge replication mechanism, one has to assure long term availability for this soure. Probably, this holds mainly for own maintained sources. For instance, the AIFB Portal (http://www.aifb.uni-karlsruhe.de) is connected to the OntoWeb.org portal in this way whereby both portals are technical maintained by the AIFB.

Bounded Integration. In many cases, there is a need to integrate knowledge from previously unknown or not influenceable sources. Therefore, the *Bounded Integration* framework has been developed providing mechanisms to integrate such information sources, whereby sources are replicated in the executing Semantic Portal. The integrated information can then be modified, evolved, etc. without changing the source. Further, to keep track of changes from the original source, it is possible to **synchronize information** between the original source and the Semantic Portal itself. For instance, this method is used for OntoWeb.org and KM-Vision.org to synchronize knowledge. Further, it is possible to integrate only Metadata of information sources into the Semantic Portal. Then the synchronization mechanism is used to update the metadata if it detects changes in the original source.

The synchronization of information leads to several problems like classical well-known problems of synchronizing files. However, synchronizing knowledge between Semantic Portals is further a question of merging and mapping Ontologies, assumed that Ontologies are used for representing the knowledge. Therefore, the bounded integration supports mappings which has to be defined for specific mapping parties.

4.2   Knowledge Processing

Knowledge can be managed by several *Semantic Processing Actions and Workflows*. In this section, we describe pre-defined methods on knowledge as a whole and on single knowledge items.

Knowledge Creation. Integrated Knowledge is *initialized* by the *Knowledge Creation* process which does (i) portal specific transformations and (ii) creates metadata for further processing and access.

The portal specific transformations (i) consists of portal specific technical transformations. Basically, we introduced such enclosure of methods to provide a generic framework. Technical details are described in [Har03].

Semantic capabilities of a portal are supported by a set of metadata(ii) which consists of general information like *creation date, author, publisher, etc.*. The used properties are based on the Dublin Core metadata[9] standard and some additional information describing relations to semantic concepts or other instances

---

[9] cf. http://www.dublincore.org/

in the portal Ontology. The metadata can be evolved by human users and machine agents under given access rights which are provided by the underlying software ZOPE[10] and Plone[11].

Knowledge Publication. One main goal of an information portal is to provide access to content dedicated to a specific community.

The framework reflects several publication methods usable for humans and machine agents. Generally, each knowledge instance of the portal holds a specific *publication state* which determines further processing or handling of the instance. Followed by a creation of a knowledge instance and its initial state following publishing workflow can be applied.

The Knowledge Input enables each user (human or machine agent) to create knowledge instances in his private user folder. To publish the knowledge a user can change the particular *state* whereby it is possible to keep the knowledge *private* or to make it explicitly *public* by submitting it to the *Review Process*.

The Review Process controls submitted knowledge instances which are examined by users which have the special role *Reviewer*. Further a Reviewer has the ability to modify the instance itself or the metadata, e.g. to prevent misclassifications.

4.3   Knowledge Representation

Ontologies are shared conceptualizations of a domain which can be seen as an agreed view of a domain for affiliated persons. We use an Ontology describing technically objects in the portal as also the knowledge of a portal. However, we support the usage of several Ontologies in a Semantic Portal.

We modelled our Ontology with OntoEdit [SSA02]. Since tools like OntoEdit supports *internationalization* of terms in an ontology, it is possible to support multi-lingual portals. Necessarily, the portal framework itself supports multilingual knowledge representations.

The knowledge is kept in an *Ontology-based Knowledge Repository* which provides general methods for storing the knowledge through a generic interface, as shown in figure 4. As a result, several different technical solutions for storing and accessing knowledge can be used. For instance, a standard relational database or, in case of using ZOPE, the Zope Object Data Base (ZODB)[12]. Reasoning facilities can be provided by Ontobroker [DEFS99].

4.4   Knowledge Organisation

We present an elaborated and practically evaluated concept for managing massive amounts of knowledge. These methods are used for Semantic Portal infrastructures located at one place, e.g. the AIFB portal is exclusively hosted at the

---

[10] cf. http://www.zope.org

[11] cf. http://www.plone.org

[12] Notice, to run a set of servers connected to one central knowledge repository it is necessary to use ZEO (Zope Enterprise Objects) instead of ZODB.

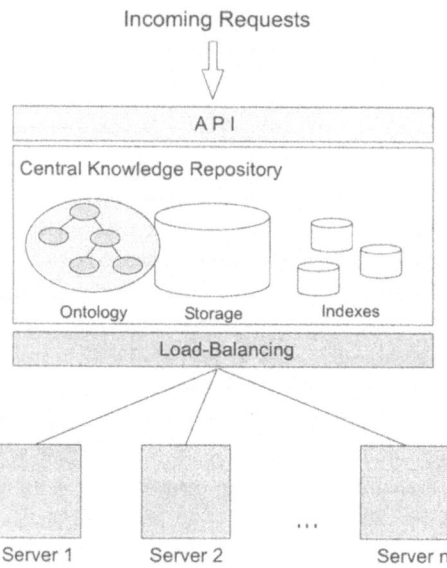

Fig. 4. Knowledge Organisation

AIFB, or to interconnect Semantic Portals across the web whereby the degree of interconnection and level of knowledge exchange can be adapted.

Based on the knowledge representation mechanism several continuative methods for organizing knowledge are developed to provide fast and effective access to knowledge.

Storage Mechanisms. Supporting large and scalable frameworks, we use a highly scalable storage mechanism which allows to set up distributed servers in a cluster for handling a large amount requests, as shown in figure 4.

Index and Search Facilities. Providing fast access methods to knowledge we provide a set of indexing facilities to create pre-processed indexes which can accelerate the access to a portal especially for search functionalities. Generally, indexes are created for concepts, relations and full-text search ability. Furthermore, one can freely define further indexes. For instance, one may create an index for a specific information source to provide an effective search and access.

4.5 Knowledge Access

This section describes the provided interfaces for accessing knowledge in a Semantic Portal. In sense of the Semantic Web, we provide interfaces for humans and machines.

Presentation. Applying *information extraction* methods combined with *knowledge integration* techniques towards an ontology-based knowledge repository *is* one difficult task of a Semantic Portal. However, presenting knowledge in an easy understandable and useful way for users, is another challenging task. Presenting knowledge to users is not one generic generation of nice HTML files rather than a sophisticated visualization of knowledge for users with different experiences. Therefore the Semantic Portal must provide several views on the stored knowledge. The presentation layer generates graphical user interfaces for users by producing HTML output. Underlying templates define where, how and when knowledge is presented to the user. The browsing interface respectively the navigation bar of the portal is dynamically generated from the Ontology.

To support users interacting with the portal we developed a context-sensitive help system providing useful tips and explanations based on the current context.

Searching and Querying the Portal. The portal offers several search and query functionalities to the user like standard fullt-text search forms as well as complex query forms, e.g. allowing to query for specific concepts or a set of them by using a simple query logic.

Personalization. As an Ontology represents a commonly shared conceptualization of a domain, an individual often comes with his own personal view. Further, different experiences requests different visualizations. Therefore, we argue that a Semantic Portal and especially community portals should provide personalization services which can become key enablers for successful portals.

Our framework supports users in describing and storing individual content in a private folder in which content can be made explicitly public available or kept for private use only. Generally, a user can store knowledge instances of the ontology in his folder. Currently, it is not possible to modify the ontology itself.

5   Related Work

Using an ontology to support the access of content has been discussed before. E.g., the so-called Yahoo-a-lizer [Erd01] transforms a knowledge base into a set of XML pages that are structured like the term hierarchy of Yahoo. These XML-files are translated via an XSL-stylesheet into ordinary HTML. Within Ontobroker-based web portals [DEFS99], a Hyperbolic View Applet allows for graphical access to an ontology and its knowledge base. Another related work is KAON Portal[13] which takes an ontology and creates a standard Web interface out of it. OntoWebber [JXD02,JDW03] also generates web interfaces based on ontologies.

Given the difficulties with managing complex Web content, several papers tried to facilitate database technology to simplify the creation and maintenance of data-intensive web-sites. OntoWeb implements our framework for a SEmantic

---

[13] cf. http://kaon.semanticweb.org/Portal

portAL, viz. SEAL [MSS+02], that relies on standard Semantic Web technologies. Other systems, such as ARANEUS [MMAC99] and AutoWeb [CFB00], take a declarative approach, i.e. they introduce their own data models and query languages, although all approaches share the idea to provide high-level descriptions of web-sites by distinct orthogonal dimensions. The idea of leveraging mediation technologies for the acquisition of data is also found in approaches like Strudel [FFLS00] and Tiramisu [ALW99], they propose a separation according to the aforementioned task profiles as well. Strudel does not concern the aspects of site maintenance and personalization. It is actually only an implementation tool, not a management system.

The importance of conceptual indexing for information retrieval has been acknowledged since quite some time in the medical information processing field [RA93,ZBB+98]. However, from our point of view the presented Semantic Portal infrastructure is rather unique with respect to the collection of methods used and the functionality provided.

6   Conclusions

Our aim is to showcase the potential value of Semantic Web applications in real-world. We presented a scalable and reliable approach for creating and maintaining Semantic Portals. We demonstrated a real-world infrastructure with a large amount of stored knowledge and a large number of users. The focus of the approach is to bring semantic technologies into real-world applications. The framework can be applied on existing information sources while the sources are kept in their original state. This solution was applied to the OntoWeb.org portals. Sophisticated portal facilities like load-balancing, mirroring and clustering provides a powerful framework to setup interconnected portals among the web. Further details on this approach can be found for the interested technical reader in [Har03].

Currently, we are developing **Web Services** interfaces for the portal to share knowledge with portals which are not based on our technical framework whereby we focus on Semantic Web Services. Further we will potentially extend our set of interconnected Semantic Portals by connecting to the KM-Vision portal which is based on our KAON technology[14]. Last, but not least, we will use advanced mapping facilities based on the usage of the OntoEdit plugin OntoMap in combination with Ontobroker to expand the knowledge exchange facilities.

Acknowledgements. We thank our colleagues at the Institute AIFB, at the VUB STAR Lab, Brussels, who provided parts of the OntoWeb.org portal, at the KMI and Queen Mary, UK, who developed the OntoWeb *Edu* portal, and at the UPM, Madrid, who developed the OntoWeb *Roadmap* portal. Part of this work was financed by the EU IST-2000-29243 OntoWeb thematic network.

---

[14] http://km.aifb.uni-karlsruhe.de/kaon/

References

[ALW99]   C. R. Anderson, A. Y. Levy, and D. S. Weld. Declarative web site management with Tiramisu. In *ACM SIGMOD Workshop on the Web and Databases - WebDB99*, pages 19–24, 1999.

[BL99]   T. Berners-Lee. *Weaving the Web*. Harper, 1999.

[CFB00]   S. Ceri, P. Fraternali, and A. Bongio. Web modeling language (WebML): a modeling language for designing web sites. In *WWW9 Conference, Amsterdam, May 2000*, 2000.

[Cha03]   S. Chakrabarti. *Mining the Web: Discovering knowledge from hypertext data*. Morgan Kaufmann, San Francisco, 2003.

[DEFS99]   S. Decker, M. Erdmann, D. Fensel, and R. Studer. Ontobroker: Ontology Based Access to Distributed and Semi-Structured Information. In R. Meersman et al., editors, *Database Semantics: Semantic Issues in Multimedia Systems*, pages 351–369. Kluwer Academic Publisher, 1999.

[Erd01]   Michael Erdmann. *Ontologien zur konzeptuellen Modellierung der Semantik von XML*. Isbn: 3831126356, University of Karlsruhe, 10 2001.

[Fen01]   D. Fensel. *Ontologies: Silver bullet for knowledge management and electronic commerce*. Springer-Verlag, Berlin, 2001.

[FFLS00]   M. F. Fernandez, D. Florescu, A. Y. Levy, and D. Suciu. Declarative specification of web sites with Strudel. *VLDB Journal*, 9(1):38–55, 2000.

[Gru95]   T. R. Gruber. Towards principles for the design of ontologies used for knowledge sharing. *International Journal of Human-Computer Studies*, 43(5/6):907–928, 1995.

[Har03]   Jens Hartmann. Technical Infrastructure for Semantic Portals. Technical report, University of Karlsruhe, Institute AIFB, 2003. To appear.

[HRGMP00]   Jun Hirai, Sriram Raghavan, Hector García-Molina, and Andreas Paepcke. WebBase: A repository of web pages. In *Proceedings of the Ninth World-Wide Web Conference*, 2000.

[HS02]   S. Handschuh and S. Staab. Authoring and annotation of web pages in CREAM. In *The Eleventh International World Wide Web Conference (WWW2002), Honolulu, Hawaii, USA 7–11 May*, 2002.

[JDW03]   Yuhui Jin, Stefan Decker, and Gio Wiederhold. Ontowebber: Building web sites using semantic web technologies. In *Twelfth International World Wide Web Conference in Budapest, HUNGARY*, May 2003.

[JXD02]   Yuhui Jin, Sichun Xu, and Stefan Decker. Ontowebber: A novel approach for managing data on the web. In *In Proceedings of the 8th International Conference on Extending Database Technology (EDBT 2002). Prague, Czech Republic.*, March 2002.

[KLW95]   M. Kifer, G. Lausen, and J. Wu. Logical foundations of object-oriented and frame-based languages. *Journal of the ACM*, 42:741–843, 1995.

[LS99]   O. Lassila and R. Swick. Resource Description Framework (RDF). Model and syntax specification. Technical report, W3C, 1999. http://www.w3.org/TR/REC-rdf-syntax.

[MMAC99]   G. Mecca, P. Merialdo, P. Atzeni, and V. Crescenzi. The (short) Araneus guide to web-site development. In *Second Intern. Workshop on the Web and Databases (WebDB'99) in conjunction with SIGMOD'99*, May 1999.

[MSS+02]   A. Maedche, S. Staab, R. Studer, Y. Sure, and R. Volz. Seal – tying up information integration and web site management by ontologies. *IEEE Data Engineering Bulletin*, 25(1):10–17, March 2002.

[MvHe03]   Deborah L. McGuinness and Frank van Harmelen (eds.). Owl web on-
            tology language. Technical report, W3C, March 2003.
[RA93]   T. Rindflesch and A. Aronson. Semantic processing in information
            retrieval. In C. Safran, editor, *Seventeenth Annual Symposium on
            Computer Applications in Medical Care (SCAMC 93)*, pages 611–615.
            McGraw-Hill Inc., New York, 1993.
[SAD+00]   S. Staab, J. Angele, S. Decker, M. Erdmann, A. Hotho, A. Maedche, H.-
            P. Schnurr, R. Studer, and Y. Sure. Semantic community web portals.
            In *WWW9 / Computer Networks (Special Issue: WWW9 – Proceedings
            of the 9th International World Wide Web Conference, Amsterdam, The
            Netherlands, May, 15–19)*, volume 33, pages 473–491. Elsevier, 2000.
[SEA+02]   Y. Sure, M. Erdmann, J. Angele, S. Staab, R. Studer, and D. Wenke.
            OntoEdit: Collaborative ontology development for the semantic web. In
            I. Horrocks and J. A. Hendler, editors, *Proceedings of the First Inter-
            national Semantic Web Conference: The Semantic Web (ISWC 2002)*,
            volume 2342 of *Lecture Notes in Computer Science (LNCS)*, pages 221–
            235, Sardinia, Italy, 2002. Springer.
[SOV+02]   P. Spyns, D. Oberle, R. Volz, J. Zheng, M. Jarrar, Y. Sure, R. Studer,
            and R. Meersman. OntoWeb – A Semantic Web Community Portal. In
            *Proceedings of the Fourth International Conference on Practical Aspects
            of Knowledge Management (PAKM02)*, pages 189–200. Springer Verlag,
            2002.
[SSA02]   Y. Sure, S. Staab, and J. Angele. OntoEdit: Guiding ontology develop-
            ment by methodology and inferencing. In R. Meersman, Z. Tari, et al.,
            editors, *Proceedings of the Confederated International Conferences: On
            the Move to Meaningful Internet Systems (CoopIS, DOA, and ODBASE
            2002)*, volume 2519 of *Lecture Notes in Computer Science (LNCS)*, pages
            1205–1222, University of California, Irvine, USA, 2002. Springer.
[SSV+01]   R. Studer, Y. Sure, R. Volz, Z. Jijuan, and R. Meersman. Seed ontology.
            OntoWeb deliverable 6.1, Institute AIFB, University of Karlsruhe &
            StarLAB, Vrije Universiteit Brussels, 2001.
[SSV02]   R. Studer, Y. Sure, and R. Volz. Managing focused access to distributed
            knowledge. *Journal of Universal Computer Science (J.UCS)*, 8(6):662–
            672, 2002.
[W3C99]   W3C. RDF Schema Specification. http://www.w3.org/TR/PR-rdf-
            schema/, 1999.
[ZBB+98]   P. Zweigenbaum, J. Bouaud, B. Bachimont, J. Charlet, B. Séroussi, and
            J.-F. Boisvieux. From text to knowledge: a unifying document-oriented
            view of analyzed medical language. *Methods of Information in Medicine*,
            37(4–5):384–393, 1998.

X-Learn: An XML-Based, Multi-agent System for Supporting "User-Device" Adaptive E-learning

Pasquale De Meo[1], Alfredo Garro[2], Giorgio Terracina[3], and Domenico Ursino[1]

[1] DIMET, Università Mediterranea di Reggio Calabria,
Via Graziella, Località Feo di Vito, 89060 Reggio Calabria, Italy,
demeo@ing.unirc.it
ursino@unirc.it
[2] DEIS, Università della Calabria,
Via Pietro Bucci, 87036 Rende (CS), Italy
garro@deis.unical.it
[3] Dipartimento di Matematica, Università della Calabria,
Via Pietro Bucci, 87036 Rende (CS), Italy
terracina@mat.unical.it

Abstract. In this paper we present *X-Learn*, an XML-based, multi-agent system for supporting "user-device" adaptive e-learning. *X-Learn* is characterized by the following features: *(i)* it is highly subjective, since it handles quite a rich and detailed user profile that plays a key role during the learning activities; *(ii)* it is dynamic and flexible, i.e., it is capable of reacting to variations of exigencies and objectives; *(iii)* it is device-adaptive, since it decides the learning objects to present to the user on the basis of the device she/he is currently exploiting; *(iv)* it is generic, i.e., it is capable of operating in a large variety of learning contexts; *(v)* it is XML based, since it exploits many facilities of XML technology for handling and exchanging information connected to e-learning activities. The paper reports also various experimental results as well as a comparison between *X-Learn* and other related e-learning management systems already presented in the literature.

1 Introduction

E-learning can be defined as the activity that supports a learning experience by either developing or applying Information & Communication Technology (ICT). It is playing a more and more relevant role in the ICT market and its importance is becoming crucial for organizing training in businesses. Indeed, market dynamism compels organizations to avoid medium-to-long term programming and to work in a project-shaped, short-to-medium term perspective.

In order to realize projects which it is involved in, an organization continuously needs new "know how" and competences; owing to the growing "skill shortage", these can be found on the external market only with a great difficulty and a high cost. As a consequence, the capability to internally construct the necessary know how has become a must for an organization.

R. Meersman et al. (Eds.): CoopIS/DOA/ODBASE 2003, LNCS 2888, pp. 739–756, 2003.
© Springer-Verlag Berlin Heidelberg 2003

E-learning is a particularly suitable solution to these exigencies. More specifically, an e-learning platform should initially determine the competence gap of the human resources assigned to a project; after this, it should fill such a gap by constructing suitable personalized and flexible learning programs that can be dinamically adapted to the feedback received by the user.

In such a context, in order to guarantee the maximum flexibility and, contemporarily, the highest efficiency to e-learning activities, it has been proposed to organize learning contents into independent units, named *learning objects*, that can be dynamically combined for constructing personalized learning programs. In order to successfully perform such an activity, an efficient and effective organization of available learning objects appears crucial. In other words, it appears necessary to define and construct a meta-knowledge that allows to classify available learning objects (documents, slides, simulations, role games, questionnaires, tests, registered lessons, etc.) on the basis of their objectives, arguments, exploited media and so on.

In order to both simplify learning object exploitation and foster platform interoperability, important international organizations have proposed to associate suitable descriptors, named LOM (Learning Object Metadata), with learning objects [3]. LOM allow information about learning objects to be obtained without the necessity to directly analyze them. More specifically, the Instruction Management System (IMS) [4], an authoritative organism for LOM standardization, has proposed to describe learning objects by means of an XML document which a suitable XML Schema is associated with. Such a proposal has been favourably accepted by the e-learning community and, presently, almost all commercial e-learning platforms support it.

LOM paradigm has largely facilitated e-learning activities, in particular the automatic construction of learning programs. However, in order to improve the efficiency and the effectiveness of e-learning activities, some important problems, often involving research areas quite far from computer science, should be faced. As an example, new didactic methodologies, based on the learning object paradigm and well suited to automatically realize learning programs, should be defined [14]. In addition, a continuous and pervasive e-learning activity should carefully consider and support the different devices that users might exploit during their learning process. With regard to this, it is worth observing that, in the Personal Digital Assistant era, limiting users to perform e-learning activities only by a Personal Computer connected to the organization's LAN unjustifiably reduces the flexibility and, consequently, both the efficiency and the effectiveness of the e-learning process.

In our opinion, some of these challenging issues can be successfully faced by exploiting the agent technology. The present paper aims at showing the feasibility of this idea; in particular, it presents *X-Learn*, an XML-based Multi-Agent System for supporting "user-device adaptive" e-learning. More specifically, X-Learn has been conceived for assisting users to learn new "know how" and competences to fill the gap between their present knowledge and that required by a new project which they have been assigned to.

In *X-Learn* user assistance is guaranteed by constructing personalized, flexible and dynamic learning programs taking into account the background knowledge of a user, her/his didactic objectives as well as devices and connection typologies she/he intends to exploit for carrying out her/his e-learning activity.

X-Learn is characterized by the following features that, in our opinion, are extremely relevant for a new e-learning system:

- *It is highly subjective*; indeed, it handles quite a rich and detailed user profile which records her/his background knowledge and future learning objectives and, consequently, plays a key role in the definition of learning programs.
- *It is dynamic and flexible* since it is provided with mechanisms for reacting to variations of both user and organization exigencies and objectives.
- *It is device adaptive* since it decides the typology (in particular, the "multimedia degree") of learning objects to present to the user on the basis of the device she/he is currently exploiting.
- *It is generic*, i.e., it is capable of operating on a large variety of learning contexts.
- *It is XML-based*, since *(i)* the agent ontologies are stored as XML documents; *(ii)* the communication language exploited by the various agents is ACML [9], a language obtained by combining XML and KQML [8]; *(iii)* the extraction of information from the various data structures is carried out by means of *XQuery* [5]; *(iv)* the manipulation of agent ontologies is performed by means of the Document Object Model (DOM) [1]; *(v)* information relative to the learning activities is represented and handled by means of the IMS standard [4] (see above).

This paper is organized as follows: the next section presents some preliminary definitions; a detailed description of all agents involved in *X-Learn* is provided in Section 3. Section 4 is devoted to describe a series of experiments we have performed for testing our system performances. In Section 5 we present related literature and compare *X-Learn* with various other systems already proposed in the past. Finally, in Section 6, we draw our conclusions.

2   Preliminaries

In this section we provide some preliminary definitions necessary to understand both the architecture and the behaviour of *X-Learn*.

Definition 1. A *skill* indicates an ability that a user wants to achieve. Examples of skills are "C++ programmer", "Webmaster", etc. Each skill requires the knowledge of a set of subjects. We say that a user acquires a skill when she/he knows all the subjects associated with it.

Definition 2. A *subject* denotes a high level topic of a skill. Examples of subjects are "C++ functions", "C++ Classes", "C++ Class Inheritance", etc. Each subject may have one or more pre-requisites; these are other subjects whose knowledge is necessary for studying it. As an example, in order to study the subject "C++ Class Inheritance", it is necessary to know the subject "C++ Classes". Analogously, a subject can be a pre-requisite for one or more subjects. We say that a subject is *basic* if it has no pre-requisites.

Definition 3. A *learning object* is an elementary learning unit relative to a specific subject. In this paper we assume that:

- each learning object is relative to only one subject;
- various learning objects could be associated with the same subject; they could differ for the associated learning methodology, for their multimedia degree, and so on. However, all learning objects associated with the same subject are considered equivalent from a didactic point of view.

A learning object consists of two components, namely the *learning object descriptor* and the *learning object content*. The former describes the characteristics of the learning object (e.g., the associated subject, the multimedia format, etc.). The latter corresponds to the actual information content associated with the learning object and that the user must study for learning the subject associated with it.

As previously mentioned, subjects can be characterized by some pre-requisites which are, in their turn, other subjects. As a consequence, a user can study a subject only if she/he knows all the corresponding pre-requisites. We have seen that studying a subject corresponds to study one of the learning objects associated with it. As a consequence, it is possible to introduce the concept of learning program which allows to formally define the (partially ordered) set of learning objects that a user must study for learning a subject starting from her/his background knowledge.

Definition 4. A *learning program LP* is a set of pairs of learning objects $(LObj_s, LObj_t)$ such that $LObj_t$ can be studied only after $LObj_s$ or, in other words, such that the subject associated with $LObj_s$ is a pre-requisite of the subject relative to $LObj_t$.

Note that, in LP, more tuples $(LObj_{s_1}, LObj_t)$, $(LObj_{s_2}, LObj_t)$, ..., $(LObj_{s_n}, LObj_t)$ could exist having $LObj_t$ as their second component; this indicates that $LObj_t$ can be studied only after $LObj_{s_1}, LObj_{s_2}, \ldots, LObj_{s_n}$ have been learned. In this way, LP specifies also a partial order according to which the learning objects must be studied.

3 The X-Learn Architecture

3.1 General Overview

X-Learn consists of three agent typologies, namely:

- a *User-Device Agent* (hereafter UDA), that handles an e-learning session carried out by a user U by means of a device D;

- a *Skill Manager Agent*, (hereafter *SMA*), that supports a user to determine the skills of her/his interest, as well as the subjects she/he has to study for attaining a given skill, on the basis of her/his background knowledge;
- a *Learning Program Agent*, (hereafter *LPA*), that generates personalized learning programs for a specific user U needing to study a particular subject S, having a certain background knowledge and exploiting a device D for her/his e-learning activity.

In addition, *X-Learn* is provided with a Learning Object Repository (*LOR*), storing all learning objects it handles.

As previously pointed out, the role of XML in *X-Learn* is crucial. Indeed:

- The agent ontologies are stored as XML documents; as a consequence, they are light, versatile, easy to be exchanged and can reside on different devices and software platforms. In spite of this simplicity, the information representation rules embodied in XML are powerful enough to allow a sophisticated information management.
- The agent communication language is ACML [9]; this is the XML encoding of FIPA Agent Communication Language [2]. The exploitation of ACML guarantees various benefits to *X-Learn*; two of the most relevant ones are the following:
  - Developing and managing tools capable of carrying out ACML message parsing is extremely simple; indeed, these tools can be constructed by exploiting the numerous off-the-shelf XML parsers available over the Internet. Vice versa, in order to construct parsers for not XML-based ACL versions, it is generally necessary to exploit a Lisp-like encoding (see [9] for all details) whose supports are more difficult to be found over the Internet.
  - Integrating Agents with a large variety of Web technologies (such as Secure Socket Layer - SSL, for handling both the authentication of agents' identities and the encryption of ACL messages) is very simple to be realized. Vice versa, addressing the same issues with a not XML-based Agent Communication Language would imply heavy constraints on the agent infrastructure (think, for example, to the great overload to be put in the ACL messages for handling these issues).
- The extraction of information from the various data structures is carried out by means of XQuery [5]. This is becoming the standard query language for the XML environment. Since it is based on the XML framework, XQuery can handle a large data variety. It has capabilities typical of database query languages as well as features typical of document management systems. Finally, it is provided with various high level constructs for simplifying querying over the Web; among them, we cite *constructors*, that allow the creation of XML structures within a query, and *FLWR expressions*, that support iteration and variable binding.
- The manipulation of agent ontologies is performed by means of the Document Object Model (DOM) [1]. This is a platform- and language-neutral interface that allows programs and scripts to dynamically access and update

Table 1. The Ontology of UDA_{ij}

DP_i		the *Profile of the Device* D_i
	DId_i	the *Identifier* of D_i
	$BMax_i$	the *Maximum Bandwidth* that D_i can guarantee for accessing or downloading data from the network
	VE_i	the *Video Enabled* field of D_i. It is set to 1 if D_i supports video data format, 0 otherwise
	AE_i	the *Audio Enabled* field of D_i. It is analogous to VE_i but for audio
	TE_i	the *Text Enabled* field of D_i. It is analogous to VE_i but for text
UP_j		the *Profile of the User* U_j
	UId_j	the *Identifier* of U_j
	$DesSkill_j$	the *Desired Skill* of U_j (i.e., the skill U_j wants to acquire)
	$AcqSkillSet_j$	the *Acquired Skill Set* of U_j
	$KnownSubjSet_j$	the *Known Subject Set* of U_j. A subject $KnownSubj_{j_l}$ of $KnownSubjSet_j$ has an identifier $SubjId_{j_l}$ and a name $SubjName_{j_l}$
	$MaxTime_j$	the *Maximum Time* U_j can spend for a learning program

the content, structure and style of XML documents. DOM makes it possible for programmers to write applications working properly on all browsers and servers as well as on a large variety of hardware and software platforms.

– Learning Object Metadata are represented and handled by means of the IMS standard [4]. As pointed out in the Introduction, such a standard describes learning objects by means of XML documents, validated with respect to an XML Schema. The exploitation of XML allows to manipulate and manage learning object descriptors using the most recent XML technologies such as DOM, for data manipulation, SAX, for data parsing, XQuery, for data querying, and so on.

In the following subsections we provide a detailed description of the various agent typologies which *X-Learn* consists of.

3.2   The User-Device Agent

A User-Device Agent UDA_{ij} is associated with a user U_j exploiting a device D_i; it supports U_j during her/his learning activities carried out by means of D_i.

Ontology. The ontology of UDA_{ij} consists of a pair $\langle DP_i, UP_j \rangle$, where:

– DP_i, the Device Profile of D_i, stores some characteristics of D_i such as the maximum bandwidth and the medium typology (e.g., video, audio, etc.) it can handle;

– UP_j, the User Profile of U_j, stores some characteristics of U_j such as the skill she/he wants to acquire, her/his background knowledge and the maximum time she/he can spend for a learning program.

Table 1 illustrates the parameters characterizing the ontology of UDA_{ij} in more detail. The corresponding XML Schema is shown in Fig. 1.

```
<?xml version="1.0" encoding="UTF-8"?>
<xs:schema xmlns:xs="http://www.w3.org/2001/XMLSchema">
    <!-- Definition of attributes -->
    <xs:attribute name="SubjId" type="xs:ID"/>
    <xs:attribute name="SubjName" type="xs:string"/>
    <xs:attribute name="DId" type="xs:ID"/>
    <xs:attribute name="BMax" type="xs:float"/>
    <xs:attribute name="VE" type="xs:integer"/>
    <xs:attribute name="AE" type="xs:integer"/>
    <xs:attribute name="TE" type="xs:integer"/>
    <xs:attribute name="UId" type="xs:ID"/>
    <xs:attribute name="DesSkill" type="xs:string"/>
    <xs:attribute name="MaxTime" type="xs:float"/>
    <!-- Definition of simple elements -->
    <xs:element name="AcqSkill" type="xs:string"/>
    <!-- Definition of complex elements -->
    <xs:element name="Subj">
        <xs:complexType>
            <xs:attribute ref="SubjId" use="required"/>
            <xs:attribute ref="SubjName" use="required"/>
        </xs:complexType>
    </xs:element>
    <xs:element name="AcqSkillSet">
        <xs:complexType>
            <xs:element ref="AcqSkill" minOccurs="0"
                                 maxOccurs="unbounded"/>
        </xs:complexType>
    </xs:element>
    <xs:element name="KnownSubjSet">
        <xs:complexType>
            <xs:element ref="KnownSubj" minOccurs="0"
                                 maxOccurs="unbounded"/>
        </xs:complexType>
    </xs:element>

    <xs:element name="DP">
        <xs:complexType>
            <xs:attribute ref="DId" use="required"/>
            <xs:attribute ref="BMax" use="required"/>
            <xs:attribute ref="VE" use="required"/>
            <xs:attribute ref="AE" use="required"/>
            <xs:attribute ref="TE" use="required"/>
        </xs:complexType>
    </xs:element>
    <xs:element name="UP">
        <xs:complexType>
            <xs:sequence>
                <xs:element ref="AcqSkillSet"/>
                <xs:element ref="KnownSubjSet"/>
            </xs:sequence>
            <xs:attribute ref="UId" use="required"/>
            <xs:attribute ref="DesSkill" />
            <xs:attribute ref="MaxTime" use="required"/>
        </xs:complexType>
    </xs:element>
    <xs:element name="UDAOntology">
        <xs:complexType>
            <xs:sequence>
                <xs:element ref="DP"/>
                <xs:element ref="UP"/>
            </xs:sequence>
        </xs:complexType>
    </xs:element>
</xs:schema>
```

Fig. 1. The XML Schema of UDA

Behaviour. UDA_{ij} is activated by U_j when she/he wants to acquire a new skill. In this case UDA_{ij} contacts SMA and sends it the set of skills already acquired by U_j. In its turn, SMA sends UDA_{ij} the list of skills U_j might acquire; these are shown to U_j who can select one of them. When this happens, UDA_{ij} adds the selected skill to UP_j and the learning session starts. In order to illustrate the exploitation of ACML, in Fig. 2 we show the ACML message that UDA_{ij} sends to SMA. In the following, due to space limitations, we cannot present the other ACML messages exchanged by the various agents; however, they are analogous to that shown in Fig. 2.

UDA_{ij} can be activated by U_j also when she/he wants to continue a previously interrupted learning program. In this case UDA_{ij} exploits information stored in its ontology for re-starting the learning program.

A learning session is carried out as follows. UDA_{ij} sends to SMA both the set of subjects already known by U_j and the skill she/he desires to acquire. SMA identifies the subjects U_j must attain for acquiring the desired skill and returns an ordered list of them to UDA_{ij}. The list order reflects the pre-requisite relationships existing among subjects. At this point, U_j can choose the next subject to learn.

After this, UDA_{ij} contacts LPA and sends it the device profile DP_i, the user profile UP_j and the subject $Subj_k$ that U_j desires to learn. LPA determines the Best Learning Program BLP_{ijk} allowing U_j to learn $Subj_k$ by means of D_i and sends it to UDA_{ij} (see Section 3.4). This extracts each learning object of BLP_{ijk} from the Learning Object Repository and presents it to U_j. When she/he ends to study a learning object of BLP_{ijk}, UDA_{ij} updates UP_j by adding the corresponding subject to the set of subjects already known by U_j.

```
<?xml version="1.0" encoding="UTF-8"?>
<!DOCTYPE fipa_acl SYSTEM "fipa_acl.dtd">
<message>
    <messagetype>
        request
    </messagetype>
    <messageparameter>
        <sender link="http://www.ing.unirc.it/user">
            UDA
        </sender>
    </messageparameter>
    <messageparameter>
        <receiver link="http://www.mat.unical.it/X-learn">
            SMA
        </receiver>
    </messageparameter>
    <messageparameter>
        <ontology link="http://www.ing.unirc.it/user/UDAontology.xml">
            Ontology of UDA
        </ontology>
    </messageparameter>
    <messageparameter>
        <content>
            Request of available skills
        </content>
    </messageparameter>
    <messageparameter>
        <reply-with>
            List of skills
        </reply-with>
    </messageparameter>
</message>
```

Fig. 2. The ACML message that UDA sends to SMA

After U_j has studied all learning objects of BLP_{ijk}, and, consequently, has acquired $Subj_k$, she/he can decide to interrupt the learning session or, alternatively, to continue it by studying a further subject relative to the current Desired Skill. In the former case, UDA_{ij} is de-activated; in the latter case, it contacts LPA for determining the new learning program.

Finally, when U_j knows all subjects associated with the current Desired Skill, UDA_{ij} updates UP_j by adding it to the set of acquired skills.

3.3   The Skill Manager Agent

A Skill Manager Agent SMA supports User-Device Agents in the selection of skills and subjects to be learned by the corresponding users.

Ontology. The ontology of SMA consists of a set of skills $SkillSet = \{Sk_1, \ldots, Sk_q\}$. Each skill Sk_l is characterized by a name $SkName_l$ and the list $SkSubjList_l$ of subjects to be learned for attaining it. Subjects in $SkSubjList_l$ are ordered on the basis of the pre-requisite relationships existing among them. The XML Schema associated with this ontology is analogous to that relative to the ontology of UDA_{ij}; due to space limitations we do not show it.

```
<SkillSet>
    for $i in document("http://www.mat.unical.it/X-learn/SMAOntology.xml)/*/Skill
    where empty (document("http://www.ing.unirc.it/user/UDAOntology.xml)
        /*/AcqSkillSet [AcqSkill eq $i/@Name]
        return
            <Skill>
                $i/@Name
            </Skill>
</SkillSet>
```

Fig. 3. The query SMA executes for selecting the skills present in *X-Learn* and not yet acquired by U_j

```
<SubjectSet>
    let $uda:=document("http://www.ing.unirc.it/user/UDAOntology.xml")
    let $skill:=document("http://www.mat.unical.it/X-learn/SMAOntology.xml")
        /*/Skill[Name eq $uda/*/@DesSkill]

    for $subject in $skill/SkSubjList/Subject
    where empty ($uda/*/KnownSubjSet [Subj/@Name eq $subject]
        return
            <Subject>
                $subject
            </Subject>
</SubjectSet>
```

Fig. 4. The query SMA executes for selecting the list of subjects of the current desired skill not already known by U_j

Behaviour. SMA is activated by a User-Device Agent UDA_{ij} when U_j wants to choose a new skill to acquire or when she/he wants to learn a new subject relative to her/his current Desired Skill.

In the former case, SMA receives from UDA_{ij} the set of skills attained by U_j in the past and returns to UDA_{ij} the skills present in *X-Learn* not yet acquired by U_j. The query for skill extraction, expressed in XQuery, is shown in Fig. 3.

In the latter case, SMA receives from UDA_{ij} the set of subjects U_j already knows and the skill she/he desires to acquire; it selects from its ontology the list of subjects necessary to be learned for attaining the current desired skill of U_j, filters out those already known by U_j and returns the remaining ones to UDA_{ij}. The associated query is illustrated in Fig. 4.

3.4   The Learning Program Agent

The Learning Program Agent LPA is activated by a User-Device Agent UDA_{ij} whenever U_j wants to study a new subject $Subj_k$. It is in charge of providing U_j with a personalized learning program for studying $Subj_k$ on the basis of her/his background knowledge and the characteristics of the device D_i she/he is currently exploiting.

Table 2. The Ontology of LPA

$SubjSet$		the *Set of Subjects* currently available in *X-Learn*
$Subj_l \in SubjSet$	$SubjId_l$	the *Identifier* of $Subj_l$
	$SubjName_l$	the *Name* of $Subj_l$
	$SubjPrereqSet_l$	the *Set of Pre-requisites* of $Subj_l$
	$SubjLObjSet_l$	the *Set of learning objects* relative to $Subj_l$
$LObjSet$		the *Set of learning objects* currently available at the e-learning system
$LObj_m \in LObjSet$	$LObjId_m$	the *Identifier* of $LObj_m$
	$LObjName_m$	the *Name* of $LObj_m$
	$LObjSubject_m$	the *Subject* which $LObj_m$ refers to
	$LObjLocation_m$	the *URI* where $LObj_m$ can be accessed
	$LObjVC_m$	the *Video Component* field of $LObj_m$. It is set to 1 if $LObj_m$ has a video component, 0 otherwise
	$LObjAC_m$	the *Audio Component* field of $LObj_m$. It is analogous to $LObjVC_m$ but for audio
	$LObjTC_m$	the *Text Component* field of $LObj_m$. It is analogous to $LObjVC_m$ but for text
	$LObjSize_m$	the *Size*, in bytes, of $LObj_m$
	$LObjDuration_m$	the *Duration* of $LObj_m$. It is defined as the time, in seconds, that $LObj_m$ takes when it is played

Ontology. The ontology of LPA consists of a pair $\langle SubjSet, LObjSet \rangle$, where:

- $SubjSet$ represents the set of subjects currently available in *X-Learn*. Each subject is characterized by a code, a name, the set of its pre-requisites and the set of learning objects associated with it.
- $LObjSet$ is the set of learning objects currently present in *X-Learn*. Each learning object is characterized by an identifier, a name, the subject it refers to[1], the URI where it can be accessed, its data format, size and duration. Metadata for describing learning objects have been defined according to IMS specifications [4]. Table 2 illustrates the parameters characterizing the ontology of LPA in more detail. The corresponding XML Schema is analogous to that relative to the ontologies of UDA_{ij} and SMA; due to space limitations we do not show it.

Behaviour. LPA is activated by UDA_{ij} whenever a user U_j wants to study a subject $Subj_k$ by means of a device D_i. LPA receives $Subj_k$, UP_j and DP_i from UDA_{ij}. It returns to UDA_{ij} the Best Learning Program BLP_{ijk} allowing U_j to study $Subj_k$ by means of D_i. The construction of BLP_{ijk} consists mainly of three steps.

Step 1. During the first step LPA constructs a support graph, named *Subject Dependency Graph* $SDG_{jk} = \langle NS_{jk}, AS_{jk} \rangle$. SDG_{jk} is constructed for guiding U_j to learn $Subj_k$ starting from basic and/or already known subjects.

As a consequence, *for each* list of subjects $\{Subj_1, Subj_2, \ldots, Subj_n\}$, such that:

---

[1] Recall that a learning object is related to only one subject but one subject might have various learning objects associated with it.

- $Subj_l$ is a pre-requisite of $Subj_{l+1}$, $1 \leq l \leq n-1$;
- $Subj_1, \ldots, Subj_n$ are not known by U_j;
- $Subj_1$ is either a basic subject or a subject whose pre-requisites are already known by U_j;
- $Subj_n = Subj_k$.

$Subj_1, \ldots, Subj_n$ are added to $NS_{jk}{}^2$ and arcs $(Subj_1, Subj_2)$, $\ldots$, $(Subj_{n-1}, Subj_n)$ are added to AS_{jk}, if not already present.

Step 2. During the second step LPA exploits SDG_{jk} for determining the Best Learning Program BLP_{ijk}. Such a task is carried out by suitably selecting a learning object for each subject in SDG_{jk}. The learning object selection is performed according to the following guidelines:

- U_j should exploit as much available bandwidth as possible. The available bandwidth for U_j is determined by computing the minimum between the bandwidth $BMax_i$ guaranteed by D_i and the bandwidth $BNet_j$ available on the network for U_j. The bandwidth required by each learning object is computed as the ratio between its size and its duration.
- The time required to U_j to learn BLP_{ijk} must be lower than $MaxTime_j$, i.e., the maximum time U_j can spend for a learning program.
- The format of each selected learning object must be compatible with the characteristics of D_i.
- In BLP_{ijk} exactly one learning object must be selected for each subject of SDG_{jk}.

The construction of BLP_{ijk} can be properly formulated as the following optimization problem:

$$
\begin{aligned}
maximize \quad & \sum_{r=1}^{|NS_{jk}|} \sum_{s=1}^{|SubjLObjSet_r|} \frac{LObjSize_{r_s}}{LObjDuration_{r_s}} x_{r_s} \\
s.t. \quad & \frac{LObjSize_{r_s}}{LObjDuration_{r_s}} x_{r_s} \leq min\{BMax_i, B_{Net_j}\} \\
& \sum_{r=1}^{|NS_{jk}|} \sum_{s=1}^{|SubjLObjSet_r|} LObjDuration_{r_s} x_{r_s} \leq MaxTime_j \\
& \sum_{s=1}^{|SubjLObjSet_r|} LObjVC_{r_s} x_{r_s} \leq VE_i, \qquad 1 \leq r \leq |NS_{jk}| \\
& \sum_{s=1}^{|SubjLObjSet_r|} LObjAC_{r_s} x_{r_s} \leq AE_i, \qquad 1 \leq r \leq |NS_{jk}| \\
& \sum_{s=1}^{|SubjLObjSet_r|} LObjTC_{r_s} x_{r_s} \leq TE_i, \qquad 1 \leq r \leq |NS_{jk}| \\
& \sum_{s=1}^{|SubjLObjSet_r|} x_{r_s} = 1, \qquad 1 \leq r \leq |NS_{jk}| \\
& x_{r_s} \in \{0, 1\}
\end{aligned}
$$

Here, the variable x_{r_s} represents the learning object $LObj_s$ associated with the subject $Subj_r$. $x_{r_s} = 1$ if $LObj_s$ belongs to BLP_{ijk}.

Step 3. During the third step LPA simply returns BLP_{ijk} to UDA_{ij}.

---

^{2} In the following we shall use the same name for indicating both a subject and the associated node in SDG_{jk}, when this is not confusing.

4   Experiments

We have carried out various experiments for verifying the performances of *X-Learn*. Most of these experiments have been conceived for verifying the capability of our system to adapt its behaviour to both bandwidth availabilities and the characteristics of the devices exploited by users.

In these experiments, 72% of learning objects *available* at the Learning Object Repository of *X-Learn* had a text component, 72% of them had an audio component and, finally, 72% of them had a video component[3].

A first experiment has been performed for measuring the fraction of *selected* learning objects having a text (resp., an audio, a video) component. Before carrying out the experiment we thought that, if the available bandwidth increases, the fraction of selected learning objects having an audio and/or a video component increases as well, whereas the percentage of selected learning objects having a text component should be quite constant and high.

The results we have obtained for this experiment are shown in Fig. 5. They confirm our intuition. Indeed, it is possible to observe that:

- The fraction of *selected* learning objects having a text component is quite constant and high; indeed, it is always greater than 80%.
- The percentage of *selected* learning objects having an audio component slightly increases when the bandwidth increases; it is quite high, since it is always greater than 60%.
- In presence of a bandwidth increase, the increase of the fraction of *selected* learning objects having a video component is enormous and rapid.

A second experiment has been carried out for verifying how the selection of learning objects depends on the device exploited by the user. In this experiment, the set of available learning objects is the same as that taken into account in the previous one.

We have considered four device typologies handling *(i)* text and audio, *(ii)* text and video, *(iii)* audio and video, *(iv)* text, audio and video. In addition, we have considered three situations for bandwidth availability, namely *(a)* low bandwidth (i.e., 9-10 kbytes/s), *(b)* medium bandwidth (i.e., 50-60 kbytes/s), *(c)* high bandwidth (i.e., over 120 kbytes/s).

Results obtained when the available bandwidth is low are shown in Table 3. In this table there is a row for each device typology; columns are associated with text, audio and video. The element corresponding to the row "Text and Audio" and to the column "Audio" specifies the fraction of learning objects, having an audio component, which are selected if a device handling only text and audio is exploited. Observe that, in case of a low bandwidth, if the device can handle text and audio (resp., video), text is preferred to audio (resp., video). Analogously, if the device can handle video and audio, audio is preferred to video. Finally, if the device can handle text, audio and video, video is totally filtered

---

[3] Remember that a learning object might contemporarily have a text, an audio and a video component.

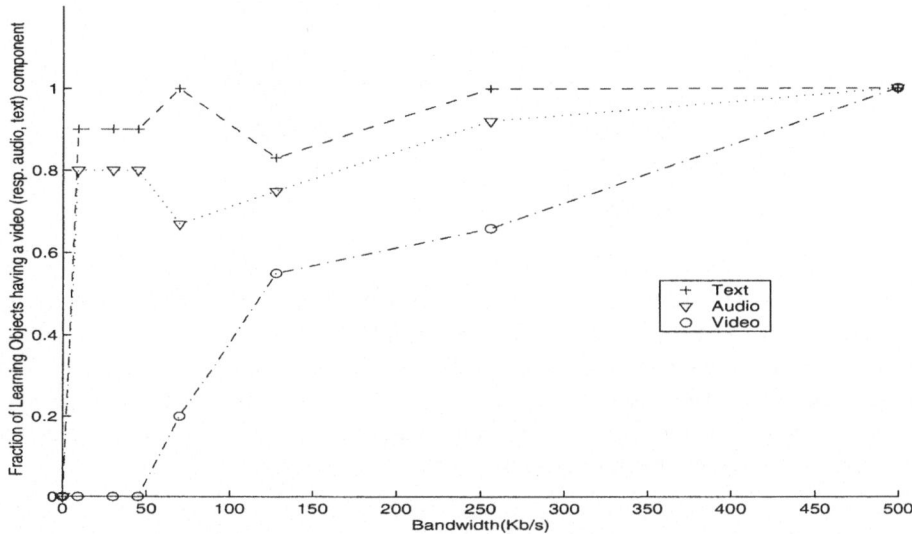

Fig. 5. Variation of the fraction of selected learning objects having a video (resp., audio, text) component against the variation of available bandwidth

Table 3. Results returned when the bandwidth is low

	Text	Audio	Video
Text and Audio	0.85	0.60	0.00
Text and Video	1.00	0.00	0.00
Audio and Video	0.00	1.00	0.00
Text, Audio and Video	0.85	0.60	0.00

Table 4. Results returned when the bandwidth is medium

	Text	Audio	Video
Text and Audio	1.00	0.80	0.00
Text and Video	1.00	0.00	0.26
Audio and Video	0.00	0.65	0.18
Text, Audio and Video	1.00	0.60	0.20

out, audio is partially considered whereas text is generally selected. These results are reasonable if we consider that, in this experiment, available bandwidth is low and video components generally require a high bandwidth.

Results returned when the available bandwidth is medium are reported in Table 4. Observe that, since available bandwidth is higher w.r.t. the previous case, the fraction of selected learning objects having an audio and/or a video component is higher than that returned previously.

Results obtained in presence of a high bandwidth are shown in Table 5. In this case, when the device is capable of handling text and audio, all selected learning

Table 5. Results returned when the bandwidth is high

	Text	Audio	Video
Text and Audio	1.00	1.00	0.00
Text and Video	1.00	0.00	0.75
Audio and Video	0.00	0.95	0.65
Text, Audio and Video	1.00	0.90	0.65

objects have both a text and an audio component. This is justified by considering that both text and audio require quite a limited bandwidth. When the device handles both video and audio, generally, audio is preferred to video even if a high percentage of selected learning objects have also a video component. Finally, when the device handles text, audio and video, a large fraction of selected learning objects has also an audio and/or a video component.

5   Related Literature

The convergence of mobile communications and handheld computers offers new interesting opportunities in e-learning activities; in this section we focus on some adaptive e-learning systems and we try to highlight their similarities and differences w.r.t our approach. More details on adaptive e-learning systems can be found in [6].

In [12] the authors propose an handheld learning device and an appropriate software infrastructure to support children education. The main components of the proposed architecture are: *(i) a learning manager*, which stores a local cache of learning objects extracted by a repository and exploits specific software agents to search and organize learning objects, *(ii) a communication manager*, which creates direct voice and data communication channels for disseminating learning materials and handles resource sharing.

Similarly to *X-Learn*, [12] develops a technology for assisting individuals and groups to *learn anytime* and *anywhere*; in addition, in both the approaches, learning materials follow the IMS standard and might have different multimedia formats. In spite of these similarities, the approach of [12] and *X-Learn* appear complementary; indeed, in [12], the authors modify an existing handheld device to support learning activities whereas *X-Learn* adapts the learning objects distribution to the device characteristics.

In [10] a multi-agent prototype called *CITS* (Confidence Intelligent Tutoring Agent) is proposed. *CITS* approach aims at being *adaptive* (i.e., it can adjust learning materials to meet user needs) and *dynamic* (i.e., it adapts the offered service to user current behaviour). *CITS* architecture consists of five kinds of agents, namely: *(i) a Cognitive Agent*, that creates a model for each learner, representing her/his level and learning style; *(ii) a Behaviour Agent*, that monitors learner behaviour during her/his interaction with the system for improving the model produced by the Cognitive Agent; *(iii) a Guide Agent*, that selects and classifies information potentially useful for the learner; *(iv)* an *Information Agent*, that searches over the Internet for extra information required by the learner and, *(v)* a *Confidence Agent*, that is in charge of strengthening the confidence between the learner and the system. In *CITS* learning information is fragmented in simple pieces called *knowledge targets*; these might have different multimedia formats.

Both *CITS* and *X-Learn* are XML-based multi-agent systems and both of them support the dissemination of learning materials having different multimedia formats. The main differences existing between them are the following: *(i) CITS* knowledge targets and *X-Learn* learning objects are different in their characteristics and purposes; *(ii) CITS* offers more "freedom degrees" in the learning program definition; *(iii) CITS* does not support device adaptivity.

[7] proposes a device-aware e-learning system as a part of a more complex e-learning platform, named *KnowledgeSea*. The core of the system proposed in [7] is a *self-organized hyperspace map*, i.e. an automatically-built map that provides a concise navigation support for a relatively large learning hyperspace. The map may help a user to find and access on-line educational resources by means of mobile wireless devices.

The approach of [7] is quite similar to *X-Learn*; indeed, both of them take into account the device a user is exploiting for accessing educational resources. The main differences existing between them are the following: *(i)* the self-organized hyperspace map provides a more flexible mechanism for selecting learning objects; however, it does not handle pre-requisite relationships possibly existing among learning objects; *(ii)* [7] does not handle the construction of a complete learning program; vice versa, in *X-Learn*, *LPA* has been conceived exactly for this purpose.

In [11] the authors propose *IDEAL* (Intelligent Distributed Environment for Active Learning), a multi-agent system for *active distance learning*. *IDEAL* consists of: *(i)* a *personal agent*, handling the profile (i.e., the background knowledge, the interests and the learning style) of a learner; *(ii)* a *course agent*, managing both the materials and the teaching technique of a course; *(iii)* a *teaching agent*, behaving as an intelligent tutor for a learner. In *IDEAL*, course materials are decomposed into small components called *Lecturelets*. These are XML documents containing JAVA code; they are dynamically assembled to cover course topics according to learner progress.

IDEAL and *X-Learn* share various similarities; indeed, both of them are XML based and exploit user modeling techniques. The main differences existing between them are the following: *(i)* the *Curriculum Sequencing Activity* of *IDEAL* and the *Best Learning Program* construction of *X-Learn* are based on different philosophies and strategies; *(ii) IDEAL* exploits non-standard and complex constructs for managing course contents (i.e. LectureLets) whereas *X-Learn* uses the concept of learning object, derived from IMS standard.

In [15] an approach for exploiting *web-mining* techniques to build a software agent supporting e-learning activities is presented. The proposed agent acts as a recommender system, i.e. it can produce both *suggestions* (helping the learner to better navigate through on-line materials) and *shortcuts* (helping the learner to quickly find needed resources). In order to perform all these activities, the system intensively exploits a user profile taking into account learner access history. *X-Learn* and [15] share some important features; in particular, both of them exploit a user profile and operate by constructing the most appropriate learning program. The main differences existing between *X-Learn* and [15] are the following: *(i)* [15] is a *single-agent* architecture whereas our approach is *multi-agent*; *(ii)* the learning program construction is based on data mining techniques in [15], whereas is performed by means of graph-based strategies in *X-Learn*.

In [13] the system *ELETROTUTOR* is proposed; this is a multi-agent system implemented on a JADE platform. *ELETROTUTOR* consists of the following agents: *(i)* a *Pedagogical Agent*, performing learning activities, such as the distribution and the dissemination of examples and exercises; *(ii)* a *Remote Agent*, managing the communication between the learner and the system; *(iii)* a *Communication Agent*, handling agent communications, and *(iv)* a *Student Model Agent*, handling a student profile and exploiting it for performing the learning activities. Both *X-Learn* and *ELETROTUTOR* are *multi-agent systems* and both of them adapt the dissemination of learning contents to user profiles. As for differences between *ELETROTUTOR* and *X-Learn*, we observe that the former does not handle device adaptivity and multimedia information that are, instead, managed by the latter.

6   Conclusions

In this paper we have proposed *X-Learn*, an XML-based multi-agent system for supporting e-learning activities.

We have seen that, in *X-Learn*, three typologies of agents are present, namely *(i)* a *User-Device Agent*, that handles an e-learning session carried out by a user U by means of a device D; *(ii)* a *Skill Manager Agent*, that supports a user U to determine the skills and the subjects she/he has to study; *(iii)* a *Learning Program Agent*, that generates personalized learning programs for a specific user U needing to study a particular subject S, having a certain background knowledge and exploiting a device D for her/his learning activities.

We have shown that *X-Learn* is adaptive w.r.t. the profile of both the customer and the device she/he is exploiting for carrying out the learning activities. Finally, we have seen that it is XML-based since: *(i)* the agent ontologies are stored as XML documents; *(ii)* the communication language exploited by the various agents is ACML; *(iii)* the extraction of information from the various data structures is carried out by means of XQuery; *(iv)* the manipulation of agent ontologies is performed by means of DOM; *(v)* learning objects are represented and handled by means of IMS standard.

As for future work, we plan to study the possibility to enrich the proposed multi-agent model with other features capable of improving its effectiveness and completeness in supporting a large variety of activities related to e-learning. As an example, it might be interesting to define various learning strategies to allow a user to specify the preferred learning strategy and, finally, to consider such a preference when the Best Learning Program is constructed.

As a second improvement, particularly interesting when *X-Learn* is exploited for managing employee learning in an organization, it could be possible to define career paths for the various employees and to relate learning programs with them.

As a final extension, it could be possible to provide *X-Learn* with a team building functionality capable of assigning employees to project teams on the basis of the skills acquired during e-learning activities.

References

1. Document Object Model. *[http://www.w3.org/DOM/]*.
2. Foundation for Intelligent Physical Agents (FIPA) Specifications. *[http://www.fipa.org]*.
3. IEEE Learning Technology Standards Committee. LOM working draft. *[http://ltsc.ieee.org/wg12/index.html]*.
4. Instructional Management System. *[http://www.imsproject.org]*.
5. World Wide Web Consortium – XML query. *[http://www.w3.org/XML/Query]*.
6. P. Brusilovsky. Adaptive and intelligent technologies for Web-based education. *Kunstliche Intelligenz-Special Issue on Intelligent Systems and Teleteaching*, 13(4):19–25, 1999.
7. P. Brusilovsky and R. Rizzo. Accessing Web educational resources from mobile wireless devices. In *Proc. of the International Workshop on Mobile Personal Information Retrieval*, pages 23–31, Tampere, Finland, 2002. ACM Press.
8. T.W. Finin, R. Fritzon, D. McKay, and R. McEntire. KQML as an agent communication language. In *Proc. of the ACM Conference on Information and Knowledge Management (CIKM'94)*, pages 456–463, Gaithersburg, Maryland, USA, 1994. ACM Press.
9. B. Grosof and Y. Labrou. An approach to using XML and a rule-based content language with an agent communication language. In *Proc. of IJCAI-99 Workshop on Agent Communication Language*, pages 96–117, Stockolm, Sweden, 1999.
10. M.A. Razek, C. Frasson, and M. Kaltenbach. Toward more effective intelligent distance learning environments. In *Proc. of the International Conference on Machine Learning and Applications (ICMLA'02)*, Las Vegas, Nevada, USA, 2002. CSREA Press.
11. Y. Shang, H. Shi, and S. Chen. An intelligent distributed environment for active learning. In *Proc. of the International Conference on World Wide Web (WWW 2001)*, pages 308–315, Hong Kong, 2001. ACM Press.
12. M. Sharples, D. Corlett, and O. Westmancott. The design and implementation of a mobile learning resource. *Personal and Ubiquitous Computing*, 6(3):220–234, 2002.
13. R.A. Silveira and R.M. Vicari. Improving interactivity in e-learning systems with multi-agent architecture. In *Proc. of the International Conference on Adaptive Hypermedia and Adaptive Web-Based Systems (AH 2002)*, pages 466–471, Malaga, Spain, 2002. Lecture Notes in Computer Science, Springer.

14. D. Wiley. Peer-to-Peer and Learning Objects: The New Potential for Collaborative Constructivist Learning Online. In *Proc. of the IEEE International Conference on Advanced Learning Technology: Issues, Achievements and Challenges (ICALT 2001)*, pages 494–498, Madison, Wisconsin, USA, 2001. IEEE Computer Society.
15. O.R. Zaiane. Building a recommender agent for e-learning systems. In *Proc. of the International Conference on Computers in Education (ICCE 2002)*, pages 55–59, Auckland, New Zealand, 2002. IEEE Press.

Mining Association Rules from Relational Data – Average Distance Based Method*

Vladimír Bartík and Jaroslav Zendulka

Brno University of Technology, Faculty of Information Technology,
Božetěchova 2, 61266 Brno, Czech Republic
{bartik,zendulka}@fit.vutbr.cz

Abstract. The paper describes a new method for association rule discovery in relational databases, which contain both quantitative and categorical attributes. Most of the methods developed in the past are based on initial equi-depth discretization of quantitative attributes. These approaches bring the loss of information. Distance-based methods are another kind of methods. They try to respect the semantics of data. The basic idea of the new method is to separate processing of categorical and quantitative attributes. The first step finds frequent itemsets containing only values of categorical attributes and then quantitative attributes are processed one by one. Discretization of values during quantitative attributes processing is distance-based. A new measure called average distance is introduced for these purposes. The paper describes the method and results of several experiments on real world data.

1 Introduction

At present, databases contain a huge amount of data and sometimes it is very difficult for people to educe some conclusions from this data. Therefore, the use of knowledge discovery techniques is necessary. Knowledge discovery in databases is a process of derivation of useful information, which is not explicitly stored in a database but may be useful in practice.

Association rules are one kind of knowledge discovered in databases. They are typically used for market basket analysis, where transactional databases are used. A transactional database is defined as a set of transactions where a transaction is a set of items. Here, the goal of mining association rules is to find rules of a form $A \Rightarrow B$ where A and B are sets of items. If this association rule is found, it means: "If a transaction contains a set of items A, it is likely to contain a set of items B". The sets A and B must be disjoint. We call them itemsets. An itemset that contains k items will be called k-itemset. Potential usefulness of a rule is usually expressed by means of two measures – support and confidence. Then, a frequent itemset is an itemset satisfying user-defined minimum support and a strong rule is a rule generated from frequent itemsets that satisfies also user-defined minimum confidence.

* This work has been supported by the Grant of FRVS MSMT, FR824/2003/G1, "Discovery of Association Rules In Relational Databases" and by the long-term grant project of Ministry of Education No. MSMT 262200012 "Research of information and control systems".

R. Meersman et al. (Eds.): CoopIS/DOA/ODBASE 2003, LNCS 2888, pp. 757–766, 2003.
© Springer-Verlag Berlin Heidelberg 2003

In the past, the research was mostly focused on methods for association rules in transactional databases. A lot of algorithms were proposed in this area. Probably the best known is Apriori algorithm [1] and its modifications [2]. The FP-tree method proposed in [3] and a graph-oriented method proposed in [4] are other examples.

The research of association rules in relational data is quite different. Here, the mining process is performed over a relational table containing only scalar values. There are two types of attributes in relational databases: categorical and quantitative. A categorical attribute (e.g. town) is an attribute the domain of which contains a finite set of values. On the other hand, the domain of a quantitative attribute (e.g. price) contains either an infinite set of values or the cardinality of the domain is "high", and the ordering must be defined on the domain.

Mining on categorical attributes is the same as in transactional databases - one row in a relational table can be considered as a transaction in a transactional database. Therefore slightly modified algorithms for mining transactional data can be used.

However, this approach cannot be applied to process quantitative attributes. The reason is that, in general, only few association rules would be generated due to a low support of individual values of a quantitative attribute. As a result, the discretization of values of the attribute must be performed the objective of which is to decrease the number of "representative values" of the attribute. In this case, the "representative values" are intervals. Minimum support and confidence, that control mining, are not considered during discretization. Equi-depth bucketing method is used very often. The intervals satisfying minimum support may be too wide in this case. It can result in high loss of information by discretization. Therefore, an additional measure for discretization "quality" should be introduced.

The paper is organized as follows: Chapter 2 contains a brief overview of methods for mining association rules in relational databases containing quantitative attributes. A new measure called the average distance, which is used to control discretization and our new method based on this measure are introduced in Chapter 3. Results of experiments that show some properties of the method are presented in Chapter 4.

2 Related Work

The term *Quantitative association rules* was defined by Srikant and Agrawal in [5]. The quantitative association rules may contain equality predicates *(Attr=val)* and range predicates (intervals). To indicate the "quality" of an interval, a metrics called K-partial completeness was introduced. It was designed to ensure that intervals are neither too big, nor too small. The basic idea is as follows: if the interval is too big, it may hide rules between the sub-intervals. The method requires an initial discretization. It is the equi-depth one. This approach does not reflect the semantics of the data, for example the distance between the data points. The initial equi-depth discretization may cause that two very near values (data points) lapse into two different intervals.

A method for mining *Optimized association rules* was proposed by Fukuda in [6]. The method uses no additional measure for the interestingness of an association rule. Because the minimum support and confidence thresholds are antipodal, either so called optimized support rules or optimized confidence rules are obtained with this method. The goal of the optimized support rules is to find rules with support as high as possible with respect to minimum confidence. Similarly, the optimized confidence rules maximize confidence of the rule while satisfying the minimum support requirement. The method proposed in [6] uses the equi-depth bucketing for the quantitative attribute discretization. The disadvantages of the method are the same as of the previous one.

The definition of association rules was extended by Zhang in [7]. The *Fuzzy Quantitative Association Rules* are introduced there. They may contain crisp values, intervals, and fuzzy terms in both antecedent and consequent. This approach combines interval partition with pre-defined fuzzy terms. Therefore, it is more general.

A *distance-based method*, in which the partitioning respects the semantics of numeric data, was proposed by Miller and Yang in [8]. The method uses a clustering method to find the intervals contained in an association rule. The algorithm works in two phases. In the first phase, the clusters over an attribute are identified using, for example, the algorithm Birch [9]. In the second phase, the clusters are combined to form rules using the classic Apriori algorithm. Frequent itemsets of clusters are the result of this phase.

A distance-based method that combines the approach of merging small intervals into larger ones with clustering was presented in [10]. This method is called *An Adaptive Method For Numerical Attribute Merging*. It takes into account both distance between data points and their density. First, each quantitative value is assigned to its own interval (containing only one value). Then, two hithermost neighboring intervals are merged together. The criterion that controls the merging process respect both distance and density of quantitative values.

In this paper, another distance-based method that reflects the distances between data points will be proposed. The association rule generated by this method contains a value of a quantitative attribute (a "representative value"), which has a sufficient number of neighbors in a sufficiently short distance from it. A new measure called an average distance controls discretization. The method and the measure will be described in the next chapter.

Most of the distance-based methods were mainly developed to mine in values of quantitative attributes. Our method processes quantitative and categorical attributes separately. This fact allows us to use faster algorithms for categorical attributes processing.

3 Average Distance Based Method

3.1 Average Distance

Assume that we have a sorted array of quantitative values. We want to find a value, which has a number of neighbors in a short distance defined by a measure. The measure will be called the *average distance* (we will use the acronym AD for it).

The average distance of a quantitative value v will is defined as:

$$AD(v) = \sum_{i=1}^{n} \frac{(v - v_i)}{n} \qquad (1)$$

where *v* is a quantitative value, v_i are the values that lie close to the value *v*, and *n* is the number of "close" values. The set of "close" values will be called a cluster. A cluster will be stored, for example, in the form of interval represented by its borders.

The number *n*, which is used to obtain AD, can be computed from the minimum support threshold. We can obtain it as

$$n = minsup * numrows, \tag{2}$$

where *minsup* is the user-defined minimum support threshold and *numrows* is the number of rows in the mined relational table. The AD of *v* is then the average distance from *v* of such number of values (data points) that satisfy the minimum support threshold.

We will introduce a maximum value of AD, which will be a parameter of a data mining task, that determines if *v* is an interesting value. If the average distance *AD(v)* does not exceed the value of maximum AD, *v* will be called an interesting value.

Besides this parameter, we assume another parameter called *precision* (we will denote it *P*) of a value in an association rule. For example, if the quantitative attribute will be Age, the value *(age=19.7647)* is not interesting for the user. If the user will enter the precision *P=1*, the result will be an integer value, either *(age=19)* or *(age=20)*. In other words, the value *P* determines the finest granularity of discretization.

Two parameters of an association rule mining task – maximum average distance *(MaxAD)* and precision *P* - defined in this chapter have to be entered by the user separately for each quantitative attribute in the table because each attribute in the table has different semantics. For example, the requirements of the user concerning an attribute *age* can differ from requirements concerning an attribute *price*.

3.2 Method Overview

Assume that there is a relational table containing both categorical and quantitative attributes. The result of the method is a set of association rules containing values of categorical and numerical attributes. An association rule may look like this:

$$(car="VW\ Golf") \Rightarrow (age\_of\_customer=32\ [MaxAD=1,\ P=1])$$

But the term *(age_of_customer=32)* does not mean that this condition satisfies the minimum support threshold. It means that there is a satisfactory number of customers whose age is near the number '32'. That's why the minimum support and confidence are not enough to say that the association rule is strong. Alternatively, the interval containing values close to the value '32' may be used in the rule instead of this specific value.

A relational table that can contain both categorical and quantitative attributes, minimum support and confidence, maximum average distance, and precision are inputs of the method. As mentioned above, the maximum average distance and precision must be entered for each quantitative attribute.

The task of mining association rules is performed in the following steps:
– **Categorical attributes processing:** Finding the frequent itemsets over the categorical attributes of the table.

– Quantitative attributes processing (getting frequent itemsets): Extending the frequent itemsets by adding quantitative items. The quantitative attributes are processed one by one. For each selected attribute and each frequent itemset from the previous step, its values are discretized first, based on the average distance measure, and the obtained interesting values are added to the itemset.

– Association rules generating: When all frequent itemsets are found, the set of strong association rules is generated by the well-known approach based on the minimum confidence entered by the user. This approach is straightforward and is described for example in [11].

3.3 Categorical Attributes Processing

The frequent itemsets over the categorical attributes can be obtained by very simple and well-known methods. In this case, we can view a row of the relational table as one transaction in a transactional database and use, for example, a slightly modified Apriori algorithm.

The result of this step is the set of all frequent itemsets over the part of the input table containing only categorical attributes. These itemsets will be extended with items of the quantitative attributes in the next step.

Notice that the categorical and quantitative attributes of the input table are processed separately. This fact significantly reduces the number of database scans because only fields in the table that are contained in categorical frequent itemsets are scanned in the following step of the process.

As a result of this step, we have a set of frequent itemsets containing only categorical values. We will call such itemsets the frequent categorical itemsets.

3.4 Quantitative Attributes Processing

Let us assume that the number of categorical items in frequent itemsets obtained in the previous step is k. We have frequent categorical itemsets, support of which is known. The quantitative attributes are processed one by one. For each frequent categorical itemset, values of a selected quantitative attribute from rows in which values of categorical attributes match the values in the actual categorical itemset are stored into an ordered number sequence. This sequence of numbers can be stored, for example, in a sorted array.

If we have this number sequence, we can find the interesting values for association rules using the average distance and precision measures. If any interesting value is found, it is added to the frequent categorical itemset, for which this sequence of numbers was constructed. The result will be a new frequent itemset.

Construction of a Number Sequence. For each frequent itemset, the algorithm scans the table. If the values in the row correspond to the values contained in the frequent itemset, the value from the quantitative column is added to the number sequence.

The algorithm looks as follows:

```
For each categorical frequent itemset FI do
     For each row R in the table do
          For each item i in FI do
               {
                    if (i.catvalue <> R.catvalue) break;
                    Insert_Into_Sequence (R.numvalue, Arr);
               }
```

The value of actual quantitative attribute is denoted as *numvalue*, the value of actual categorical attribute is denoted as *catvalue*. The procedure *Insert_Into_Sequence* will insert a new numeric value into the sorted array *Arr* of quantitative values.

Finding the interesting values. If we have the number sequence, we can find interesting values in it based on the average distance measure. The number of steps of this algorithm depends on the precision *P*.

The input of this algorithm is the sorted array *Arr*, maximum average distance *MaxAD* and the precision *P*. The output will be a set *S* of interesting quantitative values.

The algorithm can look as follows:

```
N=minsup*numrows;
Val=Round(Min_value_in_array, P);
While Val < Max_value_in_array
{
     RD=Count_AD (N, Arr, Val);
     If (AD<MaxAD) Add_To_Interesting(Val, S);
     Val=Val+P;
}
return (S);
```

At first, the algorithm sets the actual value *Val* to the lowest value in *Arr*. This value must be rounded with respect to the precision *P*. For each value, an average distance is counted by the procedure *Count_AD*. If the maximum AD threshold is satisfied, then the value *Val* is interesting and is added to *S* by the procedure *Add_To_Interesting*.

The procedure *Count_AD* can look as follows:

```
Procedure Count_AD (Arr, Val, n) {
   int p=Search_Hithermost(Val, Arr);
   int less=1; more=0; RD=0;
   for (i=0, i<=n, i++) {
       if ((Val-Arr[p-less])>=(Arr[p+more]-Val))
           { AD+=(Arr[p+more]-Val); more++; }
       else
           { AD+=(Val-Arr[p-less]); less--; }
   }
   AD/=n;
}
```

The procedure *Search_Hithermost* searches the number sequence *Arr* for the value closest to the value *Val*. It returns the index of a field in the number sequence with a higher value closest to *Val* (or equal to *Val*).

If the interesting values are added as items to the competent frequent itemset, then we have a new set of frequent itemsets, which contain values of one quantitative attribute.

3.5 Frequent Itemsets with Several Quantitative Attributes

If the input table contains more than one quantitative attribute, we have to continue computing frequent itemsets in additional iterations. Each iteration adds one interesting value of another quantitative attribute to the existing frequent itemset.

Assume that we have a frequent itemset (we will use the 2-itemset *{(car="VW Golf"), (age_of_customer=32)}* as an example). The process will be the following:

1. Let *fi* be a frequent itemset (*{(car="VW Golf"), (age_of_customer=32)}*) containing a value *v* (32 in our example) of a quantitative attribute q_1 (*age_of_customer* in our example). Let *c* be a cluster of values of the attribute represented by the value *v* (this cluster is stored together with the "representative value" *v* during the previous steps).
2. Select a quantitative attribute (for example *price*) from the attributes that have not been processed yet.
3. Construct a number sequence for the attribute q_2 containing the values of q_2 from those rows of the table the value of which in the attribute q_1 is present in the cluster *c*.
4. Find the interesting values in the number sequence constructed in step 3 for the attribute q_2 (this procedure of finding the interesting values is described in the previous section).
5. Create a new set of frequent itemsets, constructed from the itemset *fi* by adding the interesting values (from step four) to it (in our example, the new 3-itemset may be, for example, *{(car="VW Golf"), (age_of_customer=32), (price=10.000$)}*.
6. Repeat the steps 2, 3, 4 and 5 for each quantitative attribute of the table that has not been processed yet.

The processes of finding the interesting values are repeated for all frequent itemsets that contain values of quantitative attributes.

If there is no frequent (k+1)-itemset generated from a set of frequent k-itemsets, the algorithm stops and the actual set of frequent itemsets is a result of the process.

Notice that the generated quantitative items in itemsets may depend on the order of quantitative attributes processing. This implies that we can obtain different results for different orders of processing.

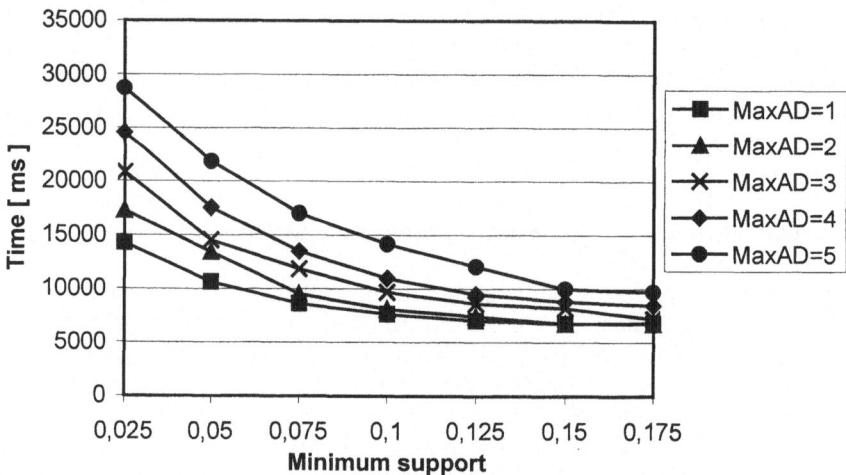

Fig. 1. Dependency between time complexity of the method, minimum support and maximum average distance (value of average distance was the same for both quantitative attributes)

4 Experimental Results

The first version of average distance based method was implemented as a part of a data mining system [12]. The implementation was made in Java. A database containing data from a medical study[1] was used for experiments.

The association rule mining task contained a relational table with four attributes. Two of them were categorical (frequency of drinking alcohol and physical activity in work) and the other two attributes were quantitative (weight and systolic blood pressure). The input relational table contained 1141 rows.

At first, we searched the dependences between time complexity and some user-defined parameters of a task (minimum support, maximum average distance and precision). These dependences are depicted in Figure 1.

The experiments confirmed the assumption that processing of categorical attributes is much faster than processing of quantitative attributes. A classic Apriori algorithm was used to process the categorical attributes. Times of processing of both kinds of attributes are shown in Figure 2. It indicates that separated processing may be advantageous.

---

[1] The study (STULONG) was realized at the 2nd Department of Medicine, 1st Faculty of Medicine of Charles University and Charles University Hospital, U nemocnice 2, Prague 2 (head. Prof. M. Aschermann, MD, SDr, FESC), under the supervision of Prof. F. Boudík, MD, ScD, with collaboration of M. Tomečková, MD, PhD and Ass. Prof. J. Bultas, MD, PhD. The data were transferred to the electronic form by the European Centre of Medical Informatics, Statistics and Epidemiology of Charles University and Academy of Sciences (head. Prof. RNDr. J. Zvárová, DrSc). The data resource is on the web pages http://euromise.vse.cz/challenge2003. At present time the data analysis is supported by the grant of the Ministry of Education CR Nr LN 00B 107.

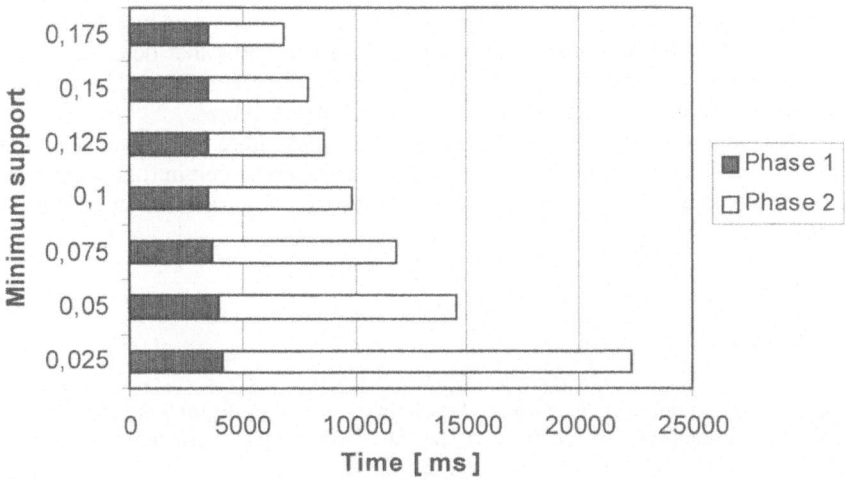

Fig. 2. Differences between time complexity of categorical (Phase 1) and quantitative attributes processing (Phase 2)

As mentioned above, the result of mining can depend on the order of processing of quantitative attributes. Therefore we tried to find out a dependency between resultant association rules, the order of processing and values of other parameters (e.g. maximum average distance). The results of these experiments showed that it is better to process first the attributes with higher maximal average distance, lower precision and lower range of values. The solution of this problem may be a heuristics, which will determine the order of attributes to be processed. This heuristics may be based on three parameters mentioned above - maximum average distance, precision and range.

5 Conclusion

A new method for discovery of association rules in relational databases, where the association rule contains both categorical and quantitative items was proposed in this paper. A new measure called average distance for interestingness of a value was introduced. The measure is used for discretization of quantitative attributes.

The presented method has two main advantages. First, the results of this method may contain association rules with quantitative items in the form *(Attr=Value)*. This expression associated with the average distance may give more useful information than an interval, which is used as a result of most of other methods. But it is possible to use intervals in the resultant association rules too.

The second advantage is the separation of categorical and quantitative attributes processing. Some advanced (and faster) methods may be used for processing of categorical attributes. This fact is of good promise to make this method more effective compared to processing both kinds of attributes together. The experiments confirmed that processing of categorical attributes takes much shorter time.

Nevertheless, there are some topics for further research. The first one concerning dependency on the order of quantitative attributes processing was briefly discussed in chapter 4. One of the possible solutions is to find heuristics that determines the best order. This heuristics may include the data mining task parameters entered by the user for the attributes and some properties of values of the attributes.

Another topic for the future research is to find more effective structure and algorithms for searching interesting values. The array presented in this paper was used only to demonstrate the principles of the method and for verification of the method functionality.

References

1. Agrawal, R., Imielinski, T., Swami, A.: Mining Association Rules Between Sets of Items In Large Databases. Proceedings of the ACM SIGMOD International Conference on Management of Data, Washington, DC, 1993.
2. Kotásek, P., Zendulka, J.: Comparison of Three Mining Algorithms For Association Rules, Proceeding of MOSIS 2000 – Information Systems Modeling ISM 2000, Rožnov pod Radhoštěm, Czech Republic, 2000, pp. 85–90
3. Han, J., Pei, J., Yin, Y.: Mining Frequent Patterns without Candidate, Proc. 2000 ACM-SIGMOD Int. Conf. on Management of Data (SIGMOD'00), Dallas, TX, May 2000.
4. Lee, G., Lee, K., L., Chen, L., P.: Efficient Graph-Based Algorithms for Discovering and Maintaining Association Rules in Large Databases, Knowledge and Information Systems, Springer-Verlag London Ltd., 2001, pp. 338–355.
5. Srikant, R., Agrawal, R.: Mining Quantitative Association Rules In Large Relational Tables. Proceedings of the 1996 ACM SIGMOD International Conference on Management of Data, 1996.
6. Fukuda, T, et al.: Mining Optimized Association Rules For Numeric Attributes. Proceedings of ACM PODS'96, Montreal, Canada, 1996, pp. 182–191.
7. Zhang, W.: Mining Fuzzy Quantitative Association Rules. Proceedings of 11th IEEE International Conference on Tools with Artificial Intelligence, IEEE Computer Society, Chicago, Illinois, 1999, pp. 99–102.
8. Miller, R. J., Yang, Y.: Association Rules Over Interval Data. Proceedings of 1997 ACM SIGMOD, Tucson, Arizona, USA, 1997, pp. 452–461.
9. Zhang, T., Ramakrishnan, R., Livny, M.: Birch: An Efficient Data Clustering Method For Very Large Databases. Proceedings of the ACM SIGMOD International Conference on Management of Data, Montreal, Canada, 1996.
10. Li, J., Shen, H., Topor, R.: An Adaptive Method of Numerical Attribute Merging for Quantitative Association Rule Mining, Proceedings of the 5th international computer science conference (ICSC), 1999, pp. 41–50, Springer.
11. Hua, Z.: On-Line Analytical Mining of Association Rules, PhD. thesis, Simon Fraser University, 1998.
12. Bartik, V.: Association Rule Discovery In Databases, Proceedings of 5th International Conference ISM'02, Roznov pod Radhostem, Czech Republic, 2002, pp. 21–27.